BUSINESS LAW IN SCOTLAND

AUSTRALIA
Law Book Co.
Sydney

CANADA and USA
Carswell
Toronto

HONG KONG
Sweet & Maxwell Asia

NEW ZEALAND
Brookers
Wellington

SINGAPORE and MALAYSIA
Sweet & Maxwell Asia
Singapore and Kuala Lumpur

Business Law in Scotland

Gillian Black
Lecturer in Law, University of Edinburgh

Josephine Bisacre
Lecturer in Business Law,
Heriot-Watt University

Andrew R. Wilson
Editor of SCOLAG Legal
Journal

Elizabeth Campbell
Lecturer in Law, University of
Aberdeen

David Cabrelli
Lecturer in Commercial Law,
University of Edinburgh,
Solicitor

James Chalmers
Senior Lecturer in Law,
University of Edinburgh

Stuart Cross
Senior Lecturer in Law,
University of Dundee

Alan Delaney
Solicitor, Maclay Murray &
Spens, LLP

Cowan Ervine
Senior Lecturer in Law,
University of Dundee

Alex Gibb
Lecturer, Aberdeen College

Greg Gordon
Lecturer in Law, University of
Aberdeen

Fiona Grant
Teaching Fellow in Law,
University of Abertay, Dundee

Angus McAllister
Solicitor, Professor of Law,
University of the West of
Scotland

Frankie McCarthy
Lecturer in Law, University of
Glasgow

Dr Catherine W. Ng
Lecturer in Law, University of
Aberdeen

Michael Plaxton
Lecturer in Law, University of
Aberdeen

Dr Hong-Lin Yu
Reader in Law, University of
Stirling

THOMSON

W. GREEN

Published in 2008 by
W. Green & Son Ltd
21 Alva Street
Edinburgh EH2 4PS

www.wgreen.thomson.com

Typeset by YHT Ltd, Hillingdon
Printed and bound in Great Britain by Athenaeum Press,
Gateshead, Tyne & Wear

No natural forests were destroyed to make this product;
only farmed timber was used and replanted

A CIP catalogue record for this book is available from
the British Library.

ISBN 978-0-414-01703-0

Foreword

A knowledge of the topics falling within the area of business law is an important requirement for individuals following or wishing to follow a career in business. It is also an important element of the Chartered Accountancy qualification offered by The Institute of Chartered Accountants of Scotland ensuring that CA Students have a broad understanding of a range of legal topics which are relevant to business and commercial situations. This breadth of knowledge is invaluable in ensuring that relevant legal matters are appropriately considered.

Business Law in Scotland will provide readers with a useful introduction to a broad range of legal topics and will be an invaluable support for those studying business law as part of a wider area of study.

Mark Allison
Executive Director, Education and International
ICAS

Introduction

Anyone in business in Scotland needs to know a little about the law. Whether you are running a web-based start-up as a sole trader or have an established company with hundreds of employees, the law will affect your business. And while the services of a solicitor may be available, it is essential to have a basic understanding of areas of law as diverse as contract, employment, data protection and insurance. This book aims to provide an introduction to those varied areas of law which are most relevant to business people in Scotland. It won't transform you into a fully qualified lawyer, but it will help you identify legal issues at an early stage—and seeking further advice in good time can save money, inconvenience and delay.

The book is organised in five sections. The first (chapters 1-3) provides an introduction to the Scottish legal system, sources of law, and a guide to business regulation. The second section (chapters 4 to 13) covers core areas of Scots private law, including contract, delict and property law. Section three (chapters 14 to 19) addresses those areas of commerce that most organisations will usually, at some time or other, have to deal with, whether it is company regulation, partnership agreements, or even insolvency. In section four (chapter 20), the focus switches to dispute resolution in Scotland—what to do if it all goes wrong. This includes seeking redress in the courts as well as alternative methods of resolving problems. The final section (chapter 21) is a guide to legal writing and problem solving, to help apply the law in problem scenarios, not least when answering exam questions.

In compiling this textbook, we have paid close attention to the "Business Law" syllabus set by the Institute of Chartered Accountants for Scotland (ICAS) for the CA programme in Scotland. We hope that *Business Law in Scotland* will provide a useful resource to those students following the ICAS programme, and we are particularly pleased that Mark Allison and Ann Lamb from ICAS have contributed the Foreword.

Finally, on behalf of all the contributors, I should like to thank Janet Campbell and the staff at W. Green for their hard work and support in bringing this book together: co-ordinating 15 authors cannot have been an easy task, and it is a tribute to their work that this book has appeared at all!

Gillian Black
Edinburgh, June 2008

Contents

Foreword.. v
Introduction... vii
Table of cases... xvii
Table of statutes.. xxxi
Table of statutory instruments....................................... xlv

CHAPTER 1: INTRODUCTION TO THE NATURE AND SOURCES OF SCOTS LAW

Chapter overview.. 1
Outcomes.. 1
Introduction.. 2
The history and development of Scots law.................... 3
Categories of law.. 9
The formal sources of Scots law.................................... 11
Legislation.. 12
Judicial precedent 22
Institutional writers.. 28
Custom... 30
Equity... 31
Chapter summary... 32
Quick quiz... 35
Further reading.. 36
Relevant weblinks.. 36

CHAPTER 2: STRUCTURE OF THE SCOTTISH LEGAL SYSTEM

Chapter overview.. 38
Outcomes.. 38
Introduction.. 38
The civil court system.. 39
The criminal court system... 46
Tribunals... 50
Ombudsmen... 53
The legal profession.. 57
Law officers... 62
Chapter summary... 64
Quick quiz... 66
Further reading.. 66
Relevant weblinks.. 66

CHAPTER 3: BUSINESS REGULATION

Chapter overview... 68
Outcomes... 68
The criminal law—its purpose and general principles................. 69
Common law crimes relevant to business............................... 79
Regulatory law and regulatory offences................................. 84
Chapter summary... 103
Quick quiz.. 105
Further reading... 106
Relevant weblinks.. 106

CHAPTER 4: THE LAW OF CONTRACT

Chapter overview... 107
Outcomes... 107
What is a contract?... 108
Formation of contracts.. 113
Contractual formalities.. 126
The contents of a contract: contractual terms......................... 126
The legal regulation of contractual terms............................... 134
Defective contracts... 139
Breach of contract.. 155
Who may sue when a contract is breached?............................ 162
Extinction of contractual obligations..................................... 164
Chapter summary... 168
Quick quiz.. 175
Further reading... 176
Relevant weblinks.. 176

CHAPTER 5: SALE AND SUPPLY OF GOODS

Chapter overview... 177
Outcomes... 177
Introduction... 178
The contract of sale.. 178
Other contracts for the supply of goods................................. 199
Exclusion of liability... 200
Chapter summary... 200
Quick quiz.. 202
Further reading... 203
Relevant weblinks.. 203

CHAPTER 6: CONSUMER PROTECTION

Chapter overview... 204
Outcomes... 204
Introduction... 205
Consumer credit... 205

The Consumer Protection from Unfair Trading Regulations
   2008... 217
Chapter summary.. 231
Quick quiz.. 232
Further reading.. 233
Relevant weblinks.. 233

CHAPTER 7: E-COMMERCE

Chapter overview.. 234
Outcomes... 234
Introduction.. 235
The electronic commerce regulations................................... 237
The distance selling regulations... 245
The legal regulation of e-commerce—other considerations......... 259
Chapter summary.. 260
Quick quiz.. 261
Further reading.. 262
Relevant weblinks.. 262

CHAPTER 8: EMPLOYMENT LAW

Chapter overview.. 263
Outcomes... 263
The contract of employment... 263
Terms and conditions of employment.................................. 267
Termination of employment and wrongful dismissal.............. 271
Unfair dismissal.. 273
Redundancy payments.. 279
Discrimination.. 282
Chapter summary.. 287
Quick quiz.. 291
Further reading.. 292
Relevant weblinks.. 292

CHAPTER 9: AGENCY

Chapter overview.. 293
Outcomes... 293
Meaning and key features of agency..................................... 294
Different kinds and examples of agency................................ 295
Creating agency.. 298
The agency relationship.. 301
Third parties... 311
Ending agency... 314
Commercial agents/Commercial Agents (Council Directive)
   Regulations 1993... 315
Chapter summary.. 319
Quick quiz.. 322

Further reading... 323
Relevant weblinks.. 323

CHAPTER 10: DELICT

Chapter overview.. 324
Outcomes.. 324
What is delict?... 325
Terminology... 325
Intentional delicts.. 325
Unintentional delicts... 329
Defences... 344
Delict in the employment context... 346
Professional liability.. 348
Breach of statutory duty... 349
Nuisance... 352
Prescription and limitation... 353
Remedies... 353
Modes of liability... 355
Chapter summary... 355
Quick quiz.. 359
Further reading.. 359

CHAPTER 11: PROPERTY

Chapter overview.. 360
Outcomes.. 360
Introduction: basic concepts... 360
Moveable and intellectual property....................................... 363
Heritable property: historical background and modern reforms.. 364
Heritable property: land registration.................................... 365
Ownership rights.. 368
Common rights... 373
Restrictions on property rights... 375
Leases.. 378
Transfer of heritable property.. 385
Chapter summary... 385
Quick quiz.. 390
Further reading.. 390
Relevant weblinks.. 390

CHAPTER 12: INTELLECTUAL PROPERTY

Chapter overview.. 392
Outcomes.. 392
Intellectual property rights... 393
The law of passing-off.. 394
Trade marks... 396
Copyright... 400

Design.. 405
Patents.. 410
Chapter summary.. 414
Quick quiz... 417
Further reading... 418
Relevant weblinks... 418

CHAPTER 13: TRUSTS

Chapter overview... 419
Outcomes.. 419
The trust concept... 419
Creation of a trust.. 422
Office of trustee.. 428
Decision-making by trustees.. 430
Duties of a trustee.. 431
Rule against *auctor in rem suam*....................................... 434
Trustee's right to reimbursement... 435
Powers of a trustee... 435
Liabilities of a trustee... 437
Variation of trust purposes.. 440
Termination of a trust... 443
Chapter summary.. 445
Quick quiz... 448
Further reading... 449
Relevant weblinks... 449

CHAPTER 14: CHOICE OF BUSINESS MEDIUM

Chapter overview... 450
Outcomes.. 450
The sole trader... 451
The partnership: an introduction.. 452
Separate legal personality and continuity............................. 453
The Partnership Act 1890.. 453
The advantages of the partnership....................................... 454
The disadvantages of the partnership................................... 454
The company: introduction.. 457
The advantages of the corporate form.................................. 458
The company: the disadvantages.. 461
The limited liability partnership: an introduction.................. 463
The limited liability partnership: advantages and disadvantages.. 464
Chapter summary.. 467
Quick quiz... 470
Further reading... 470
Relevant weblinks... 470

CHAPTER 15: THE LAW OF PARTNERSHIP

Chapter overview... 472
Outcomes.. 472
The partnership: an introduction.. 473
The partnership: the nature of a partnership............................ 473
The partnership: the relationship between the partners, the
   partnership and third parties.. 477
Partnership property... 484
Partners' duties, the relations of partners to one another and the
   regulation of the internal affairs of the partnership................ 484
The dissolution of the partnership and the distribution of its assets
   on dissolution.. 487
Partnership law reform.. 494
The limited partnership... 495
Chapter summary.. 495
Quick quiz.. 500
Further reading.. 501
Relevant weblinks... 501

CHAPTER 16: COMPANY LAW

Chapter overview... 502
Outcomes.. 503
An introduction to company law.. 504
The types of company, company names and incorporating a
   company.. 509
The constitution: the memorandum and articles of association... 516
Ongoing administrative matters... 525
Corporate decision-making and corporate governance: (i) officers
   and directors.. 531
Corporate decision-making and corporate governance: (ii)
   company meetings and resolutions...................................... 549
Corporate finance (i): share capital.. 562
Corporate finance: (ii) debentures/loan stock........................... 570
Maintenance of share capital and purchase of own shares.......... 573
Minority shareholder protection... 577
Chapter summary.. 585
Quick quiz.. 587
Further reading.. 588
Relevant weblinks... 588

CHAPTER 17: INSOLVENCY

Chapter overview... 589
Outcomes.. 589
Personal insolvency... 590
Corporate insolvency... 603
Chapter summary.. 618

Quick quiz.. 619
Further reading... 620
Relevant weblinks.. 620

CHAPTER 18: NEGOTIABLE INSTRUMENTS

Chapter overview.. 621
Outcomes... 621
Introduction... 622
Cheques.. 630
Promissory notes.. 633
Chapter summary.. 634
Quick quiz... 636
Further reading... 636
Relevant weblinks.. 636

CHAPTER 19: RIGHTS IN SECURITY

Chapter Overview.. 637
Outcomes... 637
Introduction... 638
The contract of caution (guarantee).. 638
Constitution of the guarantee.. 639
Extent of the guarantor's liability... 639
Guarantor's rights... 640
Contra proferentem rule.. 640
Grounds to invalidate a guarantee... 641
Extinction of the guarantee... 643
Real rights in security over property.. 644
Real rights in security where delivery is not required.................. 645
Floating charges... 646
Bankruptcy and Diligence etc. (Scotland) Act 2007.................... 649
Rights in security where delivery is required.............................. 650
Rights in security over heritable property................................... 650
Rights in security over corporeal moveable property................... 651
Rights in security over incorporeal moveable property................ 651
Situations where intimation is not possible—exceptions to the
  general rule.. 652
Chapter summary.. 652
Quick quiz... 655
Further reading... 656

CHAPTER 20: DISPUTE RESOLUTION

Chapter overview.. 657
Outcomes... 657
Advantages and disadvantages of ADR...................................... 657
Negotiation.. 658
Mediation.. 659

Arbitration.. 659
Arbitration agreements.. 662
Adjudication... 671
Court actions... 673
Conclusion... 676
Chapter summary... 676
Quick quiz.. 677
Further reading.. 678
Relevant weblinks.. 678

CHAPTER 21: INTRODUCTION TO LEGAL WRITING AND PROBLEM SOLVING
TECHNIQUES

Chapter overview.. 679
Writing legal essays... 679
Answering problem questions 685
Exam hints... 688

APPENDIX 1—GLOSSARY AND ABBREVIATIONS............................. 693

APPENDIX 2—QUICK QUIZ ANSWERS... 701

Index... 735

Table of Cases

A&W Hemphill Ltd v Williams; sub nom. Williams v A&W Hemphill Ltd [1966] 2 Lloyd's Rep. 101; 1966 S.C. (H.L.) 31, HL 10–34
AKZO Chemie BV v Commission of the European Communities (C62/86) [1991] E.C.R. I-3359; [1993] 5 C.M.L.R. 215, ECJ (5th Chamber) 3–53
Aberdeen Journals Ltd v Director General of Fair Trading [2003] CAT 11; [2003] Comp. A.R. 67, CCAT 3–53
Aberdeen Railway v Blaikie Bros (1854) 1 Macq. 461; (1854) 2 Eq. Rep. 1281, HL 13–40
Adams v Cape Industries Plc [1990] Ch. 433; [1990] 2 W.L.R. 657, CA (Civ Div) ... 16–06
Advocate (HM) v Cameron (Cecil Aylmer); HM Advocate v Cameron (Ruby), 1911 S.C. (J.) 110; 1911 2 S.L.T. 108, HCJ 3–19
Advocate (HM) v Kerr (1871) 2 Couper 334 3–16
Advocate (Lord) v Lappen (John Charles), 1956 S.L.T. 109, HCJ 3–16
Aerotel Ltd v Telco Holdings Ltd; Macrossan's Patent Application (No.0314464.9) [2006] EWCA Civ 1371; [2007] Bus. L.R. 634; [2007] 1 All E.R. 225, CA (Civ Div) 12–28
Aikman, Petitioners (1881) 9 R. 213 13–25
Aird's Executors v Aird, 1949 S.C. 154; 1949 S.L.T. 151, IH (1 Div) 13–20
Aitken's Trustees v Aitken, 1927 S.C. 374; 1927 S.L.T. 308, IH (1 Div) 13–21, 13–22
Akbar Khan v Attar Singh [1936] 2 All E.R. 545, PC (Ind) 18–23
Alcock v Chief Constable of South Yorkshire; Penk v Wright; Jones v Chief Constable of South Yorkshire; Copoc v Chief Constable of South Yorkshire; sub nom. Jones v Wright [1992] 1 A.C. 310; [1991] 3 W.L.R. 1057, HL 10–25
Allan (Shaw's Trustees) (1893) 1 S.L.T. 308, OH 13–16
Allan's Trustees v Lord Advocate; sub nom. Allan's Trustees v Inland Revenue Commissioners, 1971 S.C. (H.L.) 45; 1971 S.L.T. 62, HL 13–12, 13–13
Allen v Gold Reefs of West Africa Ltd [1900] 1 Ch. 656, CA 16–10
Amderson v Croall & Sons (1903) 6 F. 153 9–40
Anderson v Dundee City Council, 2000 S.L.T. (Sh Ct) 134; 1999 S.C.L.R. 518, Sh Ct (Tayside) 10–40
Anderson v Hogg, 2002 S.C. 190; 2002 S.L.T. 354, IH (Ex Div) 16–64
Anderson v Smoke (1898) 25 R. 493 13–22
Anderson's Trustees, 1921 S.C. 315; 1921 1 S.L.T. 186, IH (2 Div) 13–44
Angus's Executrix v Batchan's Trustees, 1949 S.C. 335; 1949 S.L.T. 247, IH (Ct of 7 judges) 13–16
Anstruther v Wilkie, 1856 18 D. 405 4–58
Arab Bank v Ross [1952] 2 Q.B. 216; [1952] 1 All E.R. 709, CA 18–07
Archivent Sales & Developments Ltd v Strathclyde RC, 1985 S.L.T. 154; 27 B.L.R. 98, OH 5–15
Arcos Ltd v EA Ronaasen & Son; sub nom. Ronaasen & Son v Arcos Ltd [1933] A.C. 470; (1933) 45 Ll. L. Rep. 33, HL 5–20
Arenson v Casson Beckman Rutley & Co; sub nom. Arenson v Arenson [1977] A.C. 405; [1975] 3 W.L.R. 815, HL 20–15
Argos Ltd v Office of Fair Trading; JJB Sports Plc v Office of Fair Trading [2006] EWCA Civ 1318; [2006] U.K.C.L.R. 1135; (2006) 103(42) L.S.G. 32, CA (Civ Div) 3–51
Arif v Excess Insurance Group Ltd, 1986 S.C. 317; 1987 S.L.T. 473, OH 4–33
Armagas Ltd v Mundogas SA (The Ocean Frost) 777 [1986] A.C. 717; [1986] 2 W.L.R. 1063, HL 9–22
Armour v Thyssen Edelstahlwerke AG [1991] 2 A.C. 339; [1990] 3 W.L.R. 810; [1990] 3 All E.R. 481, HL 5–08

Armour v TL Duff & Co; sub nom. Armour v Duff & Co, 1912 S.C. 120; 1911 2 S.L.T. 394, IH (2 Div) 9–37
Ashbury Railway Carriage & Iron Co Ltd v Riche; sub nom. Riche v Ashbury Railway Carriage & Iron Co Ltd (1874–75) L.R. 7 H.L. 653, HL 16–10
Attorney General's Reference (No.1 of 1991), Re [1993] Q.B. 94; [1992] 3 W.L.R. 432, CA (Crim Div) 3–43
Attridge Law (A Firm) v Coleman [2007] I.C.R. 654; [2007] I.R.L.R. 88; [2007] 2 C.M.L.R. 24, EAT 8–40
Atwool v Merryweather (1867–68) L.R. 5 Eq. 464 (Note), Ct of Chancery 16–64
Bain, Petitioner (Sequestration of Rev James Bain's Estate) (1901) 9 S.L.T. 14, Bill Chamber (SC) 13–03
Balfour Beatty Construction (Scotland) Ltd v Scottish Power Plc, 1994 S.C. (H.L.) 20; 1994 S.L.T. 807, HL 4–93
Bamford v Bamford [1970] Ch. 212; [1969] 2 W.L.R. 1107, CA (Civ Div) 16–10
Bank of Scotland v Fuller Peiser, 2002 S.L.T. 574; 2002 S.C.L.R. 255, OH 10–26
Bannatyne, Kirkwood, France & Co, Noters, 1907 S.C. 705; (1907) 14 S.L.T. 949, IH (1 Div) 9–09
Barclays Bank Plc v O'Brien [1994] 1 A.C. 180; [1993] 3 W.L.R. 786, HL 19–11
Barnett v Chelsea and Kensington Hospital Management Committee [1969] 1 Q.B. 428; [1968] 2 W.L.R. 422, QBD 10–26
Barr (Joseph) v HM Advocate, 1927 J.C. 51; 1927 S.L.T. 412, HCJ 3–25
Barrett v Duckett [1995] B.C.C. 362; [1995] 1 B.C.L.C. 243, CA (Civ Div) 16–64
Barrett McKenzie & Co Ltd v Escada (UK) Ltd; sub nom. Barret McKenzie v Escada (UK) Ltd [2001] E.C.C. 50; [2001] Eu. L.R. 567, QBD 9–51
Barry Ostlere & Shepherd Ltd v Edinburgh Cork Importing Co, 1909 S.C. 1113; 1909 1 S.L.T. 540, IH (Ex Div) 9–21
Bavins & Sims v London & South Western Bank Ltd [1900] 1 Q.B. 270, CA 18–07
Beale v Taylor [1967] 1 W.L.R. 1193; [1967] 3 All E.R. 253, CA (Civ Div) 5–20
Bedford Insurance Co Ltd v Instituto de Resseguros do Brasil [1985] Q.B. 966; [1984] 3 W.L.R. 726, QBD (Comm) 9–15
Bennett v Inveresk Paper Co (1891) 18 R. 975 9–39
Bertram's Trustees v Bertram, 1909 S.C. 1238; 1909 2 S.L.T. 86, IH (2 Div) 13–61
Bird (William Joseph) v HM Advocate, 1952 J.C. 23; 1952 S.L.T. 446, HCJ 3–07
Birmingham Vinegar Brewery Co Ltd v Powell; sub nom. Powell v Birmingham Vinegar Brewery Co [1897] A.C. 710, HL 12–05
Black v Carmichael; Carmichael v Black, 1992 S.L.T. 897; 1992 S.C.C.R. 709, HCJ Appeal 3–08, 3–10, 3–22, 3–26
Black v Cullen (1853) 15 D. 646 9–43
Blathwayt v Baron Cawley [1976] A.C. 397; [1975] 3 W.L.R. 684, HL 13–21
Bluebell Apparel Ltd v Dickinson, 1978 S.C. 16; 1980 S.L.T. 157, IH (1 Div) 4–76
Bolton v Stone; sub nom. Stone v Bolton [1951] A.C. 850; [1951] 1 All E.R. 1078, HL 10–16
Bonar v McLeod; Hogg v McLeod, 1983 S.C.C.R. 161, HCJ Appeal 3–06
Border Harvesters Ltd v Edwards Engineering (Perth) Ltd, 1985 S.L.T. 128, OH ... 5–20
Borland's Trustee v Steel Bros & Co Ltd [1901] 1 Ch. 279, Ch D 16–49, 16–51
Boston Deep Sea Fishing & Ice Co v Ansell (1888) L.R. 39 Ch. D. 339, CA 9–29
Boston Deep Sea Fishing and Ice Co v Farnham [1957] 1 W.L.R. 1051; [1957] 3 All E.R. 204, Ch D 9–15
Bourhill v Young; sub nom. Bourhill v Young's Executor [1943] A.C. 92; [1942] 2 All E.R. 396, HL 10–17
Bowman v Secular Society Ltd; sub nom. Secular Society Ltd v Bowman; Bowman, Re [1917] A.C. 406, HL 13–17, 13–18, 13–20
Brenan v Campbell's Trustees (1898) 25 R. 423 9–43
Brennan (Ian) v HM Advocate, 1977 J.C. 38; 1977 S.L.T. 151, HCJ 3–20
British Airways Plc v Starmer [2005] I.R.L.R. 863, EAT 8–36
British Bata Shoe Co Ltd v Double M Shah Ltd, 1980 S.C. 311; 1981 S.L.T. (Notes) 14, OH 9–22
British Home Stores Ltd v Burchell [1980] I.C.R. 303; [1978] I.R.L.R. 379; (1978) 13 I.T.R. 560, EAT 8–23

British Motor Trade Association v Gray, 1951 S.C. 586; 1951 S.L.T. 247, IH (1 Div) 10–9

Britvic Soft Drinks Ltd v Messer UK Ltd; sub nom. Messer UK Ltd v Britvic Soft Drinks Ltd [2002] EWCA Civ 548; [2002] 2 All E.R. (Comm) 321; [2002] 2 Lloyd's Rep. 368, CA (Civ Div) 5–22

Brown v Edinburgh Magistrates, 1931 S.L.T. 456, OH 1–09

Brown v Frame [2005] HCJAC 52; 2005 1 J.C. 320; 2005 S.L.T. 744; 2005 S.C.C.R. 400; 2005 G.W.D. 25–499, HCJ 3–14

Brown v Inland Revenue Commissioners [1965] A.C. 244; [1964] 3 W.L.R. 511, HL 9–09

Brown v Lee Constructions Ltd, 1977 S.L.T. (Notes) 61, OH 10–7

Brown v Sutherland (1875) 2 R. 615 13–52

Bruce v JM Smith Ltd (Slander to Property: Irrelevancy); JS Smith Ltd v Bruce (1898) 6 S.L.T. 247, IH (2 Div) 1–52

Bruckner v Jopp's Trustees (1887) 14 R. 1006 13–40

Bulkeley-Gavin's Trustees v Bulkeley-Gavin's Trustees (Trust: Revocation), 1971 S.C. 209, IH (2 Div) 13–61

Burgess Trustees v Crawford. *See* Murray v Crawford

Burland v Earle [1902] A.C. 83, PC (Can) 16–64

Burr v Police Commissioners of Bo'ness (1896) 24 R. 148 4–18

Bushell v Faith [1970] A.C. 1099; [1970] 2 W.L.R. 272, HL 16–46

CIN Properties Ltd v Dollar Land (Cumbernauld) Ltd, 1992 S.C. (H.L.) 104; 1992 S.L.T. 669, HL 11–60

Cannop v Highland Council [2008] CSIH 38 8–21

Caparo Industries Plc v Dickman [1990] 2 A.C. 605; [1990] 2 W.L.R. 358, HL 1–36, 10–15

Carlill v Carbolic Smoke Ball Co [1893] 1 Q.B. 256, CA 4–17, 4–18, 4–25

Carmichael v Evans [1904] 1 Ch. 486, Ch D 15–08

Carmichael v National Power Plc [1999] 1 W.L.R. 2042; [1999] 4 All E.R. 897; [1999] I.C.R. 1226; [2000] I.R.L.R. 43; (1999) 96(46) L.S.G. 38; (1999) 143 S.J.L.B. 281, HL 8–04

Cathcart's Trustees v Cathcart (1907) 15 S.L.T. 646, OH 13–51

Cawthorne (Richard Graves) v HM Advocate, 1968 J.C. 32; 1968 S.L.T. 330, HCJ 3–19

Cherry's Trustees v Patrick, 1911 2 S.L.T. 313, OH 13–23

Chief Constable of West Yorkshire v Vento (No.1) [2001] I.R.L.R. 124, EAT 8–35

Christie v Smith, 1949 S.C. 572; 1950 S.L.T. 31, IH (2 Div) 11–34

Chwee Kin Keong v Digilandmall.com Pte Ltd [2004] 2 S.L.R. 594 7–06

Clark Taylor & Co Ltd v Quality Site Development (Edinburgh) Ltd, 1981 S.C. 111; 1981 S.L.T. 308, IH (1 Div) 13–13

Clegg v Andersson (t/a Nordic Marine) [2003] EWCA Civ 320; [2003] 1 All E.R. (Comm) 721; [2003] 2 Lloyd's Rep. 32, CA (Civ Div) 5–22, 5–25, 5–26

Cleland v Morrison (1876) 6 R. 156 9–29

Clyde Industrial Training Ship Association, 1925 S.C. 676 13–59

Conlon v Simms; sub nom. Simms v Conlon [2006] EWCA Civ 1749; [2007] 3 All E.R. 802, CA (Civ Div) 15–04

Connal & Co v Loder (1868) 6 M 1095 18–10

Continental Tyre & Rubber Co Ltd v Trunk Trailer Co Ltd, 1985 S.C. 163; 1987 S.L.T. 58, IH (1 Div) 4–24

Cook v Deeks [1916] 1 A.C. 554, PC (Can) 16–64

Cooke v Falconer's Representatives (1850) 13 D. 157 9–30

Copland v Brogan, 1916 S.C. 277; 1916 1 S.L.T. 13, IH (2 Div) 9–30

Cornelius v Black (1879) 6 R. 581 9–26

Cowan v Scargill; sub nom. Mineworkers Pension Scheme Trusts, Re [1985] Ch. 270; [1984] 3 W.L.R. 501, Ch D 13–34

Cox v Coulson [1916] 2 K.B. 177, CA 15–04

Crawford (Alex) (1850) Shaw 309 3–26

Crichton v Grierson (1828) 3 W. & S. 329, HL 13–16

Crowther v Shannon Motor Co; sub nom. Crowther v Solent Motor Co [1975] 1 W.L.R. 30; [1975] 1 All E.R. 139, CA (Civ Div) 5–22

Cumana Ltd, Re [1986] B.C.L.C. 430 16–67

Cunningham v Montgomerie (1879) 6 R. 1333 13–41

Customs and Excise Commissioners v Barclays Bank Plc [2006] UKHL 28; [2006] 3
  W.L.R. 1; [2006] 4 All E.R. 256, HL 10–26
D&F Estates Ltd v Church Commissioners for England 35005 [1989] A.C. 177;
  [1988] 3 W.L.R. 368, HL 10–26
DPP v Bignall; sub nom. DPP v Bignell [1998] 1 Cr. App. R. 1; (1997) 161 J.P. 541;
  [1997–98] Info. T.L.R. 168; [1998] I.T.C.L.R. 33, QBD 3–33
Dacas v Brook Street Bureau (UK) Ltd; sub nom. Brook Street Bureau (UK) Ltd v
  Dacas [2004] EWCA Civ 217; [2004] I.C.R. 1437; [2004] I.R.L.R. 358, CA (Civ
  Div) 8–06
Daily Telegraph Co v McLaughlin [1904] A.C. 776 9–44
Dallas McMillan & Sinclair v Simpson, 1989 S.L.T. 454, OH 4–76
Daniels v Daniels [1978] Ch. 406; [1978] 2 W.L.R. 73, Ch D 16–64
Davis Contractors v Fareham Urban DC [1956] A.C. 696; [1956] 3 W.L.R. 37,
  HL 4–106
De Bussche v Alt (1878) L.R. 8 Ch. D. 286, CA 9–26
De Robeck v Inland Revenue Commissioners, 1928 S.C. (H.L.) 34; 1928 S.L.T. 222,
  HL 13–63
Dennant v Skinner and Collom [1948] 2 K.B. 164; [1948] 2 All E.R. 29; [1948] L.J.R.
  1576, KBD 5–08
Derry v Peek; sub nom. Peek v Derry (1889) L.R. 14 App. Cas. 337; (1889) 5 T.L.R.
  625, HL 4–66, 10–12
Dick v Falkirk Burgh, 1976 S.C. (H.L.) 1; 1976 S.L.T. 21, HL 1–41
Digby Brown & Co v Lyall, 1995 S.L.T. 932, OH 9–37
Dixon v Bovill (1856) 3 Macq. (HL) 1 18–07
D'Jan of London Ltd, Re; sub nom. Copp v D'Jan [1993] B.C.C. 646; [1994] 1
  B.C.L.C. 561, Ch D (Companies Ct) 16–33
Donoghue v Stevenson; sub nom. McAlister v Stevenson [1932] A.C. 562; 1932 S.C.
  (H.L.) 31, HL 1–36, 6–03, 10–15, 10–26, 10–37
Drew v Drew (1870) 9M 163 1–51
Drummond v Muirhead & Smith (1900) 7 S.L.T. 401, IH (2 Div) 9–35
Dubai Aluminium Co Ltd v Salaam; Dubai Aluminium Co Ltd v Amhurst; Dubai
  Aluminium Co Ltd v Amhurst Brown Martin & Nicholson [2002] UKHL 48;
  [2003] 2 A.C. 366; [2002] 3 W.L.R. 1913, HL 15–05, 15–11
Duncan v MFV Marigold PD 145 [2006] CSOH 128; 2006 S.L.T. 975, OH 15–08
Dundee General Hospitals Board of Management v Bell's Trustees; sub nom.
  Dundee General Hospitals v Walker [1952] 1 All E.R. 896; 1952 S.C. (H.L.) 78,
  HL 13–29
Dunlop v Higgins, 9 E.R. 805; (1848) 1 H.L. Cas. 381, QB 4–26
Dunlop Pneumatic Tyre Co Ltd v New Garage & Motor Co Ltd [1915] A.C. 79, HL   4–94
Duomatic Ltd, Re [1969] 2 Ch. 365; [1969] 2 W.L.R. 114, Ch D 16–43
Dynamco Ltd v Holland & Hannen & Cubitts (Scotland) Ltd; Dynamco v James
  Harrison & Co (Builders), 1971 S.C. 257; 1972 S.L.T. 38, IH (1 Div) 10–26
Earl of Cawdor, Petitioner [2006] CSOH 141; 2006 S.L.T. 1070; 2006 G.W.D. 30–
  662, OH 13–26
Earl of Orkney v Vinfra (1606) Mor. 16481 4–56
East Riding of Yorkshire Council v Gibson; sub nom. Gibson v East Riding of
  Yorkshire DC [2000] 3 C.M.L.R. 329; [2000] I.C.R. 890, CA (Civ Div) 8–03
Eastern Distributors v Goldring [1957] 2 Q.B. 600; [1957] 3 W.L.R. 237; [1957] 2 All
  E.R. 525, CA 5–11
Edinburgh & Dalkeith Railway v Wauchope, 8 E.R. 279; (1842) 8 Cl. & F. 710, HL   1–22
Edwards v Halliwell [1950] 2 All E.R. 1064; [1950] W.N. 537, CA 16–64
Entores Ltd v Miles Far East Corp; sub nom. Newcomb v De Roos [1955] 2 Q.B.
  327; [1955] 3 W.L.R. 48, CA 4–25
Erven Warnink BV v J Townend & Sons (Hull) Ltd (No.1) [1979] A.C. 731; [1979] 3
  W.L.R. 68, HL 10–13, 12–06
Esso Petroleum Co Ltd v Mardon [1976] Q.B. 801; [1976] 2 W.L.R. 583; [1976] 2 All
  E.R. 5; [1976] 2 Lloyd's Rep. 305; 2 B.L.R. 82; (1976) 120 S.J. 131, CA (Civ
  Div) 4–67
Express & Echo Publications Ltd v Tanton [1999] I.C.R. 693; [1999] I.R.L.R. 367;
  (1999) 96(14) L.S.G. 31, CA (Civ Div) 8–04

Fagan v Commissioner of Police of the Metropolis[1969] 1 Q.B. 439; [1968] 3 W.L.R.
1120, DC 3–06
Fairchild v Glenhaven Funeral Services Ltd (t/a GH Dovener & Son); Pendleton v
Stone & Webster Engineering Ltd; Dyson v Leeds City Council (No.2); Mat-
thews v Associated Portland Cement Manufacturers (1978) Ltd; Fox v Spousal
(Midlands) Ltd; Babcock International Ltd v National Grid Co Plc; Matthews
v British Uralite Plc [2002] UKHL 22; [2003] 1 A.C. 32; [2002] 3 W.L.R. 89,
HL 10–26
Fairlie v Carruthers, 1996 S.L.T. (Sh Ct) 56, Sh Ct (Lothian) 10–38
Farley v Skinner (No.2); sub nom. Skinner v Farley [2001] UKHL 49; [2002] 2 A.C.
732; [2001] 3 W.L.R. 899, HL 4–90
Fearn v Gordon and Craig (1893) 20 R. 352 9–24
Fernie v Robertson (1871) 9 M 437 9–16
Ferrier v Dods (1865) 3 M. 561 .... 9–38, 9–39
Findlay (Liquidator of Scottish Workmen's Assurance Co Ltd) v Waddell, 1910 S.C.
670; 1910 1 S.L.T. 315, IH (1 Div) 9–35
Finnie v Glasgow and South West Railway Co (1857) 20 D. (HL) 2 4–95
Fisher v Bell [1961] 1 Q.B. 394; [1960] 3 W.L.R. 919; [1960] 3 All E.R. 731, DC ... 4–17
Fletcher v Budgen [1974] 1 W.L.R. 1056; [1974] 2 All E.R. 1243; (1974) 59 Cr. App.
R. 234, DC 6–38
Flockhart's Trustees v Bourlet, 1934 S.N. 23 13–21
Forbes v Forbes Trustees (No.2), 1957 S.C. 325; 1957 S.L.T. 346, OH 4–58
Forman v Burns (1853) 15 D. 362 13–32
Forsyth v Royal Bank of Scotland Plc, 2000 S.L.T. 1295; 2000 S.C.L.R. 61, OH ... 19–11
Fortune v Young, 1918 S.C. 1; 1917 2 S.L.T. 150, IH (2 Div) 15–05, 19–09
Forward Trust v Hornby, 1995 S.C.L.R. 574 6–29
Foss v Harbottle, 67 E.R. 189; (1843) 2 Hare 461, Ct of Chancery 16–64
Fowler (Robert) v O'Brien, 1994 S.C.C.R. 112, HCJ Appeal 3–22
Francovich v Italy (C6/90); Bonifacti v Italy (C9/90) [1991] E.C.R. I-5357; [1993] 2
C.M.L.R. 66 1–20
Fraser v Rose (1849) 11 D. 1466 13–20
Frost v Aylesbury Dairy Co Ltd [1905] 1 K.B. 608, CA 5–21
Galbraith and Moorhead v Arethusa Ship Co Ltd (1896) 23 R. 1011 9–42
Gallemos Ltd (In Receivership) v Barratt Falkirk Ltd, 1989 S.C. 239; 1990 S.L.T. 98,
IH (Ex Div) 19–29
Gammon Ltd v Att.-Gen. of Hong Kong [1985] A.C. 1 3–15
General Accident Fire & Life Assurance Corp v Hunter; sub nom.: Hunter v General
Accident Fire & Life Assurance Corp Ltd; Hunter v General Accident Corp
[1909] A.C. 404; 1909 S.C. (H.L.) 30; 1909 2 S.L.T. 99, HL 4–18
Gibb v Cunningham & Robertson (A Firm), 1925 S.L.T. 608, OH 9–38
Gibbons v Associated British Ports [1985] I.R.L.R. 376, QBD 8–10
Gibson v Orr; sub nom. Gibson v Chief Constable of Strathclyde, 1999 S.C. 420;
1999 S.C.L.R. 661, OH 10–15
Gilford Motor Co Ltd v Horne [1933] Ch. 935, CA 16–06
Gilmour v Clark (1853) 15 D. 478 9–24
Gilmour v McGlennan, 1993 S.C.C.R. 837, HCJ Appeal 3–06
Glasgow & South Western Railway Co v Boyd & Forrest (A Firm) (No.3); sub nom.
Boyd & Forrest (A Firm) v Glasgow & South Western Railway Co (No.3)
[1915] A.C. 526; 1915 S.C. (H.L.) 20; 1915 1 S.L.T. 114, HL 4–49
Glasgow Corp v Central Land Board, 1956 S.C. (H.L.) 1; 1956 S.L.T. 41, HL 1–41
Glasgow Corp v Muir; sub nom. Muir v Glasgow Corp [1943] A.C. 448; [1943] 2 All
E.R. 44, HL 10–19
Godley v Perry [1960] 1 W.L.R. 9; [1960] 1 All E.R. 36, QBD 5–22, 5–28
Goodall v Bilsland; Cassidy v Bilsland; McLean v Bilsland, 1909 S.C. 1152; 1909 1
S.L.T. 376, IH (1 Div) 9–15
Gordon v Campbell (1842) 1 Bell 428 13–52
Gordon's Trustees v Eglinton (1851) 13 D. 1381 13–26
Goulding v James [1997] 2 All E.R. 239, CA (Civ Div) 13–55
Grace v Biagoli [2005] EWCA Civ 122; [2006] 2 B.C.L.C. 70 16–67

Graham & Co v United Turkey Red Co Ltd, 1922 S.C. 533; 1922 S.L.T. 406, IH (2
    Div) 9–24
Grant (Neil Buchan) v Allan, 1987 J.C. 71; 1988 S.L.T. 11; 1987 S.C.C.R. 402, HCJ   3–22
Grant's Trustees v Grant (1898) 25 R. 929 13–20
Great Western Railway Co v London & County Banking Co Ltd [1901] A.C. 414,
    HL 18–20
Griffiths v Dalton [1940] 2 K.B. 264, KBD 18–19
Griffiths v Peter Conway Ltd [1939] 1 All E.R. 685, CA 5–22
HD Pochin & Co v Robinows & Marjoribanks (1869) 7 M. 622 19–27
Hamilton Finance Co v Coverley Westray Walbaum & Tosetti and Portland Finance
    Co [1969] 1 Lloyd's Rep. 53, QBD (Comm) 18–15
Hamilton v Main (1823) 2 S. 356 4–72
Hamilton v Spottiswoode, 154 E.R. 1182; (1849) 4 Ex. 200, Ex Ct 18–07
Hamilton v Wright (1842) 1 Bell 574 13–40
Hardie v Morison (1899) 7 S.L.T. 42, OH 13–15
Harlingdon and Leinster Enterprises Ltd v Christopher Hull Fine Art Ltd [1991] 1
    Q.B. 564; [1990] 3 W.L.R. 13; [1990] 1 All E.R. 737, CA (Civ Div) 5–20
Harries v Church Commissioners for England; sub nom. Lord Bishop of Oxford v
    Church Commissioners of England [1992] 1 W.L.R. 1241; [1993] 2 All E.R. 300,
    Ch D 13–34
Hartley v Hyams [1920] 3 K.B. 475 5–18
Hay Memorial Judicial Factor v Hay's Trustees; sub nom. Hay v Murdoch; Hay's
    Judicial Factor v Hay's Trustees, 1952 S.C. (H.L.) 29; 1952 S.L.T. 198, HL ... 13–57
Hay v Binny (1861) 23 D. 594 13–31
Hayman & Son v McLintock; sub nom. Hayman & Son v M'lintock & Others, 1907
    S.C. 936; (1907) 15 S.L.T. 63, IH (1 Div) 19–27
Hedley Byrne & Co Ltd v Heller & Partners Ltd [1964] A.C. 465; [1963] 3 W.L.R.
    101, HL 1–38, 10–26
Henderson v Henderson's Trustees (1900) 2 F. 1295 13–51
Henderson v Merrett Syndicates Ltd (No.1); Hallam-Eames v Merrett Syndicates
    Ltd; Hughes v Merrett Syndicates Ltd; Feltrim Underwriting Agencies Ltd v
    Arbuthnott; Deeny v Gooda Walker Ltd (Duty of Care); sub nom. Gooda
    Walker Ltd v Deeny; McLarnon Deeney v Gooda Walker Ltd; Arbuthnott v
    Fagan [1995] 2 A.C. 145; [1994] 3 W.L.R. 761, HL 10–26, 10–35
Heritable Reversionary Co Ltd v Millar [1892] A.C. 598; (1892) 19 R. 43, HL 13–03
Hickman v Kent or Romney Marsh Sheepbreeders Association [1915] 1 Ch. 881, Ch
    D 16–10
High Table Ltd v Horst [1998] I.C.R. 409; [1997] I.R.L.R. 513, CA (Civ Div) 8–26
Highland Council v TGWU/UNISON, unreported, December 7, 2007 8–21
Hill v Chief Constable of West Yorkshire [1989] A.C. 53; [1988] 2 W.L.R. 1049, HL   10–17
Hodgkinson & Corby Ltd v Wards Mobility Services Ltd (No.1) [1994] 1 W.L.R.
    1564; [1995] F.S.R. 169, Ch D 12–05
Home v Pringle (1841) 2 Rob. 384 13–40
Horne v Whyte [2005] C.S.O.H. 115 4–57
Household Fire & Carriage Accident Insurance Co Ltd v Grant (1878–79) L.R. 4 Ex.
    D. 216, CA 4–26
Howard Smith Ltd v Ampol Petroleum Ltd [1974] A.C. 821; [1974] 2 W.L.R. 689, PC
    (Aus) 16–27
Hugh Stephenson & Sons Ltd v Carton Nagen Industrie AG; sub nom. Hugh Ste-
    venson & Sons Ltd v Cartonnagen-Industrie AG [1918] A.C. 239, HL 15–08
Hughes v Lord Advocate; sub nom. Hughes v Postmaster General [1963] A.C. 837;
    [1963] 2 W.L.R. 779, HL 10–16
Huisman v Soepboer, 1994 S.L.T. 682, OH 13–23
Hunter v Albancode plc, unreported, 1989 5–26
Hunter v Hanley, 1955 S.C. 200; 1955 S.L.T. 213; [1955–95] P.N.L.R. 1, IH (1 Div)   10–35
Huntingdon Copper and Sulphur Co Ltd v Henderson (1877) 4 R. 294 9–29
Hutton v Bulloch (1873–74) L.R. 9 Q.B. 572, Ex Chamber 9–39
Iceland Frozen Foods Ltd v Jones [1983] I.C.R. 17; [1982] I.R.L.R. 439; (1982) 79
    L.S.G. 1257, EAT 8–23

Industrial Development Consultants Ltd v Cooley [1972] 1 W.L.R. 443; [1972] 2 All
E.R. 162, Assizes (Birmingham) 16–30
Inglis v Inglis, 1983 S.C. 8; 1983 S.L.T. 437, IH (2 Div) 13–40
Ingmar GB Ltd v Eaton Leonard Technologies Inc (C381/98) [2001] All E.R. (EC)
57; [2001] 1 All E.R. (Comm) 329, ECJ (5th Chamber) 9–51
Inland Revenue Commissioners v Crossman; Inland Revenue Commissioners v
Mann; sub nom. Crossman, Re; Paulin, Re [1937] A.C. 26, HL 16–49
International Sponge Importers Ltd v Andrew Watt & Sons [1911] A.C. 279; 1911
S.C. (H.L.) 57; 1911 1 S.L.T. 414, HL 9–22
Ireland v Livingston (1871–72) L.R. 5 H.L. 395, HL 9–24
Irvine v Talksport [2002] F.S.R. 943 12–06
Item Software (UK) Ltd v Fassihi; sub nom. Fassihi v Item Software (UK) Ltd
[2004] EWCA Civ 1244; [2004] B.C.C. 994; [2005] 2 B.C.L.C. 91, CA (Civ Div) 16–25
James v Greenwich LBC [2007] I.R.L.R. 168; [2007] I.C.R. 577, EAT 8–06
Jamieson (Brian) v HM Advocate (No.1), 1994 J.C. 88; 1994 S.L.T. 537; 1994
S.C.C.R. 181, HCJ 3–14
Jarrett v Barclays Bank Plc; Jones v First National Bank Plc; First National Bank Plc
v Peacock [1999] Q.B. 1; [1997] 3 W.L.R. 654, CA (Civ Div) 6–29
Jeffrey (William) (1842) 1 Broun. 337 3–26
Jessop v Stevenson (Stewart), 1988 J.C. 17; 1988 S.L.T. 223, HCJ 1–46
Jewson Ltd v Boyhan; sub nom. Jewsons Ltd v Boykan; Jewson Ltd v Kelly [2003]
EWCA Civ 1030; [2004] 1 Lloyd's Rep. 505; [2004] 1 C.L.C. 87, CA (Civ Div) 5–22
John D Hope & Co v Glendinning; sub nom. Glendinning v Hope & Co; Glendin-
ning v John D Hope & Co [1911] A.C. 419; 1911 S.C. (H.L.) 73; 1911 2 S.L.T.
161, HL 9–35
Junior Books Ltd v Veitchi Co Ltd [1983] 1 A.C. 520; [1982] 3 W.L.R. 477, HL 10–26
Kay's Tutor v Ayrshire and Arran Health Board [1987] 2 All E.R. 417; 1987 S.C.
(H.L.) 145, HL 10–35
Keighley Maxsted & Co v Durant (t/a Bryan Durant & Co); sub nom. Durant & Co
v Roberts [1901] A.C. 240, HL 9–15
Kelner v Baxter (1866–67) L.R. 2 C.P. 174, CCP 9–15
Kennedy v Glass (1890) 17 R. 1085 9–33
Ker v City of Glasgow Bank (1879) 6 R. (HL) 52 13–25
Kerr's Trustees v Inland Revenue Commissioners; sub nom. Kerr's Trustees v Lord
Advocate, 1974 S.C. 115; 1974 S.L.T. 193,IH (2 Div) 13–13
Khaliq (Raja Abdul) v HM Advocate; Ahmed (Raja Ibrar) v HM Advocate, 1984
J.C. 23; 1984 S.L.T. 137, HCJ 1–53
Kimber Coal Co Ltd v Stone & Rolfe Ltd; sub nom. Owners of the Allie v Kimber
Coal Co Ltd; Stone & Rolfe Ltd v Kimber Coal Co Ltd [1926] A.C. 414; (1926)
24 Ll. L. Rep. 429, HL 9–37
King v T Tunnock Ltd, 2000 S.C. 424; 2000 S.L.T. 744, IH (Ex Div) 9–51
Kirby v National Coal Board, 1958 S.C. 514; 1959 S.L.T. 7, IH (1 Div) 10–34
Kirkham v Attenborough; Kirkham v Gill [1897] 1 Q.B. 201, CA 5–08
Krell v Henry [1903] 2 K.B. 740, CA 4–106
Kwik-Fit (GB) Ltd v Lineham [1992] I.C.R. 183; [1992] I.R.L.R. 156; (1992) 89(5)
L.S.G. 31, EAT 8–20
Lamarra v Capital Bank Plc, 2006 S.L.T. 1053; 2006 G.W.D. 33–686; 2007 S.C. 95,
IH (Ex Div) 4–82, 5–22
Lambert v Lewis; sub nom. Lexmead (Basingstoke) Ltd v Lewis [1982] A.C. 225;
[1981] 2 W.L.R. 713; [1981] 1 All E.R. 1185, HL 5–22
Lamond v Glasgow Corp, 1968 S.L.T. 291, OH 10–16
Lamont Nisbet & Co v Hamilton, 1907 S.C. 628 9–38
Latimer v AEC Ltd [1953] A.C. 643; [1953] 3 W.L.R. 259, HL 10–22
Latta v Herron (1967) S.C.C.R. Supp. 18 3–12
Leggat Bros v Gray; sub nom. Leggat Bros v Moss Empires Ltd, 1908 S.C. 67; (1907)
15 S.L.T.533, IH (1 Div) 4–98
Leitch v Leitch, 1927 S.C. 823; 1927 S.L.T. 575, IH (1 Div) 13–38
Levy v Abercorris Slate and Slab Co (1888) L.R. 37 Ch. D. 260, Ch D 16–55
Lindsay's Executor v Forsyth, 1940 S.C. 568; 1940 S.L.T. 448, IH (2 Div) 13–21

Lister v Hesley Hall Ltd [2001] UKHL 22; [2002] 1 A.C. 215; [2001] 2 W.L.R. 1311,
    HL 10–34
Littlejohn v Hadwen (1822) 20 S.L.R. 5 4–10
Liverpool Victoria Friendly Society v Houston (1900) 3 F. 42 9–28
Lloyd's Executors v Wright (1870) 7 S.L.R. 216 9–07
Lobnitz, Petitioner, 1966 S.L.T. (Notes) 81, IH (1 Div) 13–55
Lonsdale (t/a Lonsdale Agencies) v Howard & Hallam Ltd [2007] UKHL 32; [2007] 1
    W.L.R. 2055; [2007] 4 All E.R. 1, HL 9–51
Lord Advocate's Reference (No.1 of 1994) (Drugs: Supplying), 1996 J.C. 76; 1995
    S.L.T. 248, HCJ Appeal 3–07
Lord Elphinstone v Monkland Iron & Coal Co Ltd; sub nom. Lord Elphinstone v
    Markland Iron & Coal Co Ltd (1886) L.R. 11 App. Cas. 332, HL 4–94
Lothian v Jenolite Ltd, 1969 S.C. 111; 1970 S.L.T. 31, IH (2 Div) 9–27, 9–29
Lucena v Craufurd (1806) 2 Bos & P.N.R. 269 4–33
Lumsden v Buchanan (1865) 3 M. (HL) 89 13–52
Lutea Trustees Ltd v Orbis Trustees Guernsey Ltd, 1997 S.C. 255; 1998 S.L.T. 471,
    IH (2 Div) 13–50
Lynn v Scott, 1949 S.C. 442; 1949 S.L.T. 399 5–22
McCaig's Trustees v Oban Magistrates; sub nom. McCaig's Trustees v Kirk Session
    of United Free Church of Lismore, 1915 S.C. 426; 1915 1 S.L.T. 152, IH (2
    Div) 13–21
Macaura v Northern Assurance Co Ltd [1925] A.C. 619, HL 4–33, 16–06
McCosh v Moore (1905) 8 F. 31 20–13
McCrie's Trustees, 1927 S.C. 556 13–59
McCulloch v Wallace (1846) 9 D. 32 13–27
McCutcheon v David MacBrayne Ltd [1964] 1 W.L.R. 125; [1964] 1 All E.R. 430,
    HL 4–38, 4–39
McDonald v Provan (Of Scotland Street) Ltd, 1960 S.L.T. 231, OH 5–09
MacDonald (Gordon) v HM Advocate (No.2), 1996 S.L.T. 723; 1995 S.C.C.R. 663,
    HCJ Appeal 3–24
MacFarlane v Dumbarton Steamboat Co Ltd (1899) 7 S.L.T. 75, IH (2 Div) 4–76
MacFarlane v Glasgow City Council [2001] I.R.L.R. 7, EAT 8–04
McGlone v British Railways Board, 1966 S.C. 1; 1966 S.L.T. 2, HL 10–39
Macintosh v HM Advocate (Sentencing), 1999 G.W.D. 13–588, HCJ Appeal 1–44
Mackenna v City & Suburban Dairies; Mackenna v Scottish Farmers Dairy Co
    (Glasgow) Ltd; sub nom. City & Suburban Dairies v Mackenna; Scottish
    Farmers Dairy Co (Glasgow) v Mackenna, 1918 J.C. 105; 1918 2 S.L.T. 155,
    HCJ 3–17
Mackenzie v Cluny Hill Hydropathic Co Ltd, 1908 S.C. 200; (1907) 15 S.L.T. 518, IH
    (2 Div) 9–14
Mackenzie (Donald Murdo) v Skeen, 1971 J.C. 43; 1972 S.L.T. 15; [1973] Crim. L.R.
    767, HCJ 3–10, 3–24
Mackersy's Executors v St Giles Cathedral Managing Board; sub nom. Mackersy's
    Executors v Managing Board of St Giles Cathedral (1904) 12 S.L.T. 391, IH (2
    Div) 9–33
McKew v Holland & Hannen & Cubitts (Scotland) Ltd [1969] 3 All E.R. 1621; 1970
    S.C. (H.L.) 20, HL 10–27
McKillen v Barclay Curle & Co Ltd, 1967 S.L.T. 41, IH (1 Div) 10–28
Macleod v Kerr, 1965 S.C. 253; 1965 S.L.T. 358, IH (1 Div) 5–13
MacPhail v Clark, 1983 S.L.T. (Sh. Ct.) 37; 1982 S.C.C.R. 395, Sh Ct (Tayside) ... 3–06
McPherson's Trustees v Watt (1877) 5 R. (HL) 9 9–29
Macpherson v Macpherson's CB (1894) 21 R. 386 13–11
McWilliams v Sir William Arrol & Co Ltd [1962] 1 W.L.R. 295; [1962] 1 All E.R.
    623, HL 10–27
Malik v Bank of Credit and Commerce International SA (In Liquidation); sub nom.
    BCCI SA, Re; Mahmud v Bank of Credit and Commerce International SA (In
    Liquidation) [1998] A.C. 20; [1997] 3 W.L.R. 95, HL 8–14
Mann v D'Arcy [1968] 1 W.L.R. 893; [1968] 2 All E.R. 172; (1968) 112 S.J. 310, Ch
    D 15–05
Marshall & Co v Pennycock, 1908 S.C. 276 19–08

Marshall Wilson Dean and Turnbull v Feymac Properties Ltd , 1996 G.W.D. 22–
1247 9–33
Martin v Bell Ingram, 1986 S.C. 208; 1986 S.L.T. 575, IH (2 Div) 10–26
Martin v Edinburgh DC, 1988 S.L.T. 329; 1988 S.C.L.R. 90, OH 13–35
Martin v Ferguson's Trustees (1892) 19 R. 474 13–25
Mason v Coal Authority; Flaherty v Coal Authority [2001] N.P.C. 58, QBD 4–26
Mathieson Gee (Ayrshire) Ltd v Quigley, 1952 S.C. (H.L.) 38; 1952 S.L.T. 239,
HL 4–13, 4–21, 4–64
Matthews v Auld & Guild (1873) 1 R. 1224 9–38
Meier & Co v Kuchenmeister (1881) 8 R. 642 9–39
Menzies v Menzies (1893) 20 R. (HL) 108 4–64
Millar's Trustees v Polson (1897) 5 S.L.T. 94, IH (1 Div) 13–47
Miller's Trustees v Miller (1890) 18 R. 301, IH (2 Div) 13–63
Monkland v Jack Barclay Ltd [1951] 2 K.B. 252; [1951] 1 All E.R. 714, CA 5–17
Montgomery v Johnson Underwood Ltd; sub nom. Johnson Underwood Ltd v
Montgomery [2001] EWCA Civ 318; [2001] I.C.R. 819; [2001] I.R.L.R. 269;
[2001] Emp. L.R. 405; (2001) 98(20) L.S.G. 40, CA (Civ Div) 8–06
Moore v Patterson (1881) 9R 337 1–53
Morrison v Statter (1885) 12 R. 1152 9–05
Mortons Trustees v The Aged Christian Friends Society of Scotland (1899) 2 F.82 4–96
Muirhead and Turnbull v Dickson (1905) 7 F. 606 4–13
Mulvein v Murray, 1908 S.C. 528; (1908) 15 S.L.T. 807, IH (2 Div) 4–76
Murray v Cameron, 1969 S.L.T. (Notes) 76, OH 13–38
Murray v Crawford; sub nom. Burgess Trustees v Crawford, 1912 S.C. 387; 1912 1
S.L.T. 153, IH (1 Div) 13–58
Murray v Foyle Meats Ltd [2000] 1 A.C. 51; [1999] 3 W.L.R. 356, HL (NI) 8–26
NV Algemene Transport- en Expeditie Onderneming van Gend en Loos v Neder-
landse Administratie der Belastingen (26/62) [1963] E.C.R. 1; [1963] C.M.L.R.
105, ECJ 1–20
National Westminster Bank Plc v Inland Revenue Commissioners; Barclays Bank Plc
v Inland Revenue Commissioners [1995] 1 A.C. 119; [1994] 3 W.L.R. 159,
HL 16–52
Neilson v Mossend Iron Co (1885) 12 R. 499 13–27
Neilson v Skinner & Co (1890) 17 R. 1243 9–27
Nesbitt v Secretary of State for Trade and Industry [2007] I.R.L.R. 847, EAT 8–07
Neville v C&A Modes Ltd, 1945 S.C. 175; 1945 S.L.T. 189, IH (1 Div) 9–14
Nordenfelt v Maxim Nordenfelt Guns & Ammunition Co Ltd; sub nom. Maxim
Nordenfelt Guns & Ammunition Co v Nordenfelt [1894] A.C. 535, HL 4–76
North West Transportation Co Ltd v Beatty (1887) L.R. 12 App. Cas. 589, PC
(Can) 16–10
Northern Counties Securities, Ltd v Jackson & Steeple, Ltd [1974] 1 W.L.R. 1133;
[1974] 2 All E.R. 625; (1974) 118 S.J. 498, Ch D 16–10
Nouillan v Nouillan's Executors, 1991 S.L.T. 270, OH 13–38
Ocular Sciences Ltd v Aspect Vision Care Ltd (No.2) [1997] R.P.C. 289; (1997) 20(3)
I.P.D. 20022, Ch D (Patents Ct) 12–18
Office of Fair Trading v Lloyds TSB Bank Plc [2007] UKHL 48; [2007] 3 W.L.R. 733;
[2008] 1 All E.R. 205, HL 6–29
Olley v Marlborough Court Ltd [1949] 1 K.B. 532; [1949] 1 All E.R. 127, CA 4–39
O'Neill v Phillips; sub nom. Company (No.000709 of 1992), Re; Pectel Ltd, Re [1999]
1 W.L.R. 1092; [1999] 2 All E.R. 961, HL 16–67
Overseas Tankship (UK) Ltd v Morts Dock & Engineering Co (The Wagon Mound);
sub nom. Morts Dock & Engineering Co v Overseas Tankship (UK) Ltd [1961]
A.C. 388; [1961] 2 W.L.R. 126, PC (Aus) 10–28
Paal Wilson & Co A/S v Partenreederei Hannah Blumenthal (The Hannah Blu-
menthal) [1983] 1 A.C. 854; [1982] 3 W.L.R. 1149; [1983] 1 All E.R. 34, HL .. 4–107
Palazzo (Angelo) v Copeland, 1976 J.C. 52, HCJ 3–10
Paris v Stepney BC [1951] A.C. 367; [1951] 1 All E.R. 42, HL 10–21, 10–22
Parker v South Eastern Railway Co; Gabell v South Eastern Railway Co (1876–77)
L.R. 2 C.P.D. 416, CA 4–39
Paterson v Bonar (1844) 6 D. 987 19–12

Paton (Alexander Gorrie) v HM Advocate, 1936 J.C. 19; 1936 S.L.T. 298, HCJ
    Appeal 3–11
Paton (James); sub nom. HM Advocate v Paton (1858) 3 Irvine 208, HCJ Appeal   3–24
People v Fowler, 174 Pac 892 (1918) 3–07
Perrins v Bellamy [1899] 1 Ch. 797, CA 13–51
Peskin v Anderson [2001] B.C.C. 874; [2001] 1 B.C.L.C. 372, CA (Civ Div) 16–26
Petrie v Earl of Airlie (1834) 13 S. 68 4–10
Petrofina (Great Britain) Ltd v Martin [1966] Ch. 146; [1966] 2 W.L.R. 318, CA 4–77
Philip Head and Sons Ltd v Showfronts [1970] 1 Lloyds Rep. 140 5–08
Piper v JRI (Manufacturing) Ltd [2006] EWCA Civ 1344; (2006) 92 B.M.L.R. 141;
    (2006) 150 S.J.L.B. 1391, CA (Civ Div) 10–37
Polemis and Furness Withy & Co Ltd, Re; sub nom. Polemis v Furness Withy & Co
    [1921] 3 K.B. 560; (1921) 8 Ll. L. Rep. 351, CA 10–28
Polkey v AE Dayton Services Ltd; sub nom. Polkey v Edmund Walker (Holdings)
    Ltd [1988] A.C. 344; [1987] 3 W.L.R. 1153, HL 8–23
Pollock v Burns (1875) 2 R. 497 4–53
Pollok-Morris (Margaret), Petitioners, 1969 S.L.T. (Notes) 60, IH (1 Div) 13–55
Powdrill v Murrayhead Ltd, 1997 S.L.T. 1223, OH 9–35
Prain & Sons Ltd, Petitioners, 1947 S.C. 325; 1947 S.L.T. 289, IH (1 Div) 16–41
Presslie v Cochrane McGregor Group Ltd (No.1), 1996 S.C. 289; 1996 S.L.T. 988,
    IH (2 Div) 20–10
Prosoft Resources Ltd v Griffiths, 1999 S.L.T. 1255; 2000 S.C.L.R. 157, OH 4–76
Prudential Assurance Co Ltd v Newman Industries Ltd (No.2) [1982] Ch. 204; [1982]
    2 W.L.R. 31, CA (Civ Div) 16–64
Purcell Meats (Scotland) Ltd v McLeod, 1987 S.L.T. 528; 1986 S.C.C.R. 672, HCJ
    Appeal 3–18
Quinn v Leathem [1901] A.C. 495, HL (UK-Irl) 10–11
R. v Bow Street Metropolitan Stipendiary Magistrate Ex p. United States (No.2); R.
    v Governor of Brixton Prison Ex p. Allison; sub nom. R. v Bow Street
    Magistrates Court Ex p. Allison (No.2); Allison, Re [2000] 2 A.C. 216; [1999] 3
    W.L.R. 620, HL 3–33
R. v Gibbins (Walter); R. v Proctor (Edith Rose) (1919) 13 Cr. App. R. 134, CCA   3–06
R. v Gould (John Arthur) [1968] 2 Q.B. 65; [1968] 2 W.L.R. 643, CA (Crim
    Div) 3–14
R. v Instan [1893] 1 Q.B. 450, Crown Cases Reserved 3–06
R. v Jordan (James Clinton) (1956) 40 Cr. App. R. 152, CCA 3–07
R. v Local Commissioner for Administration for the North and East Area of Eng-
    land Ex p. Bradford City Council [1979] Q.B. 287; [1979] 2 W.L.R. 1, CA (Civ
    Div) 2–51
R. v Smith (Thomas Joseph) [1959] 2 Q.B. 35; [1959] 2 W.L.R. 623, CMAC 3–07
RHM Bakeries (Scotland) Ltd v Strathclyde RC, 1985 S.C. (H.L.) 17; 1985 S.L.T.
    214, HL 10–40
Rae v Donnelly, 1982 S.C.C.R. 148, HCJ Appeal 3–26
Rae v Meek; sub nom. Raes v Meek (1889) L.R. 14 App. Cas. 558; (1889) 16 R.
    (H.L.) 31, HL 13–30
Ready Mixed Concrete (South East) Ltd v Minister of Pensions and National
    Insurance; Minister for Social Security v Greenham Ready Mixed Concrete
    Ltd; Minister for Social Security v Ready Mixed Concrete (South East) Ltd
    [1968] 2 Q.B. 497; [1968] 2 W.L.R. 775; [1968] 1 All E.R. 433; 4 K.I.R. 132;
    (1967) 112 S.J. 14, QBD 8–04, 10–34
Reckitt & Colman Products Ltd v Borden Inc (No.3); sub nom. Jif Lemon case
    [1990] 1 W.L.R. 491; [1990] 1 All E.R. 873, HL 12–04, 12–07
Retail Parks Investments Ltd v Royal Bank of Scotland Plc (No.2), 1996 S.C. 227;
    1996 S.L.T. 669, IH (Ex Div) 11–60
Rigby v Ferodo Ltd [1988] I.C.R. 29; [1987] I.R.L.R. 516, HL 8–17
Roberston v Foulds (1860) 22 D. 714 9–26
Robert Barry & Co v Doyle, 1998 S.L.T. 1238; 1998 G.W.D. 6–262, OH 9–13
Robertson v Robertson's Trustees (1892) 19 R. 849 13–61
Rookes v Barnard (No.1) [1964] A.C. 1129; [1964] 2 W.L.R. 269, HL 10–10
Rose & Frank Co v JR Crompton & Bros Ltd; Rose & Frank Co v Brittains Ltd; sub

nom. Rose & Frank & Co v Crompton & Bros Ltd & Brittains Ltd [1925] A.C.
445; (1924) 20 Ll. L. Rep. 249, HL 4–09
Ross v Ross (1896) 23 R. (HL) 67 13–38
Roy v MR Pearlman Ltd, 1999 S.C. 459; 2000 S.L.T. 727; 1999 S.C.L.R. 803; [1999]
2 C.M.L.R. 1155; 1999 G.W.D. 11–486, OH 9–45
Royal Bank of Scotland Ltd v Brown, 1982 S.C. 89; 1983 S.L.T. 122, IH (2 Div) .. 19–13
Royal Bank of Scotland Plc v Bannerman Johnstone Maclay [2005] CSIH 39; 2005 1
S.C. 437; 2005 S.L.T. 579; [2006] B.C.C. 148, IH (2 Div) 1–36
Royal Bank of Scotland plc v Etridge (No.2) [2002] 2 A.C. 773 .... 4–58, 19–11
Royal Bank of Scotland Plc v Wilson, 2004 S.C. 153; 2003 S.L.T. 910, IH (2 Div)   19–11
SCM (United Kingdom) Ltd v WJ Whittall & Son Ltd [1971] 1 Q.B. 337; [1970] 3
W.L.R. 694, CA (Civ Div) 10–26
SS State of California Co Ltd v Moore (1895) 22 R. 562 9–44
Salomon v Salomon & Co Ltd; Salomon & Co Ltd v Salomon; sub nom. Broderip v
Salomon [1897] A.C. 22, HL 9–11, 14–10, 16–05
Salvesen & Co v Rederi Aktiebolaget Nordstjernan (1905) 7 F. (HL) 101 9–30
Sanderson & Son v Armour & Co Ltd; sub nom. Sanderson & Son v Armour & Co
Ltd, 1922 S.C. (H.L.) 117; 1922 S.L.T. 285, HL 20–10
Sarris v Clarke, 1995 S.L.T. 44 13–40
Sawkins v Hyperion Records Ltd; sub nom. Hyperion Records Ltd v Sawkins [2005]
EWCA Civ 565; [2005] 1 W.L.R. 3281; [2005] 3 All E.R. 636, CA (Civ Div) .. 12–14
Sayers v Harlow Urban DC [1958] 1 W.L.R. 623; [1958] 2 All E.R. 342, CA 10–27, 10–31
Scott v National Trust for Places of Historic Interest or Natural Beauty [1998] 2 All
E.R. 705, Ch D 13–29
Scott v Occidental Petroleum (Caledonia) Ltd, 1990 S.C. 201; 1990 S.L.T. 882, IH (1
Div) 13–31
Scott's Hospital Trustees, Petitioners, 1913 S.C. 289; 1912 2 S.L.T. 443, IH (2 Div)   13–44
Secretary of State for Trade and Industry v Bottrill; sub nom. Bottrill v Secretary of
State for Trade and Industry [2000] 1 All E.R. 915; [1999] B.C.C. 177, CA (Civ
Div) 8–07
Sevenoaks Stationers (Retail) Ltd, Re [1991] Ch. 164; [1990] 3 W.L.R. 1165, CA (Civ
Div) 16–25
Sharp v Highland and Islands Fire Board, 2005 S.L.T. 855; 2005 S.C.L.R. 1049, OH   10–34
Sharp v Thomson; sub nom. Sharp v Woolwich Building Society; Sharp v Joint
Receivers of Albyn Construction Ltd, 1997 S.C. (H.L.) 66; 1997 S.L.T. 636,
HL 13–03, 19–22
Short v Treasury Commissioners [1948] A.C. 534; [1948] 2 All E.R. 509; 64 T.L.R.
400, HL 16–49
Sidaway v Board of Governors of the Bethlem Royal Hospital [1985] A.C. 871;
[1985] 2 W.L.R. 480, HL 10–6
Sidebotham v Kershaw Leese & Co Ltd [1920] 1 Ch. 154, CA 16–10
Simmons v British Steel Plc [2004] UKHL 20; 2004 S.C. (H.L.) 94; 2004 S.L.T. 595,
HL 10–28
Simpson v Kidstons, Watson, Turnbull & Co, 1913 1 S.L.T. 74, OH 9–30
Simpson v Miller (1923) 39 Sh Ct. Rep. 182 10–40
Skinner (Colin) v HM Advocate, 1994 S.C.C.R. 316, HCJ Appeal 3–34
Smart (William) v HM Advocate, 1975 J.C. 30; 1975 S.L.T. 65, HCJ 3–10
Smith v Bank of Scotland; Mumford v Bank of Scotland, 1997 S.C. (H.L.) 111; 1997
S.L.T. 1061; 1997 S.C.L.R. 765, HL 19–11
Smith v Croft (No.2) [1988] Ch. 114; [1987] 3 W.L.R. 405, Ch D 16–64
Smith (John) (1871) 2 Coup. 1 3–26
Spring v Guardian Assurance Plc [1995] 2 A.C. 296; [1994] 3 W.L.R. 354, HL 10–26
St Silas Church Vestry v St Silas Church Trustees; sub nom. Vestry of St Silas
Church v Trustees of St Silas Church, 1945 S.C. 110, IH (2 Div) 13–25
Steuart's Trustees v Hart (1875) 3 R. 192, IH (1 Div) 4–63
Stevenson v Rogers [1999] Q.B. 1028; [1999] 2 W.L.R. 1064, CA (Civ Div) 5–21
Stevenson & Sons v Duncan (1842) 5 D. 167 9–34
Stewart v Chalmers (1904) 12 S.L.T. 486, IH (1 Div) 13–26
Stewart v Stewart (1899) 1 F. 1158 4–76
Struthers v Dykes (1847) 9 D. 1437 19–06

Stuart & Co v Kennedy (1885) 13 R. 221 4–64
Sturrock v Rankin's Trustees (1875) 2 R. 850, IH (2 Div) 13–20
Sugden (Edward) v HM Advocate, 1934 J.C. 103; 1934 S.L.T. 465, HCJ 1–45
Suncorp Insurance and Finance v Milano Assicurazioni SpA [1993] 2 Lloyd's Rep.
    225, QBD (Comm) 9–15
Sutcliff v Thackrah [1974] A.C. 727 20–15
Sutherland v Barnes, unreported, October 8, 1997 15–08
Taylor, Petitioners, 1932 S.C. 1; 1932 S.L.T. 29, IH (2 Div) 13–25
Taylor v Caldwell (1863) 32 L.J. Q.B. 164 4–105
Taylor v Glasgow Corp, 1952 S.C. 440; 1952 S.L.T. 399, IH (2 Div) 4–39
Templeton v Ayr Burgh Council, 1910 2 S.L.T. 12, OH 13–22
Thacker v Hardy (1878–79) L.R. 4 Q.B.D. 685, CA 9–34
Thain v Anniesland Trade Centre, 1997 S.L.T. (Sh Ct) 102; 1997 S.C.L.R. 991; 1997
    G.W.D. 32–1654, Sh Pr 5–22
Thom's Executrix v Russel & Aitken, 1983 S.L.T. 335, OH 15–08
Thomson v Jones (1855) 18 D. 4–18
Thomson v London Midland and Scottish Railway Co [1930] 1 K.B. 41 4–39
Thomson v McLachlan's Trustees (1829) 7 S. 787 13–52
Tigana Ltd v Decoro Ltd [2003] EWHC 23 (QB); [2003] E.C.C. 23; [2003] Eu. L.R.
    189, QBD 9–51
Tinnevelly Sugar Refining Co Ltd v Mirrlees Watson & Yaryan Company Ltd; sub
    nom. Tinevelly Sugar Refining Co Ltd v Mirrlees Watson Yarvan Co Ltd
    (1894) 2 S.L.T. 149, IH (1 Div) 9–15
Titchener v British Railways Board [1983] 1 W.L.R. 1427; [1983] 3 All E.R. 770, HL 10–30
Tod's Trustees, Petitioners, 1999 S.L.T. 308; 1998 G.W.D. 5–254, IH (Ex Div) 13–43
Tomlinson v Congleton BC [2003] UKHL 47; [2004] 1 A.C. 46; [2003] 3 W.L.R. 705,
    HL 10–39
Torbat v Torbat's Trustees (1906) 14 S.L.T.830, OH 9–09
Trans Barvil Agencies (UK) Ltd v John S. Baird & Co Ltd, 1988 S.C. 222 9–27
Trevor v Whitworth (1887) L.R. 12 App. Cas. 409, HL 16–60
Trustees for the United Original Secession Congregation in Stranraer, Petitioners;
    sub nom. Stranraer Original Secession Congregation, Petitioners, 1923 S.C.
    722; 1923 S.L.T. 436, IH (1 Div) 13–59
Trustees of Carnegie Park Orphanage (1892) 19 R. 605 13–59
Tsakiroglou & Co Ltd v Noblee Thorl GmbH; Albert D Gaon & Co v Societe
    Interprofessionelle des Oleagineux Fluides Alimentaires [1962] A.C. 93; [1961] 2
    W.L.R. 633, HL 4–106
Turnock v Fortune, 1989 S.L.T. (Sh. Ct.) 32, Sh Pr 5–21
Tyler v Logan (1904) 12 S.L.T. 466, IH (2 Div) 9–31
Union Music Ltd v Watson; Arias Ltd v Blacknight Ltd [2003] EWCA Civ 180;
    [2004] B.C.C. 37; [2003] 1 B.C.L.C. 453, CA (Civ Div) 16–38
United Bank v Akhtar [1989] I.R.L.R. 507, EAT 8–14
United Dominions Trust Ltd v Taylor, 1980 S.L.T. (Sh. Ct.) 28, Sh Pr 6–29
United Wholesale Grocers Ltd v Sher, 1993 S.L.T. 284, OH 10–34
University of Aberdeen v Town Council of Aberdeen (1876) 3 R. 1087 13–40
Wade v Waldron, 1909 S.C 571 4–78
Walker v Walker; sub nom. Walker v Walker's Trustees, 1911 S.C. 163; (1910) 2
    S.L.T.306, IH (1 Div) 4–73
Watt v Hertfordshire CC [1954] 1 W.L.R. 835; [1954] 2 All E.R. 368, CA 10–23
Watt v Jamieson, 1954 S.C. 56; 1954 S.L.T. 56, OH 10–40
Waugh v James K Allan Ltd [1964] 2 Lloyd's Rep. 1; 1964 S.C. (H.L.) 102; 1964
    S.L.T. 269, HL 10–19
Webster v Dominick; sub nom. Procurator Fiscal, Dunoon v Dominick, 2005 1 J.C.
    65; 2003 S.L.T. 975, HCJ 1–45
Webster v Lord Advocate, 1985 S.C. 173; 1985 S.L.T. 361, IH (2 Div) 10–40, 11–30
Whistler v Forster (1863) 14 C.B. (NS) 248 18–12
White v Jones [1995] 2 A.C. 207; [1995] 2 W.L.R. 187, HL 10–35
White & Carter (Councils) Ltd v McGregor [1962] A.C. 413; [1962] 2 W.L.R. 17,
    HL 4–79, 4–92

William Morton & Co v Muir Bros & Co, 1907 S.C. 1211; (1907) 15 S.L.T.252, IH
(Ex Div) 4–41
William S Gordon & Co Ltd v Mrs Mary Thomson Partnership, 1985 S.L.T. 122, IH
(2 Div) 15–08
Wilson v Inverness Retail & Business Park Ltd, 2003 S.L.T. 301; 2003 G.W.D. 3–60,
OH 16–64
Wilson v Rickett Cockerell & Co Ltd [1954] 1 Q.B. 598; [1954] 2 W.L.R. 629, CA   5–21
Winans v Macrae (1885) 12 R. 1051 10–7
Wolf and Wolf v Forfar Potato Co, 1984 S.L.T. 100, IH (2 Div) 4–23
Woolfson v Strathclyde RC; sub nom. Woolfson v Glasgow Corp, 1978 S.C. (H.L.)
90; 1978 S.L.T. 159; (1979) 38 P. & C.R. 521, HL 16–06
Wormell v RHM Agricultural (East) Ltd [1987] 1 W.L.R. 1091; [1987] 3 All E.R. 75,
CA (Civ Div) 5–21
Wyse v Abbott (1881) 8 R. 983 13–28
X v Schering Health Care Ltd; sub nom. XYZ v Schering Health Care Ltd [2002]
EWHC 1420; (2003) 70 B.M.L.R. 88, QBD 10–37
Young v Clydesdale Bank (1889) 17 R. 231, IH (1 Div) 19–10

Table of Statutes

1449   Leases Act (c.6) 11–57
1707   Treaty of Union with Eng-
      land Act (6 Ann. c.7)
      Art.VIII 1–09
      Art.XIX 1–09
1856   Mercantile Law Amendment
      Act (19 & 20 Vict. c.97)
      s.9 19–13
1862   Companies Act (25 & 26
      Vict. c.89) ....
      s.16 16–49
1870   Coinage Act (33 & 34 Vict.)
      s.5 18–07
1876   Appellate Jurisdiction Act
      (39 & 40 Vict. c.59)
      s.6 2–21
1878   Innkeepers Act
      s.1 19–28
1882   Bills of Exchange Act (45 &
      46 Vict. c.61) 1–09, 18–01,
                      18–07, 18–12,
                      18–17, 18–23
      s.3(1) 18–07
      (4) 18–19
      s.4(1) 18–04
      s.8(1) 18–09
      (2) 18–08
      (4) 18–08
      s.20 18–07
      s.24 18–13
      s.27(1) 18–11
      (2) 18–11
      s.29(1) 18–12
      s.31 18–10
      (2) 18–08
      (3) 18–09
      s.34(1) 18–09
      (2) 18–09
      (4) 18–09
      s.35(2) 18–09
      s.36(2) 18–12
      (5) 18–12
      s.43(2) 18–13
      s.45(2) 18–19
      (3) 18–10
      s.46(1) 18–15
      s.47 18–13
      (2) 18–13
      s.48 18–13
      s.49(12) 18–13
      s.51(2) 18–13

      s.55 18–13
      s.58 18–13
      (1) 18–13
      (2) 18–13
      (3) 18–13
      s.64(1) 18–14
      s.69 18–16
      s.73 18–17
      s.74 18–15
      s.76(2) 18–20
      s.77 18–20
      s.78 18–20
      s.79(2) 18–22
      s.80 18–22
      s.81 18–20
      (1) 18–20
      s.81A 18–22
      (1) 18–20
      s.83(1) 18–23
      s.84 18–23
      s.89(3) 18–23
      s.90 18–12
1889   Factors Act (52 & 53 Vict.
      c.45) 9–06
      s.1(1) 9–06
      s.2(1) 5–12, 9–06
1890   Partnership Act (53 & 54
      Vict. c.39) 1–09, 9–10,
                14–06, 14–09, 14–11,
                14–12, 15–01, 15–05,
                      15–09, 15–10
      s.1 15–04
      (1) 14–06, 15–04
      (2) 15–04
      ss.1–4 .... 14–06, 15–01
      s.2(1) 15–04
      (2) 15–04
      (3) 15–04
      (a) 15–04
      (b) 15–04
      (c) 15–04
      (d) 15–04
      (e) 15–04
      s.4(2) 14–05, 15–04, 15–05
      s.5 .... 9–10, 9–14, 14–12,
                      15–05, 15–08
      ss.5–9 15–05
      ss.5–18 .... 14–06, 15–01, 15–05
      s.6 15–05
      s.8 15–05
      s.9 .... 14–08, 15–05

s.10 15–05
ss.10–13 15–05
s.11 15–05
s.12 14–08
s.14(1) 15–05
    (2) 15–05
ss.14–18 15–05
s.15 15–05
s.17 15–05
    (1) 15–05
    (2) 15–05
    (3) 15–05
s.19 15–07
ss.19–31 .... 14–06, 15–01
s.20 .... 14–06, 15–01, 15–06
    (1) 15–05
s.21 15–06
s.24 14–12
    (5) 14–08
ss.24–26 15–07
s.25 .... 14–10, 14–12, 15–07
s.26 15–07
s.27 .... 15–07, 15–08
s.28 15–07
s.29 15–07
s.32(a) 15–08
    (c) 15–07, 15–08
ss.32–44 .... 14–06, 15–01
s.33(1) 14–05, 15–08
    (2) 15–08
s.35 15–08
    (b) 15–08
    (c) 15–08
    (d) 15–08
    (e) 15–08
    (f) 15–08
s.36 .... 15–05, 15–08
    (1) 9–42
    (2) 15–05
s.37 15–08
s.39 15–08
s.40 15–08
s.41 15–08
s.42 15–08
s.43 15–08
s.44 15–08
s.47 15–08
1894 Arbitration (Scotland) Act
    (56 & 57 Vict. c.13) 20–08
    s.2 20–12
    s.3 20–12
1907 Limited Partnerships Act (7
    Edw.7 c.24) 15–10
    s.5 15–10
    s.6 15–10
    s.15 15–10
Sheriff Courts (Scotland) Act
    (7 Edw.7 c.51)
    s.7 20–28

1908 Companies (Consolidation)
    Act (8 Edw.7 c.69) 16–10
1911 Parliament Act (1 & 2 Geo.5
    c.13) 1–24
1914 Entail (Scotland) Act (4 & 5
    Geo.5 c.43) 13–19
1921 Trusts (Scotland) Act (11 &
    12 Geo.5 c.58) 13–51
    s.3 13–25
        (a) 13–25
        (c) 13–28
    s.4 .... 13–42, 13–43
        (1)(ea) 13–33
        (f) 13–31
    s.4A 13–33
    s.5 .... 13–43, 13–44
    s.7 13–28
    s.22 13–25
    s.23 13–26
    s.31 13–51
    s.32 13–51
1940 Law Reform (Miscellaneous
    Provisions) (Scotland)
    Act (3 & 4 Geo.6 c.42)
    s.3(1) 10–44
1945 Law Reform (Contributory
    Negligence) Act (8 & 9
    Geo.6 c.28) 10–31
1946 Statutory Instruments Act (9
    & 10 Geo.6 c.36) 1–33
1948 Companies Act (11 & 12
    Geo.6 c.38) 16–46
    s.184 16–46
1949 Tenancy of Shops (Scotland)
    Act (12, 13 & 14 Geo.6
    c.25) 11–64
    Registered Designs Act (12,
    13 & 14 Geo.6 c.88) 12–01,
                               12–17, 12–20
    s.1 12–21
    s.1B 12–21
    s.1C 12–21
    s.1D 12–21
    s.2 12–22
    s.3 12–22
    s.7 12–23
    s.7A 12–23
        (5) 12–23
    s.8 12–23
    s.11ZA 12–24
        (4) 12–24
    s.15A 12–03
    s.15B 12–03
    s.24A 12–03
    s.45 12–03
    Parliament Act (12, 13 & 14
    Geo.6 c.103) 1–24
1950 Arbitration Act (14 Geo.6
    c.27) ....
    Pt II 20–08

1954 Landlord and Tenant Act (2
& 3 Eliz.2 c.56) 11–64
1957 Occupiers Liability Act (5 &
6 Eliz.2 c.31) 1–36
Cheques Act (5 & 6 Eliz.2
c.36) 18–01
1960 Occupiers Liability (Scot-
land) Act (8 & 9 Eliz.2
c.30) 1–36
s.2 10–39
1961 Trusts (Scotland) Act (9 &
10 Eliz.2 c.57) 13–55
s.1 13–55
(1) 13–55
s.2 13–53
s.5 13–19
1964 Succession (Scotland) Act
(11 Eliz.2 c.41) 1–52, 11–04
Hire Purchase Act (11 Eliz.2
c.53) 5–16
1966 Law Reform (Miscellaneous
Provisions) (Scotland)
Act (11 Eliz.2 c.19)
s.6 13–19
Arbitration (International
Investment Disputes)
Act (11 Eliz.2 c.41) 20–08
1967 Abortion Act (11 Eliz.2
c.87) 1–22
1968 Administration of Justice
Act (11 Eliz.2 c.5) ....
s.1(1)(a) 2–21
Trade Descriptions Act (11
Eliz.2 c.29) 6–37, 6–38,
7–16
s.2 6–42
Law Reform (Miscellaneous
Provisions) (Scotland)
Act (11 Eliz.2 c.70) ....
s.18 13–19
1969 Employers Liability (Com-
pulsory Insurance) Act
(11 Eliz.2 c.57) 4–33
1970 Conveyancing and Feudal
Reform (Scotland) Act
(11 Eliz.2 c.35) 19–26
s.40 19–26
Equal Pay Act (11 Eliz.2
c.41) 8–33, 8–34
s.1 8–34
1972 Administration of Justice
(Scotland) Act (c.59) 20–08
s.3 20–17
European Communities Act
(c.68)
s.3(1) 1–37
1973 Supply of Goods (Implied
Terms) Act (c.13) 5–01
Prescription and Limitation
(Scotland) Act (c.52) 11–08

s.6 .... 4–103, 10–41, 19–07,
19–13
(1) 18–15
s.7 11–30
s.8 11–30
s.10 4–103
s.18A(1) 10–41
Sch.1 para.1(e) 18–15
Sch.2 19–13
1974 Health and Safety at Work
etc Act (c.37) 3–29, 3–40
s.2(1) 3–31, 3–41
(2) 3–31
(3) 3–32
s.3(1) 3–33
(2) 3–33
s.7 3–34
s.10 3–40
s.20 3–40
s.21 3–40
s.22 3–40
Land Tenure Reform (Scot-
land) Act (c.38)
s.8 11–58
Consumer Credit Act (c.39) .. 4–27,
6–01, 6–04, 6–05, 6–06,
6–12, 6–14, 6–15, 6–19,
6–20, 6–29, 6–32, 6–36,
6–53, 6–54, 7–16
s.12 .... 6–08, 6–09
s.15 6–10
s.16 6–11
s.21 6–14
s.25(1) 6–14
s.51 6–18
s.56 6–28
s.57 6–24
(2) 6–24
s.58 6–21
s.60 6–20
s.61 6–22
s.62 .... 6–21, 6–22
s.63 .... 6–21, 6–22
s.64 6–21
s.65(1) 6–23
s.67 6–51
ss.67–73 6–25
s.69(1) 6–25
(7) 6–25
s.75 6–29
s.76 6–32
s.94 6–31
ss.114–122 19–27
s.129 6–34
s.132 .... 6–34, 6–36
s.133 .... 6–35, 6–36
s.134 6–36
s.135 .... 6–33, 6–36
s.136 .... 6–33, 6–36
s.140A 6–36

s.140B	6–36
s.157	6–19
s.175	6–24
1975 Arbitration Act (c.3)	20–08
Sex Discrimination Act (c.65)	8–34, 15–07
s.1(2)(a)	8–35
(b)	8–36
s.2(1)	8–34
ss.2A-4	8–34
s.4A(1)	8–37
s.6	8–34
s.7	8–35
s.11(1)(d)	15–07
s.20A	8–34
s.41	8–34
s.63A	8–38
s.76(1)-(6)	8–38
1976 Dangerous Wild Animals Act (c.38)	10–38
Licensing (Scotland) Act (c.66)	3–17
s.68(1)	3–17
s.71	3–17
Race Relations Act (c.74)	8–39, 15–07
s.1(1)(a)	8–39
(1A)	8–39
s.3(1)	8–39
ss.4A-5	8–39
s.10(1)(d)	15–07
1977 Patents Act (c.37)	12–01, 12–03, 12–25
ss.1–5	12–26
s.14	12–27
s.25	12–27
s.31	12–03
(2)	12–03
ss.31–33	19–30
s.60(5)	12–28
s.70	12–28
s.72	12–29
Unfair Contract Terms Act (c.50)	4–02, 4–45, 4–46, 4–47, 5–09, 6–03, 7–16
s.16	4–46
(1)	4–74
(a)	4–46
(b)	4–46
s.17	4–46
s.20	5–41
s.24(2)	4–46
s.25	5–17, 5–25
Sch.2	4–46
1979 Land Registration (Scotland) Act (c.33)	11–16
Estate Agents Act (c.38)	6–55, 6–55
ss.12–21	6–55
Sale of Goods Act (c.54)	4–31, 4–41, 5–01, 5–04, 5–05, 5–08, 5–09, 5–24, 5–37, 7–09, 7–09, 7–16, 11–09
Pt 5A	5–30
s.2	5–04
s.3(2)	4–52
s.6	5–17
s.7	5–17
s.12	5–09, 5–10, 5–22, 7–16
(1)	5–09
(2)	5–09
s.13	5–20, 5–22
(3)	5–20
s.14	5–20, 5–21, 5–22, 5–24, 7–11, 7–16
(1)	5–21
(2A)	5–22
(2B)	5–22
(2C)	5–21
(2D)–(2F)	5–22
(3)	5–22
s.15(2)	5–22
s.15A	5–28, 5–38
s.15B	5–25, 7–11
s.16	5–08
ss.16–18	5–08
s.17	5–08
s.18	5–08
Rule 1	5–08
Rule 2	5–08
Rule 3	5–08
Rule 4	5–08
Rule 5	5–08
s.19	5–08
s.20	5–17
(4)	5–17
s.20A	5–08
s.21	5–10, 5–11
s.24	5–14
s.25	5–14
s.27	5–18, 7–16
ss.27–29	5–16
s.29(3)	5–18
s.30	5–27
s.32	5–17
s.35	5–26
(3)	5–26
(7)	5–26
s.35A	5–27
s.36	5–26
s.39	19–28
(1)(a)	5–23
(c)	5–23
s.41	5–23
s.44	5–23
ss.44–46	5–23
s.48	5–23
s.48A(3)	5–30
s.48B	5–30

s.48C 5–30, 7–11
s.48E 5–32
s.49 5–23
s.50 5–23
   (2) 5–23
s.51 5–28
s.53A 5–28
s.61 5–08

1980 Solicitors (Scotland) Act
   (c.46)
   s.62(1) 19–17

1982 Civil Aviation Act (c.16) 11–25
   s.76(1) 11–25
   Civil Jurisdiction and Judg-
     ments Act (c.27) 20–26
   Pt I 20–26
   Pt II 20–26
   s.41(3) 20–26
   s.42(1) 20–26
     (3)-(5) 20–26
   Sch.8 20–26
     paras 3–6 20–26
     para.5 20–26
     para.6 20–26
   Supply of Goods and Ser-
     vices Act (c.29) 5–01,
                 5–04, 7–16
   Pt 1A 5–35, 5–41
   s.11A 5–35, 5–36
   s.11B 5–37
   s.11C 5–37
   s.11D 5–37
   s.11E 5–37
   s.11F 5–38
   s.11G 5–39
   s.11H 5–40
   s.11I 5–40
   s.11J 5–40
   s.11K 5–40
   Stock Transfer Act (c.41) 16–53
   Administration of Justice
     Act (c.53) ....
   s.12 10–43

1984 Dentists Act (c.24) ....
   s.80 14–04
   s.81 14–04
   Data Protection Act (c.35) .. 3–44
   s.7 6–19
   Inheritance Tax Act (c.51) ...
   Sch.4 para.2(ii) 13–24

1985 Companies Act (c.6) 14–12,
              16–03, 16–10,
              16–19, 19–18
   s.2 16–10
   s.18(3) 16–10
   s.190 16–13
   s.283(2) 16–19
   Business Names Act (c.7) ... 14–03,
         14–07, 14–08, 15–03

Companies Consolidation
   (Consequential Provi-
   sions) Act (c.9) ....
   s.1 17–47
Bankruptcy (Scotland) Act
   (c.66) 17–03, 17–06,
              17–18, 17–19
   s.1A 17–06
   s.3 17–08
   s.5 13–36
     (2)(b) 17–06
     (2A) 17–06
     (2B) 17–06
     (2C) 17–18
   s.5A 17–06
   s.7 17–05
   s.21A 17–08
   s.24 17–08
   s.31 17–09
   s.32(2) 17–09
   s.33 17–09
   s.34 17–12
   s.36 17–13
   s.37 17–14
   s.39A 17–09
   s.43A 17–15
   s.48 17–15
   s.49(6) 17–15
   s.51 17–15
   s.54 17–16
   s.56A 17–16
   s.56G 17–16
   s.73G 17–21
   s.73J 17–21
   Sch.2 17–19
   Sch.2A 17–19
   Sch.3 Pt 1 17–15
   Sch.5 17–18
     para.5 17–18
Law Reform (Miscellaneous
   Provisions) (Scotland)
   Act (c.73) 4–62
   ss.4–7 11–60
   s.8 4–62
   s.10 4–67

1986 Insolvency Act (c.45) 14–10,
     14–11, 14–12, 16–03, 16–05,
     16–06, 16–55, 17–27, 17–31,
        19–18, 19–22, 19–23
   s.1(1) 17–27
     (2) 17–28
     (3) 17–28
   s.2 17–28
   s.3 17–28
   s.4 17–29
   s.7(2) 17–30
     (3) 17–30
   s.8(1) 17–33
   s.9(1) 17–33
   s.11 17–37

s.12 17–37
s.52 17–41
   (1) 19–21
     (a) 19–21
     (b) 19–21
     (c) 19–21
     (d) 19–21
s.53 17–41
   (7) 19–22
s.60 19–21
   (1) 17–43
s.62(5) 17–44
s.64 17–41
s.65 17–41
s.72 19–23
   (B-G) 19–23
s.76 16–06
   (3) 16–06
s.84 17–54
s.85 17–54
s.86 17–54
s.89 17–55
s.91 17–55
s.94 17–55
s.95 17–55
s.96 17–55
s.98 17–56
s.99 17–56
s.100 17–56
s.101 17–56
s.105 17–56
s.106 17–56
s.120 2–12
s.122 17–46
   (1) 17–47
   (2) 17–47
s.123 17–47
s.124 17–47
s.127 17–48
s.130 17–48
s.135 17–49
s.138 17–49
s.139 17–49
s.142 17–49
s.143 17–50
s.146 17–52
s.185 17–48
s.188 17–48
s.201 .... 17–55, 17–56
s.213 16–24
s.214 16–24
ss.243–245 19–22
s.389A 17–28
Sch.1 17–38
Sch.2 17–42
Sch.4 Pt 1 17–50
   Pt 2 17–50
   Pt 3 17–50
Sch.6 17–51
Sch.B1 19–23

para.3 17–32
para.14 17–31
para.15(1) 17–35
para.18 17–35
para.26(1) 17–36
para.27 17–36
para.29 17–36
para.35 17–33
para.46 17–33
para.48 17–38
para.49 17–38
para.51 17–38
para.53 17–38
para.55 17–38
para.76 17–39
Company Directors Dis-
   qualification Act (c.46) 14–11,
                  16–03, 16–24
   s.2 16–24
     (1) 16–24
   s.3(1) 16–24
   s.4(1) 16–24
   s.5(1) 16–24
   s.6(1) 16–24
   s.10(1) 16–24
   s.11 16–20
   Sch.1 Pt 1 16–24
     Pt 2 16–24
1987 Animals (Scotland) Act 10–38
   s.1(1) 10–38
     (3)(b) 10–38
   s.2 10–38
   s.5 10–38
   Consumer Protection Act
     (c.43) 10–37
   Pt 1 6–03
   s.1(2) 10–37
   s.2(1) 10–37
   s.3(1) 10–37
   s.4 10–37
   s.5(2) 10–37
     (3) 10–37
     (4) 10–37
1988 Court of Session Act (c.36)
   s.11 2–19
   s.32(5) 2–21
   Housing (Scotland) Act
     (c.43) 11–62
   Copyright, Designs and
     Patents Act (c.48) 12–01,
      12–13, 12–16, 12–18, 12–19,
          12–20, 12–22, 12–23,
                     12–24
   s.1 12–14
     (1) 12–03
   s.3(2) 12–14
   ss.3–4 12–14
   ss.5A-6A 12–14
   s.8 12–14
   ss.9–11 12–14

ss.12–15A 12–14
ss.16–21 12–15
ss.22–27 12–15
s.29 12–15
s.30 12–15
s.51 12–19
ss.77–85 12–16
s.90 12–03
s.96 12–03
s.103 12–16
s.153 12–14
s.177 12–03
ss.205C–205N 12–16
s.213 12–18
   (1) 12–03
   (3) 12–18
s.215 12–18
s.216 12–18
s.222 12–03
s.224 12–20
s.226 12–19
s.227 12–19
s.229 12–03
s.236 12–19
s.237 12–18
s.262 12–03
Road Traffic Act (c.52) ....
  Pt VI 4–33
  s.163 3–06
1989 Finance Act (c.26) ....
  Sch.5 para.3(3) 13–24
1990 Computer Misuse Act
  (c.18) 3–43, 3–48
  s.1 3–43
     (1)(a) 3–43
  s.3 3–43
     (2) 3–43
     (3) 3–43
  s.17(5) 3–43
Law Reform (Miscellaneous
  Provisions) (Scotland)
  Act (c.40) 20–08
  s.9 13–59
     (1) 13–56, 13–58
  s.10 13–58
Environmental Protection
  Act (c.43) 11–31
  Pt IV 3–56
  s.35 3–56
  s.38 3–56
1991 Coal Mining Subsidence Act
  (c.45) 11–32
Age of Legal Capacity
  (Scotland) Act (c.50) 4–51
  s.1(1)(a) 4–51, 13–09
     (b) 4–51
  s.2(1) 4–51, 13–09
  s.3 4–51
  s.4 4–51
  s.5 4–51

s.9(f) 13–24
Agricultural Holdings (Scot-
  land) Act (c.55) 11–63
Water Industry Act 1991
  (c.56) 3–56
1992 Cheques Act (c.32) 18–01
Timeshare Act (c.35) 6–54, 7–09
  s.1A 6–54
  s.2 6–54
  s.5 6–54
  s.5B 6–54
Trade Union and Labour
  Relations (Consolida-
  tion) Act (c.52) ....
  s.179 8–10
  s.188 8–32
  s.189 8–32
1993 Prisoners and Criminal Proceedings (Scotland) Act
  (c.9)
  s.2 2–36
1994 Trade Marks Act (c.26) 12–01,
                             12–12
  s.1(1) 12–10
  s.2(2) 12–08
  s.3 12–10
  s.5 .... 12–09, 12–10
  s.10 12–09
     (4) 12–11
     (6) 12–11
  s.11(2) 12–11
  s.14 12–03
  s.22 12–03
  ss.22–24 19–30
  s.24 12–03
  s.42 12–11
  s.43 12–11
  s.46 12–12
  s.47 12–12
  s.102 12–03
Local Government etc
  (Scotland) Act (c.39) ....
  s.2 7–13
1995 Requirements of Writing
  (Scotland) Act (c.7) 4–02,
           4–03, 4–27, 4–28,
                7–04, 16–19
  s.1 11–58
     (1) 4–10, 4–28, 7–04
     (2) 4–28, 7–04
      (a) 19–05
     (2A) 7–04
     (3) 4–28
     (4) 4–28
     (7) 4–28
  s.2 .... 4–28, 13–11
  s.2A 7–04
  s.3 4–28
  s.3A 7–04
  Sch.2 para.3(1) 16–19

Pensions Act (c.26)
ss.3–6 13–24
ss.29–30 13–24
Criminal Procedure (Scot-
land) Act (c.46) ....
s.205(1) 2–36
s.211(1) 2–34
(2) 2–34
s.205(1) 2–36
s.249 3–04
s.294 3–19
Disability   Discrimination
Act (c.50) .. 8–33, 8–40, 15–07
s.1(1) 8–40
s.3A(3) 8–40
(5) 8–40
s.3B 8–40
s.6A(1)(d) 15–07
s.6B(1) 15–07
s.6C(1) 15–07
s.18B 8–40
Sch.1 8–40
1996 Employment   Rights   Act
(c.18) 8–04
s.1 8–07
s.13 .... 8–05, 8–11
s.94 8–19
s.95 8–20
s.98A 8–21
(2) 8–23
s.108 8–19
s.111 8–24
ss.112–126 8–24
s.135 8–25
s.138(2) 8–28
s.139 8–26
s.141(4) 8–28
s.155 8–25
ss.182–190 8–07
s.230(2) 8–04
Arbitration Act (c.23) ....
ss.89–91 20–08
Sch.3 20–08
Sch.4 20–08
Housing Grants, Construc-
tion and Regeneration
Act (c.53) 20–23, 20–24
s.108(1) 20–24
(1)–(4) 20–24
(2)(a) 20–24
(b) 20–24
(c) 20–24
(d) 20–24
(e) 20–24
(f) 20–24
(3) 20–24
(4) 20–24
1997 Town and Country Planning
(Scotland) Act (c.7) 11–54

Planning (Listed Buildings
and   Conservation
Areas) (Scotland) Act
(c.9) 11–54
Planning (Hazardous Sub-
stances) (Scotland) Act
(c.10) 11–54
1998 Data Protection Act (c.29) .. 3–44,
3–47, 3–48, 7–16, 8–03
s.1(1) 3–45
(d) 3–45
s.2 3–45
s.7 3–47
s.10 3–47
s.11 3–47
s.13 3–47
s.14 3–47
s.17 3–48
s.21 3–48
s.47 3–48
s.50 3–48
s.55 3–48
s.68 3–45
Sch.3 3–46
Sch.9 3–48
Sch.11 3–45
Sch.12 3–45
National   Minimum   Wage
Act (c.39) 8–11
Competition Act (c.41) 3–49,
3–54, 3–55
Ch.1 .... 3–50, 3–52
Ch.2 3–53
Human Rights Act (c.42) 1–10,
1–24, 8–03
Scotland Act (c.46) 1–10, 1–24,
1–27, 1–28, 1–33, 12–03
ss.28–30 1–27
s.29 1–10
(2) 1–27
s.33 1–28
s.36 1–28
s.48(1) 2–77
s.54 1–27
ss.95(1)–(3) 2–73
(6)–(8) 2–70
s.98 1–28
s.103 1–39
s.111 1–32
s.113(5) 1–30
(6) 1–30
s.115 1–33
Sch.5 1–27
Sch.6 1–28
Sch.7 1–33
2000 Abolition of Feudal Tenure
etc (Scotland) Act (asp
5) 1–08, 1–12, 11–13,
13–19, 14–05
ss.50–52 13–19

s.67 11–58
s.70 15–06
Electronic Communications
    Act (c.7) 7–04
    s.8 7–04
Financial Services and Mar-
    kets Act (c.8) 1–30, 2–56,
                    16–03, 16–54
    s.72(1) 16–54
    s.74(1) 16–05
    s.84 16–54
    ss.84–87R 16–54
    s.85(1) 16–54
    (2) 16–54
    (7) 16–54
    s.86 16–54
    s.87A 16–54
    (1) 16–54
    (2) 16–54
    s.87K 16–54
    s.87L 16–54
    s.87M 16–54
    ss.102A-103 16–54
    s.586 16–53
    s.761(1) 16–54
    Sch.11A 16–54
Terrorism Act (c.11) 3–08
Limited Liability Partner-
    ships Act (c.12) 14–12,
                    14–13, 15–10
    s.1(2) 14–12
    (4) 14–12
    s.2 14–12
    s.3 14–12
    s.6 14–12
    s.8 14–12
    (2) 14–12
    s.9 14–12
    s.10 14–12

2001 Housing (Scotland) Act
    (c.10) 11–62
2002 Scottish Public Services
    Ombudsman Act (asp
    11) 2–52
    Freedom of Information
    (Scotland) Act (asp 13)   2–54
    Debt Arrangement and
    Attachment (Scotland)
    Act (asp 17) 17–22
    Pt 3 17–22
    s.10(1) 17–22
    (3) 17–22
    (5) 17–22
    s.11(1) 17–22
    s.12 17–22
    s.15(1) 17–22
    (2) 17–22
    (3) 17–22
    s.18 17–22
    s.19 17–22

Employment Act (c.22)
    s.31 8–21
    s.32 8–21
    Sch.2 Pt 1 8–21
Enterprise Act (c.40) 3–55,
            17–31, 17–34, 17–40,
                    19–18, 19–23
    Pt 8 .... 6–49, 6–56, 6–57
    Pt 10 17–31
    s.18(6) 6–55
    s.23 3–55
    s.73 3–55
    s.250(2) 19–23
    s.251 19–23
    s.252 19–23
2003 Land Reform (Scotland) Act
    (asp 2) 11–13, 11–27
    Pt 1 11–27
    Building (Scotland) Act (asp
    8) 11–55
    Title Conditions (Scotland)
    Act (asp 9) 11–13, 11–49
    Agricultural Holdings (Scot-
    land) Act (asp 11) 11–63
2004 Tenements (Scotland) Act
    (asp 11) .. 11–13, 11–42, 11–44
    Patents Act (c.16) 12–01,
                    12–03, 12–25
    s.1 12–26
    s.8 12–27
    Hunting Act (c.37) 1–24
2005 Constitutional Reform Act
    (c.4) 2–23
    Charities and Trustee
    Investment (Scotland)
    Act (asp 10) ....
    s.69 13–24
    s.93(2) 13–33
    s.94 13–33
    Gambling Act (c.19) ....
    s.334 4–73
    s.335 1–04
2006 Housing (Scotland) Act (asp
    1) 11–62
    Consumer Credit Act
    (c.14) 2–56, 6–01,
                    6–02, 6–04
    Companies Act (c.46) 14–03,
            14–11, 14–12, 14–13, 16–03,
            16–04, 16–05, 16–06, 16–07,
            16–08, 16–09, 16–10, 16–10,
            16–11, 16–19, 16–51,
                    19–18
    Pt 15 16–15
    Pt 16 16–15
    Pt 18 Ch.5 16–60
    s.3(2) 14–09, 16–07
    (3) 14–09, 16–07
    s.4 14–09
    ss.7–13 .... 14–11, 16–09

ss.7–16 14–09
s.8 16–10
s.9 .... 16–08, 16–09
   (1) 16–09
   (4)(b) 14–09
   (5) 16–09
     (b) 16–09
s.10 16–09
s.11 16–09
   (3) 14–09
s.12 16–09
s.13 16–09
s.16 .... 14–09, 16–09
   (2) 16–05
s.17(a) 16–10
s.18(4) 16–10
s.20 16–09
s.21 .... 16–10, 16–18
   (1) 16–36
s.22(1) 16–45
s.25(1) 16–10
s.26(1) 16–10
s.29 16–43
s.30 16–43
   (1) 16–10
s.31(2) 16–10
s.33 .... 16–10, 16–48, 16–49
s.35(3) 16–10
s.39 .... 16–10, 16–64
s.40 16–10
   (1) 16–10
s.53 16–08
ss.58–59 16–08
ss.58–60 14–09
s.60(1)(a) 16–08
s.66 16–08
s.67 16–08
s.69 16–08
s.73 16–08
s.77(1) 16–08, 16–18
   (2) 16–08
     (a) 16–45
s.80 16–08
s.81 16–08
s.82 16–12
s.86 16–08
s.87 16–08
s.113 16–52
   (1) 16–13
s.114(1) 16–13
   (2) 16–13
   (3) 16–13
s.123(1) 16–13
s.154 14–09
   (1) 16–20
   (2) 16–20
ss.154–259 16–18
s.155 16–20
s.157(1) 16–20
s.162(3) 16–13

   (4) 16–13
ss.162–167 16–13
s.167(1) 16–13
s.168 .... 14–10, 16–05, 16–47
   (1) 16–23, 16–40,
                16–44, 16–46
s.169 14–10
   (1) 16–20
   (2) 16–23
   (3) 16–23
s.170(1) 16–26
   (2) 16–30
   (3) 16–25
   (4) 16–25
ss.170–178 16–25
s.171 .... 16–27, 16–33
   (1)(a) 16–10
ss.171–177 .... 16–26, 16–34
s.172 16–33
   (1) 16–28
    (a) 16–28
    (a)–(f) 16–28
   (3) 16–25
s.173 16–33
   (1) 16–29
   (2) 16–29
s.174 .... 16–33, 16–34
   (1) 16–33
   (2) 16–33
s.175 .... 16–30, 16–33
   (1) 16–30
   (2) 16–30
   (3) 16–30
   (4) 16–30
    (b) 16–31
   (5) 16–31
    (a) 16–30
   (7) 16–30
s.176 .... 16–31, 16–33
s.177 .... 16–30, 16–32, 16–33
   (1) 16–32
   (2) 16–32
   (4) 16–32
   (5) 16–32
   (6) 16–32
s.178 .... 16–32, 16–33, 16–34
s.179 16–25
s.180 16–30, 16–31, 16–32, 16–33
s.182 .... 16–32, 16–33
   (5) 16–32
   (6) 16–32
ss.182–187 .... 16–30, 16–32
s.183 16–32
s.184 16–32
s.185 16–32
s.187 16–33
s.188(2) 16–36
ss.188–189 16–35
s.190(1) 16–44
ss.190–196 16–35

ss.197–214 16–35
s.213 16–06
  (2) 16–06
ss.215–222 16–35
s.239 .... 16–30, 16–31, 16–34
  (1) 16–10
s.248(1) 16–13
  (3) 16–13
s.249(1) 16–13
s.250 16–20
s.251 16–20
s.265 16–66
  (4)(b) 16–66
ss.265–269 .... 16–65, 16–66
s.266(2) 16–66
  (5) 16–66
s.268(1) 16–66
  (c) 16–10
  (2) 16–66
  (3) 16–66
s.270 .... 14–09, 16–09, 16–19
  (1) 16–13, 16–19
s.271 .... 14–09, 16–19
s.273 16–19
s.275 16–13
ss.275–280 16–13
s.276(1) 16–13
s.281(1) 16–43
  (b) 16–43
  (2) 16–43
  (3) 16–43
  (4) 16–43
ss.281–361 16–18
s.282 16–43
  (1) 16–10, 16–43, 16–44
  (2) 16–44
  (3) 16–44
  (4) 16–44
  (5) 16–43
s.283 16–43
  (1) 16–10, 16–45
  (2) 16–45
  (3) 16–45
  (4) 16–45
  (5) 16–45
  (6) 16–45
s.284(1) 16–46, 16–63
  (2) 16–46
  (3) 16–46, 16–63
  (4) 16–46
s.288 16–43
  (1) 16–43
  (2) 16–47
  (b) 16–17
  (3) 16–47
s.289 16–47
  (1) 16–47
  (2) 16–47
s.291(4) 16–47
  (5) 16–47

  (7) 16–47
s.292 16–47
  (1) 16–47
  (2) 16–47
  (5) 16–47
s.293 16–47
  (1) 16–47
  (3) 16–47
  (4) 16–47
  (5) 16–47
  (7) 16–47
s.295 16–47
  (1) 16–47
s.296(3) 16–47
  (4) 16–47
s.297(1) 16–47
  (2) 16–47
s.300 16–47
s.302 16–38
s.303 .... 16–38, 16–39, 16–63
  (2) 16–38
  (3) 16–38
  (4) 16–39
  (a) 16–38
  (b) 16–38
  (5) 16–38, 16–39
s.304(1) 16–38
s.306(1) 16–38
s.307(1) 16–40
  (2) 16–40
  (a) 16–40
  (b) 16–40
  (3) 16–40
s.308 16–40
s.309 16–40
s.310(1) 16–40
  (4)(b) 16–40
s.311(1) 16–40
  (2) 16–40
s.312 16–23
  (1) 16–23, 16–40
  (2) 16–23, 16–40
  (3) 16–23, 16–40
s.318(1) 16–41
  (2) 16–41
s.319 16–41
  (1) 16–41
s.320(1) 16–41
  (2) 16–41
s.321 16–41
  (1) 16–41
s.322 16–41
s.324(1) 16–42
  (2) 16–42
s.325(1) 16–42
  (2) 16–42
  (3) 16–42
s.327(2) 16–42
s.328(1) 16–42
s.329(1) 16–41, 16–63

s.330(2)	16–42
s.331	16–42
s.336	16–37
s.337(1)	16–40
(3)	16–40
s.338	16–39
(3)	16–39
s.341	16–39
s.342	16–39
s.371	16–38
s.386	16–15
s.394	14–11, 16–15
s.410(2)	19–19
s.415	16–15
s.416(1)	16–15
s.417	16–15
s.423	16–16
s.424(2)	16–16
(3)	16–16
s.425	16–16
s.441	14–11, 16–16
s.442(2)(a)	16–16
(b)	16–16
s.448	16–11
s.451(1)	16–16
s.464(1)	19–20
s.475(1)	16–17
s.485	16–17
(1)	16–17
(4)	16–17
s.487(1)	16–17
(2)	16–17
s.489	16–17
(1)	16–17
(4)	16–17
s.491(1)	16–17
s.495	16–17
s.496	16–17
s.497	16–17
s.498	16–17
s.502(2)	16–17
s.503(1)	16–17
s.510(2)(a)	16–44
ss.510–511	16–17
s.513(2)	16–17
s.540(1)	16–49
ss.540–657	16–48
s.541	14–10, 16–10, 16–48, 16–49
s.542	16–50
(2)	16–50
(4)	16–50
s.547	16–50
ss.549–551	16–52
ss.549–616	16–52
s.550	16–52
s.551(1)	16–52
(3)	16–52
s.552	16–59
s.555	16–52
s.558	16–52
s.561	16–06
s.562	16–06, 16–52
(3)(b)	16–11
s.563(2)	16–06
ss.564–566	16–52
ss.567–573	16–52
s.570	16–45
s.571	16–45
s.610(1)	16–59
s.641(1)(a)	16–62
(6)	16–62
ss.641–651	16–62
s.642(1)(a)	16–62
s.643(1)	16–62
(2)	16–62
(4)	16–62
s.644(1)	16–62
s.645(1)	16–62
s.646(1)	16–62
s.648(1)	16–62
(2)	16–62
(3)	16–62
s.649(1)	16–62
s.658	16–60
s.677(1)(a)	16–61
(b)	16–61
(c)	16–61
s.678(1)	16–61
s.684(1)	16–60
(2)	16–60
(3)	16–60
(4)	16–60
ss.684–689	16–51
s.685(1)	16–60
(2)	16–60
s.686	16–60
(1)	16–60
s.687(1)	16–60
(2)	16–60
s.688	16–60
s.689	16–60
s.690	16–60
s.691(1)	16–60
(2)	16–60
s.692(1)	16–60
(2)	16–60
s.694(2)	16–60
s.706	16–60
s.707(1)	16–60
s.708(1)	16–60
s.719(1)	16–11
s.738	16–55
s.741(1)	16–56
s.743(1)	16–13, 16–56
(2)	16–13
(3)	16–13
(4)	16–13
ss.744–748	16–56
s.755	16–07

ss.755–760 14–09
s.761 16–53
ss.761–767 14–09
s.767(3) 16–06
    (4) 16–06
ss.770–771 16–52
ss.783–790 16–52
s.830(1) 16–59
    (2) 16–59
s.854 .... 14–11, 16–14
s.855 16–13
s.875(1) 16–13
s.876 16–13
s.877(2) 16–13
    (3) 16–13
ss.878–892 19–18
s.993 16–24
s.994 16–67
    (1) 16–67
ss.994–999 16–65
s.996 16–67
s.1000(6) 16–11
s.1003(3) 16–11
s.1061 16–11
ss.1090–1098 15–03
s.1157 16–34
s.1173(1) 16–11
ss.1200–1208 .... 14–03, 14–07
Road Safety Act (c.49)
    s.26 1–04
Legislative and Regulatory
    Reform Act (c.51) 1–30
2007 Bankruptcy and Diligence
    etc (Scotland) Act (asp
    3) 1–12, 1–29, 11–52,
                17–03, 17–06, 17–07,
                17–08, 17–09, 17–10,
                17–16, 17–18, 17–19,
                17–21, 17–23, 17–24,
                17–25, 17–26,
                19–17, 19–24
    s.1 17–16
    s.2 17–16
    s.6 17–07
    s.11(1) 17–08
    (4) 17–08
    s.14 17–06
    s.15(2) 17–06
    s.16 17–06
    s.18 17–10
    s.19 17–09
    s.20 17–18
    s.25 17–06
    s.28 17–19
    s.30 17–14
    s.34 17–16
    s.37 19–24

s.39 19–24
s.40 19–24
s.41 19–24
    (1) 19–26
s.79 17–24
s.80 17–07
s.81 17–24
s.82 17–24
s.83(2) 17–24
    (3) 17–24
s.86(5) 17–24
    (7) 17–24
s.92 17–24
s.129(2) 17–26
    (3) 17–26
    (4) 17–26
s.130 17–26
s.134(2) 17–26
s.136(4) 17–26
s.157 17–23
s.158 17–23
s.160 17–23
s.174 17–25
    (3) 17–25
s.175(1) 17–25
s.176(1) 17–25
    (2) 17–25
s.206 17–21
s.208 .... 11–60, 19–17
Legal Profession and Legal
    Aid (Scotland) Act (asp
    5) 2–54
Criminal Proceedings etc
    (Reform) (Scotland) Act
    (asp 6) 2–31
    s.43 2–33
    s.47 2–33
    s.48 2–33
    s.46 2–31
    ss.59–66 2–31
    ss.67–77 2–66
    s.74 2–31
Tribunals, Courts and
    Enforcement Act (c.15) 2–40,
                                            2–43
Consumers, Estate Agents
    and Redress Act (c.17) 6–55
Corporate Manslaughter
    and Corporate Homi-
    cide Act (c.19) 1–25, 3–41
    s.1(1) 3–41
    (3) 3–41
    (4)(b) 3–41
    (c) 3–41
s.8(2) 3–41
    (3) 3–41

Table of Statutory Instruments

1977 Consumer Credit (Credit Reference Agency) Regulations (SI 1977/329)
    reg.3 6–19

1981 Company and Business Names Regulations (SI 1981/1685) 16–08

1983 Consumer Credit (Agreements) Regulations (SI 1983/1553) 6–20

1985 Companies (Tables A to F) Regulations (SI 1985/805) 9–11, 16–10, 16–47

1987 Consumer Protection (Cancellation of Contracts Concluded away from Business Premises) Regulations (SI 1987/2117) 5–07, 6–51

1988 Consumer Protection (Cancellation of Contracts Concluded away from Business Premises) (Amendment) Regulations (SI 1988/958) 6–51

1989 Consumer Credit (Exempt Agreements) Order (SI 1989/869) ....
    art.3(1)(b) 6–11
    art.4 6–11

1992 Provision and Use of Work Equipment Regulations (SI 1998/2306) 10–36
    Health and Safety (Display Screen Equipment) Regulations (SI 1992/2792) 3–39
    reg.2 3–39
    reg.4 3–39
    reg.5 3–39
    reg.6 3–39
    Manual Handling Operations Regulations (SI 1992/2793) 3–38
    reg.4 3–38
      (1)(a) 3–38
      (b) 3–38
    Personal Protective Equipment at Work Regulations (SI 1992/2966) 10–36

Workplace (Health, Safety and Welfare) Regulations (SI 1992/3004) 10–36
Package Holidays and Package Tours Regulations (SI 1992/3288) 6–45, 7–16

1993 Act of Sederunt (Sheriff Court Ordinary Cause Rules) (SI 1993/1956) ... 20–28
    r.40.1(2)(a) 20–32
    r.40.4 20–32
    r.40.5(1) 20–32
    r.40.6 20–32
    r.40.7 20–32
    r.40.8 20–32
    r.40.10 20–32
    r.40.13 20–32
    r.40.14 20–32
    r.40.15 20–32
    Public Trusts (Reorganisation) (Scotland) Regulations (SI 1993/2036) 13–58
    Commercial Agents (Council Directive) Regulations (SI 1993/3053) 9–01, 9–02, 9–46, 9–47, 9–51
    reg.2(1) 9–46
      (i) 9–46
      (ii) 9–46
      (iii) 9–46
      (2)(a) 9–46
      (b) 9–46
    reg.3(1) 9–47
      (2)(a) 9–47
      (b) 9–47
      (c) 9–47
    reg.4(2) 9–48
      (b) 9–48
      (3) 9–48
    reg.6(1) 9–49
    reg.7(1)(a) 9–49
      (b) 9–49
    reg.10(2) 9–49
    reg.11(1) 9–49
    reg.13 .... 9–13, 9–45, 9–46
    reg.15(2)(a)-(c) 9–50
      (3) 9–50
    reg.17(2) 9–51
      (3) 17–51
      (4) 17–51

Commercial Agents (Council
    Directive) (Amend-
    ment) Regulations (SI
    1993/3173) 9–45

1994 Act of Sederunt (Rules of the
    Court of Session) (SI
    1994/1443)
    r.41.2 20–17
    r.41.5.2 20–17
    r.41.7.1 20–17
    r.41.7.2 20–17
    r.41.7.4(a) 20–17
    r.41.8.1 20–17
    r.41.8.2 20–17
    r.41.8.4 20–17
    r.41.9 20–17
    r.47.1(2) 20–32
    r.47.2 20–32
    r.47.6(1) 20–32
    r.47.11–13 20–32
    r.47.14 20–32
    r.47.16 20–32

1996 Act of Sederunt (Family
    Proceedings in the
    Sheriff Court) (SI 1996/
    2167) 20–28
    Act of Sederunt (Sheriff
    Court Ordinary Cause
    Rules Amendment)
    (Miscellaneous) (SI
    1996/2445) 20–28
    Act of Sederunt (Sheriff
    Court Ordinary Cause
    Rules Amendment)
    (Miscellaneous)
    (Amendment) (SI 1996/
    2586) 20–28

1997 Timeshare Regulations (SI
    1997/1081) 6–54

1998 Construction Contracts
    (Scotland) Exclusion
    Order (SI 1998/686) 20–24
    Scheme for Construction
    Contracts (Scotland)
    Regulations (SI 1998/
    688) 20–04
    Housing Grants, Construc-
    tion and Regeneration
    Act 1996 (Scotland)
    (Commencement No.5)
    Order (SI 1998/894) 20–24
    Working Time Regulations
    (SI 1998/1833) 8–05, 8–12
    Provision and Use of Work
    Equipment Regulations
    (SI 1998/2306) 3–37
    reg.4 3–37
    reg.5 3–37
    reg.8 3–37

Commercial Agents (Council
    Directive) (Amend-
    ment) Regulations (SI
    1998/2868) 9–45

Consumer Protection (Can-
    cellation of Contracts
    Concluded away from
    Business Premises)
    (Amendment) Regula-
    tions (SI 1998/3050) 6–51

1999 Unfair Terms in Consumer
    Contracts Regulations
    (SI 1999/2083) 4–02, 4–45,
                 4–47, 6–03, 7–16
    reg.3 4–47
    reg.5 4–47
    (1) 4–47
    (2) 4–47
    reg.7 4–47
    Sch.2 4–47
    Management of Health and
    Safety at Work Regula-
    tions (SI 1999/3242) 3–29,
                          3–36
    reg.3 3–36
    reg.5 3–36
    reg.6 3–36
    reg.8 3–36

2000 Part-time Workers (Preven-
    tion of Less Favourable
    Treatment) Regulations
    (SI 2000/1551) 8–33
    Consumer Protection (Dis-
    tance Selling) Regula-
    tions (SI 2000/2334) 5–07,
        6–45, 6–53, 7–09, 7–10,
        7–11, 7–13, 7–14, 7–15
    reg.3 .... 7–09, 7–10, 7–13
    (1) 7–09
    (2) 7–13
    reg.4 7–09
    reg.5 .... 7–09, 7–10
    reg.6 .... 7–09, 7–10
    reg.7 .... 6–53, 7–09, 7–10, 7–11
    (1) 7–10
    (a) 7–10, 7–15
    (2) 7–10
    regs 7–19(1) 7–09
    regs 7–20 7–09
    reg.8 .... 7–09, 7–10, 7–11
    (2) 7–11
    (b) 7–10, 7–11
    (d) 7–10
    regs.8–10 6–53
    reg.9 7–10
    reg.10 .... 7–09, 7–11
    (2) 7–11
    regs 10–18 7–11
    reg.11 7–12
    (1) 7–11

(3) 7–11
(5) 7–11
reg.12(2) 7–11
(3) 7–11
reg.13 .... 6–53, 7–10, 7–11
(1)(a) 7–11
reg.14 6–53
(1) 7–11
(5) 7–11
regs 14–18 7–11
reg.15 .... 6–53, 7–11
reg.16 7–11
reg.17 7–11
(2) 7–11
(4) 7–11
(7) 7–11
(8) 7–11
reg.19 6–53
reg.21 6–53
reg.25 7–13
reg.26 7–13
(1) 7–13
regs 26–29 7–13
reg.27 7–13
reg.29 7–13
Sch.1 7–09

2001 Limited Liability Partnerships (Scotland) Regulations (SI 2001/128) 14–12, 14–13
Limited Liability Partnerships Regulations (SI 2001/1090) 14–12, 14–13
reg.3 14–12
reg.4 14–12
reg.5 14–12
reg.7 14–12
(3) 14–13
reg.8 14–12

2002 Electronic Commerce (EC Directive) Regulations (SI 2002/2013) 7–05, 7–06, 7–08, 7–15
reg.2 7–05
(1) 7–06
reg.3(1)(a) 7–05
(b) 7–05
(c) 7–05
(d) 7–05
reg.4(4) 7–05
reg.6 7–07
(1) 7–06, 7–15
(b) 7–15
(c) 7–06
(2) 7–06, 7–15
regs 6–15 .... 7–05, 7–06
reg.7 .... 7–06, 7–07
reg.8 .... 7–06, 7–07
reg.9 7–06
(1) 7–07

(a) 7–06
(b) 7–06
(c) 7–06
(d) 7–06
(2) 7–06
(3) 7–06, 7–07
reg.10 7–06
reg.11 7–06
(1)(a) 7–06
(b) 7–06, 7–07
(2)(a) 7–06
(b) 7–06
reg.12 7–06
reg.13 7–07
regs 13–15 7–07
reg.14 7–07
reg.15 7–07
reg.17 7–08
regs 17–19 .... 7–05, 7–08
reg.18 7–08
(b) 7–08
reg.19 7–08
reg.20 7–08
Sch. 7–05
Fixed-term Employees (Prevention of Less Favourable Treatment) Regulations (SI 2002/2034) 8–33

2003 Employment Equality (Religion or Belief) Regulations (SI 2003/1660) 8–33, 15–07
reg.14(1)(d) 15–07
Employment Equality (Sexual Orientation) Regulations (SI 2003/1661) 8–33, 15–07
reg.14(1)(d) 15–07
Timeshare Act 1992 (Amendment) Regulations (SI 2003/1922) 6–54
Insolvency Act 1986 (Prescribed Part) Order (SI 2003/2097) 19–23
Privacy and Electronic Communications (EC Directive) Regulations (SI 2003/2426) 7–06, 7–16
Conduct of Employment Agencies and Employment Businesses Regulations (SI 2003/3319) 8–06

2004 Building (Scotland) Regulations (SI 2004/406) 11–55
Employment Act 2002 (Dispute Resolution) Regulations (SI 2004/752)
reg.3(2) 8–21
reg.4 8–21

reg.6 8–21
   (4) 8–21
reg.11 8–21
Consumer Credit (Early
   Settlement) Regulations
   (SI 2004/1483) 6–31
Financial Services (Distance
   Marketing) Regulations
   (SI 2004/2095) 7–09
reg.25 7–09
2005 Consumer Protection (Dis-
   tance Selling) (Amend-
   ment) Regulations (SI
   2005/689) 7–10, 7–11
2006 Performances (Moral
   Rights, etc.) Regula-
   tions (SI 2006/18) 12–16
Transfer of Undertakings
   (Protection of Employ-
   ment) Regulations (SI
   2006/246) 8–15
Artist's Resale Right Regulations (SI 2006/346) .. 12–16
Automated Registration of
   Title to Land (Electronic Communications)
   (Scotland) Order (SI
   2006/491) 7–04
Employment Equality (Age)
   Regulations (SI 2006/
   1031) 8–33, 15–07
reg.17(1)(d) 15–07
2007 Small Claims (Scotland)
   Amendment Order (SSI
   2007/496) 2–16
r.2(2)(a) 20–31
Sheriff Courts (Scotland) Act
   1971 (Privative Jur-
   isdiction and Summary
   Cause) Order (SSI 2007/
   507) 20–28
art.2 2–12
art.3 2–15
Company and Business
   Names (Amendment)
   (No. 2) Regulations (SI
   2007/3152) 16–08
2008 Bankruptcy (Scotland) Act
   1985 (Low Income, Low
   Asset Debtors, etc)
   Regulations (SSI 2008/
   81)
s.3 17–06

Bankruptcy (Scotland) Regulations (SSI 2008/82) .. 1–34
s.3 17–06
s.13 17–05
Protected Trust Deeds
   (Scotland) Regulations
   (SI 2008/143) 17–18
s.5 17–18
s.6 17–18
s.7 17–18
s.8 17–18
s.9 17–18
s.10 17–18
ss.12–14 17–18
Companies (Trading Dis-
   closures) Regulations
   (SI 2008/495) 16–12
reg.3 16–12
reg.4 16–12
reg.8 16–12
reg.9(1) 16–12
   (2) 16–12
reg.10(1) 16–12
Consumer Protection from
   Unfair Trading Regula-
   tions (SI 2008/1227) 6–01,
            6–15, 6–37, 6–38,
               6–50, 6–56
reg.2 .... 6–38, 6–47
   (1) 6–51
reg.3 6–39
   (1) 6–47
   (3) 6–39, 6–47
   (4) 6–49
reg.4 6–52
reg.4A 6–52
reg.5 6–41
   (4) 6–42
   (5) 6–42
reg.6 .... 6–45, 6–52
   (2) 6–45
   (4) 6–45
reg.7 6–46
   (1) 6–46
   (8) 6–52
reg.8 .... 6–49, 6–52
reg.9 6–49
reg.10 6–49
reg.11 6–49
reg.12 6–49
reg.20(4) 6–49
Sch.1 .... 6–40, 6–48, 6–49
   para.11 6–49
   para.28 6–49

Chapter 1   Introduction to the Nature and Sources of Scots Law

JOSEPHINE BISACRE[1]

► CHAPTER OVERVIEW

This chapter is concerned with the nature and sources of Scots law. It **1–01** looks first at fundamental issues of what we mean by law and the difference between legal and non-legal rules. It then traces the development of Scots law from the period before the Roman occupation to modern times, highlighting the important events that shaped the modern legal system. It explains various ways in which law can be categorised in order to understand it better. The remainder of the chapter is concerned with the formal sources of Scots law, the most important of which are legislation and case law (judicial precedent).

✓ OUTCOMES

At the end of this chapter you should be able to: **1–02**

- ✓ understand the difference between legal and non-legal rules;
- ✓ have an awareness of the historical reasons for the relationship between Scots and English law today;
- ✓ make use of different classifications of law to aid understanding of the various branches of law;
- ✓ understand the relationship between European legislation and legislation of the UK and Scottish Parliaments;
- ✓ describe the procedure for enactment of an Act of the UK Parliament and an Act of the Scottish Parliament and for the making of delegated legislation;
- ✓ describe the requirements for a precedent from an earlier court to be binding on a later court;
- ✓ display awareness of the minor formal sources of law: the institutional writers, custom and equity.
- ✓ distinguish the formal sources of Scots law from secondary sources.

---

[1] Lecturer in Business Law, Heriot-Watt University.

1

INTRODUCTION

1–03 Businesses operate within a legal framework which gives them a set of rules that are known in advance, and are kept up to date. If there are business disputes, or someone is injured by business activities, disputes can be brought before the court and remedies obtained. There are also criminal laws to try to ensure that businesses adopt safe business practices. There are legal rules which provide for different business structures, such as the partnership and the registered company described in Chapters 14 to 16. Managers and employees of businesses need some knowledge of the law: they need to know when their business is bound in a contract, and if a contract has been breached, what remedies may be sought; they need to know what the legal implications are if an employee injures a member of the public while working; and every business that takes on even one employee needs to know something about employment law. The important thing for managers of businesses to bear in mind is that while no one would expect them to have an encyclopaedic knowledge of law, they need to have a working knowledge of the most important aspects of business law, and they need to be able to ask the right questions when seeking legal advice from professional lawyers. Accountants also have a role in advising business managers on aspects of law, and are often the first port of call for such advice.

Legal rules and non-legal rules

1–04 Legal rules may appear similar to non-legal rules. For example, I may regard it as imperative that I honour an arrangement to turn up at a particular venue on a certain day and have dinner with a friend. However, if my friend decides not to turn up and goes to a football match instead, I would not be able to exercise any legal remedy, nor would the state exact any punishment. All legal systems have to draw a line between areas of behaviour that are covered by legal rules and areas of behaviour that are best regulated only by codes of moral and social behaviour. This dividing line may differ from society to society, and may change over time. For example, in Scotland, it used to be the case that gambling contracts would not be enforced by the courts as being too trivial for their consideration. However, that has now changed, and these contracts are now enforceable.[2] Talking on a mobile phone while driving a car has recently become a criminal offence for which the penalty has been increased to £60 with three penalty points on the licence.[3] The difference between a legal rule and a non-legal rule lies in whether the rule is regarded as having the authority of the state behind it: it may provide for an enforcement mechanism granting a remedy should the rule be breached (civil law), or may provide for state-backed punishment for transgression of the rule (criminal law).

---

[2] As a result of s.335 of the Gambling Act 2005.
[3] Road Safety Act 2006 s.26.

Scots law and English law

Scotland, although part of the United Kingdom, has its own distinct legal **1–05** system with many rules of law that differ from those in the rest of the United Kingdom, including separate courts. However, as this chapter goes on to discuss, in some areas of business law the law across the United Kingdom is the same or very similar. In sale and supply of goods, consumer protection, employment law, partnership and company law, and intellectual property law, the law in the different parts of the United Kingdom is largely the same. Parts of contract law and the law of delict are similar, although not identical. However, there are significant differences in criminal law, property law and in the law on rights in security, the reasons lying in their different historical development.

THE HISTORY AND DEVELOPMENT OF SCOTS LAW

The two major influences on Scots law over the centuries have been **1–06** English law and Roman law. Because of this, modern Scots law can be said to be a mixed system of law combining elements of the deductive reasoning characteristic of the civil legal systems derived from Roman law,[4] which apply principles to the solution of factual cases, with the inductive approach of the English common law,[5] which does the opposite, using inductive reasoning to develop principles from concrete cases.

The Celtic period

Little is known about the laws applying in Scotland before the Roman **1–07** occupation between AD 79 and about AD 400. Scotland at that period was inhabited by various Celtic tribes who would have had their own separate customary laws which were probably unwritten. When the Romans arrived in Scotland they made attempts to subdue the tribes, but they were never fully successful and Roman law was resisted in Scotland.

After the Roman occupation ended, Scotland was inhabited by four peoples: the Picts who inhabited the area from the Forth to the Pentland Firth; the Britons in Strathclyde; the Scots in Dalriada (modern Argyllshire); and the Angles based in the Lothians between the Tweed and the Forth. The Picts, Britons and Scots were all Celtic races who came to Scotland originally from Gaul, whereas the Angles were originally a Teutonic race who moved into Scotland from England. Around 843, Kenneth MacAlpin, King of the Scots, united the Picts and the Scots in a kingdom called Scotia. It is known that Norse invaders started to arrive in Orkney, Shetland and the Western Isles in the ninth century bringing

---

[4] Principally the countries of Western Europe, although the civil legal tradition has been exported to Louisiana in the USA and South Africa.
[5] The common law approach applies in the USA, Australia and Canada and other former colonies of the UK.

with them Norse law, traces of which remain to this day in udal law in Orkney and Shetland.[6] However, there is little evidence of lasting legal influence on modern Scots law from this period, except the office of Lord Lyon King of Arms in relation to nobiliary law, which remains to this day.[7]

The middle ages to the Union of the Parliaments

1–08 In 1016 Scotland was unified into one kingdom when Malcolm II, King of Scots, together with Owen the Bald, King of Strathclyde, defeated the Angles at the Battle of Carham.

The feudal system of land ownership arrived in Scotland around the same time as the Norman Conquest in England in 1066. This system survived in Scotland until it was recently abolished by the Abolition of Feudal Tenure etc (Scotland) Act 2000, one of the early Acts of the new Scottish Parliament. Under the feudal system, land was held by a vassal from a feudal superior, who in turn held his rights from the King. Feudal tenure involved obligations, initially including military service.

In the early Middle Ages, the King was the source of justice, which was dispensed by the King's Council, which combined the functions of a Court and a Parliament. Justiciars dispensed civil and criminal justice at twice-yearly Justice-Ayres held in spring and autumn in various locations. The modern High Court of Justiciary traces its name from the Justiciars. Sheriffs were also introduced in this period to dispense local justice in civil and criminal matters, and combined this function with that of collecting taxes. There were also barony courts as part of the feudal system. In the early mediaeval period a person could be tried by ordeal, under which an accused could face a duel, but this gave way to trial by jury during the reign of Alexander II.

In the twelfth and thirteenth centuries the burghs rose to prominence and burgh courts were introduced presided over by the Chamberlain. A legal text the *Leges Quattuor Burgorum* or Laws of the Four Burghs (Edinburgh, Berwick, Roxburgh and Stirling) was written in the thirteenth century codifying the customary and legal rules used in the four burghs to dispense justice. Other important early legal works which have survived were the *Regiam Majestatem* and the *Quoniam Attachiamenta* (both called after the first words in the text) which may date from the fourteenth century or possibly earlier.

Before the Reformation, canon law (the law of the Roman Catholic Church) was very important in Scotland. Churchmen were among the best educated in the land, and canon law was influential upon the development of family law in Scotland. It was churchmen who first travelled to continental European universities and brought back ideas borrowed from Roman law. Church courts were held in this period up to

---

[6] A system of land tenure that applied in Orkney and Shetland, and of which some aspects still survive.
[7] T.B. Smith, *A Short Commentary on the Law of Scotland* (W. Green, Edinburgh, 1962), p.4.

the Reformation, to decide on matters where canon law was influential. An example of the influence of canon law on modern Scots law is the binding nature of gratuitous promise in Scots law.

Some areas of business law can trace their origin to the middle ages. Merchants from different countries used to meet at major trade fairs across Europe, and also at the seaports. This was an opportunity for the exchange of ideas, and a European law merchant or mercantile law developed from the eleventh century onwards, as distinct from local laws. Since trade is conducted across national borders, it is important to have a degree of uniformity in commercial law. In Scotland, a Court of the Admiral of Scotland met in seaside burghs, and courts were also held at trade fairs to decide disputes between merchants. Some modern legal concepts trace their origin to this period, such as negotiable instruments, the use of simplified methods of execution for commercial documents and marine insurance.

Wars of Independence took place between Scotland and England after the death of Alexander III in 1286, ending with an uneasy peace in 1328 negotiated in the Treaty of Northampton, by which England recognised Robert the Bruce as king of an independent Scotland. The cold war between England and Scotland during and after this period meant that the only outside influence on Scots law in this period came from Roman law as taught and applied in continental Europe.

In the fifteenth century the Universities of St Andrews (1411), Glasgow (1451) and Aberdeen (1494) were founded and began to teach law. However, because the standard of law teaching was higher in continental Europe, it became common for scholars to study civil law initially at French and Italian universities and latterly at universities in the Netherlands, where they could study civil law in Latin. As a result, legal scholars returned home to Scotland bringing with them ideas from Roman law to fill in the gaps in the developing legal system. Parts of the law of obligations, and the law on corporeal moveable property derive from Roman legal concepts. Many of the legal scholars in the seventeenth and eighteenth centuries were held in such esteem that their works were elevated to the status of being considered themselves to be formal sources of law.[8] This period of rapid development of Scots law coincided with the Scottish Enlightenment, a period in Scottish history of particularly fruitful development of ideas across the fields of science, economics, philosophy and law, during which thinkers and scientists such as Adam Smith, James Watt, and David Hume were exerting an influence in Scotland and beyond.

In the sixteenth century, the most notable development was the founding of the College of Justice in 1532, (the Court of Session) which was a collegiate civil court of 15 professional judges based in Edinburgh. Law reporting began to develop in rudimentary form in Practicks from

---

[8] The most prominent example is James Dalrymple, Viscount Stair whose most authoritative work is his *Institutions of the Law of Scotland* 1681. See p.28 towards the end of this chapter where the Institutional Writers are discussed.

this period. Another decisive event was the Reformation in 1559–60, which ended the church courts and the application of canon law.

The beginning of the seventeenth century witnessed the Union of the Crowns, when James VI of Scotland became king of England in 1603. Although James desired complete union between the two kingdoms, public opinion in neither country was in favour. An important legal landmark in this period was the creation of the General Register of Sasines in 1617, which provided a single register of landownership for Scotland, a register which continued until it was gradually replaced by the Land Register only towards the end of the twentieth century. Another legal landmark was the setting up of the High Court of Justiciary in 1672 as a criminal court, replacing the Justice-Ayres. It was a circuit court, to try the most serious crimes throughout Scotland, and existed in this form until its personnel were consolidated with those of the Court of Session in the nineteenth century.

The Union of the Parliaments to the twentieth century

1–09 The Union of the Scottish and English Parliaments in 1707 was precipitated by various events: discord about the eventual succession to the throne if Queen Anne should die without surviving children; by Scotland's weak economic state after the collapse of the disastrous attempt to establish a colony in Darien, Panama; and by the likelihood of war between England and France and the undesirable prospect from the English point of view of Scotland again coming to the aid of France, under the Auld Alliance.

Acts of both Parliaments were passed to enact the provisions of the Treaty of Union. The Treaty provided that the two kingdoms would become Great Britain with a common coinage, and recognition of the Hanoverian succession to the throne. The two Parliaments were to be succeeded by one Parliament of Great Britain. There would be free trade between Scotland and England. The Treaty retained the separate system of courts in Scotland. The Treaty states that Scottish criminal cases could no longer be appealed to English courts, but does not explicitly so state in respect of civil appeals.[9] The Treaty provided that public law should be uniform throughout Great Britain, but that Scottish private law could not be altered "except for the evident utility of the subjects within Scotland".[10]

The pre-1707 Scottish Parliament was much less powerful than its English counterpart. In the middle ages, the Scottish Parliament had been made up of clergy and barons, but by the time of Robert the Bruce (1306–29) representatives from the Burghs were added (the Three Estates). However, it was never a fully democratic Parliament. It also served as a court, and as an organ of the government. From the fifteenth century it

---

[9] Article XIX of the Union with England Act 1707. The House of Lords has continued to hear appeals on civil matters on points of law from Scottish courts thereafter—see *Greenshields v Magistrates of Edinburgh* (1710–11) Rob 12.
[10] Article XVIII of the Union with England Act 1707.

was dominated by a committee called the Lords of the Articles who controlled the business of the Parliament. The Acts of the old Scots Parliament had a characteristic not shared by its successor, whereby they could lose the force of law by desuetude without having to be expressly repealed if a long period of contrary usage could be demonstrated.[11] A few statutes of the old Scots Parliament are still in force today, the oldest being the Royal Mines Act 1424 which reserves gold and silver mines to the Crown.[12] After the Union of the Parliaments, the Parliament at Westminster enacted separate statutes for Scotland in those areas of law where Scots law differed from English law, and uniform statutes, (sometimes with some separate sections for Scotland) where the law was the same or similar.

After the Treaty of Union, Scots law was increasingly influenced by English law. One of the major reasons was because civil appeals could be taken to the House of Lords, and these were often heard by a bench of English judges. However, since 1876 there has always been at least one Scottish Law Lord. Also, being a much larger legal system, England offered a fruitful source of case law, which was increasingly well documented in law reports. English influence on the law of Scotland can also be seen in the enactment of unified statutes for Scotland and England on important aspects of business law at the end of the nineteenth century relating to the sale of goods, bills of exchange and partnership.[13] The influence of Roman law also declined as continental legal systems were gradually codified, reducing the amount of Roman law taught at continental Universities, and because, during the period of the Napoleonic Wars, travel was difficult.

In the nineteenth century, Parliament became the Parliament of the United Kingdom with the inclusion of Ireland in 1800, and this was changed by a further treaty in 1920 to include Northern Ireland only, after the Republic of Ireland was created. The Court of Session was reorganised into the modern structure of the Inner and Outer House with the Inner House divided into two Divisions, and its personnel was consolidated with those of the High Court of Justiciary.[14] The Scottish Office was created in 1885 to govern Scotland in those areas of government where separate rules applied. This system continued until devolution when the Scotland Act 1998 created a Scottish Parliament and a government for Scotland.

The twentieth century saw the creation of the European Convention on Human Rights and Fundamental Freedoms, the European Community (later European Union), and the Scottish Parliament.

---

[11] Desuetude applies in some legal systems, making statutes obsolete by disuse, without having to be repealed. The last case which discussed desuetude was *Brown v Magistrates of Edinburgh*, 1931 S.L.T. 456, in which statutes from 1579 and 1661 on Sunday trading were found not to be in desuetude.

[12] Acts of the old Scots Parliament that are still in force can be found on the UK Statute Law Database at *http://www.statutelaw.gov.uk*.

[13] The Bills of Exchange Act 1882 and the Partnership Act 1890 apply to this day.

[14] See Ch.2.

The European Convention on Human Rights and Fundamental Freedoms

1–10   A major constitutional development immediately after the Second World War was the drawing up of the European Convention on Human Rights and Fundamental Freedoms by the Council of Europe in 1949.[15] The aim of this Convention was to prevent abuses of human rights by the state recurring in Europe, by providing fundamental human rights and remedies for their abuse. Although the United Kingdom has been bound by this Convention since 1950, its citizens have only since 1966 had the right to take a case to the Court of Human Rights in Strasbourg, on the grounds of violation of human rights by a public body. Because of difficulties and delays in taking a case to the court in Strasbourg, the Human Rights Act 1998 and the Scotland Act 1998 embedded the European Convention on Human Rights and Fundamental Freedoms into national law in the United Kingdom, which means that remedies against public bodies can now be sought before the domestic courts. As the courts are public bodies, their procedures must be compliant with the Convention, as must those of all other public bodies. The legislation of the new Scottish Parliament is ineffective if not compliant.[16] Because the UK Parliament is a sovereign Parliament, non-compliant legislation is not invalid, but would be a breach of the Convention. For these reasons, all legislation must be scrutinised in advance for compliance. In the case of the Westminster Parliament, there is a procedure for amendment of statutes by delegated legislation to make them compliant.

The European Union[17]

1–11   Another major legal development of the twentieth century was the creation of the European Community, which was originally concerned with European integration, and later developed into a more extensive European Union. The European Community has existed since 1956, as an economic community of six member states, which the United Kingdom joined in 1972–73. By 2008 there were 27 member states and the organisation has expanded its areas of competence so that it is now a customs union, has a foreign and security policy, provides common citizenship rights, and provides police and judicial co-operation. The organisation has an institutional infrastructure in the European Commission, the Council of the European Union, the European Parliament

---

[15] The Council of Europe, despite the similarity of its name with one of the organs if the European Union, is a different body with broader membership than the EU. It has 47 members comprising all European countries including Turkey. See *http://www.coe.int*.

[16] Section 29 of the Scotland Act 1998.

[17] See *http://europa.eu*.

and the European Court of Justice.[18] It has the power to legislate and European legislation must be applied within the member states in priority to national law, within its sphere of competence.

The Scottish Parliament

The final years of the twentieth century saw another major constitutional **1–12** change for Scotland. As has already been mentioned, after 1707 legislation for Scotland was enacted by the Westminster Parliament. Lack of parliamentary time for Scottish legislation caused dissatisfaction. Too often legislation on disparate matters was crammed into Law Reform (Miscellaneous Provisions) (Scotland) Acts, or long overdue reforms were delayed. Also, government through the Scottish Office was unpopular in periods when the government of the day did not represent the electorate of Scotland, as was the case in the 1980s. For these reasons, after the failure to secure a sufficient majority in a referendum in 1979, another referendum was held in 1997 which led to the establishment of the Scottish Parliament and a Scottish Executive (now Scottish Government). The Scottish Parliament is a unicameral Parliament and is based at Holyrood in Edinburgh. It currently has 129 Members of the Scottish Parliament (MSPs). Its power to legislate is devolved from the UK Parliament, and is limited to legislating within those powers not reserved to the Westminster Parliament, and it has a limited right to vary income tax rates by up to 3p in the pound. It is important to emphasise that the new Scottish Parliament is not a re-creation of the pre-1707 Scottish Parliament, but a completely new Parliament. Even in the few years since it came into existence, it has passed some major statutes such as the Abolition of Feudal Tenure etc (Scotland) Act 2000 which changed the system of land ownership in Scotland, and the Bankruptcy and Diligence etc (Scotland) Act 2007 which is designed to encourage an enterprise culture in Scotland by shortening the period of bankruptcy from three years to one year. Since the election in 2007 returned a narrow victory for the Scottish National Party, a debate has begun about a possible increase in devolved powers.[19]

CATEGORIES OF LAW

Law imposes itself on most areas of human activity, and even on relations **1–13** between states themselves. The branch of the law covering the treaties and conventions entered into between states is known as Public International Law.

---

[18] At the time of writing, the UK Parliament is debating the Lisbon Treaty which if approved by the member states, would introduce a longer term for the presidency than the current six months, would create a new post of High Representative on Foreign Affairs; it would reduce the membership of the European Commission, and would reform the voting system to take account of enlarged membership of the EU, reducing the scope for blocking of European legislation.

[19] For information about the Scottish Parliament see *http://www.scottish.parliament.uk*.

There are other classifications of law, some of which cut across each other and in which the same terms have different meanings, which can be confusing.

Public law and private law

1–14 Public law relates the relationship between the state and the citizen including legal persons such as partnerships and companies, while private law concerns itself with regulating relationships between citizens.

Public law can itself be divided into *constitutional law*, *administrative law* and *criminal law*. Constitutional law is concerned with a state's constitution, written or unwritten, and the operation of the organs of the state: the legislature (Parliament), the executive (government) and the judiciary (the courts). Administrative law provides a framework regulating the exercise of power by the government, to protect its citizens from abuse of power. Criminal law provides prescriptive rules to try to ensure acceptable behaviour by the citizens. A state decides which behaviour should be penalised, and this may change as society changes. If behaviour breaches these rules, the state will prosecute the alleged offender in the criminal courts and, if convicted, state-sanctioned punishment will follow.

Most of the substantive law that affects businesses covered in this book is private law. Private law includes the law of contract, law of delict, family law, law of trusts, commercial law, company law, insolvency law, parts of employment law, and the law of property, plus remedies for breach of the relevant legal rules.

Public law	Private law
Constitutional law Administrative law Criminal law	Contract Delict Family law Law of trusts Commercial law Company Law Insolvency law Parts of employment law Law of property Remedies

Civil law and criminal law

1–15 Law can also be classified into *civil and criminal law*. This distinction relates to the courts which hear the cases. Civil cases are cases where one party is in dispute with another and seeks a remedy, which is obtained from a civil court. Where a person has been charged with commission of a crime, a prosecutor will bring the case before a criminal court, seeking a sentence (punishment). This classification of law cuts across the previous one, in that cases on constitutional law in the United Kingdom are brought before the civil courts as there are no separate constitutional courts in this country, and cases on some aspects of administrative law are also brought before the civil courts, although there are some separate administrative tribunals in the United Kingdom. Cases on private law are always brought before the civil courts.[20]

Civil law and common law

This is a completely different use of the term "civil law". In this sense it refers to Roman law and the legal systems derived from it. The distinction is made between civilian legal systems and common law systems. The civil systems of law derive from Roman law, and make use of codes containing general principles of law which are applied to cases. Many of the states of western Europe developed their legal systems from Roman law, as has already been described earlier in this chapter. Common law is judge-made law and originated in England, from where it has been exported to England's colonies including the USA, Canada and Australia. Scots law is often described as being a mixed system. **1–16**

Common law and statute law

Common law is also distinguished from statute law or legislation. As will be seen in the next part of this chapter, every legal rule has a formal source from which it derives its authority as law, which may lie in a piece of primary or subordinate legislation. If it does not, it derives from the common law, which consists of legal rules which have been declared by the judges in case law, plus legal rules stemming from other minor formal sources. While the most important formal source of law in Scotland is statute law, the common law remains an important formal source of the law of contract, delict, criminal law and the law of agency. The rest of this chapter is concerned with these formal sources of law. **1–17**

THE FORMAL SOURCES OF SCOTS LAW

In order for laws to have their binding quality, rules of law must derive from a formal source. This is what differentiates legal from non-legal rules. **1–18**

---

[20] See Ch.2.

> **Key Concept**
>
> The formal sources of Scots law are:
>
> - Legislation
> - Judicial precedent
> - The Institutional Writers
> - Custom
> - Equity

There is a ranking in authority between these formal sources, with legislation in the first place, followed by judicial precedent. The other formal sources are of limited importance nowadays.

LEGISLATION

1–19 Within its area of competence, European legislation is the most authoritative formal source of law in Scotland. Nationally, legislation is enacted by the UK Parliament or by a body to whom the UK Parliament has delegated the power to legislate. The Crown also has some residual power to legislate.

> **Key Concept**
>
> Legislation that is binding in Scotland comes from four sources:
>
> - The European Union
> - The UK Parliament
> - The Scottish Parliament
> - The Royal Prerogative

European legislation

1–20 There are four types of European legislation that have binding force: Treaties, Regulations, Directives and Decisions.

Treaties are the primary legislation of the European Union and are entered into between the member states, to create the ground rules for the Union. Since the Treaty of Rome in 1957, there have been many other treaties, admitting new members and adding new spheres of competence. Provisions in the treaties themselves may have direct effect within member states, despite contrary national law.[21]

Article 249 of the EC Treaty empowers organs of the European Union to make secondary legislation in the form of *Regulations, Directives and*

---

[21] *Van Gend en Loos* Case 26/62 [1963] ECR.

Decisions. Recommendations and opinions can also be issued but these have no binding force. For the European Union to have legislative competence, authority to legislate has to be found in an article in one of the treaties. In some areas of business law, national laws have been approximated or harmonised in certain areas in order to provide a level playing field for business to prevent unfair competition and exploitation of workers.[22]

Regulations are binding on member states and their citizens and have direct effect, which means that they do not need to be enacted into national law.[23]

Directives are instructions to member states to amend their laws and are binding as to the results to be achieved. They may provide various legislative options. They have been used extensively in company law and employment law to try to make national laws comparable although not identical. If directives are not fully translated into national law, they can have direct effect, enabling affected citizens to seek a remedy from the European Court of Justice.[24] Directives take effect when notified to member states, and usually provide a period for their implementation into national law.

Decisions of the Commission or the Council are only binding upon the member states to whom they are addressed.

How European law is made

Various organs of the European Union are involved in the creation of European legislation: the European Commission, the Council of the European Union and the European Parliament. The European Commission is the 'government' of the European Union and is composed of 27 permanent Commissioners, one from every member state. It is based in Brussels. The Council of the European Union is composed of a government minister from every member state, with different ministers attending according to the topic under discussion. Currently the Presidency of the Council rotates between member states every six months, although if the Lisbon Treaty is accepted, the President will in future hold office for two-and-a-half years. The Council is based in Brussels.

1–21

The European Parliament, despite its name, is not a Parliament in the normal sense of being the body that initiates and enacts European law. Instead it is largely a forum for debate and a consultative body. It does have a role to play in voting on some of the legislation relating to the European Community, but not on the other aspects of the European Union's work. It meets in Brussels and in Strasbourg.

The ideas for secondary legislation are formulated by the European Commission. It drafts a proposal for legislation which may be circulated widely for consultation and commented upon. The proposal is then put

---

[22] Article 94 of the EC Treaty allows for the approximation of national laws to create the common market.
[23] Article 249 EC Treaty.
[24] *Frankovitch v Italy* Case 6/90 and 9/90 [1991] ECR I-5357.

to the Council, from whence it goes to the European Parliament, and is considered by a committee of the Parliament which may propose amendments, which are voted on by the Parliament. The proposal is then scrutinised by one of the working groups of the Council, and a text is either agreed by all the member states or voted on by the Council by weighted voting (according to the size of the various member states) or on some issues by unanimous vote, giving member states a veto.[25] There are some variations on this legislative procedure, which give greater or lesser powers to the European Parliament, depending on the subject of the legislation.[26]

Legislation of the United Kingdom Parliament

1–22 The United Kingdom Parliament is a sovereign Parliament, and has legislative competence over Scotland, England, Wales and Northern Ireland, despite devolved powers in differing degrees having been granted to Scotland, Wales and Northern Ireland. This means that, in theory at least, it can pass laws on anything it likes without limit. It can be argued that the UK Parliament has ceded some of its sovereignty to the European Union, since as we have seen, it has allowed some EU law to be recognised as superior to its own statutes in its areas of competence. However, the UK Parliament is still sovereign in the sense that it could repeal its own legislation that enacted the various treaties of the European Union into UK law. The legal validity of acts of the UK Parliament cannot be challenged in court.[27]

The Queen has an important ceremonial role in that all bills have to receive the Royal Assent before they can become law. The Queen also gives the Queen's Speech at the state opening of each session of Parliament in November, when she reads out the government's proposed legislative programme for the session.

The UK Parliament has two legislative chambers, the House of Commons and the House of Lords. The House of Commons is made up of 646 elected Members of Parliament (MPs), 59 of them from Scotland. The composition of the House of Lords is in the process of reform. Reform of the House of Lords has proved difficult, and the process is likely to be discussed for some time to come.

Acts of the UK Parliament can be divided into public general statutes which apply to us all, and private, local or personal statutes, which apply only to those who are the subject of the legislation. There are some hybrid bills which are a mixture of the two.

Acts of the UK Parliament all start off as bills. Most bills are proposed by government departments as part of the government's legislative programme, although in every session of Parliament some bills will come forward as private members' bills. These are public bills which are

---

[25] These will be amended by the Lisbon Treaty if it comes into force.
[26] For more information about the European Union, see *http://europa.eu*.
[27] Lord Campbell in *Edinburgh and Dalkeith Railway v Wauchope* (1842) 1 Bell App Cas 252 at p.279.

proposed by MPs of any party who are selected by ballot. [28] Although
private members' bills can be starved of Parliamentary time by the
government if it does not like them, they are nevertheless an important
part of the democratic process.

How a bill becomes an Act of the Westminster Parliament

Ideas for legislation may be included in a party's election manifesto. **1–23**
Other ideas may be a reaction to events, such as the UK's recent anti-
terrorism laws, which were enacted in the aftermath of 9/11. Some ideas
are extensively discussed in advance, to ensure that there is a measure of
assent to the legislation and that unforeseen difficulties will not arise.

A government bill will be drafted in the Parliamentary Counsel Office
of the Cabinet Office. The bill then goes through various stages in both
Houses of Parliament before it becomes an Act—the First Reading,
Second Reading, Committee Stage, Report Stage and Third Reading—
after which it will receive the Royal Assent and become an Act of Parliament. Bills may be introduced first into either House. At various stages
amendments may be proposed and voted on.

The First Reading is a formality: the short title of the bill is read out **1–24**
and a date is set for the Second Reading. The bill will be printed. Before
the Second Reading, the Minister in charge of a government bill makes a
declaration that the bill is compatible with the Human Rights Act 1998,[29]
or that the government wishes to proceed with the bill anyway.[30] At the
Second Reading there will be a debate on the general principles of the
bill. The bill then enters the Committee Stage when it goes to a Standing
Committee (House of Commons) or a Committee of the Whole House
(House of Lords). The composition of a Standing Committee is in
accordance with the share of the vote of the different parties in the House.
Bills of "first class constitutional importance" such as the bill that pre-
ceded the Scotland Act 1998 are normally heard by a Committee of the
Whole House in the House of Commons as well. At the Committee Stage
the bill is examined clause by clause, and this is the stage at which most
amendments take place. At the Report Stage, the Committee reports
back to the House, and if the Committee Stage took place before a Select
Committee, there may be further debate on the provisions of the bill, and
further amendments. The Third Reading allows for a final debate on the
principles of the bill, followed by a vote. After the bill has passed through
all these stages in one House, it then goes to the other House where it

---

[28] An example of a private members' bill is the Abortion Act 1967 which legalised abortion
in the UK, which was proposed by David Steel MP when he was a backbench MP before
becoming leader of the Liberal Party and later the Presiding Officer of the Scottish
Parliament at its inception.

[29] See earlier in this chapter, where the European Convention on Human Rights and
Fundamental Freedoms is discussed.

[30] Since the UK Parliament is a sovereign Parliament, it can proceed with non-compliant
legislation, though this is clearly undesirable.

goes through the same stages, and if approved receives the Royal Assent and becomes an Act.[31]

Acts do not generally come into force at once, but are usually brought into force later by the use of delegated legislation.

The legislative powers of the House of Lords are inferior to those of the House of Commons. Legislation on taxation and expenditure ("money bills") cannot be rejected by the House of Lords, but only delayed for one month. Under the Parliament Acts 1911 and 1949, other bills that the House of Lords does not want to pass can be delayed for two sessions of Parliament only. The Parliament Acts have not often been invoked, but were recently invoked in relation to the Hunting Act 2004.[32]

What an Act of the UK Parliament looks like

1–25 An Act of Parliament has a short title by which the Act is popularly known, e.g. "the Companies Act 2006". It has a Chapter Number, which reflects the chronological order in which statutes were enacted in a particular year. For example, the chapter number of the Companies Act 2006 is "c. 46". Acts are divided into sections and sub-divided into sub-sections. Some statutes have supplementary material in schedules at the end. Sections of statutes may be divided into parts and chapters if it is helpful to group them in that way. At the start of an Act of the UK Parliament there may be an arrangement of the sections. Acts have a long title as well as a short title to provide an indication of the purpose of the legislation. The date when the Act received the Royal Assent is given. Every section nowadays has a marginal note, though these are not part of the Act as enacted by Parliament.

Acts of the UK Parliament or sections within Acts may extend to the whole of the United Kingdom or to parts of the United Kingdom only. If a statute does not extend to the whole of the United Kingdom, it will have a section towards the end stating its extent. Even within the areas of legislative competence of the Scottish Parliament, to be discussed later in this chapter, much legislation for Scotland had already been enacted prior to the creation of the Scottish Parliament and will remain in force unless and until it is repealed. Also, the Scottish Parliament sometimes chooses to have legislation made for it by the Parliament at Westminster, generally to ensure uniformity between provisions that apply also to the rest of the United Kingdom. An example of this is the Corporate Manslaughter and Corporate Homicide Act 2007 where criminal provisions for Scotland on corporate homicide are enacted alongside provisions for the rest of the United Kingdom, despite the fact that criminal law is an area of legislative competence devolved to the Scottish Parliament.

If society's needs change, a later statute can be passed to amend parts of the earlier statute. If a statute is not needed at all, it can be repealed, whereupon all parts of that statute will cease to be a formal source of law. Acts of the UK Parliament normally continue in force unless repealed,

---

[31] You can track the progress of a bill through Parliament at *http://www.parliament.uk*.
[32] This Act does not apply to Scotland.

except where an Act specifies an expiry date (known as a "sunset provision"), which used to be the case with anti-terrorism legislation for Northern Ireland which used to have to be voted on annually.

How to find legislation

Once a statute has been enacted, it is printed and sold by the Stationery **1–26** Office. It is also published in a series called *Public General Statutes and Measures*. Legislation is also published in electronic form on the website of the Office of Public Sector Information[33] in the form in which it was enacted. However, as legislation is frequently amended it is preferable to use a database that gives an up-to-date version of the statute as amended as does the UK Statute Law Database,[34] which is free, or Westlaw, Lawtel or Justis which all require a subscription.

Legislation of the Scottish Parliament

As has been mentioned earlier in this chapter, Scotland had her own **1–27** Parliament prior to the Union of the Parliaments in 1707. A few of the Acts of that Parliament are still in force, most having ceased to apply because they were repealed, or fell into desuetude.[35]

The modern Scottish Parliament is a different institution from the pre-1707 Scottish Parliament. Its parent statute is the Scotland Act 1998, and it has been granted legislative competence in all areas not reserved to the Westminster Parliament.[36] Reserved matters include constitutional law, taxation, large parts of business law such as data protection, company law and the law of business associations generally, intellectual property law, consumer law and employment law. However, the Scottish Parliament is still left with a large area of legislative competence. This includes criminal law, legislation on the law of personal bankruptcy, the law of rights in security, the law of diligence (enforcement of claims), parts of corporate insolvency law, property law and the law of trusts. The Scottish Parliament is not a sovereign Parliament, unlike its Westminster counterpart, and can only legislate within its sphere of competence, since its legislation could be challenged for being in excess of its powers as laid out in the Scotland Act 1998.[37] All Scottish legislation is therefore really a kind of delegated legislation.[38] Not only may the Scottish Parliament not legislate in those areas reserved to the Westminster Parliament, but in addition it may not legislate in ways that are incompatible with the European Convention on Human Rights and Fundamental Freedoms or with European Community Law, it may not enact legislation with extra-

---

[33] Available at *http://www.opsi.gov.uk/legislation/about_legislation.htm*.
[34] Available at *http://www.statutelaw.gov.uk*.
[35] See earlier in this chapter under the History and Development of Scots Law.
[36] Scotland Act 1998 ss.28–30 and Sch.5.
[37] Scotland Act 1998 s.54.
[38] See later in this chapter.

territorial scope, or legislate to remove the Lord Advocate as head of the system of criminal prosecution and investigation of deaths in Scotland.[39]

The same distinction is made for Acts of the Scottish Parliament between public general Acts and private Acts.

How a bill becomes an Act of the Scottish Parliament

1–28 As in the Westminster Parliament, legislation starts off as bills which are proposed either by the Scottish Government (formerly Scottish Executive) or by individual Members of the Scottish Parliament (MSPs) (Members' bills) or by one of the Parliament's Committees (Committee bills). There is no Queen's Speech as in the Westminster Parliament, but the Scottish Government has outlined its legislative programme soon after each general election. As the Parliament is not sovereign, a bill has first to be checked in advance to ensure that it comes within its legislative competence. The proposer of the bill must so certify, and the Presiding Officer of the Scottish Parliament must also state whether or not he considers that the bill is within its legislative competence. If a bill appears not to be compliant, the Advocate-General for Scotland,[40] or the Lord Advocate[41] can refer the bill to the Judicial Committee of the Privy Council under s.33 of the Scotland Act 1998[42] for a ruling as to competence.

At stage 1 in the enactment of a bill, it goes to a lead committee which reports back to the Scottish Parliament on the general principles of the bill. A general debate takes place in the Parliament on the main points of the bill in conjunction with the committee report. If the Parliament approves the bill at this stage, it goes back to the lead committee or to another committee or a Committee of the Whole Parliament for a detailed consideration of the clauses of the bill for stage 2 and the bill is voted upon. Stage 3 is normally a formal stage at which the bill is presented to the full Parliament and will normally be passed without further discussion, although it is possible for further amendments to be made at this stage. [43]

Because of the necessity to ensure that the Parliament does not exceed its legislative competence, the Royal Assent cannot be given immediately, but is delayed for four weeks, to provide time for further checking of legislative competence. In this period the Advocate-General for Scotland, the Lord Advocate or the Attorney-General[44] may refer the bill to the Judicial Committee of the Privy Council for a decision on competence.[45]

---

[39] Scotland Act 1998 s.29(2).
[40] Law Officer for the Crown who advises the government at Westminster on matters of Scots Law. See Ch.2.
[41] Law Officer for the Crown, responsible for advice to the government in Scotland and head of the criminal prosecution service in Scotland.
[42] Eventually its function will be taken over by the proposed Supreme Court of the United Kingdom.
[43] Scotland Act 1998 s.36.
[44] The Principal Law Officer of the Crown in England.
[45] Under s.33 of the Scotland Act 1998.

The UK Government also has the power to issue an order prohibiting the Presiding Officer of the Scottish Parliament from submitting the bill for the Royal Assent if it considers that the bill has exceeded its competence.

Even once Acts of the Scottish Parliament have entered into force, they may still be challenged for having exceeded their legislative competence. "Devolution issues" i.e. issues of whether an Act of the Scottish Parliament has strayed beyond its sphere of competence may be may be raised by either the Lord Advocate or the Advocate-General for Scotland,[46] they may arise in the context of other proceedings in court, and may also be raised by affected persons who fulfil the requirements of the Scotland Act 1998 in the civil and criminal courts anywhere in the United Kingdom. Appeals concerning devolution issues may be made to the Judicial Committee of the Privy Council.

What an Act of the Scottish Parliament looks like

Acts of the Scottish Parliament look very similar to Acts of the West-   **1–29** minster Parliament. They have a short title, which includes the word "Scotland" in brackets and the date, for example the Bankruptcy and Diligence etc (Scotland) Act 2007. Each Act has a chronological serial number, in this case an "Asp Number" which stands for "Act of the Scottish Parliament". In all other respects they look the same as Acts of the UK Parliament.

As is the case with Acts of the Westminster Parliament, Acts of the Scottish Parliament continue in force unless repealed, and desuetude does not apply to them. The same rules on publication apply to Scottish primary legislation as to Acts of the Westminster Parliament.

Delegated legislation

Delegated (or subordinate or secondary) legislation is made by a body   **1–30** other than Parliament in exercise of powers given to that body by Parliament in a parent statute. Delegated legislation as a method of legislating has the following points in its favour:

(1) It saves Parliamentary time, which is limited. Parliament could never manage to legislate on all the matters covered by delegated legislation. In 2007, 31 Acts were passed by the Westminster Parliament, compared with several thousand statutory instruments. In Scotland in 2007, there were 19 Acts of the Scottish Parliament, and several hundred statutory instruments.

(2) Delegated legislation can be put in place faster than primary legislation. It can be used to the response to emergencies, such as the outbreak of foot and mouth disease in 2007, as delegated legislation can be put in place very quickly and can be amended quickly.

---

[46] Scotland Act 1998 s.98 and Sch.6.

(3) Experts can be involved in the framing of delegated legislation in areas which are technically complex.

(4) Delegated legislation can be used to phase in a large piece of new primary legislation slowly. Different parts of a statute can be introduced at different times by the relevant government minister issuing commencement orders. This is being done currently with the introduction of provisions of the Companies Act 2006.

However, the use of delegated legislation brings with it some undesirable effects as well:

(1) Delegated legislation is sometimes criticised for being undemocratic, in that there is much less advance consultation with sections of the public than is generally the case with Acts of Parliament. Most delegated legislation is issued by the government of the day, and although Parliament may be able to vote on the delegated legislation, Members of Parliament have no influence on the contents.

(3) Although the internet has been very helpful in making it easier for the public to discover the existence of delegated legislation that is relevant to them, people are generally less well aware of delegated legislation than of primary legislation.

(4) There is concern that in some cases the parent statute may itself lack detail and allow excessively wide powers of delegation. This makes the task of scrutiny of the parent statute in its passage through Parliament very hard, as Members of Parliament do not know at the time of the passage of the bill what the implications of the legislation will be. An example of this is the Financial Services and Markets Act 2000 which provides for extensive delegated legislation in implement of its provisions.

(5) Some statutes contain powers which allow the person to whom the powers are delegated to amend other pieces of legislation, which further removes the possibility for Parliamentary scrutiny—so called "Henry VIII clauses". One example is s.113(5) and (6) of the Scotland Act 1998, which delegate powers to amend other statutes. It should be noted that the Legislative and Regulatory Reform Act 2006 gives increased power to the UK government to issue legislative reform orders to amend primary legislation so as to remove "burdens" imposed by legislation, subject to certain preconditions. This wide-ranging power further removes the democratic control of Parliament over legislation.

Ultra vires and delegate legislation

1–31   Because the powers to make delegated legislation are laid down in the parent Act of Parliament or Act of the Scottish Parliament, delegated legislation may not exceed these boundaries. Like legislation of the Scottish Parliament, delegated legislation may be challenged in court if it is *ultra vires* (beyond the powers) of the body to whom legislative power was delegated.

Forms of delegated legislation

The overwhelming majority of delegated legislation is made by the gov- **1–32** ernment. The Government issues Orders, Regulations, Rules, Schemes or Directions which are all forms of delegated legislation. Local authorities also make use of delegated legislation to create bylaws or management rules for their local areas, such as the ban on drinking in public places in Glasgow. Delegated legislation is also used by the supreme courts in Scotland to make their own procedural rules by Acts of Sederunt (Court of Session) and Acts of Adjournal (High Court of Justiciary). Some statutory bodies such as railway companies have delegated powers to make their own rules. The Privy Council[47] also holds some delegated powers including delegated power to issue Orders in Council amend the constitutions of Scottish Universities, and power to issue orders in Council to regulate the fisheries on the Tweed and Esk Rivers in the borders of Scotland and England.[48]

Some delegated legislation must be in the form of a statutory instru- **1–33** ment (SI) or Scottish statutory instrument (SSI). If this is the case, the parent Act will say so. All Orders in Council must be in this form. The Statutory Instruments Act 1946 lays down rules for statutory instruments, to ensure they receive some measure of scrutiny and publicity. Statutory instruments must be dated, given a unique identifying number, printed, published and sold. Depending on the parent statute, they may have to be laid before Parliament three weeks before coming into effect and in other cases a draft must be laid before Parliament. In the Westminster Parliament, a statutory instrument may be examined by the Joint Committee on Statutory Instruments of the two Houses of Parliament to ensure compliance with these rules. Although the Committee has no power to reject a statutory instrument, it may refer it to either House on a variety of grounds, including being *ultra vires* (beyond the powers) of its parent statute. Even if it is referred, the contents of the statutory instrument may be debated but not amended. The parent statute may provide for the statutory instrument to be voted on by either or both Houses of Parliament. The vote may be either by negative or affirmative resolution. A negative resolution allows Parliament to reject the statutory instrument, while an affirmative resolution means that the statutory instrument will only come into effect if it is approved. However, although these procedures provide a veto to Parliament, they do not provide any mechanism for amendment. Some parent statutes provide for other methods of Parliamentary scrutiny.

In the case of delegated legislation in Scotland where the parent statute is an Act of the Scottish Parliament, the Scotland Act 1998 requires that

---

[47] This body is made up of certain government ministers and senior members of the opposition, and senior judges.
[48] Scotland Act 1998 s.111.

government delegated legislation takes the form of a statutory instrument. The Scotland Act 1998 lays down 11 different regimes for Parliamentary approval, depending on the subject of the delegated legislation. The different procedures call for resolutions of the Scottish Parliament and/or of both or either House of the Westminster Parliament.[49]

How to find delegated legislation

1–34 Because there is much more of it, delegated legislation is harder to locate than Acts of Parliament. As has been mentioned, every statutory instrument has a sequential number, and it is essential to know this number. As well as the name and year, every SI and SSI has a citation which contains the name and sequential number, for example the Bankruptcy (Scotland) Regulations 2008, SSI 2008/82. They can be found on the website of the Office of Public Information in unrevised form at *http://www.opsi.gov.uk/stat.htm* or on the UK Statute Law Database, also in unrevised form at *http://www.statutelaw.gov.uk* and by using subscription databases such as Westlaw, Justis or Lawtel.

Legislation under the Royal Prerogative

1–35 The Crown (the sovereign as represented by the government) has various special law-making powers which it exercises without recourse to Parliament. These include the power to ask ministers to form a government, the power to dissolve Parliament, the power to sign treaties and declare war,[50] and power to legislate for the colonies.

JUDICIAL PRECEDENT

1–36 The formal source of some parts of Scots law comes not from legislation but from prior decisions of the Scottish courts (judicial precedent). In these parts of Scots law, the decisions of past cases may be binding on later courts. The major areas of Scots business law where the formal source is in case law are the law of contract (voluntary obligations),[51] the law of delict (involuntary obligations),[52] parts of criminal law,[53] the law of agency,[54] parts of the law of property[55] and parts of the law of rights in security.[56]

It is important to draw a distinction between areas of law where judicial precedent is a formal source of law, and those areas where the formal source is statutory, but where cases are referred to court to apply

[49] Scotland Act 1998 s.115 and Sch.7.
[50] This power may be made subject to approval by Parliament in future.
[51] See Ch.4.
[52] See Ch.10.
[53] See Ch.3.
[54] See Ch.9.
[55] See Ch.11.
[56] See Ch.19.

or interpret the statute. In these circumstances the case is not the formal source of law but an application of it.

Treating judicial precedent as binding rather than as persuasive (*stare decisis* or "to stand upon decisions") is a characteristic of common law systems of law and not of the civil law systems of continental Europe or of the European Court of Justice. Before the Union of the Parliaments in 1707, precedent in Scotland used to be more loosely applied, so that it was only a tract of identical decisions that was binding on the courts and individual cases were regarded as evidence of the law rather than as a formal source of the law. However, by the nineteenth century, the Scottish courts had adopted the English doctrine of binding precedent.

T.B. Smith in his *Short Commentary on the Law of Scotland*[57] describes judicial precedent as "a good servant and a bad master". The doctrine can bring certainty, but there are dangers in over-reliance on precedents.

Stare decisis or binding precedent brings the following benefits:

(1) Going to court should not be a lottery. It accords with people's sense of justice that like cases should be treated alike.
(2) It makes for a more efficient legal system. Potential litigants can be given legal advice prior to bringing a case on the likelihood of success or failure in court, and can decide accordingly. One test case which establishes a legal precedent may allow other identical cases to be settled out of court.
(3) It provides some flexibility to the law, in enabling it to develop incrementally as society and the economy develop. For example, the delictual liability of a ginger beer manufacturer at common law was first established applying the "neighbour'" principle in the House of Lords case *Donoghue v Stevenson* 1932 SC (HL) 31. It has been extended by later courts incrementally and by analogy to other areas such as the liability of auditors to third parties for negligent misstatements in audited accounts in certain circumstances.[58]

Judicial precedent also brings with it certain disadvantages.

(1) A precedent may take the development of the law up a blind alley from which only new legislation can rescue it. An example of this comes from the law of occupiers' liability where the Occupiers' Liability Act 1957 and the Occupiers' Liability (Scotland) Act 1961 had to be enacted to overturn unsatisfactory precedents from the House of Lords.
(2) Precedents can slow the development of the law if an old precedent suitable to a by-gone age has to be followed.
(3) In a country with a relatively small population such as Scotland, there is a lack of case law on many issues. This has led to reliance

---

[57] W. Green & Son Ltd, Edinburgh, 1962, p.34.
[58] See Ch.10 and, in particular *Caparo Industries plc v Dickman* [1990] 1 A.C. 605 (HL).

on English cases in areas where the law between England and
Scotland is similar.

(4) It is sometimes hard for a court to decide when a precedent must
be applied, especially where this would lead to an undesirable
result. This is the case where there are conflicting precedents of
equal weight. This may lead to an arbitrary decision by a court
as to whether a precedent should be applied.

(5) A precedent may be hard to discover: a case may not be reported
at all or be badly reported, with important issues missing from
the law report. Or a case may be reported years after the case
was heard.

(6) All relevant precedents must be cited to the court regardless of
whether or not they have been reported. With the advent of
electronic databases of case law such as Westlaw, the courts may
at times be presented with too many cases, which may in the end
lead to a retreat from binding precedent, as is being seen in the
USA today.

When must a precedent be followed?

1-37   The European Court of Human Rights in Strasbourg and the European
Court of Justice in Luxembourg do not apply binding precedent, since
their rules are not based on the common law tradition. However, if a
court in Scotland makes a request to the European Court of Justice for a
preliminary ruling in an issue of the interpretation of European law, the
court in Scotland must apply the decision of the European Court of
Justice. Also, in cases in Scotland where an issue of the interpretation of
European law arises, the court in Scotland must apply precedents from
the European Court of Justice.[59]

Key Concept

Not every prior case has to be followed by a later court.
The precedent must be:

- in point
- binding

---

(1) *In point*

1-38   Not everything that judges say has to be followed. The binding element is
the *ratio decidendi* or reason for the decision. This is the precise issue of
law (not fact) on which the case was decided. Everything else that the
judge said that is not essential to the disposition of the case is *obiter dicta*

---

[59] European Communities Act 1972 s.3(1).

or things said by the way, which are never binding, though they may be persuasive in later courts.[60]

It is for the judges in the later case to determine the *ratio decidendi* in the earlier case. This may be difficult, as judges do not clearly signpost them as such in their judgments, and a judge may have come to his conclusion by more than one route (multiple *ratios*). Also, different judges in an appeal case may have advanced different legal arguments in their judgments. Cases may be badly reported so that it may be difficult to ascertain the *ratio*.

(2) *The precedent must also be binding*

The issue of which court in Scotland binds which other courts in Scotland **1–39** has itself been decided by precedent, and the civil courts and criminal courts form into two hierarchies.[61]

In relation to both the civil and criminal courts in Scotland, when the Judicial Committee of the Privy Council is deciding on devolution issues, its decisions are binding on the lower courts[62] but its decisions are not binding on the House of Lords which has no competence in this area. Other Privy Council decisions on civil appeals from UK colonies are persuasive only on Scottish courts in later cases.

The civil courts

Judicial precedent is strictly applied by the civil courts in Scotland. As a **1–40** general rule, appellate courts bind courts of first instance, and larger courts bind smaller.

The House of Lords

Decisions of the House of Lords in Scottish appeals bind all the civil **1–41** courts of Scotland except on devolution issues (where decisions of the Judicial Committee of the Privy Council are similarly binding). If the precedent is not a Scottish case, but is from another part of the United Kingdom, and concerns an area of law where Scots law is the same as the law applying in the earlier case, the prior decision may be binding on the later case.[63] Other House of Lords civil appeals are persuasive only.

Before 1966, the House of Lords considered itself bound by its own prior decisions. However, in that year, the Lord Chancellor issued a

---

[60] An example of a case where *obiter dicta* were highly persuasive on later courts is *Hedley Byrne & Co Ltd v Heller & Partners Ltd* [1964] A.C. 465 (HL). The case was concerned with whether a banker was liable for giving a negligent reference on the creditworthiness of a customer. The House of Lords held the banker was not liable because there had been an exclusion of liability in the reference. However, the court held that without that exclusion of liability, a banker could owe a duty of care in the making of references, and could be liable on them. This principle was *obiter dicta* in the case, but has been very influential on the development of the law of misrepresentation in later cases.
[61] For more information on the civil and criminal courts in Scotland, see Ch.2.
[62] Scotland Act 1998 s.103.
[63] *Glasgow Corporation v Central Land Board* 1956 S.C. (HL) 1.

Practice Direction, stating that although normally the House of Lords would continue to adhere to its prior decisions in the interests of certainty, it reserved the right to depart from its prior decisions, when it considered it right to do so. This power has been used sparingly, but was used by the House of Lords in the Scottish case of *Dick v Falkirk Burgh*.[64]

The Court of Session

1–42 Although this court is divided into the Inner House (a court of appeal) and the Outer House (a court of first instance) it is a collegiate court which allows for the convening of a larger court to decide difficult cases. Decisions of the House of Lords bind both the Inner House and the Outer House. A Division of the Inner House (normally three judges) is probably bound by a prior decision of either Division of the Inner House and by a court of five or more judges. A court of five or more judges can overrule a previous decision of a Division of the Inner House.

A Lord Ordinary sitting in the Outer House is bound by the House of Lords, by the Judicial Committee of the Privy Council on devolution issues, and by a Division of the Inner House, but is not bound by a decision of another Lord Ordinary, although where prior decisions are not followed, reasons are usually given.

Sheriffs are bound by decisions of the House of Lords in a Scottish Appeal and by decisions of a Division of the Inner House of the Court of Session, but there are differing views as to whether they are bound by the decision of a Lord Ordinary in the Outer House of the Court of Session. They are certainly bound by decisions of the Sheriff Principal in their own Sheriffdom, but not by other Sheriff Principals or fellow Sheriffs.

The criminal courts

1–43 Precedent is applied more flexibly in the criminal courts than in the civil courts, because liberty is potentially at stake, and also because in the case of courts that go out on circuit, it was difficult to get hold of all the law reports everywhere that the court might sit.

The House of Lords

1–44 The House of Lords has no jurisdiction to hear appeals in Scottish criminal matters.[65]

The High Court of Justiciary

1–45 The High Court of Justiciary like the Court of Session is a collegiate court, which allows for larger courts to be convened, to hear appeals on difficult legal issues. The High Court of Justiciary sitting as a Court of Criminal Appeal is not bound by its former decisions, except, perhaps,

---

[64] 1976 SC (HL) 1. Eventually the role of the Appellate Committee of the House of Lords will be taken over by the Supreme Court of the United Kingdom when it is instituted.
[65] *Macintosh v HM Advocate* (1876) 3 R. (HL) 34.

those of the full court.[66] It has the power to convene a larger court to overrule its previous decisions. In *Webster v Dominick*, 2005 1 J.C. 65, an appeal was made to the High Court of Justiciary sitting as a Court of Criminal Appeal that shameless indecency should no longer be a crime in Scots law because it contravened the European Convention on Human Rights and Fundamental Freedoms by being too ill-defined in scope. A bench of five judges was convened, which held that shameless indecency should no longer be a crime in Scotland, but the offence should be redefined as public indecency, which should be assessed not with reference to whether the behaviour was liable to deprave and corrupt others, but according to whether if, viewed objectively, the conduct would cause offence to public order, judged against the social standards of the day.

A decision of a single judge in the High Court of Justiciary (as a court of trial) is bound by the High Court of Justiciary sitting as a Court of Criminal Appeal.

The Sheriff Court

A Sheriff is bound by decisions of the High Court of Justiciary sitting as a **1–46** Court of Criminal Appeal. It used to be that Sheriffs were thought not to be bound by decisions of the High Court of Justiciary as a court of trial. However, in *Jessop v Stevenson* 1988 JC 17, the High Court of Justiciary in an appeal from the Sheriff Court held that Sheriffs were so bound.

The District Court

The District Court, as the lowest criminal court in Scotland, is concerned **1–47** with minor offences, and predominantly with questions of fact rather than law. The District Court is bound by decisions of the High Court of Justiciary as a Court of Criminal Appeal, and is probably also bound by decisions of the High Court of Justiciary as a court of trial, and possibly also the Sheriff Court.[67]

How a precedent may be handled in subsequent cases

If a precedent is both in point (as regards its point of law), and binding **1–48** (as coming from a superior court) it must be followed. If either of these elements is lacking, it need not be followed.

A court may be able to avoid having to follow a precedent by resort to the following:

> (1) It may be able to *distinguish* a precedent, which involves showing that it is not in point, perhaps because it was not fully argued in the earlier case.
> (2) If there are conflicting precedents of equal authority the court may *follow* one and not follow the other.

---

[66] *Sugden v HM Advocate*, 1934 J.C. 103.
[67] The fact that the District Court is probably bound by the Sheriff Court is asserted by D.M. Walker *Scottish Legal System* (8th edn, W. Green, 2001), p.447.

(3) Where the precedent is both a very old one and a long time has elapsed since it was last relied on, the court may *doubt* a precedent.

(4) Where the court considers that the prior decision was made *per incuriam* (i.e. in error because all the legal issues were not fully considered), it is not regarded as binding. Judges are reluctant to take this course because it reduces the certainty of the common law.

(5) Where the court considers that a legal rule has ceased to apply because the reason for the rule no longer exists (in Latin *cessante ratio cessat ipsa lex*), the precedent is not binding. Courts are reluctant to use this reason for not following a precedent, because it reduces the certainty of the common law, and feel that it is better for Parliament to legislate for a change in the law than for them to amend the law by creatively ignoring a precedent.

The role of law reporting in judicial precedent

1–49 A system of judicial precedent depends for its efficacy on a good system of law reporting, in order to be aware of all the precedents, and to weigh up whether they are in point. In the early law reports, such as Sinclair's *Practicks* (1540–1549) law reports were a few lines long and did not report the judges' words verbatim. Today cases are systematically reported both in hard copy and electronically, and are quickly available after the cases take place. However, not every case is reported.

Edited series of law reports summarise the facts and the decision of the case in headnotes at the beginning of the report. They may cover the arguments of counsel before the court. They then give the opinions of the judges verbatim, and state how the case has been disposed of.

Nowadays the courts themselves report their judgments later on the day they are issued using the World Wide Web.[68] The principal edited series of law reports in Scotland are *Session Cases*, the *Scots Law Times*, the *Scottish Civil Law Reports* and the *Scottish Criminal Case Reports*.

INSTITUTIONAL WRITERS

1–50 Although legislation and judicial precedent are by far the most important formal sources of Scots law, there are other less important formal sources, one of which consists of the works of certain very influential writers on Scots law. The debt that Scots law owes to these writers has been referred to earlier in this chapter as part of the history and development of Scots law.[69] These writers played a big part in the creation of a modern legal system in Scotland, as they did their work during a period

---

[68] Decisions of the Scottish courts are available on the Scottish Courts website at *http://www.scotcourts.gov.uk/opinionsApp/index.asp*.
House of Lords decisions are available at *http://www.publications.parliament.uk/pa/ld/ldjudgmt.htm*.
[69] See p.5 above.

of rapid development of the law when it was being crafted into a modern legal system out of the mix of customary law, mediaeval writings such as the *Regiam Majestatem*, Acts of the old Scots Parliament and the decisions of the courts as published in the Practicks, added to by borrowings from Roman law. These writers are often referred to as "institutional writers" because their works were modelled on the late Roman texts they studied, and principally Justinian's *Institutes*. They are also known as authoritative writers. Most of them were judges and/or academic lawyers. Such was their influence on the courts in the nineteenth century that their works were regarded as themselves a formal source of law, rather than as a secondary source which would be the case with a modern textbook, however eminent the author.

Whether a writer should be included among the institutional writers depends on whether his work has been treated as such by the courts, and not every work by one of these writers might so qualify, but the list would normally include the following writers and works:

Sir Thomas Craig of Riccarton (*Jus Feudale*, 1603, but published in 1655, a work on property law, published after his death).

Sir George Mackenzie (*The Laws and Customs of Scotland in Matters Criminal*, 1678). Mackenzie earned the nickname 'Bloody Mackenzie' from his career as a criminal prosecutor.

James Dalrymple, Viscount Stair (*The Institutions of the Law of Scotland*, 1681). Stair is the most influential of the institutional writers, and his work covered wide areas of civil law, including the law of obligations, property and succession. Stair had first been a lecturer at the University of Glasgow, who went on become Lord President of the Court of Session in 1671. He was forced to resign 10 years later because he refused to swear an oath recognising the supremacy of the King over the church, and fled to the Netherlands where his work was influenced by Roman law. He returned to Scotland in 1688 when William of Orange ascended the throne, and became Lord President of the Court of Session again in 1689.

Andrew McDouall, Lord Bankton (*An Institute of the Laws of Scotland*, 1751).

Henry Home, Lord Kames (*Principles of Equity*, 1760).

John Erskine of Carnock (*Principles of the Law of Scotland*, 1754, and *An Institute of the Law of Scotland*, 1773).

Baron David Hume (*Commentaries on the Law of Scotland Respecting Crimes*, 1797).

George Joseph Bell (*Commentaries on the Law of Scotland and on the Principles of Mercantile Jurisprudence*, 1810, and *Principles of the Law of Scotland*, 1829).

How much importance should be placed on the Institutional Writers?

1–51 In *Drew v Drew* Lord Benholm stated:

> "When on any point of law I find Stair's opinion uncontradicted, I look upon that opinion as ascertaining the law of Scotland."[70]

T.B. Smith, writing much later, evaluated the influence of the institutional writers as "approximately equal to that of a Division of the Inner House of the Court of Session".[71]

In any event, whatever the level of their authority might have been, it is now declining steadily with the passage of time, as the points of law for which their work was authoritative are gradually affected by legislation, or by developments in case law.

Legal writing of varying levels of authority legal writers are cited today in court and referred to in judicial opinions. However, it is important to bear in mind that modern academic writings on law are never more than secondary sources of legal rules, i.e. they are *about* the law rather than *being* the law.

CUSTOM

1–52 Before the Roman occupation of Scotland, law was largely customary and different rules will have applied in different parts of Scotland in the period before Scotland became one kingdom. Gradually customary laws were written down in works such as the *Regiam Majestatem*. In the period before the system of binding precedent was adopted in Scotland in the nineteenth century, custom was a major formal source of the law. The customs among merchants were a very important formal source of commercial law in mediaeval times.

Nowadays, custom is still regarded as a formal source of Scots law, although it has diminished greatly in importance, as it is steadily replaced by legislation and by judicial precedent.

Some customs are regarded as already being part of the law, and these customs do not need to be proved in court. These customs are more a historical source than a formal source of the legal rule, as they will have been enacted into legislation or can be found in a judicial precedent. For example the legal rights of a spouse and children to inherit part of the deceased's estate come from customary law but have been legislated for in the Succession (Scotland) Act 1964. Also, much of the common law of leases in Scotland comes from customary law, but is now found in decisions of the courts.

In cases where no legislation or judicial precedent or institutional

---

[70] (1870) 9M 163 at p.167.
[71] T.B. Smith, *A Short Commentary on the Law of Scotland* (W. Green & Son Ltd, Edinburgh, 1962), p.32.

writing can be cited as the formal source of a legal rule, it is possible to use custom as a formal source of law. To do so, the custom must be proved to the satisfaction of the court. It has to be proved that the custom: (1) has been acquiesced in for a long though undefined period of time as representing the law; (2) is definite and certain; (3) is fair and reasonable; (4) and is consistent with legal principle. In *Bruce v Smith* (1890) 17 R. 1000, landlords in Shetland failed prove a local custom by which they claimed to be entitled by customary law to one third of the caaing whales killed by their tenants on the foreshore: as the custom, though it did appear to exist, failed the test of reasonableness.

Custom can also be used as a source of contractual rules that have not been expressly provided for in the contract, though in this sense custom is not a formal source of law.

EQUITY

Scotland never had a system of equity separate from law as was the case **1–53** in England, where separate courts of equity existed at one time. However, parts of the common law of Scotland owe their origin to equitable considerations, an example being the constraints on the use of specific implement as a contractual remedy.[72]

Also, the Inner House of the Court of Session and the High Court of Justiciary both have an extraordinary equitable jurisdiction called the *nobile officium* (noble office) to fill in the gaps in the law so as to provide a remedy if one is not otherwise available. These powers are rarely used and cannot be used to defeat the intention of Parliament. The Inner House has used its powers in relation to public trusts, if the purposes have to be varied and there is no other means of doing so.

The High Court of Justiciary has a declaratory power to declare behaviour which was not hitherto regarded as criminal, to be so. A modern example is *Khaliq v HM Advocate*, 1984 J.C. 23, in which the High Court of Justiciary declared the sale of glue-sniffing kits to children to be a criminal act, as being the "wilful supply of potentially noxious substances".

Reminder on formal sources of law

In this book, the student of business law will be introduced to a range of **1–54** areas of substantive business law. When students are called on to write about the law in essays and examinations, it is essential always to give authority for every assertion about the law. Where the student is speaking about a legal rule, the formal source must be given, which will normally be a piece of legislation or a case. Students must remember that a textbook, however helpful, is not a primary source of law, and should only be referred to if the textbook writer gives a useful insight that is original and

---

[72] See *Moore v Paterson* (1881) 9 R. 337.

worth referring to in its own right. A textbook should never be referred to as a lazy substitute for a reference to a primary source.

▼ CHAPTER SUMMARY

INTRODUCTION TO LAW

1–55
1. **A working knowledge of key areas of business law is important for business managers, as decisions with legal implications are taken all the time in business. Accountants also need a good knowledge of business law, as they often have to give advice to business managers which includes legal issues.**
2. **Legal and non-legal rules often appear similar. It is essential to be able to distinguish between them, as only legal rules provide for enforcement if they are breached.**

HISTORY AND DEVELOPMENT OF SCOTS LAW

1. **The two biggest influences on Scots law over the centuries have been English law and Roman law. As a result Scots law is a mixed system between the common law and civil law traditions.**
2. **The feudal system of land ownership began in Scotland in the middle ages and continued up to the year 2000.**
3. **Some modern commercial law concepts trace their origin to the law merchant in mediaeval times. These include bills of exchange and marine insurance.**
4. **The Court of Session was founded in 1532 as a permanent civil court.**
5. **The Union of the Crowns took place in 1603, when James VI of Scotland became James I of England.**
6. **The General Register of Sasines was founded in 1617 to provide a central register of transactions relating to land. It has only recently been replaced by a new system of land registration.**
7. **The High Court of Justiciary was founded in 1672.**
8. **The Union of the Parliaments took place in 1707. The Act of Union guaranteed that separate Scottish courts should be retained and that Scots private law could not be altered "except for the evident utility of the subjects within Scotland".**
9. **The period roughly from 1600–1830 was a period of development of Scots law through the influence of the institutional writers (authoritative writers) when Roman law concepts were received into Scots law.**
10. **After 1800, the major influence on Scots law was from English law.**
11. **European legislation has been an important source of law since the United Kingdom joined the European Community (now European Union) in 1972.**

12. Since the Scotland Act 1998, Scotland has again had a separate Parliament, with power to legislate within a defined area of devolved competence, and separate government which operates within its area of devolved competence.

CATEGORIES OF LAW

1. **Public Law and Private Law:** public law regulates the relationship between the state and the citizen, while private law regulates the relationship between citizens.
2. **Civil law and Criminal Law:** civil cases are heard in the civil courts and criminal cases are heard in the criminal courts.
3. **Civil Law and Common Law:** civil systems of law are developed from Roman law, while common law systems are developed from English law.
4. **Common Law and Statute Law:** statute law = legislation. Common law consists of the legal rules that stem from the other formal sources of law: judicial precedent, the institutional writers, custom and equity.

THE FORMAL SOURCES OF SCOTS LAW

They are, in the following order: (1) Legislation (2) Judicial Precedent, (3) the Institutional Writers (4) Custom (5) Equity.

LEGISLATION

1. Legislation may be made by the European Union, by the UK Parliament, it may be made under the Royal Prerogative, it may be made by the Scottish Parliament, and delegated legislation can be made by bodies using powers delegated by Parliament.

EUROPEAN LEGISLATION

1. There are four types of European legislation that have binding force: Treaties (primary legislation), Regulations, Directives and Decisions (secondary legislation).

THE UK PARLIAMENT

1. The UK Parliament is a sovereign Parliament and can enact legislation on anything it likes.
2. A bill has to go through five stages in both Houses in order to become an Act: First Reading, Second Reading, Committee Stage,

Report Stage and Third Reading. It can then receive the Royal Assent and become an Act.

LEGISLATION BY THE SCOTTISH PARLIAMENT

1. The Scottish Parliament holds devolved power to pass Acts of the Scottish Parliament in areas of competence not reserved to the UK Parliament.
2. A bill goes through the following stages in the Scottish Parliament in order to become an Act but it must first be scrutinised to ensure it is within the Scottish Parliament's legislative competence. Stage 1—the bill goes to the lead committee, and the main points of the bill and the committee's report are debated in Parliament. Stage 2—there is a detailed consideration of the bill by committee and a vote. Stage 3—the bill is presented to the full Parliament for final consideration and a vote. Four weeks must elapse before it can then receive the Royal Assent and become an Act to allow for checking of legislative competence.
3. Acts of the Scottish Parliament can be challenged in court for exceeding their legislative competence.

DELEGATED LEGISLATION

1. Delegated (or subordinate) legislation is made by a body other than Parliament under powers delegated to it by Parliament in a parent statute.
2. Delegated legislation can be challenged in court if it has exceeded the powers delegated to it (*ultra vires*).

LEGISLATION UNDER THE ROYAL PREROGATIVE

1. The Crown holds certain residual powers to legislate.

JUDICIAL PRECEDENT

1. The formal source of parts of Scots law is judicial precedent, i.e. certain prior decisions of the courts must be followed in a later case.
2. For a later court to have to follow an earlier decision, the previous case must be (a) in point, and (b) binding.
3. The *ratio decidendi* (reason for the decision) is the exact point of law in the previous case on which the decision was based.
4. *Obiter dicta* (things said by the judge by the way) are other remarks that were not part of the *ratio decidendi* and therefore do not bind the later court.

INSTITUTIONAL WRITERS

1. The works of a select group of writers on law who wrote during a seminal period for the development of Scots law between 1600 and 1830 who are still regarded as being a formal source of law.
2. The authority of these writers is diminishing over time as the legal content of their works is gradually changed by legislation or developments in case law.
3. The works of modern writers are not regarded as being a source of law.

CUSTOM

1. A custom can be regarded as a formal source of law (a) if it has been regarded as law for a long period, (b) if it is definite and certain, (c) if it is fair and reasonable, (d) if it is consistent with legal principle.

EQUITY

1. Equitable principles can be found in Scots law, e.g. the remedy of specific implement.
2. The Court of Session and the High Court of Justiciary have an extraordinary equitable jurisdiction (*nobile officium*) to fill in gaps in the law, which they use sparingly, and the High Court of Justiciary has a declaratory power to declare immoral conduct to be a crime.

? QUICK QUIZ

- Why is it important that a business or accountancy student should know a bit about business law?
- What is the essential difference between public law and private law?
- Explain the procedure for the enactment of a public bill in the UK Parliament.
- If you wanted to look up a section of an Act of the UK Parliament, where would you look?
- What are the provisions in the Scotland Act 1998 which fix the boundaries of the legislative competence of the Scottish Parliament?
- What role do the UK Parliament and the Scottish Parliament play in relation to delegated legislation?
- What are the advantages and disadvantages of having a system of binding precedent?

- In what circumstances must a later court follow the decision of an earlier court in Scotland?
- To what extent are the institutional writers still of relevance to the decisions of the courts today?
- In what circumstances is custom regarded as a formal source of Scots law?
- Explain what is meant by the *nobile officium* of the Court of Session and High Court of Justiciary.
- When writing about the law in an essay or an examination, and you are asked to give the formal source of a legal rule, why would it not usually be correct to refer to a textbook as your authority?

📖 FURTHER READING

A book that covers most of the material in this chapter but in much more depth, and is available in an up-to-date edition is R. White and I. Willock *Scottish Legal System*, 4th edn (Tottel Publishing, Edinburgh, 2007). See also D. Walker *The Scottish Legal System* 8th edn (W. Green, Edinburgh, 2001).

The formal sources of Scots law are covered in depth in the contributions of R.B. Ferguson, G. Maher and T.B. Smith, and D. Sellar and the historical sources are covered in depth by the contributions of T.D. Fergus and G. Maher in the *Stair Memorial Encyclopaedia: The Law of Scotland*, Vol. 22 (The Law Society of Scotland / Butterworths, Edinburgh, 1987 (and updates)).

🖱 RELEVANT WEBLINKS

The UK Parliament: *http://www.parliament.uk*. You can learn about how Parliament works on this website, find out what bills are before Parliament, and track their progress.

The Scottish Parliament: *http://www.scottish.parliament.uk/*. This site is a similar resource to the UK Parliament site.

Decisions of the Scottish Courts: *http://www.scotcourts.gov.uk/opinionsApp/index.asp*

Decisions of the House of Lords: *http://www.publications.parliament.uk/pa/ld/ldjudgmt.htm*.

The European Convention of Human Rights and Fundamental Freedoms: *http://www.coe.int*. This link takes you to the Council of Europe website, where you can click on "Human Rights" which brings you to a drop-down menu where you can click on "the Convention" to bring you to the text of the Convention.

The European Union: *http://europa.eu*. This is a portal that allows you to learn all about the European Union and its various institutions, and to access European legislation.

Office of Public Sector Information—text of Acts of UK Parliament, Scottish Parliament and Statutory Instruments: *http://www.opsi.gov.uk/ legislation/about_legislation.htm*

UK Statute Law Database: *http://www.statutelaw.gov.uk*. This database gives updated texts of statutes of the UK Parliament and Scottish parliament, plus unamended statutory instruments and Scottish Statutory Instruments. It also gives unamended texts of Acts of the old Scottish Parliament where they are still in force.

Chapter 2 Structure of the Scottish Legal System

ANDREW WILSON[1]

▶ CHAPTER OVERVIEW

2–01 This chapter is concerned with the essential composition of the legal system of Scotland. It starts by detailing the two systems of our civil and criminal courts. The chapter then outlines the tribunals system and publicly appointed ombudsmen. The chapter closes by summarising the personnel working in the Scottish legal system: the two legal professions; the judiciary; and the law officers.

✓ OUTCOMES

2–02 At the end of this chapter you should be able to:

- ✓ appreciate the difference between civil and criminal courts
- ✓ identify the different courts
- ✓ understand the differences in jurisdiction between the various courts
- ✓ identify and understand the route of appeals in civil and in criminal cases
- ✓ understand the nature and function of administrative tribunals
- ✓ identify and understand the nature and function of ombudsmen
- ✓ identify the different aspects and key offices of the Scottish legal professions

INTRODUCTION

2–03 Scotland has its own system of courts legal professions, judges and law officers. These existed prior to the Treaty of Union with England in 1707, have been maintained since and, for the most part, have developed separately from the other jurisdictions in the United Kingdom.[2]

---

[1] Editor of *SCOLAG Legal Journal*.
[2] The united Kingdom has three separate jurisdictions whose laws and legal systems vary from one another: England & Wales; Northern Ireland; and Scotland.

Jurisdictions

Any court may only hear cases that fall within its jurisdiction, that is to **2–04** say, within the limits of the power it may exercise. Jurisdiction may be limited by geographical boundaries, subject matter of the legal issue in the case or the type or size of order the particular court can award.[3]

In Scotland the civil courts are empowered to hear civil law cases following civil court procedure. Similarly, criminal cases are a matter for the criminal courts following criminal procedure. Although at times they bear the same names and can even be presided over by the same judges it is important to appreciate the difference between criminal and civil law,[4] the different courts, the procedures they will follow and the powers they exercise.

Fact and law

A further distinction it is important to appreciate is the difference **2–05** between fact and law. In both civil and criminal cases the differing parties put forward arguments of fact and of law. They present evidence as to the facts in the case and set out legal arguments on their interpretation of the rules of the law with which the case is concerned. What the true facts of a case are is decided by the jury, if there is one or the judge if there is no jury. However, decisions of law are always a matter for the judge in the case.

THE CIVIL COURT SYSTEM

Civil law covers a wide range of legal issues. These relate largely to legal **2–06** issues of rights and duties between persons, as opposed to criminal matters which are between a person and the state. It is important to note here that in legal terms "person" means any one or thing with legal personality—that may be an individual, a company or other legal entity. Some writers may distinguish between "natural legal persons"—i.e. individual human beings—and "artificial legal persons" such as limited companies, trusts and unincorporated associations.

In civil cases the person bringing the action is called the pursuer. The person against whom the action is brought is the defender.

The civil courts of Scotland are the Sheriff Court, the Court of Session and the House of Lords. Both the Sheriff Court and the Court of Session are further divided into different jurisdictions and procedures. The Sheriff Court includes small claims, summary cause procedure, and ordinary cause procedure. The Court of Session comprises the Outer House and the Inner House.

---

[3] Amounts, such as maximum prison terms but particularly fines or financial limits, will change over time. They are almost always set in secondary legislation, which is easier and faster to draft and enact.

[4] See "Categories of law" above at para.1–15.

Key Concepts

Civil law relates to legal rights and duties between persons.
Person means any one or thing with legal personality.
A pursuer is the person who brings a civil action.
A defender is the person against whom an action is brought.
Privative jurisdiction: cases which can only be brought in a particular court.

Sheriff Court

2–07   The major part of civil judicial business in Scotland is conducted in the Sheriff Court. It is the only inferior court exercising first instance jurisdiction in civil matters. The Sheriff Courts exercise a civil jurisdiction within their respective territories which is very wide, being almost concurrent with that of the Court of Session.

   The Sheriff Court can be defined according to the geographical area, persons and subject matter involved in the particular case.

Organisation

2–08   Organisationally Scotland is divided into six Sheriffdoms. They are:

- Glasgow and Strathkelvin;
- Grampian Highland and Islands;
- Lothian and Borders;
- North Strathclyde;
- South Strathclyde, Dumfries and Galloway;
- Tayside, Central and Fife.

Each is presided over by its own Sheriff Principal. Sheriffdoms are generally further divided into districts, each of which is served by a particular Sheriff Court. There are currently 49 Sheriff Courts in Scotland.

Jurisdiction

2–09   The civil jurisdiction of the Sheriff Court has been repeatedly extended over the years. It can be defined by three criteria: location; persons; and subject matter. The first of these is simply the territory of the particular Sheriffdom (not just the particular Sheriff Court district).

Persons

2–10   For the court to hear a case it must have jurisdiction over the defender (*actor sequitur forum rei* – the pursuer follows the court of the defender). The Sheriff Court will have jurisdiction over the defender if they:

- are resident or domiciled within the Sheriffdom;
- carry on business in the Sheriffdom;

- own heritable property in the Sheriffdom which is the subject of the action.

Subject matter

As well as the territory of the Sheriffdom and persons within it, the **2–12** jurisdiction of the court may be determined by the subject of the case.

- In cases concerning a contract the court for the place the contract is to be performed has jurisdiction.
- In cases relating to delict the court for the place where the harmful event occurred has jurisdiction.
- In ordinary cause cases the sheriff has discretion whether to remit the cause to the Court of Session.
- Certain actions are reserved to the Court of Session: e.g. applications for Judicial Review, actions for reduction, petitions for winding up of a company if the paid-up capital exceeds £120,000.[5]
- Certain actions are reserved to specialist courts: e.g. questions over the right to bear a coat of arms are reserved to the Court of the Lord Lyon.

The Sheriff Court jurisdiction over actions for debt or damages is without financial limit. In such cases where the value does not exceed £5,000[6] the jurisdiction of the court is privative, that is to say such an action must be brought in the Sheriff Court and cannot be raised in the Court of Session.

Procedures

There is generally no jury in civil cases in the Sheriff Court and trial is **2–13** usually by a sheriff sitting alone. The only exception is in cases where an employee seeks damages against their employer in respect of injuries sustained in the course of their employment.

There are three types of proceeding conducted in the Sheriff Court. The difference between them is largely the financial value of the cause.

Ordinary cause

Ordinary cause procedure is not a distinct process defined in statute. **2–14** Rather, it is the standard form of process and procedure carried out in any civil case brought in the Sheriff Court which cannot be taken as a summary cause.

The jurisdiction of the Sheriff Court is very wide both in terms of the cases it can hear and the powers it can exercise. Actions brought before the court cover a wide range of activities including repayment of debt, claims for damages, actions in bankruptcy, implementation of a contract, orders relating to parenting, separation, divorce and adoption. Some will

---

[5] Insolvency Act 1986 s.120
[6] The Sheriff Courts (Scotland) Act 1971 (Privative Jurisdiction and Summary Cause) Order 2007, SSI 2007/507 art 2.

involve complex issues and important points of law. In ordinary cause cases the sheriff has discretion whether to remit the action to the Court of Session.

Summary cause

2–15 Summary cause procedure was introduced to simplify and speed up court actions brought in respect of relatively small amounts of money. It is applicable to any civil action for payment of money not exceeding £5,000[7] (exclusive of interest and expenses owed on the subject amount) and actions for implement of an obligation or the recovery of heritable or moveable property (unless there is an alternative or additional crave for payment of a sum exceeding £5,000).

A summary cause action does not normally involve written pleadings and evidence led at the hearing is not recorded. In undefended actions for payment the parties are not required to appear in court. A summary cause action may be raised by any person but most often are actions raised by commercial organisations, public sector creditors such as local authorities and public utilities, and debt recovery agencies.

Small claims

2–16 Small debt cause or "small claim" is a process used for a summary action where the value does not exceed £3,000.[8] It is designed to be a simple process that is less formal and easier for non-lawyers to access. It is intended to encourage the parties to appear on their own behalf rather than being represented by a lawyer and, consequently, legal aid is not available to pursue or defend a small claim. Further to this end, only limited expenses may be claimed in respect of a small claim (a maximum of £150 where the value of the claim is £1,500 or less; or 10 per cent of the value if the claim exceeds £1,500).[9]

The Scottish Courts Service produces a series of guidance notes on small claims which are available on its website at *http://www.scot courts.gov.uk/sheriff/small_claims/*.

Appeals

2–17 There are two routes of appeal from a decision of the Sheriff Court. Which route is taken will depend on the type of procedure under which the case was heard. The judgment of a sheriff may be appealed to the Sheriff Principal unless excluded by statute. However, if the case is not a summary cause then appeal may either be made to the Sheriff Principal, from whom appeal lies to the Court of Session, or be made directly to the Inner House. In most instances appeals will first be made to the Sheriff Principal as it presents a speedier and less expensive option.

---

[7] As per the Sheriff Courts (Scotland) Act 1971 (Privative Jurisdiction and Summary Cause) Order 2007, SSI 2007/507 art 3.
[8] Small Claims (Scotland) Amendment Order 2007, SSI 2007/496.
[9] Small Claims (Scotland) Amendment Order 2007, SSI 2007/496.

The Court of Session

Apart from cases in which the Sheriff Court has sole jurisdiction or where **2–18** the Court of Session has privative jurisdiction, the pursuer has a choice of initiating his claim in the appropriate Sheriff Court or in the Court of Session. The Court of Session holds jurisdiction over the whole of Scotland. Accordingly, all persons ordinarily resident in Scotland, businesses based in Scotland and contractual and delictual activity carried out in Scotland fall within the court's jurisdiction. The court also exercises the equitable power of *nobile officium* whereby, in exceptional circumstances, the court may fulfil the objects of justice by providing a remedy where none otherwise exists in law.

The Court of Session is Scotland's supreme civil court. It sits in Parliament House, in Edinburgh. It has extensive power to regulate its own practice and procedure which it does by Acts of Sederunt, a form of secondary legislation.

The court is both a court of first instance and an appellate court. For the purposes of hearing cases, the court is divided into the Outer House and the Inner House.

Outer House

The Outer House of the Court of Session is solely a court of first instance **2–19** in which the Lord Ordinary, the judge, sits alone or in some cases with a civil jury of 12 persons (e.g. in defamation cases).[10] It hears cases on practically every area of civil law including, for example, those dealt with in subsequent chapters of this book such as contract, company law, delict and property. As well as disputed cases the court considers many uncontested petitions of an administrative nature such as the appointment of new trustees or the winding up of a company.

Appeal from a decision of a Lord Ordinary may be made to the Inner House of the Court of Session. Appeals are rarely made on points of fact, most usually they are on points of law only.

Inner House

The main task of the Inner House is to sit as an appeal court, although in **2–20** a small range of cases it may act as a court of first instance.[11] The Inner House is divided into the First and Second Division. The divisions are of equal authority and presided over by the Lord President and Lord Justice Clerk respectively. Each division is made up of five judges. Occasionally, when the pressure of business demands it, an Extra Division of three judges will sit.

Generally the court will sit in basic quorum with a bench of three judges. However, if a case is particularly important or if it is necessary to

---

[10] Court of Session Act 1988 s.11.
[11] e.g. "special cases" where parties agree as to the facts and the court considers solely a question of law, or petitions to the *nobile officium*.

consider a previous decision of the court then a larger bench of five or more may be convened.

Appeal against a decision of the Inner House may be made to the House of Lords.

House of Lords

2-21 The House of Lords embodies an ancient right of ultimate appeal to Parliament that justice be done. Leave to appeal, that is permission from the Lords, is not normally required for Scottish appeals which proceed directly to an Appellate Committee provided that two counsel have certified the reasonableness of the appeal. If the case originated in the Sheriff Court then an appeal to the Lords can only be on a point of law.[12]

Those who are members of the House as a legislative chamber do not sit or vote on its judicial business, which is discharged by the Appeal Committee comprised of Lords of Appeal in Ordinary.

At present, the maximum number of Lords of Appeal in Ordinary is 12,[13] two of whom are normally appointed from Scotland (currently Lords Hope of Craighead and Rodger of Earlsferry) and one from Northern Ireland. They are appointed by the Crown on the advice of the Prime Minister. Qualification for appointment is to have held high judicial office for not less than two years or to have had right of audience in the superior courts for not less than 15 years.[14]

The House ordinarily sits as a bench of five but in exceptional cases of major political or constitutional significance a larger number may be convened. Generally both of the Scottish Law Lords will sit on an appeal from Scotland. After the Lords have delivered their judgment the case returns to the Inner House for the Court of Session to apply the judgment.

Judicial Committee of the Privy Council

2-22 The Judicial Committee of the Privy Council (JCPC) is neither a civil nor a criminal court, but one that currently serves a constitutional function in respect of devolved powers under the Scotland Act 1998. Most Scottish cases taken to the JCPC have related to the requirement that the devolved powers are exercised in compliance with the rights protected under the Human Rights Act 1998. This has had an impact in Scots criminal cases in that such devolved functions include prisons, most of our criminal law and the system of criminal prosecutions.

Future change: the Supreme Court of the United Kingdom

2-23 Both the appellate jurisdiction of the House of Lords and the devolution jurisdiction of the Judicial Committee of the Privy Council are due to be transferred to a separate Supreme Court of the United Kingdom. The

---

[12] Court of Session Act 1988 s.32(5).
[13] Administration of Justice Act 1968 s. 1(1)(a) as amended in 1994 by Order in Council.
[14] Appellate Jurisdiction Act 1876 s.6.

new court will be established when the relevant provisions of the Constitutional Reform Act 2005 are brought into force. The Act effectively creates a separation of powers between the executive, the legislature and the judiciary for the first time in British constitutional history.

The first judges of the court, who will be termed Justices of the Supreme Court, will be the 12 Lords of Appeal in Ordinary in office when the court comes into being. The criteria for appointment and removal of Justices and the conduct of court business will initially be as for the present House of Lords.

Other courts

As mentioned above, there are also a number of specialist Scottish courts **2–24** which exercise jurisdiction in specified areas of civil law. Examples of such courts are: Children's Hearings (which hear a range of civil and criminal matters relating to children); Office of the Social Security Commissioners and Child Support Commissioners (dealing with appeals against decisions made by various Tribunals in relation to the administration of Social Security benefits and child support); and Pensions Appeal Tribunals for Scotland (dealing with appeals against refusal of claims for entitlement to War Pensions).

Here is an outline of the specialist courts more relevant to businesses or corporations in Scotland.

VAT and Duties Tribunal

The VAT and Duties Tribunal deals with appeals on decisions of HM **2–25** Revenue & Customs on VAT, including penalties for tax evasion and assessment of tax etc.

Scottish Land Court

The Scottish Land Court's jurisdiction is set firmly within the context of **2–26** Scottish farming. It has authority to resolve a range of disputes, including between landlords and tenants in agriculture and crofting. The Court is based in Edinburgh, but holds hearings throughout Scotland.

Lands Tribunal for Scotland

The Lands Tribunal for Scotland has statutory power to deal with various specific types of dispute involving land or property. Its main areas of **2–27** work include: tenants' rights to purchase their public sector houses; disputed compensation for compulsory purchase of land or loss in value of land caused by public works; and valuations for rating on non-domestic premises.

Court of the Lord Lyon

No Armorial Bearings (more commonly known as a coat of arms) may be **2–28** used in Scotland unless they are on record in the Public Register of all Arms and Bearings in Scotland. The Lord Lyon King of Arms has jurisdiction on questions of heraldry and may grant Arms to Scottish people, businesses or organisations. The court administers the Public Register of All Arms and Bearings in Scotland. Appeal from a decision of the court lies with the Court of Session.

THE CRIMINAL COURT SYSTEM

2–29 Criminal law is concerned with the determination of guilt and punishment for conduct that is outlawed by the State. While civil law deals with the legal relationships between persons, criminal law is part of public law and provides a body of rules of proper behaviour for persons: both individuals and corporations. Further examination of criminal law and the aspects of it most relevant to business can be found in the following chapter "Business Regulation".

Criminal prosecutions in Scotland are almost exclusively brought on behalf of the State by the Crown Office and Procurator Fiscal Service either in the name of the Lord Advocate or local Procurator Fiscal. The person prosecuted for a crime is termed the accused or the panel.

The criminal courts of Scotland are the District Court or JP Court, Sheriff Court and the High Court of Justiciary. Both the Sheriff Court and the High Court of Justiciary are further divided into different jurisdictions and procedures. The Sheriff Court may try summary or solemn cases. The High Court of Justiciary sits both as a trial court of the most serious crimes and as the ultimate court of criminal appeal.

Criminal jurisdiction is divided into two: summary and solemn. Summary trials are heard and determined by a judge, Sheriff or justice of the peace sitting alone. Solemn cases, however, are tried by a judge or Sheriff and a jury of 15 persons. In the case of statutory offences the legislation may specify whether the offence is to be tied summarily, on indictment or either way. Most common law crimes may be tried by either procedure. Except for those crimes which are privative to the High Court, the choice of procedure and court is made by the prosecution according to the seriousness of the case and the penalty sought.

Which court tries a criminal case will depend upon where it is alleged to have been committed, the seriousness of the crime and the corresponding severity of the punishment appropriate.

Key Concepts

Criminal law is concerned with determining guilt and punishment for conduct outlawed by the State.

Criminal jurisdiction is divided into **summary** and **solemn**.

Except for crimes privative to the High Court, the **choice of procedure and court** is made by the prosecution according to the seriousness of the case and the penalty sought.

The District Court

The District Court is currently the lowest in the hierarchy of criminal **2–30** courts and deals only with summary cases. At the start of 2008 there were 30 District Courts in Scotland, administered by local councils. However, these will disappear in the coming years (2008–2012) and gradually be replaced by a new Justice of the Peace Court (see following paragraph on Summary Justice reform).

District Courts are generally presided over by a Justice of the Peace (JP) sitting alone or as a bench of three. JPs are lay judges not lawyers and are assisted on points of law and procedure by a legally qualified clerk to the court.

With the approval of the Scottish Ministers, a council may appoint a legally qualified Stipendiary Magistrate to preside over its District Court. Glasgow is the only council to have done so to date.

The jurisdiction of the District Court extends to the area covered by the local council under which it operates. In sentencing, a JP may make Probation Orders, Supervised Attendance Orders, Compensation Orders (to pay victims up to £2,500) as well as impose fines or a period of imprisonment up to a maximum of 60 days for common law offences. A Stipendiary Magistrate, on the other hand, may exercise the same sentencing powers as a Sheriff in summary sitting.

Because of the limits on sentencing powers, the District Court deals only with the most minor of crimes. Furthermore, prosecutions for some crimes are restricted to the Sherriff Court or to the High Court of Justiciary.

Appeal from the District Court, either against sentence or conviction, lies with the High Court of Justiciary sitting as a Court of Appeal.

Future change: Summary Justice Reform and Justice of the Peace Courts

The Criminal Proceedings etc. (Reform) (Scotland) Act 2007 makes a **2–31** number of changes to courts and sentencing powers. At the time of writing, its provisions are still in the process of being brought into force. The most notable changes will be: increasing the sentencing powers of the Sheriff Summary Court; replacing the District Court with a new Justice of the Peace Court; allowing for Stipendiary Magistrates to be appointed in any Sheriffdom; and allowing for increases in the maximum sentences available in the JP Court.

JP Courts will be established in each Sheriff Court district and have the same territorial jurisdiction as Sheriff Courts, i.e. the whole Sheriffdom. They will come under the authority of the relevant Sheriff Principal and be administered by the Scottish Courts Service.[15] The Act provides that the Scottish Government may, by way of a Scottish Statutory Instrument, increase the sentencing powers of JP Courts from 60 days to six

---

[15] Criminal Proceedings etc. (Reform) (Scotland) Act 2007 ss.59–66.

months.[16] Each Sheriffdom may have a Stipendiary Magistrate appointed by the Scottish Ministers on the advice of the Sheriff Principal.[17]

Courts in the Sheriffdom of Lothian and Borders will become JP Courts on March10, 2008. Courts in the Sheriffdom of Grampian Highlands and Islands will become JP courts in June 2008. For further up-to-date information see the appropriate pages of the Scottish Courts Service website.

Sheriff Court

2–32 The Sheriff Court has a criminal jurisdiction to hear both summary and solemn cases, and is the busiest of the criminal courts. Its criminal jurisdiction extends throughout the Sheriffdom but prosecutions for a number of serious crimes are reserved to the High Court of Justiciary.

Summary procedure

2–33 In summary cases the Sheriff sits alone and decides both points of law and questions of fact. In addition to a full range of statutory orders available to him, the sentencing power of a Sheriff when sitting summarily extends to imposing fines of up to £10,000[18] or a term of imprisonment of up to 12 months,[19] although sentence for statutory offences may be lower.

Solemn procedure

2–34 Solemn procedure is reserved for more serious offences. It is more costly, more time consuming and imposes harsher penalties. In solemn cases the Sheriff sits with a jury of 15 people drawn from the local community. The role of the Sheriff is to preside over the court and act as a judge of law, whereas the jury alone decides questions of fact.

Upon conviction by solemn procedure a Sheriff may impose a custodial sentence of up to three years' imprisonment, or a fine for any amount, even in excess of any limit specified for a statutory offence.[20] In addition, if a Sheriff considers his powers to be inadequate in a particular case he may refer the case to the High Court for sentencing.

In criminal appeals there is no role for the Sheriff Principal; in criminal law he has the same status as any other Sheriff. Appeal from the Sheriff Court, against sentence or verdict, lies with the High Court of Justiciary sitting as a Court of Appeal.

---

[16] Criminal Proceedings etc. (Reform) (Scotland) Act 2007 s.46.
[17] Criminal Proceedings etc. (Reform) (Scotland) Act 2007 s.74.
[18] Criminal Proceedings etc. (Reform) (Scotland) Act 2007 ss.47 and 48.
[19] Criminal Proceedings etc. (Reform) (Scotland) Act 2007 s.43.
[20] Criminal Procedure (Scotland) Act 1995 s.211(1), (2).

High Court of Justiciary

The High Court of Justiciary is Scotland's supreme criminal court. It has **2–35** jurisdiction over the whole of Scotland and over all crimes, unless expressly excluded by statute. It sits as a trial court and as a court of appeal as well as having a supervisory jurisdiction over inferior courts. Like its civil counterpart, the High Court of Justiciary has extensive power to regulate its own practice and procedure which it does by a form of secondary legislation known as Acts of Adjournal.

The trial court (first instance)

The High Court of Justiciary has privative jurisdiction to try the most **2–36** serious of crimes such as murder, culpable homicide, armed robbery, drug trafficking, rape or serious sexual offences. The trial court is a circuit court and may sit in various large towns and cities around Scotland. It also sits permanently in Edinburgh and in Glasgow.

Trials are generally conducted by a single judge with a jury of 15. In difficult cases more than one judge may sit. In sentencing a prisoner convicted in the Sheriff Court a single judge alone will usually sit.

Where the panel is convicted of a statutory offence, the maximum term of imprisonment allowed is generally limited by the relevant statute. Whether the offence is common law or statutory offences a judge may impose an unlimited fine. Similarly, there is no limit on the prison term the High Court of Justiciary may impose in relation to common law offences: it may specify a sentence of imprisonment for any fixed period or for life. A person convicted of murder must be sentenced to life imprisonment.[21] In passing a life sentence the judge must fix and state at the time of sentence the period of time ("the punishment part") the person must serve in prison before being considered for release on licence.[22]

The appeal court

The High Court of Justiciary sitting as a Court of Appeal is the ultimate **2–37** court of criminal appeal in Scotland. There is no route of appeal beyond the High Court. The appeal court sits in Edinburgh. Three judges usually sit on an appeal, although more may do so if it is an exceptionally difficult case or a particularly important point of criminal law.

In addition to hearing appeals, the Lord Advocate may refer a point of law which arises in the course of a case to the High Court for an opinion (a "Lord Advocates Reference"). This allows the High Court of Justiciary to give directions which set out the law for future similar cases.

---

[21] Criminal Procedure (Scotland) Act 1995 s.205(1).
[22] Prisoners and Criminal Proceedings (Scotland) Act 1993 s.2.

Extraordinary powers

Declaratory power

2–38   The jurisdiction of the High Court of Justiciary is unlimited at common
law and it also possesses the power to declare particular conduct to be
contrary to the criminal law. That power has never been removed by
statute, although it is doubted whether the court would seek to exercise it
today. In a modern democracy the power of declaring and defining new
offences is generally regarded as best exercised by the legislature.

Nobile officium

2–39   "The Court of Justiciary has the exclusive power of providing a remedy
for all extraordinary or unforeseen occurrences in the course of criminal
business, whether before themselves or any inferior Court. Akin to the
well known nobile officium of the Court of Session, is a similar power
enjoyed by the Justiciary Court" (Alison *Practice* (1833), p.23).

The application of this power of intervening in extraordinary circumstances for the purpose of preventing injustice or oppression is limited
and rare. It cannot be invoked when to do so would conflict with statute.

TRIBUNALS

2–40   The size and nature of the modern State has expanded considerably since
the Second World War. Whether for the provision of education, welfare
support, health services or the collection of taxation, the State intervenes
in the lives of citizens in numerous ways and on many occasions. Having
to rely on expensive and lengthy court action to resolve conflicts in all of
these areas would be impracticable, the courts simply could not deal with
the sheer volume of cases generated. Tribunals are widely utilised to
resolve disputes or apply the law as they tend to be cheaper, faster, less
formal, more expert and generally more accessible than are the courts of
law.

Tribunals operate in a number of areas of UK law, that is to say, areas
of law which are reserved to the UK Parliament under the Scotland Act
1998 and which do not differ between the three jurisdictions of the United
Kingdom. Most tribunals may be termed "administrative" as they deal
with grievances individuals have with administrative decisions of the
State, for example in awarding or withholding welfare benefits, or
granting a foreign national leave to remain in the United Kingdom. The
notable exceptions to this administrative character are employment tribunals, which deal with disputes between persons—namely employers
and their employees. Nevertheless, all tribunals are established and
defined by legislation and are largely tasked with resolving disputes
arising under legislation: hence they may also be called "statutory
tribunals".

To date, tribunals have developed unsystematically and in a rather
haphazard manner. They vary in composition and function, which is

largely determined by the statute under which the particular tribunal is established. However, pending reforms—contained in the Tribunals, Courts and Enforcement Act 2007 but yet to be brought into force—seek to create a simplified statutory framework for the various tribunals and bring them under a unified overarching structure, with greater similarity in appointments, function and appeals.

Key Concepts

Tribunals are not courts but widely used to resolve disputes or apply the law.
They are mostly **administrative** but always **statutory**.
Tribunals deal with **large numbers of cases**. They are generally speedier, less costly, less formal, more expert and more accessible than courts of law.
New reforms aim to simplify and harmonise the organisation of tribunals and their operation.

Organisation and administration

Although they exercise a judicial or quasi-judicial function, tribunals are **2–41** not part of the court system. They tend to be less adversarial in nature and more inquisitorial. Tribunals operate in fields where the adjudicating body is required to have a certain level of expertise in the subject matter. Members may be required to have certain professional qualifications and many tribunals will be presided over by a legally qualified chairperson.

Tribunals Service

The Tribunals Service is an executive agency of the Ministry of Justice of **2–42** the UK government. It provides administrative support to the major UK tribunals (there are currently 27 of them).

The Administrative Justice and Tribunals Council

Established by the Tribunals, Courts and Enforcement Act 2007, the **2–43** Administrative Justice and Tribunals Council (AJTC) replaced the Council on Tribunals. Its main functions are to keep the administrative justice system, including the various tribunals and any statutory inquiries, under review.

The Council has a Scottish Committee which is concerned with administrative justice in Scotland, including UK wide tribunals which sit in Scotland. The Committee deals directly with the Scottish government in relation to any relevant proposals coming before the Scottish Parliament and it formulates the Scottish input into UK-wide matters being considered by the Council in general.

Employment Tribunals

2–44 Employment Tribunals (ETs) are arguably the most important tribunals for businesses to be familiar with. An ET hears claims about a wide variety of matters in relation to employment brought by employees against their employer. These include unfair dismissal, redundancy, unfair discrimination and claims relating to wages.

An ET is generally comprised of a panel of three: a legally qualified chairman and two lay members. One of the lay members will have experience of employment issues in representing the interests of employees; the other will have experience of being an employer. Either party in a hearing before an ET may arrange for representation by a lawyer, trade union official or advice worker. Legal Aid may be available for an ET hearing in Scotland, but generally not in England and Wales or Northern Ireland.

For further details see Chapter 8 "Employment law". Information is also available online from the Employment Tribunals' website.

The Employment Appeal Tribunal

2–45 The Employment Appeal Tribunal (EAT) sits in London and Edinburgh. Its main function is to hear appeals from decisions made by Employment Tribunals. An appeal to the EAT must be on a point of law. The EAT will not normally re-examine issues of fact established by the ET.

EAT hearings are conducted by a judge alone or by a judge and two lay members. The judge is normally a Court of Session judge or an English High Court or circuit judge. The lay members have practical experience in employment relations: one on the employers' side and one on the employees' side.

Further appeal, from a decision of the EAT, lies to the Court of Session on any question of law arising from any decision or order of the EAT sitting in Scotland, with the leave of the tribunal or the Court of Session.

Examples of Statutory or Administrative Tribunals

2–46 The following are tribunals dealing with those aspects of administrative justice that is most relevant to commercial businesses.

The Information Tribunal

2–47 The Informal Tribunal has particular relevance to businesses as it hears appeals from notices issued by the Information Commissioner under the Data Protection Act; the Freedom of Information Act; the Privacy and Electronic Communication Regulations; and the Environmental Information Regulations. See "Information Commissioner" below.

Finance and Tax Tribunals

2–48 There are five Finance and Tax Tribunals namely:

- VAT and Duties Tribunals;
- Special Commissioners;
- Financial Services and Markets Tribunal;
- Pensions Regulator Tribunal;
- Claims Management Services Tribunal.

The five tribunals are known collectively as the Finance and Tax Tribunals, although each retains its own separate jurisdiction.

Other administrative tribunals

Other administrative tribunals include: Asylum and Immigration; **2–49** Criminal Injuries Compensation Appeals Panel; the Gender Recognition Panel; Social Security and Child Support Tribunals.

OMBUDSMEN

The use of Ombudsmen is relatively new to the United Kingdom, but has **2–50** developed significantly since the establishment of the Parliamentary Commissioner for Administration in 1969. There are an increasing number of Ombudsmen or Commissioners who perform important roles in remedying grievances. Yet Ombudsmen are not part of the courts system, nor are they part of the system of administrative justice which includes tribunals and enquiries.

The key function of Ombudsmen is the resolution of complaints made against particular bodies. An Ombudsman does not function as an advocate or representative of the complainer, nor does he simply sit in judgment over evidence presented by two sides of a complaint. An Ombudsman has significant investigatory powers and fulfils an inquisitorial role. As well as the authority to demand the presentation of evidence and documents, comparable to a court, an Ombudsman will also have powers to enter premises and search and seize any evidence thought relevant to the complaint in question.

Most Ombudsmen deal exclusively with complaints relating to administration by public bodies. A select few also have considerable powers in respect of private persons.

Major Ombudsmen

Parliamentary Ombudsman

The Parliamentary Ombudsman (PO) was the first and arguably most **2–51** significant of Ombudsmen in the United Kingdom, established by the Parliamentary Commissioner Act 1967. The PO considers complaints in respect of the administrative functions of a relevant public body, which are referred to her by a Member of Parliament on behalf of a member of the public who claims to have sustained injustice in consequence of maladministration.

The key concept in defining the jurisdiction of the PO (and other public

sector Ombudsmen) is that of "maladministration". The term is not
defined in statute. During the passage of the original bill it was suggested
that "maladministration" would cover "bias, neglect, inattention, delay,
incompetence, ineptitude, perversity, turpitude, arbitrariness and so
on".[23] While "maladministration" has been criticised for uncertainty it
has, nevertheless, also been found to be "clearly open-ended, covering the
manner in which a decision is reached or discretion is exercised; but
excluding the *merits* of the decision itself".[24]

The PO is appointed by the Monarch to hold office during good
behaviour and can only be removed from office by the Monarch at their
own request or following Addresses by both Houses of Parliament. The
Ombudsman is accountable to Parliament, producing an annual report
and on occasion special issue reports, as she sees fit. All such reports
enjoy absolute privilege. The PO is overseen by the Public Administration
Select Committee of the House of Commons.

The PO has all the investigatory power available to a court in calling
written and oral evidence under oath. However, the PO has no powers to
enforce decisions; the only sanction being the publication of the findings
and presentation to Parliament.

Scottish Public Services Ombudsman

2–52 The creation of the Scottish Parliament necessitated the creation of an
equivalent to the PO with competence over the actions of the Scottish
Executive, Administration and public bodies in devolved issues. After
consultation the Scottish Parliament decided to go considerably further
and consolidate a number of Ombudsmen into a "one-stop shop". The
Scottish Public Services Ombudsman[25] (SPSO) replaced the Scottish
Parliamentary and Health Service Ombudsman, Local Government
Ombudsman for Scotland and Housing Association Ombudsman for
Scotland.

The SPSO is appointed by the Monarch on nomination by the Parliament and deals with complaints in respect of Scottish Parliament and
Scottish Government, colleges and universities, the health services, local
government, registered social landlords and a multitude of public bodies
listed in the 2002 Act. The SPSO also works with such authorities to
promote good practice in the administration of public services in
Scotland.

In the conduct of an investigation the SPSO has the same power as the
Court of Session in calling written and oral evidence under oath.
Obstruction of an SPSO investigation is actionable on petition to the
Court of Session as contempt against the court.

The SPSO has no powers to make awards or enforce a recommendation. Its sole sanction is public publication of its report and presentation

---

[23] H.C. Deb., Vol. 754, col. 51 (1966)—Often referred to as the "Crossman catalogue" after
    the then Leader of the House, Richard Crossman MP, who introduced the bill.
[24] *R v Local Commissioner for Administration for the North and East Area of England, Ex p
    Bradford Metropolitan City Council* [1979] Q.B. 287 CA per Denning M.R. at 312.
[25] Scottish Public Services Ombudsman Act 2002.

to the Scottish Parliament, with the expectation that the matter be addressed.

Information Commissioner

The Information Commissioner (IC) is a particularly important **2–53** ombudsman with which any businesses should be familiar. It is a UK-wide independent public body set up to protect personal information and promote public access to official information. In addition to important functions in respect of public bodies regarding Freedom of Information and Environmental Information Regulations, the IC deals with Data Protection and Privacy and Electronic Communication Regulations. These latter two directly affect a great many businesses.

Data Protection relates to the gathering, holding and processing of any information by which individuals can be identified. Privacy and Electronic Communication Regulations are rules for people who wish to send electronic direct marketing, for example email and text messages. These and other areas of Business Regulation are covered in Chapter 3.

In the course of investigations the Commissioner can seek a warrant from the court to enter premises, inspect and seize any equipment found there which is used or intended for processing personal data. The IC may also issue an information notice requiring a person or business to supply information relevant to an investigation, or an enforcement notice directing them to carry out specified action to comply with data regulations. Providing a false statement or failure to comply with a notice from the IC is an offence, punishable by a fine (up to a maximum of £10,000 upon summary conviction, or unlimited fine upon solemn conviction).

Scottish Information Commissioner

The Scottish Information Commissioner exercises considerable authority **2–54** under the Freedom of Information (Scotland) Act 2002. The Commissioner has substantial powers to enforce the right of citizens to access information held by public bodies. He issues codes of practice and monitors adherence to them. He investigates and adjudicates applications from any person claiming a body has failed to comply with its duties under the Act.

The Commissioner is appointed by the Monarch on the nomination of the Scottish Parliament and reports directly to the Parliament. He can only be removed from office at his own request, being retired at the end of the year in which he reaches the age of 65, or by a resolution of the Parliament passed with a two-thirds majority.

Scottish Legal Complaints Commission

From October 2008 the Scottish Legal Complaints Commission (SLCC) **2–55** is expected to come into operation. Replacing the Scottish Legal Services Ombudsman, the SLCC will deal with complaints about legal practitioners in Scotland where the problem cannot be resolved by the professional body concerned.

Established under the Legal Profession and Legal Aid (Scotland) Act 2007, the SLCC is not a court, nor a government agency but an independent corporate body. Its members are appointed for a term of five years by the Scottish Ministers, on the advice of the Lord President of the Court of Session. The Lord President may also remove members of the SLCC.

The SLCC has the same authority as a Sheriff Court to issue an order that the practitioner rectify the error made at their own expense. Where the Commission considers that the complainer has been directly affected by the inadequate professional services, the SLCC may direct the practitioner to pay compensation of up to £20,000 to the complainer for loss, inconvenience or distress resulting from the inadequate professional services.

Financial Ombudsman Service

2–56 The Financial Ombudsman Service (FOS) is appointed and run by the Financial Services Authority (FSA) under powers conferred in the Financial Services and Markets Act 2000 and the Consumer Credit Act 2006.

The job of the Service is to help resolve individual disputes between consumers and businesses providing financial services including banks, building societies, insurance firms and financial advisers. It also covers—for their financial services activities—many businesses that offer financial services as a secondary activity to their main business (e.g. motor dealers).

The FOS lacks complete independence, in that within a particular complaint a failing may lie with the FSA itself. While it does not have the powers of investigation properly associated with an Ombudsman, the FOS may ask the court to compel a party to a complaint to produce relevant evidence. If the party cannot give reasonable excuse for its refusal to comply with the FOS request, the court will then order the evidence in question to be handed over.

In making a decision on a complaint the FOS may make an award of money to compensate a complainer for financial loss or damages, or in respect of costs incurred. If not complied with, such an award will be enforced by an order of the Court of Session.

"Non Ombudsmen"

2–57 There has been a marked tendency for many public bodies to set up their own adjudicators which are often termed "Ombudsman", much to the chagrin of the PO.[26] Generally they lack the statutory powers and independence from the subject organisation that is necessary to truly meet the notion of Ombudsmen.

For example, the Scottish Prisons Complaints Commissioner is not established by statute and is directly appointed by the Scottish Ministers.

---

[26] 1993–94 H.C. 33.

Similarly, the Prisons and Probation Ombudsman for England and Wales is directly appointed by the Home Secretary. Additionally, there are a number of state appointed offices termed Ombudsmen which deal with the private sector—for example the Housing Services Ombudsman (England and Wales). Again, many such offices may lack the political independence and/or the range of investigatory powers and statutory authority necessary for a true Ombudsman.

Key Concepts

Ombudsmen are not consumer advocates but impartial inquisitors. They mostly investigate grievances arising from **maladministration**.
True Ombudsmen are statutory, impartial, independent and have substantial powers of investigation.

THE LEGAL PROFESSION

The term "lawyer" is a generic one which covers a multitude of different **2–58** occupations of people working in and with the law. The legal profession, on the other hand, refers to legal practitioners who are accredited by and subject to the rules of a professional body, to advise and represent the legal interests of paying clients. In Scotland the legal profession is divided into two mutually exclusive branches: those of solicitors and advocates. Both branches of the profession are accorded specific responsibilities and rights, recognised in law and subject to strict regulation.

Solicitors

Solicitors are effectively the "general practitioners" of the legal profes- **2–59** sion. They may be hired directly by members of the public to provide legal advice or representation. Indeed, solicitors' offices are a regular feature of high streets in towns and cities throughout Scotland.

There are currently around 10,000 solicitors in Scotland certified to practice and regulated by the Law Society of Scotland, which is established and empowered under statute to govern the profession. Solicitors may work as sole practitioners or in partnership with other solicitors. Most work in partnerships, offering a wide range of general legal advice and services such as drafting and administering of wills and trusts, facilitating the sale of property or company formation. Solicitors may offer advice in respect of court action and represent clients in the lower courts—the District/JP Court in criminal cases or the Sheriff Court in either criminal or civil cases.

In addition to those working in private practice, large corporations may employ their own in-house solicitors to deal with much of the particular organisation's legal work. Large commercial businesses such as banks or insurance companies as well as public bodies such as local councils will often have their own legal departments, which will include a number of solicitors.

The Law Society of Scotland accredits universities awarding LLB (Bachelor of Laws) degrees in Scots law. Such degrees form part of the qualification process and exempt graduates from having to complete the Society's entrance examinations. After gaining an LLB in Scots Law or passing the Society's entrance exams, a would-be-solicitor must complete a 26-week course and attain the Diploma in Legal Practice before going on to complete a two-year traineeship with a practising solicitor in Scotland. Only upon successful completion of each of those elements of professional training will they qualify for and be granted the practising certificate necessary to work as a solicitor.

In addition to overseeing entrance to the profession, the Society also regulates the on-going training solicitors must complete throughout their career. A practising solicitor is currently required to complete a minimum of 20 hours' Continuing Professional Development (CPD) in each practice year.

Notary Public

2–60 In many other jurisdictions the position of Notary Public is a distinct legal profession. However, in Scotland only solicitors may become notaries, and most, but not all, are. The chief role of a notary is bearing witness to and certifying the validity of certain legal documents. These include where a document requires the administration of an Oath or the receipt of an Affidavit or solemn Affirmation, as well as the making of Affidavits and Affirmations, and the making or certifying of documents for use in foreign jurisdictions requiring execution or certification before a Notary.

Solicitor-Advocate

2–61 A Solicitor-Advocate is a practising solicitor who by additional training and experience has applied for and been granted rights of audience in one or more of the Supreme Courts (i.e. the Court of Session and the High Court of Justiciary).

Advocates

2–62 Advocates form the second branch of the Scottish legal profession—collectively referred to as "the bar". The bar is a specialised branch of the profession. Advocates have rights of audience in all the courts of Scotland, including the Supreme Courts (the Court of Session and the High Court of Justiciary) and the House of Lords. They represent clients in court or provide expert advice, generally in respect of litigation.

There are around 460 Advocates practising in Scotland. Counsel are self-employed, each working on their own account: partnerships or agreements to share work or profits are not allowed. Most operate within the Faculty of Advocates, headquartered in Parliament House in Edinburgh.

In order to become an Advocate it is necessary to attain a law degree and Diploma in Legal Practice, pass a year-long traineeship with a solicitor and pass an examination in evidence and procedure and then complete a nine-month period of "devilling", training as the pupil of experienced advocates the Faculty has approved as "devilmasters". A "devil" will be assessed by their devilmasters on their oral and written advocacy skills before being admitted to the Faculty and granted the right to appear before the court.

Advocates cannot be employed by members of the public directly. Traditionally and most commonly, an Advocate is instructed by a solicitor on behalf of their client. However, since 2006 wider direct access has been granted to a larger number of professional bodies and organisations. Those now able to approach and instruct counsel include foreign lawyers, professional bodies, public limited companies, voluntary organisations, public authorities, trade unions, employers' associations and any person or body on the FSA Register.

Queens Counsel

Queens Counsel (QC) is a title awarded to Advocates with at least 13 **2–63** years' experience, who are considered to have achieved distinction in full-time practice. "Taking Silk", as becoming a QC is commonly known, is in the gift of the Monarch and is exercised through the First Minister upon recommendation by the Lord Justice-General.

Advocate Deputes

Advocate Deputes are advocates employed by the Crown Office and **2–64** Procurator Fiscal Service to prosecute cases in the High Court. The Advocate Deputes, together with the Lord Advocate and Solicitor General, comprise Crown Counsel.

Judiciary

With the exception of Justices of the Peace, judges in Scotland are drawn **2–65** from the legal profession. Most appointments are made by the Monarch on the advice of the First Minister according to recommendations made to him by the Lord President and the Judicial Appointments Board for Scotland.

Justices of the Peace

Justices of the Peace are members of the local community appointed by **2–66** the Scottish government. Appointment is based on recommendation submitted to the Secretary of Commissions for Scotland by the Justice of the Peace Advisory Committee for the relevant local council. JPs in the District Court are, and in the JP Court will remain, lay justices, i.e. they are not legally qualified.

JPs currently serving in District Courts are to be reappointed to JP

Courts when they come into operation in their area.[27] JPs are to be appointed by the Scottish Ministers for a term of five years. Re-appointment is automatic unless the person declines, has reached the age of 69, is disqualified, or the Sheriff Principal recommends to the Ministers that the person not be re-appointed. A JP must live in or within 15 miles of the Sheriffdom.

A JP must retire upon reaching 70 years of age and is disqualified if they become or are bankrupt. A JP may only be removed from office by order of a tribunal appointed by the Lord President of the Court of Session.

Stipendiary Magistrates

2–67 A Stipendiary is a permanent, legally qualified judge employed to sit in the District Court or JP Court. In the District Court a Stipendiary is appointed by the local council.

In the JP Court a Stipendiary may be appointed by the Scottish Ministers if, on the advice of a Sheriff Principal, they consider that the appointment is necessary or expedient for the purposes of the efficient administration of any or all of the JP courts in that Sheriff Principal's Sheriffdom. The appointee must be a solicitor or advocate with at least five years' experience.

Part-time magistrates will be appointed for a term of five years. Full-time magistrates are to be appointed for an indefinite term.

Sheriffs

2–68 There are currently over 140 full-time Sheriffs in service. To be appointed a Sheriff a person must be and have been an advocate or solicitor for at least 10 years. Those appointed should be practitioners of standing, whether Queen's Counsel, advocates or solicitors with considerable court experience. Before appointment, the person will in many cases have some experience of the Shrieval bench as a part-time Sheriff.

Once appointed a Sheriff may remain in office until the compulsory retirement age, which is 70. Sheriffs may, if they wish, retire at any time after reaching the age of 60. A Sheriff may be required to live in or near the town in which he or she has the main or only court.

A Sheriff can only be removed from office by statutory instrument, laid before Parliament. Such instrument may only be laid following the recommendation of the Lord President of the Court of Session and the Lord Justice Clerk, having undertaken an investigation into the said Sheriff.

Sheriffs Principal

2–69 There are six Sheriffs Principal in Scotland. Each presides over a particular Sheriffdom and discharges a number of administrative functions in respect of the courts in that Sheriffdom. A Sheriff Principal sometimes

---

[27] Criminal Proceedings etc. (Reform) (Scotland) Act 2007 ss.67–77.

sits in criminal courts or conducts major fatal accident inquiries. However, a Sheriff Principal's judicial business is primarily as an appellate judge who sits alone to determine appeals from the decisions of Sheriffs in civil matters.

Appointment, service and removal for the office of Sheriff Principal is as that for Sheriffs.

Judges of the Supreme Courts of Scotland

Since 1836 the judiciary of the highest criminal and civil courts in Scot- **2–70** land have been unified. While individual judges will sometimes specialise in particular areas or types of law, as a rule a judge of the Supreme Courts in Scotland may sit on both criminal and civil cases in the respective courts. Each judge will cover a broad spectrum of cases. However, particular judges may be designated to hear cases relating to specific areas of law where certain experience or knowledge is advantageous. For example a judge may be designated to hear intellectual property, judicial review or commercial cases.

There are currently 34 judges of the Supreme Courts. Those eligible for appointment as a judge of the Supreme Courts include experienced advocates, usually QCs, or a Sheriff Principal, Sheriff or Solicitor Advocate with a minimum of five years' experience.

A judge of the Supreme Courts may resign at any time, and must retire upon reaching the age of 75. However, a judge of the Supreme Courts can only be removed from office by the Monarch upon the recommendation of the First Minister and with the agreement of the Scottish Parliament following a proper investigation and report on whether the judge is unfit for office by reason of inability, neglect of duty or misbehaviour.[28]

Senators of the College of Justice

Judges of the Court of Session are termed "Senators of the College of **2–71** Justice" or "Lords of Council and Session". A judge takes the courtesy title of "Lord" or "Lady" followed by their surname or a territorial title: for example Lord Abernethy (John Alastair Cameron); Lord Kingarth (Derek Robert Alexander Emslie). When sitting in the Outer House may also be called a Lord Ordinary.

Generally, 24 judges sit as Lords Ordinary in the Outer House. A further 10 sit in the Inner House: five, including the Lord President sit in the First Division; five, including the Lord Justice Clerk, sit in the Second Division. However, the exact numbers are subject to change according to new appointments, retirements and occasionally the formation of an extra division of the Inner House.

---

[28] Scotland Act 1998 s.95(6)–(8).

Lord Commissioners of the High Court of Justiciary

2–72 Judges of the High Court of Justiciary are called "Lord Commissioners of the High Court of Justiciary". Sitting generally reflects that of the Court of Session—Lords Ordinary presiding over criminal trials in the High Court and the members of divisions in the Inner House of the Court of Session generally forming a bench to hear appeals in the High Court of Justiciary sitting as a Court of Appeal.

Lord President and Lord Justice-General

2–73 The offices of Lord President and Lord Justice-General are the highest judicial offices in Scots civil and criminal law respectively. These two titles are now held by a single judge, dual title dates from the amalgamation of civil and criminal judiciary in the nineteenth century.

Appointment is by the Monarch, on the advice of the Prime Minister according to recommendations made by the First Minister, after consulting the serving Lord President and Lord Justice-General.[29]

Lord Justice Clerk

2–74 The Lord Justice Clerk is the second most senior Judge in Scotland, behind the Lord President of the Court of Session. The holder has the title in both the Court of Session and the High Court of Justiciary and is in charge of the Second Division of the Inner House of the Court of Session. The office is one of the Great Offices of State in Scotland.

Complaints

2–75 Complaints about practising lawyers are dealt with by the professional bodies—the Law Society of Scotland or the Faculty of Advocates. If a complainer is not satisfied with the response of the professional body they may then take their complaint further to the Scottish Legal Services Ombudsman or, when it commences operation, the Scottish Legal Complaints Commission (see above).

LAW OFFICERS

2–76 Reference to "the Scottish Law Officers" means the Lord Advocate and Solicitor General. However, as a result of devolution there is also the Advocate General—a UK law officer with dedicated powers and responsibilities of particular relevance to Scotland.

Lord Advocate

2–77 The Lord Advocate is the senior law officer in Scotland. The office dates back to at least 1483.

Today the Lord Advocate fulfils four major legal roles. As head of the

---

[29] Scotland Act 1998, s.95(1)–(3).

Crown Office and Procurator Fiscal Service (COPFS) the Lord Advocate is in charge of the system of prosecution and investigation of deaths. The Lord Advocate is also a member of the Scottish Executive and is the chief legal adviser to the Scottish government. The Lord Advocate also represents the Scottish Executive in civil proceedings and represents the public interest in a range of statutory and common law civil functions.

The Lord Advocate is appointed by the Monarch, on the advice of the First Minister with the agreement of the Scottish Parliament. Unlike other Ministers, however, they cannot be removed from office by the First Minister without the approval of the Parliament.[30]

The current Lord Advocate is the Rt Hon Elish Angiolini QC WS, who was installed as Lord Advocate on October 12, 2006.

Solicitor General

The Solicitor General is the depute of the Lord Advocate in the prose- **2–78** cution system. In the absence of a Lord Advocate in office he takes over full responsibility for the exercise of the functions of the Lord Advocate. Frank Mulholland QC was sworn in as Solicitor General on May 30, 2007.

Procurators Fiscal

Area and District Procurators Fiscal work within the Crown Office and **2–79** Procurator Fiscal Service. They prosecute crimes locally in the lower courts throughout Scotland on behalf of the Lord Advocate.

Advocate General

The office of Advocate General was established as a result of devolution. **2–80** Appointed by the Prime Minister, the Advocate General advises the UK Government on issues of Scots law with respect to UK legislation and governance not devolved to Holyrood under the Scotland Act 1998.

The Advocate General also has statutory functions under the Act relating to ensuring the devolved institutions act *intra vires*. He can refer bills of the Scottish Parliament to the Judicial Committee of the Privy Council for decisions on their competence or raise proceedings in the courts on devolution issues arising from actions of the Scottish Government or Scottish Parliament. He is also given notice of any devolution issue raised in the courts and can intervene in such cases.

The current Advocate General is Neil Davidson QC.

---

[30] Scotland Act 1998, s.48(1).

▼ CHAPTER SUMMARY

THE CIVIL COURTS

2–80
- **Sheriff Court**
  - **Ordinary cause**
  - **Summary cause**
  - **Small claims**
- **The Court of Session (Outer House)**
- **The Court of Session (Inner House)**
- **The House of Lords**

Jurisdiction can be defined according to place, person or subject matter.
The pursuer follows the defender.
The jurisdiction of the Sherriff Court and Court of Session largely overlap, but each still has its privative jurisdiction.
The choice of court and procedure will depend on the cost of the action and the nature and size of the remedy the pursuer seeks.

THE CRIMINAL COURTS

- **District Court / JP Court**
- **Sheriff Court**
  - **Summary**
  - **Solemn**
- **The High Court of Justiciary**
- **The High Court of Justiciary Court of Appeal**

Criminal law is public law.
Prosecutions are brought by the Crown Office and Procurator Fiscal Service.
The courts vary in composition, jurisdiction and gravity of penalties they can impose.
The court is chosen by the prosecution, according to the seriousness of the offence and the penalty sought.

TRIBUNALS

- **Mainly administrative, always statutory.**
- **Are utilised for certain benefits in resolving disputes:**
  - **Less costly than the courts**
  - **Speedier resolution**
  - **Expert adjudication**

- Less formal
- More accessible
- Most deal with issues of public administration, such as:
  - Social Security and Welfare
  - Asylum and Immigration
  - Care and Mental Health
- Some deal with vital business matters:
  - Information Tribunal
  - Employment Tribunals
  - Employment Appeals Tribunal
  - Finance and Tax Tribunals

OMBUDSMEN

- Established by statutes to resolve complaints in respect of maladministration by particular bodies.
- Act as impartial inquisitors.
- Most act in the public sector:
  - Parliamentary Ombudsman
  - Scottish Public Services Ombudsman
  - Scottish Information Commissioner
- Some act in the private sector or across both public and private:
  - Information Commissioner
  - Scottish Legal Complaints Commission
  - Financial Ombudsman Service
- True Ombudsmen are:
  - Statutory
  - Impartial
  - Have powers of investigation
  - Backed by the powers of court orders

THE LEGAL PROFESSION

- Divided into two branches:
  - Solicitors
  - Advocates
- Each regulated by professional bodies
- Judiciary:
  - JPs
  - Sheriff
  - Sheriff Principal

- **Senators of the College of Justice**
- **Lord Commissioners of Justiciary**
- **The Lord President and the Lord Justice-General**
- **The Lord Justice Clerk**

THE LAW OFFICERS

- **Lord Advocate**
- **Solicitor General**
- **Procurators Fiscal**
- **Advocate General**

? QUICK QUIZ

1. What does "privative jurisdiction" mean?
2. What three criteria define the civil jurisdiction of the Sheriff Court?
3. Which court hears applications for judicial review?
4. What is the maximum prison sentence that can be imposed by the District Court?
5. How many years must a JP have practised as a lawyer?
6. What is the ultimate court of civil appeal?
7. What is the ultimate court of criminal appeal?
8. What is the maximum fine a Sheriff can impose after conviction in a solemn trial?
9. How many people sit in a Scottish criminal jury?
10. What is a judge of the High Court called?
11. What does an Advocate Depute do?
12. Name the offices of the highest civil and criminal judiciary in Scotland?

FURTHER READING

Stair Memorial Encyclopaedia (Civil Procedure); (Constitutional Law); (Courts and Competency (Volume 6)); (Criminal Procedure); (Employment); (Tribunals).

R.S. Shiels, *Law Basics: Scottish Legal System*, 2nd edn (W. Green, Edinburgh, 2003).

D.M. Walker, *The Scottish Legal System*, 8th edn (W. Green, Edinburgh, 2001).

RELEVANT WEBLINKS

Courts
Scottish Courts Service *http://www.scotcourts.gov.uk.*

Scottish Justices Association *http://www.district-courts.org/*.
Summary Justice Reform *http://www.scotcourts.gov.uk/summary_justice_reform/index.asp*.
UK Supreme Court *http://www.justice.gov.uk/whatwedo/supremecourt.htm*.

Tribunals
Tribunals Service *http://www.tribunals.gov.uk/*.
Administrative Justice and Tribunals Council *http://www.ajtc.gov.uk/*.
Employment Tribunals *http://www.employmenttribunals.gov.uk*.

Ombudsmen
British and Irish Ombudsmen Association *http://www.bioa.org.uk*.
Scottish Public Services Ombudsman *http://www.scottishombudsman.org.uk*.
Information Commissioner website *http://www.ico.gov.uk*.

Legal Personnel
Law Society of Scotland *http://www.lawscot.org.uk*.
Faculty of Advocates *http://www.advocates.org.uk*.
Crown Office and Procurator Fiscal Service *http://www.copfs.gov.uk*.
Office of the Advocate General *http://www.oag.gov.uk*.

Chapter 3   Business Regulation

ELIZABETH CAMPBELL, GREG GORDON AND MICHAEL PLAXTON[1]

▶ CHAPTER OVERVIEW

3–01 This chapter is concerned with the measures adopted by the law in order to regulate businesses. It is divided into three main sections. As the criminal law is one of the most important tools used in business regulation, the chapter commences by introducing the reader to the purpose and general principles of the criminal law. It then goes on to consider a number of common law offences which are of particular relevance to business. Finally, it examines a number of regulatory regimes which parliament has enacted to control a range of business activities.

✓ OUTCOMES

3–02 By the end of this chapter you should:

- ✓ Understand the nature and purpose of the criminal law;
- ✓ Appreciate that criminal offences generally require both *actus reus* and *mens rea* while recognising that in the case of strict liability offences, only an *actus reus* is required;
- ✓ Be aware that criminal liability can in certain situations be incurred both art and part and vicariously, and understand the difference between those terms
- ✓ Appreciate the difficulties in holding corporations criminally liable, and understand the circumstances in which corporations are and are not criminally liable;
- ✓ Be able to describe the essential features of a number of common law crimes of dishonesty relevant to business, namely theft, embezzlement, fraud, uttering and extortion;
- ✓ Understand what regulatory offences are, and appreciate that criminalisation is just one of a range of responses used by the state to regulate modern business practice;
- ✓ Be in a position to describe the regulatory regimes which the state has put in place in relation to occupational health and safety, corporate homicide, the misuse of data and competition between businesses;

---

[1] All Lecturers in Law, University of Aberdeen.

✓ Have an understanding of the breath of scope of environmental regulation currently in force within the UK, and be in a position to describe some of its key features.

THE CRIMINAL LAW—ITS PURPOSE AND GENERAL PRINCIPLES

Introduction

At times, the public interest in the criminal law appears to be insatiable. **3–03** The media reports continually on the outcome of criminal trials, crime novels fill the shelves of bookshops, and crime reconstruction pro- grammes are broadcast regularly on television. Thus even readers who have never formally studied the criminal law will have built up at least some degree of awareness of its contents. It will therefore come as no surprise to learn that the criminal law prohibits forms of behaviour which society regards as serious wrongs. However, what might be less apparent is precisely *how* the criminal law defines such prohibited wrongs, and *why* certain forms of blameworthy conduct are treated as worthy of criminal prohibition while others are not. We shall consider these (and other) issues in the paragraphs which follow.

The nature of criminal law

There is a common perception that the purpose of the criminal law is to **3–04** achieve "justice for the victim"—that it aims to punish the offender in the name of the individual harmed. This, however, is a mistaken view of the criminal law's function. Such an analysis would see harmful conduct as a private wrong directed exclusively towards the victim. However, criminal law is not a branch of private law, but of public law. In other words, it is not principally concerned with the legal relationship between individuals but between the state and the individual. A crime is regarded as an affront to the community at large, not just to the individual victim. The public interest in preventing, resolving and punishing harmful behaviour that falls within the scope of the criminal law is reflected in the fact that prosecutions are generally taken on the part of the state. This is why, when the most serious criminal allegations come to court, the parties to the litigation are the accused and "Her Majesty's Advocate", the latter of whom pursues the case in the name of the sovereign and on behalf of the state.[2] None of this is to say that the victim of a crime will have no legal remedy against the wrongdoer. The Scottish criminal courts have the power to issue a compensation order, requiring the wrongdoer to make at

---

[2] Her Majesty's Advocate prosecutes all cases which take place in front of a judge and jury and which are conducted under what is known as solemn procedure: see further para.2–29, above. Less serious crimes are prosecuted by local public prosecutors known as "procurators fiscal".

least some degree of payment for the benefit of the victim.[3] Often, however, the sum which can be paid to the victim in this way will be inadequate to fully compensate him. In such cases, the victim has the right to seek further compensation through alternative branches of the law.[4]

Elements of criminal offences

3–05 A crime is generally described as comprising both an external element— typically some manner of conduct or behaviour (such as a positive act, an omission or the bringing about of a particular state of affairs)—and a mental aspect (namely a blameworthy state of mind such as intention, recklessness or the possession of knowledge). The Latin maxim *"actus non facit reum nisi mens sit rea"* encapsulates this notion, stating as it does that behaviour cannot amount to a crime unless carried out with a blameworthy state of mind. This axiom provides the terms *actus reus*, which refers to the external element of a crime, and *mens rea*, which describes the mental element. Generally speaking, an individual can only commit a criminal offence by engaging in a course of conduct which the law regards as wrongful, while simultaneously possessing a blameworthy state of mind. This proposition holds true for all common law crimes, i.e. crimes such as assault, murder, rape and theft. However, and crucially, an exception is made in the context of what are known as "strict liability" offences. These require only an *actus reus* for their commission; *mens rea* is not required. Some offences which have been created by statute or delegated legislation, known as "statutory offences", are crimes of strict liability. A variety of statutory offences which are relevant to the state's regulation of business activities are discussed at paras 3–29 to 3–56, below.

Actus Reus

3–06 The external element (*actus reus*) of a given offence may be an act or an omission. For example, the *actus reus* for assault is an "attack" (which is itself a legal term of art referring to conduct causing injury or fear of injury).[5] In the usual case, one person can attack another only by performing a positive act, for instance, by punching the victim or brandishing a knife.

Omissions may be divided into two categories: (a) pure omission; and (b) commission by omission. It can be difficult, in practice, to say that any given omission is either one or the other. In principle, though, the distinction rests upon the insight that a person may act without moving. For

---

[3] In solemn cases, the amount of compensation which can be awarded is unlimited. In summary cases, there are strict limits on the amount of compensation which the court can order: Criminal Procedure (Scotland) Act 1995 s.249.

[4] Delict, or occasionally contract law, may provide a remedy for the wronged party. Delict is discussed at Ch.10 and the law of contract is discussed at Ch.4. In certain cases, victims of physical violence may also be entitled to claim compensation from the state through the Criminal Injuries Compensation Scheme—see *http://www.cica.gov.uk* (site accessed April 14, 2008).

[5] *Gilmour v McGlennan* 1993 S.C.C.R. 837.

instance, commission by omission is evident in the English case of *Fagan
v Metropolitan Police Commissioner*,[6] where the accused inadvertently
parked his car on another's foot. When he realised what he had done, he
refused to move the vehicle. Under the circumstances, the accused's
failure to move the car may be viewed as an "attack", such that it would
satisfy the *actus reus* of assault. Broadly speaking, where the accused has
acted without moving this represents a case of "commission by omission". In such cases, the "omission" is treated as a positive act.

"Pure omission" is where the accused has not acted at all. Scots
criminal law has traditionally hesitated to impose liability on individuals
for pure omissions. The mere fact that the accused in a given case had a
moral duty to act is not enough. For example, it may be highly immoral
to stand by and permit a child to drown in a pool when he or she could be
rescued with no risk to oneself, but unless a special duty of the type
described in the following paragraph exists, it is not criminal: an accused
can satisfy the *actus reus* of a criminal offence through inaction only if he
had a legal duty to act.

At common law, courts have recognised a legal duty to act in only a
small range of circumstances: (1) where the accused has a particular kind
of relationship with the victim (for example a parental or spousal relationship);[7] (2) where the accused has assumed responsibility for the victim;[8] (3) where the accused owes a public duty by virtue of some official
position;[9] or (4) where the accused himself created the danger.[10] Beyond
this narrow range, the courts have taken the view that it should fall to
Parliament to impose positive duties to act on citizens. One example of a
statutory crime of pure omission is failing to stop a motor vehicle or
bicycle when requested to do so by a police officer.[11]

Causation

The *actus reus* of an offence may or may not require proof that the **3–07**
accused caused a certain result to occur. For example, murder requires
proof that the accused caused the death of the victim, and assault requires
proof that the accused caused injury or fear of injury. By contrast, the
crime of breaching the peace does not require proof that the accused
caused any particular result at all. Where an offence does demand proof
that the accused caused a given result, the Crown will usually discharge
that burden if it shows that, but for the accused's conduct, the result
would not have occurred. There are limits to this "but for" liability. On
occasion, something so unforeseeable will happen between the accused's
conduct and the result that it may be unjust to hold the accused liable for
that result. In such cases, there has been an intervening act (or *novus actus
interveniens*) which has "broken the chain of causation". Suppose, for

[6] [1969] 1 Q.B. 439.
[7] See *R v Gibbins and Proctor* (1918) 13 Cr App R 134.
[8] See e.g. *R v Instan* [1893] 1 Q.B. 450.
[9] See e.g. *Bonar and Hogg v MacLeod*, 1983 S.C.C.R. 161.
[10] See e.g, *MacPhail v Clark*, 1983 S.C.C.R. 395.
[11] Road Traffic Act 1988 s.163.

example, that A deliberately pushes B into a soft pile of leaves during a thunderstorm. At that moment, B is struck by a bolt of lightning, and he is killed. It seems clear that A, by pushing B, has assaulted him. It also seems clear that, but for the push, B would not have been in a position to be struck by the lightning bolt. Nonetheless, it seems wrong to say that A has caused B's death; it was so unforeseeable that a lightning bolt would strike that location at that moment, that the lightning bolt could be described as a *novus actus interveniens* which severs A's liability for B's death.

To sever the causal link the *novus actus interveniens* must supersede the original act. The circumstances in which this will occur are very limited in practice. For example, the victim's voluntary consumption of drugs does not break the chain so as to exculpate the accused who supplied the drugs for the injury/death which ensued.[12] In addition, poor or incorrect medical treatment, also known as *malregimen*, rarely breaks the chain of unless the treatment is palpably wrong or grossly negligent.[13] Moreover, intervention by a third party will not necessarily break the causal chain.[14] It seems that if the intervening act was a foreseeable one, then the causal connection is unbroken, and the initial action will be deemed to have caused the result.

The courts have also established that not every unforeseeable circumstance will break the chain of causation. Suppose that A punches B, who, unbeknownst to A, suffers from a condition which makes him unusually vulnerable to the blow, and B dies. In that case, the apparent unforeseeability of the existence of a condition capable of transforming an ordinary blow into a fatal injury will not sever the chain of causation.[15] The accused must "take his victim as he finds him", a principle sometimes referred to as the "egg-shell skull rule". It seems that such an approach is adopted on the grounds of public policy, on the basis that the initial criminal act ought not to have occurred in the first instance, and so this principle may serve as a deterrent. The rule is well-established but controversial: though we surely want to deter people from attacking each other, it can seem harsh to say that A has "caused" B's death, when we might just as easily say that it was B's condition which killed him.

Background state of affairs

3–08 Finally, the *actus reus* of an offence may require proof of some background state of affairs. For example, the *actus reus* of theft is "appropriation of corporeal property belonging to another without the owner's consent".[16] It is not enough for the Crown to show that an accused has appropriated property—it must in addition prove that the property

---

[12] *Lord Advocate's Reference (No.1 of 1994)* 1995 S.C.C.R. 117.
[13] Such criteria were satisfied in *R v Jordan* (1956) 40 Cr App R 152; *R v Smith* [1959] 2 All E.R. 193.
[14] *People v Fowler* 174 Pac 892 (1918).
[15] *Bird v Her Majesty's Advocate* 1952 J.C. 23.
[16] *Carmichael v Black* 1992 SL.T. 897.

belonged to someone else, and that the owner did not consent to the appropriation.

On occasion, the Crown may prove the *actus reus* of an offence by showing nothing more than that a state of affairs existed—i.e. without showing that the accused did anything in particular. These offences generally are what are called "status offences" in that they hold a person liable for what he *is*, rather than what he *does*. For example, the Terrorism Act 2000 makes it a criminal offence to be a member of a terrorist organisation, whether or not one advances an actual act of terrorism.

Mens rea

As we have already seen, in general, criminal liability is not attributed to **3–09** an individual merely because he has fulfilled the *actus reus* of an offence. Generally speaking, before a person is declared guilty of a particular offence, it must be proved that he had an appropriately blameworthy mental state.[17] The three types of *mens rea* that tend to arise most frequently are (a) intention, (b) recklessness, and (c) knowledge.

Intention

Some crimes require proof that the accused had a particular intention at **3–10** the time of engaging in the criminal conduct. As previously noted, assault requires proof of an intention to cause injury or fear of injury.[18] Similarly, theft requires proof of an intention to deprive the owner of his property,[19] and fraud requires proof of an intention to deceive.[20] The law generally considers someone to be acting intentionally when he acts with purpose. So, returning to the example of assault, if A walks up to B in a park and hits him in the face with a cricket bat, this would provide a strong example of A acting with criminal intent. However, if A is playing cricket in the park and, while swinging the bat to play a shot, happens to strike B in the face as he passes while walking his dog, A does not have the requisite *mens rea* for assault. He has acted deliberately only in the sense that he did mean to swing the bat. However, he did this for the purpose of hitting the ball, not for the purpose of attacking B. If, by swinging the bat when he did, A acted with a complete disregard for the consequences of his action, he will have behaved recklessly. That will not satisfy the *mens rea* requirement for assault, but is sufficient to establish the *mens rea* for the separate crime of reckless injury. The concept of recklessness is discussed in more detail below.

It should be noted, however, that although proof of intention may be required, motive is generally irrelevant to criminal liability.[21] Thus, returning to the example of A, B and the cricket bat, if the court is

---

[17] As has already been noted, offences of strict liability form an important exception to this rule. Strict liability is considered at para.3–15, below.
[18] See *Smart v HM Advocate*, 1975 S.L.T. 65.
[19] *Carmichael v Black*, 1992 S.L.T. 897.
[20] See *Mackenzie v Skeen*, 1971 J.C. 43.
[21] See *Palazzo v Copeland*, 1976 J.C. 52.

satisfied on the basis of the evidence put before it that A intended to attack B with the bat, that is enough. The prosecution do not need to prove why A acted as he did, only that the assault took place.

Recklessness

3–11 A large number of offences require or permit *mens rea* to be established through the proof of mere recklessness: for example, the offences of reckless injury, reckless endangerment or involuntary culpable homicide. To say that someone has acted "recklessly" is to say that he has not paid due regard to the consequences of his actions. However, the same could be said of someone who has acted carelessly or negligently. Recklessness is conceptually related to carelessness and negligence, but it refers to an especially inadequate regard to the consequences. Hence, recklessness has been described as "gross negligence" or a *complete* disregard for the consequences of one's actions.[22]

Knowledge

3–12 Some offences require proof that the accused had knowledge of some state of affairs. For example, the crime of reset requires proof that the accused knew that the goods he possessed were stolen.[23] This does not mean that an individual can avoid liability for knowledge-based offences simply by shutting his eyes to the circumstances around him; if the circumstances were such that it would have been blameworthy for him not to make inquiries, knowledge may be imputed to him.

Mens rea: objective or subjective?

3–13 Case law is inconsistent as to whether the Crown can establish the *mens rea* of an offence only by adducing proof of the accused's actual state of mind, or whether the Crown can do so by arguing that a reasonable man would have had that state of mind had he been in the accused's shoes at the time he acted. The former approach to proof is "subjectivist", whereas the latter is "objectivist". The subjective approach involves an examination into the state of mind of the particular accused at the time he carried out the *actus reus*, while the objective approach adopts a reasonable man standard and may involve the presumption of intention on the basis of the act.

Intention-based offences are typically subjectivist—that is, the inquiry is to whether the accused actually had the requisite intention (e.g. in cases of theft, the intention to deprive). It does not matter that, in principle, no reasonable person would have done as the accused did unless he had an intention to deprive; it remains open to the court to conclude that the accused did not himself have that intention and that he cannot, therefore, be convicted of theft. In other words, the subjectivist approach precludes

---

[22] See *Paton v HM Advocate*, 1936 J.C. 19.
[23] See *Latta v Herron* (1967) S.C.C.R. Supp. 18.

the assumption that, because the accused acted as he did, he must have had a particular intention.

Recklessness-based offences, on the other hand, are typically thought to be objectivist. This means that the Crown does not need to prove that the accused actually perceived the risk he was running by engaging in his course of conduct; it is enough that a reasonable person *would* have perceived the danger. Ultimately, this concerns the issue of whether the accused's conduct reflects a level of care falling *far below* that expected of reasonable people. (A point often missed is that the Crown must do more than show that reasonable people would not act as the accused did, since this will demonstrate only carelessness or negligence. In practice, this leaves ample room for disagreement as to whether an accused's conduct was reckless or merely negligent.) There is good reason to think that knowledge-based offences, too, are objectivist inasmuch as the trier of fact can infer knowledge from the circumstances surrounding the accused's conduct.

Error

Certain kinds of error are relevant to whether an accused has the requisite **3–14** *mens rea* for a given offence; others are not. Mistakes of fact can be relevant. Consider, for example, a case involving an accusation of rape. The *mens rea* of rape is satisfied where the accused knows that the woman is not consenting or at any rate is reckless as to whether she is consenting.[24] If the accused believed that the woman was consenting, even if he was mistaken in that belief, he lacks the *mens rea* for the offence (so long as he was not reckless in forming that belief). As a general rule, the accused's guilt is determined according to the facts as he understood them to be.

Many non-lawyers will have, at some point, heard that "ignorance of the law is no excuse". That is only partly true. An accused cannot successfully argue that he should be acquitted on the basis of an honest but mistaken belief that what he was doing was not criminal.[25] However, some errors of *civil* law may negate the *mens rea* for certain offences. For example, as we shall see at para.3–22 below, theft requires proof of an intention to deprive the owner of his property. An accused can only have such an intention if he believes that the property in question belongs to someone else; if the accused believes that the property belongs to him, then he lacks the requisite *mens rea*. Similarly, in *Gould*, the accused was acquitted of bigamy because he honestly but mistakenly believed that his first marriage had been dissolved before he entered into his second marriage.[26]

---

[24] *Jamieson v HM Advocate*, 1994 S.L.T. 537.
[25] *Brown v Frame*, 2005 S.L.T. 744.
[26] *R v Gould* [1968] 2 Q.B. 65.

Strict liability

3-15 As we have already seen,[27] all common law offences require proof of both an *actus reus* and a *mens rea*. Some statutory offences follow the same pattern and require both *actus reus* and *mens rea*, however others require only proof of *actus reus* Often the wording of the statutory provision creating the offence will itself let the reader know whether or not a particular offence is intended to be one of strict liability. If the statute states that the offence can only be committed "knowingly", "wilfully", "intentionally" or "recklessly", then it will be apparent that *mens rea* is required. Equally, if the statute expressly states that the offence is one of strict liability, or that *mens rea* is not required for the offence's commission, then again the matter is clear. However, if the statute does not expressly deal with the issue, the courts will need to determine what parliament intended. The courts will commence by presuming that *mens rea* is required. However, the presumption can be overcome if the statute creating the offence is directed towards an issue of social concern, such as public safety, and "if the creation of strict liability will be effective to promote the objects of the statute by encouraging greater vigilance to prevent the commission of the prohibited act".[28]

Key Concepts

A crime has two specific elements an *actus reus* (the physical element) and *mens rea* (the mental element). The exception to this is a strict liability crime which requires only proof of an *actus reus*.

The *actus reus* usually takes the form of an act, however, in some specific cases an omission may constitute an *actus reus*.

Mens rea (or "guilty mind") is most often defined in terms of intention, knowledge or recklessness.

Art and part liability

3-16 The principle of art and part liability concerns participation or involvement in a crime, and provides that any person who participates in the commission of an offence may be held criminally responsible. There are two requirements for art and part liability: first, there must be a common purpose,[29] and secondly, the accused must participate in the criminal enterprise.[30]

---

[27] See para.3–05, above.
[28] *Gammon Ltd v Att-Gen of Hong Kong* [1985] A.C. 1, *per* Lord Scarman at 17.
[29] *HM Advocate v Lappen* 1956 S.L.T. 109.
[30] See *H.M.A. v Kerr* (1871) 2 Couper 334.

Vicarious liability

In the criminal context,[31] vicarious liability arises when criminal liability **3–17**
is imputed to one person or company on the basis of what *another* person
did (or failed to do), even though the actors do not share a common
purpose. Vicarious liability does not arise at common law: one cannot be
held vicariously liable for a common law crime. However, vicarious liability is quite commonly imposed in statutes establishing regulatory
offences. In such offences, the employer or proprietor of a business may
be criminally liable for the criminal conduct of his employees or agents if
(and only if) the conduct takes place within the scope of the employment
or agency agreement.[32]

Vicarious liability is imposed in one of two circumstances. First, it may
be imposed by the express terms of a statute. For example, the Licensing
(Scotland) Act 1976 permits the licence-holder to be vicariously liable for
a range of offences committed by his employees or agents. For instance,
the licence-holder is guilty of an offence if the licence-holder's employee
sells alcohol to a person who is younger than 18 years of age.[33] However,
the statute also provides the licence-holder with a "due diligence"
defence—in other words, the licence-holder can escape liability if he can
persuade the court that he took appropriate steps to avoid the commission of the offence.[34] It will often be the case that the legislature will
mitigate the apparent harshness of an express provision for vicarious
liability by granting some sort of statutory defence on which the
employer or principal may rely.

Secondly, where the statute itself does not expressly permit an
employer or principal to be found vicariously liable, the courts may
nonetheless read such a possibility into the regulatory regime. This occurs
only where the employer or principal could be said to have shared
responsibility for the function performed by the employee or agent, i.e.
where the employer could be said to bear some degree of fault for the lack
of conformity to the regulations in question.[35]

Corporate liability

Corporate liability differs from vicarious liability in that it refers to **3–18**
situations where a corporate entity—generally a company, but sometimes
other entities having a legal identity separate from its consistent members—has *itself* engaged in criminal conduct and is accordingly held
criminal responsibility for its *own* acts or omissions. Thus, as outlined in
the preceding section, a corporation may in certain circumstances be
vicariously liable for the criminal conduct of its employees; alternatively,
it may be directly liable for its own criminal conduct.

---

[31] Vicarious liability also arises in other contexts, most notably in the law of delict.
[32] See *City and Suburban Dairies v Mackenna* 1918 J.C. 105 at 110.
[33] Licensing (Scotland) Act 1976 s.68(1).
[34] Licensing (Scotland) Act 1976 s.71.
[35] See the analysis by T. Jones and M. Christie, *Criminal Law* (4th edn, W. Green, 2008),
p.399.

Historically, it was believed that corporate bodies could not themselves commit criminal offences.[36] However, Scottish courts now take the view that corporate bodies can be held liable for statutory offences and some common law crimes. There are two dominant issues in the attribution of liability to a corporate entity, stemming from the fact that such an entity is not a physical person. The first issue is a simple matter of practicality: some offences can be punished only with a term of imprisonment and an incorporeal entity cannot be imprisoned. This means that a corporate entity cannot be convicted of any offence where the minimum punishment is imprisonment. Murder is the classic example of such a crime.

The second issue is more complex. As we have seen, for all common law offences, the Crown must prove both *actus reus* and *mens rea*. A corporation, however, has no brain, and therefore no mental state, of its own. Before criminal liability can be assigned to a corporation, a sensible way must be established of identifying its mental state. In Scotland, this is done by reference to the "controlling mind" of the company.[37] The "controlling mind" must be an individual person within the corporation who is in a position to set agendas and policies. The conduct and *mens rea* of the controlling mind of the company can then be attributed to the company. The problem, however, is that very often corporations act in dishonest or harmful ways not as a result of decisions being taken by senior personnel who are in a position to set agendas and policies, but as a result of the way that the company is being run by managers operating at a lower level of the corporate structure, or of employees involved in the company's day-to-day business. Thus a successful prosecution is often impossible, particularly in the case of large companies with a complex management structure, because the controlling mind of the company may be wholly uninvolved in these matters. It is generally easier for large companies to be prosecuted for breaches of regulatory offences, particularly where these are offences of strict liability. The practical difficulties associated with bringing successful prosecutions for manslaughter or culpable homicide against large companies has led to the creation of a new corporate killing offence, discussed at para.3–41, below.

Inchoate offences

3–19   Under s.294 of the Criminal Procedure (Scotland) Act 1995, any attempt to commit a crime is itself criminal. A person has "attempted" a particular offence when he has ceased to prepare to commit the offence and has begun to perpetrate it.[38] Reasonable people can disagree about whether a given accused has moved from preparation to perpetration; it certainly appears that an accused can be said to "attempt" a crime before moving to the *final* stages of perpetration.

In *Cawthorne*, the High Court held that the *mens rea* for an attempted

---

[36] See e.g. Mackenzie, *Laws and Customes of Scotland in Matters Criminal* (1678), i, i, 9.
[37] See *Purcell Meats (Scotland) Ltd v McLeod*, 1987 S.L.T. 528.
[38] See *HM Advocate v Camerons*, 1911 S.C. (J) 110.

crime is the same as the *mens rea* for the completed offence.[39] Thus, one can be convicted of attempted murder only by acting with "wicked intention" or "wicked recklessness". Likewise, one can be convicted of attempted theft only if the Crown proves an "intention to deceive". The holding in *Cawthorne* is peculiar inasmuch as it means that, in some cases, a person can be said to attempt something recklessly. This is a strange way to use the word "attempt": if A has not intended to do something, it would not ordinarily be said that he has attempted to do it at all. Nonetheless, this remains the state of the law in Scotland.

Substantive defences

Numerous defences exist in Scots law, including insanity, non-insane **3–20** automatism,[40] self-defence, coercion (the defence that the accused was forced to commit a crime against their will by another person), necessity (the defence that the accused was forced to commit a crime as a result of circumstances beyond his control) and provocation. These defences, if successful, will either lead to an outright acquittal or a conviction for a lesser offence. A further defence possibility is simple denial of some aspect of the *actus reus*, perhaps by means of the presence of an alibi, where the accused claims to be elsewhere at the time of the offence. In practice, common law defences generally are most commonly pled in the context of classic *malum in se* crimes like murder or assault in an attempt to excuse or justify the accused's actions. They occur in the business law context only relatively rarely and we will therefore pay no close attention to them here.

COMMON LAW CRIMES RELEVANT TO BUSINESS

When we read media reports about the trial for murder of an alleged **3–21** serial killer or the assault and robbery of an elderly lady, the criminal law seems quite unrelated to the world of business. However, business covers the broadest possible range of human activities and as such those engaged in business can, from time to time, come into contact with large areas of the criminal law, either as victims or the accused. Anyone conducting a business which involves interaction with the general public needs to know when he is entitled legitimately to use force to eject drunk or troublesome customers, and the degree of force which may be used. Those who are involved in potentially dangerous businesses (for instance, the transportation of passengers, or of explosive or dangerous substances) need to

---

[39] See *Cawthorne v HM Advocate*, 1968 J.C. 32.
[40] The defence of insanity is pled when an accused contends that he behaved in a way which would otherwise have been criminal as a result of "a total alienation of reason" brought about by a mental illness or mental defect: *Brennan v HM Advocate*, 1977 J.C. 38. Non-insane automatism arises where there the accused has suffered a total alienation, but not as a result of an internal factor, such as a mental illness, but as a result of an external factor: for instance, where the accused contends that someone has "spiked" his drink with hallucinogenic drugs. Voluntary intoxication is not a defence in Scots law.

know the circumstances in which they can be charged with reckless injury or even murder or culpable homicide in the event that something goes wrong and passengers or bystanders are killed or injured. It is, however, outside the scope of this work to provide a full account of all the common law crimes which businesses might possibly encounter. The common law crimes of most relevance to business are those typically categorised as crimes of dishonesty: theft, embezzlement, fraud, uttering and extortion. In this section we will briefly examine each of these common law offences.

Theft

3–22   The *actus reus* for theft is "appropriation of corporeal moveable[41] property belonging to another without the owner's consent".[42] Thus one cannot steal property belonging to oneself, and something which is not owned—for instance, a wild animal—cannot be stolen. However, the mere fact that property has been lost or apparently abandoned does not in law mean that it is ownerless: in Scots law, one can be found guilty of theft by taking possession of an item which one finds. It is not necessary for the Crown to show that the accused physically carted away property in order to prove that the accused appropriated it; the accused has "appropriated" property once he starts to make use of it as if he was its owner.[43] Moreover, the Crown need not show that the accused appropriated the goods in question for any particular length of time: temporary appropriation is sufficient.[44]

As theft applies only to corporeal property, pure knowledge or information cannot be stolen. Thus I do not steal trade secrets from my employer by remembering the information and carrying it around in my head. However, the physical media on which information is recorded can be stolen. Thus a piece of paper or a memory key may be stolen, but the information contained on the paper or the memory key cannot.

The *mens rea* for theft is an "intention to deprive". It is not necessary for the Crown to prove that the accused intended to deprive the owner permanently.[45] Thus, where the accused intends merely to "borrow" goods belonging to another, without first obtaining the owner's consent, the accused has the *mens rea* for theft.

---

[41] In *Grant v Allan*, 1988 S.L.T. 11 the accused could not be found guilty of theft as the information which he had "stolen" was not corporeal.
[42] See *Carmichael v Black*, 1992 S.L.T. 897.
[43] See Gordon (3rd edn), Vol.II, p.13.
[44] *Carmichael v Black*, 1992 S.L.T. 897; *Fowler v O'Brien*, 1994 S.C.C.R. 112.

> **Key Concept**
>
> The appropriation of another person's corporeal moveable property without his consent combined with an intention to deprive that person of his property form the key elements of the crime of theft.
>
> Temporary deprivation is sufficient to constitute the *actus reus* and satisfaction of the *mens rea* requirement does not demand proof that the accused intended to permanently deprive the owner of his property.

Embezzlement

Embezzlement is conceptually related to theft. The *actus reus* of embez- **3–23** zlement is the dishonest appropriation of property which one already possesses with the authority of another person, to whom one is bound to account. However, theft and embezzlement differ in several key respects. The most important distinction is that non-corporeal property—e.g. information—may be embezzled, but it cannot be the object of a theft. Secondly, theft can be committed by someone who was not already in possession of the goods when he appropriated them, whereas embezzlement cannot. Thirdly, embezzlement presupposes that the embezzler and the owner have some pre-existing relationship; that the owner authorised the possession of the goods ultimately appropriated. Theft does not.

The *mens rea* for embezzlement is the same as that for theft: an intention to deprive.

Fraud

The *actus reus* of fraud is the use of a false pretence that (a) deceives **3–24** another, and (b) causes a definite practical result.[46] Usually, fraudsters deceive others in order to obtain a financial benefit: for instance, a dishonest art dealer may make a false pretence by claiming that a painting he is showing to a client is by a famous artist. If the client believes him, he has been deceived, and if as a result he buys the painting for more than it is worth, then a definite practical result has been achieved and the *actus reus* of the crime has been committed. A "definite practical result" is achieved so long as the deceived party acts in a way he would not have acted but for the accused's deception. In the example given, the definite practical result is the sale of the painting for a higher price than the client would otherwise have paid. However, it is not necessary for the Crown to show that the accused derived any financial or other benefit from the deception. Thus, in the case of *James Paton*, the Court held that the accused could be convicted of fraud even though his false pretence did not produce any financial windfall for him: he had artificially manipulated the appearance of livestock which he then entered into an agricultural exhibition in order to increase his chances of winning. However,

---

[46] *MacDonald v HM Advocate*, 1996 S.L.T. 723; 1996 S.C.C.R. 663.

winning the show brought no prize money, merely the glory of victory.[47] It is important to remember that the Crown must prove that the false pretence *caused* the definite practical result: the mere fact that the accused deceived another with his false pretence will not be enough to establish fraud unless the Crown can also show that the deceived party would have otherwise acted differently. So returning to the example of the art dealer, there is fraud only if the pretence caused the purchaser to buy the picture at an inflated price; if the evidence is that he would have bought it at the price requested without knowing who it was by, causation cannot be established.

The actor has the necessary *mens rea* for fraud if he has (a) knowledge of the deception, and (b) an intention to deceive. Thus, it is not enough for the Crown to show that the accused has asserted a falsehood, that another has believed it, and that a definite practical result was caused by it; the Crown must establish that the accused knew the assertion was false, and intended to deceive others by making the assertion. This is clear from the decision in *MacKenzie v Skeen*.[48] In that case, the accused worked for a slaughterhouse which sold offal according to weight. The accused's job was to weigh the offal. The accused used a faulty system to measure the weight of the offal and, as a result, someone was presented with a false bill. The court held that, even if the false pretence deceived another and led to a definite practical result (i.e. the paying of an inappropriately high or low sum of money), the accused could not be convicted unless he knew that his method of calculating the weight of the offal was faulty.

In addition to the common law offence of fraud, there are many specific types of fraud prohibited by statute. Some of these statutory offences will be discussed as part of the general review of regulatory offences.

Uttering

3-25 The offence of uttering is committed where a person (a) deliberately exposes a forged document to another person as if it was genuine; (b) the exposure is to the prejudice of the person whose name was forged; and (c) the forged document passes beyond the control of the person uttering it. Importantly, there is no need for the Crown to show that the accused forged the document himself—it is enough that he "transmits" it.[49] Furthermore, there is no need for the Crown to show that anyone was deceived by the forgery; there is no requirement of proof of a "definite practical result". This distinguishes the offence of uttering from that of fraud.

To commit the offence of uttering, an individual must expose a forged document *as if it were genuine*; it is not enough that the accused simply showed the document to another. Thus, if the accused showed a forged cheque to another, saying "this is a forged document", she could not be

[47] *James Paton* (1858) 3 Irv. 208.
[48] 1971 J.C. 43; 1972 S.L.T. 15.
[49] See *Barr v HM Advocate*, 1927 J.C. 51.

convicted of uttering. Moreover, the act of uttering is not complete unless and until the forged document passes beyond the control of the utterer: even if the accused shows a forged cheque to another, pretending that it was genuine, she commits no offence unless and until she hands the cheque over (and therefore loses the opportunity to undo her attempt at deception). The courts have held that a document passes beyond one's control once it has been posted.[50] (This is so even though it is now quite possible for someone to expose the falsity of the document after it has been posted—for instance, by making a phone call or even driving to the addressee—but before it could possibly reach its destination.)

The case of *John Smith* states that the utterance must be to the prejudice of the person whose name has been forged.[51] Subsequent authorities do not mention this requirement. If the requirement still exists, the Crown must show that the exposure of the forged document would, *if believed*, work to the disadvantage of the person whose name was forged. The Crown does not need to show that there was any actual disadvantage. (Again, remember that the crime of uttering does not require any definite practical result.) Thus, the exposure of a forged cheque will work to the prejudice of the person whose signature has been forged, since the amount stated on the cheque will be removed from the bank account of that person.[52] On the other hand, the exposure of a forged signature on an otherwise plain piece of notepaper cannot, even if others believe that the signature is genuine, work to the detriment of the individual whose name was forged.

The *mens rea* for uttering is (a) knowledge that the document is forged, and (b) an intention to deceive another.

Extortion

Extortion is the use of a "threat to concuss a person into paying a demand".[53] This offence is more commonly known as blackmail. It is typically thought that extortion must involve a demand for money, but this is not so—the demand may be for anything. Furthermore, it does not matter whether the accused has demanded something which is lawfully owed. Consider, for example, the circumstances in *Carmichael v Black*.[54] There, a vehicle was parked on private property without permission. The accused clamped the vehicle and placed a notice on the windshield advising the owner of the car that, unless £45 was paid, the clamp would not be removed. The court held that the accused could not enforce a debt through any means other than a civil suit. The demand for £45, backed up with the threat of not unclamping the vehicle, could therefore satisfy the *actus reus* of extortion. This illustrates a second point worth noting: the threat need not be one of physical violence, and indeed can be a threat to do something which one is legally entitled to do. Thus, in *Rae v*

3–26

---

[50] *William Jeffrey* (1842) 1 Broun. 337.
[51] *John Smith* (1871) 2 Coup. 1.
[52] *John Smith* (1871) 2 Coup. 1.
[53] *Alex Crawford* (1850) Shaw 309 at 322; *Carmichael v Black*, 1992 S.L.T. 897.
[54] 1992 S.L.T. 897.

Donnelly, the accused's conviction for extortion was upheld after he threatened to expose an illicit affair between two of his employees if one of the people involved in the affair did not drop a lawsuit which she had initiated against him.[55] While the accused was legally entitled to expose the affair if he chose to, he was not entitled to *threaten to expose it* in order to force his victim to give up her claim against him.

REGULATORY LAW AND REGULATORY OFFENCES

Introduction

3–27 In the modern, highly-developed state, the criminal law is frequently used not just in the traditional sense of punishing conduct which is clearly evil, but also as a convenient means of putting in place legally enforceable rules intended to ensure that certain minimum standards and policies are adhered to. The body of law whereby public authorities seek to exercise control over activities which are of importance to the community is known as regulatory law. Much of regulatory law is directed towards business. Thus, those who engage in the sale of food, medical drugs and alcohol have certain positive duties designed to insulate the public from some of the risks attached to the consumption of such products; those who drive motor vehicles are subject to various positive duties which protect pedestrians and other drivers from the risks attached to the dangerous use of such vehicles; landlords have positive duties designed to mitigate the risks associated with living in unsafe living spaces; employers have a range of duties to insulate employees from the risks associated with certain working environments; companies engaged in industrial activities bear positive duties designed to minimise detrimental environmental impact.

The criminal law is by no means the only vehicle used to enforce regulatory law. A variety of approaches are taken. Occasionally, the state takes the view that "self-regulation" is appropriate. This is the approach which has traditionally been utilised for the regulation of the professions: for instance, complaints of professional misconduct against professional people are commonly investigated by the relevant professional body, and then adjudicated upon by an independent tribunal.[56] Alternatively, the state may require that a licence be obtained before one can undertake certain activities. Thus individuals need a licence to drive, and businesses large and small require a range of licences to undertake activities as run-of-the-mill as operating a taxi or selling alcohol, or as sophisticated as operating a telecommunications network or drilling for oil. Sometimes, legislation establishes a public body with the specific remit of overseeing

---

[55] *Rae v Donnelly*, 1982 S.C.C.R. 148.

[56] In the case of solicitors, for instance, the relevant professional body is the Law Society of Scotland and the independent tribunal (made up of both solicitors and non-lawyers) is the Scottish Solicitors Disciplinary Tribunal. The Tribunal has a range of powers which include striking a solicitor off the roll (which makes it impossible for him to continue to practice as a solicitor) and ordering the payment of compensation or a "fine" payable to the Law Society.

and enforcing a given area of regulatory law. Thus occupational health and safety law is enforced by the Health and Safety Executive and Data Protection law by the Information Commissioner's Office.

Even where these other approaches are utilised, however, the criminal law is generally seen lurking in the background. Where licences are required, operating without one is almost invariably a criminal offence, and operating with a licence but in breach of its terms is also an offence. Lying to, or otherwise obstructing the investigations of, members of statutory inspectorates is often criminal, as is failing to comply with any orders which they make.

Regulatory offences are commonly (but by no means invariably) "strict liability offences". In such instances, the Crown can establish guilt without proof of *mens rea*. The Crown need only adduce evidence that the accused person or company failed to discharge its duty to act: criminal liability will follow directly from the establishment of that fact (unless the accused is entitled to a defence).

Selected regulatory regimes and regulatory offences

It would be a mistake to imagine that regulatory law is an entirely new **3–28** thing. Germany's laws governing the purity of beer dated back to 1516,[57] while the United Kingdom has regulated workplace health, safety and welfare since 1802, when the first of the Factories Acts was introduced.[58] However, the number of regulatory laws with which businesses have to comply has expanded dramatically over the last 50 years or so. Indeed, organisations which represent the interests of businesses in the United Kingdom frequently protest that the law has become too bureaucratic: they contend that there is simply too much regulation, and that the costs associated with complying with it are out of proportion to any benefits the regulation brings. The British Chambers of Commerce estimate that the total cost of the major sets of regulations with which businesses require to comply exceeded £55 billion in the period between 1998 and 2007.[59] On the day when Gordon Brown succeeded Tony Blair, a former chairman of the Confederation of British Industry identified the reduction of the regulatory burden as one of the most important tasks facing the new Prime Minister.[60] It is not possible in this section to detail all of the regulatory provisions with which businesses require to comply. However, a selection of the more important regulatory provisions are discussed below.

---

[57] The *Reinheitsgebot*; this was abolished in 1987 and replaced with a new set of regulations as the old law was unduly restrictive and contravened EU law.
[58] Albeit the level of protection afforded by the Factories Act 1802 looks very minimal by modern standards.
[59] British Chambers of Commerce, *Burdens Barometer*, available for download from *http://www.britishchambers.org.uk* [Accessed April 12, 2008].
[60] "From day one, it is vital that simpler and better regulation of wealth and job creation takes the place of excessive red tape. Bureaucracy is a serious problem in the private sector" Sir Digby Jones, *The Independent*, "A Manifesto for Gordon Brown", June 28, 2007.

Regulatory provisions designed to secure health and safety

Health and safety at work

3–29 Health and safety law in the United Kingdom adopts what might be described as a two-step approach. First, the leading piece of legislation in the field, the Health and Safety at Work etc Act 1974 (HSWA), sets out a number of over-arching duties. These are expressed in very general terms and all employers have to comply with them. However, the detailed regulations which make up the greater part of UK health and safety law are set out in a large number of Statutory Instruments. Some of the regulations contained in these SIs are of broad application—for instance, every employer and self-employed person in the United Kingdom has to comply with the Management of Health and Safety Regulations 1999, which, as we shall see, require risk assessments to be carried out. Other regulations, however, are sector-specific—they apply only to businesses engaged in a particular industry. As one might expect, potentially hazardous industries are subjected to a greater degree of sector-specific health and safety regulation than more mundane activities. For instance, the construction and offshore oil and gas industries are subjected to especially close regulation.

Principal duties imposed by HSWA upon employers

3–30 HSWA imposes a number of principal duties upon employers. Breaching these duties is a criminal offence and may alternatively, or in addition to prosecution give rise to enforcement proceedings against the employer.[61]

Employer's duty to ensure the health, safety and welfare of employees

3–31 Section 2(1) of the HSWA provides that "it shall be the duty of every employer to ensure, so far as is reasonably practicable, the health, safety and welfare at work of all his employees". Section 2(2) of the HSWA lists five areas to which this duty extends in particular. These are:

    (a) the provision and maintenance of plant and systems of work that are, so far as is reasonably practicable, safe and without risks to health;

    (b) arrangements for ensuring, so far as is reasonably practicable, safety and absence of risks to health in connection with the use, handling, storage and transport of articles and substances;

    (c) the provision of such information, instruction, training and supervision as is necessary to ensure, so far as is reasonably practicable, the health and safety at work of his employees;

    (d) so far as is reasonably practicable as regards any place of work under the employer's control, the maintenance of it in a condition that is safe and without risks to health and the provision

---

[61] See para.3–40, below.

and maintenance of means of access to and egress from it that are safe and without such risks;

(e) the provision and maintenance of a working environment for his employees that is, so far as is reasonably practicable, safe, without risks to health, and adequate as regards facilities and arrangements for their welfare at work.

Employer's duty to prepare a written health and safety at work policy

Section 2(3) of the HSWA requires anyone who employs more than five **3–32** persons to prepare and keep updated a written statement of his general policy with respect to the health and safety at work of his employees and the organisation and arrangements for carrying out that policy, and to bring the statement and any revision of it to the notice of all his employees.

Employer's duty to ensure the health and safety of non-employees

Section 3(1) of the HSWA provides that it shall be the duty of every **3–33** employer to ensure, so far as is reasonably practicable, that persons not in his employment who may be affected by things done in the course of the thereby are not thereby exposed to risks to their health or safety. Section 3(2) of the HSWA imposes similar duties on the self-employed.

Employee's own responsibilities under HSWA

It is not just the employer who is made subject to responsibilities by the **3–34** HSWA; the Act also imposes some duties upon employees. In particular, s.7 provides that every employee is, while at work, under an obligation:

(a) to take reasonable care for the health and safety of himself and of other persons who may be affected by his acts or omissions at work; and

(b) as regards any duty or requirement imposed on his employer or any other person by or under any of the relevant statutory provisions, to cooperate with him so far as is necessary to enable that duty or requirement to be performed or complied with.

As is the case with the obligations imposed upon employers, it is a criminal offence to breach these obligations. Thus employees can be prosecuted for jeopardising the health and safety of either themselves, their colleagues or others who may be affected by their actions at work.[62] In practice, however, such prosecutions are very rare.

---

[62] See *Skinner v HM Advocate* 1994 S.C.C.R. 316. In this case, an employee who had overall responsibility for the undertaking of a particular set of roadworks was convicted of a breach of s.7 when he failed to adequately warn motorists of the existence of the roadworks.

Health and safety regulations

3–35 There are so many health and safety regulations in force regulating so many different aspects of the operation of businesses that it is impossible to describe them all here. We will, however, briefly cover a selection of the more commonly encountered regulations.

The Management of Health and Safety at Work Regulations 1999

3–36 Regulation 3 of the Management of Health and Safety at Work Regulations 1999 (usually described as the "Management Regulations") is one of the cornerstones of UK health and safety law. This regulation requires every employer and self-employed person to undertake (and, when necessary, repeat the undertaking of) a suitable and sufficient assessment of the risks which his business poses to the health and safety of his employees and anyone else who might be affected by it. Other important duties imposed upon employers by the Management Regulations are the obligations to plan, organise, control, monitor and review their health and safety provision (reg.5); to appropriately survey the health of his employees (reg.6) and to establish appropriate procedures to be followed in the event of serious and imminent danger to persons in the workplace (reg.8).

The Provision and Use of Work Equipment Regulations 1998

3–37 These regulations are designed to prevent employees from being injured by being provided with dangerous equipment. They require employers to ensure that equipment provided to workers is suitable for its intended purpose, maintained in efficient working order and in good repair (reg.4), that maintenance is appropriately recorded (reg.5) and that equipment is regularly inspected to ensure its safety (reg.8).

The Manual Handling Operations Regulations 1992

3–38 These regulations place employers under an obligation, so far as is reasonably practicable, to avoid the need for his employees to undertake any manual handling operations at work which involve a risk of their being injured.[63] Regulation 4 also stipulates that where it is not reasonably practicable to avoid such manual handling of work altogether, the employer is under an obligation to make a suitable and sufficient risk assessment of the handling operation,[64] to take appropriate steps to reduce the risk of injury to his employees,[65] and to provide information to employees about the total weight and weight distribution of each load.[66]

---

[63] reg.4(1)(a).
[64] reg.4(1)(b)(i).
[65] reg.4(1)(b)(ii).
[66] reg.4(1)(b)(iii).

The Health and Safety (Display Screen Equipment) Regulations 1992

These regulations oblige employers to assess the suitability of work-sta- **3–39** tions (reg.2) and train users on their safe use (reg.6), permit workers who use computer screens in the course of their employment to demand free eye tests and any necessary treatment (reg.5), and state that the work patterns of workers using computer screens must be planned so as to ensure that they are given periodic breaks and changes of activity (reg.4).

Enforcement

Section 10 of the HSWA created the Health and Safety Commission and **3–40** the Health and Safety Executive. Initially, the Commission was tasked with overseeing occupational health and safety policy from a strategic standpoint and the Executive was involved in the day-to-day enforcement of the health and safety regime. Since April 1, 2008, however, the two bodies have been merged and both of these functions are now undertaken by the Health and Safety Executive. The HSWA provides the Executive's inspectorate with extensive powers: for instance, inspectors may enter premises, examine premises and their contents, take measurements and photographs, remove samples of substances found, dismantle or test any apparently dangerous equipment, interview witnesses and make copies books or documents.[67] If an inspector reaches the conclusion that health and safety law is being breached, he can serve an improvement notice requiring that the contravention be remedied within a given period.[68] Moreover, if an inspector forms the conclusion that there is an immediate risk of serious personal injury, he may issue a prohibition notice, directing that the dangerous activity be stopped immediately.[69] Alter- natively, the inspector can choose not to utilise either the improvement or prohibition notice process and to instead report the employer to the procurator fiscal, recommending prosecution for the breach of health and safety law. This is commonly done in the case of a serious breach of the law. Failing to implement either an improvement or prohibition notice is also a criminal offence.

The courts take the contravention of health and safety law seriously, particularly when the risks taken by the wrongdoer were obvious or where death or serious injury has resulted. Some of the largest fines ever handed down by courts in United Kingdom have been for breaches of health and safety law.[70]

---

[67] HSWA s.20.
[68] HSWA s.21.
[69] HSWA s.22.
[70] In 2004, Thames Trains were fined £2 million for health and safety breaches which resulted in the Ladbroke Grove rail disaster in which 31 people were killed. In 2005, Transco plc, the company which administers the gas pipelines network in the United Kingdom, was fined £15 million for a series of health and safety failings which led to the death of a family of four in a gas explosion.

> **Key Concept**
>
> The Health and Safety at Work etc. Act 1974 imposes a number of
> principal duties upon employers. A breach of these duties will con-
> stitute a criminal offence and may result in proceedings against the
> employer.

Corporate homicide

3–41 The problems which have been experienced in convicting corporations—
particularly large companies—of the common law offence of corporate
homicide have already been discussed.[71] In an attempt to address these
difficulties, the Corporate Manslaughter and Corporate Homicide Act
2007 creates a new offence of corporate homicide. A corporation commits
this offence if "the way in which its activities are managed or organised
... (a) causes a person's death, and (b) amounts to a gross breach of a
relevant duty of care owed by the organisation to the deceased".[72] The
fatality must be substantially attributable to the policies and strategies
devised by the entity's senior management;[73] i.e. those who make "decisions about how the whole or a substantial part of [the corporation's]
activities are to be managed or organised' or manage or organise all or a
substantial part of those activities.[74] The legislation continues to attribute
liability to the corporation on the basis of the conduct and *mens rea* of
those who function as its "controlling mind".[75]

The Crown must prove that the corporation caused death by breaching
"a relevant duty of care". Section 2(1) stipulates that the relevant duties
of care include those owed to "employees or to other persons working for
the organisation or performing services for it"; to persons for whose
safety the organisation is responsible as an occupier of premises; and
those owed in connection with the supply of goods or services, construction or maintenance operations, any other activity on a commercial
basis, and the use or keeping of any plant, vehicle or other thing. The
breach of such a duty must be "gross", that is, falling "far below what can
reasonably be expected of the organisation in the circumstances".[76] The
test, in other words, is one of recklessness.

In determining whether the corporation was criminally reckless, the
jury may have regard to whether it failed to comply with health and
safety legislation, and decide whether any such violation was serious or
especially risky.[77] The jury may also consider whether the corporation

---

[71] See para.3–18, above.
[72] Corporate Manslaughter and Corporate Homicide Act 2007 c.17, s.1(1) (Corporate
Homicide Act).
[73] s.1(3).
[74] s.1(4)(c).
[75] See the commentary by Peter Ferguson, QC, "Corporate Manslaughter and Corporate
Homicide Act 2007" 2007 S.L.T. (News) 251 at 252–253.
[76] Corporate Homicide Act s.1(4)(b).
[77] Corporate Homicide Act s.8(2).

failed to actively foster a culture in which compliance with heath and safety laws are treated by employees as something to be encouraged and enforced.[78]

Key Concept

The Corporate Manslaughter and Corporate Homicide Act 2007 was introduced in order to increase the chances of a corporation incurring a form of criminal liability which the public will recognise as seriously blameworthy in relation to a death.

Liability will be attributed to the corporation based on the actions and *mens rea* of those identified as its "controlling mind".

The protection of consumers from misleading information

We have already seen that the common law crime of fraud is committed **3–42** when a person makes a false pretence and causes a definite practical result. There are, in addition, a number of statutory provisions which also prohibit certain kinds of false pretence. These are fully discussed in Chapter 6, below.

Regulatory requirements relative to the misuse of data

Computer Misuse Act 1990

Section 1 of the Computer Misuse Act 1990 (CMA) states: **3–43**

"(1) A person is guilty of an offence if—
    (a) he causes a computer to perform any function with intent to secure access to any program or data held in any computer;
    (b) the access he intends to secure is unauthorised; and
    (c) he knows at the time when he causes the computer to perform the function that that is the case.
(2) The intent a person has to have to commit an offence under this section need not be directed at—
    (a) any particular program or data;
    (b) a program or data of a particular kind; or
    (c) a program or data held in any particular computer."

Though the CMA was primarily designed to thwart computer hacking, one can commit the offence simply by physically standing at another person's computer and causing the computer to perform any function with intent to access, without authorisation, programs or data contained

---

[78] Corporate Homicide Act s.8(3).

in that computer.[79] The wording of s.1(1)(a) suggests that actual access to the program or data is not required; it is enough that the accused causes the computer to perform a function in an attempt to access that program or data. Access to any program or data is "unauthorised" if it is accessed by a person who is not entitled to control access to it or has not been given access by someone so entitled.[80] The question in a given case will be whether the accused had authorisation to access the *actual* data or programs involved, not whether he had authorisation to access the *kind* of data or programs involved. Thus, a person who has authorisation to access the computer files of a particular group of customers does not necessarily have authorisation to access the computer files of other customers even though all the files contain the same kind of information.[81] If the accused has authorisation to access the program or data in question, however, it appears that he does not lose that authorisation merely because he has an inappropriate reason for accessing it.[82]

In addition, s.3 provides that:

"A person is guilty of an offence if—

> (a) he does any act which causes an unauthorised modification of the contents of any computer; and
> (b) at the time when he does the act he has the requisite intent and the requisite knowledge."

The accused has the requisite intent if he intends to modify the contents of a computer program for the purpose of impairing the operation of the computer, preventing or impairing access to any program or data on the computer, or impairing the operation of any program or the reliability of data.[83] The accused has the requisite knowledge if he knows that the modifications in question are unauthorised.[84]

Data Protection Act 1998

3–44 Following concern among both the public and the legislature at UK and EU level about the possibility that the growing amount of personal data held on computer databases could be misused, laws regulating the retention and use of personal data were first introduced in the United Kingdom by the Data Protection Act 1984. This Act was replaced by the Data Protection Act 1998 (DPA) which implements the EU's Data Protection Directive (94/96/EC) and which both expands the scope of the UK's data protection regime (meaning that for the first time some paper-

---

[79] *Attorney-General's Reference (No.1 of 1991)* [1992] 3 W.L.R. 432 (CA).
[80] CMA s.17(5).
[81] See *R v Bow Street Metropolitan Magistrates, ex parte US Government* [1999] 3 W.L.R. 620.
[82] See *DPP v Bignell* (1998) 1 Cr. App. R. 1, approved in *Bow Street Magistrates* (above).
[83] CMA s.3(2).
[84] CMA s.3(3).

based records, as well as those held electronically, are regulated) and
fortifies the rights available to individuals.

Definitions

The DPA is ultimately concerned with the regulation of the processing of **3–45**
personal data. Broadly speaking, data is "processed" when it is obtained,
recorded, held or when a variety of operations are carried out upon it:
examples include organising, accessing, altering, disclosing or erasing the
data. The definition of "data" is complex[85] but in practice it generally
refers to information deliberately held on computer as part of some kind
of filing system—typically, but not necessarily, a database. The DPA
defines "data" primarily as information held by equipment operating
automatically in response to instructions given for that purpose (in
practice, this means information held on computer and accessible by
programs).[86] The person about whom the information is held is known as
the "data subject". The person holding the information about the data
subject is known as the "data controller". "Personal data" is data which
relates to a living person who can be identified either directly from those
data, or from those data and other information held or likely to come
into the possession of the data controller. Information such as a person's
name, address, age and the like will be "personal data". "Sensitive personal data" is also defined by the DPA—it needs to be, as this is given
some specific protections not afforded to regular personal data. "Sensitive
personal data" is defined as information which relates to a data subject's
racial or ethnic origin, political opinions, religious or similar beliefs,
membership (or non-membership) of a trade union, physical or mental
health or condition, sexual life and police or criminal record.[87]

This multitude of definitions serves to demonstrate that the DPA is
drafted in a rather convoluted and technical manner. This is unfortunate,
given that its purpose is to provide "the man in the street" with a set of
rights. Despite the Act's apparent complexity, once the definitions which
it uses are understood, its core principles can be set out reasonably briefly.

The data protection principles

The DPA contains eight data protection principles which apply to all **3–46**
instances of processing of data, other than processing that falls within the
scope of the exemption. (In practice, the majority of the exemptions relate

---

[85] See DPA s.1(1): "data" means information which—
    (a) is being processed by means of equipment operating automatically in response
        to instructions given for that purpose,
    (b) is recorded with the intention that it should be processed by means of such
        equipment,
    (c) is recorded as part of a relevant filing system or with the intention that it should
        form part of a relevant filing system.
[86] Certain public records, including health and education records, are also included in the
    definition whether held on computer or not. See DPA s.1(1)(d) read with s.68 and Schs
    11 and 12.
[87] DPA s.2.

to the domestic use of information and the public sector and a limited number of professions, including the legal profession and journalism; exemptions are not generally available in the business context.) The principles are:

(1) Personal data shall be processed fairly and lawfully and, in particular, shall not be processed unless one or more of the following conditions is met:

- the data subject has given his consent to the processing;[88] or
- the processing is necessary for the performance of a contract to which the data subject is a party or for the taking of steps at the request of the data subject with a view to entering into a contract; or
- the processing is necessary for compliance with any legal obligation to which the data controller is subject, other than an obligation imposed by contract; or
- the processing is necessary in order to protect the vital interests of the data subject; or
- the processing is necessary for the administration of justice, for the exercise of any functions conferred on any person by or under any enactment, for the exercise of any functions of the Crown, a Minister of the Crown or a government department, or for the exercise of any other functions of a public nature exercised in the public interest by any person; or
- the processing is necessary for the purposes of legitimate interests pursued by the data controller or by the third party or parties to whom the data are disclosed, except where the processing is unwarranted in any particular case by reason of prejudice to the rights and freedoms or legitimate interests of the data subject; the Secretary of State may by order specify particular circumstances in which this condition is, or is not, to be taken to be satisfied.

Given the lack of certainty inherent in some of the above conditions,[89] in practice a sensible data controller will always seek to obtain the consent of a data subject to the controller's proposed processing. It is for this reason that when, for instance, one is purchasing goods off the internet, immediately before to completing the purchase, one will generally be presented with a set of "tick boxes," offering one the option to change to agree or not agree to what the seller proposes to do with your personal data.

---

[88] As we shall see, in practice this is the easiest and safest way for a data controller to comply with the DPA.

[89] It can be difficult, for example, for a data controller to demonstrate that it was "necessary" to process information, as opposed to it being merely "desirable" or "convenient" for him to do so.

In the case of "sensitive personal data" only, in addition to one of the above conditions, one of a further set of additional conditions must also be met if the first principle is to be satisfied. Among this additional set of conditions are the following:

- The data subject has given his explicit consent to the processing of the personal data.
- The processing is necessary for the purposes of exercising or performing any right or obligation which is conferred or imposed by law on the data controller in connection with employment.
- The information contained in the personal data has been made public as a result of steps deliberately taken by the data subject.
- The processing is necessary for the purpose of, or in connection with, any legal proceedings or the obtaining of legal advice.
- The processing is necessary for medical purposes and is undertaken by a health professional, or other person owing the data subject an effectual duty of confidentiality.
- The processing is of sensitive personal data consisting of information as to racial or ethnic origin and is necessary for the purpose of identifying or keeping under review the existence or absence of equality of opportunity or treatment between persons of different racial or ethnic origins, with a view to enabling such equality to be promoted or maintained.[90]

(2) Personal data shall be obtained only for one or more specified and lawful purposes, and shall not be further processed in any manner incompatible with that purpose or those purposes.

(3) Personal data shall be adequate, relevant and not excessive in relation to the purpose or purposes for which they are processed.

(4) Personal data shall be accurate and, where necessary, kept up to date.

(5) Personal data processed for any purpose or purposes shall not be kept for longer than is necessary for that purpose or those purposes.

(6) Personal data shall be processed in accordance with the rights of data subjects under this Act.

(7) Appropriate technical and organisational measures shall be taken against unauthorised or unlawful processing of personal data and against accidental loss or destruction of, or damage to, personal data.

(8) Personal data shall not be transferred to a country or territory outside the European Economic Area unless that country or territory ensures an adequate level of protection for the rights

---

[90] The full list of conditions can be found in Sch.3 to the DPA.

and freedoms of data subjects in relation to the processing of
personal data.[91]

Enforcement (1): The rights of data subjects

3–47 Data subjects have a variety of rights under the DPA; these can be used
by the individual in order to enforce the data protection principles. In
particular, data subjects have the right to know whether any personal
data relating to them is held by a particular data controller and, if so, to
receive a copy of it.[92] If the personal data held by the data controller is
inaccurate, the data subject is entitled to have the information corrected,
blocked, erased or destroyed and may go to court for an order to that
effect if the data controller will not voluntarily alter the information
held.[93] If the data subject is likely to suffer substantial and unwarranted
distress or damage through the processing of their personal information,
he is entitled to serve a notice on the data controller, demanding that he
stop processing the data.[94] Data subjects are also entitled to demand that
data controllers stop sending direct marketing materials to them.[95] Data
controllers who breach any of the data subject's rights and thereby cause
a data subject to suffer a loss are liable to pay compensation to the data
subject.[96]

Enforcement (2): Enforcement by the state

3–48 In addition to the data subject's own right to take an interest in the
personal data held about him, the DPA provides the Information
Commissioner's Office (ICO) with a broad range of powers designed to
enforce compliance with the Act. Any organisation which is not exempt
must register with the ICO before processing personal data;[97] failure to
do so is a criminal offence. In addition, the ICO has the power to:

- enter upon premises and conduct searches to ensure that organisations are complying with the Act;[98]
- serve information notices requiring organisations to provide the
  ICO with specified information within a certain time period with a
  view to assessing whether the data protection principles are being
  properly complied with;
- serve enforcement notices where there has been a breach of the
  Act, compelling organisations to take action in order to comply
  with the law;

[91] The European Economic Area comprises the member states of the EU and the states of
Iceland, Norway and Lichtenstein.
[92] DPA s.7. The data controller is entitled to demand that the request be made in writing
and to levy a small fee for providing the copy.
[93] DPA s.14.
[94] DPA s.10.
[95] DPA s.11.
[96] DPA s.13.
[97] DPA s.17.
[98] DPA s.50 read together with Sch.9.

- prosecute those who commit criminal offences under the Act. Breaching a data protection principle is not of itself a criminal offence: however the DPA does create a number of criminal offences. For instance, failing to register with the ICO is an offence of strict liability;[99] failing to comply with an enforcement or other notice issued by the ICO is also an offence of strict liability, albeit the data controller has the benefit of a "due diligence" defence;[100] and it is an offence to knowingly or recklessly obtain or disclose personal data without the consent of the relevant data controller, or to procure another to do so;[101]
- conduct audits to assess whether an organisation's processing of personal data follows good practice;
- report to Parliament on data protection issues of concern.

Key Concept

The use of data in the commercial environment is regulated by the Computer Misuse Act 1990 and the Data Protection Act 1998.

Competition law

Not that long ago, we lived in a society which was at least somewhat **3–49** uncertain about the benefits of competition between rival businesses. There always was competition between companies in the private sector, but large numbers of important activities were carried out not by private companies, but by public corporations or other emanations of the state.[102] The pendulum has now swung very much the other way. The old monopolies have been broken up and sold off—it is now possible to buy gas or electricity, for example, from a broad range of providers, all of whom compete for the consumer's business. Competition between businesses is widely believed to be a good thing. The fact that businesses have to fight amongst each other for customers is believed to lead to the "survival of the fittest" and to act as an incentive to businesses to lower prices (because if they don't, consumers will buy from their rivals that do), increase quality (as otherwise consumers will buy better goods from their rivals) and generally reduce waste and perform efficiently: factors which are thought to work to the benefit both of the economy and the individual consumer.

Competition might be good for the consumer and the economy in general, but it can be bad for individual businesses who may find that in a competitive marketplace they require to work harder and for less profit

---

[99] DPA s.17 read together with s.21.
[100] DPA s.47.
[101] DPA s.55.
[102] This was particularly so in the case of public utilities—the telecommunications network, rail transport, natural gas, coal mining and water supplies, to name but a few, were all in public ownership.

than would be the case in a less competitive marketplace. There is, therefore, a natural temptation for businesses to seek to reduce the amount of competition which they face. However, given the benefits which competition is thought to bring, it will come as no surprise to learn that attempts to eradicate competition or distort the free market are taken very seriously, and most jurisdictions have developed a body of law that regulates such behaviour.[103] Both domestic UK and EU laws exist to prohibit such anti-competitive practices. UK law is currently governed principally by the Competition Act 1998; EU Law by Articles 81 and 82 the Treaty of Rome.[104] There were formerly significant differences between UK and EU competition law but the sets of law have by and large become harmonised into one set of rules.[105] Both UK and EU law contain two main prohibitions: businesses[106] must not to engage in anti-competitive agreements or practices, and they must not seek to abuse a dominant market position. In addition, competition law seeks to control mergers between large corporations which would have the effect of threatening competition.

The regulation of anti-competitive agreements and behaviour

3–50 Chapter 1 of the Competition Act 1998 and Art.81 of the Treaty of Rome both prohibit arrangements between businesses which:

- have the capacity to affect trade in the United Kingdom or EU; and
- have, as their object or effect, the restriction of competition in the United Kingdom or EU.

A variety of such agreements have been found to exist over the years. Perhaps the classic examples of such agreements are price-fixing and market-sharing agreements, but others also exist: orchestrated customer boycotts, trade association rules and mergers which have the effect of significantly impeding competition have all on occasion breached Ch.1 or Art.81. For our purposes it is sufficient to focus on price-fixing and market-sharing agreements.

Price fixing

3–51 Price fixing occurs when trade competitors agree that they will set either the purchase or selling price of goods or services, or that they will similarly fix other important terms on which they do business. For obvious

---

[103] In America, where modern competition law first emerged, this body of law is known as "antitrust" law.

[104] i.e. the treaty which founded the European Economic Community in 1957.

[105] Some differences of detail remain, particularly with regard to investigatory powers and the procedure for dealing with complaints about competition, but it is outside the scope of this work to discuss them.

[106] In fact, the prohibition is imposed upon "undertakings", a term which includes all vehicles commonly used for business purposes in this country and also includes state bodies and trade organisations.

reasons, the price is usually set at a level which is higher than would be achievable in a truly competitive market. Such agreements will not breach competition law if they will have only a minimal effect upon competition.[107] In all other cases, they are prohibited.

There have been a number of notable examples of such agreements over the years. In 2006, the Court of Appeal concluded that the well-known sports shop, JJB Sports, had been involved in fixing the price of Umbro football shirts.[108] In the same case, the toy and game manufacturer Hasbro and retailers Argos and Littlewoods were found to have entered into an agreement fixing the retail sale price of a number of Hasbro products.[109] Civil penalties of £6.7 million had been imposed on JJB and £17.28 million on Argos. The Court of Appeal found that these penalties were appropriate and refused to over-turn them on appeal.

Market-sharing agreements

The most straightforward example of a market-sharing agreement is **3–52** where two competitors agree that they will stay out of a particular area: e.g. that one will operate within the Highlands of Scotland and the east coast, and the other within the south-west and the Borders. This sort of arrangement may be efficient from the standpoint of the businesses, because it may save them from the expense of setting up a sales infrastructure in areas where they have not traditionally done business. It is, however, inefficient from the standpoint of the consumer, as it means that he does not have the opportunity to buy from the company who has agreed not to sell within the part of the country in which he resides. Again, such agreements breach Ch.1 of the Competition Act 1998 and Art.81 of the Treaty of Rome.

Abuse of a dominant market position

Chapter 2 of the Competition Act 1998 and Art.82 of the Treaty of Rome **3–53** both prohibit conduct which:

- amounts to abuse of a dominant position; and
- affects trade in the United Kingdom or EU.

By definition, businesses can only contravene this rule by having a dominant position. Dominance is assessed by considering the business's market power: this in turn usually involves having regard to the business's level of market share. Generally, a company with a market share of

---

[107] In the case of trade competitors, if the aggregate market share of all the parties involved in the agreement is less than 10% of the market affected by the agreement, it will be considered to fall outside the ambit of the prohibition on the basis that it is "Agreement of Minor Importance".

[108] *Argos Ltd and JJB Sports Ltd v Office of Fair Trading*, 2006 UKCLR 1135. The investigation into the price-fixing practices was reportedly triggered by a tip-off provided by the chief executive of a rival sports shop company after he was told by a senior executive of JJB that "there is a club in the north, son, and you're not part of it".

[109] Ironically, one of the products concerned was the board-game, Monopoly.

40 per cent is at risk of being found to be in a dominant position; a company with a market share of 50 per cent will be presumed to be in a dominant position, although this presumption may be rebutted by the leading of evidence.[110]

It is not, however, the mere possession of a dominant market position which is problematic, but the *abuse* of that dominance. Abuse of a dominant position may occur in a number of ways: predatory pricing (i.e. the practice of selling goods or services at a lower price than they are worth in order to "kill off" competition) and offering rebates to loyal customers are examples of the kind of conduct which will be seen as abusive. A good example of such conduct occurred in the case of *Aberdeen Journals Ltd v Director General of Fair Trading*.[111] Here, Aberdeen Journals was found to have abused the dominant position which it held within the newspaper advertising market in Aberdeen by greatly reducing the cost of advertising in its newspapers to below cost price in advance of the launch of a new competitor newspaper, the *Aberdeen Independent*.

Enforcement of prohibitions on anti-competitive agreements and abuses a dominant market position

3-54 In the United Kingdom, investigations into anti-competitive agreements and abuses of dominant positions (whether under UK or EU law) are now carried out by the Office of Fair Trading and the Competition Commission. These authorities have extensive powers to carry out investigations, including the right to enter into and search business premises. If anti-competitive behaviour in breach of the Competition Act 1998 or the Treaty of Rome is established, the principal enforcement mechanism is the imposition of a penalty, similar to a fine but in fact recoverable under civil law and procedure, rather than under the criminal law. Such a penalty will be imposed in the first instance by the Office of Fair Trading (OFT) but if the penalised business believes the penalty to be excessive it may appeal to the Competition Appeals Tribunal (CAT). The OFT is empowered to impose penalties as high as 10 per cent of a company's worldwide turnover. In addition, while the criminal law has not traditionally played a role in the enforcement of UK competition law, individuals who are guilty of the most serious anti-competitive practices such as price-fixing commit an offence and, if convicted, a maximum sentence of five years' imprisonment and/or an unlimited fine. Company directors found to have been involved in anti-competitive practices may be disqualified for up to 15 years.

---

[110] See case 62/86, *AKZO Chemie BV v Commission* [1991] ECR I-3359.
[111] [2003] CAT 11.

Merger control

The merger of large corporate entities can also have an impact upon **3–55**
competition, even if that is not the main reason why the parties have
decided to enter into the merger. Mergers which have a "Community
Dimension"—generally speaking, mergers of business organisations
having very large turnovers (i.e. those measured in many thousands of
millions of Euros) will be governed by the EU under and in terms of the
Merger Regulation (Regulation 139/2004). Smaller UK mergers will be
dealt with under UK law, which is now contained in the Enterprise Act
2002 (EA). This provides that the OFT has a duty to investigate any
proposed merger where the company targeted for acquisition has an
annual turnover in excess of £70 million, and/or the merged companies
would between them supply at least 25 per cent of the goods of services of
a particular type either within the United Kingdom, or within part of the
United Kingdom.[112] If the OFT concludes that such a merger may have
the effect of causing a "substantial lessening in competition", it must
either refer the matter to the Competition Commission (CC) or receive
undertakings from the companies who intend to merge which satisfy it
that the reconfigured company would not substantially lessen competition.[113] If the matter is referred to the CC and it is satisfied that the
merger will substantially lessen competition, it may prohibit the merger,
approve it subject to conditions or approve it subject to the receipt of
undertakings from the companies party to the merger. For instance, in
the case of the takeover of the supermarket chain Safeway in 2003, the
CC refused to permit the bids by the largest supermarket chains Tesco,
Sainsbury and Asda to go ahead on the basis that these supermarket
chains already had a very large market share and it would substantially
lessen competition if any of them were to take over Safeway's business.
Morrisons, however, had a smaller market share and their bid was permitted to go ahead, subject to the requirement that they sell 53 of the
newly acquired stores.[114]

Key Concept

Anti-competitive practices are currently governed principally in
domestic law by the Competition Act 1998 and in EU Law by Arts 81
and 82 the Treaty of Rome.[115]

---

[112] EA s.23.
[113] EA s.73.
[114] Competition Commission, Report on the Mergers in Contemplation (Safeway plc),
available for download from *http://www.competition-commission.org.uk/rep_pub/reports/
2003/481safeway.htm* (visited April 22, 2008).
[115] i.e. the treaty which founded the European Economic Community in 1957.

Environmental law

3–56 Environmental regulation is a very substantial body of law which encompasses a wide range of situations ranging from the unauthorised release of genetically modified organisms[116] to the protection of rare offshore marine habitats.[117] Given the scope of the subject, it is not possible here to offer more than a brief introduction.[118] A broad range of regulatory approaches are also taken within the field, ranging right along the spectrum from what is known as "procedural regulation" through a licensing/permissioning approach up to the imposition of criminal liability.

"Procedural regulation" is where the law is not concerned with the outcome of a given regulatory process, but requires only that a particular process be gone through before a decision is reached. This is a feature of environmental impact law. Certain large-scale projects of a nature such that they are likely to have a significant effect upon the environment must be the subject of an environmental impact assessment (EIA) before the state is permitted to approve them. However, matters end there. The law does not prescribe what is to happen in the event that the EIA suggests that the project should not go ahead. Instead, it seeks to ensure that the potential impact upon the environment is borne in mind when the decision on whether or not to proceed with the project is being taken.[119]

So far as licensing is concerned, those involved in the waste disposal business require a licence authorising their operations from the local waste regulation authority.[120] Such licences may be suspended or revoked if the holder ceases to be a fit and proper person to hold such a licence, or if the continuation of the activities authorised by the licence would cause serious levels of pollution.[121]

Criminal liability is imposed in a number of environmental law regulations. For instance, it is an offence for a company which supplies water to provide water that is unfit for human consumption. The offence is one of strict liability, but the water company is entitled to a due diligence defence; it is also a defence for it to prove that it had no reasonable grounds for suspecting that the water would be used for human consumption.[122]

---

[116] Regulated by Part IV of the Environmental Protection Act 1990.
[117] On which see the Habitats Directive (92/43/EC) and the Offshore Petroleum Activities (Conservation of Habitats) Regulations 2001.
[118] For an excellent account of environmental law and policy see S. Bell and D. McGillivray *Environmental Law* (6th edn, Oxford University Press, 2006).
[119] See C. Reid *Nature Conservation Law* (2nd edn, 2002), at para.8.3.14.
[120] Environmental Protection Act 1990 s.35.
[121] Environmental Protection Act 1990 s.38.
[122] Water Industry Act 1991 s.7.

▼ CHAPTER SUMMARY

THE CRIMINAL LAW

1. Generally an individual can only commit a criminal offence by 3–57 engaging in a course of conduct which the law regards as wrongful (the *actus reus*) while simultaneously possessing a blameworthy state of mind (the required *mens rea*).
2. An important exception to this is a strict liability crime where proof of the relevant *actus reus* is sufficient to secure a conviction.
3. The *actus reus* usually takes the form of an action but in some specific cases may result from an omission.
4. Where an offence requires proof that the accused caused the given result (the requirement of causation), the Crown must prove that "but for" the accused's actions the result would not have occurred.
5. Where an intervening act (*novus actus interveniens*) occurs between the accused's conduct and the result this may "break the chain of causation" thereby making it unjust to hold the accused liable for the result.
6. The three types of *mens rea* that tend to arise most frequently are (a) intention, (b) recklessness, and (c) knowledge.
7. A corporate body can be guilty of a criminal offence. Where an offence requires *mens rea* it must be proved that those identified as the "controlling mind" of the company possessed the necessary "guilty mind".
8. Art and part liability concerns participation or involvement in a crime. Any person who participates in the commission of an offence may be held criminally responsible.
9. Vicarious liability arises when criminal liability is imputed to one person or company on the basis of what *another* person did (or failed to do), even though the actors do not share a common purpose.

THEFT

1. The appropriation of another person's corporeal moveable property without his consent combined with an intention to deprive that person of his property form the *actus reus* and *mens rea* of theft.
2. Temporary deprivation is sufficient to constitute the *actus reus* and satisfaction of the *mens rea* requirement does not demand proof that the accused intended to permanently deprive the owner of his property.

EMBEZZLEMENT

1. The *actus reus* of embezzlement is the dishonest appropriation of property which, while belonging to another, is already in one's possession. The *mens rea* of the crime is the intention to deprive the owner of his property.
2. Non-corporeal property, such as information, may be embezzled, but it cannot be the object of a theft.

FRAUD

1. The *actus reus* of fraud is the use of a false pretence that deceives another and causes a definite practical result.
2. The *mens rea* is satisfied by proof of knowledge of the deception along with an intention to deceive.

UTTERING

1. In the crime of uttering it is not necessary for the Crown to prove that the accused forged the document himself. It is sufficient to show that the accused transmitted the document in the knowledge that the document was forged and with the intention of deceiving another.

EXTORTION

1. Extortion is constituted by the use of a threat in pursuit of a demand.
2. The demand may be for something other than money.

REGULATORY LAW

1. The criminal law is only one method used to enforce regulatory law. Other approaches include:

   - self-regulation through a professional body;
   - requirement for state controlled licences;
   - regulation through by a public body established by legislation.

HEALTH AND SAFETY AT WORK

1. An important piece of legislation which impacts on all businesses is the Health and Safety at Work etc. Act 1974 (HSWA)

2. The HWSA imposes a number of principal duties upon employers. A breach of these duties will constitute a criminal offence and may result in proceedings against the employer.

CORPORATE HOMICIDE

1. The Corporate Manslaughter and Corporate Homicide Act 2007 was introduced in order to increase the chances of a corporation incurring a form of criminal liability which the public will recognise as seriously blameworthy in relation to a death.
2. The *actus reus* of the crime is causing a person's death; its *mens rea* is doing so through a gross breach of a relevant duty of care. This in turn requires recklessness.
3. Liability will be attributed to the corporation based on the actions and *mens rea* of those identified as its "controlling mind".

MISUSE OF DATA

1. The use of data in the commercial environment is regulated by the Computer Misuse Act 1990 and the Data Protection Act 1998.

COMPETITION LAW

1. Anti-competitive practices in the United Kingdom are currently governed principally by the Competition Act 1998 and by EU law through Arts 81 and 82 of the Treaty of Rome

ENVIRONMENTAL LAW

1. Regulation in this area of the law extends from licensing requirements to imposition of criminal liability through strict liability crimes.

? QUICK QUIZ

- Is the criminal law a branch of public or private law?
- What are the elements of a common law offence?
- What kinds of state of mind are capable of satisfying the requirement of *mens rea*?
- What is strict liability?
- What is vicarious liability?
- Can corporations be found guilty of a crime?
- What is the mens rea of theft?

- What are the elements of the crime of fraud?
- What does the expression "regulatory law" mean?
- The Health and Safety At Work etc Act 1974 is the main piece of occupational health legislation in the UK. What are the essential features of HSWA?
- What is the purpose of the Corporate Manslaughter and Corporate Homicide Act 2007?
- What are the essential features of the Data Protection Act 1998?
- Why do we regulate competition between businesses? Which anti-competitive behaviours are regulated by competition law? What are the consequences of breaching the prohibitions?

FURTHER READING

T. Jones and M. Christie, *Criminal Law*, 4th edn (W. Green Edinburgh, 2008) (an excellent concise guide).

G. Gordn and M. Christie, *The Criminal Law of Scotland*, 3rd edn (W. Green Edinburgh, 2005) (the most authoritative modern text but complex, detailed and quite theoretical in points).

R. Baldwin and M. Cave, *Understanding Regulation* (OUP, 1999) (theoretical in approach but very thought provoking).

M. Tyler and Others, *Tolley's Health and Safety at Work Handbook 2008*, 20th edn (LexisNexis, 2008) (provides a good practical account of health and safety law in practice).

V. Korah, *An Introductory Guide to EC Competition Law and Practice* (Hart, 2007) (a good introductory account).

S. Bell and D. McGillivray, *Environmental Law*, 6th edn (OUP, 2006) (an excellent introductory account).

RELEVANT WEBLINKS

Health and Safety Executive: *www.hse.cov.uk*.
Office of Fair Trading: *www.oft.gov.uk* and the Competition Commission: *www.competition-commission.org.uk*.

Chapter 4   The Law of Contract

Greg Gordon[1]

▶ CHAPTER OVERVIEW

This chapter is concerned with the law of contract. It begins by looking at **4–01** the definition of a contract and then examines the process through which contracts are formed. The chapter then proceeds to consider important aspects relating to the legal content of a contract and then turns to the issue of defective contracts. Remedies for breach of contract are then considered and finally the various circumstances under which contractual obligations may become extinct are discussed.

✓ OUTCOMES

After studying this chapter you should: **4–02**

- ✓ be able to describe what a contract is and be able to differentiate contracts from:
  - non-binding agreements; and
  - unilateral gratuitous promises;
- ✓ understand the process by which contracts are formed and, in particular, be aware of the legal significance of both *consensus in idem* and the following concepts:
  - offer;
  - acceptance (including the problems associated with the communication of acceptance);
  - counter-offer;
  - battle of the forms;
- ✓ appreciate that while formalities are not normally required for the creation of a contract there are exceptions to this general rule, most notably, those contained in the Requirements of Writing (Scotland) Act 1995;
- ✓ be aware that the legal content of a contract are contained in its terms and have some appreciation of some of the key terms of some of the more important contracts encountered in business;

---

[1] Lecturer in Law, University of Aberdeen.

✓ understand that terms may be

- expressly agreed
- incorporated by reference or by a course of dealing
- implied by the law
- and, in the case of the latter two bullet points, understand the legal rules used to effect those processes;

✓ be aware that the Unfair Contract Terms Act 1977 and the Unfair Terms in Consumer Contracts Regulations 1999 regulate the use of unfair terms in contracts, and understand the key features of both of those regulatory instruments;

✓ appreciate that not all attempts to enter into a contract will be successful and understand the meaning and significance of the terms "void", "voidable" and "unenforceable" contract;

✓ be aware of the circumstances in which a person will lack legal capacity to enter into a contract and understand the meaning and significance of the terms "force and fear", "facility and circumvention" and "undue influence";

✓ understand the principal categories of error (including induced error, or misrepresentation) and the effect that these various different sorts of error have upon parties' attempts to enter contractual relations.

✓ understand what is meant by, and what sorts of situations will qualify as, *pacta illicita*;

- in connection with the above, be able to describe when a court will and will not enforce a restrictive covenant or solus agreement;

✓ understand what a "breach of contract" is, differentiate the various different types of breach (anticipatory, material, simple) from each other and be able to describe the main remedies available in the event of breach;

✓ recognise that only the parties to a contract may usually sue or be sued for a breach of contract, but that in exceptional circumstances a *jus quaesitum tertio* (third party right) will exist;

✓ understand the circumstances in which contractual obligations come to an end.

WHAT IS A CONTRACT?

4–03 "Business" could be defined in many ways, but at the heart of the process is the provision of goods and services with a view towards profit. Contract law is the legal underpin of those activities. It is therefore important for students of business law to have a firm grasp of the essential features of the law of contract.

Even if one has never previously given a moment's thought to the law of contract, the fact remains that, since attaining the age of legal capacity,[2] we have all been entering into contracts on a daily basis. Every time we travel by bus or pay to park a car, the law of contract is involved. Similarly, we conclude a contract every time we buy ourselves a newspaper, pay to watch a sporting event or rent a property to stay in. The same principles of the law of contract are also involved when we carry out less commonplace transactions, like when we buy insurance or purchase a home.[3] Without us ever necessarily giving active thought to it, contract law is part of the everyday flow of our lives.

In what is perhaps the classic book on the Scots law of contract, Gloag defined contract as "an agreement which creates or is intended to create a legal obligation between the parties to it".[4] This definition could arguably be criticised as being somewhat simplistic: other writers have defined contract at greater length.[5] However, the great strength of Gloag's definition is that it allows us to focus on two concepts which lie at the heart of contract law: agreement, and the need for an intention to create legal obligations.

Agreement

The need for two or more parties

Contracts are by their nature bilateral or multi-lateral: there needs to **4–04** more than one party to a contract. This is just as one would expect: contracts are ultimately about agreement and it is a nonsense to talk about "agreeing" with oneself.

The general lack of need for particular formality

In Scots law there is in general no need for an agreement to take a **4–05** particular form before it will be a legally enforceable contract. In particular, there is in general no need for a contract to be in writing.[6] One sometimes hears a friend or relation say something like "the roofer who fixed my roof ripped me off but there's nothing I can do about it because I didn't have a contract". This is not correct. If a tradesman has accepted

---

[2] Legal capacity is discussed at paras 4–50—4–54, below.

[3] Note that although the general principles of contract remain the same, these principles are supplemented by the addition of further legal rules in the case of certain types of contracts. For instance, contracts for the purchase of land (including houses) are made subject to the Requirements of Writing (Scotland) Act 1995, discussed further at para.4–28, below.

[4] W. Gloag, *The Law of Contract*, 2nd end (W. Green, Edinburgh, 1929) ("Gloag") p.8.

[5] H. MacQueen and J. Thomson, *Contract Law in Scotland*, 2nd edn (Tottel), with revisions 2005 ("MacQueen and Thomson") at para 1.9: "Contract can be defined as an agreement between two or more parties having the capacity to make it in the form demanded by law to perform on one side or both acts which are not trifling, indeterminate, impossible or illegal."

[6] There are a limited number of exceptions to this general rule. The most important such exception relates to contracts for the transfer of land; these are discussed at para.4–28, below. Certain types of consumer credit agreement also require to be in a particular form before they will be fully legally enforceable: see Ch.6, below.

an instruction to attend at a householder's home, go onto his roof, assess what is wrong and fix it, then there most certainly is a contract in place. It is not necessarily the most advantageous contract that the householder could have entered into, and the householder may find it difficult to exercise his or her rights under the contract. No doubt it would have been better for the householder if the contract had been in writing, or if there had at least been more specific agreement on exactly what the roofer was supposed to be doing and how much he was going to charge. But none of this affects the fact that a contract has, as a matter of law, come into existence.

In addition, the "doctrine of consideration", which adds a range of technical complications to English contract law, is not recognised in Scots law. The doctrine states that for an enforceable contract to come into effect between the parties what is known as "valuable consideration" must pass between them. Valuable consideration means money or money's worth. In practice, this means that agreements entered into without consideration on both sides—for instance, an agreement to donate money to a charity—cannot be considered to be contracts in English law. This doctrine forms no part of Scots law.

When is agreement reached?

4–06 The particular circumstances in which the courts will hold that an agreement has been reached will be discussed in greater detail at paras 4–11 to 4–28, below.

Intention to create legal obligations

4–07 As we have seen, before a contract can be formed, there must be an agreement between two or more people. However, not *all* agreements are contractual in nature: only those which are intended to create legal obligations will constitute a contract. Perhaps the most common examples of an agreement not intended to create legal relations are social and domestic arrangements.

Social and domestic arrangements

4–08 If two friends agree to meet in order to play squash and one of them changes his mind and fails to turn up, this will not ordinarily be a breach of contract. The law presumes that people who enter into arrangements of this kind intend them not to be legally binding. A similar presumption is made in the case of domestic arrangements.[7] Thus if a husband and wife agree that he will do the ironing if she dusts the house, these obligations will not ordinarily be legally enforceable. In such situations, we generally go ahead and do the thing that we agreed to do not because the law says we must, but because we think it is the right thing to do, perhaps

---

[7] This presumption is, however, rebuttable: if it is clear that the parties both accepted that the agreement was to be legally binding, then even a social or domestic arrangement can be the subject of an enforceable contract.

because we actively want to or perhaps because we have promised to do so and do not want to go back on our word.

Agreements made in the commercial context

By contrast, when we move from the social sphere to the business or **4–09** commercial context—for instance, when we agree to buy or sell things, or to provide services in exchange for payment—the law assumes that we do intend our agreements to be legally binding. Thus such agreements are generally contracts. Again, however, this is not a binding rule of law but merely a rebuttable presumption, and there are certain types of commercial agreement which will not be intended to be binding. For instance, when a business decides that it wishes to lease commercial premises such as an industrial unit or an office block from a landlord, the parties will commonly enter into a "heads of terms" agreement. This is done because contracts of commercial lease are generally very lengthy documents and negotiations relating to them can become very time-consuming and complicated. It is generally thought to assist the parties' negotiations if they are able to agree some key principles of the deal at a relatively early stage of the process. Such "heads of terms" agreement are not generally intended to be legally binding, although they can be made to be, if the parties so desire. Outside of this particular context, non-binding commercial agreements are rare. However, the courts will occasionally be persuaded that a commercial agreement was not intended to be legally binding. A notable instance where this occurred is discussed below.

Rose and Frank Company v J.R. Crompton and Brothers Limited
[1925] A.C. 445

An American firm (RF) entered into an agreement with an English company (C) whereby RF were appointed the only company permitted to sell C's products in North America. C became dissatisfied with the level of service provided by RF and decided to terminate the agreement with immediate effect and appoint other American agents. RF sued, contending that they had a binding contract and that C could only lawfully end it by doing so in accordance with its termination clause. If RF had been correct in this, it would have meant that C would have been held to have breached the contract, and RF would have been entitled to damages. However, the House of Lords held that the agreement between the parties was not a contract, and was therefore not legally enforceable. This was so because the contract contained a provision expressly stating that it was not a "a formal or legal agreement" but was "only a definite expression and record of the purpose and intention of the parties concerned, to which they each honourably pledge themselves, with the fullest confidence that it will be carried through with mutual loyalty and friendly co-operation".

> **Key Concepts**
>
> A contract is an agreement entered into between two or more par-
> ties, which the parties intend to be legally binding.
>   The courts will presume that the parties to social or domestic
> agreements do not intend their agreement to be binding, and will
> assume that parties to commercial or business-related agreements
> do intend their agreements to constitute contracts. In both cases,
> however, these presumptions are rebuttable in the face of clear
> evidence to the contrary.

Unilateral gratuitous promise

4–10   As we have already seen at para.4–05, above, Scots law does not recognise the doctrine of consideration. As a consequence, in Scots law, contracts whereby one party gives a benefit and in exchange receives nothing
of financial value are enforceable. Moreover, it means that a unilateral
promise to do something is also binding in Scots law, but only if the
promise is made:

- in formal writing;[8] or
- in the course of business.[9]

Declaring that one will make a gift at a future time is the classic example
of a promise. Such a declaration will be binding in Scotland as long as
one of the two criteria set out immediately above is satisfied. Thus if A
promises to give his sister B a television, he will not be legally bound to
do so unless he commits the promise to writing. By contrast, if C, the
owner of a television shop, broadcasts a radio advertisement offering to
give a free TV to the 100th person to enter his shop on a particular day,
that customer is legally entitled to demand delivery of the TV. An offer to
pay a reward in exchange for the provision of information or the return
of an item of property can also be characterised as a promise,[10] as can an
undertaking to keep an offer open for a period of time in order to allow
the person to whom the offer has been made to have some time in which
to consider it.[11]
   The distinction between a promise and a contract can sometimes be

---

[8] i.e. in writing and signed by the promiser. For a further discussion of what is meant by
"formal writing", see para.4–28, below.
[9] The Requirements of Writing (Scotland) Act 1995 (RWSA) s.1(1).
[10] *Petrie v Earl of Airlie* (1834) 13 S. 68. In this case, a sign was anonymously posted
attacking the Earl's character after he refused to support a particular bill before parliament. The Earl issued a proclamation offering a reward for information leading to the
conviction of the people who had produced the sign. Petrie provided information
implicating his brother and another. The Court of Session held that it the Earl was
legally bound to pay the reward.
[11] *Littlejohn v Hadwen* (1822) 20 S.L.R. 5.

elusive. Woolman and Lake provide a useful analysis of the essential distinctions:

- A contract arises out of the will of two parties. A promise is the product of one person's intention alone. No acceptance is required to create a binding obligation.
- An offer is revocable until accepted. A promise is binding and irrevocable from the moment it is made.
- A promise places an obligation on one person alone. By contrast, contracts place obligations on both parties to the contract. In theory this is true even of gratuitous contracts. For instance, if A offers to gift a statue to his local council and it accepts, the council is under an obligation to take the statue. In the case of a promise, the council would always have a right to reject the statue.[12]

Key Concept

A unilateral gratuitous promise is not a contract as it is not an agreement made between two or more parties. However, such promises are legally binding in Scots law either if they are written down and signed by the promisor, or if they are made in a business context.

FORMATION OF CONTRACTS

Introduction

Contracts are formed by a process of offer and acceptance. In the simplest of cases, one party makes an offer and the other accepts it. Through this process, the parties reach what is known as *consensus in idem* or a "meeting of the minds". At that moment a contract comes into existence.[13] We shall commence this section by considering *consensus in idem* in greater detail before expanding on what we mean by "offer" and "acceptance" and concluding by examining some important issues that arise as a result of the law's conceptualisation of contract in terms of offer and acceptance.

4–11

Key Concept

A contract is formed when an *offer* is met by an *unconditional acceptance* leading to *consensus in idem* – a meeting of the minds.

---

[12] S. Woolman and J. Lake, *Contract* (3rd edn, W. Green, Edinburgh, 2001) ("Woolman and Lake"), para.4.2.
[13] Always assuming that there is no incapacity preventing the parties from entering into contractual relation: see para.4–50, below.

Consensus in idem (1): What needs to be agreed before consensus is reached?

4–12 It is important to understand exactly what needs to be agreed between the parties before it can be said that a *consensus in idem* has been achieved. It is not the case that every minute detail of the contract requires to be specifically agreed. For a contract to be constituted, only its essential elements need to have been settled upon. What is "essential" will vary as between different types of contract, but in the case of contracts for the sale of goods, for example, the subject-matter of what is being sold and its price will be considered to be essential.

Consensus in idem (2): Resolving disputes about essentials—the objective nature of the test

4–13 Sometimes, a dispute will arise between the parties about one of the essentials of the contract. One might think that this would automatically mean that there was no agreement: how can there be *consensus* if the parties are locked in dispute about an essential matter? Nevertheless, a contract may very well still exist in such circumstances. The courts assess the question of whether consensus in idem has been reached not *subjectively*, but *objectively*. In other words, the courts determine the matter not by assessing what the parties actually thought they had agreed (which would be a subjective approach) but by considering what an objective person who happened to witness the parties' contractual negotiations would have understood the parties to have agreed. *Muirhead and Turnbull v Dickson*[14] provides a good example of the objective approach in operation.

Muirhead and Turnbull v Dickson
(1905) 7 F. 606

Muirhead and Turnbull (MT) were piano sellers who entered into an agreement with Dickson (D) that he would take a piano from them at a price of £26, payable in monthly instalments. D took delivery of the piano and paid his first five instalments. He then stopped paying. MT sued, arguing that the contract between it and D was one of hire purchase and that as a result D was under an obligation to return the piano, which was still owned by MT, and that MT were entitled to treat the money paid by D as payments towards the hire of the piano. D defended the action on the basis that it was not a contract of hire purchase at all, but a credit sale. On that analysis, ownership of the piano had passed to D upon delivery: as such, while MT could claim the balance due on the purchase price, they could not reclaim the piano from him. When the case was argued in court, there was evidence that MT's usual practice was to sell on

---

[14] (1905) 7 F. 606.

hire purchase terms. However, MT was not able to establish that D had been made aware that this was what they intended in this particular case. Indeed, there had been no express agreement between the parties and it appeared that MT and D were at cross-purposes as to the nature of the agreement which they were entering into. Nevertheless, the court held that that there had been *consensus in idem* between the parties. In emphasising the objective nature of the test which is used, Lord President Dunedin stated that "commercial contracts cannot be arranged by what people think in their inmost minds. Commercial contracts are made according to what people say". The parties had said and done enough to lead an objective bystander to conclude that they were agreeing a credit sale.

The objective nature of the test also means that there will be occasions where courts will hold that there is no contract, even when the parties thought there was one and have proceeded to implement the obligations that they thought had been agreed. This is exemplified by *Mathieson Gee (Ayrshire) Ltd v Quigley*.[15]

Mathieson Gee (MG) offered to hire Quigley (Q) equipment for the removal of silt which had built up in a large pond at his home. Q purported to accept their offer to remove and dispose of the silt. The equipment was delivered and a part-payment of the contractual price was made. A dispute then arose as to what precisely had been agreed, and the parties went to court. There, the parties contended that there was a contract between them and asked the court to adjudicate on whether it was one for the provision of equipment only, or one for the carrying out of the job of removing the silt. The court declined to do so, on the basis that an analysis of the evidence in the case demonstrated that the acceptance did not meet the terms of the offer: as such, there had therefore been no consensus in idem, and no contract could therefore have come into existence.

Thus if a party delivers goods, performs work or incurs expense in the erroneous belief that a contract has come into existence, it can make no use of the law of contract, as no contract has come into effect. It may, however, be able to establish a remedy under a separate branch of law known as unjustified enrichment.[16]

[15] 1952 S.L.T. 239.
[16] Unjustified enrichment is a highly technical area of law which falls outside the scope of this book. An introductory account can be found in H. MacQueen *Law Basics: Unjustified Enrichment* (W. Green, Edinburgh, 2004).

Key Concept

Consensus in idem is reached when an objective bystander observing the parties' discussions, correspondence and behaviour would come to the conclusion that they had agreed on all of the essential elements of the contract.

Offers

4-14 An offer is both a proposal by one party to enter into a legally binding agreement with another and a statement of the terms which the offeror (i.e. the person making the offer) proposes should govern that agreement. The essential feature of an offer, and the thing which distinguishes from certain other types of proposal which may also be involved in the lead-up to a contract, is that it must "contemplate acceptance". This means that, to qualify as an offer, the proposal must be of such a nature that if it were met with an unqualified acceptance, a contract would be formed without the need for further negotiation. In other words, to qualify as an offer, a proposal must contain at least the essential terms on which the offeror intends to do the deal.

Offers may come in many forms. In general, they can be written or verbal or, in some instances, they can be inferred from the circumstances.[17] For instance, a customer may go into a newsagents, pick up a magazine, proceed to the check-out, give the magazine over to be scanned, see the purchase price appear on the till's display screen, hand over the price and exit with the magazine. In this example, not a word has been exchanged. However no-one would seriously dispute the fact that the customer has made a purchase. Thus, somewhere within that exchange, an offer has both been made and accepted.[18]

Non-offers

4-15 Not every statement or proposal concerning a potential supply of goods or services will in law constitute an offer. It is important to be able to distinguish between offers and other proposals which, while they may superficially resemble offers, are not considered by the courts to contain an offer's essential legal characteristics.

Statements of future intent

4-16 A broad statement of future intent will not be considered to be an offer. Thus the statement "I am going to sell my car" is not an offer as it does not contemplate acceptance. Which car is being spoken about? When will

---

[17] This is the general principle; however, the law imposes some formalities concerning the form which both an offer and an acceptance must take in some, limited, situations. See paras 4–27—4–28, below.
[18] In the example given, the offer would come when the shop assistant scans the magazine and the price pops up on the till. The acceptance comes when the price is handed over.

the transaction take place? What will the price be? We do not know. The essential features of an offer are therefore absent.

Invitations to treat

Invitations to treat more closely resemble offers and require fuller con- **4–17** sideration.[19] An invitation to treat is not an offer but merely an announcement that one would like others to come forward and make an offer. For instance, invitations to tender are commonly used in major construction and engineering projects. In such a case, a party will announce that it wants certain works to do be carried out, and invites interested parties to tender the price they would charge for the job, and the terms and conditions on which they would do it. Invitations to tender are generally invitations to treat. Where this is so, the party hosting the tender will be under no liability to accept the best-value tender received.[20] Consequently, the tenders received as a result the exercise will not be acceptances concluding a contract, but merely offers which the party who announced the tender is at liberty to accept or decline as he chooses. Advertisements, too, are presumed to be invitations to treat, although this presumption will be overcome (and the advertisement therefore treated as an offer) if the advertisement makes it clear that the advertiser intends to be bound by an acceptance. The case of *Carlill v Carbolic Smoke Ball Company*[21] provides a famous example of such an advertisement.

Carlill v Carbolic Smoke Ball Company
[1893] 1 Q.B. 256

The Carbolic Smoke Ball Company (CSBC) took out a number of newspaper advertisements extolling the virtues of its "carbolic smoke ball", a product which, when lit, gave off fumes which CSBC claimed had medical benefits. CSBC's advertisement offered to pay £100 to anyone who contracted flu after buying and using one of their carbolic smoke balls in accordance with its printed instructions. CSBC also stated that it had deposited £1,000 with a named bank "in order to demonstrate their sincerity in the matter". Impressed by the advertisement, Mrs Carlill purchased one of the balls from her local chemist and diligently used it. She caught the flu and sued CSBC, arguing that their advertisement was an offer

---

[19] "Treat" in this context has a rather archaic legal meaning. "To treat" in this sense means "to enter into a contract". "Treaty"—meaning an agreement between two or more governments—also stems from this sense of the word.

[20] This does, however, depend on the precise terms of the invitation to tender. If this contains a clear undertaking to accept the best bid, then in Scots law at least the inviting party will be bound, not under the law of contract, but promise, discussed earlier at para.4–10, above.

[21] [1893] 1 Q.B. 256.

which she had impliedly accepted by purchasing one of the balls.
The court concluded that, in the very particular circumstances of
the case, CSBC's advertisement was indeed an offer. In practice,
advertisements in such terms are very rarely encountered nowadays[22] and in the majority of cases an advert will constitute an
invitation to treat.

Further examples of an invitation to treat are the exhibition of items for
viewing in advance of an auction sale or the display of goods in a shop or
on the internet. An unusual but striking example of this is seen in *Fisher v
Bell*.[23] Here, a shopkeeper displayed a flick-knife for sale in his shop
window with a price-tag next to it. He was prosecuted under legislation
which made it an offence to "sell or offer to sell a flick-knife". The
shopkeeper was acquitted on the basis that displaying the flick-knife was
not an offer to sell, but merely an invitation to treat.

Communication of offers

4–18   Offers must be communicated before they become effectual: "an offer is
nothing until it is communicated to the offeree".[24] Thus if an offer is
formulated in a person's mind but not articulated, or written down but
not passed to the offeree, it is ineffectual. Additionally, if an offer is
transmitted to an offeree without the offeror's authorisation, that, too, is
ineffectual.

In *Burr v Police Commissioners of Bo'ness*,[25] B was employed by the
Commissioners as a sanitary inspector. Following a dispute between the
parties about work which B contended he had been required to carry out
without adequate payment, the Commissioners passed a resolution
increasing B's salary but requiring him to work under the supervision of
another. The Commissioners did not intimate this resolution to B, but
news of it was it was informally "leaked" to him. B protested at being
required to work under supervision. The Commissioners responded by
cancelling the part of the resolution which increased B's salary. B sued,
contending he was entitled to be paid at the higher rate, but lost his claim
on the basis that the offer had never been legally communicated to him.

Offers can be (and frequently are) made only towards a specified person. Where this is so, others are not entitled to intercept the offer and
accept it; it may only be accepted by the person to whom it was
addressed. Offerers can, however, make offers on a more open basis if
they choose, stating that they can be accepted by a particular class of
persons (for instance, members of a particular trade union or alumni of a
particular college or university). Indeed, in appropriate cases the courts

[22] Not least because of the effect of the consumer protection legislation discussed in Ch.6,
below.
[23] [1961] 1 Q.B. 394.
[24] *Thomson v Jones* (1855) 18 D. 1 *per* the Lord President (McNeill) at 10.
[25] (1896) 24 R. 148.

will hold that an offer has been addressed to the world at large, and that anyone is entitled to accept it if they so choose: see *Carlill v Carbolic Smoke Ball Company*[26] and *Hunter v General Accident Fire and Life Assurance Corporation*,[27] in which the court stated:

> "... when a general offer addressed to the public is appropriated to himself by a distinct acceptance by one person, then it is to be read in exactly the same way as if it had been addressed to the individual originally."

Key Concept

Not all discussions or proposals made during the course of a contractual negotiation are offers. The identifying feature of an offer is that it must "contemplate acceptance". Statements of future intent and invitations to treat are not offers and therefore cannot be accepted by the offeree.

An offer is not effectual until it is communicated to the offeree.

Offers may only be accepted by the person to whom they are addressed but it is possible for an offeror to address an offer to one person, a category of people or the world at large.

Revocation of offer

Unlike a unilateral promise, which takes legal effect as soon as it is made,[28] offers can be revoked or withdrawn at any time before acceptance unless the offeror provides otherwise.[29] However, the revocation of the offer must be communicated to the person to whom the offer was made.   **4–19**

Lapse of offer

Quite apart from the possibility of revocation, offers will automatically lapse in certain circumstances. Once an offer has lapsed, it no longer legally exists and the offeree is therefore no longer able to accept it. The circumstances in which an offer will lapse are: **4–20**

- through passage of time. If a time-limit imposed by the offeror passes without the offer being accepted, the offer lapses. If no time-limit is imposed by the offeror, the offer will remain open for a reasonable period of time. What is reasonable will depend on the facts and circumstances of the case: for instance, where the

---

[26] [1893] 1 Q.B. 256, discussed at para.4–17, above.
[27] 1909 S.C. (HL) 30.
[28] See para.4–10, above.
[29] The offeror can, if he or she chooses, state that the offer is open for a certain period of time, or indeed that it is irrevocable—in other words that the offer cannot be withdrawn by the offeror, and will only fall when it lapses through the operation of law (discussed in the following paragraph).

offer concerns perishable goods such as a truck-load of cut
flowers, the offer may very well lapse more quickly than if it
concerns goods which are not subject to the risk of deterioration,
such as a lorry load of cement. Similarly, offers concerning
commodities with volatile prices will stay open for a shorter
period than those the price of which is more stable; or
- upon rejection of the offer, or the making of a counter-offer;[30] or
- upon the death of either party or in the event of the offeror
  becoming bankrupt or insane; or
- upon the destruction or material alteration of the subject-matter
  of the offer; or
- in the event of supervening illegality.[31]

Acceptance

4–21 MacQueen and Thomson define acceptance particularly succinctly:

> "An acceptance is the final unqualified assent by the offeree to the
> terms stipulated in the offer."[32]

As we have already seen, an acceptance will only give rise to *consensus in
idem* if it coincides with the offer. Thus if (as in *Mathieson Gee (Ayrshire)
Ltd v Quigley*,[33] discussed at para.4–13, above) the offeree purports to
accept something that the offeror did not offer, no contract is formed. In
addition, a purported "acceptance" which seeks to introduce new terms
into the contract is not an acceptance at all, but a counter-offer.[34]

Key Concept

The identifying feature of an acceptance is that it must be an
unqualified agreement to the offer put forward by the offeree.

As with offers, acceptances come in a variety of guises. Express acceptances may be made verbally or in writing.[35] Silence *on its own* is not
sufficient to serve as an acceptance. Thus if a self-employed gardener puts
notes through various householder's letter boxes saying that unless he
hears from them by 5.00 p.m. the following day, he will proceed to mow
their lawn at a cost of £20, and hears nothing from them, he cannot insist
upon payment. The courts will, however, be willing in appropriate cases
to infer an implied acceptance from an offeree's behaviour. We have
already seen an example of such an acceptance: the newsagent example

---

[30] Counter-offers are discussed at para.4–23, below.
[31] For a discussion of what is meant by "supervening illegality" see para.4–107, below.
[32] MacQueen and Thomson, para.2.23.
[33] 1952 S.L.T. 239.
[34] Counter-offers are discussed below at para.4–23.
[35] i.e. either in traditional writing, or by modern equivalent means such as by fax or email.

given at para.4–14, above. Such acceptance—known as acceptance by performance—occurs frequently, particularly in the context of simple, low-value contracts concluded without negotiation.[36]

In general, any of these forms of acceptance is valid, and there is no need for the acceptance to be in the same medium as the offer: a written offer does not, as a matter of law, have to be accepted in writing. However, the offeror is entitled to stipulate the form of acceptance in the offer itself, and where this is done, the offeree must accept in the medium demanded.

Non-acceptance

Rejection

The rejection of an offer causes it to lapse. As a lapsed offer ceases to be, **4–22** rejection cannot be undone. If the offeree subsequently regrets rejecting an offer, he cannot change his mind and issue a legally binding acceptance; he can do no more than go back to the offeror and ask him to renew the offer. Such a request would constitute an invitation to treat.

Counter-offer

A response to an offer which, while not expressly rejecting the offer, seeks **4–23** to qualify it by deleting some of the offer's terms and/or imposing new conditions is known as a "counter-offer" or "qualified acceptance". Despite the fact that it is not expressed, an outright rejection of a counter-offer has the effect, first, of rejecting the offer to which it is a response and then of making a fresh offer for the party who was originally the offeror to consider. A good example of counter-offer in operation is seen in *Wolf and Wolf v Forfar Potato Co Ltd*.[37]

Wolf and Wolf v Forfar Potato Co Ltd
1984 S.L.T. 100

FPC offered to sell a consignment of potatoes to WW, a firm of potato merchants. The offer was open for acceptance by 5 p.m. the following day. On the following morning, WW sent what purported to be an acceptance of FPC's offer. However, this so-called acceptance sought to add a number of new terms and conditions to those which had been proposed by FPC. During a telephone conversation, FPC made it clear that the new conditions were not acceptable and thereafter WW sent a further document, purporting to accept FPC's original offer. FPC did not respond and did not supply the potatoes. WW sued, arguing that FPC were in breach of

---

[36] Examples of such contracts could be the purchase of a pub lunch where the order constitutes an offer and the delivery of the food acceptance, or travelling by bus, where the customer makes the offer by tendering the fare and the bus driver accepts by issuing a ticket.

[37] 1984 S.L.T. 100.

contract. The court held that WW's first "acceptance" was a counter-offer. As a matter of law, this rejected FPC's offer, and put in place a fresh offer which FPC had rejected. As FPC's offer had lapsed upon rejection, WW's second attempt at issuing an "acceptance" could not conclude the contract either. Instead, it was a fresh offer which FPC had chosen not to accept. There was therefore no contract between the parties.

The battle of the forms

4–24 As some contractual negotiations can be quite protracted it is possible for there to be a large number of counter-offers before a contract is eventually concluded by a simple acceptance. This can lead to a particular problem known as the "battle of the forms". This occurs when two parties agree that they wish to enter into a contract with each other, but where each wants their own standard terms and conditions to govern the contract. This is most readily illustrated by way of example. Company A orders goods from Company B. A wants the contract to proceed on the basis of its standard terms and conditions of purchase, so it incorporates them into the purchase order which it sends to B.[38] B receives the order. It wants to sell the goods to A because selling goods is how B makes its money. However, B wants to use its own standard terms and conditions of business.[39] It sends an order confirmation form in which it incorporates its own standard terms and conditions. A couple of days later, it despatches the goods, which are accepted by Company A. It is clear that the parties wish to contract with each other, but how does the law ascertain which set of terms and conditions prevail? The answer is that the law does not look at this matter from the standpoint of what would be an acceptance compromise to impose upon the parties. It looks at the matter in terms of offer, counter-offer (or counter-offers) and acceptance. The party who wins the battle of the forms is the one which succeeds in making the last counter-offer before acceptance. It is sometimes said that that party has "fired the last shot" in the battle of the forms, but this is potentially misleading. It must be stressed that it is the last set of conditions proffered *before acceptance* which wins the "battle". Thus any sets of conditions put forward once the contract has been concluded by acceptance are irrelevant. The point is well illustrated in *Continental Tyre and Rubber Co Ltd v Trunk Trailer Co Ltd*.[40]

---

[38] Company A may wish to do this because it is familiar with what its legal rights and liabilities are under its own standard terms and conditions. It may also be that A has slanted its standard conditions of purchase in its own favour. For instance, these terms might seek to impose strict obligations on the seller about the quality of the goods, or to give A an unusually long time in which to pay for the goods.

[39] It may want to do this because B's conditions are biased in B's favour: for instance, B may wish to restrict A's rights to the lowest allowable under the law, or to be able to choose when he delivers the goods, or to compel A to pay for the goods very quickly.

[40] 1987 S.C.L.R. 58.

TTCL placed an order for tyres from CTRC. The order was printed on TTCL's standard order form, which contained the company's standard terms and conditions of business. CTRC proceeded to supply the tyres in a number of batches. Each batch was accompanied by a delivery note and followed a few days later by an invoice. Both the delivery note and the invoice contained CTRC's terms and conditions, which differed markedly from those of TTCL. TTCL became dissatisfied with the tyres, which they considered wore out more quickly than should be the case, and sued. CTRC defended the action on the basis that the contract has been concluded on their terms and conditions, and measured against those, there was no breach. The court found in favour of TTCL: the contract had been concluded by performance when the first batch of tyres was delivered. CTRC's attempts to have their own terms and conditions govern the contract therefore came too late.

Communication of acceptance

As with offers, acceptances must usually be communicated before they **4–25** take effect, although the offeror can, if he chooses, frame his offer in such a way that the requirement for communication of acceptance is dispensed with.[41]

Sometimes, it is important to know at which particular moment in time the law will consider an acceptance to have been communicated. This is particularly so when the offeror seeks to revoke his offer at or around the same time that the offeree purports to accept the offer, or where an offer is subject to a time-limit and a dispute arises as to whether or not the offeree's acceptance has come in on time.

In relation to contracts concluded in Scotland or between a party located in Scotland and another located elsewhere in the United Kingdom, the law recognises two distinct categories of communication: instantaneous and delayed.[42] Very different sets of rules apply to each, so it is important to be able to differentiate between the two.

Instantaneous communication

The classic example of instantaneous communication is meeting someone face to face and speaking to them in live time. Telephone conversations are also instantaneous (give or take a couple of seconds satellite delay if

---

[41] This is competent, but occurs only rarely. In *Carlill v Carbolic Smoke Ball Company* [1893] 1 Q.B. 256 (discussed at para.4–17, above), CSBC argued that, even if their advertisement were to be considered an offer, there could be no contract as C had never communicated an acceptance to them. The court held that by wording their advertisement as they did, CSBC had dispensed with the need for communication: acceptance took place when C purchased the smoke ball and used it in accordance with its instructions.

[42] This distinction is not widely recognised outside the Anglo-American legal world. Most continental systems operate on the basis of the rules for instantaneous communication. This can make resolving these questions in cross-border contracts rather difficult, but such considerations fall outside the scope of this work.

one happens to be talking with someone on the other side of the world.) Although they take time to prepare, telexes and faxes are also considered to be instantaneous because, at the moment when they are sent, one is in direct communication with the other party, and so if anything goes wrong with the attempted transmission one realises that more or less instantly and can attempt to transmit the information again. Similarly, live-time chat conversations using systems such as MSM messenger and sharing information over the internet in order to make a purchase from a fully integrated sales website like those operated by the major airlines and companies such as Amazon or iTunes are also considered to be instantaneous forms of communication.

For all of these forms of communication, the rule is as set out in *Entores Limited v Miles Far East Corporation*. There, Lord Denning observed:

> "Suppose that I make an offer to a man by telephone and, in the middle of his reply, the line goes 'dead' so that I do not hear his words of acceptance. There is no contract at that moment. The other man may not know the precise moment when the line failed. But he will know that the telephone conversation was abruptly broken off.... If he wishes to make a contract, he must therefore get through again so as to make sure that I heard. Suppose next, that the line does not go dead, but it is nevertheless so indistinct that I do not catch what he says and I ask him to repeat it. He then repeats it and I hear his acceptance. The contract is made, not on the first time when I do not hear, but only the second time when I do hear."[43]

It is not enough, therefore, to try to communicate an acceptance and fail. The acceptance must be received. It is the person who is trying to communicate the acceptance who has the burden of ensuring that the message has got through.

Delayed communication

4–26 The rules concerning delayed communication evolved to accommodate the widespread use of the postal system in contractual negotiations from the 1800s onwards. Even assuming that one's letter is not lost or unduly delayed, once committed to the post it will not be delivered instantly but will take at least a day to work its way through the system. Similarly, sending a telegram is a delayed communication. Email is also thought of as a delayed communication. Although email systems will often deliver messages very quickly, one is not in direct communication with the recipient of the message and, when for some reason a message is not successfully delivered, it can take a significant period of time for the system to generate a message warning the sender of that fact.

When the rule on delayed communications was being formulated, the courts had to attempt to balance the competing interests of the person

---

[43] *Entores Limited v Miles Far East Corporation* [1955] 2 Q.B. 327 at 332–333.

sending an acceptance by post with those of the person receiving it. Once the sender has posted his acceptance, he has no control over what happens to it: it therefore seems unfair if a delay which is outside of his control acts to his prejudice. Equally, however, it may be harsh upon someone awaiting an acceptance if he is deemed to receive the acceptance days or even weeks before it actually lands on his doorstep. In *Dunlop v Higgins*[44] it was held that the interests of the sender should be preferred to that of the recipient: the rule on delayed communications is therefore that the acceptance is "effective on dispatch". Once a properly-addressed letter is placed into the post-box, the acceptance takes effect, even if the letter is delayed, although in Scots law it appears that if the letter is lost in the postal system, the acceptance will not be deemed to have been effectual.[45]

The rule has been subjected to criticism and can have some fairly startling consequences. For example, if an offer must be accepted by 5.00 p.m. on a particular day, the acceptance is effectual if it got into the post-box at 4.57 p.m. notwithstanding the fact that the other party is not going to receive the letter until early on the following day at the earliest. On the other hand, if one continually tries to phone through an acceptance from at 4.45 p.m. onwards but cannot get through as the other party's phone is engaged until 5.05 p.m., the deadline has been missed. For this reason offerors will commonly dis-apply the postal rule by stating that their offer "is only for acceptance to be received by the offeror before [*whenever they set the deadline to be*.]" Similarly, the fact that offers and revocations of offers are not subject to the postal rule but are effectual only upon receipt also has the potential to produce peculiar results: if an offeror decides to revoke his offer and puts a letter to that effect in the post, the revocation does not take effect until received by the offeree. So if the offeree gets a letter of acceptance into the post before the revocation of offer is delivered to him, the contract is concluded, even if the letter of acceptance was dispatched hours or days after the dispatch of the revocation.

Key Concepts

An acceptance, like an offer, does not take effect until it is communicated. In the case of instantaneous methods of communication an acceptance will not be communicated until it is actually heard by the other party. In the case of delayed methods of communication, communication is "effective on despatch".

---

[44] (1848) 6 Bell's App. 195.
[45] *Mason v Benhar Coal* (1882) 9 R. 883. The position in England is to the contrary: even if the letter is lost in the post and never makes its way to the offeror, the contract is nevertheless concluded: *Household Fire Insurance v Grant* (1879) Ex. D. 216.

Contractual Formalities

Introduction

4–27 As has already been explained, there is, in general, no requirement for particular formalities to be attended to when one is making a contract. So in the ordinary course of events contracts may be concluded verbally, in writing, by implication or through some combination of these.

There are, however, a limited number of exceptions to this rule. Situations therefore exist where the law imposes particular formalities. The most significant set of technical formalities is contained in the Requirements of Writing (Scotland) Act 1995 (discussed immediately below). Other examples also exist.[46]

The Requirements of Writing (Scotland) Act 1995 (RWSA)

4–28 The RWSA commences by confirming the general principle that subject to the provisions of RWSA itself and any other enactment, writing is not required for the constitution of a contract, unilateral obligation or trust.[47] It then goes on to list in s.1(2) the particular types of contracts and other legal instruments which do require formal writing in order to be legally valid. These are:

> "(a) the constitution of—
>
>> (i) a contract or unilateral obligation for the creation, transfer, variation or extinction of an interest in land;
>> (ii) a gratuitous unilateral obligation except an obligation undertaken in the course of business; and
>> (iii) a trust whereby a person declares himself to be sole trustee of his own property or any property which he may acquire;
>
>> (b) the creation, transfer, variation or extinction of an interest in land otherwise than by the operation of a court decree, enactment or rule of law; and
>> (c) the making of any will, testamentary trust disposition and settlement or codicil.

Thus contracts and promises relative to land,[48] gratuitous unilateral obligations, "sole trustee" trusts and wills all need to be constituted in accordance with the formalities demanded by RWSA if they are to be binding.[49] What, then, are the Act's formalities? Any legal instrument of the type set out in s.1(2) of the Act need to be both in writing and signed at the end of the document ("subscribed") by all the persons intended to

---

[46] See e.g. the requirements of the Consumer Credit Act 1974, discussed in Ch.6, below.
[47] RWSA s.1(1).
[48] But not the creation of leases for less than one year: these are excluded by RWSA s.1(7).
[49] Gratuitous unilateral obligations (promises) have already been discussed at para.4–10, above. Trust law is discussed in Ch.13, below. Wills are the legal writings whereby a person specifies what they wish to happen to their property upon their death.

be bound by it.[50] If the document is intended to be "probative"—in other words, if it is to be regarded as authentic without the need for producing evidence on matters such as the fact that the signature on the document truly is that of the person who purports to have signed it—the document should also be signed by a witness.[51] Thus it is not, as a matter of pure law, necessary for the subscription to be witnessed but if it is not, then evidence will have to be led to the effect that the signature is that of the person who purported to sign. This is potentially expensive and time-consuming and (if, in the interim, the grantor disappears, becomes insane or dies) may become practically impossible to do.

The only exception to the need for the legal instruments listed in s.1(2) to be in writing and subscribed is contained in s.1(3) and (4) of the RWSA. These provide that where an agreement exists which is not in the correct form (e.g. it is verbal; or it is in writing but not signed) the obligor (i.e. the party obliged to perform under the agreement) will be legally bound by the agreement if the obligee (the person getting the benefit of the obligation under the defective agreement) has:

- acted or refrained from acting in reliance upon the contract and with the knowledge or acquiescence of the obligor (the person giving the obligation); and
- that as a result, the obligee has had a material change of position; and
- the interests of the obligee would be adversely affected to a material extent if the other party were allowed to withdraw from the obligation.

THE CONTENTS OF A CONTRACT: CONTRACTUAL TERMS

Introduction

Just as important as a consideration of how a contract comes to be **4–29** formed is the question, what are the contents of this agreement, once it comes into existence? Or to put matters another way, what legal rights and given, and which legal duties imposed, by the contract? The rights and obligations imposed by a contract are known as its *terms* (or sometimes, terms and conditions).

Illustrative examples of typical contractual terms

Contracts cover the whole range of commercial activities: different types **4–30** of contract will contain different terms, and we cannot possibly list and discuss the kind of terms that one would expect to see in each and every type of contract. Nevertheless, it is still useful to consider some

---

[50] RWSA s.2.
[51] RWSA s.3. This presumption can be overcome, but the burden of proof lies on the party challenging the authenticity of the signature.

illustrative examples of the terms which one encounters in certain types of contract.

Sale of goods

4–31 Perhaps the most important business contract—certainly the most commonly-encountered contract in practice—is a contract for the sale and purchase of goods. Such contracts need to deal with a range of issues such as:

- What is the identity of the goods being sold?
- Price: at what price are the goods being sold? In a lump sum, or by instalments? When is it payable?
- Delivery: when are the goods being handed over the purchaser? If in the future, when? What are the rights and obligations of the parties if the goods are delayed, lost or damaged in transit?
- What are the rights and obligations of the parties if the goods turn out to be unfit for the purpose for which they are sold, defective, or if, on reflection, the purchaser decides that he simply doesn't want them?

The Sale of Goods Act 1979 (SGA) governs the vast majority of such contracts. The SGA is considered in detail at Ch.5, below.

Contracts for the provision of services

4–32 Another commonly-encountered business contract is a contract for the provision of services. These differ from sales in that they are not concerned with the transfer of items of corporeal property, but with the carrying out of work by one person for another. Contracts with professionals such as accountants or lawyers are contracts for the provision of services; so, too, are the contracts we make with airlines or railway operators to carry us from one place to another[52] and contracts with tradesmen for the carrying out of activities such as fitting a kitchen. Such contracts will contain terms intended to answer the following kinds of questions:

- What is the nature of the service being provided?
- Does it have to be carried out personally, or can the service provider delegate the provision of the service to someone else?
- How much will the services cost? Is the job being carried out for a fixed price, or at an hourly or daily rate?
- When must the job be finished? What are the legal consequences if it is not finished in time?

---

[52] Such contracts are commonly described as contracts of carriage, but they are just a particular type of contract for the provision of services.

- To what standard are the services to be carried out? What are the rights and obligations of the parties if the services are not carried out to that standard?

Contracts of insurance

A contract of insurance is a contract whereby the insurer assumes the risk **4–33** that a particular event will occur in the future, and accepts that it will pay money or provide goods and/or services to the insured if the insured event occurred. Businesses will almost inevitably require at least some insurance cover: it is compulsory for any private sector business having any employees to maintain a policy of insurance which complies with the provisions of the Employer's Liability (Compulsory Insurance) Act 1969 against which employees or members of the public can claim if the employer negligently injures them. Similarly, anyone, whether a business or a private individual, who uses or causes or permits anyone else to use, a motor vehicle on a public road is required by Part VI of the Road Traffic Act 1998 to maintain insurance for the benefit of any other persons who may be injured by the vehicle. In addition to compulsory insurances, businesses will usually voluntarily insure against a broad range of risks which have the potential to damage their commercial interests. Businesses will often carry insurance against the risk that a fire, flood or other accident will damage buildings or other property which they own or lease, or against the risk that a key employee fundamental to the success of the business is killed or seriously injured.

Central to the creation of a contract of insurance is the proposal form.[53] This will generally take the form of a questionnaire issued by the insurance company which the insured must complete. The act of returning the completed proposal form to the insurer will generally constitute the making of an offer to purchase insurance from the insurer and the issue of an insurance policy by the insured will generally act as the acceptance of that offer.

One can only insure something in respect of which one has an insurable interest. In general, a person has an insurable interest in something when they "have some relation to or concern in the subject of the insurance".[54] The application of this rule can become complicated when dealing with artificial persons. For instance, the legal entity of the company has the insurable interest in property owned by the company, not its shareholders. Even a major shareholder will therefore be unable to enter into an effectual contract of insurance relative to the company's property.[55] Similarly, in *Arif v Excess Insurance Group Ltd,*[56] A took out fire insurance in his sole name relative to a hotel. However, the hotel was not owned by A, but by his brother, and it was operated as a hotel business

---

[53] A growing number of insurance contracts are not completed over the telephone. In such cases, the questions which would generally appear on the proposal form will be put to the insured verbally and his answers noted or recorded.
[54] *Lucena v Craufurd* (1806) 2 Bos & PNR 269.
[55] *Macaura v Northern Assurance Co Ltd* [1925] All E.R. 51.
[56] 1986 S.C. 317.

by a partnership comprising of the two brothers. There was a serious fire at the hotel. A claimed under his contract of insurance, but the insurer refused to make payment. The court held that the insurer was entitled to decline the claim: as A did not own the hotel, he could not have an insurable interest.

Insurance contracts are contracts *uberrima fides*: contracts "of the utmost good faith". This means that at the time of entering into the contract of insurance the parties to the contract are each required to disclose to the other "all material facts within their knowledge which the other party does not know or is not deemed to know".[57] This obligation arises even if the other party does not ask for the information. Thus an insured party does not comply with the obligation simply by honestly completing the proposal form: if the form omits to ask something material, the insured is under an obligation to volunteer that information. Someone who lives in a house which is prone to flooding who is looking to purchase insurance against the risk of accidental damage to buildings and contents will therefore be under an obligation to disclose the increased risk of flood, whether the insurer asks about it or not. If he fails to do so, the insurer will be entitled to deny liability. More than this, the insurer will often include clauses in the insurance contract which expand the disclosure obligation yet further. The insured will often be required to warrant that even any non-material facts provided are true. This is a controversial area of the law as it can permit insurers to avoid making payment under the policy on very insubstantial and technical grounds.[58] If one is ever in any doubt about whether a particular fact should be disclosed to an insurer, the only safe course is to make disclosure and to leave it to the insurer to decide if the fact is relevant or not.

An insurer who makes payment under a policy of insurance is entitled to make use of the legal doctrine of subrogation. This means that the insurer is entitled to "stand in the shoes" of the insured and exercise any rights and remedies to which the insured would have been entitled. So if A has a contract of fire insurance with B and A's house is burnt down as a result of the negligence of A's neighbour C, A is entitled to demand payment from B under the insurance policy. B must make payment to A, but is then entitled to claim back from C the money paid out under the contract of insurance.

How do terms find their way into contracts?

4-34   There are three ways in which terms can find their way into a contract. These are by:

---

[57] J. Birds, *Birds' Modern Insurance Law* (4th edn, Sweet and Maxwell), p.101. A fact is material when it is one which a prudent insurer would give consideration to when fixing the premium to be paid for the insurance, or determining whether to offer cover.

[58] For instance, if someone answers a question common in life insurance proposal forms by saying that he attended his doctor's surgery one time in the last year when in fact he miscounted and went twice, the insurers may refuse to make payment under the policy on the basis that information warranted by the insured was false.

- express agreement;
- incorporation from an outside source; and
- implication.

Each will be considered in turn.

Express agreement

The most obvious way in which terms can find their way into a contract is **4–35**
for them to be expressly agreed by the parties. Subject to any restrictions
imposed by parliament,[59] such agreement may be verbal or in writing. As
we shall see below, there are some number of statutory provisions and
rules of common law which restrict the legal enforceability of certain
types of contractual terms. Generally speaking, however, the courts will
enforce terms which have been expressly agreed between the parties.
Where the contract is a written one which the offeree has signed, the
offeree will in general be held to have agreed to the terms of the contract,
even if he has not read or understood them.

The incorporation of terms

Terms may be incorporated into a contract either by reference or through **4–36**
a prior course of dealings.

Incorporation by reference

Instead of producing a lengthy written contract expressly setting out the **4–37**
terms at length, a company which provides goods and services might offer
to enter into contract with a customer on the basis of a brief document
which identifies the goods to be provided, describes the services to be
carried out and the price of the goods and the services, and fixes a date
when the goods will be delivered and the works will start, but which
otherwise refers the customer to standard terms and conditions of business not expressly set out in the document itself but which it states are
available elsewhere: perhaps from a website, or by post, on request from
the company's head office. Is an attempt to incorporate terms in this way
valid? In a series of decisions, the courts have held that terms can by
incorporated into a contract by reference, but only if certain conditions
are met.

Incorporation by signature. Where the reference to the terms is con- **4–38**
tained in a document signed by the offeree at or before the point of
creation of the contract, then the courts have traditionally held (albeit
sometimes with considerable reluctance[60]) that he will be bound by the
terms even if he has neither read them nor had a ready opportunity to do
so. Signature in such cases is considered to act as agreement to the terms.

---

[59] Such as the Requirements of Writing (Scotland) Act 1995, discussed above.
[60] As in *McCutcheon v MacBrayne* 1964 S.C. (HL) 28. See, in particular, the comments of
Lord Devlin at 39–40.

4-39 Incorporation in other cases. Where the reference is not contained in a document signed by the offeree, a number of conditions require to be met before the courts will accept that the conditions have been validly incorporated into the contract:

- The offeror must bring the offeree's attention to the conditions timeously, which is to say, at or before the time contract was concluded. This may be done by way of a notice displayed or in a document given to the offeree. Any attempt to impose terms after the contract has been concluded will be unsuccessful. In *Olley v Marlborough Court Hotel*,[61] Mrs Olley, a guest at the hotel, left her fur coat in a locked store room for safe keeping. The coat was stolen. She sued the hotel, who defended on the basis that, in every room of the hotel, there was a notice stating that the hotel would not be liable in the event that guests' property was stolen. The court held that the hotel's reference to the notice came too late to be effectual: the contract had been concluded at the reception desk.
- If the terms and conditions are contained in a document presented to the offeree, as opposed to a public notice, then the document must be one which the offeree would reasonably have understood to be contractual in nature. Not every piece of paper handed over during the course of a contractual negotiation is of such a nature. Invoices, receipts and acceptance notes for goods supplied have been held in a string of cases not to be contractual in nature, and, while tickets issued in contracts of carriage[62] are viewed as contractual, not all tickets are: some are viewed as mere receipts or vouchers. In *Taylor v Glasgow Corporation*,[63] Mrs Taylor slipped and fell down the stairs when visiting public baths run by the Corporation. In defending the action, the Corporation sought to rely upon a clause printed on the ticket which T had received when paying her admission fee: this notice disclaimed liability for "any loss, injury or damage sustained by persons entering ... this establishment." The court held that this ticket was no more than a voucher—a receipt indicating that the holder had paid the requisite price and was entitled to make use of the facility. As such, it could not impose contractual terms.
- The offeror must in addition take adequate steps to bring the terms to the notice of the offeree. A notice stating that the terms on which services are being provided may be obtained from the offeror's head office will probably be valid if printed on the front of a contractual document, but not if printed on the back.[64] Similarly, a public notice posted up in the offeror's office stating

---

[61] [1949] 1 K.B. 532.
[62] i.e. contracts for the transportation of a person from one place to another. See e.g. *Thomson v London Midland and Scottish Railway Co* [1930] 1 K.B. 41.
[63] 1952 S.C. 440.
[64] *Parker v SE Railway Co* (1877) 2 C.P.D. 416.

the terms on which he does business will be sufficient only if the offeree has been in the office at or before the acceptance of the contract, and then only if it was plainly visible from the parts of the office open to the public.[65]

Key Concepts

In the case of terms incorporated by reference, if the offeree signs a legal document which states on the face of it that the contract is to be governed by terms which can be seen elsewhere, the courts will usually hold that the offeree is bound by those terms. If the offeree has not signed such a document, a number of conditions must be satisfied before a court will hold the terms incorporated into the contract. The terms must be:

- brought to the offeree's attention at or before the conclusion of the contract;
- contained in a document which the offeree would reasonably have understood to be contractual in nature; and
- adequately brought to the attention of the offeree.

Incorporation by a course of dealing

Quite apart from incorporation by reference, it is also possible for terms **4–40** to be incorporated into a contract by a prior course of dealing. For this to occur, the hypothetical objective observer must be in a position to conclude that when these parties do business, they invariably do so on a particular set of terms. There must therefore be a number of prior transactions between the parties and evidence that a set of conditions has been both consistently referred to and accepted (or at least, not objected to).

Terms implied by law

Not all contractual terms find their way into contracts because they have **4–41** been expressly agreed to, or even incorporated into the contract by the parties. Terms may also be implied into the contract. This is necessary because often the parties will say very little about what the terms of the agreement are going to be. Taking the example of a contract of sale, sometimes the only things expressly agreed between the parties are what is being sold, who is selling it to whom and the price. Everything else may be left unsaid. However, this does not mean that such a contract will contain no terms: a whole host of detailed provisions are implied into the contract by the Sale of Goods Act 1979.[66] Terms can also be implied into contracts by the common law. At common law, a term will be implied

---

[65] *McCutcheon v MacBrayne* 1964 S.C. (HL) 28.
[66] The Sale of Goods Act 1979 is discussed in detail in Ch.5, below.

into a contract in the circumstances described in *William Morton & Co v Muir Brothers & Co.*[67]

> "If the condition is such that every reasonable man on the one part would desire for his own protection to stipulate for the condition, and that no reasonable man on the other part would refuse to accede to it, then it is not unnatural that the conditions should be taken for granted in all contracts of the class without the necessity of giving it formal expression."

For example, when a professional person such as a solicitor or an accountant agrees to do some work for a client, a contract for the provision of services is formed under which the law will imply a duty on the part of the professional person to carry out the services in accordance with the degree of care which could reasonably be expected of a member of that profession.

THE LEGAL REGULATION OF CONTRACTUAL TERMS

Introduction

4-42 Contracts are ultimately about agreement. One might therefore think that the purpose of contract law would be to give effect to what the parties have agreed, and often the law does just that. However, the law has also come to recognise that there are situations where it is profoundly unfair to give effect to the terms of the contract as agreed by the parties. This is particularly so in consumer contracts.[68] These are contracts where a consumer of goods or services contracts with an entity whose business it is to provide goods or services. In some cases, the contract may be made between a 17-year-old and one of the largest companies in the world.[69] In such cases, there is clearly a disparity in the sophistication and bargaining power of the two parties. Indeed, on a daily basis, consumers face contract by ultimatum: they will be presented with the company's standard terms contract and told that these are the only terms on which the company does business; the consumer must "take it or leave it".

Exemption clauses

4-43 Sometimes, contracts will contain what are known as exemption clauses. These are clauses by which one party seeks to exclude or limit liability it would otherwise incur to the other. A contractual term stating that a

---

[67] 1907 S.C. 1211 *per* Lord McLaren at 1224.

[68] It also has the potential to occur in other contexts too, such as where a large and sophisticated business organisation enters into a contract on standard terms with a much smaller business.

[69] As when a school-leaver buys an airline ticket from, e.g., British Airways in order to travel to university for the first time. Such contracts have something of the flavour of David and Goliath but—unless the law does something to protect the interests of the consumer—are rather less likely to feature a happy ending.

hotel does not accept liability for the theft of guests' property is an example of an *exclusion* clause. A term stating that in the event of theft, the hotel will not be liable for damages in excess of £100 would be a *limitation* clause. Such clauses have a legitimate place when knowingly entered into by sophisticated business organisations in order to implement informed choices which they have made on how best to allocate risk. However, in other contexts—such as when they are incorporated by signature into a contract by a consumer who has not read, far less understood what he is signing—they have the potential to be grossly unfair.

Common law regulation of unfair contract terms

The common law provided some measure of protection for the unwary by **4–44** imposing rules on the circumstances in which terms could be incorporated into a contract. It also developed a rule which stated that, in the event that an exemption clause was ambiguous, it would be interpreted in the way least favourable to the interests of the party who had imposed the clause upon the other.[70] However, the courts were unwilling to declare unambiguous, properly-incorporated terms unenforceable.[71]

Statutory regulation of unfair contracts

In the middle part of the twentieth century there developed a growing **4–45** awareness that the common law's response was not adequate in itself to address the problem.[72] The Unfair Contract Terms Act was enacted in 1977 in order to control the use of exemption clauses. The Act was followed in due course by the Unfair Terms in Consumer Contracts Regulations 1999, which broaden the scope of the statutory protections beyond exemption clauses. Each will be discussed in turn.

The Unfair Contract Terms Act 1977 (UCTA)

UCTA's primary function is to regulate attempts by businesses to exclude **4–46** or limit their liabilities through the use of exemption clauses. UCTA applies to a broad range of contracts, including contracts for the sale or supply of goods, employment contracts, contracts for the provision of services and contracts permitting persons to enter onto land.[73] However, it should be noted that some significant types of contract are excluded from the Act's ambit. In particular, UCTA does not apply to contracts of insurance, contracts for the sale of land or contracts relative to the formation of dissolution of any form of business organisation.

Section 16 of the UCTA contains two important provisions which apply not just in contracts between businesses and consumers but also in

---

[70] This is known as the *contra proferentem* rule.
[71] See MacQueen and Thomson, para.7.1.
[72] The common law approach has not been abolished, but is now supplemented by the statutory provisions discussed in the paragraphs which follow.
[73] An example of the last-mentioned form of contract is the one by which a football club permits a spectator to enter a stadium to watch a football match.

contracts between businesses. Section 16(1)(a) of UCTA provides that any exemption clause which limits or excludes a business's liability for death or personal injury resulting from its negligence or other breach of duty is void and unenforceable. This is so because Parliament considered that the most abusive use of such clauses was to seek to evade or limit lawful liability for unlawfully causing injury to others. By contrast, s.16(1)(b) of the UCTA states that any other exemption clause which limits or excludes a business's liability for negligence or other breach of duty is enforceable only if it is fair and reasonable for the term to have been included in the contract and for it to be relied upon in the circumstances. Thus, if a business's negligence or breach of duty has not caused someone to be injured or killed but has, for instance, caused property to be lost or damaged, the exemption clause will be ineffectual only if unfair and unreasonable. Among the range of factors which the court will take into account in determining whether the clause is fair and reasonable is the relative strength of the bargaining position of the parties.[74]

Section 17 of UCTA provides a further set of protections for the benefit of (a) consumers entering into contracts with businesses, and (b) businesses forced, due to their poor bargaining power relative to another business, to enter into a contract on another party's standard terms. Section 17 provides that, in such situations, any term of a contract which either allows a party to exclude or restrict liability for breach of contract or permits a party to render no performance or to render a performance substantially different from that which was reasonably expected from the contract will be enforceable only if fair and reasonable. The provisions of s.17 differ from those of s.16 in that they are provided even where (as will often be the case) the breach or different performance of the contract has nothing to do with negligence or fault.[75]

Key Concepts

UCTA is concerned principally with a particular class of unfair terms known as exemption clauses. Its provisions have the potential to apply to most contracts, and:

- render unenforceable exemption clauses which purport to exclude or limit liability for death or personal injury caused as a result of negligence or other breach of duty; and
- state that exemption clauses which exclude or limit liability for other sorts of losses caused as a result of negligence or other

---

[74] UCTA s.24(2) and Sch.2.

[75] As Woolman and Lake note, if a builder fails to complete a job in the time agreed, or if a wedding photographer fails to turn up to the church, they will have breached a contract irrespective of whether or not they have been negligent. The builder may have been delayed by poor weather; the photographer may have been involved in a road traffic accident that was not his fault: Woolman and Lake, para.9.9.

> breach of duty will only be enforceable if they satisfy a fair and reasonable test; and
> - make all exemption clauses contained in consumer or standard-form contracts subject to a fair and reasonable test.

The Unfair Terms in Consumer Contracts Regulations 1999 (UTCCR)

UCTA provides a number of valuable protections, but the Act is rela- **4–47** tively narrow in its scope: there are many terms which have the potential to be unfair, but which are not covered by UCTA. UTCCR provides a more general set of protections.

UTCCR applies to contractual terms in consumer contracts.[76] In broad terms, UTCCR have two main purposes: to encourage the use of plain and intelligible language in written consumer contracts; and to regulate the use in consumer contracts of terms which have not been individually negotiated. The first of these objectives is implemented by reg.7, which provides that businesses must ensure that any written contractual term is expressed in plain, intelligible language, and that if there is any doubt about the meaning of a written term, the interpretation which is most favourable to the consumer shall prevail. The main provision on the regulation of terms which have not been individually negotiated is reg.5. This provides that such a term shall be regarded as unfair if it "causes a significant imbalance in the parties' rights and obligations arising under the contract" to the detriment of the consumer.[77] Any term which has been drafted in advance is deemed to be one which has not been individually negotiated.[78] Schedule 2 to UTCCR contains a lengthy illustrative list of the kind of contractual term likely to be regarded as unfair. As well as the kind of exemption clause already regulated by UCTA, these include clauses which:

- permit the seller or supplier to retain sums paid by the consumer where the latter decides not to conclude or perform the contract; or
- enable the seller or supplier to terminate a contract of indeterminate duration without reasonable notice except where there are serious grounds for doing so; or
- irrevocably bind the consumer to terms with which he had no real opportunity of becoming acquainted before the conclusion of the contract; or
- enable the business to alter the terms of the contract unilaterally without a valid reason which is specified in the contract; or

---

[76] Unlike most of the provisions of UCTA, UTCCR applies to consumer contracts only. Consumer is defined by reg.3 of UTCCR as any natural person acting for purposes which are outside his trade, business or profession.

[77] UCTA reg.5(1).

[78] UCTA reg.5(2).

- exclude or hinder the consumer's right to take legal action or exercise any other legal remedy.

Terms which are found to be unfair shall not be binding on the consumer. However, the rest of the contract shall continue to have legal effect if it is capable of continuing in existence without the unfair term.

An important feature of UTCCR is the appointment of the Director General of the Office of Fair Trading (OFT) as an overseer of the effectiveness of the Regulations and potential "consumer's champion". The Director is obliged by the Regulations to consider complaints about contractual terms which are in general use and, if he considers any of the terms to be unfair, to take court action preventing the continued use of these terms. This is an important innovation. One of the weaknesses of UCTA is that, while as a matter of law it makes certain types of exclusion clause unenforceable, it does not contain a mechanism preventing businesses from purporting to include such clauses in their contracts. Thus consumers in a dispute with a business may see the clause in their contract and, unaware of the existence of UCTA and UTCCR, form the mistaken impression that the clause is binding. The appointment of the OFT to an overseeing role has the potential to "clean up" contracting practice by ensuring that the legal effect of clauses of dubious legality are tested, and unenforceable clauses removed from consumer contracts. The OFT's overseeing role has the potential to change the face of contracting practice in the UK.[79]

Key Concepts

Unlike UCTA, UTCCR provides protection only for the benefit of consumers contracting with businesses. Also unlike UCTA, UTCCR does not focus on exemption clauses but instead seeks to regulate any form of unfairness which may act to the detriment of the consumer. UTCCR:

- provides incentives for businesses to contract in plain and readily understandable language;
- provides that unfair terms not individually negotiated by the parties shall not be binding on the consumer; and
- has the potential to "clean up" commercial organisations' contracting practice by giving the OFT an overseeing role and permitting that body to take court action demanding that organisations stop using unfair terms in their contracts.

---

[79] At time of writing, the OFT is engaged in litigation challenging the fairness of the contractual terms used by banks to permit administrative charges to be levied against their customers. If the OFT is successful in this action, it will result in a substantial rewriting of the majority of the personal banking contracts in current use in the United Kingdom.

DEFECTIVE CONTRACTS

Introduction

As we have already seen, contracts come about when the parties agree to **4-48** enter into a legally binding arrangement between themselves. Sometimes, however, an attempt by the parties to enter into a contract may go wrong in some way. There may be some sort of defect or impediment which makes a contract "void", "voidable" or "legally unenforceable". It is important to appreciate that these expressions are not interchangeable. They mean quite distinct things.

"Void", "voidable" and "unenforceable" explained

A "void contract" is an absolute nullity; it has no legal effect whatsoever. **4-49** Nothing requires to be done to bring a void contract to an end as it never came into being in the first place. Contracts will generally be considered void if they suffer from a fundamental defect, for instance, if one or more of the parties does not have legal capacity to enter into a contract.

A "voidable contract", on the other hand, does come into existence, but suffers from an underlying defect which means that either of the parties can petition the court, asking for it to be "annulled" or "reduced". As we shall see below, a contract will be declared voidable if someone has been tricked into entering it by the provision of false information, or if there is a problem (other than a fundamental problem) with a party's legal capacity. Crucially, however, the right to reduce a contract will be lost if:

- the party seeking to reduce the contract has delayed unreasonably before commencing proceedings to have the contract set aside, or behaves in such a way as to lead the other party to believe that the contract is not going to be challenged; or
- a third party has since innocently acquired rights which it would be unfair for the court to interfere with; or
- *restitutio in integram* can no longer be effected. The law requires that if a contract is going to be reduced, it must be physically possible to put the parties back in the position that they occupied before the contract was entered into. This cannot always be done.

Boyd and Forrest v Glasgow and South West Railway Company
1915 S.C. (HL) 20

BF entered into a contract with GSWRC to build a railway line. BF duly started the job, and proceeded to blast railway cuttings into the countryside, move earth and commence laying the line. Having done so, they discovered that information they had received from GSWRC about the geological characteristics of the area in which they were working was incorrect; the contract was therefore voidable. They attempted to reduce the contract, but the court held that they could not do so. The engineering work which they had carried out could not readily be undone. *Restitutio in integram* was therefore impossible.

An "unenforceable agreement" is different again; here the courts, without giving consideration to whether the contract is void or voidable, simply say that the contract is of a nature that they will not enforce it. Courts will commonly hold contracts unenforceable if the contract is contrary to public policy or pursues an immoral objective.

The distinction between these expressions can have significant consequences. As we have already seen, the right to annul a voidable contract may be lost; void or unenforceable contracts, by contrast, remain void or unenforceable come what may. Another particularly important consequence is seen in the context of contracts for the sale of goods. If a void contract purports to transfer property, no title to that property passes and any subsequent sale or disposal is ineffectual. With a voidable contract, the position would be different. As a voidable contract exists until such time as it is reduced by the court, if property is transferred under a voidable contract that has not yet been set aside then a good title to the property is passed. This in turn means that the person who purchased the property can pass a valid title on to a third party.

Key Concepts

Not all attempts to create a contract will be successful. Defects may emerge which render either a contract or a particular term within a contract void, voidable or unenforceable.

There is legal significance in the distinction between void, voidable or unenforceable contracts. In particular, the right to reduce a voidable contract can be lost in certain circumstances. This issue does not arise with void or unenforceable contracts.

Instances of defects in contracts

Lack of legal capacity

As a matter of law, certain categories of people are not permitted to enter **4–50** into contracts. Such people are said to lack legal capacity to enter into agreements. Any purported contract entered into by a person lacking legal capacity will be void. There are a number of situations where a person will lack legal capacity. Each will be considered in turn.

Non-age

The law seeks to protect the interests of children and young persons by **4–51** providing that before they attain a certain age, they cannot enter into a legally binding contract. There is no automatic cut-off point in place after which an elderly person automatically loses legal capacity, but as we shall see, vulnerable elderly people are protected in other ways.[80] The rules related to non-age in Scotland are contained in the Age of Legal Capacity (Scotland) Act 1991 (ALSCA). The Act divides the young person's capacity to act into three periods, namely:

1. A period from birth to the last day on which a young person is aged 15.
    During this period, a young person is in general deemed to have no capacity to enter into a contract,[81] and any contracts relating to the young person will generally require to be entered into by his or her legal guardian (generally, his or her parents).[82] The only exception to this rule is that a young person may enter into a binding agreement so long as:

    a. it relates to a transaction is of a kind commonly entered into by persons of that age; and
    b. the terms of the transaction are reasonable.[83]

2. A period lasting from the day when the age of 16 is attained until the last day on which a young person is aged 17.
    Upon reaching the age of 16, a person is deemed to be capable of looking after his own legal affairs and therefore attains legal capacity.[84] He or she may therefore enter into binding legal contracts. 16 and 17-year-olds are, however, given the benefit of a statutory protection from prejudicial transactions. If such a person enters into a prejudicial transaction, he is entitled to make an application to the court to have that transaction set aside. The Act defines a "prejudicial transaction" as one which a reasonably prudent adult would not have entered into, and which has caused or is likely to cause substantial prejudice to the

---

[80] See para.4–57.
[81] ALSCA s.1(1)(a).
[82] ALSCA s.5.
[83] ALSCA s.2(1).
[84] ALSCA s.1(1)(b).

young person.[85] Any such application must be presented to the
court before the young person reaches 21 years of age. The Act
also contains a provision which allows an application to be made
to the court to have a transaction made by someone between 16
and 18 ratified by the court.[86] If the court is satisfied that the
transaction is not prejudicial, then it will issue a judgment confirming this. Any transaction so confirmed cannot later be
challenged on the grounds that it was prejudicial.

3.   A period commencing upon the attainment of 18 years of age.
     On one's 18th birthday, one continues to have legal capacity but
     ceases to enjoy the benefit of the protection provided by s.3 of
     the ACLA.[87]

Insanity

4-52 The law also seeks to protect the interests of the insane by stating that
such persons too lack legal capacity; any contracts entered into by such
persons are therefore void.[88] This does not mean that every person suffering to a greater or lesser extent from a mental illness is prevented from
entering into a contract. Before someone will be said to lack mental
capacity as a result of insanity, he must be suffering from a mental illness
or disorder sufficiently severe to mean that he has no understanding of
the nature of the obligations which he is offering to undertake. Procedures exist for the appointment of guardians to look after the interests of
insane persons. As the law is concerned with the mental state of the
person at the time that he entered into the contract, not at other points, it
is believed that someone who suffers from a mental condition the effects
of which come and go may enter into a contract during a lucid interval.
Arguably, the law does not at present do enough to protect the legal
interests of people who suffer from mental illnesses which produce
symptoms falling short of the present test for insanity.[89]

---

[85] ALCSA s.3. Any such application must be presented to the court before the young
person reaches 21 years of age.

[86] ALSCA s.4.

[87] i.e. the court's protection can still be sought in relation to contracts entered into while
one was 16 or 17, but no protection is afforded for contracts entered into from one's 18th
birthday onwards.

[88] As an exception to this general rule, someone providing the necessities of life to an insane
person may recover a reasonable price (which may not necessarily be the contract price,
particularly if the provider is profiteering at the expense of the insane person) for so
doing: Sale of Goods Act 1979 s.3(2).

[89] Bipolar disorder, for instance, can lead to periods of intense excitement during which a
person may, while still aware at some level of what they are doing, act in a disinhibited
way. This may cause such a person to enter into contracts which he would not generally
have wished to enter into.

Intoxication

If someone is so intoxicated by drink or (presumably[90]) drugs that they **4–53** are unaware of the nature of the obligations which they are offering to undertake, then they will lack the capacity to enter into a contract. Any contracts which they purport to enter into whilst in that condition will therefore be void. However, the law will not lightly permit people to escape their contractual obligations by pleading intoxication and if such an argument is to be successful there must be compelling evidence that the contract was entered into in a state of extremely advanced intoxication. In *Pollock v Burns*,[91] P signed a document committing him to pay a sum of money to B in relation to a race-horse which P had bought from him. A dispute arose as to the enforceability of the document and the court was asked to rule on its validity. P led evidence that he had been drinking heavily for days prior to signing the document and that he had no recollection of signing it. However, there was other evidence which showed that although he had been drinking, P was still in a position to converse with B, sign the bill and then to help B put on his coat as he was leaving. The court held that in these circumstances it was not satisfied that P had been utterly intoxicated, and the obligation therefore stood.

Corporations

Corporations such as companies have legal personalities separate from **4–54** those of their members. However, as corporations are persons in only legal, and not a natural sense, they are generally established by documents which set out and determine the extent of their legal powers. At common law, any act on the part of the corporation which goes outside those powers is void. However, these common-law rules have, at least for companies, been somewhat overtaken by statutory provisions which provide at least some measure of protection for persons entering into contractual relations with companies. These are discussed in Ch.16, below.

Improper negotiations and abuse of position

Scots law recognises that sometimes conduct on the part of one of the **4–55** parties unfairly induces the other party to enter into an agreement that they would not otherwise have concluded. It permits such contracts to be challenged in certain circumstances. These are discussed below.

Force and fear

A contract will be rendered null and void if it was entered into in cir- **4–56** cumstances so extreme that a person was entirely unable to exercise free will as a result of his fear of the threat or use of force. In such circumstances, the objective bystander would take the view that there was no

---

[90] The reported cases, almost all of which come from the Victorian era, are concerned with the effects of alcohol rather than illicit or prescription drugs but in principle the rules developed in the one context would appear to be application in the other.
[91] (1875) 2 R. 497.

Business Law in Scotland

real *consensus in idem*. History provides us with some colourful examples
of force and fear. Perhaps the most celebrated is *Earl of Orkney v Vinfra*,[92] in which the Earl took offence at V's refusal to sign a legally binding
document and threatened to stab him through the head if he did not sign.
V duly signed but the Earl's triumph was short-lived; the court held that
the document was null and void. Such practices, while less common in the
21st century, have not necessarily been wholly eradicated from modern
business practice.[93] However, of greater day-to-day relevance today is the
fact that other, lesser threats will be sufficient to have a contract rendered
voidable if the pressure exerted by the threats is sufficient to mean that
the consent was given only reluctantly. In order to establish this, a party
must show that an illegitimate threat has been made which is of such a
nature that the objective bystander would conclude that the victim's
consent was not freely given. The threat may be against the victim or
someone closely connected to him. However, only threats which are
unlawful will be considered to be illegitimate. Threats of physical violence
clearly qualify, but so, too, do threats to spread malicious and untrue
rumours about someone,[94] or a threat to breach a pre-existing contract.
By contrast, a threat to put someone into insolvency in respect of a debt
which is lawfully due is not illegitimate.

Facility and circumvention

4–57 The expression "facility" describes a weakened state of mind. A facile
person continues to have some understanding of his actions, but is sug-
gestible and susceptible to influence. Facility may arise in many ways, for
instance as a result of old age, mental illness short of insanity,[95] or
physical frailty leading a person to be psychologically dependant upon
another.[96] "Facility" need not be a permanent state of mind but can be a
transient condition: someone recovering from the administration of a
general anaesthetic may be facile today but in a more robust frame of
mind tomorrow. "Circumvention" occurs when someone:

- takes dishonest advantage of the other person's facile condition
  and thereby induces him to enter into a contract with him, or
  make a promise; and
- the transaction causes the facile person a loss.

---

[92] (1606) Mor. 16481.
[93] In 2006, seven men were charged with punching and threatening at gunpoint a director of
Queens Park Rangers FC in an alleged attempt to force him to sign a document
resigning as a director, albeit the charges were not established and all were acquitted after
trial: see *http://news.bbc.co.uk/1/hi/england/london/5124508.stm* [Accessed April 15,
2008].
[94] Such threats constitute the delict of defamation.
[95] As we have already seen, if someone is insane, he will in any event lack legal capacity on
that ground.
[96] See e.g. *Horne and Another v Whyte* [2005] C.S.O.H. 115.

A contract entered into as a result of facility and circumvention is voidable.

Undue influence

A contract may be attacked on the basis of undue influence where: **4–58**

- the person alleged to have exercised an undue influence is in a relationship of trust or influence over the other party; and
- the party in that position of trust or influence abuses it and thereby induces the other party to enter into an arrangement to the detriment of the trusting party.

When established, the plea of undue influence permits a party to reduce a contract. In practice, undue influence arises most commonly in relationships of parent and child,[97] between spouses,[98] or as between professional persons and their clients.[99]

Error

Parties sometimes purport to enter into a contract whilst one or more of **4–59** them are labouring under some kind of misapprehension. In such cases, the courts have to steer an awkward course between the competing interests of the parties. Considerations of fairness might lead the court to wish to release the party who has erred from the (possibly very onerous) consequences of its mistake. By contrast, it would be undesirable if large numbers of contracts were capable of being challenged on the basis that one of the parties did not fully understand what it was doing when it entered into it: considerations of certainty, therefore, would make the courts lean towards upholding the contract notwithstanding the error. Against this background, the law has sought (and sometimes struggled[100]) to evolve a system of categorisation whereby different treatment is offered to different types of error. The major categories are:

- error of law;
- uninduced error as to fact;
- induced error as to fact (misrepresentation).

We shall discuss the major categories below.

---

[97] See e.g. *Forbes v Forbes' Trs*, 1957 S.C. 325.
[98] See e.g. *Royal Bank of Scotland plc v Etridge (No.2)* [2002] 2 A.C. 773.
[99] See e.g. *Anstruther v Wilkie* (1856) 18 D. 405.
[100] The courts have found it difficult to lay down a coherent and consistent set of rules relative to error. Some of the elderly cases on this area have to be treated with great care.

Error of law

4–60 Where the error which has been made is one which relates to the legal effect of the contract, then, at least from the standpoint of the law of contract,[101] the error will have no legal effect. One is presumed to know the law of the land: ignorance of the law is no excuse.

Uninduced error of fact

4–61 The position concerning error of fact is far more complicated that that relating to errors of law. Errors of fact are sub-categorised into a variety of different classes of error. The major sub-categories are:

- error in expression;
- unilateral uninduced error of intention;
- bilateral uninduced error of intention.

Each produces different legal consequences and each shall be discussed in turn.

4–62 Error in expression. An error in expression occurs when the parties to a verbal agreement then attempt to put that agreement into writing, but make an error in recording the terms of the contract. The Law Reform (Miscellaneous Provisions) (Scotland) Act 1985 introduced a process known as rectification. This empowers the court to correct any document which was intended to express or give effect to an agreement but which failed to express accurately the common intention of the parties.[102]

4–63 Unilateral, uninduced error in intention. An error which is:

- made by only one of the parties; and
- not made because of false statements made by or on behalf of the other party; and
- related to facts, not law

may be categorised a unilateral, uninduced error in intention. The courts will normally consider such an error to be a legal irrelevance, and will decline to reduce a contract entered into as a result of this kind of mistake, even if it goes to the essentials of the contract.[103] So if a man seeks to impress his wife by purchasing two seats for her favourite show off e-Bay at an inflated price, mistakenly believing the "Grand Circle" to contain the best seats in the house when it in fact contains very poor views and

---

[101] In some limited circumstances, money which has been paid as a result of an error as to the law can be recovered, but under the law of unjustified enrichment. For a discussion of this area of the law, see H. MacQueen, *Unjustified Enrichment* (Law Basics series, W. Green, Edinburgh, 2004).

[102] The Law Reform (Miscellaneous Provisions) (Scotland) Act 1985 s.8.

[103] For a discussion on the essentials of the contract, see para.4–64, below.

worse leg-room, he cannot take any action to reduce the contract.[104] There is some authority for the proposition that a contract entered into as a result of a unilateral uninduced error can be reduced where the party not making the error is aware of the party's mistake and deliberately took advantage of it in order to "snap up a bargain",[105] but the existence and scope of this possible exception to the rule has not been authoritatively settled and therefore remains unclear.

Bilateral, uninduced error in intention. Bilateral errors involve both **4–64** parties (or, where there are more than two parties, all parties) to the contract. Bilateral errors are frequently sub-categorised as "common" or "mutual" errors and, although little turns on the distinction, we will follow this practice here.

An error is "common" when all parties to the contract make the same mistake. For instance, in a contract for the sale of a painting, if both parties think the painting continues to be in existence whereas in fact it was destroyed by a fire moments before the contract came into existence, that would be a case of a common error.[106] In such a case, if the common error relates to an essential element of the contract, the contract will be void. It is likely that any other common error has no effect upon the validity of the contract.[107] What, then, is an essential error? An error is essential if it goes to the root of the contract: in other words, if it can be demonstrated that, were it not for the error, one or more of the parties would have declined to enter into the contract.[108]

A bilateral error is described as "mutual" when each party misunderstands the other party's intentions. If this occurs in relation to an essential element of the contract, then, while the parties may believe that their negotiations have led them to agreement, in reality, they are at cross-purposes in relation to a matter which goes to the heart of the contract. As a result, no consensus in idem has ever been achieved and the contract has not come into existence. We have already seen one example of such a case when discussing *consensus*;[109] another example is *Stuart & Co v Kennedy*,[110] in which a quantity of stone was being sold at a price "per foot". However, the prospective purchaser was offering to buying by the linear foot, while the seller was offering to sell by the square foot. The price per square foot was more than double the price per linear foot. It was held that there was no consensus between the parties. It is likely that a mutual error which does not relate to the essentials of the contract will have no effect upon the validity of the contract.

---

[104] This example is taken from bitter personal experience.
[105] *Steuart's Trs v Hart* (1875) 3 R. 192.
[106] This example was given by Woolman and Lake at para.6.21.
[107] (1885) 13 R. 225.
[108] *Menzies v Menzies* (1893) 20 R. (HL) 108.
[109] *Mathieson Gee v Quigley*, discussed at para.4–13, above.
[110] (1885) 13 R. 221.

Induced errors as to fact (misrepresentation)

4–65 The law of misrepresentation developed significantly throughout the 20th century and most cases on error are now pursued on this ground. A misrepresentation is a misleading statement made by one person to another. A person who is induced to enter into a contract as a result of a misrepresentation will be entitled to some manner of legal remedy if:

- the statement complained of was made by the other contracting party or someone acting on his behalf;[111] and
- the misrepresentation was not trivial and was made in a context where the objective observer would conclude it was intended to be a serious statement of fact.

The precise nature of the remedy available will depend upon two further factors:

- the degree of blameworthiness attaching to which the person who made it: in other words, did they mislead the other party fraudulently, negligently or innocently?; and
- the significance of the misrepresentation: does it relate to a material matter, or to an essential one?[112]

4–66 Fraudulent misrepresentation. A fraudulent misrepresentation is one which is made with a deliberate intention to deceive.[113] In practice, it is difficult to prove a dishonest intent in all but the most extreme of circumstances and cases of fraudulent misrepresentation are relatively rare. Where fraud is established, the legal effect of the misrepresentation will depend upon whether the misrepresentation relates to an essential or merely a material matter.[114] If the misrepresentation induces an essential error, the contract will be void. If the misrepresentation brings about a material error, the contract will be voidable. In both cases, damages will in addition be available to the party to whom the misrepresentation was made if it can prove it has suffered a loss as a result of the misrepresentation.

4–67 Negligent misrepresentation. A negligent misrepresentation occurs when a person makes a misleading statement having failed to take reasonable care to ensure its accuracy. Such misrepresentations only give rise to legal consequences if the misrepresenter owes a "duty of care"[115] to the

---

[111] Thus if I enter into a mortgage agreement with a particular bank because a friend says that they have a mortgage with that bank because they offer the best rates available, when in fact a mortgage with that bank is offered only on very expensive terms, my contract with the bank is not capable of being annulled.

[112] Essential error is discussed at para.4–64, above.

[113] *Derry v Peek* (1889) 44 App. Cas. 337.

[114] As we have already seen, if the misrepresentation relates only to a trivial matter, it is of no legal significance and no remedy is available at all.

[115] The legal concept of "duty of care" is discussed in greater detail in Ch.10, below.

party to whom the misrepresentation is made; this criterion will usually be established when the parties are engaged in contractual negotiations.[116] If a negligent misrepresentation induces an essential error, the contract will be void. If it brings about a material error, the contract will be voidable. In both cases, damages will in addition be available to the party to whom the misrepresentation was made if it can prove it has suffered a loss as a result.[117]

Innocent misrepresentation. A statement will be considered an inno- 4-68 cent misrepresentation if its maker honestly but mistakenly believed it to be true, and if he made the statement in circumstances which would not entitle the court to conclude he had been negligent in saying what he did. Innocent misrepresentations render a contract voidable, but damages are never available where a misrepresentation is innocent. Thus the only remedy available to a person who enters into a contract as a result of an innocent misrepresentation is to reduce the contract and, as we have already seen, the right to reduce a contract can in certain circumstances be lost.

Key Concepts

Parties sometimes enter into contracts on the basis of some kind of misapprehension (error). The legal effect of an error on a contract depends upon a combination of factors: the nature of the error, its legal significance, and whether it was made by the party themselves or as a result of a misrepresentation by the other party. Taking all these factors together we can say:

No remedy is given to a party who enters into a contract as a result of an error of law. "Ignorance of the law is no excuse."

The category of uninduced errors of fact can be sub-divided further into:

- **errors of expression**. Here the parties may take a court action to correct a document which incorrectly records the terms of a verbal agreement;
- **unilateral uninduced error of intention**. Such errors are generally irrelevant; i.e. the law generally provides no legal remedy; and
- **bilateral uninduced error of intention**. These render a contract void on the basis of dissensus if made in relation to an essential term of the contract. In other circumstances their effect is not wholly clear, but it is believed that other such errors will have no effect upon the validity of the contract.

---

[116] *Esso Petroleum Co v Mardon* [1976] Q.B. 801.
[117] Law Reform (Miscellaneous Provisions) (Scotland) Act 1985 s.10.

The category of misrepresentation, or induced errors of fact, is sub-categorised as follows:

- Fraudulent misrepresentation. This is a misrepresentation made with the deliberate intention to deceive. If this induces an essential error, the contact is void; if the error is only material, the contract will be voidable. In addition, damages are also recoverable to compensate for any loss suffered.
- Negligent misrepresentation. As in the case of fraud, if this induces an essential error, the contact is void; if the error is only material, the contract will be voidable. In addition, since the enactment of legislation in 1985, damages are also recoverable to compensate for any loss suffered.
- Innocent misrepresentation. This arises when incorrect information is passed to the offeree by the offeror in circumstances where the offeror cannot be blamed for the inaccuracy. Such a misrepresentation renders a contract made in reliance upon it voidable, but damages are not recoverable.

Pacta Illicita
Introduction

4-69 There are certain contracts which the courts will not enforce, even if the parties themselves intend them to be enforceable. At common law, at least, such contracts are not void or voidable; the courts simply take the view that they will not allow the parties to enforce them.[118] These contracts are known by the latin expression *pacta illicita*. The direct translation of this expression is "illegal contracts" but as we shall see in practice the term is used more broadly than this would suggest: the term encompasses not just contracts to carry out unlawful acts, but also contracts which would be contrary to the public interest, possibly on the grounds that the contract promotes immorality or is an unjustifiable restraint of free trade. The principal examples of *pacta illicita* are outlined below.

Contracts to commit crimes

4-70 The clearest example of *pacta illicita* is an agreement to commit a crime. An agreement to carry out a murder entered into between a mafia boss and a contract killer will not be enforceable in the courts; nor will a contract for the purchase of cocaine entered into between a drug user and his dealer. For the very obvious reason that to pursue a claim under such a contract would necessarily involve publicly confessing that one has at the very least engaged in a criminal conspiracy, such cases very rarely appear before the courts.

---

[118] The position can be different in the case of statutory *pacta illicita*: see para.4-74, below.

Contracts to commit delicts

Contravening the criminal law is not the only way one can commit a legal 4–71
wrong. The commission of a delict, too, is unlawful.[119] A contract
whereby the parties agree that one of them will breach the law of delict is
therefore also *pactum illicitum*. Examples might be if the parties agreed to
commit the delict of trespass, or conspired to induce the customers of a
trade competitor to breach existing contracts with that competitor and
instead pass their business to the conspirators.

Contracts which promote immorality

The court will not give effect to agreements which promote or further 4–72
immoral behaviour. A contract for the provision of sexual services by
way of prostitution, for instance, will not be enforceable. In *Hamilton v
Main*,[120] H granted a bill of exchange—essentially a cheque—for £60 to
M, an inn-keeper, in order to pay for the drink consumed by him and the
hire of a prostitute provided by M during what appears to have been a
rather boisterous stay at M's inn.[121] The court held that the bill of
exchange was not enforceable in full: M was entitled to charge a reasonable price for the alcohol which had been consumed, but could not
receive payment for the services of the prostitute.

Contracts which are contrary to public policy

The courts will also decline to enforce any contract which is contrary to 4–73
public policy. Numerous contracts have been declared contrary to public
policy, for example contracts to perpetrate a fraud against a court.[122] For
a long time *sponsiones ludicrae* – contracts relating to gambling—were
also considered to be contrary to public policy. However, the rule against
such contracts was abolished when the law relating to gambling was
modernised in 2005.[123] Gambling agreements now are therefore generally
legally enforceable. Attempts to unjustifiably interfere with free trade are
also, strictly speaking, examples of contracts which are unenforceable
because they are contrary to public policy but these are of such great
practical importance that they deserve to be given separate treatment.
They are discussed at paras 4–75 to 4–77, below.

Statutory pacta illicita

Parliament may declare by statute that certain types of contract, or 4–74
certain terms within a contract, are illegal. Sometimes parliament will
state that such terms or contracts are unenforceable; sometimes it will

---

[119] The law of delict is discussed in some detail in Ch.10, below.
[120] (1823) 2 S. 356.
[121] According to the case report, during the seven days that M and his lady friend lodged at
the inn, they between them consumed "113 bottles of port and madeira wine, besides a
large quantity of spirituous and malt liqueurs".
[122] *Walker v Walker* 1911 S.C. 163.
[123] Gambling Act 2005 s.334.

state that they are "null" or "void". We have already seen an example of such a provision when discussing s.16(1) of the Unfair Contract Terms Act 1977, which makes clauses which purport to exclude liability for death or personal injury as a result of negligence, void.[124]

Contracts and contractual terms in restraint of free trade

4–75 The courts are, in general, hostile to contracts which restrict one of the party's ability to work to earn a living, or otherwise act as a restraint upon free trade. This is because, in this country, at least, there is believed to be a very strong public interest in free trade. We will examine the court's approach to two particular types of contract which have the effect of restricting free trade: restrictive covenants and *solus* agreements.

4–76 **Restrictive covenants.** A restrictive covenant is a term by which one party to the contract agrees that for a period of time he will refrain from doing certain things which would involve him commercially competing with the other party. Restrictive covenants are commonly inserted into contracts for the sale of a business or contracts of employment. In the context of the sale of a business, the seller of the business might enter into a covenant in something like the following terms:

> "Seller hereby undertakes and covenants not to set up any business within [X] miles of [the location of the business sold] for a period of [Y] years from the date hereof."

A restrictive covenant in an employment contract intended to prevent the employee from working for a trade competitor might look something like this:

> "Employee hereby undertakes and agrees that he will not accept any work, whether as an employee, contractor or in any other manner whatever, for a business which is:
>
> (a) to any extent whatever a competitor of Employer; and
> (b) located within [X] miles of [the location of Employee's present place of employment]
>
> for a period of [X] months/years after the date of termination of this agreement."

A contract of employment might alternatively or in addition contain a separate restrictive covenant designed to prevent the employee from undertaking work for the customers of his former employer.

The leading case of *Nordenfelt v Maxim Nordenfelt*[125] provides that a restrictive covenant will be unenforceable unless the person seeking to enforce the restriction can demonstrate that the clause:

---

[124] See para.4–46, above.
[125] [1894] A.C. 535.

- protects a legitimate interest of his. The desire to protect trade secrets is a commonly given example of a legitimate interest.[126] Other examples could be given, but the courts will never consider a desire to avoid fair competition to be legitimate; and
- is reasonable in the circumstances. What is "reasonable" will depend upon a range of factors including the length of the restriction, the geographical area involved and the precise nature of the restriction imposed. The issue of whether the clause was reasonable is determined by considering the facts and state of knowledge of the parties at the time that the contract was entered into, not with the benefit of hindsight; and
- is in the public interest. In practice, when the first two criteria are satisfied, it is most unusual for the courts to hold that the restriction is contrary to the public interest.

The courts apply this test somewhat differently as between restrictive covenants imposed relative to the sale of a business and those imposed in contracts of employment. Each will be discussed separately, below. In the meantime, it should be noted that when assessing the reasonableness of a restrictive covenant, the court will look at the covenant as it stands. The court will not "water down" an unreasonable covenant to the point where it becomes reasonable—they will either enforce the covenant as it stands, or strike it out. So if a restrictive covenant is stated in an agreement to last for five years and to cover a radius of 50 miles from the employer's place of business and the court considers that only a six-month duration relative to a radius of one mile was justified, the covenant will be declared unenforceable.[127] However, if there are a number of separate restrictive covenants within a contract, the court may take the view that some of them are unenforceable while some others are capable of being enforced.[128]

In general, the courts will be rather more accepting of a broad restriction in a contract for the sale of a business than it will be in the context of an employment context. Where someone is selling his business and the purchaser has paid money for the good-will of the business, the purchaser obviously has a strong interest in ensuring that his investment is protected. This is dramatically demonstrated by *Nordenfelt v Maxim Nordenfelt*.[129]

N sold his arms business to a new limited company (MN) for a very significant price. It was agreed that he would act as the new company's Managing Director for five years, and N also entered into a restrictive covenant under which he undertook that, for a 25-year period, he would not "engage except on behalf of the company either directly or indirectly in the trade or business of a manufacturer of

---

[126] See e.g. *Bluebell Apparel v Dickinson*, 1980 S.L.T. 158.
[127] See e.g. *MacFarlane v Dumbarton Steamboat Co Ltd* (1899) 1 F. 993 discussed below.
[128] *Mulvein v Murray*, 1908 S.C. 528.
[129] [1894] A.C. 535.

guns, gun mountings or gunpowder, explosives or ammunition".
The clause therefore had no geographical limit whatever and, if it
was enforceable, effectively meant that N could not engage in the
arms trade anywhere in the world for the rest of his working life. In
due course, N left the new company and started selling guns, in
apparent breach of his covenant. Relying upon the restrictive
covenant, MN took N to court, seeking an order to prevent him
continuing to trade. The House of Lords upheld the covenant. N's
business was a world-wide one—"he had upon his books almost
every monarch in every state of any note in the habitable globe"—
and as he had received a good price for the transfer of his business,
the restraint was reasonable.

However, the court will not always uphold a restriction contained in a
contract for the sale of a business. In *MacFarlane v Dumbarton Steamboat Co Ltd*[130] a restrictive covenant which sought to prevent the seller of
a business which carried goods between Dumbarton and Glasgow from
operating as carriers anywhere within the United Kingdom within 10
years of the date of the sale was struck down. The court held that as the
scope of the business was inherently local, a nationwide restriction was
wholly unreasonable.

As was noted above, the courts will in general be less accepting of a
broad restriction in an employment contract than in one for the sale of a
business. This is so because, while the courts are prepared to order
someone who has sold his business for a large sum of money not to work
in direct competition to the purchaser of that business, it is rather less
willing to prevent employees from earning a living. However, if the
employee has worked in a senior position and has been privy to sensitive
trade secrets and/or has had an opportunity to build up close personal
relationships with the employer's customer base, the courts may be prepared to recognise that the employer has a legitimate interest to protect.[131] Where this is so, a skilfully prepared clause which imposes only the
minimum restrictions necessary to protect the employer's legitimate
interests will be upheld.[132]

4–77 **Solus agreements.** A *solus* agreement is one whereby a seller of goods
agrees to sell only or predominantly the products of a particular supplier.
This restriction is normally granted in exchange for some degree of
financial support from the supplier, typically to offset the start-up costs of
the business, and these arrangements are most commonly seen in the
public house and petrol retail businesses. Like restrictive covenants, *solus*

---

[130] (1899) 1 F. 993.
[131] See e.g. *Dallas MacMillan & Sinclair v Simpson*, 1989 S.L.T. 454; *Prosoft Resources v
Griffiths*, 1999 S.L.T. 1255.
[132] See e.g. *Stewart v Stewart* (1899) 1 F. 1158; *Dallas MacMillan & Sinclair v Simpson*, 1989
S.L.T. 454.

agreements will be declared unenforceable unless the restrictions upon free trade which they impose are reasonable in all the circumstances.[133]

BREACH OF CONTRACT

Introduction

If either party fails without justification to fulfil an obligation it has **4–78** undertaken in the contract, then that party is in breach of contract.[134] The party not in breach is generally referred to as the innocent party.

Breaches of contract can take many forms. By way of example, in a contract for the sale of goods, if the purchaser fails to pay the price on time, he is in breach of contract. If the seller fails to deliver the goods, or if delivers them and they are not of the same quality as was described in the contract, then that too would be a breach of contract.

Some breaches are more significant than others. A significant breach of contract—one which "goes to the root of the contract"[135]—is known as a material breach. Examples of a material breach would be failing to perform one's obligations under a contract at all, or performing them in a seriously defective way, for instance by delivering goods significantly different from what the parties had contracted for: for instance, A orders a new "state of the art" fridge freezer; B delivers a second-hand budget model. Less significant breaches are not material, and may be referred to as "ancillary" or "simple" breaches. The distinction between material breaches and simple breaches is important and has a bearing on the legal remedies for breach of contract which the innocent party may seek from the party in breach. Remedies for breach of contract are discussed at paras 4–80 to 4–94 below.

Key Concept

If either party fails without justification to fulfil an obligation it has undertaken in the contract, that party is in breach of contract. Particularly significant breaches—material breaches—give the innocent party a greater range of legal remedies than less significant breaches of contract.

---

[133] *Petrofina (Great Britain) Ltd v Martin* [1966] Ch. 146.
[134] The best example of a situation where a party is justified in not carrying out an obligation under the contract is where the other party has itself already failed to carry out one or more of its obligations under the contract. This topic will be discussed further under the heading of retention, at para.4–83, below.
[135] *Wade v Waldron*, 1909 S.C. 571, *per* the Lord President (Dunedin) at 576.

Anticipatory breach

4–79 A type of breach of contract which requires particular consideration is anticipatory breach (sometimes known as repudiation). This occurs when the party who is due to make performance under a contract informs the innocent party that he is not going to fulfil his side of the bargain. An innocent party faced with such a declaration from the repudiating party may elect to do one of three things:

- the innocent party is entitled to take the other party's statement at face value, accept that the contract is not going to be performed, declare the repudiating party in material breach of contract, rescind the contract[136] and, always assuming that the repudiating party's decision not to perform has caused the innocent party a loss, bring a court action for damages; or
- the innocent party may decide to simply wait for the time for performance to come around. If the repudiating party decides, on reflection, to go ahead and carry out its obligations under the contract, there is no breach. However, if the repudiating party fails to perform its obligations at the appointed time, the innocent party is then entitled to declare a material breach, rescind and sue for damages; or
- if the innocent party is in a position to carry out its side of the bargain without any further co-operation from the repudiating party, it can choose to ignore the repudiation, carry out its obligations under the contract, and demand payment of the price under the contract.[137]

Note, however, that the third option will only rarely be open to the innocent party, as in the usual course of events the innocent party will not be able to carry out its obligations without at least some measure of co-operation from the repudiating party.[138] Consider the following examples:

- A agrees to buy a television from B with delivery to be in a week's time.
- C agrees to fit a kitchen in D's house a month from now.

Neither A, B, C or D will be able to unilaterally carry out their side of the bargain in the event that the other party repudiates the contract. A cannot physically get ahold of the TV without B's co-operation; similarly

---

[136] Rescission is discussed at para.4–82, below.

[137] *White and Carter (Councils) Ltd v McGregor*, 1962 S.C. (HL) 1.

[138] In *White and Carter (Councils)*, the facts were unusual. The pursuer was an advertising agency. It entered into a contract with the defender to post certain advertisements on his behalf. The defender changed his mind almost immediately after concluding the contract, and repudiated. The pursuers refused to accept his repudiation and, as they required no assistance from the defender in order to post the advertisements up around the town, went ahead and carried out their obligations under the contract. They were held to be entitled to recover the full contract price.

B cannot physically compel A to take delivery of the TV if A refuses to; C cannot get into D's house to carry out the work unless D unlocks the door; and D cannot physically make C carry out the work against C's will.

Remedies for breach of contract

Where a contract has been breached, the innocent party will be able to **4–80** pursue one or more remedies against the party who has breached the contract.

Self-help remedies

Self-help (sometimes called "defensive") remedies are ones which the **4–81** innocent party is entitled to take without having to have recourse to the courts. These remedies are available only in the case of material breach. Only the courts can provide remedies for simple breaches of contract. The principal self-help remedies are discussed below.

Rescission

Rescission occurs when the innocent party, faced with a material breach **4–82** by the other party to the contract, decides not to continue with the contract and brings it to an end (rescinds it). A person who buys a new car which is found to be suffering from significant defects is entitled to rescind the contract and demand the repayment of the purchase price.[139] This is often the most powerful remedy available to the innocent party and, if the innocent party suffers a loss which is not adequately compensated by rescission alone, he will in addition be entitled to sue for damages.

Retention

Retention is where the innocent party withholds payment or performance **4–83** of its obligations until the party in breach performs its obligations under the contract. A "rent-strike" is a good example of retention. If a landlord permits a property let to a tenant under a contract of lease to fall into a dilapidated state, the tenant may choose to withhold payment of a proportion of the rent until such time as the landlord effects the necessary repairs. The remedy is only partial, in the sense that the innocent party continues to be under a legal liability to carry out its obligations once the party in breach performs its obligations.[140] It can nevertheless be a very useful way of encouraging the breaching party to remedy its breach.

---

[139] *Lamara v Capital Bank Plc* [2006] C.S.I.H. 49. If the defects are not significant but trivial then rescission is not available as the breach will not be material.

[140] i.e. in the example given, the tenant will have to pay the arrears of rent to the landlord once the property has been adequately repaired.

Lien

4-84 When an innocent party happens to have lawfully within its possession goods or documents belonging to the party in breach, it may retain possession of that property (exercise a lien over it) until the party in breach performs its obligations under the contract. Solicitors who are owed money by a client can generally refuse to deliver to the client any legal documents which they hold on his behalf until such time as they are paid. Similarly, mechanics who have carried out repairs upon a car or jewellers who have carried out repairs on a customer's property are entitled to decline to return the items until their bill is paid.

Judicial remedies

4-85 Judicial remedies are available only by order of the court. The principal judicial remedies are discussed below.

Action for debt

4-86 One of the most commonly encountered breaches of contract is a failure to pay money due under the contract. The classic example of this concerns the purchase of goods[141] on credit terms. The purchaser buys goods which are delivered; the contract states that the purchaser has a period of, say, 30 days in which to pay; the purchaser does not make payment. Upon the expiry of the period of credit, the purchaser is in breach of contract and the seller may raise a court action demanding payment of the purchase price.

Specific implement

4-87 Conceptually, specific implement is similar to an action for debt in so far as the innocent party raises a court action demanding that the party in breach carries through a contractual obligation. The difference between the two remedies is that the specific implement concerns situations arising where "a positive act of performance other than the payment of money is sought from the contract breaker".[142] Perhaps the classic example of specific implement is an action for delivery of an item bought but not yet delivered.

Parties are not always entitled to demand specific implement. In particular, the courts will not grant a decree of specific implement if:

- performance is impossible, perhaps because the subject matter of the contract has been stolen or accidentally destroyed; or
- the insistence upon specific implement would cause the party in breach hardship or loss out of all proportion to the benefit which would accrue to the innocent party; or

[141] The same principle is equally applicable to contracts for the provision of services.
[142] MacQueen and Thomson, para.6.6.

- the subject matter of the contract is of no particular significance and damages would provide adequate compensation. This would be the case, for example, where the seller of readily available, mass-produced consumer goods such as a TV set fails to deliver the goods contracted for. However, this rule would not prevent someone from seeking delivery of a rare or unusual item such as an antique, a work of art or a specially commissioned item of furniture; or
- the contract involves a significant degree of personal relationship. Contracts of employment and partnership fall into this category. If an employee walks out on a contract of employment without giving the notice period required by the contract, the courts will not insist that he or she returns to their place of work to see the contract out.

The fact that the court will not allow specific implement in these circumstances does not mean that someone can just breach their contract and "get away with it". Other remedies—for instance, damages—will continue to be available to the innocent party.

Interdict

An interdict is essentially the converse of a decree for specific implement. **4–88** Whereas a decree of specific implement is a judicial demand that someone does something, an interdict is an order not to do something. Interdicts are used to prevent the occurrence of legal wrongs which are about to be committed, or to bring an end to ongoing legal wrongs. In the contractual context, interdict is most commonly used in an attempt to prevent or stop parties from breaching restrictive covenants.[143]

Damages

Actions for the payment of damages rank along with actions for the **4–89** recovery of debt as the most commonly utilised judicial remedies for breach of contract. When an innocent party raises an action for damages against the party in breach, he in effect asks the court to award a sum of money in order payable by the party in breach in order to make good the losses suffered by the innocent party as a result of the breach. Depending on the circumstances of the breach, damages may be:

- available in conjunction with another remedy (for instance, an innocent party may rescind and demand damages, or seek interdict and damages); or
- pursued as an alternative to another remedy (an innocent party unsure if she is as a matter of law entitled to specific implement may demand that remedy which failing, damages); or
- the only remedy available.

---

[143] For a discussion on restrictive covenants, see para.4–76, above.

4–90 The compensatory nature of damages. In Scots law, at least, the purpose of damages is invariably to compensate the innocent party for losses suffered as a result of the breach.[144] The purpose is not to punish the party who is in breach. As a result, the damages awarded by the court are intended to put the innocent party back in the position that he or she would have been in, had the breach not occurred. However, only certain types of losses are recognised as legally recoverable. In general, damages are available only to compensate personal injuries, damage to property and economic losses. In a standard commercial contract, the courts will not award damages for any hurt feelings, annoyance or distress occasioned by the breach of contract.[145]

4–91 The requirement of causation. Damages are only recoverable for loss which can be proved to have been caused by the breach of contract. In other words, the person claiming damages must be able to link the breach of contract complained about to the loss suffered. If, while a building is being renovated, a houses collapses after a builder knocks down an internal wall which he had not been asked to demolish, the owner cannot sue the builder *just because* he breached the terms of his contract. The home owner must be able to prove on the balance of probabilities that the building fell down as a direct result of the builder's breach of contract.

4–92 The duty to mitigate loss. When a contract is breached, the innocent party is, in general, under a legal obligation to take steps to mitigate his or her loss.[146] However, this is a relatively "soft" duty: the innocent party is not under an obligation to take all steps which could conceivably be taken to mitigate his or her loss. The obligation is to take reasonable steps only. Thus the innocent party will not be expected to incur substantial expenses or take large commercial risks in order to mitigate his or her loss, but where the innocent party does incur the expenses associated with taking appropriate steps to re-advertise goods or services refused by the party in breach, such expenses are recoverable.

4–93 Remoteness of loss. A further limitation which the law places on the damages that can be recovered by the innocent party is that damages will not be awarded for any loss which is "too remote". The classic statement of remoteness is found in the English case of *Hadley v Baxendale*.[147] Here, it was held that damages payable under contract:

---

[144] This is not the case in every legal system. Many American legal systems, for example, permit an innocent party to seek punitive damages when the breach is a particularly flagrant or disgraceful one. In these cases, the party in breach is made to pay significantly more than the innocent party lost, as a deterrent and a punishment.
[145] However, in contracts which are essentially about relaxation or enjoyment rather than commerce, this rule will not apply: *Fairley v Skinner* [2001] 3 W.L.R. 899. The courts have therefore held that damages for distress, annoyance and hurt feelings are available when contracts for the provision of holidays or wedding services are breached.
[146] The rule in *White and Carter (Councils) Ltd v McGregor* 1962 S.C. (HL) 1, discussed at para.4–79, above, provides an exception to this rule.
[147] (1854) 9 Exch. 341.

"should be such as may fairly and reasonably be considered as either arising naturally ie according to the usual cause of things, from such breach of contract itself or such as may reasonably supposed to have been in the contemplation of both parties at the time they made the contract as the probable result of the breach."

Thus damages are recoverable for losses which either arise naturally from the breach, or for losses which, while not normally arising from breaches of this type, can in the particular circumstances of a given case be seen to have been in the contemplation of the parties as reasonably likely. The Scottish case of *Balfour Beatty Construction v Scottish Power plc*[148] provides a good example of the test in operation.

Balfour Beatty Construction v Scottish Power plc
1994 S.C. (HL) 20

BB won a tender to build a length of road using concrete. BB operated a work-site next to the road at which preparatory construction works were carried out, and entered into a contract with SP for the provision of electricity to the site. BB needed to build a concrete "flyover" bridge to carry part of the road. In order to be structurally sound, the flyover needed to be created in one continuous pour of concrete. This is turn required an uninterrupted electricity supply. However, the electricity supply failed during the course of the pour and as a result the first attempt at building the flyover had to be demolished and reconstructed at significant cost. BB sued SP for damages for breach of contract. SP defended on the basis that while they had been in breach, they could not be expected to forsee the unusually severe consequences of failing to maintain the power supply. The House of Lords held that they were not liable for this loss. The consequences did not naturally flow from the failure of an electricity supply, and SP had not at the time of entering into the contract been made aware that this damage would occur if the supply were interrupted, so it could not be said that it was within BB's contemplation at the time of entering into the contract.

Liquidate damages. A liquidate damages clause is one which attempts **4–94** to set out at the start of the parties' contractual relationship the level of damages which will be paid upon the occurrence of a specified type of breach of contract. Such clauses are often used in, for example, the construction or engineering industry to determine the amount of damages which will be payable to the innocent party if the contract is not completed on time.

The courts will enforce a liquidate damages clause if they are satisfied

---

[148] 1994 S.C. (HL) 20.

that the clause represented a genuine and reasonable pre-estimate of the innocent party's loss.[149] However, because, as was noted above, the Scottish courts view damages as essentially compensatory in nature, the courts will not enforce a liquidate damages clause if it is a penalty. In assessing whether a clause is a penalty, the courts will have regard to the true nature of the clause, not the label attached to it by the parties.[150] It is therefore quite possible that a clause which the parties describe as a "penalty clause" will be enforced, and that a clause described by the parties as a "liquidate damages clause" will to be ruled unenforceable. The courts will use a number of tests in order to ascertain the true nature of the clause. These were set out in *Dunlop Pneumatic Tyre Co v New Grange Motor Co*[151] as follows:

- A clause will be held to be a penalty if the amount stipulated to be paid is "extravagant and unconscionable".
- A clause will be penal if the breach consists only in not paying a sum of money, and the clause stipulates for a sum greater than the sum which was originally due to be paid.
- A clause is presumed penal when a single lump sum is made payable by way of compensation on the occurrence of one or more or all of several events, some of which may occasion serious damage but others of which are of little significance.
- A clause will not be penal simply because the consequences of the breach cannot be easily ascertained. Indeed, the courts accept that "that is just the situation when it is probable that pre-estimated damage was the true bargain between the parties".

WHO MAY SUE WHEN A CONTRACT IS BREACHED?

The general rule: privity of contract

4–95 Contracts create legal relations between the parties to the contract, not between those parties and the world at large. This concept is sometimes described as the doctrine of privity of contract. In general, therefore, only a party to the contract may sue or be sued in the event of a breach.[152] We can illustrate this point by way of example. Suppose A, a supplier of computer processors, enters into a contract with B, one of the world's largest computer manufacturers, to supply components at a fraction of the normal price. If the contract is honoured, it will enable B to pass on a significant saving to customers all over the world. However, in the event, A breaches the contract and fails to supply the processors. B can sue A for A's breach of contract. However, the many thousands of consumers who, instead of being able to buy computers at a reduced price, are going

---

[149] *Dunlop Pneumatic Tyre Co v New Grange Motor Co* (1915) A.C. 79.
[150] *Lord Elphinstone v The Monkland Iron and Coal Co Ltd* (1883) 13 R. (HL) 98.
[151] (1915) A.C. 79 at 86.
[152] *Finnie v Glasgow and South West Rly Co* (1857) 20 D. (HL) 2.

to have to pay the full price for them are unable to sue, as they were not party to the contract between A and B.

An exception to the rule: *jus quaesitum tertio*

As an exception to the rule that only parties to the contract may sue or be **4–96** sued in the event of a breach, Scots law will permit third parties (i.e. someone not party to the contract) to acquire the right to enforce the contract if certain qualifying criteria are satisfied. The law does this because, occasionally, parties will enter into a contract which is not for their own purposes, but for the benefit of a third party (i.e. someone who is not party to the contract). When this occurs, the courts will give effect to the intentions of the parties. Enforceable third party rights are known by the latin expression, *jus quaesitum tertio*.

Two very important points need to be recognised in relation to *jus quaesitum tertio*:

- The courts will only permit the parties to a contract to convey a *benefit* upon a third party. *Jus quaesitum tertio* cannot be used to impose a *burden* upon it. Thus parties A and B may between them agree that A is going to pay B to carry out work for C's benefit, and if B is duly paid by A and does not carry out the work, then C may sue him. However, A and B cannot agree that B will carry out work for A's benefit and C will pay.
- The courts will only recognise a *jus quaesitum tertio* if it is clear that the contracting parties intended to be firmly bound by their agreement. If it appears to the court that the contracting parties wished to be in a position to change their minds about the arrangement, then no *jus quaesitum tertio* will come into existence. The seriousness of the parties' intent will be confirmed by their carrying out actions such as, for example, delivering a copy of the contract to the third party, so it can see the nature of the right for itself, or publicly registering the document.

An example of *jus quaesitum tertio* in operation may be found in the case of *Mortons Trustees v The Aged Christian Friends Society of Scotland*.[153] Here, M wished to make a donation to a charity. However, the situation was complicated by the fact that the charity had not yet legally come into existence. M therefore entered into a contract with the members of a provisional committee involved in setting up the charity. The contract clearly stated that M would pay annual instalments to the charitable society for a period of 10 years. During M's lifetime, the obligation was honoured. However, when M died, the trustees on her estate refused to continue to make the payment. The charity successfully sued for payment: in the circumstances, it enjoyed a clear *jus quaesistum tertio*.

---

[153] (1899) 2 F. 82.

EXTINCTION OF CONTRACTUAL OBLIGATIONS

Introduction

4-97 Contractual obligations do not last for ever. It would clearly be non-sensical, 10 years after the day when a newsagent sold you a newspaper, to say that the two of you are in a contractual relationship relative to that sale. Contractual obligations come to an end in a number of ways. We shall consider the most common instances below

Performance

4-98 One of the most commonplace ways in which a contractual relationship will come to an end is upon performance. Once the obligations on both sides of the contract have been performed in full, the contract's purpose is at an end and it simply "withers away" into legal nothingness. So if A takes out a contract of loan with B in order to buy a car, the contract will ordinarily come to an end when A makes his or her final repayment. Similarly, if C purchases a new television which comes with a two-year warranty from D, then the contract between the parties will come to an end when the warranty period expires. It is, however, possible for a contract apparently brought to an end by performance to revive if the apparent performance proves to be defective. Thus in *Leggat Bros v Gray*,[154] the defender paid a debt due under a contract by cheque, which subsequently "bounced". The court held that despite the apparent performance by the defender at the point of time, the debt revived when the cheque was dishonoured.

Discharge by consent

4-99 A contract may be brought to an end by discharge by consent. This occurs when the parties agree that all existing performance and obligations under the contract is to be waived. This may occur for a number of reasons: for instance, if A owes B a sum of money under a contract, B may agree to write off the debt either as a gesture of goodwill or because A has recommended B's services to someone else. In either such case, A's initial obligation to pay the purchase price is discharged by consent.

Compensation

4-100 Another way in which certain forms of obligations can come to an end is through a process called compensation. The law's use of the term "compensation" is perhaps unfortunate, because that expression is used in other legal contexts to mean something quite different. In this context, compensation describes the setting off of one obligation against another. If A owes B £100 in relation to one transaction and B owes A £150 in relation to another, the two obligations can be set off against each other with the net effect that B would owe A £50.

---

[154] 1908 S.C. 67.

Compensation applies only to monetary obligations and so if an electrician and a plumber agree that the electrician will rewire the plumber's house in exchange for the plumber installing a new bathroom at the electrician's, the law will not permit set-off of the obligations. In that case, the law would require each party to pay the other for the work which has been done. Moreover, for compensation to operate, both of the monetary obligations must be both "current" and "liquid". The requirement that both obligations be current means that one cannot set an existing obligation off against one which has not yet come into being. The word "liquid" is used here not in its popular sense but in much the same way when the term is used in the expression "liquidate damages": in other words, the money obligation must be one which is for a certain, or at least, readily ascertainable, sum of money. The purchase price of goods bought under a contract of sale is a good example of a liquid debt: one knows precisely what the price is; it has been the subject of agreement between the parties. A claim for damages for breach of contract, by contrast, is a claim for an illiquid sum of money, as the precise value of the claim is not readily ascertainable. Until the court rules on the matter and fixes the amount of damages due, it is impossible for the parties to say exactly how much one is due to the other.

Novation

Novation occurs where an original obligation is extinguished and **4–101** replaced by a new obligation. This occurs commonly in practice. Parties to a contract may find that it is not working to their satisfaction and decide to re-negotiate its terms. Where this occurs, the new set of contractual obligations will supersede the old set.

Confusion

Confusion occurs when the same person becomes both the debtor and the **4–102** creditor in relation to a legal obligation. A person cannot be under an obligation to his or herself; where the same legal person simultaneously has both the right to enforce and the obligation to perform an obligation, the obligation itself cases to be. One might wonder how confusion could ever occur in practice: people are hardly likely to try to enter into contracts with themselves. However, confusion can occur because in practice the right to enforce obligations under contracts are sometimes sold or otherwise transferred. For instance, A, a company which is experiencing cash-flow problems and which is in immediate need of a large lump sum, might sell all of the debts which it is entitled to recover from its customers to B, a financial institution, in exchange for, say, 60 per cent of those debts' aggregate value. If one of the debts transferred is one which was originally owed by B to A, then we can see that as a result of this transaction, B has become both the debtor and the creditor in this obligation. The obligation will therefore be extinguished by confusion.

Prescription

4–103 Prescription is the branch of law which is concerned with the creation or extinction of legal obligations through the passage of time. This is a complex area of the law relevant not only to contract but also delict and property law. Prescription is relevant to contract law as it provides one of the circumstances in which contractual obligations to pay a debt may be extinguished. People who are owed money for performing obligations under a contract have only a finite amount of time in order to take action to recover the debt due to them. Two prescriptive periods are potentially relevant to contractual obligations: the so-called short negative prescription period of five years from the date when the obligation became enforceable[155] and the long negative prescription of 20 years.[156] The great majority of contractual obligations fall into the five-year period, but the 20-year period is the relevant one for contracts relating to land. The period stops running either on the date when a writ asserting the pursuer's claim is stamped by the court and then legally served upon the defender, or if the defender makes a "relevant acknowledgement" of the claim.[157]

Frustration (impossibility)

4–104 The obligations under a contract will be brought to an end as a result of the doctrine of frustration if, after the contract has been concluded but before the contract is performed, an event which is outside the control of the parties makes performance either:

- physically impossible; or
- practically impossible; or
- impossible to perform without breaking the law.

Each category of impossibility shall be discussed in turn.

Physical impossibility—rei interitus

4–105 Frustration by physical impossibility (sometimes known as "*rei interitus*") will arise when a supervening event outside the control of either party destroys the subject matter of the contract. A good example of this occurred in *Taylor v Caldwell*.[158] C, the owner of the premises used as a music hall, agreed to let it to a theatrical impresario, T, for four dates. T arranged for impressive programmes of entertainment to take place on

---

[155] The Prescription and Limitation (Scotland) Act 1973 (PLSA) s.6.

[156] PLSA s.7.

[157] A relevant acknowledgement takes place where there has either been part-performance of the obligation such as "clearly indicates" that the obligation still exists, or where the debtor has provided an "unequivocal written admission clearly acknowledging" that the obligation is still in existence: PLSA s.10. These are restrictive criteria and if the creditor is any doubt about whether they have been satisfied, the only safe course of action is to serve appropriate court papers upon the defender before the prescriptive period expires.

[158] (1863) 3 B&S 826.

each of the dates. However, one week before the first concert, the music hall burned down through no fault of either of the parties. T sued for the loss of the profit which he would have made had the venture proceeded as planned. The court held, however, that the parties' obligations under the contract had been brought to an end by the destruction of the subject matter of the contract.

A contract will also be brought to an end by frustration by physical impossibility upon the death of a party who has been chosen to carry out a contract because of his personal characteristics or skills. Such contracts are known as contracts *delectus personae*. Not all contracts are of this nature: the purchase of standard consumer products, for example, does not raise such issues. However, if one specifically commissions someone to manufacture a stained glass window or a one-off, hand-made item of furniture, *delectus personae* is present. Contracts of employment are commonly encountered examples of contracts *delectus personae*.

Practical impossibility

Practical impossibility is another event which can frustrate a contract. **4–106** This arises when an event has occurred which, while not inevitably making the contract physically impossible to perform, makes performance "something radically different from what the parties contemplated when they entered into it.[159]. The most famous example of a contract being frustrated for practical impossibility is the so-called "coronation case," *Krell v Henry*.[160] Here, rooms affording a clear view of Pall Mall were let out at high prices to permit affluent members of the public to see the procession marking Edward VII's coronation. In the event, however, the King fell ill and the coronation was cancelled. It was held that the contract had been frustrated: its commercial purpose was not the hire of the room, but the hire of a location from which to see the parade. However, the courts will not lightly accept that performance of a contract has become practically impossible, and in particular, the mere fact that the change in circumstances makes it impossible for someone selling goods or providing a service to make a profit is irrelevant.[161] In *Tsakiroglou & Co Ltd v Noblee Thorl GmbH*,[162] the parties entered into a charter of a boat to carry a cargo of nuts from Port Sudan on the east coast of Africa to Hamburg, in Germany's northern coast. In entering into the contract, both parties assumed that the ship would proceed by the shortest route, which involved passing through the Suez Canal, but nothing about the route was expressly stated in the contract. The Suez crisis of 1956 intervened and the Egyptian government closed the canal. This meant that the ship would have to undertake its voyage round the Cape of Good Hope, adding thousands of miles to the distance the ship would have to travel and more than doubling the cost of fuel and crewing

---

[159] *Paal Wilson & Co v Blumenthal* [1983] 1 A.C. 854.
[160] [1903] 2 K.B. 740.
[161] *Davis Contractors v Fareham Urban District Council* [1956] A.C. 696.
[162] [1962] A.C. 93.

costs of the vessel. The court held that the contract had not been frustrated; although the voyage was longer and more expensive than was envisaged, an alternative route existed; the contract therefore stood.

Supervening illegality

4–107 A contract will also be frustrated if its performance becomes illegal after the contract has been formed, but before it is performed. This may occur, for instance, if legislation is passed in the intervening time which makes it illegal for a person situated within the jurisdiction to trade with certain named individuals, organisations or states.[163] It can also occur as a result of the outbreak of war. In *Cantiere San Rocco SA v Clyde Shipbuilding & Engineering Co Ltd*,[164] a Scottish engineering company entered into a contract with an Austrian company for the provision of ship's engines. Before the contract could be fully performed, the First World War was declared. As the United Kingdom was at war with (among other nations), Austria, it was illegal (under the common law doctrine of enemy alien) for UK-based companies to maintain trading arrangements with Austrian-based organisations. The contract was therefore declared frustrated as a result of supervening illegality.

▼ CHAPTER SUMMARY

WHAT IS A CONTRACT?

4–108 **A contract is an agreement entered into between two or more parties, which the parties intend to be legally binding.**

The courts will presume that the parties to social or domestic agreements do not intend their agreement to be binding, and will assume that parties to commercial or business-related agreements do intend their agreements to constitute contracts. In both cases, however, these presumptions are rebuttable in the face of clear evidence to the contrary.

A unilateral gratuitous promise is not a contract as it is not an agreement made between two or more parties. However, such promises are legally binding in Scots law either if they are written down and signed by the promisor, or if they are made in a business context.

HOW IS A CONTRACT FORMED?

A contract is formed when an *offer* is met by an *unconditional acceptance* leading to *consensus in idem*—a meeting of the minds.

***Consensus in idem* is reached when an objective bystander observing the**

---

[163] A time of writing, UK financial institutions are prevented by statutory instrument from providing a range of financial services to a range of people and organisations associated with, e.g., Al-Quaeda and the Taliban, Zimbabwe and parts of the former Soviet Union: see *http://www.lloyds.com/Lloyds_Worldwide/Sanctions/What_are_sanctions.htm*.
[164] 1923 S.C. (HL) 105.

parties' discussions, correspondence and behaviour would come to the conclusion that they had agreed on all of the essential elements of the contract.

In general, the law does not require contracts to be in a particular form (e.g. in writing). As a result, offers may generally be made orally, in writing or even by implication from the factual circumstances. Exceptionally, the law requires that some contracts need to be in a particular form (i.e. in writing) before they will be valid.

Not all discussions or proposals made during the course of a contractual negotiation are offers. The identifying feature of an offer is that it must "contemplate acceptance". Statements of future intent and invitations to treat are not offers and therefore cannot be accepted by the offeree.

An offer is not effectual until it is communicated to the offeree.

Offers may only be accepted by the person to whom they are addressed but it is possible for an offeror to address an offer to one person, a category of people or the world at large.

An offer may be revoked before acceptance unless the offeror has undertaken to leave his offer open for acceptance for a period of time: where the offeror does so, the undertaking will be enforceable if it satisfies the criteria for the making of a unilateral promise.

Offers automatically lapse upon the occurrence of a number of events, namely: passage of time, rejection (including the making of a counter-offer), death of either party or the bankruptcy or insanity of the offeror, the destruction or material alteration of the subject matter of the contract or in the event of supervening illegality.

Unless (a) the offeror has demanded that acceptance has to be made in a particular way, or (b) the contract is one of the few types of agreement which the law demands be made in a particular form, an acceptance may be communicated in any medium of the offeree's choosing.

The identifying feature of an acceptance is that it must be an unqualified agreement to the offer put forward by the offeree.

A reply to an offer which agrees to some or even most of the terms advanced by the offeror but which seeks to introduce new legal terms into the deal is a counter-offer, not an acceptance.

A counter-offer has the legal effect of rejecting the initial offer and presenting a new offer which may in its turn be either accepted or rejected by the other party.

A "battle of the forms" can occur when both parties to a negotiation seek to contract upon their preferred own terms and conditions. The "battle" will be won by the party who presents the final set of terms and conditions before legal acceptance.

An acceptance, like an offer, does not take effect until it is communicated. In the case of instantaneous methods of communication an acceptance will not be communicated until it is actually heard by the other party. In the case of delayed methods of communication, communication is "effective on despatch".

FORMALITIES: RWSA

Contrary to the general rule (which states that formalities do not need to be observed when one enters into a contract), some contracts do require to be entered into in a particular way if they are to be effectual. The most important practical example is a contract for the sale or transfer of ownership of land. RWSA provides that such contracts need to be made in writing and require to be signed. It is strongly advisable for them to in addition be witnessed.

CONTRACTUAL TERMS

The content of a contract is found in its terms. Contracts cover a broad range of commercial activities, and different types of contract will contain different types of terms. But in general, the terms of a contract will set out the obligations that each party is to undertake: who is doing what for who, when, how and in exchange for what?

Terms may find their way into contract by express agreement, by incorporation from an external source either by reference or by a prior course of dealings, or by implication.

In the case of terms incorporated by reference, if the offeree signs a legal document which states on the face of it that the contract is to be governed by terms which can be seen elsewhere, the courts will usually hold that the offeree is bound by those terms. If the offeree has not signed such a document, a number of conditions must be satisfied before a court will hold the terms incorporated into the contract. The terms must be:

- brought to the offeree's attention at or before the conclusion of the contract;
- contained in a document which the offeree would reasonably have understood to be contractual in nature; and
- adequately brought to the attention of the offeree.

Terms are commonly implied into contracts by the law, rather than the parties themselves. This may be done by statute (e.g. the Sale of Goods Act 1979) or by the common law. A term will be incorporated at common law if it is of such a nature that a reasonable man would himself want for his own protection, and no reasonable man would refuse to accept it.

STATUTORY REGULATION OF UNFAIR TERMS

Historically, many parties have adopted the practice of contracting on terms and conditions which are heavily biased in their favour. Over the years, this led to much unfairness. The problem was seen at its most acute when consumers contracted with large commercial organisations. The common law's response to this problem came to be seen as inadequate.

There now exist statutory controls (in the form of UCTA and UTCCR) to regulate the use of unfair terms.

UCTA is concerned principally with a particular class of unfair terms known as exemption clauses. Its provisions have the potential to apply to most contracts, and:

- render unenforceable exemption clauses which purport to exclude or limit liability for death or personal injury caused as a result of negligence or other breach of duty; and
- state that exemption clauses which exclude or limit liability for other sorts of losses caused as a result of negligence or other breach of duty will only be enforceable if they satisfy a fair and reasonable test; and
- make all exemption clauses contained in consumer or standard-form contracts subject to a fair and reasonable test.

Unlike UCTA, UTCCR provides protection only for the benefit of consumers contracting with businesses. Also unlike UCTA, UTCCR does not focus on exemption clauses but instead seeks to regulate any form of unfairness which may act to the detriment of the consumer. UTCCR:

- provides incentives for businesses to contract in plain and readily understandable language;
- provides that unfair terms not individually negotiated by the parties shall not be binding on the consumer; and
- has the potential to "clean up" commercial organisations' contracting practice by giving the OFT an overseeing role and permitting that body to take court action demanding that organisations stop using unfair terms in their contracts.

DEFECTIVE CONTRACTS

Not all attempts to create a contract will be successful. Defects may emerge which render either a contract or a particular term within a contract void, voidable or unenforceable.

There is legal significance in the distinction between void, voidable or unenforceable contracts. In particular, the right to reduce a voidable contract can be lost in certain circumstances. This issue does not arise with void or unenforceable contracts.

A contract will be void if it is entered into by someone who lacks legal capacity. A person may lack legal capacity by reason of:

- non-age;
- insanity;
- intoxication;
- being a corporation; corporations are legal persons established for certain purposes and do not, in general, have the legal capacity to enter into contracts outwith those purposes (albeit certain statutory

protections exist to protect innocent third parties dealing with companies).

A contract will also be void if entered into by someone unable to exercise free will as he was in immediate peril of his life. This is the most extreme form of the doctrine of force and fear.

In other, lesser, examples of force and fear, a contract will be voidable. A contract will also be voidable if entered into as a result of facility and circumvention or the undue influence of another.

Parties sometimes enter into contracts on the basis of some kind of mis-apprehension (error). The legal effect of an error on a contract depends upon a combination of factors: the nature of the error, its legal significance, and whether it was made by the party themselves or as a result of a mis-representation by the other party. Taking all these factors together we can say:

> No remedy is given to a party who enters into a contract as a result of an error of law. "Ignorance of the law is no excuse."

The category of uninduced errors of fact can be sub-divided further into:

- errors of expression. Here the parties may take a court action to correct a document which incorrectly records the terms of a verbal agreement;
- unilateral uninduced error of intention. Such errors are generally irrelevant; i.e. the law generally provides no legal remedy; and
- bilateral uninduced error of intention. These render a contract void on the basis of dissensus if made in relation to an essential term of the contract. In other circumstances their effect is not wholly clear, but it is believed that other such errors will have no effect upon the validity of the contract.

The category of misrepresentation, or induced errors of fact, is sub-cate-gorised as follows:

- Fraudulent misrepresentation. This is a misrepresentation made with the deliberate intention to deceive. If this induces an essential error, the contact is void; if the error is only material, the contract will be voidable. In addition, damages are also recoverable to compensate for any loss suffered.
- Negligent misrepresentation. As in the case of fraud, if this induces an essential error, the contact is void; if the error is only material, the contract will be voidable. In addition, since the enactment of legislation in 1985, damages are also recoverable to compensate for any loss suffered.
- Innocent misrepresentation. This arises when incorrect information is passed to the offeree by the offeror in circumstances where the

offeror cannot be blamed for the inaccuracy. Such a mis-representation renders a contract made in reliance upon it voidable, but damages are not recoverable.

A further category of defective contract is *pacta illicita*. These are illegal contracts. Such contracts are unenforceable. Some examples of *pacta illicita* are:

- contracts to commit crimes;
- contracts to commit delicts;
- contracts which promote immorality;
- contracts which are contrary to public policy;
- contracts rendered illegal by statute. Contrary to the general rule, these will not always simply render a contract unenforcerable but may declare a particular contract or term of a contract void.

Contractual terms in restraint of trade require separate discussion. Such contractual terms may be public policy. However, not all such terms will be considered unenforceable: these clauses are assessed on a case-by-case by the courts. In particular, a restrictive covenant (an especially important example of a contractual term in restraint of trade) will be upheld by the court if it:

- protects a legitimate interest of the party seeking to enforce it; and
- is reasonable in the circumstances; and
- is in the public interest.

A restrictive covenant which cannot satisfy these criteria will be declared unenforceable.

BREACH OF CONTRACT

If either party fails without justification to fulfil an obligation it has undertaken in the contract, that party is in breach of contract. Particularly significant breaches—material breaches—give the innocent party a greater range of legal remedies than less significant breaches of contract.

A variety of self-help and judicial remedies are available to the innocent party in the event of breach. Self-help remedies are available only in the case of a material breach. Judicial remedies are not subject to this restriction.

Among the main self-help remedies are rescission, retention and lien. The main judicial remedies are actions for the recovery of debt, specific implement, interdict, damages and liquidate damages.

Damages are imposed solely for the purpose of compensating the innocent party, not to punish the party in breach. In contract law, damages are generally available only to compensate personal injuries, and damage to property and economic losses.

In order to claim damages, the innocent party must be in a position to demonstrate that the breach of contract has caused him loss. The innocent party must also take reasonable steps to mitigate his loss, and will not be able to recover damages in respect of losses which the law deems to be too remotely connected to the breach of contract for it to be reasonable to merit compensation.

Liquidate damages are awards of damages made in accordance with a clause in the parties' contract which specifies the level of damages which will be paid upon the occurrence of a specified type of breach of contract. Such a clause is unenforceable if its true purpose is to punish the party in breach. However, if its true purpose is to provide a reasonable pre-estimate of what the innocent party stands to lose in the event of breach, the clause will be enforceable.

Who May Sue When a Contract is Breached?

In general, Scots law follows the doctrine of privity of contract. This is means that generally only the parties to a contract may sue or be sued on it.

An important exception to this principle is made in the case of *jus quaesitum tertio*, which provides that a person not party to the contract will have the right to sue (but not be sued) under it if the parties to the contract clearly intended that person to have an enforceable legal right.

Extinction of Contractual Obligations

Contractual obligations do not last for ever but come to an end in a number of different ways.

- When the obligations due to be performed under the contract are carried out, the contract itself ceases to exist.
- In addition, obligations may be discharged by:

  - mutual consent;
  - compensation (or "set-off");
  - novation; or
  - confusion.

- After a certain period of time (usually five years in the case of contractual obligations), an obligation will expire unless the innocent party initiates court proceedings relative to the obligation or receives a relevant acknowledgement of claim.
- Finally, a contract may also be brought to an end by frustration. This occurs when, after the contract has been concluded but before the contract is performed, an event which is outside the control of the parties makes performance either:

  - physically impossible; or
  - practically impossible; or
  - impossible to perform without breaking the law.

? QUICK QUIZ

- What is a contract?
- Are all agreements contractually binding?
- Is a unilateral gratuitous promise a contract?
- What is *consensus in idem*? What is its legal significance?
- What kind of test do the courts use to assess if a *consensus in idem* has been reached?
- What is the identifying feature of an offer?
- What is an intention to treat? Give examples of common invitations to treat.
- Does an offer not stated to be subject to a time-limit remain open indefinitely?
- What is the identifying feature of an acceptance?
- What is the legal effect of a counter-offer?
- When will the law consider an acceptance to have been effectually communicated to the offeror?
- "Contracts relating to ____ form the most significant exception to the rule that contracts do not require to be in writing." What is the missing word?
- A and B intend to enter into a contract. B is worried that A may try to include terms contrary to B's interests, but reckons that if he doesn't sign anything, he will be safe enough. Is B's analysis correct?
- Name the two major statutory regimes which regulate contractual terms. Outline their essential features.
- Is a contract entered into between a major record company and an eight-year-old child prodigy legally binding? What about a 17-year-old?
- If a person suffering from a mental illness, while on a euphoric high, decides to spend £100,000 on designer clothes, is the contract of purchase he has apparently entered into legally binding?
- A is a fan of the band Pink Floyd. On hearing that "Floyd" is to be appearing live at SECC, A buys a ticket for the event. It transpires that the event is a cooking demonstration by the celebrity chef, Keith Floyd. Is A bound by the contract?
- A places a large bet on a horse-race. His horse loses. Disappointed, he decides to cheer himself up by buying a knighthood from a corrupt public official. Happy now, he celebrates by buying a case of vintage champagne and hiring a prostitute. How many binding contracts has A entered into in this sequence of events?
- What is a restrictive covenant? Will such contractual terms be enforced by the courts?
- What is a material breach of contract? Which contractual remedies available to someone suffering a material breach of contract are not available to the innocent party in the case of a non-material breach?

- What is meant by "the duty to mitigate loss"?
- What is meant by "remoteness of damages"?
- What are liquidate damages, and are they legally enforceable?
- After what period of time will the right to enforce a contractual obligation be lost?
- In which circumstances will a contract be brought to an end by "frustration"?

📖 FURTHER READING

S. Woolman and J. Lake, *Contract*, 3rd edn (W. Green, 2001) (an excellent introductory text).

H. MacQueen and J. Thomson, *Contract Law in Scotland*, 2nd edn (Tottel, with revisions, 2005 (more detailed than Woolman and Lake; a superb intermediate text).

W. McBryde, *The Law of Contract in Scotland*, 3rd edn (W. Green, 2007) (an excellent reference work but very detailed and complex).

J. Huntley et al., *Contract: Cases and Materials*, 2nd edn (W. Green, 2003) (a useful source of legal cases and authorities)

🖱 USEFUL WEBLINKS

Office of Fair Trading, Unfair Terms in Consumer Contracts: *http://www.oft.gov.uk/advice_and_resources/resource_base/legal/unfair-terms/*

Chapter 5   Sale and Supply of Goods

COWAN ERVINE[1]

► CHAPTER OVERVIEW

This chapter deals with various contracts by which goods can be trans- **5–01**
ferred from one person to another. The commonest is known as the
contract of sale. This is a contract governed by the Sale of Goods Act
1979 and involves the transfer of ownership of goods for a money consideration called the price. There are other ways in which goods can be
transferred such as hire-purchase, barter or where services are also being
provided as when a car is being serviced and a part is replaced. These
have in common that the buyer becomes the owner. These are regulated
by other pieces of legislation such as the Supply of Goods (Implied
Terms) Act 1973 and the Supply of Goods and Services Act 1982. Most
attention will be paid to the contract of sale. There are rules about when
ownership is transferred which are also connected with who takes the risk
of the goods being lost or damaged during the transaction. A key part of
the contract of sale is the terms about description and quality which are
implied in all such contracts. Similar terms are also implied into the other
contracts for the supply of goods. Both seller and buyer have legal
obligations and there are remedies available if one party breaches an
obligation. These contracts have in common that the buyer becomes the
owner. The contract of hire is different in that the customer only gets
temporary possession of the goods. It is governed by the Supply of Goods
and Services Act 1982. It has similar implied terms about description and
quality.

✓ OUTCOMES

After studying this chapter you should know: **5–02**

   ✓   which contracts involve the supply of goods;
   ✓   the main characteristics of the contract of sale;
   ✓   the terms implied in various contracts for the supply of goods;
   ✓   the right and duties of suppliers and buyers of goods.

---

[1] Senior Lecturer in Law, University of Dundee.

INTRODUCTION

5–03 This chapter is called *Supply of Goods* because there are several different ways in which someone can acquire goods. The most common type of contract is the contract of sale and we shall concentrate on it. However, goods can be bought by paying instalments and one way of doing that is to buy on hire purchase. Goods may also be obtained by hiring them as where someone wishes to rent a car for a short period. Hire in the form of a finance lease is often used in business where the economic effect is very similar to sale. Though it is not very common, goods are sometimes bartered with one product being exchanged for another or in part exchange where a product and cash are exchanged for a product. In addition, goods may be obtained in return for a voucher such as the now not so common trading stamp. And, of course, goods may be acquired as gifts. Legally these transactions involve different types of contract and different Acts of Parliament apply to them. As the contract of sale is the most important we shall concentrate on it but reference will also be made to the others.

THE CONTRACT OF SALE

5–04 For more than a century the contract of sale has been governed by an Act of Parliament. The current version is the Sale of Goods Act 1979. Section 2 of the Act defines a contract of sale as:

> "a contract by which the seller transfers or agrees to transfer the property in goods to the buyer for a monetary consideration, called the price."

There are several points to notice about this definition:

- **"transfers or agrees to transfer":** the Act applies not just where the goods are being handed over but also where there is only an agreement to do so in the future. In other words, there can still be a contract of sale where the buyer and seller have only agreed to hand over the goods in exchange for payment at some time in the future.
- **"property":** in this context property means legal title or ownership.
- **"monetary consideration":** this is what distinguishes sale from barter or a gift. Cases where a person directly swaps one good for another are covered by the Supply of Goods and Services Act 1982. Monetary consideration includes not just cash but cheques and payment by credit card.
- **"transfer the property":** the hiring of goods is not covered because the definition refers to the transfer of title (ownership) whereas goods that are on hire do not belong to the person using them but to the person who is hiring them out.

The definition of "goods"

Goods, for the purposes of the Sale of Goods Act are defined as: **5–05**

> "all corporeal moveables except money; and in particular 'goods' includes ... industrial growing crops and things attached to or forming part of the land, which are agreed to be severed before sale or under the contact of sale".

This definition means that property such as houses and flats are not goods nor are the fixtures, but the fittings are goods. Goods include all tangible things and whilst money itself is not goods, coins or banknotes that have a greater value than their legal tender value are. Goods include crops, which are sown and intended to be harvested, but not wild crops.

Section 5 states that the goods that are the subject of a contract may be existing goods, owned or possessed by the seller, or goods to be manufactured or acquired by the seller after the contract of sale. Goods not already in existence or requiring to be manufactured are called *future goods* in the Act. A contract where the seller is trying to sell future goods at that moment operates as an agreement to sell.

So we can see that "goods" covers a huge range of things from books to buses and a great deal in between.

Key Concept

Goods in the context of SOGA 1979 are defined as corporeal moveables including things growing on or in the land. Property and land are not goods for the purposes of the Act. Money is also excluded from this definition except in relation to antique coins and banknotes.

Price

A monetary consideration called the price distinguishes sale from some **5–06** other transactions. The price can be fixed by the contract or can be determined in a manner agreed by both parties, for example a valuation by a third party. If no price is agreed between buyer and seller, the buyer must pay a "reasonable" price.

Formation of the contract

The normal rules about the formation of contracts apply to the contract **5–07** of sale and there are usually no special formalities that need be complied with. However, the Consumer Protection (Cancellation of Contracts Concluded Away From Business Premises) Regulations 1987 and the Consumer Protection (Distance Selling) Regulations 2000 both require information to be given to the consumer buyer. Failure to do so can result in the contract being unenforceable.

When does property pass from the seller to the buyer?

5–08 Sale is about transferring the "property" or ownership in the goods and the Sale of Goods Act defines when that occurs. It is important to know when this happens particularly if either the seller or buyer has become insolvent. If the seller has become insolvent before he has given up ownership of goods those goods are assets of his which are available to pay his creditors. Knowing when ownership has been transferred can also be important in deciding whether it is the buyer or seller who bears the risk of the goods being damaged or lost. Sections 16–18 of the Act deal with this issue.

To understand these sections it is first essential to know what "specific goods" and "unascertained goods" are. Section 61 defines "specific goods" as "goods identified and agreed on at the time a contract of sale is made". In a consumer context an obvious example would be a product selected by the consumer in a shop. "Unascertained goods" are not defined in the Act but it is clear that the term is used in contradistinction to specific goods. It covers three situations.

- goods are to be manufactured or grown;
- generic goods, e.g. a ton of coal;
- an unidentified part of a specific whole, e.g. a case of Beaujolais Nouveau from the shipment in a particular wine merchant's warehouse.

The starting point for working out when ownership passes is s.16 which states that until goods are "ascertained" ownership cannot be transferred. Goods are unascertained until they are allocated to a particular contract. An example might be a roll of carpet—the goods are unascertained until the correct length is cut off the roll for a particular order.

There is one exception to this rule and it applies to sales from part of an identified bulk. It is quite common for traders in commodities such as oil or cereals to buy and pay for part of a cargo or a consignment being stored in a warehouse which would be known as a sale from bulk. Until that part has been identified it is not *ascertained*. To avoid unfairness that could arise in these situations if the seller became insolvent before the goods were ascertained, the law was altered in this situation. Section 20A of the Act provides that traders who have paid in advance for a specified quantity of goods which are part of a bulk which has been identified acquire an undivided share in the bulk and become owners in common with the other buyers or with the seller.

For goods that are ascertained or specified, s.17 states that property in the goods passes when the buyer and seller intend it should pass. The trouble is that it may be far from clear what they intended. If that is the case, s.18 of the Act comes to the rescue by setting out a number of rules to assist in working out what their intention must have been. These rules are set out in s.18.

Rule 1   In an unconditional contract for specific goods in a deliverable state, property passes when the contract is made, and it is immaterial whether the time of payment or the time of delivery, or both, be postponed.

An example of this is *Dennant v Skinner*[2] where at an auction a bid was accepted by the auctioneer. The buyer was then given a form saying that ownership would not pass until the buyer's cheque cleared. It was held this was not a term of the contract and Rule 1 applied.

Rule 2 In a contract for specific goods where the seller has to do something to the goods before delivery (put them in a deliverable state), property passes when that has been done and the buyer has been informed.

Rule 3 In a contract for the sale of specific goods where they are in a deliverable state but the seller has to weigh, measure, test etc. to find the price, property does not pass until that is done and the buyer is informed.

Rule 4 If goods are sent on approval or sale or return, property passes when buyers show their approval or acceptance or do something inconsistent with someone else's ownership, or if buyers retain the goods and there is no fixed time for the return then property passes after a reasonable length of time.

For example, in *Kirkham v Attenborough*,[3] a manufacturer of jewellery sent some pieces on a sale or return basis to X who then pawned them to Attenborough and did not pay Kirkham. It was held under Rule 4 that property had passed to X when he had pawned the jewellery because this was a way of showing that he was accepting the goods.

Rule 5 Where there is a contract for the sale of unascertained or future goods by description, and goods of that description and in a deliverable state are unconditionally appropriated to the contract, either by the seller with the assent of the buyer, or by the buyer with the assent of the seller, the property in the goods thereupon passes to the buyer. Such assent may be express or implied, and may be given either before or after the appropriation is made.

Philip Head and Sons Ltd v Shop Fronts
[1970] 1 Lloyds Rep. 140

Philip Head Ltd had agreed to supply and lay some carpet in a new office development. They arranged for the delivery of the carpet to the site but before they could lay it someone stole it. Who was to bear the loss? Was it Philip Head Ltd or their customer? Whoever was the owner would have to bear the loss. The judge decided that it was Philip Head Ltd and he reached this conclusion by applying this rule. He said that lying on site but not fitted it could not be said to be in a deliverable state.

---

[2] [1948] 2 K.B. 164.
[3] [1897] 1 Q.B. 201.

> **Key Concept**
>
> Where goods are unascertained, no property in the goods can be
> transferred to the buyer until the goods are ascertained — SOGA
> s.16. Where goods are specific or ascertained property in the goods
> passes when the parties intended the property to pass — SOGA
> s.17. In the absence of clear evidence of the intention of the parties
> to the contract the rules contained in SOGA s.18 will be applied.

Section 19 allows the seller to impose terms governing when property will
pass under a contract and property will not pass until they are fulfilled.
This permits retention of title clauses which allow a seller to protect himself
against the danger of the buyer becoming insolvent before payment has
been made. This was established in *Armour v Thyssen Edelstahlwerke AG*.[4]

Does the seller have the right to sell?

5–09   Questions may arise about the right of the seller to sell the goods and
difficult questions may arise involving the buyer, the person from whom
the goods were acquired, and the true owner. Such problems often arise
where the original owner has been tricked into parting with his goods by a
rogue. In contracts of sale the starting point is the implied terms that are at
the heart of the Sale of Goods Act. Section 12 of the Act has terms relating
to title or ownership. It is important to note that as a result of the Unfair
Contract Terms Act 1977, they cannot be excluded in consumer contracts.

Section 12(1) provides that there is an implied term that the seller has a
right to sell the goods. Section 12(2) provides that there is also an implied
term that the goods are free from any charge or encumbrance not disclosed or known to the buyer before the contract is made and that the
buyer will enjoy quiet possession of the goods except so far as it may be
disturbed by the owner or other person entitled to the benefit of any
charge or encumbrance which was disclosed.

> ### McDonald v Provan (of Scotland Street) Ltd
> #### 1960 S.L.T. 231
>
> *McDonald v Provan (of Scotland Street) Ltd* demonstrates the
> operation of s.12. McDonald bought a car from Provan Ltd, who in
> turn had bought it in good faith. Three months after the sale the car
> was taken from McDonald by the police because at least part of it
> was stolen property. It appeared that the car consisted of parts of
> two separate cars, one of which had been stolen, that had been
> welded together. McDonald sued for damages for breach of the
> implied term about title in s.12 and it was held that he was entitled
> to succeed if he could prove the assertions on which he relied.

---

[4] [1991] 2 A.C. 339.

The seller does not have the right to sell: nemo dat quod non habet

Section 12 protects the buyer from someone who has not had the right to **5–10** sell the goods. If the true owner takes back the goods he or she can sue for breach of this implied term. Often in these situations the seller cannot be traced so it becomes important to try to show that the buyer did get a good title. The barrier to this is the general principle that those who transfer goods to others cannot confer a better title than they themselves have. For example, a thief has no title to what has been stolen so when he or she purports to sell the goods the buyer, however innocent, does not become the owner. This principle is set out in s. 21 of the Act. However, it can work very unfairly so a number of exceptions have grown up often referred to as the exceptions to the *nemo dat* rule. This is a reference to the Latin phrase at the top of this paragraph which means: you cannot give a title that you do not have.

The exceptions

Personal bar

This exception is found in s.21 just after it states the general rule. The **5–11** section goes on that the owner of goods can be precluded from denying the seller's authority to sell because of his conduct. An example comes from the English case of *Eastern Distributors Ltd v Goldring*.[5] Mr Murphy, the owner of a van, signed hire purchase forms in blank, so that a car dealer who was assisting him to finance the purchase of a Chrysler car could sell it to a hire purchase company. It had been agreed between them that the dealer would only sell the van if the dealer was able to arrange finance for the purchase of the Chrysler from the hire purchase company. This did not prove to be possible but the dealer still sold the van to the hire purchase company, Eastern Distributors Ltd. Meantime, the Mr Murphy who still had possession of the van sold it to Mr Goldring. So now he and Eastern Distributors claimed to be the owners. It was held that Eastern Distributors, not Mr Goldring, were the true owners because they had bought in good faith from the car dealer whom Mr Murphy had put in a position to sell his van.

Sale by a mercantile agent

Section 2(1) of the Factors Act 1889 states that: **5–12**

> "Where a mercantile agent is, with the consent of the owner, in possession of goods or of the documents of title to goods, any sale, pledge, or other disposition of the goods, made by him when acting in the ordinary course of business of a mercantile agent, shall, subject to the provisions of this Act, be as valid as if he were expressly authorised by the owner of the goods to make the same;

---

[5] [1957] 2 Q.B. 600.

provided that the person taking under the disposition acts in good faith, and has not at the time of the disposition notice that the person making the disposition has not authority to make the same."

Examples of mercantile agents are shops, auctioneers and warehousemen so this exception is of considerable everyday importance.

Sale under a voidable title

5–13 Where a seller has a voidable title the person in possession of the goods can pass a good title until steps have been taken by the true owner to avoid that title. A classic example is provided by the case of *MacLeod v Kerr*.[6]

> **MacLeod v Kerr**
> **1965 S.C. 253**
>
> Kerr had advertised his car for sale in a newspaper and sold it to a man who came to see it. He accepted a cheque in payment and permitted the man to take the car away together with the registration document. The man had given a false name and paid with a cheque from a stolen cheque book. On discovering that he had been tricked Kerr immediately informed the police. Meanwhile, the rogue sold the car to a Mr Gibson who knew nothing of these events. The rogue was not worth suing and the question in the case was which of two people who had been duped by him was the legal owner of the car. It was held by the Court of Session that the rogue's fraudulent misrepresentation resulted in him obtaining a voidable title. Informing the police was not sufficient to upset this title so the rogue was still able to give Gibson ownership.

Sale by a seller in possession after a sale

5–14 It will sometimes happen that after a sale has been completed and the buyer has become the owner of the goods they will remain in the possession of the seller. Should the seller purport to sell them to someone else that person will get a good title. This is the effect of s.24 of the Act which applies where the person to whom the goods were sold the second time does not know of the original sale and is acting in good faith.

Sale by a buyer in possession after a sale

5–15 This is the converse of the previous situation. Before becoming the legal owner the buyer has obtained possession of the goods. Nevertheless, as a result of s.25 of the Act such a person can give a good title to someone acting in good faith who does not know of the original seller's rights. A good example comes from the case of *Archivent Sales & Development Ltd*

---

[6] 1965 S.C. 253.

v Strathclyde Regional Council[7] which also demonstrates that this exception can override a retention of title clause.

Archivent delivered building materials to the site where a contractor was building a school for the regional council. The contract between Archivent and the contractor included a clause reserving title in the materials to them until payment was made in full. The contract between the contractor and the council provided that the materials should become the property of the council when they were delivered to the site. The contractor became insolvent before Archivent had been paid. The council had acted in good faith throughout and had been unaware of the clause reserving title until after the insolvency. The issue was who owned the goods and in the circumstances it was decided that it was the council by virtue of s.25.

Sales of motor vehicles subject to hire purchase or conditional sale

Someone who buys goods by means of hire-purchase or conditional sale, **5–16** which is very similar, does not become the owner of them until all the instalments have been paid and thus cannot pass a good title to anyone else. Unfortunately, it is not uncommon for those buying cars on hire purchase and conditional sale to try to do so. To combat the hardship to unsuspecting purchasers from such people ss.27–29 of the Hire Purchase Act 1964 were passed. These apply only to motor vehicles and result in a private purchaser acting in good faith and without notice of the hire purchase or conditional sale agreement getting as good a title as the true owner (usually a finance company) has. It should be emphasised that this applies only to hire purchase and conditional sale and not to pure hire.

When does the risk pass?

Various problems may arise where the goods have been destroyed or **5–17** damaged around the time of the contract. Section 6 of the Sale of Goods Act 1979 provides that where there is a contract for the sale of specific goods, and the goods without the knowledge of the seller have perished at the time when the contract is made, the contract is void. This might apply where the seller and buyer have agreed that the seller will sell a specific car identified by make and registration number. If, unknown to either, it was destroyed in a fire on the day before the contract was made the contract would be a nullity.

Section 7 deals with a slightly different situation. Like s.6 it applies to a sale of specific goods, but here the destruction occurs, without any fault on the part of the seller or buyer, after the contract has been entered into but before risk passes to the buyer. In this situation the sale is avoided.

In the case of unascertained goods the scope for them to perish in a legal sense is more limited. An agreement to sell purely generic goods cannot be frustrated by the destruction of the goods and it is of no

---

[7] 1985 S.L.T. 154.

concern to the buyer that the seller had a particular source in mind as Asquith L.J. explained in *Monkland v Jack Barclay Ltd* [8]:

> "Suppose A has contracted to sell to B unascertained goods by description for example, 'a' Bentley Mark VI (not 'this' Bentley Mark VI), and suppose, further, that the seller expects to acquire the goods from a particular source, which may, indeed, be the only source available, the bare fact, without more, that when the time for delivery comes that source has dried up and that the seller cannot draw on it, does not absolve the seller. He is still, in the absence of some contractual term excusing him, liable for non-delivery."

Other situations are covered by s.20 of the Act. This provides that the risk of damage to or destruction of the goods is with the owner. This is another reason why the rules discussed earlier about when ownership passes are important. This rule is subject to some important exceptions. First, the parties may have decided otherwise. It is common in retention of title clauses to provide that though the goods remain in the ownership of the seller the buyer bears the risk of damage or destruction. Also, where delivery has been delayed because of the fault of one of the parties the party responsible for the delay bears the risk of loss which would not have occurred had delivery been on time.

There is also an important exception for the benefit of consumers. Section 20(4) states that where there is a consumer contract in which the buyer is a consumer the goods remain at the seller's risk until they are delivered to the consumer. A consumer contract for this purpose is defined by s.25 of the Unfair Contract Terms Act 1977 and means a contract between an individual and a trader involving goods ordinarily supplied for private use or consumption. This change is complemented by another to s.32 of the Sale of Goods Act 1979. That section contains the general rule that where the seller is authorised or required to send the goods to the buyer delivery to a carrier is "prima facie deemed to be delivery of the goods to the buyer". This too does not apply to consumer contracts so the result of these changes is that until the goods are delivered to a consumer the risk is on the seller.

Duties of the seller

(a) Delivery

5–18 Section 27 provides that it is the seller's duty to deliver the goods and s.29 explains that whether it is up to the seller to send the goods or the buyer to take delivery depends on the interpretation of the contract. If the contract does not say where delivery is to be made the same section provides that it is to be the seller's place of business or, where he or she has no place of business, his or her residence. However, if the contract is for the sale of specific goods which the parties knew at the time of the contract were somewhere else delivery should be made at that other place.

---

[8] [1951] 2 K.B. 252.

If the contract requires the seller to send the goods to the buyer but does not say when this is to be done, s.29(3) provides that this must be done within a reasonable time and delivery must be at a reasonable hour. In *Hartley v Hyams*[9] it was held that time is *prima facie* of the essence in a commercial contract and so failure to deliver on time will justify the buyer in rescinding the contract.

Section 30 deals with delivery of the wrong quantity of goods. Where too few goods are delivered but the shortfall is not material the buyer may not reject the delivery but must pay for what is delivered at the contract rate. If too many goods are delivered the buyer may only reject the delivery if the excess is material. If it is material the buyer may choose to reject only the excess, or keep the whole delivery, paying at the contract rate.

(b) Duty to pass a good title

This has already been discussed under the heading of the right to sell. **5–19**

(c) Duty to provide goods of the correct description

Section 13 of 1979 Act provides that where there is a sale by description **5–20** there is an implied term that the goods will correspond with the description. If the sale is by sample, as well as by description, it is not sufficient that the bulk of the goods correspond with the sample if the goods do not also correspond with the description. Sales are by description in a wide range of situations. An obvious example is provided by mail order purchasing where the buyer relies on the description in a catalogue or an advertisement in a newspaper or magazine. As s.13(3) makes clear, the fact that the goods are seen and selected by the buyer does not prevent the sale being one by description. Many goods are packaged and the buyer relies on the label or packaging for identification of the product. *Beale v Taylor*[10] extended this to a situation where the purchaser had examined the goods.

Beale v Taylor
[1967] 1 W.L.R. 1193

Mr Taylor had placed an advertisement for a car in a newspaper, describing the car as "Herald, convertible, white, 1961". After examining the car, Mr Beale decided to buy it. In fact, the car was an amalgamation of a 1961 Herald and another of a different year which had been welded together and was in a very dangerous condition. As this was a private sale, Mr Beale could not rely on the quality terms in s.14, so he had to resort to s.13. The English Court of Appeal held that the words "1961 Herald" formed part of the description which had not been complied with.

---

[9] [1920] 3 K.B. 475.
[10] [1967] 1 W.L.R. 1193.

The modern tendency is to draw a distinction between disputes about quality, which should be reserved for s.14, and those about the identity of the goods, which are appropriate to s.13. This point was made in *Border Harvesters Ltd v Edwards Engineering (Perth) Ltd*[11] where the buyers were dissatisfied with the performance of a drying machine. Their attempt to argue that this could be brought within s.13 failed the judge pointing out that they got what they bargained for namely, a drying machine of a certain type.

As *Beale v Taylor*[12] demonstrates, almost any words describing the goods will be regarded as part of the description. Strict compliance with description has been enforced in some cases.[13] However, as the unusual facts of *Harlingdon and Leinster Enterprises Ltd v Christopher Hull Fine Art Ltd*[14] demonstrate, there are limits. This case resulted from the sale of a painting which the defendants had purchased some time earlier when it had been described as being by the German artist, Munter. On the claimant, a specialist in German art, expressing interest in it the defendant emphasised that he did not know much about it, his particular expertise being in a different school of painting. The Court of Appeal held that it must be the intention of the parties that the description should be relied on. On the facts of this case that could not be said to have occurred.

(d) Duty to provide goods of satisfactory quality

5–21 A central aspect of any contract for the sale of goods will be the quality of the goods. Section 14 provides that there is an implied term that goods must be of satisfactory quality. Before looking at what exactly this means some preliminary points need to be noted. This implied term only applies to sales in the course of a business: private sales are not covered. A wide meaning is given to a sale in the course of a business as *Stevenson v Rogers*[15] demonstrates.

> **Stevenson v Rogers**
> **[1999] Q.B. 1028**
>
> Mr Rogers was a commercial fisherman who decided to sell his fishing boat and buy another one. The buyer alleged that there was a defect in the boat and Mr Rogers countered by arguing that as the sale was not in the course of a business the implied quality term did not apply. The English Court of Appeal disagreed. They pointed out that the boat was part of Mr Rogers' equipment as a fisherman and thus when he sold he was doing so in the course of his business.

---

[11] 1985 S.L.T. 128
[12] [1967] 1 W.L.R. 1193.
[13] See *Arcos v E. A. Ronaasen & Son* [1933] A.C. 470.
[14] [1990] 1 All E.R. 737.
[15] [1999] Q.B. 1028.

Another important point is that it does not matter that the seller was not in any way to blame for the defect. A classic example is *Frost v Aylesbury Dairy*.[16]

Frost v Aylesbury Dairy
[1905] 1 K.B. 608

The dairy had supplied Mr Frost and his family with milk which contained typhoid germs which caused the death of his wife. The evidence showed that the dairy's processes were extremely careful and that typhoid germs could only be detected by prolonged investigation. Nevertheless, it was held that there was an implied term that the milk would be reasonably fit for consumption. It was irrelevant that the defect could not have been discovered at the time of sale.

It can also be important that the term applies, to quote s.14(1), to "goods supplied under a contract of sale". This means that the labelling and packaging of goods are part of the product as are instructions. This was important in *Wormell v RHM Agricultural (East) Ltd*[17] where it was deficiencies in the instructions that rendered the product of unsatisfactory quality. It also means that material that was not intended to be included with the goods can also render them unsatisfactory. For example, in *Wilson v Rickett Cockerell & Co*[18] a bag of coal which contained a detonator rendered the consignment of unsatisfactory quality.

Section 14(2C) sets out two situations where the test of satisfactory quality does not apply. These are:

(1) Defects "specifically drawn to the buyer's attention before the contract is made". It is important to note that the factor must be specifically brought to the buyer's attention. In *Turnock v Fortune*[19] it was held by the Sheriff Principal that a strong recommendation from a third party not to buy a car did not amount to specifically drawing attention to its unroadworthiness, and thus did not prevent the car from being regarded as unmerchantable, the predecessor of satisfactory quality.

(2) If a buyer has examined the goods before the contract was made nothing which "that examination ought to reveal" can be relied on to demonstrate that the goods are not of satisfactory quality.

The definition of satisfactory quality

Section 14(2A) of the Act starts with a general definition of satisfactory **5–22** quality and then later subsections go on to set out some criteria for judging when goods are of satisfactory quality. Section 14(2A) states:

---

[16] [1905] 1 K.B. 608.
[17] [1986] 1 All E.R. 769.
[18] [1954] Q.B. 598.
[19] 1989 S.L.T. (Sh. Ct.) 32.

"For the purposes of this Act, goods are of satisfactory quality if they meet the standard that a reasonable person would regard as satisfactory, taking account of any description of the goods, the price (if relevant) and all the other relevant circumstances.

The standard is objective: not what the particular buyer considers but what the hypothetical reasonable person would consider reasonable. The reasonable person is not an expert, to quote the English Court of Appeal in *Jewson Ltd v Boyhan*.[20] In coming to a decision such a person must take into account the description attached to the goods. One cannot expect a second-hand car to be in as good a condition as a new one; but if a product is described as designed to the highest standards one is entitled to expect more from it than from a run-of-the-mill product. In *Clegg v Andersson* Hale L.J. pointed out that the buyer of a very expensive, brand new, ocean-going yacht is entitled to expect it to be "perfect or nearly so".[21]

Price is an ambiguous indicator of quality so it is to be taken into account only if relevant. Sometimes a lower price indicates lower quality but it may simply indicate a desire to sell items faster. In *Thain v Anniesland Trade Centre*,[22] for example, stress was put on the price together with the fact that the car was second-hand, not new, and had a high mileage as factors that lowered the level of quality that could be expected. At the other end of the scale, payment of a high price, as the observation of Hale L.J. in the previous paragraph demonstrates, will raise the standard of quality that can be expected.

In addition to these factors, "all the other relevant circumstances" are to be considered. In *Britvic v Messer*[23] this seems to have been important. The case involved the sale of carbon dioxide by the manufacturer to a soft drinks firm that added it to its products. It had been contaminated with minute traces of benzene which is carcinogenic. Despite the fact that the levels were well below the levels that were considered unsafe it was decided that the benzene was not of satisfactory quality because of the commercial fact that consumers would not be prepared to buy products to which it had been added.

Although it was probably unnecessary, subss.(2D)–(2F) were recently added to the section making it clear that public statements by "seller, the producer or his representative, particularly in advertising or on labelling" are relevant circumstances. *Lamarra v Capital Bank plc*[24] makes it clear that the fact that new cars come with a manufacturer's warranty is not a relevant circumstance.

In addition to the general definition, s.14(2B) states that:

---

[20] [2003] EWCA Civ. 1030, para.78.
[21] [2003] 1 All E.R. (Comm) 721, para.73.
[22] 1997 S.L.T. (Sh. Ct.) 102.
[23] [2002] EWCA Civ. 548.
[24] 2007 S.C. 95.

"the following (among others) are in appropriate cases aspects of the quality of goods—

    (a) fitness for all the purposes for which goods of the kind in question are commonly supplied,

    (b) appearance and finish,

    (c) freedom from minor defects,

    (d) safety, and

    (e) durability."

The first factor is that the goods are fit for all the purposes for which goods of the kind in question are commonly supplied. This is clearly an important factor. If a kettle does not boil water or a car breaks down frequently, no-one would think it of satisfactory quality. If goods have more than one purpose and the seller intends his product to fulfil only one of those purposes it will be necessary to make this clear. This may be done explicitly or, in some circumstances, other factors such as the price may indicate this fact.

The case of *Jewson Ltd v Boyhan*[25] shows that the implied term of satisfactory quality is not the appropriate one where the buyer has a particular purpose in mind.

Jewson Ltd v Boyhan
[2003] EWCA Civ. 1030

The buyer was a property developer who purchased from Jewsons a number of electric central heating boilers for installation in flats that he was constructing. He discovered that these boilers had poor energy ratings according to government approved tests and feared that the flats would therefore be difficult or impossible to sell. This caused him to abandon the project and when Jewsons sued him for the price of the boilers he counterclaimed for several hundred thousand pounds based on his loss of profit and increased costs resulting from the installation of the boilers, as opposed to boilers with better energy ratings. He argued that among the purposes for which the boilers had to be fit was ensuring that they would not render the flats in which they were to be installed difficult or impossible to sell. In effect, the Court of Appeal did not accept that this was one of "the purposes for which goods of the kind in question are commonly supplied". As one of the judges put it: "[The buyer] got exactly what he had bargained for: twelve boilers which worked perfectly well".[26]

Appearance and finish, and freedom from minor defects are also to be taken into account in determining whether goods are of satisfactory quality. The application of this test will, of course, depend on the facts. Second-hand goods may be expected to have some minor marks or defects while,

---

[25] [2003] EWCA Civ. 1030.

[26] [2003] EWCA Civ. 1030, para.79.

usually, new goods should not. Hale L.J. pointed out in *Clegg v Andersson*, a consumer case, that: "In some cases, such as a high priced quality product, the customer may be entitled to expect that it is free from even minor defects, in other words perfect or nearly so".[27] However, certain kinds of product such as earthenware, pottery or natural products may be expected to have minor inconsistencies and blemishes and these may well not render them of unsatisfactory quality. In some cases this test will have no application at all as in the case of cars sold as scrap and loads of manure.

There has never been any doubt that unsafe goods were not of the quality demanded by law[28] and this is explicitly recognised in the definition. Safety was the central factor in *Clegg v Andersson*.[29] A new ocean-going yacht costing £250,000 was delivered to the buyer with a keel which was substantially heavier than the manufacturer's specification. Technical evidence showed that this would render the rigging unsafe and, in the circumstances, the Court of Appeal had no difficulty in finding that the yacht did not meet the standard of satisfactory quality.[30]

The final factor is durability. It is important to realise that this term is to be satisfied at the time of delivery and not at some later date. Later events may be relevant in determining whether, at the time of sale, the goods were durable.[31] This factor was important in the first case to discuss the new satisfactory quality term, *Thain v Anniesland Trade Centre*.[32]

Thain v Anniesland Trade Centre
1997 S.L.T. (Sh Ct) 102

Ms Thain had paid £2,995 for a second-hand Renault 19 car which had travelled about 80,000 miles and was about six years old. Two weeks after she purchased it an intermittent droning noise was noticed and this proved to be a failing differential bearing in the automatic gear box. The sellers refused to replace the gear box. Eventually, after about nine to ten weeks, the car was unusable and Ms Thain rejected it. The Sheriff Principal upheld the Sheriff's decision that the car was of satisfactory quality observing:

"The sheriff's conclusion can only be described as that of the reasonable person. Even a negligible degree of durability may not represent unsatisfactory quality where the second-hand car supplied is as old and as heavily used as the Renault had been. The plain fact is that, given the Renault's age and mileage when supplied, its durability was a matter of luck. Durability, in all the circumstances, was simply not a quality that a reasonable person would demand of it."[33]

---

[27] [2003] 1 All E.R. (Comm) 721; [2003] EWCA Civ. 320; [2003] 2 Lloyd's Rep. 32, para.72.
[28] *Godley v Perry* [1960] 1 WL.R. 9, CA; *Lambert v Lewis* [1982] A.C. 225.
[29] [2003] 1 All E.R. (Comm) 721; [2003] EWCA Civ. 320; [2003] 2 Lloyd's Rep. 32.
[30] [2003] 1 All E.R. (Comm) 721, paras 49 and 73.
[31] *Crowther v Shannon Motor Co Ltd* [1975] 1 WL.R. 30.
[32] 1997 S.L.T. (Sh. Ct.) 102; 1997 S.C.L.R. 991.
[33] 1997 S.L.T. (Sh. Ct.) 102 at 106.

(e) Duty to provide goods to fit a particular purpose specified by the buyer

Section 14 of the Act has another separate implied term about quality in s.14(3). This states that where goods are sold in the course of a business and the seller "expressly or by implication, makes known" to the seller "any particular purpose for which the goods are being bought, there is an implied term that the goods supplied under the contract are reasonably fit for that purpose, whether or not that is a purpose for which such goods are commonly supplied, except where the circumstances show that the buyer does not rely, or that it is unreasonable for him to rely, on the skill or judgment of the seller ..."

This term only applies if the buyer has made it clear that the goods are wanted for a particular purpose. That does not have to be spelt out in the case of goods which have only one purpose such as a kettle or a hot water bottle. Where goods might be used for several purposes the term can only be relied on if that particular purpose that the buyer has in mind has been made clear to the seller. The result may then be that goods which are of satisfactory quality will not satisfy this term. Take the example of someone who needs paint to paint a wooden fence. He or she asks the seller for suitable paint for this job and is advised to buy a certain tin of paint. On applying the paint it soon peels off. It turns out that this is because it is paint which is suitable only for painting metal work. The seller would be in breach of this implied term although the paint is perfectly good paint for its proper purpose.

Flynn v Scott[34] makes clear that the particular purpose must be clearly specified. There, the subject of the sale was a lorry which could have been used for a number of different functions, though the buyer intended to use it to transport furniture and livestock. A claim for breach of the implied term of fitness for purpose failed because it was not shown that the buyer had communicated his particular purpose.

If the customer has some susceptibility, this must be communicated to the seller. *Griffiths v Peter Conway Ltd*[35] is an example.

Griffiths v Peter Conway Ltd
[1939] 1 All E.R. 685

Mrs Griffith developed a very severe attack of dermatitis as a result of wearing a tweed coat purchased from the defendants. Her skin was unusually sensitive and the evidence showed that there was nothing in the cloth that would have affected a normal person's skin. As Mrs Griffiths had not informed the sellers of her sensitivity they were not liable.

---

[34] 1949 S.C. 442; 1949 S.L.T. 399.
[35] [1939] 1 All E.R. 685, approved in *Slater v Finning Ltd*, 1996 S.L.T. 912; [1996] 3 All E.R. 398, HL.

(f) Duty to provide goods matching sample

Goods may often be sold by reference to a sample. Consumer sales of wallpaper and carpets are examples where the buyer chooses the particular design from a book of samples. In this situation s.15(2) provides that:

> "In the case of a contract for sale by sample there is an implied term—
>
> (a) that the bulk will correspond with the sample in quality;
>
> (c) that the goods will be free from any defect, making their quality unsatisfactory, which would not be apparent on reasonable examination of the sample."

Key Concept

In contracts of sale there are usually *express* terms which are clearly spelled out in the contract and *implied* terms which are not.

SOGA ss.12, 13, 14 and 15 provide for implied terms in relation to the duties of the seller. These terms apply whether the seller has been at fault or not, *Frost v Aylesbury Diary* (1905).

Seller's remedies

(i) Action for the price—s.49

5–23 If the property in the goods has passed to the buyer and he has not paid the seller's principal remedy is to sue for the price.

(ii) Damages for non-acceptance—s.50

Section 50 deals with the situation where the buyer refuses to take delivery of the goods. The seller can sue for non-acceptance and s.50(2) states that the measure of damages (i.e. how damages are assessed) is, in principle, "the estimated loss directly and naturally resulting, in the ordinary course of events, from the buyer's breach of contract". If there is a market for the goods in question, this will be the difference between the contract price and the market price.

(iii) Other remedies

In commercial transactions the sellers may discover that they are not going to be paid at a point where they still have control of the goods. This gives them useful powers as follows:

(a) Right of lien over goods—ss.39(1)(a) and 41

This is a right to retain the goods until they have been paid for.

(b) Stoppage in transit—ss 44–46

If the seller learns that the buyer has become insolvent while the goods are being transported, s.44 gives a right to retake possession of them and keep them until payment is received.

(c) Right of resale—ss.39(1)(c) and 48

Where goods are perishable or the unpaid seller gives notice of intention to resell, this may be done within a reasonable time.

Buyer's remedies

If it is the seller who is in breach of the contract, the buyer has a number **5–24** of possible remedies. Remember that the seller must be able to demonstrate that in some way the seller has failed to carry out the terms of the contract. This may be a failure to honour an express term or one of the implied terms. For example, if the buyer considers that the goods are not of good quality, it is necessary to show that they do not meet the standard of satisfactory quality in s.14. It is only then that the buyer can start to consider which of the following remedies he or she wishes to pursue.

Consumer buyers now have a choice of two sets of remedies. In addition to the set of remedies available to all buyers whether they are consumers or trade buyers, consumers can opt for a set of "additional remedies" as the Act calls them. The set of remedies available to all kinds of buyers will be referred to as the "original remedies" and those available only to consumers as the "additional consumer remedies".

The original remedies

Right to reject

Section 15B of the Sale of Goods Act 1979 provides that, where the seller **5–25** is in breach of any term of a contract the buyer is entitled to claim damages and, if the breach is material, to reject the goods and treat the contract as repudiated. This is what was called "rescission".

As Hale L.J pointed out in the English case of *Clegg v Andersson* (2003):

"... the customer has a right to reject goods which are not of satisfactory quality. He does not have to act reasonably in choosing rejection rather than damages or cure" [and the fact that this remedy] ... may be thought to be disproportionate by some is irrelevant ..."

While the customer does not have to act reasonably, he or she must show that there was a "material" breach and act fairly quickly. What is "material" depends on the circumstances of the particular case.

However, the section goes further in the case of consumer contracts. Consumer contracts mean those meeting the definition in s.25 of the Unfair Contract Terms Act 1977. In these contracts, breach of any express or implied terms about the quality or fitness of goods for a purpose and correspondence with description or sample, is deemed to be a material breach. This makes clear that the primary remedy of a consumer for the common breaches of contract is rejection of the goods. Section 15B does not deem breach of the implied term about title to be material. It is difficult to conceive of circumstances where this would not be so.

Conditions for rejecting

5–26   (i) You must tell the seller that you are rejecting, though, unless the contract says so, you need not return the goods—see s.36.

(ii) The goods must not have been accepted. The right to reject ceases to be available when the consumer has accepted the goods in the legal sense. When goods are accepted is defined in s.35 of the Sale of Goods Act 1979. It occurs in three circumstances:

(1) The buyer has intimated to the seller that he has accepted the goods. If the buyer says that the goods have been accepted, rejection is no longer possible. Note that consumers often are asked to sign "acceptance notes" which could have this effect. The effect of s.35(3) is that signing an acceptance note can no longer sign away the consumer's rights to reject the goods.

(2) On receiving delivery, the buyer does an act inconsistent with the seller's ownership. In commercial transactions, the most common situation where this arises is in the re-sale of goods. For a Scottish case involving a consumer, see:

> **Hunter v Albancode plc**
> (1989)
>
> Mrs Hunter bought a suite of furniture which proved to be defective and she purported to reject it. When it was not uplifted by Albancode, Mrs Hunter continued to use it as she could not afford to replace it until she obtained a refund. The Sheriff held that continuing to use the goods amounted to an act inconsistent with the seller's ownership and thus the right to reject had been lost.

Section 35(7) makes clear that agreeing to a repair does not amount to an act inconsistent with the seller's ownership.

(3) After the lapse of a reasonable time, the buyer retains the goods without intimating to the seller that he has rejected them. What is a reasonable time is a question of fact and will vary from product to product, being longer for more complex products. In *Clegg v Andersson* which we looked at on

another point above, the buyer of the yacht took delivery in August. He did not reject the goods until the following March. This was not too late. This lengthy period is explained by the fact that he was entitled to delay his decision to accept or reject the yacht until the seller had provided him with the necessary technical information to make a decision. When he got that information he then made up his mind to reject with three weeks after consulting his technical advisers.

Other aspects of rejection

Section 35A of the Sale of Goods Act 1979 deals with partial rejection. **5–27** Where a buyer has the right to reject goods but is prepared to retain some of them and reject only the remainder, the right to reject is not lost by retaining some of them. Where goods are delivered by instalments, the right to reject a non-conforming instalment is not lost by having accepted another instalment.

Where the seller delivers too few goods, or too many, s.30 provides that rejection is only possible where the excess or shortfall is material.

Damages

Section 15A provides that damages is also a remedy where a contract of **5–28** sale is breached. This may be the only remedy for the non-material breach of an express term, or may be the remedy which must be used where the right to reject has been lost through acceptance.

The Sale of Goods Act applies the normal contract rule that the damages should be such as result naturally from the breach in the ordinary course of events. Where the breach is the failure of the seller to deliver the goods, s.51 goes on to say that where there is an available market for the goods, the measure of damages is, *prima facie*, to be ascertained by the difference between the contract price and the market or current price of the goods at the time that they ought to have been delivered.

Where the seller delivers the goods but is in breach of one of the terms of the contract regarding quality, s.53A states how the consumer's loss is to be calculated. It is "the difference between the value of the goods at the time of delivery to the buyer and the value they would have had if they had fulfilled the contract". In addition, other damage may have resulted to the buyer or his or her property. In *Godley v Perry* a defective catapult resulted in the purchaser losing an eye, and the claim for breach of contract was mainly for damages for this injury.

Specific implement

Recall your general contract law. From that it will be clear that this **5–29** remedy will rarely be of any importance as one of the original remedies in contracts for sale of goods. Notice the different position under the new additional consumer remedies.

The additional consumer remedies

5–30 Consumers, and only consumers, may invoke a different set of remedies. They can, however, choose to use the original remedies. The additional remedies are set out in Part 5A of the Sale of Goods Act 1979. Remember, before these remedies can come into play you must be able to show that there is a breach of some term of the contract express or implied. Notice the very useful provision in s.48A(3):

> "... goods which do not conform to the contract of sale at any time within the period of six months starting with the date on which the goods were delivered to the buyer must be taken not to have so conformed at that date."

The additional remedies are:

- repair or replacement—s.48B;
- reduction in price—s.48C;
- rescission of the contract—s.48C.

The remedies are available in that order. So notice that under this new system of remedies the primary remedy is repair or replacement.

Repair or replacement—who Decides?

5–31 The consumer decides (subject to some qualifications) and it must be

- done within a reasonable time;
- without significant inconvenience to the buyer;
- at the seller's expense (includes labour, cost of materials and postage).

Repair or replacement must be possible, not be "disproportionate" to the other remedy and neither must be disproportionate to price reduction or rescission.

Reduction in price or rescission

5–32 These are the second and third remedies but only come into play if repair and replacement:

- are not possible;
- are too expensive (disproportionate);
- cannot be achieved within a reasonable time and without significant inconvenience to the buyer.

Where rescission is the remedy any reimbursement can include a deduction for use. So, if you have had a washing machine for six months when it develops a serious fault which cannot be repaired and the machine cannot be replaced you might choose to rescind the contract.

That is the same as rejecting the goods. The seller can say that as you have had six months' use of the machine you should not get a full refund. A proportion of the price should be deducted to take account of six months' use.

Enforcing the new rights—s.48E

The new rights can be enforced by an order of specific implement. This is a court order requiring someone to do something, in this case to repair goods, offer a replacement or a price reduction.

5–33

The buyer's duties

- To pay.
- To take delivery.
- To accept the goods.

5–34

OTHER CONTRACTS FOR THE SUPPLY OF GOODS

Part 1A of the Supply of Goods and Services Act 1982 provides implied terms and remedies for certain types of contract by which goods can be obtained.

5–35

The categories of contracts affected

(a) Contracts for the transfer of goods (s.11A)

Section 11A defines these as those "under which one person transfers or agrees to transfer to another the property in goods, whether or not services are also provided, other than an excepted contract", i.e.:

5–36

- contract of sale;
- hire purchase contract;
- contract where there is no consideration;
- contract operating by way of mortgage, pledge, charge or security.

Examples of contracts within this definition would be: barter; contracts for work and materials; goods exchanged for tokens or coupons.

What terms are implied?

- s.11B—Terms about title.
- s.11C—A term about description.
- s.11D—Terms about quality and fitness for purpose.
- s.11E—Correspondence of sample with bulk.

5–37

As these are virtually a carbon copy of those found in the Sale of Goods Act 1979, they are not reproduced here.

Remedies

5–38 Section 11F sets out the remedies in language appropriate to Scots law. It is a copy of s.15A of the Sale of Goods Act 1979.

(b) Contracts of hire

5–39 Contracts of hire are defined by s.11G of the Supply of Goods and Services Act 1982 as contracts "under which one person ('the supplier') hires or agrees to hire goods to another whether or not services are also to be provided whatever the nature of the consideration other than hire purchase contracts".

Examples are rentals, e.g. television or short-term car hire, leasing, finance leasing, and contract hire.

What terms are implied?

5–40
- s.11H—Terms about title.
- s.11I—A term about description.
- s.11J—Terms about quality and fitness for purpose.
- S.11K—Correspondence of sample with bulk.

Remedies

These are not set out in the Act. The common law remedies therefore apply.

EXCLUSION OF LIABILITY

5–41 Suppliers of goods will often attempt to exclude or limit their legal liability to the buyer. This topic is covered in detail in Chapter 4 on Contract Law to which reference should be made and is only briefly dealt with here. Section 20 of the Unfair Contract Terms Act 1977 provides that in contracts of sale, hire purchase and contracts governed by Part 1A of the Supply of Goods and Services Act 1982 terms purporting to exclude or limit the implied terms about title are void. Where the other implied terms are concerned, greater protection is given to consumers than to commercial buyers. The various terms about description, quality, fitness for purpose and sale by sample cannot be excluded in consumer contracts. In other contracts their exclusion will only be effective if it can be shown to be fair and reasonable.

▼ CHAPTER SUMMARY

5–42
1. One of several contracts can be involved when goods are supplied. These include sale, hire-purchase, barter and goods supplied when services are also performed.
2. The most common supply of goods contract is the contract of sale and it is governed by the Sale of Goods Act 1979.

3. A contract of sale is one the seller transfers or agrees to transfer the property in goods to the buyer for a monetary consideration, called the price (Sale of Goods Act 1979 s.2(1)).
4. The Act has rules about when legal title to the goods passes from the seller to the buyer (Sale of Goods Act 1979 ss.16–18).
5. These rules are also important in deciding who bears the risk if something goes wrong during a transaction.
6. A seller can only sell what he owns and if he tries to sell something that is not his the buyer generally does not become the owner (Sale of Goods Act 1979 s.21).
7. To this rule there are several exceptions:

   (a) personal bar;
   (b) sale by a mercantile agent;
   (c) if a seller has a voidable title, and that title is not reduced by the time of sale to a purchaser who buys in good faith without notice of the defect in title, the purchaser may keep the goods;
   (d) Sale of Goods Act 1979 s.23— *Macleod v Kerr* (1965);
   (e) buyer or seller in possession after sale (Sale of Goods Act 1979 ss.24 and 25)—*Archivent Sales and Developments Ltd v Strathclyde Regional Council* (1985).
   (f) sales of motor vehicles subject to hire purchase or conditional sale (Hire Purchase Act 1964 ss.27–29).

8. The heart of the Sale of Goods Act 1979 is a series of sections which implies various terms into all contracts of sale.)Note that these terms apply whether the seller has been at fault or not, see *Frost v Aylesbury Dairy* (1905)). They are:

   • The seller has the right to sell the goods (s.12(1)).
   • There is no charge or encumbrance over the goods (s.12(2)(a)).
   • The buyer will enjoy quiet possession of the goods (s.12(2)(b)).
   • The seller will not be liable for the charge or encumbrance if the charge or encumbrance is disclosed (s.12(3), (4) and (5)).
   • Goods will correspond with their description (s.13). See *Beale v Taylor* (1967).
   • Goods sold must be of satisfactory quality (s.14(2)).

   Important cases on satisfactory quality are *Clegg v Andersson* (2003), *Thain v Anniesland Trade Centre* (1997) and *Lamarra v Capital Bank plc* (2007).

   • Goods must be reasonably fit for a purpose which has been specified by the buyer (s.14(3)). See *Griffiths v Peter Conway* (1939).
   • The terms in s.14 apply only to sales in the course of a business. See *Stevenson v Rogers* (1999).
   • The bulk will correspond with any sample (s.15).

9. Breach by the seller of these implied terms entitles a purchaser to various remedies. These are:

EITHER

(a) **to reject the goods and get his or her money back**
(b) **damages**
(c) **specific performance (rare)**

Rejection must be made fairly quickly (Sale of Goods Act 1979 s. 35).

OR alternatively (Sale of Goods Act 1979 Part 5A)

(a) **repair or replacement**
(b) **compensation to make up for the defect**
(c) **reject the goods and get money back**

Damages is a sum of money that represents the loss to the person making the claim (Sale of Goods Act 1979 s.53A). Normal contract rules about damages apply.

10. **If it is the buyer who has broken the contract the seller has the following remedies:**

    (i)   **action for the price—s.49**
    (ii) **damages for non-acceptance—s.50**
    (iii) **other remedies**

        (a) **right of lien over goods—ss.39(1)(a) and 41**
        (b) **stoppage in transit—ss.44–46**
        (c) **right of resale—ss.39(1)(c) and 48**

11. **Other contracts for the supply of goods.**

    (a) **There are similar implied terms in the contracts of barter or where goods are transferred when services are also being rendered (Sale and Supply of Goods Act 1982 Part 1A).**
    (b) **The Contract of Hire. The Supply of Goods and Services Act 1982 ss.11H–11K implies terms into hire contracts.**

? QUICK QUIZ

- Name three types of contract dealing with the supply of goods.
- Which Act of Parliament governs contracts of sale?
- How is a contract of sale different from other contracts for the supply of goods?
- There are exceptions to the rule that someone who is not the legal owner of goods cannot pass on a good title to them. State two of them.
- What terms are implied in contracts of sale?
- When are goods of satisfactory quality?
- When does the satisfactory quality test not apply?
- What remedies are available to a purchaser who buys defective goods?

- What remedies are available to a seller if the buyer breaks the contract?
- What terms are implied in contracts for the transfer of goods governed by the Supply of Goods and Services Act 1982?

📖 FURTHER READING

Atiyah, Adams and MacQueen, *The Sale of Goods Act* (11th edn, Pearson, 2005).
Ervine, *Consumer Law in Scotland* (4th edn, W. Green, 2008).

🖰 RELEVANT WEBLINKS

Department of Business, Enterprise and Regulatory Reform: *http://www.berr.gov.uk/*.

Chapter 6   Consumer Protection

Cowan Ervine[1]

▶ OVERVIEW OF THE CHAPTER

6–01 This chapter deals with two major aspects of consumer protection. After pointing out that other chapters deal with some facets of the topic it deals first with consumer credit. The various methods by which credit can be provided are explained. Consumer credit is largely governed by the Consumer Credit Act 1974 which has been updated by the Consumer Credit Act 2006. The special terminology that the Act uses are discussed and then the various methods by which consumers are protected. This involves a licensing system and requirements to provide consumers with information so that they know what they are letting themselves in for. There are some special protections for consumers of credit such as connected lender liability where the credit provider can be liable for the failings of the supplier of the goods or services. The courts have special powers to deal with consumers who run into difficulties with their credit agreements.

The second part of the chapter deals with the control of various trade practices. This section concentrates on the new Consumer Protection from Unfair Trading Regulations 2008 which implement the EC's Unfair Commercial Practices Directive. This is designed to deal with various practices which may harm consumers. These may appear in advertising or sales promotions. The regulations create a duty not to trade unfairly. There is a general ban on unfair trade practices as well as bans on misleading actions, misleading omissions and aggressive practices. In addition there is a list of specific practices which are always deemed unfair. The Office of Fair Trading and local trading standards officers enforce these regulations using various methods both criminal and civil.

✓ OUTCOMES

6–02 After studying this chapter you should:

- ✓ be aware of the range of ways in which consumers are protected;
- ✓ know in more detail how consumer credit and trade practices are controlled;

---

[1] Senior Lecturer in Law, University of Dundee.

✓ in relation to credit know that:

- the major statute is the Consumer Credit Act 1974;
- the licensing system is important;
- consumers are entitled to information before making credit agreements;
- there are special protections during the agreement;
- credit granters can be liable for what the suppliers of goods and services say;
- Sheriffs have wide powers to deal with breaches of agreements.

✓ In relation to trade practices know that:

- there are new regulations making major changes in their control;
- these regulations introduce a duty not to trade unfairly;
- they are enforced in a number of ways.

INTRODUCTION

The term consumer protection is a convenient name for a range of legal **6–03** rules which are designed to protect individuals who purchase goods or services for their own personal use or consumption. Some of its rules are closely related to areas of law that you will have touched on in other chapters of this book. For example, in the chapter on the Law of Contract you will have seen that the control of exclusion clauses and other potentially unfair terms are controlled by the Unfair Contract Terms Act 1977 and the Unfair Terms in Consumer Contracts Regulations 1999. The contract rules about misrepresentation and undue influence can also be important in the protection of consumers. In Chapter 10 "Law of Delict" the important case of *Donoghue v Stevenson* was discussed at length. This is one of the most important consumer protection cases of all time. The same chapter discusses strict liability for defective products contained in Part 1 of the Consumer Protection Act 1987, another very important piece of consumer protection legislation. This chapter deals with two other important areas of consumer protection: consumer credit and the control of unfair trading practices.

CONSUMER CREDIT

As a walk down any high street will show, credit is very important. On all **6–04** sides consumers are being urged to borrow money or purchase goods on credit. Credit comes in many forms. Banks and finance companies offer overdrafts and personal loans, shops sell goods on hire purchase and other forms of credit and goods and services can be paid for by credit cards. Pawnbrokers and moneylenders are also sources of credit. Because of its importance economically and the problems that it can cause for consumers, credit is heavily regulated by law. The principal controls are found in the Consumer Credit Act 1974 which has recently been amended by the Consumer Credit Act 2006.

The Consumer Credit Act 1974

6–05 The Consumer Credit Act 1974 (the 1974 Act) regulates a wide range of credit transactions. However, it should be realised that aspects of the ordinary law of contract, such as the law on formation and mis-representation still apply, and the 1974 Act does not apply to all credit contracts, as we shall see below.

The 1974 Act applies to two types of agreement:

- credit agreements;
- hire agreements.

> **Key Concept**
>
> Consumer credit is governed by the Consumer Credit Act 1974. It covers both consumer credit and consumer hire agreements. A key idea in the Act is that of the "regulated agreement". With few exceptions, it is only regulated agreements that are covered by the Act.

Credit agreements

6–06 The Act applies to what it calls "regulated" credit agreements. To qualify an agreement must be:

    (i) with an individual;
    (ii) either:

        a debtor-creditor-supplier agreement, or
        a debtor-creditor agreement;

    (iii) not be exempt.

(i) Individuals

6–07 "Individual" here means human beings as well as partnerships of not more than three partners (not more than one of whom is a limited company) and unincorporated bodies such as clubs as long as they do not consist entirely of bodies corporate and are not partnerships.

(ii) Debtor-creditor-supplier agreements

6–08 A debtor-creditor-supplier agreement can arise in three ways.[2] It occurs where a restricted use credit agreement is made to finance a transaction

---

[2] Consumer Credit Act 1974 s.12.

between a debtor and a creditor. An example would be a hire purchase or credit sale agreement where the supplier provides the finance. Where, as is probably more common, a third party provides restricted use finance this, too, is a debtor-creditor-supplier agreement if made under pre-existing arrangements, or in contemplation of future arrangements between the creditor and the supplier. The typical hire purchase arrangement, where the finance is provided by a finance company, is a good example, but credit card and check trading transactions provide further examples. The third situation deals with the case where a third party provides unrestricted use credit under pre-existing arrangements with the supplier in the knowledge that the credit is to be used to finance a transaction between the debtor and the supplier. This brings within the ambit of debtor-creditor-supplier agreements situations where a supplier, such as a retailer, has agreed to refer customers to a finance company which will provide them with loans which, although technically not limited to the purchase of a specific product, all parties know will be so used.

(iii) Debtor-creditor agreements

Restricted use credit agreements which would be debtor-creditor-supplier **6–09** agreements but for the fact that there are no pre-existing arrangements between the creditor and the supplier are known as debtor-creditor agreements. Restricted use credit arrangements to refinance any existing indebtedness of the debtor are in the same category. So are unrestricted use credit agreements which are not made by the creditor under pre-existing arrangements with a supplier.[3] Examples are bank overdrafts, moneylenders' advances and loans from pawnbrokers.

Consumer hire agreements

Section 15 of the 1974 Act defines a consumer hire agreement. It is **6–10**

- made by an individual (the "hirer");
- for the hiring of goods to the hirer;
- not a hire purchase agreement;
- capable of lasting for more than three months.

Typical examples of hire agreements are TV rentals. Cars are sometimes acquired in this way through what are known as finance leases. Short-term car hire for a weekend or a holiday will not be included because of the requirement to be capable of lasting for more than three months.

Exempt agreements

Agreements which would come within the definition are exempt. Most of **6–11** these are set out in s.16 of the Act and its related orders. They are:

---

[3] Consumer Credit Act 1974 s.12.

(1) Agreements where the creditor is a local authority, building society or one of a number of other organisations listed in the section where the loan is secured on land.

(2) Agreements financing purchases of land which do not gain exemption under the previous exemptions will be exempt if the number of payments to be made does not exceed four.[4]

(3) A debtor-creditor-supplier agreement for fixed sum credit which is not hire purchase or conditional sale where the number of payments to be made by the debtor in respect of the credit does not exceed four and must be made within 12 months of the date of the agreement.

(4) A debtor-creditor-supplier agreement which is not for hire purchase or conditional sale and provides running account credit where the whole of the credit is repayable in one instalment.

(5) A low interest exemption for debtor-creditor agreements, low being defined as an annual percentage rate which does not exceed 1 per cent above the highest base rate of an English or Scottish clearing bank in the 28 days prior to the making of the agreement.[5]

(6) An agreement with a "high net worth" person. This allows someone who is wealthy to agree not to have the protections of the Act presumably because they are thought to know how to look after themselves.

(7) Credit exceeds £25,000 or hire payments are more than £25,000 if the agreement is entered into by the debtor or hirer wholly or predominantly for the purposes of a business.

Partially regulated agreements

Small agreements

6–12 A consumer credit agreement for credit not exceeding £50 which is not a hire purchase or conditional sale agreement, a regulated consumer hire agreement which does not require the hirer to make payments exceeding £50 and a non-commercial agreement are only subject to some of the controls in the Act.

Controlling business activities

6–13 Various parts of the Act regulate the way in which those in the credit industry can carry on their businesses. In addition to the licensing system there are controls on advertising, canvassing for business, the marketing of credit cards and the operation of credit reference agencies.

---

[4] Consumer Credit (Exempt Agreements) Order 1989 (SI 1989/869) art.3(1)(b).
[5] Consumer Credit (Exempt Agreements) Order 1989 (SI 1989/869) art.4.

The licensing system

One of the most important aspects of the 1974 Act is the licensing system **6–14**
that it set up. It is operated by the Office of Fair Trading (OFT). The
overall effect is that almost anyone involved in the credit industry must
have a licence though local authorities and bodies corporate with statutory powers to carry on business are not required to have them. Section
21 of the 1974 Act provides that licences are required to carry on a
consumer credit or consumer hire business which involves any of the
following activities:

(1) credit brokerage;
(2) debt-adjusting;
(3) debt counselling;
(4) debt collection;
(5) debt administration;
(6) credit information services;
(7) credit reference agency.

Credit brokerage includes not only businesses acting as brokers in the
ordinary sense of the term but many dealers and services providers.
Retailers, for example, even though they themselves do not provide
credit, must have a licence, because they introduce customers to sources
of finance such as hire purchase companies.

There are two types of licence: a "standard licence" which can be issued
to sole traders, partnerships and companies, and "group licences" which
are issued where the OFT considers that it is in the public interest to do
so, rather than require those affected to apply individually. Group
licences, of which there are currently 14, have been issued to the Law
Society of Scotland and Citizens' Advice Scotland.

To obtain a licence an applicant must show that the name which the
business will use is not misleading or otherwise improper; and that "he is
a fit person to engage in activities covered by the licence".[6] The fitness test
involves not only the honesty and integrity of the applicant but also its
experience and competence.

In addition to the power to refuse a licence, the OFT may revoke or
suspend one that has been issued if the holder has done things that would
have prevented a licence being granted in the first place. Alternatively,
financial penalties can be imposed.

Advertising controls

Credit advertising is subject to the controls in the Consumer Protection **6–15**
from Unfair Trading Regulations 2008 discussed later. In addition, regulations made under powers in the 1974 Act prescribe information that
must be included in advertisements. This can included so-called "wealth

---

[6] Consumer Credit Act 1974 s.25(1).

warnings" and the Annual Percentage Rate (APR) showing the cost of credit.

Canvassing

6–16 Canvassing debtor-creditor agreements (of which the most common type will be personal loans) off trade premises is a criminal offence. So is soliciting the entry of an individual into such an agreement during a visit carried out in response to a request made on a previous occasion, if the request was not in writing and signed by the person making it.

Circulars to minors

6–17 In line with the policy of protecting vulnerable consumers, the Act makes it a criminal offence to send to a person under 18 years old, with a view to financial gain, any document inviting him or her to borrow money, obtain goods or services on credit, hire goods, or even apply for information about doing any of these things.

Distribution of credit tokens

6–18 Credit tokens, such as credit cards, may only be distributed in response to a written and signed request though there are exceptions in the case of renewals. Otherwise s.51 makes it a criminal offence to supply one.

Credit reference agencies

6–19 Credit reference agencies play an important part in the credit industry by providing information to credit granters about consumers. This often involves a credit score based on this information. Given the importance of credit scoring and access to credit, the accuracy of the information held by credit reference agencies is vital. Their existence also raises other issues related to privacy. For this reason the Act contains protections for consumers. Section 157 imposes a duty on a creditor, owner or negotiator to respond within seven working days[7] to a written request for the name and address of any credit reference agency from which information has been sought about the customer's financial standing. This obligation is complemented by s.7 of the Data Protection Act 1998 which allows consumers to see files relating to them.

Key Concept

The ways in which those in the credit industry do business is heavily regulated. Of the methods used the most important is the licensing system.

---

[7] See Consumer Credit (Credit Reference Agency) Regulations 1977 (SI 1977/329) reg.3.

Form and content of agreements

In a further attempt to ensure that consumers know exactly what they are **6–20**
doing, the form and content of regulated agreements are closely regulated.[8] The debtor or hirer must be made aware of:

- the rights and duties conferred or imposed on him by the
  agreement;
- the cost of credit;
- the protection and remedies available under the 1974 Act;
- any other matters which it is desirable that creditors should know.

The Consumer Credit (Agreement) Regulations 1983[9] set out in great
detail the form, content, legibility and signature of documents containing
regulated consumer credit and hire agreements. Different types of
agreement require different types of information to be given and the
Regulations set out the requirements for each type in schedules. These
have in common the fact that the kind of information which must be
given falls into five main categories:

(1) heading on the first page of the document prominently stating
    the legal nature of the agreement;
(2) name and address of each party;
(3) financial information, such as the timing and amount of
    payments;
(4) the cost of credit, including the annual percentage rate (APR);
(5) other information such as details of any security provided and
    charges payable on default;
(6) remedies available under the Act.

The Regulations also require that there should be a signature box in an
agreement and go into detail on exactly how this is to be set out. In the
case of credit-token agreements the name, address and telephone number
of the person to whom notice is to be given of loss or misuse must be
included.

Proper execution of an agreement

Execution of an agreement is the technical term for the signing of it by **6–21**
both parties. To be properly executed, as the Act calls it, the following
requirements must be complied with:

(1) the document must be in the prescribed form containing all the
    prescribed terms and conform to the agreement regulations;
(2) it must contain all the terms of the agreement apart from the
    implied terms;

---

[8] Consumer Credit Act 1974 s.60.
[9] SI 1983/1553.

(3) it must be legible;

(4) the requirements of ss.62 and 63 about supplying copies;

(5) the cancellation provisions of s.64 or the special provisions of s.58 for a consideration period where there is a heritable security;

(6) it must be signed in the prescribed manner by the debtor and the creditor or owner.[10]

Copies of the agreement

6–22 The debtor or hirer must get at least one copy of an agreement and ss.62 and 63 of the Act have detailed rules about this. If the debtor signs an agreement at the same time as the creditor, a copy of the executed agreement must be given to the debtor then and there. Where an unexecuted agreement is presented to the debtor and he or she signs it but the creditor does not sign at that time, the debtor must then and there be given a copy of the unexecuted agreement. In addition, within seven days of the agreement being signed by the creditor a further copy must be sent. Where an agreement is sent to the debtor a copy must also accompany it. If the agreement has already been signed by the creditor and so becomes an executed agreement on the debtor signing it, no further copy need be sent. If, however, the creditor has not signed it at that stage a copy of the executed agreement must be sent within seven days of being signed by the creditor.

Consequences of improper execution

6–23 Where an agreement has not been properly executed it can only be enforced against a creditor or hirer by an order of the Sheriff Court.[11]

Withdrawal

6–24 Where the debtor or hirer has signed the agreement before the creditor has done so he or she will have an opportunity to withdraw what is, legally speaking, an offer. Section 57 says that no special wording is required; all that is required is that it "indicates the intention of the [consumer] to withdraw from a prospective regulated agreement".[12] The notice of withdrawal can be written or oral and can be given to the creditor or hirer, a credit-broker or supplier who is the negotiator in antecedent negotiations and any person who, in the course of a business carried on by him, acts on behalf of the debtor or hirer in any negotiations for the agreement.[13] Withdrawal has the same effect as cancellation and is discussed below.

---

[10] Requirements 1–3 and 6 are found in the Consumer Credit Act 1974 s.61.

[11] Consumer Credit Act 1974 s.65(1).

[12] Consumer Credit Act 1974 s.57(2).

[13] Consumer Credit Act 1974 s.175 provides that the deemed agent is under a contractual duty to the creditor or owner to transmit the notice to him forthwith.

Cancellation

In some circumstances someone who has entered into a consumer credit **6–25**
or hire agreement may cancel it. The period during which an agreement
may be cancelled is popularly known as the "cooling off" period. The
cancellation rules are set out in ss.67–73 of the 1974 Act. A regulated
consumer credit or hire agreement may be cancelled if two conditions are
met:

- oral representations have been made in the presence of the debtor
  or hirer during the course of antecedent negotiations;
- the subsequent agreement must not have been signed by the
  debtor or hirer at trade premises.

The "cooling-off" period begins when the debtor or hirer signs the
unexecuted agreement. It ends five days after the second statutory notice
or copy is received by the debtor or hirer. To exercise the right to cancel,
a notice must be served within the cancellation period on one of a number
of people. This notice, unlike a notice that one is withdrawing from a
prospective agreement, must be in writing. If it is posted it is deemed to
be served on the recipient at the time of posting, whether or not it ever
arrives.[14] The notice can be given to the same people to whom an
intention to withdraw from a prospective agreement may be sent, as well
as anyone specified in the statutory cancellation notice.[15] The effect of a
notice of cancellation is to cancel the agreement and any linked transaction; and to withdraw any offer by the debtor or hirer, or a relative, to
enter into a linked transaction.

During the agreement

Implied terms

Credit contracts relating to goods will be contracts of sale or contracts **6–26**
governed by one of the other statutes discussed in the chapter on Supply
of Goods. The terms implied by those statutes will therefore apply.

Connected lender liability

When consumers are buying goods on credit they will often deal only **6–27**
with the supplier, for example a shop. They will not have any contact
with the finance company or bank providing the credit. Despite this,
where there is a relationship between the supplier and the provider of the
credit the latter may be liable for the acts or omissions of the supplier.

---

[14] Consumer Credit Act 1974 s.69(7).
[15] Consumer Credit Act 1974 s.69(1).

Section 56: Liability for antecedent negotiations

6–28 Section 56 makes the finance provider liable for the statements of the supplier of the goods. It applies where a debtor-creditor-supplier trans-action is involved. A typical example would arise where the consumer buy using hire purchase. The consumer will see the goods in a shop and if he or she decides to buy using hire purchase the goods are sold to the finance company and, technically, it is the finance company that sells them to the consumer. The shop drops out of the transaction. Although it will probably have known nothing about the transaction in the shop the finance company is liable for any claims made there.

Section 75: Equal liability

6–29 Section 75 gives consumers valuable protection in certain situations. Where it applies the consumer can make the same claims against the company providing the credit claims for breach of contract and mis-representation that it can make against the supplier of the goods or services. However, four conditions must be met:

- the cash price of the goods or service being supplied must exceed £100 but not be more than £30,000 (including VAT);
- there must be a debtor-creditor-supplier agreement regulated by the 1974 Act, an agreement where credit of not more than £25,000 is advanced to an individual and which is not exempt under the Act;
- the provider of the credit is in the business of giving credit and the credit agreement is made in the course of that business; and
- the credit is advanced under pre-existing arrangements, or in contemplation of future arrangements, between the provider of credit and the supplier.

One of the most common situations where connected lender liability applies is a credit card transaction such as Access or Visa. Suppose that someone arranges a package holiday but after the cost has been paid but before the holiday has been taken the holiday company becomes insol-vent. If the cost has been paid by credit card the consumer can look to the credit card company for reimbursement. It would also apply where a consumer wished to buy a car from a motor dealer and the dealer arranged finance with a finance company with whom he had pre-existing arrangements. It would not apply where the consumer wished to buy the car and went to his bank and arranged a personal loan, even where the bank was aware that the loan was specifically for the purchase of the car. In this case the credit is not advanced under pre-existing arrangements between the supplier and the bank and there is not a debtor-creditor-supplier agreement.

It has been decided by the House of Lords in *OFT v Lloyds TSB Bank plc*[16] that this protection applies where a credit card is used abroad.

What is not clear is what exactly is meant by "a like claim". In *United Dominions Trust Ltd v Taylor*[17] it was decided that this meant that the consumer could not only rescind the supply contract but also the credit contract. This has been doubted by the English Court of Appeal.[18]

Termination

Regulated hire purchase and conditional sale agreements may be termi- **6–30** nated by the debtor at any time before the final payment falls due by giving notice to anyone who is entitled to receive payments under the agreement. To this right there are two exceptions, both relating to conditional sale agreements. Such an agreement relating to land, title to which has passed to the buyer, or one relating to goods where the property has vested in the debtor who has transferred the goods to someone else, cannot be terminated. On termination the debtor must pay the difference between what has been paid and half the total price of the goods. In making this calculation any installation charge is deducted first and the whole of that charge added as it is clearly reasonable that such a charge should be payable. It is possible that the amount due could be less if it can be shown that the creditor's loss is less.

In the case of a consumer hire agreement there is also a right to terminate, but the earliest time at which this can occur is 18 months after the making of the agreement. Notice of not less than the shorter of the shortest payment interval or three months must be given. Because early termination can cause hardship to the owner there are three circumstances in which the right is not available. These are: where the total payments, ignoring sums payable on breach, exceed £1,000 in any year; where the goods are let out for the hirer's business and were selected by him and acquired by the owner at his request from a third party; and, finally, where the hirer requires the goods to re-let them in the course of business.

Early settlement

At any time during a regulated consumer credit agreement the debtor **6–31** may give notice to the creditor of an intention to complete payments early.[19] This is only economic if there is a rebate on the total charge for credit and the regulations prescribe how this is to be calculated.[20]

---

[16] [2007] UKHL 48.
[17] 1980 S.L.T. (Sh. Ct.) 28. Followed in *Forward Trust v Hornby*, 1995 S.C.L.R. 574.
[18] *Jarrett v Barclays Bank plc* [1999] Q.B. 1.
[19] Consumer Credit Act 1974 s.94.
[20] See Consumer Credit (Rebate on Early Settlement) Regulations 2004 (SI 2004/1483).

Default

6–32 A consumer who breaks the terms of a credit agreement is said to be in default. A simple example would be where the buyer paying for goods on hire purchase fails to keep up the instalments. As credit agreements often have harsh terms which come into operation in this situation there are various protections for consumers in the 1974 Act.

Before a creditor can take action against a debtor, s.76 states that a default notice must be served specifying:

- the breach;
- what action needs to be taken to remedy it;
- if it is not capable of remedy the compensation required;
- the date by which this must be paid has to be stated.

Where a debtor has paid one-third or more of the total price of the goods, and the property in the goods remains in the creditor, the goods are known as "protected goods". This means that the creditor is not entitled to recover possession from the debtor except on an order of the Sheriff Court.

Judicial control

Enforcement orders

6–33 In some cases a credit agreement can only be enforced by the creditor by getting a court order. When this has to be done ss.135 and 136 give wide powers to the Sheriff to vary agreements.

Time orders

6–34 Where a creditor is taking action to enforce a credit agreement, s.129 of the Act gives wide powers to the Sheriff to make time orders. These are orders which permit the Sheriff to adjust the rate and time of payments of instalments by debtors, hirers or sureties. In addition, they can be used to specify the time within which a breach of an agreement, other than non-payment of money, should be rectified. There are parallel powers in relation to hire agreements in s.132.

Special powers relating to hire purchase and conditional sale agreements

6–35 In cases of hire purchase or conditional sale agreements, s.133 of the Act contains special provisions involving "return orders" and "transfer orders". Such orders may be made where an application for an enforcement order or time order has been made, or where the creditor has brought an action to recover possession of goods. They allow a Sheriff to adjust the transaction where more than one product is being bought and payments covering at least part of them have been made.

Unfair credit relationships

The power in the original Consumer Credit Act to reopen extortionate **6–36** credit bargains has been replaced by new provisions dealing with unfair credit relationships. From April 6, 2008 powers in ss.140A and 140B will apply where the relationship is unfair because of its terms, the way the creditor has exercised its rights or in any other way. A Sheriff will have wide powers to alter the original agreement.

> **Key Concept**
>
> The Consumer Credit Act provides sheriffs with wide powers to deal with breaches of credit and hire agreements (ss.132–136). In addition to these provisions, ss.140A–140D enable sheriffs to reopen unfair credit bargains.

THE CONSUMER PROTECTION FROM UNFAIR TRADING REGULATIONS 2008

Overview of the regulations

The Consumer Protection from Unfair Trading Regulations 2008[21] bring **6–37** about a major change in the way that UK law deals with unfair trade practices directed at consumers. These practices cover a wide range of things such as misleading advertisements, high pressure selling and various scams such as misleading and dishonest mailings to people informing them that they have won prizes in lotteries. The regulations are necessary to implement an EC Directive, the Unfair Commercial Practices Directive.[22] Some idea of the scale of the change may be gained by noting that it has been necessary to repeal several important pieces of existing legislation. Of these the best known is the Trade Descriptions Act 1968.

The approach of the directive is to create what may be called a duty on traders not to trade unfairly. The directive and the implementing regulations start by creating a general duty prohibiting unfair practices. This is expected to act as a safety net because there are more specific rules in the directive which are expected to catch most unfair practices. The purpose of the general prohibition is to ensure that resourceful traders do not get away with dubious practices that do not fall within the letter of the other parts of the regulations. In addition to the general duty, the regulations ban misleading acts and misleading omissions as well as aggressive practices. There is in addition a list of 31 practices which are regarded as so serious that they are always to be considered to be unfair.

---

[21] SI 2008/1277.
[22] 2005/29/EC.

Scope of the regulations

6-38 The regulations protect only consumers not businesses against unfair commercial practices. A consumer is an individual who is acting for purposes which are outside his business.[23] A commercial practice

> "means any act, omission, course of conduct, representation or commercial communication (including advertising and marketing) by a trader, which is directly connected with the promotion, sale or supply of a product to or from a consumer, whether occurring before, during or after a commercial transaction in relation to a product."

It should be noted that "product" means not just goods but also immovable property and services. The definition covers practices occurring before, during and after the purchase of a product. For example, high pressure selling techniques are used by some sellers and will be covered by this definition. Practices occurring after a product has been acquired such as after sales services promised on the sale of a car or the activities of debt collectors are covered. Because the practice is to be "directly connected" to the promotion, sale or supply of a product, manufacturers' practices can be caught. The Office of Fair Trading's draft guidance on the regulations gave the following example:

Example

A trader makes and sells processed cheese slices to supermarkets. Although the trader does not sell directly to consumers, any labels he produces must be compliant with the CPRs as they are directly connected with the promotion and sale of the cheese slices to consumers.

The regulations cover not only the sale or supply of a product *to* a consumer they also cover sale or supply by a consumer to a trader. This would catch the situation which arose in the Trade Descriptions Act 1968 case of *Fletcher v Budgen*[24] where a second-hand car dealer made false statements about a car which was traded-in in order to offer a lower price for it. The purpose of the regulations is to protect the economic interests of consumers. They are not concerned with questions of taste or decency.

Key Concept

The Consumer Protection from Unfair Trading Practices Regulations 2008 protects consumers rather than businesses against unfair commercial practices. A consumer is an individual who is acting for purposes which are outside business.

---

[23] Consumer Protection from Unfair Trading Regulations 2008 reg.2.
[24] [1974] 1 W.L.R. 1056.

Unfair practices

Regulation 3 is the key to the regulations. It states that "Unfair com- **6–39** mercial practices are prohibited" and then goes on to set out four situations when practices are unfair. These are:

- breaches of the general prohibition (reg.3(3));
- misleading actions;
- misleading omissions;
- banned practices.

Because the general prohibition is the least likely to be relevant in practice and the practices on the banned list the most likely it is useful to look at these categories in reverse order.

Schedule 1: Banned practices

Schedule 1 to the regulations sets out 31 practices which are considered **6–40** unfair in all circumstances. There is an outright ban on these practices. The first four involve false claims about involvement in trade organisations or schemes such as being a member of a code of conduct, that a code has been endorsed by a public body when it has not or that the trader or its products have been endorsed by someone when they have not. An example would be a claim by a plumber that he was a member of CORGI (the Council of Registered Gas Installers) when he was not.

"Bait advertising" and "bait and switch" advertising are on the list. These are advertisements about products which the seller does not intend to sell. Also included are false claims that a product can legally be sold, that it will be available for only a limited time, that consumers' legal rights are a distinctive feature of an offer or that the trader is about to close down. Various marketing scams are included such as pyramid schemes, bogus prize schemes and "free" gifts which involve further payments beyond the cost of responding or collecting the product. False claims that a product can facilitate winning at games of chance, cure illnesses, dysfunctions or malformations or that an after sales service is available outside the state in which it has been sold or will be available are all banned as is failing to honour an undertaking to provide after-sales service to consumers in a language other than that in which the trader has communicated with those consumers.

Direct appeals to children to buy advertised products or persuade their parents to do so are banned. Creating the impression that the consumer cannot leave the premises until a contract is formed, a practice associated with time-share marketing, conducting personal visits to the consumer's home, ignoring the consumer's request to leave or not to return, and making persistent and unwanted solicitations by telephone, fax, email or other remote means are also prohibited. Traders pretending not to be selling as traders are also included as are unsolicited product scams where goods are sent to someone who has not ordered them and then followed up with demands for payment. Using editorial content in the media to promote a product where a trader has paid for the promotion without making that clear, sometimes referred to as "advertorials", and promoting a product of a particular manufacturer in such a way as to mislead consumers to think that it is that of another manufacturer are also on the banned list.

Misleading practices

Misleading actions (reg.5)

6–41 Misleading action occurs when a practice misleads through the information it contains, or its deceptive presentation, and causes or is likely to cause the average consumer to take a different decision. For instance, if a trader falsely tells a consumer that his boiler cannot be repaired and he will need a new one, he will have committed a misleading action.

There are three ways in which actions can be misleading:

    (i) misleading information generally;
    (ii) creating confusion with competitors' products;
    (iii) failing to honour firm commitments made in a code of conduct.

(i) Misleading information generally. These are actions that mislead because:

- they contain false information or they deceive or are likely to deceive the average consumer (even if the information they contain is factually correct);
- the false information, or deception, relates to one or more pieces of information in a list (see below);
- the average consumer takes, or is likely to take, a different decision as a result. This is called a "transactional decision" in the regulations.

The false information must relate to various things set out in reg.5(4). The most important of these are likely to be the price and the main characteristics of the product. The "main characteristics" comprise a long list set out in sub-reg.(5) which is not unlike the list of features of a trade description contained in s.2 of the Trade Descriptions Act 1968. These include such things as the availability of the product, its benefits, risks, composition and accessories, fitness for purpose, quantity, origin, expected results from use and the results of tests carried out on it.

This is the part of the regulations which will catch the common practice of "clocking" a car, that is turning back the odometer or mileage recorder. This could come under "usage" in reg.5(5) or could more generally be within the general meaning of "main characteristic". Remembering that the regulations cover services as well as goods, another example could involve a package holiday. Suppose that a holiday brochure says that the hotel has a swimming pool and that when customers arrive there it is still under construction. This will be an example of false information about a main characteristic.

A claim does not have to be false if the overall effect is deceptive. An example could be a jar of moisturising cream sold in jars which have false bottoms and are substantially larger in appearance than required to hold the amount of cream. Even though the weight of the contents is accurately printed on the jar it could well be that this form of packaging would amount to a misleading practice.

(ii) Creating confusion with competitors' products. The second way **6–43** in which a practice may amount to a misleading action is where it is marketed in a way which creates confusion with any products, trade marks, trade names or other distinguishing marks of a competitor. This is designed to deal with practices such as copycat marketing where a manufacturer tries to benefit from the popularity of a successful product by producing one that looks similar to it. Again it must be shown that the average consumer would be likely to take a different decision.

(iii) Failing to honour firm commitments made in a code of con- **6–44** **duct.** The third kind of misleading actions arise where a trader who has undertaken to be bound by a code of conduct indicates that he is bound by it but fails to comply with a firm and verifiable commitment in it.

Example[25]

A trader who is a member of a code of practice that promotes the sustainable use of wood and uses the code's logo in an advertising campaign. The code of practice contains a commitment that its members will not use hardwood from unsustainable sources. However, it is found that the product advertised by the trader contains hardwood from endangered rainforests. This practice is a breach of a firm and verifiable commitment.

This misleading action must be likely to cause the average consumer to make a different decision.

Misleading omissions (reg.6)

Practices may be misleading not only because they positively mislead by **6–45** giving false information but also by failing to give consumers the information they need to make an informed choice. Regulation 6 deals with this aspect of unfair practices. A practice will be misleading by omission if it:

- omits material information;
- hides material information;
- provides material information in a manner which is unclear, unintelligible, ambiguous or untimely; or
- fails to identify its commercial intent.

---

[25] From OFT's Draft Guidance on the Regulations

It must also be shown that the average consumer would take a different decision as a result.

When deciding whether a practice misleads by omission, the courts will take account of the context and reg.6(2) says that certain factors be taken into account. These are the features and circumstances of the commercial practice, the limitations of the medium used to communicate the commercial practice, and where the medium used to communicate the commercial practice imposes limitations of space or time, any measures taken by the trader to make the information available to consumers by other means. Where, for example, a cereal bar wrapper contained an offer of a T-shirt at a low price as a promotional offer it might be difficult to include comprehensive information. An indication that full details of the offer could be found on the manufacturer's website might prevent a breach of the regulations.

The missing information must be "material" which means information that the average consumer needs, in the context, to make informed decisions. It includes any information required by European derived (EC) law, such as the Package Travel, Package Holidays and Package Tours Regulations and the Consumer Protection (Distance Selling) Regulations. What information is required may range from a very small amount of information for simple products, to more information for complex products.

If a commercial practice is what is called an "invitation to purchase" it must provide certain information or there will be a misleading omission. An "invitation to purchase" is, "a commercial communication which indicates characteristics of the product and the price in a way appropriate to the means of that commercial communication and thereby enables the consumer to make a purchase". It is not to be confused with the idea of an invitation to treat found in contract law though in some circumstances there may be overlap.

There will be many kinds of invitations to purchase. Newspaper advertisements containing prices will be examples as would an interactive TV advertisement through which consumers can place orders and restaurant menus. On the other hand, many advertisements which are designed to promote the trader's brand will not be. Newspapers, magazines and billboards often contain advertisements which merely draw attention to a product or company without giving specific details about price or the characteristics of products.

Where an advertisement is an invitation to purchase, reg.6(4) requires further information to be provided. Subject to the same considerations about the context and the limitations of the communication medium as we have seen apply to misleading omissions generally, the information must be provided in a clear, unambiguous, intelligible and timely manner.

The information that is deemed to be material in invitations to purchase includes:

- the main characteristics of the product;
- the identity of the trader;
- the trader's address;

- the price of the product (including taxes);
- any arrangements for payment, delivery or performance;
- complaint handling that differ from consumers' reasonable expectations.

Aggressive practices (reg.7)

Regulation 7 sets out the circumstances in which a practice will be **6–46** regarded as aggressive. There are three requirements:

- that harassment, coercion or undue influence has been used by a trader;
- that this has significantly impaired or is likely significantly to impair the average consumer's freedom of choice;
- that this has caused or is likely to cause the average consumer to take a different decision.[26]

The aggressive practices which might be regarded as aggressive will be numerous and varied. The draft guidance on the regulations given by the OFT cites the example of a mechanic who has a consumer's car at his garage and has done more work than agreed, and who refuses to return the car to the consumer until he is paid in full for the work. The mechanic did not check with the consumer before he went ahead with the extra work. As he has the car, he has power over the consumer's decision to pay for the unauthorised work. He has exploited his position of power, by demanding payment for doing more than was agreed and refusing to return the vehicle until the consumer has paid for all the work.

The exploitation of specific misfortune is one of the factors to be taken into account in deciding if a practice is aggressive. This could arise where staff working in a funeral parlour put pressure on a recently bereaved relative, who is deciding on a coffin, to buy a more expensive coffin as a better mark of respect. This might be seen as coercion or undue influence. An example of harassment might arise where a debt collector persistently telephones a debtor late at night or telephones the debtor at his workplace.

The general clause

Regulation 3(1) and (3) of the regulations set out the general prohibition **6–47** on unfair business to consumer commercial practices. This can catch practices which are neither misleading nor aggressive and are not on the list of banned practices.

To come within the general prohibition a practice must

- contravene the requirements of professional diligence; and
- materially distort the economic behaviour of the average consumer.

---

[26] reg.7(1).

Professional diligence is defined (in reg.2) as:

> "the standard of special skill and care which a trader may reasonably be expected to exercise towards consumers which is commensurate with either
>
> (a) honest market practice in the trader's field of activity, or
> (b) the general principle of good faith in the trader's field of activity, or both."

This general clause is designed as a safety net to catch practices which cannot be brought within one of the other categories. In this way it is hoped that the regulations will not be circumvented by devious traders.

Who is the "average" consumer?

6–48 Whether commercial practices are generally unfair or unfair because they are misleading or aggressive depends on their effect on the "average consumer". It has no application to the practices in the banned list in Sch.1. It is important, therefore, to know what is meant by the "average consumer". There are three different applications of the test. First, it means the "average consumer whom it reaches or to whom it is addressed", to quote the directive on which the regulations are based. We know from the recitals to the directive that this means someone "who is reasonably well-informed and reasonably observant and circumspect, taking into account social, cultural and linguistic factors".

This might not work very fairly in some circumstances so "when a commercial practice is directed to a particular group of consumers" it is the average member of that group which is to be taken as the benchmark. For example, if a television advertisement were shown during a children's programme the test would be its effect on an average child.

Another variation of the test applies where a practice is aimed at "a clearly identifiable group of consumers who are particularly vulnerable to the practice or the underlying product because of their mental or physical infirmity, age or credulity in a way which the trader could reasonably be expected to foresee". An example might be elderly infirm people in relation to advertisements about stair lifts. In that case the test would be the effect on the average elderly consumer.

Key Concept

Commercial practices are unfair if they are misleading actions, misleading omissions or one of those on the list of banned practices. In addition, a practice can be unfair because it contravenes the requirements of professional diligence. With the exception of the practices on the banned list unfairness is judged by the effect on the "average customer".

Enforcement

The regulations will be enforced using a number of techniques invoking **6–49** both civil and criminal law. In the least serious cases no formal action may be necessary and it may be more a matter of guidance and education or issuing warning letters. In more serious cases enforcers have formal options. Regulation 20(4) directs enforcers to "have regard to the desirability of encouraging control of unfair commercial practices by such established means as it considers appropriate having regard to all the circumstances of the particular case". For example, if an enforcer is satisfied that a problem with an advertisement can be adequately dealt with by the Advertising Standards Authority which has a well-established record of dealing with complaints about advertisements it could refer the complaint to that body.

Where an informal approach or reference to established means is not appropriate, enforcers may take civil enforcement action in respect of any breach of the regulations as Community Infringements under Part 8 of the Enterprise Act 2002. Under this procedure, enforcers may apply to a court for an enforcement order to prevent Community or Domestic infringements. Breach of an enforcement order could be contempt of court which could lead to up to two years' imprisonment and/or an unlimited fine. This procedure is discussed in detail later in this chapter.

Breach of the regulations in almost all cases will be criminal offences. They fall into two broad categories: those involving proof of mens rea (guilty intent) and those which are strict liability offences. Regulation 8 is the mens rea offence making traders criminally liable for breach of the general duty not to trade unfairly contained in reg.3. To prove this offence it must be shown that the trader "knowingly or recklessly" engaged in a commercial practice which contravenes the requirements of professional diligence; and "the practice materially distorts or is likely to materially distort the economic behaviour of the average consumer (within the meaning of reg.3(4)) with regard to the product".

The other offences are strict liability offences of the kind that have been common in consumer protection statutes. All that is required is that the prohibited conduct is proved; it is not necessary to show any form of mens rea or guilty mind. The apparent harshness of this is ameliorated by providing certain due diligence defences. Regulation 9 makes it an offence to engage in a commercial practice which is a misleading action except for breaches of commitments in codes of conduct. Misleading omissions are offences under reg.10 and reg.11 makes aggressive practices criminal offences as well. Regulation 12 makes most of the commercial practices listed in Sch.1 criminal offences. The exceptions are the offence in para.11 of the Schedule of promoting a product in editorial content in the media without revealing that the material has been paid for and, somewhat surprisingly, the offence in para.28 of including in an advertisement a direct exhortation to children to buy advertised products or persuade their parents or other adults to buy advertised products for them.

Enforcement action can only be taken by the Office of Fair Trading and District Councils. Private consumers and consumers cannot do so.

Other trade practices

6–50 Although the Consumer Protection from Unfair Trade Practices Regulations 2008 largely replace more specific legislation on unfair practices there are several other pieces of legislation which are still in force and these are described below.

Doorstep selling

6–51 Stories about high pressure methods used by some sales representatives who call at people's home are common. Some have been known to stay for hours and to leave only when the consumer agrees to sign a contract. To combat this sort of practice the Consumer Protection (Cancellation of Contracts Concluded away from Business Premises) Regulations 1987[27] were passed. They implement The EC's Doorstep Selling Directive.[28] Where they apply a consumer has a right to cancel the contract (a cooling-off period) within seven days.

The regulations apply where a contract relating to goods or services is made:

> (a) during an unsolicited visit to the home of a consumer,[29] or to another person's home, and also to a person's workplace;
> (b) during a visit which was requested if it results in a contract to supply goods or services other than those concerning which the consumer requested the visit and the consumer did not or could not reasonably have known, when the visit was requested, that the supply of those goods or services formed part of the trader's business activities;
> (c) during an excursion organised by a trader away from trade premises;
> (d) after an offer was made by the consumer in the above situations.

The regulations do not normally apply where the visit is at the request of the consumer. A visit is considered to be unsolicited if it follows an earlier unsolicited visit during which a trader indicates that he or some other trader is prepared to make a subsequent visit to the consumer. They also cover a visit following an unsolicited telephone call where the person who visits the consumer is not the same as the person who made the telephone call.

Contracts outside the regulations:

> • for the sale of land, or for a lease or land mortgage;

---

[27] SI 1987/2117 (as amended by Consumer Protection (Cancellation of Contracts Concluded away from Business Premises) (Amendment) Regulations 1988 (SI 1988/958); and Consumer Protection (Cancellation of Contracts Concluded away from Business Premises) (Amendment) Regulations 1998 (SI 1998/3050)).

[28] Directive to Protect the Consumer in Respect of Contracts Negotiated away from Business Premises, Dir. 85/577; [1985] O.J. L372/31.

[29] "Consumer" means a person, other than a body corporate, who, in making a contract is acting for purposes which can be regarded as outside his business: see reg.2(1).

- to finance the purchase of land;
- bridging loans for the purchase of land;
- building contracts;
- any contract for the supply of food, drink or other goods intended for current consumption in the household and supplied by regular roundsmen;
- contracts of insurance;
- Contracts resulting from catalogues;
- any agreement the making or performance of which by either party constitutes a relevant regulated activity;
- the total payments to be made by the consumer do not exceed £35;
- credit contracts with a right of withdrawal under s.67 of the Consumer Credit Act 1974 (see section on credit above);

Cancellation

Consumers have a cooling-off period of seven days from the making of **6–52** the contract during which they may cancel the contract by giving written notice of cancellation. This need be in no particular form as long as it indicates the intention of the consumer to cancel the contract. The fact that there is a cooling-off period must be brought to the attention of consumers by an easily legible notice which must be given at least as much prominence as any other information in the document. The notice must be given to the consumer at the time of making the contract or, where consumers offer to enter into a contract in their homes, when they make that offer. Failure to comply with this requirement means that the contract is not enforceable and that the trader commits a criminal offence.[30]

Where consumers exercise their rights to cancel, any money that they have paid becomes repayable and there is a lien (a right to retain the goods) for its repayment over any goods supplied under the contract which may be in the possession of a consumer. Subject to this lien, consumers who are in possession of goods are under a duty to take reasonable care of them pending their return to the supplier. Although under no obligation to deliver the goods to the supplier other than at their own homes, consumers may choose to return them to the person on whom a cancellation notice could have been served. These duties to take reasonable care of the goods and to return them are statutory duties and are actionable as such.[31] There are detailed provisions in the Regulations dealing with the return of goods given in part exchange[32] and the repayment of credit.[33]

---

[30] regs 4, 4A.
[31] reg.7(8).
[32] reg.8.
[33] reg.6.

Distance selling[34]

6–53 Goods and services are often bought without face to face contact. Mail order is a long-standing example but now sales over the internet or by telephone or teleshopping are very common. Special rules for the protection of consumers are contained in the Consumer Protection (Distance Selling) Regulations 2000.[35] This implements the EC's Distance Selling Directive[36]

The Regulations apply to contracts for goods or services to be supplied to a consumer where the contract is made exclusively by means of distance communication such as fax, email or telephone. There are a number of exceptions for contracts relating to the supply of financial services, certain contracts relating to land, those concluded through automated vending machines, auctions and those concluded through a telecommunications operator using a public pay-phone. The Regulations have limited application to contracts for the supply of groceries by regular delivery and contracts for the provision of accommodation, transport, catering or leisure services.

The Regulations require the supplier to provide the consumer with various pieces of information prior to the conclusion of the contract. This includes information on the right to cancel the contract, the main characteristics of the goods or services, delivery costs where appropriate and the seller's geographical address.

A cooling-off period enables the consumer to cancel the contract by giving notice of cancellation to the supplier. The effect of giving notice of cancellation is that the contract is treated as if it had not been made. Where the supplier supplies the information to the consumer on time, the cooling-off period is seven working days from the day after the date of the contract, in the case of services, or from the day after the date of delivery of the goods. Where the supplier fails to comply with the information requirement at all, the cooling-off period is extended by three months. Where the supplier complies with the information requirement later than he should have done but within three months the cooling-off begins from the date he provided the information.[37]

Certain contracts are excluded from the right to cancel unless the parties agree otherwise, such as a contract for the supply of goods made to the consumer's specifications.[38] If consumers cancel, they must be reimbursed within a maximum period of 30 days[39] and any related credit agreement is automatically cancelled.[40] On cancellation of the contract the consumer is under a duty to restore goods to the supplier if he collects them and in the meantime to take reasonable care of them. The Regulations do not require the consumer to return goods but if he is required

---

[34] For a more detailed discussion of distance selling regulation, see Ch.7 on E-commerce.
[35] SI 2000/2334, which came into effect on October 31, 2000.
[36] Dir. 97/7; [1997] O.J. L144/4, p.19.
[37] SI 2000/2334, regs 8–10.
[38] reg.13.
[39] reg.14.
[40] reg.15.

to under the contract and does not do so, he must pay the cost to the supplier of recovering them.

Unless otherwise agreed the supplier must perform the contract within 30 days beginning with the day after the day on which the consumer sent the order to the supplier. However, where the supplier is not able to provide the goods or service ordered, substitutes may be offered provided this possibility was included in the contract and formed part of the information supplied to the consumer and this was done in accordance with reg.7.[41]

Regulation 21 amends the Consumer Credit Act 1974 by removing the potential liability of the debtor under a regulated consumer credit agreement for the first £50 of loss to the creditor from misuse of a credit-token in connection with a distance contract where the consumer's payment card is used fraudulently. Where the consumer's payment card is used fraudulently in connection with a distance contract the consumer will be entitled to cancel the payment.

Timeshare

Timeshare is a right to use accommodation at a holiday development or **6–54** resort for a specified number of weeks each year over a specified period of time or in perpetuity. To acquire this right an "owner" pays a lump sum to a "developer". In addition, there are usually annual service charges and there may also be optional annual fees for participation in a scheme to exchange timeshares with others. There have been many complaints about sharp practice in the timeshare market and as a result the Time-share Act 1992 was passed. It has been extensively amended[42] to implement the EC's Timeshare Directive.[43]

The approach of the 1992 Act is first to try to ensure that consumers make a properly informed decision to buy a timeshare, and then to give a period for reflection during which they can cancel the arrangement. To further the first objective s.1A requires a timeshare operator to provide anyone who requests it with information about the accommodation. Failure to do so is a criminal offence. If the consumer purchases a timeshare this information is deemed to be a term of the contract. To combat the many complaints about high pressure selling methods s.5 provides that a cooling-off period must be provided during which the consumer can choose to cancel the contract. Consumers who have entered into a timeshare agreement must be given a notice informing them of this right and the cooling-off period must be at least 14 days from the date of the contract.[44] Not only may consumers withdraw from the contract during the cooling-off period, the operator cannot enforce the agreement during that period. That means, for example, that the seller

---

[41] reg.19.
[42] Timeshare Regulations 1997 (SI 1997/1081), with effect from April 29, 1997. Further amendments were made by Timeshare Act 1992 (Amendment) Regulations 2003 (SI 2003/1922), with effect from September 1, 2003.
[43] [1994] O.J. L.280/83.
[44] Timeshare Act 1992 s.2.

may not ask for or accept any money from the consumer during it.[45] The 14-day cooling-off period will be extended to three months and 10 days if the operator fails to include certain information which must be given under s.1A about the timeshare. The 1992 Act also covers "timeshare credit agreements" which are those financed by credit but which do not come within the cooling off provisions of the Consumer Credit Act 1974. Here the same notice of cancellation rights must be given.

Estate agency

6–55 Estate agency has been the subject of much criticism over many years because of the sharp practices of a minority of those involved in it.[46] The Estate Agents Act 1979 controls certain aspects of the work of estate agents and it is enforced by the OFT and district councils. The 1979 Act does not control entry into the profession: instead, it creates a system of negativing licensing. The OFT is given powers to ban persons from acting as estate agents if it finds that they are unfit to do so. The grounds which may render a person unfit include convictions for fraud, dishonesty or violence; convictions for breach of the 1979 Act; failure to comply with other obligations under the 1979 Act; and discrimination.

In addition, ss.12–21 impose duties on estate agents. They must give certain information about their charges and when these are payable. There is a duty to declare any conflict of interest or personal interest in the transaction. Where deposits are taken from a purchaser, there are duties relating to keeping the money in a clients' account. Failure to observe the duty to provide the client with information about charges results in the contract being unenforceable without the approval of the sheriff.[47] As a result of the Consumers, Estates Agents and Redress Act 2007 estate agents must belong to a redress scheme. That Act will shortly amend the Estate Agents Act 1979 to tighten up the controls on estate agents.

Enforcement orders

6–56 Under Part 8 of the Enterprise Act 2002, the Office of Fair Trading, Trading standards authorities, regulators of particular industries such as gas, electricity and telecommunications and other designated enforcement bodies such as the consumer organisation *Which?*, can apply to the courts to stop traders infringing a wide range of consumer protection legislation. This power is not designed to deal with the complaints of individual consumers. To obtain an enforcement order it must be shown that the conduct of the trader is harming the "collective interests of consumers". These orders are known as Enforcement Orders. Breach of an Enforcement Order is a contempt of court and could result in a fine or imprisonment.

Enforcers can also use Enforcement Orders to clamp down on traders

---

[45] Timeshare Act 1992 s.5B.
[46] See *Estate Agency: A report by the Director-General of Fair Trading* (OFT, March 1990).
[47] Estate Agents Act 1979 s.18(6).

who fail to carry out a service with reasonable care and skill. The Office of Fair Trading is responsible for co-ordinating enforcement action under the Regulations.

Who can seek enforcement orders?

Under Part 8 of the Act there are three types of enforcers, outlined below. **6–57**

(i) General enforcers

In addition to the OFT, the Trading Standards Service.

(ii) Designated enforcers

- the Civil Aviation Authority;
- the Director General of Electricity Supply for Northern Ireland;
- The Director General of Gas for Northern Ireland;
- Ofcom;
- the Water Services Regulation Authority;
- the Gas and Electricity Markets Authority;
- the Information Commissioner;
  the Office of Rail Regulation;
- the Financial Services Authority;
- Consumers' Association (Which?).

(iii) Community enforcers

Community enforcers are entities from other EEA states that are listed in the Official Journal of the European Communities. These enforcers may apply for injunctions in other member states.

▼ CHAPTER SUMMARY

1. **Consumer credit is governed by the Consumer Credit Act 1974. It** **6–58**
   covers both consumer credit and consumer hire agreements
2. **A key idea in the Act is that of the "regulated agreement". With**
   few exceptions, it is only regulated agreements that are covered by
   the Act.
3. **A regulated consumer credit agreement is (see s.15) one:**

   i. with an individual
   ii. either:
      a debtor-creditor-supplier agreement, or
      a debtor-creditor agreement, and
   iii. Not exempt.
   'Individual' here means human beings as well as small
   partnerships.
4. **A regulated consumer hire agreement (see s.16) is:**

   - **made by an individual (the "hirer");**

- **for the hiring of goods to the hirer;**
- **not a hire purchase agreement;**
- **capable of lasting for more than three months.**

5. **Consumers are protected in several ways.**

   (a) **Control of business practices**

   - **Those in the credit industry must have a licence.**
   - **Advertising is controlled.**
   - **Loans cannot be sold door-to-door.**
   - **Credit cards can only be sent to those who request them.**

   (b) **Controls on making a credit agreement**

   - **Credit documents must be in the right form.**
   - **Copies must be given to the consumer.**
   - **In some cases there is a cooling-off period allowing a consumer to have second thoughts (ss.67–73).**

   (c) **Protection during the agreement**

   - **Connected lender liability—see ss.56 and 75.**
   - **On s.75 see *OFT v Lloyds TSB Bank plc* (2007).**
   - **Right to terminate (ss.99–104).**
   - **Early settlement (ss.94–97).**

   (d) **Protection of those in financial difficulty**

   - **Goods on hire purcahse cannot be repossessed if "protected" (s.90).**
   - **Creditors can only take action against a consumer who is in breach of an agreement if a default notice has been served.**
   - **Sheriffs have wide powers to deal with breaches of credit and hire agreements (ss.132–136).**
   - **These include power to reopen unfair credit bargains (ss.140A–140D).**

? QUICK QUIZ

- Which is the main statute governing consumer credit?
- Which two categories of agreement does the Act referred to in the previous question cover?
- Name two ways in which the activities of traders in the credit industry are controlled.
- Who runs the credit licensing system?
- What is connected lender liability?
- Why were the Consumer Protection from Unfair Trading Regulations 2008 introduced?
- As well as a general ban on unfair practices the regulations ban four different types of unfair practice. Name them.

- Describe a specific practice banned by the regulations.
- What is meant in the regulations by the "average consumer"?
- What methods are used to enforce the Consumer Protection from Unfair Trading Regulations 2008?
- Name other legislation controlling a trade practice.

📖 FURTHER READING

Ervine, *Consumer Law in Scotland*, 4th edn (W. Green, Edinburgh, 2008).

🖰 RELEVANT WEBLINKS

Department for Business Enterprise and Regulatory Reform: *http://www.berr.gov.uk/*.
Office of Fair Trading: *http://www.oft.gov.uk/*.

Chapter 7 E-Commerce

GILLIAN BLACK[1]

▶ CHAPTER OVERVIEW

7–01 Electronic commerce, or e-commerce, is the term usually applied to commercial transactions concluded online or by way of email. Typically this will refer to buying and selling goods and services over the internet, and this chapter will focus on the legal regulation of such transactions. These regulations apply both where the goods or services are provided online, such as software or music downloads, and where they are provided in real-time, such as the physical delivery of books, DVDs or other purchases ordered online. The chapter will start with a short introduction to e-commerce and the need to regulate it, and then look at three areas: (i) the Electronic Commerce Regulations, (ii) the Distance Selling Regulations, and (iii) a brief summary of other legislation which impacts on online transactions.

✓ OUTCOMES

7–02 By the end of this chapter you should be able to:

- ✓ understand the significance of e-commerce in an economic and political context;
- ✓ understand the legal regulation of contracts concluded online;
- ✓ be familiar with the obligations imposed on service providers by the Electronic Commerce Regulations;
- ✓ know what suppliers must do to comply with their obligations under the Distance Selling Regulations;
- ✓ understand the protection given to consumers under the Distance Selling Regulations; and
- ✓ be aware of other areas of law, such as data protection and sale of goods, which affect e-commerce.

---

[1] Lecturer in Law, University of Edinburgh.

Introduction

Why regulate E-commerce?

When the internet first came to prominence (in the early to mid-1990s) **7–03** there was some question as to whether it was possible or desirable to regulate its use, particularly the World Wide Web.[2] Early users of the internet saw it as a global, unregulated space. However, with increasing use of the internet in everyday life, especially in commerce, the need for regulation increased. Governments had a vested interest in ensuring safe access to the internet, in order to promote business interests and protect consumers. Recognising the excellent opportunity provided by the internet to promote the freedoms of the Community, particularly regarding the provision of goods and services, the European Community has led the way in promoting consumer confidence and opening up the Internal Market online. Thus, a small trader in rural Spain can now access nearly 500 million people in 27 member states. The same trader can combine traditional retail practices with online e-tailing (known as "bricks and clicks") or can operate purely online, either independently or through a third party site, such as eBay, for example.

The main advantages of trading online for businesses are access to a wider (and far-flung) customer base; the opportunity to offer more specialised or tailored goods or services; the low start-up costs, especially with regard to physical premises; and the ability to market and promote products and services at a relatively low cost. For consumers, the primary benefits are the much wider range of goods and services available, which can be accessed with ease through online searches; the quantity of information and ability to compare different goods and services, and to compare the same goods and services provided by different e-tailers; and the "open all hours" availability of the web.

Although figures for the value of e-commerce vary widely, a recent review by the Office of Fair Trading (OFT) indicates that consumer spending online in the United Kingdom in 2005 was just over £21 billion, four times the £5 billion that was spent online in the United Kingdom in 2002.[3] Only 10 per cent of this online spend was incurred in cross-border transactions, however.[4] Further, despite the high value of online shopping in 2005 in the United Kingdom, it amounted to only 3 per cent of UK retail sales.[5] Both these figures illustrate that there is a considerable way to go to before online retail and cross-border sales are of greater economic significance in the United Kingdom.

---

[2] The internet is the term for the world-wide network which enables computers to communicate, and which hosts, among other things, the World Wide Web. The internet also enables email communication. The Web, or WWW, is probably the best known element of the internet, and consists of billions of webpages which provide information, and enable global research and commerce on an unprecedented scale.

[3] "Internet Shopping", An OFT Market Study, June 2007, pp.9 and 17.

[4] "Internet Shopping", An OFT Market Study, p.5.

[5] "Internet Shopping", An OFT Market Study, p.6.

> **Key Concepts**
>
> Online trading (or e-tailing) allows traders to reach a much wider market, and enables consumers to choose from a wider range of goods and services at more competitive prices.

Concluding contracts electronically

7–04 If persons are to trade electronically, the most important question to consider is whether, and if so, how, contracts can be concluded electronically. Scots contract law only requires a formal written contract in limited situations, most notably contracts relating to land.[6] However, the Requirements of Writing (Scotland) Act 1995 has now been amended to provide that contracts which require formal validity can be concluded electronically, where the granter has authenticated the electronic document by adding his digital signature, and this digital signature is certified in accordance with the Act.[7] This means that all contracts under Scots law can be entered into electronically, where there has been compliance with the provisions of the 1995 Act as amended.

In all other cases, a wholly or partially verbal contract is sufficient in Scots law. Email, being similar to a telephone conversation which is written down, or a fax, is therefore sufficient to conclude a contract, albeit not one that requires formal validity.

In addition to these specific provisions regarding conclusion of contracts electronically, it is important to remember that all other principles of contract law still apply in the online world. Thus, both parties to the contract must have capacity, and the validity of the contract could be challenged where there is evidence of force and fear or undue influence, for example.[8]

However, life is undeniably more complex in online transactions. There are two European Directives which regulate commercial transactions executed online, and impose additional obligations on traders who wish to take advantage of the internet. The next section of the chapter will examine the Electronic Commerce Directive, while the following section will consider the Distance Selling Directive.

---

[6] The Requirements of Writing (Scotland) Act 1995, s.1(1) and (2), and Chapter 4 Contract Law.

[7] See ss.1(2A), 2A and 3A of the Requirements of Writing (Scotland) Act 1995, as amended by the Automated Registration of Title to Land (Electronic Communications) (Scotland) Order 2006 (SSI 2006/491), made under s.8 of the Electronic Communications Act 2000.

[8] For further detail on these principles, see Chapter 4 Contract Law.

> **Key Concepts**
>
> Electronic contracts are still contracts: the basic principles of contract law continue to apply. Scots law has been amended to recognise the validity of electronic writing where formal writing is required.

THE ELECTRONIC COMMERCE REGULATIONS

1. Introductory matters and defined terms

The Electronic Commerce Directive[9] has been implemented in the United Kingdom as the Electronic Commerce (EC Directive) Regulations 2002[10] ("E-Commerce Regulations"). These regulations are undeniably complex to interpret and apply, partly because they are heavily reliant on a number of defined terms, which are not immediately familiar to Scots lawyers. For example, the E-Commerce Regulations regulate providers of "information society services", a rather wide-ranging term which covers **7–05**

> "any service normally provided for remuneration, at a distance, by means of electronic equipment for the processing (including digital compression) and storage of data, and at the individual request of a recipient of the service."[11]

This broad concept covers most online commercial activities, including: (i) the online sale of goods and services; (ii) the activities of internet service providers (ISPs) and email providers, who enable access to the internet and email; and (iii) online or email advertising. However, for the E-Commerce Regulations to apply, all elements of this definition must be fulfilled. Face-to-face transactions will therefore be excluded by virtue of the need for the "distance" service provision. Services which are not provided at the individual request of the recipient will also be excluded, such as those broadcast television channels which are provided to all users simultaneously and not on demand.

It is very important to note that the E-Commerce Regulations extend to commercial contracts between businesses ("B2B") as well as between businesses and consumers ("B2C"). Any B2B contracts will therefore be protected, as well as B2C contracts. Service providers must ensure they comply with the E-Commerce Regulations in all their dealings, not merely consumer contracts.

However, the E-Commerce Regulations do not apply to all electronic

---

[9] Directive 2000/31/EC of the European Parliament and of the Council of June 8, 2000 on certain legal aspects of information society services, in particular electronic commerce, in the Internal Market.

[10] SI 2002/2013.

[11] As defined in E-Commerce Regulations, reg.2, with reference to recital 17 of the Electronic Commerce Directive.

activities conducted at a distance. The activities of a public notary and
the defence of a client's interests before the courts are excluded, as are
betting, gaming or lotteries where there is a financial stake involved.[12] In
addition, the E-Commerce Regulations do not apply in respect of taxation, data protection matters, or any practices governed by cartel law.[13]

A further introductory point is that the E-Commerce Regulations aim
to ensure that member states do not hinder the creation of an internal
market by imposing legal barriers to cross-border online activities.
Accordingly, the E-Commerce Regulations create a "coordinated field",
and operate within that field. This coordinated field is defined as the field
of legal regulation relating to online provision of information, advertising, shopping and contracting, and those legal requirements which concern the behaviour of the service provider and its services. However, the
coordinated field does not include legal requirements directed towards
"goods as such", for example the regulation of the sale of goods or safety
standards.

Regulation 4 states that where a service provider is affected by legal
requirements in the coordinated field then the applicable legal requirement shall be that of its home jurisdiction, irrespective of where the actual
information society services are provided.[14] Under this provision, a service provider based in Scotland would come under the jurisdiction of
Scots law, even where the services were provided in France or Italy, for
example. However, reg.4(4) states that this rule shall not apply to those
fields listed in the Schedule to the E-Commerce Regulations, and the
Schedule includes consumer contracts.[15] Accordingly, consumer contracts
must comply with the relevant laws in the *consumer's* home state,
regardless of whether the activities of the service provider fall within the
coordinated field.

In regulating service providers, the E-Commerce Regulations do two
things. First, they impose obligations as to the provision of information
and related communications (regs 6–15) and, secondly, they exempt
service providers from liability in certain circumstances relating to the
transfer, caching and hosting of third party information (regs 17–19).

---

[12] reg.3(1)(d).
[13] reg.3(1)(a), (b) and (c).
[14] This is known as the "country of origin" principle, that is to say the governing law is that
of the supplier's home state. Matters of jurisdiction and choice of law are very complex in
cross-border transactions, because each party usually wishes to litigate in his home state.
The area of law which deals with jurisdiction and choice of law is known as "International Private Law". This chapter will not deal with this in any detail, except to note
specific principles in the various laws, where relevant.
[15] The other excluded areas under the Schedule are: "Copyright, neighbouring rights, rights
referred to in Directive 87/54/EEC and Directive 96/9/EC and industrial property rights;
The freedom of the parties to a contract to choose the applicable law; ... Formal validity
of contracts creating or transferring rights in real estate where such contracts are subject
to mandatory formal requirements of the law of the member State where the real estate is
situated; The permissibility of unsolicited commercial communications by electronic
mail."

The obligations of service providers (regs 6–15)

One of the concerns with online trading is that the trader is (or can be) **7–06** largely anonymous. Consumers and other businesses may not be able to discern whether the online business is a multi-national firm or is being run out of someone's kitchen.[16] Similarly, it is not always possible to tell where the online business is based.[17] The European Community response to this has been to require those trading online to provide certain information to their customers, to increase transparency and accountability, and therefore increase consumer confidence.

> **Key Concept**
>
> Service providers must make certain information available to customers under the E-Commerce Regulations, and this information must be provided clearly and unambiguously, in a form which is easily and permanently accessible. The main thrust of this information is to allow the customer to identify and locate the trader.

The necessary information specified in reg.6(1) of the E-Commerce Regulations is:

1. the name of the service provider;
2. the geographic address at which the service provider is established;
3. contact details of the service provider, including email address, which make it possible to "contact him rapidly and communicate with him in a direct and effective manner";[18]
4. details of any trade register in which the service provider is registered and means of identifying him in that register;
5. details of the relevant supervisory authority where the service provider is subject to authorisation;
6. where the service provider exercises a regulated profession, details must be provided informing the customer of any professional body with which the service provider is registered, including jurisdiction, and reference to the professional rules applicable in that jurisdiction. Thus, an accountant registered in Scotland would need to make reference on his website or in commercial communications to the Institute of Chartered Accountants of Scotland, as the relevant professional body; and

---

[16] In the words of the famous New Yorker cartoon by Peter Steiner, "On the Internet, nobody knows you're a dog".

[17] The "top-level" domain, the .uk, or .ie or .ca part of the url indicates where the url was registered, but does not necessarily mean the business is located there. For example, the top-level domain of Tuvalu is popular with television stations, as it is .tv.

[18] reg.6(1)(c).

7. finally, where the service provider is VAT registered, its identi-
    fication number must be stated.

Obviously, the precise information to be provided by a service provider
will depend on its circumstances, so that items 4–7 above will not be
applicable in all cases. The information required by items 1–3 will,
however, be relevant to all service providers, as will the further requirement in reg.6(2), which requires any pricing information to be indicated
clearly and unambiguously. Specifically, the service provider must make
it clear whether the price stated includes any taxes and delivery costs.

In making this information available, the service provider must comply
with the terms of reg.6, which require the information to be provided
"clearly and unambiguously" and in a form which is "easily, directly and
permanently accessible". This may require the service provider to provide
the information separately from, or in different format to, the information society services. For example, the services may be provided by text
message, but this is unlikely to fulfil the separate requirement of "permanent accessibility" in this regulation. Service providers may therefore
have to take further steps to provide the reg.6 information in a form that
complies with the E-Commerce Regulations.

Regulations 7 and 8 also impose requirements in relation to "commercial communications". These are defined in the E-Commerce Regulations as a communication "in any form, designed to promote, directly
or indirectly, the goods, services or image of any person pursuing a
commercial... activity".[19] This would cover, for example, an email to
previous customers to promote a new product. Regulation 7 requires that
all commercial communications must be clearly identifiable as such and
identify the person on whose behalf it is made, together with any promotional offers and the terms and conditions of that offer. Where it is an
unsolicited commercial communication (e.g. "spam" emails), it must be
"clearly and unambiguously identifiable as such as soon as it is received"
according to reg.8.[20] Anyone who receives spam regularly will testify to
the fact that this provision is not regularly observed, perhaps due to the
large proportion of spam which originates from outside the EEA.

Perhaps the most critical regulation in the E-Commerce Regulations is
that which relates to the conclusion of electronic contracts, under reg.9.
This applies to all B2C contracts, and to those B2B contracts where the
parties have not agreed otherwise. It is therefore possible for a service
provider to contract out of the regulations in its B2B dealings, but not its
B2C contracts. Where the E-Commerce Regulations do apply, however,

---

[19] reg.2(1). Where the communication consists only of an address or webpage address or
where it has been prepared independently of (and not at the expense of) the person that it
promotes, then it is excluded from the definition of commercial communication, and is
not regulated by the E-Commerce Regulations.

[20] Unsolicited commercial communications, typically spam, are also regulated by The
Privacy and Electronic Communications (EC Directive) Regulations 2003 (SI 2003/
2426).

and where a contract can be concluded online, then the service provider is under a number of obligations pre- and post-conclusion.

To deal with the pre-contractual obligations first, these constitute a further information requirement. The most important of these is the obligation in reg.9(1)(a) to provide the customer with details of "the different technical steps to follow to conclude the contract". This is an attempt to provide some certainty as to when both parties become bound by legal obligations. In the past, this has been notoriously difficult, as witnessed by a number of high profile disputes in the last decade between consumers and e-tailers. These typically arise where goods are displayed online at incorrect prices, which offer consumers a bargain. Examples include TVs offered for sale by Argos at £2.99 instead of £299, and cameras advertised at low prices from Kodak. Where a customer orders one (or, frequently, several) of these erroneously priced goods, and the e-tailer then refuses to deliver, the question then arises whether the initial order was sufficient to conclude a contract, creating a legal obligation, or whether it was simply an offer by the customer capable of rejection by the e-tailer.[21]

However, although e-tailers must make the contractual steps clear, no further guidance is given in the E-Commerce Regulations as to when this moment of conclusion occurs. Issues of principle therefore remain unresolved. For example, a standard online transaction can be broken into four constituent parts, as follows:

Consumer browses website

↓

Consumer places order for goods and submits credit card details

↓

Supplier acknowledges order

↓

Supplier takes payment and despatches goods

In legal terms, these facts and actions could be analysed in a number of ways, such as:

---

[21] This has recently been the subject of litigation in Singapore, where purchasers tried unsuccessfully to take advantage of erroneously posted prices online: *Chwee Kin Keong v Digilandmall.com Pte Ltd* [2004] 2 SLR 594.

Fact/Action	Legal Analysis I	Legal Analysis II	Legal Analysis III
Website on public display	Invitation to treat	Invitation to treat	Offer
Consumer places order	Offer	Offer	Acceptance of offer: **Contract Concluded**
Supplier acknowledges order	Acceptance of offer: **Contract Concluded**	—	
Supplier performs: takes payment and despatches goods		Acceptance of offer: **Contract Concluded**	

From this, it can be seen that the different legal steps could be met by a number of different actions: the offer could be constituted by the website or the consumer's order. Conversely, the legal status of these different elements remains unclear: are goods offered for sale on a website an invitation to treat or an offer? Is the consumer's order an offer or an acceptance of prior offer?

The E-Commerce Regulations do not clarify the legal consequences of each step, but they do place the onus on the supplier to make the contractual steps known to the consumer. The legal provision in the E-Commerce Regulations is therefore not as effective as it might otherwise have been, and can be seen as a lost opportunity to clarify legislatively the moment at which an online contract is concluded.

As well as making clear the mode of concluding a contract, the service provider must also inform the customer whether or not the concluded contract will be filed by the service provider and whether it will be accessible (reg.9(1(b)); how any input errors can be identified and corrected prior to the placing of the order (reg.9(1)(c)); and the languages offered for the conclusion of the contract (reg.9(1)(d)). Where the service provider subscribes to any codes of conduct, he must make these known to the customer, together with details of how to consult those codes (reg.9(2)). Where the terms and conditions which govern the contract are made available by the service provider, they must be accessible to the customer, such that the customer can store and reproduce them (reg.9(3)).

Many of these requirements can be met by an automated email sent to the customer following the receipt of the order, which provides the information in a clear and unambiguous manner. However, the most critical element of reg.9 will require some consideration by the service provider, to ensure that the steps to be followed to conclude the contract are made explicitly clear prior to the customer placing the order.

Service providers should also note that reg.10 expressly states that the provisions of reg.9 are supplemental to other information requirements under Community law, and are not optional extras. Thus, e-tailers must also take account of the Distance Selling Regulations, discussed below, for example.

Once the order has been placed, the requirements of reg.11 take effect, to oblige service providers to acknowledge receipt of the order "without undue delay" (reg.11(1)(a)), while reg.11(1)(b) reiterates the requirement to enable the customer to identify and correct any input errors prior to the placing of an order by technological means. Regulation 11 also clears up any doubt over when "receipt" happens electronically: the order and acknowledgement shall "be deemed to be received when the parties to whom they are addressed are able to access them" (reg.11(2)(a)). It is therefore not sufficient to show that the order or acknowledgment was sent: it must have been *received* to take effect.[22] However, in the case of an electronic order for information society services, such as ISP services, the acknowledgement can take the form of the provision of the service that has been paid for (reg.11(2)(b)).

Both regs 9 and 11 confirm that their information provisions do not apply where the contracts are concluded exclusively by email (or its technical equivalent). This would exclude email negotiations, but would apply to online purchases made using the e-tailer's standard order form. Further technical legal clarification is given by reg.12 which confirms that the "order" placed by the customer may equate to the formal "offer" for the purposes of contract law, but that it need not. Thus, the service provider is free to stipulate which stage of the electronic communication constitutes the offer and acceptance in the contract formation process, which accords with the terms of reg.9, allowing the service provider to stipulate the steps necessary to conclude the contract.

Liability of service providers

Regulations 13–15 deal with aspects of liability and compliance. Reg- **7–07** ulation 13 states that any recipient of the information society services may raise an action against the service provider for damages for breach of statutory duty, in order to enforce regs 6, 7, 8, 9(1) and 11(1)(a). Although direct action against the service provider is often the most persuasive remedy for recipients, this right is limited to breach of the listed regulations only. In addition, it may prove impractical for recipients (especially consumer recipients) to raise a court action when the service provider is located in a different jurisdiction.

Where the service provider fails to comply with reg.9(3), the recipient shall be entitled to seek a court order to enforce this provision, in accordance with reg.14. Regulation 9(3) would be breached where the supplier provides terms and conditions but fails to make them available for storage and reproduction by the recipient. Although the right under reg.14 does have the benefit of direct redress for the customer, it is

---

[22] Contrast this with the rules on delayed acceptance in Ch.4, para.4–26.

difficult to envisage many customers (whether business or consumer) taking the necessary court action, with its associated expense, to enforce it, simply to gain access to the terms and conditions. Further, there is no suggestion that any compensation for resulting loss will be available.

Perhaps the most practical remedy, and the one with the most serious consequences for the service provider, is set out in reg.15, which provides the customer with an opportunity to rescind the contract where there has been a breach of reg.11(1)(b). (Regulation 11(1)(b) obliges the service provider to give the customer the opportunity to identify and correct any input errors prior to placing the order.) Although this is a powerful remedy for the customer, it is severely limited because it can only be exercised for breach of one sub-regulation.

Protection for Intermediaries (regs 17–19)

7–08 In recognition of the fact that many service providers (such as ISPs) may well act as intermediaries, and deal with information and data for which they are not directly responsible, the E-Commerce Regulations provide a number of safeguards for these providers.[23] Although these safeguards are not necessarily an integral part of online commerce, they are an important part of the E-Commerce Regulations and it is helpful to mention them briefly.

> **Key Concept**
>
> Intermediaries who are responsible for transferring, caching or hosting information may avoid liability for any wrong arising from the information, if they were not responsible for its content.

Regulation 17 deals with the transmission of information by the service provider, where this is done on behalf of the ISS recipient, and the service provider is a "mere conduit". Where the service provider simply transmits information provided by a recipient of the service, the service provider shall not be liable for any damages (or indeed any criminal sanction) which results from the transmission of this information. An example would be where a defamatory statement is sent by email: the ISP or email provider will not be liable for the defamation that results from this information. The service provider can only take advantage of this exclusion of liability if it can show that it was not responsible for: initiating the transmission; selecting the receiver of the transmission; and selecting or modifying the information transmitted. Effectively, the service provider must be acting as a "mere conduit" for the information, and where the pursuer can show that there was a more active involvement by the service provider, liability will arise.

---

[23] reg.20, however, provides that the parties can contract out of these safeguards, and agree other terms if they wish to do so.

Similarly, reg.18 deals with the problems faced by service providers who temporarily cache information—usually to improve the speed and efficiency of their service. Search engines or ISPs, for example, may make a temporary cache of webpages to enable faster retrieval the next time the page is searched for. Caching is therefore a temporary storage of data, and service providers will not be liable for any damages or criminal sanctions resulting from their cache of information, where this storage is automatic, temporary and undertaken solely for the purpose of improving the efficiency of the service for future users. The exclusion from liability is not absolute, however: a service provider can only take advantage of the exclusion where it has not modified the cached information and where it has acted expeditiously to remove the cached information once it obtains actual knowledge that the original information has been removed.[24]

Regulation 19 provides the third category of relief from liability, which arises where the service provider has provided hosting or storage services. Examples of hosting or storage services might be a blog site and a webspace hosting site. Where a recipient has used this service to upload material in breach of copyright, perhaps to his blog or personal website for example, the service provider will not be liable so long as it was unaware of the breach, or acted expeditiously to remove the offending information once the breach comes to its attention.

THE DISTANCE SELLING REGULATIONS

1. Defining "distance selling"

When trading online, suppliers need to be aware of their obligations **7–09** under the Distance Selling Directive,[25] implemented in the United Kingdom as the Consumer Protection (Distance Selling) Regulations 2000 ("DS Regulations").[26] The protection given to consumers by the DS Regulations, and the obligations it imposes on traders, are additional to other rights and obligations imposed by law: it does not replace or supplant other legislative protection.

---

[24] The detailed terms of the qualification for exclusion are set out in reg.18(b).
[25] Directive 97/7/EC of the European Parliament and the Council of May 20, 1997 on the protection of consumers in relation to distance contracts.
[26] SI 2000/2334.

> **Key Concepts**
>
> The DS Regulations impose certain obligations on suppliers under any contract for goods or services which is concluded "at a distance", i.e. where the buyer and seller are not face-to-face.
>
> However, not all contracts are covered. Contracts for financial services for example are covered by other legislation. Further, the DS Regulations only apply in part to contracts for a range of goods and services, including accommodation and travel services to be provided within a specific period.

The DS Regulations impose obligations on suppliers who enter into "distance contracts". The first step in interpreting and applying these regulations is therefore to understand what a "distance contract" is. Regulation 3 provides a number of key definitions, including the following:

> "'distance contract' means any contract concerning goods or services concluded between a supplier and a consumer under an organised distance sales or service provision scheme run by the supplier who, for the purpose of the contract, makes exclusive use of one or more means of distance communication up to and including the moment at which the contract is concluded."

This definition has five elements, all of which must be fulfilled before the DS Regulations will apply to the contract.

In the first place, there must be a contract. Thus, the provisions of contract law (such as offer and acceptance, and capacity) must be fulfilled. In the case of online contracts, the E-Commerce Regulations must also be adhered to, as discussed above.

Secondly, the contract must be for goods or services. Neither goods nor services are defined under the DS Regulations, but most contracts entered into online will be for goods or for services. Software and electronic music is potentially difficult to classify as a good (as evidenced by the debate arising under the Sale of Goods Act 1979[27]), but even if software is not categorised as goods, the electronic provision of software or music by download is likely to constitute the provision of services. Consequently, the DS Regulations will still apply, although the application of the Sale of Goods Act 1979 may be less certain.

The third element of this definition requires that the contract must be between a supplier and a consumer. A supplier is defined by reg.3 as any person (whether natural or legal) who is acting in his commercial or professional capacity. The regulations will not apply to an individual who

---

[27] The Sale of Goods Act 1979 only applies to goods, leading to the question whether software is a good or a service: if it is the latter it will be excluded from the scope of the 1979 Act. See further, Ch.5 on sale and supply of goods.

sells something in a private capacity, for example an accountant who wishes to sell her car through a used car website. A consumer is a natural person (that is, not a company or partnership) who is acting for purposes which are outside his business. Thus, B2B contracts do not fall within the DS Regulations and the requirements of the DS Regulations do not need to be observed in non-consumer contracts.[28] The fourth requirement under this definition is that the distance sales or service scheme must be "organised". This is to prevent one-off or occasional transactions by traders being caught by the DS Regulations.

Finally, the contract must be concluded exclusively by means of one or more methods of distance communication. This means that up to the moment of conclusion of the contract, the supplier (or any agent) and the consumer cannot be simultaneously physically present. However, this requirement only applies until the moment of conclusion of the contract, from which it can be inferred that any face-to-face contact thereafter does not affect the distance selling status of the contract.

Schedule 1 provides an indicative list of the methods of distance communication covered by the DS Regulations. The list is non-exhaustive, so that it would be possible for other methods to qualify as distance communications. One advantage of this is that the DS Regulations are to some extent future-proofed. That is to say, if a new method of distance communication is developed in the future, it will still be covered by the DS Regulations without the need for any legislative intervention. The methods listed in Sch.1 include printed matter (including junk mail), letters, press advertising with order form, telephone, radio or television communication, email and fax. For the purposes of this chapter, the focus will be on internet and email communication, but it should be remembered that the scope of the DS Regulations is much wider than this, and includes a range of more traditional means of communication, including letter, telephone and fax.

Even where a contract meets these five elements in reg.3, however, the DS Regulations do not automatically apply. Regulation 4 states that the DS Regulations apply to distance contracts other than "excepted contracts", and reg.5 goes on to define such excepted contracts. Accordingly, the DS Regulations will *not* apply to these contracts, even when concluded by means of distance communication. The definition of "excepted contract" covers the following types of contract:

1. Contracts for the sale or other disposition of an interest in land (except for a rental agreement) including contracts for the construction of a building which includes an element of sale or disposition of an interest in land (again except for rental agreements). Thus, leases concluded by means of distance communication will be covered by the DS Regulations, but

---

[28] From a practical point of view, it is often difficult for an online supplier to distinguish easily between a consumer and non-consumer purchaser online. Accordingly, suppliers may choose to comply with the DS Regulations in all their online dealings, to avoid any errors.

selling land or buildings, whether for the construction of another building or not, will be excluded.
2. Contracts relating to financial services. Financial services are defined in reg.3(1) of the DS Regulations[29] as "any service of a banking, credit, insurance, personal pension, investment or payment nature". However, it should be noted that the distance marketing of financial services is regulated by a specific set of regulations: the Financial Services (Distance Marketing) Regulations 2004.[30]
3. Contracts concluded by an automated vending machine or automated commercial premises. The sort of thing covered by this exception would be standard vending machines and auto-mated car-parking services, for example.
4. Contracts concluded with a telecommunications operator through the use of a public pay-phone, such as making a phone call from a payphone via the operator.
5. Contracts concluded at an auction.

This last category potentially creates a problem for consumers who wish to rely upon the DS Regulations, yet have bought via an online auction site, such as eBay. At first sight, online auction transactions will not be covered by the DS Regulations. In fact, whether or not eBay and similar "auction" sites fall within the scope of the DS Regulations is dependent on a number of factors. In the first place, the DS Regulations only apply where the seller is a "supplier" in terms of the definition, which means the seller must be acting in a commercial or professional capacity as a sup-plier, i.e. they must be engaged in a course of dealing. Thus, private individuals selling on eBay for non-commercial or non-professional purposes will be excluded from the scope of the DS Regulations, regardless of whether or not eBay is a "true" auction under reg.5. Where, however, a private individual is using an online auction site to conduct a regular series of sales as a business, the DS Regulations may apply. The second issue is whether or not the sale is by way of auction or the "buy it now" facility. Where the seller offers the goods under a "buy it now" scheme, the transaction is not an auction but is a straightforward sale and purchase, and it will therefore be covered by the DS Regulations (so long as all other elements of the definition are fulfilled). Where the transaction is conducted through the standard auction facility, however, then the DS Regulations may not apply. The view has been expressed, however, that online auctions are not true "auctions", since there is typically no auc-tioneer involvement: the goods go to the highest bidder when the bidding

---

[29] As amended by the Financial Services (Distance Marketing) Regulations 2004 (SI 2004/2095), reg 25.
[30] SI 2004/2095. These Regulations are on much the same terms as the DS Regulations, in respect of financial services. Thus, suppliers must provide certain information to con-sumers prior to the conclusion of any distance contract, and as with the DS Regulations, this information includes the geographical address of the supplier and details of any supervisory authority. Similarly, the consumer under a distance contract for financial services also has a right to cancel the contract, subject to certain limitations.

period closes. If this analysis is accepted, then online auctions are unlikely to be true auctions, and the DS Regulations will therefore apply in the normal way.[31]

Unless this is the case, however, auctions, together with contracts for the sale of land, contracts relating to financial services, vending machine contracts and telecommunications operator contracts will all be excluded from the DS Regulations, by virtue of reg.5. Even for those contracts which are not excepted contracts, and which are therefore covered by the DS Regulations, it is possible that the DS Regulations will only apply in part. For example, reg.6 excludes the bulk of the DS Regulations in relation to contracts for: (i) timeshares;[32] (ii) contracts for food, drink or goods intended for everyday consumption supplied to the consumer's residence or work by "regular roundsmen"—this covers supermarket home delivery services (as least as far they deliver food, drink or goods for everyday consumption), and presumably also the morning delivery by the paperboy and milkman; and (iii) contracts for accommodation, transport, catering or leisure services where the services are to be provided on a specific date or within a specific period. This last is a critical provision in light of the popularity of online bookings of holidays or concert tickets, for example. Where consumers do buy flights, accommodation or tickets for entertainment events, the DS Regulations will only apply in part. In the case of timeshare contracts, regs 7–20 are excluded, while for contracts for the supply of food etc. or for accommodation and transport etc. (i.e. ii and iii) regs 7–19(1) are excluded. In either case, the key provisions of regs 7, 8 and 10 are denied to consumers in these situations.

The information requirements

At this stage, after clearing the definitional hurdles in regs 3, 5 and 6, it is **7–10** possible to consider the substantive elements of the DS Regulations. As far as the consumer is concerned, the main thrust of the DS Regulations is in the provision of information and the right to cancel, also known as the cooling off period. To take the information provision obligation first, suppliers must ensure they comply with regs 7 and 8.

Key Concepts

Traders must supply the consumer with pre- and post-contract information. The purpose of this information is to provide details of the supplier's place of business, and the nature of the goods or services, including any guarantees. Importantly, the consumer is also entitled to know about the right of cancellation.

---

[31] This argument is put forward by Annette Nordhausen in "Distance Marketing in the European Union" in Edwards (ed.) *The New Legal Framework for E-Commerce in Europe* (2005), p.247.
[32] As defined in the Timeshare Act 1992.

These two regulations attempt to break down the provision of information into two categories: (i) that which must be provided prior to the conclusion of the contract, and (ii) that which must be provided at some point before or during performance of the contract. However, the information in each category largely overlaps, and the rules regarding post-contractual delivery of information are somewhat confusing. There is therefore something to be said for traders providing all the necessary information up front, to avoid future complications and the risk of falling foul of the DS Regulations.

The more straightforward element is the information which must be provided "in good time" prior to the conclusion of the contract, in terms of reg.7. This means that it has to be given in time for it to be useful to the consumer, for example, to allow him to make an informed decision. What constitutes "good time" is likely to depend on the circumstances of each transaction. In order to comply with regulation 7, the trader must:

"(a) provide to the consumer the following information—

    (i) the identity of the supplier and, where the contract requires payment in advance, the supplier's address;

    (ii) a description of the main characteristics of the goods or services;

    (iii) the price of the goods or services including all taxes;

    (iv) delivery costs where appropriate;

    (v) the arrangements for payment, delivery or performance;

    (vi) the existence of a right of cancellation except in the cases referred to in regulation 13;

    (vii) the cost of using the means of distance communication where it is calculated other than at the basic rate;

    (viii) the period for which the offer or the price remains valid; and

    (ix) where appropriate, the minimum duration of the contract, in the case of contracts for the supply of goods or services to be performed permanently or recurrently;

(b) inform the consumer if he proposes, in the event of the goods or services ordered by the consumer being unavailable, to provide substitute goods or services (as the case may be) of equivalent quality and price; and

(c) inform the consumer that the cost of returning any such substitute goods to the supplier in the event of cancellation by the consumer would be met by the supplier."

In addition to providing this information under reg.7(1), the supplier must ensure it is provided in a "clear and comprehensible manner", which suggests that including it in small print or hiding it in the midst of a lengthy contract would not suffice. However, some latitude is allowed depending on the means of communication. For example, it would not often be possible to communicate all of this information in a 30-second radio or television advertisement. However, it would be possible to include an address or web page to allow consumers to obtain further details themselves. In any event, regardless of how suppliers choose to fulfil their obligations under this regulation, they must do so "with due regard to the principles of good faith in commercial transactions".[33] It is not entirely clear that Scots commercial law recognises principles of good faith in commercial transactions, and this phrase owes much to the European origins of the original Directive.

Once this information has been duly provided "in good time prior to the conclusion of the contract", the supplier must also remember to provide the post-contractual information as stipulated in reg.8. Although some of this information should already have been provided under reg.7, the additional requirement to be fulfilled under reg.8 is that the information must be provided in writing "or in another durable medium which is available and accessible to the consumer". It is thought that email would fulfil this requirement, as would a fax, but that a text message is probably not sufficiently durable. Further, the supplier should take note of the obligation to provide the information in a manner which is accessible to the consumer: a supplier that only provides this information by email will fail to meet its reg.8 obligations in the case of a consumer who does not have an email address.

The information required under reg.8 must be provided prior to the conclusion of the contract or thereafter "in good time". Again, this concept of "good time" remains unclear. However, to ensure that there is a longstop date for the provision of this information, reg.8(1)(b) obliges the supplier to provide the information no later than (i) during the performance of the services to be supplied, or (ii) when the goods are delivered to the consumer.[34] Thus, a supplier of goods could fulfil its obligations under reg.8 by including a printed sheet containing the necessary information with the goods, when they are packaged for delivery.

In order to meet the reg.8 requirements, the supplier must provide the information in paras (i) to (vi) of reg.7(1)(a), i.e. details as to the nature of the goods or services, including price, details of the supplier, including address, and details of the right of cancellation. As this information must already have been provided to the consumer prior to the contract, the only additional obligation on the supplier under reg.8 is to provide that information in writing. If the supplier fulfils the pre-contractual obligation by providing the information in writing which is available and accessible to the consumer in terms of reg.8, there is presumably no need to provide the information a second time.

Even where this has been given to the consumer, however, the supplier must also provide further information, which falls into two distinct categories. First, the consumer is entitled to receive more detailed

[33] reg.7(2).
[34] Where goods are to be delivered to third parties, the DS Regulations are not entirely clear when this information is to be provided. In order to ensure compliance, it is suggested that suppliers provide the reg.8 information prior to, or at the time of, the conclusion of the contract.

information regarding the right to cancel, including the procedure for exercising this right. The consumer is entitled to know of any limitations to the right, and reg.8 specifically obliges the supplier to inform the consumer of the following points:

(i) where the consumer must return the goods to the supplier if the consumer cancels the contract, the consumer must be notified of that requirement (reg.8(2)(b)(i));

(ii) again, in relation to cancellation of a contract for the supply of goods, the consumer must be informed who will bear responsibility for the cost of returning the goods to the supplier (reg.8(2)(b)(ii)). Since it would be in the supplier's interests to ensure that any costs are borne by the consumer, this is something that must be made explicit to the consumer under reg.8; and

(iii) where the contract is one for services rather than goods, the consumer must be told that the right to cancel will expire when the services have been provided within the seven-day cooling-off period, where the consumer has given his agreement to performance in this period.[35]

The second category of information to be provided under reg.8 is in relation to after-sales matters, including the address to which complaints should be addressed and details of any after-sales services or guarantees.[36]

The need for written terms under reg.8 does not apply in the rather specialised situation outlined in reg.9. This arises where the services are supplied on only one occasion through the means of distance communication, and where the cost of the services is invoiced by the operator of the distance communication. Thus, where a mobile phone company provides a ring tone to a mobile phone and renders an invoice for it on the owner's monthly contract, there is no need to comply with the terms of reg.8. Of course, the other obligations under the DS Regulations will continue to apply.

The primary requirement of the DS Regulations is therefore the obligation to provide information to the consumer, typically information which allows the consumer to identify and contact the supplier, and to provide a cooling-off period in which the consumer may change his mind about receiving the goods or services. One of the advantages of providing written information to the consumer is to convey the formality of what he has done by entering into the agreement. A written statement of the nature and cost of the goods or services, together with other details as to his legal rights, may bring home to the consumer the nature of his actions and allow him to reflect on whether or not he wishes to proceed. These measures are therefore designed to prevent suppliers from taking advantage of consumers, particularly through the use of high-pressure

---

[35] This amendment was added by the Consumer Protection (Distance Selling) (Amendment) Regulations 2005 (SI 2005/0689).
[36] reg.8(2)(d).

sales pitches: consumers can always cancel the services before performance or return the goods.

3. The right of cancellation

Following the information obligations in regs 7 and 8, regs 10–18 deal **7–11**
with cancellation and related matters, such as cancellation of ancillary
credit agreements and return of the goods. The right to cancel is arguably
the strongest measure of protection given to consumers under the DS
Regulations and one of their most effective remedies, as will be seen. It
can be seen as an extension of the information requirements in regs 7 and
8, in that both measures are intended to provide protection for an
uninformed consumer, by giving him greater information including the
chance to inspect the goods before he is finally committed.

The basic right is that all consumers are entitled to cancel the contract,
in its entirety, within the cancellation period. The cancellation period
depends on a number of factors, the first of which is whether the contract
is for goods or for services.

Key Concepts

The right of cancellation allows the consumer to change his mind,
even if there is nothing wrong with the goods. The length of the
cancellation period depends on whether the contract is for goods or
services, and on when the consumer is told of the right to cancel. At
its longest, the right will last for three months and seven days following delivery of the goods.

In the case of contracts for *goods*, the period within which the consumer
can exercise his right of cancellation begins on the day the contract is
concluded and ends seven working days beginning on the day after
delivery of the goods.[37] Thus, if the contract was concluded on Monday
and the goods were delivered two days later, on Wednesday, the right to
cancel would begin on the Monday on which the contract was concluded
and would end on the Friday of the following week.

In some cases, however, the consumer will be entitled to a longer
cooling-off period. Where the supplier fails to tell the consumer of the
right to cancel, that is, where the supplier is in breach of its obligations
under reg.8(2)(b), then the cancellation period continues until the consumer is given notice of the right to cancel, at which point the seven
working days deadline again becomes operative. In this situation, the
consumer may have received the goods and even be using them before he
is notified of the right to cancel. Where this happens, the right to cancel
will continue and can only be brought to an end by the supplier giving
notice of the existence of the right, at which point the consumer has a

---

[37] reg.11(1).

further seven working days beginning on the day following receipt of this notice.[38] Where the supplier fails to give the consumer any notice at all of this cancellation right, the right continues in existence for three months and seven days following the day on which the consumer received the goods, as per reg.11(3). In all cases, therefore, the longest duration of the cancellation period is three months and seven days *following delivery of the goods*.[39]

This extensive cancellation period is disadvantageous to traders, who run the risk that goods are returned several weeks after delivery, but the means to avoid this risk lie firmly with the trader, who can minimise the cancellation period by giving due notice in accordance with reg.8. Accordingly, the extended right to cancel forms one of the consumer's strongest remedies for breach of the DS Regulations, as it enables him to walk away from the contract without the need for any court action. Unfortunately for consumers, the extended right only comes into operation on breach of one particular requirement (the notice of the cancellation provision, in reg.8(2)): it does not apply where the supplier breaches any other provision.

Further, the right to cancel cannot be used where the goods supplied under the contract fall into one of the listed categories in reg.13. These situations are:

- where the price of the goods is dependent on fluctuations in the financial market outwith the trader's control;
- where the goods have been made to the customer's specification or personalised, or some element of them means they cannot be returned, or they are liable to deteriorate or expire rapidly— examples of such goods include (a favourite present for children) pencils or stationery marked with their name or initials; items which cannot be returned for reasons of hygiene, such as earrings; and date specific items, such as foodstuffs or perhaps calendars;
- where audio or video recordings have been unsealed by the consumer;
- where the goods are newspapers, periodicals or magazines; or
- gaming, betting or lottery services.[40]

In the case of distance contracts for *services*, slightly different rules apply, reflecting the problems inherent in "returning" services after they have been provided. Thus, reg.12(2) stipulates that the cancellation period for services is seven working days beginning on the day following the conclusion of the contract. If the supplier has failed to comply with its reg.8(2) requirement to tell the consumer of this right, the cancellation

---

[38] reg.11(3).

[39] reg.11(5) clarifies that where goods are ordered by the consumer for delivery to a third party, the cancellation period shall operate from the day following receipt by that third party, rather than the consumer.

[40] Allowing gamblers to "return" their chance for a refund of their stake would rather defeat the purpose of gambling on an unknown outcome.

period is seven working days from the day after the consumer eventually receives this notification, as per reg.12(3). However, regs 8 and 12 have been amended from their original form[41] to take account of the situation where the supplier starts the provision of services within this cancellation period. It is therefore the case that the cancellation period will end on the day when performance is completed, if (a) this is before the end of the seven working day period, and (b) the consumer has consented to this performance.

Regulation 13 has been amended to confirm that the seven working day cancellation period does not apply where the consumer has consented to the early performance of the services under the contract.[42] In this case, the consumer will have no right to cancel a contract for services, so long as the necessary reg.8(2) information has been provided and the consumer has agreed to the performance before the end of the cancellation period. Another exception to the right to cancel a contract for services is also listed in reg.13, being where the price of the services is dependent on fluctuations in the financial market outwith the trader's control.

Where the consumer exercises his right to cancel, whether in relation to goods or services, the contract is treated as if it had not been made.[43] The implication of this is that the consumer must cancel the whole contract, and cannot opt for partial cancellation. This would potentially undermine the value of the right to the consumer, by forcing him into an "all or nothing" situation. However, there is no judicial guidance on this point and it may be that traders would accept a partial cancellation where relevant.

In order to cancel the contract, the consumer must comply with the terms of reg.10, which requires the notice of cancellation to be given in writing or another durable medium. There is no prescribed form of words, so long as the intention of the consumer is clear. Regulation 10(4) sets out a number of ways in which the notice of cancellation can be given, such as delivery or post to the supplier's last known address, or by email to the last known email address.

Regulations 14 to 18 deal with a number of ancillary matters in the event the contract is cancelled. Regulation 14(1) provides that the supplier shall reimburse any sums paid by the consumer, although reg.14(5) allows the supplier to make a charge to cover the direct costs of recovering the goods supplied to the consumer, where a term in the contract obliges the consumer to return the goods in the event of cancellation. Importantly, the right to charge the consumer for the return costs does not apply where the consumer is entitled to reject the goods for some other reason, such as where the goods breach the requirement of satisfactory quality under s.14 of the Sale of Goods Act 1979, for example.

Where the goods have been supplied together with a related credit

---

[41] By the Consumer Protection (Distance Selling) (Amendment) Regulations 2005 (SI 2005/0689).

[42] reg.13(1)(a), as amended.

[43] reg.10(2).

agreement, then cancellation under reg.10 also operates to cancel any related credit agreement, in terms of reg.15, while reg.16 confirms that no interest shall be payable on any credit provided under such an agreement which is then cancelled.

Regulation 17 deals with the return of the goods to the supplier following cancellation. Under reg.17(2), the consumer is placed under a duty to retain possession of the goods and take reasonable care of them, in the period prior to cancellation. Following cancellation, he is under a duty to restore the goods to the supplier, although this does not equate to a duty to deliver them: rather, reg.17(4) simply requires the goods to be kept at the consumer's premises to await collection by the supplier. However, reg.17(8) and reg.14(5), when read together, imply that the supplier may, by contractual term, oblige the consumer to return the goods to the supplier, at the consumer's expense.[44] In order to take advantage of this, suppliers would need to ensure the appropriate contractual provision is made in their terms and conditions. There is, however, a possibility that the intention of the original Directive is thwarted by the drafting of reg.17(8), which refers to reg.17(7) and, in so doing, it appears to offer the consumer the option to refuse to return the goods at his own expense, and simply retain them for a six-month period. The right to cancel does not affect any other legal right the consumer has to reject the goods, for example under ss 15B or 48C of the Sale of Goods Act 1979.

Performance of the contract

7–12 If the contract is not cancelled, the supplier is obliged, in accordance with reg.19(1), to perform the contract, i.e. to supply the goods or services contracted for, within a 30-day period, which starts the day after the consumer sent his order to the supplier. This is a rather curious obligation, since there is no obligation on the supplier to accept the order received from the consumer, and there is therefore no certainty as to when, if at all, the contract will be concluded. Further, the obligation arises the day after the order was sent, without making reference to the receipt by the supplier of the order: there is no guarantee that the supplier will receive the order the day after it has been sent by the consumer, and the risk of delay or non-delivery applies to almost all methods of communication used by the consumer. This also conflicts with reg.11 in the E-Commerce Regulations, which states that any correspondence, including orders, takes effect from the date of receipt. It would have been preferable for both these sets of regulations to adopt a consistent approach. Nonetheless, where a contract is concluded, it would appear that the 30-day period for performance starts ticking from the day after the consumer's order was sent, regardless of when the contract was concluded.

---

[44] This would certainly reflect the clear statement enabling suppliers to charge for the costs of return which is contained in the original Directive (97/7/EC), in art.6(2).

Enforcement of the Distance Selling Regulations

> **Key Concept**
>
> The DS Regulations are enforced by the Office of Fair Trading. The supplier is not allowed to avoid the DS Regulations by contracting out of them.

Given that the DS Regulations impose a number of duties on the sup- **7–13** plier, for the benefit of the consumer, it is important to look at the enforcement of the DS Regulations. The Regulations will only protect consumers if they can be enforced for their benefit, and this is where one of the problems with the Regulations arises. It is not obvious that the Regulations can be or are being rigorously enforced. For the year April 1, 2006 to March 31, 2007, OFT statistics show that it investigated 129 complaints or enquiries made under these Regulations.[45] This would seem a relatively small amount of problems in light of the high value of distance selling transactions: those on the internet alone totalled £21 billion in 2005. Part of the problem may be simply that consumers are unaware of their rights or how to enforce them. The OFT market study, "Internet Shopping", published in June 2007, indicated that 28 per cent of UK-based suppliers who trade online were not aware of specific laws regulating internet trading, while 56 per cent of consumers were oblivious to their right to cancel an online contract.[46] Although there may be relatively low levels of awareness or enforcement of the DS Regulations, the success or otherwise of these Regulations depends on the success of enforcement.

Regulations 26 to 29 deal with the critical matter of enforcement. The first point to note is that individual consumers have no right of redress or standing to raise an action under the DS Regulations. Regulation 26 empowers an "enforcement authority" to consider any complaint made to it about a breach of the DS Regulations.[47] An enforcement authority is deemed to be the Director General of Fair Trading, together with all weights and measures authorities in the United Kingdom.[48] In Scotland, such functions are exercised by the local council.[49] Where a valid complaint is made, the enforcement authority or the Director General of Fair Trading may apply for an interdict[50] (or an injunction in England and Wales) against any person who is, or appears to be, responsible for the

---

[45] "Internet Shopping", An OFT Market Study, June 2007.
[46] The report is available at: http://www.oft.gov.uk/shared_oft/reports/consumer_protection/oft921.pdf (November 2, 2007).
[47] Regulation 26(1) provides that the enforcement authority does not have to consider a frivolous or vexatious complaint, or one where another enforcement authority has notified the Director General of Fair Trading that it will investigate the same complaint.
[48] According to reg.3, Definitions.
[49] In accordance with the Local Government etc (Scotland) Act 1994 s.2.
[50] This includes an interim interdict. Regulation 27 governs the application and grant of an injunction. Regulation 3(2) confirms that "injunction" is to be read as including an interdict in Scotland.

breach. Where the court is satisfied that an interdict is necessary to secure compliance with the DS Regulations, it may grant the order. The Director General also has the power to order publicity under reg.29, to alert the public to any court order against a supplier or any undertaking given by a supplier in relation to the breach.

Finally, reg.25 expressly stipulates that the supplier may not contract out of the DS Regulations. It is therefore impossible for the supplier under a distance contract to avoid its obligations to consumers under the DS Regulations.

Conclusion

7–14 A closing observation on the DS Regulations is to question whether the aim of increasing consumer confidence is actually achieved. The evidence of a widespread lack of awareness would suggest that most consumers trade online even without the reassurance provided by the legislation. It is also not clear how much comfort can be derived from the provision of information, which is the primary obligation of the DS Regulations. The cooling-off period does redress the balance, by allowing a consumer to change his mind, yet even this has its drawbacks, most notably the complications involved in returning goods after they have been delivered. Further, the lack of direct consumer redress may reduce its value even further: a right to complain to the OFT is not necessarily a notable enhancement of consumers' rights. Websites such as eBay show that consumer confidence can be built and maintained through non-legal methods, such as the famous eBay feedback and rating system. In many cases, consumer confidence is generated through experience and familiarity, rather than legislative intervention.

The relationship between the DS Regulations and the E-Commerce Regulations

7–15 Both sets of Regulations discussed above impose information obligations upon suppliers, such that they must provide consumers with certain information. How do these two sets of Regulations interact?

The first thing to note is that some (but not all) of the information to be provided is the same. For example, where goods or services are supplied, the cost of the goods, including taxes and delivery costs, must be stated clearly and unambiguously.[51] Similarly, both sets of Regulations require the supplier to state its geographical address[52] although the DS Regulations only require this where the supplier requires payment in advance.

However, there are differences in the scope and obligations in each set of regulations. Suppliers cannot assume that compliance with one set of Regulations will result in compliance with the other. For example, even where all the information required under the E-Commerce Regulations has been provided, the supplier will still need to provide additional

---

[51] reg.6(2) of the E-Commerce Regulations and reg.7(1)(a)(iii) and (iv) of the DS Regulations.

[52] reg.6(1)(b) of the E-Commerce Regulations and reg.7(1)(a)(i) of the DS Regulations.

information to comply with the DS Regulations, such as a description of the main characteristics of the goods and information regarding the right to cancel.[53] Conversely, even where all the information under the DS Regulations has been provided, this will not encompass the need to inform the customer of any authorisation scheme or professional body, as required under reg.6(1) of the E-Commerce Regulations.

Further, the two sets of Regulations apply to different situations. The E-Commerce Regulations only deal with online commerce, but cover B2B as well as B2C relationships. In contrast, the DS Regulations are much wider in scope, since they apply to more than online contracts: they also apply to mail, telephone, fax and other distance contracts. At the same time, however, the DS Regulations are narrower in a different sense, since they only apply to B2C transactions and not B2B dealings.

THE LEGAL REGULATION OF E-COMMERCE—OTHER CONSIDERATIONS

It is important to remember that national law will still apply to online **7–16** transactions. Thus, where goods are bought online in the United Kingdom, the Sale of Goods Act 1979 will regulate the quality of goods (s.14), together with the seller's obligations to give good title (s.12) and the buyer's obligations to accept and pay for them (s.27).[54]

On matters of privacy, consumers are entitled to have their personal data held and processed in accordance with the Data Protection Act 1998.[55]

Key Concept

Other pieces of legislation, most notably the Sale of Goods Act 1979 and the Data Protection Act 1998, will also provide consumers with a range of rights when buying online.

In any online transaction, the Unfair Commercial Practices Directive[56] will apply. This has been implemented in the United Kingdom as the Consumer Protection from Unfair Trading Regulations 2008, which came into force on May 26, 2008.[57] The Directive, and consequent Regulations, regulate business-to-consumer commercial practices which are unfair, in that they cause the consumer to take a decision to purchase or not to purchase, which he would not otherwise have taken.

In addition to the above-mentioned pieces of legislation, there are a

---

[53] reg.7(1)(a)(ii) and (vi).
[54] See Ch.5 on sale and supply of goods.
[55] See Ch.3, para.3–44.
[56] Directive 2005/29/EC concerning unfair business-to-consumer commercial transactions.
[57] See Ch.6 on consumer protection.

number of other legislative provisions which impact on consumers and online suppliers, as follows:

1. the Trade Descriptions Act 1968;
2. the Consumer Credit Act 1974;
3. the Unfair Contract Terms Act 1977;
4. the Supply of Goods and Services Act 1982;
5. the Unfair Terms in Consumer Contracts Regulations 1999;
6. the Privacy and Electronic Communications (EC Directive) Regulations 2003;
7. the Package Travel, Package Holiday and Package Tours Regulations 1992.

▼ CHAPTER SUMMARY

7–17 The key points from this chapter on e-commerce are:

WHY REGULATE E-COMMERCE?

1. **Government and European Community recognition of e-commerce is necessary to help boost consumer confidence and open up the internal market for both suppliers and customers.**
2. **Trading online brings advantages for both suppliers and customers, including greater choice, wider markets and cost savings.**

CONCLUDING CONTRACTS ELECTRONICALLY

1. **The Requirements of Writing (Scotland) Act 1995 (as amended) enables all contracts in Scots law to be formally concluded electronically.**

THE ELECTRONIC COMMERCE REGULATIONS

1. **The Electronic Commerce Directive (2000/31/EC on certain legal aspects of information society services, in particular electronic commerce) has been implemented in the United Kingdom as the Electronic Commerce (EC Directive) Regulations 2002 (SI 2002/2013).**
2. **The E-Commerce Regulations govern the provision of "information society services" and cover B2B and B2C contracts.**
3. **Under the E-Commerce Regulations, the service provider may choose to have his contracts governed by the laws of his home jurisdiction, unless the customer is a consumer, in which case the laws of the consumer's jurisdiction apply.**

4. The E-Commerce Regulations impose information requirements on service providers, in regs 6–15.
5. Part of the information that suppliers are required to provide is details of how the contract is concluded online, as per regs 9–11.
6. Regulations 17–19 provide protection for intermediaries who transmit, cache, host or store information which gives rise to liability, for example defamatory statements.

THE DISTANCE SELLING REGULATIONS

1. The Consumer Protection (Distance Selling) Regulations 2000 (SI 2000/2334) implement the Distance Selling Directive (97/7/EC on the protection of consumers in relation to distance contracts).
2. The Distance Selling Regulations govern any B2C contracts for goods or services concluded at a distance.
3. Regulations 7 and 8 impose pre- and post-contractual information obligations on the supplier.
4. Regulation 10 gives consumers the right to cancel the contract within a seven-day period, although this period can be extended if they are not notified of this right by the supplier.
5. Enforcement of the Distance Selling Regulations is the responsibility of the OFT and local authorities: consumers have no direct right of redress.

THE LEGAL REGULATION OF E-COMMERCE—OTHER CONSIDERATIONS

1. Other legal provisions may regulate e-commerce, including the Sale of Goods Act 1979, the Data Protection Act 1998, and the Consumer Protection From Unfair Trading Regulations 2008.

? QUICK QUIZ

- Can a contract be concluded electronically in Scots law? What is your authority for this?
- What are "information society services"?
- What legislation regulates the provision of information society services?
- What obligations are imposed on providers of information society services? (Hint: what information is required?)
- What is a "distance selling" contract? (Your definition should contain five elements.)
- What legislation regulates distance selling contracts?
- What information must be provided by sellers under a distance selling contract?

- When does the consumer's right to cancel arise? How does this cancellation affect a related credit agreement?
- How can these regulations be enforced by a consumer?
- What other legislation might affect suppliers and customers trading online?

📖 FURTHER READING

Atiyah, Adams, and MacQueen, *The Sale of Goods* 11th edn (Pearson and Longman, 2005).
Lilian Edwards and Charlotte Waelde (eds), *Law and the Internet*, 2nd edn (Hart Publishing, 2000).
Lilian Edwards (ed.), *The New Legal Framework for E-Commerce in Europe* (Hart Publishing, 2005).
Chris Reed, *Internet Law Texts and Materials* 2nd edn (Cambridge University Press, 2004).

🖱 RELEVANT WEBLINKS

The OFT: *http://www.oft.gov.uk/*.
The OFT's Consumer Direct website: *http://www.consumerdirect.gov.uk/*.
The OFT's publications: *http://www.oft.gov.uk/advice_and_resources/ publications/*.
UK legislation: *www.opsi.gov.uk*.

Chapter 8   Employment Law

ALAN DELANEY[1]

▶ CHAPTER OVERVIEW

This chapter is concerned with employment law. It begins by looking at **8–01** the appropriate test to identify a contract of employment. Terms and conditions are considered before moving onto the termination of employment. The chapter then turns to look at rights in relation to unfair dismissal and redundancy payments, before concluding with a brief overview of the key anti-discrimination statutes on grounds of sex, race and disability.

✓ OUTCOMES

By the end of this chapter, you should be able to: **8–02**

- ✓ identify the key ingredients for a contract of employment;
- ✓ discuss the main sources of terms and conditions of employment;
- ✓ explain the means by which an employment contract might be terminated;
- ✓ understand the key principles of unfair dismissal;
- ✓ outline what is meant by direct and indirect discrimination and harassment.

THE CONTRACT OF EMPLOYMENT

Introduction

Modern-day employment law is essentially a mixture of common law **8–03** (especially contract law) and a minimum level of statutory employment rights. Generally employment tribunals have exclusive jurisdiction to hear claims based on statutory rights. Claims based on a breach of contract must usually be brought before the civil courts (although the employment tribunal has limited jurisdiction for certain breach of contract claims). It should also be noted that European Community law has played an increasingly important role in setting minimum employment standards, particularly in the discrimination field. Those employed by

---

[1] Solicitor, Maclay Murray & Spens, LLP.

"emanations of the State" may also be able to rely directly on the provisions of a Directive, so long as they are unconditional and sufficiently precise.[2] Other legislation such as the Human Rights Act 1998 and the Data Protection Act 1998 are also having a gradual influence on employment law which is likely to continue in the future.

Identifying a contract of employment

8–04 Many significant employment rights are restricted to employees (including, for example, rights to maternity benefits, redundancy payments and not to be unfairly dismissed). It is therefore important to be able to identify a contract of employment.

It should be a simple matter to identify a contract of employment. In practice, however, it can be difficult in some cases. The starting point is the Employment Rights Act 1996 which defines an "employee" as an individual who has entered into or works under a "contract of employment". This in turn is defined as a contract of service or apprenticeship, whether express or implied, and (if it is express) whether oral or in writing.[3] The focus in most cases will be on being able to establish a "contract of service".

Over the years, courts and employment tribunals have grappled with the question of what gives rise to a "contract of service". Various tests have been applied at times, none of which has emerged as pre-eminent, other than what is sometimes known as the "multiple" test, requiring consideration of a variety of different factors. Essentially, there is a need to consider (a) whether certain fundamental criteria are satisfied on the facts, and (b) all other relevant characteristics of the relationship, to ascertain if they are consistent or not with a "contract of service".[4]

First, a minimum level of mutual obligations between the parties requires to be demonstrated. An employee needs to establish that the employer is under an obligation to provide work to them, and that they are under an equivalent obligation to perform that work. Without this "mutuality", a contract of employment does not arise.

> ### Carmichael v National Power
> #### [2000] I.R.L.R. 43 (HL)
>
> Mrs C worked as a power station guide for N on a "casual as required" basis. She was paid only for the hours worked by her from time to time. There were occasions where N offered work to Mrs C which she chose not to accept. Along with another guide, Mrs L, they brought claims alleging a failure to provide written statements of employment particulars. This in turn required them to

---

[2] *Gibson v East Riding of Yorkshire Council* [2000] I.R.L.R. 598.
[3] Employment Rights Act 1996 ("ERA") s.230(2) .
[4] *Ready Mixed Concrete (South East) Ltd v Minister of Pensions and National Insurance* [1968] 2 Q.B. 487 HC.

establish that they were employed over the course of their work for N.

HELD: the House of Lords found that as both Mrs C and Mrs L were able to choose not to work when contacted by N and had done so on various occasions, there were insufficient mutual obligations to create a contract of service. The tribunal had been entitled to find from the documents and surrounding circumstances that the intention of the parties was not to have their relationship governed by contract during the periods when the tour guides were not working.

Mutuality by itself, however, is not enough. The employee in most cases will also have to perform the work personally in exchange for wages or remuneration, under the control or supervision of the employer. The ability to arrange for a substitute to perform the work will usually be fatal, unless there are exceptional circumstances.[5]

Finally, the other provisions of the contract need to be consistent with employment. Certain provisions can point towards this, including fixed hours of work, eligibility for benefits generally reserved for employees (such as sick pay, maternity pay and pensions), application of disciplinary and grievance procedures, statutory notice provisions, and other similar obligations.

As well as the above, employment tribunals and courts will have regard to a number of factors including:

- how the parties view the relationship (the "label" given to the relationship by the parties will be taken into account but will not be determinative);
- who assumes the financial risk (does the employer assume the financial risk and the reward of the business—apart from any employee incentive benefits);
- whether equipment is provided by the employer or not (provision of equipment by an employee is fairly uncommon); and
- payment of tax and national insurance (seldom a key factor, since this will be determined by HMRC obligations).

[5] Compare *Express & Echo Publications Ltd v Tanton* [1999] I.R.L.R. 367 (CA) (right to provide substitute inconsistent with contract of employment) with *Macfarlane v Glasgow City Council* [2001] I.R.L.R. 7 (gymnastic instructor with limited right if unable to attend to arrange replacement from employer-maintained list could still be consistent with employment).

Key Concept

Employee status

- Establishing a "contract of service" generally requires demonstrating certain fundamental criteria.
- There has to be mutuality of obligations between the parties to the contract (typically an obligation on the employer to provide work and on the individual to perform that work personally — although some very limited right to arrange a substitute may not be fatal).
- There also needs to be a sufficient level of control by the employer over the individual in relation to the work performed.
- Other characteristics of the relationship (e.g. terms of the contract) should be consistent with a "contract of service".

Workers

8–05 Some statutory rights go further and benefit "workers", a wider category which includes employees, but also extends to others who work under a contract (whether express or implied, oral or in writing) to personally undertake work or services for another party, whose status is not that of a client or customer of the person's profession or business. In other words, the law seeks to exclude from these rights only those who are genuinely self-employed. Examples of legislation extending to workers includes the right not to suffer unauthorised deductions from wages[6] and rights that arise in relation to working time and paid annual leave under the Working Time Regulations 1998. It should be similarly noted that discrimination law extends to those in "employment" which goes beyond employees and is defined such that most workers are protected, as with certain other categories of person.

Agency workers

8–06 The status of "agency workers" has been a specific problem area in recent years. This often tripartite relationship is at its most straightforward where an individual (A) contracts with an agency (B) to provide work to an end-user (C). Such individuals can be engaged on fairly long-term arrangements yet deprived of the basic employment rights which require employee status, leading to a fundamental absence of job security.

Most attempts in this scenario to assert unfair dismissal rights by an individual against the agency have been unsuccessful, on the ground that the agency typically assumes no obligation to offer work to the individual, and where an offer of work is made, it does not need to be accepted or performed by the person. In the absence of mutuality (as well as sufficient day-to-day control or supervision), it is difficult to establish employment.[7]

---

[6] ERA s.13.
[7] *Montgomery v Johnson Underwood Ltd* [2001] I.R.L.R. 269 (CA).

Similarly, the fundamental problem faced by the individual seeking to argue employment by the end-user is typically the lack of any direct legal obligations between them. Whilst one recent case sought to imply a contract of employment as between the individual and end-user, this challenge to the status quo appears not to have established itself.[8] Subsequent cases have stressed the need for there to be "necessity" before a contract will be implied. This is unlikely to arise where the existing relationship can be adequately explained by the contracts already in place (usually between the individual and the agency and separately between the agency and the end-user). Whilst the courts recognise that this places agency workers in a vulnerable position, they have generally stressed that this is a matter for Parliament to address. [9]

Whilst there is some relevant legislation in place—including the Conduct of Employment Agencies and Employment Businesses Regulations 2003 (which sets down certain minimum requirements including an obligation to provide information to individuals and end-users as to employment status)—the expectation is to see stronger protections introduced in the near future, whether at the UK or at the EC level.

Company directors

The other group of individuals who can give rise to uncertainty as to **8–07** "employment status" is that of executive directors. It is not inconsistent to be both a director and an employee (often such directors will work under a "service agreement"). The extent of shareholding is a relevant but not a decisive matter. Even a controlling shareholding can still be consistent with employment, if this genuinely reflects the reality of the situation and is not a sham.[10] This issue is most commonly encountered in the context of insolvency, when a director wishes to claim payments from the National Insurance Fund, which requires "employee" status to be established.[11]

TERMS AND CONDITIONS OF EMPLOYMENT

Formation

There is no need for a contract of employment to be in writing, although **8–08** this is highly advisable for reasons of clarity and evidence. Terms can be oral or in writing, and express or implied by custom and practice.

---

[8] *Dacas v Brook Street Bureau (UK) Ltd* [2004] I.R.L.R. 358.

[9] *James v London Borough of Greenwich* [2007] I.R.L.R. 168 (recently upheld by the Court of Appeal [2008] EWCA 35).

[10] *Secretary of State for Trade and Industry v Bottrill* [1999] I.C.R. 592; *Nesbitt & Nesbitt v Secretary of State for Trade and Industry* [2007] I.R.L.R. 847.

[11] ERA ss.182–190.

Written statement of particulars

8–09 An employer is required by statute to provide a written statement of employment particulars to an employee within two months of employment commencing.[12] This statement must contain:

- names of the employer and employee;
- date when employment began (as well the date from which any continuous service is recognised);
- remuneration details (rate/scale and when payment is to be made);
- hours of work;
- terms and conditions in relation to holidays, sick pay, pension entitlement;
- notice entitlements;
- job title or a description of duties;
- place or places of work;
- if a fixed-term contract, when it is envisaged to end;
- details of any collective agreement which applies to the employment;
- details of disciplinary or grievance procedures which apply (or reference to where they can be found); and
- certain further information where work requires to be performed outside the United Kingdom for more than one month

Some of this information can be provided via other documents. An employee who does not receive a statement can bring a claim to an employment tribunal, which has power to confirm or amend particulars. An employer is generally required to update changes to this statement within one month of the change having effect. Whilst the written statement is unilaterally given by the employer and therefore not contractual, it can of course be influential in establishing what the agreed terms are between the parties.

Collective agreements

8–10 Collective agreements can be a further source of terms and conditions. Such agreements are made by or on behalf of one or more trade unions with one or more employers or employers' associations and relate to one or more of the following:

- terms and conditions of employment or the physical conditions in which any workers are required to work;
- engagement or non-engagement, or termination or suspension of employment or the duties of employment, of one or more workers;
- matters of discipline;

---

[12] ERA s.1.

- a worker's membership or non-membership of a trade union;
- facilities for officials of trade unions; and
- machinery for negotiation or consultation, and other procedures relating to any of the above matters.

Whilst collective agreements are presumed by law to be unenforceable between the parties[13] (i.e. trade union and employer) this does not prevent terms within a collective agreement, which relate to terms and conditions of individual employees, from becoming incorporated within contracts of employment and as such enforceable within that contract. Once incorporated within contracts of employment, such terms will survive the termination of the underlying collective agreement.[14]

Wages

The contract of employment will determine the level and extent of wages **8–11** payable by the employer to the employee. In addition, employers must comply with the National Minimum Wage Act 1998 which currently requires employers to pay a standard rate of £5.52 per hour (for those aged 22 or above) or a development rate of £4.60 per hour (for those aged 18–21 or 22 or over but undergoing accredited training in the first six months of employment). These rates are correct as at October 1, 2007 but are subject to annual review in October each year.

Workers are given statutory protection against unlawful deductions from their wages.[15] Employers can only make deductions where (a) required or authorised by statute or a relevant provision of the contract of employment, or (b) the worker has given prior written consent to the deduction being made. Exceptions apply where there has been an overpayment of wages or expenses, and in certain other narrow circumstances. The onus is on an employer to consider the circumstances in which they may require to make a deduction from wages and to get written consent in advance from workers. Those working in retail employment receive some additional protection as to the level of deductions that can be made which arise from cash shortages or stock deficiency, even where consent has been obtained. Where an unlawful deduction has taken place, workers can complain to an employment tribunal within three months of the relevant deduction (or series of deductions).

Hours

Hours are regulated by the contract of employment subject to statutory **8–12** limits set out in the Working Time Regulations 1998. The Regulations provide for an average maximum weekly limit of 48 hours across a standard reference period of 17 weeks. Failure to comply with this limit is a criminal offence for employers. It is open to employers to either

---

[13] Trade Union and Labour Relations (Consolidation) Act 1992 ("TULR(C)A") s.179.
[14] *Gibbons v Associated British Ports* [1985] I.R.L.R. 376.
[15] ERA s.13.

negotiate a change to the length of the reference period with workforce representatives, or to enter into individual opt-out agreements with workers in relation to this upper limit on average working hours. Other key provisions of the Regulations include entitlement to paid annual leave (currently 4.8 weeks rising to 5.6 weeks from April 1, 2009), daily rest of 11 hours in each 24-hour period, weekly rest of 24 hours in every 7-day period (or at the employer's option 48 consecutive hours in a 14-day period), and the right to a rest break of 20 minutes where an employee is working a shift longer than six hours. There are also provisions in relation to night work and in relation to young workers. Some entitlements can be varied either by collective or workforce agreements and certain exemptions apply in relation to particular activities (e.g. where there is a need for continuity of service or production).

Maternity and family-friendly rights

8–13 It is not possible to provide detailed coverage of the many family-friendly statutory employment rights that are relevant to the contract of employment. The main rights can be summarised as follows, some of which require specific eligibility criteria to be met:

- A right to 26 weeks' ordinary maternity leave and a further 26 weeks of additional maternity leave (all employees eligible, subject to notification requirements).
- A right to 39 weeks' statutory maternity pay (which the Government aims to increase to 52 weeks in due course).
- A right to return from maternity leave to the same job (or, where the full 52 weeks has been taken and this is not practicable, to an alternative which is suitable and appropriate and on no less favourable terms and conditions).
- A right of up to two weeks' paternity leave and paternity pay.
- A right of up to 13 weeks' unpaid parental leave.
- A right to ordinary/additional adoption leave and adoption pay.
- A right to request flexible working for childcare purposes in relation to a child under six (or under 18 if the child is disabled) or for the purpose of caring for an adult aged 18 or over who is in need of care.
- A right to reasonable time off for dependants in certain circumstances.

Implied duties

8–14 Certain obligations are implied by common law into every contract of employment. An employee, for example, is under a duty to give faithful service, to obey lawful and reasonable orders and to exercise reasonable skill and care. Similarly, an employer is under an implied duty to provide work, take reasonable care in relation to health and safety at work, and not to exercise a discretion under the contract (e.g. in relation to a flexibility or mobility clause) in such a manner as to render performance of the contract impossible. Similarly, a key implied term is that the employer is required not to engage in conduct likely to undermine mutual trust and confidence, without reasonable and proper cause for doing so.

> ### United Bank v Akhtar
> ### [1989] I.R.L.R. 507
>
> A was employed by U as a clerical worker in Leeds. Relying on a mobility clause in his contract of employment, U required A to transfer from Leeds to Birmingham on six days' notice and without financial assistance. A's request for a three-month postponement to make personal arrangements was refused and he ultimately resigned and claimed constructive dismissal.
>
> HELD: U had breached A's contract of employment—there is an implied duty to give reasonable notice in such circumstances and by failing to do so U had made it impossible for A to move. Employers are under a duty not to exercise contractual terms in such a manner as would be likely to breach mutual trust and confidence without reasonable or proper cause.
>
> See also: *Malik v Bank of Credit and Commerce International SA* [1997] I.R.L.R. 462 (HL).

Transfer of undertakings

It should also be noted that there is specific statutory protection of terms **8–15** and conditions of employment in relation to a transfer of an undertaking or a service provision change in terms of the Transfer of Undertakings (Protection of Employment) Regulations 2006.

TERMINATION OF EMPLOYMENT AND WRONGFUL DISMISSAL

Notice rights

The parties to a contract of employment will generally agree appropriate **8–16** notice periods to apply. If no specific provision is made, a reasonable period of notice can be implied at common law, based on the employee's role and seniority. In any event, every employee who has been continuously employed for one month or more is entitled to a statutory minimum period of notice, when an employer wishes to terminate the contract of employment. A sliding scale applies as follows:

- one week's notice where continuous employment is between one month and two years;
- one week's notice per year where continuous service is between two years and 12 years; and
- 12 weeks' notice where continuous service is 12 years or longer.

An employer is entitled to only one week's statutory notice from an employee who has been continuously employed for one month or more (contractually, more notice is usually required). An employee may also elect to receive a payment in lieu of statutory notice entitlement.

Breach of contract and wrongful dismissal

8–17 The rights to contractual or statutory minimum notice do not apply where a party is entitled to terminate the contract because of the other party's conduct. Thus, an employer might opt to summarily dismiss an employee who is guilty of serious misconduct or other act which amounts to a material or fundamental breach of contract. Where an employer terminates the contract in breach of contract, for example by not giving proper notice, or failing to follow a contractual disciplinary procedure, an employee will be able to claim damages for wrongful dismissal. Similarly, an employee might choose to resign without giving notice in circumstances where an employer has acted in a manner which amounts to a material or fundamental breach of contract. This may arise from breach of either an express term (such as the duty to pay wages) or an implied term (such as the duty not to damage mutual trust and confidence without reasonable or proper cause). An employer can also pursue damages from an employee who resigns without giving notice in circumstances which do not involve a material or fundamental breach of contract. It should also be noted that aside from cases involving termination of employment, a breach of contract by the employer will not itself operate to terminate the employment contract, and the employee in such cases may be able to continue working and pursue damages for breach of contract from the employer (or a claim for wages, if appropriate).[16]

Other termination

8–18 An employment contract can become "frustrated" and terminate automatically by operation of law, where unforeseen circumstances arise which render future performance impossible. Examples include the death of either party and historically have included the imposition of a substantial custodial sentence, or a sudden medical trauma which renders the employee permanently unable to work. As courts and employment tribunals tend to be reluctant to find an employment contract to be frustrated, the argument tends to be little used in practice.

Similarly, a contract of employment is terminated in certain but not all insolvency situations (a court order winding up a company is the main example of an order which does operate to terminate such contracts).

---

[16] *Rigby v Ferodo Ltd* [1987] I.R.L.R. 516 (HL).

Unfair Dismissal

Who has the right?

Section 94 of the Employment Rights Act 1996 confers one of the most **8–19** important rights within employment law: not to be unfairly dismissed. The right is generally restricted to employees who have minimum continuous service of one year with their employer. There are exceptions to this service requirement—which apply in relation to dismissals for certain automatically unfair reasons, including those relating to pregnancy, childbirth, maternity or other statutory family-related leave, as well as dismissals arising from making protected disclosures (whistle-blowing) or taking certain actions in relation to health and safety or trade union activities.[17]

What is a dismissal?

"Dismissal" is given a statutory meaning, and extends beyond termina- **8–20** tion of an employment contract by an employer. Section 95 provides that a dismissal arises in relation to:

- termination by the employer (with or without notice);
- termination of a limited-term contract by virtue of the limiting event and which is not renewed (the expiry of a fixed-term contract is the main example); and
- termination by the employee in circumstances where he is entitled to do so without notice by reason of the employer's conduct (i.e. "constructive" dismissal)

Constructive dismissal requires an employee to have resigned in response to a fundamental or material breach of contract by the employer, as discussed above. It should be noted that where an employer is too hasty in accepting the resignation of an employee which is either ambiguous or which is unambiguous but given in the "heat of the moment" or in circumstances of apparent emotional stress, this may amount to termination by the employer, rather than constructive dismissal.[18]

Statutory dispute resolution procedures

From October 1, 2004, the Government introduced statutory procedures **8–21** which employers are required to comply with in relation to dismissals (and certain other disciplinary action) to avoid them being automatically unfair.[19] A failure to comply with these procedures by an employer (or an employee) allows a tribunal to uplift or decrease compensation by between 10 and 50 per cent.[20] Following a recent review by the

---

[17] ERA s.108.
[18] *Kwik-Fit Ltd v Lineham* [1992] I.R.L.R. 156 (EAT).
[19] ERA s.98A.
[20] Employment Act 2002 s.31.

Government, the procedures are expected to be repealed in April 2009.[21] They have not achieved their stated purpose, to encourage resolution of disputes at the workplace level and reduce the number of tribunal claims. In the meantime, they must be followed by an employer as part of a dismissal procedure, apart from in relation to certain types of dismissal (the main exclusions are retirement dismissals, redundancy dismissals where statutory collective consultation requirements apply and dismissals which involve re-engagement on new terms and conditions).[22] There are also exceptional circumstances where the procedures need not be complied with (the main exclusions being where doing so would lead to a significant threat to persons/property, further harassment (where harassment has already taken place) or where it is not reasonably practicable to comply with the procedures).[23]

The "standard" procedure is as follows[24]:

- STEP ONE: the employer must set out in writing the alleged conduct or other circumstances which lead him to contemplate dismissal and send a copy of this statement to the employee and invite him to a meeting to discuss the matter.
- STEP TWO: the meeting must take place before any action is taken (except suspension) and must not take place unless the employer has informed the employee of the basis for including the ground or grounds for contemplating dismissal in the step one statement—the employee must have a reasonable opportunity to consider his response to that information and is under a duty to take all reasonable steps to attend the meeting—the employer then must inform the employee of his decision and provide a right to appeal.
- STEP THREE: if the employee wishes to appeal, he must inform the employer, who must arrange a further meeting which the employee has to take reasonable steps to attend—after the meeting the employee must be notified of the final decision.

A "modified" dismissal procedure also exists, which appears to have been designed for circumstances where an employer dismisses more or less "on the spot" in circumstances where it is reasonable to do so.[25] As an employment tribunal is very unlikely to consider such a dismissal to be fair, save in the most exceptional circumstances, it is thought that the modified procedure will have little impact, if any, in practice.

In cases of constructive dismissal (as well as in relation to the majority of other statutory employment claims), an employee must generally

---

[21] The DTI (now DBERR) consultation *Success at work: Resolving disputes in the workplace* closed on June 20, 2007. The employment bill abolishing the procedures at the time of writing is before Parliament.
[22] Employment Act 2002 (Dispute Resolution) Regulations 2004 reg.4.
[23] regs 6(4) and 11.
[24] Part 1, Sch. 2 to Employment Act 2002.
[25] Part 1, Sch. 2 to Employment Act 2002 and Employment Act 2002 (Dispute Resolution) Regulations 2004 reg.3(2).

follow requirements in relation to a standard grievance procedure or, where the employee has left employment and the procedure has not been started or completed and the employer agrees, a modified grievance procedure.[26]

The standard procedure again involves three steps:

- STEP ONE—the employee must set out the grievance in writing and send a copy of it to the employer.
- STEP TWO—the employer must invite the employee to a meeting to discuss the grievance—this meeting must not take place unless the employee has informed the employer of the basis for the grievance in the step one statement and the employer has had a reasonable opportunity to consider his response—the employee must then take reasonable steps to attend the meeting, after which the employer must advise of his decision and provide a right of appeal.
- STEP THREE—if the employee wishes to appeal, he must inform the employer, who must arrange a further meeting which the employee has to take reasonable steps to attend—after the meeting the employee must be notified of the final decision.

The modified grievance procedure is simpler insofar as it requires only at step one for the employee to set out the grievance and basis for it in writing to the employer and at step two the employer writes back responding in writing to the grievance. There is no right of appeal. Much controversy has arisen over exactly how much detail an employee must provide at each stage. Suffice to say that employees would be well advised to provide as much detailed information as possible, to support a grievance, referring to any potential claims the employee might be considering bringing against the employer.[27] In most cases, a tribunal will not have jurisdiction to hear a claim unless a statutory grievance has been lodged and the employee has waited 28 days before bringing a claim, underlining the importance of compliance.[28] Raising a grievance may also allow the employee an automatic extension of time in which to bring certain claims. There are also similar provisions regarding the uplift and decrease of tribunal awards by between 10 and 50 per cent for non-compliance by either party.[29]

Potentially fair reasons for dismissal

Unless an employee establishes dismissal for an automatically unfair **8–22** reason (in which case a finding of unfair dismissal is made), the employer is under an onus to establish that the dismissal was for one (or more) of six potentially fair reasons. These relate to:

---

[26] reg.6.
[27] See *Cannop v Highland Council* [2008] CSIH 38.
[28] Employment Act 2002 s.32.
[29] Employment Act 2002 s.31.

- capability or qualifications (e.g. the employee is no longer capable or qualified to perform the role);
- conduct of the employee (e.g. the employee is guilty of gross misconduct or has been dismissed for further misconduct after a series of warnings);
- retirement (this requires an employer to have followed a statutory retirement procedure which gives the employee advance warning of impending retirement and an ability to request to continue working);
- redundancy;
- inability to continue working without contravening an enactment (e.g. a person employed as a driver who is subsequently banned from driving); or
- some other substantial reason of a kind such as to justify the dismissal (this is intended to be a residual category to cover dismissals for other substantial reasons not falling within the other headings).

The employer needs to provide a minimum level of evidence in each case before a tribunal will accept a potentially fair reason to exist. For example, in a redundancy case, the employer is required to establish at this stage that a genuine redundancy situation existed and that this was the potentially fair reason for dismissal.

Reasonableness

8–23 Once an employer establishes a potentially fair reason, a tribunal must determine whether or not the dismissal was fair or unfair. Except in relation to retirement dismissals (where specific provisions apply) this requires the tribunal to have regard to whether in the circumstances (including the size and administrative resources of the employer) it has acted reasonably or unreasonably in treating the reason for dismissal as sufficient. Courts have interpreted this requirement such that a tribunal has to ask whether the decision to dismiss fell within the "band of reasonable responses" open to a reasonable employer faced with the same circumstances. It is not appropriate for a tribunal to substitute its own view as to what action it would have taken.[30] It must objectively assess the decision to dismiss against the scope for one reasonable employer to take one approach but another reasonable employer to take a different approach. Only where the dismissal is outside the "band of reasonable responses" will the dismissal be unfair.

What a tribunal will generally look for will depend on the potentially fair reason being relied upon. In a capability dismissal, it will usually be necessary as a minimum to show that the employee was given sufficient warning of shortcomings and a genuine opportunity to improve (or in cases of ill-health that there has been adequate investigation of the medical position and regular consultation with the employee

---

[30] *Iceland Frozen Food v Jones* [1993] I.C.R. 17.

throughout). In a conduct dismissal, as a minimum, unless guilt is admitted, the employer will have to reasonably believe the employee is guilty, on reasonable grounds, after as much investigation as is reasonable.[31] Employers are also expected to follow a procedure which, over and above the statutory minimum, is fair and reasonable. However, it is open to an employer to argue that not following procedures which are in addition to the statutory minimum requirements (e.g. extra provisions within a contractual disciplinary policy) made no difference to the outcome, such that dismissal would have taken place even if additional procedures had been followed.[32] In redundancy cases, tribunals will consider issues such as the selection process for redundancy, the consultation process with employees, and whether means of avoiding the redundancy dismissal (such as alternative employment) were explored by the employer.

Polkey v A E Dayton Services Ltd
[1988] I.C.R. 142 (HL)

This case has long been a key decision in stressing the importance of procedural safeguards as part of a fair dismissal process. The case involved a redundancy which was unfair due to a lack of consultation with the employee before the decision was made by the employer. Lord Bridge in his judgement referred to the potentially fair reasons and said this:

"...an employer having prima facie grounds to dismiss for one of these reasons will in the great majority of cases not act reasonably in treating the reason as a sufficient reason for dismissal unless and until he has taken the steps, conveniently classified in most of the authorities as 'procedural,' which are necessary in the circumstances of the case to justify that course of action. Thus, in the case of incapacity, the employer will normally not act reasonably unless he gives the employee fair warning and an opportunity to mend his ways and show that he can do the job; in the case of misconduct, the employer will normally not act reasonably unless he investigates the complaint of misconduct fully and fairly and hears whatever the employee wishes to say in his defence or in explanation or mitigation; in the case of redundancy, the employer will normally not act reasonably unless he warns and consults any employees affected or their representative, adopts a fair basis on which to select for redundancy and takes such steps as may be reasonable to avoid or minimise redundancy by redeployment within his own organisation".

---

[31] *British Home Stores v Burchell* [1978] I.R.L.R. 379.
[32] ERA s.98A(2).

Complaints

8–24 A claim of unfair dismissal requires to be lodged within three months of the effective date of termination of employment.[33] On upholding a claim of unfair dismissal the tribunal can order (a) such compensation as is just and equitable in the circumstances, and/or (b) reinstatement, or (c) re-engagement.[34] Compensation for unfair dismissal breaks down into two elements—(i) a basic award (which is equivalent to a statutory redundancy payment—capped from February 1, 2008 at £9,900), and (ii) a compensatory award (which is generally design to reflect loss of earnings—capped from February 1, 2008 at £63,000). No maximum limit on the compensatory element applies to a dismissal for certain health and safety reasons or on the grounds of making a protected disclosure (whistle-blowing). In cases where an employer fails to comply with a reinstatement or re-engagement order, a further "additional award" can be made (capped from February 1, 2008 at £17,160). It is open to employers to argue that re-employment is not practicable in the circumstances. In practice, compensation tends to be the main remedy for unfair dismissals.

Key Concepts

Unfair dismissal

- The statutory meaning of "dismissal" includes (a) termination by the employer, (b) the expiry of a limited-term contract, and (c) resignation by the employee in circumstances where the employee is entitled to do so by reason of the employer's conduct ("constructive dismissal").
- The right to claim unfair dismissal is restricted to employees who generally must establish continuous service of one year with the employer.
- There are exceptions to the minimum service requirement for certain automatically unfair reasons, including those relating to pregnancy, childbirth, maternity or other statutory-related leave, as well as dismissals arising from making protected disclosures or taking certain actions in relation to health and safety or trade union activities.
- Employers must follow a minimum statutory procedure in relation to dismissals — a failure to do so renders the dismissal unfair. "The procedure" is expected to be repealed in April 2009.
- In addition, any dismissal requires to be "potentially fair" reason and otherwise reasonable in the circumstances in terms of s.98 of the Employment Rights Act 1996.

---

[33] ERA s.111.
[34] ERA ss.112–126.

> • The remedies for unfair dismissal are compensation, re-
> instatement and re-engagement.

REDUNDANCY PAYMENTS

Who has the right?

The right to a redundancy payment arises where an employee is dismissed **8–25**
on grounds of redundancy, or alternatively, in certain other limited
situations involving lay-off or short-time working.[35] To be eligible, an
employee needs to have two years' continuous service as at the relevant
date of termination.[36] Those who volunteer in redundancy situations are
generally looked upon as being dismissed on redundancy grounds, unless
there is evidence to the contrary.

What is redundancy?

For the purpose of redundancy payments, a dismissal on grounds of **8–26**
redundancy will be established where the dismissal is wholly or mainly
attributable to[37]:

- the fact that an employer has ceased or intends to cease (a) to
  carry on the business for the purposes of which the employee was
  employed, or (b) to carry on that business in the place where the
  employee was employed; or
- the fact that the requirements of that business (a) for employees to
  carry out work of a particular kind, or (b) for employees to carry
  out work of a particular kind in the place where the employee was
  employed, has in either case, ceased or diminished, or are
  expected to cease or diminish.

The focus can be seen to be on a disappearing role, workplace or a
cessation or diminution of work. Note that the definition of redundancy
is sufficient to permit what is known as "bumping", typically where one
employee with long experience but whose role no longer exists, displaces
a newer employee who has recently joined. The reason for dismissing the
newer employee is still on grounds of redundancy.[38] Place of employment
is generally approached by looking at where the employee actually
worked in practice, rather than looking at where their contract might
oblige them to work, if requested by the employer.[39]

---

[35] ERA s.135.
[36] ERA s.155.
[37] ERA s.139.
[38] *Murray v Foyle Meats* [1999] I.R.L.R. 563.
[39] *High Table v Horst* [1997] I.R.L.R. 513.

How is a redundancy payment calculated?

8–27 A statutory redundancy payment is calculated by reference to weekly pay, age and length of service. A maximum limit is placed on "weekly pay" for this purpose (currently £330 from February 1, 2008). Essentially, the payment is calculated at the rate of 1½ weeks' pay for a year of employment when the employee was aged not less than 41; otherwise at the rate of one week's pay for a year of employment when the employee was aged not less than 22 and finally at the rate of a ½ week's pay for each year of employment below this age. The maximum period for calculation purposes is 20 years, with no account taken of any earlier year.

> **Example:**
>
> X is made redundant from XYZ Limited on February 1, 2008 after 25 complete years employment, aged 45 and earning £800 per week. His payment is calculated as follows:
>
> Years not less than 41 = 4 × £330 (maximum weekly pay) × 1.5 (multiplication factor) = £1980
>
> Years between 22 and 41 = 16 (limited to last 20 years) × £330 × 1 = £5280
>
> Total = £1980 + £5280 = £7260

Alternative employment

8–28 An employee who receives an offer of alternative employment in a redundancy situation is entitled to a statutory four-week trial period (which can be extended by agreement between the parties where training is required) to determine whether the job is suitable, without losing the right to claim a redundancy payment.[40] Conversely, an employee who unreasonably refuses an offer of suitable alternative employment made prior to the date on which the dismissal for redundancy takes effect (or within four weeks of that date) will lose their right to a redundancy payment.[41]

Right to time off

8–29 An employee who is given notice of dismissal on grounds of redundancy is entitled to be permitted by an employer to take reasonable paid time off during working hours in the notice period to (a) look for new employment, or (b) make arrangements for training for future employment. An employee not afforded such rights can bring an employment tribunal claim within three months of the failure.

---

[40] ERA s.138(2).
[41] ERA s.141(4).

Claim for redundancy payment

Where an employer has failed to make a statutory redundancy payment, **8–30** an employee can bring a claim to an employment tribunal for such a payment within six months of the relevant date (usually termination of employment).

Other considerations

Enhanced redundancy

An employee may be contractually entitled to a payment over and above **8–31** the minimum statutory redundancy payment. Many employers offer more generous schemes which offer payments which are inclusive of the statutory element. The employee needs to establish a contractual right to the payment, rather than simply one-off or ad-hoc situations in the past where the employer has chosen to pay more than the statutory minimum. A failure by an employer to pay an enhanced redundancy payment will entitle an employee to bring a claim for breach of contract. This can be brought in an employment tribunal (subject to an upper limit of £25,000 damages) or can be brought in the ordinary civil courts within the normal limitation period for breach of contract claims.

Collective consultation requirements

A statutory duty arises to consult trade union or other elected repre- **8–32** sentatives where an employer is proposing to dismiss as redundant 20 or more employees at one establishment within a period of 90 days or less.[42] Such consultation must begin in good time and at least 30 days before the first of the dismissals takes effect unless the employer proposes to dismiss 100 or more within that period, in which case it must begin in good time and at least 90 days before the first of the dismissals takes effect. There are detailed statutory provisions which set out various obligations in relation to this requirement to collectively consult with representatives. A failure to comply by an employer may on application to an employment tribunal trigger a protective award being made of up to 90 days pay per employee.[43] An employer is also required in collective redundancy situations to notify the Secretary of State in advance within similar prescribed periods (commonly done in practice on a HR1 form).

---

[42] TULR(C)A s.188.
[43] TULR(C)A s.189.

DISCRIMINATION

Introduction

8-33   This chapter can do no more than scratch the surface of existing discrimination law and provide a very brief outline of the three main forms of unlawful discrimination relevant to employment—on grounds of sex, race and disability.

It is important to note that other legislation renders discrimination unlawful on other grounds including, part-time status,[44] fixed-term status,[45] religion or belief,[46] sexual orientation,[47] age,[48] as well as specific legislation on equal pay.[49] The Government has consulted on plans to introduce a Single Equality Act in the Parliamentary Session 2008–2009. This forms part of a general approach to joining up the strands of discrimination law, illustrated recently by the Equality Act 2006, which established the Commission for Equality and Human Rights in place of the separate equality commissions. It is also important to note that national legislation is required to implement EC law in this area, which has been recently consolidated within the new Equal Treatment Directive (2006/54).

Key Concept

Discrimination law

- It is unlawful to discriminate on grounds of sex, race, disability, part-time or fixed-term status, religion or belief, sexual orientation or age.
- Most discrimination legislation prohibits "direct" discrimination, "indirect" discrimination and "harassment" on discriminatory grounds.
- The Disability Discrimination Act 1995 is different in some respects and includes additional obligations, such as the duty on employers to make reasonable adjustments for disabled persons.
- Where an employment tribunal finds a complaint to be well-founded, it has power to award compensation, including for injury to feelings. There is no limit on the compensation award that can be made.
- Claims relating to equal pay as between men and women require to be raised separately under the Equal Pay Act 1970.

---

[44] Part-Time Workers (Prevention of Less Favourable Treatment) Regulations 2000 (SI 2000/1551).
[45] Fixed-Term Employees (Prevention of Less Favourable Treatment) Regulations 2002 (SI 2002/2034).
[46] Employment Equality (Religion or Belief) Regulations 2003 (SI 2003/1660).
[47] Employment Equality (Sexual Orientation) Regulations 2003 (SI 2003/1661).
[48] Employment Equality (Age) Regulations 2006 (SI 2006/1031).
[49] Equal Pay Act 1970.

> • EC law is an important source of rights under discrimination law, which national legislation must comply with (and which can sometimes be relied upon directly). There is a stated intention in future to consolidate the existing strands of discrimination law under the Single Equity Act.

Sex discrimination

The Sex Discrimination Act 1975 can be considered as rendering **8–34** unlawful three main types of discrimination on grounds of gender within the employment field: direct discrimination, indirect discrimination and harassment. Each of these three categories requires to be considered in turn. Whilst the wording of the legislation deals with discrimination against women, it is equally applied to equivalent discrimination against men.[50]

In relation to job applicants, it is unlawful for an employer to discriminate against a woman on various grounds, including in relation to arrangements made for determining who should be offered employment, in the terms on which employment is offered, or by refusing or deliberately omitting to offer her employment. Similarly, in relation to employment, it is unlawful to discriminate against a woman in relation to access to opportunities for promotion, transfer or training, or any other benefits, facilities, services or by subjecting her to any detriment, or dismissal from employment.[51] There is also protection from post-employment detriment, which may include, for example, the provision of a reference.[52] For liability purposes, anything done by a person in the course of their employment is treated by the Act as being done by the employer, unless the employer can establish having taken such steps as were reasonably practicable to prevent the employee doing the relevant act or acts in question.[53] As indicated earlier in the chapter, the scope of discrimination law generally extends beyond "employees" in the narrow sense and protects most workers and certain other persons.

The Act prohibits discrimination on the grounds of gender reassignment, marital status, civil partnership, pregnancy or maternity leave. Those bringing claims or asserting rights under the Act (or assisting others in doing so) are protected from victimisation occurring because they have done so.[54]

The legislation generally excludes claims relating to the provision of contractual financial benefits, which are instead dealt with by the Equal Pay Act 1970. That legislation requires equality of pay as between men and women in relation to (a) like work, (b) work rated as equivalent, or (c) work of equal value. It is open to an employer to defend an equal pay

---

[50] Sex Discrimination Act 1975 ("SDA") s.2(1).
[51] SDA s.6.
[52] SDA s.20A.
[53] SDA s.41.
[54] SDA ss.2A–4.

claim by showing that the difference in pay is due to a genuine material factor between the man and the woman, other than gender.[55]

Direct discrimination

8–35 Direct discrimination occurs where a person, on the ground of a woman's sex, treats her less favourably than he treats or would treat a man.[56] A woman does not need to show an actual comparator, a hypothetical comparator will suffice. Thus, where a female probationer police officer was not offered a permanent role, in circumstances where the evidence established that a hypothetical male in similar circumstances would have been, direct discrimination was found to have taken place.[57] In cases involving discrimination on grounds of pregnancy or maternity leave no comparator is required. There is no ability to seek to justify direct sex discrimination. There are, however, very narrow exceptions where sex is considered to be a "genuine occupational qualification" or GOQ, where employment opportunities can be limited to one gender.[58] Examples include "decency or privacy" reasons where a job is likely to involve physical contact with the opposite sex, where objection might reasonably be taken (e.g. a bra-fitting service), or where the holder of a job provides personal welfare or education services which can most effectively be provided by one gender (e.g. a rape counselling service for women).

Indirect discrimination

8–36 Indirect discrimination occurs where a person applies to a woman a "provision, criteria or practice" which he applies or would apply equally to a man, but:

- which puts, or would put women at a particular disadvantage when compared with men;
- which puts her at that disadvantage; and
- which he cannot show to be a proportionate means of achieving a legitimate aim.[59]

Typically this arises where an apparently "gender neutral" requirement is applied across the board but which disadvantages one sex, including the victim, and which cannot be objectively justified. An example of such discrimination can be seen in a recent case involving a female airline pilot, employed by British Airways, who refused her request to reduce her flying hours by 50 per cent and would allow only a reduction of 25 per cent. There was sufficient evidence to establish that a provision requiring those requesting to work part-time to move only to 75 per cent of normal

---

[55] Equal Pay Act 1970 s.1.
[56] SDA s.1(2)(a).
[57] *Chief Constable of West Yorkshire v Vento* [2001] I.R.L.R. 124 (EAT). For the appeal as to remedy see the decision of the Court of Appeal at [2003] I.R.L.R. 102.
[58] SDA s.7.
[59] SDA s.1(2)(b).

hours would be to the detriment of a considerably larger proportion of women than men. The reasons put forward by the employer in this case were held to be insufficient to objectively justify the provision as being a proportionate means of achieving a legitimate aim.[60]

Harassment

A woman is subjected to unlawful harassment where, on the ground of **8–37** her sex, a person engages in unwanted conduct or any form of unwanted verbal, non-verbal or physical conduct of a sexual nature which has the purpose or effect of (a) violating her dignity, or (b) creating an intimidating, hostile, degrading, humiliating or offensive environment for her. Protection is also given where a woman is treated less favourably for rejecting or submitting to such conduct.[61] This definition of harassment seeks to be expansive. The conduct in question need not be intended to harass; it is sufficient that the conduct has that effect. This will be established where, having regard to all the circumstances, including the perception of the victim, it is reasonable to consider the conduct as having that effect. Whilst the feelings of the victim are taken into account, this is not determinative—it still needs to be considered whether it is reasonable to conclude that conduct had the effect of violating dignity or creating such an environment.

Complaint

A complaint lies to an employment tribunal, within three months of an **8–38** unlawful act (or where the act extends over a period, the end of the period).[62] Where a claimant proves facts from which the tribunal could infer discrimination, the burden of proof shifts to the employer to prove that unlawful discrimination has not occurred.[63] A tribunal who finds a complaint to be well-founded has power to make an order upholding the claim and can award compensation. There is no upper limit on discrimination awards, which can include sums in relation to financial loss, injury to feelings, personal injury, and interest. In addition, a tribunal can make a recommendation that the employer take certain action to avoid or reduce the adverse effect of any act of discrimination to which the complaint relates.

Race discrimination

Equivalent provisions can be found in the Race Relations Act 1976. It is **8–39** unlawful on racial grounds to treat a person less favourably than other persons are or would be treated (direct discrimination).[64] This can include discrimination against a person on the racial grounds of another (where,

---

[60] *British Airways Plc v Starmer* [2005] I.R.L.R. 863.
[61] SDA s.4A(1).
[62] SDA s.76(1)–(6). The requirement to raise a statutory grievance applies until such time as these procedures are repealed.
[63] SDA s.63A.
[64] Race Relations Act 1976 ("RRA") s.1(1)(a)

for example, an employer instructs an employee to racially discriminate). For the purposes of the Act, "racial grounds" includes colour, race, nationality or ethnic or national origins.[65] The situations in which a "genuine occupational requirement" can be established are significantly narrower.[66] Similarly, it is unlawful to apply a provision, criteria or practice to a person, which is or would be applied to persons not of the same race or ethnic or national origins, but which puts persons (including the victim) of the same race or ethnic or national origins at a particular disadvantage, and which cannot be shown to be a proportionate means of achieving a legitimate aim (indirect discrimination).[67] Harassment is also unlawful on the ground of race or ethnic or national origins. Similar provisions relating to victimisation as well as in relation to complaints to an employment tribunal and its remedies apply.

Disability discrimination

8–40   The Disability Discrimination Act 1995 prohibits discrimination against disabled persons, more specifically those who have a physical or mental impairment which has a substantial and long-term adverse effect on their ability to carry out normal day-to-day activities.[68] Severe disfigurements are automatically covered. Progressive conditions (such as cancer, multiple sclerosis or HIV) can also be deemed to amount to disabilities where the impairment is not yet substantial.[69] The focus is on what the person cannot do rather than on what the person can do. There is detailed guidance issued by the Secretary of State for Work and Pensions which is to be taken into account for the purpose of determining questions relating to the definition of "disability", which can often be a complex matter.[70] This should be read alongside the detailed Code of Practice on Employment and Occupation published by the (then) Disability Rights Commission in 2004, which remains the key source of advice for employers on complying with the Act. The ECJ is expected to rule later this year on whether EC law prohibits discrimination on the grounds of another person's disability.[71]

The legislation has certain key distinguishing features from other discrimination legislation. As well as prohibiting direct discrimination—less favourable treatment on the ground of a person's disability[72]—it also prohibits two other types of discrimination which are not dealt with by sex or race discrimination.

The first is known as "disability-related discrimination" which arises

---

[65] RRA s.3(1).
[66] RRA ss.4A–5.
[67] RRA s.1(1A).
[68] Disability Discrimination Act 1995 ("DDA") s.1(1).
[69] DDA Sch.1.
[70] (2006) available at *www.dwp.gov.uk*.
[71] *Coleman v Attridge Law* (Case C-303/06). The Advocate-General has already given a preliminary opinion that EC law requires this protection (31/01/2008) but the ECJ is not bound to follow his opinion.
[72] DDA s.3A(5).

where a person subjects a disabled person to less favourable treatment for a reason *which relates* to the disabled person's disability, where such treatment is not justified. In such a case, treatment shall only be justified where the reason for it is material to the circumstances of the particular case and substantial.[73] Cases might arise under this heading, for example, in relation to how employers operate sickness absence policies in the workplace. There is also a specific prohibition on disability-related harassment.[74]

The second is a duty on employers to make reasonable adjustments where a physical feature of premises, or a provision, criteria or practice places a disabled person at a substantial disadvantage compared with persons who are not disabled and where it is reasonable for the employer to take steps to prevent such effect. A variety of factors are to be considered in determining whether it is reasonable for adjustments to be made or not, including the extent to which doing so would prevent the effect, the practicability of the measure, the financial and other costs involved and resources of the employer, and the availability of financial assistance.[75] The legislation also gives examples of the kind of steps that may need to be taken so as to comply with the duty including:

- making adjustments to premises;
- allocating duties to others;
- transferring to an existing vacancy;
- altering hours of work;
- allowing absence from the workplace for assessment, treatment or rehabilitation;
- providing training or mentoring;
- acquiring or modifying equipment;
- modifying instructions or manuals;
- providing a reader or interpreter; or
- providing supervision or other support.

The duty to make reasonable adjustments has to date significantly added to the protections afforded to disabled persons at work and is likely to continue to do so in future.

▼ CHAPTER SUMMARY

THE CONTRACT OF EMPLOYMENT

1. **It is important to be able to identify a contract of employment as** 8–41 **certain rights are restricted to employees only.**

---

[73] DDA s.3A(3).
[74] DDA s.3B.
[75] DDA s.18B.

2. A minimum level of obligation needs to exist between the parties before a contract of service will arise. This will include mutual obligations to provide and perform work.
3. An obligation to perform the work personally will usually also have to exist and there has to be sufficient control.
4. Other provisions within the contract should be consistent with that of employment.
5. Workers may also qualify for certain rights arising under employment law, including in relation to the Working Time Regulations 1998.

TERMS AND CONDITIONS OF EMPLOYMENT

1. Contracts of employment do not require to be in writing—terms can be written or oral and express or implied.
2. An employer is required to give an employee a written statement of terms and conditions within two months of employment commencing—this is not contractual but can evidence what the contractual terms are;

   ➢ ERA s.1.

3. Collective agreements may also be a source of terms and conditions through becoming incorporated in contracts of employment.
4. Employees have a right not to be subjected to unlawful deductions from wages;

   ➢ ERA s.13.

5. Minimum rights exist in relation to wages and working hours/rest periods;

   ➢ National Minimum Wage Act 1998 & Working Time Regulations 1998.

6. Important terms are implied in all contracts of employment, including the duty of the employer not to engage in conduct likely to undermine trust and confidence without reasonable or proper cause;

   ➢ *United Bank v Akhtar* [1989] I.R.L.R. 507; *Malik v Bank of Credit and Commerce International SA* [1997] I.R.L.R. 462 (HL).

TERMINATION OF EMPLOYMENT AND WRONGFUL DISMISSAL

1. Statutory minimum notice rights exist for employers and employees;

   ➢ ERA s.86.

2. **A fundamental or material breach of contract will generally permit the party not in default to terminate the contract.**
3. **If an employer dismisses in breach of contract, an employee will be able to bring a claim of wrongful dismissal seeking damages. An employer may also bring a similar breach of contract claim against an employee who resigns and fails to give notice, in circumstances not involving a fundamental or material breach of contract.**
4. **A contract of employment can also terminate by operation of law where an unforeseen event or circumstances renders all future performance of the contract impossible. This is known as "frustration".**

UNFAIR DISMISSAL

1. **The right to claim unfair dismissal is generally restricted to employees with at least one year's continuous service;**

    ➤ ERA s.108.

2. **Exceptions apply to this general rule in relation to certain dismissals which are also automatically unfair, for example, dismissals on grounds of pregnancy, childbirth, maternity or certain health and safety grounds.**
3. **Dismissal is a statutory concept and includes termination of a fixed-term contract which is not renewed and also termination of the contract by an employee in circumstances where they are entitled to do so because of the employer's conduct (constructive dismissal);**

    ➤ ERA s.95.

4. **At present, employers are required to follow certain statutory procedures in relation to dismissals, which are designed to provide a minimum level of procedural fairness (expected to be repealed in April 2009). Failure to comply renders a dismissal unfair;**

    ➤ Employment Act 2002 s.98A.

5. **Similarly, employees need to comply with requirements in relation to minimum statutory grievance procedures prior to bringing most statutory employment claims, including constructive dismissal (also expected to be repealed in April 2009);**

    ➤ Employment Act 2002.

6. **There are six potentially fair reasons for dismissal: capability/qualifications, conduct, retirement, redundancy, inability to work without contravening an enactment, and some other substantial reason;**

    ➤ ERA s.98(2).

7. **Once a potentially fair reason is established, a tribunal must determine whether the employer acted reasonably or unreasonably in treating that reason as sufficient to dismiss the employee in the circumstances;**

   ➤ ERA s.98(4).

8. **A complaint of unfair dismissal requires to be raised to an employment within three months of the effective date of termination.**

9. **Remedies for unfair dismissal include compensation, reinstatement and re-engagement. A cap on compensation exists, unless the dismissal is on the ground of certain health and safety reasons or a protected disclosure (whistle-blowing)**

REDUNDANCY PAYMENTS

1. **An employee requires two years service to be eligible for a redundancy payment;**

   ➤ ERA s.155.

2. **Redundancy arises where there is a disappearing role, workplace or a cessation or diminution of work.**

3. **A redundancy payment is calculated by reference to weekly pay, age and length of service. A limit on "weekly pay" is applied for this purpose.**

4. **An employee is entitled to a four-week trial period if alternative employment is offered, without losing a right to a redundancy payment.**

5. **A redundancy payment may be lost if an employee unreasonably refuses suitable alternative employment.**

6. **Employees may also be entitled under their contracts of employment to enhanced redundancy terms.**

7. **Detailed requirements in relation to collective consultation apply where an employer is proposing to dismiss as redundant 20 or more employees at one establishment within a period of 90 days;**

   ➤ TULR(C)A s.188.

DISCRIMINATION

1. **Anti-discrimination law exists on grounds of sex, race, disability, part-time status, fixed-term status, religion or belief, sexual orientation, age, as well as specific legislation dealing with equal pay;**

   ➤ Sex Discrimination Act 1975; Equal Pay Act 1970; Race Relations Act 1976; Disability Discrimination Act 1995; Part-Time Workers (Prevention of Less Favourable

Treatment) Regulations 2000; Fixed-Term Employees (Prevention of Less Favourable Treatment) Regulations 2002; Employment Equality (Religion or Belief) Regulations 2003; Employment Equality (Sexual Orientation) Regulations 2003; Employment Equality (Age) Regulations 2006.

2. **Much discrimination law now focuses on three separate types of discrimination: direct, indirect and harassment.**
3. **Direct discrimination will generally arise where an employer subjects a person to less favourable treatment on a discriminatory ground.**
4. **Indirect discrimination will generally arise where an employer applies an apparently "neutral" provision, criteria or practice to everyone, but which is one that places one group (including the victim) at a particular disadvantage, and which cannot be shown to be proportionate means of achieving a legitimate aim.**
5. **Harassment will generally arise where a person is subjected, on a discriminatory ground, to unwanted conduct which has the purpose or effect of violating dignity or creating an intimidating, hostile, degrading, humiliating or offensive environment. The perception of the victim is taken into account in considering whether or not it is reasonable to consider that harassment has taken place in the circumstances.**
6. **A complaint in relation to unlawful discrimination can be brought to an employment tribunal within three months, which has power to award compensation, including for injury to feelings. There is no limit on the compensation that may be awarded.**
7. **The Disability Discrimination Act 1995 applies to disabled persons—this generally requires a claimant to establish a physical or mental impairment which has a long-term substantial adverse effect on normal day-to-day activities.**
8. **The Act also prohibits its own unique types of discrimination: "disability-related" discrimination and a failure to make reasonable adjustments.**

? QUICK QUIZ

- What are the key ingredients for a contract of service?
- Can a director who is a controlling shareholder also be an employee?
- When does a written statement of employment particulars have to be provided by an employer?
- What is a collective agreement? How can such agreements be sources of terms and conditions of employment?
- What limit does the Working Time Regulations 1998 place on maximum weekly working hours? Can employees waive their rights to this limit?

- What is wrongful dismissal and how is this different from unfair dismissal?
- What are the six potentially fair reasons for dismissal in unfair dismissal law?
- How much continuous service is required to be eligible to claim a redundancy payment?
- Can direct sex discrimination ever be justified?
- What is the general test for "disability" under the Disability Discrimination Act 1995?

📖 FURTHER READING

V. Craig and S. Walker, *Employment Law: An Introduction* 3rd edn (Edinburgh, W. Green, 2007)—useful, concise and up-to-date guide to employment law.

V. Craig and K. Miller, *Employment Law in Scotland* 3rd edn, (Tottel, 2004)—coverage of all aspects of employment law in Scotland.

Harvey on Industrial Relations and Employment Law (looseleaf, ongoing, Butterworths)—authoritative commentary designed for the practitioner.

✓ RELEVANT WEBLINKS

Acas: *http://www.acas.org.uk*.
Department for Business, Enterprise and Regulatory Reform: *http://www.berr.gov.uk/*.
Equality and Human Rights Commission: *http://www.equalityhumanrights.com*.

Chapter 9   Agency

Stuart Cross[1]

► CHAPTER OVERVIEW

This chapter is concerned with the law of agency. It starts by looking at   **9–01**
what is meant by agency and the key features or characteristics of an
agency relationship. Different kinds of agency relationships and examples
of common types of agency are examined which demonstrate how
important agency is to the effective operation of business and in commercial law generally. The ways of creating agency relationships are
discussed along with the legal consequences for each of the parties to the
agency. The chapter goes on to consider how third parties are affected by
an agency situation and how agency may be brought to an end. The
chapter concludes by looking at commercial agents and the impact of the
Commercial Agents (Council Directive) Regulations 1993 on the Scots
law of agency.

✓ OUTCOMES

At the end of this chapter you should be able to: **9–02**

- ✓ identify an agency relationship;
- ✓ recognise differing types and forms of agency;
- ✓ recognise and understand the various ways in which agency can
    be brought into existence;
- ✓ recognise the different parties involved in agency and understand
    the nature and extent of their legal relationship with each other;
- ✓ understand the duties owed by an agent to their principal;
- ✓ understand the duties owed by a principal to their agent;
- ✓ appreciate the impact agency can have on third parties and
    understand the rights third parties may have against agents and
    principals;
- ✓ understand how agency may be brought to an end;
- ✓ identify commercial agents and understand how they are pro-
    tected by the Commercial Agents (Council Directive) Regula-
    tions 1993.

---

[1] Senior Lecturer in Law, University of Dundee.

MEANING AND KEY FEATURES OF AGENCY

9–03 In the commercial world it is common to encounter situations where business and transactions are entered into or concluded via intermediaries. This may come about because the main parties to the transaction are too busy, do not have the necessary expertise or simply prefer that someone else concludes their commercial arrangements on their behalf. Whatever the reason for using someone else to act on your behalf, the relationship which is being created and relied upon is known as agency. Legally, agency is the contract which exists when one person instructs or allows another person to act for them in what will be a binding legal arrangement with a third party. This means that there are three parties involved in an agency relationship and two contracts. The three parties are the agent, the principal and the third party. The agent acts on behalf of the principal and brings the principal into a binding relationship with the third party and normally the agent will have no involvement in that contract. The two contracts are, therefore, the relationship between the principal and the agent in the first instance and the relationship between the principal and the third party which results from the agent's actions.

There is no single or precise definition of agency in Scots law and the courts are more concerned with the consequences of a commercial relationship and the effect on the parties rather than the description given to a particular relationship. Agency is a vital tool in business and it has been commented that:

"Commerce would literally come to a standstill if businessmen and merchants could not employ the services of factors, brokers, estate agents ... and the like and were expected to do everything themselves."[2]

Key Concept

There are three parties involved in an agency relationship. The agent, the principal and the third party. The agent acts on behalf of the principal and binds the principal to the third party in a contractual relationship without himself necessarily becoming a legal part of that relationship.

---

[2] B.S. Markesinis and R.J.C. Munday, *An Outline of the Law of Agency* (1992), p.3.

DIFFERENT KINDS AND EXAMPLES OF AGENCY

Kinds of agents

There are many different types of agents and many differing names and **9–04**
labels are used to describe agency relationships. The use of a particular
name or description to describe a relationship is not always a conclusive
guide as to what the actual legal relationship is between the parties
involved. What all the varying descriptions and categories have in common is usefulness in showing what the intentions of the parties involved
may have been in creating the relationship in question and what is the
actual legal nature of the relationship. There are a number of relatively
well understood and long established broad categories or kinds of agency
in Scots law. These are:

  (a) general and special agents;
  (b) mercantile agents;
  (c) *del credere* agents.

A further more recent category, commercial agents, is looked at later in
this chapter.

General and special agents

A general agent is an agent who has been engaged to conduct all of the **9–05**
business for a particular principal or, at a minimum, all of the business of
the principal of a particular sort. A special agent has a different kind of
relationship with the principal and is only engaged by the principal to
carry out a particular transaction or piece of business. The differing
relationship between the principal and a general or special agent will
shape the type and extent of authority which the agent has to act on
behalf of the principal and bind the principal to third parties. Normally,
third parties will be able to assume that a general agent has all the powers
that an agent of that kind would normally have whereas a special agent
would only have the powers and authority needed to carry out the particular transaction. A family solicitor who looks after all the legal affairs
for a family would usually be treated as a general agent[3] while a solicitor
appointed by a new client to look after a single transaction could be
considered to be acting as a special agent.[4]

Mercantile agents

A mercantile agent is a very particular kind of agent and the agency **9–06**
relationship is defined in the Factors Acts of 1889 and 1890. A mercantile
agent is defined as someone who "in the customary course of business as
such agent" has "authority either to sell goods or consign goods for the

---

[3] See *Morrison v Statter* (1885) 12 R.1152.
[4] See the position outlined in Bell, *Principles*, s.219(7) where a solicitor is treated as a
special agent.

purpose of sale, or to buy goods, or to raise money on the security of goods".[5] So, in establishing whether mercantile agency exists it is important to consider all the facts surrounding the type of business and relationship in assessing the "customary course of business" of the particular agent. The crucial feature of the relationship between a mercantile agent and the principal is that because of the Factors Acts the agent has the authority and ability to transfer title to the principal's goods where the principal has not given consent to the transfer and where the principal would not have given permission for the transaction entered into by the agent. This means that a third party transacting with a mercantile agent can transact with the agent with few concerns over the extent of the agent's authority provided the third party enters into the transaction in good faith and does not know of any restriction on the agent's authority relating to the transaction.[6]

Del credere agency

9–07 This is a long-established but not very common and fairly specialised form of agency. When an agent acts on behalf of a principal it is not normal or common practice for the agent to give any form of guarantee or indemnity to the principal as to the solvency or ability to pay of the third party the agent has introduced to the principal. When the agent does provide a guarantee or indemnity to the principal then the agent is described to be acting as a *del credere* agent.[7] The agent would charge a fee for this additional service to the principal but in all other aspects the agency relationship between the agent and principal is like other forms of agency. The *del credere* agency is usually a mercantile agent and this type of relationship was often used where goods were being sold abroad and the principal wished to minimise any risk of not being paid for the goods. This type of agency arrangement is far less common now as far more sophisticated mechanisms such as credit guarantee schemes are available. These schemes are often state or government supported.

Examples of agency

9–08 Looking at different examples of agency relationships can be a useful way to identify not only the parties to the agency but also the types of authority which can be given to an agent or deemed to have been given to an agent by a principal. Many commonly encountered business relationships are simple examples of agency. The relationship between a client (principal) and an estate agent, accountant, surveyor or stockbroker (all agents) is a simple agency relationship. Other common examples of agency relationships are as follows:

---

[5] Factors Act 1889 s.1(1) as applied in Scotland by the Factors Act 1890.
[6] Factors Act 1889 s.2(1).
[7] *Lloyd's Exrs v Wright* (1870) 7 S.L.R 216.

Solicitors

A solicitor can be both a general and a special agent and the true nature **9–09** of the relationship will depend on the facts and circumstances of each case. Traditionally, the "law agent" was engaged in Scotland on a broad basis, looking after the general interests of clients. There is now much more variety in the manner in which solicitors are engaged, with specialist practitioners often now engaged by clients solely for a particular piece of work. Whether the relationship is special or general, it is in all respects fiduciary in nature[8] and, as such, the solicitor must carry out the instructions given by the client (principal). The other elements of the fiduciary relationship between a solicitor and client mean that a solicitor should not make a secret profit from his client as a result of a transaction in which the solicitor is a party.[9] Various other features apply in relation to a solicitor/client relationship which mainly relate to the type of authority a solicitor has to act on behalf of the client. For example, a solicitor engaged in a court matter has authority to take all necessary steps to pursue the court process including the instruction of a local solicitor[10] and the implied authority to instruct Counsel (an advocate).[11] In Scotland the Law Society of Scotland is the professional body for solicitors and it regulates the activities of solicitors. Law Society rules reflect the fiduciary nature of the solicitor/client relationship and solicitors would not be expected to act for more than one principal where their interests conflict.

Partners

An important and very clear example of a commonly used business **9–10** structure which involves an agency relationship is partnership. In Scotland partnership is regulated by the Partnership Act 1890 and s.5 of that Act states that: "Every partner is an agent of the firm and his other partners for the purpose of the business of the partnership...".

This means that the partnership (the firm) and the fellow partners are bound by actions taken by any of their other partners. There are restrictions on what partners can do which will bind their fellow partners and the firm and the main condition is that the action taken must have been carried out in the course of the partnership's normal business.[12] The type of authority which individual partners can have may also vary. In some situations their authority will be implied but in others (as will be seen later in the chapter) it will be actual.

---

[8] *Brown v Inland revenue Comrs*, 1964 S.C. (HL) 180.
[9] See *Brown v Inland Revenue Comrs* at 197.
[10] *Bannatyne, Kirkwood, France & Co*, 1907 S.C. 705.
[11] *Torbat v Torbat's Trs* (1906) 14 S.L.T. 830.
[12] Partnership Act 1890 s.5.

Company directors

9–11 In the United Kingdom registered companies, of which the limited company is by far the most common, are treated by the law as having a separate legal personality from those who are the shareholders and directors of the company[13]. This means that registered companies are recognised as legal persons in their own right but that personality is entirely artificial. Companies need human beings to act on their behalf. The responsibility for acting on behalf of companies is normally delegated to the directors of the company. The internal rules of a company are to be found in its articles of association and these deal with the delegation of authority from the company to directors. That delegation of authority to the directors to act on the company's behalf places the directors in the role of agents for the company.

CREATING AGENCY

9–12 Agency is a contractual relationship and in similar fashion to most other types of contract an agency relationship can be brought into existence in a variety of ways. The main ways that agency can be created are:

- express creation;
- implied creation
- creation by ratification;
- creation by necessity;
- creation by holding out.

Express creation of agency

9–13 The express creation of agency simply means that there has been a deliberate and conscious act on the part of the principal to appoint someone as their agent. There is no special form or process required for express creation and it can be done either orally or in writing.[14] Differing types of documents may be used to create agency and the extent of the formality involved can vary. In a commercial agency relationship both the agent and principal are entitled to request a signed written document setting out the terms of the agency arrangement.[15] Sometimes where the agency relationship is of particular importance the document creating the agency will itself be formal and the nature and extent of the agency clearly stated. A good example of such an arrangement is where one party (the principal) grants a power of attorney in favour of another (the agent) which permits the principal's affairs to be looked after by the agent.

In the majority of instances agency will be created by less formal means. This may be orally, or by other informal means. Provided issues of proof can be dealt with satisfactorily there is no reason why agency

---

[13] See the case of *Salomon v Salomon & Co* [1897] A.C. 22.
[14] *Robert Barry & Co v Doyle*, 1998 S.L.T. 1238.
[15] Commercial Agents (Council Directive) Regulations 1993 (SI 1993/3053), reg.13.

cannot be created by more modern means of communication such as e-mail or text messages.

Implied creation of agency

An agency relationship can be brought into existence because the actions **9–14** of the parties involved imply that this is what they actually intended to happen even though there is no express appointment of the agent by the principal. In many cases this will be obvious from the circumstances involved. This might simply involve looking at the facts and the actions of the various parties involved. It is also possible that agency will be implied as a result of a particular rule of law. A good example arises in partnerships. In the case of a partnership, s.5 of the Partnership Act 1890 states that every partner is "deemed or implied" to be an agent of the firm and the other partners. Combining the factual position that someone is a partner with the rule of law in s.5 gives rise to an implied agency relationship. In other factual situations such as employment the seniority of an employee or manager or the circumstances of employment may imply an agency relationship.[16]

Creation by ratification

It will normally be the case that an agency agreement or relationship is **9–15** brought into existence between the agent and the principal before the agent takes any action on the principal's behalf. In some situations this may not happen and may not even be possible and "an agent" takes action on behalf of "a principal" when the principal may be completely unaware of the agent's actions. This does not mean that an agency cannot exist or be brought into existence. The critical issue is what happens when the "principal" becomes aware of the action taken by the "agent". At that stage it is possible for the principal to ratify the actions which have already been taken by the agent. The principal can ratify the agent's actions either expressly (i.e by taking some form of positive action) or by implication (e.g. by some form of action or course of conduct). In working out whether ratification has taken place the factual position is crucial and any act, behaviour or statement by the principal which is clear enough to show an intention to ratify will be enough. Before it can be shown that ratification has been effective and taken place, a number of conditions have to be met:

- The agent must have been acting in the capacity of an agent and disclosed this to the third party.[17]
- The principal must have been in existence at the time of the "agent's" actions;[18]

---

[16] See *Neville v C and A Modes*, 1945 S.C. 175 and *Mackenzie v Cluny Hill Hydro*, 1908 S.C. 200.

[17] *Keighley, Maxsted & Co v Durant* [1901] A.C. 240 HL.

[18] *Tinnevelly Sugar Refining Co Ltd v Mirrlees Watson and Yaryan Co Ltd* (1894) 21 R. 1009; *Kelner v Baxter* (1866) LR CP 174.

**Tinnevelly Sugar Refining Co Ltd v Mirrlees Watson
and Yaryan Co Ltd**
(1894) 21 R. 1009; (1894) 2 S.L.T. 149, IH

Two men bought machinery from Mirrlees Watson, saying
that they were acting on behalf of the Tinnevelly company. In
fact the company wasn't formed until two weeks later. The
machinery supplied turned out to be defective and the Tinnevelly company (which had by now been registered)
attempted to sue on the basis of the defects. It was held that
Tinnevelly had no rights under the original "contract"
because it could not be a party to that contract. It had not
existed at the time the original "contract" was entered into
and it could therefore not subsequently ratify the actions of
the two "agents".

- The principal must have had the necessary legal capacity to take the action in question.[19]
- The principal must have been informed of or known of all the relevant facts behind the agent's actions at the stage the principal elects to ratify unless it can be shown that the principal was willing to ratify whatever the circumstances.[20]
- The ratification by the principal must take place within any relevant timescales, so that any action taken by a principal which is outwith, for example the statutory time limit for the lodging of an appeal will not amount to valid ratification even though the appeal may have been successfully lodged on time by the "agent".[21]
- The action being ratified must itself have been legal.[22]

The overall effect of ratification is to put the agent and principal in the same position they would have been in had agency been agreed in the conventional way before anything was done by the agent. If the "prin-cipal" opts not to take any action to ratify the action which has already been taken by the "agent" then the "agent" will be personally liable for the action they have taken.

---

[19] *Boston Deep Sea Fishing and Ice Co Ltd v Farnham* [1957] 3 All E.R. 204.
[20] *Suncorp Insurance and Finance v Milano Assecurazioni SpA* [1992] 2 Lloyd's Rep. 225, QBD (Comm).
[21] *Goodall v Bilsland*, 1909 S.C. 1152; 1 S.L.T. 376 IH (1 Div).
[22] *Bedford Insurance Co Ltd v Instituto de Resseguros do Brasil* [1985] Q.B. 966; [1984] 3 W.L.R. 726, QBD (Comm).

Creation by necessity

Agency can be created in situations of necessity where in an emergency or **9–16**
critical situation an agent carries out essential actions for a principal
without having been instructed to do so. In Scots law this notion of
agency of necessity sits within the doctrine of *negotiorum gestio*. All of
this takes place in circumstances where it is impossible to communicate
with the person on whose behalf action is being taken. The situations in
which this is likely to occur are now far less common with the advent of
modern means of instantaneous communication such as mobile and
satellite telephones and computer-based communication such as email,
but unforeseen and uncontrollable circumstances involving civil disturbance, war or extreme weather events could still provide opportunities
for the effective operation of agency by necessity. Situations of ill-health
leading to an inability to give instructions which forces someone to act on
behalf of the infirm person can also trigger agency by necessity.[23] When
agency of necessity is relied upon the actions taken should be taken in
good faith, should be reasonable and should be in the best interests of the
person on whose behalf they are taken.

Creation by holding out

This type of agency arises when a third party receives the impression that **9–17**
someone is an agent or acting as an agent because of either positive
encouragement of that impression by the principal or the fact that the
principal takes no action to contradict the impression that agency actually exists. In this situation the action or inaction of the principal results
in someone being "held out" or represented as being an agent. Agency by
holding out often arises from situations where agency proper did in fact
exist at some stage between the principal and the agent but the agent's
earlier authority to act has been withdrawn and third parties have not
been told.

Key Concept

Agency can be brought into existence in a whole variety of ways.
Whatever the route to agency, provided the required conditions in
each instance have been met the contractual relationship in each
instance will be binding on the principal and agent.

THE AGENCY RELATIONSHIP

The nature of the relationship between a principal and an agent will **9–18**
largely be shaped by the following:

- the nature and extent of the agent's authority;

---

[23] *Fernie v Robertson* (1871) 9 M. 437.

- the agent's duties and the principal's rights;
- the agent's rights and the principal's duties.

Each of these is now considered in turn.

The agent's authority

9–19   The extent of an agent's authority is a critical part of the relationship between an agent and a principal. Normally an agent will act within the limits of the authority given by the principal and in those situations the principal will be bound to third parties by the agent's actions. More problematic issues arise when an agent is unclear as to the nature and extent of authority given by a principal. Authority is, therefore, crucial to the successful operation of agency. There are three broadly recognised categories used to identify types of authority given to an agent. These are:

- express;
- implied;
- apparent or ostensible.

Express authority

9–20   In an ideal situation the extent of the authority given to an agent will be set out in the agreement between the agent and the principal. If an agent exceeds the extent of the authority given by the principal then that can jeopardise the validity of the contract which the agent has tried to enter into. If there is no other type of authority open to an agent and the principal opts not to ratify an action by an agent which exceeds the express authority the agent has then the principal will normally not be liable to the third party.

Implied authority

9–21   For a variety of reasons it is common to find that the exact boundaries of an agent's authority have not been clearly recorded as part of the agreement between the agent and the principal. This absence of express authority does not mean that the agent has no authority to act. Commonly, an agent's authority is implied. This may be because of the particular facts and circumstances surrounding the relationship between the agent and the principal, or because of the particular type of transaction or because the agent is a member of a particular profession and a particular level or type of authority is afforded to members of that profession when acting as an agent. A good example of the professional situation is a solicitor who has implied powers to take certain actions without the express authority of his or her principal. In other situations the nature of the relationship between the agent and the principal will imply a certain type and level of authority. For example, a member of staff responsible for sales will have implied authority to take an order. In *Barry, Ostlere &*

Shepherd Ltd v Edinburgh Cork Importing Co[24] an order was placed by Barry, Ostlere and Shepherd with Edinburgh Cork for a supply of cork shavings. The order was placed via one of Edinburgh Cork's salesmen. The order wasn't fulfilled and B, O and S brought an action against Edinburgh Cork for breach of contract. The defence was to the effect that the salesman had no authority to conclude the contract. It was held that B, O and S were entitled to assume that the salesman did have the necessary authority to accept the order.

Apparent or ostensible authority

This type of authority arises in situations where the behaviour of the **9–22** principal gives rise to an impression that the agent has been given authority to act. These instances tend to arise because of the way the principal has acted or because the principal has allowed a particular set of circumstances to continue which give the impression to a third party that the principal has in fact granted authority to an agent to act on the principal's behalf. There must be a clear linkage between the various elements. First, the principal must have created a particular impression, usually by means of some form of direct representation or allowing a set of circumstances to continue. Secondly, the third party has to believe that the agent was authorised to act on the basis of the principal's behaviour or representation. Finally, the third party has to have placed some form of reliance on the principal's behaviour or representation and suffered a loss as a result. This type of authority can operate to render a transaction valid even where the agent did not in fact have the necessary authority from the principal at the outset to carry out the transaction. There are two common situations where this type of authority can operate to validate an otherwise unauthorised transaction. The first example is when a principal has given authority to an agent at some stage but has, at a later date, withdrawn that authority without having told third parties. To make the later withdrawal of authority effective the principal should have told the third parties of the change in the agent's authority. The second example of a situation when this type of authority comes about is when the principal has an agreement with the agent which places a limit on the extent of the agent's authority but the agent exceeds that authority when dealing with third parties. If the third parties dealing with the agent continue to believe that the agent has the original level of authority they experienced in their previous dealings with the agent then that level of "apparent" authority will continue to exist until they are properly told otherwise by the principal.

---

[24] 1909 S.C. 1113.

International Sponge Importers Ltd v Andrew Watt & Sons
[1911] A.C. 279; 1911 S.C. (HL) 57

Cohen, a commercial travelling salesman was authorised to sell sponges on behalf of International Sponge Importers Ltd. Cohen was a regular caller to Watt & Sons and he had sold them sponges on a number of occasions in the past. Normally Watt & Sons made payment directly to International Sponge Importers (ISI) by sending them a cheque. On a few occasions Cohen had collected cheques from Watt which were payable to ISI and which Cohen had then passed on to ISI. On four instances Cohen had also persuaded Watt & Sons to pay with cheques made out to Cohen or by means of cash. Cohen eventually absconded with money owing to ISI. Both the Court of Session and the House of Lords held that ISI could not recover the missing money from the customers who had paid Cohen. They were entitled to conclude from the earlier course of dealings that Cohen did have authority to accept payment personally.

The whole concept of apparent or ostensible authority is closely linked to the principle of personal bar and the net effect of apparent or ostensible authority is to place the principal in a position where the principal cannot deny that the agent has authority to act[25].

Key Concept

An agent's authority is critical in determining whether his principal will be bound to a third party by the agent's actions and to what extent. If the agent has acted within the boundaries of the authority given by the principal then the principal will be liable for all the agent's actions. In the same way, if the principal ratifies the agent's actions the principal is liable in exactly the same way as if the agent had full authority in the first place.

The agent's duties/principal's rights

9–23   In an ideal situation there will be a contract between the principal and agent which deals not only with the obvious issue of the agent's authority but also sets out the duties the agent has to the principal and the rights the principal enjoys in the agency relationship. Unfortunately it is surprisingly common to encounter agency arrangements when no clear agreement exists setting out the terms of the agency relationship or, if it does exist, it is silent about some or all of the agent's duties and

---

[25] *British Bata Shoe Co Ltd v Double M Shah Ltd*, 1980 S.C. 311; *Armagus Ltd v Mundogas* [1986] 1 A.C. 717.

principal's rights. In such situations the law will imply a number of duties to apply between the principal and agent. These are as follows:

- the duty to perform instructions;
- good faith/fiduciary duty;
- the duty to exercise skill and care;
- the duty to keep accounts.

These are each considered in turn.

The duty to perform instructions

An agent is obliged to do what he or she has been asked to do by the **9–24** principal in terms of the agency agreement. In a situation where the agent has only been given general instructions by the principal or there are no instructions then the agent is expected to act in a way which reflects their best judgment and the generally accepted customs of their profession.[26] If the principal's instructions are not clear then the principal cannot hold the agent responsible for any loss flowing from the poor instructions.[27]

When an agent does not comply with the principal's clear instructions then the agent will be personally liable to the principal for any losses arising as a consequence of the non-compliance.

Gilmour v Clark
(1853) 15 D. 478

Gilmour, an Edinburgh merchant, gave instructions to a local carrier to take a consignment of goods to Leith docks to be loaded onto a specifically identified ship, the *Earl of Zetland*. For apparently legitimate reasons the goods were loaded onto another ship, the *Magnet*. This ship sank en route and Gilmour's cargo was lost. It was held that Clark was liable to Gilmour for the loss of the goods even though the change in ship was well intentioned.

An agent who does not follow instructions also loses the right to claim any payment or commission so long as the non-compliance continues.[28]

Good faith/fiduciary duty

A key element of the relationship between an agent and a principal is the **9–25** fiduciary duty which is owed by the agent to the principal. An agent is bound to act in good faith and in the best interests of the principal.[29] This duty stands as a clear duty in its own right but it is often seen more clearly

---

[26] Bell, *Commentaries*, I, 517; *Fearn v Gordon and Craig* (1893) 20 R. 352.
[27] *Ireland v Livingston* (1872) L.R. 5 H.L. 395.
[28] *Alexander Graham & Co v United Turkey Red Co Ltd*, 1922 S.C. 533.
[29] Bell, *Principles*, s.222.

in operation in the range of other duties to be observed by an agent which are influenced by the good faith obligation. These duties are:

(1) the duty to act personally;
(2) the duty to account;
(3) the duty not to disclose confidential information;
(4) the duty to avoid conflicts of interest.

Each of these duties is considered in turn.

(1) The duty to act personally

9–26 The starting assumption in an agency relationship is that because the principal has selected the agent to act the agent must not delegate the work to anyone else.[30] While this is the generally accepted rule it is also recognised and accepted that there are many situations where there can be exceptions to the rule and delegation can take place. Delegation may be expressly permitted by the agency agreement itself. It is also possible that delegation may be implied from the particular facts and circumstances of the particular agency situation or because it may be common or accepted practice in particular industries, trades and professions. It is accepted practice that architects can delegate certain types of work to a surveyor[31] and that solicitors can instruct a local solicitor to act when the original case is being heard in another part of the country.[32] When delegation is allowed then the sub-agent will also owe duties to the principal. In the case of *De Bussche v Alt*[33] DE Bussche had been appointed as an agent to sell a ship for a particular price. Permission had been given for the appointment of a sub-agent and Alt had been given that appointment and was instructed to sell the ship in Japan. In a dispute over the sale and appointment of the sub-agent it was held that Alt's appointment was valid and there was a contractual relationship between the principal and Alt. However, even when delegation is allowed the original agent may remain liable for acts and omissions of the sub-agent. In instances where delegation is not permissible but the agent has purported to delegate the agent will be liable to the principal for breach of the agency agreement.

---

[30] Two Latin phrases are often used in this connection. The first is *delectus personae* which simply refers to the fact that the agent has been chosen by the principal on the basis of special skills or attributes. The second phrase, *delegatus non potest delegare* is more direct and simply translates as meaning that an agent cannot delegate.

[31] *Cornelius v Black* (1879) 6 R. 581.

[32] *Robertson v Foulds* (1860) 22 D. 714.

[33] (1878) 8 Ch. D. 286.

(2) The duty to account

An agent must account to the principal for all benefits received by the **9–27** agent during the period of the agency.[34] This duty is concerned with potential secret profits or benefits earned or retained by an agent and should not be confused with the quite separate obligation on an agent to keep accounts of the transactions occurring during the agency. The duty to account does not stop an agent from acting for another principal at the same time, even if the two or more principals are in competition.[35]

(3) The duty not to disclose confidential information

It is commonly the case that an agent will receive confidential or sensitive **9–28** information from a principal during an agency relationship. In such situations the agent is under a duty not to disclose or to make use of that information.

Liverpool Victoria Friendly Society v Houston
(1900) 3 F. 42

For four years Houston was an insurance agent for Liverpool Victoria. Over that time he saw detailed lists of people insured by the company. After being dismissed by the company Houston offered the customer lists to a competing society which then made approaches to the people on the lists. It was held that Houston had a duty to treat the customer information as confidential and was liable in damages for the loss of business suffered by Liverpool Victoria.

(4) The duty to avoid conflicts of interest

The general position is that an agent should avoid situations where the **9–29** agent's interests conflict with the principal's interests.[36] This does not mean that an agent cannot act at the same time for more than one principal who may have directly competing interests. In *Lothian v Jenolite Ltd*[37] Lothian agreed to sell some of Jenolite's products in Scotland and to be paid on commission. The initial agreement covered a four-year period but it was ended by Jenolite after just over a year. Lothian claimed damages for breach of contract. Lothian counterclaimed and argued that as Lothian had bought and sold products from competitors that was itself a breach of contract. It has held that because the original contract had not said that Lothian could only sell Jenolite's products then he was permitted to sell other products.

---

[34] *Neilson v Skinner & Co* (1890) 17 R. 1243; *Trans Barvil Agencies (UK) Ltd v John S. Baird & Co Ltd*, 1988 S.C. 222.
[35] *Lothian v Jenolite Ltd* 1969 S.C 111.
[36] *Huntingdon Copper and Sulphur Co Ltd v Henderson* (1877) 4 R. 294.
[37] 1969 S.C. 111.

If an agent does not avoid potentially conflicting situations then the risk is that anything the agent does which creates a benefit for the agent may be seen as the agent generating what is often referred to as a secret profit and being liable to account to the principle for that profit. A conflict of interest will not always generate a secret profit but it is the most commonly encountered example of how a conflict of interest can affect the relationship between a principal and agent.

> ### McPherson's Trustees v Watt
> ### (1877) 5 R. (HL) 9
>
> Watt was a solicitor who acted on behalf of the trustees in relation to the sale of four houses. Without telling the trustees he had arranged for his brother to be the purchaser of the houses and Watt intended to buy the other two for himself by paying half the purchase price to his brother. The transaction was set aside by the court. The court also pointed out that it was of no consequence that the transaction might have been a good bargain; the sale could be set aside even if the price was a fair one.

While it is possible that if the agent tells the principal about any additional benefit and the principal agrees to the benefit being retained the agent may be able to retain the benefit it is still possible, especially in situations such as a solicitor/client relationship, that even with disclosure of a conflict this may still amount to a breach of the duty.[38] If the principal discovers a secret profit which the agent has not disclosed then the principal is entitled to terminate the contract[39] and the agent will lose any entitlement to be paid for the period of the contract during which the breach continues.

The duty to exercise skill and care

9–30 An agent must perform the agency arrangement with skill and care. The nature and extent of that duty may vary. If the agent is not a member of a particular profession then the level of skill and care which can be expected is that which is associated with an ordinary prudent man managing his own affairs.[40] If the agent is a member of a particular profession or trade then the level of skill and care to be expected is that of a reasonably competent member of that trade or profession.[41] An agent from a particular trade or profession who makes an error of judgment will not be held to have breached the duty of skill and care if they can

---

[38] *Cleland v Morrison* (1876) 6 R. 156
[39] *Boston Deep Sea Fishing Co Ltd v Ansell* (1888) L.R. 39 Ch. D. 339, CA.
[40] Bell, *Commentaries*, I, 516.
[41] *Cooke v Falconer's Representatives* (1850) 13 D. 157.

establish that they acted in a way which showed reasonable knowledge, skill and care.[42]

In cases where the agent is not receiving any payment the agent is still expected to act with due care and skill.[43] An agent will be liable to the principal for damages for breach of contract if the agent breaches the duty of skill and care.[44] The agent will not be liable where an action taken turns out not to be in the interests of the principal but it was taken on the basis of instructions issued by the principal.

The duty to keep accounts

The agent must keep accounts. Although there is no fundamental **9–31** requirement that these be written, most agency agreements require that they are in fact in writing. If there is any discrepancy which the agent is unable to explain then this has to be made good by the agent even in the absence of any suggestion of dishonesty. In *Tyler v Logan* there was a shortfall of £362 when stocktaking was taken in a Dundee shoe shop. Logan was the manager of the shop and he was held liable to pay the shortfall even though there was no suggestion of dishonesty.

Key Concept

The concept of good faith lies at the heart of the agency relationship and shapes the main duty owed by an agent to a principal. The good faith duty to act in the best interest of the principal shapes and informs other duties owed by an agent.

The agent's rights/principal's duties

The main rights an agent can expect to flow from agency and which the **9–32** agent will expect the principal to observe centre around ensuring that the agent is properly rewarded and not out of pocket and is in a position to secure those entitlements. This can be seen in each of the main rights, which are:

- to be remunerated and reimbursed;
- to be relieved of liabilities;
- to enjoy rights of lien and security.

These are considered in turn:

---

[42] *Simpson v Kidstons, Watson, Turnbull & Co*, 1913 S.L.T. 74.
[43] *Copland v Brogan*, 1916 S.C. 277.
[44] *Salvesen & Co v Rederi Aktiebolaget Nordstjernan* (1905) 7 F. (HL) 101.

Remuneration and reimbursement

9–33 Hopefully, the agency agreement will set out that the agent is entitled to remuneration and the basis upon which the agent is to be remunerated by the principal. If the agreement says nothing or it is not clear then there is a rebuttable presumption that an agent is entitled to be remunerated if the work the agent has done forms part of the agent's livelihood.[45] If the agreement is silent or unclear about the level of remuneration then the normal practice is for the courts to consider what is customary in the particular trade or profession and attempt to set a level of payment on this basis. If this cannot be done or the agent is not part of a recognised trade or profession then the remuneration will be worked out on the basis of the work done and the amount the agent has actually earned.[46] An agent also has a right to be reimbursed by the principal for expenses which the agent has incurred in properly carrying out the work of the agency contract.[47]

To be relieved of liabilities

9–34 An agent has the right to be relieved by the principal of all liabilities which have been incurred by the agent because of the proper performance of the agency contract.[48] The principal will not be obliged to provide relief to the principal when the agent has not acted in accordance with the agency agreement or has acted in a way which is illegal or negligent.[49]

To enjoy rights of lien and security

9–35 If an agent is not paid or is not reimbursed for expenses when they are entitled to payment then the agent is entitled to exercise certain rights in relation to the principal's assets. These rights are by way of security and are referred to as rights of lien or security. There are two types of lien: general and special. General lien allows an agent to retain the principal's goods or assets in relation to a particular agency transaction even though the retained goods may not have been involved in the particular transaction. Certain professions such as solicitors, bankers,[50] stockbrokers[51] and particular types of agents such as mercantile agents[52] are recognised as being able to exercise a general lien. The right to use a general lien is not automatic in all cases of agency and where it does not exist the type of lien is known as a special lien. This right only allows the agent to retain assets which are involved in the transaction which has given rise to the

---

[45] *Mackersy's Executors v St. Giles Cathedral Managing Board* (1904) 12 S.L.T. 391.
[46] This way of calculating the payment is referred to as being *quantum meruit*, i.e. the amount which has been earned. See *Kennedy v Glass* (1890) 17 R. 1085.
[47] *Marshall Wilson Dean and Turnbull v Feymac Properties Ltd*, 1996 G.W.D. 22-1247.
[48] *Stevenson & Sons v Duncan* (1842) 5 D. 167.
[49] *Thacker v Hardy* (1878) Q.B.D. 685.
[50] *Drummond v Muirhead and Guthrie Smith* (1900) 2 F. 585.
[51] *Glendinning v John D. Hope & Co*, 1911 S.C. (HL) 73.
[52] *Powdrill v Murrayhead*, 1996 G.W.D. 34-2011.

agent's entitlement to be paid. Accountants are only entitled to use the special lien.[53]

The right of lien is only a security right. Unless there has been agreement with the principal the right of lien does not allow the agent to sell the assets belonging to the principal which have been retained.

THIRD PARTIES

The aim of agency is to provide a way for agents to enter into transactions which contractually binds the principal and third party together but does not create any liability for the agent. Whether this situation comes about will depend on a range of factors but the most significant of these is the way the agent has behaved during the course of the agency transactions. There are two main ways in which an agent can act. These are as follows: **9–36**

- the agent acts as an agent;
- the agent exceeds his/her authority.

Each of these is now considered.

The agent acts as an agent

In this situation the information that the agent has disclosed to the third party is of particular importance. The three types of situations which are likely to occur are:

(1) the agent discloses that there is a principal and names the principal;
(2) the agent discloses that there is a principal but does not name the principal; and
(3) the agent does not disclose that there is a principal.

Each of these situations is now considered.

(1) The principal is disclosed and named

The general rule is that when the agent discloses that there is an agency involved and names the principal the contract is between the third party and the principal and the agent has no part in the contract and incurs no personal liability.[54] There will be the same outcome where the principal's actual name has not been disclosed but the principal can be easily identified by the third party.[55] There can be exceptions to this general rule and an agent can be held liable to third parties if the parties to the agency intend that this should happen or the agreement makes it clear that is **9–37**

---

[53] *Finlay (Liquidator of Scottish Workmen's Assurance Co Ltd) v Waddell*, 1910 S.C. 670.
[54] *Stone and Rolfe Ltd v Kimber Coal Co Ltd*, 1926 S.C. (HL) 45.
[55] *Armour v T.L. Duff & Co*, 1912 S.C. 120.

what was intended. In some trades and professions the agent will still be personally liable to third parties even though clearly acting as an agent for a named and disclosed principal. One of the clearest examples of this practice is solicitors, who can be held personally liable for obligations they grant during the course of a transaction.[56]

(2) The principal is disclosed but not named

9-38 In this situation the fact there is a principal involved is known to the third party but the name of the principal is not disclosed. There is very little clear authority on this situation in Scots law. If it is possible by other means to identify the principal then the outcome will be similar to that when the principal is named and the agent has no liability to the third party.[57] If easy identification is not possible then the third party may have to choose or elect whether to hold the principal or the agent liable under the contract.[58] The position is simpler when the agent refuses to identify the undisclosed principal. To do this is to deny the third party any remedy against the principal and the agent can be held personally liable.[59]

(3) The agent does not disclose that there is a principal

9-39 If an agent acts without disclosing that the actions are on behalf of a principal then the likelihood is that third parties will believe that the agent is in fact acting as a principal. There is nothing to suggest agency even exists as far as the third party is concerned. In such situations the agent runs the risk that the third party will consider that they have entered into a contract with the agent and hold the agent liable under the contract. The normal position is that in situations where the existence of a principal remains undisclosed then the agent may be sued by the third party. Once a contract has been concluded by the agent it is open to the principal to disclose his/her identity. Provided the agent has acted within the limits of his/her authority then the principal may sue the third party.[60] Once the identity of the principal has been disclosed then the third party also has the option to sue the principal. This is an optional process. The third party must select to sue the principal or the agent and cannot pursue both.

---

[56] Digby Brown & Co v Lyall 1995 S.L.T. 932.
[57] *Matthews v Auld & Guild* (1873) 1 R. 1224.
[58] See *Lamont Nisbet & Co v Hamilton*, 1907 S.C. 628 and *Ferrier v Dods* (1865) 3 M. 561
[59] *Gibb v Cunningham and Robertson*, 1925 S.L.T. 608.
[60] *Hutton v Bulloch* (1874) L.R. 9 QB 572.

> ### Bennett v Inveresk Paper Co
> ### (1891) 18 R. 975
>
> Bennett owned an Australian newspaper and instructed his agent in London to make arrangements for the supply of paper for the newspaper. The agent contracted with Inveresk to supply the paper and transport it to Australia. Inveresk knew nothing about Bennett's existence at this stage. The paper arrived in Australia but was damaged. Bennett raised an action against Inveresk for breach of contract. It was held that he had title to sue.

Once an agent has elected who to sue then the choice is final.[61] There can be confusion as to whether or not a clear election has been made by the third party. This can be evidenced in a variety of ways but the common element is that the choice must have been clear. Raising a court action alone will not be enough to establish that a clear election has taken place.[62]

The agent exceeds his/her authority

If an agent acts in a way which exceeds the authority given by the principal then there will be no binding contract between the principal and the third party unless the principal chooses to ratify the agent's actions or the doctrine of apparent/ostensible authority can be relied on. While there is no absolute rule that an agent acting outside the authority given by a principal will be bound into a contract with the third party the agent will almost certainly have some sort of personal liability to the third party. So, in situations where the agent has acted fraudulently or has negligently misrepresented the extent of the authority given by the principal the third party will have a right of action in delict. Even if the agent's actions are innocent the third party may still have a right of action and the agent may still be liable for damages. This type of liability arises because the agent is considered as a matter of law as having given an implied warranty to the third party that the agent had the authority needed to contract when in fact that was not the case. The agent can be held liable for having breached that authority.[63]

9–40

---

[61] *Ferrier v Dods* (1865) 3 M. 561.
[62] *Meier & Co v Kuchenmeister* (1881) 8 R. 642.
[63] *Anderson v Croall & Sons* (1903) 6 F. 153.

Key Concept

Agency will operate in such a way as to bind the third party to the
principal in a valid contract when the agent acts within the level of
authority given by the principal. When the agent acts outwith the
authority given by the principal or does not properly disclose the
existence or identity of the principal to the third party then the agent
runs the risk of incurring some form of personal liability.

ENDING AGENCY

9–41 An agency can be brought to an end in a variety of ways. Many of the
ways relied upon to bring an agency to an end simply rely on principles of
common law. The most common ways that an agency arrangement may
be ended are as follows:

- termination by the agent or principal;
- termination under the agency contract;
- termination by frustration.

Each of these methods is now considered.

Termination by the agent or principal

9–42 Both the agent and the principal can agree together that the agency
relationship should be terminated. In some situations, such as partnership, even an agreed termination will not be effective unless notice is given
to third parties who may be affected by the termination.[64] The principal
may also attempt to unilaterally terminate the agency without the agent's
consent. If this is possible within the terms of the agency agreement then
the principal must give notice to third parties to ensure that there is no
potential for ongoing liability on the basis of apparent/ostensible
authority. When a principal attempts to unilaterally end an agency when
that is not permitted then the principal may be liable to the agent for
damages.[65] An agent may also be permitted to unilaterally terminate
within the terms of the agency arrangement. An agent may also be liable
to the principal for any delays in telling the principal that the agency is
being terminated or for terminating the agency at a critical moment.[66]

Termination under contract

9–43 If the agency contract itself has provisions on termination then these will
bring the agency relationship to an end. The simplest situation which will
bring about termination is the end of a fixed period of time which is set

---

[64] See s.36(1) of the Partnership Act 1890.
[65] *Galbraith and Moorhead v Arethusa Ship Co Ltd* (1896) 23 R. 1011.
[66] Erskine, *Institute*, III, 3, 40.

out in the contract as the duration of the agency relationship.[67] Agency will also come to an end if a specified purpose for which the agency was established has been fulfilled or come to an end.[68]

Termination by frustration

As with any other contract, agency can be brought to an end through **9–44** frustration. This simply refers to the occurrence of unexpected events which are outwith the control of the parties to the agency. Once the relationship is terminated on the basis of frustration then the agent and principal have no further or ongoing obligations under the contract.

Subject to very limited exceptions the death of the principal or agent will terminate the agency relationship. The personal bankruptcy (sequestration) or insolvency (for corporate bodies) of either the principal or agent will normally also bring the agency to an end. An agent's insanity will bring the agency to an end and the principal's insanity will also bring the agency to an end if the insanity is permanent.[69] If the principal's business is discontinued then the agency relationship is also terminated.[70]

Key Concepts

Agency can be brought to an end in a variety of ways. This can be on the basis of terms in the contract of agency or as a matter of law, which can include termination by mutual agreement, termination by revocation or frustration.

COMMERCIAL AGENTS/COMMERCIAL AGENTS (COUNCIL DIRECTIVE) REGULATIONS 1993

The Commercial Agents (Council Directive) Regulations 1993[71] imple- **9–45** mented the Commercial Agents Directive 1986. They defined a new class of commercial agents who are bound by a set of special rules which are in many respects different from the normal rules of agency in Scots and English law. One of the key aims of the directive was to harmonise the conditions for commercial agents across Europe and to provide standard levels of protection for commercial agents. While there is some scope for agents and principals to negotiate and agree changes to the application of the Regulations most of the Regulations cannot be changed or excluded and they will operate in priority to common law rules of agency.[72]

---

[67] *Brenan v Campbell's Trustees* (1898) 25 R. 423.
[68] *Black v Cullen* (1853) 15 D. 646.
[69] *Daily Telegraph Co v McLaughlin* [1904] A.C. 776.
[70] *SS State of California Co Ltd v Moore* (1895) 22 R. 562.
[71] SI 1993/3053 (as amended in 1993 and 1998 by SI 1993/3173 and SI 1998/2868).
[72] *Roy v M.R. Pearlman*, 1999 S.C. 459.

Meaning of commercial agents

9–46 The Regulations define a commercial agent as:

> "a self-employed intermediary who has continuing authority to negotiate the sale or purchase of goods on behalf of another person (the 'principal'), or to negotiate and conclude the sale or purchase of goods on behalf of and in the name of that principal."[73]

This definition is important in that it creates a classification of agency which includes certain people who would not normally be treated by Scots law as being agents but also excludes others who would normally have been recognised as agents in Scots law. Being an employee is an express exclusion so anyone acting in that capacity is excluded from the application of the Regulations. Anyone who is a partner in a firm or a company director is excluded[74] and also excluded are insolvency practitioners,[75] commercial agents who are unpaid[76] and a range of specialist agents involved in commodity exchanges and markets.[77] However it is possible that a company can be a commercial agent. The Regulations will not apply where there is only a single transaction involved which is not repeated or where the agent is acting for an undisclosed principal. The Regulations will also not apply where the transactions involve services.

Duties owed by commercial agents

9–47 Commercial agents owe their principals a general duty to act dutifully and in good faith and to look after the interests of the principal.[78] The Regulations elaborate on this and give further non-exhaustive indications of what a commercial agent must do. This includes:

- making proper efforts to negotiate and, if appropriate, conclude transactions which the agent has been instructed to take care of;[79]
- communicating to the principal all the necessary information available to the agent;[80] and
- complying with all reasonable instructions given by the principal.[81]

---

[73] See reg.2(1).
[74] reg.2(1)(i) and (ii).
[75] reg.2(1)(iii).
[76] reg.2(2)(a).
[77] reg.2(2)(b).
[78] reg.3(1).
[79] reg.3(2)(a).
[80] reg.3(2)(b).
[81] reg.3(2)(c).

Duties owed by principals to commercial agents

The principal in a relationship governed by the Regulations must also act **9–48**
dutifully and in good faith towards the commercial agent. The Regulations approach this duty in the same way as the agent's duties are treated
and a series of non-exhaustive "good faith" duties are listed. These
include:

- obliging the principal to provide the agent with all necessary
  documentation relating to the goods involved;[82]
- obtaining for the agent any information which is needed to perform the contract;[83]
- notifying the agent within a reasonable time if it is anticipated
  that the volume of transactions will be significantly lower than the
  agent could reasonably have expected;[84] and
- informing the agent within a reasonable time of the principal's
  acceptance or refusal or non-performance of a transaction which
  the agent has arranged.[85]

Remuneration and commission

As with conventional agency arrangements, it is open to the agent and **9–49**
principal to agree levels of payment. If there is no provision for remuneration then the agent is entitled to be paid what is customarily paid to
agents who are appointed in relation to the type of goods involved in the
agency. If there is no such customary practice then the agent is entitled to
a reasonable level of remuneration which takes into account all elements
of the transaction.[86]

An agent will be entitled to commission when:

- the transaction has taken place because of the agent's actions;[87] or
- the transaction has been concluded with a third party who the
  agent had previously acquired as a customer for similar
  transactions.[88]

The agent is given a degree of protection in relation to the payment of
commission. Commission must be paid to the agent at the very latest
when the third party has completed his part of the transaction or would
have completed the transaction had the principal also completed his part
of the transaction.[89] The agent's entitlement to commission ends if it can
be shown that the contract between the principal and the third party will

---

[82] reg.4(2).
[83] reg.4(2)(b).
[84] reg.4(2)(b).
[85] reg.4(3).
[86] reg.6(1).
[87] reg.7(1)(a).
[88] reg.7(1)(b).
[89] reg.10(2).

not be completed because of circumstances for which the principal is not to blame.[90]

Termination of agency

9–50   The Regulations contain detailed provisions about the termination of agency arrangements which are covered by the Regulations. The key provisions on termination relate to the period of notice which has to be given. When the contract is for an indefinite period then either the agent or principal can terminate the contract. The notice periods that they must give are:

- one month during the first year of the contract;
- two months in the second year; and
- three months in the third and any subsequent years.[91]

The agent and principal cannot opt out of these minimum periods but they can agree on longer notice periods. If longer notice periods are agreed then the principal has to give at least the same notice to the agent as the agent has to give to the principal.[92]

Compensation and indemnity

9–51   The Regulations set out the circumstances in which compensation may be payable to the agent on termination and when an indemnity may be available to the agent. The starting position is that the agent and principal cannot agree to opt out of payment of compensation of the grant of an indemnity.[93] If the agreement says nothing then compensation is the option that is available to the agent and an indemnity is not available. Compensation is intended to compensate the agent for damage suffered as a result of the termination of the contract. The most difficult part of the compensation mechanism as applied in the United Kingdom has been the way the compensation is calculated. Until 2007 the position was that the Scottish courts calculated levels of compensation on the basis of French principles which had informed the 1986 Directive on which the Regulations are based.[94] The House of Lords case of *Lonsdale v Howard and Hallam Ltd*[95] has now made it clear that the agent is entitled to compensation for loss which is calculated by valuing the level of income which the agency would have generated.

The right to an indemnity is intended to give the agent the benefit of any work the agent has done before the agency is ended, the benefit of

---

[90] reg.11(1).
[91] reg.15(2)(a)–(c).
[92] reg.15(3).
[93] reg.17(2).
[94] See *King v Tunnock Ltd*, 2000 S.C. 424, as discussed in *Barrett McKenzie v Escada (UK) Ltd* [2001] All E.R. (D) 78; *Ingmar GB Ltd v Eaton Leonard Inc* [2001] All E.R. (D) 448 and *Tigana Ltd v Decoro Ltd* [2003] E.W.H.C. 23 (QB).
[95] [2007] UKHL 32; [2007] 4 All E.R. 1.

which would go to the principal. The right to indemnity comes about when:

- the agent has brought the principal new customers or has significantly increased the level of business with current customers and the principal continues to enjoy the benefit of those customers; and
- the payment of an indemnity is seen as equitable taking into account all the circumstances, especially any commission lost by the agent on business with these customers.[96]

There is a maximum level of indemnity which amounts to the equivalent of one year's commission, which is worked out on the basis of an average of the last five years or if the agency has been less than that, the average of the period of the agency.[97]

Key Concepts

The Commercial Agents (Council Directive) Regulations 1993 regulate the very particular form of agency involved when a self-employed agent is involved in negotiating the sale and/or purchase of goods for a principal. The Regulations provide particular rules to deal with such matters as reciprocal duties, remuneration, commission and termination.

▼ CHAPTER SUMMARY

MEANING AND KEY FEATURES OF AGENCY

1. **Agency is a three way relationship by which an agent acts on behalf of a principal and legally binds the principal to the third party involved in the relationship.**
2. **There are many differing names and labels given to differing types of agency. What the courts are concerned with is establishing whether agency in fact exists and who the parties are.**
3. **Agency can be created in a variety of ways:**

   - Express (i.e. deliberate or conscious) creation;
   - Implied creation;
   - Creation by ratification;
   - Creation by necessity;
   - Creation by holding out.

---

[96] reg.17(3).
[97] reg.17(4).

4. **Express creation of agency means that there has been a conscious or deliberate set of actions involving the principal and agent which shows their intention to set up an agency relationship. There is no set or special form or process required;**

   - *Robert Barry & Co v Doyle* (1998)

5. **Implied agency arises because the actions of the parties imply that agency was intended even although the principal has not made an express appointment.**

6. **Agency is created by ratification when the principal ratifies action taken by an 'agent' after the actions have already been taken. The principal has to have existed at the time the ratified actions took place, know all the relevant facts and satisfy a number of other conditions;**

   - *Tinnevelly Sugar Refining Co Ltd v Mirrlees Watson and Yaryan Co Ltd* (1894)

7. **Agency by necessity is created when it is impossible to communicate with the principal.**

8. **Agency by holding out is created when the principal's actions create the impression that the agent has been appointed and given authority to act even although that has not actually happened.**

THE AGENCY RELATIONSHIP

1. **The nature and extent of the authority given to an agent by a principal is a crucial element of the relationship between the agent and principal. There are three broad categories of authority;**

   - Express Authority;
   - Implied Authority;
   - Apparent or ostensible authority.

2. **The principal will normally be liable for the actions of an agent who acts within their authority.**

3. **Express authority will be clearly agreed between the agent and principal and, ideally, will appear in the agreement between them.**

4. **Implied authority often exists in the absence of express authority and arises because the facts and circumstances of the transaction or relationship imply that the principal has given a level of authority to the agent;**

   - *Barry, Ostlere & Shepherd Ltd v Edinburgh Cork Importing Co.* (1909).

5. **Apparent or ostensible arises where the principal's behaviour gives the impression that the agent has been given authority to act;**

   - *International Sponge Importers Ltd v Andrew Watt & Sons* [1911] A.C. 279 and (1911)

6. **An agent owes various duties to the principal. The key duties are;**

- To perform instructions;
- To act in good faith (the fiduciary duty);
- To exercise skill and care;
- To keep accounts.

7. **An agent who does not follow instructions will be personally liable for losses flowing from the actions taken;**

- *Gilmour v Clark* (1853)

8. **The fiduciary duty can be seen in a range of specific examples, which include:**

- The duty to act personally;
  De Bussche v Alt (1878).
- The duty to account;
- The duty not to disclose confidential information;
  Liverpool Victoria Friendly Society v Houston (1903).
- The duty to avoid conflicts of interest;
  McPherson's Trustees v Watt (1877).

9. **An agent is owed certain duties by the principal and enjoys a number of rights. The main rights are;**

- To be remunerated and reimbursed;
- To be relieved of liabilities
- To enjoy rights of lien and security.

10. **If agency works properly then normally third parties will be legally bound to the principal and there will be no rights or liabilities in place between the agent and the third party. When the agent acts as agent the key issue which affect potential rights and liabilities with third parties is disclosure of the agency relationship.**

11. **If the agent discloses the existence and name of the principal then the principal is bound to the third party.**

12. **If the existence of the principal is disclosed but not the name then normally the principal will be bound to the third party.**

13. **When the very existence of the principal is not disclosed then the agent will normally be bound to and liable to the third party. Once the identity of the principal has been revealed then the third party has the option to sue the principal or the agent;**

- *Bennett v Inveresk Paper Co.* (1891)

14. **If an agent exceeds their authority then the agent will be liable and there will be no binding contract with the principal unless the principal opts to ratify.**

ENDING AGENCY

1. **Agency can be ended in a variety of ways, many of which are based on common law principles. The most common ways are;**

    ● Termination by the agent or principal;
    ● Termination in terms of the agency agreement;
    ● Termination by frustration.

COMMERCIAL AGENTS

1. **The Commercial Agents (Council Directive) Regulations 1993 provide a range of rights and safeguards for 'commercial agents' which are not subject to change or exclusion by common law.**
2. **A commercial agent is someone who is self employed and acts for a principal in buying or selling goods.**
3. **A commercial agent must act dutifully for the principal and act in good faith and look after the principal's interests.**
4. **A principal must also act dutifully and in good faith towards a commercial agent and observe the particular good faith duties contained in the regulations.**
5. **If remuneration levels are not agreed between the principal and agent then the agent is entitled to what is customary, failing which, what is reasonable for the work done.**
6. **Agents are entitled to minimum periods of notice of termination of their agency arrangement and to potential compensation on termination.**

? QUICK QUIZ

● What is the purpose of agency?
● What are the main categories and types of agency?
● What are the main ways that agency can be created?
● Give an example of agency created by implication
● What are the conditions needed to establish agency by ratification?
● What is needed for agency to exist on the basis of holding out?
● What are the main types of authority an agent may have?
● How does apparent or ostensible authority differ from implied authority?
● What are the duties owed by an agent to a principal?
● What rights does an agent enjoy?
● When might an agent become liable to a third party?
● What happens if an agent exceeds the authority given by a principal?
● What is a commercial agent?

- What rights do the Commercial Agents (Council Directive) Regulations give to a commercial agent?
- What duties are owed to a principal by a commercial agent?
- How can commercial agency be terminated?

📖 FURTHER READING

Davidson and MacGregor, *Commercial Law in Scotland*, 2nd edn (W.Green, Edinburgh, 2008), Ch.2.

Gloag and Henderson, *The Law of Scotland*, 12th edn (W. Green, Edinburgh, 2007), Ch.19.

Busby, Clark, Paisley and Spink, *Scots Law: A Student Guide* (Tottel, 2006) Ch.6.

MacGregor, "Agency and Mandate" in *Stair Memorial Encyclopaedia* (Law Society of Scotland/Butterworths, 1995), Vol.1 as re-issued December 31, 2001.

🖱 RELEVANT WEBLINKS

The Department for Business Enterprise and Regulatory Reform (BERR) has two areas which deal with the Commercial Agents Regulations.

BERR's first link simply explains the purpose of the Regulations.
www.berr.gov.uk/consumers/business/commercial-agents/index.html

BERR's second link is more useful and contains a series of Quick Facts about the Regulations.
www.berr.gov.uk/consumers/fact-sheets/page38098.html

The Office of Public Sector Information has links to the full text of the Regulations:
www.opsi.gov.uk/si/si1993/Uksi_19933053_en_1.htm#end

Chapter 10   Delict

FRANKIE MCCARTHY[1]

► CHAPTER OVERVIEW

10–01 A delict is a civil wrong. The law of delict details when a person will be legally responsible for a wrong they have committed, whether intentionally or accidentally. The chapter looks first at how to define and remedy intentional delicts. It then considers negligent or unintentional delicts, and details the five steps that must be taken in order to establish liability for unintentional harm. The chapter goes on to look at examples of delict in specific contexts such as between employee and employer, for professionals and where the rules are regulated by statute. Finally, the remedies available in respect of a delict once proved are explained and evaluated.

✓ OUTCOMES

10–02 At the conclusion of this chapter, you should be able to:

- ✓ explain the overarching principle of the law of delict using the maxim *damnum injuria datum*;
- ✓ identify and explain intentional delicts including assault, trespass, the economic delicts, fraud and passing off;
- ✓ list the five key steps in establishing a case of liability for unintentional harm;
- ✓ explain and apply the tripartite test of duty of care;
- ✓ explain and apply the calculus of risk used to determine whether a duty of care has been breached;
- ✓ discuss the different types of loss that will give rise to a remedy in delict;
- ✓ understand and apply the tests of causation and remoteness of injury;
- ✓ outline the specific rules of delict that apply in the employment context, for professional liability, for breach of statutory duty and for nuisance;
- ✓ explain the different remedies available for delictual claims and evaluate which is most appropriate in different situations.

---

[1] Lecturer in Private and Commercial Law, University of Glasgow.

WHAT IS DELICT?

Delict is the area of law which details when a person will be responsible **10–03** for their intentional or negligent acts which cause loss to others. In England, this is known as the law of tort. Unlike contractual obligations, delictual responsibilities have not been voluntarily assumed, but rather are imposed on every person by the law itself. Unlike criminal law, delict does not define offences which are punishable by the state on behalf of society, but rather regulates the relationship between individuals, often awarding damages (financial compensation) to make up for a loss suffered by one individual as a result of the negligence of another. For example, if Tony has an accident whilst driving and bumps Gina's car, he will have to pay the cost of repairing her car. This is not because he signed a contract beforehand agreeing that he would pay for Gina's car if he damaged it, but because the law says he must take responsibility for his actions, even though they were accidental.

Delict can be summed up by the Latin maxim *damnum injuria datum*. *Damnum* means a loss, which could be a physical injury, damage to property or a financial loss. *Injuria* means a legal wrong, the intentional or accidental act of one party which has caused loss to another. *Datum* means a connection between these two elements—in other words, a loss caused by a legal wrong.

A delict can be intentional, where harm is deliberately caused, such as when an individual is assaulted. It can also be unintentional, as in the example of Tony hitting Gina's car; Tony did not intend to cause any damage, but the law says he must be responsible nonetheless.

TERMINOLOGY

The person who has suffered harm at the hands of another can seek a **10–04** legal remedy (discussed below) for his loss. This person is called the pursuer. The other party, who is allegedly responsible for the loss, is called the defender. In English legal terminology, the pursuer is known as the plaintiff and the defender as the defendant.

INTENTIONAL DELICTS

Where one person deliberately causes harm to another, they will be **10–05** responsible for that loss in delict. Five key intentional delicts are outlined below.

1. Assault

Imagine Phil and Grant have a disagreement, and then Phil punches **10–06** Grant in the face. A physical attack of this kind will constitute an assault, and is likely to lead to Phil being charged with a criminal offence. However, the attack may also have civil consequences. Grant may wish

to seek damages as recompense for the injury he has suffered, which he
would do by making a civil claim for the delict of assault.

In addition to a physical attack, assault can also take the form of
threats or verbal abuse. Delictual liability will arise if the victim has
suffered physical or psychiatric harm as a result of the attack.

In order to qualify as assault, the invasion of the pursuer's bodily
integrity must be non-consensual. So, if Phil had tackled Grant to the
ground in a game of rugby, there is unlikely to be any claim in delict,
since tackles of this kind are part and parcel of the game Grant has
consented to play. This principle is important in medical situations,
where a patient must give consent before treatment can be carried out. In
Sidaway v Board of Governors of the Bethlehem Royal Hospital,[2] the court
ruled that a patient must be advised of all the risks of the procedure
which are regarded by a reasonable body of medical opinion as proper to
disclose, or else the patient's consent will not be valid.

The remedy for assault will usually be damages, although interdict can
also be granted if the conduct is likely to be repeated.[3]

2. Trespass

10–07   The delict of trespass occurs when a person temporarily intrudes onto
another person's property without consent.[4] Land in Scotland is owned
from the heavens to the centre of the Earth, so trespass will not only
include, for example, an individual walking across private property
without the owner's consent, but will also cover an intrusion under a
person's land or through their airspace. In *Brown v Lee Construction*,[5] the
defenders were building developers who had set up a crane which passed
above the pursuer's property. The court was satisfied that this constituted
trespass.

One remedy for trespass is interdict, to prevent the behaviour being
repeated. It is important that the conduct appear *likely* to recur before
this order will be granted, however. In *Winans v Macrae*,[6] the pursuer
sought an interdict in respect of the defender's pet lamb, which kept
straying into his fields and eating grass. By the time of the case, the
defender no longer owned the lamb, and no interdict was granted. If the
trespasser has damaged the property in some way, compensation in the
form of damages can also be sought.

As a side note, it is important to differentiate trespass from
encroachment, which is the name for a permanent intrusion, such as
extending a building onto another person's land. Encroachment is dealt
with under the rules of property law.

---

[2] [1985] A.C. 871.
[3] See the discussion of remedies at paras 10–42 *et seq.*
[4] In Scotland, extensive rights of access to land are available. See the Scottish Outdoor
Access Code at *www.outdooraccess-scotland.com*.
[5] 1977 S.L.T. (Notes) 61.
[6] (1885) 12 R. 1051.

3. Economic delicts

As a general rule, the law will not interfere in the conduct of business. **10–08**
The market operates in such a way that some businesses succeed while
others fail. However, in certain very specific situations, the law will regard
use of extreme forms of economic duress as amounting to a delictual act.
The three principal examples of this doctrine are induced breach of
contract, intimidation and conspiracy.

Induced breach of contract

Imagine that Phil runs a cafe and Ian supplies him with barrels of beer. **10–09**
Grant, who is opening a rival bar, tells Ian he'll give him £1,000 if he
"forgets" to make the barrel delivery to Phil on the day Grant's bar is
opening for the first time. Ian, desperate for the money, fails to deliver
that day, and therefore breaches his contract with Phil. Phil could sue Ian
for straightforward breach of contract. However, the law says Phil can
also sue Grant in delict, since Grant induced Ian to break the contract.

There are various elements required to make a successful claim under
this head, first recognised in *British Motor Trade Association v Gray*.[7] The
defender (Grant, in our example) must know of the contract between the
pursuer (Phil) and the third party (Ian). The defender must induce the
breach with the intention of harming the pursuer. Finally, the pursuer
must actually have suffered a loss as a result of the breach; in our
example, Phil may have lost profits because he was unable to sell beer
that day. If all these elements are present, the defender will be liable in
damages to the pursuer for the loss suffered.

If the defender's duress does not cause a breach of contract, but does
compromise the third party's performance of their contractual obligations to the extent that the pursuer suffers a loss, that may still be sufficient for a remedy in delict. More generally, where the mode of duress
applied is unlawful, but there is no specific contractual interference, there
may be a remedy for the separate delict of adverse affect on a business
interest.

Intimidation

The second economic delict is intimidation. This arises where one party **10–10**
threatens another with some unlawful action unless they harm a third
economically. Grant, for example, might tell Ian he will beat him up
unless Ian brings his beer supply contract with Phil to an end. This delict
was first set out in the case of *Rookes v Barnard (No.1)*.[8] Rookes was a
draftsman who had left the draftsman's union. Prior to his departure, the
union had operated the factory where Rookes worked as a closed shop,
and wished to continue to do so. Union representatives therefore told the
employers of Rookes that they had three days to dismiss him, failing
which the union would call a strike of their members in breach of the

---

[7] 1951 S.C. 586.
[8] [1964] A.C. 1129.

terms of their contracts of employment. Rookes was sacked, and then successfully sued the union for intimidation. Their threat of unlawful strike action had caused Rookes to lose his job.

Intimidation can cross over with induced breach of contract, where the inducement is of a type that may amount to intimidation.

Conspiracy

10–11 The third economic delict is conspiracy, first recognised in *Quinn v Leathem*.[9] This occurs where two parties join together in order to harm the economic interests of a third. Grant and Ian, for example, might agree to drop their beer prices in order to cut Phil out of the market. The mechanism used to harm the third party is important. If the conspired conduct is legal, such as Grant and Ian's agreement to cut prices, the aim of damaging the third party must be the primary motive of the conspiracy before a delict will be found to exist. If the conspired conduct is unlawful, for example if Grant and Ian kidnap Phil's bar staff so that the pub cannot open, the intention to harm Phil as a result of their actions need only be a secondary motivation for a delict to be shown.

Remedies

The remedy for any economic delict will usually be damages in recompense for the economic harm suffered. Interdict may also be appropriate if the conduct is likely to be repeated.

4. Fraud

10–12 The classic definition of fraud is "a machination or contrivance to deceive".[10] One party makes a statement or takes some other action to represent something as a fact. The party is telling a straightforward lie, or at least does not believe what he is saying is true.[11] The intention of making this representation is to cause a loss to another party. For example, Grant might tell Phil that Ian is selling very high quality champagne at a very cheap price with the aim of convincing Phil to waste a lot of money buying bottles. If Grant knows the so-called champagne is actually supermarket cava relabelled, or else suspects it must be based on dodgy dealings he has had with Ian in the past, Grant has committed the delict of fraud. If Grant honestly believes the champagne is excellent and at a cheap price, even though his belief might be inaccurate, there is no intentional delict.

The remedy for fraud will usually be damages for any losses suffered as a result.[12]

---

[9] [1901] A.C. 495.
[10] Erskine *Institute* III, 1, 16.
[11] *Derry v Peek* (1889) LR 14 App Cas 337.
[12] However, see the discussion regarding liability for pure economic loss resulting from misrepresentation at para.10–26.

5. Passing off

The delict of passing off is concerned with protecting the "goodwill" of a **10–13** business. Goodwill is the term given to what might be considered the good name of a business, its reputation, the marketability of the brand. Imagine that Grant opens a coffee shop in the East End of Glasgow. He furnishes it with comfortable armchairs and pine furniture, plays jazz music and sells muffins and panini. He calls the shop Starstrucks, and writes the sign in a white font on a green background. Customers may well become confused by the similarities and think that Grant's shop is, in fact, a branch of Starbucks. This confusion is the essence of the delict of passing off; Grant is attempting to pass off his coffee shop as being a Starbucks in order to take advantage of their popularity.

The criteria for this delict are set out in the case of *Erven Warnink BV v J Townend & Sons (Hull) Ltd (No.1)*.[13] The five criteria are:

(i) a misrepresentation (in our example, the way in which Grant has set up his shop and the name are likely to amount to misrepresentations);

(ii) made by a trader in the course of a trade (if Grant had simply set up his living room like a coffee shop, there would be no delict);

(iii) to prospective customers or to the ultimate consumers of the good or services;

(iv) which is calculated to injure the goodwill of another;

(v) which caused actual damage to the business or goodwill of the trader by whom the action is brought. This is likely to be the most difficult aspect to prove in our example. (Starbucks would have to show they had lost profit as a result of the confusion caused by Grant's café.)

The usual remedy for passing off will be interdict, although a damages claim may also be possible if losses can be proved and accurately quantified.

Unintentional Delicts

The concept of liability for intentional harm is easy to understand; a **10–14** person who deliberately hurts another should be responsible for repairing that damage. However, the law does not restrict liability in delict to situations where the harm has been caused deliberately. Damage caused accidentally still requires repair; personal injury suffered at the hands of another is incapacitating whether that person intended it to be so or not. The law says that, where a person causes harm as a result of not taking enough care, they will be responsible for that harm, even though it was accidental. In other words, where an individual has been negligent, they will be liable for any unintentional delicts which occur as a result.

---

[13] [1979] A.C. 731.

When is a person responsible for an act of unintentional harm? The law answers this question as follows:

1. There must be a duty of care between the pursuer and defender.
2. The defender must have breached this duty of care, by falling below the standard of care exercised by the reasonable man.
3. The pursuer must have sustained a loss.
4. The breach of duty of care must have been the factual and legal cause of the loss to the pursuer.
5. The loss must not be too remote.

In any situation where one person has accidentally suffered harm as a result of the actions of another, these five criteria must be fulfilled for a case in delict to be made out.

1. There must be a duty of care
What is a duty of care?

10–15   Each person has a responsibility to take care in their acts (and omissions to act) so as to avoid causing harm to others. That is the essence of the duty of care.

Imagine that Tony decides to park his car at the top of a hill while he goes into a shop to buy a newspaper. He forgets to put on his handbrake. While he is in the shop, the car is disturbed by passing traffic and rolls down the hill until it collides with Gina's car. Obviously the damage here is accidental. Tony did not want to damage Gina's car, and he will have damaged his own vehicle in the process. However, the accident is still Tony's fault, since it was him who forgot to put on the handbrake. His thoughtlessness—or lack of care—is the reason for the accident. Tony had a duty to take care to apply his handbrake when parking his car.

This idea of duty of care was first described in the case of *Donoghue v Stevenson*,[14] often called the "snail in the bottle" case.

Donoghue v Stevenson
1932 S.C. (HL) 31

Mrs Donoghue went to a café with a friend. The friend bought her a bottle of ginger beer, and poured half the bottle into a glass, which Mrs Donoghue then drank. When she poured the rest of the drink into the glass, the remainder of a decomposing snail appeared along with it. Mrs Donoghue became ill as a result, and wished to make a claim against the manufacturers of the drink. However, she had no contract on which to base such a legal claim; it had been her friend who had bought the drink, and therefore her friend who had a contract with the drink makers. The court decided that, even in the absence of a contractual relationship, there was still a legal

---

[14] 1932 S.C. (HL) 31.

basis on which Mrs Donoghue could make a claim. The drink manufacturers should have been able to foresee that someone other than the person who bought the drink might ultimately be the consumer of the drink. They should also have been able to foresee that finding half a snail in the bottle would make the consumer of the drink fall ill. The court was of the view that the drink manufacturer therefore had a duty towards the eventual consumer of the drink to take reasonable care to prevent snails falling into their bottles. Mrs Donoghue was, on that basis of that delictual duty, entitled to make a claim against the drink manufacturer.

In *Donoghue*, Lord Atkin explained the idea of duty of care using what has become known as the "neighbourhood principle".

> "The rule that you are to love your neighbour becomes in law that you must not injure your neighbour ... Who, then in law is my neighbour? The answer seems to be—persons who are so closely and directly affected by my act that I ought reasonably to have them in contemplation as being so affected when I am directing my mind to the acts or omissions which are called into question."[15]

Essentially, Lord Atkin is saying that we owe a duty of care to anyone who we can reasonably foresee might be affected by the way we act.

This principle has been refined and extended over time, most importantly in *Caparo Industries plc v Dickman*.[16]

Caparo Industries Plc v Dickman
[1990] 2 A.C. 605.

The plaintiff was an auditor who had produced a set of figures suggesting a company was in a stronger financial position than it actually was. Investors bought shares in the company as a result, and then lost money. The auditor had no contract with the investors; his contract was with the company. However, the court was satisfied that he owed a duty of care to the investors. The court set out three criteria that had to be fulfilled before a duty of care could exist in a given situation. In the first place, the harm suffered by the pursuer must be foreseeable. In the second place, there must be proximity between the pursuer and the defender. Finally, it must be fair, just and reasonable to impose a duty in the particular circumstances of the case. This is now known as the "tripartite test" of duty of care, and has been adopted in a number of subsequent cases.[17]

---

[15] 1932 S.C. (HL) 31 at 44.
[16] [1990] 2 A.C. 605.
[17] *Gibson v Orr* 1999 S.C. 420.

Foreseeability of harm

10–16 A duty of care will be owed by one person to another when it is reasonably foreseeable that the actions of the first will cause harm to the second. So when is harm reasonably foreseeable? The answer to this is largely a matter of common sense. Take the example of our motorist, Tony. If, whilst driving, he decides to make a right turn, but does not use his indicator to show he intends to do so, what might happen? The car travelling behind him might run into him, since the driver is not expecting Tony to slow down for the turn. A car travelling in the lane of traffic Tony must cross to make his turn might collide with Tony, since the driver of that car is not anticipating Tony's manoeuvre across the lane. Tony might hit a pedestrian crossing the road he is turning into, since the pedestrian may not be alerted of Tony's intention to enter the road. The possibility that these things may happen is obvious. They are foreseeable consequences of Tony's failure to use his indicator.

Not every possible consequence will be foreseeable, however. If a parachutist descended on to the road in front of Tony as he made his right turn, Tony would hit the parachutist. This is a possible consequence of Tony's failure to indicate, but it is not a foreseeable one. Foreseeable consequences have to be the reasonable and probable outcome of the pursuer's conduct.

This distinction is illustrated by two similar cases involving sporting accidents. In *Bolton v Stone*,[18] a cricket ball was struck right out of a cricket ground where it injured a person around 100 yards from the wicket. Balls had been struck out of the ground on only six occasions in the previous 30 years. The harm to the pursuer was not considered foreseeable, as the risk of injury was so unlikely it could not be considered a reasonable and probable consequence of hitting the ball. Conversely, in *Lamond v Glasgow Corporation*,[19] a golf ball was struck out into a footpath which ran alongside the golf course, where it hit the pursuer in the head. On average, 6,000 golf balls were played onto the footpath every year, although there was no evidence of anyone having been struck before. Given the frequency with which balls entered the footpath, it was considered to be reasonable and probable that a passer-by would be struck eventually, and the harm was therefore foreseeable.

Where a certain type of loss is a reasonable and probable outcome of the pursuer's actions, the exact chain of circumstances leading to that loss may not have to be foreseeable. *Hughes v Lord Advocate*[20] concerned two young boys who were burned following an explosion of paraffin. They had been investigating a work site, where employees of the Post Office had uncovered a manhole and left it unattended, with a canvas tent protecting the manhole and two paraffin lamps set outside as a warning. The boys took the lamps inside the tent, at which point one was knocked over and exploded on contact with air. The court found it to be

---

[18] [1951] A.C. 850.
[19] 1968 S.L.T. 291.
[20] 1963 S.C. (HL) 31.

foreseeable that leaving paraffin lamps unattended would lead to burning injuries. The fact the burns had been caused by an explosion rather than by straightforward contact with the flames in the lamp was irrelevant. The nature of the harm was foreseeable.

Proximity

This criterion is concerned with the identity of the persons who may be **10–17** affected by the conduct of another. It is not enough to say that the pursuer's actions may reasonably and probably cause harm to somebody, somewhere. A particular class or category of people must be in mind.

Return to our example of Tony with his careless car parking at the top of the hill. It is clear that other road users, such as Gina, may be affected by his carelessness. It is also possible that Chet, watching CCTV footage of the accident over the internet in California, might laugh so much at the Tony's car rolling down the hill that he ruptures his spleen. Chet's injury is possible, but it is not reasonably foreseeable. It is not within the normal range of consequences of Tony's actions. Chet is not proximate to Tony, so he is not Tony's neighbour in law.

A useful illustration of this concept comes in the case of *Bourhill v Young*.[21] A motorcyclist, Young, crashed into a car and died as a result of his own negligence. Mrs Bourhill was a pedestrian who happened to be in the vicinity at the time. She did not see the accident, but heard the noise of the collision and witnessed blood on the road. She claimed to have suffered "nervous shock" as a result which lead to a miscarriage. The court was satisfied that the defender owed a duty of care to nearby road users. However, Mrs Bourhill had not been at risk of physical injury from the accident, and had not even seen it happening. Although it was possible she could be affected by the defender's negligence, it was not probable. She was not proximate to the defender, and so no duty of care could arise.

A very different example of this doctrine is shown in *Hill v Chief Constable of West Yorkshire*.[22]

Hill v Chief Constable of West Yorkshire
[1989] A.C. 53.

The mother of the final victim of Peter Sutcliffe, the Yorkshire Ripper, sued the police. She argued the police were negligent in failing to find Sutcliffe sooner, and it was reasonably foreseeable that because they had not found him, he would murder again. The case failed for lack of proximity. All of Sutcliffe's victims had been women in the Leeds area, and the argument was that the police owed a duty of care to this limited class of people—the women of Leeds—to catch Sutcliffe. However, the court was of the view that,

---

[21] 1942 S.C. (HL) 78.
[22] [1989] A.C. 53.

although this category was limited, it was still too wide for a relationship of proximity to exist between the police and this group of
women. No duty of care could be said to exist.

"Fair, just and reasonable"

10–18 A duty of care can only be found to exist where it is fair, just and
reasonable in the circumstances of the case. This is a type of catch-all
provision which allows the court to take into account broader economic
or policy arguments when determining if a duty of care should be
imposed.

Again, *Hill*[23] provides assistance. If the police were under a duty of care
to every victim of crime, even if limited to every victim of a recidivist, this
could give rise to an enormous number of claims in delict. Defending
such claims and paying damages would cost a huge amount of money,
which in turn would make police funding an impossible issue for government. Additionally, it would be extremely difficult for the police to
investigate reported crimes with the threat of legal action looming at all
times. Ultimately, recognising a duty of care in situations of this type
would impact negatively on society as a whole. These are the types of
considerations the court may take into account under this head of the
tripartite test.

In many cases, it is settled law that a duty of care exists. There is no
real question that a motorist owes a duty of care to pedestrians and other
road users, for example, or that an employer owes a duty of care to his
employees. The tripartite test is particularly useful for establishing the
existence of a duty of care (or otherwise) in novel situations.

Key Concept

A duty of care is owed to anyone who it can be reasonably foreseen
will be affected by the defender's conduct. This is assessed using
the tripartite test:

- Is the harm of a type that was reasonably foreseeable?
- Is the pursuer proximate to the defender?
- Is it fair, just & reasonable to impose a duty of care in this
  situation?

---

[23] [1989] A.C. 53.

2. The defender must have breached his duty of care

We have seen that every person has a duty to take care in the way they act **10–19**
so as to avoid causing harm to others. This duty is breached when a
person fails to take the requisite amount of care, or, in other words, when
a person is negligent.

In the first place, for a breach of duty to occur, the defender must have
been acting voluntarily. Imagine Kerry is standing on a bus which lurches
suddenly, causing her to lose her footing and fall into Karim, bruising his
arm. In a technical sense, Kerry is the cause of Karim's injury. However,
she could not have taken care to avoid the accident; it was beyond her
control. In *Waugh v James K Allan Ltd*,[24] a lorry driver suffered the onset
of coronary thrombosis at the wheel and died. In so doing, the lorry
swerved and hit a pedestrian, causing serious injury. The court held that
the lorry driver had not breached his duty of care, since the onset of
illness was beyond his control, and he could not have known it was about
to happen.

For a voluntary act, then, how much care is enough? In law, we call
this the standard of care. A person is expected to display the standard of
care a reasonable man would display in the same situation. If a heart
surgeon is carrying out heart surgery, they will be expected to take the
same amount of care as a reasonable heart surgeon performing the same
operation. This is discussed in *Muir v Glasgow Corporation (No.2)*,[25] in
which some schoolchildren, having lunch in a tea shop operated by the
defenders, were scalded when a tea urn being carried by employees of the
defenders was upset. The court held that the defenders had demonstrated
the standard of care to be expected of reasonable café owners. The urn
required to be transported through the café, and was being carried by
competent members of staff. It is impossible to prevent every accident
from happening, and the defenders had done everything they could
reasonably be expected to do in the circumstances.

In ascertaining the standard of care expected of a reasonable man in a
given situation, and deciding whether this standard has been met, the
court will give weight to a number of factors known as the calculus of
risk. This is made up of four main questions.

(i) How likely was it that the defender's conduct would cause an injury?

If the defender's act or omission was very likely to cause harm, then it is **10–20**
more likely that he will be found to fall below the standard of care
expected.

(ii) How serious was the injury likely to be?

The risk of a serious injury or major property damage is more likely to **10–21**
lead the court to the conclusion that the appropriate standard of care has
not been reached. The severity of any injury will be looked at in the

---

[24] 1964 S.C. (HL) 102.
[25] 1943 S.C. (HL) 3.

circumstances of the case in question. For example, *Paris v Stepney Borough Council*[26] concerned an accident in a garage where a mechanic was struck in the eye by a chip of metal from a car he had been working on. The mechanic was blind in one eye, and the metal chip hit his remaining good eye, resulting in total blindness. Safety goggles had not been supplied. The standard of care expected of the mechanic's employers was higher than it would have been for a fully sighted mechanic, precisely because the result of the accident was so serious for the pursuer.

(iii) How difficult/expensive would it have been to take precautions against the accident?

10–22 Again, if a cheap and easy precaution which would have prevented the accident was not taken, it is more likely that the necessary standard of care will not have been reached. In *Paris*, the defenders could have supplied safety goggles to their employees cheaply and easily, but failed to do so. Conversely, in *Latimer v AEC Ltd*,[27] an employee who slipped on a flooded factory floor argued that the factory should have been closed down. The court thought such an inconvenient and expensive precaution was unnecessary in the circumstances, and considered that the defenders had successfully met the required standard of care by spreading sawdust on the floor.

(iv) What was the purpose of the defender's conduct?

10–23 The basic idea behind this question is that, if the defender was doing something particularly important which perhaps required him to act quickly, a lower standard of care could reasonably be expected. A helpful example is *Watt v Hertfordshire County Council*,[28] in which a fireman was injured by a heavy jack which fell into him as the fire engine was rushing to the scene of an accident. The fire engine was not adapted to carry the particular jack, but the fire crew had taken it from the station because they knew it was needed urgently to rescue a woman trapped under a car. The court was of the view that the risk to the plaintiff had to be weighed against the cost of the woman's life. In the circumstances, the requisite standard of care had been displayed.

In addition to the four questions set out above, the court will also consider anything else relevant in deciding whether the standard of care has been breached, including previous case law which may be in point. Ultimately, the decision should be largely a matter of common sense.

---

[26] [1951] A.C. 367.
[27] [1953] A.C. 643.
[28] [1954] 1 W.L.R. 835.

> **Key Concept**
>
> - Only a voluntary act can breach the duty of care.
> - The standard of care expected is that of a reasonable man in the same situation.
> - Whether the standard of care has been reached will be assessed using the calculus of risk.

3. The pursuer must have sustained a loss

In order for a claim to be made in delict, the pursuer must have suffered **10–24** some loss. Consider again Tony's car, parked at the top of the hill without application of the handbrake. Say his car rolls down the hill, but bypasses Gina's car, and instead comes to a rest harmlessly at the bottom of the hill, out of the way of traffic. Tony still owes Gina a duty of care; he has still breached this duty by failing to meet the requisite standard of care. But Gina has not suffered any loss as a result of the breach. She cannot make a claim, and no successful action in delict could be established.

Many different types of loss can give rise to a delictual claim. Most obviously, a person suffering a physical injury can claim for the pain and suffering they have endured, known as *solatium*. They may also claim for any losses following on that injury, such as loss of income if they have been unable to work. Damage to property, such as the dent in Gina's car, can also be recovered.

Not all forms of loss are so straightforward, however. We will consider two types of loss which have additional complications: psychiatric injury and pure economic loss.

Psychiatric injury

A psychiatric injury will constitute a loss for the purposes of an action in **10–25** delict, provided that it is a diagnosable condition, and not simply ordinary distress or upset.

A person suffering from a psychiatric illness caused by negligence will be categorised by the law as either a primary or a secondary victim, following *Page v Smith*.[29] A primary victim is defined as someone who was at risk of physical injury as a result of the breach, whether they actually suffered physical injury or not. A primary victim is always entitled to claim for psychiatric harm.

The position of a secondary victim is more complex. Secondary victims are those who suffer psychiatric harm as a result of witnessing another person suffering injury in an accident caused through negligence. The rules on secondary victims were first established in *Bourhill v Young*,[30]

---

[29] [1996] A.C. 155.
[30] 1942 S.C. (HL) 78.

discussed above,[31] in which the pursuer was categorised as a secondary victim, having been at no risk of physical harm herself.

The doctrine was developed in *Alcock v Chief Constable of South Yorkshire Police.*[32]

Alcock v Chief Constable of South Yorkshire Police
[1992] 1 AC 310

This case arose from the tragedy at Hillsborough football stadium in which dozens of supporters were killed in a crush caused by overcrowding. Friends and relatives of the victims sought damages for psychiatric harm caused by viewing television footage of the incident. The court set out three criteria which had to be fulfilled before a secondary victim would be entitled to recover damages:

(1) There must have been a close tie of love and affection between the primary and secondary victims.
(2) The secondary victim must have been present at the accident or its immediate aftermath.
(3) The secondary victim must have had direct perception of the accident with his unaided senses.

So, for example, if a mother is advised by telephone that her daughter has been in an accident, and attends the scene of the accident, witnessing her child in distress, it is likely she will be entitled to recover for any psychiatric injury which results. However, if she was simply advised by telephone that her child had died, and did not attend the scene, she will be unlikely to have a claim.

Pure economic loss

10–26   As mentioned above, economic loss which is consequent on a physical injury (such as loss of earnings) or property damage can usually be recovered in delict. However, a loss which is purely financial—in other words, does not result from some other direct damage to a person or property—is not usually recoverable. The reason for this is simple practicality. If Tony's car hits Gina's, there is likely to be a hold-up in the traffic on the road. Many cars will be stuck, and every one of those drivers will have to pay for petrol they have burned whilst sitting in a traffic jam which could have been avoided. If Tony were liable for the costs of all that extra petrol, it would be a heavy burden—too heavy, in the eyes of the law.

A useful illustration is provided by the contrast of two cases involving power cuts. In *Dynamco Ltd v Holland & Hannen & Cubitts (Scotland)*

[31] See para.10–17.
[32] [1992] 1 A.C. 310.

Ltd,[33] the defenders negligently severed an electricity cable, with the result that the pursuer's factory was out of operation for a period of time since its machinery could not operate without power. The court held that no recovery was possible. The physical damage had been done to the power cable, owned by the electricity company. The pursuer's loss was purely financial. In *SCM (UK) Ltd v WJ Whittall & Son Ltd*,[34] a power cable was again cut, causing molten metal in the plaintiff's mixing machines to solidify, effectively destroying the machines. The plaintiff was entitled to recover the cost of replacing the machines, since the property had been damaged directly by the power cut.

There are, however, a few limited exceptions to this principle regarding pure economic loss.

The first exception concerns loss resulting from a misrepresentation, or negligent statement. If a person makes a statement which is false, but which they reasonably believed to be true, and a second person acts on that statement to their economic loss, the first will be liable in damages.[35] This principle was established in the case of *Hedley Byrne & Co Ltd v Heller & Partners Ltd*.[36] The plaintiffs here had begun acting as agents for a third party company based on advice as to its reliability given by the defendants. The third party then went into liquidation, causing the plaintiffs to lose a substantial sum of money. The court held that the defendants should have known that the plaintiffs would reply on their statement, and on that basis a "special duty of care" arose between the parties which allowed recovery for pure economic loss.

This "special" duty of care will only arise in relationships where there are additional proximity factors between the parties, a situation which most often arises where one party is offering advice in a professional capacity and should know the other will rely on that advice. One example in case law is that of a surveyor who made critical errors in a survey instructed by the mortgage lender. The surveyor was held liable to the house buyer who relied on that survey when purchasing the house.[37]

This proposition was expanded into a more general rule in *Henderson v Merrett Syndicates Ltd*.[38]

Henderson v Merrett Syndicates Ltd
[1995] 2 AC 145

Lloyds' "names" provided funds to investment syndicates for speculation on the stock market and elsewhere. The "names" then sued the managing agents of the syndicates for loss of profit through negligent investment. The court set out a principle that a

---

[33] 1971 S.C. 257.
[34] [1971] 1 Q.B. 337.
[35] A deliberate false statement will be the intentional delict of fraud, as discussed above.
[36] [1964] A.C. 465.
[37] *Martin v Bell-Ingram*, 1986 S.C. 208.
[38] [1995] 2 A.C. 145.

duty of care for economic loss would arise if the defender had voluntarily assumed responsibility for the economic interests of the pursuer and knew that the pursuer would be relying on his advice. In this case, the agents had assumed responsibility for the return on the investment of the "names", and so a duty of care was held to exist.

Whether responsibility has been voluntarily assumed will depend on the facts of the case. An employer agreeing to write a reference for an employee has been held to have voluntarily assumed responsibility for his economic interests, since the employee is relying on the reference being accurate and timeously provided.[39] However, an exemption clause was enough to demonstrate no responsibility had been assumed by the defender in *Bank of Scotland v Fuller Peiser*,[40] where the defenders, a firm of surveyors, stated on the valuation report that they took no responsibility for anyone other than the purchaser. The mortgage lender later tried to make a claim against them, but the court held that the disclaimer prevented the *Henderson v Merrett Syndicates Ltd* test from being satisfied. A focus on the exact circumstances of every case has recently been affirmed by the court as the correct approach to determining the existence of a duty of care in these situations.[41]

One other limited exception to the principle that pure economic loss cannot be recovered is what has come to be known as *Junior Books* liability.[42] Junior Books was a company who had engaged architects to remodel factory premises. The architects subcontracted the job of laying the floor to Veitchi Co Ltd, who did the work to a very poor standard, leaving Junior Books with no option but to rip up the floor and replace it, at obvious expense. Junior Books had no contract with Veitchi; both parties had contracts only with the architect. Junior Books therefore sued Veitchi in delict. The floor had not directly harmed Junior Books, so there was no straightforward *Donoghue v Stevenson* duty of care. The loss was the purely economic cost of replacing the floor. None the less, the House of Lords held that, in the circumstances, there was sufficient proximity between the parties for a duty of care to arise. They set out an exacting list of requirements to be met before liability of this kind could arise, in particular that the defender must know the identity of the pursuer and that the pursuer must be relying on the defender's expertise to prevent an economic loss. At one time, it was thought that *Junior Books* set out a general duty of care for economic loss arising from defective buildings, but more recent judicial analysis suggests it is actually

---

[39] *Spring v Guardian Assurance Plc* [1995] 2 A.C. 296.
[40] 2002 S.L.T. 574.
[41] *Customs and Excise Commissioners v Barclays Bank Plc* [2007] 1 A.C. 181.
[42] *Junior Books Ltd v Veitchi Co Ltd* 1982 S.C. (HL) 244.

authority only for a duty arising from defective performance of contract in the very specific circumstances of the case.[43]

4. The pursuer's loss must have been caused by the defender's breach of duty of care

This is the crucial link between the pursuer and the defender. The pursuer's loss must have been caused by the defender's breach of duty of care. In law, this is often described as the "but for" test. But for the defender's breach, the pursuer would not have suffered a loss. **10–27**

There are two different types of causation. Factual causation deals with whether, as a matter of simple fact, the defender's breach caused the pursuer's loss. Of course, there could be several factual causes for one accident. Think again of Tony's parked car. Imagine the road was icy at the time, and that Gina had parked her own car dangerously far out from the kerb. All the elements have combined to cause the accident. All that matters, for the test of factual causation to be satisfied, is that the defender's breach was *one* such factor. In law, we say that it was a *causa sine qua non* of the pursuer's loss.

Legal causation deals with the effective, dominant or immediate cause of the loss. What was the primary cause, or *causa causans*, of the pursuer's injury? If the answer to that question is the defender's breach of duty, only then is the test of legal causation satisfied, and the defender will be liable for the pursuer's losses.

The concept of causation is usefully illustrated by *McWilliams v Sir William Arrol & Co, Lithgows, Ltd*,[44] in which a steel erector fell to his death. The defenders, his employers, were held to be in breach of duty of care by failing to provide him with a safety belt. However, the evidence was that, even if the belt had been provided, the pursuer would not have worn it. Provision of the belt would not have stopped the accident, and so the test of causation was not satisfied. More dramatically, in *Barnett v Chelsea and Kensington Hospital Management Committee*,[45] a man attended the casualty department of the defendant's hospital complaining of sickness and vomiting. This should have marked him as a priority patient, but in fact he was not seen by a doctor, and instead he was sent home, where he died later that night. The defendant had clearly breached its duty of care. However, the evidence was that the man's death was the result of arsenic poisoning. Even if he had been seen by a doctor as soon as he arrived at casualty, there would have been nothing the doctor could have done to help him. He would have died anyway. The breach of duty was therefore not the legal cause of his death.

In limited circumstances, the test of causation can be satisfied provided the defender's breach of duty made a material contribution to the pursuer's loss, or else materially increased the risk of the pursuer's loss. This doctrine has so far only been used in cases in which the harm to the

---

[43] *D & F Estates Ltd v Church Commissioners for England* [1989] A.C. 177.
[44] 1962 S.C. (HL) 70.
[45] [1969] 1 Q.B. 428.

defender was the contraction of a disease, and the courts have said that material increase in risk can only satisfy the causation test where science is unable to identify the exact cause of an illness. These rules were set out by *Fairchild v Glenhaven Funeral Services Ltd*,[46] in which the pursuer contracted terminal lung cancer as a result of exposure to asbestos. Scientific evidence suggested that the cancer could be caused by inhalation of one single fibre of asbestos dust. The pursuer had been negligently exposed by two different employers, and it was impossible to say during which of these employments he might have inhaled the particular fibre. The court held that, since both employers had materially increased his risk of contracting the disease, and since there was no other possible way the disease could have developed, the test of causation was satisfied. Both employers were held to be at fault.

The chain of causation leading from the defender's breach to the pursuer's loss can be broken by a natural event, the actions of other people, or by the actions of the pursuer himself. Any action or event which causes a break in the chain is known as a *novus actus interveniens*, which means "new act intervening". In *McKew v Holland & Hannen & Cubitts (Scotland) Ltd*,[47] the pursuer had injured his ankle in consequence of the defender's negligence, with the result that his leg was liable to give way on occasion. Shortly afterwards, the pursuer was descending a steep staircase with no handrail. His leg gave way, and he panicked and jumped down ten steps, causing further injury to his leg. The court said that the original injury was a *causa sine qua non* of the second injury, but not the *causa causans*. The pursuer's own act, in panicking and jumping down the steps, constituted a *novus actus interveniens*. The second injury was the pursuer's own fault.

It is important to note, however, that conduct on the part of the pursuer which might reasonably be foreseen as a result of the initial breach will not break the causal chain. In *Sayers v Harlow Urban District Council*,[48] the pursuer found herself locked in a public toilet as the result of a faulty lock. Panicking, she attempted to escape over the top of the cubicle wall and put her foot on the toilet roll holder, which snapped, causing her to fall to her injury. The court was not satisfied that her actions in trying to escape constituted a *novus actus interveniens*, since it was foreseeable that a person, on becoming trapped, would try to escape.

---

[46] [2003] 1 A.C. 32.
[47] 1970 S.C. (HL) 20.
[48] [1958] 1 W.L.R. 623.

> **Key Concept**
>
> - The pursuer's loss must have been caused by the defender's breach of duty of care.
> - The "but for" test must be satisfied to show that the defender's breach was the effective, dominant or immediate cause of the loss.
> - The chain of causation can be broken by a *novus actus interveniens*.

5. The loss must not be too remote

Accidents can have far-reaching consequences. Think of Tony's car, **10–28** which has collided with Gina's car, damaging it so that it cannot be driven. Gina calls the AA, but by the time they have arrived to deal with the problem, she has missed the job interview she was going to, and does not get the job she really wanted. Bitter about missing out, she goes home and has a fight with her husband, which turns into a series of fights and eventually they divorce. In one way this all leads back to the accident. Should Tony have to pay compensation for all of it?

The law says you have to draw the line somewhere. This is where the concept of remoteness of damage comes in. The concept of foreseeability is again important; if the losses are not foreseeable, the defender should not be held liable for them.

What is the test of foreseeability in this context? The law is not entirely clear. Two leading cases offer conflicting viewpoints. The first of these is the "direct consequences" test, set out in *Re Polemis, Furness Withy & Co Ltd.*[49] A ship was destroyed in a fire caused when a stevedore negligently knocked a timber board into the hold of a ship. The board collided with another object, causing a spark which ignited petrol vapour in the hold. The court admitted that the fire itself was not foreseeable. However, it was foreseeable that some type of harm to the ship would result from the negligence of the stevedore, and so the loss was recoverable on the basis that the fire was a direct consequence of a foreseeable harm. In other words, if it can be foreseen that something bad will happen, the defender will be liable for anything bad which actually happens as a direct consequence of the breach.

The *Polemis* test was rejected by the Privy Council in *Overseas Tankship (UK) Ltd v Morts Dock & Engineering Co Ltd (The Wagon Mound)*,[50] another case involving an unusual fire. The *Wagon Mound*, a ship, was docked and being refuelled when some of the fuel oil was negligently allowed to leak into the water in the bay. The leaked oil travelled on the water to a wharf, where repair work was being carried out on another vessel. A piece of molten metal fell from the repair works onto cotton waste floating on top of the oil, setting the cotton alight.

---

[49] [1921] 3 K.B. 560.
[50] [1961] A.C. 388.

This, in turn, led to the oil catching light and a huge fire taking place. The Privy Council said "direct consequences" was not the proper test of remoteness, and the loss should rather be a reasonably foreseeable consequence of the breach. Here, it was foreseeable that the wharf might be fouled by the oil, but damage by fire was not foreseeable, because oil on water would not usually ignite.

Which of these two approaches is the correct test in Scots law is not certain. The courts have vacillated between the two, and on occasion have used what appears to be a combination of both. Recent authority, however, seems to come down more strongly in favour of the *Wagon Mound* test of reasonable foreseeability. In *Simmons v British Steel Plc*,[51] it was held that the defender should be liable for harm of a kind that was reasonably foreseeable, even though the harm was greater than could have been foreseen, or where it was caused in a way that could not have been foreseen.

What is clear from the case law is that, where the harm is foreseeable, the defender must "take his victim as he finds him". This is known as the "eggshell skull" rule. If the defender accidentally trips the pursuer, and the pursuer suffers from osteoporosis and breaks several bones as a result of a fall which would, for most people, have no serious consequences, that is simply the defender's bad luck. Liability persists. This rule was first established in *McKillen v Barclay Curle & Co Ltd*,[52] in which the pursuer's rib was broken in an accident causing a reactivation of dormant tuberculosis.

DEFENCES

10–29 If a pursuer is able to successfully negotiate the five steps of liability for unintentional harm, he will have proved his case. The defender may, however, have a defence to the claim that will defeat or reduce the pursuer's right to damages.

Volenti

10–30 One potential line of defence is *volenti non fit injuria*, which translates to mean that no harm can be done to someone who consents. *Volenti* will be a defence where the defender can prove the pursuer consented to the risk inherent in the defender's behaviour. If *volenti* can be established, it will relieve the defender of all liability for the harm. For example, say Gina is out drinking with Tony, and then agrees to let Tony drive her home despite the fact she is aware that Tony is several drinks over the limit. Tony will not be liable to her for crashing his car and killing her.

The classic example of *volenti* is *Titchener v British Railways Board*.[53]

---

[51] [2004] S.C. (HL) 94.
[52] 1967 S.L.T. 41.
[53] 1984 S.C. (HL) 34.

Titchener v British Railways Board
1984 SC (HL) 34

A girl climbed through the hole in a protective fence in order to cross a railway line and was hit by a train. No duty of care was found to exist, but the court also commented that, in any event, the pursuer was *volens* to the risks of being on the train line. The fence was there to prevent passers-by straying on to the track. The pursuer had deliberately ignored that protection, demonstrating her willingness to accept the risk of injury inherent in being on a train line.

Contributory negligence

In some cases, the accident may have been partly caused or exacerbated **10–31** by the pursuer's own actions. In this case, the defender can argue that the pursuer was contributorily negligent, based on the Law Reform (Contributory Negligence) (Scotland) Act 1945. For example, if Tony (sober this time) is driving Gina home and negligently crashes his car, he will be responsible for her injuries. But if her injuries are exacerbated by the fact she did not bother to put on her seatbelt when she got into the car, she will have contributed to the loss through her own failure to take reasonable care of herself.

If the defender can successfully argue for contributory negligence, this will not relieve him of all liability for the accident, but will reduce the amount of damages he has to pay by the percentage of liability the courts attribute to the pursuer. The percentage will depend entirely on the facts and circumstances of the case. For example, a deduction of 25 per cent is often applied for failure to wear a seatbelt. In S*ayers v Harlow Urban District Council*, discussed above,[54] the pursuer's dangerous escape route from the toilet cubicle was considered to have contributed to the accident and her damages were reduced by 25 per cent.

Sole fault/joint fault

Where a loss is the result of breaches of duty of care by two different **10–32** persons, the responsibility for the accident will be attributed between them in the appropriate percentages. Equally, the pursuer can be considered the sole cause of the loss, or the author of his own misfortune. This may be the case where his actions constitute a *novus actus interveniens* between his loss and the defender's breach of duty of care.

---

[54] See para.10–27.

DELICT IN THE EMPLOYMENT CONTEXT

Employers' liability

10–33 Every employer owes his employee a duty to take reasonable care for the employee's safety. This will include more specific duties to provide the employee with a safe workplace, to devise a safe system of working and to provide appropriate plant and equipment for the employee's tasks. At common law, the employer's duty is to take reasonable care, and the usual calculus of risk will be applied in determining whether that standard of care has been reached in a particular case. However, the law in this area is heavily regulated by a statutory regime implementing a range of EU directives which tend to impose a much higher standard of care on the employer. A full examination of the statutory scheme is beyond the scope of this book.[55]

Vicarious liability

10–34 Vicarious liability is the doctrine by which one person can be held responsible for the actions of another. An employer will be vicariously liable for the actions of his employee during the course of employment. In simple terms, this means that if Ewan's car is damaged by Jasmine whilst out driving on a business errand for her employers, Nowhere City Council, Ewan is entitled to make a claim against Jasmine's employers rather than against Jasmine personally. Often this will make sound economic sense, since Jasmine's employers will be likely to have more money than Jasmine.

For an employer to be vicariously liable, two conditions must be fulfilled:

(1) a contract of employment must exist between the two parties;
(2) the employee must have been acting in the course of his employment at the time the delictual act took place.

In some situations, the fact of employment will be easy to ascertain, but the modern working environment has resulted in employment relationships growing increasingly complex. The court will not place too much reliance on how the parties describe their relationship, but rather will look at the circumstances in order to ascertain whether one party was employed, or was merely providing services to the other. One concept which has traditionally been important is that of control; if the purported employer is able to direct specifically how the other party carries out his duties, that tends to suggest the contract is one of employment. For example, if Jasmine employs someone to cook her meals at home, she can specify what she wants to eat and how she wants it to be cooked, and can stand over the chef in the kitchen if she so wishes; that is a contract of

---

[55] Further information is available at the website of the Health and Safety Executive: *www.hse.gov.uk*.

employment. However, if Jasmine goes to a restaurant, she will usually be limited in her choice to what appears on the menu and will have very little say in how exactly her meal is prepared; that is merely a contract for services. The court will also look at factors such as the role the employee plays in a large organisation, who paid for the tools required to carry out the work (be they tools in the traditional sense or, for example, IT facilities) and whether the "employee" requires to take an economic risk in the course of carrying out the duties assigned, which will tend to suggest he is independent. This multiple factor approach, first discussed in the English case of *Ready Mixed Concrete (South East) Ltd v Minister of Pensions and National Insurance*,[56] has been affirmed as the correct approach in Scotland in recent cases including *United Wholesale Grocers Ltd v Sher*.[57]

Similarly, the question of whether an employee was acting in the course of his employment, or was "off on a frolic of his own", must be decided with reference to all the circumstances of the case. In *Kirby v National Coal Board*,[58] the Court stated that if an employee was carrying out his master's work, even in a way in which the employer may not have envisaged that work being carried out, the employer will be vicariously liable. For example, in *Williams v A&W Hemphill Ltd*,[59] a bus driver was persuaded by his passengers to drive his bus from Argyll back to Glasgow taking a circuitous route through Stirling so that they could be dropped off nearer home. The bus was then involved in an accident. The court was of the view that, although the driver had taken a different route to that authorised by his employer, he was still performing the task he was employed to do, and so his employer was vicariously liable. More recently, a trainee fireman participating in a football game traditionally staged at the end of the 16-week residential induction course for new recruits was held to be acting in the course of his employment, since the game was one of the activities associated with the course in which recruits were expected to participate.[60]

On the other hand, if an employee acts outwith the scope of his employment, or uses his employer's tools and time to embark on a project of his own, his employer has no liability. This was the situation in *Kirby v National Coal Board*,[61] where a coal miner caused an explosion whilst smoking a cigarette on his break in an area where smoking was expressly prohibited. His employer was not considered vicariously liable, since this action could not be said to have been carried out in the scope of his employment.

Difficult cases often arise. One recent example is *Lister v Hesley Hall Ltd*,[62] in which the warden of a residential care home was found to have

---

[56] [1968] 2 Q.B. 497.
[57] 1993 S.L.T. 284.
[58] 1958 S.C. 514.
[59] 1966 S.C. (HL) 31.
[60] *Sharp v Highland and Islands Fire Board*, 2005 S.L.T. 855.
[61] 1958 S.C. 514.
[62] [2002] 1 A.C. 215.

been abusing children in his care during the course of his night time duties. The defender argued that this could not possibly be said to be an unauthorised mode of the employee carrying out his work; his actions were in fact contrary to the whole purpose of his employment. However, the court was of the view that his actions were so closely connected with the nature of his employment that imposition of vicarious liability was justified. It seems that the court was influenced here by the particularly tragic circumstances of the case and the obvious undesirability of an alternative outcome. The extent to which this decision will translate into other employment contexts is unclear.

PROFESSIONAL LIABILITY

10–35 On most occasions where a person provides a service in a professional capacity (e.g. as a doctor, lawyer, accountant or surveyor) there will be a contract between the professional and their client. Any loss which results can be remedied under contract in the usual way. However, this does not prevent a separate liability in delict arising, as we have seen in cases such as *Henderson v Merrett Syndicates Ltd.*[63]

The test for breach of professional duty is set very high. A pursuer seeking to prove that a professional has breached his duty of care must show that the professional took a course of action that no reasonable professional person in the same circumstances would have taken. This rule was first elaborated in the case of *Hunter v Hanley*,[64] in which a patient sued his doctor for using a needle which the patient alleged was not strong enough for the injection for which it was being used. Although there was a body of medical opinion that regarded the doctor's treatment as wrong, there was also a body of opinion which considered it reasonable in the circumstances. The court considered the doctor's duty of care had been fulfilled. The court's approach was confirmed as correct in the Scottish context in *Kay v Ayrshire and Arran Health Board.*[65]

Any situation in which a professional is required to exercise professional judgment will share this high standard of proof.

In the case of solicitors, there can be an additional complication. The solicitor obviously has a duty of care towards his client in contract, and in delict as outlined above. However, the solicitor's negligence may not impact only on his client. Say a client instructs his solicitor to change his will, so that all his money rather than being left to Jasmine is now to be left to Ewan. The solicitor does not carry out the instructions in good time. The client then dies. It is Ewan who has lost out here, since the solicitor's failure to act will result in the inheritance going to Jasmine. Ewan is known in this situation as the "disappointed legatee". *White v Jones*[66] is authority for the premise that, in this situation, the solicitor

---

[63] [1995] 2 A.C. 145.
[64] 1955 S.C. 200.
[65] S.C. (HL) 145.
[66] [1995] 2 A.C. 207.

owes a duty of care to the disappointed legatee to carry out the alterations to the will timeously.

BREACH OF STATUTORY DUTY

Certain pieces of legislation impose their own duty of care in respect of **10–36** acts which result in loss to other people. The steps for proving liability as a result of breach of a statutory duty are essentially the same as for proof of liability through negligence; it must be shown that the pursuer has breached a duty of care towards the defender causing a loss. The difference is that the content of the duty will be defined by the statute rather than by the usual rules on foreseeability, and the exact definition of the duty set out in a given statute, or what is required to satisfy the duty can be a matter of considerable debate in practice. Statutory duties often import strict liability, which means the element of "reasonableness" is removed from any discussion. If the duty has been breached, the pursuer is automatically liable, no matter how unexpected the result. This is commonplace in the Regulations on workplace safety, for example.[67] A statute will often expressly provide whether breach of its terms will give rise to civil liability or otherwise. If it is silent on the matter, it will be left to the Courts to interpret the intention of Parliament as regards liability.

We will now look at three specific instances of statutory liability: product liability, liability for animals and occupiers' liability.

Product liability

At common law, producers obviously have a liability to their ultimate **10–37** consumer in terms of *Donoghue v Stevenson*.[68] This common law duty is backed up by the Consumer Protection Act 1987, which is significantly more exacting on the producer. Under s.2(1) of the Act, the producer of a defective product *will* be liable for any damage caused wholly or partly by the defect. This means that, where personal injury or damage to property is caused, the producer of the product will be required to make payment of damages even though there may have been no fault on his part. The Act does not apply to the damage to the product itself,[69] or to losses under £275.[70] The product must also be a "consumer" product, loosely defined to mean something you would use in the home rather than a product designed for business use.[71] "Producer" is given a wide meaning, to include not only the manufacturer of the product, but anyone in the supply chain, including wholesalers, retailers and any person who

---

[67] See the Workplace (Health, Safety and Welfare) Regulations 1992, Provision and Use of Work Equipment Regulations 1998 and the Personal Equipment at Work Regulations 1992 for examples.

[68] 1932 S.C. (HL) 31.

[69] s.5(2).

[70] s.5(4).

[71] s.5(3).

markets the item as their "own brand" (such as a supermarket).[72] "Product" is also widely defined to include any goods or electricity, in addition to components or materials which make up a larger product.[73]

So what is considered a "defect" for the purposes of the Act? Essentially anything that falls below the standard the consumer is entitled to expect;[74] a much higher standard than that of negligence at common law. It also includes products which are inherently dangerous, such as drugs, if they are not labelled appropriately with adequate warnings as to their risks.[75]

Certain defences are available to producers under s.4 of the 1987 Act, the most problematic of which is that there will be no liability if the defect did not exist at the "relevant time" (broadly speaking, the time at which the producer in question had control of the product). This defence should be based on straightforward factual evidence of when the defect came into being. However, often clear evidence is not available, and the court is left trying to ascertain the existence of a defect at a given time on a balance of probabilities. In the recent case of *Piper v JRI (Manufacturing) Ltd,*[76] where a prosthetic hip had split inside the patient only 18 months after the replacement operation, the court used evidence of the producer's inspection procedures to draw the conclusion that the defect most probably had not existed at the time the prosthesis left the factory. This decision harks back to common law negligence with the idea of whether everything "reasonable" had been done to prevent a defect arising. In some senses, this could be said to undermine the point of the legislation altogether.

Liability for animals

10–38 The Animals (Scotland) Act 1987 provides that the keeper of an animal shall be liable for any injury or damage caused by that animal.[77] Again, the statutory regime imposes strict liability, so there is no need to show negligence on the part of the defender. "Keeper" is defined in s.5 of the Act and will normally mean the owner or person in possession of the animal. Liability is imposed on two different groups of animals: first, dogs and dangerous wild animals[78] who are likely to kill or severely injure persons or other animals or damage property; and secondly, animals listed in s.1(3)(b) (principally farmyard animals) who are likely to cause property damage by foraging.

In relation to the first category, the keeper will be liable only if the harm is caused by the animal attacking a person or another animal in some way. The fact of the animal's mere presence, for example in the middle of the road, will not be enough. However, there could be ordinary

---

[72] s.1(2).
[73] s.1(2).
[74] s.3(1).
[75] *X v Schering Health Care Ltd* [2002] EWHC 1420.
[76] (2006) 92 BMLR 141.
[77] s.1(1).
[78] As defined by the Dangerous Wild Animals Act 1976.

negligence-based common law liability in a situation of that kind. In *Fairlie v Carruthers*,[79] the elderly pursuer was knocked over by the defender's over-enthusiastic retriever. The court did not find liability under the Act to be established, since the dog had not attacked, chased or harried the pursuer.

Defences to liability are set out in s.2 of the Act. These focus on the pursuer's own responsibility towards the animal. If the accident was caused by the pursuer, or the pursuer was *volens* to the risk, there will be no liability. Equally, trespassers will not be protected by the Act.

Occupiers' liability

Unlike the other statutory schemes we have considered, liability for **10–39** occupiers is not strict. Section 2 of the Occupiers' Liability (Scotland) Act 1960 provides that the occupiers of land or premises should take reasonable care to avoid damage to persons entering onto the property as a result of the state of the property, or anything done or omitted to be done there. This will include temporary hazards, such as a spilled drink on the floor which has not been cleaned up, or more permanent dangers such as a hole in the ground.

The occupier will be the person who is in possession of the premises at the time of the accident. Their duty is to take positive steps to ensure the premises are kept safe. However, it is for the pursuer to show that not all reasonable steps have been taken, for example, that the defender did not have in place a system for cleaning up spilled drinks. Whether or not reasonable care has been taken will be a matter for the court to decide in applying the calculus of risk, in the same way as it would do in a regular case of liability for unintentional harm. In *McGlone v British Railways Board*,[80] a 12-year-old boy was burned on a transformer with live wires at 2,500 volts after climbing through the defender's ill-maintained fence. The pursuer argued that the defender had not taken reasonable care to protect the boy from the transformer by allowing the fence to fall into disrepair. The court disagreed. The boy was aware the fence was there to keep him from the transformer, which was dangerous, and had climbed through it anyway. It would not be reasonable to expect the defenders to erect an impenetrable fence. *Tomlinson v Congleton BC*[81] is authority for the proposition that a defender is not under a duty to protect against a danger arising from a natural feature of his property, such a steep hill or a lake.

Various defences are also set out in s.2. The defence of *volenti* will apply, and it is also possible for a pursuer's damages to be reduced on grounds of contributory negligence.

---

[79] 1996 S.L.T. (Sh Ct) 56.
[80] 1966 S.C. 1.
[81] [2004] 1 A.C. 46.

NUISANCE

10-40 A general principle of Scots law is that an owner of property is entitled to do whatever he wants on that property. However, in reality, the actions of one property owner can impact on his neighbours. If Ewan plays loud music all through the night, or allows his rubbish to build up so that noxious odours permeate the atmosphere and vermin are attracted, these actions will obviously have a negative effect on those living next to him. This negative impact on his neighbours is the focus of the delict of nuisance.

Nuisance was defined by Lord President Cooper in *Watt v Jamieson*[82]:

> "If any person so uses his property as to occasion serious disturbance or substantial inconvenience to his neighbour or material damage to his neighbour's property, it is in the general case irrelevant to plead merely that he was making a normal and familiar use of his own property ... The critical question is whether what he was exposed to was *plus quam tolerabile* [more than is tolerable] when due weight has been given to all the surrounding circumstances of the offensive conduct and its effects."

An important balancing exercise has to be carried out: the owner's right to enjoy his property must be balanced against the neighbour's right to enjoy *his* property. Is the neighbour being asked to put up with more than is reasonable? There is no clear and simple line to be drawn here. What is reasonable in a large house in the countryside is likely to be different than what is reasonable in a tenement flat in Glasgow city centre. The conduct must be beyond tolerance for an action of nuisance to apply; conduct which is simply annoying will not be enough.[83] The court will consider what would be tolerable for a reasonable person. In *Simpson v Miller*,[84] the pursuer complained that the noise of bread mixing machines in the basement of her building was intolerable, but several witnesses gave evidence to the effect the noise and vibrations were virtually imperceptible in the pursuer's premises. The court held that the pursuer was unusually sensitive, and no finding of nuisance could be made in those circumstances. The court will also take account of the purpose of the disturbance. It seems that if the disturbance is caused for the public benefit, no remedy in delict will be available, such as in the case of *Webster v Lord Advocate*[85] where no remedy was available to a neighbour inconvenienced by the noise of the Edinburgh Military Tattoo.

Liability for nuisance is usually strict, so that no fault has to be shown on the part of the defender for a finding in delict to be made. The remedy will usually be interdict, obliging the defender to cease the conduct causing the nuisance. However, if the conduct has actually caused

---

[82] 1954 S.C. 56.
[83] *Anderson v Dundee City Council*, 2000 S.L.T. (Sh Ct) 134.
[84] (1923) 39 Sh. Ct. Rep. 182.
[85] 1985 S.C. 173.

damage to the pursuer's property such that damages are sought, in that case fault must be shown. This was decided by the case of *RHM Bakeries (Scotland) Ltd v Strathclyde Regional Council*,[86] in which the pursuer's premises and goods were damaged when a sewer collapsed. Although it was admitted that maintenance of the sewer was the responsibility of the defenders, the pursuer had not made any argument that the defenders had, in fact, failed to maintain it, or to show that this failure was the reason for the collapse. In the absence of any proof of fault, no finding of nuisance could be made.

PRESCRIPTION AND LIMITATION

A pursuer who has suffered must make his claim within a specified time **10–41** limit or he will lose the right to do so. In general, a case in delict must be brought within five years of the date of the loss, or the pursuer's right to action will prescribe.[87] If the claim is for personal injury, the pursuer cannot enforce his claim more than three years after the loss date.[88] The rationale behind these time limits is that, as time passes, it becomes increasingly difficult to obtain clear evidence of what happened and who may have been responsible. It is in the interests of justice to have cases come before the court before they become stale.

REMEDIES

Interdict

An interdict is a court decree ordering a person to cease a particular type **10–42** of conduct, for example trespassing on another person's land. In English legal terminology, this type of order is known as an injunction.

Interdict can be sought to bring ongoing conduct to an end, or to prevent an anticipated wrong before it occurs. It is important that any order for interdict is framed in very clear and specific terms so that there is no question of the order being breached accidentally. If a person continues the conduct in breach of interdict, they could be liable to a fine or imprisonment.

Damages

Damages is the legal term for financial compensation awarded to a **10–43** pursuer who has successfully established a claim. The key principle underlying delictual damages is that they should put the pursuer in the position he would have been in had the accident never happened. If the loss in the case is a straightforward matter of damage to property, the damages awarded by the court will simply be the cost of the repair. In

---

[86] 1985 S.C. (HL) 17.
[87] Prescription and Limitation (Scotland) Act 1973 s.6.
[88] Prescription and Limitation (Scotland) Act 1973 s.18A(1).

personal injury cases, the pursuer will be awarded damages for *sola-tium*—the pain and suffering they have endured—in addition to financial losses following on from the injury, such as lost wages, the price of a cancelled holiday or childcare expenses. If the injury is likely to have long-term consequences, future damages will be calculated to take account of further losses likely to be incurred.

Damages can also be awarded on either a provisional or interim basis. Provisional damages are awarded in personal injury cases where there is a possibility that the pursuer's condition may substantially deteriorate in the future. An assessment of damages will be made on the basis of the pursuer's condition at the time of proof, and the option will be left open for the pursuer to return for a second payment if they deteriorate. For example, if a child is injured in an accident and suffers brain damage, it may be impossible for doctors to ascertain the full extent of the injury until the child is closer to adulthood. Provisional damages could be awarded after the accident, and the child could return to the court at a later stage when their condition was fully known. Provisional damages are regulated by s.12 of the Administration of Justice Act 1982.

Interim damages may be awarded prior to proof in a case where the defender has admitted that he was liable in delict for the harm. In some cases, although there is clear evidence of negligence, it may still take some time to resolve matters while the necessary evidence is gathered to fully quantify the claim. However, the pursuer may be in financial hardship in the meantime. For example, if a pursuer is seriously injured in a car crash caused by a drunk driver, it is likely that the defender will have admitted his liability for the accident. It may take months or even years for the solicitors acting for each party to obtain the necessary medical reports and other evidence to allow a full quantification of the financial loss to the pursuer for the rest of his life. In the meantime, however, the pursuer must still pay his bills and may be incapable of working. In such a situation, the pursuer may apply for an award of interim damages to "tide him over" until the case is finally resolved. Interim damages will be a lump sum paid immediately by the defender, which will then be deducted from the total damages awarded to the pursuer on the con-clusion of the case.

Key Concept

- The primary remedies in delict are interdict and damages.
- An interdict can be granted only in respect of clear and specific conduct.
- Damages can be awarded for solatium and patrimonial loss, and can be assessed on a provisional or interim basis where appropriate.

Modes of Liability

A loss may be caused by more than one person. In such cases, the courts **10–44** will often find all the defenders "joint and severally liable".[89] What this means is that each defender is liable to the pursuer for the whole amount of damages awarded. The pursuer, if they so choose, can recover the full amount from one defender, and that defender is left with a "right of recovery", meaning they are then entitled to recover the appropriate share of the damages from each of the other defenders.

▼ CHAPTER SUMMARY

What is Delict?

1. **A delict is a civil wrong. The law of delict determines when a** **10–45** **remedy will be available for a loss caused by one person to another.**
2. **The basic principle of delict can be summed up by the maxim** ***damnum injuria datum*: **a loss caused by a legal wrong.**

Intentional Delicts

1. **An intentional delict is a deliberate act causing harm to another.**
2. **An assault, whether physical or verbal, which causes loss will give rise to liability in delict.**
3. **An assault must be non-consensual.**

   > *Sidaway v Board of Governors of Bethlehem Royal Hospital*: a patient must be advised of all the risks of a treatment to give valid consent.

4. **Trespass is the temporary intrusion onto, over or under another person's property.**
5. **The remedy for trespass will be interdict, provided the trespass is likely to be repeated.**
6. **Extreme forms of economic duress will give rise to a claim in delict.**
7. **The principal economic delicts are induced breach of contract, intimidation and conspiracy.**
8. **Fraud is a misrepresentation made with the intention of causing a loss to another person.**
9. **Passing off is the delict of taking advantage of the goodwill in another person's business.**

---

[89] Law Reform (Miscellaneous Provisions) (Scotland) Act 1940 s.3(1).

> *Erven Warnink BV v J Townend & Sons (Hull) Ltd (No.1)*: sets out the five criteria which must be fulfilled to establish a case of passing off.

UNINTENTIONAL DELICTS

1. **Where a person causes a loss to another through a lack of care, or negligence, this will give rise to liability in delict.**
2. **A duty of care must exist between pursuer and defender.**

   > *Donoghue v Stevenson*: the "snail in a bottle case" which established the "neighbourhood principle".

3. **The existence of a duty can be established through the tripartite test of foreseeability of harm, proximity and the requirement that a duty be "fair, just and reasonable".**

   > *Caparo Industries Plc v Dickman*: authority for the tripartite test.
   > *Hill v Chief Constable of West Yorkshire*: the Yorkshire Ripper case in which it was not considered fair, just and reasonable to impose a duty of care.

4. **The defender must have breached his duty of care.**
5. **To breach his duty, the defender's conduct must have been voluntary.**

   > *Waugh v James K Allan*: a driver who suffered the onset of thrombosis at the wheel did not voluntarily cause an accident.

6. **A duty will be breached if the defender's conduct falls below the standard of care expected of a reasonable man in the same situation.**

   > *Muir v Glasgow Corporation (No.2)*: it is impossible to prevent every accident from happening, and a defender can only do what is reasonable in the circumstances.

7. **Whether the standard of care has been reached will be assessed by applying the calculus of risk.**
8. **The pursuer must have sustained a loss to their person or property.**
9. **Psychiatric loss will give rise to recovery for primary victims, and for secondary victims only where they satisfy the test set out in *Alcock v Chief Constable of South Yorkshire Police*.**
10. **Pure economic loss cannot generally be recovered. However, recovery will be available where the loss results from a misrepresentation, where the defender had voluntarily assumed responsibility for the pursuer's economic interests, or where a *Junior Books* duty of care arises.**

> *Henderson v Merrett Syndicates Ltd:* the Lloyds' names case, which established a duty of care for economic loss where the defender had voluntarily assumed responsibility for the pursuer's economic well-being.

11. **The defender's breach of duty must have been the *casua causans* of the pursuer's loss.**

> *Barnett v Chelsea & Kensington Hospital Management Committee*: set out the "but for" test of causation.

12. **The chain of causation can be broken by a *novus actus interveniens*.**
13. **The pursuer's loss must not be too remote from the pursuer's conduct for recovery to be allowed.**

> *Simmons v British Steel*: the type of losses sustained must be a reasonably foreseeable consequence of the breach of duty.

14. **The loss will not be too remote where the harm is of a kind that was reasonably foreseeable, even though the harm was greater than could have been foreseen, or was caused in a way that could not have been foreseen.**
15. **The defender can defend a claim for liability for unintentional harm using the plea of *volenti non fit injuria* if the pursuer was or should have been aware of the risks of the activity.**
16. **The pursuer's damages may be reduced if he was contributorily negligent.**

DELICT IN THE EMPLOYMENT CONTEXT

1. **Employers owe a duty to their employees to take reasonable care for their safety in the workplace.**
2. **An employer will be vicariously liable for the actions of his employee during the course of his employment.**
3. **For vicarious liability to arise, a contract of employment must exist between the two parties, and the employee must have been acting in the course of his duties at the time the delictual conduct occurred.**

> *Kirby v National Coal Board*: an employee smoking a cigarette during his break in a designated no-smoking zone was not acting in the course of his employment.

PROFESSIONAL LIABILITY

1. **A person providing a service in a professional capacity will owe a delictual as well as a contractual duty to his client.**

2. The test for breach of professional duty is that no other reasonable professional in the same circumstances would have acted in the way the defender acted, established in *Hunter v Hanley*.
3. A solicitor will also owe a duty of care to a disappointed beneficiary, set out in *White v Jones*.

BREACH OF STATUTORY DUTY

1. Where a duty of care is imposed in a particular situation by a statute, the content of that duty will be defined by the wording of the statute and not by the usual tripartite test.
2. Where a statute imposes strict liability, there will be no need to prove negligence.
3. Product liability is regulated by the Consumer Protection Act 1987. Section 2 of the Act provides that a producer of a defective product will be strictly liable for any damage caused by the defect.
4. A "defect" is defined as anything that falls below the standard the consumer is entitled to expect.
5. Certain remedies are available to producers under s.4 of the Act, particularly that there is no remedy if the defect did not exist at the "relevant time", meaning at the time when the product was within the producer's control.
6. Liability for animals is regulated by the Animals (Scotland) Act 1987. Section 1 provides that the keeper of an animal will be strictly liable for injury or damage caused by that animal.
7. Liability is imposed on wild animals who are likely to kill or severely injure persons, animals or property, and on farmyard animals who are likely to cause damage by foraging.
8. Defences are set out in s.2 of the Act.
9. Occupiers' liability is regulated by the Occupiers' Liability (Scotland) Act 1960. Liability under this statute is not strict, but requires owners or occupiers of premises to take reasonable care for the safety of people in or on their property.
10. It is for the pursuer to show that the occupier has failed to take all reasonable steps.
11. Defences are set out in s.2 of the Act. In particular, the defence of *volenti* can be used.

NUISANCE

1. Where one person uses his property in such a way that it negatively impacts on his neighbours to an intolerable extent, this will constitute the delict of nuisance.
2. Liability for nuisance is strict, unless damages are sought, in which case fault must be shown.

PRESCRIPTION AND LIMITATION

1. **An action for personal injury must be brought within three years.**
2. **An action for property damage must be brought within five years.**

REMEDIES

1. **Interdict is a court order prohibiting a certain type of conduct from continuing.**
2. **Breach of interdict can result in a fine or prison sentence.**
3. **Damages are financial compensation for loss designed to put the pursuer in the position he would have been in if the delict had not occurred.**
4. **Damages can be claimed for *solatium* and financial loss.**
5. **Damages may be awarded on a provisional basis, if the pursuer's condition is likely to deteriorate, or on an interim basis where liability on the part of the defender has been admitted and the pursuer is likely to suffer financial hardship while agreement on final damages is reached.**

? QUICK QUIZ

- Explain what is meant by *damnum injuria datum*?
- Which case set out the criteria for the delict of passing off?
- State the five steps used to establish a case of liability for unintentional harm?
- What is a duty of care and what is the test for identifying whether a duty exists?
- How will the court determine whether a duty of care has been breached?
- What types of loss will give rise to recovery in delict?
- Explain the meaning of the term *causa causans*?
- What is the correct test for remoteness of damage?
- What will be the effect of a finding of contributory negligence in a case of liability for unintentional harm?
- Name the two conditions which must be satisfied before an employer will be found vicariously liable for the actions of his employee?
- What rule was set out by the case of *Hunter v Hanley*?
- What is an interdict?

📖 FURTHER READING

J. Thomson, *Delictual Liability*, 3rd edn (LexisNexis Butterworths, 2004.
G. Cameron, *Law Basics: Delict*, 3rd edn (W. Green, Edinburgh, 2008).
W.J. Stewart, *Delict*, 4th edn (W. Green, Edinburgh, 2004).

Chapter 11   Property

Angus McAllister[1]

▶ OVERVIEW OF CHAPTER

11–01 This chapter describes the main concepts relating to heritable and moveable property, though the main emphasis will be upon heritable property. Consideration will be given to the abolition of feudal tenure, land registration, rights of ownership and restrictions upon property rights. An overview will be given of the law of leases, and the chapter will end with a brief outline of the procedure for the transfer of ownership of heritable property.

✓ OUTCOMES

11–02 At the end of this chapter you should be able to:

✓ understand some basic concepts of property law;
✓ have some appreciation of the historical background to land ownership;
✓ understand the function of the Land Register;
✓ know what the main rights are attaching to the ownership of property;
✓ appreciate the main restrictions upon property ownership, whether these are undertaken voluntarily or imposed by law;
✓ understand the main principles of the law of leases, including commercial leases;
✓ have an overview of how ownership in heritable property is transferred.

Introduction: Basic Concepts

Nature of property

11–03 The word "property" is somewhat ambiguous. It is regularly used in several senses, both legal and colloquial. It is therefore desirable to be clear at the outset about these various meanings.

In the first place, "property" is commonly used to mean anything that

---

[1] Angus McAllister, Solicitor, Professor of Law at the University of the West of Scotland.

can be owned. A TV set, a car, company shares, a house are all property in this sense. However, the term is also understood in other, slightly different ways. We talk about property rights to describe the various legal interests that a person may have in a piece of property, such as the right of an owner or of a tenant. We also use the word "property" to denote ownership itself, the legal right enjoyed by a property owner. The word will be used in all of these senses at various points in this chapter.

"Property" in the first sense is also commonly used in a much narrower sense, to refer to land and buildings (or, in England or America, "real property" or "real estate"). In a strict legal sense, this is only one type of property (known as "heritable property"), and the general term "property" also includes other things that can be owned, such as moveable or intellectual property. These other aspects will briefly be discussed in this chapter, though the main emphasis will be upon heritable property.

Classification of property

Heritable and moveable property

This is by far the most important way in which different types of property **11–04** may be classified. The most convenient way to formulate the distinction is that heritable property consists of land and anything (including buildings) permanently attached to the land. Heritable property also includes rights over, or connected with, land and buildings, such as the right of a tenant, or a right in security; the latter is colloquially known as a "mortgage" though in Scotland that is not the correct legal term.

Moveable property, on the other hand, is simply every kind of property other than heritable property, such as a book, a car or a TV set.

Unfortunately, this formulation is not completely accurate. The word "heritable" does not simply mean "immoveable". Historically the term derives from the law of succession as it used to be before radical reforms were made to the system in 1964.[2] Under the old system of succession, heritable property was the property which, after a person's death, passed entirely to the heir, usually the eldest son. This mainly included land and buildings. However, in strict law, the scope of the term heritable property extends a little wider than this to include, for example, pensions, annuities, interest-bearing bonds and titles of honour.

Corporeal and incorporeal property

Another way in which property can be classified is into corporeal and **11–05** incorporeal property. Corporeal property consists of things that exist in the physical world and can be seen or touched, such as a car or a house. Incorporeal property, on the other hand, consists of rights, such as company shares, or intellectual property such as patents, copyright etc.

---

[2] By the Succession (Scotland) Act 1964.

Ownership

11–06 We saw above that "ownership" is one of the common meanings of the word "property". One of the best definitions of this is by the institutional writer Erskine, one of several historical figures who made a key contribution to the development of Scots Law. Erskine defined ownership (or property) as "the right of using and disposing of a subject as our own, except in so far as we are restrained by law or paction".[3] "Paction" means "agreement" or "contract". In other words, there are restrictions imposed upon the absolute rights of an owner, which may be imposed upon the owner by the law or may be incurred voluntarily.

Erskine's definition is useful because, as well as being concise, it draws to our attention two fundamental aspects of ownership. It recognises that, although ownership is still the largest right a person can have in a thing, there are many ways in which the rights of an owner are qualified by the law. Some of these, mainly those which apply to heritable property, are considered briefly below.

Owners may also, of their own free will, further restrict their right of ownership by granting subsidiary property rights to others, such as servitude rights (like a right of way) or a lease. These will also be discussed later in the chapter.

Real and personal rights

11–07 This distinction has a general significance within the law of obligations, but has particular importance within the law of property. A real right is one that can be enforced against anyone in the world, whereas a personal right can only be exacted against a particular person, the one who owes the corresponding obligation. A real right is typically (though not exclusively) completed by some kind of formality, such as the registration of a document in the Land Register.

The most obvious, and most easily understood, real right is that of ownership. If I own a piece of property I may defend my right against anyone at all, not just against a particular person. Some subsidiary property rights are also real rights, such as the right of a tenant, or the rights of a creditor (such as a bank or building society) under a heritable security. An important feature of such real rights is that they "run with the land". This means that they attach to a property right rather than to the person who has that right at a particular time. For example, if a property owner enjoys a servitude right of way over another property, that right will transfer to the new owner when the property is sold.

Prescription

11–08 Prescription is a process whereby rights (including rights of ownership) may either be acquired or lost as a result of the passage of time. The period of time required varies depending upon the type of right involved. A right (e.g. a right to claim damages, or a servitude right) is lost by

---

[3] Erskine *An Institute of the Law of Scotland* (8th edn 1871) II, 2, 1.

negative prescription if it is not exercised within the relevant time period. Certain rights may be acquired by positive prescription, such as servitude rights (if exercised for 20 years) and even ownership (10 years). However, for the 10-year prescription to operate, a registered title deed will also be required.

Positive prescription used to be very important in relation to the acquisition of heritable property, as it operated to cure defects in older title deeds. It is less important now that there is a system of registration of title backed by a government guarantee. However, prescription may still be important in eventually curing defects in a title where the Keeper of the Land Register has initially withheld indemnity. This is discussed further below in the section relating to land registration.

The law relating to prescription, which is somewhat complex, is governed by the Prescription and Limitation (Scotland) Act 1973.

MOVEABLE AND INTELLECTUAL PROPERTY

Corporeal moveable property

Ownership of corporeal moveable property can be acquired by acquisition (where it has not been owned before) or by transfer from another owner. The existing owner must intend to transfer ownership, with the result that a thief (for example) will not acquire ownership. Evidence of an owner's intention to transfer may be contained in some kind of written agreement. Transfer of ownership will be completed (and a real right of ownership acquired by the new owner) when the property has been delivered. This may involve a physical transfer, but not necessarily so. **11–09**

The sale of goods is governed by the Sale of Goods Act 1979. Where that act applies, it is sometimes possible for ownership to pass without delivery.

Incorporeal moveable property

Incorporeal moveable property effectively means the ownership of a right, as opposed to something tangible. Examples include company shares and insurance policies. Another example is intellectual property, which concerns rights in original and creative works, such as patents, copyright, trade marks and designs. This important category is dealt with in Chapter 12. **11–10**

Moveable property is transferred by assignation, which may or may not be in writing. However, the new owner will not acquire a real right unless the assignation has been intimated. This means that the person against whom the right can be enforced must be informed of the transfer. For example, the assignation of an insurance policy will only become effective when the insurance company has been notified of the change.

> **Key Concepts**
>
> - The most fundamental distinction is between heritable property (land and buildings) and moveable property (everything else).
> - Moveable property can be divided between corporeal moveable property (things that can be seen or touched) and incorporeal property (rights).
> - There are restrictions upon the absolute right of ownership, which may be imposed upon an owner by law or be incurred voluntarily.
> - A real right (such as ownership) can be defended against anyone in the world, whereas a personal right (such as a contractual right) can only be enforced against a particular person.
> - Property rights (and other rights) can either be acquired or lost by the passage of time by the processes of positive and negative prescription.

HERITABLE PROPERTY: HISTORICAL BACKGROUND AND
MODERN REFORMS

The feudal system

11–11 Until recently the system of landholding in Scotland was based upon the feudal system, though it survived in a form that had been greatly modified over the centuries. Although the feudal system of landholding is no longer with us, its demise is still so recent that something needs to be said about it to explain the many references to it that still crop up in legal documents and elsewhere.

The feudal system was a pyramid-like structure, at the top of which was the king, the ultimate feudal superior. Grants of land were made to subjects (or "vassals") in return for military service or other favours. These vassals had the power to make sub-grants (to subfeu) and there was, in theory, no limit to the number of times this process could be repeated.

11–12 The modern version of this was that in Scotland land was not owned outright, but there were different layers of ownership. Above the vassal, who actually occupied the land, there would be one or more feudal superiors. The superior had no right to occupy the land, but enjoyed a number of powers that could be exercised over the vassal. These included the right to charge the vassal an annual sum (known as "feuduty") and the right to impose and enforce conditions upon the vassal's title. These feuing conditions would not normally be arbitrary exercises of power, but typically would regulate the amenity of the area by placing restrictions upon the way the vassal could build upon and use the land.

Even in its evolved form, the feudal system was difficult to defend in modern times. Regulation of land use had properly become the function of the town and country planning system. There was a case for title

conditions that protected amenity being enforced by neighbouring proprietors against one another, but not by a superior. The imposition of
feuduty was difficult to justify at all.

Reform and abolition

In the second half of the 20th century a number of reforms were made to **11–13**
the system. These included machinery for the gradual redemption of
feuduties, usually when a property was sold. Finally, in the early years of
the present century, a series of statutes passed by the Scottish Parliament
completed a virtual revolution in Scottish land law.[4] The effect of these
various statutes will be noted at various points in this chapter. Notably,
the feudal system was abolished entirely, as from November 28, 2004.
The last feuduties were redeemed and superiors were stripped entirely of
their powers, though they were entitled to compensation. Feudal layers of
ownership were swept away and all land in Scotland was now owned
outright. Title conditions survived in a modified form, but could now
only be enforced by neighbouring owners against each other, when they
could demonstrate an interest to do so.

Key Concept

- Land ownership in Scotland was formerly based upon the feudal
  system, but feudal tenure was abolished as from November 28,
  2004.

HERITABLE PROPERTY: LAND REGISTRATION

The Register of Sasines

For many centuries there has been a public register of deeds relating to **11–14**
heritable property. The Register of Sasines was established in 1617. In it
there could be recorded all types of legal document relating to heritable
property, including those creating feudal rights, transferring ownership,
creating security rights etc. By preserving transcripts of these deeds and
making them accessible to the public, the legal rights of the parties
involved (owners, creditors etc) were protected. The title deeds of a
property, which provided legal evidence of ownership, comprised all of
the deeds relating to that property to have been recorded in the Register
of Sasines.

The registration of title deeds in the Register of Sasines was an effective **11–15**
system, but had a number of disadvantages. In particular:

---

[4] Abolition of Feudal Tenure etc (Scotland) Act 2000; Title Conditions (Scotland) Act
2003; Land Reform (Scotland) Act 2003; Tenements (Scotland) Act 2004.

- Transfer of ownership was cumbersome. The purchaser's solicitor had to examine the title deeds for validity. The process of positive prescription (see above) reduced the number of deeds that had to be examined by making flaws in older deeds irrelevant, but it was still a considerable task. This process had to be repeated every time the property changed hands.
- The description of the relevant property contained in the title deeds was often vague or inaccurate, mainly due to the passage of time, sometimes making it difficult to identify the property precisely. This made disputes over ownership or boundaries more likely.

The Land Register

11–16   The Land Register for Scotland was set up by the Land Registration (Scotland) Act 1979. Since the passing of that Act, the Land Register has gradually been superseding the Register of Sasines, a process which is now nearing completion. The Land Register built upon the system created by the Register of Sasines, but took it much further by creating a system of registration of title. Effectively, this dealt with the above criticisms in the following ways:

- The Land Register records, not individual documents, but the title as a whole. All the information relevant to ownership is now contained in a computer record (the title sheet). The title sheet is amended after every sale of the property, or other transaction (such as the creation of a security) that may affect it. The validity of the title is backed by a government guarantee, which makes repeated examination of the title deeds unnecessary.
- Each property is mapped on to a master Ordnance Survey plan, thereby enabling it to be precisely identified.

First registration

11–17   The changeover to the new system could not happen overnight. Each individual property in Scotland had first of all to undergo a process of first registration. This involved the Keeper of the Registers (or a member of his staff) performing the task formerly undertaken by a purchaser's solicitor. In other words, the title deeds of the property had to be examined for one last time, so as to ensure that the title was valid and a guarantee could be given. At the same time, the boundaries of the property had to be mapped on to the Ordnance Survey plan, using the description in the title deeds. If the title contained any flaws or uncertainties, the Keeper could proceed to registration, but withhold his indemnity until such time as the process of positive prescription could cure any defects.

The divisions of the General Register of Sasines were based upon the old Scottish counties. The process of first registration was introduced piecemeal, one or two counties at a time. The first operational county was the County of Renfrew, which became open for registration in 1981, and other counties gradually followed. First registration took place whenever a property in an operational division changed hands. Once its title had been registered, future sales or other transactions relating to that property became much more straightforward.

The process of transfer to the new system is now nearing completion.

The Land Certificate

When a person becomes the owner of heritable property, their title **11–18** documentation now consists, not of a bundle of legal deeds, but of a single, compact document. The Land Certificate is an updated printout of the title sheet relating to the property in question. It has four sections, outlined below.

(1) Property section

This states briefly the property interest being registered, e.g. that of **11–19** owner, or perhaps tenant. It also identifies the property very briefly by its address and a reference to the Keeper's title plan. An extract from the title plan will also be included, on which the boundaries of the property will be marked.

(2) Proprietorship section

This will include the name of the person whose interest is being recorded, **11–20** the date of registration, the price and the date of entry.

(3) Charges section

This will specify any heritable securities over the property, e.g. in favour **11–21** of a bank that granted a loan over it. The creditor will be issued with a separate certificate, known as a charge certificate.

(4) Burdens section

This is the only section that normally extends to any length. In it are **11–22** gathered together the conditions from all of the deeds that contained burdens over the property.

Automated registration of title to land

Automated registration of title to land (ARTL) is a system which will **11–23** replace paper-based documentation relating to transactions on the Land Register with documents that have been electronically created and communicated. Its purpose is to simplify and considerably speed up the process of registration.

It will only be available to authorised users (mainly firms of solicitors and lending institutions such as banks and building societies) who have applied for and been granted a licence to use ARTL.

A pilot scheme, which only related to the creation and discharge of standard securities, was introduced in 2007. From 2008, the system will begin to handle transfers of ownership and other kinds of transaction. As with first registrations, it will gradually be extended across the whole of Scotland in a piecemeal fashion, one or two counties at a time.

Key Concepts

- Real rights in heritable property (including ownership) are completed by registration in the Land Register for Scotland.
- When a title has been registered, the property is identified upon a master Ordnance Survey plan and the title is backed by a government guarantee.
- Records in the register are held electronically, and a new system is currently being introduced which will allow transactions to take place electronically also.

OWNERSHIP RIGHTS

11–24 In our definition of "ownership" above, we emphasised the restrictions upon the absolute right of ownership. However, before looking at a few of these restrictions in a little more detail, we will consider some of the rights that go along with ownership. In other words, we will consider what is involved in the right "to use a subject as our own". These rights are mainly relevant to the ownership of heritable rather than moveable property.

Right to exclusive possession

11–25 Owners normally have the sole right to occupy their property and have the legal right to defend themselves against anyone who encroaches upon this right in any way

Within the boundaries of their land, the right of owners to exclusive possession is, in theory, without limit. Traditionally it is said to extend *a coelo usque ad centrum* (from the sky to the centre of the earth). For practical purposes, there are a number of qualifications to this right, notably by the Civil Aviation Act 1982,[5] which permits flights over another person's property at a reasonable height. Without this, airline companies would be guilty of multiple trespass on a daily basis.

There is another common exception in relation to mineral rights. Under the feudal system, these were normally reserved to the superior in feudal grants, and are likely to have survived the abolition of that system in separate ownership

---

[5] s.76(1).

Trespass

This is where an owner's right to exclusive possession has been encroa- **11–26**
ched upon by the temporary presence of a person or persons who have no
right to be there. Despite the prevalence of notices threatening prosecution for trespassers, trespass as such is not a crime (unless some crime is
committed in the process, such as breaking and entering upon a dwellinghouse or other building).

However, an owner is entitled to ask a trespasser to leave the property.
Also, if the trespass is a regular occurrence, or if there is any other good
reason to believe that it might be repeated, the owner may obtain an
interdict from the court to prevent a recurrence. An interdict is a court
order forbidding a person from carrying out an illegal act that has been
occurring on a regular basis. It is the Scottish equivalent of the English
remedy known as an injunction.

Access rights

The law of trespass was modified by Part I of the Land Reform (Scot- **11–27**
land) Act 2003, which came into force on February 9, 2005. This gives
everyone a right of access to land for recreational, educational and, in
some cases, commercial purposes. It also confers a right to cross land. A
person has such rights only if they are exercised responsibly. There is a
reciprocal obligation upon every owner of land to use and manage the
land and otherwise conduct the ownership of it in a responsible way in
relation to those rights.

There are certain types of property to which the access rights do not
apply. These include buildings and their surroundings, building sites and
sites of mineral workings, sports grounds and schools, and land where
there are crops.

Guidance about the responsible exercise of access rights and the
responsible management of ownership can be found in the *Scottish
Outdoor Access Code* (2004) drawn up by Scottish Natural Heritage,
under powers granted by the 2003 Act.

Unlawful possession

This is where the encroachment is not temporary, but the property has in **11–28**
fact been occupied by someone having no right to do so. In such a case
the owner may take a civil court action to evict the occupant. There are
several variants of this court action, which are known collectively as
possessory remedies.

Right to freedom from interference by neighbours

There are several categories of harmful action by a neighbour to which a **11–29**
property owner may take legal exception. Here we will focus upon the
one known as nuisance. Others include malicious action and non-natural
use of property.

Nuisance

11–30 The most common types of nuisance are noise, vibration, smoke, fumes etc, though the categories of nuisance are in theory unlimited. The most common (though not all) cases of nuisance arise between neighbours, not necessarily owners, where the activities of one neighbour interferes with the other's peaceful enjoyment of his or her property. For this reason, nuisance is also often known as the law of the neighbourhood.

A nuisance is something that happens on a regular basis, and there can be no liability for a one-off occurrence. It must be substantial and not of a trivial nature. Also, it is irrelevant that the nuisance may have predated the arrival of the complaining owner, and it is no defence for the per-petrator to say that the party complaining willingly moved into the area where the nuisance already existed. However, failure to object over a period of time may bar an owner from taking action under the principle of acquiescence, and any right of action (including that of future owners of the property) will be extinguished by the long negative prescription if the nuisance has continued unchallenged for 20 years or more.[6] The main legal remedy for nuisance is a court action of interdict, to restrain the offending party from carrying on the nuisance in future. Damages may also be claimed if the nuisance has had a detrimental effect upon the pursuer's health or upon the value of the pursuer's property. However, unlike interdict (which automatically becomes available if the nuisance occurs) damages can only be claimed where the pursuer can establish negligence or other form of *culpa* (blame) on the part of the defender.

Webster v Lord Advocate
1985 S.C. 173

The owner of a flat adjoining the esplanade of Edinburgh Castle raised an action of nuisance in respect of the annual military tattoo and, more particularly, the noise caused by the erection and dis-mantling of the scaffolding for the seating, a process which con-tinued throughout a considerable portion of the year.

It was held that the neither the tattoo itself nor the rehearsals for it amounted to a nuisance, since they only occurred for a brief period during the year. However, the noise caused by the erection and dismantling of the scaffolding did amount to a nuisance. It made no difference that the tattoo had existed for many years prior to the date when the pursuer bought her flat. Nor did it matter that the tattoo might be considered to be in the public interest.

The court granted an interdict. However, its effect was sus-pended for a period of six months in order to allow that year's tattoo to go ahead and to allow the organisers the opportunity to devise quieter ways of carrying out the work.

---

[6] Prescription and Limitation (Scotland) Act 1973, ss.7 and 8.

Statutory nuisance

The above discussion relates to the traditional law of nuisance under the **11–31** common law. A number of activities are also categorised as nuisances by the Environmental Protection Act 1990. These place a particular emphasis on activities that are prejudicial to health. They duplicate the main types of common law nuisance, but also extend much further to include, for example, nuisances arising from accumulations or deposits, or the keeping of animals. The main responsibility for dealing with statutory nuisances lies with local authorities, who are under a duty to detect statutory nuisances and investigate complaints about them.

The most convenient way for a member of the public to take action against a statutory nuisance will normally be to complain to the local authority. However, it is also possible for a member of the public to apply directly to the Sheriff Court in order to bring about the abatement of a statutory nuisance.

Right of support

There is an automatic right of support for land that is in its natural state **11–32** and, in the vast majority of cases, a right of support is also implied where there are buildings on the ground. This gives property owners a right to claim damages from the person responsible in respect of damage caused by subsidence.

Most disputes regarding support arise as a result of mineral workings, where the minerals are in separate ownership. Under the Coal Mining (Subsidence) Act 1991 the licensed operator or the Coal Authority are required to carry out remedial work (or in some cases pay compensation instead) in respect of damage caused to land or buildings from lawful coal-mining operations.

Questions of support can also arise between the owners of buildings in multiple ownership. This is dealt with below under the Law of the Tenement.

Fixtures

When talking of heritable property, it is natural to think mainly of **11–33** buildings rather than the land on which they are built. This is because, unless we are talking of large tracts of land, buildings are likely to be the most valuable element in the property. In strict law, however, what is owned is land and anything attached to the land. Questions relating to fixtures arise when there is some dubiety about an article that is attached to the land. Has it become so attached that it has become part of the heritable property, or is it still a moveable item?

There are a number of situations where disputes about fixtures may arise, but not all of them can be discussed here. Disputes may arise between a seller and purchaser. A prospective purchaser of a house is likely to view it while the seller is still living there. It will contain items such as curtains, fitted carpets, light bulbs, fitted cupboards and shelves, a central heating system etc. Which of these are moveable items, that can be removed by the seller, and which have become part of the heritable property and will pass to the purchaser? Another example is a tenant who spends money improving a property. To what extent will these improvements pass to the landlord as a windfall at the end of the lease?

Determination of fixtures

11–34 There is no hard-and-fast rule determining what is and what is not a fixture, but a number of guidlelines have been established. In any particular case, one or more of them may be enough to decide the matter:

- An article will not be a fixture if it can be removed either without destroying itself as a separate entity or damaging the soil or building to which it is attached.
- If an article was intended to be a permanent attachment, it is more likely to be a fixture.
- If the building or land has been specially adapted to the use of the article, it is probably a fixture.
- The extent to which the use and enjoyment of the building or land would be affected by the article's removal will help to determine whether or not it is a fixture.
- A particularly heavy article may be a fixture, even if it is not physically attached.

Christie v Smith's Executrix
1949 S.C. 572

A two-ton summerhouse, which rested on its own weight on a prepared site, was removed by a seller. Its removal left a gap in the garden wall.

It was held that the summerhouse was a fixture and should have been left (a) because of its weight; and (b) because the property had been specially adapted to it.

Examples of fixtures

11–35 Things growing in the soil, e.g. trees, shrubs, turf, crops etc are generally fixtures.

Articles in a house which are generally considered to be fixtures include doors and windows, tiles, fireplaces, grates, chandeliers, picture rods, build-in cupboards and wardrobes, built-in kitchen units and electric light flexes down to the bulb holder. Carpets (even though fitted), lino, pictures and mirrors (even if screwed to the wall) are generally considered *not* to be fixtures.

Constructive fixtures

Certain items, which are not physically annexed, qualify as fixtures **11–36** because they are necessary accessories to the heritable property. Examples include the keys of a house, and the loose parts which are necessary for the operation of fixed machinery.

Contracting out

There are many cases where it will be convenient for the parties involved **11–37** to contract out of the law of fixtures. For example, when parties conclude missives for the sale of a house or other property, it is common to override the law of fixtures by specifying which items should be included in the sale. Thus, things like fitted carpets or curtains, although they are moveable, will often be left as part of the deal.

Similarly, a lease document may allow certain fixtures to be removed by the tenant when the lease comes to an end.

Trade fixtures

A tenant may remove fixtures (such as heavy machinery) at the end of the **11–38** lease, provided that they have been annexed for the purpose of the tenant's trade or business. This only applies if the articles can be removed without material injury to the heritable property and without themselves being destroyed in the process, or losing their essential character or value.

COMMON RIGHTS

Under this heading we will look at several situations where two or more **11–39** people may have some sort of legal interest in the same property:

Common property

Where there is common property (or co-ownership) a single piece of **11–40** heritable property has more than one owner. Each co-owner has a separate title to a share of the property. All co-owners have a right to an equal say in the management or control of the common property.

We will consider examples of common property below in relation to the law of the tenement.

Joint property

This is also a situation where a single piece of heritable property has more **11–41** than one owner. The difference is that, unlike a co-owner, a joint owner cannot sell his or her share separately or will it to a third party. A common example of joint property is the property of a club. A member automatically becomes a joint owner of the club property when joining, and ceases in that ownership on resignation. The same is true of trustees in relation to trust property.

Law of the tenement

11–42 This applies mainly to blocks of flats, but may also apply to other properties (such as office blocks) where there is multiple occupation within one building. In the vast majority of cases, the situation will be governed contractually, within the titles of the various owners, and the relevant information will be found in their Land Certificates.[7] In the case of blocks of flats, the close, stairs, landings, division walls, roof, solum (the land beneath the building) garden ground etc will all be common property. Maintenance will be equal, or perhaps in proportion to the size of each property. There will be provision for the appointment of a common factor to manage the building.

If the titles do not contain such provisions, or there is an insufficient provision, it was formerly the case that the gap or gaps would be filled in by the common law of the tenement. However, this old law was generally thought to operate unfairly in modern times (e.g. by making top-floor owners entirely responsible for the maintenance of the roof). The new law of the tenement (which still operates only in default of a sufficient title provision) can be found in the Tenements (Scotland) Act 2004.

Ownership

11–43 The following are the main default provisions regarding ownership:

- The boundary between adjacent flats, between flats and the close, and between a lower and upper flat, is the mid point.
- A door or window serving one flat only is the sole property of that flat's owner.
- A top flat includes the roof over that flat and the air space up to the roof's highest point.
- A bottom flat includes the solum (the site) under the flat.
- The close, stair and landings are common property.
- A lift is common property, unless it serves one flat only.
- Ground is owned by the owner of the immediately adjacent bottom flat.
- Chimney stacks are common property.

Any parts not listed will be common property if they serve more than one flat, but otherwise will be owned exclusively by the individual owners whose flats they serve.

Management and maintenance

11–44 The 2004 Act sets out a Tenement Management Scheme, which also operates in default of relevant title provisions. However, since the scheme is more comprehensive than many title provisions are likely to be, particularly in the case of older properties, the scheme will very often apply, in part at least, to plug any gaps in the title provision.

---

[7] See paras 11–14 to 11–23.

Strategic parts of the tenement are to be maintained by everyone on an equitable basis, whether they are common property or not. Strategic parts include the solum (site), foundations, external walls, the roof, mutual gables, mutual gable walls to the mid-point, and load-bearing walls, beams or columns.

Thus (for example) parts of the roof and solum, while individually owned, will have to be maintained by everyone. Any parts not included in the list that are common property (e.g. the close and stairs) will of course be maintainable by the co-owners.

Key Concepts

- In principle, a landowner has a right to exclusive possession from the sky to the centre of the earth.
- An owner's right to exclusive possession is protected by the law of trespass.
- The law of trespass has now been modified by certain access rights of the public to private land, guidance about which can be found in the *Scottish Outdoor Access Code*.
- A property owner's right to peaceful enjoyment of his or her property and to freedom from interference by neighbours is protected by the law of nuisance, both under the common law and by statute.
- Property owners enjoy certain rights of support, and often may be entitled to compensation for damage caused by subsidence.
- A heritable fixture is an item which has become attached to land or a building in a sufficiently permanent way to become part of the heritable property.
- When a building is in multiple ownership, the rights and obligations of the various owners are generally set out in the titles of the various properties, but any gaps in this provision are filled in by a statutory law of the tenement.

RESTRICTIONS ON PROPERTY RIGHTS

The following are some of the ways in which the rights of an owner may **11–45** be qualified "by law or paction". In some cases (such as servitudes or real burdens, where the obligation runs with the land) the current owner may be bound by the agreement of a previous owner. Most of these refer to heritable property, but securities over moveable property are also briefly considered.

Servitudes

A servitude is a right (such as a right of way) which an owner of heritable **11–46** property has over another property. Servitude rights are not personal to the respective owners of the properties in question, but they run with the land. They are therefore real rights. In other words, they can be exercised, or must be suffered, not only by the current owners of the properties in question, but also by any future owners who may succeed them. Servitude rights cannot therefore be separated from the ownership of the properties in question. In this way they resemble real burdens (see below) though there are important differences between the two.

The property whose owner enjoys the servitude right is known as the "dominant tenement" and its owner is known as the "dominant owner". The property subject to the servitude right is known as the "servient tenement" and its owner is known as the "servient owner". The word "tenement" is not here being used in its colloquial sense of a block of flats, but in a technical legal sense. It simply means a piece of heritable property that may be separately owned, or be the subject of some other property right.

Types of servitude

11–47 Recognised servitude rights include:

- **Support**: The right for a building to be supported, in certain respects, by an adjoining building.
- **Way**: The dominant owner is allowed to pass over the servient tenement. Traditionally, a right of way can be either a footpath, a horse road or a carriage road (in modern times, a road for motor vehicles).
- **Aqueduct**: The right to convey water through the servient tenement by means of a pipe or canal.

Creation of servitudes

11–48 Servitudes may be created between two properties that already exist, and also when a single property is being divided in two for the first time. For example, when a property is subdivided, it may be necessary or convenient for one of the owners to have a servitude (such as a right of way) over the other property.

Real burdens

11–49 Real burdens resemble servitudes and also run with the land. They are obligations that appear in a property title and bind the owner for the time being of that property. They are there for the benefit of a neighbouring property or properties. Before the abolition of the feudal system, real burdens were regularly inserted by superiors in feudal titles and would be enforceable by superiors. Now the only people who can enforce real burdens are property owners who can demonstrate both a title and an interest to enforce the burden. This will normally mean that the burden was created for the benefit of that owner's property and that the other property would be adversely affected to a material extent if the burden were not enforced.

Real burdens may be affirmative, which means that the burdened owner is bound to carry out a positive action or actions, such as maintaining a boundary wall. Real burdens may also be negative. This means that the burdened owner is obliged to refrain from doing something, such as using a residential property for commercial purposes.

Real burdens are used for such purposes as regulating the amenity of an area, or for setting out the mutual rights and obligations of the proprietors of a building (such as a tenement) that is in multiple ownership.

The law relating to real burdens is contained in the Title Conditions (Scotland) Act 2003.

Securities[8]

A security is a right over a piece of property which is granted to a creditor **11–50** in order to safeguard the repayment of a loan. The creation of a security gives a creditor certain legal rights, including the right to recover the debt by selling the property if the debtor should default.

A common type of security over moveable property is *pledge*, which takes effect by the delivery of the security property to the creditor, probably a pawnbroker.

A security over heritable property (colloquially known as a mortgage) **11–51** is called a *standard security*. It is a formal document signed by the debtor and delivered to the creditor (probably a bank or building society). It takes effect by registration in the Land Register.

A *floating charge* is a security that can only be granted by limited **11–52** companies. It covers all the property, heritable and moveable, which the company owns at any particular time. It takes effect on the occurrence of a particular event, such as the winding up of the company. At that time it is said to crystallise, which means that it attaches to all the property then owned by the company, thereby conferring a preference upon the creditor. A floating charge may be granted by a company to a bank, for example, in order to secure an overdraft. The law relating to floating charges is now found in the Bankruptcy and Diligence etc (Scotland) Act 2007.

Statutory controls

There are a wide variety of statutory controls over heritable property, **11–53** including legislation relating to health and safety at work, environmental protection, local authority housing controls, compulsory purchase and many others. Two of them, outlined below, perhaps merit particular mention.

Planning control

Local authorities regulate land use and development under a statutory **11–54** framework laid down by central government. Planning permission is required for material changes of use and new building projects of a substantial nature. Councils also have enforcement powers in relation to

---

[8] For a fuller account of rights in security see Ch.19.

unauthorised development. There are special, more stringent controls in relation to (among others) listed buildings (buildings of special architectural or historical interest), conservation areas, tree preservation, advertisements, hazardous substances and projects of an environmentally sensitive nature (which may require an environmental assessment).

The current planning legislation is mainly embodied in the Town and Country Planning (Scotland) Act 1997, the Planning (Listed Buildings and Conservation Areas) (Scotland) Act 1997 and the Planning (Hazardous Substances) (Scotland) Act 1997.

Building control

11-55 Building control is also a function of local authorities. Unlike planning controls (which are concerned with the way in which property is used) building control relates to the technical standards in relation to health, safety etc to which buildings must conform, in accordance with building standards regulations. Building permission is required for new buildings or for substantial alterations to existing ones.

The current building control legislation is embodied in the Building (Scotland) Act 2003 and the Building (Scotland) Regulations 2004.

Key Concepts

- A servitude is a right (such as a right of way) which an owner of heritable property has over another property.
- Real burdens are obligations which appear in a property title and bind the owner for the time being of that property.
- A security is a right over a piece of property which is granted to a creditor in order to safeguard the repayment of a loan.
- Land use and development is regulated by local authorities under powers granted by the legislation on town and country planning.
- Building control in relation to the health and safety aspects of buildings is also regulated by local authorities under statutory powers.

LEASES

Nature of leases

11-56 A lease is a contract by which a person (a tenant) is allowed to occupy someone else's heritable property for a finite period. In return the tenant pays the owner (the landlord) a periodical sum of money as rent. The equivalent contract in relation to moveable property is that of hire.

In one sense, a lease may be regarded as a restriction upon ownership, which the property owner (the landlord) has granted voluntarily. However, a tenant's right is in itself a right of property and it is more convenient to classify it in this way.

Since a lease is a contract, the general law of contract applies to leases **11–57** in the same way as it applies to any other contract. However, in several respects the rights of a tenant transcend those normally conferred by a contract, with the result that a tenant also acquires a right of property:

- **A lease confers a real right**. Under a very old statute (the Leases Act 1449) a tenant's right is protected if the landlord sells the property to a new owner. Even although the new owner did not have a contract with the tenant, he or she will normally have to recognise the lease and allow the tenant to continue in occupation at the same rent until the lease is due to end. This only applies if the lease is for 20 years or less. For longer leases, the tenant acquires a real right by registration of the lease in the Land Register.
- **Length of tenure**. If a lease is for a sufficiently long period, a tenant's legal right will acquire a capital value and become a marketable asset. If the lease is sufficiently long (e.g. 99 years), the market price payable on transfer (assignation) may be as high as that obtainable by an outright sale of the property. One common type of long lease is a *ground lease* under which the landlord leases the ground only, at a comparatively modest rent, and the tenant erects (or pays for) the building. As the building is a fixture and will revert to the landlord at the end of the lease, a tenant is unlikely to take on such a lease without a substantial period of tenure. However, where a ground lease has a long unexpired term the tenant's interest can be sold for a substantial capital sum.
- **Registration**. A lease of more than 20 years may be registered in the Land Register. This strengthens a tenant's rights considerably. In particular, it allows the lease to be used as security for a loan.
- **Statutory protection**. In relation to certain types of lease (e.g. residential leases or farm leases) a lease may be extended by statute beyond the period contracted for.

Essential elements in leases

Lease documents (particularly commercial leases) may be long and **11–58** complex and contain many provisions, but only four elements are essential for a valid lease at common law:

- **Parties**. The landlord and tenant must be named and properly identified (usually by the inclusion of an address).
- **Subjects**. The property being leased must be accurately described. Sometimes an address will be sufficient, but often a longer description and/or a plan will be used.
- **Rent**. There must be a rent. Usually the lease document will also specify how it should be paid (e.g. weekly, monthly or quarterly, or whether it is payable in advance or in arrear).

- **Duration**. A lease must have a definite duration, though if this is accidentally omitted, a period of one year will be implied. The maximum duration of a residential lease is 20 years.[9] For all other leases, it is 175 years.[10]

Leases of more than one year must be in writing.[11] A lease for one year or less may be entered orally, though this is not recommended.

Rights and obligations of the parties

11–59 The contractual rights and obligations of the landlord and tenant will be set out in the lease document. In relation to residential leases and farm leases, certain rights and obligations are also conferred by statute (e.g. a residential landlord's obligation to carry out repairs). A number of rights and obligations also apply automatically at common law, unless the lease document provides otherwise:

- The tenant must enter into possession, and continue to occupy and use the property.
- The tenant must pay the rent when it is due.
- The tenant must use the property only for the purpose for which it is let.
- The tenant must take reasonable care of the property.
- The tenant must plenish the property, i.e. keep enough moveable property there to provide security for the rent.
- The landlord must give the tenant full possession of the property, and thereafter maintain the tenant in full possession, without encroaching upon it in any way.
- The landlord warrants that the property will be in a tenantable or habitable condition at entry, i.e. it should be wind and watertight, free from damp and in a safe condition.
- The landlord will maintain the property in a tenantable or habitable condition throughout the duration of the lease, though only after notification by the tenant that a repair is necessary. In commercial leases (though *not* residential leases) this obligation is normally contracted out of and all repairing obligations transferred to the tenant.

Legal remedies of the parties

11–60 If either the landlord or tenant is in breach of a lease obligation, the other party has a number of legal remedies. These include the normal remedies for breach of contract, with certain additional remedies being available to the landlord. The following are the main ones:

---

[9] Land Tenure Reform (Scotland) Act 1974, s.8.
[10] Abolition of Feudal Tenure etc (Scotland) Act 2000, s.67.
[11] Requirements of Writing (Scotland) Act 1995, s.1.

- **Implement.** Either the landlord or tenant may force compliance with a lease term by means of court action. If the obligation is a positive one (e.g. to carry out repairs) the appropriate action is called specific implement. If the obligation is a negative one (e.g. not to use the property for an unauthorised use) the action is known as an interdict (the Scottish equivalent of the English injunction).
- **Court action for debt.** This is appropriate where the obligation is to pay money (e.g. rent).
- **Rescission.** If the breach is material, the injured party may withdraw from the lease.
- **Damages.** The injured party is entitled to claim compensation for any loss caused by the breach.
- **Rent retention.** If the landlord is in breach, the tenant may withhold rent until such time as the breach has been remedied. This right may be contracted out of by a lease provision.
- **Landlord's hypothec.** The landlord has a right in security over moveable property on the leased premises in order to recover his rent. This gives the landlord a preferential claim if the tenant should go bankrupt or (if the tenant is a limited company) go into receivership or liquidation.[12]
- **Irritancy.** In commercial leases, there is normally a provision entitling the landlord to terminate the lease for non-payment of rent and for other specified breaches. This right may only be exercised (for non-payment of rent) after the tenant has been given 14 days' notice to pay and (for other breaches) where the court considers the landlord to be acting fairly and reasonably.[13] This remedy has been controversial in recent years, as it may seem disproportionately severe in relation to the tenant's breach, particularly in the case of long leases where the tenant's interest may be a valuable one.

Retail Parks Investments Ltd v Royal Bank of Scotland (No.2)
1996 S.L.T. 669

The Royal Bank proposed to close their branch in the Sauchiehall Centre in Glasgow on economic grounds. As the landlords would not release them from the lease, they wanted to minimise their overheads, while continuing to pay rent.

The court granted an order of specific implement, requiring the tenants to use the premises as bank offices during all normal business hours for the remaining seven years of the lease.

---

[12] Bankruptcy and Diligence etc (Scotland) Act 2007 s.208.
[13] Law Reform (Miscellaneous Provisions) (Scotland) Act 1985 ss.4–7.

CIN Properties Ltd v Dollar Land (Cumbernauld) Ltd
1992 S.L.T. 669

This concerned a 99-year ground lease of 6.73 acres, comprising a substantial proportion of Cumbernauld Town Centre. The tenants had purchased the lease from the former tenants at a price of £2.2 million. The tenants failed to pay the quarter's rent due on November 11, 1988. The landlords sent a notice on December 15 requiring the rent to be paid by January 4, which the tenants failed to do.

The House of Lords held that the landlords were entitled to irritate the lease. The tenants lost a substantial property interest and the landlords received a considerable windfall.

Termination of leases

11–61   A lease may be terminated prematurely if it contains a break clause, or otherwise by the mutual agreement of the parties. It may also be terminated by rescission, irritancy, accidental damage or destruction of the premises or (in certain circumstances) by the death or insolvency of the tenant.

When a lease is due to terminate it does not end automatically. It will only end if either the landlord or tenant sends the other a notice to quit. The minimum period of notice for commercial leases is normally 40 days, and for residential leases there is a statutory minimum period of 28 days.

If no notice to quit is sent, the lease will continue automatically on the same terms by a process known as *tacit relocation* (silent renewal). For leases of up to one year, it will be renewed for the same period as before. For leases of a year or more, it will be continued for one year. The same will apply at the end of the renewed period, and this process can continue indefinitely until such time as a notice to quit is sent.

Types of lease

Residential leases

11–62   Leases of houses and flats are heavily regulated by statute, mainly designed to protect the rights of tenants. The overall situation is complex, but residential leases can be very broadly divided into two categories:

- **Private sector lets**. These are lets by private landlords. The most common categories are Assured Tenancies and Short Assured Tenancies. The main relevant statutes are the Housing Scotland Acts 1988 and 2006.
- **Social tenancies**. These are lets by social landlords such as housing associations or councils. The main category is the Scottish Secure Tenancy and the main relevant statute is the Housing (Scotland) Act 2001.

There are provisions in relation to matters like rents, repairs and other tenancy conditions. Assured tenants (but not Short Assured tenants) and Scottish Secure tenants generally have security of tenure. This means that they can only be evicted on certain specified grounds, whether or not the contractual term of the lease is due to come to an end.

Agricultural leases

For well over 100 years farm leases have been regulated by a series of **11–63** statutes, the most recent being the Agricultural Holdings (Scotland) Acts 1991 and 2003. In many cases, farm tenants enjoy security of tenure beyond the contractual terms of their leases. Alternatively, if evicted, they may be entitled to compensation for improvements etc.

There is separate legislation relating to crofts and small landholdings.

Commercial leases

This is the title normally given to leases of shops, offices, factories and **11–64** other business premises. Unlike other types of lease, commercial leases are largely unaffected by statute, and the terms of the lease will be governed by the lease document, with the common law filling in any gaps. There is a minor exception that only applies to shops. Under the Tenancy of Shops (Scotland) Act 1949, a shop tenant whose lease is about to expire may apply to the Sheriff Court for an extension of up to one year.

The situation is different in England, where there is more statutory regulation. In particular, the purely English Landlord and Tenant Act 1954 gives the courts power to extend business leases for up to 14 years.

Commercial landlords are generally financial institutions (such as banks, insurance companies or pension funds) which purchase commercial properties as an investment. Business concerns often prefer to rent rather than buy their premises in order to minimise their capital investment. The traditional investment lease was for 25 years, though market pressure from tenants in recent years has led to much shorter commercial leases.

Lease provisions. Commercial lease documents tend to be long and **11–65** complex, but the following are a few of the provisions likely to be encountered:

- **Alienation**. The tenant will not normally be entitled to assign (transfer the tenancy to another tenant) or sublet without the landlord's consent. Often it is stated that the landlord's consent will not be unreasonably withheld.
- **Rent**. This will generally be payable quarterly in advance
- **Use**. The lease will state how the property should be used. This will often limit the tenant to a specific business, particularly in shopping centres, where the landlord will want to control the trade mix.
- **Insurance**. The tenant will normally have to meet the cost of insurance.

- **Repairs**. The most common type of commercial lease is the tenant's FRI (Full Repairing and Insuring) lease. This means that the tenant will normally have to carry out all repairs as well as pay for the insurance. This contracts out of the landlord's common law repairing obligation.
- **Service charges**. Where there is a building in multiple occupation (such as a shopping centre or office block) the landlord will normally take responsibility for repairs to the common parts, insurance and common services such as heating, car parking, toilets, cleaning etc. The cost will then be recovered from each tenant in proportion to the size of their premises, in the form of a periodic service charge.
- **Rent reviews**. The landlord will require the rent to be reviewed at regular intervals, most often every five years. Rent review clauses are often complex and have been subject to much litigation.

Key Concepts

- A lease is a contract, but also confers rights of property upon the tenant.
- The four essential elements in a lease are the parties, the subjects, the rent and the duration.
- A lease for more than one year must be in writing.
- The legal rights and obligations of the landlord and tenant are set out in the common law, in the lease document and (in some cases) imposed by statute.
- Both parties under a lease are entitled to the usual remedies for breach of contract, but the landlord also enjoys some additional rights, such as the right to terminate the lease by irritancy.
- The main types of lease are residential leases (houses and flats), agricultural leases (farms) and commercial leases (business premises).
- Leases may terminate prematurely in a number of circumstances, and also at the end of the lease.
- Leases do not end automatically at their termination date, but only if either party sends the other a notice to quit. Otherwise the lease will be renewed for up to one year on the same terms and conditions, by a process known as tacit relocation (silent renewal).
- Residential and agricultural leases are largely regulated by statute, but commercial leases in Scotland are mainly free from statutory control.
- Shop tenants may apply to the Sheriff Court at the end of their lease for an extension of up to one year.

TRANSFER OF HERITABLE PROPERTY

The first stage of this procedure is the completion of a contract (or **11–66** missives). This gives the purchaser a personal right against the seller, which confers the right to claim breach of contract remedies if the seller fails in any contractual obligations; these remedies include damages and, in extreme cases, the right to withdraw from the contract entirely. However, such a personal right does not safeguard the purchaser's entitlement to the actual property in the face of, for example, the rights of a competing owner. Nor does it correct any flaws there may be in the seller's title.

The second stage is for the seller to fulfil this personal obligation by taking the necessary steps to transfer ownership to the purchaser. This includes signing and handing over a formal document of transfer (a disposition), which the purchaser will register in the Land Register. At the end of this process the purchaser's personal right will be converted into a real right of ownership.

A purchaser of heritable property will not normally be able to purchase the property outright, but will need to obtain a loan from a bank, building society or other lender. The lender will require to have the loan secured by a standard security, which will be registered in the Land Register at the same time as the disposition transferring ownership.

It is normal for both purchaser and seller to be represented by a solicitor or other agent.

Key Concepts

- Personal rights of contract between the purchaser and seller are created by completion of missives of sale.
- A purchaser obtains a real right of ownership by registration of a disposition in the Land Register.
- A creditor obtains a real right in security by the registration in the Land Register of a standard security, signed by the debtor.

▼ CHAPTER SUMMARY

INTRODUCTION: BASIC CONCEPTS

1. The word "property" has several meanings. It can mean anything **11–67** that is owned, the rights a person can have in a piece of property, and it can mean "ownership".
2. Property can be classified between:

    (a) Heritable (land and buildings) and moveable (everything else).
    (b) Corporeal (things in the physical world) and incorporeal (rights).

3. **Property in the sense of ownership may be defined as "the right of using and disposing of a subject as our own, except in so far as we are restrained by law or paction".**

    ➤ Erskine *An Institute of the Law of Scotland* (8th edn 1871) II, 2, 1.

4. **Prescription is a process by which rights may be acquired (positive prescription) or lost (negative prescription) as a result of the passage of time.**

    ➤ Prescription and Limitation (Scotland) Act 1973

MOVEABLE AND INTELLECTUAL PROPERTY

1. **Ownership of corporeal moveable property can be acquired by acquisition (where it has not been owned before) or by transfer from another owner.**
2. **The sale of goods is governed by statute.**

    ➤ Sale of Goods Act 1979

3. **Incorporeal moveable property (e.g. company shares or insurance policies) is transferred by assignation, which must be intimated.**

HERITABLE PROPERTY: HISTORICAL BACKGROUND AND MODERN REFORMS

1. **The system of landholding in Scotland was formerly based upon the feudal system, which was abolished as from November 28, 2004.**

    ➤ Abolition of Feudal Tenure etc (Scotland) Act 2000

2. **The Crown still owns some rights in land, which are known as "regalia".**

HERITABLE PROPERTY: LAND REGISTRATION

1. **Real rights in heritable property were formerly acquired by the registration of the relevant deed in the Register of Sasines.**
2. **The Register of Sasines has now almost completely been replaced by the Land Register for Scotland, in which the title to a property is registered as an entity.**

    ➤ Land Registration (Scotland) Act 1979

3. **When a title has been registered, it is identified on a master Ordnance Survey plan and backed by a government guarantee.**

4. An owner's title documentation is a Land Certificate, which is a printout of the title sheet to the property contained in the land register.
5. The creditor under a Standard Security to which the property is subject receives a charge certificate.
6. Paper-based transactions on the Land Register are now being replaced by an electronic system known as Automated Registration of Title to Land (ARTL).

OWNERSHIP RIGHTS

1. Owners normally have a right of exclusive possession to their property, which is protected by the law of trespass.
2. The law of trespass has been modified by public access rights to private land.

   ➢ Land Reform (Scotland) Act 2003
   ➢ *Scottish Outdoor Access Code* (2004)

3. The rights of an owner (or other occupier) to freedom from interference by neighbours is protected by the law of nuisance, under both common law and statute.

   ➢ *Webster v Lord Advocate* (1985)
   ➢ Environmental Protection Act 1990

4. Landowners normally have a right of support to their property and can claim compensation for subsidence damage.

   ➢ Coal Mining (Subsidence) Act 1991

5. A heritable fixture is an item which has become attached to land or a building in a sufficiently permanent way to become part of the heritable property.

   ➢ *Christie v Smith's Executrix* (1949)

6. When heritable property is sold, the law of fixtures is generally modified by contract under the missives of sale.
7. A tenant may remove trade fixtures at the end of the lease.
8. The main distinction between common property and joint property is that the former can sell his or her share of the property separately, whereas a joint owner can not.
9. When a building is in multiple ownership, the rights and obligations of the various owners are generally contained in the titles to the property.
10. Any necessary provisions not covered in the titles can be found in a statutory law of the tenement.

    ➢ Tenements (Scotland) Act 2004

RESTRICTIONS ON PROPERTY RIGHTS

1. **A servitude is a right which an owner of heritable property has over another property.**
2. **Servitude rights include rights of support, rights of way and rights of aqueduct (the right to convey water across another property by a pipe or canal).**
3. **Real burdens are obligations which appear in a property title and bind the owner for the time being of that property.**

   ➤ Title Conditions (Scotland) Act 2003

4. **A security is a right over a piece of property which is granted to a creditor in order to safeguard the repayment of a loan.**
5. **Three common types of security are pledge, standard securities and floating charges.**

   ➤ Bankruptcy and Diligence etc (Scotland) Act 2007

6. **There are many statutory controls over heritable property, including planning control and building control.**

   ➤ Town and Country Planning (Scotland) Act 1997
   ➤ Planning (Listed Buildings and Conservation Areas) (Scotland) Act 1997
   ➤ Planning (Hazardous Substances) (Scotland) Act 1997.
   ➤ Building (Scotland) Act 2003
   ➤ Building (Scotland) Regulations 2004

LEASES

1. **A lease is a contract, but it also confers a right of property upon a tenant.**
2. **An important element in a tenant's property right is that a tenant enjoys a real right. This means that, should the landlord sell the property, the lease can be enforced against the new owner.**

   ➤ Leases Act 1449

3. **The four essential elements in a lease are the parties, the subjects, the rent and the duration.**
4. **A lease for more than one year must be in writing.**
5. **The maximum duration of a residential lease is 20 years. For all other leases it is 175 years.**

   ➤ Land Tenure Reform (Scotland) Act 1974
   ➤ Abolition of Feudal Tenure etc (Scotland) Act 2000

6. **The legal rights and obligations of the landlord and tenant are set out in the common law, in the lease document and (in some cases) imposed by statute.**

7. The common law obligations of a landlord include the obligation to carry out repairs. This is normally contracted out of in commercial, but not in residential, leases.

8. Both parties under a lease are entitled to the usual remedies for breach of contract. These are implement, court action for debt, rescission, damages and rent retention.

   ➤ *Retail Parks Investments Ltd v Royal Bank of Scotland (No.2)* (1996)

9. A landlord also enjoys important additional rights. These include the landlord's right of hypothec and the right to terminate the lease by irritancy.

   ➤ *CIN Properties Ltd v Dollar Land (Cumbernauld) Ltd* (1992)

10. Leases may terminate prematurely in a number of circumstances, and also at the end of the lease.

11. Leases do not end automatically at their termination date, but only if either party sends the other a notice to quit. Otherwise the lease will be renewed for up to one year on the same terms and conditions by a process known as tacit relocation (silent renewal).

12. The main types of lease are residential leases (houses and flats), agricultural leases (farms) and commercial leases (business premises).

13. The main types of residential lease are assured and short assured tenancies (private sector) and Scottish secure tenancies (social tenancies).

   ➤ Housing (Scotland) Act 1988
   ➤ Housing (Scotland) Act 2006
   ➤ Housing (Scotland) Act 2001

14. Agricultural leases are extensively regulated by statute.

   ➤ Agricultural Holdings (Scotland) Act 1991
   ➤ Agricultural Holdings (Scotland) Act 2003

15. Commercial leases in Scotland are largely free from statutory control.

16. Commercial lease documents tend to be long and complex, but generally include provisions relating to alienation (assignation and subletting), rental payment dates, the use of the premises, insurance, repairs, service charges (if the property is in multiple occupation) and rent review.

17. Shop tenants may apply to the Sheriff Court at the end of their lease for an extension of up to one year.

   ➤ Tenancy of Shops (Scotland) Act 1949

TRANSFER OF HERITABLE PROPERTY

1. **Personal rights of contract between the purchaser and seller are created by completion of missives of sale.**
2. **A purchaser obtains a real right of ownership by registration of a disposition in the Land Register.**
3. **A creditor obtains a real right in security by the registration in the Land Register of a Standard Security, signed by the debtor.**

? QUICK QUIZ

- What are the main ways in which property can be classified?
- What is the difference between real rights and personal rights?
- What are the main characteristics of registration of title?
- What are the main rights of ownership?
- In what circumstances can a person raise an action under the common law of nuisance and what remedies may be available to him or her?
- In what respects has the law of trespass been modified by the Land Reform (Scotland) Act 2003?
- What are the rules for determining whether or not an item is an heritable fixture?
- What are the main rules of the law of the tenement?
- What are the main legal restrictions upon ownership?
- What is meant by saying that a lease confers a real right upon a tenant?
- What are the main legal remedies of the parties to a lease in the event of a breach of the lease contract?
- What are the main categories of lease and the statutes regulating them?

📖 FURTHER READING

A. McAllister, *Scottish Law of Leases*, 3rd edn (Tottel, 2002).
T. Guthrie, *Scottish Property Law*, 2nd edn (Tottel, 2005).
Busby et al., *Scots Law: A Student Guide*, 3rd edn (Tottel 2006).
Gloag and Henderson, *The Law of Scotland*, Part III 12th edn (W. Green, Edinburgh, 2007).
D. Brand, *Understanding Scots Law* (W. Green, Edinburgh, 2007), Ch.12.
D. McFadzean (ed.), *Scots Law for Students: An Introduction* (Dundee University Press, 2007), Ch.12.

🖱 RELEVANT WEBLINKS

Scottish Courts: *www.scotcourts.gov.uk*.
Scottish Parliament: *www.scottish.parliament.uk*.

Scottish Executive: *www.scotland.gov.uk*.
Scottish Law Online: *www.scottishlaw.org.uk*.
Scottish Outdoor Access Code: *www.outdooraccess-scotland.com*.
Registers of Scotland: *www.ros.gov.uk*. Includes information about the Land Register.
Office of Public Sector Information (formerly HMSO): *www.opsi.gov.uk*. Includes full text of Scottish and UK statutes and statutory instruments.

Chapter 12   Intellectual Property

Dr Catherine W. Ng[1]

► CHAPTER OVERVIEW

12–01 Intellectual property law is an important aspect of business both as a going-concern and as the object of sale or acquisition. Intellectual property rights protect certain products of the human mind.

This chapter will begin with an overview of some common characteristics of intellectual property rights and then outline five types of intellectual property rights:

1.   the right against passing-off;
2.   trade mark rights (as set out in the Trade Marks Act 1994 (hereafter, TMA));
3.   copyright and moral rights (as set out in the Copyright, Designs and Patents Act 1988 (hereafter, CDPA));
4.   design rights (as set out in the CDPA and the Registered Designs Act 1949 (the latter hereafter, RDA)); and
5.   patents (as set out in the Patents Acts 1977 and 2004 (hereafter, PA 1977 and PA 2004 respectively)).

Trade mark rights and the right against passing-off relate to the identification of a trader's goods and services. The publisher's mark, for example, can be found on the spine of this book. Copyright including moral rights relates to creative works. An example of the assertion of these rights can be found on the copyright page of this book, beginning with "© **W. Green & Son Ltd 2008**". Design rights relate to the design or appearance of an object or a part of it. Finally, patents relate to inventions, such as mechanical devices and medicines. This chapter will outline these rights.

✓ OUTCOMES

12–02 At the end of this chapter, you should be able to:

✓   identify some common characteristics among intellectual property rights;

---

[1] Lecturer in Law, University of Aberdeen.

✓ understand the principles relating to the law of passing-off;
✓ understand the principles relating to trade marks;
✓ understand the principles relating to copyright including moral rights;
✓ understand the principles relating to design rights;
✓ understand the principles relating to patents; and
✓ identify the remedies for enforcing intellectual property rights.

INTELLECTUAL PROPERTY RIGHTS

Intellectual property rights share some characteristics which are useful in **12–03** conceptualising these rights in a business context:

1. Registered trade marks, registered designs and applications for registered designs, patents and application for patents are incorporeal moveable properties. Copyright and design right are property rights.[2] These properties and rights can be licensed, assigned and the subject of a security interest.[3]

2. Each intellectual property right has its discrete legal existence. For example, while a painting may be sold as an object, the copyright to it may remain with the vendor or traded separately, and the moral rights to it remain with the artist.

3. Intellectual property rights may be exploited by several parties at any one time. For example, the copyright to a painting may be licensed to one trader for printing posters and to another trader for printing postcards. It may also be licensed to different traders for printing the same postcards in different parts of the world.

4. International conventions, treaties and European Directives, among other international instruments, influence domestic laws which govern intellectual property rights. Intellectual property is generally a reserved matter under the Scotland Act 1998.

5. Public interests are often at stake. For example, a patentee can determine how his patented medicines may be made available to the public.

6. A breach of intellectual property rights may incur severe harm to the right-holder. Right-holders may therefore have the offending activity cease immediately by the relief of an interdict. Right-holders may also have the offending materials delivered or destroyed, and the right to recover the loss caused by the offending activity or to have the defender's profits from the

---

[2] Trade marks: TMA s.22; Copyright: CDPA s.1(1); Designs: CDPA s.213(1), RDA s.15A; Patents: PA 1977 s.31(2).
[3] Trade marks: TMA ss.24 et seq; Copyright: CDPA ss.90 *et seq.* (moral rights: see the section detailed below); Designs: CDPA ss.222 *et seq.*, RDA 1949 ss.15B *et seq.*; Patents: PA 1977 s.31.

activity accounted and paid.[4] Criminal sanctions are also available.

THE LAW OF PASSING-OFF

12–04 The basic principle of the law of passing-off is to protect traders from the use of (registered and unregistered) trade marks and other representations to misrepresent their goods or services as someone else's.

> **Reckitt & Colman Products Ltd v Borden Inc**
> **[1990] 1 W.L.R. 491 (HL(E))**
>
> The defendant proposed to supply lemon juice in packaging broadly similar to the plaintiffs' packaging: plastic containers in the shape and size of a lemon. The court established that to succeed in an action of passing-off, three elements must be proven: (1) A goodwill or reputation associated in the mind of the purchasing public such that the public would recognise the get-up as distinctive of the plaintiffs' goods or services; (2) misrepresentation by the defendant to the public (whether or not intentional) leading or likely to lead the public to believe that his goods or services were those of the plaintiffs; and (3) damage or likelihood of damage as a result of the misrepresentation.

Goodwill

12–05 The trader pursuer must establish that a representation, be it a trade mark or other means, has been so used in association with the goods or services of the pursuer in the market place that the representation has come to distinguish the goods or services as the pursuer's. For example, the publisher W. Green has developed a goodwill associated with its name in relation to its books such that by this mark the relevant public can distinguish this publisher's books from those of other publishers. The more unique the representation as an identifier, and the less descriptive it is of its goods or services (e.g. GREEN, rather than PUBLISHER—a generic term[5] for publishers), the easier it is for the trader to establish this goodwill and the greater the protection it attracts under the law. Nonetheless, where a trader has used a generic or a descriptive term consistently such that it becomes uniquely identified with that trader, goodwill may be established by such use. The term would have acquired a secondary meaning to denote that trader. The relevant public need not

---

[4] Trade marks: TMA ss.14 et seq, s.102; Copyright: CDPA ss.96 et seq, s.177 (moral rights: see the section detailed below); Designs: CDPA ss.229 et seq, s.262, RDA ss.24A et seq, s.45; Patents: PA 1977 as amended by PA 2004 ss.61 et seq.

[5] The word mark is, however, registered for copying paper for use with photocopier machines by Xerox Corporation under Trade Mark 2025039. See *http://www.ipo.gov.uk*.

know the exact identity of the trader represented by a distinctive mark, but only that all goods and services bearing the mark originate from one same source, the pursuer trader.[6] Where a distinctive feature (e.g. the shape of a cushion for wheelchairs) serves a practical purpose (to prevent pressure sores) as a part of the goods or services, however, the feature alone may not necessarily serve as a source identifier for the trader.[7]

The protection against passing-off is limited by the scope of goodwill. It extends geographically only where the pursuer has established goodwill. It extinguishes with the pursuer's goodwill. Businesses must therefore be vigilant in keeping their identifying representations unique in the mind of their relevant public.

Misrepresentation

The second element is misrepresentation. The trader pursuer must **12–06** establish that the use of the representation is misleading or likely to mislead the public to believe that the goods or services offered by the defender are those of the pursuer. This element has been extended to include misrepresentation that the defender's goods or services share the same distinctive characteristics as those of the pursuer.[8] It has been further extended to include misrepresentation that the defender or the defender's goods or services are in some way connected or associated with the pursuer[9] because trade marks are often used to indicate this connection or association. For example, the affiliation of W. Green with the Thomson Group was illustrated by the use of the THOMSON mark together with the W. GREEN mark for this book:

The defender's innocent intentions do not prevent a successful passing-off action where the misrepresentation leads to confusion or likelihood of confusion within a significant portion of the relevant public.

Damage

The third element is damage or a likelihood of damage accrued to the **12–07** pursuer as a result of the erroneous belief engendered by the defender's misrepresentation. The damage that usually results is a diversion of custom to the defender. The pursuer may also suffer from damage to its reputation as a result of public confusion in the perception of the pursuer's goods or services, its endorsement of others' goods or services, or its business affiliations. The damage may affect the pursuer's existing and prospective custom as well as business relations.

[6] *Birmingham Vinegar Brewery Co v Powell* [1870] A.C. 710.
[7] *Hodgkinson and Corby Ltd v Wards Mobility Services Ltd* [1995] F.S.R. 169.
[8] *Erven Warnink Besloten Vennootschap v J Townend & Sons (Hull) Ltd* [1979] A.C. 731.
[9] *Irvine v Talksport* [2002] F.S.R. 943.

Businesses must act without delay in a passing-off action. Where a pursuer may be construed to have consented to the defender's activities, the passing-off action would fail.

Key Concepts

Passing-off: The basic principal set out in *Reckitt & Colman Products Ltd v Borden Inc* (1990) is that no one may pass-off one's goods as those of another's. The pursuer must establish three elements:

- Goodwill
- Misrepresentation
- Damage

TRADE MARKS

12–08   Traders may register their marks to gain additional protection. They may also avoid the cost and uncertainty of establishing the elements required to constitute the law of passing-off at each action. Trade marks in the United Kingdom can be protected UK-wide by domestic registration with the UK Intellectual Property Office, European Community-wide by registration with the Office for Harmonisation in the Internal Markets,[10] and internationally by registration with the World Intellectual Property Organisation.[11] This chapter will focus on domestic registrations under the TMA. Under the TMA, the registered mark owner's rights under the law of passing-off remain unaffected.[12]

Protection

12–09   A registered mark is protected from the later conflicting registration or infringing use of a mark.[13] Conflict and infringement in the following circumstances:

1.   Where a mark is identical with an earlier mark and the goods or services for which an application for registration of the mark is made or for which the mark is used are identical with the goods or services for which the earlier mark is protected. (For example, a third-party registration or use of the Golden Arches logo,

---

[10] Council Regulation (EC) No 40/94 of December 20, 1993 on the Community trade mark.
[11] Protocol relating to the Madrid Agreement Concerning the International Registration of Marks adopted June 27, 1989.
[12] TMA s.2(2).
[13] Conflicting registration: TMA s.5; infringing use: TMA s.10.

registered earlier by McDonald's for goods and services associated with fast food restaurants,[14] for a fast food restaurant.)

2. Where a mark is identical with an earlier mark and is to be registered or used for goods or services similar to those for which the earlier mark is protected, or where a mark is similar to an earlier mark and is to be registered or used for goods or services identical with or similar to those for which the earlier trade mark is protected. In both cases, there must be a likelihood of public confusion, which includes the likelihood of association with the earlier mark. (For example, a third-party registration or use of the aforesaid McDonald's Golden Arches logo for a tuck shop.)

3. Where a mark is identical with or similar to an earlier mark and where the earlier mark has a reputation in the United Kingdom (or in the EC if a Community mark or an international mark for the EC) and the use of the later mark without due cause would take unfair advantage of, or be detrimental to, the distinctive character or the repute of the earlier mark. (For example, a third-party registration or use of the aforesaid McDonald's Golden Arches logo for cigarettes.)

Registration

To qualify for registration, a "trade mark" must be a "sign capable of **12–10** being represented graphically which is capable of distinguishing goods or services of one undertaking from those of other undertakings".[15] As an example, for this book, the mark

THOMSON

is a registered design mark.[16] THOMSON itself is a registered word mark.[17]

To be registered, a mark must fall outwith the absolute grounds for refusal of registration.[18] These grounds reflect the requirements in the definition of a trade mark. Marks which are non-distinctive, descriptive of their underlying goods or services, or which are customary expressions of the trade are absolutely barred from registration as trade marks. For example, while APPLE for use on apples would be absolutely barred for non-distinctiveness, it would not be barred for use on computers.[19] Where these marks have acquired a distinctive character for their traders through consistent use in the relevant market, they can overcome this bar. Falling within other absolute grounds for refusal are marks which

---

[14] Trade Marks 1320744, 1320745 and 1320746 by McDonald's International Property Company Limited. *http://www.ipo.gov.uk.*

[15] TMA s.1(1).

[16] Trade Mark 2355910 by Thomson Finance S.A.

[17] Trade Mark 2355911 by Thomson Finance S.A.

[18] TMA s.3.

[19] e.g. Trade Marks 1158659, 1246443 and E6313316 by Apple Inc. *http://www.ipo.gov.uk.*

consist exclusively of shapes which result from the nature of the goods themselves, which are necessary to obtain a technical result, or which give substantial value to the goods, and marks which are deceptive to the public or contrary to public policy or morality.

A mark must also fall outwith the relative grounds for refusal of registration.[20] These grounds relate to trade marks with earlier application dates for registration or to claims for marks registered earlier UK-wide, Community-wide, or internationally for the United Kingdom or the EC, or marks entitled to international protection as a well-known mark. The four relative grounds for refusal to register include the three circumstances of conflicting registration mentioned at para.12–09 and the fourth ground where the use of the mark would be prevented by any rule of law (particularly the law of passing-off) or by an earlier right (particularly under the law of copyright, design right or registered designs).

The UK Intellectual Property Office will search for earlier conflicting UK trade marks, EC trade marks or international trade marks that are protected in the United Kingdom or the EC as a whole and notify the applicant and the qualified prior registrants. The applicant may then decide whether or not to continue the application and whether or not to amend it or to seek consent to register from the prior registrants before the application is subject to opposition.

Infringement and defences

12–11   Once registered, a mark is under protection from the above-mentioned conflicting registration and infringing use of future marks identical or similar to the protected mark for a period of 10 years, renewable for further periods of 10 years.[21] Infringing use further includes affixing such identical or similar mark to goods or their packaging, stocking goods, offering goods or services for sale under such mark, importing or exporting goods under such mark or using such mark on business papers or in advertising.[22]

No infringement would be found, however, where a mark is used in accordance with honest practices in industrial or commercial matters by a person of his own name or address, or to indicate the kind, quality, quantity, intended purpose, value, geographical origin or other characteristics of goods or services.[23] It is therefore not an infringement to use another's registered mark to indicate the compatibility of a product or service with the goods or services provided under that registered mark. It is likewise not an infringement to use another's registered mark for the purpose of identifying the goods or services as those of the registrant or a licensee.[24] This would permit rival and complementary traders to use each others' marks for comparative or compatibility advertising purposes, so long as such use falls within honest practices in industrial or commercial

---

[20] TMA s.5.
[21] TMA ss.42, 43.
[22] TMA s.10(4).
[23] TMA s.11(2).
[24] TMA s.10(6).

matters and does not take unfair advantage of and is not detrimental to the distinctive character or repute of the registered mark without due cause.

Revocation and invalidity

A registration may be revoked where the mark has not been in genuine **12–12** use for a period of five years without a proper reason for non-use or where the use of the mark is liable to mislead the public as a result of certain use made by the owner or with his consent. The registration may also be declared invalid where the mark has been registered contrary to the absolute grounds for refusal of registration. Given public interest in maintaining a current registry system, anyone may challenge a trade mark registration in these ways.[25]

Key Concepts

Trade Marks: Under the Trade Marks Act 1994, to gain registration, a trade mark must be:

- a sign (word, design, numeral or shape, among other possibilities);
- capable of being represented graphically; and
- capable of distinguishing goods or services of one undertaking from those of other undertakings.

Registered marks are entitled to:

- protection against the later conflicting registration or infringing use of a mark:
  - where the marks are identical, and their goods and services are identical;
  - where the marks are identical, and their goods and services are similar, or where the marks are similar and their goods and services are identical or similar. In both cases, public confusion must be likely;
  - where the marks are identical or similar and the earlier registered mark has a reputation and the use of the later mark would, without due cause, take unfair advantage of or be detrimental to the distinctiveness or repute of the mark;
- protection for initial period of 10 years, renewable for periods of 10 years.

---

[25] TMA s.46, 47.

Copyright

12–13 Copyright consists of two aspects: economic rights and moral rights. Both are set out in the CDPA. Economic rights are the more commonly recognised aspect of copyright. They purport to encourage and to reward creativity by permitting the copyright holder (not necessarily the creator) to exploit a work for gain for a limited period. Moral rights are intended to protect the creator's reputation and rights in the work. Moral rights are set out in para.12–16, below.

In a work such as this book, the copyright page sets out some of the key economic and moral rights to the work:

> "No part of this publication may be reproduced or transmitted in any form, or by any means as amended, stored in any retrieval system of any nature without prior written permission, except for permitted fair dealing under the Copyright, Designs and Patents Act 1988, or in accordance with the terms of a licence issued by the Copyright Licensing Agency in respect of photocopying and/or reprographic reproduction. Application for permission for other use of copyright material including permission to reproduce extracts in other published works shall be made to the publishers. Full acknowledgment of author, publisher and source must be given."

Protection

12–14 Copyright covers a wide scope of works[26]:

- original literary, dramatic, musical or artistic works;[27]
- sound recordings, films or broadcasts;[28] and
- typographical arrangements of published works.[29]

Literary works, for example, include computer programs and databases as set out in the legislation.

Copyright protection is conferred automatically when the requirements under the legislation are fulfilled. Literary, dramatic, musical or artistic works first need to be original. The originality requirement is low. The works need not be unique or meritorious, but need simply to have originated from their claimed creators. These works must also be recorded to attract protection.[30] Copyright protects this recorded expression. Finally, the creator or the work must have sufficient connection with the United Kingdom or a country with which the United Kingdom has certain international obligations. This connection may be established either by reference to the creator of the work or by reference to the country of first publication or first transmission, for example where the

---

[26] CDPA s.1.
[27] CDPA ss.3–4.
[28] CDPA ss.5A–6A.
[29] CDPA s.8.
[30] CDPA s.3(2).

author was at the material time a British citizen, or a UK domicile or resident, or where the literary, dramatic, musical or artistic work, sound recording or film is first published in the United Kingdom.[31]

As an example, this book attracts copyright because it is a literary work, original, written and thus recorded, and first published in the United Kingdom.

Hyperion Records Ltd v Sawkins
[2005] EWCA Civ 565

Sawkins, a musicologist, edited and corrected the music scores of Lalande, a baroque composer. Sawkins' aim was to reproduce Lalande's music as faithfully as possible by way of an edition close to the composer's intentions. Hyperion recorded the music performed using Sawkins' edition. The court stated that the general policy of copyright was to prevent the unauthorised copying of certain material forms of expression which resulted from intellectual exertions of the human mind. In this case, the court found Sawkins exerted sufficient skill and labour to constitute original musical work in his edition, and to fulfil the public policy of encouraging similar contribution to music for copyright to subsist in the edition.

Generally the creator of the work is the first owner of the copyright. However, where a literary, dramatic, musical or artistic work, or a film is made by an employee in the course of employment, the employer is the first owner of the right subject to any agreement to the contrary.[32]

The duration of copyright varies depending on the type of work under protection. For a literary, dramatic, musical or artistic work, the copyright expires at the end of 70 years from the end of the calendar year in which the known author dies. The same period holds for copyright in films, but from the last to die among the known principal director, the author of the screenplay, the author of the dialogue, and the composer of music specially created for and used in the film. Copyright in sound recordings, however, expires at the end of 50 years from the end of the calendar year in which the recording is first made, or if authorised release by publication or performance is made to the public during that time, 50 years from the end of the calendar year in which the release is first made. Copyright in broadcasts generally expires at the end of 50 years from the end of the calendar year of the initial broadcast.[33]

---

[31] CDPA ss.153 *et seq.*
[32] CDPA ss.9–11.
[33] CDPA ss.12–15A.

Infringement and defences

12–15 Copyright protects from two types of acts: primary infringement and secondary infringement.

Primary infringements are infringements against the owner's and the licensee's exclusive right to perform or to authorise another to perform the following restricted acts within the United Kingdom[34]:

1. to copy the work (including, for an artistic work, to make a copy in three dimensions of a two-dimensional work, and to make a copy in two dimensions of a three-dimensional work);
2. to issue copies of the work to the public;
3. to rent or lend the work to the public;
4. to perform, show, or play the work in public;
5. to communicate the work to the public; or
6. to make an adaptation of the work or do any of the above in relation to an adaptation.

The right is infringed where these restricted acts are performed without consent on the whole or a substantial part of a copyright work, directly or indirectly. So the copyright page of this book cautions:

> "No part of this publication may be reproduced or transmitted in any form, or by any means stored in any retrieval system of any nature without prior written permission, except ... in accordance with the terms of a licence issued by the Copyright Licensing Agency in respect of photocopying and/or reprographic reproduction. Application for permission for other use of copyright material including permission to reproduce extracts in other published works shall be made to the publishers."

In practice, copyright holders often license a collecting society such as the Copyright Licensing Agency or the Performing Rights Society to collect royalties from the public on behalf of the copyright holders. For example, the Copyright Licensing Agency's licence permits an organisation such as an educational institution to photocopy, scan and e-mail articles from certain publications without having to seek permission from each copyright holder each time a copy is made. In exchange, the Agency collects from the organisation a single annual payment of royalties. The Agency then undertakes surveys and audits to determine how the royalties should be distributed among the copyright holders.

Secondary infringement of copyright occurs where a person who, without the licence of the copyright owner, knowingly deals or has reason to believe he is dealing with an infringing copy or performance[35]:

---

[34] CDPA ss.16–21.
[35] CDPA ss.22–27.

1. imports the infringing copy into the United Kingdom other than for his private and domestic use;
2. sells or lets for hire or offers or exposes for sale or hire an infringing copy, in the course of a business possesses or exhibits in public or distributes an infringing copy, or otherwise than in the course of a business distributes an infringing copy to such an extent as to prejudicially affect the copyright owner;
3. makes, imports into the United Kingdom, possesses in the course of a business, or sells or lets for hire, or offers or exposes for sale or hire an article specifically designed or adapted for making infringing copies of a copyright work;
4. permits the use of a place of public entertainment for the performance of a literary, dramatic or musical work; or
5. permits the use of certain facilities (equipment and/or premises) for playing sound recordings, showing films or receiving visual images or sounds conveyed by electronic means.

However, some permitted uses by non-copyright holders are set out in the legislation. They include, of particular importance to students: (1) the fair dealing with a literary, dramatic, musical or artistic work for the purposes of research for a non-commercial purpose if the use is accompanied by sufficient acknowledgement where practicable, or for private study; and (2) the fair dealing of a work already available to the public, for the purpose of criticism or review or for reporting current events. In these cases, the use must also be accompanied by sufficient acknowledgment, wherever possible in the cases of sound recording, film or broadcast.[36]

Moral rights

Moral rights are intended to protect the creators of certain copyright **12–16** works. Five types of moral rights are recognised in the United Kingdom:

First is the right to be identified as the author of a copyright literary, dramatic, musical, artistic work or work of architecture in the form of a building, or the director of a copyright film. This right is not infringed unless it has been asserted in accordance with the statute, for example by printing on the copyright page of a book: "The moral rights of the authors have been asserted".[37] Second is the right to object to the derogatory treatment of a copyright literary, dramatic, musical or artistic work or work of architecture in the form of a building, or a copyright film. The treatment of a work is derogatory if it distorts or mutilates the work or otherwise prejudices the honour or reputation of the author or director of the work. Third is the right against the false attribution to a person other than the true author or director of a copyright literary, dramatic, musical or artistic work or a film. Fourth is the right of the commissioner of photographs or films taken or made for private and domestic purposes, where copyright subsists in those works, not to have

---

[36] CDPA ss.29, 30.
[37] RRM Paisley *Land Law* (Edinburgh: W. Green & Son 2000).

copies of the work issued, shown or communicated to the public.[38]
Finally, the resale right for artists of works of graphic or plastic art such
as paintings, sculptures, or photographs gives the artists a right to royalty
on any sale of their works after the initial transfer from them.[39]

Unlike economic rights, moral rights cannot be transferred except
upon the death of the persons entitled to the rights. These rights, other
than the resale right, may be waived. All moral rights other than the right
against false attribution last for the same duration as the economic rights.
The right against false attribution lasts for 20 years after the author's or
the director's death. Exceptions, such as use of a copyright work for the
reporting of current events, apply to certain moral rights. A person
entitled to a moral right can take action against any infringement as a
breach of a statutory duty. In the case of the right to object to derogatory
treatment of a work, the court may grant an interdict unless a disclaimer
is made to dissociate the author or director from the treatment of the
work.[40]

Key Concepts

Copyright: Under the CDPA, copyright automatically subsists in:

- original literary, dramatic, musical or artistic works, where
  recorded;
- sound recordings, films or broadcasts; and
- typographical arrangements of published works,

where the creator or the work has established sufficient connection
with the United Kingdom or a country with which the United Kingdom
has certain international obligations.

A copyright holder is entitled to:

- protection of qualifying work from being
  - copied,
  - issued to the public,
  - rented or lent to the public,
  - performed, shown or played in public,
  - communicated to the public, or
  - adapted, or from having any of the above done in relation to an
    adapted work.
- protection against third-party facilitation of the foregoing acts;
- a duration of protection which varies depending on the type of
  work protected.

---

[38] CDPA ss.77–85. For performers' moral rights, see CDPA s.205C–N, as amended by the
Performances (Moral Rights, etc.) Regulations 2006 (SI 2006/18).
[39] Artist's Resale Right Regulations 2006 (SI 2006/346).
[40] CDPA s.103.

However, certain acts, such as the fair dealing of a literary, dramatic, musical or artistic work for non-commercial research or private study or for the criticism or review of a work already available to the public are permitted as defences against infringement.

Moral Rights: In addition to economic rights, five types of moral rights are recognised in the United Kingdom:

- the right to be identified as the author or director;
- the right to object to any derogatory treatment of the copyright work;
- the right against false attribution;
- the right to privacy of certain photographs and films; and
- the artist's resale right.

Moral right holders are entitled to:

- protection against infringement as a breach of statutory duty;
- protection for the same duration as economic rights, except the right against false attribution which lasts for 20 years after the author's or director's death.

Moral rights other than resale right can be waived, but not transferred.

DESIGN

"Design", in intellectual property terms, refers to the design or appear- **12–17** ance of an object or a part of it, resulting from lines, contours, colours, shapes, textures or materials. The design may be for a functional article. One example is:

41

Within the United Kingdom, designs are protected under the copyright legislation (CDPA) automatically when all legislative requirements are

---

[41] Design No. 3012578, courtesy of its proprietor Scottish & Newcastle plc. *http://www.ipo.gov.uk*.

met, and may be further protected under the Registered Designs Act 1949. As the title of this latter legislation suggests, the statute concerns the registration of designs. The two types of protection have different requirements. Another level of registered and unregistered Community design rights exists. The protection offered varies between jurisdictional levels, and between registered and unregistered designs. This chapter will again focus on the United Kingdom.

CDPA design rights

Protection

12–18 In the United Kingdom, design rights arise automatically, without registration, under the CDPA where the design is: the design of any aspect of the shape or configuration (internal or external—thus unlike registered designs, no eye appeal is required) of a whole or a part of an article, that is original and not commonplace, and recorded in a design document or an article has been made to the design. Furthermore, the designer or the commissioner of the design must be a qualifying individual or person, for example a UK resident.[42]

However, CDPA design rights do not subsist in surface decorations, methods or principles of construction, or features of shape or configuration of an article which enable the article to fit with another article so that either may perform its function, or which must match another article in appearance to form an integral part of that article as intended by the designer.[43] These last two exclusions permit third party manufacture of spare parts or accessories to a protected article or portion of the article.

> ### Ocular Sciences Ltd v Vision Care
> #### [1997] R.P.C. 289
>
> The court found that even though the minute details in the design of a contact lens would require "sophisticated measuring equipment in the hands of a skilled technician to tell them apart", they might nonetheless qualify as designs protected under CDPA. However, some features of the contact lens in question were designed to enable the lens to fit onto the eye so as to achieve in-eye stability and were therefore excluded from protection under the "must fit" exception. In any event, the court found the designs as a whole commonplace and did not attract unregistered design protection.

CDPA design rights last 15 years from the end of the calendar year in which the design is first recorded in a document or an article is first made to the design, whichever is earlier. However, where the article made to the design is available for sale or hire within five years from the end of that

---

[42] CDPA s.213.
[43] CDPA s.213(3).

calendar year, the rights expire 10 years from the end of the calendar year in which that availability first occurs.[44] Furthermore, any person may be entitled to a license of a design within the last five years of the protection.[45] So, in effect, the right holder may only enjoy five years of exclusivity from the commencement of his exploitation of the design right.

The designer or, where applicable, the commissioner of the design, is generally the first owner of the design.[46]

Infringement and defences

CDPA design rights may be infringed by the exact or substantial making **12–19** or copying of articles with a protected design, or by the making of a design document recording the design so that the article may be made.[47] These rights are also secondarily infringed where a person imports an infringing article into the United Kingdom or possesses it for commercial purposes, or sells, lets for hire, or offers for sale or hire in the course of a business an article where that person knows or has reason to know that the article is infringing.[48]

Unlike copyright, the protection of designs under the CDPA is limited to that against commercial use only. Where a work attracts copyright as well as design right, it is not an infringement of design right to do anything which is an infringement of the copyright in that work.[49] In that case, only an action in copyright would lie. The copyright legislation also stipulates that copyright is not infringed for design documents or models recording designs for anything other than an artistic work or typeface.[50] So, for example, the production of an exhaust pipe from its blueprint would not infringe the copyright in the blueprint because it is a design document rather than an artistic work. The same result attains in the reproduction of an exhaust pipe from another.

Registered design rights

While CDPA design rights and registered design rights overlap, they do **12–20** not protect the same designs nor do they confer the same rights. Registered design rights last longer and are stronger. These rights are set out in the Registered Designs Act 1949. The 1664 glass illustrated at the beginning of this section (para.12–17) is an example of a registered design. Where registered and CDPA design rights coincide in a design and both rights are owned by one party, the CDPA raises a presumption that an assignment of registered design right be taken as an assignment of the design right also.[51]

---

[44] CDPA s.216.
[45] CDPA s.237.
[46] CDPA s.215.
[47] CDPA s.226.
[48] CDPA s.227.
[49] CDPA s.236.
[50] CDPA s.51.
[51] CDPA s.224.

Protection

12-21 Registered design rights protect the appearance of the whole or a part of an industrial or handicraft item, including the lines, contours, colours, shapes, textures or materials of the item or its ornamentation.[52] The protected design must be new such that no identical design or design which varies only in immaterial detail has been made available to the public before the design registration application date (or the deemed application date). This design must have an individual character; it must produce on the informed user a different overall impression of the item from the overall impression produced by any other designs.[53] In short, registered designs must have an "eye-appeal" to the consuming public. These designs must be capable of being seen. Furthermore, designs which are solely dictated by the technical function do not attract registered design rights. Parallel to the "must fit" exception for CDPA design rights (see para.12–18), no registered design right subsists in a design necessary to permit the product bearing the design to fit another product so that either may perform its function.[54] Designs which are contrary to public policy or morality also do not attract registered design rights.[55]

Registration

12-22 As with CDPA designs generally, the creator or, where applicable, the commissioner of a design is considered the original proprietor of the design.[56] The person claiming to be the proprietor of a design or the owner of CDPA design rights to the design may apply for the design to be registered.[57]

Infringement and defences

12-23 Once registered, the proprietor has the exclusive right to use the design and any other design which does not produce on the informed user a different overall impression.[58] This use includes the making, offering, putting on the market, importing, exporting or using, or stocking for these purposes, a product in which the design is incorporated or to which the design is applied. The use of a product bearing the design for private or teaching or experimental purposes is therefore not an infringement where the source is mentioned and the use is compatible with fair trade practice and does not unduly prejudice the normal exploitation of the design.[59] Reflecting the "must match" exception to CDPA design rights (see para.12–18), registered design rights are not infringed where the design of a component part is used for the purpose of the repair of a

---

[52] RDA s.1.
[53] RDA s.1B.
[54] RDA s.1C.
[55] RDA s.1D.
[56] RDA s.2.
[57] RDA s.3.
[58] RDA s.7.
[59] RDA s.7A.

complex product to restore to its original appearance.[60] Other exceptions to infringement are set out in the statute. The registered rights last for an initial period of five years, and are renewable for up to four additional periods of five years.[61]

Revocation and invalidity

As with trade mark rights, registered design rights may be invalidated if **12–24** the registration has not been properly granted.[62] Where the design registration constitutes an unauthorised use of a work protected by UK copyright law, the registration may also be invalidated based on an objection by the owner of the copyright.[63]

Key Concepts

Design Rights: there are two types of design rights under UK domestic law: CDPA design rights and registered design rights.

CDPA design rights subsist:

- in a shape or configuration,
- which is original and not common place,
- which is recorded or made into an article, and
- where the designer or the commissioner of the design is a qualifying person.

CDPA design rights do not subsist:

- in surface decoration,
- in method or principle of construction,
- where it must fit another article for either article to function, or
- where it must match another article in appearance.

CDPA design right holders are entitled to:

- protection against the exact or substantial making or copying of articles to the protected design, or the making of a design document recording the protected design to enable such article to be made;
- protection for up to 15 years from the year the design is first recorded or made, or 10 years from the year the recorded design is first made available for sale or hire, whichever expires earlier. In any event, anyone may license the design right during the last five years.

---

[60] RDA s.7A(5).
[61] RDA s.8.
[62] RDA s.11ZA.
[63] RDA s.11ZA(4).

Registered design rights subsist:

- in the appearance of the whole or a part of an industrial or handicraft item,
- where the design is new, and
- where the design has individual character,

Registered design rights do not subsist:

- where the designs are dictated solely by function (including those which "must fit"), or
- where the designs are contrary to public policy or morality.

Registered design right holders are entitled to:

- the exclusive commercial use of the design and any design which does not produce on the informed user a different overall impression. Certain uses of a product bearing the registered design for private, teaching, experimental or "must match" purposes are not infringements;
- protection for an initial period of five years, renewable every five years, up to 25 years in total.

PATENTS

12–25 Patents are granted for inventions, be they life-saving medicines or toys for leisure. One example for the latter is the Lego toy:

Abstract of **GB1065932**

1,065,932. Toy building elements. LEGO SYSTEMS A.S.
Feb. 14, 1966 [March 1, 1965], No. 6453/66. Heading A6S.
Toy building elements comprise hollow parallel sided blocks adapted to be interconnected by uniformly spaced projections P by axial distances constituting a module q, and cog-wheel elements having teeth in accordance with the formula $r = cq$, where c is an integer and r is half the pitch diameter D.

FIG. 5.

64

Data supplied from the *esp@cenet* database - Worldwide

The UK legislation, Patents Acts 1997 and 2004, incorporates the requirements of the Patent Cooperation Treaty (PCT) 1970 and the European Patent Convention (EPC) 1973 as revised in 2000. The PCT provides for a single international application and an international search by an international searching authority before the application is sent for full consideration at the designated contracting states in which the patent is sought. The EPC has established the European Patent Office which provides a single entry point for lodging one patent application and following one examination process for a grant of patent with full effect in designated countries. While the European Patent Office may grant patents, it has no enforcement power. An application may be made at the UK Intellectual Property Office for a UK patent, a patent for designated member states of the EPC, and/or a patent for the designated contracting states of the PCT.

Protection

Patents may only be granted for inventions where they are new, involve **12–26** an inventive step and are capable of industrial application, and where their commercial exploitation would not be contrary to public policy or morality. An invention is new if, at the priority date—normally the filing date of the application, it is not yet part of the state of the art, publicly disclosed or anticipated in an invention or publication which would enable a person skilled in the art to put the invention into effect. It is therefore prudent to file a patent application before anyone, including the inventor, discloses the invention. An invention must also involve an inventive step, such that it is not obvious to a person skilled in that art, having regard to the state of the art. It must add a new idea to the existing stock of knowledge. The invention must also be capable of industrial application such that it can be readily made or used in any kind of industry, including agriculture. It must be able to produce a technical effect or serve a useful purpose.

The legislation specifies that a patentable invention cannot be a discovery, scientific theory or mathematical method, a method of therapeutic or surgical treatment or a method of diagnosis for humans or animals, a literary, dramatic, musical or artistic work or any other aesthethic creation or any scheme, rule or method for performing a mental act, playing a game or doing business, or a program for a computer.[65]

Registration

A patent application must contain (1) a request for the grant of a patent, **12–27** (2) a specification which contains a description of the invention, a claim or claims and any drawing referred to in the description or claim, and (3) an abstract.[66] The specification must disclose the invention in a manner clear and complete enough for a person skilled in the art to work the

---

[65] PA 1997 ss.1–5 as amended by PA 2004 s.1.
[66] PA 1997 s.14.

invention. Within this specification, the claim will define the essence of the invention and the boundaries of the protection claimed. These boundaries should correspond with those of the contribution of the invention. The claim may be for a product such as a Lego toy, or a process of production such as a process for deacidizing a gas with washing of the hydrocarbons desorbed upon regeneration of the solvent.[67]

Once filed at the UK Intellectual Property Office, the domestic patent application is first subject to a preliminary examination to ensure that the application requirements are fulfilled. The application will then be published and a substantive examination of it made by a skilled examiner before the patent is granted and published in its final form.

A patent may be granted to the inventor or to any person who is by virtue of domestic, foreign or international law entitled to it in the United Kingdom. Once granted, a patent will be effective for a period of up to 20 years, usually from the date of filing the patent application.[68]

Infringement and defences

12–28   Essentially, a product patent grants a patentee an exclusive right to make, dispose of, offer to dispose of, use or import the product or keep the product. The exclusive right in a process patent lies in using the process or offering it for use in the United Kingdom. Anyone who uses it or offers it for use in the United Kingdom would infringe the patent when he knows or it is obvious to a reasonable person that such use without the consent of the patent owner would infringe the patent. Furthermore, anyone who disposes of, offers to dispose of, uses or imports any product obtained directly through the patented process or keeps any such product would infringe the patent. The unauthorised supply or offer to supply in the United Kingdom of means relating to an essential element of the invention (other than a staple commercial product) to work the invention when the supplier knows or it is obvious to a reasonable person that the means are suitable and intended for working the invention in the United Kingdom may also constitute an infringement of the patent. Exceptions to infringement include the private and non-commercial use of an invention, and experimental use relating to the subject matter of the invention.[69]

To prove infringement, the patentee's claims are compared with the defender's product or process. The defender's product or process need not be identical with the patentee's claims. The determination of infringement may depend on how the claims are interpreted and the tests applied by the courts for the interpretation.

Where groundless threats of infringement proceedings are made, statutory remedies are available.[70]

---

[67] Application No. GB0202177.2, Publication No. GB2375544. *http://www.ipo.gov.uk*.
[68] PA 1977 s.25 as amended by PA 2004 s.8.
[69] PA 1977 s.60(5).
[70] PA 1977 s.70.

Aerotel v Telco Holdings
[2006] EWCA Civ 1371

At issue were computer-implemented inventions. One was a tele-phone call handling system. The court analysed the case in four steps:

(1) properly construe the claim;
(2) identify the actual contribution;
(3) ask whether it falls solely within the excluded subject matter;
(4) check whether the actual or alleged contribution is actually technical in nature.

The exclusions of schemes, rules and methods for performing mental acts, playing games or doing business, and programs for computers from being patentable subject matters was found not to apply in this case because the contribution consisted of a new combination of hardware resulting in a new system. Aerotel retained its patent as a result of this finding.

Revocation and invalidity

The validity of a patent may be challenged as to whether the patent has **12–29** been properly granted.[71] Thus, where the claims of the patent are too broad, the patent may be revoked or partially revoked if it includes non-patentable materials. Where the claims of the patent are too narrow, they would limit the patentee's protection.

Key Concepts

Patents: To be patentable an invention, which may be a product or a process, must:

- be new;
- involve an inventive step; and
- be capable of industrial application.

Furthermore, the commercial exploitation of the patent must not be contrary to public policy or morality.

A patentee is entitled to:

- protection in respect of:
  - product patents—an exclusive right to make, dispose of, offer to dispose of, use or import the product or keep the product;

---

[71] PA 1977 ss.72 *et seq.*

- process patents—an exclusive right to use the process or offer it for use in the United Kingdom, and an exclusive right to dispose of, offer to dispose of, use or import any product obtained directly through the patented process or to keep any such product. Exceptions include the private and non-commercial use of an invention, and experimental use relating to the subject matter of the invention;
- protection against unauthorised supply or offer to supply in the United Kingdom of means relating to an essential element of the invention (other than a staple commercial product) to work the invention when the supplier knows or it is obvious to a reasonable person that the means are suitable and intended for working the invention in the United Kingdom;
- protection up to 20 years.

▼ CHAPTER SUMMARY

12–30
1. **Intellectual property rights protect certain products of the human mind.**
2. **A breach of intellectual property rights may be remedied by the relief of an interdict, having the offending materials delivered or destroyed, and recovering the loss caused by the offending activity or having the defender's profits from the activity accounted and paid. Criminal sanctions are also available.**
3. **Save for the law of passing-off, the four other major types of intellectual property rights—trade marks, copyright, designs and patents, are set out in statutes.**

PASSING-OFF

1. **The basic principle for the law of passing-off is that no one may pass-off one's goods as those of another's. It is therefore often applied to protect registered and unregistered trade marks;**

   ➢ *Reckitt & Colman Products Ltd v Borden Inc* (1990): three elements must be proven to constitute passing-off—goodwill, misrepresentation and damage.

TRADE MARKS

1. **To gain registration, a trade mark must be a sign capable of being represented graphically and capable of distinguishing the goods and services of one undertaking from those of other undertakings;**

➢ Trade Marks Act 1994.

2. **A registered mark is protected from future conflicting registration or infringing use: where identical marks are to be registered or used for identical goods and services; where identical marks are to be registered or used for similar goods and services or where similar marks are to be registered or used for identical or similar goods and services, and where public confusion is likely; or where identical or similar marks are to be registered or used and the earlier registered mark has a reputation and the use of the later mark would, without due cause, take unfair advantage of or be detrimental to the distinctive character or repute of the earlier mark.**

3. **A trade mark registration lasts 10 years, renewable for periods of 10 years. The registration may nonetheless be revoked or invalidated.**

COPYRIGHT

➢ Copyright, Designs and Patents Act 1988.

1. **Copyright is automatically conferred on original literary, dramatic, musical or artistic works where recorded, sound recordings, films or broadcasts, and typographical arrangements of published works. In all cases, the creator or the work must have sufficient connection with the United Kingdom or a country with which the United Kingdom has certain international obligations;**

➢ *Hyperion Records Ltd v Sawkins* (2005): The general policy of copyright is to prevent the unauthorised copying of certain material forms of expression which result from the intellectual exertions of the human mind, requiring sufficient skill and labour to constitute an original work, and to fulfil the public policy of encouraging similar contribution.

2. **The copyright holder can protect a qualifying work and its adaptation from being copied, issued to the public, rented or lent to the public, performed, shown or played in the public, communicated to the public or adapted. The copyright holder may also take action against third parties who facilitate these activities. Exceptions include certain fair dealing with a copyright work.**

3. **The duration of copyright protection varies depending on the type of protected work.**

4. **In addition to economic rights, five types of moral rights are recognised in the United Kingdom—the right to be identified as the author or director, the right to object to any derogatory treatment of the copyright work, the right against false attribution, the right to privacy of certain photographs and films, and the artist's resale right. These rights, other than resale right, can be waived but not transferred.**

Designs

1. **There are two types of design rights under UK domestic law: CDPA design rights and registered design rights.**
2. **CDPA design rights arise automatically under the statute;**

   ➤ Copyright, Designs and Patents Act 1988.

3. **CDPA design rights subsist in a shape or configuration which is original and which is recorded or made into an article and where the designer or the commissioner of the design is a qualifying person;**

   ➤ *Ocular Sciences Ltd v Vision Care* (1997): eye appeal is not required.

4. **CDPA design rights do not subsist in surface decorations, methods or principles of construction, where the design must fit or must match with another article.**
5. **CDPA design right holders are protected from the exact or substantial making or copying of articles to the protected design, or the making of a design document recording the protected design to enable such article to be made. Their rights last for up to 15 years. Other provisions apply to vary this length of protection.**
6. **Registered design rights are set out in legislation;**

   ➤ Registered Designs Act 1949.

7. **Registered design rights subsist in the appearance of the whole or a part of an industrial or handicraft item where the design is new, and where the design has individual character.**
8. **Registered design rights do not subsist where the designs are dictated solely by function (including those which "must fit") or where the designs are contrary to public policy or morality.**
9. **Registered design right holders are entitled to the exclusive commercial use of the design and any design which does not produce on the informed user a different overall impression. However, certain uses of a product bearing the registered design for private, teaching, experimental or "must match" purposes are not infringements.**
10. **Design registrations initially last for five years, and are renewable every five years, up to 25 years in total.**

Patents

1. **The provisions for the grant of patent are set out in legislation;**

   ➤ Patents Act 1977 as amended by Patents Act 2004.

2. **To be patentable an invention, which may be a product or a process, must be new, involve an inventive step, and be capable of**

industrial application. The commercial exploitation of the patent must not be contrary to public policy or morality;

> *Aerotel v Telco Holdings* (2006): steps in a structured analysis:

(1) properly construe the claim;
(2) identify the actual contribution;
(3) ask whether it falls solely within the excluded subject matter;
(4) check whether the actual or alleged contribution is actually technical in nature.

3. Patentees have an exclusive right to make, dispose of, offer to dispose of, use or import the patented product or keep the product, and an exclusive right to use the patented process or offer it for use in the United Kingdom, and an exclusive right to dispose of, offer to dispose of, use or import any product obtained directly through the patented process or to keep any such product. Exceptions include the private and non-commercial use of an invention, and experimental use relating to the subject matter of the invention.
4. Patentees have a right of action against the unauthorised supply or offer to supply in the United Kingdom of means relating to an essential element of the invention (other than a staple commercial product) to work the invention when the supplier knows or it is obvious to a reasonable person that the means are suitable and intended for working the invention in the United Kingdom.
5. Patent protection lasts up to 20 years.

? QUICK QUIZ

- What are the elements that a pursuer must establish to constitute the action of passing-off?
- What are the advantages of registering trade marks?
- Are written responses to this quick quiz protected by copyright? How?
- What intellectual property right may accrue in the THOMSON design mark?
- What moral rights subsist in the written responses to this quick quiz?
- Can an invention which is the subject of a patent attract registered trade mark rights?
- Can a copyright work also attract design rights?
- What are the advantages to registering design rights?
- What are the basic criteria in determining the patentability of an invention?
- What are two basic types of patent claims?

📖 FURTHER READING

D.I. Bainbridge, *Intellectual Property*, 6th edn (Pearson Education
Limited, 2007).
L. Bently and B. Sherman, *Intellectual Property Law*, 2nd edn (Oxford
University Press, 2004).
A. Christie and S. Gare, *Blackstone's Statutes on Intellectual Property*,
8th edn, (Oxford University Press, 2006).
W. Cornish and D. Llewelyn, *Intellectual Property: Patents, Copyright,
Trade Marks and Allied Rights*, 5th edn (Sweet & Maxwell, 2003).
H. MacQueen, C. Waelde and G. Laurie, *Contemporary Intellectual
Property: Law and Policy* (Oxford University Press, 2008).
P.L. Torremans, *Intellectual Property Law*, 4th edn (Oxford University
Press, 2005).

🖱 RELEVANT WEBLINKS

Centre for Intellectual Property and Information Law: *http://www.ci-
pil.law.cam.ac.uk/*.
Office for Harmonisation in the Internal Market: *http://oami.europa.eu/*.
Oxford Intellectual Property Research Centre: *http://www.oiprc.ox.ac.uk/*.
UK Intellectual Property Office: *http://www.ipo.gov.uk/*.
World Intellectual Property Organisation: *http://www.wipo.int/*.
World Trade Organisation: *http://www.wto.org/*.

Chapter 13   Trusts

JAMES CHALMERS[1]

▶ CHAPTER OVERVIEW

This chapter is concerned with the law of trusts. It starts by explaining **13–01**
the concept of the trust as it is recognised in Scots law. The chapter goes
on to explain how trusts are created and administered, and sets out the
duties, powers and potential liabilities of trustees. It then considers how
trust purposes may be varied and how trusts may be brought to an end
(terminated).

✓ OUTCOMES

At the end of the chapter, you should be able to explain and apply the **13–02**
following:

- ✓ what a trust is and how one can be created;
- ✓ how trusts are administered;
- ✓ the general duties and powers of trustees;
- ✓ the rule against *auctor in rem suam* (conflict of interest);
- ✓ the potential liabilities of trustees to beneficiaries and third
  parties;
- ✓ the rules and procedures for varying trust purposes;
- ✓ the means by which a trust may be terminated.

THE TRUST CONCEPT

A trust may be most easily understood as a tripartite relationship, **13–03**
involving three roles:

- the truster (the person who creates the trust and is the owner of
  the trust property before its creation);
- the trustee (who is the owner of the trust property after the trust is
  created and is responsible for administering the trust); and
- the beneficiary (the person for whose benefit the trust property is
  held by the trustee).

---

[1] Senior Lecturer in Law, University of Edinburgh.

In other words, a trust is created when one person (the truster) transfers property to a second person (the trustee) who is then under an obligation to apply the property for the benefit of a third person (the beneficiary).

It is possible for there to be more than one truster, trustee or beneficiary, and it is possible for one person to hold more than one of those roles (except that a sole trustee cannot be a sole beneficiary).

Trust property is owned by the trustee.[2] However, if the trustee becomes insolvent, the trust property is not available to satisfy the claims of his creditors.[3] Nor is it available to satisfy the claims of the truster's creditors. This "insolvency effect" is the most important—and often the most useful—feature of the trust. The trust can *itself* become insolvent and be sequestrated, however.[4]

Consequences of a trust

13–04 The trust is a versatile device and its use is not restricted to any one particular context. Six useful features of the trust may be noted:

- it can divorce the right to benefit from property from the right of ownership—and the control and administration—of that property;
- it can split the right to benefit from property between two or more individuals;
- it can place restrictions on the right to benefit from trust property, or lay down conditions which must be fulfilled before an individual is entitled to become owner of that property;
- it can be used to postpone a decision on who is to benefit from that property;
- it can be used to place property in the hands of persons who are regarded as more appropriate to administer it than the truster—perhaps because they are better qualified to do so, or are able to devote more time to the role; and
- as noted earlier, trust property is protected from the insolvency of either the truster or the trustee.

Why create a trust?

13–05 Trusts may be created for any number of reasons. Some of the more common are as follows:

- *Protection of the incompetent or the vulnerable.* A truster may wish to set up a trust for a beneficiary who is legally incapable of managing property, or whom the truster believes would not manage the property sensibly.
- *Trusts for the benefit of the public.* A truster may set up a trust fund to be applied to specified public purposes.

---

[2] See *Sharp v Thomson*, 1995 S.C. 455, *per* the Lord President (Hope) at 474–475.
[3] *Heritable Reversionary Co Ltd v Millar* (1892) 19 R. (HL) 43.
[4] *Bain, Petr* (1901) 9 S.L.T. 14.

- *Collective investment purposes.* Trusts provide a convenient means of administering collective investment schemes (such as pension funds), which allow for professional management and diversification of investment to a degree which would not normally be available to individual investors.
- *Tax efficiency.* Manipulation of ownership and control by means of the trust device may be used by a truster in order to minimise liability to taxation.

Classifications of trusts

Trusts are frequently classified in various ways. The following are the two **13–06** most important classifications:

Public and private trusts

Public trusts are those set up for the benefit of the public in general, or a **13–07** specified class of the public. Private trusts are those set up for a specified individual or group of individuals.[5] The most important consequence of this distinction is the procedure for varying trust purposes, as the relevant law differs for the two types of trust.[6]

Inter vivos and mortis causa trusts

An *inter vivos* trust takes effect during the truster's lifetime; a *mortis causa* **13–08** (or "testamentary") trust takes effect on the truster's death.

Key Concepts

A **trust** is created when one person (the truster) transfers property to a second person (the trustee) who is then under an obligation to apply the property for the benefit of a third person (the beneficiary).

It is possible for there to be more than one truster, trustee or beneficiary.

The trustee is the owner of trust property.

Trust property is protected from the insolvency of either the truster or the trustee.

Trusts may be either **private trusts** (for the benefit of individuals or a specified group of individuals) or **public trusts** (for the benefit of the general public or a specified class of the public).

Trusts may be also be either *inter vivos* (taking effect during the truster's lifetime) or *mortis causa* (taking effect on the death of the truster).

---

[5] K.McK. Norrie and E.M. Scobbie, *Trusts* (1991), 17–18.
[6] See below, paras 13–54—13–59 *et seq.*

CREATION OF A TRUST

13–09 The law does not place any specific restrictions on the type of person who may create a trust. The general rules of legal capacity apply, and therefore children under 16—who normally have no legal capacity to enter into any transaction—cannot normally be trusters.[7] Nor are there any legal restrictions on the type of property which can be subject to a trust.

Trusts may be divided into two types—those created voluntarily and those created by legal implication. There are different rules governing the creation of each type of trust.

How to create a trust: voluntarily created trusts

13–10 Two requirements must be satisfied for the creation of a voluntary trust. There must be (a) a declaration of trust, and (b) a transfer of property from the truster to the trustee.

Declaration of trust

13–11 In order to create a trust, A must transfer property to B accompanied by a declaration that B is to apply the property for specified purposes.

The crucial question is this. Did A (i) intend to make an outright gift of the property to B coupled with a recommendation as to how the property should be applied, but ultimately leaving it up to B as to what he chose to do with the property—in which case no trust is created? Or, did A (ii) intend to bind B to apply the property to specified purposes, thus creating a trust?

For example, in one case a woman left money in her will "to Katherine Alexandrina Macpherson, for the benefit of herself and her sister Jane Macpherson". The court held that this was a trust and that Katherine had to administer the money as a trust for herself and Jane (who was mentally incapable).[8] One judge remarked that no "special or technical" form of words was required to create a trust.[9]

The declaration may be verbal—except in the following three cases, where a written document subscribed by the truster is required[10]:

- a trust whereby a person declares himself to be sole trustee of his own property or any property which he may require;
- a trust of an interest in land (except where created by court decree, statute or rule of law);
- a *mortis causa* trust (i.e. one created by a will).

---

[7] Age of Legal Capacity (Scotland) Act 1991, ss.1(1)(a) and 2(1).
[8] *Macpherson v Macpherson's CB* (1894) 21 R. 386.
[9] *Macpherson v Macpherson's CB* (1894) 21 R. 386, *per* Lord McLaren at 387.
[10] See Requirements of Writing (Scotland) Act 1995, s.2.

Transfer of property

A trust will not be effective until the trust property is transferred to the **13–12** trustee. The requirement of a transfer of property is necessary to prevent fraudulent misuse of the trust device:

> ### Allan's Trs v Inland Revenue
> ### 1971 S.L.T. 62
>
> Lord Reid: "I reject the argument ... that a mere proved intention to make a trust coupled with the execution of a declaration of trust can suffice. If that were so it would be easy to execute such a declaration, keep it in reserve, use it in case of bankruptcy to defeat the claims of creditors, but if all went well and the trustee desired to regain control of the fund simply suppress the declaration of trust."

Problem of the truster as trustee

It is possible for a truster to declare himself to be sole trustee of his own **13–13** property. In such a case, it is impossible to transfer property from the truster and the trustee. The recognised alternative is intimation to the beneficiaries (or their representatives) of their rights under the trust.[11]

The intimation must take place simultaneously with, or subsequent to, the execution of the declaration of trust.[12] If it takes place before the declaration of trust, it is merely an expression of an intention to create a trust and is not legally effective. Furthermore, a declaration of trust cannot be made unless there is actually a trust fund in existence. In other words, a person cannot declare themselves trustee of property they intend to acquire in the future.[13]

Validity of the trust purposes

The declaration of trust must specify the purposes of the trust in order to **13–14** be effective. Trust purposes may be invalid for three reasons. First, they may be void from uncertainty. Secondly, they may be overly wide and therefore ineffective. Thirdly, they may be illegal.

Purposes void from uncertainty

Purposes will be void from uncertainty if it is impossible to establish their **13–15** meaning. For example, in one case the purposes of establishing "a shop in which one of the objects is the sale of books dealing with the subject of free thought" was held to be too vague, because the term "free thought" had no "recognised or determinate meaning".[14]

---

[11] *Allan's Trs v Inland Revenue*, 1971 S.L.T. 62.
[12] *Kerr's Trs v Inland Revenue*, 1974 S.L.T. 193.
[13] *Clark Taylor & Co Ltd v Quality Site Development (Edinburgh) Ltd*, 1981 S.C. 111.
[14] *Hardie v Morison* (1899) 7 S.L.T. 42.

Overly wide purposes

13–16 It is not essential for a truster to specify down to the last detail how his trustees should distribute or apply his property. He can choose a "particular class" of individuals or purposes and give his trustees discretion to select between them.[15]

Two things are required for this to work. First, there must be a selection of a "particular individual" (or individuals) as trustee(s). Secondly, the truster must select a "particular class" of individuals and objects.

The selection of a "particular individual" may be problematic in *mortis causa* trusts (those created by a will). In such cases, the trustees named in the testator's will may have died before the testator or may decline office—or the testator may simply fail to name an executor in his will. In such cases, although a person can be appointed to administer the estate for other purposes, the trust purposes will be invalid as being overly wide, and the trust will fail.[16]

Secondly, the "particular class", which should not be so wide as to prevent a reasonable man from knowing who the truster meant to benefit, must be specified by the trustee. It is not enough for a testator to say, for example, that his property should be disposed of "in such way or ways as my trustees shall deem best".[17]

Illegal purposes

13–17 There are four types of purpose which will be held invalid due to illegality, which are as follows[18]:

- criminal purposes;
- directly prohibited purposes;
- purposes which are *contra bonos mores*; and
- purposes which are contrary to public policy.

Each of these will be dealt with in turn.

(i) Criminal purposes

13–18 There is an almost total absence of authority on this issue, and it is doubtful that it is of much practical importance. It is clear, however, that a trust for criminal purposes is void.[19]

(ii) Directly prohibited purposes

13–19 There are three forms of trust purpose which are directly prohibited by statute, as follows:

---

[15] See *Crichton v Grierson* (1828) 3 W. & S. 329.
[16] *Angus's Exrx v Batchan's Trs*, 1949 S.C. 335.
[17] *Allan (Shaw's Trs)* (1893) 1 S.L.T. 308.
[18] *Bowman v Secular Society Ltd* [1917] A.C. 406, *per* Lord Dunedin at 434.
[19] This was accepted in *Bowman v Secular Society Ltd* [1917] A.C. 406.

(a) *Entails*. An entail is a device which was historically used to keep heritable property in the same family indefinitely. The owner would normally be obliged to pass the property to his eldest son on his death, and the son on to his eldest son, and so on. It has not been possible to create entails since 1914,[20] and any entails which continued to exist until recently were finally brought to an end by the Abolition of Feudal Tenure etc. (Scotland) Act 2000.[21]

(b) *Successive liferents*. Successive liferents are similar to entails but can be used in relation to moveable property. A truster might, for example, direct that the trustee is to receive a liferent of the property and hold the fee in trust for his (the trustee's) eldest son, who is then to receive a liferent of the property and hold the fee in trust for his eldest son, and so on. While successive liferents can still be created, their duration can no longer be indefinite thanks to statutory restrictions.[22]

(c) *Excessive accumulations of income*. A truster may not create a trust where the trust income is simply added to the trust fund and not spent for longer than certain periods of time. The applicable period of time is generally 21 years, but there are a number of other possibilities depending on the applicability of certain rather complex statutory provisions.[23]

(iii) Purposes which are *contra bonos mores*

Trust purposes may be invalid as being *contra bonos mores* (an "offence **13–20** against what may be termed the natural moral sense"[24]). This head of invalidity has most commonly been used to hold that conditions attached to bequests in wills are invalid. The cases may be divided into three categories, as follows:

(a) *Conditions relating to living arrangements*. In *Fraser v Rose*,[25] a testator left money to his (adult) daughter on the condition that she should leave her mother within four weeks of his death and never live with her again. It was held that the condition was invalid.

(b) *Conditions relating to marriage*. A condition that a person may only take a benefit under a trust if they remain unmarried is generally thought to be invalid.[26] However, it is competent to

---

[20] Entail (Scotland) Act 1914.
[21] ss.50–52.
[22] For the relevant rules, see the Law Reform (Miscellaneous Provisions) (Scotland) Act 1968 s.18.
[23] Trusts (Scotland) Act 1961 s.5 and the Law Reform (Miscellaneous Provisions) (Scotland) Act 1966 s.6.
[24] *Bowman v Secular Society Ltd* [1917] A.C. 406, *per* Lord Dunedin at 434.
[25] (1849) 11 D. 1466. See also *Grant's Trs v Grant* (1898) 25 R. 929.
[26] *Aird's Exrs v Aird*, 1949 S.C. 154.

establish a trust to provide financial support for a person for as
long as they remain unmarried.[27]

(c) *Conditions relating to religion*. Although there has been some
debate on the point, a truster may provide that a person may
only benefit under a trust if he adheres (or refrains from
adhering) to a particular religion.[28]

Where a condition is held invalid, the beneficiary will normally take the
benefit without being required to comply with the condition.

(iv) Purposes which are contrary to public policy

13–21 The term "public policy" refers here to a very narrow doctrine, which is
that if trust purposes "are unreasonable as conferring neither a patrimonial benefit upon anybody nor a benefit upon the public or any section
thereof, the directions are invalid".[29]

> ## McCaig's Trs v Kirk-Session of United Free Church of Lismore
> ### 1915 S.C. 426
>
> In her will, Catherine McCaig directed that her trustees should
> convert the McCaig Tower in Oban into a private enclosure, and
> should erect bronze statues within the tower of members of her
> family, each of which was to cost not less than £1,000. The trustees
> were to be bound in all time coming not to sell the tower and
> statutes. It was held that these purposes were invalid as conferring
> no benefit on any person: the incidental benefit which might be
> received by workmen in constructing the enclosure was
> insufficient.

There are two exceptional cases, however, where trust purposes may be
valid despite the fact that they do not confer any benefit upon particular
individuals or the general public. These are trusts for memorials,[30] and
trusts for the maintenance of particular animals.[31] Trusts for the benefit
of a class of animals or the prevention of cruelty to animals are regarded
as conferring a benefit upon the general public.[32]

---

[27] See, e.g., *Sturrock v Rankin's Trs* (1875) 2 R. 850.
[28] *Blathwayt v Baron Cawley* [1976] A.C. 397.
[29] *Aitken's Trs v Aitken*, 1927 S.C. 374, *per* Lord Sands at 381.
[30] *Lindsay's Exr v Forsyth*, 1940 S.C. 568, *per* the Lord Justice-Clerk (Aitchison) at 572.
[31] See, e.g., *Flockhart's Trs v Bourlet*, 1934 S.N. 23.
[32] *Aitken's Trs v Aitken*, 1927 S.C. 374, *per* Lord Sands at 381.

How to create a trust: legally implied trusts

Resulting trusts

A resulting trust will arise where the purposes of an existing trust fail to **13–22** dispose of all the trust property. In such a case, the trustees will hold the trust property in a resulting trust for the benefit of the truster or his representatives.

A resulting trust may arise in two principal types of case. First, the trust purposes may be void or impossible to fulfil.[33] Secondly, the trust purposes may not exhaust the full trust estate, as in *Anderson v Smoke*[34] where a trust was created for the benefit of Mr Anderson's son, who died before the fund had been spent.

Constructive trusts

Scots law only recognises "constructive trusts" to a very limited extent. It **13–23** is commonly thought that such trusts will be created in two situations[35]:

(a) *Where a person in a fiduciary position gains an advantage by virtue of that position.* That is, a trustee who in some way profits from his position will be obliged to return any benefit obtained to the trust.[36]

(b) *Where a person who is a stranger to an existing trust is to his knowledge in possession of property belonging to the trust.*[37]

> ### Key Concepts
>
> There are no specific restrictions on the persons who may create a trust or the type of property which may be subject to a trust. The general rules of property and legal capacity apply.
>
> A **voluntarily created trust** is created by (a) a **declaration of trust** accompanied by (b) a **transfer of property** from the truster to the trustee.
>
> Where the truster and the trustee are the same person, there can be no transfer of property. In such cases, **intimation to the beneficiaries** of their rights under the trust is required for the creation of the trust.
>
> Trust purposes may be **invalid** for the following reasons:

[33] See, e.g. *Templeton v Burgh of Ayr*, 1910 2 S.L.T. 12.
[34] (1898) 25 R. 493.
[35] See W.A. Wilson and A.G.M. Duncan, *Trusts, Trustees and Executors* (2nd edn, 1995), para.6–61. This is the orthodox view, but there is considerable debate as to whether "constructive trusts" really exist in Scots law at all: see G.L. Gretton, "Constructive Trusts" (1997) 1 Edin. L.R. 281.
[36] See, e.g. *Cherry's Trs v Patrick*, 1911 2 S.L.T. 313.
[37] One case is *Huisman v Soepboer*, 1994 S.L.T. 682.

- they may be too uncertain (i.e. the truster's meaning cannot be ascertained);
- they may be overly wide;
- they may be illegal as being:
  - contrary to the criminal law;
  - directly prohibited (entails, accumulations of income and successive liferents);
  - *contra bonos mores* (an offence against the "natural moral sense"); or
  - contrary to public policy (if they confer no benefit upon any person).

A **resulting trust** is a type of legally implied trust. It will arise where the purposes of an existing trust fail to dispose of all the trust property. In such a case, the trustees will hold the remaining property in trust for the original truster or his representatives.

A **constructive trust** will be created where:

- a person in a fiduciary position gains an advantage by virtue of that position; or
- a person who is a stranger to a trust is to his knowledge in possession of property belonging to the trust.

In such cases, the constructive trustee will be required to communicate the relevant property to the trust estate.

OFFICE OF TRUSTEE

Who can be a trustee?

13–24 The law does not generally place any specific restrictions on the type of person who may act as trustees. The general rules of legal capacity apply, and therefore children under 16—who, as noted earlier, normally have no legal capacity to enter into any transaction—cannot normally be trustees.[38] Bankruptcy or insolvency is not normally a barrier. There are, however, specific statutory restrictions regarding certain types of trust, particularly charitable trusts.[39]

---

[38] Age of Legal Capacity (Scotland) Act 1991 s.9(f).
[39] Charities and Trustee Investment (Scotland) Act 2005 s.69. See also Pensions Act 1995, ss.3–6 and 29–30 (pension trusts); Finance Act 1989 Sch.5, para.3(3)(c) (employee share ownership trusts) and the Inheritance Tax Act 1984 Sch.4, para.2(ii).

Appointment, assumption, acceptance and resignation of trustees

Trustees will generally be appointed in the trust deed. They may be **13–25** named as individuals, or identified *ex officio* (as the holder of an office). Essentially, any description which is sufficient to identify the relevant individual is enough.[40]

The trustee must accept office. No trustee can be forced to accept office against his will.[41] Acceptance need not necessarily be express but can be inferred from actions.[42]

Trustees always have a power to assume additional trustees unless this is excluded by the terms of the trust deed.[43]

The court has a statutory power to appoint trustees where there is no power to assume additional trustees under the trust deed, or where a sole trustee is or has become insane or incapable, or has been absent from the United Kingdom for six months or has disappeared for that period.[44] The court may also appoint new trustees at common law in exceptional cases. This power has been used where two trustees were unable to work together and the appointment of a third was required to resolve the deadlock.[45]

Trustees normally have a power to resign office unless the trust deed provides otherwise,[46] although a sole trustee is not entitled to resign unless new trustees are appointed.[47]

Removal and death of trustees

The court has a statutory power to remove a trustee who is insane; **13–26** "incapable of acting by reason of physical or mental disability"; has been absent from the United Kingdom continuously for at least six months; or who has disappeared for at least six months.[48] The court also has a common law power to remove a trustee for misconduct in office,[49] but this will only be exercised in exceptional circumstances.[50] Where one of several trustees dies, his share in the trust property passes automatically to the other trustees.[51] The position is more complex where a sole trustee dies. In such cases, the title remains with the sole trustee "and has to be taken out of him by process of conveyancing".[52]

---

[40] See, e.g. *Martin v Ferguson's Trs* (1892) 19 R. 474.
[41] *Vestry of St Silas Church v Trs of St Silas Church*, 1945 S.C. 110, *per* the Lord Justice-Clerk (Cooper) at 121.
[42] *Ker v City of Glasgow Bank* (1879) 6 R. (HL) 52.
[43] Trusts (Scotland) Act 1921 s.3.
[44] Trusts (Scotland) Act 1921 s.22.
[45] *Aikman, Petr* (1881) 9 R. 213; *Taylor, Petr*, 1932 S.C. 1.
[46] Trusts (Scotland) Act 1921 s.3(a).
[47] Trusts (Scotland) Act 1921 s.3.
[48] Trusts (Scotland) Act 1921 s.23.
[49] *Stewart v Chalmers* (1904) 7 F. 163.
[50] *Earl of Cawdor, Petr*, 2006 S.L.T. 1070.
[51] *Gordon's Trs v Eglinton* (1851) 13 D. 1381.
[52] A.J.P. Menzies, *The Law of Scotland Affecting Trustees*, 2nd edn (1913), para.153.

Key Concepts

Trustees may be **appointed** by any description which is sufficient to identify the relevant individual. They must **accept** office; they cannot be forced to do so. Acceptance may be either express or implied.

Trustees always have the power to **assume additional trustees** unless this is excluded by the terms of the trust deed. The court has the power to **appoint additional trustees** in certain cases.

Trustees always have a power to **resign office** unless the trust deed provides otherwise.

The court has the power to **remove** trustees who are insane, incapable, have been absent from the United Kingdom or who have disappeared for at least six months, or who have misconducted themselves in office.

DECISION-MAKING BY TRUSTEES

13–27 As a general rule, trust decisions may validly be made by a majority of trustees.[53]

Importance of a quorum

13–28 A "quorum" is the minimum number of trustees who must participate in trust decision-making for any decisions taken to be valid. Unless the trust deed provides otherwise, the quorum is a "majority of the trustees accepting and surviving".[54]

All trustees have a right to be consulted in trust decision-making. A failure to consult a trustee will render a decision taken by the remaining trustees void.[55] Third parties are, however, protected in such a situation by two factors: (a) the personal liability of trustees who make contracts on behalf of the trust;[56] and (b) s.7 of the Trusts (Scotland) Act 1921, which states that a deed which bears to be granted by trustees but is "in fact executed by a quorum of such trustees in favour of any person other than a beneficiary or co-trustee" shall not normally be challengeable for lack of consultation or other irregularity of procedure.

---

[53] *McCulloch v Wallace* (1846) 9 D. 32. One-half of the body of trustees is insufficient: *Neilson v Mossend Iron Co* (1885) 12 R. 499.
[54] Trusts (Scotland) Act 1921 s.3(c).
[55] *Wyse v Abbott* (1881) 8 R. 983.
[56] See below, para.13–52.

Can the courts interfere in the trustees' exercise of discretion?

The courts will not normally interfere with decisions taken by trustees 13–29
except in very limited circumstances, such as where trustees considered
the wrong question or acted in bad faith.[57] Trustees are not obliged to
give reasons for their decisions.[58]

Key Concepts

Trust decisions may validly be made by a **majority** of trustees.

A **quorum** is a majority of the trustees unless the trust deed
provides otherwise. This is the minimum number of trustees who
must participate in decision-making for any decisions taken to be
valid.

All trustees have a **right to be consulted** in trust decision-
making.

The courts will not **interfere with decisions taken by trustees**
unless it can be shown that they have considered the wrong
question or have acted in bad faith.

DUTIES OF A TRUSTEE

General duty of care

Trustees must, in all cases, exercise due care in their dealings with the 13–30
trust estate. The standard of care required is that of the "ordinary prudent man".[59] A trustee who fails to live up to this standard will be liable
for any loss caused thereby even if he has acted in good faith and to the
best of his abilities.

Duty not to delegate the trust

Trustees must take responsibility for trust decision-making themselves 13–31
and cannot delegate this responsibility to a third party.[60] They are,
however, entitled to employ agents when a person of reasonable prudence
would do so.[61]

Duty to secure trust property

A trustee is responsible for ingathering and securing trust property.[62] 13–32

---

[57] *Board of Management for Dundee General Hospital v Bell's Trs*, 1952 S.C. (HL) 78.
[58] *Scott v National Trust* [1998] 2 All E.R. 705.
[59] *Raes v Meek* (1889) 16 R. (HL) 31.
[60] *Scott v Occidental Petroleum (Caledonia) Ltd*, 1990 S.L.T. 882.
[61] *Hay v Binny* (1861) 23 D. 594. See also Trusts (Scotland) Act 1921 s.4(1)(f).
[62] *Forman v Burns* (1853) 15 D. 362.

Investment duties

13–33 When trustees hold the trust estate for any period of time, they must consider investing the estate to protect its value.

> ### Melville v Noble's Trs
> #### (1896) 24 R. 243
>
> Trustees left a substantial trust fund on deposit-receipt with a bank for 19 years without considering the question of investment. If it had been invested properly, a return of 3 per cent per annum could have been received. It was held that they were liable to make up this 3 per cent return personally.

Trustee investment was until recently subject to restrictive statutory rules. Trustees now have a general power to "make any kind of investment of the trust estate".[63] They must consider whether the investment is a suitable one, and consider the need for diversification of the trust investments. They must also obtain and consider proper advice, except where they reasonably consider that such advice is unnecessary or inappropriate.[64]

The problem of "ethical" investment

13–34 In taking investment decisions, trustees must act in the best interests of the trust beneficiaries. They are not entitled to disregard those interests in favour of other considerations, as the following case demonstrates:

> ### Cowan v Scargill
> #### [1985] Ch. 270
>
> A mineworkers' pension scheme was established under statute. There were 10 trustees, five of which were appointed by the National Union of Mineworkers. The NUM trustees objected to the investment plan on the basis that it involved investment overseas and investment in energies in competition with coal, both of which conflicted with NUM policy. The other trustees sought a declaration that the NUM trustees were in breach of their duties as trustees by demanding that investment decisions be made in accordance with NUM policy. The declaration was granted.

[63] Trusts (Scotland) Act 1921 s.4(1)(ea), as inserted by the Charities and Trustee Investment (Scotland) Act 2005 s.93(2).
[64] Trusts (Scotland) Act 1921 s.4A, as inserted by the Charities and Trustee Investment (Scotland) Act 2005 s.94. There is also a common law duty to take advice: see below, para.13–35.

This decision does not necessarily prevent trustees from taking into account what might be termed "ethical" considerations in making investment decisions. If two investments are equally attractive, there is nothing to stop trustees choosing the one which they consider to be most "ethical".[65] But what they cannot do is choose a *less* attractive investment on the basis of "ethical" factors.

Duty to take advice

It was noted earlier that trustees must administer the trust-estate to the standard that a man of ordinary prudence would exercise in the management of his own affairs. The man of ordinary prudence, of course, recognises that he is not an expert in all matters and must seek professional advice in appropriate cases. A failure to seek such advice may leave the decision open to challenge.[66] **13–35**

Duties regarding existing debts and obligations

While it is unusual for an *inter vivos* trust to have existing debts and obligations, these will exist as a matter of course in *mortis causa* trusts. In such cases, trustees are required to pay off the debts of the deceased, but are not personally liable for those debts.[67] **13–36**

Duties regarding new debts and obligations

In most cases, in order to discharge their duties, trustees will have to enter into contracts with third parties. The general rule is that they incur personal liability in respect of any such contracts, unless they explicitly contract out of such liability.[68] They are, of course, entitled to be reimbursed from the trust-estate.[69] **13–37**

Duty to keep accounts

Trustees must keep accounts which detail their dealings with the trust estate.[70] A beneficiary has a right to see the trust accounts and supporting documentation.[71] Exceptionally, the truster may be regarded as having excluded any duty to keep accounts.[72] **13–38**

---

[65] See *Harries v Church Commissioners for England* [1992] 1 W.L.R. 1241, *per* Nicholls V.C. at 1247–1248.
[66] *Martin v City of Edinburgh District Council*, 1988 S.L.T. 329.
[67] Bankruptcy (Scotland) Act 1985 s.5.
[68] See below, para.13–52.
[69] See below, para.13–41.
[70] *Ross v Ross* (1896) 23 R. (HL) 67.
[71] *Murray v Cameron*, 1969 S.L.T. (Notes) 76; *Nouillan v Nouillan's Exrs*, 1991 S.L.T. 270.
[72] *Leitch v Leitch*, 1927 S.C. 823.

Duty to pay the correct beneficiaries

13–39 A trustee must pay out funds to the correct beneficiaries. If a trustee pays out funds to the wrong beneficiaries, he is obliged to make payment to the correct beneficiary out of his own funds.

Key Concepts

Trustees have the following duties:

- The duty to **exercise due care** in their dealings with the trust estate. The standard of care required is that of the "ordinary prudent man".
- The duty **not to delegate the trust** and to take responsibility for trust decision-making themselves.
- The duty to **secure trust property**.
- The duty to **invest the trust estate** if they hold it for any period of time.
- The duty to **take advice** where it is prudent to do so, particularly in relation to investment matters.
- The duty to **meet trust debts and obligations**.
- The duty to **keep accounts**.
- The duty to **pay the correct beneficiaries**.

RULE AGAINST AUCTOR IN REM SUAM

13–40 *Auctor in rem suam* may be translated as "actor in his own cause". This rule prohibits a trustee from placing himself in a position where his position as trustee conflicts with his interests as an individual.

If a trustee enters into a transaction in breach of the rule, the transaction is voidable regardless of whether he was acting in good faith or whether or not the transaction was a fair one.[73] If he profits from a breach of the rule, he must hand over those profits to the trust-estate regardless of whether the trust-estate has in fact suffered any loss.[74]

The rule has three main consequences:

- Trustees may not enter into transactions with the trust estate.[75]
- Trustees may not use their position to obtain a personal advantage (e.g. if a trustee is given a discretion, he may not exercise it in his favour).[76]
- Trustees may not charge fees for work done for the trust.[77]

---

[73] *Aberdeen Railway Co v Blaikie Bros* (1854) 1 Macq. 461.
[74] *Hamilton v Wright* (1842) 1 Bell 574.
[75] *University of Aberdeen v Town Council of Aberdeen* (1876) 3 R. 1087.
[76] *Inglis v Inglis*, 1983 S.C. 8.
[77] *Home v Pringle* (1841) 2 Rob. 384.

A trustee may, however, be *auctor in rem suam* where this is permitted by the trust deed. The sanction should normally be express, but may be implied.[78] A trustee may also be *auctor in rem suam* if this is permitted by the beneficiaries.[79]

Key Concepts

A trustee may not be ***auctor in rem suam***. This means that he may not place himself in a position where his interests as trustee conflicts with his interests as an individual.

The rule has three main consequences:

● trustees may not enter into transactions with the trust estate;
● trustees may not use their position to obtain a personal advantage; and
● trustees may not charge fees for work done for the trust.

A trustee may, however, be *auctor in rem suam* if this is **sanctioned** in the trust deed or by the beneficiaries.

Trustee's Right to Reimbursement

Trustees are entitled to be reimbursed for monies legitimately spent on **13–41** trust business. They can, of course, apply the trust funds directly to payments which are necessary for the trust—they are not required to pay such expenses themselves and claim reimbursement later.[80]

Key Concept

A trustee is entitled to be **reimbursed** for any expenses properly incurred in administering the trust.

Powers of a Trustee

Trustees may not do any act in furtherance of the trust purposes unless **13–42** they have the power to perform such an act (e.g. a power to sell the trust estate; a power to pay debts, etc.) Trustees' powers may be divided into three categories, as follows:

---

[78] *Sarris v Clark*, 1995 S.L.T. 44.
[79] *Bruckner v Jopp's Trs* (1887) 14 R. 1006.
[80] *Cunningham v Montgomerie* (1879) 6 R. 1333.

- powers granted in the trust deed;
- powers conferred by statutory provisions; and
- common law powers which may be granted upon an application to the court.

The trust-deed must be examined in all instances to establish any other powers it confers upon trustees (and also whether it excludes any of the powers which are otherwise conferred by s.4 of the 1921 Act).

Powers conferred by statutory provisions

13–43 Section 4 of the Trusts (Scotland) Act 1921, as amended by later legislation, contains a list of general powers which all trustees have unless to so act would be "at variance with the terms or purposes of the trust". The principal powers conferred by this section are as follows:

- to sell the trust estate or any part thereof;
- to grant leases of the trust estate or any part thereof;
- to acquire or invest in heritable property;
- to appoint factors and law agents and pay them suitable remuneration;
- to uplift, discharge or assign debts due to the trust estate;
- to grant all deeds necessary for carrying into effect the powers vested in the trustees; and
- to pay trust debts without requiring the creditors to constitute such debts.

Trustees may, of course, only exercise these powers if to do so would further the purposes of the trust.

Occasionally, some of these powers may be specifically excluded by the trust deed. In such cases, the trustees may petition the court under s.5 of the 1921 Act for power to do the relevant act. The court may grant the power if it is "satisfied that such act is in all the circumstances expedient for the execution of the trust".[81]

Common law powers with court application

13–44 Aside from s.5 of the 1921 Act, the court cannot normally grant additional powers to trustees.[82] In exceptional cases, however, where it would be impossible to fulfil the trust purposes without additional powers being granted, the court may be able to intervene.[83]

---

[81] For an example, see *Tod's Trs, Petrs*, 1999 S.L.T. 308.
[82] *Scott's Hospital Trs*, 1913 S.C. 289, *per* the Lord Justice Clerk (Macdonald) at 290–291.
[83] *Anderson's Trs*, 1921 S.C. 315.

Key Concepts

The trust deed is the principal source of trustees' powers, although **there are a number of powers which are conferred by statute upon all trustees** unless they are "at variance with the terms or purposes of the trust". The principal statutory powers are as follows:

- to sell the trust estate or any part thereof;
- to grant leases of the trust estate or any part thereof;
- to acquire with trust funds any interest in residential accommodation "reasonably required to enable the trustees to provide a suitable residence for occupation by any of the beneficiaries";
- to appoint factors and law agents and pay them suitable remuneration;
- to uplift, discharge or assign debts due to the trust estate;
- to grant all deeds necessary for carrying into effect the powers vested in the trustees; and
- to pay trust debts without requiring the creditors to constitute such debts.

If one of these powers is excluded by the trust deed, the trustees may **petition the court** for authority to exercise it.

LIABILITIES OF A TRUSTEE

Liability to beneficiaries

Where a trustee has committed or appears likely to commit a breach of **13–45** trust, various remedies may be open to the beneficiary. The principal remedies for breach of trust are as follows:

(a) Interdict

Where a trustee proposes to do something which a beneficiary believes to **13–46** be a breach of trust, the beneficiary is entitled to seek an interdict. An interdict is a court order prohibiting a person from doing a specified act. If the breach of trust has already taken place, interdict is useless and will not be granted.

(b) Damages

Where a breach of trust has caused a loss to the trust estate, a beneficiary **13–47** may take a court action to require the offending trustee to make up the loss in damages. It is a defence for the trustee(s) to show that the loss would have occurred even if the breach had not taken place.[84]

---

[84] See, e.g. *Millar's Trs v Polson* (1897) 24 R. 1038.

(c) Accounting (count, reckoning and payment)

13–48 A beneficiary may also bring an action of "count, reckoning and pay-ment" (commonly referred to as an action for accounting), calling upon the trustee to produce trust accounts and to make up any shortfall.[85] This should generally have the same practical result as an action for damages, but it may provide a means of ascertaining the amount of any loss where this cannot be otherwise done.

Protecting trustees from liability

13–49 Trustees may receive some protection from liability for breach of trust through an immunity clause in the trust deed or under statute, as follows.

(a) Immunity clauses

13–50 An attempt is sometimes made to protect trustees from liability for breach of trust by inserting an immunity clause into the trust deed stating that they will not be liable for errors or neglect of management. It is thought that such clauses will protect trustees from liability for negli-gence, but not from liability from gross negligence.[86]

(b) Statutory protections

13–51 There are two principal statutory protections from liability under the Trusts (Scotland) Act 1921.

(i) Trustees who have acted "honestly and reasonably". Section 32 of the 1921 Act gives the court a discretion to relieve a trustee from personal liability for a breach of trust if he "has acted honestly and reasonably" and "ought fairly to be excused". Where a trustee has acted honestly and reasonably, it will normally be assumed that it is fair to grant relief.[87]

(ii) Trustees who have committed a breach of trust with the ben-eficiary's consent. Under s.31 of the 1921 Act, if a trustee has com-mitted a breach of trust at the instigation or request or with the written consent of a beneficiary, the court is entitled to apply or of any part of that beneficiary's interest in the trust estate to indemnify the trustee. For s.31 to operate, the beneficiary must have been aware of the facts which made the proposed action a breach of trust.[88]

---

[85] On the duty to keep accounts, see above, para.13–38.
[86] *Lutea Trs Ltd v Orbis Trs Guernsey Ltd*, 1997 S.C.L.R. 735.
[87] *Perrins v Bellamy* [1898] 2 Ch. 521, *per* Kekewich J. at 528.
[88] See *Cathcart's Trs v Cathcart* (1907) 15 S.L.T. 646; *Henderson v Henderson's Trs* (1900) 2 F. 1295.

Liability to third parties

Trustees will commonly, in order to discharge their responsibilities as **13–52** trustees, enter into contracts with third parties. As a general rule, they are personally liable on such contracts unless there is an agreement to exclude such liability.[89] Where a person signs a contract "as trustee", this will generally be taken as indicating such an agreement.[90] The mere use of the word "trustee" is not sufficient, as this may be intended only to describe or identify the signatory.[91] Personal liability is generally only of importance if the trust fund is or becomes insolvent.

Third parties who acquire trust property

Where a trustee, acting in breach of trust, sells trust property to a third **13–53** party, that third party will acquire a good title to the property provided that he purchased the property in good faith and for value.[92]

Key Concepts

Where a trustee has committed or appears likely to commit a breach of trust, the following remedies may be open to the beneficiaries:

- interdict (a court order preventing the trustee from doing a particular act);
- an action for damages; and
- an action for accounting (a combination of an action to produce accounts and for payment of any shortfall in the trust funds).

Trustees may be protected from liability by **immunity clauses** in the trust deed providing that they are not to be liable for negligence.

Trustees who commit a breach of trust but who have acted **honestly and reasonably** may apply to the court to be relieved from the consequences of their breach of trust.

Trustees who commit a breach of trust at the request of or with the consent of a beneficiary may apply to the court to be **indemnified** by that beneficiary's interest in the trust estate.

Trustees will be **personally liable to third parties** on contracts which they make on behalf of the trust unless they have contracted out of such liability.

Third parties who acquire trust property **in good faith and for value** will receive a good title to the property even if the trustee was acting in breach of trust.

---

[89] *Brown v Sutherland* (1875) 2 R. 615.
[90] *Gordon v Campbell* (1842) 1 Bell 428.
[91] *Thomson v McLachlan's Trs* (1829) 7 S. 787; *Lumsden v Buchanan* (1865) 3 M. (HL) 89.
[92] Hume, *Lectures* (1821–1822) (G.C.H. Paton ed., Stair Society, Vol.17, 1952), Vol.IV, 315; Trusts (Scotland) Act 1961 s.2.

VARIATION OF TRUST PURPOSES

13–54 A trust, by its very nature, severely limits the manner in which the property which is subject to it may be held and applied. Circumstances change, and what appears appropriate when the trust is established may cease to be appropriate with the passage of time. The scope which exists for varying the terms of the trust differs according to whether the trust is private or public.[93]

Private trusts

13–55 At common law, variation of the terms of a private trust is competent if all the beneficiaries consented to the variation. However, not all the beneficiaries may be capable of consenting. For example, the beneficiaries may include children, or the trust deed may even make provision for persons who have not yet been born (and who may never be).

The matter is now dealt with by the Trusts (Scotland) Act 1961. Section 1 of the Trusts (Scotland) Act 1961 enables the court to give consent to a variation on behalf of:

  (a) any person who is incapable of consenting by reason of nonage or other disability;
  (b) any person who is not currently a beneficiary but may become one on the happening of a future event or on a particular date, unless that person is currently ascertained and is capable of assenting; or
  (c) any unborn person.

The court is not entitled to approve the arrangement on behalf of any person "unless it is of the opinion that the carrying out thereof would not be prejudicial to that person".[94]

The court is not obliged to grant approval simply because a proposed variation is shown not to be prejudicial.[95] The court has a discretion and will take into account all relevant circumstances including the relative benefits which the various parties would gain from the variation.[96]

Public trusts

13–56 There are two mechanisms available for varying the terms of a public trust. These are, first, the common law *cy-près* jurisdiction, and secondly, variation under s.9(1) of the Law Reform (Miscellaneous Provisions) (Scotland) Act 1990. Variation under the 1990 Act is only possible where the trust has already taken effect in some form. It is not permitted where it is impossible to give any effect to the terms of the trust. *Cy-près* is

---

[93] On this distinction generally, see above, para.13–07.
[94] Trusts (Scotland) Act 1961 s.1(1). For an application of this rule, see *Pollok-Morris, Petrs*, 1969 S.L.T. (Notes) 60.
[95] *Lobnitz, Petr*, 1966 S.L.T. (Notes) 81.
[96] *Goulding v James* [1997] 2 All E.R. 239; *Lobnitz, Petr*, 1966 S.L.T. (Notes) 81.

available in both cases, but much stricter criteria must be met for this power to be available.

The criteria which must be satisfied in order for the court to sanction variation are therefore different depending on whether the case involves "initial failure" (where it was never possible to give effect to the trust) or "subsequent failure" (where the trust was initially given effect to but later failed).

Initial failure

Variation in such cases must be under the *cy-près* jurisdiction. In such **13–57** cases, two factors must be established for variation to be permissible:

- a "general charitable intention" on the part of the truster; and
- failure of the trust purposes (impossibility).

In determining whether the truster had a "general charitable intention", the court must ask whether his object was "to establish a charity for the benefit of a certain class with a particular mode of doing it? Or was the mode of application such an essential part of the gift that it is not possible to distinguish any general purpose of charity?"[97] The distinction is illustrated by the following case:

Hay's J.F. v Hay's Trs
1952 S.C. (HL) 29

A testatrix directed in her will that her trustees should maintain a mansion-house "under the style and designation of 'The Hay Memorial'" as a hospital on Shetland. The funds available under the trust-deed were insufficient to maintain the house for this purpose. The trustees applied to the court for a variation of the trust purposes under the *cy-près* jurisdiction. Held, that *cy-près* was not available as no general charitable intention existed. It was clear that the use of the house as the "Hay Memorial" was an essential part of the testatrix's intention. If this was not possible, there was no general purpose of charity to fall back on.

Subsequent failure

In cases of subsequent failure, it is not necessary to establish a general **13–58** charitable intention. It is only necessary to establish impossibility (in which case *cy-près* may be invoked) or one of the statutory grounds under s.9(1) of the Law Reform (Miscellaneous Provisions) (Scotland) Act 1990, which are:

---

[97] *Burgess' Trs v Crawford*, 1912 S.C. 387, *per* Lord Mackenzie at 398.

"(a) that the purposes of the trust, whether in whole or in part—

    (i) have been fulfilled as far as it is possible to do so; or

    (ii) can no longer be given effect to, whether in accordance with the directions or spirit of the trust deed or other document constituting the trust or otherwise;

(b) that the purposes of the trust provide a use for only part of the property available under the trust;

(c) that the purposes of the trust were expressed by reference to—

    (i) an area which has, since the trust was constituted, ceased to have effect for the purpose described expressly or by implication in the trust deed or other document constituting the trust; or

    (ii) a class of persons or area which has ceased to be suitable or appropriate, having regard to the spirit of the trust deed or other document constituting the trust, or as regards which it has ceased to be practicable to administer the property available under the trust; or

(d) that the purpose of the trust, whether in whole or in part, have, since the trust was constituted—

    (i) been adequately provided for by other means; or

    (ii) ceased to be such as would enable the trust to become a recognised body [a charity]; or

    (iii) ceased in any other way to provide a suitable and effective method of using the property available under the trust, having regard to the spirit of the trust deed or other document constituting the trust."

In cases involving small public trusts (those having an annual income not exceeding £5,000) where one of these conditions is satisfied, the trustees may vary the purposes of such a trust, transfer its assets to another public trust, or amalgamate it with one or more public trusts without the necessity of court application, provided that the Lord Advocate does not object.[98]

What can the court do once the variation jurisdiction is triggered?

13–59 Once the criteria for variation have been met, the court may approve a scheme for the variation of the trust. In doing so, the court will adhere to the "principle of approximation". This means that the objects of the varied trust must "approximate as closely as may be" to those which were originally selected by the truster.[99] As part of variation, the court may

---

[98] Law Reform (Miscellaneous Provisions) (Scotland) Act 1990 s.10; Public Trusts (Reorganisation) (Scotland) (No.2) Regulations 1993 (SI 1993/2036).
[99] *Stranraer Original Secession Corporation*, 1923 S.C. 722, *per* the Lord President (Clyde) at 725.

transfer trust funds to another body,[100] widen the class of persons who are entitled to benefit from the trust,[101] or extend the powers of the trustees.[102]

Key Concepts

In some cases, it may be desirable to **vary the purposes** of a trust.

In **private trusts**, the basic principle is that variation is possible with the consent of all the beneficiaries. Where a person who is or may be a beneficiary is unable to consent to a variation, the court may consent on their behalf provided that it is satisfied the variation would not be **prejudicial** to that person.

Where it has never been possible to give effect to the terms of a **public trust** (**initial failure**), the court may apply *cy-près* to vary the terms of the trust provided that a **general charitable intention** on the part of the truster can be shown and that it is **impossible** to give effect to the trust purposes.

Where it has been possible initially to give effect to the terms of a public trust (cases of **subsequent failure**), *cy-près* may be applied if it has become **impossible** to give effect to the trust purposes. It is not necessary to show a general charitable intention in such cases. Variation may also be possible under s.9 of the Law Reform (Miscellaneous Provisions) (Scotland) Act 1990 if the trust purposes have become in some way inappropriate—s.9 lays down criteria which must be satisfied for variation under this section.

Where grounds for variation of a public trust have been established, the court may **vary the purposes** of the trust, **transfer trust funds** to another body, or **extend the powers** of the trustees.

TERMINATION OF A TRUST

This section considers the circumstances in which a trust may be brought **13–60** to an end.

Revocation by the truster

Because a *mortis causa* trust is not effective until the testator's death, it is **13–61** open to the testator to revoke his will and prevent the trust from even taking effect.

An *inter vivos* trust is only irrevocable if the following conditions are satisfied:

---

[100] See, e.g. *Clyde Industrial Training Ship Association*, 1925 S.C. 676.
[101] See, e.g. *Trs of Carnegie Park Orphanage* (1892) 19 R. 605.
[102] *McCrie's Trs*, 1927 S.C. 556.

- there must be an ascertained beneficiary (if the only ascertained beneficiary is the truster himself, the trust remains revocable);[103] and
- the beneficiary must have an "immediate beneficial interest" (called a *jus quaesitium*). If the beneficiary's interest depends on a particular event taking place, then the trust is revocable,[104] unless all that is required is that the beneficiary survive to a specified date.[105]

If these conditions are not satisfied, the truster is entitled to revoke the trust.

Termination by the trustees

13–62 The trustees may bring the trust to an end by fulfilling the trust purposes and distributing the trust estate.

Termination by the beneficiaries

13–63 There are two relevant principles here. First, if all the beneficiaries in a private trust consent to the termination of a trust, the trustees must normally comply, except where termination would prejudice the proper administration of the trust.[106] Secondly, according to the case of *Miller's Trs v Miller*,[107] a beneficiary who has acquired a right in fee to property is entitled to insist that the trustees transfer the property to him absolutely, even if they have instructions to the contrary.

Key Concepts

Trusts may be **terminated** in a number of ways.
  By the **truster**:

- Because a *mortis causa* trust does not take effect until the testator's death, it is normally open to the testator to revoke his will at any time before his death and prevent the trust ever taking effect.
- An *inter vivos* trust may be revoked by the truster unless (a) there is an ascertained beneficiary (other than the truster himself), and (b) that beneficiary has an "immediate beneficial interest".

---

[103] *Bertram's Trs v Bertram*, 1909 S.C. 1238.
[104] *Bulkeley-Gavin's Trs v Bulkeley-Gavin's Trs*, 1971 S.C. 209 (benefit contingent on the wholesale nationalisation of land).
[105] *Robertson v Robertson's Trs* (1892) 19 R. 849.
[106] See, e.g. *De Robeck v Inland Revenue*, 1928 S.C. (HL) 34 (termination would have prejudiced taxation arrangements).
[107] (1890) 18 R. 301.

By the **trustees**: the **trustees** may terminate a trust by fulfilling the trust purposes and distributing the trust estate.
By the **beneficiaries**:

- In a private trust, all the beneficiaries acting together may compel the termination of a trust.
- A beneficiary who has acquired a right in fee to property is normally entitled to insist that the trustees pass the property to him absolutely.

▼ CHAPTER SUMMARY

THE TRUST CONCEPT

1. A trust involves three roles: a truster, trustee and a beneficiary.   **13–63**
2. The truster is the person who sets up the trust; the trustee is the person who owns and administers the property; the beneficiary is the person for whose benefit the property is administered.
3. These are *roles* rather than *persons*: the same person can hold more than one of these roles, and there can be more than one person in each role.
4. There are various practical advantages to the trust device, mainly because it allows a separation of *benefit* from property from the *control* of that property. Some of these advantages could be achieved by other legal devices, but the one unique advantage of the trust is that it protects against insolvency: if the trustee is made bankrupt, the trust property cannot be used to pay off his debts.

PUBLIC AND PRIVATE TRUSTS

1. Trusts may be either public or private: that is, for the benefit of the public as whole (or a specific section of the public), or for a defined group of individuals.

CREATING A TRUST

1. A trust is created by (a) declaring the trust, and (b) transferring property from the truster to the trustee. Trusts can also be created by "legal implication" in some circumstances.

    ➤ *Allan's Trs v Inland Revenue* (1971): to create a trust, delivery of the property, or some equivalent to delivery, is essential.

2. Where the truster and trustee are the same person, there must be some "equivalent of delivery" to create the trust. This will

normally take the form of intimating the rights created by the trust
to the beneficiaries.

3. In order to be valid, trust purposes must not be (a) too uncertain,
    (b) too wide, or (c) illegal.

    ➤ *McCaig's Trs v Kirk-Session of United Free Church of Lis-
      more* (1915): a trust to create a private enclosure with inor-
      dinately expensive statutes was invalid because it conferred
      no benefit on anyone.

TRUST ADMINISTRATION

1. Trust decision-making is by a majority of trustees, unless the trust
    deed provides otherwise.

DUTIES AND POWERS OF TRUSTEES

1. Trustees have a number of general duties which are implied by law.
    The most important of these is to exercise due care in their deal-
    ings with the trust estate.
2. Trustees are also under a duty not to delegate the trust (that is, to
    take responsibility for decision-making themselves); to secure trust
    property; to invest trust property; to take advice where appro-
    priate; to meet trust debts and obligations; to keep accounts; and to
    pay the correct beneficiaries.

    ➤ *Melville v Noble's Trs* (1896): trustees who failed to invest
      trust property were liable personally to pay the money that
      could have been earned if it had been invested.

3. Trustees must not be *auctor in rem suam* (actors in their own
    cause). This means they must not put themselves in a position
    where their personal interests are in conflict with their position as
    trustee. Specifically, this means they (a) cannot contract with the
    trust estate; (b) cannot obtain a personal advantage from their
    position as trustee; and (c) cannot charge for work done for the
    trust.

    ➤ *Cowan v Scargill* (1985): pension fund trustees could not use
      their position to further the aims of the National Union of
      Mineworkers, but had to restrict their considerations to the
      best interests of the beneficiaries.

4. A trustee may be *auctor in rem suam* if this is sanctioned in the
    trust deed or by the beneficiaries.
5. The powers of a trustee may be set out in the trust deed, or the
    trustee may rely on general powers which are set out in s.4 of the
    Trusts (Scotland) Act 1921. These general powers may, however,
    be excluded by the terms of the trust deed.

> Trusts (Scotland) Act 1921, s.4: sets out various general powers which all trustees have unless they would be "at variance with the terms and purposes of the trust".

REMEDIES FOR BREACH OF TRUST

1. **Where trustees are in breach of trust or plan to do something which would be a breach, the principal remedies open to the beneficiaries are: (a) interdict (a court order which prohibits a person from a specific act); (b) an action for damages; or (c) an action for "accounting".**

TRUSTEES' LIABILITY TO THIRD PARTIES

1. **If trustees enter into contracts on behalf of the trust, they are personally liable on these contracts unless there is an agreement to the contrary. Signing contracts "as trustee" is enough to imply such an agreement.**

VARIATION OF TRUSTS

1. **The purposes of a private trust may be varied by consent of all the beneficiaries. Where a beneficiary is unable to consent, the court may be asked to consent on their behalf. The court cannot do this unless satisfied that the variation would not be "prejudicial" to that person.**

   > Trusts (Scotland) Act 1961, s.1: where a beneficiary (or potential beneficiary) is unable to consent to a proposed variation of a private trust, this section gives the court a discretionary power to consent on their behalf.

2. **The purposes of a public trust may be varied by way of a court application. Where the trust is a small one, it may be possible to avoid the need for a court application by following alternative statutory procedures.**

3. **Where it has never been possible to give effect to the purposes of a public trust, an application for variation must be under the *cy-près* jurisdiction. It must be shown that (a) the truster had a "general charitable intention", and (b) that the purposes set out in the trust are impossible.**

   > *Hay's J.F. v Hay's Trs* (1952): where Ms Hay wished her trustees to maintain a mansion-house as a hospital named the "Hay Memorial", but there were insufficient funds to do this, there was no "general charitable intention". This is

because it was clear that the use of the house as the "Hay Memorial" was an essential part of her intention.

4. **Where it has been possible to give effect to the purposes of a public trust, an application for variation may be made under the broader grounds set out in the statute.**

> ➤ Law Reform (Miscellaneous Provisions) (Scotland) Act 1990 s.9: makes statutory provision for the variation of the purposes of a public trust.

TERMINATION OF TRUSTS

1. **A trust may be terminated primarily by (a) the trustees fulfilling the trust purposes and bringing the trust to an end, or (b) by the beneficiaries acting together to compel its termination.**

? QUICK QUIZ

Basic concepts and the creation of a trust

- What is a trust?
- Who owns trust property?
- How is a voluntary trust created?
- What restrictions does Scots law place on the validity of trust purposes?

Trustees and trust management

- Must trust decisions be taken unanimously?
- What general duties does the law impose on trustees?
- What is meant by the rule against *auctor in rem suam*?
- What are the sources of trustees' powers?

Trustees' liabilities

- When a trustee has been in breach of trust, what remedies are open to the beneficiaries?
- How may trustees be protected from liability for breach of trust?
- Are trustees personally liable on trust contracts?

Variation of trust purposes

- What requirements must be satisfied before the terms of a private trust can be varied? To what extent is the court involved in this process?

📖 FURTHER READING

The leading textbook on the Scottish law of trusts is W.A. Wilson and A.G.M. Duncan, *Trusts, Trustees and Executors,* 2nd edn (1995). It is a detailed reference work but is generally unsuitable for someone who is approaching the subject for the first time. There are relatively few student textbooks on the subject. The most recent is a cases and materials book: J. Chalmers, *Trusts: Cases and Materials* (2002). There is one textbook: K.McK. Norrie and E.M. Scobbie, *Trusts* (1991). R.R.M. Paisley, *Trusts LawBasics* (1999) is a very brief introduction to the subject.

🖱 RELEVANT WEBLINKS

The Scottish Law Commission (*http://www.scotlawcom.gov.uk*) currently regards the reform of the law of trusts as a long-term project and has published six discussion papers and one report on various aspects of the law of trusts between 2003 and 2008.

Chapter 14   Choice of Business Medium

DAVID CABRELLI[1]

▶ CHAPTER OVERVIEW

14–01 This chapter concentrates on the legal forms which are available to a person who is seeking to carry on a business. First, we consider the concept of the sole trader and the implications of running a business through this medium. The chapter goes on to consider the principal characteristics of business forms provided by the law which enable more than one person to come together to carry on a business, e.g. the partnership or "firm", the registered company and the Limited Liability Partnership ("LLP"). Finally, the chapter examines the advantages and disadvantages of each of these business forms and offers insights into the approach a person or persons should take when deciding which form to select.

✓ OUTCOMES

14–02 At the end of this chapter you should be able to understand:

- ✓ the implications of conducting business as, and the principal characteristics of, a sole trader;
- ✓ the implications of conducting business as, and the principal characteristics of, a partnership or LLP;
- ✓ the implications of conducting business as, and the principal characteristics of, a registered company;
- ✓ the differences between conducting business as a sole trader, partnership, LLP and registered company;
- ✓ the merits and demerits of conducting business as a sole trader, partnership or registered company; and
- ✓ the meaning and importance of concepts such as personal liability, limited liability, separate legal personality, the division between ownership and control and perpetual succession.

---

[1] Lecturer in Commerical Law, University of Edinburgh.

THE SOLE TRADER

An individual who wishes to carry on a business may choose to run his/ **14–03**
her business as a sole trader. By definition, it is only that individual
person which is involved in the management and control of the business.
Thus, the sole trader business form is not suitable where a group of
persons wish to come together to carry on a business and, by definition, a
sole trader will be a small business. Only the sole trader has the right to
manage the business and only he or she is the owner of the capital of the
business. So there is no separation between the ownership and the control
of the business of the sole trader. Thus, if the business is valued by the
sole trader's accountant at £50,000, it is only the sole trader who will have
the right to receive that sum in the event that the business of the sole
trader is sold at that price to a third party on the open market. The sole
trader also has the sole right to participate in the profits of the business.
However, if the business makes a loss in a particular financial year, it is
the sole trader who will require to bear those losses—no-one else. The
debts of the business are not separated from the sole trader's own personal debts and income. That is because the individual can in no way be
separated from the business: the two are indissoluble and the sole trader
business form possesses no separate legal personality. This means that the
sole trader is personally liable for the debts of the business. So if the
business has debts of £50,000 owing to its creditors, the sole trader is
personally liable for those debts. For example, if the business has only
£10,000 of funds and assets, the sole trader will be required to meet the
shortfall of £40,000 from his own personal funds. If the sole trader refuses
or is unable to meet that shortfall, the creditors of the sole trader's
business have the power to petition the court for the sequestration of the
sole trader. In such circumstances, the personal assets of the sole trader
can be secured and sold by the trustee in sequestration (appointed to the
estate of the sole trader) in order to meet the debts of the business.

The sole trader business form is characterised by a large degree of
informality and privacy. There are no registration requirements or other
formalities involved in operating as a sole trader. The law imposes no
such initial or continuing requirements. Moreover, there is no legal
requirement for a sole trader to produce or publish accounts and financial records. Depending on the size of the sole trader's annual turnover
(i.e. its annual total sales), it may or may not require to keep records for
the purposes of VAT. Finally, when the individual sole trader dies, the
assets of the business are distributed alongside the personal assets of the
individual in accordance with the law of succession contained in the
Succession (Scotland) Act 1964. The death of the sole trader heralds the
automatic cessation of the business.

One area where formalities are imposed on sole traders by law is in the
area of business names. The Business Names Act 1985 ("BNA") applies
to sole traders who are trading under a name other than their own personal name. For example, an electrician called Albert Winkle trading
under the name "Sparks Flying" would fall within the compass of the
BNA, but John Winterton the florist trading under the name "John

Winterton's Blossoms" would not require to comply with the BNA's requirements. Under s.4 of the BNA, traders must specify their name and address on all business letters, written orders for goods or services to be supplied to the business, invoices and receipts issued in the course of the business and written demands for payment of debts arising in the course of the business. Both civil and criminal liability attaches to those sole traders who fail to comply. The purpose of s.4 of the BNA is to enable the creditors, suppliers and contractors of the sole trader to identify the "owners" of the business. It is worth noting that the BNA will be replaced by the provisions of ss.1200–1208 of the Companies Act 2006 when the latter finally come into force. The provisions in the Companies act 2006 are broadly similar to those contained in the BNA. At the time of writing, the anticipated implementation date of the relevant sections of the Companies Act 2006 was October 1, 2009.

Key Concepts

A sole trader is an individual who carries on a business on an individual basis in his own name or some other name. The sole trader owns and manages the business, enjoys the profits of the business and bears the losses of the business. The sole trader is personally liable for the debts of the business.

THE PARTNERSHIP: AN INTRODUCTION

14–04 Unlike the sole trader, the partnership vehicle is well-suited towards the joining together of a number of persons for the purposes of carrying on a business. In the case of a partnership, a number of individuals, namely the partners, voluntarily agree to combine for a common purpose and thus form a partnership business. Each of those individuals will contribute capital investment, skills, know-how, expertise and contacts and pool those resources as a means of selling products or services. Each partner has the right to participate in the business of the partnership and is an agent of the partnership firm, with the ability to bind the firm in law. Partnership businesses range from very small organisations, such as two partners running a local store, to large international firms of solicitors and accountants. Some regulatory bodies require that their members operate through a partnership, such as dentists.[2]

---

[2] Dentists Act 1984 ss.80 and 81.

SEPARATE LEGAL PERSONALITY AND CONTINUITY

For the purposes of Scots law, s.4(2) of the Partnership Act 1890 provides **14–05** that a partnership firm possesses separate legal personality, i.e. that it is a legal body distinct from its constituent partners.[3] Since the firm enjoys separate legal personality, it can enter into binding contracts in its own name and it has the power to sue and be sued in its own name. It can commit delicts and own property, taking title to heritable property in its own name in terms of s.70 of the Abolition of Feudal Tenure (Scotland) Act 2000. Since the partnership is a separate legal personality, one might assume that it would survive the death or bankruptcy of any of its constituent partners. However, this is not the case. Section 33(1) of the Partnership Act 1890 provides that the death or bankruptcy of a partner automatically dissolves the partnership.[4] Moreover, whether the partnership continues to exist on a change in the membership of its partners, e.g. the assumption of a new partner or the retiral or resignation of an existing partner, is not altogether wholly clear.[5]

THE PARTNERSHIP ACT 1890

The partnership is regulated by the Partnership Act 1890 ("the Act"). The **14–06** Act provides a definition of a partnership and provides for various legal relationships and scenarios which, while resembling a partnership, are excluded from the definition. The basic definition of a partnership is contained in s.1(1) of the Act which provides that a partnership "is the relation which subsists between persons carrying on a business in common with a view of profit". Thus, the parties must have the objective of realising a profit in coming together to form a business. However, the Act includes exceptions and these exceptions will be analysed in more detail in Chapter 15. The Act contains rules which govern and regulate partnerships. Those rules can be divided into the following broad categories:

- the nature of a partnership—ss.1–4;
- the relationship between the partnership and third parties and the liability of the partners to third parties—ss.5–18;
- property owned by the partnership—s.20;
- the duties of partners, the relations of partners to one another and the regulation of the internal affairs of the partnership—ss.19–31; and
- the dissolution of the partnership and the distribution of assets on dissolution—ss.32–44.

---

[3] The position in English law is different.
[4] However, this is subject to agreement to the contrary in the partnership agreement. See the terms of s.33(1) of the Partnership Act 1890.
[5] See F. Davidson and L. MacGregor, *Commercial Law in Scotland*, 2nd edn (W. Green, 2008), p.393 and Joint Law Commission and Scottish Law Commission Report, Partnership Law (Cm 6015) (Law Com 283 and Scot Law Com No. 192) at para.8.7, p.107.

THE ADVANTAGES OF THE PARTNERSHIP

14–07 One of the advantages of running a business through the medium of a partnership is that there are very few formalities or administrative requirements involved in its creation or continuing operation. For example, there is no requirement for a partnership to be constituted in writing. Moreover, there is no need to notify any public registry of any changes in the composition of the membership of a partnership. A partnership does not require to file accounts or details of its financial affairs on a continuing basis. However, there is one exception. That is to say that a partnership must comply with the provisions of the Business Names Act 1985 where the partnership is trading under a name other than the personal names of the partners. Thus, the names and addresses of all partners of the partnership must be stated in legible characters on all business letters, written orders for goods or services to be supplied to the business, invoices and receipts issued in the course of the business and written demands for payment of debts arising in the course of the business. If a partner fails to comply with the provisions of the BNA, they are subject to civil and criminal sanctions if found liable. The BNA will be replaced by ss.1200 to 1208 of the Companies Act 2006 when the latter comes into force. At the time of writing the anticipated implementation date of the relevant sections of the Companies Act 2006 was October 1, 2009.

Allied to the lack of formalities and administration is the advantage of privacy. There is no requirement for a partnership to publicise the management of its internal affairs, e.g. how the votes of partners on partnership matters are to be weighted, how profits are shared by the partners (e.g. the profit percentages per partner), etc. A partnership is not obliged to disclose its financial affairs. One of the causes of the advantage of privacy is the lack of complexity of partnership law. In comparison with the limited liability company incorporated under the Companies Acts, the partnership is regulated very loosely. The light touch regulation of the Act is complemented by the fact that a partnership may disapply all or some of the provisions of that Act by agreement. The lack of complexity leads to low compliance costs and expenses which is another advantage over the incorporated company. It also ensures that the partnership model benefits from the advantage of flexibility. In other words, given the absence of formalities, the partnership vehicle is more responsive to changes in underlying economic or market conditions.

THE DISADVANTAGES OF THE PARTNERSHIP

14–08 Of course, the benefits associated with the partnership model are offset, and one might argue overshadowed, by certain disadvantages. The first disadvantage is the absence of any division between its ownership and control. The provisions of the Act countenance little scope for such an innovation. The chief culprit is s.24(5) of the Act which states that every partner is entitled to take part in the management of the partnership.

Thus, a partner who contributes capital to the firm has a prima facie entitlement to participate in management. The effect is that the introduction of a passive investor who does not intend to involve himself in the day-to-day affairs of the partnership requires the partnership to oust the terms of s.24(5) of the Act at cost. This can be contrasted with a limited liability company where there is a natural division between ownership, i.e. investors and control, i.e. management. Companies can offer shares in return for capital investment with no requirement for the investor to take part in the management of the company. This is difficult to achieve in the case of a partnership as a result of (i) the provisions of s.24(5) of the Act, and (ii) the inability of partnerships to issue transferable shares to investors. Transferable shares make a company attractive to investors since they can purchase shares and sell them to third parties at market value as and when they please. Another consequence of the absence of a division between ownership and control in the case of a partnership is that it is more difficult for a partnership to introduce specialised outside management to control its affairs. This is the case since partners can only be introduced to manage a partnership in return for a contribution to the capital of the firm. In the case of a company, it is not necessary for new management to make a capital contribution.

A second disadvantage of the partnership is the absence of limited liability of the partners for the debts of the partnership. Sections 9 and 12 of the Act provide that the partners are jointly and severally liable for the debts of the partnership. In practice, what this means is that a creditor who is owed £100,000 from the partnership in the following scenario can sue all of the partners or some or one of the partners (of the creditor's own choice) to recover the shortfall of £90,000:

- Partnership assets—worth £10,000;
- Partner 1—personal assets worth £40,000;
- Partner 2—personal assets worth £50,000; and
- Partner 3—personal assets worth £230,000.

Meanwhile, the members of a company incorporated under the Companies Acts would have limited liability in the above scenario, the extent of their liability being limited to the value of (i) any value remaining unpaid on their shares (in an incorporated company limited by shares); or (ii) guarantee (in the case of an incorporated company limited by guarantee). A consequence of the lack of limited liability in the case of the partnership is that partners and their personal assets are left exposed to attack from the creditors of the partnership, whereas in the case of a company, the members do not have such concerns.[6]

Another disadvantage of the partnership is that it does not possess the benefit of perpetual succession. Whenever a partner dies or becomes bankrupt, the partnership ceases to exist. If the remaining partners

---

[6] Although, in practice, more sophisticated creditors of a company (such as banks and other lenders) will demand and obtain personal guarantees from certain members of the company in respect of the company's indebtedness towards them.

continue to trade, the law treats a new partnership as having been created. This can be distinguished from the position in the case of an incorporated company. The incorporated company continues to exist notwithstanding any change in the composition of its membership or management (i.e. the identity of its shareholders or directors). On the face of it, the cessation of a partnership and the constitution of a new partnership on the death or bankruptcy of a partner may seem inconsequential. However, this overlooks the significance of such an event. Of most importance is the accounting and taxation treatment of the old and new partnership and, in turn, the financial and tax position of the partners. The interruption of continuity in the affairs of the partnership results in extra costs and complications from an accountancy and taxation perspective which would not have arisen in the case of a change of membership or management in a company.

The final disadvantage of the partnership is its inability to grant a floating charge. A company can grant a floating charge to a creditor as a security for loans advanced to it by creditors and debts owed by it to creditors. Essentially, a floating charge is a security which is granted over the whole assets and undertaking of the company. When it is created, the charge "hovers" over those assets and the company can sell its assets in the ordinary course of business without the consent of the creditor/chargeholder. It is only when a liquidator or receiver is appointed over the assets and undertaking of the company that the charge is said to "crystallise". When the charge crystallises, the charge becomes fixed and the liquidator or receiver is entitled to ingather and sell the assets in order to meet the debts which the company owed to the creditor/chargeholder. Since partnerships are not permitted to grant a floating charge, there is the possibility that a creditor may decide not to advance funding to a partnership on the same terms and conditions as a company which makes the cost of borrowing more expensive.

Key Concepts

Advantages of the partnership: (1) the lack of formalities in constituting and operating a partnership; (2) no requirement to make public the internal affairs and financial performance of the partnership; (3) lack of complexity in managing the partnership; (4) low costs of compliance with law; and (5) flexibility in the affairs and management of the partnership.

Disadvantages of the partnership: (1) the lack of a separation between ownership and control in the partnership; (2) the absence of transferable shares which can be issued to investors; (3) the difficulty in removing existing management and introducing specialised management to run the partnership; (4) the joint and several liability of the partners for the debts of the partnership; (5) the lack of perpetual succession; and (6) the inability of a partnership to grant a floating charge.

THE COMPANY: AN INTRODUCTION

Like a partnership governed by the Partnership Act 1890, a company is **14–09** well-suited towards the joining together of a number of persons for the purposes of carrying on a business. In the case of a company, a number of individuals, namely the members, voluntarily agree to combine for a common purpose and thus form a company as a means of carrying on business. Each of those individuals will contribute capital investment, skills, know-how, expertise and contacts and pool those resources as a means of selling products or services. In terms of ss.7–16 of the Companies Act 2006 ("CA 2006"), a company is formed by registration with the Registrar of Companies and is incorporated when the Registrar has issued a document to the company called a certificate of incorporation. Section 16 of the CA 2006 also provides that a company is a body corporate. This can be contrasted with sole traders and partnerships which are not bodies corporate.

There are many types of company. By far the most common form of company is the company incorporated under the Companies Acts with limited liability. All references in this chapter are to such limited liability companies.[7] Limited liability companies can be divided in terms of two distinctions, namely (i) the limited liability company by shares or guarantee, and (ii) the private limited liability company and the public limited liability company. In the case of a limited liability company by shares, the members are referred to as "shareholders" and in terms of s.3(2) of the CA 2006 the extent of their liability for the debts of the company is limited to any value which remains unpaid on their shares. Thus, if their shareholding is 100 ordinary shares of £1 each, the full extent of their liability to the company for its debts is £100. If a shareholder has paid £30 to the company towards their liability of £100, their liability would be limited to £70 for the company's debts. Meanwhile, if the shareholder has paid £100, their residual liability to the company and its creditors for the company's debts would be zero.

Shareholders can be distinguished from the members of limited liability companies by guarantee. Here, the liability of the members for the debts of the company is not limited to the value of any shares in the company (since a company limited by guarantee will not usually have any shares) but to the value of the contribution which they have agreed to make towards the assets of the company on its winding up.[8] The company and the members agree the extent of the guarantee in the memorandum of association of the company[9] and the specified amount must be outlined in the company's application for registration when it applies to the Registrar of Companies to be incorporated.[10] The effect of the above is that if a company owes £100,000 to a creditor when it is wound up, the member

---

[7] As explored in Ch.16, there are also unlimited liability companies.
[8] CA 2006 s.3(3).
[9] In practice, it is common for the contribution to be limited to £5.
[10] CA 2006 ss.9(4)(b) and 11(3).

can only be called upon to pay the value of his/her agreed contribution towards the debts of the company.

Companies can also be divided into the private limited liability company and the public limited liability company ("plc"). Section 4 of the CA 2006 provides that a private company is a company which is not a public company and that a plc is a company (i) limited by shares, or (ii) limited by guarantee whose certificate of incorporation states that it is a plc. Although s.4 of the CA 2006 is particularly unilluminating regarding the nature of the principal differences between a private company and a plc, the other provisions of the CA 2006 serve to underline them. For example, ss.755–760 of the CA 2006 prohibit a private limited company from offering its shares or debentures to the public. In contrast, a plc is permitted to do so. Another distinction is that s.271 of the CA 2006 requires every public limited company to have a company secretary, whereas s.270 of the CA 2006 gives a private limited company the choice to appoint a company secretary. A third distinction is that s.154 of the CA 2006 provides that a private company must have a minimum of one director, whereas a public company must have at least two directors. Public companies must also comply with the minimum authorised share capital requirements in terms of ss.761–767 of the CA 2006. These provisions provide that every public company is not permitted to do business or borrow money unless it has a trading certificate and it can only obtain a trading certificate from the Registrar of Companies if the nominal value of the company's allotted share capital is not less than the authorised minimum of £50,000. Meanwhile, there are no such restrictions on private companies. Another difference between private and public companies is apparent from the terms of ss.58–60 of the CA 2006. The name of every public limited company must end with the words "public limited company" or the abbreviation "plc", whereas the name of every private limited company must end with the word "limited" or the abbreviation "ltd".

THE ADVANTAGES OF THE CORPORATE FORM

14–10 The case of *Salomon v A. Salomon & Co Ltd* [1897] A.C. 22 is the most important of all company law cases. It settled once and for all that the shareholders of limited liability companies enjoy limited liability for the debts of the company. It also established that a company is a body corporate having separate legal personality distinct from its constituent members. The effect of the rule that a company is a separate legal person is that it can be sued, sue third parties in its own name, enter into contracts, own property in its own name, etc.

Salomon v A. Salomon & Co Ltd
[1897] A.C. 22

Concerning: The liability of the members of a private limited liability company for the debts of the company and the separate legal personality of a company.

Facts: Mr Salomon was a leather merchant running a wholesale boot manufacturing business as a sole trader. He decided to convert his business from a sole trader to a limited liability company. Mr Salomon took 20,001 shares of £1 each in the share capital of the company with his wife and five children each taking one share of £1 each. Mr Salomon's business was transferred to the company in exchange for those 20,001 shares. Mr Salomon also received £1,000 in cash and £10,000 worth of debentures (debt instruments issued by the company) from the company in return for the transfer of his business to the company. In essence, Mr Salomon controlled the company and it was a "one-man" company. Subsequent to the transfer, the company continued the leather manufacturing trade, but eventually fell on hard times. Mr Salomon cancelled his debentures and reissued them to a Mr Broderip in return for an advance of £5,000 which Mr Salomon then applied towards the company's debts. Unfortunately, this did not resolve the financial difficulties of the company. A liquidator was appointed over the company, who realised the company's assets and held the proceeds of sale. When the proceeds of sale were distributed amongst the company's creditors, the effect was that there was enough money to repay only part of the debt due to Mr Broderip, but the company's unsecured trade creditors received nothing. Mr Broderip challenged the distribution of the proceeds of sale on a number of grounds, ultimately seeking recovery of funds from Mr Salomon in respect of the shortfall on his debentures. The trial judge held that Mr Broderip had a right to be indemnified from Mr Salomon who was an agent of the company. The case was appealed all the way to the House of Lords.

Decision: The House of Lords held that Mr Salomon did not require to indemnify the company or its creditors in respect of the debts of the company. The requirements of the Companies Act 1862 had been complied with in full and the effect of that Act was clear, namely that members have limited liability for the debts of the company and that the company has its own legal personality which is distinct from its members. So the decision of the trial judge was set aside and the Law Lords ruled that Mr Broderip could not recover from Mr Salomon.

As the case of *Salomon* demonstrates, separate legal personality and the limited liability of the membership of the company are major benefits of the corporate form. Another advantage which limited liability companies have over other business forms (such as partnership, sole traders, etc.) is the ability to issue transferable shares as investments to shareholders/ investors.[11] This enables the company to raise finance from investors/ shareholders in return for the allotment and issue of its own shares to the investor/shareholder. Only limited liability companies by shares can raise this form of finance, which is referred to as "equity finance". Companies limited by guarantee do not have the facility to offer shares to investors, since generally they are not permitted to issue such shares. Moreover, other business vehicles such as sole traders and partnerships do not have the ability to raise money by issuing shares and if such organisations wish to raise finance from outside third parties, debt finance (i.e. a loan-based arrangement) is the only available option. When shares are allotted and issued to investors in return for finance, the shares are treated as property owned by the investors. Section 541 of the CA 2006 provides that shares are moveable property belonging to the investor in terms of Scots law. Shares represent a measure of the shareholder's liability and interest in the company, consisting of a bundle of rights in favour of them and obligations imposed on them. In other words, they have an open market value, representing a percentage of the overall value of the company.[12] A great benefit of shares is the ease with which they may be transferred to third parties or offered to a lender as a security in return for borrowing.

A related benefit of the corporate form is the distinction between ownership of the company and its control. If an individual owns shares in a company, they have no obligation or right to manage the affairs of the company. In other words, simply because a person owns shares does not mean that they are required to participate in management. This enables a company to introduce passive investors who have no intention of administering the day-to-day affairs of the company. On the other hand, if an individual wishes to enter into the management of a company or is identified by the company as someone suitable for appointment as a director, it is not a prerequisite of acting as a director that the individual must invest money in the company in return for shares and become a shareholder. Since shareholders do not require to be directors of a company, the company can introduce specialised management to run the business of the company without offering them shares in the company. The company can thus seek out the best managers for their business on the open market. The contrast with the partnership where no division exists between control and ownership of the company is abundantly stark. By the same token that management can be readily introduced to a company, ss.168 and 169 of the Companies Act 2006 also provide for a readily accessible means of removing the management of a company. A

---

[11] Of course, this advantage applies only to share companies and not to companies limited by guarantee.

[12] However, for the purposes of the valuation of shareholdings, accounting conventions and practices do not adopt the practice whereby a 15% shareholding in a company is automatically valued at 15% of the overall value of the company. Discounts are commonly applied for minority shareholdings and premiums applied in respect of majority shareholdings.

director can be removed by the shareholders passing an ordinary resolution, namely 50 per cent or more of the members who vote in person or by proxy on a show of hands or on a poll at a general meeting. This can be contrasted with a partnership where the general rule (subject to contrary agreement) is that unanimity of the partners is required to expel a partner in terms of s.25 of the Partnership Act 1890.

Companies are also advantageous in the sense that they outlive their constituent members and directors. In other words, one of their attributes is perpetual succession. The "life" of a company can only be terminated by the process of liquidation in terms of the Insolvency Act 1986. Until liquidation, the company will continue to subsist, regardless of any changes in the composition of its members or directors.

A final advantage is the power of a company to grant a floating charge. As mentioned in the context of the discussion of partnerships, a floating charge is a form of security which can be granted over the entirety of the assets and undertaking of a company to a lender in exchange for debt funding. Sole traders and partnerships cannot grant floating charges and so there is the potential that the borrowing costs of such business organisations will be higher.

The Disadvantages of the Corporate Form

One of the dominant features of the CA 2006 is the requirement for **14–11** companies to comply with a number of initial and continuing administrative and filing obligations. For example, there are various formalities which must be fulfilled before a company can be formed. In terms of ss.7–13 of the CA 2006, a company must submit a memorandum of association, articles of association, an application for registration and a statement of compliance to the Registrar of Companies. In return for such documents and a cheque in respect of registration dues, the Registrar of Companies will issue the company with a certificate of incorporation which amounts to conclusive evidence that the formalities of the CA 2006 as regards formation have been complied with and that the company is registered under the CA 2006 as a body corporate. Once the company is incorporated, there are various continuing obligations which are imposed on companies. For example, in terms of ss.394 and 441 of the CA 2006, companies must prepare individual accounts and file their annual accounts with the Registrar of Companies. Likewise, every year, a company must prepare and file a document containing information about the company called an annual return in terms of s.854 of the CA 2006. A common feature of most of these formalities is that they are generally administrative. Furthermore, the formalities and registration requirements are imposed in the public interest. The public interest is served by casting the light of publicity on certain aspects of the organisation of the company. Any member of the public can consult and review details about a particular company from the website of the Registrar of Companies. Of course, whilst such publicity is necessary given the limited liability enjoyed by the members of the company and the economic and social power wielded by companies, it does result in disadvantages for the company and its directors and members. It is impossible for the company to keep certain matters secret and, for obvious reasons, this may sometimes be undesirable from a commercial perspective.

Another downside of running a business as a company is that companies, their directors and members must grapple with the complexities of the Companies Act 2006, the Insolvency Act 1986, the Company Directors Disqualification Act 1986 and other legislation. It is common for companies to seek out external professional advice to assist them in navigating around the intricacies of the legislation and regulatory requirements. An outcome of the complexity of company law is the fourth disadvantage of adopting the corporate form, namely the costs and expenses which must be borne in order to ensure compliance with the statutory requirements. Finally, a large chunk of the legislation is prescriptive to the extent that it erodes some of the flexibility which lies at the heart of the corporation. That is not to say that the internal organisation of companies is completely inflexible, but that the freedom of autonomy of the corporate actors, namely the company, the directors and the members to contract and agree amongst themselves is circumscribed and controlled by the provisions of the legislation. This can be contrasted with the partnership form where the rules contained in the Partnership Act 1890 are mainly default rules. In other words, the partnership and the partners can choose to disapply or adopt the rules contained in the Partnership Act 1890 as they wish in terms of a partnership agreement— not so in the case of the company.

Key Concepts

Advantages of the company: (1) separate legal personality; (2) limited liability of members for the debts of the company; (3) the separation between ownership and control in the company; (4) the ease with which a company can issue transferable shares to investors; (5) the ease with which existing management may be removed and specialised management introduced to run the company; (6) perpetual succession; and (7) the ability of the company to grant a floating charge.

Disadvantages of the company: (1) the formalities which must be complied with in order to form a company and in respect of the continuing management of the company; (2) the requirement to make public the internal affairs and financial performance of the company; (3) the complexity of company rules in relation to the management and ownership structure of the company; (4) the costs of legal compliance; and (5) the lack of flexibility in the affairs and management of the company, which are conditioned by the terms of the Companies Act 2006.

THE LIMITED LIABILITY PARTNERSHIP: AN INTRODUCTION

Another vehicle which a collection of persons can adopt for the purposes **14–12** of running a business is the limited liability partnership. The limited liability partnership is governed by the Limited Liability Partnerships Act 2000, the Limited Liability Partnerships Regulations 2001[13] and the Limited Liability Partnerships (Scotland) Regulations 2001.[14] The limited liability partnership is a hybrid form of business vehicle, representing a cross between a partnership and a company registered under the CA 2006. Like the partnership form, the limited liability partnership ("LLP") enables more than two persons to come together for the purposes of carrying on a lawful business with a view to profit. Section 1(2) of the Limited Liability Partnerships Act 2000 makes it abundantly clear that the LLP is a body corporate with separate legal personality distinct from its constituent members. Moreover, the members of the LLP enjoy limited liability for the debts of the LLP in terms of ss.1(4) and 10 of the Limited Liability Partnerships Act 2000. The members are liable to contribute towards the assets of the LLP on its winding up to the extent stipulated in the limited liability partnership agreement. It is the corporate nature of the LLP and the limited liability of the members of an LLP for the debts of the LLP which signal it as a radical departure from partnership law.

The LLP is similar to the partnership in that there must be two members or more which combine to form the LLP. Moreover, their purpose in forming the LLP must be with a view to achieving a profit. Another similarity between the LLP and the partnership arises in connection with the ability of members of an LLP to bind the LLP in contract. Thus, in terms of s.6 of the Limited Liability Partnerships Act 2000, members are deemed to be the agents of the LLP and can bind it in contract. However, there is an exception which is more or less identical to the exception contained in the Partnership Act 1890. That is to say that the LLP is not bound by a contract concluded with a third party on its behalf by a member, where the member is exceeding their authority to bind the LLP and the third party knows that he has no authority or does not know or believe him to be a member of the LLP. Thus, s.6 of the Limited Liability Partnerships Act 2000 reflects the terms of s.5 of the Partnership Act 1890. LLPs also resemble partnerships in relation to the manner in which the profits of the LLP are taxed. Thus the taxation rules which apply to partnerships are deemed to apply to LLPs in terms of s.10 of the Limited Liability Partnerships Act 2000. Finally, the Partnership Act 1890 and the Limited Liability Partnerships Act 2000 apply the same techniques to regulate the internal affairs of the partnership and the LLP. Therefore, we find that ss.24 and 25 of the Partnership Act 1890 and regs 7 and 8 of the Limited Liability Partnerships Regulations 2001[15] mirror each other to the effect that they both provide that the internal affairs of

---

[13] SI 2001/1090.
[14] SSI 2001/128.
[15] SI 2001/1090.

the partnership and the LLP are to be regulated by the partnership agreement. In the absence of any provision in the partnership agreement, the relevant default rules in the Partnership Act 1890 or the Limited Liability Partnerships Regulations 2001[16] will apply.

Nevertheless, there are crucial differences between the partnership and the LLP. First, in terms of s.8(2) of the Limited Liability Partnerships Act 2000, every LLP must have at least two designated members. Otherwise, if there would appear to be no designated members or only one designated member, s.8(2) of the Limited Liability Partnerships Act 2000 provides that every member is deemed to be a designated member and there is a requirement to give notice to the Registrar of Companies of the identity of designated members. Of course, partnerships do not require to have designated members. The second difference between the LLP and the partnership is the demands which the Limited Liability Partnerships Act 2000 imposes on LLPs by way of formalities, publicity and the registration of particulars. For example, in terms of ss.2 and 3 of the Limited Liability Partnerships Act 2000, there are various registration requirements which must be complied with before an LLP can be formed. Not so in the case of a partnership. Thirdly, unlike the partnership, by virtue of s.8 of the Limited Liability Partnerships Act 2000, notices of the identity of designated members and changes in composition of designated members must be notified to the Registrar of Companies by the filing of appropriate documentation. On a similar note, s.9 of the Limited Liability Partnerships Act 2000 requires the registration of changes in the composition of the membership of an LLP to be notified to the Registrar of Companies. Finally, regs 3, 4 and 5 of the Limited Liability Partnerships Regulations 2001[17] incorporate many provisions from the Companies Act 1985 and the Insolvency Act 1986 into the Limited Liability Partnerships Act 2000. Therefore, for example, it is possible for an LLP to grant a floating charge to a lender in return for funding in the same manner as a company registered under the Companies Acts and an LLP must file an annual return and annual accounts with the Registrar of Companies. At the time of writing, it was the Government's intention to apply to LLPs those provisions in the CA 2006 which correspond to provisions in the Companies Act 1985 that were applied to LLPs, with such modifications as are needed. The relevant dates for such application were projected to be October 1, 2008 in relation to audit and accounts of LLPs, and October 1, 2009 in respect of the remaining provisions of the CA 2006.

THE LIMITED LIABILITY PARTNERSHIP: ADVANTAGES AND DISADVANTAGES

14–13 The following statement is perhaps simplistic but it is nevertheless true: that is to say that the advantages and disadvantages of the LLP closely

---

[16] SI 2001/1090.
[17] SI 2001/1090.

mirror the benefits and demerits of a company registered under the Companies Acts. Thus, the LLP enjoys separate legal personality and the liability of members for the debts of the LLP is limited to the making of a contribution towards the assets of the LLP on winding up to the extent stipulated in the limited liability partnership agreement. Moreover, since an LLP possesses separate legal personality, it has the benefit of perpetual succession. The LLP also has the advantage that it is able to grant a floating charge over the whole of its assets and undertaking with the potential for lower costs of borrowing. Moreover, in the case of an LLP, the members are able to keep secret the details regarding the internal affairs of the LLP. There is no requirement under the Limited Liability Partnerships Act 2000 to publicise the limited liability partnership agreement—only details of the financial performance of the LLP, namely the financial accounts and reports (e.g. profit and loss account and balance sheet) need be registered in a public register.

However, a disadvantage of the LLP is that there is no separation between ownership and control. Here, the LLP resembles the partnership in that it is difficult for outside investors to contribute capital towards the company without taking a management position. The relevant regulation is reg.7(3) of the Limited Liability Regulations 2001 which provides that every member of an LLP is entitled to participate in its management.[18] Although it is possible to disapply reg.7(3) in terms of the limited liability partnership agreement, the inherent structure of the LLP is nevertheless geared towards the absence of a division between ownership and control. Another difficulty with the LLP is that it is impossible for an LLP to issue transferable shares as a means of attracting outside capital investment. Moreover, there are also various formalities which must be complied with in exactly the same mould as the incorporated company, e.g. the initial and continuing registration requirements which were outlined above. Like the company, the LLP has the disadvantage that various matters concerning its affairs must be made public. However, the publicity is more limited than in the case of the company, since it is only the accounts of the LLP which must be disclosed and the limited liability partnership agreement which specifies the details of the internal control and management of the LLP does not require to be registered. This can be contrasted with the company where the articles of association of the company (which are the equivalent of the limited liability partnership agreement), do indeed require to be registered. Another disadvantage of the LLP is the complexity surrounding its management and administration. The regulation of the LLP closely resembles the regulation of the company. This is the case since the Limited Liability Partnerships Act 2000, the Limited Liability Partnerships Regulations 2001[19] and the

---

[18] SI 2001/1090.
[19] SI 2001/1090.

Limited Liability Partnerships (Scotland) Regulations 2001[20] incorporate the majority of the Companies Act 1985, the Insolvency Act 1986 and other company legislation[21] into the management and administration of the LLP by reference. This means that the complexity of company law and insolvency law is incorporated into the regulation of the LLP form by implication, with all of the costs and expenses of compliance which that entails. The lack of flexibility inherent in the structure of the LLP is another drawback of this business form. Moreover, a difficulty of the LLP is that unanimity is required to expel a member, unless the limited liability partnership agreement provides otherwise. Therefore, it is not always straightforward to remove management and replace them with specialised management.

Key Concepts

Advantages of the LLP: (1) separate legal personality; (2) limited liability of members for the debts of the LLP; (3) perpetual succession; (4) the ability to keep secret the details regarding the internal affairs of the LLP, namely the voting rights of the members of the LLP and the profit sharing (and loss-bearing) rights of the members of the LLP; and (5) the ability of the LLP to grant a floating charge.

Disadvantages of the LLP: (1) the lack of any separation between ownership and control of the LLP; (2) the inability of the LLP to issue transferable shares to shareholders in return for outside capital investment; (3) the formalities which must be complied with in order to form an LLP and in respect of the continued management of the LLP; (4) the requirement to make public the accounts and details of the financial performance of the LLP, namely the financial accounts and reports, e.g. profit-and-loss account and balance sheet; (5) the complexity of the company law and insolvency law rules in relation to the management and ownership structure of the LLP which are specifically applied to the LLP; (6) the costs of legal compliance; (7) the lack of flexibility in the affairs and management of the LLP, which are conditioned by the terms of the Limited Liability Partnerships Act 2000, the Limited Liability Partnerships Regulations 2001 and the Limited Liability Partnerships (Scotland) Regulations 2001; and (8) the difficulties involved in (i) removing the existing management of the LLP and (ii) introducing specialised management to run the LLP.

---

[20] SSI 2001/128.
[21] The majority of the provisions of the Companies Act 2006 will be incorporated into the regulation of the LLP business form by subordinate legislation of the UK Parliament (and possibly the Scottish Parliament) when this Act comes into force.

▼ CHAPTER SUMMARY

SOLE TRADER   14–14

1. A sole trader is an individual involved in the management and control of his/her own business.
2. There is no separation between the ownership and the control of the business of the sole trader and only the sole trader has the sole right to participate in the profits of the business or bear the losses of that business.
3. The sole trader business form possesses no separate legal personality and the sole trader is personally liable for the debts of the business.

PARTNERSHIPS

Main Attributes

1. A partnership is the relation which subsists between persons carrying on a business in common with a view of profit—s.1(1) of the Partnership Act 1890;
2. It is a vehicle which is well-suited towards the joining together of a number of persons for the purposes of carrying on a business;
3. Each partner of the partnership contributes capital investment, skills, know-how, expertise and contacts and pools those resources; and
4. Each partner in the partnership has the right to participate in the business of the partnership and is an agent of the partnership firm, with the ability to bind the firm in law—ss.5 and 24(5) of the Partnership Act 1890.

Main Advantages & Disadvantages of a Partnership

1. Advantages:
   - the lack of formalities in constituting and operating a partnership;
   - lack of publicity in respect of the internal affairs and financial performance of the partnership;
   - lack of complexity involved in the management of the partnership;
   - low costs of compliance of partnership law; and
   - large degree of flexibility in connection with the affairs and management of the partnership.

2. Disadvantages:

- the lack of a separation between ownership and control in the partnership;
- the absence of transferable shares which can be issued to shareholders in return for capital investment;
- difficulties involved in removing existing management and introducing specialised management to run the partnership;
- the partners are jointly and severally liable for the debts of the partnership—ss.9 and 12 of the Partnership Act 1890;
- the lack of perpetual succession; and
- the inability of a partnership to grant a floating charge.

INCORPORATED COMPANIES

Main attributes

1. A company has separate legal personality distinct from its members or directors—*Salomon v A. Salomon & Co. Ltd* [1897] AC 22;
2. A company consists of a number of individuals, namely the members, who voluntarily agree to combine for a common purpose and thus, form a company as a means of carrying on business;
3. Each member will contribute capital investment, skills, know-how, expertise and contacts to the company and pool those resources;
4. A company is formed when it has been registered with the Registrar of Companies and the Registrar has issued a document called a certificate of incorporation—ss.7–16 of the Companies Act 2006; and
5. In the case of a limited liability company, the liability of the members for the debts of the company is limited to;

   (i) (in the case of a company limited by shares) the value remaining unpaid on their shares or
   (ii) (in the case of a company limited by guarantee) the contribution which they have agreed to make towards the assets of the company on its winding up in terms of the memorandum of association of the company—s.3(2) and (3) of the Companies Act 2006.

Main Advantages and Disadvantages of a Company

1. Advantages of the company:

- a company has separate legal personality;
- the members have limited liability for the debts of the company;
- there is a clear separation between ownership and control in the company;

- companies can issue transferable shares to shareholders in return for capital investment;
- the ease with which existing management may be removed and specialised management introduced to run the company;
- perpetual succession of the company; and
- the ability of the company to grant a floating charge.

2. **Disadvantages of the company:**

- the formalities which must be complied with in order to form a company and in respect of the continued management of the company;
- the requirement to make public the internal affairs and financial performance of the company;
- the complexity of company rules in relation to the management and ownership structure of the company;
- the costs of legal compliance in relation to the Companies Act 2006 and other legislation; and
- the lack of flexibility in the affairs and management of the company, which are conditioned by the terms of the Companies Act 2006.

Main advantages and disadvantages of conducting business as a sole trader, partnership or incorporated company

1. See the table.

Advantage/ Disadvantage	Sole Trader	Partnership	LLP	Company
Advantages				
Separate legal personality	✗	✓	✓	✓
Body corporate	✗	✗	✓	✓
Limited liability of members/ partners/owners	✗	✗	✓	✓
Perpetual succession	✗	✗	✓	✓
Division between ownership and control	✗	✗	✗	✓
Can issue transferable shares in return for capital investment	✗	✗	✗	✓

Ease of removal of management and introduction of outside specialised management	x	x	x	✓
Ability to grant floating charge	x	x	✓	✓
Disadvantages				
Publicity	x	x	x – but no need to disclose LLP agreement	✓
Formalities	x	x	✓	✓
Expense	x	x	✓	✓
Complexity	x	x	Some	✓
Lack of flexibility	x	x	Some	✓
Personal liability of owners or joint and several liability of owners/partners/members	✓	✓	x	x

? QUICK QUIZ

- What is a sole trader?
- What is a partnership?
- What is meant by personal liability in this context?
- What is meant by limited liability?
- What does separate legal personality mean?
- Explain the concept of perpetual succession?
- Explain what is meant by a division between ownership and control?

📖 FURTHER READING

Busby et al., *Scots Law: A Student Guide*, 3rd edn (Tottel Publishing, 2006), Ch.12.

F. Davidson and L. MacGregor, *Commercial Law in Scotland*, 2nd edn (W. Green, Edinburgh, 2008), Ch.9.

A. Forte, *Scots Commercial Law* (LexisNexis/Butterworths, Edinburgh, 1997), Ch.9.

H. MacQueen, Lord Coulsfield et al., *Gloag and Henderson's The Law of Scotland*, 12th edn (Edinburgh, W. Green, 2007), Chs 46–47.

S. Mayson, D. French and C. Ryan, *Company Law*, 25th edn (Oxford University Press, 2008), Ch.1.

⌐₿ RELEVANT WEBLINKS

Business Gateway: *http://www.bgateway.com/bdotg/action/layer?r.ll = 1073858805&topicId= 1073865730&site = 202&r.l2 = 1073859131&r.s = tl.*
Business Link: *http://www.businesslink.gov.uk/bdotg/action/layer?r.ll = 1073858805&topicId= 1073859131&r.l2 = 1073859137&r.s = m.*

Chapter 15   The Law of Partnership

DAVID CABRELLI[1]

► CHAPTER OVERVIEW

15–01 This chapter concentrates on the law and regulation of partnerships. As stated in Chapter 14, a partnership[2] is a legal form which is available to persons who are seeking to come together to carry on a business. In Chapter 14, the main characteristics of the partnership as a business vehicle were explored, together with the advantages and disadvantages of the partnership over other business forms. In this chapter, the partnership will be analysed in much more detail. For this purpose, the chapter is divided into the following five categories which closely follow the architecture and flow of the Partnership Act 1890 ("the Act"):

- the nature of a partnership (dealt with by ss.1–4 of the Act);
- the relationship between the partnership and third parties and the liability of the partners to third parties (considered by ss.5–18 of the Act);
- property owned by the partnership (dealt with by s.20 of the Act);
- the duties of the partners, their relations to one another and the regulation of the internal affairs of the partnership (dealt with by ss.19–31 of the Act); and
- the dissolution of the partnership and the distribution of its assets on dissolution (considered in detail in ss.32–44 of the Act).

✓ OUTCOMES

15–02 At the end of this chapter you should be able to understand:

- ✓ that a partnership in Scots law is a separate legal person distinct from its partners;
- ✓ the rules for determining whether the relationship which arises between individuals amounts to a partnership;
- ✓ the relevant rules which determine whether a partner has bound the partnership in contract with a third party;

---

[1] Lecturer in Commercial Law, University of Edinburgh.
[2] References in this chapter to a "firm" are synonymous with references to a "partnership".

✓ the relevant rules which ascertain whether the partnership or other partners are liable for wrongs, delicts or omissions of a partner which have caused injury or loss to a third party;

✓ how partnership property is regulated;

✓ the principles which regulate the internal affairs of the partnership, e.g. the duties of the partners towards each other and the partnership and the co-relative rights which they enjoy against each other and the partnership itself; and

✓ how a partnership may come to be terminated or expire and the principles which must be applied towards the distribution of the assets of the partnership on its dissolution and winding up.

THE PARTNERSHIP: AN INTRODUCTION

As explored in Chapter 14, the partnership vehicle is well-suited towards **15–03** the joining together of a number of persons for the purposes of carrying on a business. Partnerships range from large accountancy firms to small businesses. The partnership is regulated by the Act and in connection with the control of the trading name of a partnership, the Business Names Act 1985 and ss.1192–1198 of the Companies Act 2006 (when it comes into force) apply. It is crucial to stress that the Act provides default rules for the regulation of the partnership. This is significant since it means that the partners can oust or modify the rules of partnership law contained in the Act by providing for alternative rules in a partnership agreement. Thus, the Act is subject to the terms of the partnership agreement entered into between the partners and/or the partnership.

One of the most important issues which the law must decide is how the relationship between individuals in business can be categorised. In other words, how is a partnership defined and what relationships which are similar to partnerships are excluded?

THE NATURE OF A PARTNERSHIP

In this first section of this chapter, the rules for the constitution of the **15–04** partnership, its legal nature, the duties of the partners on the constitution of the partnership and, most importantly, the statutory definition of a partnership in the Act, will be explored each in turn. First, a partnership can be constituted in writing or orally. It may also be inferred from the actions of the parties and in particular the nature of their relationship towards each other. The important issue is to ascertain the intention of the parties from all of the circumstances of the case. Secondly, for the purposes of Scots law, s.4(2) of the Act provides that a partnership firm possesses separate legal personality, i.e. that it is a legal body distinct from its constituent partners.[3] Since the firm enjoys separate legal

---

[3] The position in English law is different.

personality, it can enter into binding contracts in its own name and it has the power to sue and be sued in its own name. It can commit delicts and own property. The separate legal personality of the partnership is important in relation to matters such as the prescription of rights of the partnership, diligence and ranking in sequestration.

When persons combine to form a partnership, they owe certain duties towards each other which cannot be displaced. As will become evident later in this chapter, the partners are in a fiduciary relationship to each other and the partnership itself and thus owe a duty of good faith towards each other during the course of the partnership.[4] However, the duty of good faith also exists at the inception of their relationship when they are about to form the partnership. A good example of this premise is provided by the case of *Conlon v Simms*.

Conlon v Simms
[2007] 3 All E.R. 802

Concerning: The duties which partners owe towards each other when they initially come together to form a partnership.

Facts: Conlon was a partner and Simms was the senior partner in a firm of solicitors which was composed of eight partners. Six of the partners joined another firm and all of the partners entered into a deed of dissolution which dissolved the original partnership. Conlon and Simms decided to enter into a new partnership and some months later a Mr Harris joined this new partnership. The Law Society of England and Wales commenced disciplinary proceedings against Mr Simms on the grounds of suspected dishonesty, the outcome of which was a conclusion that Mr Simms should be struck off from the roll of solicitors. Conlon, Harris and Simms entered into an agreement to deal with the position of Simms' suspension from practice and Conlon and Harris raised court proceedings against Simms claiming damages for negligence and misrepresentation. Conlon and Harris' claim was that Simms owed them a duty to disclose anything which might affect his status as a solicitor and his ability to enter into partnership agreements. Simms had failed to do so and, if he had, Conlon and Harris claimed that they would not have entered into the partnership agreement. Simms argued that there was no such duty of disclosure and no dishonesty on his part and that Conlon and Harris had believed in his innocence.

Decision: The Court of Appeal held that in negotiating a partnership agreement, a prospective partner owed a duty to the other negotiating partners to disclose all material facts of which he had knowledge and in respect of which the other negotiating partners

---

[4] H. MacQueen, Lord Coulsfield et al., *Gloag and Henderson's The Law of Scotland*, 12th edn (W. Green, Edinburgh, 2007), para.46.18.

might not be aware. Thus, prospective partners had a duty to disclose material facts to each other and in the event of a fraudulent breach of such duty, the innocent partners who suffered loss as a result of the breach might be able to recover damages in respect of such loss.

Conlon v Simms demonstrates the nature of the duties which partners owe towards each other when a partnership is formed. But it is not always straightforward to ascertain whether a partnership exists and, to this end, it is critical to consider the definition of a partnership which is contained in s.1 of the Act. So s.1(1) of the Act provides that a partnership "is the relation which subsists between persons carrying on a business in common with a view of profit". The effect of this definition is that the parties must have the objective of realising a profit in coming together to form a business. The fact that the relevant persons realise a loss is irrelevant, provided that their aim is to be profitable.

The Act also provides for various organisations, legal relationships and scenarios which, while resembling a partnership, are excluded from the definition. First, s.1(2) of the Act provides that the relationship between members of a company or association which is an incorporated company or company formed by Act of Parliament or Royal Charter is deemed not to be a partnership under the Act. Secondly, s.2(1) of the Act states that the owners of joint property or common property are not to be considered partners without more, regardless of the profit sharing arrangements which exist between them. Thirdly, where persons share in gross returns, this does not of itself constitute a partnership. A good example of this point is provided by the case of *Cox v Coulson*.

Cox v Coulson
[1916] 2 K.B. 177

Concerning: The nature of the relationship between the lessee and manager of a theatre and whether they were partners.

Facts: Coulson was the lessee and manager of a theatre. The manager of a touring theatrical company named Mill provided actors and scenery for a theatrical production and Coulson provided the theatre, the lighting and the playbills. Coulson and Mill agreed to share in the gross receipts taken from the box office on a 60/40 basis. Cox attended the play at the theatre one night. During the performance, one of the actors fired a pistol which ought to have contained a blank cartridge. However, for some reason, the barrel of the pistol was loaded with a live cartridge that night and when it was fired it struck Cox on the wrist and as a result he was wounded. Cox sued Coulson and, during the proceedings, a question was raised as to the relationship between Coulson and Mill.

Decision: In the Court of Appeal, two of the judges specifically stated that the sharing of gross receipts by individuals does not constitute a partnership between them.

So *Cox v Coulson* is a case which exemplifies the rule in s.2(2) of the Act that the sharing of a proportion of gross returns does not of itself create a partnership between individuals. This makes sense since it will be recalled that s.1(1) of the Act enunciates the principle that individuals must be involved in a relationship whose purpose is the achievement of a profit.

Section 2(3) of the Act goes on to provide for five scenarios where the mere objective of attaining a profit will not of itself amount to a presumption of a relationship of partnership. Thus, in certain circumstances, the Act provides that persons who are sharing in profits will be deemed not to be partners. For example, s.2(3)(a) states that the receipt by a person of a debt or other liquidated amount by instalments or otherwise out of the accruing profits of a business does not of itself make him a partner in the business or liable as such. This provision seeks to ensure that a debtor who is paid a debt by a creditor in instalments out of the profits of the business of the creditor does not qualify the debtor as a partner of the creditor. Section 2(3)(b) of the Act states that employees or agents who are remunerated out of the profits of the business of their employers or principals are not partners of the latter. Section 2(3)(c) of the Act creates the presumption that widows, widowers, children and surviving civil partners who receive a share of the profits of the business in which the deceased was a partner prior to his/her death are deemed not to be partners of that business without further factors present. Likewise, s.2(3)(d) of the Act seeks to ensure that creditors are deemed not to be partners of their debtors where (i) the capital or interest which they receive from debtors is paid out of, or varies with, the profits of the business of the debtor, or (ii) the creditors receive a share of the profits of the business of the debtor. Finally, where a person sells his/her goodwill in a business and receives an annuity or share in the profits of that business as the consideration for the sale, s.2(3)(e) of the Act states that the seller will be deemed not to be a partner. Therefore, in ascertaining whether persons are engaged in a partnership, care must be taken to ensure that the principles in s.2(3) are considered, since the mere aim of realising a profit on the part of the parties will not always be a factor which tips the balance in favour of a conclusion tending towards a partnership relationship.

Key Concepts

A partnership is defined as "the relation which subsists between persons carrying on a business in common with a view of profit" and it may be constituted orally or in writing or may be inferred from the conduct of the parties. A partnership possesses separate legal personality distinct from its partners in terms of Scots law. On the constitution of a partnership, the partners owe each other duties of good faith and in particular duties to disclose any material facts of which they have knowledge and in respect of which the other partners might not be aware.

THE RELATIONSHIP BETWEEN THE PARTNERS, THE PARTNERSHIP AND THIRD PARTIES

The relevant provisions of the Act which deal with the relationship of the **15–05** partnership and the partners to the outside world are contained in ss.5–18 of the Act. In analysing ss.5–18 of the Act, matters are divided into three portions. First, we will deal with ss.5–9. Secondly, consideration will be given to ss.10–13 and, finally, ss.14–18 will be reviewed.

Sections 5 to 9 of the Act deal with the liability of the partnership and the partners to third parties in contract. Section 5 of the Act states that every partner is deemed to be an agent of the partnership and of the other partners. In this context, it is worth setting out the terms of s. 5 of the Act in full:

> "Every partner is an agent of the firm and his other partners for the purpose of the business of the partnership; and the acts of every partner who does any act for carrying on in the usual way business of the kind carried on by the firm of which he is a member bind the firm and the partners, unless the partner so acting has in fact no authority to act for the firm in the particular matter, and the person with whom he is dealing either knows that he has no authority, or does not know or believe him to be a partner."

Thus, a partner has the power to bind the partnership in contract with third parties where the partner engages in acts "for carrying on in the usual way business of the kind carried on by the" partnership. For example, where the partner enters into a contract with a third party which falls in the ordinary course of business of the partnership, the partnership will be bound by that contract. However, s.5 of the Act provides for two situations where the partnership will not be liable under such a contract. First, where the partner has no authority to bind the partnership and the third party knows that the partner has no such authority, the partnership will not be bound. Secondly, the partnership will have no liability under a contract with a third party where the partner has no authority to bind the partnership and the third party does not know or believe him to be a partner.

The authority of the partners to bind the partnership is commonly controlled by a partnership agreement. For example, where a partnership agreement is clear that a partner has the power to enter into contracts with third parties having a value of no more than £500,000, the partner who acts in contravention of such express authority is said to have "exceeded their authority". Nevertheless, even in those circumstances where the partnership agreement is silent regarding the authority of the partners, or there is no partnership agreement at all, the common law doctrines of implied authority and ostensible authority may apply to bind the partnership where a partner purports to enter into a contract with a third party in the name of that partnership. A partner, being a manager and owner of a partnership, will enjoy a broad canvass to bind the partnership in contract by virtue of the doctrine of implied authority. However, where it is arguable that the partner does not possess such implicit authority, there may be circumstances in which the partnership has represented to third parties, by their own words or conduct that the partner has authority to act on their behalf. In the latter circumstance, the partner is said to have ostensible authority to bind the partnership. The effect of s.5 of the Act is that the partnership will be bound by the actions of a partner where that partner possesses express, implied or ostensible authority, subject to the two exceptions outlined above.

One of the difficulties with s.5 of the Act is that it is not clear when the actions of the partners are such that they are "carrying on in the usual way business of the kind carried on by the" partnership. A useful case is *Mann v D'Arcy* which provides an example of a situation where a partner was held by a court to be engaged in carrying on in the usual way business of the kind carried on by the partnership.

Mann v D'Arcy
[1968] 1 W.L.R. 893

Concerning: Whether a partnership was bound by a single venture with a Mr Mann as a result of the actions of a partner of the partnership.

Facts: An oral agreement was entered into between Mann and D'Arcy whereby D'Arcy would go on "joint account" with Mann on the purchase and re-sale of approximately 350 tons of potatoes which formed part of the cargo of a vessel. D'Arcy was the active partner in a partnership of produce merchants carried on under the name of D'Arcy & Co and the arrangement between Mann and D'Arcy envisaged a partnership between D'Arcy & Co and Mann. In other words, D'Arcy had purported to bind the partnership in contract with Mann for a single venture. The question arose whether D'Arcy had implied authority to bind the partnership, D'Arcy & Co, to a partnership with Mann for the joint venture. This depended on whether D'Arcy had acted "for carrying on in the usual way business of the kind carried on by the firm of which the partner is a member" in accordance with s.5 of the Act.

Decision: The High Court ruled that the arrangement entered into between Mann and D'Arcy, being an arrangement for sharing profit and loss on a transaction of purchase and re-sale of potatoes, was something done for carrying on "in the usual way business of the kind carried on by" the partnership. D'Arcy & Co were produce merchants and a significant part of such a business was the purchase and re-sale of potatoes. Thus, even though a partner has no implied authority to make his co-partners partners with another person in another business, D'Arcy had authority to bind, and did bind, the partnership D'Arcy & Co to a partnership with Mann for the single venture.

If the court had held that the actions of D'Arcy did not fall within the ordinary course of business of the partnership, the result would have been very different. First, the partnership would not have been liable on the contract to Mann. Secondly, and most importantly, D'Arcy would have been personally liable on the contract to Mann. Thus, if there was a breach of the contract which caused loss to Mann, D'Arcy would have been liable to Mann. As Lord Justice-Clerk Scott Dickson stated in the case of *Fortune v Young* 1918 S.C. 1:

> "A partner who signs an obligatory document outwith the scope of his copartnery does not bind the firm, but he undoubtedly binds himself. Therefore in this case I think it is quite clear in law that the [partner], while he did not bind his copartnery, did bind himself by signing this document."[5]

Section 6 of the Act enunciates another rule which deals with the partners, the partnership and third parties. It provides that any act or instrument executed by a partner or authorised person relating to the business of the partnership which is done or executed in the name of the partnership, or in any other manner showing an intention to bind the partnership, is deemed to be duly binding on the partnership and all the partners. Moreover, s.8 of the Act supplements s.6 by detailing the legal position where the partners agree that a restriction is to be placed on the power of any one or more of them to bind the partnership. In such circumstances, any act done in contravention of the agreement is not binding on the partnership with respect to any persons having notice of the agreement. Most importantly, s.9 of the Act provides that persons are jointly and severally liable for the debts of the partnership which are incurred by the partnership whilst such persons are partners of the partnership. Moreover, s.9 of the Act provides that the estate of a deceased partner is also jointly and severally liable for the partnership's debts and s.17(2) of the Act sets out the position regarding a partner who has retired whereby they do not cease to be liable for the debts or obligations of the partnership which were incurred when he/she was a partner. The joint and several liability rule is significant since it means that a creditor of the partnership can choose to sue one partner, some partners

---

[5] 1918 S.C. 1, 6 *per* Lord Justice-Clerk Scott Dickson. Writer's annotations are shown in square brackets.

or all of the partners for the recovery of debts due to them by the partnership. The creditor can also choose to sue such partners for different amounts. If the creditor does seek to call the partners to account for the debt due to them by the partnership in differing amounts, s.4(2) of the Act imparts the rule that the partner who has paid the debt of the partnership to the third party is entitled to pro rata relief from the remaining partners. For example, if the debt due by the partnership to the third party is £26,000 and the third party recovers £20,000 from partner 1 and £6,000 from partner 2, partner 1 has the right to be reimbursed £7,000 from partner 2.

Sections 10–13 of the Act cover the liability of the partnership and partners for wrongs committed against third parties. Section 10 provides as follows:

> "Where, by any wrongful act or omission of any partner acting in the ordinary course of the business of the firm, or with the authority of his co-partners, loss or injury is caused to any person not being a partner in the firm, or any penalty is incurred, the firm is liable therefor to the same extent as the partner so acting or omitting to act."

For the purposes of the above, it is beneficial to make a distinction between two different scenarios:

(1) where a partner acts in the ordinary course of business; and
(2) where a partner acts with the authority of his co-partners.

In the case of (1), the partnership will be liable for delicts and defaults to the same degree as the partner who has committed the wrongful act or omission. With regard to (2), again, the partnership will be liable for wrongs committed by a partner where the partner has acted with the authority of his fellow partners. This rule applies regardless of whether the partner is acting in the ordinary course of business or not. However, an exception applies where a wrong committed by a partner acting on behalf of the partnership results in a negligent injury to another partner. Here, the case of *Mair v Wood*[6] ruled that the partnership will not be liable for the negligence of the partner.

As in the case of s.5 of the Act, in the case of (1) above, difficulties arise in ascertaining whether the partner is actually acting in the ordinary course of business of the partnership. The case of *Dubai Aluminium v Salaam*[7] establishes how the courts will tackle this issue.

---

[6] 1948 S.C. 83.
[7] [2003] 2 A.C. 366.

Dubai Aluminium v Salaam
[2003] 2 A.C. 366

Concerning: Whether a partnership was liable to third parties as a result of the activities of a partner who dishonestly assisted one of his clients in perpetrating a fraud.

Facts: A senior partner in a firm of solicitors dishonestly assisted a client in perpetrating a fraud against Dubai Aluminium which resulted in the latter paying out $US50m in terms of a fake consultancy agreement. Dubai Aluminium sued the partnership on the basis that the senior partner was acting in his capacity as a partner when he assisted his client in perpetrating the fraud by drafting certain contracts and agreements. The question was whether the senior partner was acting in the ordinary course of business of the partnership in drafting the agreements. The Court of Appeal held that the activities of the senior partner had been done outwith the ordinary course of business of the partnership.

Decision: The House of Lords ruled that the Court of Appeal had erred in holding that the senior partner's acts had not been done in the ordinary course of business of the partnership. For the wrongful activities of a partner to have been conducted in the ordinary course of a partnership's business, they must be so closely connected with acts he or she was authorised to do that, for the purpose of the liability of the firm to third parties, it might fairly and properly be considered as done by the partner whilst acting in the ordinary course of the firm's business. In this particular case, it was ruled that the drafting of agreements and contracts for clients was part and portion of the role of a firm of solicitors practising law. As such, the partner's wrongful conduct in assisting in the perpetration of the fraud was such that it amounted to actions conducted in the ordinary course of the business of the partnership and so the partnership was liable to Dubai Aluminium.

Section 10 of the Act is complemented by s.11 which applies to a fact-specific situation. That is to say that the partnership will be liable for financial losses suffered by third parties where a partner misapplies money or property received from such third party which is held in the custody of the firm. Section 12 of the Act mirrors the terms of s.9 of the Act. That is to say that all of the partners are jointly and severally liable to the extent that the partnership is liable to third parties who suffer injury or loss as a result of the wrongful actions or omissions of one of the partners. Again, what this means is that an injured third party may sue one partner, some partners or all of the partners to recover damages or compensation which is due to them by the partnership. The injured third party also has the right to sue such partners for different amounts and, if they do so, s.4(2) of the Act applies to settle matters amongst the partners. Thus, a partner who has paid sums to the third party on behalf of the partnership in damages or compensation is entitled to pro rata relief from the remaining partners.

Finally, we turn to ss.14 to 18 of the Act which deal with various miscellaneous matters which arise where the partners and/or the partnership interact with third parties. First, s.14(1) of the Act ascertains the legal position where an individual who is not legally a partner holds himself/herself out as a partner to a third party. It is provided that any person who represents himself/herself as a partner is liable as a partner to a third party who has on the faith of such representation given credit to the firm. This rule applies regardless of whether the representation has or has not been made or communicated to the third party who gives credit by or with the knowledge of the apparent partner making the representation. The Act makes specific provision for the situation where after a partner's death the business of the partnership is continued in the name of the old partnership. Hence, by virtue of s.14(2) of the Act, the continued use of that name or of the deceased partner's name as part thereof does not of itself make his executors or his estate or effects liable for any partnership debts contracted after his death. Thus, in such circumstances, the executors and/or estate of the deceased partner are not held out as being a partner of the partnership and the general rule in s.14(1) does not apply.

Another rule of partnership law is contained in s.15 of the Act whereby an admission or representation made by any partner concerning the partnership affairs, and in the ordinary course of its business, is evidence against the firm. Moreover, notice to any partner who habitually acts in the partnership business of any matter relating to partnership affairs operates as notice to the firm. However, an exception applies in the case of a fraud on the firm committed by or with the consent of that partner.

In terms of s.17 of the Act, there are essentially two circumstances in which the partners of the partnership may change. First, where a new partner is admitted to the partnership. Here, s.17(1) of the Act sets out the position regarding the liability of such new partner for the debts of the partnership which were incurred prior to that new partner's assumption. It is provided that such a new partner does not become liable to the creditors of the firm for anything done before he became a partner. Secondly, the composition of a partnership will change when a partner retires from the partnership. On retiral, s.17(2) of the Act stipulates that a partner does not automatically cease to be liable for the debts or obligations of the partnership which were incurred before his retirement. If the partnership wishes to relieve the retiring partner of such liability, s.17(3) of the Act narrates that this must be specified in an agreement entered into between the retiring partner, the remaining partners of the partnership as newly constituted and the creditors of the partnership. Such agreement may be either constituted orally or in writing or inferred as a fact from the course of dealing between the creditors and the partnership as newly constituted. The liability of retiring partners is also considered by s.36 of the Act. Here, it is stated that a retiring partner who has not provided creditors of the partnership with notice of his retiral may be liable for debts incurred by the partnership after his retirement.

However, a partner who has not given notice of his retirement will not be liable for partnership debts incurred after the date of his retirement if he was not known to be a partner by the third party dealing with the firm. Section 36(2) of the Act clarifies the position regarding notice to parties who had not dealt with the partnership whereby an advertisement in the *Edinburgh Gazette* will be deemed to be proper notice of a partner's retirement to all such persons who had no prior dealings with the partnership. However, in the case of third parties who have had such dealings with the partnership, the publication of an advertisement in the *Edinburgh Gazette* will not amount to sufficient notice. Unless there has been an amendment to the name of the partnership or specific notice has been given to the third party, the retiring partner will continue to be liable post-retirement.

Key Concepts

Every partner is deemed to be an agent of the partnership and of the other partners.

The acts of every partner who does any act for carrying on in the usual way business of the kind carried on by the firm will bind the firm and the partners. However, the partnership will not be liable on such a third party contract where (i) the partner has in fact no authority to act for the firm in the particular matter, and the person with whom he is dealing knows that he has no authority, or (ii) or the partner has no authority to bind the partnership and the third party does not know or believe him to be a partner.

If the partnership is not liable on a contract entered into with a third party, the partner will be personally liable. But, if the partnership is liable, the partners are jointly and severally liable to the third party for the debts of the partnership.

If a partner commits a wrongful act or omission when acting in the ordinary course of business of the partnership, or with the authority of his co-partners, the firm is liable to a third party who has suffered injury or loss as a result of such a wrongful act or omission. In such circumstances, the partners are jointly and severally liable for any debt incurred by the partnership pursuant to the partnership's liability to third parties to make good the injury or loss which the latter has suffered. However, if the third party who has sustained an injury or loss is a partner, the partnership is not liable and it is only the partner who has committed the wrongful act who is liable.

An individual who is not a partner but holds himself out to a third party as a partner is personally liable on that contract.

PARTNERSHIP PROPERTY

15–06 If property is purchased with the money of the partnership or on account of the partnership in the ordinary course of the business of the partnership, such property is deemed to be partnership property. In terms of s.20(1) of the Act, partnership property must be held by the partners exclusively for the purposes of the partnership and in accordance with the partnership agreement. Section 21 of the Act creates a presumption of law whereby unless the contrary intention appears, property bought with money belonging to a partnership is deemed to have been bought on account of the firm. The practice used to be that a partnership would take title to heritable property in the name of the partners in trust for the firm. However, since the coming into force of s.70 of the Abolition of Feudal Tenure (Scotland) Act 2000, it is now competent for title to partnership property to be taken in the name of the partnership, rather in the name of the partners in trust. The effect of ss.20 and 21 of the Act is that the rights of each partner in partnership property amounts to a right to a *pro indiviso* share of the assets of the partnership.

PARTNERS' DUTIES, THE RELATIONS OF PARTNERS TO ONE ANOTHER AND THE REGULATION OF THE INTERNAL AFFAIRS OF THE PARTNERSHIP

15–07 At the beginning of this chapter, it was mentioned that the partners may depart from the rules of partnership law contained in the Act by providing for their own set of tailor-made rules in a partnership agreement. Regardless of whether the regulations which govern the partnership are adopted from the Act or ousted by virtue of the terms of a partnership agreement, by virtue of s.19 of the Act, the partners have the power to vary the terms and conditions which regulate the partnership either orally or in writing or such variation may be inferred from a course of dealing.

Partners are fiduciaries and owe each other fiduciary duties. This means that the partners owe each other duties of good faith in their accounts with each other and third parties. Since partners owe fiduciary duties of good faith to one another, we find sections of the Act such as s.28 which provides that the partners are bound to render true accounts and full information of all things affecting the partnership to the other partners or their legal representatives. Moreover, s.29 states that every partner must account to the partnership for any benefit derived by him without the consent of the other partners from any transaction concerning the partnership, or from any use by him of the partnership property name or business connection. In other words, partners must not make a personal profit. If they do, they must account to the partnership for that private profit. Another aspect of the duty of good faith is detailed in s.30 of the Act to the effect that if a partner, without the consent of the other partners, carries on any business of the same nature as and competing with that of the firm, he must account for and pay over to the firm all profits made by him in that business.

Sections 24–26 of the Act provide for a number of default rules which regulate the interests, duties and rights of the partners in the partnership. Thus, these rules may be disapplied by the partners by express or implied agreement. The rules are as follows:

- All the partners are entitled to share equally in the capital and profits of the business, and must contribute equally towards the losses whether of capital or otherwise sustained by the firm.[8]
- The firm must indemnify every partner in respect of payments made and personal liabilities incurred by him:

  - In the ordinary and proper conduct of the business of the firm; or
  - In or about anything necessarily done for the preservation of the business or property of the firm.

- A partner making, for the purpose of the partnership, any actual payment or advance beyond the amount of capital which he has agreed to subscribe, is entitled to interest at the rate of 5 per cent per annum from the date of the payment or advance.
- A partner is not entitled, before the ascertainment of profits, to interest on the capital subscribed by him.
- Every partner may take part in the management of the partnership business.[9]
- No partner shall be entitled to remuneration for acting in the partnership business.[10]
- No person may be introduced as a partner without the consent of all existing partners.
- Any difference arising as to ordinary matters connected with the partnership business may be decided by a majority of the partners, but no change may be made in the nature of the partnership business without the consent of all existing partners.[11]
- The partnership books are to be kept at the place of business of the partnership (or the principal place, if there is more than one), and every partner may, when he thinks fit, have access to and inspect and copy any of them.

Section 25 of the Act goes on to impose a default rule to the effect that no majority of the partners has the power to expel any partner unless a power to do so has been conferred by express agreement between the partners. If the partnership does include such a power of majority expulsion in terms of the partnership agreement, the courts have

---

[8] This rule is commonly displaced by the partners in the partnership agreement.

[9] In the case of "silent" partners, this rule will be disapplied.

[10] For obvious reasons, this default rule will be removed to ensure that the partners are entitled to remuneration.

[11] This rule introduces what amounts to a distinction between ordinary and significant matters of partnership business and for the reason that it is not always straightforward to distinguish between the two, it is a rule which is routinely modified or ousted in the partnership agreement.

demonstrated that they will police such a power very stringently and will on occasion refuse the partners the power to insist on such a power. Moreover, in terms of the Sex Discrimination Act 1975,[12] the Race Relations Act 1976,[13] the Disability Discrimination Act 1995,[14] the Employment Equality (Religion or Belief) Regulations 2003,[15] the Employment Equality (Sexual Orientation) Regulations 2003[16] and the Employment Equality (Age) Regulations 2006,[17] it is unlawful for the partners to remove a partner on the basis of prohibited grounds, such as the partner's sex, race, disability, religious belief, philosophical belief, sexual orientation and/or age.

In the case of a partnership of an indefinite duration, s.26 sets out the rule that any partner may determine the partnership at any time on giving notice of his intention so to do to all the other partners. In such a case, where the retiring partner intimates his intention to dissolve the partnership, this will be effective in terms of s.32(c) of the Act. Where the partnership has originally been constituted by deed, a notice in writing, signed by the partner giving it, shall be sufficient for this purpose. However, it is common for a partnership agreement to state that the partnership will not be terminated without the consent of all of the partners. As regards the partners, this will be valid in law. As regards third parties, Scots common law is to the effect that the partnership will not be determined provided notice is given to them.[18] In such circumstances, third parties will be bound by such a notice.[19]

Meanwhile, in terms of s.27 of the Act, if a partnership for a fixed duration is continued after the term has expired, and without any express new agreement, the rights and duties of the partners remain the same as they were at the expiration of the term, so far as is consistent with the incidents of a partnership at will. The precise legal terminology for such continuation of the partnership is "tacit relocation". If the business of the partnership is continued by the partners or such of them as habitually acted therein during the term, without any settlement or liquidation of the partnership affairs, a presumption to the effect that the partnership is continued duly applies. However, there must remain at least two partners at the date of expiry. Otherwise, the presumption in s.27 will not apply and the partnership will terminate on expiry with a new partnership coming into being.

---

[12] s.11(1)(d).
[13] s.10(1)(d). Although the prohibition here only applies when the partnership consists of six partners or more.
[14] ss.6A(1)(d), 6B(1) and 6C(1).
[15] SI 2003/1660, reg.14(1)(d).
[16] SI 2003/1661, reg.14(1)(d).
[17] SI 2006/1031, reg.17(1)(d).
[18] This is despite what may be stipulated in the partnership deed, e.g. a provision to the effect that the partnership is dissolved after the passage of a fixed term.
[19] Bell, *Commentaries*, II, 530.

Key Concepts

The rules of partnership law contained in the Act are subject to the terms and conditions expressly agreed upon by the parties.

Partners are fiduciaries and owe each other fiduciary duties. They owe each other duties of good faith in their accounts with each other and third parties. Partners must account to the partnership for any benefit which they have derived without the consent of the other partners from any partnership transaction, or from any use of the partnership property name or business connection. A partner who competes with the partnership must account for and pay over to the firm all profits made by him in that business.

Sections 24–26 of the Act provide for a number of default rules which regulate the interests, duties and rights of the partners in the partnership. So, all the partners are entitled to share equally in the capital and profits of the business, and must contribute equally towards the losses whether of capital or otherwise sustained by the firm. Every partner may take part in the management of the partnership business and no partner is entitled to remuneration for acting in the partnership business. Moreover, no majority of the partners has the power to expel any partner unless a power to do so has been conferred by express agreement between the partners.

In the case of a partnership of unlimited duration, any partner may determine the partnership at any time on giving notice of his intention so to do to all the other partners. However, it is common for a partnership agreement to state that the partnership will not be terminated without the consent of all of the partners and as regards the partners and third parties, this will be valid in law. If a partnership for a fixed duration is continued after the term has expired, and without any express new agreement, the doctrine of "tacit relocation" applies, to the effect that the partnership continues.

THE DISSOLUTION OF THE PARTNERSHIP AND THE DISTRIBUTION OF ITS ASSETS ON DISSOLUTION

At this juncture, it is opportune to consider the principles which apply in **15–08** the case of the determination and dissolution of a partnership. Essentially, there are two mechanisms by which the partnership may be dissolved. First, it may be dissolved without the intervention of the courts. Secondly, it may be dissolved under the superintendence and approval of the courts. Each of these methods for dissolution will be considered in turn.

First, in connection with the dissolution of the partnership without court approval, the first way in which this may be achieved is by agreement of all the partners. A second method is specified in s.32(a) of the Act. This states that subject to (i) what is provided in the partnership agreement, and (ii) what was stated above in connection with the tacit relocation of a fixed-term partnership in terms of s.27 of the Act, the general rule is that a fixed-term partnership is dissolved by expiration of that term. Meanwhile, s.32(c) of the Act covers the position as regards determination in the context of a partnership of unlimited duration. Here, it is stated that any partner can dissolve the partnership by providing notice to the other partners of his intention to do so. Moreover, in terms of s.33(1) of the Act, the death or bankruptcy of a partner automatically dissolves the partnership. However, this is subject to agreement to the contrary in the partnership agreement. The case of *W S Gordon & Co Ltd v Thomson Partnership* is a case in point.[20]

W S Gordon & Co Ltd v Thomson Partnership
1985 S.L.T. 122

Concerning: Whether a partnership dissolves on the death or bankruptcy of one of the partners where the partnership agreement specifically provides that it does not.

Facts: A partnership agreement stated that in the event of the death or incapacity of any of the partners, the remaining partners were required to decide within two months of such date either (i) to wind up the business of the partnership, or (ii) to assume the estate and assets of the business of the partnership and to carry on the business of the partnership to the exclusion of the representatives of the deceased or incapacitated partner with exclusive right to the goodwill and use of the partnership name. When one of the partners died, the owners of a farm leased to the partnership raised proceedings to eject the remaining partners on the basis that the partnership had dissolved when the partner died.

Decision: The Inner House of the Court of Session ruled that the partnership agreement incorporated tailor-made provisions into the relationship of the parties to the effect that the death of a partner did not function so as to dissolve the partnership.

As well as the dissolution of the partnership on the death or bankruptcy of one of the partners, s.33(2) of the Act provides that a partnership may, at the option of the other partners, be dissolved if any partner arranges for his share of the partnership property to be charged under the Act for his own personal debts. A partnership may also be dissolved by the occurrence of an event which makes it unlawful for the business of the partnership to be continued, e.g. for reasons of illegality. In the case of *Hugh Stevenson & Sons v AG Fur Cartonnagen-Industrie*,[21] the House of Lords ruled that the outbreak of war between the United Kingdom and Germany dissolved a partnership between a UK company and German

---

[20] 1985 S.L.T. 122.
[21] [1918] A.C. 239 (HL).

company on the basis that it was illegal to trade with the enemy in terms of UK legislation. Finally, a partnership may be dissolved outwith the superintendence of the courts by rescission of the partnership agreement. A partner may rescind the partnership on the basis that one of the partners has perpetrated a fraud or has misrepresented the position. In terms of s.41 of the Act, it is provided that the partner who seeks to rescind on the basis of fraud or misrepresentation is entitled to a lien on the surplus of the partnership assets, to stand in the place of the creditors of the firm for any payments made by him in respect of the liabilities of the partnership and to be indemnified by the person guilty of fraud or making the misrepresentation against all debts and liabilities of the partnership.

As mentioned above, the partnership may be dissolved with the authority of the court. Section 35 of the Act sets out the bases on which the court may sanction the dissolution of the partnership. First, s.35(b) specifies that the court may dissolve the partnership when one of the partners is permanently incapable of performing his part of the partnership contract. Moreover, conduct by one of the partners which is prejudicial to the carrying on of the partnership's business will give the court the authority to dissolve the partnership in terms of s.35(c) of the Act. An example of the kind of conduct of a partner which will be prejudicial to the partnership is provided by the case of *Carmichael v Evans*.[22]

Carmichael v Evans
[1904] 1 Ch. 486

Concerning: Whether the conduct of a partner in being convicted of travelling on a train without a ticket amounted to conduct prejudicial to the business of the partnership.

Facts: A partnership agreement provided that where a junior partner had been "addicted to scandalous conduct detrimental to the partnership business," or had been found guilty of "any flagrant breach of the duties of a partner", the senior partner might give the offending partner six days' notice of expulsion from the partnership. One of the junior partners was convicted of travelling on a train without a ticket with intent to avoid payment, and fined the full penalty. The senior partner served the offending partner with notice of expulsion.

Decision: The court held that the junior partner had been found guilty of a crime of dishonesty. Accordingly it was valid for him to be expelled and for the partnership to be dissolved.

Where a partner is in breach of contract or conducts himself in a manner which renders it not reasonably practicable for the other partners to carry

---

[22] [1904] 1 Ch. 486.

on the business in partnership with him, it is lawful for the other partners to dissolve the partnership. This is provided for in s.35(d) of the Act. Moreover, in terms of s.35(e) of the Act, the partnership may be dissolved by the court where the business of the partnership can only be carried on at a loss. Finally, the court has the power to dissolve a partnership where it is just and equitable to do so in terms of s.35(f) of the Act. The "just and equitable" ground is very wide in scope and a case such as *Sutherland v Barnes* exemplifies the circumstances in which the court will be prepared to dissolve a partnership on this particular basis.[23]

> ### Sutherland v Barnes
> Unreported, 8 October 1997, Vinelott J. (CA)
>
> Concerning: Whether it was just and equitable that a partnership be dissolved by the court.
>
> Facts: The case concerned a general medical practice. One of the partners of the partnership, namely a Dr Barnes, consistently refused to (i) take part in necessary discussions concerning the future of the partnership, in particular the acquisition of new and more commodious premises, and (ii) consider the terms of a new partnership agreement.
>
> Decision: The Court of Appeal in England ruled that Dr Barnes' refusal to take part in discussions regarding the partnership's future had been intransigent and unreasonable. His failure to take part in discussions concerning the terms of a new partnership agreement in the face of a deed which was no longer appropriate, having regard to the changes in the structure and membership of the partnership and in the nature of the practice since 1973, was equally unreasonable. In light of such factors, the court held that the relationship of trust and confidence between Dr Barnes and his co-partners had irrevocably broken down. Consequently, it was just and equitable that the partnership be dissolved.

In connection with the dissolution of a partnership by the court or otherwise, issues concerning notification of the dissolution are covered by the Act. In this context, it is important to distinguish between two different scenarios. First, there is the situation where the partnership is dissolved and the partners cease to trade. Secondly, consider the case where the partnership is dissolved and the remaining partners continue to trade as a new partnership after dissolution in the old name. As regards third parties who trade with the partnership, they will obviously be anxious to know of the composition of the partners after dissolution in the latter case, since the partnership will continue to trade and the creditworthiness of the partners will be a paramount concern. However, in the first case, the creditors will be less concerned since there will be an

---

[23] Unreported, October 8, 1997, Vinelott J. (CA).

accounting, winding up and distribution of assets in accordance with the Act and the creditworthiness of the partners going forward is less of an issue. The general rule regarding notification contained in s.36 of the Act is that there is a requirement for notice to be given in order to extinguish the liability of partners following dissolution of the firm where the business is carried on in the old name. Having said that, there are three exceptions which apply. First, the estate of a partner who dies is not liable for partnership debts contracted after the date of his/her death. Secondly, the same rule applies in the case of the estate of a partner who is made bankrupt, i.e. a partner who enters into sequestration. Finally, as out-lined above, the estate of a dormant partner is not liable on his retiral from the firm for partnership debts after the date of his retirement.

Once it has been clarified that the partnership is to be dissolved with or without the intervention of the court, there are various consequences which follow thereon. First, under s.37 of the Act, the partners may intimate publicly the fact of dissolution of the partnership or the retire-ment of a partner from the partnership. The partners making such notification may require the other partner or partners to participate for that purpose in all necessary or proper acts, if any, which cannot be done without his or their participation. Section 37 is intended to allow the partners to protect themselves by ensuring that notice is given of dis-solution or retirement of a partner. Once the partnership has been dis-solved, the general authority of the partners to bind the partnership in terms of s.5 of the Act ceases to be effective. However, s.38 of the Act clarifies that the authority of each partner to bind the firm, and the other rights and obligations of the partners, both continue for certain purposes only notwithstanding its dissolution. Such authority continues so far as may be necessary to wind up the affairs of the partnership, and to complete transactions begun but unfinished at the time of the dissolution, but not otherwise. Nevertheless, the partnership will not by bound by the acts of a partner who has become bankrupt. But this exception does not affect the liability of any person who has after the bankruptcy represented himself or knowingly suffered himself to be represented as a partner of the bankrupt in terms of s.47 of the Act.

Once the partnership has been dissolved, s.39 (which is set out in full below) of the Act provides that every partner or representative has the right to apply to the court to have the business and affairs of the part-nership wound up:

> "On the dissolution of a partnership every partner is entitled, as against the other partners in the firm, and all persons claiming through them in respect of their interests as partners, to have the property of the partnership applied in payment of the debts and liabilities of the firm, and to have the surplus assets after such payment applied in payment of what may be due to the partners respectively after deducting what may be due from them as partners to the firm; and for that purpose any partner or his representatives may on the termination of the partnership apply to the Court to wind up the business and affairs of the firm."

In terms of the common law, it was and continues to be the practice for the surviving partners to take charge of the winding up of the affairs of the partnership. However, on application to the court, the court has the discretion to appoint a judicial factor to the estate of the partnership to organise and arrange for the winding up of the partnership. The appointment of a judicial factor may be desirable where a partner or partners die, partners are made bankrupt or a partner is seeking an impartial agent to administer the winding up of the partnership in order to protect himself/herself from the influence and interests of the remaining surviving partners. In such circumstances, rather than apply personally to the court for the business and affairs of the partnership to be wound up, the partner may prefer to apply to the court for the appointment of an independent judicial factor to oversee the winding up of the partnership.

Section 40 of the Act governs the situation where a partner has paid a premium on entering a fixed-term partnership and the partnership has been dissolved before the expiration of the fixed term otherwise than by the death of a partner. It is provided that the court may order the whole or any part of the repayment of the premium to the partner as it thinks is just. The court must take into account the terms and conditions of the partnership agreement and have regard to the length of time during which the partnership has continued. However, the court may refuse an order to repay the premium where the dissolution of the partnership was wholly due to the misconduct of the partner who paid the premium or the partnership was dissolved by an agreement containing no provision for a return of any part of the premium.

Where a partner has died or otherwise ceased to be a partner, and the surviving or continuing partners carry on the partnership's business with its capital or assets without any final settlement of accounts as between the partnership and the outgoing partner or his estate, unless there is any agreement to the contrary, or an option to purchase the share of the deceased or outgoing partner has been exercised in terms of the partnership agreement or otherwise, s.42 of the Act will apply. Section 42 of the Act states that the outgoing partner or his estate is entitled to receive either a share of any profits made after dissolution from use of that partner's share in the partnership assets, or, at the option of the outgoing partner or his representatives, interest at the rate of 5 per cent per annum on the amount of his share in the partnership assets. So where a partner dies and the surviving partners continue the business of the partnership without accounting for the share of the deceased, s.42 of the Act will apply. Section 42 of the Act will also be applicable where a partner becomes bankrupt and the remaining solvent partners carry on the business without paying out the bankrupt partner's share. Section 43 of the Act stipulates that the amount due from surviving or continuing partners to an outgoing partner or the representatives of a deceased partner in respect of the outgoing or deceased partner's share is a debt accruing at the date of the dissolution or death. However, the case of *Duncan v The MFV Marigold PD145*[24] ruled

---

[24] 2006 S.L.T. 975.

that cessation accounts drawn up as at the date of dissolution by a partnership's accountants which purported to represent a deceased's share of the capital in the partnership did not represent, unless otherwise agreed, the measure of the amount due to the estate of a deceased partner. Instead, the balance due must be ascertained by winding up the affairs of the partnership and following the specific rules described in s.44 of the Act.

Turning now to s.44 of the Act, this sets out the rules to be applied in settling accounts between the partners after the dissolution of a partnership which are as follows:

- Losses, including losses and deficiencies of capital, are to be paid first out of profits, next out of capital, and lastly, if necessary, by the partners individually in the proportion in which they are entitled to share profits.
- The assets of the firm including the sums, if any, contributed by the partners to make up losses or deficiencies of capital, are applied in the following manner and order:
    - in paying the debts and liabilities of the firm to persons who are not partners therein;
    - in paying to each partner rateably what is due from the firm to him for advances as distinguished from capital;
    - in paying to each partner rateably what is due from the firm to him in respect of capital;
    - the ultimate residue, if any, is to be divided among the partners in the proportion in which profits are divisible. With regard to rights in capital which require to be ascertained pursuant to valuations in accounts or balance sheets, a fair market valuation of the assets should be entered.

It is worth stressing that the above rules are inapplicable where the partnership agreement provides otherwise. An example is provided by the case of *Thom's Executrix v Russel & Aitken*.[25]

Thom's Executrix v Russel and Aitken
1983 S.L.T. 335 (OH).

Concerning: How the share of a deceased partner in the assets of a partnership should be valued.

Facts: A partnership agreement provided that on the death of a partner no accounts up to the date of death were to be made up but that his representatives were to be entitled to receive "(one) the share standing at his credit in the capital of the firm as the amount thereof may be determined by the partnership's auditors and (two) the share of profits up to the date of his death" calculated by

---

[25] 1983 S.L.T. 335 (OH).

applying the share to which the partner had been entitled to the proportion of annual profits represented by the period up to his death. The representatives of the deceased partner argued that there should be a revaluation of assets. The remaining partners argued that the share of capital was restricted to the book values.

Decision: The court ruled that the partnership deed provided that payment of a deceased partner's share was restricted to book value of capital and that the actings of the parties demonstrated that they had agreed that a retiring partner or the representatives of a deceased partner would receive only a share calculated by reference to book value.

PARTNERSHIP LAW REFORM

15–09 The Law Commission and the Scottish Law Commission published a joint paper on partnership law on November 18, 2003.[26] Their recommendation was for the introduction of legislation to amend the Scots and English law of partnership. Essentially, the proposals were that the English law of partnership ought to be re-aligned so that it was more in line with the Scots law of partnership, e.g. that a partnership constituted under English law should have separate legal personality and be able to enter into contracts and hold property in its own name, etc. Moreover, the joint proposals envisaged the implementation of a new Partnership Act with an emphasis on flexible default rules which could be adopted or displaced by a partnership in a partnership agreement. Moreover, partnership law would be altered so that its default rules were more geared towards small firms and the rules for the determination and winding up of a solvent partnership would be made simpler, fairer, quicker and more cost effective.

Ian McCartney, a Minister in the Department of Trade and Industry (now the Department for Business, Enterprise and Regulatory Reform) issued a written statement on July 20, 2006 regarding the Government's intentions regarding partnership law reform. He stated that the Government did not intend to take forward the proposed reforms for general partnership law at that particular point in time. So, whilst there is the possibility that the proposed reforms might be introduced by the Government in the future, they are unlikely to be implemented in the near future.

---

[26] Joint Law Commission and Scottish Law Commission Report, Partnership Law (Cm 6015) (Law Com 283 and Scot Law Com No. 192) (available at *http://www.lawcom.-gov.uk/docs/lc283.pdf*).

THE LIMITED PARTNERSHIP

As noted earlier in this chapter, one of the defining characteristics of a **15–10** partnership is that the partners are jointly and severally liable for the debts of the partnership. However, it is open to businesspersons to form a limited partnership under the Limited Partnerships Act 1907 ("the 1907 Act"). A limited partnership is a different creature from the limited liability partnership incorporated under the Limited Liability Partnerships Act 2000 which we explored in Chapter 14. In the case of a limited partnership, one or more persons are referred to as "general partners" and one or more persons are called "limited partners". A general partner in a limited partnership is personally liable to contribute towards the debts and obligations of the limited partnership. However, a limited partner will contribute capital towards the limited partnership when he or she enters the limited partnership but will not be personally liable for the debts or obligations of the limited partnership in terms of s.4(2) of the 1907 Act. If the limited partnership is not registered with the Registrar of Companies, the limited partner will be deemed to be a general partner and will not enjoy limited liability in terms of ss.5 and 15 of the 1907 Act. Moreover, a limited partner has no power to bind the limited partnership.[27] So a general partner is responsible for the day-to-day management of the limited partnership and the limited partners are essentially anonymous in the sense that their names do not require to be included in the firm name. Like a partnership, there will be a (limited) partnership agreement which sets out the rights and obligations of the general and limited partners. There are very few limited partnerships registered in the United Kingdom. Where they exist, they tend to be formed and used to take the benefit of tax advantages. They are encountered particularly in the fund management area of the financial services sector. In Scotland, they were also encountered in the field of agricultural leases, but much less so since the coming into force of the Agricultural Holdings (Scotland) Act 2003. A final point to make is that the general law of partnership in terms of the Partnership Act 1890 applies to the limited partnership save where the 1907 Act provides otherwise.

▼ CHAPTER SUMMARY

1. **A partnership is a separate legal person distinct from its partners** **15–11** **in terms of Scots law—s.4(2) of the Act. A partnership can be constituted orally or in writing. It may also be inferred from the actions of the parties and in particular the nature of their relationship towards each other. Where the relationship between partners amounts to a partnership, they are deemed to be fiduciaries.**

---

[27] 1907 Act s.6.

2. **The rules which determine whether the relationship which arises between individuals amounts to a partnership are as follows:**

   (i) **A partnership is the relation which subsists between persons carrying on a business in common with a view of profit—s.1(1) of the Act.**

   (ii) **But the owners of joint property or common property are not to be considered partners without more, regardless of the profit sharing arrangements which exist between them—s.2(1) of the Act.**

   (iii) **The sharing of gross returns by parties does not of itself create a partnership—s.2(2) of the Act and *Cox v Coulson* [1916] 2 K.B. 177.**

   (iv) **If a person receives a share of the profits of a business, this is prima facie evidence that he is a partner in the business—s.2(3) of the Act. However, there are exceptions where profit-sharing does not necessarily amount to a partnership:**

      a) **The receipt by a person of a debt or other liquidated amount by instalments or otherwise out of the accruing profits of a business does not of itself make him a partner in the business, e.g. a creditor who is paid a debt by a debtor in instalments out of the profits of the business of the debtor does not qualify the creditor as a partner of the debtor—s.2(3)(a) of the Act.**

      b) **Where an employee or agent is remunerated out of the profits of the business of his employer or principal, he is not a partner of either of the latter—s.2(3)(b) of the Act.**

      c) **Widows, widowers, children and surviving civil partners who receive a share of the profits of the business in which the deceased was a partner prior to his/her death are deemed not to be partners of that business without more—s.2(3)(c) of the Act.**

      d) **Creditors are deemed not to be partners of their debtors where (i) the capital or interest which they receive from their debtors is paid out of, or varies with, the profits of the business of the debtor or (ii) the creditors receive a share of the profits of the business of the debtor—s.2(3)(d) of the Act.**

      e) **Where a person sells his/her goodwill in a business and receives an annuity or share in the profits of that business as the consideration for the sale, s.2(3)(e) of the Act states that the seller will not necessarily be a partner.**

3. **The following rules determine whether a partner has bound the partnership in contract with a third party:**

   (i) **Where a partners engages in acts "for carrying on in the usual way business of the kind carried on by the" partnership, the partnership will be bound in contract with a third party as a result of the actions of the partner—s.5 of the Act.**

(ii) However, the partnership will not be liable under such a contract with a third party where:

    a) the partner has no authority to bind the partnership and the third party knows that the partner has no such authority, or

    b) the partner has no authority to bind the partnership and the third party does not know or believe him to be a partner.

4. The rules for determining whether the partnership or other partners are liable for wrongs, delicts or omissions of a partner which have caused injury or loss to a third party are as follows:

    (i) Where a partner commits a wrongful act or omits to act in the ordinary course of the business of the partnership, or with the authority of his co-partners, loss or injury is caused to a third party, or any penalty is incurred, the partnership is liable to the same extent as the partner so acting or omitting to act.

    (ii) Where a partner in a firm of solicitors dishonestly assists a client in perpetrating a fraud by drafting bogus agreements, this will amount to the ordinary course of the business of the partnership, since drafting and advising on agreements is part and portion of the business of a firm of solicitors: *Dubai Aluminium v Salaam* [2003] 2 A.C. 366.

5. The following rules in the Act regulate partnership property:

    (i) Property purchased with the money of the partnership or on account of the partnership in the ordinary course of the business of the partnership, is deemed to be partnership property. Such property must be held by the partners exclusively for the purposes of the partnership and in accordance with the partnership agreement — s. 20(1) of the Act.

6. The principles which regulate the internal affairs of the partnership are as follows:

    (i) The partners are bound to render true accounts and full information of all things affecting the partnership to the other partners or their legal representatives—s.28 of the Act.

    (ii) Every partner must account to the partnership for any benefit derived by him without the consent of the other partners from any transaction concerning the partnership, or from any use by him of the partnership property name or business connection. In other words, partners must not make a personal profit and any breach of this duty will result in the partnership accounting for the profit—s.29 of the Act.

    (iii) If a partner engages in business of the same nature as and competing with that of the firm, he must account for and pay over to the firm all profits made by him in that business—s.30 of the Act.

(iv) A number of default rules regulate the interests, duties and rights of the partners in the partnership, some of which are as follows:

a) All the partners are entitled to share equally in the capital and profits of the business, and must contribute equally towards the losses whether of capital or otherwise sustained by the firm;

b) A partner is not entitled, before the ascertainment of profits, to interest on the capital subscribed by him;

c) Every partner may take part in the management of the partnership business;

d) No partner shall be entitled to remuneration for acting in the partnership business;

e) No person may be introduced as a partner without the consent of all existing partners;

f) no majority of the partners has the power to expel any partner unless a power to do so has been conferred by express agreement between the partners;

g) In the case of a partnership of an indefinite duration, any partner may determine the partnership at any time on giving notice of his intention so to do to all the other partners; and

h) If a partnership for a fixed duration is continued after the term has expired, and without any express new agreement, the rights and duties of the partners remain the same as they were at the expiration of the term, so far as is consistent with the incidents of a partnership at will, i.e. "tacit relocation" applies—see ss.24–27 of the Act.

7. There are several ways in which a partnership may come to be terminated or expire:

(i) A partnership may be dissolved with or without the intervention of the courts on different grounds.

First, dissolution may be effected on the following grounds without court approval:

- by agreement of all the partners;
- In the case of a partnership for a fixed duration, by expiration of that term—s.32(a) of the Act;
- For a partnership of unlimited duration, by a partner providing notice to the other partners of his intention to do so – s. 32(c) of the Act;
- Subject to contrary agreement, the death or bankruptcy of a partner—s.33(1) of the Act;

- If a partner arranges for his share of the partnership property to be charged under the Act for his own personal debts—s.33(2) of the Act.
- If an event occurs which makes it unlawful for the business of the partnership to be continued, e.g. for reasons of illegality—s.34 of the Act; or
- Where the partnership agreement is rescinded by a partner on the basis that one of the partners has perpetrated a fraud or has misrepresented the position—s.41 of the Act.

Secondly, the partnership may be dissolved with the authority of the court in the following circumstances:
- When one of the partners is permanently incapable of performing his part of the partnership contract—s.35(b) of the Act;
- Where a partner is guilty of conduct which is prejudicial to the carrying on of the partnership's business—s.35(c) of the Act;
- If a partner is in breach of contract or conducts himself in a manner which renders it not reasonably practicable for the other partners to carry on the business in partnership with him—s.35(d) of the Act;
- If the business of the partnership can only be carried on at a loss—s.35(e) of the Act; or
- If it is just and equitable to dissolve the partnership—s.35(f) of the Act.

8. The following principles are applied towards the distribution of the assets of the partnership on its dissolution and winding up.

   (i) Once a partnership has been dissolved, every partner or representative has the right to apply to the court to have the business and affairs of the partnership wound up—s.39 of the Act;
   (ii) Where a partner has died or otherwise ceased to be a partner, and the surviving or continuing partners carry on the partnership's business with its capital or assets without any final settlement between the partnership and the outgoing partner or his estate, unless there is any agreement to the contrary, or an option to purchase the share of the deceased or outgoing partner has been exercised in terms of the partnership agreement or otherwise, then the outgoing partner or his estate is entitled to receive either a share of any profits made after dissolution from use of that partner's share in the partnership assets, or, at the option of the outgoing partner or his representatives, interest at the rate of 5 per cent per annum on the amount of his share in the partnership assets—s.42 of the Act;

(iii) **The rules for settling accounts between the partners after the dissolution of a partnership are as follows:**

   a) **Losses, including losses and deficiencies of capital, are paid first out of profits, next out of capital, and lastly, if necessary, by the partners individually in the proportion in which they were entitled to share profits.**

   b) **The assets of the firm including the sums, if any, contributed by the partners to make up losses or deficiencies of capital, are applied in the following manner and order:**
   - **In paying the debts and liabilities of the firm to persons who are not partners therein:**
   - **In paying to each partner rateably what is due from the firm to him for advances as distinguished from capital:**
   - **In paying to each partner rateably what is due from the firm to him in respect of capital:**
   - **The ultimate residue, if any, is divided among the partners in the proportion in which profits are divisible. With regard to rights in capital which require to be ascertained pursuant to valuations in accounts or balance sheets, a fair market valuation of the assets should be entered—s.44 of the Act.**

? QUICK QUIZ

- What is a partnership and what are its main attributes?
- What are the rules for determining whether the partnership or other partners are liable for wrongs, delicts or omissions of a partner which have caused injury or loss to a third party?
- Which rules in the Act regulate partnership property?
- Can the partners dismiss a partner by majority vote?
- Is a partnership legally bound where a third party enters into a contract with the partnership knowing that the partner has no authority to bind the partnership?
- Is a partner entitled to retain a personal profit?
- Is a provision in the partnership agreement which provides that the partnership will continue notwithstanding the death of a partner a lawful provision which will be upheld by the courts?
- Section 35(f) of the Act stipulates that a partnership can be dissolved by the court where it is "just and equitable"'. What does this mean?
- I don't understand the case of *Dubai Aluminium v Salaam* [2003] 2 A.C. 366. How can it be logical that a partnership is liable to third parties under s.10 of the Act for the fraudulent activities of a partner?
- What is joint and several liability?

📖 FURTHER READING:

D. Bennett, *An introduction to the Law of Partnership in Scotland* (W. Green, Edinburgh, 1995).

G. Brough, *Miller on Partnership in Scotland,* 2nd edn (W. Green, Edinburgh, 1994).

Busby et al., *Scots Law: A Student Guide,* 3rd edn (Tottel Publishing, 2006), Ch.12.

F. Davidson and L. MacGregor, *Commercial Law in Scotland*, 2nd edn (W. Green, Edinburgh, 2008), Ch.9.

A. Forte, *Scots Commercial Law* (LexisNexis/Butterworths, 1997), Ch.9.

H. MacQueen, Lord Coulsfield et al., *Gloag and Henderson's Introduction to the Law of Scotland,* 12th edn (W. Green, Edinburgh, 2007), Ch.46.

🖰 RELEVANT WEBLINKS

Business Gateway:
http://www.bgateway.com/bdotg/action/layer?r.l1 = 1073858805&topicId = 1073865730&site = 202&r.l2 = 1073859131&r.s = tl.

Business Link:
http://www.businesslink.gov.uk/bdotg/action/layer?r.l1 = 1073858805& topicId = 1073859131&r.l2 = 1073859137&r.s = m.

Joint Law Commission and Scottish Law Commission Report: Partnership Law (Cm 6015) (Law Com 283 and Scot Law Com No. 192): *http:// www.lawcom.gov.uk/docs/lc283.pdf.*

Written Ministerial Statement of Ian McCartney, Minister: *http:// www.dti.gov.uk/files/file32331.doc.*

Chapter 16   Company Law

DAVID CABRELLI[1]

▶ CHAPTER OVERVIEW

16–01 This chapter is designed to introduce students to the law which governs the creation and operation of companies registered under the Companies Acts. Like a partnership, a registered company is a form of business vehicle which persons can deploy as a means of combining together to carry on a business. The main attributes of the company as a business vehicle were explored in Chapter 14, together with the advantages and disadvantages of the company over other business forms. In this chapter, the company will be analysed in much more detail. For this purpose, the aim of this chapter is to consider the general principles (including case law and statutory material) relating to the following aspects of company law:

- the sources, purposes and core features of company law and the consequences of incorporation;
- the types of company, the regulation of company names and administrative requirements in connection with the incorporation of a company;
- the basic constitutional documents of a company, the memorandum and articles of association, and the legal effect and significance of these;
- the continuing regulation of companies, the reason for, the nature of, and the formal requirements for accounts, audits and auditors;
- corporate decision-making and corporate governance: (i) officers and directors. The appointment, eligibility, powers, types, removal, disqualification and duties of directors and their position *vis-à-vis* the company and shareholders;
- corporate decision-making and corporate governance: (ii) company meetings and resolutions. The nature and purpose of company meetings, and how they are called and run. The types of resolutions and how they are passed;
- the nature and types of shares; how shares can be allotted, issued and transferred; the rights that ownership of a share confers on the member of the company; how a company can raise capital,

---

[1] Lecturer in Commercial Law, University of Edinburgh.

"offers to the public" via a prospectus and the law of prospectuses;

- the issuance of debt instruments by the company as a means of raising loan capital;
- the legal requirement to maintain capital and what this means in terms of company law, including the rules governing the repurchase by a company of its own shares, the rules prohibiting "financial assistance" by a company for the purchase of its shares, and the distribution of dividends; and
- the position of a minority shareholder, and the protection that a minority shareholder may seek in the event of "unfairness".

✓ OUTCOMES

At the end of this chapter you should be able to understand: **16–02**

- ✓ the legislation which governs company law;
- ✓ the importance of the concepts of separate legal personality, limited liability and the corporate veil;
- ✓ the different types of registered company which exist under company legislation, how company names are regulated and the requirements for incorporating companies;
- ✓ the law governing the constitutional documentation of the company and the rules which govern the amendment of the articles of association of a company;
- ✓ the nature of the continuing disclosure and administrative requirements in terms of company law and the rationales for these rules;
- ✓ that decision-making on behalf of a company is divided between the board of directors and the shareholders in general meeting under company law;
- ✓ how directors are appointed, their powers and duties and the applicable rules for their disqualification and removal;
- ✓ the law relating to company meetings and resolutions, including how and why company meetings are called and run and the types of resolutions and how they are passed.
- ✓ issues relating to corporate finance, and in particular the nature of shares and share capital. How companies raise finance, the rules for raising finance and the requirement for a prospectus;
- ✓ what is meant by "debentures" and how these can be used by companies as an alternative to equity finance to raise capital to finance the strategy and objectives of the company;
- ✓ how the share capital of a company can be altered or reduced and the rules on the maintenance of a company's capital; and
- ✓ what routes are available for a shareholder to seek redress against (i) directors who are in breach of duty, breach of trust or are negligent, or (ii) majority shareholders and the nature of the redress which is available to a shareholder in such circumstances.

AN INTRODUCTION TO COMPANY LAW

Sources of company law

16–03 Company law has recently undergone a degree of material change. Companies were regulated by the Companies Act 1985 until relatively recently, and in a number of important respects, at the time of writing, it was envisaged that companies would continue to be governed by this legislation until October 2009. This chapter proceeds on the basis that the entirety of the Companies Act 2006, which replaces the Companies Act 1985, is in force. So all of the references in this chapter to company legislation will be to the Companies Act 2006 ("the Act"). The Act applies to England, Wales, Scotland and Northern Ireland. There is little company law which can be referred to as "Scottish". Most company law is national in scope and so company law is a classic example of "British law".

Companies are also regulated by the Insolvency Act 1986. The Insolvency Act 1986 applies to govern the affairs of companies in financial difficulty when they have entered into administration, liquidation, receivership or a company voluntary arrangement. Other legislation of the UK Parliament will be referred to from time to time in this chapter including in particular the Company Directors Disqualification Act 1986 ("CDDA") and the Financial Services and Markets Act 2000 ("FSMA"). Both of these Acts contain concepts and principles which are largely incidental to company law and so will be routinely mentioned in passing, rather than in any specific detail. The former Act of Parliament controls the disqualification of directors. The latter Act of Parliament is primarily concerned with the regulation of firms engaged in the business of providing financial services. However, certain parts of the FSMA are extremely important for the purposes of company law.

Together with the legislation mentioned above, there is much subordinate legislation, e.g. statutory instruments, regulations and orders in council, which regulate companies and company law. Although company law is heavily controlled by statute and subordinate legislation, this does not by any means signify the absence of a role for the common law. For example, the rules which concern the duties of shareholders in applying their mind to a vote on a special resolution purporting to alter the company's articles of association lie within the territory of the common law.

The purposes of company law

16–04 Company law is concerned with the regulation of the power, rights, duties and liabilities of companies and constituencies which are closely connected with the company. In Chapter 14, we were introduced to one of the fundamental features of the company. That is to say, that the company, once properly incorporated and registered in terms of the Act, possesses a separate legal personality which is distinct from its owners, managers and other third parties. Much of company law is about regulating the relationship between:

- the company and its managers, namely the board of directors. The company is an artificial person and so cannot act of its own accord and must act through certain designated persons. The articles of association of companies commonly provide that the board of directors are agents of the company, may exercise all of the powers of the company and take the majority of the decisions on behalf of the company.[2] Since the board of directors may act in the name of the company, company law promulgates principles and rules which seek to harness the freedom of action of the board, whilst ensuring that the company is not prejudiced at the hands of the same directors.
- the company and its owners, namely the members or the shareholders (in the case of a company limited by shares). The principles of company law seek to ensure that members are protected from the activities of the majority shareholders of the company and that the company is not held to ransom by the actions or decisions of the minority shareholders;
- the owners (i.e. the members or the shareholders) and the managers (i.e. the board of directors). As expressed above, the lion's share of decisions are taken for the company by the board of directors. However, company law proscribes the directors from taking certain decisions unless they have obtained the approval of the owners by members' resolution. Such decisions are deemed so important that the shareholders must be consulted and vote on them beforehand. Moreover, a number of principles of company law are designed to protect owners from self-serving directors, e.g. directors who breach their duties towards the company, or directors who put their own interests before that of the company which they represent; and
- the protection of creditors. Creditors are affected by the actions or omissions of the company and its directors and members. Whilst the law of corporate insolvency is principally concerned with the fair treatment of the creditors of a company when the latter enters into some form of insolvency procedure (e.g. liquidation, administration, receivership, etc.), company law also performs a residual role for the protection of creditors. Some rules of company law seek to safeguard creditors' interests, amounting to pre-insolvency or preventive regulation. This can be contrasted with corporate insolvency laws which represent post-insolvency, protective regulation of creditors, whereby the interests of creditors are upheld once the company has entered into financial difficulties.

---

[2] For example, see Art.3 of the draft model articles for (i) private companies limited by shares, (ii) private companies limited by guarantee, (iii) public companies in Schs 1, 2 and 3 to the Draft Companies (Model Articles) Regulations 2008 (not yet finalised, expected to come into force on October 1, 2009 and available at *http://www.berr.gov.uk/files/file45533.doc*).

Seven core features of company law

16–05 In Chapter 14, the significant case of *Salomon v A. Salomon & Co Ltd*[3] was analysed in detail. This case ruled that (i) the shareholders of limited liability companies enjoy limited liability for the debts of the company, and (ii) a company is a body corporate having separate legal personality distinct from its constituent members.[4] It was stated that the effect of this rule is that a company can be sued, sue third parties in its own name, enter into contracts, own property in its own name, etc. The separate legal personality of the company is otherwise known as the "corporate veil", whereby the creditors of the company are unable to obtain redress from its members, managers, directors, employees or other third parties in respect of the debts, obligations and/or liabilities of the company.

Another core characteristic of limited liability companies is that they have the power to issue transferable shares as investments to shareholders/investors.[5] So a company can raise corporate finance known as equity finance from investors/shareholders in return for the allotment and issue of its own shares to the investor/shareholder. Shareholders can alienate their shares like any other piece of property which they own and thus realise their equity stake in the company, which will equate to a proportion (broadly equivalent to the percentage which their shares bears to the overall issued share capital of the company) of (i) the overall market capitalisation of the company in the case of a public limited company whose shares are admitted to trading on the Official List maintained by the Financial Services Authority ("the FSA") as the UK Listing Authority,[6] or (ii) the open market value of the company (taking into account factors such as marketability, liquidity and transferability which will be governed by the articles of association of the company and the market) in the case of a private company.

Another principal feature of company law is the manner in which it naturally distinguishes between ownership of the company and its control. One of the consequences of such a division is that a company may (i) with significant ease introduce passive investors as shareholders who have no intention of administering the day-to-day affairs of the company, and/ or (ii) introduce specialised management to run the business of the company without any prerequisite that they be offered or take up shares in the company or invest money in the company in return for shares. The company can thus seek out the best managers for their business on the open market and (in theory, at least) readily remove them from the management of the company.[7]

---

[3] [1897] A.C. 22.

[4] In addition, see s.16(2) of the Act (unless otherwise stated, all references to sections of an Act in the footnotes to this chapter are to the Companies Act 2006).

[5] Of course, this applies only to share companies and not to companies limited by guarantee.

[6] FSMA s.74(1).

[7] A director can be removed by the shareholders passing an ordinary resolution, namely 50% or more of the members who vote in person or by proxy on a show of hands or on a poll in terms of s.168 of the Act.

Moreover, since company law dictates that the company is a legal person which is separate from its members or managers, another characteristic which defines it is perpetual succession. Only the application of the liquidation processes in terms of the Insolvency Act 1986 can bring the company to an end. Finally, the company is characterised by the power which it has to grant a floating charge. The floating charge is a form of security which can be granted over the entirety of the assets and undertaking of a company to a lender in exchange for debt funding.

Consequences of incorporation: the corporate veil

The fundamental premise of company law that a company is a distinct **16–06** legal person has the effect of erecting a natural barrier between the managers and owners of a company and the company itself. The metaphorical legal term for this barrier or cloak is the "corporate veil". It is rare for the corporate veil to be lifted. For example in the case of *MacAura v Northern Assurance Ltd*,[8] Macaura was the owner of a timber estate and he sold the whole of the timber on the estate to a company of which he was the sole shareholder and a substantial creditor. He insured the timber against fire in his own name with several insurance companies. When the majority of the timber was destroyed by fire, he sued the insurance companies to recover the loss. The House of Lords ruled that Macaura stood in no "legal or equitable relation to" the timber at all, that he had no "concern in" the timber insured since it was owned by the company and that the insurance company was legally entitled to refuse to indemnify him in respect of the loss. The House of Lords were not prepared to pierce the corporate veil between Macaura and the company to enable him to recover.

Since it is evident that the courts will lift the veil sparingly, it is crucial to understand the general common law tests which apply. What emerges from the cases is that the courts will only lift the veil where:

- the laws concerning trading with the enemy in times of war apply; or
- special circumstances exist which demonstrate that the company is a mere façade or sham concealing the true facts.[9] In other words, that the company was incorporated as a device, sham or cloak for the achievement of grave impropriety, with the motive of the incorporation being relevant.[10] Thus, where a corporate group structure has been used or exploited whereby a new company within the group has been specifically incorporated ("Specific company") as a means of ensuring that the legal liability (if any) in respect of particular future activities of the group (and correspondingly the risk of enforcement of that liability) will fall on the Specific company rather than other companies within the

---

[8] [1925] A.C. 619.
[9] *Woolfson v Strathclyde Regional Council* 1978 S.L.T. 159, 161 *per* Lord Keith.
[10] *Adams v Cape Industries plc* [1990] Ch. 433, 542 *per* Slade LJ.

group, this is perfectly legitimate and the court will not be entitled to lift the corporate veil as against the other companies in the group or the group itself;[11] or

- the company has been incorporated with the specific objective of facilitating fraud or evading its legal obligations.

Gilford Motor Co v Horne
[1933] Ch. 935

Concerning: Whether the court was entitled to lift the corporate veil where an individual incorporated a company purely as a means of defeating the terms and enforceability of a restrictive covenant.

Facts: Mr Horne entered into a restrictive covenant which restricted him from soliciting or dealing with customers of his former employer for a period of five years subsequent to the termination of a contract appointing him as a managing director. When his employment terminated, he solicited and entered into contracts with third parties, but channelled such contracts through a company of which he and his wife were the principal shareholders. That company had been incorporated only seven days after he had originally entered into the contract of appointment. The reason he channelled the third party contracts through the company was that he recognised that he would be in patent breach of the restrictive covenants in his contract of appointment if he entered into the contracts with the third parties on a personal basis.

Decision: Lord Hanworth M.R. ruled that the company was formed as a device, a stratagem, in order to mask the effective carrying on of a business of Horne and to avoid a perfectly valid, personal legal obligation incumbent on Horne. The purpose of it was to try to enable him to avoid the application of the restrictive covenant. So the court was prepared to pierce the corporate veil to make both Horne and the company liable on the covenants to the former employer.

Whilst the common law demonstrates that the courts are far from enthusiastic about piercing the corporate veil to enable creditors or other third parties to obtain a remedy against the members or directors, the corporate veil is not impregnable. Provisions in the Act and the Insolvency Act 1986 impose liability on the directors and the members of a company in certain circumstances for the debts, obligations or liabilities of the company. Section 767(3) and (4) of the Act stipulates that every director or officer of a public company which does business or exercises borrowing powers without having been issued a trading certificate from the Registrar of Companies is jointly and severally liable to indemnify any third party who has suffered loss or damage as a result of such a

---

[11] *Adams v Cape Industries plc* [1990] Ch. 433, 544 *per* Slade LJ.

failure. Likewise, s.563(2) of the Act provides that any officer of a company who knowingly authorises or permits the contravention of the rules in ss.561 and 562 of the Act (which concern the rights of pre-emption of existing shareholders on an allotment of shares) is jointly and severally liable to compensate any third party to whom an offer of shares ought to have been made in respect of any loss, damage or expenses that third party might have incurred as a result of that contravention. Personal liability is also imposed on members of a company in terms of ss.213 and 76 of the Insolvency Act 1986. For example, in terms of s.213(2), the court may declare any person to be liable to make a contribution to the assets of a company, including the members or the directors, where the company is guilty of fraudulent trading. Furthermore, s.76(3) of the Insolvency Act 1986 provides for circumstances in which past members of a company may be liable to make a personal contribution to the assets of the company. The Act and other statutes also provide for circumstances in which directors will be made criminally liable.

> **Key Concept**
>
> A core feature of company law is the separate legal personality of the company. A company is a person distinct from its directors, members and creditors. This barrier is referred to as the "corporate veil". In limited circumstances, the common law and statute can be used to enjoin the courts to pierce the "corporate veil" and thus enable third parties to seek redress personally against the directors or members for the debts of the company.

> **Key Concept**
>
> In the case of a limited liability company, the members of that company know in advance that their liability for the debts of the company are restricted to the amount they have invested in the company or the amount which they are prepared to so invest. The worst case scenario is that they will lose their investment, but their personal assets are not at risk.

THE TYPES OF COMPANY, COMPANY NAMES AND INCORPORATING A COMPANY

Types of company

By virtue of the Act, companies come in many shapes and sizes. Leaving **16–07** aside the obvious distinction between companies which can be described as small businesses and those which are so large that they display a not insignificant degree of economic power, companies can be classified according to three particular categories as follows:

- limited liability companies v unlimited companies;
- companies limited by shares v companies limited by guarantee; and
- private companies v public companies.

The distinction between each of the above will be considered in turn.

First, a company can be one in which the liability of the members for the debts of the company is (i) limited, or (ii) unlimited. By far the most common form of company is the company incorporated under the Companies Acts with limited liability. The reasons for such a factual phenomenon are obvious. Members of a limited liability company can go into business safe in the knowledge that their personal assets are not subject to attack if the company gets into financial difficulties and folds with debts remaining to be paid to creditors. Notwithstanding this, that is not to say that all companies are incorporated with limited liability status. In certain circumstances, members may be more attracted to the unlimited liability form of company. Whilst such members are personally liable for the debts of the company, the unlimited company possesses the potentially attractive characteristic that the affairs of the company do not require to be publicised, e.g. disclosure of (i) the internal affairs of the company, such as allocation of voting rights, entitlements to profits and a return of capital on winding up, (ii) the composition of its management and membership, and (iii) its financial performance.

Secondly, limited liability companies can be divided into two camps, namely (i) the limited liability company by shares, and (ii) the limited liability company by guarantee. In Chapter 14, the distinction between these two categories was explored. To recap, in terms of s.3(2) of the Act, the extent of a shareholder's liability for the debts of a company limited by shares is limited to any value which remains unpaid on his shares. Meanwhile, the liability of the members of a company limited by guarantee is limited to the value of the contribution which they have agreed to make towards the assets of the company on its winding up in terms of the memorandum of association of the company.[12]

Thirdly, companies can also be divided between the private limited liability company and the public limited liability company categories. The major differences between these classifications were considered in detail in Chapter 14 and suffice to say at this juncture that public limited companies are entitled to offer shares and seek membership from the public whereas private limited companies are prohibited in the Act from doing so.[13] Public companies have the benefit of access to the capital markets such as the London Stock Exchange ("LSE") or the Alternative Investment Market ("AIM") to finance their activities and so are more heavily

---

[12] s.3(3).
[13] s.755.

regulated under the Act, the common law, subordinate legislation and extra-legal regulation (such as the FSA's Handbook, the Combined Code on Corporate Governance and the Takeover Code) than private limited companies. The Act represents a further piece of legislation which has perpetuated the increasing trend in recent years towards the de-regulation of private companies.

Figure 16.1: Overview of the different types of company

	Limited by shares	Limited by guarantee	Unlimited
Public	Yes	Yes (new innovation— see s.4(2) of the Act)	No
Private	Yes	Yes	Yes

The regulation of company names and the registered office

Every company must choose a name and there are controls in the Act on the words can be used as part of a company's name. The restrictions on company names can be divided into the following four camps:

16-08

- prohibited names;
- sensitive words or expressions;
- required indications for limited companies; and
- Similar Names and the Company Names Adjudicator.

Section 53 of the Act provides that a company cannot be registered with a name which, in the opinion of the Secretary of State, is offensive or its use would constitute an offence. At the time of writing, subordinate legislation detailing the words and phrases which are prohibited had not been published.[14] Meanwhile, ss.54 and 55 of the Act state that the approval of the Secretary of State is required for a company to use certain words or phrases which (i) are likely to give the impression that the company is connected with the Government, the Scottish Government, a local authority or the NHS, or (ii) are deemed by subordinate legislation to be "sensitive".[15] However, an indication of the types of words and phrases which may be prohibited by the Secretary of State by subordinate legislation is provided by the Company and Business Names Regulations 1981.[16] Some examples of words or phrases which are deemed to be sensitive are "abortion", "association", "assurance" and "assurer".

---

[14] At the time of writing, s.53 of the Act was scheduled to come into force on October 1, 2009 — see reg.3(e) of the draft Companies Act 2006 (Commencement No.8, Transitional Provisions and Savings) Order 2008 available at *http://www.berr.gov.uk/files/file46678.doc*.

[15] At the time of writing, the relevant subordinate legislation listing the relevant words and phrases are contained in the Company and Business Names Regulations 1981 (SI 1981/1685) and the Company and Business Names (Amendment) Regulations 2007 (SI 2007/3152).

[16] SI 1981/1685.

Sections 58–59 of the Act narrate the fact that the names of private limited companies must end with the word "limited" or "ltd". However, private companies which are charities are exempt from using the word "limited" or "ltd" in terms of s.60(1)(a) of the Act. Meanwhile, the names of public limited companies must end with the words "public limited company" or "plc". When a company applies for registration with a name which is the same as another name appearing in the index of names of companies maintained by the Registrar of Companies, s.66 of the Act states that the application must be refused. If the name is not identical to an existing name and is duly registered by the Registrar of Companies, the Secretary of State has power under s.67 of the Act to direct a company to change its name if in his opinion it is the same or too like the name of an existing company appearing in the index of names of companies. Moreover, s.69 provides that a person may make an objection to a Company Names Adjudicator if that person believes that the name of a company is (i) the same as, or (ii) sufficiently similar, to a name associated with him/her in which he/she has goodwill. So this provision enables an individual having an association with a company to object to another company's name which is the same as, or very similar to, the former. For example, if an individual is associated with a company with the name "Clothes For You Ltd" and has goodwill in such a name, they may seek to object to another company listed in the Registrar of Companies' index of names which has the name "Clothes 4 U Ltd". Interestingly, the Act does not specify the criteria which the Company Names Adjudicator must apply in making a decision. However, at the time of writing, guidance was contained in the draft Company Names Adjudicator Rules 2008. If the Company Names Adjudicator upholds the applicant's objection, he has the power to make an order requiring the name of the respondent company to be changed to one that is no longer offending.[17]

The Act confers a power in favour of the company to change its name. Section 77(1) of the Act provides that a special resolution of the shareholders is required to effect such a name change.[18] Another option specified in s.77(2) of the Act is for the company to change its name in conformity with a procedure already provided for by the company's articles. However, by definition, this option is available only where the company already has a change of name procedure narrated in its articles of association. So if there is no such procedure in the company's articles, the change of name will require to be effected by the shareholders passing a special resolution. When a company changes its name, notice of that fact must be given to the Registrar of Companies under s.80 of the Act, together with a copy of the special resolution. In return, the Registrar of Companies will issue a certificate of incorporation on change of name if he is convinced that the new name complies with the requirements of the

---

[17] s.73.
[18] A special resolution is a resolution passed by a majority of not less than 75% of the shareholders (i) in general meeting in the case of a plc, or (ii) by written resolution procedure or in general meeting in the case of a private company.

Act and the company's articles of association.[19] The change of name has effect from the date on which the certificate of incorporation on change of name is issued by the Registrar of Companies.[20]

In addition to a name, every company must have a registered office.[21] The location of the registered office must be detailed on the initial application for registration in terms of s.9 of the Act. If a company wishes to change its registered office, this is a decision for the board of directors and not the shareholders of the company. Section 87 states that a company may change the address of its registered office by giving notice to the Registrar of Companies.

Incorporating a company and the necessary documentation

All companies in the UK are registered with the Registrar of Companies **16–09** at Companies House. There are three offices. The principal office for companies incorporated in England and Wales is based in Cardiff. The second office which deals with companies incorporated in Scotland is located at Castle Terrace in Edinburgh. The Northern Ireland office of Companies House is in Belfast. A number of documents are required to incorporate a company, which must be submitted to Companies House. First, a company must prepare and submit its memorandum of association and articles of association in terms of s.9(1) and (5) of the Act. However, s.9(5)(b) of the Act narrates that the articles do not require to be delivered to the Registrar where the company is proposing to adopt the model articles of association referred to in s.20.[22] A statement of compliance and an application for registration must also be submitted to the Registrar of Companies under the terms of s.9. Section 13 explains the nature of the statement of compliance in that it is a statement to the effect that the requirements of the Act as to registration have been observed. The contents of the application for registration are dictated by ss.9, 10, 11 and 12 of the Act and are as follows:

(1) a statement of the company's proposed name;
(2) confirmation as to whether the company's registered office is to be situated in England and Wales, in Scotland or in Northern Ireland;
(3) confirmation as to whether the liability of the members is to be limited and, if so, whether it is limited by shares or guarantee;
(4) confirmation as to whether the company is private or public;
(5) a statement of the name and address of the agent of the company in the incorporation;

---

[19] s.80.
[20] s.81.
[21] s.86.
[22] At the time of writing, the model form of the Articles of Association pursuant to the Companies Act 2006 had not yet been published by statutory instrument, but a draft is found in the Companies (Model Articles) Regulations 2008 (available at *http:// www.berr.gov.uk/files/file45533.doc*) which were published in March 2008.

(6) a statement of capital and initial shareholdings which itself will contain:

- a note of the total number of shares of the company to be taken on formation by the subscribers to the memorandum of association;
- a note of the aggregate nominal value of those shares;
- for each class of shares:

  (a) "prescribed particulars" of the rights attached to those shares;
  (b) the total number of shares of that class; and
  (c) the aggregate nominal value of shares of that class;

- a note of the amount to be paid up and the amount (if any) to be unpaid on each share (whether on account of the nominal value of the share or by way of a premium);
- such information as may be prescribed for the purpose of identifying the subscribers to the memorandum of association;
- a statement, with respect to each subscriber to the memorandum providing details of (a) the number, nominal value (of each share) and class of shares to be taken by him on formation, and (b) the amount to be paid up and the amount (if any) unpaid on each share (whether on account of the nominal value of the share or by way of premium); and/or

(7) a statement of guarantee *if the company is to be formed as a company limited by guarantee* containing the following information:

- such information as may be prescribed for the purpose of identifying the subscribers to the memorandum of association;
- a statement that each member undertakes that, if the company is wound up while he is a member, or within one year after he ceases to be a member, he will contribute to the assets of the company such amount as may be required for (i) payment of the debts and liabilities of the company contracted before he ceases to be a member, (ii) payment of the costs, charges and expenses of winding up, and (iii) adjustment of the rights of the contributories among themselves, not exceeding a specified amount; and

(8) a statement of the company's proposed officers which will contain the following:

- particulars of the person who is, or persons who are, to be the first director or directors of the company; and

- in the case of a company that is to be a private company, particulars of the person who is, or persons who are, to be the first secretary (or joint secretaries) of the company;[23] and
- in the case of a company that is to be a plc, particulars of the person who is or the persons who are to be the first secretary (or joint secretaries) of the company; and
- a consent to act as a director or secretary (box to be signed); and

(9) a statement of the intended address of the registered office of the company.

Provided that the Registrar of Companies is satisfied that the requirements of ss.7–13 of the Act have been followed, then in return for such documents, the Registrar will issue a certificate of incorporation, which will look something like the following:

CERTIFICATE OF INCORPORATION

No. 8888888

I hereby certify that

RAZORS "R" US LIMITED

is this day incorporated under the Companies Act 2006 and that the company is a [private] OR [public] company limited [by shares] OR [by guarantee] with a registered office situated in [Scotland] OR [England and Wales] OR [Northern Ireland].

Given under my hand at [Cardiff] OR [Edinburgh] OR [Belfast] on the 23rd day of November, 2010

Donald Mambo Smith Registrar of Companies

In terms of s.16 of the Act, the effect of the issuance of the certificate of incorporation is that the subscribers to the memorandum, together with future members of the company, are deemed to be a body corporate by the name stated in the certificate and with effect from the date of incorporation (also specified on the certificate).

It is worthwhile clarifying that although the Act envisages that companies will be incorporated specifically by individuals coming together for the purposes of setting up a business who have drawn up the initial documentation with their own specific requirements in mind, in practical reality, this is a rare occurrence indeed. Sealy and Worthington estimate that approximately 60 per cent of all companies incorporated in the United Kingdom are initially formed as what are called "shelf

---

[23] That is, if the private company chooses to have a company secretary, since there is no legal requirement for a company to do so—see s.270.

companies" by company formation agents, law firms or accountancy firms.[24] Such agents and firms form a number of these shelf companies at the same time, with the subscribers and officers of such companies being employees of the agents or firms. The office of the agent or firm is commonly narrated as the registered office of the shelf company, with the company name picked at random. The shelf companies do not trade, thus lying dormant until one of the clients of the agent or firm makes an "order" for a company. At this point, the members, officers, name, registered office and share capital of the company are altered, with the memorandum of association and articles of association being tailored to the needs of the client in accordance with their instructions. The documentation effecting such changes are signed and registered and the customer can then use the company to trade.

THE CONSTITUTION: THE MEMORANDUM AND ARTICLES OF ASSOCIATION

Introduction

16–10 The most important legal documents which describes the powers, rights, duties, and liabilities of the company, its directors and members are:

- the memorandum of association; and
- the articles of association.

In s.8 of the Act, the memorandum of association of a company is described as a document which states that the subscribers (i) wish to form a company under the Act, and (ii) agree to become members of the company and, in the case of a company that is to have a share capital, to take at least one share each. It must be subscribed by each member on incorporation of the company. To that extent, s.8 clarifies that the memorandum states very little.[25] At the time of writing, the UK Government had not finalised the form of the Memorandum of Association under the Act, but it is anticipated that it will look something like the following:

---

[24] L. Sealy and S. Worthington, *Cases and Materials in Company Law* (8th edn, Oxford University Press, 2007), p.28.

[25] The Form of the Memorandum of Association pursuant to the Companies Act 2006 has not yet been published by statutory instrument, but a draft statutory instrument entitled The Companies (Registration) Regulations 2008 was published by the Department for Business, Enterprise and Regulatory Reform in February 2008 prescribing the forms of memorandum for a company having a share capital and for a company not having a share capital.

Memorandum of Association of Razors "R" Us Limited

We, the subscribers to this memorandum of association, wish to form a company under the Companies Act 2006 and agree to become members of the company and to take at least one share each.

(1) *H. Brocklebank*
Hector Brocklebank
2 Marchmont Terrace
Edinburgh

(2) *H. B. Fash*
Harriet Birchard Fash
5 Strathearn Place
Edinburgh

Dated 31st November, 2009

Witness to the above signatures
Jenny McLeod
Jenny McLeod
22 Earl Street
Edinburgh

In the Companies Acts enacted prior to the Act, the purpose of the memorandum of association was clear. It functioned to inform the general public of the nature of the objectives and purposes of the company, e.g. whether it was a property letting company, a manufacturing company, distribution company, mining company, etc.[26] A particular portion of the memorandum provided notice of the company's objectives to the public. This particular section of the memorandum of association was referred to as its "objects" clause. In addition, the memorandum of association would include the powers which the company could use as a means of enabling them to achieve the "objects". For example, that the company would have the power to borrow money, purchase property, sell property, etc. all of which powers would be exercised by the directors. In strict company law, if a company entered into transactions which fell outwith the activities specified in the objects clause, then they would be deemed to be acting "*ultra vires*", that is to say beyond their capacity to contract. Where a company entered into a transaction on the basis of activities which were *ultra vires*, the general law was that the contract would be invalid and neither the third party nor the company would be bound.[27] Moreover, the contract could not be ratified by the company's shareholders.

Under existing law, it is crucial to draw a distinction between contracts

---

[26] See Companies Act 1985, s.2.
[27] See *Ashbury Railway Carriage and Iron Co Ltd v Riche* [1875] L.R. HL 653.

which are entered into between third parties and the company in circumstances where (i) the directors or the company have exceeded or
abused the *company's* constitutional powers, e.g. have entered into a
transaction or done something which is beyond the objects clause, and (ii)
the directors have exceeded or abused *their own* powers (in terms of the
company's constitution). With regard to the capacity of the company, i.e.
(i) above, it is now provided in s.39 of the Act that the company has the
capacity to enter into a contract or that such capacity can be assumed. So
as regards third parties and the company, a contract is binding whether it
involves the corporate powers being exceeded or abused or not. However,
for internal purposes, where the directors have abused the powers of the
company, whether (a) the actions of the director may be ratified by the
company by resolution, or (b) a director may be relieved from liability by
resolution of the shareholders,[28] are two issues which are not wholly clear.

With regard to the situation where the directors exceed or abuse the
powers afforded to them to act on behalf of the company in terms of the
company's constitution, the position is different. First, in so far as a third
party deals with a company in good faith, the power of the directors to
bind the company (i.e. (ii) above) is deemed to be free of any limitation
under the company's constitution, which will include any objects clause.[29]
In such circumstances, the company and the third party will be bound by
the contract where the directors have exceeded their powers. Internally,
the shareholders may ratify the director's abuse of their constitutional
powers by ordinary resolution.[30] Where a director exceeds or abuses their
powers, they will also be in breach of their statutory duty to observe the
company's constitution.[31] Such an ordinary resolution of the shareholder
may also absolve the director of such a breach.[32] Where such an ordinary
resolution is passed, the court must refuse an aggrieved shareholder leave
to raise derivative proceedings against a director that the director's
breach of the constitution (i) has caused the company loss, or (ii) has
resulted in a gain in the hands of the director which should be restored to
the company.[33]

In terms of s.8 of the Act, the memorandum of association of a
company incorporated under the Act no longer contains objects clauses
or details concerning the powers of the company or its capacity to contract. That is not to say that ss.39 and 40 of the Act and the rules
regarding shareholder ratification are irrelevant. There are two reasons
for this. First, the memoranda of association of many companies incorporated under the Companies Acts prior to the coming into force of the

---

[28] In terms of the Companies Act 1985, s.35(3), the shareholders could so ratify by passing
a special resolution.
[29] s.40(1) of the Act.
[30] *Bamford v Bamford* [1970] Ch. 212. An ordinary resolution is a resolution of the
shareholders passed by a simple majority, i.e. 51% of the shareholders (s.282(1)) (i) in
general meeting in the case of a public limited company, or (ii) by written resolution
procedure or in general meeting in the case of a private limited company.
[31] s.171(1)(a).
[32] s.239(1).
[33] s.268(1)(c)(ii).

Act will continue to have objects clauses and provisions regulating the powers and capacity of the company. Section 28 of the Act states that these provisions are deemed to be provisions of the company's articles of association and will be regulated by ss.39 and 40 of the Act (and the rules on ratification). Moreover, if a company (an existing company incorporated under the Companies Acts in force prior to the Act, or in circumstances where a company is incorporated under the Act with an objects clause) has an objects clause in its articles of association, its objects are deemed to be unrestricted. Secondly, although no such provisions are permitted in the memoranda of association of companies formed under the Act, such companies may include identical or broadly similar provisions in their articles of association. Where this is done, ss.39 and 40 of the Act will have a bearing on matters.

> **Key Concept**
>
> A company's memorandum of association is a public document which states that the subscribers (i) wish to form a company under the Act, and (ii) agree to become members of the company and, in the case of a company that is to have a share capital, to take at least one share each.

Whilst the memorandum of association was a document which traditionally intimated to the world the nature of the activities undertaken by the company, the articles of association would regulate the internal affairs of the company, its directors and members. The articles of association continue to perform that role. In s.17(a) of the Act, the articles are referred to as the "constitution of the company" and s.33 of the Act provides that the articles represent a "contract" entered into between the members and the company and the members *inter se*:

> "the provisions of a company's constitution bind the company and its members to the same extent as if there were covenants on the part of the company and of each member to observe these provisions."

Accordingly, the members of the company can enforce the articles as a "contract" against the company and the company can enforce the articles against the members.

Hickman v Kent or Romney March Sheep Breeders Association
[1915] 1 Ch. 881

Concerning: Whether a member was contractually bound by an article in the articles of association of the company which provided that any disputes or differences between the members and the company regarding the "true intent or construction or the incidents or consequences" of the articles of association or the Companies (Consolidation) Act, 1908 (8 Edw. 7, c. 69) would be referred to arbitration.

Facts: A company was formed with articles of association which contained an article providing that any disputes or differences between the members and the company regarding the "true intent or construction or the incidents or consequences" of the articles of association or the Companies (Consolidation) Act, 1908 (8 Edw. 7, c. 69) required to be referred to arbitration. A dispute emerged between Hickman, the company and its company secretary. Hickman raised court proceedings seeking (amongst other orders) (i) an interdict to restrain the company from taking any steps to expel him from the company, and (ii) a declaration that Hickman was entitled to have the resolutions and proceedings of the company and of any committee thereof truly and accurately entered in its minutes. The company issued a summons requesting that all further proceedings in the action be stopped and that the matters in question in the proceedings be referred to arbitration in accordance with the provisions of the relevant article.

Decision: Astbury J. held that the proceedings should be stopped and that the matters at issue ought to proceed to arbitration in terms of the relevant article. The articles constituted a contract between the company and the members, creating rights and obligations between them and the company respectively. He also held that no article can constitute a contract between the company and a third party and that no right purporting to be given by an article to a person, whether a member or not, in a capacity other than that of a member, as, for instance, as solicitor, promoter, director, can be enforced against the company.

The articles of association must be contained in a single document and divided into paragraphs numbered consecutively.[34] The Companies Act 1985 prescribed a form of model articles of association for use by companies which were known as "Table A".[35] When they were formed, companies would base their articles of association on Table A by adopting it in full, or adopting it subject to amendments. The Companies

---

[34] s.18(3).
[35] The Companies (Tables A to F) Regulations 1985 (SI 1985/805).

Act 2006 provides for an equivalent set of model articles of association. As mentioned above, at the time of writing, the model articles had not yet been finalised by the UK Government by subordinate legislation. However, a draft statutory instrument specifying the model articles for the purposes of the Act was published by the UK Government in March 2008.[36] This document gives some indication of the likely content of the model articles for private limited companies by shares, public limited companies by guarantee and public limited companies by shares. The Model Articles contain provisions on shares and distributions, the organisation of, and voting at, general meetings and the regulation of (i) directors' powers and responsibilities, (ii) decision-making by directors, and (iii) the appointment of directors. For public companies limited by shares, a greater number of matters are catered for in the Model Articles given the more complex nature of that form of company and the fact that certain issues apply to them which are irrelevant to private companies, e.g. AGMs.

When the subscribers to the memorandum of association apply to the Registrar of Companies to form a company, they must register the articles of association of the company. However, there is an exception if the subscribers are adopting the Model articles of association without any amendment. In such circumstances, there is no need to register a copy of the company's articles.[37]

Section 21 of the Act stipulates that a company may amend its articles of association by special resolution, that is to say a resolution passed by a majority of not less than 75 per cent of the members of the company (i) in general meeting in the case of a public limited company, or (ii) by written resolution procedure or in general meeting in the case of a private limited company.[38] Once passed by special resolution, the alteration takes immediate effect. But if the alteration to the articles is such that it is adding, removing or altering a statement of the company's objects, notice of such an alteration must be given to the Registrar of Companies and the amendment of the company's objects is not effective until the notice is entered on the register.[39] Moreover, if the alteration of the articles of association (i) purports to require a member to take or subscribe for more shares than the number held by him at the date on which the alteration was made, or (ii) in any way increases a members' liability as at the date of the alteration to contribute to the company's share capital or otherwise to pay money to the company, then the member is not bound by the alteration.[40] Once the special resolution amending the articles of association has been passed, the company has 15 days from the amendment taking effect to lodge with the Registrar of Companies (i) a copy of the

---

[36] The Companies (Model Articles) Regulations 2008 (Draft), available at *http://www.berr.gov.uk/files/file45533.doc*. Throughout this chapter, references to the model articles will be to such draft model articles, which are hereinafter referred to as the "Model Articles".

[37] s.18(4).

[38] s.283(1).

[39] s.31(2).

[40] s.25(1).

special resolution or a written memorandum of its terms, and (ii) a new copy of the articles of association incorporating the amendments.[41] The Registrar of Companies may take action against a company if the company fails to lodge the necessary documentation.

An important control exerted by company law arises where the members of a company pass a special resolution to alter the articles of association and the amendment introduced is likely to result in harm or loss to the company. In such circumstances, the question is whether company law should develop rules to enable an aggrieved shareholder (e.g. a minority shareholder) to take action against the company or the 75 per cent or more of the voting shareholders who voted in favour of the amendment on the premise that it is not in the best interests of the company? Another way of looking at this issue is to contemplate whether shareholders should have the right to freely cast their votes as they wish when voting on a resolution of the company. It may be that company law might reject any notion that it ought to evolve rules to enable aggrieved shareholders to take action against the company in such circumstances on the basis that this would amount to an unwarranted curtailment of the individual freedom, liberty and autonomy of shareholders to vote their shares as they please. Indeed, the general rule of company law is that a share is a property right[42] and that members have the right to cast their votes in any way they please.[43] In doing so, the member can vote in a way which advances his personal interests and he is not bound to consider the effect of the vote on the interests of the company or any third party for that matter.

Company law responds to the matters raised by this issue by forging a common law principle that on a special resolution to alter the articles of association there is an exception to the general rule that members can exercise their vote in any way they think fit. So when a member is confronted with a special resolution, the wide scope of manoeuvre afforded to him by the general rule is curtailed to the effect that he must exercise his vote in a way which is "bona fide" for the benefit of the company as a whole. The key case enunciating this principle is *Allen v Gold Reefs of West Africa Ltd.*[44]

Allen v Gold Reefs of West Africa Ltd
[1900] 1 Ch. 656

Concerning: Whether an amendment to the articles of association of a company authorised by the members by special resolution was lawful.

Facts: A company amended its articles of association by

---

[41] ss.30(1) and 26(1).
[42] s.541.
[43] *North-West Transportation Co Ltd v Beatty* (1887) 12 App Cas 589 (Privy Council) and *Northern Counties Securities Ltd v Jackson & Steeple Ltd* [1974] 1 W.L.R. 1133.
[44] [1900] 1 Ch. 656.

removing the words "(not being fully paid)" from a provision in a company's articles which provided that a company had a lien "upon all shares (not being fully paid) held by such members". So the effect of the original provision was that the company had a lien over shares which were not fully paid up, whereas the effect of the amendment was to give the company a lien over all shares whether they were fully paid or not. Only one member had fully paid up shares in the company and when he died his executors challenged the company when they sought to claim a lien on his shares pursuant to the amended articles.

Decision: Lindley M.R. in the Court of Appeal ruled that the company had the power to exercise the lien over the deceased member's shares. The special resolution which amended the articles of association of the company was valid. However, in coming to this view, Lindley M.R. introduced the principle that the members must exercise their vote in a way which is likely to be "bona fide" for the benefit of the company as a whole. So if the members vote against the proposed alteration, they must do so on the basis that they are of the view that the proposed alteration is not for the benefit of the company. Conversely, if they vote in favour, they must be satisfied that the proposed alteration is for the good of the company.

The difficulty with the "'bona fide' for the benefit of the company as a whole" test is that it is a concept which is inherently subjective and vague. What is the content of such a rule? For example, when the proposed amendment to the articles of association is such that it enables one section of the membership of the company or the directors for that matter to expropriate the shares of another section of the membership of the company, is that necessarily disadvantageous to the company? Here the argument is that the amendment is nothing but an attempt by those members who vote in favour to compel those who vote against to forfeit their shares. The concern of the court is to ensure that the amendment will not tear a rupture in the established constitutional balance of power in the company. A prime example is where the majority shareholders pass a special resolution which amends the articles to insert a provision forcing the minority shareholders or a particular body of shareholders to sell their shares to the majority shareholders on the occurrence of a particular event, e.g. a takeover bid for the company, the minority shareholders proposing to sell to an outsider, etc.[45] A prime example is the case of *Sidebotham v Kershaw Leese & Co Ltd*.[46] In such circumstances, the difficulty facing a court is how they are to ascertain whether the amendments which introduce the power of expropriation or forfeiture are nevertheless "'bona fide' for the benefit of the company as a whole".

[45] Such clauses are generally known as "compulsory transfer" provisions.
[46] [1920] 1 Ch. 154.

Sidebotham v Kershaw Leese & Co Ltd
[1920] 1 Ch. 154

Concerning: Whether an amendment to the articles of association of a company authorised by the members by special resolution was lawful.

Facts: A company's articles of association were amended to provide that the directors would be given the power to purchase the shares of any members at a fair price who had been found to be competing with the business of the company. Minority shareholders in the company who ran a business which competed with the company sought to challenge the amendment of the alteration on the basis that it was not "'bona fide' for the benefit of the company as a whole". They argued that the amendment was nothing more than an attempt by the majority shareholders and the directors to expropriate their shares.

Decision: Lord Sterndale M.R. in the Court of Appeal held that the amendment was clearly "'bona fide' for the benefit of the company as a whole". He stated that it was "very much to the benefit of the company to get rid of members who are in competing businesses ... I think there can be no doubt that a member of a competing business or an owner of a competing business who is a member of the company has a much better chance of knowing what is going on in the business of the company, and of thereby helping his own competition with it, than if he were a non-member ... I think, looking at the alteration broadly, that it is for the benefit of the company that they should not be obliged to have amongst them as members persons who are competing with them in business, and who may get knowledge from their membership which would enable them to compete better."

Key Concept

A company's articles of association represent its internal constitution, detailing how shares may be transferred, directors appointed, meetings of directors held, etc. If a company proposes to alter its articles of association, it must obtain the approval of its members by special resolution. Where an alteration is authorised by special resolution, it may nevertheless be challenged in terms of the common law if it is not "bona fide" for the benefit of the company as a whole.

Ongoing Administrative Matters

Introduction to disclosure and administration

As earlier sections of this chapter have shown, a number of formal steps **16–11** are required to form a limited liability company which involve registration of documents and the disclosure of information about the company at the point in time at which it is formed. However, such formal requirements are not restricted to the formation stage. Hence, the Act imposes a number of ongoing administrative requirements on companies subsequent to their incorporation. The rationale for such requirements— which generally involve registration and disclosure of information about the company with the Registrar of Companies—is that the members of limited liability companies enjoy the privilege of limited liability for the debts of the company.[47] To the extent that members are protected by limited liability, the creditors are prejudiced. In return for such a privilege, members must make ongoing disclosure of information about the company. Disclosure offsets (to some extent) the dangers faced by creditors, since the quality of the information about the company which the company is compelled by the Act to introduce into the public domain enables creditors to assess the (i) competency of the management team at the helm of the company, and (ii) the capital position and so the relative financial health of the company. Therefore, limited liability comes hand in hand with disclosure and the registration of information.

Ongoing disclosure is effected under the Act by four mechanisms, namely (i) the provision of information about the company on business correspondence and other media (generally referred to as "trading disclosures"), (ii) the provision of information about the company at its registered office, (iii) publication of information about the company on its website, electronically and in newspapers such as the *London Gazette*, the *Edinburgh Gazette* and the *Belfast Gazette*,[48] and (iv) the submission of certain information about the company to the Registrar of Companies.[49] In this section, consideration will be limited to (i), (ii) and (iv) in particular. Information published in the respective Gazettes is commonly encountered in the Act in the case of topic-specific contexts, e.g. alterations in the share capital position of the company[50] or in the context of the dissolution or striking off[51] of companies. Reference will be made to such disclosure throughout this chapter when such topics are being considered in more detail.

---

[47] An example of this principle is found in s.448 which provides that unlimited liability companies are exempt from publishing their accounts provided certain conditions are met.

[48] See s.1173(1).

[49] The Registrar of Companies is the relevant authority to which disclosure should be made for the purposes of the Act, see s.1061.

[50] See ss.562(3)(b) (pre-emption rights on the allotment of ordinary shares) and 719(1) (redemption or repurchase of shares out of capital).

[51] See ss.1000(6) and 1003(3).

Trading disclosures

16–12 The first ongoing administrative requirements which will be analysed are the provisions in the Act and subordinate legislation which oblige companies to make certain trading disclosures. Therefore, s.82 of the Act states that the Secretary of State may pass subordinate legislation obliging a company to display, state and provide information about itself in certain locations and communications, including its name and registered office. There are civil and criminal consequences for a company where they fail to comply with such requirements. To discover the nature of such obligations, consideration must be given to the subordinate legislation promulgated by the Secretary of State, namely the Companies (Trading Disclosures) Regulations 2008.[52] Regulations 3 and 4 provide that a company must display its registered name at its registered office, any place at which the company carries on its business and any other place at which its statutory registers (i.e. the register of members, register of directors, register of company secretaries, register of charges, etc.), information (e.g. board minutes, copies of member resolutions, etc.) and records about it are kept. Regulation 6 goes on to impose obligations on a company to disclose its registered name on all business letters, notices and other official publications, bills of exchange, promissory notes, cheques signed by or on behalf of the company, invoices, other demands for payment, receipts, letters of credit, licences, business correspondence, business documentation, and websites. Regulation 7 is crafted in similar terms to the effect that every company must disclose information regarding the part of the United Kingdom in which it is registered, its registered number and the address of its registered office on its website and all business letters and order forms. If a company discloses its share capital on its business letters, order forms or website, that reference must be to the paid up share capital of the company. A company may also disclose the identity of a director on its business letters, but if it does so, reg.8 enjoins the company to disclose the names of all directors—not just one. Finally, a person who deals with the company in the course of its business has the right to request details from the company regarding the address of its registered office, the address of any place at which at which its statutory registers and other records are kept and the nature of those records.[53] The company has five working days of the receipt of the request to provide such information.[54] If a company fails to comply with the above requirements in the absence of a reasonable excuse, the company and every officer of the company in default will be deemed to have committed a criminal offence.[55]

---

[52] SI 2008/495.
[53] reg.9(1) of the Companies (Trading Disclosures) Regulations 2008.
[54] reg.9(2) of the Companies (Trading Disclosures) Regulations 2008.
[55] reg.10(1) of the Companies (Trading Disclosures) Regulations 2008.

Maintenance of statutory registers

Trading disclosures are only one of the ongoing administrative require- **16–13**
ments imposed on companies. In terms of ss.162–167 of the Act, every
company must keep a register of directors at its registered office or some
other place notified to the Registrar of Companies. This register must be
kept available for inspection.[56] If the company does not keep the register
of directors at their registered office, they must intimate that fact to the
Registrar of Companies.[57] Any changes to this register must be notified to
the Registrar of Companies within 14 days.[58] A company must take
minutes of any proceedings of the board of directors and keep them for a
period of at least 10 years from the date of that meeting.[59] Otherwise, a
criminal offence will have been committed.[60] Such minutes are important
for evidential purposes, i.e. as evidence of decisions taken by the board.[61]
Sections 275–280 of the Act provide that every public limited company
must keep a register of company secretaries available for inspection at its
registered office or some other place notified to the Registrar of Companies, and any changes to this register must be notified to the Registrar
of Companies within 14 days.[62] There is no requirement for a private
company to have a company secretary,[63] and thus, no requirement to
keep a register of secretaries. However, if a private company does choose
to have a company secretary, it is under a legal duty to keep a register of
secretaries in terms of s.275 of the Act. Companies must also keep a
register of members.[64] Every company must keep its register of members
available for inspection at its registered office or some other place notified
to the Registrar of Companies.[65] If the company does not keep the register of members at its registered office, they must intimate that fact to the
Registrar of Companies.[66] In the case of a single member company, a
statement must be provided in the register of members to the effect that
there is only one member of the company, together with the name and
address of that sole member.[67] A register of charges containing details
about charges and floating charges granted by a limited company must be
maintained by that company in terms of s.876 of the Act and kept
available at its registered office or some other place notified to the
Registrar of Companies.[68] A copy of the instrument creating the charge
must be also kept available for inspection at its registered office or some

---

[56] s.162(3).
[57] s.162(4).
[58] s.167(1).
[59] s.248(1).
[60] s.248(3).
[61] s.249(1).
[62] s.276(1).
[63] s.270(1).
[64] s.113(1).
[65] s.114(1).
[66] s.114(2) and (3).
[67] s.123(1).
[68] s.877(2) and (3).

other place notified to the Registrar of Companies.[69] Finally, in relation
to the maintenance of a register of debenture holders, a close inspection
of the language of s.743 of the Act reveals that there is no equivalent of
s.190 of the Companies Act 1985 which compelled a company to maintain a register of debenture holders. Section 743(1) of the Act stipulates
that a company has a choice whether to keep such a register of debenture
holders. If the company chooses to keep such a register, then it must be
kept available for inspection (i) at its registered office, or (ii) some other
place.[70] If the company does not keep the register of debenture holders at
its registered office, it must intimate that fact to the Register of Companies in terms of s.743(2) of the Act. Section 743(4) of the Act states
that, if a company makes default for 14 days in complying with its duty to
provide notice to the Registrar, an offence is committed by the company
and every officer in default.

The annual return

16–14　Coupled with trading disclosures and the requirement to make certain
information available at its registered office, companies must submit an
annual return to the Registrar of Companies in compliance with its
obligations contained in s.854 of the Act. The annual return amounts to a
"snapshot" of the company taken annually on a specific date. Section 855
of the Act states that the annual return must be delivered to the Registrar
of Companies within 28 days after the date to which it is made up. The
information which must be provided includes the registered office address
of the company, the nature of the company, e.g. whether it is private or
public, its principal business activities, details of the directors and company secretary of the company, details of any changes in the members of
the company and the share capital of the company (including details of
transfers of shares in the company) since the last annual return date.
Information must also be provided regarding classes of shares, e.g. the
rights attached to those shares, the total number of shares of that class,
the aggregate nominal value of shares of that class and a note of the paid
and unpaid amount on the shares.

Annual accounts: Introduction

16–15　The fourth and most important administrative requirements which are
imposed on companies on an ongoing basis are contained in Parts 15 and
16 of the Act which deal with the accounts of companies and their audit.
Part 15 deals with the regulation of annual accounts which must be
submitted by companies to the Registrar of Companies. Section 386 of
the Act obliges companies to keep adequate accounting records. Such
records are defined as records which are sufficient (i) to show and explain
the company's transactions, (ii) to disclose with reasonable accuracy, at
any time, the financial position of the company at that time, and (iii) to

---

[69]　ss.875(1) and 877(2) and (3).
[70]　s.743(1) and (2) of the Act.

enable the directors to ensure that any accounts required to be prepared comply with the requirements of the Act. Section 394 of the Act compels the directors of a company to prepare individual accounts in respect of each of its financial years. Once compiled, the company's annual accounts must be approved by the board of directors and signed on behalf of the board by a director of the company on the balance sheet. A director is under a duty to produce a directors' report for each financial year in terms of s.415 of the Act. It must narrate the names of each person who was a director of the company during the relevant financial year and the principal activities of the company in that financial year.[71] In terms of s.417 of the Act, the directors' report must also contain a business review. The business review enjoins the directors to apply their mind to the overall strategic objectives of the company and the effects of implementing those objectives over time. Finally, the directors' report must be approved by the board of directors and signed on behalf of the board by a director or the secretary of the company.

Annual accounts: Submission and laying of accounts

In terms of s.423 of the Act, every company must send a copy of its **16–16** annual accounts and reports for each financial year to every member of the company, every holder of debentures of the company and to every person who is entitled to receive notice of general meetings of the company. A private company has until the date for filing its annual accounts with the Registrar of Companies to send out copies of its annual accounts and reports to its members, debenture-holders, etc.[72] In the case of a public company, the period for sending the annual accounts and reports is before 21 days of the date of the general meeting of the company at which the accounts are to be laid.[73] A failure to comply with such requirements to send out copies of the annual accounts in accordance with s.423 of the Act is a criminal offence and the company and its officers are liable to criminal penalties.[74] Once the annual accounts and reports have been prepared and duly signed by the directors or company secretary they must be filed with the Registrar of Companies.[75] A private company has a period of nine months from the end of the relevant financial year to file the accounts.[76] In the case of a public limited company, the period is six months from the financial year end.[77] If the directors fail to file the annual accounts and reports with the Registrar, the directors are deemed to have committed a criminal offence.[78]

---

[71] s.416(1).
[72] s.424(2).
[73] s.424(3).
[74] s.425.
[75] s.441(1).
[76] s.442(2)(a).
[77] s.442(2)(b).
[78] s.451(1).

Annual accounts: Audit and auditors

16–17 Every company must ensure that its annual accounts for a financial year are audited.[79] In terms of ss.485 and 489 of the Act, all companies must appoint an auditor by ordinary resolution of the members.[80] However, in the case of private limited companies, the directors may resolve not to appoint auditors "on the ground that audited accounts are unlikely to be required".[81] The same rules apply in respect of public limited companies.[82] There can only be one auditor of a private company or public company at any one point in time.[83] In the case of a private company, subject to certain exceptions, where an auditor has not been re-appointed in respect of the next financial year, the auditor in office in the previous financial year is deemed to be re-appointed.[84]

The duties of the auditors are spelt out in ss.495, 496, 497, 498 et seq. of the Act. This requires the auditors to investigate matters in order to form an opinion on the adequacy of the company's accounting records, whether the company's individual accounts agree with those accounting records. The auditors must compile an auditor's report which will state whether the annual accounts give a true and fair view of the state of affairs of the company as represented in the balance sheet and the profit and loss of the company. Moreover, the auditors must state in the auditor's report whether the information provided by the directors in the directors' report is consistent with the details in the annual accounts. An auditor has the right to (i) receive all notices and communications relating to a general meeting of the company, (ii) attend any general meeting of the company, and (iii) be heard at any general meeting which he attends on any part of the business of the meeting which concerns him as an auditor.[85] The auditor's report must state the name of the auditor and be signed and dated.[86] A final point to make is that the auditors may be removed by ordinary resolution of the members by special notice procedure in accordance with ss.510–511 of the Act. At any meeting proposing to remove him or her as an auditor, the auditor has the right to be heard.[87] An auditor cannot be removed by the members of a private company by written resolution procedure.[88]

---

[79] s.475(1).
[80] s.485(1) and (4).
[81] s.485(1).
[82] s.489(1) and (4).
[83] ss.487(1) and 491(1).
[84] s.487(2).
[85] s.502(2).
[86] s.503(1).
[87] s.513(2).
[88] s.288(2)(b).

CORPORATE DECISION-MAKING AND CORPORATE GOVERNANCE:
(I) OFFICERS AND DIRECTORS

Introduction: The constitutional balance of power between the directors and members

Since a company is an artificial person, it can only act and take decisions **16–18** through its human actors. The two organs which take decisions for the company and steer the direction of a company are (i) the board of directors, and (ii) the members in (a) general meeting or (b) in the case of a private company, outwith general meeting by written resolution procedure under the Act. The regulation of the board of directors and directors generally are to be found in ss.154–259 of the Act and Arts 3–20 and 53–54 of the Model Articles in the case of a private limited company by shares, Arts 3–20 and 38–39 of the Model Articles in the case of a private company limited by guarantee and Articles 3–27 and 85–86 of the Model Articles in respect of public limited companies. Meanwhile, the rules regarding general meetings and the written resolution procedure in the case of private companies are detailed in ss.281–361 of the Act and Arts 38–48 of the Model Articles in the case of a private limited company by shares, Arts 23–33 of the Model Articles in the case of a private company limited by guarantee and Arts 28–42 of the Model Articles in respect of public limited companies. The Model Articles set out the division of responsibility for decision-making between the board of directors and the members. The principal articles which embody such a distribution of decision-making authority are Arts 3 and 4 of the Model Articles in the case of private limited companies by shares, private companies limited by guarantee and public limited companies. Article 3 gives wide powers to the board of directors in the following terms:

- "Subject to the articles, the directors are responsible for the management of the company's business, for which purpose they may exercise all the powers of the company."

So the board of directors has the full power to manage and take decisions for the company. Articles 5 and 6 of the Model Articles give the directors the authority to delegate to managers or committees as they think fit. For example, certain decisions may be allocated to managing directors or the chairman.

However, Art.4 of the Model Articles reserve certain powers of instruction and initiation in favour of the members as follows:

"The shareholders/members may, by special resolution, direct the directors to take, or refrain from taking, specified action."

Hence, by special resolution, the members may direct the board of directors to take action or omit to act by special resolution. This provision demonstrates that the originating power of company law is vested in the members rather than the directors by virtue of the articles of association. Since s.21 of the Act empowers the members to alter the articles of association, the Act entrenches the right of members to remove Art.3 of the Model Articles and thus repatriate decision-making powers from the directors to the members.

Moreover, the Act provides that certain corporate decisions are so important or influential that only the members may sanction them. The board have no authority in such circumstances to proceed to take these decisions without the approval of the members. For example, s.77(1) of the Act narrates the fact that only the members can alter the name of the company by special resolution. The directors have no such power of their own to change the company's name. So whenever the Act provides that an ordinary resolution or special resolution is required before a company can take a certain course of action or decision, the directors are dis-empowered in such contexts.

The above discourse presents an abridged exposition of the constitu-tional balance of power in the company. What is clear is that the board of directors generally has a free hand to guide the course which a company takes. However, the members have residual "step in" rights. Provided that the members can meet the relevant threshold attached to a special resolution, they can instruct the directors how to act. Moreover, there are certain decisions which the directors are disqualified from making. Here, the Act draws the contours of the constitutional settlement between the directors and members. It does so by stipulating that certain decisions or actions must not be taken forward without the requisite degree of shareholder approval. The degree of shareholder approval required varies, depending on the decision at hand.

The company secretary

16–19   Prior to any detailed consideration of the role of the directors in the governance of the company, it is important not to lose sight of the pivotal role played by the company secretary. The company secretary performs an administrative role, dealing with official correspondence on behalf of the company, maintaining the statutory registers and ensuring that the filing and other administrative obligations imposed on the company are complied with in accordance with the terms of the Act. So it will com-monly be the company secretary who arranges for all notifications to be made to the Registrar of Companies in accordance with the Act or by law generally. Company secretaries commonly sit in on meetings of the board of directors and take the minutes of the deliberations. They will also produce draft board minutes,[89] briefing papers, draft resolutions and other documents for approval or consideration by the directors. Com-pany secretaries have the power to sign contracts and documents on behalf of the company in terms of the Requirements of Writing (Scot-land) Act 1995.[90] So they have the power to bind the company.

---

[89] In other words, minutes in conformance with the company's obligation in terms of s.248(1).
[90] Sch.2, para.3(1) to the Requirements of Writing (Scotland) Act 1995.

Section 270(1) of the Act states that a private company does not require to have a company secretary. Nevertheless, many private companies have and will continue to have company secretaries, since the administrative requirements imposed by the Act and the law generally will continue to be required to be fulfilled. In contrast, a public company must have a secretary at all times.[91] So it is unlawful for a public company not to have a company secretary in office at any particular point in time. A director may be a company secretary. In terms of the Companies Act 1985, where a company had only one director, that individual could not also be the secretary of the company.[92] Thus, it was not possible to have one director and secretary, the identities of which were the same. However, there is no equivalent provision in the Act. Therefore, where a private company has a sole director and opts to appoint a company secretary (which it is not required to do in terms of s.270 of the Act), there is no legal impediment to that director also acting as the company secretary.

There are various eligibility requirements regarding the qualifications of the company secretaries of public companies which must be satisfied before someone can be appointed a secretary of a public company in terms of s.273 of the Act. The company must keep a register of secretaries at its registered office or some other place notified to the Registrar of Companies. The details about company secretaries which must be kept in the register are his/her name, former name and address. Any change in (i) the identity of the company secretary, or (ii) the particulars contained in the company's register of secretaries, must be intimated to the Registrar of Companies within 14 days of the alteration.

The directors: General

This section of the book considers the appointment, eligibility, powers, **16–20** types, removal, disqualification and duties of directors and their position *vis-à-vis* the company and its members. Directors are the agents of the company. They are not the agents of the members of the company. In terms of s.250 of the Act, a director is defined as a "person occupying the position of director, by whatever name called". This definition includes a "shadow director" which is someone who has not been officially appointed as a director, but is a person in accordance with whose instructions the board of directors is accustomed to act.[93] Every private company must have at least one director,[94] and a public company must have no less than two directors.[95] In all cases, at least one director must be a natural person.[96] The Act contains various restrictions on the eligibility of persons to be a director. For example, persons under 16 years of age

---

[91] s.271.
[92] Companies Act 1985 s.283(2).
[93] s.251.
[94] s.154(1).
[95] s.154(2).
[96] s.155.

are not eligible for appointment as a director.[97] Moreover, s.11 of the CDDA states that an undischarged bankrupt cannot be appointed as a director of a company without the prior leave of the court.

The directors: Appointment

16–21   Article 17 of the Model Articles in the case of a private company limited by shares states that a director may be appointed to the board by ordinary resolution of the members or by co-option by the directors. A person will cease to be a director where they are made bankrupt, are prohibited from being a director by law, e.g. where they are disqualified from being a director, are declared to be physically or mentally incapable of acting as a director by medics or a court makes an order that the person is mentally ill.[98]

The directors: Types of director

16–22   There are essentially two types of directors. First, there are executive directors. Executive directors are involved in the "day-to-day" management of the business, take executive decisions on behalf of the company and usually have a service contract with the company which details their terms and conditions of service, including their contractual duties, obligations and powers. Meanwhile, non-executive directors do not directly run or manage the business of the company. They attend meetings of the board of directors and act as a check on the executive directors, principally performing a supervisory function over the executive members of the board. Decisions of the directors may be taken by unanimity or by a majority decision.[99] However, this rule does not apply in the case where the company has a sole director.[100]

The directors: Removal

16–23   Directors may be removed in terms of s.168(1) of the Act by an ordinary resolution of the members of the company. The power of the members to remove a director arises "notwithstanding anything in any agreement between [the company] and [the director]". A member proposing to remove a director must proceed by special notice procedure in terms of s.312 of the Act. The special notice procedure envisages the member providing notice to the company of their intention to remove a director at least 28 days before the general meeting at which the resolution is moved.[101] The company is then under an obligation to give notice to the members of any such ordinary resolution in the same manner and at the same time as it gives notice of the meeting.[102] If it is impracticable for the company to give notice within the said 28-day timescale, the company

---

[97] s.157(1).
[98] Art.18 of the Model Articles.
[99] Art.7(1) of the Model Articles.
[100] Art.7(2) of the Model Articles.
[101] s.312(1).
[102] s.312(2).

must give its members notice at least 14 days before the meeting by advertisement in a newspaper having an appropriate circulation or in any other manner permitted by the company's articles of association.[103] Moreover, when the company receives notice from a member intending to remove a director, the company must forthwith send a copy of that notice to the director concerned.[104] At the meeting, the director has the right to protest his or her removal and has a right to be heard.[105] If the director provides the company with representations in writing regarding his proposed removal, if time will allow, the company must send a copy of those representations to each of the members with the notice of the resolution given to the members of the company.[106]

The directors: Disqualification

Notwithstanding the rules in the Act concerning the removal of directors, **16–24** individuals may be disqualified from acting as a director. The relevant legislation is the CDDA. The CDDA outlines a number of grounds on which a natural person may be disqualified from taking up a directorship or shadow directorship without judicial consent. The intervention of the court is required and where any of the statutory grounds are satisfied, the court may, and in certain circumstances must, grant what is called a disqualification order. Section 2 of the CDDA states that the court may make a disqualification order against a person where any of the following grounds have been fulfilled:

- an individual is convicted of an indictable offence in connection with the promotion, formation, management, liquidation or striking off of a company;[107]
- an individual is found to be in persistent breach of his obligations under company law;[108]
- an individual has been found guilty of fraudulent trading in terms of s.993 of the Act which manifested itself in the context of a winding up, that is to say that the directors have traded in a manner which demonstrates an intention on their part to defraud creditors of the company or creditors of any other person;[109]
- an individual is convicted of a summary offence in consequence of a contravention of, or a failure to comply with, any provision of the companies legislation requiring a return, account or other document to be filed with the Registrar of Companies;[110]

---

[103] s.312(3).
[104] s.169(1).
[105] s.169(2).
[106] s.169(3).
[107] CDDA s.2(1).
[108] CDDA s.3(1).
[109] CDDA s.4(1).
[110] CDDA s.5(1).

- a court has made a declaration finding an individual to have participated in fraudulent trading or wrongful trading in contravention of s.213 or s.214 of the Insolvency Act 1986.[111]

Where a company has gone into insolvent liquidation and a director is ruled to be unfit to be a director, the court must make a disqualification order in respect of that individual.[112] Parts 1 and 2 of Sch.1 to the CDDA provide a non-exhaustive list of the circumstances in which an individual will be deemed to be unfit. For example, an individual will be unfit where he or she is found to be in breach of fiduciary duty or breach of trust. Likewise, where an individual engages in conduct which gives rise to an obligation to account for any money or other property of the company. An individual will also be ruled to be unfit where they have failed to satisfy various requirements regarding the keeping of records and registers at the registered office of the company and the filing of documents such as the company's annual return with the Registrar of Companies. The director may be disqualified for a period of up to 15 years for serious misconduct and up to five years in cases of a less serious nature.[113]

The directors: Powers and duties

16–25 Turning to the powers of directors, as mentioned above, the default rule in terms of Art.3 of the Model Articles is that the directors have the right to exercise all of the powers of the company. Thus decision-making authority and responsibility for steering the company in a particular direction is conferred upon the directors. Given the wide potential for directors to self-deal at the company's expense or to apply the funds and resources of the company for their own personal benefit, company law has developed rules over the years to inhibit such conduct. Such rules which are designed to stymie the potential for directors to abuse their powers are derived from the law of trusts and so historically, in developing the law here, an analogy was made by the English courts of Chancery between a trustee and a director. In the case of the law of trusts, the courts imposed duties on trustees as regards the property of the trust. Likewise, in the case of the company, the common law courts imposed duties on directors as regards the direction of the company, corporate decision-making and the application of the company's assets. The common law duties established by the courts can be broadly divided into two categories. First, a director owes a fiduciary duty of loyalty towards the company, that is to say that the large degree of trust and confidence inherent within the relationship between the company and the director is such that the director must not use corporate assets, or deal with the company, as to benefit himself at the expense of the company and its shareholders. Secondly, the directors owe a duty of care and skill to the company in respect of their actions and decision-making. The duty

---

[111] CDDA s.10(1).
[112] CDDA s.6(1).
[113] *Re Sevenoaks Stationers (Retail) Ltd* [1991] Ch. 164.

of loyalty is the basis upon which the courts test the impartiality of a decision taken by the director and the duty of care and skill is the means by which the law lays down its expectations about the degree of competence and care which directors should exercise in taking a decision.

The common law rules which give expression to the duties of loyalty and care owed by directors have now been superseded by the terms of ss.170–178 of the Act. Section 170(3) of the Act clarifies that the statutory duties "have effect in place of" the common law rules as regards the duties owed to a company by a director. However, the common law rules have not simply "gone away". The statutory statement of director's duties in the Act do not offer a complete codification of the existing common law rules. This is partly due to simple gaps, such as the common law duty of directors to consider the interests of creditors when insolvency is threatened, which are not separately addressed in the Act and are clearly expressed in s.172(3) of the Act to be found in the common law. Likewise, it is not clear that the duty of a director to disclose his own misconduct to the company is codified in the Act.[114] The partial nature of the codification exercise is also evident from the terms of s.170(4) of the Act. This provision states that the statutory duties must be interpreted and applied in the same way as the common rules which they replace and regard must be had to the corresponding common law rules in interpreting and applying the statutory duties. What this means is that the case law which was relevant prior to the coming into force of the Act will continue to command importance for the purposes of construing the meaning and application of the statutory duties. For that reason, recourse will be made to case law from time to time during the ensuing discussion to enhance understanding of the relevant statutory duty to which that case law corresponds. Another point to stress is that there is more than one duty. Thus, in a particular case, more than one duty may apply and this is recognised by s.179 of the Act. To that extent, there may be an overlap between the duties in any given case.

The directors: To whom are the duties owed?

Prior to initiating a discussion of the content of the duties, it is beneficial **16–26** to clarify to whom a director owes those duties. Section 170(1) of the Act answers this question in terms that the duties are owed by a director to the company. But to what extent and in what circumstances does a director owe duties to an individual shareholder? As is clear from the case of *Peskin v Anderson*,[115] it will only be in special factual circumstances that third parties will be able to demonstrate to a court that a director owes them duties of the nature enumerated in ss.171 to 177 of the Act.

---

[114] In other words, the rule in *Item Software (UK) Ltd v Fassihi* [2005] 2 B.C.L.C. 91.
[115] [2001] 1 B.C.L.C. 372.

Peskin v Anderson
[2001] 1 B.C.L.C. 372

Concerning: Whether the directors of a company owed duties to a particular shareholder of the company.

Facts: In terms of a company's articles of association, profits generated by the commercial activities of the company could not be distributed to its members. The company entered into negotiations with, and agreed to sell its business to, a third party. The sale and purchase arrangements involved the alteration of the company's articles to permit the distribution of some of the sale proceeds to the members. Members who had resigned their membership approximately three years prior to the announcement of the sale of the company's business to the third party sued the directors for breach of their duties as directors. The former members' claim against the directors was formulated on the basis that had the directors disclosed to them that the company was in negotiations to sell its business to the third party, those members would not have decided to resign as members when they did. So the members claimed that the directors breached a duty which the directors owed to them as members.

Decision: The Court of Appeal recognised that there are circumstances in which the directors of a company will owe fiduciary duties to members, e.g. where the directors make direct approaches to, and deal with, the shareholders in relation to a specific transaction and hold themselves out as agents for them in connection with the acquisition or disposal of shares. Likewise, the directors may owe duties to members where the former make material representations to the latter, where the former fail to make material disclosure to the latter of insider information in the context of negotiations for a take-over of the company's business or where the former supply to the latter specific information and advice on which the latter have relied. But absent such circumstances, generally, directors will owe their duties to the company only. In this particular case, the Court of Appeal ruled that there was nothing special in the factual relationship between the directors and the members to give rise to a fiduciary duty of disclosure. In particular there were no relevant dealings, negotiations, communications or other contact directly between the directors and the members. The actions of the directors had not caused the members to sell their shares when they did and, probably most important of all, at the beginning of the year in which the business of the company was sold, there was nothing sufficiently concrete and specific, either in existence or in contemplation, for the directors to disclose to the members.

The directors: Duty to obey the constitution and act for a proper purpose

The first duty of a director to consider is the duty in s.171 which provides **16–27** that directors must act in accordance with a company's constitution and that they must only exercise the powers which they are conferred under the constitution for the purposes for which they were conferred. The duty to obey the constitution means that the directors must not attempt to do something which it is not in the power of the company to undertake. As for the duty that a director must not use their powers for an improper purpose, examples of what are meant by this duty are provided by the case law.

Howard Smith Ltd v Ampol Petroleum Ltd
[1974] A.C. 821 (Privy Council)

Concerning: Whether the directors of a company had breached their duty not to exercise their powers for an improper purpose where they used their constitutional power to issue shares in the company to one preferred bidder over another in the context of a takeover battle for the company.

Facts: Two companies, Ampol and Bulkships, held 30 per cent and 25 per cent respectively of the issued shares of RW Miller ("Holdings") Ltd ("Millers"), which required more capital. Ampol made an offer for all the issued shares of Millers, and another company, Howard Smith, announced an intention to make a higher offer for those shares. Millers' directors considered Ampol's offer to be too low and decided to recommend that the offer be rejected. Ampol and Bulkships then stated that they intended to act jointly in the future operations of Millers and would reject any offer for their shares. Howard Smith then applied to Millers for an allotment of 4½ million ordinary shares. Millers' directors decided by a majority to make the allotment and immediately issued the shares. The effect of that issue was that Millers secured the much needed capital, Ampol and Bulkship's respective shareholdings were reduced to 36.6 per cent of the issued shares and Howard Smith was in a position to make an effective takeover offer. Ampol challenged the validity of the issue of the shares to Howard Smith and sought an order for the rectification of Millers' share register by the removal of Howard Smith as a member of Millers in respect of the allotted shares. Millers' directors contended that the primary reason for the issue of the shares to Howard was to obtain more capital. Ampol argued that the reason for the issue of the shares was to destroy their majority shareholding, which was an improper purpose.

Decision: The Privy Council ruled that it is unconstitutional and a breach of duty for a director to use his fiduciary powers over the shares in the company purely for the purpose of destroying an existing majority shareholding, or creating a new majority which did

> not previously exist. To do so is to disturb that element of the company's constitution which is separate from and set against their powers. If there is added to this immediate purpose, an ulterior purpose to enable an offer for shares to proceed which the existing majority was in a position to block, the departure from the legitimate use of the fiduciary power becomes not less, but all the greater. The right to dispose of shares at a given price is essentially an individual right to be exercised on individual decision and on which a majority, in the absence of oppression or similar impropriety, is entitled to prevail. So for directors to use their fiduciary powers solely for the purpose of upsetting the balance of power to decide to whom and at what price shares are to be sold cannot be related to any purpose for which the power over the share capital was conferred upon them.

So, in the case of *Howard Smith*, where the directors issue shares in order to raise capital, that should not be undertaken in a manner which is designed to upset the existing constitutional balance of shareholder power.

The directors: Duty to promote the success of the company

16–28 The second statutory duty to examine is the duty of a director to promote the success of the company. Section 172(1) of the Act is as follows:

"A director of a company must act in the way he considers, in good faith, would be most likely to promote the success of the company for the benefit of its members as a whole, and in doing so have regard (amongst other matters) to—

(a) the likely consequences of any decision in the long term,
(b) the interests of the company's employees,
(c) the need to foster the company's business relationships with suppliers, customers and others,
(d) the impact of the company's operations on the community and the environment,
(e) the desirability of the company maintaining a reputation for high standards of business conduct, and
(f) the need to act fairly as between members of the company."

This is the overarching fiduciary duty owed by directors by virtue of the Act. What is clear from s.172(1) of the Act is that a subjective test is applied to the director's decision. So provided the director acts in good faith and genuinely believes the decision he takes will promote the success of the company, what only matters is that director's view, not that of the court—and the court will be unable to substitute its own judgment for that of the director. Moreover, the duty of the director is "to promote the success of the company for the benefit of its members as a whole". In practice, this will enjoin the director to take decisions which attain the objectives for which the company has been established and in the case of commercial non-charitable companies, this will be a decision which results in a long-term increase in value for the company.[116] From s.172(1) of the Act, it is clear that the primary obligation of the director is to promote the success of the company. So the interests of the company and its members are paramount and the other six constituencies and factors listed in subs.(1)(a)–(f),[117] e.g. the interests of employees, suppliers, customers, the community, the environment, etc. which the directors must have regard to in taking a decision,[118] are subordinate. Hence, if a director takes a decision which is in the interests of the company, but contrary to the interests of one of the other constituencies, the director will not be in breach of duty. So long as a director can show that he did actually consider these statutory factors, even if he ultimately decided that they were less important than other factors, he will probably have discharged his duty. A further important point to make is that s.172(1)(a) of the Act imposes a requirement on the directors to consider the likely long-term consequences of their decision. This represents a departure from the common law which was predominantly concerned with the short-term consequences of decisions. However, the concern is that the Act does not provide the directors with any particular direction as to how they are supposed to reconcile long-term and short-term interests where they are clearly incompatible with each other. In certain cases, it may be commercially sensible for a director to accept a loan from a lender which resolves the short-term financial difficulties of the company. However, in the long term, that decision may be disadvantageous to the company. So in such a situation is the director bound to forgo the offer of loan? It is not particularly clear how the director ought to proceed in such a case and the courts may be asked to adjudicate on such a matter.

The directors: Duty to exercise independent judgment

Turning to the third duty of directors, the duty in s.173(1) of the Act **16–29** imposes a requirement on directors to exercise independent judgment. This is particularly relevant in the context of the exercise of their decision-making powers. This duty compels a director to approach matters with an open mind and without bias when they are exercising their discretionary decision-making powers. Therefore, in circumstances where a director has legally bound themselves in advance to take a certain course of action, they will be ostensibly in breach of such a duty. However, s.173(2) provides two exceptions to the general rule. First, where a

[116] See the statement of Lord Goldsmith, Lords Grand Committee, February 6, 2006, cols 255–258, *Hansard*.
[117] Which list is not intended to be exhaustive of the matters which the directors "must have regard to" in forming their decision.
[118] In the view of Margaret Hodge MP, Minister of State for Industry and the Regions at the time of the passage of the Companies Bill, "have regard to" will mean "think about" or "give proper consideration to", see Commons Report, October 17, 2006, col.789, Hansard.

director has entered into a contractual agreement which restricts the future exercise of their discretionary powers of decision-making, they will not be in breach of such duty. So the Act recognises that there may be circumstances in which the company has bound itself in contract to a course of action which may fetter the discretion of the directors in the future and that this will not be unlawful. Secondly, a director will not be in breach of duty where the company's articles of association enable a director to restrict their independent judgment. Hence, a director will not be prevented from exercising a power to delegate conferred by the company's articles provided that its exercise is in accordance with the company's articles.

The directors: Duty to avoid conflicts of interest

16–30 One of the principal ramifications of the loyalty obligation is that a director must avoid conflicts between his/her interests and the company's interests. Section 175(1) of the Act provides as follows:

> "A director of a company must avoid a situation in which he has, or can have, a direct or indirect interest that conflicts, or possibly may conflict, with the interests of the company."

In terms of s.175(7) of the Act, the scope of s.175(1) covers both conflicts of interest and duty and conflicts of duties. The conflicting interest of the director may be direct or indirect, e.g. the interest of a director may be indirect where the director has been appointed by a major shareholder to serve their interests and those interests are contrary to the interests of the company. Section 175(2) of the Act provides in particular that the duty applies to the exploitation of property, information or opportunities by the director. So if a director comes across information in the capacity of director and then seeks to use that information for his own personal advantage, the director will be in breach. Most importantly, s.175(2) of the Act states that it is immaterial that the company could not itself take advantage of the information, opportunity or property. That is to say, that a director will not be able to defend a claim of breach of duty by arguing that the property, information or opportunity which the director sought to exploit was one which the company could not take advantage for itself.

Section 175(4) of the Act makes it clear that the duty to avoid conflicts of interest in s.175(1) will not be breached if the situation cannot reasonably be regarded as likely to give rise to a conflict of interest. Furthermore, a director will not be in breach of duty in circumstances where the breach has been authorised in advance. Section 175(5)(a) of the Act states that the conflict of interest may be authorised in advance by the directors. For such prior authorisation by the directors to be valid, in the case of a private company there must be nothing in the company's articles which invalidates such authorisation, and in the case of a public company there must be specific provision in the company's articles which entitles the directors to authorise conflicts and the directors must follow that particular procedure for authorising conflicts. If the directors do not authorise the conflict in advance, it is open to the members of the company to ratify any infringement of the duty in accordance with ss.180 and 239 of the Act.

An important exception to the duty to avoid conflicts of interest and duty is spelled out in s.175(3) of the Act. Here, it is provided that s.175 does not apply to a conflict of interest arising in relation to a transaction or arrangement with the company. Sections 177 and 182–187 of the Act apply where such a conflict of interest arises and consideration will be given to the specific rules which apply shortly. Moreover, the duty to avoid conflicts of interest applies to a limited extent in relation to directors who have resigned and thus ceased to be a director and are no longer in office by virtue of the terms of s.170(2) of the Act. There have been a number of cases in which the common law considered the culpability of directors for breach of the duty to avoid conflicts of interest in circumstances where they had resigned from office. One such case is *Industrial Development Consultants Ltd v Cooley*.

Industrial Development Consultants Ltd v Cooley
[1972] 1 W.L.R. 443

Concerning: Whether a director who had resigned from office and had taken advantage of an opportunity presented to him in his capacity as a director was in breach of duty to avoid conflicts of interest.

Facts: Cooley was an architect and managing director of a building and development consultancy company. In his capacity as a director, he entered into negotiations with the Eastern Gas Board ("EGB"). His remit was to secure contracts for the company from EGB. However, EGB refused to enter into contracts with consultants and so the company could not take advantage of the opportunity. However, EGB were happy to offer the work to private architects and so offered contracts to Cooley in a private capacity. Cooley was released from office as a director on the false basis of ill-health and then took advantage of the contract offered by EGB. When the company sued Cooley for recovery of the benefits which he had personally derived from the contract with EGB, he sought to defend his conduct by arguing that (i) he was no longer a director of the company when he had taken the contractual opportunity, and (ii) the opportunity was one which the company could not take advantage of itself.

Decision: Roskill J. in the High Court held that while Cooley was a managing director of the company, a fiduciary relationship existed between him and the company. Accordingly, information which came to him while he was managing director and was of concern to the company, was information which it was his duty to disclose to the company. He was under a duty therefore to disclose all information which he received in the course of his dealings with EGB.

Instead he had embarked on a deliberate course of conduct which had put his personal interests as a potential contracting party with EGB in direct conflict with his pre-existing and continuing duty as managing director to the company. He was therefore in breach of his fiduciary duty to the company in failing to pass on to them all the relevant information received in the course of his dealings with EGB and in guarding it for his own personal purposes and profit. Moreover, it was irrelevant that he was no longer a director when he had exploited the contractual opportunity with EGB and the question whether the benefit of the contract would have been obtained for the company but for Cooley's breach of fiduciary duty was irrelevant.

The directors: Duty not to accept benefits from third parties

16–31 Coupled with the duty of a director to avoid conflicts of interest, s.176 of the Act provides that a director must not accept benefits from third parties. So it stands to reason that directors must not accept bribes or commissions from clients or potential clients. The duty not to accept benefits is not breached if the acceptance of the benefit cannot reasonably be regarded as likely to give rise to a conflict of interest. So this provision covers minor gifts and benefits received by directors which are of a trivial nature. However, unlike s.175(4)(b) and (5) of the Act, there is no specific provision empowering the directors to authorise a director's breach of the duty not to accept benefits from third parties. Having said that, ss.180 and 239 enable the members to authorise or ratify breaches of this duty.

The directors: Duty to declare interest in proposed or existing transaction or arrangement with the company

16–32 As mentioned above, where the conflict of interest concerns a transaction or arrangement arising between the director and the company, ss.177 and 182–187 of the Act will apply. Section 177 applies in the case of a proposed transaction or arrangement between the director and the company, while ss.182 to 187 of the Act are the relevant provisions in the context of an existing transaction or arrangement. First, s.177 recognises that directors may be directly or indirectly interested in a proposed transaction or arrangement with the company. Rather than prohibit the entering into of such conflicted transactions, s.177(1), (2) and (4) of the Act provides that a director has an obligation to declare that interest to the directors at a board meeting or by notice in advance of the transaction or arrangement being concluded or entered into. If the director fails to comply with the duty in s.177, the contract, transaction or arrangement is voidable if it is entered into. That is to say that it is not invalidated, but that it may be set aside at the instance or option of the company. Moreover, there are other remedies available, which are narrated in s.178 of the Act. It is stipulated in s.177(5) and (6) that a director need not declare an interest in a proposed transaction if he could not reasonably be aware of it, or it could not be reasonably regarded as likely to give rise to a conflict of interest. A director is also relieved from making disclosure where the other directors are already aware of the transaction. Section 180 of the Act provides that, subject to the company's articles of association, if the directors observe their duty to declare their interest in accordance with s.177 of the Act, the transaction is not liable to be set aside on the basis of the common law rule that the consent of the members is also required.

Section 182 of the Act states that where a director is directly or indirectly interested in an existing (rather than proposed) transaction or arrangement that has been entered into by a company, the director must declare that interest to the other directors as soon as reasonably practicable at a board meeting, by written notice in terms of s.184 of the Act or by general notice in accordance with s.185 of the Act. Moreover, where a director fails to comply with his duty to declare his interest in a proposed transaction or arrangement with the company of which he ought reasonably to have been aware in accordance with s.177 of the Act and subsequently enters into the transaction with the company, not only will he be in breach of his duty to disclose under s.177 of the Act, but he must make separate disclosure in accordance with the terms of s.182 of the Act. Breach of the duty in s.182 of the Act to disclose an interest in an existing transaction or arrangement is an offence in terms of s.183 of the Act. Again, it is narrated in s.182(5) and (6) that a director need not declare an interest in an existing transaction if he could not reasonably be aware of it, or it could not be reasonably regarded as likely to give rise to a conflict of interest. A director is also relieved from making disclosure where the other directors are already aware of the transaction.

The directors: Duty of care, skill and diligence

It should be stressed that each of the duties of directors which have been **16–33** considered so far are fiduciary duties; that is to say, the duty to obey the constitution and not to act for an improper purpose,[119] the duty to promote the success of the company,[120] the duty to exercise independent judgment,[121] the duty to avoid conflicts of interest,[122] the duty not to accept benefits from third parties,[123] and the duties of disclosure in respect of proposed or existing transactions or arrangements entered into between the director and the company.[124] This is important since it explains the loyalty obligation which underpins those particular duties and, as will become apparent in the ensuing discussion of s.178 of the Act, it is important to make the classification between fiduciary duties and non-fiduciary duties for the purposes of ascertaining the nature of the remedies open to parties seeking to challenge a director for breach of

---

[119] s.171.
[120] s.172.
[121] s.173.
[122] s.175.
[123] s.176
[124] ss.177, 180 and 182 to 187.

duty. One duty which is not fiduciary in nature is the duty in s.174 of the Act.[125] Section 174(1) states that a director must exercise reasonable care, skill and diligence. An exploration of the content of such a duty is made in s.174(2) where the duty is taken to signify the care, skill and diligence that would be exercised by a reasonably diligent person with (a) the general knowledge, skill and experience that may reasonably be expected of a person carrying out the functions carried out by the director in relation to the company, and (b) the general knowledge, skill and experience that the director has. Thus, in determining whether a director has breached his duty of care and skill in terms of s.174, the court must apply a mixture of an objective and subjective test. Therefore, what the reasonable person would regard as the knowledge, skill and experience to be expected of the hypothetical director sets the lowest acceptable standard (this is the objective assessment) with the actual director's knowledge, skill and experience operating to lift that threshold where it is clear that the attributes of the actual director are higher than the reasonable, hypothetical standard (this is the subjective assessment). Section 174 codifies the existing common law, a good example of which is provided by the case of *Re D'Jan of London Ltd.*

Re D'Jan of London Ltd
[1994] 1 B.C.L.C. 561

Concerning: Whether a director who had failed to read an insurance policy proposal form before signing it was in breach of his duty of care, skill and diligence.

Facts: Mr D'Jan was a director. He failed to read an insurance policy proposal form in taking out insurance on behalf of the company of which he was a director. The effect of his signature was that certain questions which had been answered in the negative by his insurance broker were in fact true. When the company's premises and stock to the value of £174,000 were destroyed by fire, the insurance company avoided the insurance policy on the basis of breach of warranty. The result was that the company was insolvent and the liquidator of the company brought proceedings for the benefit of the unsecured creditors on the basis of a breach of the director's duty of care, skill and diligence.

Decision: The High Court in England ruled that Mr D'Jan had been negligent. In failing to read the insurance policy proposal form before signing it on behalf of the company, he had failed to discharge the duty of care, skill and diligence which he owed to the company on an objective assessment (i.e. the standard which the reasonable person would regard as the knowledge, skill and experience to be expected of the hypothetical director) and a subjective assessment (i.e. the standard of knowledge, skill and

---

[125] Lord Goldsmith, Lords Grand Committee, February 9, 2006, col.334, *Hansard.*

experience which the actual director possessed). So he was in breach of duty.

The relevance of the duty of care, skill and diligence lies in the fact that it must be observed by a director in applying his mind to his fiduciary duties in the context of decision-making. So this duty will apply in connection with the duty to promote the success of the company under s.172 of the Act, i.e. to any good faith assessment as to which of the factors are relevant to a business decision and to what extent they need to be taken into account. If the good faith assessment turns out to be wrong, the decision could be open to challenge if the directors fail either the subjective or the objective test in s.174 of the Act, which underscores the importance of directors taking care and exercising the appropriate standard of diligence in undertaking a consideration of the list of statutory factors enumerated in s.172 of the Act.

The directors: Remedies for breach of duty

The consequences of a director breaching the duties in ss.171 to 177 of **16–34** the Act are set out in s.178 of the Act which provides as follows:

"(1) The consequences of breach (or threatened breach) of sections 171 to 177 are the same as would apply if the corresponding common law rule or equitable principle applied.
(2) The duties in those sections (with the exception of section 174 (duty to exercise reasonable care, skill and diligence)) are, accordingly, enforceable in the same way as any other fiduciary duty owed to a company by its directors."

Therefore, in the case of fiduciary duties (i.e. all of the statutory duties with the exception of s.174), the consequences of breach may include:

- damages or compensation where the company has suffered loss;
- restoration of the company's property;
- an account of profits made by the director; and/or
- rescission of a contract where the director failed to disclose an interest.

In the case of a breach of s.174, i.e. the non-fiduciary duty of care, skill and diligence, only the damages remedy from the above list will be available and the other remedies in the bullet-points above will be irrelevant.

However, the company may wish to ratify a director's conduct which amounts to a breach of the duties in ss.171–177. Section 239 of the Act permits this to be achieved by the members passing an ordinary resolution in general meeting. There are certain anti-avoidance provisions which apply whereby any votes held by a director in breach, or any member connected with him, are not to be taken into account. Bodies corporate in which the director and any persons connected with him together have broadly a 20 per cent interest in the equity or the voting rights are connected with a director for this purpose. Ratification may not be possible where a holding company is asked to ratify the acts of a director of its subsidiary company and the director has a material interest in the holding company. Finally, if a director is found to be in breach of duty by a court, the court has a discretion to grant relief to that director under s.1157 of the Act, if they are satisfied that the director acted "honestly and reasonably and ... having regard to all the circumstances of the case ... he ought fairly to be excused."

The directors: Statutory obligations

16–35 Notwithstanding the statutory statement of general duties owed by the directors to the company expressed in ss.171–177 of the Act, there are further statutory restrictions contained in the Act in respect of contracts, transactions and arrangements entered into between the company and a director. The restrictions are imposed in connection with:

- long-term service contracts entered into between the company and a director;[126]
- transactions where the company sells or buys a substantial non-cash asset to or from a director of the company;[127]
- loan and similar type transactions by companies to their directors;[128] and
- payments by companies to directors for loss of office.[129]

Each of the above transactions or payments must be approved by an ordinary resolution of the members to be effective.

Key Concept

A director is an officer of the company who is responsible for the day-to-day management of the company. The law imposes duties on directors in an effort to control self-dealing and opportunistic behaviour on the part of directors. Such duties can be divided into fiduciary duties, embodying a director's (i) duty of loyalty and fidelity towards the company, and (ii) duties of care, skill and diligence in decision-making.

---

[126] ss.188–189.
[127] ss.190–196.
[128] ss.197–214.
[129] ss.215–222.

Corporate Decision-making and Corporate Governance: (ii) Company Meetings and Resolutions

Introduction

The general meeting is the forum at which the members of the company **16–36** can come together to consider the performance of the directors of the company and vote on matters which the Act and the articles of association of the company specify must be passed by resolution of the members. For example, in terms of s.188(2) of the Act, it is at the general meeting that the members can consider whether to pass an ordinary resolution (or not as the case may be) to approve a long-term service contract entered into between the company and a director. Likewise, a decision to amend the company's articles of association by special resolution in terms of s.21(1) of the Act will be considered at a general meeting. As will be explored shortly, there are three types of resolutions, each with different consequences and each required in differing contexts as prescribed by the Act or the company's articles of association.

General meetings: General

In undertaking any examination of the rules in the Act concerning general **16–37** meetings, it is salutary to keep in mind the distinction between private companies and public companies. This is so, since there is no legal requirement for a private limited company to hold a general meeting as a matter of course. By contrast, plcs (whether quoted or not) are under a statutory obligation to hold an annual general meeting ("AGM") in terms of s.336 of the Act, that is to say a general meeting which takes place once a year. The AGM of the public company must be held within 6 months of its financial year end.[130] However, public companies may call and hold general meetings other than AGMs where there is a requirement to undertake and complete business which is so pressing or urgent that it is impracticable to wait until the next AGM.

General meetings: Power to call general meetings

If a public company wishes to hold a general meeting (other than an **16–38** AGM) or a private company proposes to call and hold a general meeting,[131] the company must opt in to the holding of general meetings through the relevant procedures in the Act.[132] Section 302 enables the directors of a private company or public company to call a general meeting. Section 303 of the Act contains a separate members' requisition procedure. Where a member or members holding:

- at least 10 per cent of the paid up capital of the company as carries the right of voting at general meetings; or

---

[130] s.336.
[131] There is no such thing as an AGM in the case of a private company.
[132] For example, by applying the procedure in ss.302 or 303 of the Act.

- in the case of a non-share company, at least 10 per cent[133] of the total voting rights of all the members having a right to vote at general meetings,

request a general meeting, the directors are required to call such a meeting:

- within 21 days from the date on which they become subject to the requirement; and
- to be held on a date not more than 28 days after the date of the notice convening the meeting.[134]

In relation to private companies, the threshold of 10 per cent referred to above may be changed to 5 per cent where more than 12 months have elapsed since the end of the last general meeting.[135] The member(s)' request under s.303(2) of the Act may be in hard copy or electronic form and must be authenticated by the member or members and state the general nature of the business to be dealt with at the general meeting.[136] It may also include the text of a resolution that may be properly moved and is intended to be moved at the meeting.[137] As regards the proposed resolution, any resolution may be moved by a member or members unless:

- it would, if passed, be ineffective—whether by reason of inconsistency with any enactment or the company's constitution or otherwise; or
- it is defamatory of any person; or
- it is frivolous or vexatious.[138]

As a complete stop gap, the court has the power to order a general meeting where it is impracticable to call the meeting of a company in any manner in which meetings of that company may be called or to conduct the meeting in the manner prescribed by the company's articles or the Act.[139] This is on the application of a director or any member who would be entitled to vote at the meeting. The intervention of the court to order the calling of a meeting will be appropriate in circumstances where there has been an irretrievable breakdown in relations between the members and there is a clear deadlock.

---

[133] ss.302 or 303 of the Act.
[134] ss.303(2) and (3) and 304(1).
[135] s.303(3).
[136] s.303(4)(a).
[137] s.303(4)(b).
[138] s.303(5).
[139] s.306(1).

Union Music Ltd v Watson
[2003] EWCA Civ 180; [2003] 1 B.C.L.C. 453

Concerning: The circumstances in which the court should exercise its discretion under s.306(1) of the Act to order the calling of a general meeting.

Facts: Union Music Ltd ("UML") was the majority shareholder of the company and Russell Watson, the opera singer, was the minority shareholder. A shareholders' agreement entered into between UML and Watson provided that both shareholders' prior written consent was required for the holding of a general meeting of the members of the company. There was a breakdown in the relationship between the two members, UML refused to attend meetings of the company and one of the directors of the company resigned. UML applied to the court seeking an order for the calling of a general meeting in order to appoint a new director. At first instance, it was ruled that the court had no authority to exercise its discretion to call a meeting where a shareholders' agreement provided expressly that the consent of both members was required for any general meeting. UML appealed to the Court of Appeal.

Decision: The Court of Appeal granted the appeal. Section 371 of the Act was a procedural section intended to enable company business that needed to be conducted at a meeting of the company to be so conducted, and to allow a company not to be frustrated in its affairs by the impracticability of calling a meeting in the manner prescribed by its articles. Where, as in the instant case, there were unequal shareholdings the court was under no obligation to assume that the parties had intended that a veto had been intended on the part of either shareholder, much less the minority shareholder. The shareholders' agreement had to be read against that situation, and it was not to be viewed as giving one party a veto over another from calling any meeting at all. Instead, it should be viewed as a provision relating to a quorum. In those circumstances, it was plain that the court should exercise its discretion to make an order for a meeting under the Act.

General meetings: AGMs of public companies

Every plc must hold an AGM in each period of six months beginning **16–39** with the day following its accounting reference date. The procedures for holding an AGM of a public company are distinct from the conventions in the Act which apply in the context of a general meeting of a plc (which were considered above). The effect of a failure to hold such an AGM is that each officer of the public company is deemed to have committed a criminal offence. In practice, it is commonly the directors who will take the necessary steps to arrange the AGM and the business and resolutions to be considered. The members have a separate power under s.338 of the Act to require the company to circulate resolutions for AGMs—over and above the right they have under s.303(4) and (5) of the Act to call a general meeting. However, there are crucial differences. Under s.303 of the Act, the threshold is 10 per cent of the members for the calling of an EGM, whereas under s.338 (3), the threshold is:

- 5 per cent of the total voting rights of all of the members of the plc who have a right to vote on the resolution at the AGM to which the requests relate (excluding voting rights attached to any shares in the company which are held as treasury shares); or
- at least 100 members who have a right to vote on the resolution at the AGM to which the requests relate and hold shares in the company on which there has been paid up an average sum, per member, of at least £100.

Any resolution may be moved by a member at an AGM unless:

- it would, if passed, be ineffective—whether by reason of inconsistency with any enactment or the company's constitution or otherwise; or
- it is defamatory of any person; or
- it is frivolous or vexatious.

Additional requirements are imposed on quoted companies as follows:

- there is a requirement to publish poll results online;[140] and
- shareholders (100 in number or representing 5 per cent of more of the voting rights) have the power to require a report on a poll to be procured from an independent assessor, but only where a poll is to be taken at a meeting of which notice was given on or after October 1, 2007.[141]

General meetings: Notice of general meetings

16–40 Subject to any longer period of notice stipulated in the articles,[142] a general meeting of a private company requires 14 days' prior notice to the members.[143] In the case of a plc, a general meeting must be called by 21 days' prior notice to the members in the case of an AGM[144] or 14 days' prior notice to the members in the case of any other general meeting.[145] In the case of an AGM of a public company, it is a legal requirement for the plc to specify in the notice that the meeting is an annual general meeting.[146]

Notwithstanding the periods for the provision of notice, there is a

---

[140] s.341.
[141] s.342.
[142] s.307(3).
[143] s.307(1).
[144] s.307(2)(a).
[145] s.307(2)(b). This is subject to any longer period of notice stipulated in the articles.
[146] s.337(1).

procedure in the Act whereby a general meeting may be held on short notice. The threshold for members' consent to short notice in the case of a private company limited by shares is 90 per cent in nominal value of the shares of the company which give a right to attend and vote at the meeting—subject to the right of the company in its articles to increase this threshold to a maximum of 95 per cent. In the case of a private company limited by guarantee, the requisite percentage of the members requiring to give consent to short notice is 90 per cent of the total voting rights at a meeting of all the members—subject to the right of the company in its articles to increase this threshold to a maximum of 95 per cent. In the case of a plc, the consent to short notice procedure is slightly more complicated. First, one must make a distinction between a general meeting and an AGM. In the case of a general meeting, the requisite percentage of the members of a plc limited by shares requiring to give consent to short notice is 95 per cent in nominal value of the shares of the company which give a right to attend and vote at the meeting. Meanwhile, in the case of a general meeting of a plc limited by guarantee the requisite percentage of the members requiring to give consent to short notice is 95 per cent of the total voting rights at a meeting of all the members. As for the AGMs of a plc, the regime is different. Section 337(3) of the Act provides that an AGM may be called by short notice if all the members entitled to attend and vote at the meeting agree to the shorter notice.

Sections 308 and 309 of the Act dictate the manner in which the notice of a general meeting must be given, namely hard copy form, electronic form or by means of a website. The notice must be served on every member and every director of the company.[147] However, the company's articles may validly provide otherwise.[148] It is a requirement for the notice of a general meeting to provide the following information:

- the time and date of the meeting; and
- the place of the meeting.[149]

The notice must also state the general nature of the business to be dealt with at the meeting, but this is subject to any provision in the company's articles.[150]

Where the Act requires special notice of a resolution,[151] the resolution will not be effective unless notice of the intention to move it has been given to the company at least 28 days before the meeting at which it is to be moved.[152] The company must, where practicable, give its members notice of any such resolution in the same manner and at the same time as

---

[147] s.310(1).
[148] s.310(4)(b).
[149] s.311(1).
[150] s.311(2).
[151] For example, in the context of an ordinary resolution to remove a director in terms of s.168(1).
[152] s.312(1).

it gives notice of the meeting.[153] Where that is not practicable, the company must give its members notice at least 14 days before the meeting:

- by advertisement in a newspaper having an appropriate circulation; or
- in any other manner allowed by the company's articles.[154]

General meetings: Procedure at general meetings

16–41 If a general meeting is not quorate, any business or resolutions conducted or passed at that meeting are invalid.[155] A quorum for a single member private company is one member[156] and, as a default, a quorum are two "qualifying persons" in any other case.[157] A member, corporate representative or proxy present at the meeting may all be "qualifying persons", but the Act excludes the possibility of two or more corporate representatives or proxies of the same member comprising a quorum. As for the election of a chairman to a meeting, s.319 of the Act provides that where the articles are silent, a member may be elected to be the chairman of a general meeting by a resolution of the company passed at the meeting.[158] When the members vote on a resolution tabled at a general meeting, their votes may be counted on (i) a show of hands, or (ii) a poll. As will become apparent, on a show of hands each member has one vote, whereas on a poll, each member has one vote for each share which they hold. The chairman's declaration of a vote taken on a show hands is conclusive evidence of the resolution being passed or lost without further proof being provided, unless a poll is demanded on the resolution.[159] The minutes of the meeting also provide conclusive evidence of the chairman's declaration.[160] These provisions are designed to provide certainty by preventing members from challenging a declaration of the chairman as to the votes cast on a resolution at a meeting otherwise than by calling a poll. In relation to voting on a poll, s.321 of the Act states that any provision in a company's articles which restricts the right of a member to demand a poll at a general meeting is void other than a question regarding (i) the election of the chairman of the meeting, or (ii) the adjournment of the meeting.[161] On a poll, a member entitled to more than one vote need not, if he votes, use all his votes or cast all the votes he uses in the same way.[162] Therefore, this provision recognises that a member may hold shares on behalf of third parties and allows that member to cast votes in different ways according to instructions from third party clients.

---

[153] s.312(2).
[154] s.312(3).
[155] *Prain & Sons Ltd, Petitioners*, 1947 S.C. 325.
[156] s.318(1).
[157] s.318(2).
[158] s.319(1).
[159] s.320(1).
[160] s.320(2).
[161] s.321(1).
[162] s.322.

A poll may be demanded by the chairman of the meeting, a proxy, any director of the company, at least two shareholders having the right to vote or a person or persons representing not less than one-tenth of the total voting rights of all the shareholders having the right to vote on the resolution.[163]

General meetings: Proxies

A proxy is a person who attends a general meeting on behalf of a **16–42** member. Proxies are commonly appointed where a member is unable to attend a meeting due to illness or other commitments. Members of both private companies and plcs have the right to appoint more than one proxy, provided that each proxy is appointed to exercise the rights attached to a different share or shares held by him.[164] All proxies are able to attend, to speak and to vote at a general meeting on behalf of their appointing member on a show of hands or on a poll.[165] A proxy also has the right to demand a vote on a poll.[166] The effect of all of the provisions relating to proxies is that, where a member appoints more than one proxy, each proxy will have a vote. The articles may restrict the number of votes of the proxies, provided that they still have at least one vote between them.

Every notice calling a meeting must contain a statement informing the member of his right to appoint one or more proxies and any more extensive rights conferred upon that member by the articles of association of the company.[167] Failure to include such a statement will not invalidate the meeting, but is an offence attracting a fine for every officer of the company found in default.[168] The minimum period for notice to the company of the appointment of a proxy is 48 hours.[169] A proxy may be appointed chairman of a general meeting,[170] but this is subject to the terms of the company's articles. The Act also provides that an appointed proxy's actions at a meeting are valid unless notice of termination of the proxy's authority is given before the meeting starts.[171] Finally, the Act makes it clear that the company's articles may confer more extensive rights than are provided for under the provisions in the Act on members and their proxies.[172]

---

[163] See s.329(1) of the Act and Art.45(2) of the Model Articles in the case of a private limited company by shares, Art.30(2) of the Model Articles in the case of a private company limited by guarantee and Art.36(2) of the Model Articles in respect of public limited companies.
[164] s.324(2).
[165] s.324(1).
[166] s.329(1).
[167] s.325(1).
[168] s.325(2) and (3).
[169] s.327(2).
[170] s.328(1).
[171] s.330(2).
[172] s.331.

Resolutions: General

16–43 As has been stipulated elsewhere in this chapter, the power of the company to take decisions is divided amongst the board of directors of the company and the members of the company. The members exercise their decision-making prerogative by voting on resolutions. Section 281(1) of the Act empowers a private company to pass a resolution of its members either as a written resolution or at a general meeting of the members. Section 282(1) of the Act provides that a plc will only be entitled to pass a resolution at a meeting of the members. The unanimous consent rule of the common law, i.e. the rule in *Re Duomatic*[173] is preserved by s.281(4) of the Act which provides that the rules on resolutions in the Act do not affect any enactment or rule of law as to the circumstances in which a resolution is or is not treated as having been passed or cases in which a person is precluded from alleging that a resolution has not been duly passed. The unanimous consent rule confers a discretion on the court to rule that where it is clear that a decision taken by the company commanded the unanimous approval of the members, it is binding on a company notwithstanding the fact that the members of the company failed to pass any resolution required in accordance with the Act or the company's articles. So the unanimous consent rule disentitles a person from seeking to challenge the validity of the decision for the want of a resolution.

Section 281(3) of the Act states that any reference to a resolution in the Act is taken to be a reference to an ordinary resolution, unless the company's articles specify a higher majority. There are only three types of resolution valid under the Act, as follows:

- ordinary resolutions;
- special resolutions; and
- written resolutions.[174]

An ordinary resolution or a special resolution may be passed at a general meeting of the company.[175] In the case of a private company only, an ordinary resolution or a special resolution may be also passed as a written resolution in terms of the written resolution procedure under the Act.[176] When a resolution has been passed, a copy of it must be sent to the company's auditors. Sections 29 and 30 of the Act make it clear that copies of resolutions duly passed by the members of the company must be filed with the Registrar of Companies within 15 days of them having been passed or made. The Act provides that anything that may be done by ordinary resolution may also be done by special resolution.[177]

---

[173] [1969] 1 All E.R. 161.
[174] ss.282, 283 and 288.
[175] s.281(1)(b) and (2).
[176] ss.281(2) and 288(1).
[177] s.282(5).

Resolutions: Ordinary resolutions

Section 282(1) of the Act provides that an ordinary resolution of the **16–44** members of a company or of a class of members of a company means a resolution that is passed by a simple majority of the members. Section 282(2) states that if an ordinary resolution is passed as a written resolution it will be passed by the members of the company representing a simple majority of the total voting rights of eligible members. Moreover, s.282(3) goes on to provide that a resolution passed at a meeting on a show of hands is passed by a simple majority if it is passed by a simple majority of the members who, being entitled to do so, vote in person on the resolution or their appointed proxies. A resolution passed on a poll taken at a meeting is passed by a simple majority in terms of s.282(4) if it is passed by members representing a simple majority of the total voting rights of members who (being entitled to do so) vote in person or by proxy on the resolution. The Act specifies a number of decisions which require an ordinary resolution to be passed validly, e.g. an ordinary resolution is required to remove the auditors of the company,[178] to remove a director[179] or to approve a substantial property transaction entered into between the director and the company.[180]

Resolutions: Special resolutions

In terms of s.283(1) of the Act, a special resolution of the members of a **16–45** company or of a class of members of a company means a resolution that is passed by a majority of not less than 75 per cent. Section 283(2) of the Act is to the effect that a special resolution is passed validly as a written resolution if it is passed by a majority of the members of the company representing not less than 75 per cent of the total voting rights of eligible members. Moreover, s.283(3) states that where a resolution of a private company is passed as a written resolution (a) the resolution is not a special resolution unless it states that it was proposed as a special resolution, and (b) if the resolution is so framed, it may only be passed as a special resolution.

The effect of s.283(4) is that a resolution passed at a meeting on a show of hands is passed by a majority of not less than 75 per cent if it is passed by not less than 75 per cent of the members who, being entitled to do so, vote in person on the resolution or by proxy. A resolution passed on a poll taken at a meeting is passed by a majority of not less than 75 per cent in terms of s.283(5) if it is passed by members representing a majority of not less than 75 per cent of the total voting rights of members who (being entitled to do so) vote in person or by proxy on the resolution. Finally, s.283(6) states that where a resolution is passed at a meeting (i) the resolution is not a special resolution unless the notice of the meeting includes the text of the resolution and specifies the intention to propose the resolution as a special resolution, and (ii) if the notice of the meeting

---

[178] s.510(2)(a).
[179] s.168(1).
[180] s.190(1).

so specifies, the resolution may only be passed as a special resolution. Some of the decisions which the Act specifies must be passed by special resolution in order to be valid are as follows:

- the alteration of the articles of association of the company;[181]
- to change the company's name;[182] and
- to disapply the statutory pre-emption rights on the allotment of shares.[183]

Resolutions: Voting of members on resolutions

16–46 Where the members are voting on a written resolution:

- in the case of a company having a share capital, every member has one vote in respect of each share which they own or each £10 of stock held by them; and
- in any other case, every member has one vote.[184]

Where the members are voting on a show of hands at a general meeting:

- every member present has one vote; and
- every proxy present who has been duly appointed by a member entitled to vote on the resolution has one vote.[185]

Where the members are voting on a poll at a general meeting:

- in the case of a company having a share capital, every member has one vote in respect of each share which they own or each £10 of stock held by them; and
- in any other case, every member has one vote.[186]

However, s.284(4) of the Act clarifies that all of the above is subject to any provisions to the contrary contained in the articles of association of the company. So the Act expressly recognises that the articles of association may alter the voting rights attaching to shares. A prime example is the case of *Bushell v Faith*.

---

[181] s.22(1).
[182] s.77(2)(a).
[183] ss.570 and 571.
[184] s.284(1).
[185] s.284(2).
[186] s.284(3).

Bushell v Faith
[1970] A.C. 1099

Concerning: Whether it is competent for a member to have "weighted" voting rights in terms of the articles of association of a company.

Facts: Mr Bushell was a director of Bush Court (Southgate) Ltd and held one-third in total of the shares of the company. His two sisters owned the remaining two-thirds of the shares. Article 9 of the articles of association of the company provided that any director would have three votes per share on a poll at a general meeting in respect of a resolution to remove him/her as a director of the company. His two sisters proposed a resolution to remove him as a director and Mr Bushell demanded a poll on the resolution at the general meeting. When a vote was taken on a poll, he was able to defeat the resolution since he had three votes per share. The sisters challenged article 9 of the articles of association which purported to give Mr Bushell weighted voting rights on the basis that s.184 of the Companies Act 1948 (the equivalent of what is now s.168(1) of the Act) provided that every director may be removed by passing an ordinary resolution of the members, i.e. 50 per cent of the members having the right to vote on the resolution.

Decision: The House of Lords decided that there was nothing in the Companies Act 1948 which precluded the company from providing for weighted voting rights in its articles of association. Parliament could easily have provided that weighted voting rights were prohibited in the case of a resolution to remove a director, but they didn't. Thus, the vote which defeated the resolution to remove Mr Bushell as a director could not be set aside and was valid.

Resolutions: Written resolutions

The Act contains a procedure called the written resolution procedure **16–47** which enables ordinary resolutions and special resolutions to be passed otherwise than at a general meeting of the company. The Act includes specific provisions dealing with the competence, circulation and effect of written resolutions. However, s.288(2) of the Act specifies certain resolutions which may not be proposed and passed as a written resolution, e.g.:

- a resolution removing a director from office prior to the expiration of his period of office in terms of s.168 of the Act; and
- a resolution removing an auditor from office prior to the expiration of his term of office in terms of s.510 of the Act.

It is competent for the directors or the members of a private company to propose and pass a written resolution.[187] A written resolution has effect as if passed by the company in general meeting or by a meeting of a class of members of the company. However, written resolutions can only be passed under the Act. It is no longer competent to pass written resolutions pursuant to a company's articles.[188] Since the Act prohibits public limited companies from passing written resolutions, the effect is that any attempt by a public company to pass a written resolution post October 1, 2007 will be ineffective.

Section 289 of the Act identities the members who are eligible to vote on written resolutions. The eligible members are the members who would have been entitled to vote on the resolution on the *circulation date* of the resolution.[189] The circulation date of the written resolution is the date on which copies of it are sent or submitted to members. If copies are sent or submitted to members on different days, then the first of those days is deemed to be the relevant circulation date.

As outlined above, a written resolution may be proposed by the directors or the members. As regards the director-initiated procedure, it is stated that the company must send or submit a copy of the resolution to every eligible member.[190] When the company sends the copy of the written resolution to the eligible members it must be accompanied by a statement informing the member:

- how to signify agreement to the resolution; and
- as to the date by which the resolution must be passed if it is not to lapse.[191]

A failure to follow the above procedure is a criminal offence.[192] However, somewhat interestingly, the Act provides that the validity of a resolution which fails to comply with the above is not to be questioned where it is passed.[193]

The written resolution procedure also enables members (rather than the directors) to propose and move a written resolution.[194] Any written resolution may be proposed and moved by the members, unless:

- it would, if passed, be ineffective (whether by reason of inconsistency with any enactment or the company's constitution or otherwise);

---

[187] s.288(3). The procedures differ depending on whether the written resolution is initiated by the directors or the members—see below.
[188] Article 53 of the model articles of association for a company incorporated under the Companies Act 1985 in Table A (the Schedule to the Companies (Tables A–F) Regulations 1985 (SI 1985/805) purported to enable companies to pass written resolutions).
[189] s.289(1).
[190] s.291(2).
[191] s.291(4).
[192] s.291(5).
[193] s.291(7).
[194] s.292(1).

- it is defamatory of any person; or
- it is frivolous or vexatious.[195]

The percentage of members required to compel the company to propose and circulate the written resolution is 5 per cent of the total voting rights of all members entitled to vote on the resolution.[196] Where the requisite percentage of members have proposed the written resolution, the company is bound to send or submit a copy of the written resolution to every eligible member.[197]

The company has no more than 21 days from the date of the requisite percentage member(s)' request (proposing the written resolution and requiring the company to circulate it in accordance with s.292 of the Act) to send or submit the copies of the written resolution to the eligible members.[198] When the company sends the copy of the written resolution to an eligible member it must be accompanied by guidance informing the member:

- how he must signify his agreement to the resolution; and
- the date by which the resolution must be passed if it is not to lapse—which is 28 days beginning with the circulation date of the written resolution (i.e. the date on which copies of it were sent or submitted to members), or some other period specified in the company's articles.[199]

Any failure to follow the above procedure is a criminal offence.[200] However, somewhat interestingly, the Act provides that the validity of a resolution which fails to comply with the above is not to be questioned where it is passed.[201]

A final point to make is that s.295 of the Act contains an objection procedure where the requisite percentage of members utilise their power to propose and move a written resolution.[202] Section 295 of the Act provides that a company is not required to circulate a members' statement under s.293 of the Act if, on the application by the company or another person who claims to be aggrieved, the court is satisfied that the right of the members to propose a written resolution is being abused.

It is provided in the Act that a written resolution is passed when the required majority of eligible members have signified their agreement to it.[203] A member's agreement is irrevocable once he has signified his agreement to it.[204] A written resolution automatically lapses if it has not

---

[195] s.292(2).
[196] s.292(5). The company's articles of association may specify a lower percentage.
[197] s.293(1).
[198] s.293(3).
[199] ss.293(4) and 297(1).
[200] s.293(5).
[201] s.293(7).
[202] s.295(1).
[203] s.296(4).
[204] s.296(3).

been passed by the period stipulated in the written resolution or 28 days beginning with the circulation date if no particular period is stipulated.[205] The agreement of a member to a written resolution is ineffective if signified after the expiry of the period for agreeing to the written resolution.[206] A final point to make is that the articles of association of a company cannot remove the ability of a private company and its members to propose and pass a resolution using the statutory written resolution procedures.[207]

CORPORATE FINANCE (I): SHARE CAPITAL

Share capital: General

16–48 In return for "risk" investment or "risk" capital, a company limited by shares has the power to issue shares to investors. On investing in the company and obtaining such shares from the company, the investors become members of the company. As noted earlier in this chapter, the effect of a person becoming a member is that they are bound by the articles of association of the company which form a contract between the company and the members *inter se*.[208] When shares are issued to investors in return for the introduction of finance into the company, the shares are treated as property owned by the investors. Section 541 of the Act provides that shares are moveable property belonging to the investor in terms of Scots law. The relevant statutory provisions governing the share capital of companies are contained in ss.540–657 of the Act inclusive. In this section of this chapter, consideration will be given to the central areas surrounding shares and share capital which require particular attention.

Share capital: Definition of the nature of a share

16–49 What is the juridical nature of a "share"? Section 540(1) of the Act defines a "share" as a "share in the company's share capital". Such a statutory definition is not particularly helpful as it fails to craft the precise contours of a share and so it is worthwhile looking to case law for some further guidance. What is clear from the case law is that a share does not confer a member with real rights or other property rights in the assets of the company. Nor does a member have any rights as a beneficiary in the assets of the company in the sense of the company owning the underlying assets but holding them in trust for the members.[209] This must be accurate since the company has a separate legal personality and so owns its own assets. In the case of *Borland's Trustee v Steel Bros & Co Ltd*,[210] Farwell J.

---

[205] s.297(1).
[206] s.297(2).
[207] s.300.
[208] s.33.
[209] See *Commissioners of Inland Revenue v Crossman* [1937] A.C. 26 and *Short v Treasury Commissioners* [1948] 1 K.B. 116, affd [1948] A.C. 534 HL.
[210] [1901] 1 Ch. 279.

gave the following description of a share, which is generally considered to be the most revealing exposition of the nature of a share in a company:

> "A share is the interest of a shareholder in the company measured by a sum of money, for the purpose of liability in the first place, and of interest in the second, but also consisting of a series of mutual covenants entered into by all the shareholders inter se in accordance with s. 16 of the Companies Act, 1862 [now section 33 of the Act].[211] The contract contained in the articles of association is one of the original incidents of the share. A share is not a sum of money settled in the way suggested, but is an interest measured by a sum of money and made up of various rights contained in the contract, including the right to a sum of money of a more or less amount."[212]

In terms of the excerpt above from Farwell J.'s judgment, shares represent a measure of a shareholder's liability to contribute monies on a call in the winding up of the company and his interest in the company, such interest consisting of a bundle of rights in favour of him and imposing concomitant obligations upon him. A share also conceives of the rights of a member as the owner of a type of property and in terms of s.541 of the Act, it is clear that the share falls within the incorporeal moveable classification of property in Scots law. So shares have an open market value, representing a percentage of the overall value of the company.

Share capital: Nominal value, "paid-up" and "called up" share capital

Section 542 of the Act stipulates that every share must have a nominal value and have a number attached to it, that is to say that it must have a particular monetary value attached to it and be numbered.[213] Thus, it is incompetent for a company to issue 100 ordinary shares. Such shares must be issued as 100 ordinary shares of so many Pounds Sterling or Pence each (e.g. 100 ordinary shares of £1 each or 100 ordinary shares of 10p each). The same point applies regardless of the class of shares involved. **16–50**

A distinction is made in the Act between paid up capital, called up capital and unpaid/uncalled capital.[214] To explain these concepts, some examples might be of assistance. Let us imagine that X subscribes for 100 shares in a company at £1 each. In such circumstances, X's total stake is worth £100, i.e., 100 shares at a nominal value of £1 each. X's total liability is, thus, £100. If X has paid £100 to the company, then X has no further liability and so the shares are fully paid-up and fully called up. Since X's share capital is fully paid up, no further calls may be made on X by the company for a capital contribution and so X cannot be asked to

---

[211] Writer's annotation in square brackets.
[212] [1901] 1 Ch. 279, 288.
[213] If a share is allotted without a nominal value, the allotment is void and every officer of the company has committed a criminal offence—see s.542(2) and (4).
[214] See s.547.

pay any more, even if the company has debts of £1 million. However, if X has not paid for all his shares, the shares are partly paid-up and the company may seek the outstanding balance from him to pay creditors. Thus, if X has only paid 60p for each share, making a stake of £60, £60 of the share capital is paid up and the company may seek the remaining £40 from X to help pay its debts by making a "call". The £60 that has been paid is X's paid up/called up share capital, while the outstanding £40 is uncalled capital. However, the overall sum of £100 is the total extent of X's liability. X cannot be asked to pay any more, even if the company has debts of £1 million. If X transfers his shares to Y, then Y is liable for the remaining 40p per share (£40), but nothing more. So £40 is the total extent of Y's liability to the company for the debts of the company. The sale price of the shares is irrelevant to Y's liability. X "pockets" the sale price, with Y now assuming whatever liabilities X had (if any) concerning the nominal value of the shares.

Share capital: Classes of shares

16–51 In above extract from the judgment of Farwell J. in the case of *Borland's Trustee v Steel Bros & Co Ltd*,[215] it was remarked that a share represents an interest measured by a sum of money and made up of various rights contained in the articles of association. Hence, company law and the Act enables the members to attach various rights to shares in the articles of association and this is commonly achieved by creating different classes of shares with different rights. There are no restrictions on the kinds of classes of shares which may be created and so there is no such thing as a "closed list" of classes of shares, but it is common to find certain classes of shares in practice which are as follows:

- ordinary shares;
- preference shares;
- redeemable shares;
- convertible shares; and
- cumulative shares.[216]

The above classes of shares can be analysed by concentrating on the nature of the rights which attach to them. The most important rights which a member will have as an incident of their shareholding are the rights to (i) vote on a resolution (a) in general meeting and/or (b) by written resolution procedure, (ii) a dividend out of the annual profits of the company, and (iii) a return of capital on a winding-up of the company. An examination of the above classes of shares, duly mapped against such rights and other important rights would reveal the following table:

---

[215] [1901] 1 Ch. 279.
[216] This list is not intended to be exhaustive.

Class	Right to vote	Right to be paid a dividend	Right to a return of capital	Right to have shares bought back	Right to convert shares into debentures/ debt instruments
Ordinary share	✓	✓	✓	✗	✗
Preference share	✗	✓ (preferential over all other classes)	✓ (preferential over all other classes)	✗	✗
Redeemable share	Possibly	✓	✓	✓	✗
Convertible share	Possibly	✓	✓	✗	✓
Cumulative share	Possibly	✓ (if the dividend is not paid in a particular year, it becomes a debt payable in the following year)	✓	✗	✗

Ordinary shares are by far the most common class of shares, which entitle the member to vote on resolutions, the right to be paid a dividend and to a return of capital on a winding up. Preferential shareholders do not usually have the right to vote. In return for relinquishing the right to vote, preferential shareholders have a preferential right to (i) be paid a dividend, and (ii) a return of capital on a winding up, in priority to other classes of shareholders. Redeemable shareholders may have the right to vote and are usually given the right to be paid a dividend and a return of capital on a winding up on an equal par with the ordinary shareholders. By virtue of the nature of the class, the redeemable shareholders are entitled to have their shares bought back by the company. The articles of association and ss.684–689 of the Act will govern the terms, conditions and the manner of the redemption of the shares by the company. It is open to the company to stipulate that the convertible shareholders will have a right to vote on resolutions. Convertible shareholders may also be given a right to be paid a dividend and a return of capital on a winding up and by definition will be given a right to convert their shares into a debenture or other debt instrument issued by the company, thereby converting their equity stake into a debt stake. Cumulative shares share many of the affinities of preference shares. The main difference is that cumulative shares confer a right to be paid a dividend as a debt, whereby if the company is unable to declare a dividend in a particular year, it is nevertheless cumulative and must be paid in the following year. Finally, since the nature of the rights attaching to different classes of shares are governed by the principle of freedom of contract, it is possible by appropriate drafting of the articles of association to "mix and match" the above rights and indeed the classes of shares. So it is a not uncommon occurrence to encounter preference redeemable convertible cumulative shares. Alternatively, the articles of association may create an ordinary redeemable share or ordinary convertible share.

Share capital: Acquisition of shares

16–52   Shares may be acquired by original acquisition or derivative acquisition. Original acquisition occurs when fresh shares are newly issued by a company, referred to as an allotment and issue of shares in terms of the Act. Meanwhile derivative acquisition takes place where issued shares are acquired from an existing shareholder by another person which is referred to as a transfer of shares in the Act. First, in this section, consideration will be given to the mechanics of original acquisition, namely the allotment and issue of shares. Secondly, the rules on derivative acquisition and in particular the transfer of shares from an existing shareholder to a transferee will be examined.

Sections 549–616 of the Act cover the rules on the allotment and issue of shares. Shares may be issued by rights issue or pursuant to a bonus issue. A rights issue describes the situation where the company issues shares in return for cash or kind as a means of raising corporate finance. This can be contrasted with a bonus issue. Where a company issues shares to persons without payment in cash or in kind in lieu of a distribution of annual profits by way of dividend, this is referred to as a bonus issue. The power to allot shares resides in the company. However, the Act provides that such power may be devolved to directors. Thus, prior to an allotment of shares, the directors must have the authority from the company to allot such shares in terms of ss.549 to 551 of the Act. However, if the company is a private company with only one class of shares, the directors may allot shares without first seeking the authority of the members of the company.[217] The general rule is that the authority to allot may be conferred on directors in the articles of association or by ordinary resolution of the members.[218] Such authority may be generally conferred on the directors or granted for a specific exercise of the power only. The terms of the authorisation must state (i) the maximum amount of shares that may be allotted under it, and (ii) the duration of the authority which cannot be for more than five years.[219] In terms of s.561 of the Act, existing shareholders have a right of pre-emption on allotment, that is to say that any shares to be allotted must first be offered to the existing shareholders in proportion to their holdings at the time of the

---

[217] s.550. This is subject to any prohibition in the articles of association.
[218] s.551(1).
[219] s.551(3).

proposed allotment.[220] The purpose of such a provision is to protect a shareholder from the dilution of their shares. Nevertheless, there are a number of exceptions which apply to the general pre-emption rights of members[221] and it is possible to disapply pre-emption rights in the articles of association or by special resolution, depending on the nature of the authority to allot conferred upon the directors and whether the company is a private or public company.[222]

The mechanics of an allotment are, first, that the directors will publicise their intention to have a rights issue. Pre-printed letters of application for the allotment of shares are sent by the company to potentially interested parties (which may include existing shareholders of the company, depending on whether the statutory pre-exemption rights on allotment have been disapplied or not as the case may be). When a person signs a letter of application for the allotment of shares and transfers cash to the company, the company and that person enter into a contractual relationship. Section 558 of the Act explains the nature and effect of an allotment. It is provided that a share is allotted when a person acquires an unconditional right to be entered into the register of members of the company, i.e. at the point when a person has a contractual right to be issued with shares in the capital of the company. Within one month of the shares having been allotted, the company is under an obligation to make a return of allotment to the Registrar of Companies in terms of s.555 of the Act. The difference between an allotment and an issue of shares is revealed by s.113 of the Act which states that a share is only issued when the name of the person to whom shares have been allotted has been entered into the company's register of members. It is only at that point that the person is a shareholder of the company and the owner of shares in the company duly entitled to a share certificate.[223]

One of the great benefits of shares is the ease with which they may be transferred to third parties or offered to a lender as security in return for borrowing. Where shares are transferred from an existing shareholder to a third party, this is the most common form of derivative acquisition. Another form of derivative acquisition is the situation where the shares of a member are involuntarily assigned to another person, which is otherwise known as the transmission of shares. Transmission occurs where a member dies or is made bankrupt and their shares are transmitted to their personal representatives (such as an executor or a trustee in sequestration) in accordance with the articles of association of the company.

Very few restrictions on the transferability of shares are contained in the Act. For example, ss.770–771 of the Act provide that the company may not register a transfer of shares in the register of members of the company unless it has received a properly completed and executed stock transfer form in accordance with the Stock Transfer Act 1982. A person becomes a member of the company when the stock transfer form is

---

[220] The procedure is outlined in s.562.
[221] See ss.564 to 566.
[222] See ss.567–573 of the Act.
[223] See *National Westminster Bank plc v Inland Revenue Commissioners* [1995] 1 A.C. 119.

forwarded to the directors of the company and their name is entered by the directors into the company's register of members. But there are some restrictions on share transfers. For example, reg.26(5) of the Model Articles of association in the case of a private limited company by shares[224] provided the directors with a discretion to refuse to register a transfer of shares. If the directors refuse to register, s.771 of the Act stipulates that the company must specify the reasons for the decision to refuse to register. The notification of the reasons for the refusal will have to be given as soon as practicable, and s.771(1) sets a final deadline of two months from the date that the stock transfer form was lodged with the company. The transferee is entitled to receive such information as he may reasonably require regarding the reasons for the directors' refusal to register the transfer, but such information does not extend to minutes of meetings with directors. Moreover, the articles of association of private limited companies commonly include pre-emption rights in favour of existing shareholders which are applicable to a proposed transfer of shares, which like pre-emption rights on allotment, operate as an anti-dilution protection. Sections 783–790 of the Act enable the transfer of shares without a written instrument of transfer, i.e. stock transfer form. Thus, shares subject to the Crest system may be transferred without written instrument by electronic means.

Share capital: Minimum capital requirements

16–53　Minimum capital requirements apply in the case of public companies. Such rules are premised on the need to protect creditors and stem from the obligations imposed on the United Kingdom by Art.6 of the Second EU Company Law Directive.[225] Hence, s.761 of the Act narrates that a public company must not do business or exercise any borrowing powers unless the Registrar of Companies has issued it with a trading certificate.[226] A trading certificate will be issued by the Registrar of Companies if it is satisfied that the nominal value of the company's allotted share capital is not less than £50,000. However, only one-quarter of the minimum capital requires to be paid up. Thus, a public company will be able to obtain the trading certificate which it requires if it is able to confirm that £12,500 of investment has been introduced into the capital of the company.[227]

Prospectuses

16–54　Various requirements are imposed on public companies which seek finance from the public in return for the issue of shares in the context of (i) an initial public offering of shares, i.e. the situation where shares of a public company are admitted to listing on a regulated market such as the

---

[224] See reg.63(5) of the Model Articles in respect of public limited companies.
[225] 77/91/EEC and see Directive 2006/68/EC amending the Second Company Law Directive.
[226] s.761(1).
[227] s.586.

LSE or the AIM, and/or (ii) a rights issue. These requirements stem from the Prospectus Directive.[228] The United Kingdom implemented its obligations in terms of ss.84–87R and 102A–103 of and Sch.11A to the FSMA. Moreover, the terms of the Financial Services Handbook issued by the FSA as the United Kingdom's competent authority in terms of s.72(1) of the FSMA were amended to ensure compliance with the Prospectus Directive. The relevant section of the FSA's Handbook is the detailed Prospectus Rules which must be observed by public companies.[229]

The Prospectus Directive requires disclosure of information (i) regarding the issuer, i.e. the company, and (ii) the transferable securities of the issuer with annual updating of information regarding the issuer, i.e. (i). The Prospectus may be divided into two documents, namely (i) the Registration Document which contains information about the issuer which is valid for a period of 12 months, and (ii) the Securities Note which contains information about the securities to be issued. It applies to an "offer of securities to the public", i.e. a "communication to persons in any form and by any means, presenting sufficient information on the terms of the offer and the securities to be offered so as to enable an investor to decide to purchase or subscribe to the securities".[230]

The principal obligation of the public company seeking to offer its shares to the public is to issue a document called a "prospectus". The main rules as regards the content and presentation of prospectuses are contained in the Prospectus Rules, which are given the force of legal recognition by s.84 of the FSMA. It is a criminal offence for a company to offer transferable securities, i.e. shares and other instruments issued by companies, to the public unless a prospectus approved by the FSA[231] has been made available to the public before the offer is made.[232] It is also an offence for a company to request the admission of transferable securities to trading on a regulated market in the United Kingdom, e.g. the LSE or AIM, unless an approved prospectus has been made available to the public before the offer is made.[233] Thus, the terms of the relevant sections of the FSMA above and the Prospectus Rules must be followed by a company where it seeks to (i) admit its shares/securities to listing, and (ii) make an offer of shares/securities to the public (e.g. non-admission arrangements such as rights issues).

The relevant sections of the FSMA and the Prospectus Rules regulate the content and presentation of prospectuses which are made available to

---

[228] 2003/71/EC.
[229] See *http://fsahandbook.info/FSA/html/handbook/PR*.
[230] Art.2.1(d).
[231] See s.85(7) of and Sch.11A to the FSMA for a list of transferable securities subject to the Act.
[232] FSMA s.85(1). However, there are exceptions to these requirements which may apply in terms of s.86 of the FSMA, e.g. (a) 'qualifying investors' such as banks, insurance companies, collective investment schemes (see Prospectus Rule 5.4) and (b) where the offer is being made to less than 100 persons.
[233] FSMA s.85(2).

the public[234] and impose a requirement for regulatory approval of prospectuses by the FSA. For example, s.87A(1) of the FSMA provides that the FSA must not approve a prospectus unless it is satisfied that the United Kingdom is the home state in relation to the issuer of transferable shares/securities to which it relates, the prospectus contains the necessary information and the requirements of the Prospectus Directive have been complied with.[235] Section 87A of the FSMA goes on to state that the "necessary information" is the information necessary to enable investors to make an informed assessment of the assets and liabilities, financial position, profits and losses and prospects of the issuer of the transferable securities and the rights attaching to those shares/securities.[236] The Prospectus must contain a summary which in a brief manner and non-technical language conveys the essential characteristics and risks associated with the issuer and the securities. The FSMA and the Prospectus Rules also deal with the filing and the actual publication of the prospectus,[237] advertising in connection with the prospectus,[238] administrative sanctions for non-compliance[239] and liability for misstatements in the prospectus. The relevant provisions of the FSMA and the Prospectus Rules do not impose continuing obligations of information disclosure. Instead, continuing obligations are governed by the Market Abuse Directive,[240] the Transparency Directive[241] and other EU Directives.

CORPORATE FINANCE: (II) DEBENTURES/LOAN STOCK

Introduction

16–55 As explored above, one particular route open to a company to raise money is to issue shares in return for capital investment. Such capital is risk capital and so an investor stands to gain on their investment through capital growth or to lose the entirety of their original investment. That is the risk which they take. When they invest in the company, they become shareholders. An alternative source of finance available to a company is to raise loan finance by issuing debt instruments to investors. Such investment is loan capital and the investor is not a shareholder. Instead, they are a creditor of the company. In the capital markets, such loan capital comes in a variety of shapes, sizes and names. For example, a company may issue tradable debt instruments, sometimes known as bonds, loan stock, loan notes, etc. Section 738 of the Act collectively refers to such debt instruments as "debentures" and the common law

---

[234] FSMA ss.84 and 87A and Prospectus Rules 2.1–2.5.
[235] Prospectus Rule 3.1 is also important here.
[236] FSMA s.87A(2).
[237] Prospectus Rule 3.2.
[238] Prospectus Rule 3.3.
[239] FSMA ss.87K, 87L and 87M.
[240] 2003/6/EC and amending Directives 2003/124/EC and 2004/72/EC.
[241] 2004/109/EC and amending Directive 2007/14/EC of 8 March 2007.

treats any document evidencing a debt of any kind as a debenture.[242] By their very nature, these debt instruments are tradable, that is to say that they may be transferred or traded on or off a recognised exchange, such as a public bond market. Debt may also be non-tradable, that is to say it amounts to debt which cannot be transferred on or off a recognised exchange or market.

One of the advantages of issuing debentures as opposed to shares in return for capital investment is that a company does not require to comply with the capital maintenance requirements in the Act which are considered in the next section of this chapter. Thus, debentures may be issued at a discount to their nominal value and may be bought back from investors without requiring to comply with company laws. Another benefit of issuing debentures is that such financing exercises are generally considered to be cheaper than issuing shares through a rights issue or a public offer. Another difference between equity share capital and debt capital is that the owners of the latter are creditors and thus rank behind shareholders on the distribution of assets of the company on a winding up in terms of the Insolvency Act 1986. Moreover, whilst shareholders have a right to vote, a right to income and a right to the return of their capital on a winding up (and sometimes a trade sale, depending on the terms of the articles of association and/or investment agreement entered into with the company), debenture holders enjoy no such rights in terms of company law. The taxation position also differs, depending on whether the investor's stake in the company is a share or a debenture.

A debenture-holder will enter into a debenture instrument with the company. The terms of the debenture are settled by negotiation and are subject to freedom of contract and the general tenets of contract law. A well-framed debenture instrument will settle the level of the debt, i.e. the outstanding capital sum. The terms and conditions and manner of payment of interest will be outlined in detail, together with the applicable interest rate. Provision will usually be made for the levy of penalty interest in the event that an interest and/or capital repayment is missed by the company. Moreover, various financial covenants and "events of default" will be set out in the debenture. Where an "event of default" occurs, the debenture will stipulate that the investor/debenture-holder will have the right to call for the full repayment of the outstanding capital and interest, i.e. an accelerated payment provision.

Register of debenture-holders

Where debentures are allotted to investors in return for debt finance, the **16–56** company must lodge an allotment of debentures as soon as reasonably practicable and in any event within two months after the date of allotment.[243] Thus, notification must be made of the allotment on the company's public register maintained by the Registrar of Companies at Companies House. The Act provides that the company may maintain a

---

[242] *Levy v Abercorris Slate and Slab Co* (1887) 37 Ch.D 260.
[243] s.741(1).

register of debenture-holders. If the company chooses to keep a register, it must keep it available for inspection. The register must be kept at the registered office of the company or some other place notified to the Registrar of Companies.[244] Debenture holders and the public have a right to inspect the register in accordance with the requirements in the Act and to request copies of the register from the company.[245]

Secured debentures

16–57 Debentures may be secured or unsecured by the assets, property and/or undertaking of the company. However, it is extremely common for debentures to be secured since if the company defaults in discharging its monetary or non-monetary obligations stipulated in the debenture, the debenture-holder may "call up" its security and the sell the secured assets and property of the company as a means of realising the outstanding indebtedness owed to them. For example, if there is £340,000 of debt capital outstanding in terms of the debenture and the company defaults in the interest and capital payments which it is obliged to make to the investor in accordance with the terms of the debenture, the investor may choose to exercise the powers of sale and entry conferred upon him under the rights in security granted by the company at the time the debenture was granted. This enables the investor to sell the assets and realise the outstanding indebtedness of the £340,000 owed to him.

In terms of Scots law, the rights in security which may be granted by the company include standard securities over heritage, floating charges over part or the entirety of the company's assets, property and under-taking, together with assignations of debts/receivables, life assurance policies and other incorporeal moveables owned by the company in security. Where more than one security has been granted by the company, a ranking agreement will commonly be concluded between the security-holders and the company which settles the priority of payment in the event that the securities are called up in an effort to realise the out-standing indebtedness owed to the security-holders. In the case of most rights in security, various registration requirements must be followed. Otherwise, the failure to register may invalidate the security. For a more detailed treatment of rights in security, Chapter 19 should be consulted.

Key Concept

A "debenture" is a document issued by a company evidencing a debt of any kind which is owed by the company to an "investor".

---

[244] s.743(1).
[245] ss.744–748.

Maintenance of Share Capital and Purchase of Own Shares

Capital maintenance: General

A fundamental premise of company law is that once capital has been **16–58** advanced to a company, it should be maintained—the so-called capital maintenance principle. Thus, capital, assets or funds must not be returned to shareholders and should be maintained by the company. A number of rules of company law stem from this principle. For example, a company is generally prohibited from repurchasing its shares, reducing its capital and granting financial assistance to a third party for the acquisition of its own shares. Each of these rules are concerned with ensuring that capital is not given back to the members by direct or indirect means. Nevertheless, as company law has developed over time, a number of innovations have been introduced to relax the strict effect of the principle.

Capital maintenance: General restrictions

First, s.552 of the Act provides that a company may not issue shares at a **16–59** discount.[246] Shares are issued at a discount when they are issued at less than their nominal value. So if 100 ordinary shares of £1 each have been issued at 50p each in return for £50 of investment, this is a contravention of s.552 of the Act. However, there is a distinction between issuing shares at a discount and issuing shares which are partly paid up. In the previous example, it is competent for the company to issue 100 ordinary shares of £1 each partly paid up 50 per cent to £50. In such a case, the shares have not been issued at a discount, but are half paid up. The company has the option to call on the shareholders to pay up the remaining £50 on their shares.

Another rule which emerges from the capital maintenance principle is that dividends can only be paid to shareholders out of the company's annual distributable profits.[247] A company's distributable profits are its accumulated, realised profits, so far as not previously utilised by distribution or capitalisation, less its accumulated, realised losses, so far as not previously written off in a reduction or reorganisation of capital duly made.[248] Dividends are payments which are made to members on an annual basis based on a percentage of the nominal value of their shares. So if a company achieves no profits in a financial year, it will be unable to declare a dividend and issue a payment to the shareholders. Since the rule in s.830(2) of the Act is that losses accumulated from previous years are taking into account in each year, in the following examples, the company

---

[246] Shares may be issued at a premium, that is to say that shares are issued at more than their nominal value, e.g. to issue 100 ordinary shares of £1 each at £5 each. In such an example, the excess over the nominal value of £4 is referred to as a "premium", £5 representing the market value of the share. However, if shares are issued at a premium, the premium must be shown in the company's balance sheet as a share premium account in terms of s.610(1).

[247] s.830(1).

[248] s.830(2).

would not be able to pay a dividend to its members in financial years four and five.

Financial Year	Profit
1	(£200,000)
2	(£100,000)
3	£0
4	£55,000
5	£185,000

Capital maintenance: Acquisition of own shares

16–60 In the case of *Trevor v Whitworth*,[249] the common law enunciated a principle that a company could not buy back it own shares whether by purchase, subscription or otherwise, since this would represent a return of capital to shareholders which was contrary to the capital maintenance principle. Parliament codified this rule in subsequent Companies Acts. In the Act, the rule is now found in s.658 which states that a failure to observe the prohibition on the acquisition of shares is a criminal offence.

However, over time, the Companies Acts progressively relaxed the rule against a company acquiring its own shares. Thus, it is now possible for a company to issue shares which by definition may be repurchased by the company. Such shares represent a particular class of shares and are known as redeemable shares. Section 684(1) and (2) of the Act empowers every company to issue redeemable shares unless the articles of association of the company prohibit or restrict the same. The shares may be redeemed at the option of the shareholder or the company. A public company may only issue redeemable shares if it is authorised to do so in terms of its articles of association.[250] No redeemable shares may be issued at a time when there are no issued shares of the company that are not redeemable.[251] The terms, conditions and manner of redemption may be (i) contained in the articles of association of the company, or (ii) determined by the directors if they are authorised to do so by the articles or an ordinary resolution of the members.[252] The redeemable shares must be fully paid when the company repurchases them.[253] Payment for the redemption of the redeemable shares may be made by the company on a date later than the redemption date if the terms and conditions of redemption permit this.[254] Redemption of redeemable shares may be made out of (i) distributable profits, and/or (ii) a fresh issue of shares.[255]

---

[249] (1887) 12 App. Cas. 409.
[250] s.684(3).
[251] s.684(4).
[252] s.685(1) and (4).
[253] s.686(1).
[254] s.686.
[255] s.687(1).

Private companies also have the option to repurchase redeemable shares out of capital (but only if the strict requirements narrated in Chapter 5 of Part 18 of the Act are complied with).[256] Once the company has purchased the redeemed shares, the redeemed shares must be cancelled and notice of the redemption must be given to the Registrar of Companies.[257]

A company also has the power to repurchase shares other than redeemable shares in terms of the Act. Section 690 provides that every company may buy back its own shares unless the articles of association of the company prohibit or restrict this. A resolution of the members approving the purchase is required and the nature of the resolution depends on whether the repurchase is "off-market" or on the market. If it is "off-market", then the contract embodying the repurchase must be authorised by a special resolution[258] and if it is on market (i.e. a trade on a recognised investment exchange such as the LSE, AIM, etc.), then an ordinary resolution is required.[259] When a company repurchases shares, those shares must be fully paid up.[260] Shares may be repurchased out of (i) distributable profits; and/or (ii) a fresh issue of shares.[261] Private companies may also repurchase their shares out of capital (but only if the strict requirements narrated in Chapter 5 of Part 18 of the Act are complied with).[262] Unlike the repurchase of redeemable shares, the company must make payment for the repurchase of the shares on the repurchase date—and not later.[263] The repurchased shares must be cancelled or held by the company in treasury.[264] If the company chooses to cancel the shares, notice must be given to the Registrar of Companies to that effect.[265] Whether the shares are cancelled or not, the company must give notice of the repurchase within 28 days of it being effected to the Registrar of Companies.[266]

Capital maintenance: Prohibition against financial assistance

A public company is prohibited from providing financial assistance to a **16–61** third party to enable that third party to purchase the company's shares.[267] However, a private company is not precluded from giving such financial assistance. So it is unlawful for public company A to provide cash or exchange value to party B to enable party B to acquire the shares of company A. Such a rule is a manifestation of the capital maintenance principle and complements the general rule which precludes a company from repurchasing its shares otherwise than in accordance with the Act.

---

[256] s.687(2).
[257] ss.688 and 689.
[258] s.694(2).
[259] s.701(1).
[260] s.691(1).
[261] s.692(2).
[262] s.692(1).
[263] s.691(2).
[264] s.706.
[265] s.708(1).
[266] s.707(1).
[267] s.678(1).

The prohibition against financial assistance is paramount since in its absence a company could easily circumvent the "no-repurchase of shares" rule by effecting a return of capital to shareholders indirectly by routing the capital into the hands of a third party who subsequently becomes a shareholder. This rule in effect seeks to counter what is known as "asset-stripping".

The definition of "financial assistance" is wide-ranging and covers more than the simple transfer of cash or property. For example, a gift or loan may amount to financial assistance.[268] Furthermore, the grant of a guarantee, security, indemnity, release, waiver or novation may fall within the scope of the definition of financial assistance.[269] So if a company grants a security such as a standard security or a floating charge to a bank over its heritage and/or assets generally to enable a third party to obtain finance from that bank to acquire the shares of the company, the standard security and floating charge will amount to unlawful financial assistance, since the assistance will be given for the purpose of the acquisition.

Capital maintenance: Reduction of capital

16–62 Sections 641–651 of the Act enable a company to reduce its capital in accordance with certain procedures. A company does not need to have the power in its articles to reduce its capital—the Act stipulates that the company will have this power, unless the company's articles themselves prohibit or restrict the reduction of the company's share capital.[270] A private company may reduce its capital by passing a special resolution of its shareholders and the directors making a solvency statement not more than 15 days before the date on which the special resolution is passed.[271] A solvency statement is a declaration by each of the directors of the private company to the effect that each of them has formed the opinion:

    (i) as regards the company's situation at the date of the statement, that there is no ground on which the company could then be found to be unable to pay (or otherwise discharge) its debts; and

    (ii) if it is intended to commence the winding up of the company within 12 months of that date, that the company will be able to pay (or otherwise discharge) its debts in full within 12 months of the commencement of the winding up; or

    (iii) in any other case, that the company will be able to pay (or otherwise discharge) its debts as they fall due during the year immediately following that date.[272]

---

[268] s.677(1)(a) and (c)(i).
[269] s.677(1)(b)(i), (ii) and (c)(ii).
[270] s.641(6).
[271] ss.641(1)(a) and 642(1)(a).
[272] s.643(1).

In forming these opinions, the directors must take into account all of the company's liabilities (including any contingent or prospective liabilities).[273] If the directors make a solvency statement without having reasonable grounds for the opinions expressed in it, and the statement is delivered to the registrar, an offence is committed by every director who is in default.[274] Within 15 days of the special resolution having been passed, a copy of the resolution, the solvency statement and a statement of capital must be lodged with the Registrar of Companies.[275]

A public company, or a private company for that matter, may apply to the court for an order confirming a reduction of capital where the company has passed a special resolution to reduce it share capital.[276] Every creditor of the company who at the date fixed by the court is entitled to any debt or claim that, if that date were the commencement of the winding up of the company would be admissible in proof against the company, is entitled to object to the reduction of capital.[277] The court has the power to make an order confirming the reduction of capital on such terms and conditions as it thinks fit.[278] Before confirming the reduction, the court must be satisfied, with respect to every creditor of the company who is entitled to object to the reduction of capital that either his consent to the reduction has been obtained, or his debt or claim has been discharged, or has determined or has been secured.[279] Where the court confirms the reduction, it may order the company to publish (as the court directs) the reasons for reduction of capital, or such other information in regard to it as the court thinks expedient with a view to giving proper information to the public, and (if the court thinks fit) the causes that led to the reduction.[280] On the production of an order of the court confirming the reduction of a company's share capital and the delivery of a copy of the order and of a statement of capital (approved by the court), the Registrar of Companies must register the order and statement.[281]

MINORITY SHAREHOLDER PROTECTION

Introduction

As noted in prior sections of this chapter, the general rule is that each **16–63** shareholder is entitled to one vote per share on a vote on (i) a poll in a general meeting, or (ii) a written resolution (in the case of a private company).[282] Since a poll may be demanded by the chairman of the

---

[273] s.643(2).
[274] s.643(4).
[275] s.644(1).
[276] s.645(1).
[277] s.646(1).
[278] s.648(1).
[279] s.648(2).
[280] s.648(3).
[281] s.649(1).
[282] s.284(1) and (3).

meeting, a proxy, any director of the company, at least two shareholders having the right to vote, or a person or persons representing not less than one-tenth of the total voting rights of all the shareholders having the right to vote on the resolution,[283] and there is no restriction on the number of shareholders which a company may have, it is inevitable that some members will be in the majority and others in the minority. Minority shareholders are essentially shareholders or a body of shareholders who are unable to exert sufficient influence over the direction of the affairs of the company by virtue of the voting rights attached to their shares. Since company law provides that the general authority to direct the affairs of the company is vested in the (i) directors and (ii) shareholders who are able to command sufficient votes to pass ordinary and special resolutions, the effect is that shareholders or groupings of shareholders possessing less than 25 per cent of the voting base of the company will be minority shareholders. Whilst it is accurate to say that shareholders may (i) request that the company hold a general meeting, and (ii) table a resolution to be considered at such general meeting, with 10 per cent of the voting shares,[284] unless the minority shareholders are able to rally support for the resolution amongst the other shareholders of the company, it is unlikely that the resolution will be carried, since 10 per cent will be insufficient.

On the face of matters, one might assume that minority shareholders have no influence or control over the affairs of the company since they are susceptible to be outvoted at every turn. However, such an assumption would be mistaken. For example, minority shareholders may protect themselves by bargaining with the company for specific rights in order to safeguard their interests. Such contractual protections are commonly inserted into the articles of association of the company or a shareholders' agreement concluded between the members and the company. For example, specific voting rights, such as weighted voting rights may be included in the articles in favour of a particular minority shareholder. Alternatively, a minority shareholder may insist on the inclusion of a provision in a shareholders' agreement to the effect that certain decisions cannot be taken by the directors or the majority shareholders without the approval or consent of the minority shareholder. Whilst such contractual mechanisms are an extremely effective means of protection, for obvious reasons, not all minority shareholders will be in a position of sufficient bargaining strength to secure such concessions from the company. Thus, these forms of protection will not usually be available to the vast majority of minority shareholders. So, in most cases, minority shareholders will be required to rely on the principles and techniques of company law which are specifically designed to safeguard their interests.

---

[283] See s.329(1) of the Act and Art.45(2) of the Model Articles in the case of a private limited company by shares, Art.30(2) of the Model Articles in the case of a private company limited by guarantee and Art.36(2) of the Model Articles in respect of public limited companies.
[284] s.303 of the Act.

Common law derivative proceedings

In the 19th century, the courts in England recognised the need to intro- **16–64** duce certain rules to tackle subversive action taken by directors or majority shareholders which may have damaging consequences for the interests of minority shareholders. A distinction should be made at this point between actions taken by third parties which result in loss, prejudice or damage to (i) the minority shareholder himself or herself, and (ii) the company. Traditionally, absent any tailored rights in favour of the minority shareholder in the articles of association or a contract, there was no means of recovering for loss in respect of (i) under the principles or rules of company law. However, loss of the kind described in (ii) is an altogether different proposition and was and is something which the common law considered. Consideration of (ii) takes us to the classic rule in the case of *Foss v Harbottle*[285] which provided that where a wrong has been done to the company, only the company itself may initiate an action to recover any loss which it has sustained as a result of that wrong. This is the so-called "proper plaintiff" principle. However, a company is an artificial person and can only act through its organs, namely the board of directors or the shareholders in general meeting. So, if a majority of the shareholders of the company have voted on an ordinary resolution not to take action against a third party who has perpetrated a wrong on the company, a minority shareholder who is aggrieved at that decision is precluded from raising a "derivative" action of his/her own initiative. A "derivative" action is said to derive from the company since it represents an action taken by the minority shareholder in his/her own personal name on behalf of the company to recover loss suffered by the company as a result of the suffering of the particular wrong. The "proper plaintiff" principle (to which the derivative action is an exception) recognises the force of "majority rule" and where the majority have spoken, no minority has any standing to seek recovery. Generally, a court will not interfere in matters of internal management which have been sanctioned by a majority of the members.

However, the courts recognised that such a principle, while sensible, may result in prejudice. It may be harsh on minority shareholders, especially in a situation where a director has perpetrated a wrong on the company and the majority shareholders, in the throng of the directors, have voted to protect that director by denying the company the ability to sue the director to effect a recovery. Thus, in the case of *Edwards v Halliwell*,[286] the court established four exceptions to the "proper plaintiff" and "majority rule" principles, which established circumstances in which derivative proceedings may be raised, as follows:

(1) where the personal rights of a member have been infringed, then that member can sue to seek recovery of any loss suffered;

---

[285] (1843) 2 Hare 461.
[286] [1950] 2 All E.R. 1064.

(2) where a company proposes to do something which is *ultra vires*, i.e. beyond its constitutional powers or purpose, then a shareholder can raise an action to prevent the *ultra vires* act. Since the abolition of the *ultra vires* rule,[287] for obvious reasons, this particular exception has become of little significance;

(3) where a resolution required to be passed by special majority and it was not so passed then a member can object; and

(4) where the majority shareholders perpetrate a fraud on the minority.

The fourth exception was the most important exception in practice. Derivative proceedings have been raised to seek recovery of assets, funds and property where there has been a "fraud on the minority". The difficulty with this exception is that it is clear what is meant by "fraud on the minority". The common law was clear that the majority shareholders or a director would have committed a fraud on the minority where either of the former had committed a fraud,[288] misappropriated or misapplied the assets or funds of the company for their own personal benefit[289] or engaged in self-serving negligence, i.e. the negligent sale of an asset at undervalue which indirectly benefits the majority shareholder or director who has sanctioned the transaction.[290] However, beyond these particular circumstances, it was not particularly easy to understand the nature and content of the fraud on the minority exception. Another difficulty with the fraud on the minority exception was the potential for the shareholders to ratify the conduct after the event. Another requirement was imposed on minority shareholders to demonstrate to a court that the "wrongdoers" were in control of the company, i.e. that the wrongdoers had command of the majority of votes and had exercised such votes to stifle the opportunity to initiate proceedings for recovery.[291] Even where there was evidence of wrongdoer control, a minority shareholder would not succeed in their derivative action where the evidence demonstrated that the remaining shareholders, independent of the wrongdoers, were opposed to the raising of proceedings.[292] Other hurdles placed before the minority shareholder were that he must demonstrate that (i) the derivative action was being raised for a proper purpose, and (ii) he had no other remedy available.[293] In short, the common law "fraud on the minority"

---

[287] See s.39 and above for a wider discussion.

[288] *Atwool v Merryweather* (1867) LR 5 Eq 464n.

[289] *Cook v Deeks* [1916] 1 A.C. 554 (PC); and *Burland v Earle* [1902] A.C. 83 (PC).

[290] See *Daniels v Daniels* [1978] Ch. 406.

[291] See *Prudential Assurance Co Ltd v Newman Industries Ltd (No.2)* [1981] Ch. 257. Although whether the Court of Appeal in *Prudential Assurance Co Ltd v Newman Industries Ltd (No.2)* [1982] Ch. 204 endorsed the requirement to show wrongdoer control outlined by Vinelott J. in the High Court is not altogether clear.

[292] *Smith v Croft (No.2)* [1988] Ch. 114.

[293] *Barrett v Duckett* [1995] 1 B.C.L.C. 243. However, (ii) may not be a rule forming part of Scots law, see *Anderson v Hogg* 2002 S.L.T. 354 and *Wilson v Inverness Retail and Business Park Ltd*, 2003 S.L.T. 301.

exception was and is so difficult to enforce that the likelihood of a minority shareholder being successful was and is slim.

Statutory intervention

Since the common law avenues to obtain relief were and are restricted, Parliament has intervened to protect minority shareholders. First, ss.265–269 of the Act enable shareholders to raise statutory derivative proceedings to recover losses sustained by the company in certain circumstances. Secondly, ss.994–999 of the Act provide that a shareholder may present a petition to the court to obtain certain remedies where the affairs of the company are being conducted in a manner which is unfairly prejudicial to their interests. Each of these statutory innovations will be considered in turn. **16–65**

Statutory derivative proceedings

Sections 265–269 of the Act introduce a right to raise derivative proceedings in Scots law. This process enables a minority shareholder to seek redress against a director (rather than a majority shareholder) where the conduct of the director results in the company sustaining a loss. So, if the statutory claim is successful, the damages awarded flow to the company. Section 265 provides that a member[294] of a company may raise an action in respect of certain acts or omissions in order to protect the interests of the company and obtain a remedy on its behalf. The specified actions or omissions may be actual or proposed[295] and are as follows: negligence, default, breach of duty or breach of trust by a director[296] of the company. **16–66**

The statutory provisions enable a minority shareholder to raise proceedings in the name of the company against a director or "another person".[297] The import is that derivative proceedings can be taken against persons who are implicated in a director's breach of duty. For example, in proceedings concerning the transfer of funds by a director in breach of trust, the proceedings may also be brought against the recipient who has colluded with the director and has knowledge of their source or nature.

Members may only raise derivative proceedings if they have obtained the leave of the court. An application for the leave of the court must:

- specify the cause of action; and
- summarise the facts on which the derivative proceedings are to be based.[298]

The Court may:

---

[294] "Member of a company" in this context includes a person who is not a member but to whom shares in the company have been transferred or transmitted by operation of law.
[295] The actions or omissions are defined in the Act as the "cause of action".
[296] "Director" includes former directors or shadow directors.
[297] s.265(4)(b).
[298] s.266(2).

- grant the application on such terms as it thinks fit;
- refuse the application; or
- adjourn the proceedings on the application and make such order as to further procedure as it thinks fit.[299]

The Act provides that the court must refuse leave to raise derivative proceedings if it is satisfied that:

- a person acting in accordance with the director's duty to promote the success of the company for the benefit of its members as a whole, would not seek to raise or continue the claim; or
- where the cause of action is an act or omission that is yet to occur, that the act or omission has been authorised by the company; or
- where the cause of action is an act or omission that has already occurred, that the act or omission (i) was authorised by the company before it occurred, or (ii) has been ratified by the company since it occurred.[300]

In considering whether to grant leave to raise derivative proceedings, the court must take into account the following criteria:

- whether the member is acting in good faith in seeking to raise the proceedings;
- the importance that a person acting in good faith in accordance with the director's duty to promote the success of the company for the benefit of its members as a whole, would attach to raising or continuing it;
- where the cause of action is an act or omission that is yet to occur, whether the act or omission could be, and in the circumstances would likely to be (i) authorised by the company before it occurs, or (ii) ratified by the company after it occurs;
- where the cause of action is an act or omission that has already occurred, whether the act or omission could be, and in the circumstances would be likely to be, ratified by the company;
- whether the company has decided not to raise proceedings in respect of the same cause of action or to persist in the proceedings (as the case may be); and
- whether the cause of action is one in respect of which the member could raise an action in his own right rather than on behalf of the company.[301]

Finally, in considering whether to grant leave to raise derivative proceedings, the court must have regard to any evidence before it as to the

---

[299] s.266(5).
[300] s.268(1).
[301] s.268(2).

views of members of the company who have no personal interest, direct or indirect, in the matter (i.e. the passive members).[302]

The statutory "unfair prejudice" remedy

Section 994(1) of the Act enables a member to petition the court to **16–67** declare that the company's affairs are being conducted in an unfairly prejudicial manner to the members generally or to particular members. Section 994 of the Act differs from the statutory derivative proceedings in that (i) the remedies available are wider, (ii) the remedies may be awarded to the successful petitioner rather than the company, and (iii) unlike the statutory derivative proceedings, the wrongdoing may have been perpetrated by persons other than the directors, e.g. the majority shareholders. The precise terms of s.994 are as follows:

> "A member of a company may apply to the court by petition for an order ... on the ground—
>
> (a) that the company's affairs are being or have been conducted in a manner that is unfairly prejudicial to the interests of members generally or of some part of its members (including at least himself), or
> (b) that an actual or proposed act or omission of the company (including an act or omission on its behalf) is or would be so prejudicial."

If the petition is successful, the court has the power to:

- order the company to carry out certain acts or refrain from doing or continuing an act—including ordering the company to sue for a wrong done;
- prevent the company from carrying out certain acts;
- order members of the company to buy the shares of the prejudiced members, at a fair price; or
- make any order which it sees fit.[303]

In practice, the lion's share of minority shareholders presenting a petition before the court will be seeking an exit from the company by obtaining an order from the court for their shares to be bought by the majority shareholders or the company at a fair price. In the case law, the courts have provided a number of examples of unfair prejudice, e.g. the non-payment of dividends, the exclusion of a shareholder from the management of the company without offering a reasonable fair value for his/her shares, the payment of excessive remuneration to directors and the sanctioning of a rights issue which the minority are unable to afford.[304]

---

[302] s.268(3).
[303] s.996.
[304] See *Grace v Biagoli* [2005] EWCA Civ 122; [2006] 2 B.C.L.C. 70; *O'Neill v Phillips* [1999] 1 W.L.R. 1092 and *Re Cumana Ltd* [1986] B.C.L.C. 430.

The most important case on the width of the court's jurisdiction is the House of Lords case of *O'Neill v Phillips*.[305]

O'Neill v Phillips
[1999] 1 W.L.R. 1092

Concerning: The kinds of conduct which amount to "unfair prejudice".

Facts: Phillips owned the entire issued share capital of Pectel Ltd, namely 100 ordinary shares of £1 each. O'Neill was employed by the company as a manual worker and, after two years, Phillips gave O'Neill 25 shares in the company and appointed him as a director. At that time, Phillips resigned as a director. Pectel Ltd performed well under O'Neill's stewardship and he was credited with half the profits of the business. This was drawn as salary and dividends and some money was left in the company. As regards Phillip's dividend, he decided to waive a third of his 75 per cent entitlement in favour of O'Neill in order to produce equality. In one particular year, the retained profits which amounted to O'Neill's undrawn entitlement were capitalised as bonus shares to increase the issued share capital of the company to £50,000. The bonus shares were allotted in the same proportions as their existing shareholdings. Various discussions ensued with regard to O'Neill obtaining a 50 per cent shareholding. However, negotiations were never concluded. The onset of economic recession had a detrimental impact upon the fortunes of the company. Phillips became concerned about the financial performance of the company and O'Neill's management. Finally, he decided to resume personal command of the company and gave O'Neill the option of managing the UK or German branches of the business under his overall stewardship. O'Neill chose to manage the German side of the business and remain on the board as a director under the overall command of Phillips. Phillips determined that O'Neill would be paid only his salary and any dividends payable upon his 25 per cent shareholding. This was the final straw for O'Neill who decided to cut all ties with the company. He presented a petition to the court seeking an order that the company's affairs were being conducted in a manner which was unfairly prejudicial to his interests. The Court of Appeal ruled that unfair prejudice had been established and ordered Phillips to purchase O'Neill's shares. Phillips appealed to the House of Lords.

Decision: The House of Lords ruled that Phillips' appeal would be allowed and the petition dismissed. In s.994 of the Act Parliament had chosen fairness as the criterion by which the court had to decide whether it had jurisdiction to grant relief. For the purposes of that section, a member of a company would not ordinarily be

---

entitled to complain of unfairness unless there had been some breach of the terms on which he had agreed that the company should be conducted. Although the answer would normally be found in the understandings between the members at the time they entered into association, there might be later promises, by words or conduct, which it would be unfair to allow a member to ignore, and it was not necessary that such promises should be independently enforceable as a matter of contract. In addition, unfairness might arise not from what the parties had positively agreed but from a majority using its legal powers to maintain the association in circumstances to which the minority could reasonably say it did not agree. In the instant case, the real question was whether in fairness or in equity O'Neill had a right to the shares or to 50 per cent of the profits. Since the judge had found that Phillips had made no promises, there was no basis, consistent with the principles of equity, for a court to hold that Phillips was behaving unfairly in withdrawing from negotiations.

▼ CHAPTER SUMMARY

1. **Companies are regulated by the Companies Act 2006 and the common law.** 16.68
2. **The main features of company law are that limited companies have their own legal personality and the members are not responsible for their companies' debts, except to the extent of the capital they have contributed or have agreed to contribute.**
3. **The main case authorities for the separate legal personality of the company are:**

   ➢ *Salomon v A Salomon & Co Ltd* (1897).
   ➢ *MacAura v Northern Assurance Co Ltd* (1925).

4. **Where the position is a mere sham or façade concealing the true situation or statute empowers the courts to intervene, the courts may lift the "corporate veil" to enable a creditor to sue the directors or members;**

   ➢ *Gilford Motor Co v Horne* [1933] Ch. 935.

5. **Companies can be classified according to three particular categories as follows:**

   ● **Limited liability companies v unlimited companies;**
   ● **Companies limited by shares v companies limited by guarantee; and**
   ● **Private companies v public companies.**

6. **To incorporate a company, an application for registration and a statement of compliance must be completed and sent to the**

Registrar of Companies together with the company's memorandum
and articles of association.

7. A company's memorandum of association is a public document
    which states that the subscribers (i) wish to form a company under
    the Act, and (ii) agree to become members of the company and, in
    the case of a company that is to have a share capital, to take at
    least one share each;

    ➢ s.8 of the Act.

8. A company's articles of association are its internal constitution,
    detailing how shares may be transferred, directors appointed,
    meetings of directors held, etc. The articles represent a "contract"
    entered into between the members and the company and the
    members *inter se*. If a company proposes to alter its articles of
    association, it must obtain the approval of its members by special
    resolution. Where an alteration is authorised by special resolution,
    it may nevertheless be challenged in terms of the common law if it
    is not "bona fide" for the benefit of the company as a whole;

    ➢ ss.17(a), 21 and 33 of the Act.
    ➢ *Allen v Gold Reefs of West Africa Ltd* [1900] 1 Ch. 656.
    ➢ *Sidebotham v Kershaw Leese & Co Ltd* [1920] 1 Ch. 154.

9. Directors manage the company, but are still subject to certain
    restraints imposed by the law, the company's articles and contracts
    with shareholders.

10. (a) Directors owe various duties to their company, the most
    important being the statutory fiduciary duties;

    ➢ ss.170–173, 175–177 and 182–187 of the Act.

    (b) The duty of care, skill and diligence;

    ➢ s.174 of the Act.

    (c) and various statutory duties;

    ➢ ss.188–222 of the Act.

11. There are three types of resolutions which the members may pass:

    • ordinary resolutions;
    • special resolutions; and
    • written resolutions—see ss.282, 283 and 288 of the Act.

12. Shareholders of public limited companies may meet to review the
    directors' performance at annual general meetings. A director, the
    court or members representing at least 10 per cent of the paid up
    capital of the company as carries the right of voting at general
    meetings may request a general meeting to be held;

    ➢ ss.302, 303 and 306 of the Act.

13. A share is a unit of ownership in a company, measured by a sum of
    money, for the purpose of liability in the first place, and of interest

in the second, but also consisting of a series of mutual covenants entered into by all the shareholders *inter se* in accordance with the Act;

➢ *Borland"s Trustee v Steel Bros & Co Ltd* [1901] 1 Ch. 279.

14. Shares may be acquired by members by original acquisition or derivative acquisition. The original acquisition of shares is referred to as an allotment and issue of shares. The derivative acquisition of shares may take place by transfer or transmission.

15. Once capital has been advanced to a company, it should be maintained: the so-called capital maintenance principle. Thus, capital, assets or funds must not be returned to shareholders and should be maintained by the company.

16. A shareholder may raise derivative proceedings in the name of the company against directors or other persons to recover losses sustained by the company as a result of the negligence, default, breach of duty or breach of trust of a director or directors of the company;

➢ ss.265–269 of the Act.

17. A shareholder has the right to present a petition to the court alleging that the affairs of the company are being or have been conducted in a manner which is unfairly prejudicial to the interests of the shareholders generally or some particular shareholder or shareholders;

➢ s.994 of the Act.

? QUICK QUIZ

- What are the sources of company law?
- What are the objectives and purposes of company law?
- What are the core features of companies?
- What are the main types of company?
- What documentation is required to incorporate a company?
- What are the constitutional documents of the company?
- What is the memorandum of association?
- What are the articles of association of the company?
- What is the legal effect of the articles of association?
- What are trading disclosures?
- What is an annual return?
- Through which organs can a company act?
- Explain the role of the company secretary?
- What is the role of a company director?
- How many directors must a company have?
- Are there any restrictions on who can be a director?
- List the different types of directors.
- Explain how directors can be removed in terms of the law?
- To whom do directors owe their duties?

- What is the general meeting and what is its purpose?
- Who has the power to call general meetings?
- How much notice must be given of general meetings?
- What information must be included in a notice of a general meeting?
- What is a proxy?
- What is an ordinary resolution?
- What is a special resolution?
- What is a written resolution?
- What is a share?
- What is meant by different classes of shares?
- How can shares be acquired?
- What is a prospectus?
- What is a debenture?
- What protections are available to minority shareholders?

📖 FURTHER READING

Busby et al. *Scots Law: A Student Guide,* 3rd edn (Tottel Publishing, 2006), Ch.13.
D. French, S. Mayson and C. Ryan, *Mayson, French & Ryan on Company Law* 24th (Oxford University Press, 2007/2008).
L.S. Sealy and S. Worthington, *Cases and Materials in Company Law,* 8th edn (Oxford University Press, 2007).
P. Davies, *Introduction to Company Law* (Oxford University Press, 2002).
A. Hicks and S. Goo, *Cases and Materials on Company Law,* 6th edn (Oxford University Press, 2008).

🖱 RELEVANT WEBLINKS

Department for Business, Enterprise and Regulatory Reform site on Companies Act 2006: *http://www.berr.gov.uk/bbf/co-act-2006/index.html*
Company Law Forum: *http://www.companylawforum.co.uk/.*

Business Gateway:
http://www.bgateway.com/bdotg/action/layer?r.ll = 1073858805& topicId = 1073865730&site = 202&r.l2 = 1073859131&r.s = tl.

Business Link:
http://www.businesslink.gov.uk/bdotg/action/layer?r.ll = 1073858805& topicId = 1073859131&r.l2 = 1073859137&r.s = m.

Chapter 17   Insolvency

Alex Gibb[1]

▶ CHAPTER OVERVIEW

Insolvency is the state of affairs in which an individual (or any legal **17–01**
entity, such as a company) is unable to pay his, her or its debts. From an
accounting point of view, insolvency can be viewed as the situation where
an individual's *liabilities* outweigh his *assets*.

This chapter discusses personal insolvency and corporate insolvency.
The material on personal insolvency is divided into three sections:
sequestration, alternative procedures and diligence. The material on
corporate insolvency is divided into four sections: company voluntary
arrangements, administration, receivership and liquidation.

✓ OUTCOMES

At the end of this chapter you should be able to: **17–02**

- ✓ explain what is meant by bankruptcy and sequestration;
- ✓ describe how sequestration affects a debtor's estate;
- ✓ outline how a debtor's estate is distributed among his creditors;
- ✓ explain some alternatives to sequestration;
- ✓ explain what is meant by arrestment, attachment and inhibition;
- ✓ outline how company voluntary arrangements operate;
- ✓ explain what is meant by administration, and outline how this
  procedure operates;
- ✓ explain what is meant by receivership, and outline how this
  procedure operates;
- ✓ explain what is meant by liquidation and winding up;
- ✓ distinguish between compulsory and voluntary winding up, and
  outline how these procedures operate.

---

[1] Lecturer, Aberdeen College.

PERSONAL INSOLVENCY

Sequestration

17–03 A great number of people have debts. Indeed, it is difficult to exist in modern society without incurring personal debts at some point in one's life. A far lesser—though still considerable—number of people will encounter difficulty in repaying these debts. The reasons for suffering such crises of cash flow are many and varied, and the majority of people who experience debt problems are able to remedy the situation amicably with their creditors. However, others are not so fortunate, and are faced with the difficult decision to accept legal intervention in an effort to address the problem.

When an individual can be legally declared as unable to pay his debts, the term commonly used to describe this is "bankruptcy". The legal mechanism by which a person is declared bankrupt and his assets are disposed of in payment of his debts is called "sequestration". An individual whose estate is to be sequestrated is known as the "debtor".

> **Key Concept**
>
> Sequestration is the legal process by which a bankrupt person's estate is disposed of in payment of his debts.

The law of bankruptcy is primarily found in the Bankruptcy (Scotland) Act 1985, as amended.[2] However, the new Bankruptcy and Diligence etc. (Scotland) Act,[3] which received Royal Assent in January 2007, is gradually being brought into force. Although at the time of writing many of the provisions of the 2007 Act have yet to be brought in, attempts will be made to comment on the changes that are most likely to be introduced.

The Accountant in Bankruptcy

17–04 The Accountant in Bankruptcy[4] is an Executive Agency of the Scottish Ministers, and is responsible for the supervision and registration of sequestrations in Scotland. The AiB may also have an active role in the process of sequestrations, it being legitimate for the AiB to act as trustee (see below). Indeed, according to the agency's website,[5] the AiB is appointed as trustee in around 90 per cent of all sequestrations.

---

[2] Hereafter referred to as BSA 1985.
[3] Hereafter referred to as BDSA 2007.
[4] Hereafter referred to as the AiB.
[5] *http://www.aib.gov.uk.*

Absolute insolvency and apparent insolvency

A person is deemed to be in "absolute insolvency" if, on any given date, **17–05**
his total liabilities outweigh his total assets. However, an individual does
not need to be in absolute insolvency in order for his estate to be
sequestrated. There also exists a state of "apparent insolvency", which
gives a creditor the right to petition the court for sequestration of the
debtor. There are a number of ways in which apparent insolvency can be
constituted, including:

(a) if the debtor's estate is sequestrated or he is declared bankrupt;
(b) if the debtor gives written notice to his business creditors that he
   has ceased paying his debts;
(c) if the debtor grants a trust deed;
(d) if the debtor fails to pay a debt (or aggregated debts) amounting
   to £1,500[6] within three weeks of a demand for payment.[7]

Commencement of sequestration

The sequestration process can be commenced by a number of parties. The **17–06**
debtor himself can apply for the sequestration of his own estate. Previously, this involved the presentation of a petition to the court but such
an application will now be made to the AiB.[8] The debtor can apply for
sequestration provided that:

(a) the total amount of his debts is not less than £3,000[9];
(b) there has been no previous award of sequestration within the last
   five years; and
(c) the debtor is apparently insolvent, qualifies as a "low income,
   low asset" debtor, or has granted a trust deed which cannot be
   converted into a protected trust deed (see below).[10]

The "low income, low asset" debtor application is a new creation of the
BDSA 2007. It is intended to provide a simple application option for
debtors who have little income or assets. A debtor will qualify if:

(a) his weekly income does not exceed the national minimum wage
   for a full-time worker;
(b) he owns no land;
(c) the total value of his assets (not considering liabilities) is £10,000
   or less[11]; and

---

[6] Increased from £750 by the Bankruptcy (Scotland) Regulations 2008 s.13.
[7] BSA 1985 s.7.
[8] BSA 1985 s.1A, amended by BDSA 2007 s.14.
[9] Increased from £1,500 by BDSA 2007 s.25.
[10] BSA 1985 s.5(2B).
[11] BSA 1985 s.5A, inserted by BDSA 2007, s.15(2).

(d) he does not own any single asset with a value in excess of £1,000.[12]

If a debtor cannot satisfy the above criteria, he may still apply for sequestration with the concurrence (agreement) of a "qualified creditor".[13] This means a creditor who is owed at least £3,000[14] or a group of creditors who together are owed at least £3,000.

Creditors by themselves might also be able to commence a sequestration, but this must still be done by petition to the court.[15] Any qualified creditor (or group of creditors who together qualify) can present a petition, but only if the debtor is apparently insolvent as outlined above. Previously, a petition for sequestration could be presented to either the Sheriff Court or the Court of Session, but the BDSA 2007 removes the jurisdiction of the Court of Session in this area.[16] Therefore, the petition must be made to the Sheriff Court.

On debtor applications, the sequestration will be granted as long as the AiB is satisfied that the provisions of the BSA 1985 have been complied with. Where a creditor petitions for sequestration, the debtor will be cited to appear in court to show cause as to why the petition should not be granted. If the debtor fails to appear, or if the grounds for the petition are upheld, the court will grant the sequestration.

The trustee in sequestration

17-07 Upon a successful application or petition for sequestration, a trustee must be appointed to take control of the debtor's estate. Previously, an interim trustee would be appointed immediately upon sequestration being granted, and would be replaced in due course by a permanent trustee. However, the BDSA 2007 amalgamates these two offices into one, that of the trustee in sequestration.[17] An interim trustee might still be appointed when a petition is presented to the court, with the responsibility of safeguarding the debtor's estate pending the court's decision, but upon the petition being granted he will still be replaced by a trustee in sequestration.

Key Concept

When a debtor is sequestrated, his estate is placed under the control of a trustee in sequestration, to be distributed amongst his creditors.

---

[12] Bankruptcy (Scotland) Act 1985 (Low Income, Low Assets Debtors, etc.) Regulations 2008 s.3.
[13] BSA 1985 s.5(2A).
[14] Also increased from £1,500 by BDSA 2007.
[15] BSA 1985 s.5(2)(b).
[16] BDSA 2007 s.16.
[17] BDSA 2007 s.6.

Notice of the sequestration must also be registered. This is done by a copy of the order being sent to the keeper of the Register of Inhibitions (formerly the Register of Inhibitions and Adjudications)[18] and, if necessary, to the AiB. The sequestration will also be advertised in the *Edinburgh Gazette*.

Duties of the trustee in sequestration

The trustee in sequestration has a range of general functions. Among **17–08** these are:

    (a) to recover, manage and realise (sell off) the debtor's estate;
    (b) to distribute the estate among the debtor's creditors according to their respective entitlements;
    (c) to ascertain the state of the debtor's liabilities and assets.[19]

Within 60 days of the date of sequestration, the trustee must give notice to every known creditor as to whether or not he intends to hold a statutory meeting of creditors. (Previously, this was an obligation imposed on the interim trustee, but is at the trustee's discretion under the BDSA 2007.[20]) If he does intend to hold such a meeting, it must be called within 28 days of the notice. If he does not intend to hold a meeting any creditor can, within seven days, request that a meeting be held. The trustee cannot refuse if a request is made by creditors representing one-quarter of the debtor's liabilities.[21]

Where a statutory meeting of creditors is held, a vote will be taken whereby the creditors may elect an alternative trustee in sequestration, or confirm the appointment of the original trustee.[22]

Vesting of the debtor's estate

Once a trustee has been elected (or confirmed) the debtor's estate vests in **17–09** the trustee, subject to certain rules.[23] The trustee is then required to administer the estate for the benefit of the debtor's creditors.

Any assets that are necessary for the maintenance of the debtor's family life do not vest in the trustee. This would include home furnishings such as beds and kitchen appliances. Any tools that are necessary for the operation of a business can also be kept by the debtor, but the value of such tools cannot exceed £1,000.[24]

The debtor's heritable property (and so, potentially, his home) will also vest in the trustee. The trustee must register a notice of title, and can potentially require the debtor to leave the property in order that it can be

---

[18] Renamed under BDSA 2007 s.80.
[19] BSA 1985 s.3.
[20] BDSA 2007 s.11(1).
[21] BSA 1985 s.21A.
[22] BSA 1985 s.24, amended by BDSA 2007 s.11(4).
[23] BSA 1985 s.31.
[24] BSA 1985 s.33.

sold. Under the BDSA 2007, however, the trustee has only a limited time
to do this; if he has not taken steps towards selling the debtor's family
home within three years, the property must be returned to the debtor.[25]

Income received after sequestration

17–10 Any ordinary income that the debtor receives after sequestration is
generally kept by him. However, the trustee can apply for a court order
under which any income surplus to that required for reasonable support
of the debtor and his family must be given over to the trustee.[26]

The BDSA 2007 introduces two new arrangements in this area: income
payment orders (IPOs) and income payment agreements (IPAs).[27] These
are schemes by which the debtor pays a portion of any income he receives
after sequestration to the trustee. The period for which either scheme will
be in place must be decided at the outset, but can be for a maximum of
three years. This is significant in light of the fact that, under the BDSA
2007, the debtor will be discharged (i.e. his sequestration will end) after a
period of one year. These new provisions therefore allow a trustee to
continue recouping income from the debtor beyond the date of his
discharge.

An IPO is imposed by way of the trustee making an application to the
court. As well as stipulating the terms of the order, an IPO can require
that any income owed to the debtor by a third party be paid instead
directly to the trustee. Subject to the exception outlined below, an IPO
must be applied for before the date of the debtor's discharge. Failure to
comply with an IPO is a criminal offence.

An IPA is a formal written agreement between the debtor and the
trustee, which has the same effect as an IPO but does not require court
involvement. If a debtor fails to honour the terms of an IPA, the trustee
can apply to the court for the outstanding payments to be converted to an
IPO; this can be done even after the date of discharge.

Transactions made prior to sequestration

17–11 An important role of the trustee in sequestration is to protect the interests
of the debtor's creditors. This is straightforward in terms of property that
has vested in the trustee, but is more difficult in respect of property that
the debtor disposes of before his sequestration. Therefore, the trustee has
the right to examine transactions entered into by the debtor prior to
sequestration and, if sufficient reasons exist, such transactions can be
challenged and reduced.

Parties having the right to challenge include the trustee in sequestration, a trustee acting under a trust deed (see below), and any creditor
owed a debt as of the date of sequestration.

---

[25] BSA 1985 s.39A, inserted by BDSA 2007 s.19.
[26] BSA 1985 s.32(2).
[27] BDSA 2007 s.18.

Challengeable transactions 1: gratuitous alienations

A gratuitous alienation is a transaction whereby the debtor has given **17–12** over assets, or surrendered a right, without receiving a reasonable value in return. A common example would be where a debtor decides to give his possessions away to friends and family, rather than see them given over to his creditors. Clearly this is unfair on creditors who have a legitimate claim to the property.

Such a disposal can be challenged if it took place within a two-year period prior to sequestration, or within a period of five years if the recipient is an associate of the debtor such as a family member or business partner. Gifts such as birthday, Christmas and wedding presents are exempted, as long as they are reasonable.[28]

If the challenge is successful, the alienation will be reduced. The recipient will be required to return the property to the debtor's estate, or pay the value of the property. The property must be returned even if the recipient did pay some value for the item, although he can claim against the estate as a creditor in respect of what he has lost.

Challengeable transactions 2: unfair preferences

An unfair preference is created by a transaction that places certain **17–13** creditors in an advantageous position over other creditors, without justification. An example would be where a debtor purposefully settles a debt before it is due, in an effort to retain the creditor's goodwill in the future. A transaction can be challenged as an unfair preference if it was agreed within a six-month period prior to the date of sequestration. A number of transactions are exempt from challenge, namely: transactions made in the ordinary course of business; payments made in respect of debts that have become due; transactions involving reciprocal obligations (unless there is evidence of collusion); and the granting of a mandate to pay over arrested funds.[29]

If the challenge is successful, the transaction will be reduced. The subject of the transaction must be returned to the debtor's estate, or if this is not possible another form of redress will be directed by the court.

Challengeable transactions 3: equalisation of diligence

Diligence is a process in which a creditor enforces his right to payment by **17–14** appropriating certain assets of the debtor, following a court order in his favour or on the strength of certain instruments of debt.

Following sequestration, creditors are prevented from carrying out diligence against the debtor. A problem can occur where certain creditors have commenced diligence proceedings in the period immediately preceding the debtor's sequestration, as this would place them in a favourable position compared to other creditors who have been less aggressive in the pursuit of their debt.

---

[28] BSA 1985 s.34.
[29] BSA 1985 s.36.

To avoid such inequalities, rules exist regarding the "equalisation" of diligence.[30] The effect of these is that all diligence procedures commenced during the 60 days preceding sequestration will be deemed to have been effected on the same day, and will rank equally with each other. Any property obtained as a result of such diligences must be given over to the trustee.

Management and distribution of the debtor's estate

17–15   After the trustee has ingathered the debtor's assets, and carried out any of the above procedures as are appropriate, he is responsible for the management of the debtor's estate. This might include the closing down of the debtor's business (or the continuance of it if this will raise more funds for the creditors) or the raising of court actions if this would benefit the estate. For the debtor's part, he must act in good faith with the trustee and can be required by the trustee to give regular accounts of his income and expenditure.[31]

If they have not already done so, creditors will submit their claims to the trustee and, if necessary, provide supporting evidence. The trustee will assess the validity of each claim and, if it is accepted, the creditor will be entitled to receive a dividend from the debtor's estate.[32] A creditor whose claim is rejected can appeal to the court.[33]

In distributing the debtor's estate, the trustee must pay debts according to a statutory order. This order does not include secured debts, since secured creditors might have the right to be paid first out of the secured property. Other than these, the order in which debts will be met is as follows:

(a) the outlays and remuneration of the interim trustee (if appointed);

(b) the outlays and remuneration of the trustee in sequestration;

(c) where the debtor is deceased, the reasonable expenses of his funeral and of the administration of his estate;

(d) where a creditor has petitioned for sequestration, his reasonable expenses incurred in making the petition;

(e) preferred debts;[34]

(f) ordinary debts (those of unsecured creditors);

(g) interest on preferred and ordinary debts;

(h) any postponed debt (e.g. loans made to a spouse or business, or the value of a challenged gratuitous alienation).[35]

---

[30] BSA 1985 s.37.

[31] BSA 1985 s.43A, inserted by BDSA 2007 s.30.

[32] BSA 1985 s.48.

[33] BSA 1985 s.49(6).

[34] As outlined by BSA 1985 Sch.3 Part 1.

[35] BSA 1985 s.51.

Discharge of the debtor

A debtor will be discharged from bankruptcy if, at any time, his financial **17–16** position allows an acceptable offer to be made to the whole of his creditors. The more common scenario, however, is that the debtor's discharge will be effected automatically by the passing of time.

Under the BDSA 2007, the debtor shall be discharged after one year.[36] However, as mentioned above, this Act also introduces a number of schemes that can be applied to the debtor, which will continue for a set period after his discharge. In addition to the IPO and IPA arrangements explained above, s.2 of the BDSA 2007 introduces "bankruptcy restrictions orders"[37] (BROs) and "bankruptcy restrictions undertakings"[38] (BRUs).

A BRO application must be made to the court by the AiB, and will be granted where the court agrees that the debtor's conduct during the sequestration warrants the placement of restrictions after his discharge. Examples of such conduct would be failure to co-operate with the trustee, and the making of gratuitous alienations or the creation of unfair preferences. The application must be made after sequestration but before the date of discharge, except where the sheriff is willing to permit an application after discharge. If a BRO is granted, it will place certain restrictions on the debtor for a period of anything between two and 15 years.

A BRU operates in the same way as a BRO, but is agreed between the debtor and the AiB, without the need to go to court.

Once discharged, the debtor is freed from all debts and obligations that existed at the time of his sequestration, with certain exceptions such as fines and any liabilities incurred through fraud. Student loans also remain unaffected by sequestration and discharge.[39] The debtor may then, subject to any orders or agreements as outlined above, acquire assets and property, and effectively continue with his life.

Key Concept

Once a sequestration is complete, the debtor is "discharged" and is freed from most of his previous debts. However, measures can be put in place that will affect him even after he is discharged.

Alternative procedures

Sequestration can be a lengthy process, and certainly has important **17–17** implications for a person's life. As with other areas of insolvency, it might be possible to remedy an individual's problematic situation without recourse to such an onerous procedure. It is possible, therefore, for an

---

[36] BSA 1985 s.54, amended by BDSA 2007 s.1.
[37] BSA 1985 s.56A, inserted by BDSA 2007 s.2.
[38] BSA 1985 s.56G, inserted by BDSA 2007 s.2.
[39] BDSA 2007 s.34.

insolvent individual to enter into certain voluntary arrangements with his creditors, as an alternative to sequestration proceedings.

Trust deeds

17–18   A trust deed is an arrangement entered into between a debtor and his creditors, whereby an agreed portion of the debtor's estate is put in the hands of a trustee, to be administered for the benefit of the creditors. If the debtor fails to comply with the conditions of a trust deed, the trustee can petition for the debtor's estate to be sequestrated.[40]

Key Concept

A trust deed is an alternative to sequestration, and involves an agreement being made between the debtor and his creditors. It is a less formal process, with fewer legal implications for the debtor.

The most significant drawback of a trust deed is that its success depends largely on all creditors acceding (agreeing) to it. This is because any creditors who do not accede to the trust deed are not bound by its terms, and neither are new creditors bound by it. Such creditors may still effect diligence against the debtor, which is clearly to the disadvantage of the creditors who are party to the trust deed.

As a result of such failings, voluntary trust deeds have proved unpopular in practice. However, a more favourable alternative exists in the form of the protected trust deed. This is a deed which, provided it conforms to statutory criteria, will provide additional layers of protection against action by creditors.

Since April 2008, protected trust deeds have been regulated by the Protected Trust Deeds (Scotland) Regulations 2008.[41] Deeds created before April 1, 2008 continue to be regulated by the BSA 1985 as amended.[42]

Under the new regime, a trust deed can become protected if the following conditions are satisfied:

  (a) the trustee must not be disqualified from acting as a trustee in sequestration[43];
  (b) the trust deed must state that all the debtor's estate, other than that excluded under statute, is conveyed to the trustee[44];
  (c) the trustee must publish a notice of the trust deed in the *Edinburgh Gazette*[45];

---

[40] BSA 1985 s.5(2C).
[41] Hereafter referred to as PTDSR 2008.
[42] See BSA 1985 Sch.5.
[43] PTDSR 2008 s.5.
[44] PTDSR 2008 s.6.
[45] PTDSR 2008 s.7.

(d) the trustee must, within seven days of the notice being published, send to every known creditor a copy of the trust deed, a copy of the notice a statement of the debtor's affairs, and a creditor's claim form[46];

(e) the creditors must accede to the trust deed, which will be presumed to be the case unless a majority in number or one-third in value of creditors give written notice to the trustee of their objection[47]; and

(f) finally, as soon as is reasonably practicable, the trustee must register the trust deed with the AiB.[48]

The effect of a trust deed becoming protected is that creditors are prevented from taking action against the debtor to enforce their debts, except in very limited circumstances.[49]

Simplified procedures

Two simplified sequestration procedures also exist. The first is known as **17–19** the "Schedule 2 procedure", as it is regulated by Sch.2 to the BSA 1985. This procedure can be employed in a number of situations, most commonly where the debtor's estate is relatively small. It allows for a simplified sequestration in which the AiB will act as trustee, and will have wide authority to administer the estate and distribute assets to creditors.

There is also the "summary administration procedure", introduced by the Bankruptcy (Scotland) Act 1993 and governed by Sch.2A to the BSA 1985. This is a process available where the debtor's unsecured liabilities total less than £20,000, and allows for a more straightforward procedure whereby the trustee is absolved of certain responsibilities towards the estate; instead, his only responsibility is to the creditors. However, it was noted in a 2005 Scottish Parliament Information Centre Briefing[50] that a certificate of summary administration had not at that time been applied for in five years, and in the opinion of the Scottish Executive the procedure was defunct and ought to be abolished. This indeed is the case under the BDSA 2007, which repeals various provisions relating to summary administration.[51]

Diligence

Under the law of diligence, creditors are provided with a range of legal **17–20** procedures under which debts can be enforced. All forms of diligence involve exercising control over certain assets of the debtor, and are

---

[46] PTDSR 2008 s.8.
[47] PTDSR 2008 s.9.
[48] PTDSR 2008 s.10.
[49] See PTDSR 2008 ss.12–14.
[50] Dewer, J. *Bankruptcy and Diligence etc (Scotland) Bill: Bankruptcy*, SPICe Briefing 05/73.
[51] BDSA 2007 s.28.

commenced on the authority of a court order or, perhaps less commonly, on the terms of an instrument of debt.

Key Concept

Diligence is an area of the law that provides a range of procedures under which a creditor can force payment of a debt.

Arrestment

17–21 Arrestment is a process of diligence executed against property that belongs to the debtor, but is in the hands of a third party. A common example would be the funds in a debtor's bank account; these belong to the debtor, but are of course under the immediate control of the bank.

The effect of arrestment is that the arrested assets are "frozen", and can be disposed of by neither the debtor nor the third party (who is known as the "arrestee"). The arrested assets remain in the possession of the arrestee, and will be given over to the creditor either upon the signing of a mandate to this effect by the debtor, or upon the raising of a successful action of furthcoming by the creditor. An action of furthcoming is an application made by the creditor to the court, for the passing of arrested assets into his ownership, or for the selling of arrested assets so that the proceeds can be given over to him.

Arrestment as it is currently regulated is open to a number of criticisms.[52] First, creditors face difficulty in ascertaining the value of the arrested assets, or indeed in ascertaining whether any assets have been arrested at all; for example, a debtor's bank account might already be devoid of funds. Secondly, the process is somewhat cumbersome, as it potentially involves two separate legal actions.

These issues are addressed by the BDSA 2007. In terms of creditor uncertainty regarding arrested assets, a new duty of disclosure is placed on the arrestee. Under this duty the arrestee must inform the creditor of the nature and value of the arrested assets.[53] In addition, actions of furthcoming may no longer be required, due to new provisions allowing funds to be released to a creditor automatically after 14 weeks.[54]

Attachment

17–22 Attachment is a form of diligence executed against goods that are in the possession of the debtor. It was introduced in 2002[55] as a replacement for the widely criticised "poinding and sale" procedure which, as well as being objectionable to many by its nature, was largely an ineffective

---

[52] See e.g. Baijal, E. *The Bankruptcy and Diligence etc (Scotland) Act 2007: The New Jewell in the Creditor's Crown*, 2007 S.L.T., 9, 55–59.

[53] BSA 1985 s.73G, inserted by BDSA 2007 s.206.

[54] BSA 1985 s.73J, inserted by BDSA 2007 s.206.

[55] By the Debt Arrangement and Attachment (Scotland) Act 2002, hereafter referred to as DAA 2002.

method of recovering a debt.[56] A crucial difference between attachment and poinding is that attachment is less likely to involve the removal of property from a debtor's home which was a central aspect of poinding's unpopularity.

Before a creditor can proceed with attachment, two conditions must be met. These are:

(a) that the debtor has been charged to pay the sum specified, together with any interest; *and*
(b) that the creditor has provided the debtor with a debt advice and information package.[57]

A debt advice and information package is a document (or collection of documents) providing the debtor with relevant information, such as the availability of debt advice in his locality, plus any other information as is stipulated by the Scottish Ministers.[58]

Certain restrictions apply to attachment. The procedure is only relevant in respect of corporeal moveable property,[59] though this should not be confused with the new diligence of "land attachment" (see below). In addition, a range of items are exempt from attachment, including:

(a) tools and other items that are necessary for the debtor's profession, up to a combined value of £1,000;
(b) any vehicle reasonably required by the debtor, again up to a value of £1,000;
(c) a mobile home that is the debtor's only or primary residence;
(d) any tools or equipment reasonably required for keeping the garden or yard of a dwellinghouse in good order.[60]

It is not generally competent to execute attachment on a Sunday, or on a public holiday, or outwith the times of 8am and 8pm.[61]

As mentioned above, attachment does not tend to involve the removal of property from a debtor's home, though this is possible in exceptional circumstances.[62] It is far more common for attachment to be executed against items being kept outwith the debtor's home. Entry can be gained to the premises where the property is being kept, and may be forced if necessary.[63]

Once attached, the property will then be valued, by a suitably skilled person if necessary, within 14 days.[64] The property may be "redeemed"

---

[56] See e.g. Nichols, D. *Poinding and Sale: Effective Enforcement and Debtor Protection*, 1999 Scot. Law Com. No. 110.
[57] DAA 2002 s.10(3).
[58] DAA 2002 s.10(5).
[59] DAA 2002 s.10(1).
[60] DAA 2002 s.11(1).
[61] DAA 2002 s.12.
[62] DAA 2002 Part 3.
[63] DAA 2002 s.15(1).
[64] DAA 2002 s.15(2) and (3).

(bought back) by the debtor at the valuation reached upon,[65] else the property will be removed and put up for auction.[66]

Inhibition

17–23   Inhibition is a form of diligence executed against a debtor's heritable property. It differs significantly from arrestment and attachment in that it does not involve the creditor taking control of the debtor's assets. Instead, it puts restrictions on the debtor's use of the inhibited property. It is therefore perhaps better viewed as a defensive measure to encourage settlement of a debt by the debtor, rather than as a positive remedy exercised by the creditor to recover his debt.

The effect of an inhibition is that the debtor is prohibited from voluntarily selling the property, and from using it for certain purposes, e.g. as security. If the debtor does undertake any prohibited act in respect of the inhibited property, he will be held in breach of the inhibition.[67]

The BDSA 2007 makes it clear that an inhibition will cease to have effect if the amount due (plus interest and expenses) is paid in full,[68] or if any other relevant obligation is complied with.[69]

Land attachment

17–24   This is a new form of diligence, introduced by the BDSA 2007[70] to replace the older (and of late rarely seen) diligence of adjudication, which is thereafter abolished.[71] The process is similar to that of attachment of moveable property as explained above, but instead here the subject of the attachment is land, be it land owned by the debtor, or land of which the debtor is a tenant under an assignable long lease.[72] Land attachment is only competent to enforce a debt exceeding £3,000.[73]

The effect of land attachment is that the creditor is given a subordinate real right over the land, as security for the outstanding debt plus any accrued interest and expenses.[74] After a period of six months has elapsed since registration of the notice of land attachment, if the outstanding debt is still in excess of £3,000, the creditor can apply for a warrant to sell the attached land.[75]

---

[65]   DAA 2002 s.18.
[66]   DAA 2002 s.19.
[67]   BDSA 2007 s.160.
[68]   BDSA 2007 s.157.
[69]   BDSA 2007 s.158.
[70]   BDSA 2007 s.81.
[71]   BDSA 2007 s.79.
[72]   BDSA 2007 s.82.
[73]   BDSA 2007 s.83(2) and (3).
[74]   BDSA 2007 s.86(5) and (6).
[75]   BDSA 2007 s.92.

Money attachment

This is another new diligence introduced by the BDSA 2007,[76] which **17–25** allows for the attachment of money owned by the debtor. "Money" for these purposes is taken to mean cash in any currency, or banking instruments such as cheques and promissory notes.[77] An important exception is that any coins or banknotes that have a higher intrinsic value than their face value (i.e. those that are collectable) cannot be attached.[78]

A number of other restrictions apply to money attachment. It is not possible to attach money that is being kept within a dwelling,[79] and it is also not competent to attach money that would be capable of being arrested.[80] Similarly with attachment of corporeal moveable property, money attachment generally cannot be carried out on a Sunday, on a public holiday or outwith the times of 8am and 8pm.[81]

Residual attachment

A final new form of diligence introduced by the BDSA 2007 is that of **17–26** residual attachment. The intention here is to allow the attachment of certain types of property that cannot be attached by any other form of diligence. The Act gives power to the Scottish Ministers to specify what property may be attached in this way,[82] subject to certain rules and exemptions.[83]

If a creditor wishes to execute residual attachment, he must apply to the court for sanction.[84] If a residual attachment order is granted, this will confer on the creditor a right in security over the attached property.[85] If the debt (plus interest and expenses) remains unpaid, the creditor can then apply to the court for a satisfaction order. If granted, this will allow provisions to be made for satisfaction of the debt by, for example, sale of the property, or transfer of the property to the creditor.[86]

CORPORATE INSOLVENCY

Company voluntary arrangements

When a company is facing serious financial difficulty—or indeed if it is **17–27** already insolvent—steps can be taken in an attempt to remedy the situation and prevent the company from being wound up (see below).

---

[76] BDSA 2007 s.174.
[77] BDSA 2007 s.175(1).
[78] BDSA 2007 s.175(1).
[79] BDSA 2007 s.174(3).
[80] BDSA 2007 s.174(3).
[81] BDSA 2007 s.176(1) and (2).
[82] BDSA 2007 s.129(2) and (3).
[83] BDSA 2007 s.129(4).
[84] BDSA 2007 s.130.
[85] BDSA 2007 s.134(2).
[86] BDSA 2007 s.136(4).

Under the Insolvency Act 1986,[87] an agreement can be entered into between the company and its creditors, whereby existing debts are frozen, and the company is allowed to continue trading. Over a stipulated time period, which is commonly between three and five years, regular payments are made to creditors, with a view to eventually repaying the outstanding debts. These agreements are known as "company voluntary arrangements", although they are sometimes referred to as CVAs or, simply, voluntary arrangements.

Key Concept

A company voluntary arrangement is where a company enters an agreement with its creditors outlining how debts are to be repaid.

Initiating the procedure

17–28 A proposal for voluntary arrangements can be made by the company's directors,[88] regardless of whether or not the company is insolvent, but not if the company is already in liquidation or administration (see below). In the latter situation, a liquidator or administrator is empowered to make the proposal.[89]

In either case, the voluntary arrangement must be supervised by a "nominee".[90] Where the directors have made the proposal, they will appoint the nominee, who must be a licensed insolvency practitioner or a member of a body recognised for this purpose.[91] If a liquidator or administrator makes the proposal, he will act as nominee.

After investigating the proposals the nominee must, within 28 days, make a report to the court giving his opinion as to whether the scheme is viable.[92] (A court report is not required if the nominee is already a liquidator or an administrator.) The nominee will then order separate meetings of the company members and the creditors, so that the proposals can be considered and voted on.[93]

Approval of the scheme

17–29 At the meeting of the company members, approval of the scheme requires a simple majority in value; i.e. members representing more than half of the total votes must be in favour of the proposals. At the meeting of company creditors, approval requires a qualified majority of three-quarters support.

---

[87] Hereafter referred to as IA 1986.
[88] IA 1986 s.1(1).
[89] IA 1986 s.1(3).
[90] IA 1986 s.1(2).
[91] IA 1986 s.389A.
[92] IA 1986 s.2.
[93] IA 1986 s.3.

If the scheme is approved, the arrangement will be binding on all ordinary creditors. The arrangement cannot involve any proposal affecting the rights of secured and preferential creditors, unless they agree to the contrary.[94]

Subsequent procedure

If the scheme is approved, the nominee's function is to act as supervisor **17–30** of the scheme and to oversee its implementation.[95] As supervisor, the nominee has a range of decision-making powers, but any decisions he makes are subject to potential challenge by the creditors.[96]

The intention behind these voluntary arrangements is, as outlined above, that debts are repaid, thus preventing the company from being wound up. It is possible, of course, that in spite of the scheme being put in place, the company's financial position will not improve, and it will ultimately be forced into winding up regardless.

Administration

Administration is a process by which a specialist individual is given the **17–31** task of managing a company's affairs, with a view to improving the company's financial position. The primary function of this "administrator" is to rescue the company from financial difficulty, allowing it to continue as a going concern. However, if this is not possible, then there are a number of secondary functions, which involve facilitating a more favourable position for the company's creditors.

> **Key Concept**
>
> Administration is where a specialist takes control of a company's affairs, usually in an effort to rescue it from insolvency.

The area of administration is governed largely by the IA 1986, although significant additions to this Act were made by the Enterprise Act 2002.[97] Under the IA 1986, the courts have the power to make an administration order in relation to any company that is already insolvent, or is likely to soon become insolvent. The EA 2002 introduced an additional simpler process, by which an administrator could be appointed without the need to go to court.

The EA 2002 also introduced two important new concepts relating to floating charges (see Ch.19). These are the "qualifying floating charge" (QFC) and the "qualifying floating charge holder" (QFCH).[98] A QFC is

---

[94] IA 1986 s.4.
[95] IA 1986 s.7(2).
[96] IA 1986 s.7(3).
[97] Hereafter referred to as EA 2002.
[98] EA 2002 Pt 10.

one to which the EA 2002 applies, while a QFCH is a person who holds a QFC that relates to the whole or substantially the whole of the company's property.[99]

The purposes of administration

17–32 As stated above, the primary function of an administrator is to improve the company's financial position. However, the purpose of an administration order can go beyond this remit, and indeed it may not be possible to rescue the company from insolvency at all. An administrator must therefore perform his functions with the following objectives:

(a) to rescue the company as a going concern;
(b) to achieve a better result for the company's creditors as a whole than would be likely if the company were wound up; *or*
(c) to realise property in order to make a distribution to one or more secured or preferential creditors, provided this can be done without unnecessarily harming the interests of the creditors as a whole.[100]

Court appointment of an administrator

17–33 The court route to administration is commenced by petition to court, which can be presented by the company members, the directors or any creditor.[101] The court will grant the order if:

(a) it is satisfied that the company is unable to pay its debts, or likely to soon become unable to pay its debts; *and*
(b) it is of the opinion that the order would be likely to achieve at least one of the statutory purposes of administration.[102]

It is also possible for a QFCH to make the petition. In this case the court need only be satisfied that the charge is indeed a QFC, and that it is enforceable.[103]

Upon successful application, an administrator will be appointed. He must, as soon as is reasonably practicable, send notice of his appointment to the company and each of its creditors, and must advertise his appointment. He must also, within seven days, give notice of the court order to the Registrar of Companies.[104]

---

[99] IA 1986 Sch.B1, para.14.
[100] IA 1986 Sch.B1, para.3.
[101] IA 1986 s.9(1).
[102] IA 1986 s.8(1).
[103] IA 1986 Sch.B1, para.35.
[104] IA 1986 Sch.B1, para.46.

Out of court appointment

The EA 2002 also introduced provisions allowing an administrator to be **17–34** appointed without the need to go to court. This simplifies the process somewhat, and also avoids the expense of a court application. The purposes of administration remain the same when an out of court appointment is made.

An out of court appointment can be made by either a QFCH, or by the company or its directors. The procedure to be followed differs depending on who is making the appointment.

Out of court appointment by a QFCH

When a QFCH intends to appoint an administrator using the out of **17–35** court route, he must give two business days' written notice to (or otherwise secure the consent of) any QFCH who has priority.[105] The QFCH must then file with the court the following:

(a) a notice of appointment;
(b) a relevant statutory declaration; and
(c) a statement of consent made by the administrator.[106]

Upon satisfaction of the above requirements, the appointment is effective.

Out of court appointment by the company or the directors

Where an out of court appointment is to be made by the company or **17–36** directors, at least five business days' notice in writing must be given to any person who is entitled to appoint an administrator as a QFCH.[107] This written notice must be filed with the court as soon as is reasonably practicable, and must be accompanied by a statutory declaration by the person who proposes to make the appointment that:

(a) the company is or is likely to become unable to pay its debts;
(b) the company is not in liquidation; and
(c) as far as can be ascertained, appointment of an administrator is not otherwise prevented.[108]

Upon expiry of the notice period, the person seeking to make the appointment must then file with the court a notice of the appointment and a statutory declaration of compliance. The notice of appointment must identify the administrator, and must be accompanied by a statement of consent made by him.[109]

---

[105] IA 1986 Sch.B1, para.15(1).
[106] IA 1986 Sch.B1, para.18.
[107] IA 1986 Sch.B1, para.26(1).
[108] IA 1986 Sch.B1, para.27.
[109] IA 1986 Sch.B1, para.29.

Upon satisfaction of the above requirements, the appointment is effective.

Effect of administrator's appointment

17–37   Regardless of how the administrator has been appointed, once the relevant procedure has been completed, the company is said to be "in administration". This fact must be publicised on every business document issued by or on behalf of the company.[110]

The appointment of an administrator also affords the company certain protections against action by its creditors. In particular, the administration order has the following effects:

(a) the company cannot be put into liquidation;
(b) any administrative receiver must vacate office;
(c) a receiver appointed under a floating charge relating to only part of the company's property must vacate office if required to do so by the administrator;
(d) no steps may be taken to enforce any security over the company's property without the consent of either the administrator or the court;
(e) no legal proceedings may be commenced nor any diligence done against the company's property without the consent of either the administrator or the court.[111]

These restrictions on creditor action remain in place for the duration of the administration.

The administration process

17–38   Following his appointment, the administrator will request of the company's officers a statement of the company's affairs. This statement of affairs is the starting point for the administration, and must be supplied within 11 days of the administrator making the request.[112] The statement details the company's assets and liabilities, and will often have been prepared by the company's accountant.

The administrator is then generally empowered to do anything he feels is necessary to achieve the purpose of the administration. This includes the power to:

(a) sell company property;
(b) raise or borrow money on behalf of the company;
(c) bring or defend legal action in the company's name;
(d) call meetings of the creditors or members;
(e) remove and appoint directors as appropriate.[113]

---

[110] IA 1986 s.12.
[111] IA 1986 s.11.
[112] IA 1986 Sch.B1, para.48.
[113] IA 1986 Sch.1.

Within eight weeks of the administration order having been made, the administrator must make a statement of his proposals as to how the purpose of the administration order is to be achieved. This must be sent to the Registrar of Companies, the members of the company and to all creditors of whom the administrator is aware.[114]

The proposals must also be laid before a meeting of the creditors, to be held within 10 weeks of the company going into administration.[115] At this meeting, the creditors will vote, by a simple majority in value, on whether or not they wish to approve the proposals.[116]

The administrator must report the result of the meeting to the court and must also notify the Registrar of Companies. If the creditors refuse to approve the proposals, the court may either discharge the administration order or make any other order as it sees fit in the circumstances.[117]

Ending of the administration

The administrator must complete the administration within 12 months of **17–39** the date of appointment, at which time his appointment will automatically come to an end. This date may be extended once by a further six months with the consent of the creditors, or by any such period as is deemed necessary by the court.[118]

The most desirable scenario is, of course, that the purpose of the administration order will have been achieved. If the administrator is of the opinion that this is the case, he must file a notice with the court, and intimate the same to the Registrar of Companies. He must also send copies of this notice to the creditors. Upon filing of the notice in court, the administration ends. If, on the other hand, the administrator is ever of the opinion that the purpose of the administration *cannot* be achieved, he may apply to the court for a discharge of the order. If the company cannot be rescued, it is likely that it will pass into liquidation (see below).

Receivership

Receivership is not a procedure that seeks to rescue the company, as **17–40** administration or company voluntary arrangements might. Instead, receivership is a process initiated by a creditor who holds a floating charge over the company's assets. These assets are then seized, and sold off ("realised") with a view to repaying the floating charge holder. The individual appointed to seize and realise these assets is known as a "receiver".

---

[114] IA 1986 Sch.B1, para.49.
[115] IA 1986 Sch.B1, para.51.
[116] IA 1986 Sch.B1, para.53.
[117] IA 1986 Sch.B1, para.55.
[118] IA 1986 Sch.B1, para.76.

> **Key Concept**
>
> Receivership is where an individual takes control of certain company assets, which he will sell with a view to repaying the creditor who appointed him.

The law of receivership was changed significantly by the EA 2002, which came into force in September 2003 and generally prohibits the appointment of receivers in respect of charges created after this date. However, it is still legitimate to appoint a receiver in respect of charges created before the EA 2002 came into force.

Appointment of a receiver

17–41 A receiver may be appointed by a creditor who holds a floating charge over any part of a company's assets. It is also possible for the court to appoint a receiver on application from a floating charge holder.

A floating charge holder is justified in appointing a receiver on the happening of any event specified in the Instrument of Charge as entitling such an appointment. A common example of such an event would be failure by the company to repay a debt by a specified date. It is also possible for a receiver to be appointed on the following statutory grounds:

(a) the expiry of 21 days after the making of a demand for payment, without payment being made;
(b) the expiry of two months during the whole of which interest due under the charge has been in arrears;
(c) the making of an order or the passing of a resolution to wind up the company;
(d) the appointment of a receiver by virtue of any other floating charge created by the company.[119]

Notification must be given to the Registrar of Companies within seven days of the appointment.[120]

When a receiver is appointed, he must immediately notify the company and publish the fact that he has been appointed. He must also, within 28 days, notify all the company's creditors of his appointment.[121] In addition, every business document issued by or on behalf of the company must include a statement that a receiver has been appointed.[122]

---

[119] IA 1986 s.52.
[120] IA 1986 s.53.
[121] IA 1986 s.65.
[122] IA 1986 s.64.

Receiver's powers

A receiver's powers are essentially limited to those outlined in the **17–42** Instrument of Charge, and those powers granted by statute. Among a receiver's most significant statutory powers are:

(a) to take possession of company property;
(b) to sell company property;
(c) to appoint a solicitor or accountant, or other professional person to assist him in performance of his functions;
(d) to do all such things as may be necessary for the realisation of the property;
(e) to call up any uncalled capital of the company.[123]

Distribution of monies

Although the receiver's duty is to the creditor who appointed him, and **17–43** indeed his function is to repay that creditor, he cannot be ignorant as to the rights of other creditors. Some of these creditors will have debts that rank higher than that of the floating charge holder and, when distributing realised assets, the receiver is bound to recognise these prior-ranking claims before paying over any monies to the floating charge holder who appointed him. Therefore, the distribution of monies must be made in the following order:

(a) any creditor who holds a fixed security over property which is also the subject of the floating charge and which ranks prior to, or equally with, the floating charge;
(b) any creditor who, before the receiver's appointment, has effectually executed diligence against property of the company that is also the subject of the floating charge;
(c) debts incurred by the receiver in the course of the receivership;
(d) expenses of the receivership and the remuneration of the receiver;
(e) preferential creditors who have intimated their claims within six months;
(f) the holder of the floating charge by virtue of which the receiver was appointed.[124]

Termination of receivership

Once the receiver has completed the purpose for which he was appointed, **17–44** the receivership will come to an end. Notice of termination of the receivership must be given, within 14 days, to the Registrar of Companies.[125]

---

[123] IA 1986 Sch.2.
[124] IA 1986 s.60(1).
[125] IA 1986 s.62(5).

Liquidation

17–45 Liquidation is the process by which all of a company's assets are ingathered, and used to repay existing debts. The company's affairs are "wound up" and, after the process is complete and notice has been given to the Registrar of Companies, the company is dissolved and ceases to exist. Any outstanding debts not satisfied by the distribution of the company's assets will expire along with the company.

> **Key Concept**
>
> Liquidation is where a company's assets are sold off, after which the company is dissolved and ceases to exist.

It is most commonly the case that a company is wound up because it cannot be rescued from insolvency. In such a case, circumstance more than choice has determined the company's fate. However, there are various other reasons why a company might be wound up, so it is worth bearing in mind that insolvency is *not* a pre-requisite of liquidation.

Broadly, a company may be wound up by one of two methods: compulsory liquidation and voluntary liquidation. In practice, voluntary liquidation is more common.

Liquidation 1: Compulsory winding up

17–46 A compulsory liquidation is commenced by the presentation of a petition for a winding up to the court. There are a number of situations that justify such a petition being presented,[126] the most common ground being that the company is unable to pay its debts. The court is not bound to grant the petition, regardless of the reason for it being presented.

Making the petition

17–47 A petition for winding up can be presented by any of the following:

(a) the company or directors;
(b) the Department of Business, Enterprise and Regulatory Reform,[127] in certain situations;
(c) any creditor or creditors;
(d) any "contributory", i.e. any person who is liable to contribute to the assets of the company upon winding up.[128]

Such a petition may be presented if:

---

[126] IA 1986 s.122.
[127] Formerly the Department of Trade and Industry.
[128] IA 1986 s.124.

   (a) the company has passed a special resolution to that effect;

   (b) the company is a plc that has failed to obtain a trading certificate within 12 months of incorporation;

   (c) the company is an "old" public company;[129]

   (d) the company has not commenced its business within one year of incorporation, or has suspended its business for an entire year;

   (e) the membership of a public limited company falls below two persons;

   (f) the company is unable to pay its debts;

   (g) the court is of the opinion that it is just and equitable that the company should be wound up.[130]

In addition to these grounds, it is also possible to present a petition for winding up of a Scottish company if there is a floating charge over the company's assets, and the court is satisfied that the security of the creditor is in jeopardy.[131]

A company is deemed to be unable to pay its debts if it can be proved that the value of its assets is less than the extent of its liabilities, or if:

   (a) a creditor for £750 or more serves a written demand for payment, and the debt is not satisfied within three weeks;

   (b) payment is not made within the time allowed following a court order to repay the debts;

   (c) it is proved to the satisfaction of the court that the company is unable to pay its debts as they fall due.[132]

Effects of a winding up order

Upon the making of a winding up order by the court, the company is said **17–48** to be "in liquidation", as from the date on which the petition was presented. The company must immediately notify the Registrar of Companies as to this fact, which has a number of important consequences, for example:

   (a) no legal action may be commenced against the company without the leave of the court;[133]

   (b) all sales or other dispositions of the company's property and all transfers of the company's shares are void unless the court orders otherwise;[134]

   (c) all diligences executed within 60 days prior to the winding up order being made are rendered ineffectual.[135]

---

[129] As defined by the Companies Consolidation (Consequential Provisions) Act 1985 s.1.
[130] IA 1986 s.122(1).
[131] IA 1986 s.122(2).
[132] IA 1986 s.123.
[133] IA 1986 s.130.
[134] IA 1986 s.127.
[135] IA 1986 s.185.

Once the Registrar has been notified that the company is in liquidation, he will enter this information in all records pertaining to the company, and will also publicise the fact. All business documents issued from then on by or on behalf of the company must state that the company is in liquidation.[136]

Appointment of the liquidator

17–49 It is open to the courts, upon the presentation of a petition for winding up, to take charge of the company's affairs by appointing a "provisional" liquidator. His function is to protect the interests of the creditors, pending the outcome of the court hearing. To this end, he will have such powers as are conferred on him by the court.[137]

Where the court makes a winding up order, it will at the same time appoint an "interim" liquidator, who must hold a meeting of the creditors and, if appropriate, a meeting of the contributories.[138] The purpose of this meeting is to select a person to take over as the company's "liquidator" and oversee the winding up in full. If no appropriate person is identified at the meeting, the courts will appoint a liquidator.[139]

It is also possible for a liquidation committee to be established, to advise and assist the liquidator in his functions, and to sanction certain powers the liquidator might wish to exercise. The committee may consist of both creditors and contributories, except where the company is being wound up due to an inability to pay its debts, in which case the committee will be composed entirely of creditors.[140]

Liquidator's function and powers

17–50 The primary functions of the liquidator are to ingather the company's assets, and apply those assets in satisfaction of the company's liabilities.[141] The liquidator has a range of powers, which are divided broadly into those that can be exercised without prior sanction of the court (or liquidation committee, if applicable), and those that do require prior sanction.

Powers that require sanction include:

(a) the power to pay any class of creditor in full;
(b) the power to bring or defend certain legal proceedings;
(c) the power to carry on the business of the company so far as may be necessary for its beneficial winding up.[142]

---

[136] IA 1986 s.188.
[137] IA 1986 s.135.
[138] IA 1986 s.138.
[139] IA 1986 s.139.
[140] IA 1986 s.142.
[141] IA 1986 s.143.
[142] IA 1986 Sch.4 Parts 1 and 2.

(The powers to defend legal actions and to carry on company business require no prior sanction in a voluntary winding up—see below.)

Powers that require no prior sanction include:

(a) the power to sell any of the company's property;
(b) the power to raise money on the security of the company's assets;
(c) the power to do all such other things as may be necessary for winding up the company's affairs and distributing its assets.[143]

Distribution of monies

Once the liquidator has ingathered all the company's assets, he must then **17–51** apply those assets to the company's debts. All proven creditor claims must be ranked against each other to determine the order of payment. The liquidator must apply assets according to the following ranking:

(a) holders of fixed securities;
(b) costs of liquidation, including the liquidator's remuneration;
(c) preferential creditors (most commonly, unpaid employees of the company);[144]
(d) floating charge holders, subject to the rule that any floating charge created within 12 months prior to commencement of the winding up is void;
(e) ordinary creditors.

Ordinary creditors rank equally with each other, and might not be paid at all if the funds by this point have been exhausted.

Dissolution of the company

Once all assets have been applied to proven debts, and any surplus **17–52** monies distributed among the company members, the liquidation is complete. The liquidator, having held a final meeting of the creditors to present his report on the winding up, must inform the Registrar of Companies. After a period of three months the company is dissolved and ceases to exist.[145]

Liquidation 2: Voluntary winding up

The process of going to court can be expensive and time consuming. **17–53** Therefore, a more straightforward procedure can be utilised when there is a broad agreement that the company has no viable future. This procedure is available in the form of voluntary winding up, which allows the company's affairs to be settled without the formality of petitioning the court.

---

[143] IA 1986 Sch.4 Part 3.
[144] IA 1986 Sch.6.
[145] IA 1986 s.146.

There are two distinct situations in which a company might be wound up voluntarily. The first is where there is no doubt as to the company's solvency. In this situation, the creditors need not be involved, as there is no risk of their debts being left unsatisfied. The liquidation can therefore proceed as a "members' voluntary winding up". However, if there *is* some doubt as to whether all debts of the company will be paid, the creditors will likely wish to supervise the process, and so the liquidation must proceed as a "creditors' voluntary winding up".

Key Concept

If a solvent company is to be wound up voluntarily, this can be done as a members' voluntary winding up. If the company is not solvent, the procedure employed must be a creditors' voluntary winding up.

Other than where specifically highlighted, the rules outlined above for compulsory winding up (e.g. the effects of the winding up and the ranking of creditors' claims) remain the same.

Commencement of a voluntary winding up

17–54 Regardless of whether or not the creditors will supervise the liquidation, a voluntary winding up is commenced by the passing of a resolution to that effect by the members of the company at a general meeting. A company can be wound up voluntarily on:

  (a) the expiry of a fixed period for the duration of the company, or on the occurrence of a specified event;
  (b) the passing of a special resolution, subject to certain rules;
  (c) the passing of a resolution to the effect that the company cannot, by reason of its liabilities, continue its business.[146]

Within 14 days of passing the resolution, the company must give notice in the *Edinburgh Gazette*.[147] The winding up is deemed to have commenced at the time of the passing of the resolution.[148]

Members' voluntary winding up

17–55 The essential feature of a members' voluntary winding up is that the company must be in a position to pay off all outstanding debts. The directors must make a "declaration of solvency" to this effect, stating that they have made a full investigation of the company's affairs and are of the

---

[146] IA 1986 s.84.
[147] IA 1986 s.85.
[148] IA 1986 s.86.

opinion that the company will, within a period not exceeding 12 months, be able to pay all its debts.[149]

The liquidator in this case is appointed by the members,[150] and there is no liquidation committee. The liquidator must keep the members informed as to the progress of the winding up, and must call meetings for this purpose. If at any point the liquidator becomes of the opinion that the company will *not* after all be able to pay its debts in full, he must call a meeting of the creditors to notify them of this;[151] from the date of the meeting, the liquidation will proceed as a creditors' voluntary winding up.[152]

Once the winding up is complete, a final meeting of the members must be called by the liquidator.[153] His final report and accounts will be given at this meeting, after which he must notify the Registrar that the company's affairs have been wound up. The company will then be dissolved as of three months from the date of notification.[154]

Creditors' voluntary winding up

If there is any doubt as to the company's ability to repay its debts the **17–56** directors will, of course, be unable to make a statutory declaration of solvency. In such a case, the winding up must proceed as a creditors' voluntary winding up. The decision to commence a winding up must still be taken by the company members at a general meeting, but there must be an additional meeting of the creditors called within 14 days of the resolution being passed.[155]

At this meeting, a full statement of the company's affairs must be placed before the creditors.[156] The creditors may appoint a liquidator, or may accept a nominee of the company as liquidator.[157] They may also establish a liquidation committee.[158]

The liquidator in this case is answerable to the creditors, and must hold meetings to keep them informed of the progress of the winding up.[159] Once the winding up is complete and a final meeting of the creditors has been called,[160] the Registrar must be notified that the company has been wound up. The company will then be dissolved as of three months from the date of notification.[161]

---

[149] IA 1986 s.89.
[150] IA 1986 s.91.
[151] IA 1986 s.95.
[152] IA 1986 s.96.
[153] IA 1986 s.94.
[154] IA 1986 s.201.
[155] IA 1986 s.98.
[156] IA 1986 s.99.
[157] IA 1986 s.100.
[158] IA 1986 s.101.
[159] IA 1986 s.105.
[160] IA 1986 s.106.
[161] IA 1986 s.201.

▼ CHAPTER SUMMARY

PERSONAL INSOLVENCY

17–57   1. Sequestration of a debtor's estate can be commenced by the debtor, his creditors, or a trustee acting under a trust deed.

2. A trustee in sequestration is appointed to recover, manage and realise the debtor's assets, and distribute them amongst the debtor's creditors.

3. Property that is essential for the maintenance of the debtor's family life, or for the operation of the debtor's business (up to £1,000), do not vest in the trustee.

4. To protect creditors, certain transactions of the debtor prior to his sequestration can be challenged by the trustee. Challengeable transactions include gratuitous alienations, unfair preferences and diligences commenced within 60 days prior to sequestration.

5. The trustee must pay debts according to a statutory order, laid down by the Bankruptcy (Scotland) Act 1985 s.51.

6. One year after the debtor's estate is sequestrated, he will be discharged from bankruptcy.

7. As an alternative to sequestration, a debtor can enter into a trust deed with his creditors, or employ an appropriate simplified procedure.

8. Arrestment is where assets of the debtor being held by third parties are "frozen", and in time are handed over to the creditor to be sold for repayment of a debt.

9. Attachment is where assets of the debtor that are in his possession are removed, valued and sold for repayment of a debt.

10. Inhibition is where restrictions are put on the debtor's use of his property, to encourage repayment of a debt.

CORPORATE INSOLVENCY

1. A company facing financial difficulty can enter into a voluntary arrangement with its creditors whereby a schedule for repayment of debts is agreed.

2. Administration is a process whereby a specialist takes control of a company's affairs, in an effort to improve its financial position.

3. An administrator can be appointed either by the court, or by a qualifying floating charge holder, or by the company.

4. When a company is in administration, it is protected against a range of legal proceedings that might otherwise be taken by creditors.

5. An administrator has a wide range of powers, including the power to sell company property, and raise or borrow money on the company's behalf.

6. Receivership is a process by which a creditor who holds a floating charge can appoint a receiver to take control of the charged assets, and sell them with a view to recovering a debt.
7. A receiver has a range of powers, but he must exercise these powers subject to the rights of any prior-ranking creditors.
8. Liquidation is a process by which the assets of a company are sold off, and the money used to repay as much of the company's debt as possible. At the end of this "winding up" process the company will be dissolved and will cease to exist.
9. Winding up can either be compulsory, which requires a petition to the court, or voluntary, where the company members decide that the company should be wound up.
10. If the company is solvent when the decision is made to commence a voluntary winding up, this can be done as a members' voluntary winding up. If the company is insolvent, the procedure will proceed as a creditors' voluntary winding up.

? QUICK QUIZ

- Explain briefly what is meant by insolvency.
- What is a trustee in sequestration's main function?
- After what period of time will a debtor be discharged from bankruptcy?
- Explain briefly the diligences of arrestment, attachment and inhibition.
- What are the benefits of a company voluntary arrangement to a company that is facing financial difficulty?
- What is the main purpose of administration?
- Under what circumstances can a creditor of a company appoint a receiver?
- In terms of insolvency procedures, why is administration often seen as a preferable alternative to receivership?
- Briefly outline any *two* circumstances that might justify a company being put into liquidation.
- What is the essential difference between a members' voluntary winding up and a creditors' voluntary winding up?

📖 FURTHER READING

Books: Personal Insolvency

Adie, *Bankruptcy* (W. Green, due October 2008).

Davidson and MacGregor, *Commercial Law in Scotland*, 2nd edn (W. Green, Edinburgh, 2008).

McBryde, *Bankruptcy* (W. Green, Edinburgh, 1995).

Maher, *The Law and Practice of Diligence* (Butterworths, 1990).

Books: Corporate Insolvency

Grier, *Company Law* (W. Green, Edinburgh, 2002).

Keenan and Bisacre, *Smith and Keenan's Company Law (Scottish Edition)* (Pearson/Longman, 2005).

MacKenzie-Skene, *Insolvency Law in Scotland* (Butterworths, 1999).

Sealy and Milman, *Annotated Guide to the Insolvency Legislation* (Sweet & Maxwell, 2005).

Sealy, *Cases and Materials in Company Law* (Butterworths, 2001).

St Clair and Lord Drummond Young, *The Law of Corporate Insolvency in Scotland* (W. Green, Edinburgh, 2004).

⏻ RELEVANT WEBLINKS

The Accountant in Bankruptcy: *www.aib.gov.uk*.

The Registrar of Companies: *www.companieshouse.gov.uk*.

The Department for Business, Enterprise and Regulatory Reform (formerly the Department of Trade and Industry): *www.berr.gov.uk*.

The UK Statute Law Database: *www.statutelaw.gov.uk*.

The Office of Public Sector Information: *www.opsi.gov.uk*.

Chapter 18   Negotiable Instruments

Fiona Grant[1]

▶ CHAPTER OVERVIEW

This chapter explains the law on negotiable instruments. A negotiable **18–01** instrument is a signed document detailing the ownership of a debt which can be used by debtors as a method of paying for goods or services. A negotiable instrument may be used as an alternative to payment in cash or via electronic transfer of funds. The benefit of settling a debt by means of a negotiable instrument is that the signed document in question can be *negotiated* which means that it can be transferred from one person to another before the debt is to be paid. In essence, a negotiable instrument is equivalent to cash, given that it can change hands in exactly the same way as money. Although negotiable instruments are not used as frequently as they were in the past, they still play a part in commercial transactions where other methods of payment may not be desirable. Negotiable instruments include: bills of exchange, cheques (which are a type of bill of exchange) and promissory notes. The law relating to negotiable instruments is mainly found in the Bills of Exchange Act 1882 (hereinafter referred to as the BOEA) as amended by the Cheques Act 1957 and the Cheques Act 1992.

✓ OUTCOMES

By the end of this chapter you will be able to;   **18–02**

- ✓ recognise the essential features of a bill of exchange;
- ✓ recognise the parties to a bill of exchange;
- ✓ understand who is liable on a bill of exchange;
- ✓ understand how a bill of exchange is negotiated;
- ✓ recognise when and why cheques and promissory notes differ from bills of exchange used in commerce.

---

[1] Teaching Fellow in Law, University of Abertay, Dundee.

Introduction

Origins of bills of exchange

18–03 The origins of such an enterprising instrument to facilitate and pay a debt can be traced back to the Knights Templar in the 12th century. A holy order sanctioned by the Pope, the Templars devised the concept of the transfer of funds by *note of hand*. One duty undertaken by the Templars was to house and protect pilgrims on their way to and from the Holy Land. For obvious reasons, a pilgrim navigating unknown and hostile territory would not wish to travel thousands of miles and back carrying large sums of cash. So, before the journey began, funds would be deposited with the Templars in his homeland and, in return, the pilgrim would receive a coded note. At each stop along the way, the pilgrim would hand this note to the local Templar representative who would then pay over cash in local currency and record the transaction, again in code, on the note. When the pilgrim returned home, the note was presented to the Templar who had first issued it, with any balance being returned or overspend cleared at that time. Bills of exchange, as we understand them today, were popularised on a commercial scale by the business practices of Lombardy businessmen in Italy in the 14th century who, when faced with a rising volume of overseas trade, wished to avoid the perils of sending large sums of cash to and from foreign shores.

Benefits of bills of exchange

18–04 A bill of exchange may be the preferred method of payment for goods or services if payment will take place at some point after the goods or services have been provided. For example, the seller of goods may operate an open trading account with either a domestic or foreign buyer, with usual practice being that an invoice for payment is sent after the goods have been shipped. If the buyer fails to pay, the seller's only recourse is to raise a court action to seek payment. If, however, the seller has been provided with a properly constituted bill of exchange from the buyer, ordering a third party to make payment, this would have ensured payment, irrespective of the solvency or otherwise of the buyer at the time payment fell due. The main benefit of being paid via a bill of exchange is that the seller can *negotiate* the bill, that is to say, sell the bill on to another party for less than its face value and get paid sooner if the bill falls due weeks or months hence. The profit of the person buying the negotiated bill is the difference between what was paid to the seller and the face value of the bill. An obvious advantage of making payment with a bill which falls due at some future point in time is that it allows a trader to carry on his business on credit.

The following examples illustrate how a bill of exchange operates in practice:

Example 1

Denis is a trader based in Perth.Helen is a trader based in Inverness. Alain is a trader based in Brussels.

Alain owes Denis £10,000. Helen owes Alain £10,000.

Instead of Alain sending cash to Denis and Helen sending cash to Alain, Alain will *draw a bill* for £10,000 on his debtor who is Helen.

If Helen accepts the bill it will be sent to Denis, Alain's creditor.

Denis will then obtain payment from Helen at the time stipulated on the face of the bill.

In this way both transactions are settled without any cash being sent to or from Brussels.

Such a bill is known as a *foreign bill*, given one of the parties is based overseas, which is of significance should the bill be dishonoured, that is to say, the party accepting the bill ultimately fails to pay. Dishonourment of a bill is discussed below at para.18–13.

Example 2

Alice, Neil and Gavin are all traders based in Scotland.

Alice buys goods from Neil for £2,000.

Alice is experiencing cash-flow problems and cannot pay for the goods on the date of purchase. However she is owed £2,500 by Gavin two months hence.

If Neil agrees to wait for payment, Alice can draw a bill ordering Gavin to pay Neil £2,000 in two months time. If Gavin accepts the bill it will be delivered to Neil and Gavin will pay the £2,000 he owes Alice two months hence to Neil instead.

However, if Neil requires to realise funds before the bill falls due for payment, he can *negotiate* the bill; that is to say, sell it on to Kevin for £1,700. Kevin in turn can negotiate the bill by selling it on to Liam. Liam will then present the bill to Gavin for payment on the due date.

Such a bill is known as an *inland bill* given all the parties are domiciled in the same country.[2]

Parties to a bill

The party drawing the bill is known as the *drawer* (debtor).The party ordered to pay the specified sum is known as the *drawee*. This could be a bank or a private individual. If a bank is the drawee the document is known as a bank draft.The party who is due the sum specified in the bill is known as the *payee* (creditor). **18–05**

---

[2] Bills of Exchange Act 1882 (BOEA) s.4(1).

Terminology

18–06 The reader will quickly become aware of alternative names for the parties, depending upon the stage the transaction has reached. To properly explain the legal significance of such designations, the use of these alternatives is unavoidable.

Definition of a bill of exchange—BOEA, as amended

18–07 The BOEA dictates whether a document ordering a party to make payment *upon demand* or *on sight* or at some stated time in the future is a valid bill of exchange.[3] To be such, the document must conform with the relevant sections of the Act, primarily its *negotiability* which is the ability to transfer the bill between parties.

Section 3(1) of the BOEA states that a bill of exchange is:

> "an unconditional order in writing, addressed by one person to another, signed by the person giving it, requiring the person to whom it is addressed to pay on demand, or at a fixed or determinable future time a sum certain in money, or to the order of a specified person or to bearer."

It is therefore clear that the bill must:

- be an unconditional order to pay, meaning that the words used must emphatically instruct payment[4] and there must be no conditions on the face of the bill restricting the right to payment;[5]
- be in writing in any recognised language[6] and on any durable medium[7];
- be addressed by one person to another, that is by the drawer to the drawee, and signed by the person drawing the bill;
- be payable on demand or at a fixed or determinable future time[8];
- be a sum certain in money[9];
- be payable to the order of a specified person or to the *bearer* who is the person in possession of the bill when it falls due for payment.

---

[3] A bill may also become payable upon the occurrence of an event which is certain to happen, e.g. death, but not marriage.

[4] In *Hamilton v Spottiswoode* (1849) 154 E.R. 1182 it was held that the words "We hereby authorise you to pay" was not an order to pay *per* s.3(1) of the BOEA.

[5] In *Bavins Jnr & Sims v London & South Western Bank Ltd* [1901] 1 Q.B. 270 a stipulation that the payee was to sign a receipt prior to receiving payment appeared on the face of the bill. This condition meant the document was not a bill of exchange *per* s.3(1) of the BOEA.

[6] *Arab Bank Ltd v Ross* [1952] 2 Q.B. 216 where both Arabic and English words were used on the face of the bills which were in the form of promissory notes.

[7] Except metal to comply with the terms of s.5 of the Coinage Act 1870.

[8] Bills payable at a future date are generally made payable in periods of 30 days. If a bill is undated, s.12 of the BOEA permits the payee to insert a date.

[9] *Dixon v Bovill* (1856) 3 Macq. (HL) 1.

A document which fails to comply with *all* the requirements of s.3(1) is not a bill of exchange and, accordingly, cannot be negotiated.

Form of the bill

There is no statutory form of bill of exchange but a bill as in Example 1 **18–08** above would look like this:

£10,000   Brussels, April 6, 2008

At thirty (30) days after date pay Denis Smith or order the sum of ten thousand pounds Sterling for value received.

To Helen Jones   (Signed) Alain DuBois
3 Anywhere Road,
Inverness

The bill will be sent by Alain to Helen who will write *accepted* on the face of the bill and add her signature. The bill is said to be *drawn upon* Helen, who is now called the *acceptor* of the bill.[10]

£10,000   Brussels, April 6, 2008

At thirty (30) days after date pay Denis Smith or order the sum of ten thousand pounds Sterling for value received.

To Helen Jones   (Signed) Alain DuBois
3 Anywhere Road,
Inverness

ACCEPTED H Jones

The bill will then be sent to Denis, who can if he so chooses negotiate the bill, that is, to sell the bill to another party who will then be entitled to payment from Helen on the due date. A bill made out *to order*, as the one above is, is transferred by *indorsement and delivery*. In the above example the words *or order* appear after Denis's name. However, if the words had been omitted Denis could still sell the bill on as the law deems a bill made payable to a named individual should be read as to include the words *or order*.[11] Where a bill is made out *to bearer* the bill is transferred from party to party purely by delivery.[12] The word bearer simply means the party who has possession of the bill.

---

[10] The drawee does not need to accept at this point, but it is clearly wise to confirm that the drawee will pay the debt. Upon acceptance, the acceptor becomes the principal debtor under the bill

[11] BOEA s.8(2), (4).

[12] BOEA s.31(2).

Indorsement

18–09 To transfer a bill made payable to order the payee will sign his name on the back of the bill. His signature acts as indorsement, signifying that a new payee has been nominated. The name of the new payee, now known as the *indorsee*, can also be written on the back of the bill. This is known as a *special indorsement*.[13]

Example of a Special Indorsement

Brian King (existing payee/indorser)
Pay Pauline Henderson (new payee/indorsee)

Although at this point the transfer of the bill is restricted to Pauline Henderson, she is not prohibited from indorsing the bill herself and transferring it to a new indorsee thereafter. A special indorsement is to be distinguished from a *restrictive indorsement*. This is achieved by adding the word *only* after the name of the new indorsee. If this happens, the bill cannot be negotiated beyond the named indorsee. [14]

Example of a Restrictive Indorsement

Brian King
Pay Pauline Henderson only

If the name of the indorsee is not stated a *blank indorsement* has been given by the indorser. The bill then automatically becomes a bearer bill which can be negotiated by delivery alone.[15] However, the recipient of a blank indorsement is entitled to sign his name above that of the indorser's. If this is done, the blank indorsement is converted into a special indorsement which can then be negotiated by future indorsement in favour of a new indorsee or bearer.[16] Negotiation is complete when the indorsee receives the bill.[17] For obvious reasons, an order bill is always to be preferred to a bearer bill given that a thief in possession of a bearer bill can sell it on without indorsement or simply present it for payment to the acceptor.

Holders

18–10 When the bill is transferred, either by indorsement and delivery, or by delivery alone, in the case of a bearer bill, the recipient is then known as the *holder* of the bill. Only the holder is entitled to negotiate the bill[18] and this status also enables him/her to present the bill to the drawee/acceptor

---

[13] BOEA s.34(2).
[14] BOEA ss.8(1), 35(2).
[15] BOEA s.34(1).
[16] BOEA s.34(4).
[17] BOEA s.31(3).
[18] BOEA s.31.

for payment when it falls due.[19] However, to be sure of realising payment a holder must also be both a *holder for value* and a *holder in due course*.

Before explaining the meaning of the above terms it is necessary to further explore the legal effect of negotiability.

The ability to transfer a bill of exchange from party to party without the knowledge or agreement of the drawee/acceptor stems from the fact that the bill is treated as a cash equivalent, as stated in para.18–01 above. Accordingly, a bill *stands on its own two feet* and differs from other forms of incorporeal moveable property, such as shares or rights under an insurance policy, where to effect a legally enforceable transfer of the benefit of the property between the parties, *assignation and intimation* must occur.[20] If this does not happen, the assignee gains no right to or benefit in the property at all.

> "The privilege of a negotiable document is that it passes in its own corpus the thing it represents without intimation" (*Connal & Co v Loder* (1868) 6 M 1095 at 1102 *per* Lord Neaves).

However, if a bill of exchange is negotiated for value and the indorsee holds it in good faith and in ignorance of any defect attaching to it, for example the bill was stolen by the party who indorsed it in his favour, he is in the fortunate position of being a holder for value and a holder in due course respectively.

Holder for value

The requirement that the indorsee has actually paid for the bill, rather than have been given it as a gift, must be met to satisfy a rule of English, not Scots, contract law.[21] As the BOEA applies throughout the United Kingdom this requirement must be met in Scotland too if the indorsee is to enforce payment of the bill. **18–11**

Holder in due course

To meet the requirements of the BOEA the bill must appear on the face of things to have been executed in proper form,[22] taken in good faith from the previous holder by the holder for value[23] whilst unaware of any defect in the title of the bill at that time or previous dishonour of the bill.[24] The bill must also not be overdue.[25] If it is overdue the indorsee who takes such a bill gets no better title than the indorser who negotiated it to him. Dishonoured bills and overdue bills are discussed at para.18–13. **18–12**

If these stipulations are met, a holder in due course is entitled to be

---

[19] BOEA s.45(3).
[20] See para.19–29.
[21] BOEA s.27(1) and (2). English law requires consideration. See para.4–05.
[22] BOEA s.29(1).
[23] BOEA s.90.
[24] BOEA s.36(5).
[25] BOEA s.36(2).

paid by the drawee/acceptor notwithstanding the fact that the title of the previous indorsee is defective because the bill was obtained by him though nefarious means such as theft, duress, force or fear or by fraud.

Key Concept

For a holder to gain good title to the debt, irrespective of any defect in his title, he must also be a holder for value and a holder in due course.

The legal protection afforded by a negotiable instrument as a means of receiving payment of a debt is succinctly stated by Willes J. in *Whistler v Forster*[26]:

> "The general rule of law is undoubted that no-one can acquire a better title than he himself possesses.[27] To this there are some exceptions, one of which arises out of the rule of ... law ... as to negotiable instruments. These ... are subject to the same rule as money and if such an instrument be transferred in good faith, for value, before it is overdue, it becomes available in the hands of the holder, notwithstanding fraud which would have rendered it unavailable in the hands of a previous holder."

Parties liable on a bill

18–13   In an ideal world the drawee will have accepted the bill in advance of the due date for payment. The holder will then simply present it and get paid. However, as stated above, a drawee may not have accepted the bill and until he does so, which may be as late as the time it is presented for payment, he is not a party to the bill. If the drawee refuses to accept the bill this is known as *dishonour by non-acceptance* and the drawer of the bill is liable to make payment to the holder. In addition, if the bill has been negotiated by indorsement each indorsee is also potentially liable to the holder.[28] This liability is clearly stated in BOEA s.43(2) and elaborated on in s.55:

> "(1) The drawer of a bill by drawing it—
>
>> (a) Engages that on due presentment it shall be accepted and paid according to its tenor, and that if it be dishonoured he will compensate the holder or any indorser who is compelled to pay it, provided that the requisite proceedings on dishonour be duly taken;

---

[26] (1863) 14 C.B. (NS) 248 at 257.
[27] This is expressed in the Latin maxim *Nemo dat quem non habet* which roughly translated means "you cannot give that which you do not have".
[28] BOEA s.43(2).

(2) The indorser of a bill by indorsing it—

> (a) Engages that on due presentment it shall be accepted and paid according to its tenor, and that if it be dishonoured he will compensate the holder or a subsequent indorser who is compelled to pay it, provided that the requisite proceedings on dishonour be duly taken."

If, however, the acceptor has insufficient funds to pay the bill or refuses to pay the bill it is said to be *dishonoured by non-payment*.[29] The holder must inform the drawer and every endorser that the bill has been dishonoured in this way.[30] If the bill is a foreign bill, it must also be *noted and protested* which means that a notary public[31] must certify that the acceptor has failed to honour the bill. This should be done no later than the next business day after the bill has been dishonoured. [32] An Inland bill may be noted and protested but this is not a requirement under the BOEA.

The drawer and any party who indorses a bill may be held liable to the holder if the acceptor refuses to honour the bill when it is presented for payment, unless, that is, any individual's signature has been forged.[33] However, as stated in para.18–12, the holder for value gains good title to have the debt discharged irrespective of any fraud or irregularity. Thus if one indorser's signature has been forged and/or the bill was transferred to the holder by another indorser, who himself did not hold good title, the bill remains valid and the holder for value can sue any party for payment save the party whose signature has been forged. Section 58 of the BOEA states that where the holder of a bill payable to bearer negotiates it by delivery without indorsing it he is not liable on the instrument.[34]

Material alterations to a bill

If a bill has been *materially altered* in some way without the agreement of all the parties liable on the bill, for example the sum payable on the face of the bill has been changed from £5,000 to £50,000, parties to the bill *before* the material alteration occurred are not liable to pay the £50,000 fraudulently stated on the bill.[35] They are, however, potentially liable for the original sum of £5,000 if the alteration was not apparent to the **18–14**

---

[29] BOEA s.47.

[30] BOEA s.48.

[31] BOEA s.51(2). Noting is achieved by the notary stating the date of dishonour on the bill with the addition of his initials and the letters NP to mark his office. Notaries are solicitors who have authority from the Court of Session to, amongst other duties, administer oaths and witness and authenticate documents.

[32] BOEA s.49(12).

[33] BOEA ss.47(2) and 24.

[34] Where the holder of a bill payable to bearer negotiates it by delivery without indorsing it he is called a transferor by delivery. However, a transferor by delivery who negotiates a bill thereby warrants to his immediate transferee being a holder for value that the bill is what it purports to be, that he has a right to transfer it, and that at the time of transfer he is not aware of any fact which renders it valueless (s.58(1), (2), (3)).

[35] BOEA s.64(1).

holder. The party who actually altered the bill and subsequent indorsers are all potentially liable to pay £50,000 to the holder.

Overdue bills

18–15 When a bill falls due for payment the holder must present it to the drawer or acceptor for payment on the day it actually falls due. Failure to do this sees the holder lose the right to claim against the drawer and any indorsers, unless the delay in making presentation is beyond his control.[36] In *Hamilton Finance Co Ltd v Coverley Westray Walbaum & Tosetti Ltd*[37] the court accepted that a bill delayed for presentment by the inefficiency of the postal service met the terms of s.46(1) of the BOEA. A bill payable on demand is held to be overdue when it has been in circulation for an unreasonable length of time. In determining what is reasonable a court will look to the facts of the individual case and also usual trade practice. If a bill payable on demand is held to be overdue the drawer and indorsers are discharged from making payment.[38]

In any event, if a bill is not presented for payment within five years it will *prescribe*.[39] This means that if five years from the appropriate date of payment have elapsed without the bill being presented to the acceptor for payment, or any *relevant claim* being made in connection to the bill via a court action, the holder has no further mechanism by which to enforce payment.

Lost bills

18–16 If a bill is lost before it is overdue the person who was the holder of it at the relevant time may require the drawer to provide a duplicate bill for the purpose of indemnifying the holder in case the missing bill subsequently reappears in the hands of another person.[40]

CHEQUES

18–17 The reader will no doubt have been surprised to discover that a cheque is a bill of exchange. Section 73 of the BOEA states that a cheque is a bill of exchange "drawn on a banker and payable on demand". In essence, a cheque is a written document giving an order to a bank from one of its customers to pay money, held by the bank on behalf of the customer, to a third party, or to the customer herself if she wishes to withdraw cash. Whilst it is still true to say that a cheque is the most commonly used bill of exchange, the availability of near instant payment by means of electronic transfer of cash via debit cards has led to some domestic traders, most notably supermarkets, advising customers that payment by cheque

---

[36] BOEA s.45(1); s.46(1). However, the acceptor will still be liable to the drawer.
[37] [1969] 1 L.R. 53.
[38] BOEA s.74.
[39] The Prescription and Limitation (Scotland) Act 1973 s.6(1), Sch.1, para.1(e).
[40] BOEA s.69.

will no longer be accepted. Whilst it is premature to suggest that making payment by cheque will become obsolete, it is highly likely that this method of making payment for goods or services will continue to decline. The BOEA applies to cheques in the same way as bills, albeit with some minor differences. These differences are highlighted in the following paragraphs.

Parties to a cheque

The parties to a cheque comprise the drawer, the person who signs the **18–18** cheque, the drawee, the bank or building society to whom the cheque is addressed and the payee, the party to whom, or to whose order, the money is to be paid. The first discernible difference between a bill of exchange as detailed in the preceding paragraphs and a cheque is that a cheque is payable on demand, thus the bank, the drawee, does not need to accept the cheque which will only ever be presented to it for the purpose of payment.

Stale and undated cheques

As with an ordinary bill of exchange, the cheque must be delivered to the **18–19** payee before it reaches the status of a negotiable instrument and s.45(2) of the BOEA states that the drawer and any indorser will be discharged if the cheque is not presented for payment within a reasonable time. However, banking practice dictates that a cheque will not be honoured if it is presented for payment six months after it was signed by the drawer. Banks treat such cheques as *stale*. In addition, although under s.3(4) of the BOEA a cheque is valid even if it is undated, in practice banks refuse to pay such cheques. This practice has been upheld by the courts.

Griffiths v Dalton
[1940] 2 K.B. 264

Dalton gave Griffiths an undated cheque which 18 months later Griffiths filled in the date as February 20, 1933, however by that date Dalton was dead and Griffiths raised an action to recover the sum through Dalton's executors. The court held that a bill, in incomplete form, must be rectified (the date added) within a reasonable time, per s.20(2) of the BOEA and that by February 20, 1933 that period had expired. Accordingly, Dalton's estate was not liable on the cheque.

Crossed cheques

The main distinction between a bill and a cheque is that a cheque may be **18–20** *crossed*. Crossing a cheque is achieved by drawing two parallel across the face of the cheque. A *general crossing* occurs when the words *account payee* or *account payee only* are added. A generally crossed cheque must be presented for payment via the payee's bank account. Modern banking practice dictates that cheques are now pre-printed, and supplied to customers pre-crossed which means that such a cheque cannot be transferred by indorsement and is thus only valid between the parties concerned.[41] Section 78 of the BOEA states that a crossing is a material part of the cheque and that it is unlawful for any person to obliterate or, except as authorised by the act, to add to or alter the crossing. However, the drawer can *open* the crossing, that is to say, *before delivery* to the payee, write the words *Pay Cash* on the face of the cheque and add his initials or signature next to the words. This does not amount to a material alteration and the payee can then present the cheque for cash payment or transfer it by indorsement and delivery in the usual way. It will be recalled that until a cheque, as a species of bill of exchange, does not achieve that status until it has been delivered to the payee.

A *special crossing* is given if the name of the bank at which payment will be made is stipulated on the face of the cheque.[42] Special crossings are rare in practice. In the event that a signed cheque is uncrossed it may be crossed by the drawer or any holder.[43] In addition, if a cheque is crossed and the words *not negotiable* alone appear on the face of the cheque, the cheque may be transferred, but not negotiated. Thus the holder can assign the right to another party to receive the sum stated on the face of the cheque. However, the assignee will only obtain as good a title to the cheque as the assignor had himself.[44] If there is any taint attached to the cheque the assignee will not qualify as a holder in due course, making his right to payment void.[45]

> ### Key Concept
>
> A cheque is to be regarded as a negotiable instrument so long as it contains no words or markings prohibiting its transfer or indicating an intention that it should not be transferred.
>
> Section 81(1) of the BOEA makes it clear that where a cheque is crossed and the words "account payee" or "a/c payee" are added either with or without the word "only" the cheque is not transferable.

Clearing

18–21 Upon presentment of the cheque, the paying bank will pay the proceeds to the holder's bank once the cheque has *cleared*. Clearing is the process by which banks resolve their indebtedness to one another. Once a cheque has been presented to a bank for payment the bank will send it, in a batch along with other cheques which have been presented to it, to a *clearing house*. There, debits and credits between specific banks are recorded and

---

[41] BOEA s.81A(1).
[42] BOEA s.76(2).
[43] BOEA s.77.
[44] *Great Western Railway Co v London and County Banking Co* [1900] 2 Q.B. 464.
[45] BOEA s.81.

settled. In this way, banks avoid the cumbersome process of presenting a single cheque to one another for individual attention.

Liability of the parties

The rationale behind issuing crossed cheques is simply to better protect **18–22** the parties against fraud given that an uncrossed cheque obtained by theft could simply be presented for payment in cash. If a bank pays in cash a cheque bearing the words a/c payee only when presented by a thief, the bank is liable to the true owner of cheque and will have to reimburse that party.[46] On the other hand, if a bank pays a cheque into an account, in accord with its crossing and does so without being negligent and in good faith, s.80 of the BOEA states that the bank is deemed to have paid the cheque to its lawful owner notwithstanding the fact that the cheque was non-transferable under s.81A. Accordingly, the drawer's bank account can be lawfully debited, even if it transpires that the cheque has been stolen. In similar vein, if a bank credits a customer account with a cheque received by it but which the customer has no title to (a stolen cheque) and thereafter debits any charges due by the customer to the bank, the bank will not be held liable to the lawful owner of the cheque.

PROMISSORY NOTES

The BOEA recognises one further form of negotiable instrument—the **18–23** promissory note. A promissory note is defined in s.83(1) of the BOEA as:

> "an unconditional promise in writing made by one person to another signed by the maker, engaging to pay, on demand or at a fixed or determinable future time, a sum certain in money, to, or to the order of, a specified person or to bearer."

It is clear from the above that a promissory note is a personal *promise* to pay with no order being given to a third party to make payment to the promissee. As there is no drawer or acceptor, s.89(3) of the BOEA states that any provisions within the act dealing with acceptance do not apply to promissory notes. As with bills and cheques, delivery is necessary[47] and a note may be negotiated in exactly the same way as a bill. The promissor is primarily liable on the note and any indorser is in exactly the same legal position as an indorser to a bill of exchange. There is no statutory form of promissory note and the word "promise" need not appear at all on the face of the document. However, the words used must give rise to an inference that a promise to pay has been made.[48] It is the unequivocal promise to pay that distinguishes a promissory note from an IOU—

---

[46] BOEA s.79(2).
[47] BOEA s.84.
[48] *Akbar Khan v Attar Singh* [1936] 2 All E.R. 545.

which is simply a document stating that a certain sum of money is owed by one party to another.

▼ CHAPTER SUMMARY

18–24 **A negotiable instrument is a signed document detailing the ownership of a debt. The benefit of settling a debt by means of a negotiable instrument is that the signed document in question can be negotiated meaning that it can be transferred from one person to another before the debt is due to be paid. Negotiable instruments include: bills of exchange, cheques and promissory notes. The law relating to negotiable instruments is mainly found in the BOEA, as amended by the Cheques Act 1957 and the Cheques Act 1992.**

1. **The party drawing the bill is known as the *drawer*, the party ordered to pay the specified sum is known as the *drawee* and the party who is due the sum specified in the bill is known as the *payee* (creditor).**

2. **To qualify as a bill of exchange the signed document in question must be an unconditional order in writing, addressed by one person to another, signed by the person giving it, requiring the person to whom it is addressed to pay on demand, or at a fixed or determinable future time a sum certain in money, or to the order of a specified person (an order bill) or to bearer (a bearer bill);**

   ➢ s.3(1) BOEA; *Hamilton v Spottiswoode* (1849) 154 E.R. 1182; *Bavins Jnr & Sims v London & South Western Bank Ltd* [1901] 1 Q.B. 270; *Arab Bank Ltd v Ross* [1952] 2 Q.B. 216.

3. **To transfer a bill made payable to order the current payee will sign his name on the back of the bill. His signature acts as a special indorsement, signifying that a new named payee has been nominated. Negotiation is complete when the indorsee receives the bill. A bearer bill is transferred by delivery alone;**

   ➢ BOEA ss.31(2), 34(2).

4. **If the name of the indorsee is not stated a blank indorsement has been given and the bill then automatically becomes a bearer bill;**

   ➢ BOEA s.34(1).

5. **When the bill is transferred, either by indorsement and delivery, or by delivery alone, in the case of a bearer bill, the recipient is then known as the holder of the bill. Only the holder is entitled to negotiate the bill;**

   ➢ BOEA s.31.

6. **To be entitled to payment a holder must also be a holder for value (having paid for the bill) and a holder in due course; the bill must appear to have been executed in proper form, taken in good faith whilst unaware of any defect in the title of the bill at that time. If**

these stipulations are met, the holder is entitled to be paid by the drawee/acceptor notwithstanding the fact that the title of the previous indorsee is defective;

> ➤ BOEA ss.27(1) and (2), 29(1), 36(5), 90; *Connal & Co v Loder* (1868) 6 M. 1095; *Whistler v Forster* (1863) 14 C.B. (NS) 248.

7. If the drawee refuses to accept the bill this is known as dishonour by non-acceptance and the drawer of the bill is liable to make payment to the holder. In addition, if the bill has been negotiated by indorsement each indorsee is potentially liable to the holder;

> ➤ BOEA ss.43(2) and 55.

8. If the bill has been accepted and the acceptor refuses to pay the bill it is said to be dishonoured by non-payment. The holder must inform the drawer and every endorser that the bill has been dishonoured in this way. If the bill is a foreign bill, it must also be noted and protested. The drawer and any indorser of the bill are potentially liable to the holder;

> ➤ BOEA ss.24, 47(2), 48, 51(2).

9. When a bill falls due for payment the holder must present it to the drawer or acceptor for payment on the day it actually falls due. Failure to do this sees the holder lose the right to claim against the drawer and any indorsers, unless the delay in making presentation is beyond his control;

> ➤ BOEA s.46(1); *Hamilton Finance Co Ltd v Coverley Westray Walbaum & Tosetti Ltd* [1969] 1 L.R. 53.

10. A cheque is a bill of exchange drawn on a banker and payable on demand;

> ➤ BOEA s.73.

11. The parties to a cheque comprise the drawer, the drawee and the payee.

12. Banking practice dictates that a cheque will be treated as stale if not presented for payment within six months of being signed by the drawer. This practice has been upheld by the courts;

> ➤ *Griffiths v Dalton* [1940] 2 K.B. 264.

13. An undated cheque will not be honoured by a bank irrespective of the fact that s.3(4) of the BOEA states an undated cheque is valid.

14. If a cheque is crossed it must be paid into the payee's bank account and cannot be transferred by indorsement. It is valid between the drawer and payee only;

> ➤ BOEA s.81A(1).

15. A promissory note is an unconditional promise in writing made by one person to another signed by the maker, engaging to pay on

demand or at a specified time in the future a sum certain in money
to, or to the order of, a specified person or to bearer;

> ➤ BOEA s.83(1).

16. As a promissory note is a personal promise to pay another person
there is no drawer or acceptor thus s.89(3) of the BOEA does not
apply to promissory notes.
17. A promissory note can be negotiated in exactly the same way as a
bill.

? QUICK QUIZ

True or False?

- A bill of exchange is always payable on demand.
- A bearer bill cannot be negotiated.
- A holder who is also a holder for value and a holder in due course
is entitled to be paid even if the person he bought the bill from
came by it dishonestly.
- Overdue bills cannot be paid in any circumstance.
- A crossed cheque must be paid into the payee's bank account.

📖 FURTHER READING

Ashton et al., *Understanding Scots Law* (W. Green, Edinburgh, 2007),
Ch.10.
Davidson and MacGregor, *Commercial Law in Scotland*, 2nd edn (W.
Green, Edinburgh, 2008), Ch.5.
Forte (ed.), *Scots Commercial Law* (Butterworths, 1997), Ch.5.
Mays et al., *Scots Law, A Student Guide* (Tottel, 2006), Ch.10.

🖱 RELEVANT WEBLINKS

A fully revised version of the Bills of Exchange Act 1882 can be accessed
at: *http://www.legislation.gov.uk/RevisedStatutes/Acts/ukpga/1882/
cukpga_18820061_en_5*

Chapter 19   Rights in Security

Fiona Grant[1]

▶ CHAPTER OVERVIEW

This chapter is concerned with rights in security for the repayment of   **19–01**
debt. A right in security confers an additional legal right which the
creditor may enforce should the debtor fail to pay the sum(s) owed and
exists in tandem with, but is distinct from, the creditor's right of action
against the debtor under the debtor's contractual obligation to repay the
debt. Rights in security can be sub-divided into personal rights, which are
traditionally known as cautionary obligations (pronounced kay-shun-
ary) and real rights. This chapter begins by outlining the key difference
between the two types of right. It then explains how a cautionary obligation is constituted and how it operates. It then details real rights in
security over heritage (land and buildings) and moveable property.
Moveable property may be either corporeal, something that has a physical existence and can be moved from one place to another, or incorporeal, for example shares in a company, the existence of which may be
proved by the issue of a share certificate but otherwise has no tangible
existence.

✓ OUTCOMES

At the end of this chapter you should be able to: **19–02**

- ✓   understand the difference between a personal right and a real
  right in security;
- ✓   understand the rules underpinning the creation of a contract of
  caution or guarantee;
- ✓   distinguish the respective rights and duties of the creditor, debtor
  and guarantor;
- ✓   appreciate the general principles underpinning the creation of a
  real right
- ✓   in security;
- ✓   understand the different methods by which a real right can be
  created and enforced;

---

[1] Teaching Fellow in Law, University of Abertay, Dundee.

   ✓ distinguish heritable, corporeal and incorporeal moveable property;
   ✓ develop your understanding of core principles of contract law.

INTRODUCTION

19–03 A creditor may demand a right in security for a debt to increase the likelihood that he will recover his outlay should the debtor fail to make payment when it falls due. In Scots law, a right in security gives rise to either a personal right (*ius in personam*) or a real right (*ius in re*). The distinction is important.

Where the right in security is a personal right this allows the creditor to recover the debt from some specified person other than the debtor, or to force that other person to carry out some other obligation on behalf of the debtor. The obligation is generally to pay the sum(s) due by the debtor. If the guarantor becomes insolvent, however, the creditor has no preferential right to any property or assets belonging to the guarantor and is thus in no better position than any of the guarantor's ordinary creditors.

Where the right in security is a real right, this gives the creditor the right to claim identified property belonging to the debtor, or the right to withhold certain property from him, in satisfaction of the debt. In most cases, the holder of a real right in security will defeat the claims of all other creditors to the property in question.

> **Key Concept**
>
> A personal right in security is inferior to that of a real right, given it is only of any practical effect if the guarantor is solvent and in a position to honour the debtor's liability to the creditor.

THE CONTRACT OF CAUTION (GUARANTEE)

19–04 A cautionary obligation is a personal right in security that gives the creditor the right to recover the sum(s) owed him by the debtor, who is known as the *principal debtor*, from another person who has undertaken to pay the debt if the debtor fails to do so. This other person is known traditionally in Scots law as the cautioner but now, more commonly, as the guarantor. A contract of guarantee is an accessory obligation which means that the principal debt must exist or be in the contemplation of the parties, before it can be enforced against the guarantor. It follows that the guarantor's liability to the creditor is *in addition* to that of the principal debtor and can only be enforced if the debtor fails to pay. Guarantees are generally sought and drafted by financial institutions.

CONSTITUTION OF THE GUARANTEE

A contract of guarantee need not be in writing unless it is gratuitous and **19–05** unilateral and entered into in a private, rather than business, capacity.[2] A gratuitous unilateral obligation arises where one party undertakes to do something for another party with the other party having no corresponding obligation to do or give anything in return. In most cases, the guarantor and debtor are clearly identifiable as such—this is known as *proper caution*. This enables the creditor to enforce the guarantee against the guarantor as soon as the debtor defaults, unless a contractual term states otherwise. *Improper caution*, on the other hand, arises where the two parties appear, on the face of things, to be *co-debtors* of the creditor thus *jointly and severally* liable for the debt, enabling the creditor to proceed against a co-debtor of choice for the whole sum due. This may occur where the creditor is unaware that the two parties have agreed between themselves that one will act as guarantor, the other being the debtor. However, if the true nature of the relationship between the two parties can be determined then the party identified as the guarantor will be entitled to exercise the legal rights, such a designation confers. These rights are discussed in paras 19–07; 19–08.

EXTENT OF THE GUARANTOR'S LIABILITY

It is in order for the guarantor to agree with the debtor alone that he will **19–06** guarantee debts to unspecified creditors, either for a fixed period of time or for a stated sum of money. If this is the case, the creditors concerned must subsequently show that they knew of the existence of the guarantee at the time the contract was entered into with the debtor and that they placed reliance on it, otherwise the guarantor will not be bound.

Key Concepts

- As a guarantee is an accessory obligation the guarantor cannot be held liable for more than the principal debt itself.[3]
- If the debtor dies, the guarantor will only be liable for any debt due at the date of the debtor's death.
- If the creditor dies, the position of the guarantor remains unchanged in relation to the guarantee he originally entered into.
- If the guarantor dies, his liability to existing creditors lives on and will be charged as a debt on his estate.

---

[2] Requirements of Writing (Scotland) Act 1995 s.1(2)(a)(ii).
[3] *Struthers v Dykes* (1847) 9 D. 1437.

GUARANTOR'S RIGHTS

(a) Right of relief against the debtor

19–07 The guarantor who has paid the debt has a right of relief, which is to claim the sum paid, including expenses, from the debtor. This right will exist for a period of five years after the debt has been paid. Thereafter, it will prescribe, meaning that the guarantor is no longer able to raise a court action against the debtor to recover the sum paid to the creditor.[4]

(b) Right of relief against co-guarantors

19–08 Where there are several guarantors, each is generally only liable for his pro rata (proportionate) share of the debt if all co-guarantors are solvent. If any co-guarantor is insolvent the deficit is made up by the other co-guarantors. This is known as the *benefit of division*. It is important to note that a co-guarantor cannot be asked to pay his pro rata share unless the creditor requires all co-guarantors to do likewise. However, if the contract states that co-guarantors are bound jointly and severally the creditor may proceed against a co-guarantor of choice for the whole sum due. If a co-guarantor is required to pay more than his pro rata share, he can subsequently claim pro rata relief from his co-guarantor(s) for any additional sum he has paid to the creditor or loss incurred. Joint and several liability is to be avoided.

Marshall & Co v Pennycook
1908 S.C. 276

Messrs Marshall and Pennycook agreed to be bound jointly and severally as co-guarantors for Mr McDonald who had entered into an engineering contract with a local authority. When Mr McDonald found himself unable to complete the contract, Mr Marshall, with the agreement of Mr Pennycook, took over the contract and completed the works, but at a loss. Applying the principle that co-guarantors are only liable pro rata, the court held that Mr Pennycook was liable to pay Mr Marshall 50 per cent of the loss he had incurred.

CONTRA PROFERENTEM RULE

19–09 Most contracts of guarantee will set out clearly the extent of the guarantor's liability and also include a clause allowing for immediate steps to be taken against the guarantor (do summary diligence) to recover the sum(s) owed without the need for the creditor to go back to court. However, if the guarantee is worded imprecisely or is ambiguous in any

---

[4] Prescription and Limitation (Scotland) Act 1973 s.6.

way, a court will invoke the *contra proferentem* rule which means that it will interpret ambiguous phrases or words *contrary to the interests of* the party seeking to rely upon any ambiguity. This will invariably be the creditor.

Fortune v Young
1917 2 S.L.T. 150

Mr Young wrote a letter which stated:

> "The bearer, Mr Fortune, we have known for a long number of years, and have pleasure in testifying as to his good and straightforward character, and guarantee that his financial standing is all in order, in accordance with his statement to the extent of from sixteen to eighteen hundred pounds stg." [5]

Young subsequently disputed that the letter gave a guarantee arguing that it was merely a testimonial as to Fortune's credit-worthiness. The court disagreed.

> "... From the terms of the document itself ... I think the evidence makes it abundantly clear, that the defender having given what was a perfectly good testimonial was asked if he could not say something more, and he accordingly added the words 'and guarantee that his financial standing is all in order in accordance with his statement to the extent of from sixteen to eighteen hundred pounds'. I cannot read that as amounting to anything else than a very clear, distinct, and specific guarantee to the extent of from sixteen to eighteen hundred pounds." [6]

GROUNDS TO INVALIDATE A GUARANTEE

(a) Void or voidable guarantees

If the guarantee is held to be invalid due to the creditor or debtor lacking **19–10** contractual capacity or the substance of the contract is or becomes illegal (*pacta illicitum*) the guarantee will be *void*, meaning the contract is viewed as never having come into existence. A guarantee may also be void or *voidable*,[7] if the guarantor entered into the contract on the basis of a misrepresentation made by the creditor or was put under pressure to do so. However, a contract of guarantee is not considered a contract of

---

[5] *per* L.J.C. Dickson at 154.
[6] *per* Lord (Ordinary) Hunter quoted at 151.
[7] Meaning the court may set the guarantee aside if challenged by one of the parties to it.

utmost good faith (*uberrimae fidei*) therefore there is no general duty placed on the creditor to disclose all material facts concerning the debtor's affairs or financial standing to the guarantor.

> ### Young v Clydesdale Bank
> ### (1889) 17 R. 231
>
> Young gave guarantee on behalf of his brother for "... payment of any advances made and which may hereafter be made".
>
> The bank did not inform Young that his brother's account was heavily overdrawn at the time and Young failed to read the guarantee before he signed it.
>
> "It is well settled that it is not the duty of the bank to give any information to a proposed cautioner as to the state of the accounts with the principal.
>
> If the cautioner desires to know ... it is his duty to ask and inform himself, but no duty lies upon a party seeking security to give any information of that kind."[8]

If, however, the guarantor actively seeks information from the creditor about the debtor's financial standing the creditor must answer all questions posed truthfully. If the creditor fails to do so by misrepresenting, even innocently, the facts, and the guarantor then relies on his response to enter into the guarantee, the guarantor has the right to withdraw from the contract by *resiling* which means he can treat the guarantee as at an end, without going to court. The debtor is also under an obligation not to mislead the guarantor by misrepresenting his actual financial situation. If the misrepresentation is fraudulent, the guarantor may seek to have the guarantee set aside, if he is aware of the fraud. Otherwise, the guarantee will stand. However, there is an exception to this general rule.

(b) Creditors' duty of good faith

19–11 In *Smith v Bank of Scotland*[9] it was held by the House of Lords that where a *proximate relationship*[10] exists between the debtor and the guarantor and the *creditor is aware* of the nature of the relationship between the parties, then the creditor is under a duty to act in *good faith* and to take reasonable steps to enquire whether the party with no financial interest in the venture guaranteed (there the wife) has entered into the guarantee in full knowledge of the risk involved and without undue influence being exerted, or through any misrepresentation made, by the debtor:

---

[8] (1889) 17 R. 231 at 240.
[9] 1997 S.C. (HL) 111.
[10] The debtor and guarantor are connected by close personal (non-commercial) relationship.

"... he (the creditor) should take reasonable steps to secure that in relation to the proposed contract he acts throughout in good faith ... it seems to me that it would be sufficient for the creditor to warn the potential cautioner of the consequences of entering into the proposed cautionary obligation and to advise him or her to take independent advice. But apart from that it seems to me that the giving of the warning and the advice should be sufficient so far as Scots law is concerned to fulfil the duty on the creditor and secure that he remains in good faith in relation to the proposed transaction."[11]

In *Smith* the guarantee was set aside by the court as the creditor had failed to take the steps outlined by Lord Clyde.

(c) Unenforceable guarantees

If there is more than one guarantor it is imperative that the creditor has **19–12** ensured that all co-guarantors have agreed to undertake liability. The law implies, as a condition of the contract, that each guarantor has agreed to undertake liability on the basis that his co-guarantors have also accepted liability.[12]

EXTINCTION OF THE GUARANTEE

The guarantee will expire if any of the following occur: **19–13**

- the principal debt is repaid;
- the debtor dies (the guarantor will only be held liable for debts due at the date of death);
- where joint and several liability applies, if a co-guarantor is discharged (relieved of liability) without the consent of the other co-guarantors or without them also being relieved of liability all guarantors are deemed to be discharged also;[13]
- the guarantee prescribes. Section 6 of the Prescription and Limitation (Scotland) Act 1973 states that a cautionary obligation prescribes five years after the appropriate date, if no claim has been made by the creditor before that time. Appropriate dates for certain types of obligations are listed in Sch.2 to the 1973 Act; however, it is silent on the appropriate date for a guarantee. In general, the courts have taken the view that the appropriate date

---

[11] *per* Lord Clyde at 122. English law requires a creditor to go further and ensure that a would-be guarantor in a proximate relationship takes independent legal advice. See *Barclays Bank plc v O'Brien* [1994] 1 A.C. 180. See also *Royal Bank of Scotland plc v Etridge (No.2)* [2002] 2 A.C. 773 HL; *Forsyth v Royal Bank of Scotland plc* 2000 S.L.T 1295; *Royal Bank of Scotland v Wilson* 2004 S.C. 153.

[12] *Paterson v Bonar* (1844) 6 D. 987.

[13] Mercantile Law Amendment (S) Act 1856 s.9. However, the guarantee may dictate otherwise avoiding the effect of s.9.

for a guarantee to prescribe is five years from the date of default by the debtor. If the creditor fails to raise a court action or do diligence against the guarantor within this period, he loses his right to recompense. On the other hand, if a guarantee is worded in such a way as to be payable on demand the prescriptive period will only begin to run when the creditor demands payment.

> **Royal Bank of Scotland Ltd v Brown**
> 1982 S.C. 89
>
> The bank raised an action on May 23, 1979 against co-guarantors for a loan made to a company which went into liquidation in 1969. The bank argued that the prescriptive period did not start running until May 27, 1974 which was the day the bank contacted the co-guarantors, demanding payment. The co-guarantors argued that their obligation had prescribed given that the "appropriate date" was September 1, 1969 when the bank first raised a claim in the liquidation of the company. The court held that such payment on demand guarantees prescribe five years from the date of demand not the date of the debtor's default.
>
> As the appropriate date was held to be the date of demand, the bank was entitled to enforce the guarantee as it had demanded payment four years and 361 days before the expiry of the five-year prescriptive period!

REAL RIGHTS IN SECURITY OVER PROPERTY

> **Key Concept**
>
> **19–14**
>
> A real right in security differs from a personal right in that it gives the creditor a right, often referred to as a *nexus* or a *bond*, over heritable property (land and buildings) or moveable property belonging to the debtor if the debt remains unpaid, or some specified event occurs. The holder of a real right will, in general terms, defeat the claims of the debtor's other creditors to the property concerned if the debtor is sequestrated or, in the case of a company, becomes insolvent.

A real right in security, as with a contract of guarantee, is an accessory obligation. However, a real right can only be created if there is *delivery* from the debtor to the creditor of the property that is subject to the security. It is not sufficient for the debtor to identify a particular item of property then set it aside for the benefit of the creditor at some point in the future. However, there are exceptions to this general principle and these exceptions will be discussed first.

Real Rights in Security where Delivery is not required

Hypothecs

Hypothec is the legal term used to describe a right in security over cor- **19–15** poreal moveable property where delivery is not required. At common law, hypothecs may either be created by contract, these are known as *conventional* hypothecs, or created by the operation of law where the term *legal* hypothecs is used.

Conventional hypothecs

Conventional hypothecs are restricted to *bonds of bottomry* and *bonds of* **19–16** *respondentia* which can be granted over, respectively, a ship or its cargo. Such hypothecs can be granted either by the owner of the ship, the owner of the cargo or an agent of either party to raise funds, which cannot be found by any other means, to enable the ship to reach its destination. The law will also imply that the master of a ship who is unable to make contact with the owner of the ship/cargo it is carrying may, if the ship is berthed in a foreign port, grant a bond of either type to enable the ship to reach its home port. The holder of either type of bond who remains unpaid when the ship reaches its destination can apply to the court for an order to sell either the ship or its cargo. Conventional hypothecs are now likely to be of historic interest given modern methods of communication.

Legal hypothecs

(a) The *solicitor's hypothec* may be exercised in relation to outlays **19–17** incurred whilst bringing a court action on behalf of a client. The hypothec, at common law, is over the award of any damages or costs to the client and, under statute, to property belonging to the client which is recovered during litigation.[14]

(b) At common law, a *landlord's hypothec* previously enabled the landlord to raise an action in the Sheriff Court known as sequestration for rent to claim the value of up to one year's rent due by seeking to take possession of certain *moveable property of the tenant* located within the leased property. If the court action succeeded, the landlord could lawfully remove the goods then sell them. The Bankruptcy and Diligence etc. (Scotland) Act 2007 abolished both the common law diligence of sequestration for rent and the landlord's hypothec over goods in dwelling-houses or kept on agricultural land or in a croft.[15] Although the landlord's hypothec has been retained by the 2007 Act its effect is now somewhat limited.[16]

---

[14] Solicitors (Scotland) Act 1980 s.62(1).

[15] Bankruptcy and Diligence etc. (Scotland) Act 2007 s.208.

[16] Moveable property kept in residential garages, lock-ups, sheds, outbuildings etc. and property in commercial premises only will now be subject to landlord's hypothec. The hypothec is now not limited to one year's rent thus it subsists for as long as rent due remains unpaid.

FLOATING CHARGES

19–18 A *floating charge* is a statutory form of security granted over the heritable and moveable property of a registered company but not those of individuals or partnerships. The applicable law is contained in the Companies Act 1985,[17] the Insolvency Act 1986 and the Enterprise Act 2002. A floating charge is just that—it *floats* over the assets of a company and if the repayments to the charge holder are up to date the charge will continue to float undisturbed enabling the company to use the property, dispose of it or add further assets to its holdings.

As of September 15, 2003, when the relevant sections of the Enterprise Act 2002 came into force, the law relating to floating charges has to be understood with regard to charges granted before and on or after that date.

Charges granted before September 15, 2003

19–19 To be valid, a floating charge granted before September 15, 2003 must be in writing and registered with the Registrar of Companies in Scotland within 21 days of the date of the execution (creation) of the deed.[18] However, the floating charge would actually have taken effect from the date of execution if registration was completed within the statutory period. A pre-Enterprise Act floating charge will *crystallise* (attach to the assets in the company's ownership at that time) if the company goes into liquidation[19] or the floating charge holder appoints a receiver. It is at the point of crystallisation that the real right in security is constituted. In essence, the charge becomes a fixed one.

Company in liquidation

19–20 When a company goes into liquidation a floating charge *attaches* to the relevant property, subject to the legal rights of any person who has:

    (i) executed diligence on the property; or
    (ii) holds a fixed security over the property; or
    (iii) holds over the property a floating charge with prior ranking. Ranking is determined in order of the date of execution of the deed creating the charge.[20] Section 464(1) of the Companies Act 1985 allows, however, for a deed executing a floating charge to contain a ranking agreement setting out the actual and agreed ranking of the floating charge in relation to any future securities granted over the same property. Where a ranking agreement

---

[17] The relevant provisions of the Companies Act 2006 will apply in due course. At the time of writing, this Act is not in force. Sections 878–892 of the 2006 Act, which are not yet in force, will apply to floating charges in due course; current estimates suggest by 2009.
[18] Currently Companies Act 1985 s.410(2).
[19] Currently Companies Act 1985 s.463(1).
[20] Currently Companies Act 1985 s.464(3), (4).

exists a fixed security arising by the operation of law,[21] such as a hypothec, will have priority over the claim of the floating charge holder concerned.

Appointment of a receiver

A receiver may be appointed if a contractually specified event occurs, **19–21** usually non-payment of the debt, or an event stipulated in s.52 (1) of the Insolvency Act 1986 comes to pass. A floating charge will crystallise under s.52 (1) if any of the following occur;

- when asked to do so by the floating charge holder the company fails to repay the sum due within 21 days[22];
- the company is two months in arrears of interest due[23];
- the company is wound up[24];
- another holder of a floating charge over the same property appoints a receiver.[25]

The role of the receiver is to act primarily in the interests of the floating charge holder who appointed him to ensure the repayment of the debt. This can be achieved by keeping the company running as a going concern or by selling all or part of the company. To discharge the duty owed to the charge holder the receiver will ingather all monies or assets owed to the company prior to settling the claims of debtors, according to their ranking. Section 60 of the Insolvency Act 1986 details the ranking of creditors.

The ranking is as follows:

(1) the holder of any fixed charge which is over property subject to the floating charge and which ranks prior to or pari passu (equal to) the floating charge.
(2) individuals or bodies who have executed diligence on any part of the property of the company which is subject to the charge
(3) creditors in respect of all liabilities, charges and expenses incurred by or on behalf of the receiver
(4) the receiver in respect of his liabilities, expenses and remuneration
(5) preferential creditors entitled to payment such as HM Revenue and Customs per outstanding taxes and employees owed wages/salaries

Only after the above 5 categories of creditor have been paid can the receiver lawfully pay the holder of the floating charge who appointed him.

---

[21] A pre-existing implied legal right that cannot be negated by a subsequent agreement.
[22] Insolvency Act 1986 s.52 (1)(a).
[23] Insolvency Act 1986 s.52(1)(b).
[24] Insolvency Act 1986 s.52(1)(c).
[25] Insolvency Act 1986 s.52(1)(d).

Limitations on the receiver's powers

19–22 Certain statutory and non-statutory rules of law may restrict the receiver's powers to satisfy the claim of the floating charge holder who appointed him, for example:

> (a) the floating charge was not registered within the 21-day statutory period;
> (b) the floating charge was created or granted in breach of ss.243 to 245 of the Insolvency Act 1986;
> (c) the House of Lords ruling in *Sharp v Thomson*.[26]

In *Sharp*, a company granted a floating charge over certain property and thereafter entered into missives for the sale of a flat, subject to the floating charge. A disposition was delivered to the purchasers but the following day a receiver was appointed. The disposition was not recorded in the Register of Sasines at that point. The receiver argued that at the time of crystallisation the flat *still belonged to the company* given heritage in Scotland only passes to the buyer when the disposition is recorded. Although the House of Lords agreed that delivery of a disposition cannot create a real right in property, it held that the Insolvency Act 1986 did not allow the receiver to lay claim to the flat. If the receiver had been entitled to the flat he would have been granted legal authority to do something which, if it had been carried out by the company, would amount to fraud given that the purchasers had paid for the flat. The House concluded by stating that the heritable property to which a floating charge attaches is the *beneficial interest* in the property and *not the title* to it. Therefore, once a disposition is delivered the seller loses beneficial interest.

Charges granted on or after September 15, 2003

19–23 Section 250(2) of the Enterprise Act 2002 inserts a new section into the Insolvency Act 1986[27] that stipulates that the holder of a floating charge *may not* appoint a receiver unless one of the exceptions detailed in ss.72(B–G) of the amended 1986 Act apply. Instead, an *administrator* will be appointed who is under a statutory duty to manage the company's affairs, business and property with the objective of *rescuing the company as a going concern*, or, if that proves impossible, achieving a better result for *all* the company's creditors than would be likely if the company were to be wound up immediately, not just the holder of the floating charge who appointed him.[28] The Enterprise Act 2002 also removes the preferential status of HM Revenue & Customs excepting the preferential right of employees for unpaid wages.[29] These debts will now rank alongside other unsecured debts. Section 252 of the 2002 Act also introduces a procedure under which a set percentage of the company's

---

[26] 1997 S.C. (HL) 66.
[27] Insolvency Act 1986 1986 s.72.
[28] Insolvency Act 1986 Sch.B1.
[29] Enterprise Act 2002 s.251.

net property is to be set aside for distribution to unsecured creditors and the administrator is prohibited from distributing this prescribed part to the holder of a floating charge unless it exceeds the amount required for the satisfaction of unsecured debts.[30]

Bankruptcy and Diligence etc. (Scotland) Act 2007

The relevant sections of the Bankruptcy and Diligence etc. (Scotland) Act **19–24** 2007 are not yet in force but will have an impact upon the registration and ranking of floating charges created on or after September 15, 2003. Section 37 of the 2007 Act provides for a new registration regime under the auspices of the Keeper of the Registers of Scotland. The date of registration of the floating charge will be when the relevant registration documents or notice of registration[31] is received by the Keeper, rather than when the floating charge is executed as is presently the case. Until this provision is in force, floating charges will still require to be registered with the Registrar of Companies. Section 40 of the 2007 Act amends the law as follows:

- A floating charge will rank with any other floating charge which has attached to that property or any fixed security over that property or any part of it according to date of creation, which is the date of registration with the Keeper.
- A floating charge will also rank equally with a floating charge or fixed security which was created on the same date as the floating charge.
- Section 40 also restates the rule that where the property is subject to both a floating charge and a security arising by operation of law, such as a hypothec, the fixed security has priority over any floating charge.
- The Act also restates, at s.41, that ranking agreements may displace the statutory ranking contained within s.40 with the exception that a security arising by the operation of law cannot be displaced by such an agreement.

---

[30] The Insolvency Act 1986 (Prescribed Part) Order 2003 (SI 2003/2097) details how the prescribed part is to be calculated.

[31] Bankruptcy and Diligence etc (Scotland) Act 2007 s.39 allows a creditor and debtor to jointly lodge an advance notice of a floating charge. If the charge is registered within 21 days of advance notice being received by the Keeper, the date of the creation of the floating charge will be that of the date of the registration of the advance notice. This means that there will no longer be a period during which a floating charge exists but its existence is not within the public domain.

RIGHTS IN SECURITY WHERE DELIVERY IS REQUIRED

19–25 With the exception of hypothecs and floating charges, it is a general principle of Scots law that a real right can only be created if there is delivery, from the debtor to the creditor, of the property that is subject to the security. It is the act of delivery, putting the property beyond the reach of the debtor, that creates the real right to the property itself and confers on the creditor an additional and more secure right to payment if the debtor defaults. The latin maxim *traditionibus, non nudis pactis, transferunter rerum dominia* (by delivery not mere agreements are real rights in property transferred) applies, although in certain cases actual delivery of the property will not be possible so symbolic or constructive delivery of the property will be sufficient to effect the security.

RIGHTS IN SECURITY OVER HERITABLE PROPERTY

The standard security

19–26 Since 1970 the only competent means of granting a right of security over heritable property is by entering into a contract of *standard security* which must be in the form prescribed by the Conveyancing and Feudal Reform Act 1970 and registered in the Land Register or the Register of Sasines kept by the Keeper. Registration amounts to constructive delivery of the property. On registration, the creditor, usually a bank or building society, gains a real right to the property and is known as the *standard security holder*. If the debtor fails to make the loan repayments as agreed or abide by other conditions set out in the standard security the holder can ultimately enforce the sale of the property. The holder of a standard security (heritable creditor) also currently has the comfort of knowing that his security acts as a *fixed charge*, meaning that if the debtor is sequestrated or goes into liquidation and the property is sold, all proceeds of the sale will be made over to him in preference to all other creditors.

However, as detailed in para.19–24, when s.40 of the Bankruptcy and Diligence etc. (Scotland) Act 2007 comes into force, a floating charge will rank with any fixed security over that property or any part of it according to date of creation, which is the date of registration with the Keeper. A floating charge will also rank equally with a fixed security which was created on the same date as the floating charge. However, a ranking agreement between charge holders may displace the statutory ranking contained within s.40, with the exception that a security arising by the operation of law cannot be displaced.[32]

---

[32] Bankruptcy and Diligence etc. (Scotland) Act 2007 s.41(1).

RIGHTS IN SECURITY OVER CORPOREAL MOVEABLE PROPERTY

(a) Pledge

It is generally a straightforward matter to effect delivery of corporeal **19–27** moveable property by simply handing it over to the creditor. Where this is possible the security created is known as *pledge* and the *pledger* is under a contractual obligation to deliver the property to the *pledgee* as security for the personal obligation he has entered into. When the obligation is fulfilled, usually the repayment of a loan, the pledgee must return the property to the pledger. Most contracts of pledge will permit the pledgee to sell the property if the pledger defaults. Pawn broking is a form of pledge and is regulated by ss.114–122 of the Consumer Credit Act 1974. Pledge can also be created by constructive[33] or symbolic[34] delivery of the property to the pledgee.

(b) Lien

A lien (pronounced lean) is a right of security created by the operation of **19–28** law and enables the party in possession of the property to retain it until the owner of the property fulfils his obligation, which is generally to pay money. Liens are classified as either *general* or *special* liens. A general lien allows the person holding the property to exercise it in relation to *all* his transactions with the debtor. An innkeeper, as defined in s.1 of the Innkeepers Act 1878, has a general lien over property (except clothing) brought into his establishment by a guest who fails to pay his bill, as does a solicitor over the property of a client who has failed to pay fees and expenses incurred on his behalf. A special lien, on the other hand, may only be exercised in relation to a single transaction with the debtor. A special lien will arise, for example, when property has been handed over for repair or safekeeping. The party in possession of the property has no right to sell the property, unless he is successful in seeking a court order to dispose of it or s.39 of the Sale of Goods Act 1979, applies.[35]

RIGHTS IN SECURITY OVER INCORPOREAL MOVEABLE PROPERTY

Incorporeal moveable property, which includes royalties, shares, patents, **19–29** copyright, trademarks and rights arising under insurance policies, has in itself no physical existence, therefore mere delivery to the creditor of a document detailing the existence and extent of the right concerned does

---

[33] For example, where the property is in the safekeeping of a third party who has been made aware that he is holding the goods on behalf of the pledgee: *HD Pochin & Co v Robinows & Marjoribanks* (1869) 7 M. 622.

[34] A bill of lading, which indicates that goods have been shipped, is a pledge of the goods themselves if it has been delivered to the pledgee: *Hayman & Son v McLintock* 1907 S.C. 936.

[35] If the seller remains unpaid he may resell the goods if he gives the debtor reasonable notice of his intention to do so.

not create a real right in security. To effect delivery of such a property right a two-stage process must be followed:

- *assignation* of the right by the property owner (assignor) to the party providing the security (assignee);
- *intimation* to the debtor that the property has been assigned and that all benefits arising from it are now payable to the assignee.

Assignation by itself only creates a contractual thus personal right against the assignor who is borrowing money on the strength of the value of, or the income generated by, the property concerned. Generally, for a real right to be created in favour of the assignee, the assignor's debtor must be informed that assignation has taken place. It is when this step has been carried out by the assignee that delivery is effected.[36]

SITUATIONS WHERE INTIMATION IS NOT POSSIBLE—EXCEPTIONS TO THE GENERAL RULE

19–30 The bare act of assignation of certain types of incorporeal property, for example patents and shares is capable of creating a real right. This exception arises because there is no actual debtor to inform that assignation has taken place! However, the real right will not be constituted until the assignation is registered, if registration is required by law. Thus to effect a valid assignation of a patent this must be registered in the Register of Patents[37] and the assignation of shares in a company will only be effected when the transfer of the shares is registered in that company's register of shareholders.

▼ CHAPTER SUMMARY

19–31 **A creditor may demand a right in security for a debt to increase the likelihood that he will recover his outlay should the debtor fail to make payment when it falls due. In Scots law, a right in security gives rise to either a personal right (*ius in personam*) or a real right (*ius in re*).**

PERSONAL RIGHTS IN SECURITY

1. **A cautionary obligation is a personal right in security which gives the creditor the right to recover the sum owed him by the debtor from another person.**

---

[36] *Gallemos Ltd v Barratt Falkirk Ltd*, 1990 S.L.T. 98.
[37] Patents Act 1977 ss.31–33. There is also a register for trademarks under the terms of ss.22–24 of the Trade Marks Act 1994.

2. A contract of guarantee is an accessory obligation which means that the debt must exist before it can be enforced against the guarantor.

3. The guarantor cannot be held liable for more than the principal debt itself

   ➢ *Struthers v Dykes*

4. If the guarantor has paid the debt he has a right of relief, which is to claim the sum paid, including expenses, from the debtor.

5. Where there are several guarantors, each is only liable for his pro rata share of the debt if all co-guarantors are solvent and joint and several liability does not apply. If any co-guarantor is insolvent the deficit is made up by the other co-guarantors.

6. If the guarantee states that guarantors are bound jointly and severally the creditor may proceed against a co-guarantor of choice for payment. If a co-guarantor is required to pay more than his pro rata share, he can subsequently claim pro rata relief from his co-guarantors;

   ➢ *Marshall & Co v Pennycook* 1908 S.C. 276.

7. If the guarantee is worded imprecisely or is ambiguous a court will apply the *contra proferentem* rule;

   ➢ *Fortune v Young* 1917 2 S.L.T. 150.

8. A contract of guarantee is not considered a contract *uberrimae fidei* therefore there is no general duty on the creditor to disclose all material facts concerning the debtor's affairs to the guarantor;

   ➢ *Young v Clydesdale Bank* (1889) 17 R. 231.

   The exception to this rule is where a proximate relationship exists between the debtor and the guarantor. If the creditor is aware of the nature of the relationship between the parties, there exists a duty to act in good faith;

   ➢ *Smith v Bank of Scotland* 1997 S.C (HL) 111.

REAL RIGHTS IN SECURITY OVER PROPERTY

A real right in security differs from a personal right in that it gives the creditor a right, often referred to as a *nexus* or a *bond*, over heritable property or moveable property belonging to the debtor. A real right can generally only be created if there is delivery from the debtor to the creditor of the property that is subject to the security. The exceptions to this rule are as follows:

Hypothecs

1. Hypothecs are either conventional, or implied by law where the term legal hypothecs is used. Conventional hypothecs are restricted

to *bonds of bottomry* and *bonds of respondentia.* **Legal hypothecs include the solicitor's hypothec which, at common law, is over the award of any damages or costs to the client and, under statute, to property belonging to the client which is recovered during litigation;**

> Solicitor's (S) Act 1980 s.62(1).

2. **The landlord's legal hypothec can now only be exercised in relation to goods kept outwith domestic premises and those in commercial premises;**

> Bankruptcy and Diligence etc. (Scotland) Act 2007 s.208.

Floating charges

A floating charge is a statutory form of security which can be created by contract over the heritable and moveable property of a registered company but not those of individuals or partnerships. The charge "floats" over the assets of a company and if the repayments to the charge holder are up to date the charge will continue to float undisturbed. If the debt is not repaid the charge is said to crystallise.

1. **A charge granted before September 15, 2003 enables the charge holder to appoint a receiver to recover the debt.**
2. **A charge granted on or after September15, 2003 requires the charge holder to appoint an administrator, who unlike a receiver, is under a statutory duty to achieve the best result for all the company's creditors.**

> Companies Act 1985; the Insolvency Act 1986; the Enterprise Act 2002.

3. **The relevant sections of the Bankruptcy and Diligence etc. (Scotland) Act 2007 are not yet in force but will have an impact upon the registration and ranking of floating charges.**

RIGHTS IN SECURITY WHERE DELIVERY IS REQUIRED

With the exception of hypothecs and floating charges, it is a general principle of Scots law that a real right can only be created if there is delivery from the debtor to the creditor, of the property that is subject to the security. In certain cases physical delivery of the property will not be possible, so symbolic or constructive delivery of the property will suffice.

STANDARD SECURITY

1. **Since 1970 the only competent means of granting a right of security over heritable property is by entering into a contract of standard security;**

➤ Conveyancing and Feudal Reform Act 1970.

2. **If the debtor fails to make the loan repayments as agreed the standard security holder can ultimately enforce the sale of the property.**

RIGHTS IN SECURITY OVER CORPOREAL MOVEABLE PROPERTY

1. **Pledge occurs where corporeal moveable property is delivered to the creditor. Pledge can also be created by actual, constructive or symbolic delivery of the property to the pledgee;**

➤ *HD Pochin & Co v Robinows & Marjoribanks* (1869) 7 M. 622; *Hayman & Son v McLintock* 1907 S.C. 936.

2. **A lien is created by the operation of law enabling the party in possession of the property to retain it until the owner of the property fulfils his obligation which is generally to pay money. Liens are classified as either general or special.**

RIGHTS IN SECURITY OVER INCORPOREAL MOVEABLE PROPERTY

1. **Incorporeal moveable property enjoys no physical existence and mere delivery to the creditor of a document detailing the existence and extent of the right concerned will not generally create a real right in security. To effect delivery of such a property right assignation and intimation are required, excepting rights in shares, patents, trademarks and copyright.**

? QUICK QUIZ

True or False?

- A real right in security is always to be preferred to a personal right.
- A contract of guarantee is a principal obligation.
- The guarantor enjoys no right of relief against the debtor if required to pay the creditor on his behalf.
- A guarantee is considered a contract *uberrimae fidei*.
- A real right in security can only be created where there is delivery of the property subject to the security.
- A floating charge is said to crystallise if the company concerned goes into liquidation or a receiver is appointed.
- Pledge may only be constituted by actual delivery of the property concerned.
- A real right in security over incorporeal moveable property can only be created via assignation and intimation.

Business Law in Scotland

📖 **FURTHER READING**

Ashton et al., *Understanding Scots Law* (W. Green, 2007), Ch.10.
Davidson and MacGregor, *Commercial Law in Scotland*, 2nd edn
  (W. Green, 2008), Ch.6.
Forte (ed.) Scots, *Commercial Law* (Butterworths, 1997), Ch.6.
N. Grier, *Commercial Law* (W. Green, Edinburgh, 2006), Ch.10.
Mays et al., *Scots Law, A Student Guide* (Tottel, 2006), Ch.10.

🖱 **RELEVANT WEBLINKS**

http://www.ros.gov.uk/registration/floating_charges.html.

Chapter 20   Dispute Resolution

Dr Hong-Lin Yu[1]

▶ CHAPTER OVERVIEW

This chapter is concerned with different forms of dispute resolution in **20–01**
business, both domestic and international in nature. It starts by presenting the practice of negotiation and mediation. The chapter goes on to
discuss the operation of commercial arbitration involving Scottish businesses. The chapter then turns to consider the use of adjudication in
construction disputes. Finally, the topic of court actions will be
examined.

✓ OUTCOMES

At the end of this chapter you should be able to: **20–02**

- ✓ understand the reasons for the popularity of alternative dispute
  resolution;
- ✓ identify the advantages and disadvantages of different forms of
  dispute resolution;
- ✓ understand the practice of negotiation;
- ✓ understand the practice of mediation;
- ✓ understand the different aspects of commercial arbitration;
- ✓ appreciate the different rules governing commercial arbitration
  involving a Scottish company in foreign trade;
- ✓ understand the laws relating to adjudication;
- ✓ identify the courts to which disputes can be submitted.

ADVANTAGES AND DISADVANTAGES OF ADR

In the business world, disputes arise every day and various ways have **20–03**
been devised to resolve them. These methods fall into two broad categories; public resolution through the civil courts and private dispute
resolution through devices such as negotiation, mediation, arbitration
and adjudication, collectively known as alternative dispute resolution
(ADR). While court processes are public, ADR is private. The

---

[1] Reader in Law, University of Stirling.

advantages of a public resolution are that the parties will receive a binding decision from the court and the court can exercise coercive powers over the parties or relevant third parties. However, this method may cause difficulties such as slow process and exposure of the disputes in the public domain.

The second type of dispute resolution which is popular in business is to resolve the dispute in a closed-door environment. Frequently, alternative dispute resolution covers the areas of negotiation, mediation, arbitration and adjudication. The advantages of ADR are privacy, speed, specialised decision makers, confidentiality and flexibility. However, due to its private nature, ADR is often criticised for its lack of coercive powers and lack of binding force decision (apart from arbitration).

In Scotland, the importance of the role played by ADR has increased. It is revealed in the consultation paper on the Scottish Civil Court Review that the review team, led by Lord Gill, will look into "the role of mediation and other methods of dispute resolution in assisting people to resolve disputes with resort to the courts".[2] Therefore, it is essential to discuss different types of dispute resolution in this chapter. They include negotiation, mediation, arbitration, adjudication, and finally, traditional court actions.

NEGOTIATION

20–04 Negotiation is a form of ADR "which can be informal, economic and quick, and which encourages the parties to work out a resolution for themselves".[3] Negotiation sees the parties discussing means of settling a dispute that will lead to a satisfactory outcome for both parties. It is often the first step parties may take to resolve a dispute. It may take the form of telephone calls, face-to-face meetings between the parties or, more formally, meetings between the parties' lawyers.

Frequently, disputes will end after the parties engage in negotiation. However it is said that whatever type of negotiation one is involved in:

> "There must be thorough preparation and careful assessment of the different issues. The presentation involves knowing your own case, your opponent's case, how the process will develop, what conventions will apply, where they will take place and who should make the opening offer."[4]

Yet sometimes negotiations will break down, so that parties may look to a third party to determine the disputes. This leaves the parties to choose between mediation, arbitration, adjudication or litigation, all of which will be discussed in detail in the following sections.

---

[2] Scottish Civil Court Review Consultation Paper November 2007, para.2.6.
[3] Moody and Mackay (eds) *Green's Guide to Alternative Dispute Resolution in Scotland* (Edinburgh, W. Green, 1995), p.2.
[4] Bevan, *Alternative Dispute Resolution* (London, Sweet and Maxwell, 1992), pp.4–5.

MEDIATION

Introduction

Mediation involves an independent third party —a mediator—whose job **20–05**
is to help the parties resolve their dispute. A mediator may help the
parties evaluate their position, and can often be proactive in suggesting
ways in which the dispute might be resolved.

Mediation process

It is said that "Mediation is forward-looking; the goal is for all parties to **20–06**
work out a solution they can live with and trust. It focuses on solving
problems, not uncovering the truth or imposing legal rules. This, of
course, is a far different approach than courts take. In court, a judge or
jury looks back to determine who was right and who was wrong, then
imposes a penalty or award based on its decision."[5]

This emphasises the fact that the process focuses not on the legal rights
of the parties, but on their interests and thus looks to arrive at a resolution which is mutually beneficial. While going to court (or indeed
arbitration) produces a winner and a loser, mediation allows both parties
to emerge as winners.

During the mediation process the parties can either choose to represent
themselves or send representatives with their full authority to resolve the
dispute. It is not unusual to have lawyers acting on behalf of their clients
participate in the proceedings. Once the mediation starts, parties will be
asked to explain the case and their positions to the mediator who may
probe in order to find out what the parties really want out of the process.
While sometimes mediators are little more than intermediaries, or do
little more than point out the strengths and weaknesses of the respective
positions, others may seize the initiative and offer innovative solutions to
the parties' problems. It is important to understand that even if a mediator puts forward a specific solution, the parties are free to take it or
leave it. In other words, mediation is not binding, although if the parties
reach a formal agreement as a result of the mediation, that is binding.
The non-binding character of mediation is sometimes seen as a weakness,
since although it is private, flexible, speedy and informal, if mediation
fails then the parties will not have a resolution for their dispute. For that
reason many prefer to resort to a process which results in the imposition
of a binding decision, such as going to court or arbitration.

ARBITRATION

Arbitration sees parties submit their dispute to an impartial third person, **20–07**
called an arbiter, who will adjudicate upon that dispute. One main
strength of arbitration is that the arbiter's decision is binding and

---

[5] *http://www.nolo.com* [accessed January 17, 2008].

enforceable against the losing party, therefore the dispute is sure to be resolved. Other advantages include privacy, confidentiality, flexibility and the fact that the parties can choose the arbiter means that arbitration can (sometimes) be quicker and cheaper than going to court.

Legal framework

> **Key Concept**
>
> Scotland operates a dual track of arbitration law.

20–08 Leaving aside international commercial arbitration, the law of arbitration in Scotland is based almost entirely on the common law with isolated statutory provisions dealing with specific points. These include:

- the 25th Act of the Articles of Regulation 1695 which lays down grounds on which the validity of awards may be challenged;
- the Arbitration (Scotland) Act 1894 which regulates the naming of arbitrators and the court's power to appoint arbitrators;
- the Administration of Justice (Scotland) Act 1972 which stipulates the stated case procedure;
- the Arbitration Act 1996, ss.89–91 and Schs 3 and 4.

The law governing international commercial arbitration in Scotland is listed as follows:

- Part II of the Arbitration Act 1950 which gives effect to the 1927 Geneva Convention for the Execution of Foreign Arbitral Awards and the 1923 Protocol;
- the Arbitration (International Investment Disputes) Act 1966 which gives effect to the 1965 Washington Convention on the Settlement of Investment Disputes between States and the Nationals of Other States;
- the Arbitration Act 1975 which gives effect to the 1958 New York Convention on the Recognition and Enforcement of Foreign Arbitral Awards; and
- the Law Reform (Miscellaneous Provisions) (Scotland) Act 1990 which applies the UNCITRAL Model Law to International Commercial Arbitrations in Scotland.

Accordingly, Art.1(3) of the Model Law stipulates that an arbitration is international, even if the disputes are between two Scottish parties, if:

"a. the parties to an arbitration agreement have, at the time of the conclusion of that agreement, their places of business in different States; or

b.   one of the following places is situated outside the State in which the parties have their places of business:

   (i)   the place of arbitration if determined in, or pursuant to, the arbitration agreement;
   (ii)   any place where a substantial part of the obligations of the commercial relationship is to be performed or the place with which the subject-matter of the dispute is most closely connected; or

c.   the parties have expressly agreed that the subject-matter of the arbitration agreement relates to more than one country."

The doctrine of party autonomy

The parties' freedom to have their disputes resolved by arbitration is well **20–09** recognised. This freedom is based on the doctrine of party autonomy, which originated from the idea of "freedom of contract". Freedom of contract in the United Kingdom originated in the 18th century. At that time the individual was granted the maximum freedom to pursue his objectives and an inalienable right to enter into contracts for his own benefit. Later on, in the early 19th century, the philosophy of *laissez-faire*, that is, the doctrine invoking unrestricted freedom in commerce, flourished and similarly indicated that the law should interfere with people as little as possible.[6]

Following the economic and social changes since the 19th century, the classical contract theory no longer accords with the modern world in many respects. For instance the classical concept of freedom of contract takes little account of social and economic pressures which might virtually force a man to enter into a contract which is obviously unfair to him. In addition, the classical concept of freedom of contract ignores the possible inequalities of the bargaining powers between the contracting parties. Considering the criticisms mentioned above and the possible involvement of third parties, the issues of monopolies, restrictive agreements, consumer protection and compensation for the workmen, freedom of contract is more restricted than it was previously claimed to be.

Although freedom of contract is restricted on the grounds of public policy and mandatory rules, it still significantly influences the design of commercial arbitration. Based on freedom of contract, commercial arbitration develops the doctrine of party autonomy which is said to be the pillar of commercial arbitration. This can be observed in various aspects of commercial arbitration such as the appointment of arbiters, choice of place of arbitration, choice of language, choice of applicable laws ... and so on.

---

[6] Atiyah, *An Introduction to the Law of Contract*, 3rd edn (Oxford University Press, 1989), p.7.

ARBITRATION AGREEMENTS

20–10 | **Key Concept**

An arbitration agreement is the foundation stone of commercial arbitration. "If the parties have contracted to arbitrate then they must go" (*Sanderson v Armour & Co*).

An arbitration agreement is said to be the foundation stone of commercial arbitration.[7] Without a valid arbitration agreement between the parties, no arbitration can be initiated. This is because an arbitration agreement is a symbol of the parties' consent to subject their dispute to the jurisdiction of arbitration and an arbitral tribunal. Due to its importance, the principle of the autonomy of arbitration agreement has developed to ensure the smooth operation of commercial arbitration. According to this principle, an arbitration agreement is independent from the main contract (e.g. sale of goods contract), consequently, an arbitration agreement will survive even if the main contract is declared as null and void for other reasons.

According to Art.8(1) of the Model Law, courts have to decline jurisdiction and refer the parties to arbitration if a valid arbitration agreement between the parties is found. It reads:

> "A court before which an action is brought in a matter which is the subject of an arbitration agreement shall, if a party so requests not later than when submitting his first statement on the substance of the dispute, refer the parties to arbitration unless it finds that the agreement is null and void, inoperative or incapable of being performed."

Under the Scottish law even if the dispute has been submitted to and pending before the court, the arbitral proceedings can still be commenced and the tribunal can make a binding award.[8] This attitude can be observed in *Sanderson v Armour & Co* in which the court decided that if the parties have contracted to arbitrate then they must go.[9]

In general, no arbitration agreement can be unilaterally withdrawn by an unwilling participating party. However, if one party failed to insist on his right to arbitrate but participated in the substance of debates when the other party raised the court proceeding, the court may regard this as waiver of rights to arbitrate.[10]

---

[7] Redfern and Hunter *International Commercial Arbitration*, 4th edn (Sweet and Maxwell, London, 2004), para.3-01.
[8] Art.8(2).
[9] 1922 S.C. (HL) 117 at 126.
[10] *Presslie v Cochrane Mcgregor Group Ltd*, 1996 S.L.T. 514.

Choice of applicable laws

> ### Key Concept 20–11
>
> Three steps to be followed by an arbiter to determine the proper law governing the main contract between the parties: express choice of law test, implied test and the closest and most real test.

Based on the doctrine of party autonomy, parties have the freedom to choose the relevant applicable laws. In the choice of procedural law, the parties' are subject to the public policy and the mandatory rules of the relevant Scottish law. Regarding the parties' choice of proper law governing the rights and obligations of the parties to the disputes, according to Art.28(1) of the Model Law, the arbitral tribunal is required to apply the rules of law expressly chosen by the parties to determine the disputes. If the parties' fail to agree on the proper law, the arbitral tribunal shall apply the law determined by the conflict of laws rules that it considers applicable,[11] which include the implied choice of law test and the closest and most real choice of law test. It also needs to be noted that trade usages applicable to the dispute shall be taken into consideration by the arbitral tribunal.[12] Furthermore, with parties' expressed authorisation the arbitral tribunal is allowed to decide *ex aequo et bono* or amiable composition (meaning: arbitrator can decide the case according to what he believes is just and fair) by considering what is fair and just in their opinions.[13]

Appointment of arbiters / arbitral tribunal[14]

One of the reasons that arbitration enjoys such success is because the **20–12** parties have the freedom to choose an arbiter or arbitral tribunal specialising in the area where the disputes have arising from. The appointment of arbiter is the first step after the proceedings are initiated, therefore the importance of appointing a skilled and experienced arbiter to ensure an efficient and successful arbitration should not be underestimated.

According to Art.11(2) of the Model Law, parties are free to determine the method of appointment. This freedom can be exercised by the parties jointly or independently in the case of arbitral tribunal or exercised by a third party delegated by the parties. The choice can be made in the arbitration agreement before the dispute arises or left until the disputes arise. For a single arbitrator the parties have to agree to his/her appointment jointly. For a three-member arbitral tribunal the parties

---

[11] Art.28(2).
[12] Art.28(4).
[13] Art.28(3).
[14] The term "arbiter" is used in the Scottish statutes and the term "arbitrator" is used in the Model Law and relevant international instruments.

may agree to appoint one arbitrator each, and the third will be appointed by the two-party appointed arbitrators.

In the absence of such an agreement, under Art.11(3) of the Model Law, it is default that in an arbitration with three arbitrators, each party shall appoint one arbitrator, and the two arbitrators thus appointed shall appoint the third arbitrator. Moreover, 30 days after the parties fail to appoint or compose the tribunal, a party can request the court or other authority to make appointment.

Under the Scottish law, if the parties failed to agree or appoint the arbiter, the parties may ask the court to provide assistance in the appointment of arbiters. According to ss.2 and 3 of the Arbitration (Scotland) Act 1894, the sheriff or the Court of Session may appoint an arbiter in the event of a failure of the parties to agree the nomination of a single arbiter, or in the case of a reference to two arbiters where one party failed to appoint his arbiter. Similar provision is also stipulated in Art.11(4) of the Model Law. Furthermore, such appointment made by the court cannot be appealed.[15]

Jurisdiction of arbiters

20–13   To ensure the smooth operation of commercial arbitration proceedings, it is well established that an arbiter/ arbitral tribunal has the power to rule on it own jurisdiction. This also includes the power to rule on the existence or validity of the arbitration agreement.[16] This is the so-called doctrine of competence/competence.

However, a plea has to be raised no later than the submission of the statement of defence if either party wish to challenge the jurisdiction of the arbiter / arbitral tribunal. If the party raised the issue of lack of jurisdiction after he conducting a substantive defence then it will be regarded as a waiver on the party's part. If it becomes apparent to the parties that the arbiter / arbitral tribunal has exceeded the scope of his/ its authority, parties have to raise this issue as soon as the matter alleged has come to their attention.[17]

Under the Scottish law an arbiter is allowed to decide the issue of his jurisdiction in the first instance, however, courts may be called upon to make the final decision on the issue of jurisdiction.[18]

The power enjoyed by the arbiter /arbitral tribunal originate from the arbitration agreement between the parties and from the relevant laws. The powers conferred by the parties can be expressed or implied powers, however they are subject to mandatory rules and public policy. For instance, the parties may agree that the arbiter/ arbitral tribunal has the powers to award interest. The arbiter /arbitral tribunal can only exercise such powers if the level of interest rate is within the tolerance of the mandatory rules.

---

[15] Art.28(5).
[16] Art.16(1).
[17] Art.16(2).
[18] *McCosh v Moore* (1905) 8 F. 31.

Duties of arbiters

While arbiter/arbitral tribunals possess certain powers to carry out the **20–14** arbitration proceedings, certain duties are also imposed on them. These include duties to act with due care, duties to act with due diligence, ethical duties to carry out the task with competence and the duty to remain independent and impartial.[19] Under the Scottish law, having accepted the appointment the arbiter is under a duty to resolve the dispute between the parties, unless he can prove that there is a good reason for resignation. In breach of this duty a penalty or imprisonment may be enforced.

While it remains difficult to define the exact contents for such moral duties as an arbiter has, the IBA Rules of Ethics for International Arbitrators have provided useful guidelines. According to the Rules:

1. Arbitrators shall proceed diligently and efficiently to provide the parties with a just and effective resolution of their disputes, and shall be and shall remain free from bias.
2. A prospective arbitrator shall accept an appointment only if he is satisfied that he is competent, can give full attention and has an adequate knowledge of the issue and language of arbitration.
3. An arbitrator shall remain independent and impartial.
4. A prospective arbitrator shall disclose all facts which may give rise to justifiable doubt as to his impartiality or independence.[20]
5. In general, an arbitrator shall make no unilateral arrangements for fees or expenses.
6. An arbitrator shall not discuss the possible settlement proposals with one party in the absence of the other party.
7. There must be confidentiality of deliberation.[21]

Similar provisions can also be seen in Arts 12 and 18 of the Model Law, which give the parties the grounds for challenge of arbitrators.[22]

Immunity of arbiters[23]

The immunity of arbiters is predicated upon the generally accepted **20–15** proposition that they enjoy quasi-judicial status in that it has its basis in the fact that the functions performed by the arbiters are compared to the acts performed by judges. It has further been submitted that absence of immunity for arbiters could compromise their integrity in such a way that they would be inclined to make an award in favour of a party who is more likely to sue them. With immunity, arbiters can do their work

---

[19] Art.18.
[20] Art.12.
[21] *http://www.ibanet.org* [accessed January 17, 2008].
[22] Art.12(2).
[23] Detailed discussion on this issue, see Yu and Shore "Independence, impartiality and immunity of arbitrators" (2003) 52 I.C.L.Q. 935.

without constantly looking over their shoulders in the fear of being forced to defend themselves in the courts.

While the issue of immunity remains undecided in Scotland, England has already decided this issue in favour of arbitrators in the decisions made by the House of Lords in *Sutcliff v Thackrah*[24] and *Arenson v Casson Beckman Rutley & Co.*[25] In *Sutcliff*, the House of Lords established the need for such immunity by saying:

> "I think that the immunity of arbitrators from liability for negligence must be based on the belief—probably well founded—that with such immunity arbitrators would be harassed by actions which would have very little chance of success. And it may also have been thought that an arbitrator might be influenced by the thought that he was more likely to be sued if his decision went one way than if it went the other way, or that in some way the immunity put him in a more independent position to reach the decision which he thought right."[26]

Finally, "Since arbitrators are in much the same position as judges, in that they carry out more or less the same functions, the law has for generations recognised that public policy requires that they too shall be accorded the immunity to which I have referred."[27]

Relationship between arbitration and courts

20–16 | **Key concept**

Courts have powers to assist or supervise arbitration procedures.

The relationship between arbitration and the courts is always one of a love-hate relationship. Believing in party autonomy, the design of arbitration is to move away from court supervision, however at the same time, arbitration may not function well without the support from national courts, especially at the stage of recognition and enforcement of arbitral awards and the necessary involvement of third party.

Regarding the supporting role played by the Scottish courts, according to the Scottish Council for International Commercial Arbitration the Scottish courts provides assistance to arbitration:

> "(1) before the commencement of the arbitration to obtain assistance in the appointment of the arbiter or arbiters;
> (2) to obtain interim measures of protection;

---

[24] [1974] A.C. 727.
[25] [1977] A.C. 405.
[26] [1974] A.C. 727 at 757.
[27] Ibid at 758.

(3) to obtain assistance in compelling the production of documents, or the attendance of witnesses;

(4) during the course of the arbitration to obtain an opinion on a point of law arising from a decision in the arbitration; and

(5) at the conclusion of the arbitration to obtain assistance in enforcement of the arbiter's award."[28]

As far as the supervisory functions exercised by the Scottish courts, they can be observed in different stages of arbitration such as general supervision of arbitration process, the stated case procedure and recognition of enforcement awards which will be discussed in the following section.

The stated case procedure

Key Concept   20–17

The stated case procedure only applies to domestic arbitration.

If any arbitrations fall into the scope of the Model Law, the practice of stated case procedure does not apply. In domestic arbitration this procedure is one special feature of commercial arbitration in Scotland. This procedure, grounded in s.3 of the Administration of Justice (Scotland) Act 1972, introduced a procedure under which a party may require an arbiter or a tribunal to state a case (at any stage during the course of the arbitration) for the opinion of the court, the Court of Session, on any question of law arising in the arbitration.

Unless the enactment allowing the appeal requires the application to be made to the court or it is impracticable or impossible to apply to the tribunal, an application for such leave shall be made, in the first instance, to the tribunal which made the decision sought to be appealed against.[29] Before the tribunal makes the final decision, the party applying for the stated case sends a minute setting out the question on which the case is applied for to the clerk of the tribunal. [30]

Within 21 days after the expiry of the period for lodging a minute, an arbiter can agree to state a case on some or all questions the party has raised, refuse to state a case or decide to ascertain the facts before disposing the application.[31] If the tribunal has deferred a decision, it shall, within 14 days after it has ascertained the facts, decide whether to state or refuse to state a case.[32] However, an intimation containing the date of the decision of the tribunal and the reasons for refusal must be submitted to the court if the arbiter refuses to state the case.[33] After the tribunal has

---

[28] *http://www.scia.co.uk* [accessed January 17, 2008].
[29] RSC r. 41.2.
[30] RSC r.41.5.2
[31] RSC r. 41.7.1.
[32] RSC r. 41.7.2.
[33] RSC r. 41.7.4(a).

refused to state a case on any question, the party whose application has been refused may, within 14 days after the date on which intimation of the refusal was made, lodge in the General Department an application by note stating briefly the grounds on which the application is made[34] to the Inner House for an order to require the other party to show cause why a case should not be stated.[35] Under this procedure a tribunal can be ordained to state a case.[36]

In any case, if the tribunal has decided or is ordered to state a case, the tribunal shall within 14 days after the date of intimation of its decision to the parties, have the case prepared and copies of it submitted in draft to each party.[37] As the stated case is sometimes abused to slow down arbitration process, the Scottish Council for International Arbitration advises the parties to contract out this practice in their agreement in order to avoid this slow cumbersome procedure.

The award

20–18 | **Key Concept**

Arbitral awards are final and have binding force on the parties.

Types of awards

20–19 The main purpose of submitting disputes to arbitration is to resolve the disputes with a binding decision made in arbitral awards. The decision made by arbitral tribunal is called arbitral awards. There are different types of arbitral awards: interim awards, partial award and final award. With parties' authorisation, the tribunal can make an interim award dealing with preliminary issues, such as the issue of jurisdiction. The tribunal can also make partial awards dealing with some, not all, issues raised by the parties. A final award is an award containing the decisions made by the tribunal which exhausts all the issues raised by the parties. The contents of a final award shall include both interim awards and partial awards.

Once the award is made by the arbitral tribunal, arbitral awards will enjoy the effect of *res judicata* and can be enforced by the winning party against the losing party for the recognition and enforcement of the arbitral awards. On the other hand, the awards may be subject to a legal challenge raised by the losing party. This is the so-called setting aside.

---

[34] RSC r.41.8.2.
[35] RSC r.41.8.1.
[36] RSC r.41.8.4.
[37] RSC r.41.9.

Setting aside of an award

Although the stated case procedure provides the parties with an oppor- **20–20**
tunity to question the arbiter's decision in general, under the Scottish law,
arbitral awards cannot be appealed against in the court system and no
review of the merits of the arbitral awards is allowed. The only way for
the losing party to challenge the arbitral awards made by the arbiter is to
actively apply for an order of the court to set aside the arbitral award.
Alternatively, the similar effects can also be achieved by raising a defence
to an action for recognition or enforcement of the arbitral award.
According to Art.25 of the Articles of Regulation 1695, grounds for
challenging the arbitral awards are limited to "corruption, bribery or
falsehood". Apart from Statutes, common law also allows challenge on
the grounds that:

(1) the arbiter decides the case beyond the scope of his jurisdiction
    the parties conferred or decides the case based on the power he
    never had;
(2) the arbiter fails to decide all the disputes submitted to him in the
    final award;
(3) the contents of the award are uncertain;
(4) the arbiter has been guilty of misconduct such as breach of due
    process, failing to follow the procedures agreed between the
    parties, to ignoring the court's opinions on certain points of law
    issues;
(5) fraudulent methods were applied to obtain the award;
(6) grounds for disqualification of arbiters have been established.
    For instance, the arbiter does not have the necessary qualifica-
    tions specified by the parties or the arbiter breaches his duties.

For international commercial arbitration in Scotland, seven grounds
were listed in Art.34(2) of the Model Law. They are:
Article 34(2)(a):

(i) incapacity of a party to the arbitration agreement or invalidity
    of the agreement;
(ii) breach of due process;
(iii) that the award deals with dispute beyond the scope of
    submission;
(iv) that the composition of the tribunal or the arbitral procedure
    was not in accordance with the parties' agreement or not in
    accordance with the Model Law;
(v) that the award was procured by fraud, bribery or corruption,

Article 34(2)(b):

(i) inarbitrability of the disputes; and
(ii) breach public policy.

Recognition or enforcement of an award

20–21 One advantage of submitting disputes to arbitration is that there will be a
binding decision made by the arbiter or arbitral tribunal at the end of the
proceedings. However, not every losing party carries out the award
voluntarily. Consequently, the role played by national court will become
extremely important at the stage of the recognition or enforcement of
arbitral awards. The court will be asked by the enforcing party to be
involved if the losing party refuses to perform the arbitral award
voluntarily. The party seeking recognition or enforcement of the arbitral
award can apply to the Sheriff Court or the Court of Session for assistance. It is the same for international commercial arbitration governed by
the Model Law under Arts 35 and 36 of the Model Law.[38]

The Scottish Arbitration Code and Arbitration (Scotland) Bill

20–22
> **Key Concept**
>
> The Scottish Arbitration Code is a voluntary code. The Arbitration
> (Scotland) Bill is an attempt to bring a single-track arbitration law to
> Scotland.

Concerned by the enactments of new arbitration laws in different countries, particularly England and Ireland, and the fear that Scotland is
being seen as outdated arbitration forum, the practitioners are of the
opinion that there is a need for a single track of arbitration law in
Scotland. With an intention to promote Scotland as the place of arbitration, in 1997, the Dervaird Committee was set up to achieve such a
goal. The Committee is of the opinion that a new legislation is needed in
order to (1) put virtually the whole of arbitration law in Scotland into a
single statute, (2) find in one place the principles governing the law of
arbitration in Scotland in a language which can be readily understood.
The Committee made recommendations and produced a draft Arbitration (Scotland) Bill in order to consolidate existing enactments and
render the arbitration process speedier and more effective. This draft Bill
contains 75 sections, five parts and five Schedules. The general principles
of the bill are:

- to obtain the fair resolution of disputes by an impartial tribunal
  without unnecessary delay or expense;
- the parties should be free to agree how their disputes are resolved
  subject only to such safeguards as are necessary in the public
  interest;
- the court should not intervene except as provided by Part I.[39]

---

[38] The grounds for refusal of recognition or enforcement of arbitral award listed in Art.36
of the Model Law are similar to those grounds listed in Art.34 of the Model Law.

[39] Draft Arbitration (Scotland) Bill s.1.

Under the Bill, arbitrators are given the powers to award damages, make an award of interest, order security for expenses and order rectification of the contract. Arbiters will be obliged to disclose any circumstances giving rise to justified doubts as to their impartiality as well as take all necessary steps to resolve disputes without delay. The procedures for challenge and removal are clearly set out. The arbitrator's immunity from being sued in civil courts for his acts or omissions is also included. The arbitrator is also given wide powers to deal with the case, in the situation where parties fail to corporate and afford remedies to the parties if parties agree so.

Since Mr Alex Salmond, of the Scottish National Party, became the First Minister of Scotland in May 2007, promoting commercial status of Scotland is one of the aims of the Government. It is hoped that a new Arbitration Bill prepared by the Justice Department will be given Parliamentary time and reaches the statute books in 2009.

Apart from the efforts of bringing a single track of arbitration law, the Scottish Arbitration Code, is produced and first launched in 1999, amended in 2007, by the joint force of the Scottish Council for International Arbitration and the Chartered Institute of Arbitrators (Scottish Branch). The Code is designed to be voluntary in nature and adopted by ad hoc arbitration. Despite that the Code "Is only a voluntary code requiring all parties to agree to its adoption. Nor can it deal adequately with many matters which can only be done by statute. It is fair to say that the Code was regarded by its framers as a stop-gap pending the introduction of legislation",[40] it is welcomed by the practitioners involved in commercial arbitration before the enactment of the Arbitration (Scotland) Bill.

ADJUDICATION

> **Key Concept** 20–23
>
> Adjudication is widely used in construction disputes under the Housing Grants, Construction and Regeneration Act 1996.

Adjudication is a decision-making process involving a neutral third party, called an adjudicator, with the authority to make a binding decision on the parties. To reduce the caseloads of the courts and arbitration, since May 1, 1998, adjudication as an ADR to resolve disputes arising under the construction, telecommunications, security installation and engineering contracts has been introduced by the Housing Grants, Construction and Regeneration Act 1996. Since then adjudication has been receiving full support from the construction industry. Based on its

---

[40] Memorandum and overview of the draft Bill, Lord Dervaird Committee and the Joint Working Group.

mandatory provision, adjudication has become a standard form of dispute resolution settling differences between parties to a construction contract. According to the Act, to submit disputes arising from the contract to adjudication, the construction contract between the parties must be in writing, made by exchange of correspondence or otherwise evidenced in writing. Different types of dispute which can be submitted to adjudication include money claims, delay and disruption, extension of time, declarations, specific performance and defect claims.

Legal framework

20–24 Alongside the Housing Grants, Construction and Regeneration Act 1996 (HGCRA), in Scotland, there are statutes affecting the adjudication process. They are:

- the Scheme for Construction Contracts (Scotland) Regulations 1998;
- the Construction Contracts (Scotland) Exclusion Order 1998;
- the Housing Grants, Construction and Regeneration Act 1996 (Scotland) (Commencement No.5) Order 1998.

Section 108(1) of the HGCRA sets out the right to refer disputes to adjudication. It reads: "A party to a construction contract has the right to refer a dispute arising under the contract for adjudication under a procedure complying with this section. For this purpose 'dispute' includes any difference." Following this provision, the parties have the right to give notice of intention to refer a dispute to adjudication,[41] and the dispute must be referred to the adjudicator so appointed within seven days of such notice.[42] Once the dispute is submitted to the adjudicator, he is required to reach a decision within 28 days,[43] extendable to 42 days in total.[44] The appointed adjudicator is required by law to act in an impartial manner[45] and take his initiative in ascertaining the facts and the law.[46] The binding nature of adjudicator's decision is usually upheld by arbitral tribunal or the courts.[47] It is furthermore enforced by the courts by means of summary proceedings. Once the decision turns into a court order, then the court, upon the application of the party, will be able to enforce the award against the losing party. It is also noted that the right to adjudication is not affected by the discharge or termination of the main contract. Unless acting in bad faith, the adjudicator is not liable for anything done or omitted in the discharge or purported discharge of his

---

[41] HGCRA s.108(2)(a).
[42] HGCRA s.108(2)(b).
[43] HGCRA s.108(2)(c).
[44] HGCRA s.108(2)(d).
[45] HGCRA s.108(2)(e).
[46] HGCRA s.108(2)(f).
[47] HGCRA s.108(3).

function as adjudicator.[48] Similar protection is also afforded to the agents or employee of the adjudicator.[49]

COURT ACTIONS

Key Concept   **20–25**

The value of the claim determines which court the pursuer shall submit the dispute to. Court of Session—£5,000 or above; Sheriff Court—ordinary causes action—£5,000 or above, summary causes action—above £3,000 and below £5,000, small claim action—below £3,000.

Jurisdiction under the Civil Jurisdiction and Judgments Act 1982

If the parties decide to resolve their business disputes in Scotland, it is **20–26** paramount for the parties to find out whether the Scottish courts have jurisdiction over the dispute. The general principle to determine whether a court has jurisdiction over the dispute depends on whether the individual or the corporate is domiciled within the court jurisdiction. An individual is domiciled in Scotland if and only if (a) he is resident in Scotland, and (b) the nature and circumstances of his residence indicate that he has a substantial connection with Scotland.[50] For a legal person, the seat of a corporation or association shall be treated as its domicile in Scotland[51] if it was incorporated or formed under the Scottish law, or its central management and control is exercised in Scotland, or it has its registered office or some other official address in Scotland, or it has a place of business in Scotland.[52]

Subject to Parts I and II of the Civil Jurisdiction and Judgments Act 1982, Sch.8 has effects to determine in what circumstances a person may be sued in civil proceedings in the Court of Session or in a Sheriff Court in Scotland. Under Sch.8, if the parties agree in writing that a court is to have jurisdiction to settle any disputes which have arisen or which may arise in connection with a particular legal relationship, that court shall have jurisdiction.[53] A Scottish court also has exclusive jurisdiction: (a) in proceedings which have as their object rights *in rem* in, or tenancies of, immovable property, the courts for the place where the property is

---

[48] HGCRA s.108(4).
[49] In any case, if the contract does not comply with the requirements of s.108(1)–(4), the parties to a construction contract are unable to reach agreement regarding entitlement to stage payment, notice of intention to withhold payment and prohibition of conditional payment, or a construction contract does not make provisions about date of payment, the provisions of the Scheme for Construction Contracts apply to adjudication.
[50] Civil Jurisdiction and Judgments Act 1982 s.41(3).
[51] Civil Jurisdiction and Judgments Act 1982 s.42(1).
[52] Civil Jurisdiction and Judgments Act 1982 s.42(3)–(5).
[53] Civil Jurisdiction and Judgments Act 1982 s.41(3) Sch.8, r.6.

situated in Scotland; (b) in proceedings which have as their object the validity of the constitution, the nullity or the dissolution of companies or other legal persons or associations of natural or legal persons, the courts for the place where the company, legal person or association has its seat in Scotland; (c) in proceedings which have as their object the validity of entries in public registers, the courts for the place where the register is kept in Scotland; (d) in proceedings concerned with the enforcement of judgments, the courts for the place where the judgment has been or is to be enforced in Scotland.[54] Regarding jurisdiction over consumer contracts, such as a contract for sale of goods on instalment credit term or a contract for a loan repayable by instalments or other financial arrangements or other similar types consumer contract, the Scottish court has jurisdiction if the consumer or the defender or both of them is domiciled in Scotland.[55]

Value of the claim determining which court has the jurisdiction[56]

20–27 Apart from the issue of domicile, the value of the claims the purser raises is also a factor to consider about which court has jurisdiction over the dispute.

Court of Session

20–28 According to s.7 of the Sheriff Courts (Scotland) Act 1907,[57] a claim over £5,000 (see SSI 2007/507) excluding expenses and interest, the parties can submit to either the Court of Session or the Sheriff Court.

Sheriff Court

Ordinary cause actions

20–29 If the pursuer seeks a sum above £5,000, then the appropriate form of procedure is ordinary cause. There is no upper limit for ordinary cause actions.

Summary cause action

20–30 If the purser seeks a sum above £3,000, but not above £5,000, then the appropriate form of procedure is summary cause.

Small claims actions

20–31 Since January 14, 2008, for the claims below £3,000, the pursuer can raised a small claim procedure in the Sheriff Court.[58]

---

[54] Civil Jurisdiction and Judgments Act 1982 s.41(3) Sch.8, r.5.
[55] Civil Jurisdiction and Judgments Act 1982 s.41(3) Sch.8, rr.3–6. The Civil Jurisdiction and Judgments Act 1982 also lists the grounds where a person may be sued in Scottish courts.
[56] For detailed discussion, see Chapter 2 "Structure of the Scottish Legal System".
[57] For actions commenced on or after January 1, 1994, the issue will be regulated by SI 1993/1956 as amended by SI 1996/2167, SI 1996/2445 and SI 1996/2586.
[58] Small Claims (Scotland) Amendment Order 2007 (SSI 2007/496) r.2(2)(a).

Commercial litigation

Both r.47.1(2) of the Rules of the Court of Session 1994 and r.40.1(2)(a) **20–32** of the Ordinary Cause Rule 1993 define commercial action as an action arising out of, or concerned with, any transaction or dispute of a commercial or business nature including, but not limited to, actions relating to the construction of a commercial document, the sale or hire purchase of goods, the export or import of merchandise, the carriage of goods by land, air or sea, insurance, banking, the provision of services, building, engineering or construction contract, or a commercial lease.

In the Court of Session, all commercial actions shall be brought to the commercial judges in the Outer House.[59] The defender has the right to defend himself, however, the defences in a commercial action shall be in the form of answers to the summons with any additional statement of facts or legal grounds on which it is intended to rely.[60] Both preliminary and procedural hearing will be arranged then a debate will be ordered by the judge.[61] Also, any document required for any proof in a commercial action shall be lodged as a production not less than seven days before the date fixed for the proof.[62] Finally, the judge may: (a) refuse to extend any period for compliance with a provision in these Rules or an order of the court; (b) dismiss the action or counterclaim, as the case may be, in whole or in part; (c) grant a decree in respect of all or any of the conclusions of the summons or counterclaim, as the case may be; or (d) make an award of expenses if any party fails to comply with the Rules or any order made by the judge.[63]

For a commercial action raised in the Sheriff Court, it was regulated in the Ordinary Cause Rule 1993 where similar definition is provided in r.40.1(2)(a). In the appropriate cases, the proceeding can be initiated by the pursuer electing to adopt the commercial action procedure by bringing an action[64] or providing no election by the pursuer, based on the application made by any party to have the cause appointed as commercial action.[65] Alternatively, the Sheriff Court may, on its own initiative, order the case to be decided in commercial action to achieve justice or transfer the dispute to commercial action on the basis of the joint motion between the parties. [66] To commence a commercial action proceeding in a Sheriff Court, a writ must be submitted by the pursuer to the court.[67] The defender must lodge defence within seven days after a notice of intention to defend is lodged with the Sheriff clerk if he wishes to challenge the jurisdiction of the court, state a defence or make a counterclaim.[68] On the

---

[59] Rules of the Court of Session 1994 r.47.2.
[60] Rules of the Court of Session 1994 r.47.6(1).
[61] Rules of the Court of Session 1994 r.47.11–13.
[62] Rules of the Court of Session 1994 r.47.14.
[63] Rules of the Court of Session 1994 r.47.16.
[64] Ordinary Cause Rules 1993 r.40.4.
[65] Ordinary Cause Rules 1993 r.40.5(1).
[66] Ordinary Cause Rules 1993 r.40.6.
[67] Ordinary Cause Rules 1993 r.40.7.
[68] Ordinary Cause Rules 1993 r.40.8.

lodging of defences, the Sheriff clerk shall fix a date and time and the first
suitable court day shall be not sooner than 14 days, nor later than 28
days, after the date of expiry of the period of notice.[69] The parties shall
lodge any proofs which are necessary for the judge to decide the case[70]
and the judge can arrange a hearing if he deems it necessary.[71] Any failure
of a party to comply with the Rules or any order made by the Sheriff, the
Sheriff has the power to: (a) refuse to extend any period for compliance
with a provision in these Rules or an order of the court; (b) dismiss the
action or counterclaim, as the case may be, in whole or in part; (c) grant
decree in respect of all or any of the craves of the initial writ or counterclaim, as the case may be; or (d) make an award of expenses.[72]

CONCLUSION

20–33   ADR such as negotiation and mediation, has the advantages of low costs,
speed, flexibility and confidentiality in terms of resolving disputes.
However, they do not provide the parties with a binding decision. This
may leave the parties involved in such types of ADR in a vulnerable
situation. To obtain a binding decision, the parties will have to consider
the possibilities of arbitration and court actions. The parties shall consider the types of dispute and their expectations and needs before
deciding which mechanism is the most suitable choice for them.

▼ CHAPTER SUMMARY

NEGOTIATION

20–34   **Negotiation is the first step to take to resolve disputes. It can be carried out
by the parties or their legal representatives.**

MEDIATION

**Mediation is an informal method of ADR, where a third party is appointed
as a mediator. His task is to guide the parties to reach a mutually acceptable resolution without damaging the business relationship. The main
advantages of mediation are informality and lower costs. The disadvantages
of mediation include the facts that the parties can leave the process at any
time, the agreement is not binding and the evidence used in the mediation
process may compromise the case if the parties submit their disputes to the
court or arbitration at a later stage.**

---

[69] Ordinary Cause Rules 1993 r.40.10.
[70] Ordinary Cause Rules 1993 r.40.13.
[71] Ordinary Cause Rules 1993 r.40.14.
[72] Ordinary Cause Rules 1993 r.40.15.

ARBITRATION

Commercial arbitration is a more formal form of ADR used in business. In Scotland, domestic arbitration is based on common law and statutes while international commercial arbitration is governed by the UNCITRAL Model Law by virtue of the Law Reform (Miscellaneous Provisions) (Scotland) Act 1991. The arbitration process is private, confidential, speedy and can be controlled by parties' agreement. Parties are given control over the choice of law, language, place, arbitrators and applicability. The arbitral award is binding.

ADJUDICATION

Adjudication is a decision-making process involving a neutral third party with the authority to make a binding decision on the parties. It is the main dispute resolution method used in construction disputes under the Housing Grants, Construction and Regeneration Act 1996.

COURT ACTIONS

Apart from ADR, parties can also submit to the Scottish courts. For a claim over £5,000, excluding expenses and interest, the parties can submit to the Court of Session (SSI 2007/507). For Sheriff Courts, the pursuer can raise an ordinary cause action for a claim over £5,000. For a claim over £3,000 but below £5,000, the appropriate form of action is a summary cause action. For any claims below £3,000, the pursuer can raise a small claim procedure in the Sheriff Court.

? QUICK QUIZ

- Do the parties to a business dispute have to hire lawyers in the negotiation process?
- What are the main features of mediation?
- What are the advantages and disadvantages of using commercial arbitration to resolve business disputes?
- What are the statutes regulating domestic arbitration in Scotland?
- What duties does an arbiter have?
- What is the legal effect of an arbitral award?
- Which form of alternative dispute resolution is widely adopted for construction disputes and which statute provides the legal framework for such method?
- What is the limit of claim for the Court of Session?
- What is the limit of claim for an ordinary cause action in a Sheriff Court?
- What is the limit of claim for a summary cause action?
- What is the limit of claim for a small claim procedure?

📖 FURTHER READING

Bevan, *Alternative Dispute Resolution* (Sweet & Maxwell, London, 1992).
Davidson and MacGregor, *Commercial Law in Scotland*, 2nd edn (Edinburgh, W. Green, 2008).
Forte, *Scots Commercial Law* (Butterworths, Edinburgh, 1997).
Moody and Mackay (eds) *Green's Guide to Alternative Dispute Resolution in Scotland* (W. Green, 1995).
Mruk research, *Civil & International Analytical Team within Scottish Government*, ISBN 978 0 7559 6888 6, Scottish Parliament Publication, December 2007.
Redfern and Hunter, *International Commercial Arbitration*, 4th edn (London, Sweet & Maxwell, 2004).
John Sturrock, "Reflections on Commercial Mediation in Scotland Arbitration", *Journal of the Chartered Institute of Arbitrators*, 73(1), 2007, pp.77–83.

🖱 RELEVANT WEBLINKS

http://www.scottishlaw.org.uk/scotlaw/
http://www.a-negotiation-skills.co.uk/
http://www.scottishmediation.org.uk/
http://www.scia.co.uk
http://www.scottish-arbitrators.org/adjudication/resources.html
http://www.uncitral.org/
http://www.kluwerarbitration.com
http://www.scotland.gov.uk/consultations/industry/iaci-00.asp
http://www.scotland.gov.uk/Publications/2004/05/19360/37122
http://www.scotcourts.gov.uk/

Chapter 21   Introduction to Legal Writing and Problem Solving Techniques

GILLIAN BLACK[1]

▶ CHAPTER OVERVIEW

This chapter is intended to help students with the demands of legal essay **21–01** writing and exams. Writing essays and sitting exams can be daunting tasks, especially in a new subject which has its own vocabulary and rules. Citing legal authority, using the right terminology, and dealing with different types of questions present problems and pitfalls for students who are new to the study of law. The following guide aims to provide some advice and suggest ways to help you demonstrate and communicate your legal knowledge as clearly and confidently as possible.

The guide is split into three sections:

> Writing legal essays
> Answering problem questions
> Exam hints

WRITING LEGAL ESSAYS

In any law course, it is likely that you will have to write essays. These may **21–02** be non-assessed, assessed or part of the final exam. The guide below is intended to help with essay structure and to explain some technical elements of legal authorities, which are critically important in any legal work.

Essays in law are expected to exhibit:

- good structure: have a clear beginning, middle and end—state the problem, argue for an answer, refute counter-arguments then state your conclusion;
- relevance: stick to the point in issue and do not digress;
- clarity: avoid obscurity and undue complexity;

---

[1] Many thanks to Professor George Gretton, Mr Burkhard Schafer and Mr Scott Wortley for their generous consent to use their study technique guide as a basis for this chapter, the glossary and abbreviations in Appendix 1. The original guide was produced for the Legal Reasoning and Legal System course offered by the School of Law at the University of Edinburgh, and has been modified for this chapter.

- good style: observe the tone and register of language that you find in good law journals and textbooks, and stick to plain English;
- proper citation of legal authorities (cases and statutes) and of academic or other sources that support key points you are making. Also cite any work you have used in building up your argument (but note that the course handout is not an acceptable reference work).

In all prepared written work (but much less formally in unseen examinations) it is obligatory to acknowledge the authorship of quotations, and to refer to any authority on which some statement is based. Both in relation to cases and statutes and in relation to textbooks and articles you need to develop the skill of presenting in a concise way and in your own words your understanding of the main point of authorities or learned works on which you base your own argument. This is true whether you take a critical or a supportive line towards the material you are using. Careful and accurate acknowledgement of sources, and appropriate marking of quotations, helps to ensure you keep clear of all suspicion of plagiarism.

Using correct methods for referencing and citation is a crucial part of writing an essay. You have to master two skills for this: *what* to reference, and *how* to do it.

(1) *What* to reference

21–03 To get this question right is crucial to avoid accusations of plagiarism, which in minor cases can cost you marks, and in more serious cases may even result in disciplinary proceedings. Not everything you write will need referencing though. Some facts are so generally known that it is not necessary to attribute a source. You may have read for instance that Scotland has trial by jury. If you want to use this information in an essay, you would not need to find out where you first read it. However, if you come across an academic article that states: "Trial by jury never developed the same social significance in Scotland as it did in England or the US" and you want to use this idea, you have to acknowledge where it came from. If in doubt, reference it.

For students on a law course, using the right *legal authority* is of crucial importance to make a valid legal argument. In most cases in Scots law, the appropriate legal authority for a statement of law will be a statute or a judicial decision (case law). When you write a legal essay, you will have to show which authority you are using. To know that the age of legal capacity in Scots law is 16 years is not enough. You will also have to state what the authority for this rule is, in this particular case a statute (Act of Parliament). Examples on how to do this properly are given below.

(2) *How* to reference

21–04 Unfortunately, there are several different standards for referencing in existence, which often creates confusion. They are created by influential journals, universities or academic societies. Whichever one you use though, you must use consistently. Once you have chosen a style, all references in that essay should follow it.

All these standards have something in common. They tell the reader:

- **who** wrote the work;
- **when** the book or article was written, or the case was decided;
- **what** is the title of the work;
- **where** it can be found.

In addition to acknowledging the author, they therefore allow the readers to find or check for themselves the sources you use, in as easy a way as possible. Giving a date also ensures that the reader can check if your information is up to date.

There are two very different ways in which you can use ideas, facts or theories from other authors. BOTH of them need referencing.

(i) Direct quotations

Sometimes an idea is so crucial, or so well worded by the original author, **21–05** that you want to *quote* it word by word. If you want to quote a passage directly, you have to put it into quotation marks and, especially with longer quotations, it is helpful to indent it. If you wish to omit a section from the passage you are quoting, you can do this with an ellipsis: ... These three dots mark the place of the omitted text.

You can see examples of direct quotations throughout this textbook.

(ii) Paraphrasing

Alternatively, you may want to rephrase the author's statement in your **21–06** own words. This is perfectly acceptable, but it STILL requires a reference.

Note that only minor changes, e.g. from "uncivilised and inhuman" to "inhumane and uncivilised", or simply replacing words by synonyms, e.g. "... have been wrongly sentenced" changed to "... have been mistakenly sentenced" is not a paraphrase. You should either quote literally, or express the idea entirely in your own words.

Case citations

A case name should be given as it appears in the most authoritative **21–07** report of the case, and should be printed in italics, with the "v" roman (i.e., not in italics). Thus Donoghue v Stevenson would be written as *Donoghue* v *Stevenson*. Citations should follow the conventions established in the Oxford Standard Citation of Legal Authorities. A full citation need only be given at the first reference to the case, which should also provide the shorthand reference to be used in subsequent citations, e.g.

Junior Books Ltd v *The Veitchi Co Ltd* 1982 SC (HL) 244 (henceforth *Junior Books*).

Such shorthand references should enable ready recognition of the case referred to.

If you refer to dicta (judicial speeches) within the case, your footnote should state the page number and the name of the judge who made that speech. For example:

> *Robertson* v *Forth Road Bridge Joint Board* 1996 SLT 263 at 265 per Lord President Hope.

Where a neutral case citation (such as [2007] UKHL 21) is available, this should be given, and paragraph rather than page numbering should be used to identify dicta within the case.

Cite ECJ cases thus:

> Case 6/60 *Humblet* v *Belgium* [1960] ECR 559
> Case C-213/89 *R* v *Secretary of State for Transport, ex parte Factortame* [1991] ECR I-3905

Statute citations

21–08 Statutes should normally be referred to by their short titles only, together with the calendar year, as in the example below. No comma should be inserted between the word "Act" and the date. The following abbreviations are permissible:

1. "Section" becomes "s", except where it is the first word in a sentence or footnote.
2. "Sections" can be abbreviated as "ss"
3. "Schedule" becomes "Sch" unless the Act contains only one Schedule
4. "chapter" is abbreviated as "ch".

"Part" is not abbreviated.

To show these in practice, two examples are given:

> Finance Act 1965, s 19(1), Sch 7
> Companies Act 1985, part V, ch VI

Cite Acts of the Scottish Parliament thus:

> Mental Health (Public Safety and Appeals) (Scotland) Act 1999 asp 1

Statutory instruments should be referred to by name and date, followed by their number, thus:

> Duration of Copyright and Rights in Performances Regulations 1995, SI 1995/3297
> The Parking Attendants (Wearing of Uniforms) (City of Glasgow Parking Area) Regulations 1999, SSI 1999/62

European Community legislation

Cite Treaty Articles thus: **21–09**

>   Article 234 EC Treaty

This may also be cited, in order to incorporate reference to the previous Article number, as Article 234 EC Treaty (ex Art.177).
   Paragraphs of Articles should be cited thus: Article 177(5) EC Treaty.
   Cite Directives thus:

>   Council Directive 2001/89/EC of 23 October 2001 on Community measures for the control of classical swine fever OJ 2001 L 316/5

Cite Decisions thus:

>   Commission Decision 239/96/EC on emergency measures to protect against bovine spongiform encephalopathy OJ 1996 L78/47

Cite Regulations thus:

>   Commission Regulation (EC) 3223/94/EC of 21 December 1994 on detailed rules for the application of the import arrangements for fruit and vegetables OJ 1994 L 337/66

Note that OJ stands for the Official Journal.

Citation of the Stair Memorial Encyclopaedia

The first reference to this work in an article should be as follows: **21–10**
   The Laws of Scotland: Stair Memorial Encyclopaedia (henceforth SME)
   Citation should then be by volume number (vol 18), year of publication in brackets, and paragraph number (para 16). The names of editors and authors in this work should not be cited, although they may be referred to in the text as holding the views expressed in their contributions to the Encyclopaedia. Similar principles should be applied to other encyclopaedic works.

Citation of books

Give the author's initial(s) and surname, the title (in italics) and the year **21–11** of publication in round brackets. If it is not the first edition, you should also state to which edition number you are referring ("edition" is usually abbreviated as "edn"):

>   T B Smith, *A Short Commentary on the Law of Scotland* (1962)
>   E M Clive, *The Law of Husband and Wife in Scotland*, 4th edn (1997)

For edited books, give the editor's name(s) as above for the author, with "ed" or "eds" following immediately in round brackets.

> D L Carey Miller and D W Meyers (eds), *Comparative and Historical Essays in Scots Law: a Tribute to Sir Thomas Smith QC* (1992)

At the first of repeated references to a book, give a shorthand reference consisting of author's surname and keywords from the title, introduced by "hereafter referred to as":

> T B Smith, *A Short Commentary on the Law of Scotland* (1962) (hereafter referred to as Smith, *Short Commentary*).

Citation of articles

21–12 Give the author's initials and surname, the full title of the article within double quotation marks but with minimum necessary capitalisation, the year of publication (in round brackets unless there is no volume number), the volume number in Arabic numerals, the full name of the journal in italics, the first page of the article:

> A D M Forte, "Marine insurance and risk distribution in Scotland before 1800" (1987) 4 *Law and History Review* 394.

If a more specific page reference is being given, include the page number(s) in the form "at 397", for example

> A D M Forte, "Marine insurance and risk distribution in Scotland before 1800" (1987) 4 *Law and History Review* 394 at 397.

At the first of repeated references to an article, give a shorthand reference consisting of author's surname and keywords from the title, introduced by "hereafter referred to as", as with book citations above.

Multiple authors

21–13 For publications that have multiple authors, you should use the last name and initial(s) for up to three authors, separated by a comma and "and", thus:

E P Ellinger, E Lomnicka and R Hooley, *Modern Banking Law* (2002)

For more than three authors use the last name and initials of the first author, and then et al, thus:

> A Anderson, et al, *Universal Access to E-mail: Feasibility and Societal Implications* (1995).

Citation from websites

21–14 URLs should be italicised and placed within brackets. You should always include the date when you last visited the website.

When a case or article available in printed form is cited, reference should always be made to the printed source. If there is no printed equivalent, e.g. for a recent case obtained from the Scottish Courts Administration website, give the date of the judgment and the relevant URL.

Health Warning: websites can be a useful source of information, but they are not always accurate or up to date. It is also likely that an online search for material will produce legal material *for other jurisdictions*: remember that your authority must usually be relevant to the jurisdiction that you have been asked to write about (e.g. Scotland or England).

ANSWERING PROBLEM QUESTIONS

Broadly, a legal "problem question" involves a scenario containing a given set of facts, followed by an instruction to advise the respective parties on their rights and any remedies they may have. Problem questions really test students' understanding of a particular section of law. This is because problems force you to *apply* the law that you have learnt to those facts.   **21–15**

As with essay writing, there are varied approaches to legal problem solving. In general examiners want to see that you are alive to all the possibilities that a set of facts throws up. This means that you are able to see all the issues that arise for consideration and are able to deal with them in a legally accurate and structured way. This ability generally is what distinguishes a good student from an average one. The aim of this guide is to give you a suggested framework to help you develop your legal skills in answering problem questions.

It is helpful to take a relatively simple four-step structure when approaching legal problems: Issue, Law, Application and Conclusion (ILAC). What do these steps entail?

1. The issue

The first step to solving a legal problem is to work out what the issues are that arise out of the set of facts. Of course the better you know the law the easier it is to spot the issues.   **21–16**

You should first read the problem *carefully* to get an overall idea of the area(s) of law involved. You should pay close attention to the question that is posed at the end of the problem. In general you will be asked to advise one or more of the respective parties that appear in the problem. If that is the case, ask yourself what that party would really want to know. The answer to this question will reveal the legal issue for determination. It is vitally important for your own clarity (and it usually impresses the examiners) if you can accurately and clearly identify the issues in this way.

When writing your answer, there is no need to start by repeating the facts: instead, you should set out in the introduction the salient points that you will address in the rest of your response and the area(s) of law involved.

2. The applicable law

21–17 Once you have identified the issues for determination, the next step is to set out the law applicable to these issues. You will need to cite the relevant authority in support of the current legal position in respect of the issues raised. *It cannot be stressed strongly enough how important it is for you to cite authority for your statements relating to the law.* In general this entails citing one of the authoritative sources of law, such as case law or statute. Where there is no authoritative source then you should state this and cite one of the persuasive sources such as an *obiter dicta* judgment or a textbook/article.

Although there is frequently a clear and settled point of law that will decide a case, this is not always so. Sometimes there is conflicting authority with the result that the law is unclear. In these situations it is usually helpful if you acknowledge this lack of clarity and argue the point both ways when it comes to applying the law to the facts. Don't be afraid to express your (substantiated) opinion if you think that one view is preferable to another.

3. Applying the law to the facts

21–18 After you have identified the issues and clearly set out the applicable law, you then need to apply the law to the facts of the problem at hand. Sometimes the facts of the problem will closely track a particular case and this will provide you with a clear starting point (and sometimes a suggested conclusion) when applying the law to the facts. However, where this is not the case, you will have to argue by analogy, or reason from scratch, and come to a decision as to how the current problem should be decided. You should try to find evidence in the facts given to you which support your conclusions.

It is not unusual for the problem question to provide an incomplete set of facts. This lack of detail may well make it impossible to say for certain what the outcome of a particular problem might be. For example, a question on contract issues might disclose that the defender had been drinking alcohol, but not specify how much or whether this resulted in the defender lacking capacity at the point of conclusion of contract. Whether or not the defender had capacity is therefore unclear. In these situations you need to explain what information is missing, and what you would need to give a definitive answer. In the absence of such information, you should also mount contingency arguments. This means you should explore the reasonable possibilities. So, in the example just given, you would ideally argue the point both ways, and say (a) if the party had drunk 25 shots of vodka, then he would be likely to lack capacity by reason of intoxication, but you would also have to point out that (b) if it was proved that the defender had only had one glass of wine then he would be likely to have full capacity.

Another manifestation of this problem arises where you are given all the facts, but it is difficult to reach a conclusion as to the *impact* of these facts. To take another example from the field of contract law, the law of contract tells us that a contract can be terminated only if a breach is material. The law also states that a breach is material if it is serious (or goes to the root of the contract). Whether a breach is material may be unclear from the facts that have been given to you in the problem question. Again, in this situation you would have to argue (a) that should the court find that the breach is material then *x* ... but (b) in the event that the court should find that the breach is not material then *y*. ... However, if the facts lean a particular way or if you think you can substantiate one or other conclusion, then you should not shy away from saying so.

4. Conclusion

Once you have (i) identified the issue, (ii) set out the law, and (iii) applied **21–19** the law to the facts, you need to conclude. In general it is useful to frame the conclusion in relation to the issues that you have identified, as well as in relation to the question that you have been asked. For example, if you have said that the issue for determination is whether there is a valid contract between X and Y and you have been asked to advise X, you might conclude that there is a valid contract between X and Y and, accordingly, you advise X to sue Y on the contract.

The most important thing is to remember to answer the question you have been asked.

5. Tackling problem questions in an exam

Remember, the examiners are looking for the ability to *apply* legal **21–20** knowledge, not a *recitation* of that knowledge. When you look at a law book or a statute it seems that law is a set of rules, and therefore that to learn the law is to learn those rules. In a sense that is true. But in reality there are far too many rules for anyone to learn. In addition, lawyers and judges do not start with the rules, but with problems. Law is largely about problem-solving.

The following pointers should help you apply your legal knowledge to solve the problem you are faced with in the exam:

1. Sometimes a problem has a clear answer, and sometimes no clear answer, and sometimes partly both. Identifying where the law is clear and where it is not is one of the skills being tested.
2. Sometimes a problem question will contain *irrelevant facts*. That is like real life. One of the skills of a lawyer is to perceive which facts are legally relevant and which are not.
3. Conversely, a problem question may leave out some vital piece of information. Again, this is like real life. One of the skills of the lawyer is to identify missing information which will enable him to solve a problem.
4. Credit is given for identifying relevant issues, even if the wrong answer is given. This is probably the single most important skill

in tackling a law exam. You may know everything there is to
know about directors' duties in company law, for example, but
your knowledge is useless if you cannot spot such an issue hiding
in a set of facts.

5. Do not *waffle*. Irrelevancy counts against you. To put in back-
    ground information is legitimate. Learning to draw the line
    between background information and sheer waffle is one of the
    skills being tested.
6. However, if some aspect of the problem might be relevant but in
    your view is in fact irrelevant, you should of course say why.

Address the question that is posed. If you are asked whether Smith is liable
to Robertson, answer that question, whether your answer is a yes or a no
or a maybe. This may seem obvious, but each year numerous students get
nowhere near actually offering an answer to the question asked. You may
be reluctant to give an answer in case it is the wrong answer, but the truth
is that nothing can be worse than no answer at all.

EXAM HINTS

21-21   The chances are that you will not be sitting an exam on Business Law:
you will be sitting an exam on Business Law as taught in your University/
College/course by Ms A, Dr B, Professor C and so on. The lecturer has a
limited time to decide what to teach and what to leave out, and also a
limited time in which to examine the course. Inevitably the exam will tend
to be an exam on the course as taught. (Which is not to say that questions
will not sometimes require knowledge beyond that which was covered in
lectures and tutorials.)
Exam questions can comprise a number of different types:

- problem questions;
- essay questions;
- "notes" questions;
- multiple choice questions.

This section will contain some general hints on improving your exam
performance. It will also contain a brief section on notes questions and
multiple choice questions: for guidance on problems and essays you
should refer to the sections above.

General exam advice

21-22   *Time management is crucial.* No matter how much you know, you cannot
and will not get a good mark if you do not leave yourself enough time to
answer the necessary questions. If you are required to write three essays,
then composing two excellent ones will not compensate for running out
of time before the third one. You should know before you start the exam

how much time you have for each question—and make sure you stick to it.

One of the most important elements in any exam is the ability to communicate. You need to be able to communicate your answer *clearly, concisely, correctly and unambiguously*. Don't forget presentation, especially:

- spelling;
- grammar;
- punctuation;
- handwriting (examiners cannot give marks for what they cannot read).

Poor English makes a bad impression and may make it difficult to understand what you are trying to say. Thus: "The contract between A and B is subject to C's right. So he can sue." Who can sue? A, B or C?

How many mistakes can you spot in the following?

"Bank of Edinburgh credits a/c when they recieve the cheque so b/c a banker has lien & so becomes holder if it's customer has got an overdraft, (s 2 of 1882 act) he may be able to sue, b/c he does have overdraft there is a lien therefore the chq must be payed, this is, basically an unsatisfactary senario if they get liquidated."

Here it is again, with the errors highlighted in bold:

"Bank of Edinburgh credits a/c when they **recieve** the cheque so **b/c** a banker has lien & so becomes holder if **it's** customer has got an overdraft, (s 2 of 1882 **act**) **he** [who?] may be able to sue, **b/c he** [who?] does have **[an]** overdraft there is a lien therefore the **chq** must be **payed**, this is, basically an **unsatisfactary senario** if **they** [who?] get liquidated."

Beware of abbreviations. Conventional abbreviations are acceptable. Thus in the above example "a/c" for "account" is acceptable, as is "&" for "and". But unconventional abbreviations, such as "b/c" for "because" make a bad impression and sometimes entirely baffle the examiner as to their meaning, especially if the handwriting is poor.

Beware of colloquialisms: you are supposed to be writing a legal brief. Write complete sentences, in formal English. Do not write notes. Do not use txt spk.

In a problem question there will usually be various parties. If you mean "Jones" do not write "Smith". This may seem obvious, but it is a common error. The examiner can judge you only on what you have written.

Perhaps the worst error to make is to talk of Scot's law. Or Scots' law. Or scots law. Or Scott's law. **The term is "Scots law"**. No apostrophes. Only one t. And an upper case initial S.

It helps the examiner if you <u>underline</u> cases and statutes.

Re-read your answers, to correct blunders. Many students feel an overwhelming disinclination to do this: they cannot bear to look again at what they have said. Do it. It can save many lost marks.

Give authority. You have to tread a middle path in this respect. Excessive citation of authority is often a symptom of irrelevance, and is often an attempt to cover up a failure to understand the issues. But equally an answer on company law which suggests that you have not heard of the Companies Act 2006 is likely to attract a fail mark. If the exam is an open-folder one, you do not need to cite authority merely to impress. Cite authority where it is needed in the development of your argument or analysis, but not otherwise.

Look at exam papers for the same course for the past three or four years to get an idea of the format and of the sort of questions that are likely to be asked.

Students often fear that if they develop a line of reasoning not given in the lectures they will make fools of themselves. On the contrary, *you should not be afraid to argue.* An interesting line of argument will often attract several additional marks even if the examiner disagrees with it.

Spend time reading the exam questions carefully. Do not be intimidated by the fact that the person at the next desk is already on page two of the answer book before you have started writing.

Leading on from the last point, examiners are looking for quality rather than quantity. You are not marked by the number of pages you have managed to fill up. Shorter answers can attract a higher mark than longer ones.

It is usually helpful to make notes on a question before answering it. If you do this, do not forget to cross out your notes at the end, for otherwise the examiner has to assume that your notes form part of your answer.

If part of a question baffles you, you should nevertheless write something about it. For silence you can be awarded no marks, but even a bad answer will normally pick up a few marks.

Read the instructions on the front of the script book. This will often advise you to start each answer on a new page, for example, and complete the front of the script book. FOLLOW THESE INSTRUCTIONS.

Do not begin by copying out the question or narrating the facts of the problem. This is a sheer waste of time. The examiner has the question paper beside him while he marks.

Likewise, there is normally no point in copying out a statutory provision, unless it is very brief. In general, a simple reference is enough. Longer quotation from a statutory provision makes sense only if you need to discuss its precise wording.

Avoid non-sequiturs. Avoid self-contradictions. What happens all too often is that a student says one thing in one sentence and the opposite a few lines later. Sometimes this is because he has changed his mind in the course of writing. You can lessen the danger of this by making notes for an answer first. You can also save yourself by re-reading what you have written to pick up errors and contradictions.

In an open-folder exam, no credit is given just for copying out chunks of the handouts or lectures. In other exams (the majority) some credit is given for memory work, but it is not the most important aspect of the examination.

Finally, remember the guidance of Eric Blair (George Orwell) who in an essay on "Politics and the English Language" (available in his collected essays) proposed five rules for clear writing:

> "(i) Never use a metaphor, simile, or other figure of speech which you are used to seeing in print.
> (ii) Never use a long word where a short one will do.
> (iii) If it is possible to cut a word out, always cut it out.
> (iv) Never use the passive where you can use the active.
> (v) Never use a foreign phrase, a scientific word, or a jargon word if you can think of an everyday English equivalent.
> (vi) Break any of these rules sooner than say anything outright barbarous."

Notes questions

A notes style question will ask you to write short notes on a particular **21–23** case or statutory provision, or perhaps a particular legal doctrine. Typically, it will ask you to write short notes on a number of these, not just one.

It can be too easy to answer these questions by simply repeating the facts of the case or the effect of the statutory provision. This may attract some marks, but it is unlikely that it will be enough to pass.

Instead, you need to tell the examiner not only what the case/statute/doctrine says, but also why it is so important. Think about why the examiner might have selected that case/statutory provision etc. for inclusion in the exam paper, instead of another. The sort of things you may wish to comment on are:

- Has it changed a previous rule of law?
- Have there been subsequent cases regarding it?
- Is it controversial?
- How does it interact with other legal provisions?

A good answer will discuss wider issues—perhaps not in too much detail, but it will certainly not be restricted to only the precise point on which you have been asked to comment.

Multiple choice questions

There are two secrets to success with multiple choice questions: know the **21–24** law and read the question and answers carefully. If you have not learnt the relevant law, then this type of exam question will really catch you out: you cannot hide partial or incomplete knowledge in waffle. All you can do is pick one answer, and you need to make sure its the right one.

However, even if you know the law, its all too easy to get it wrong by mis-reading the question and the choice of answers. Examiners will usually select the wrong answers (known as "distractors") very carefully.

For example, if you are asked to calculate the value of unpaid shares in a given scenario, the choice of wrong answers may well be plausible figures, such as the total value of the shareholding, or the value of the paid shares instead. Not only do you need to know how to calculate the value of the unpaid shares, you need to make sure you are not distracted by the distractors.

A final tip is to be clear whether the multiple choice questions will be negatively marked or not. Negative marking is where you lose marks if you give the wrong answer: a common scheme might be +2 marks for a correct answer, 0 marks for no answer, and −1 marks for a wrong answer. In this case, it is often better not to answer a question (thus attracting 0 marks), rather than guessing and getting it wrong (thereby losing 1 mark). (However, you cannot pass the exam without answering some of the questions, so you cannot play safe by leaving them all blank!) Where negative marking does not apply, then it is common to get +1 mark for a correct answer and 0 marks for a blank or a wrong answer. In these exams, there is more to be gained by guessing, even if you are not sure. However, whichever tactical approach you take, you must be 100 per cent sure of the marking scheme, i.e. whether it is negatively marked or not.

Appendix 1   Glossary and Abbreviations

This is only a selection of terms which you may come across and be puzzled by. If you encounter unfamiliar terms and do not find them here, there are various books that will help, for instance the *Glossary: Scottish and European Union Legal Terms* and *Trayner's Latin Maxims*.

Glossary

ADVOCATE Member of Faculty of Advocates, specialising in Court of Session and High Court work. Similar to English barrister.

AUDIENCE If a lawyer has the "right of audience" in a court that means s/he can appear there for a client. Advocates and solicitor-advocates have a right of audience in all courts. Other solicitors only have a right of audience in lower courts.

APPELLANT Person appealing to higher court from decision of lower court.

AVER To aver is to claim the truth of certain facts. Noun is averment.

AVIZANDUM If a court "makes avizandum" that means that it will not give judgment at once but will take time to consider.

BARRISTER English equivalent of advocate.

BLACKLETTER LAW Blackletter law means technical legal doctrine as opposed, for example, to questions of public policy or legal philosophy. So called because law texts were formerly often printed in blackletter typeface.

BONA FIDES Good faith. (*Fide* is the ablative form e.g. "The purchaser was *in bona fide*".) To be in good faith is to act honestly, to be unaware of any irregularity or wrongdoing. For example, a purchaser from a thief is in good faith if he has no reason to suspect that the goods are stolen.

CAPACITY The ability to have rights and enter into juristic acts. Some persons have restricted capacity. Thus a person with severe mental handicap could own property (passive capacity) but not, on his own, sell it. Again, a company has legal capacity for most things but not, for example, marriage.

CAUTION (Pronounced "cayshun".) A guarantee for someone else's debt.

CIVIL As well as being the opposite of criminal, civil also means Roman: "Civil law" = Roman law. A "civilian" legal system is one much influenced by Roman law.

CLAIMANT Modern English term for plaintiff.

CODE (1) Part of the *Corpus Juris Civilis*. (2) A statute which system-atically sets forth the whole of a large area of law. The two most famous codes are the French *Code Civil* (also called the *Code Napoleon*) and the German *Bürgerliches Gesetzbuch* (the BGB). They have had international influence.

COMMON LAW (1) Unenacted law. (2) A collective term for the Anglo-American legal systems.

CONSENSUS IN [or AD] IDEM PLACITUM Agreement on the same proposition. In a contract, the two parties must understand each other aright.

CORPORATION Any juristic person other than a partnership.

COUNSEL An advocate. Senior counsel = Queen's Counsel. Junior counsel = any advocate other than a QC.

COURT OF SESSION Established 1532. Sits in Edinburgh only. Divided into Outer House and Inner House. Outer House is a court of first instance. Inner House hears appeals from Outer House and other lower courts. Judges are called "Lords of Council and Session" or "Senators of the College of Justice".

CROWN Term used to mean the state, which the Queen personifies.

CULPA Fault.

CURATOR BONIS A type of judicial factor, appointed to look after the affairs of an incapax.

DAMAGES (always plural) means not harm but the right to compen-sation for harm.

DAMNUM Loss. *Damnum injuria datum* means loss caused by wrong-doing (that is, by another person).

DECLARATOR Decree setting forth existence of rights without neces-sarily seeking to enforce them.

DECREE (Stress is on first syllable.) The order of a court disposing of a case, in favour of the pursuer or the defender. The three main types of decree are (a) condemnator, in which the pursuer's case is upheld, (b) absolivitor, in which the defender's case is upheld, and (c) dismissal, in which no decision is reached, for example because the pursuer has abandoned the action or because the pursuer has sued in the wrong court etc. Dismissal is decree effectively in favour of defender but since no determination of the dispute, it is not *res judicata*. A decree in absence is where defender has not appeared. Decree *in foro contentioso* is where defender has appeared.

DEFENDANT English term for defender.

DEFENDER Person against whom an action is raised, opposite of pursuer.

DELEGATED LEGISLATION See Statutory Instrument.

DELICT A civil wrong other than breach of contract. Also called law of reparation.

DISTINGUISH To distinguish a precedent is to show that the precedent in fact deals with a different situation and so is not a true precedent.

EQUITY Slippery word with many meanings. (1) Special branch of English law. (2) Fairness, to be applied where law is silent or too rigid. (3) Share capital of company. (4) Value of land or buildings minus debt secured thereon.

GOOD FAITH See *bona fides.*

HERITABLE Heritable or immoveable property means land and buildings. Everything else is moveable property. Heritable security means a security over heritable property, securing a loan. (It is often referred to by its name in English law: a mortgage.)

HIGH COURT OF JUSTICIARY Highest criminal court, which hears both trials and appeals. Based in Edinburgh but goes "on circuit". The judges (Commissioners of Justiciary) are same persons as Court of Session judges.

HOUSE OF LORDS (1) The upper house of Parliament, whose members are unelected. Limited powers since House of Commons can override its veto. (2) Highest court of appeal in civil matters (and, in England, criminal also). In theory (2) is a committee of (1). As a court it is being replaced by the Supreme Court. Often abbreviated to HL.

INCAPAX Someone not able to look after their affairs; lacking in full legal capacity, e.g. through insanity or mental handicap.

INJURIA Wrongdoing, delict. Does not mean "injury".

INNER HOUSE of Court of Session. Highest appeal court (except HL and ECJ) for civil matters. Normally sits in two "divisions" to double throughput. Occasionally a third "extra" division is added.

INTER VIVOS Between living persons. Opposite of *mortis causa.*

INTERDICT A court order forbidding someone from doing something.

INTERLOCUTOR Any order made by court. The final interlocutor disposing of the case is called the decree. A court is said to "pronounce" an interlocutor.

JOINT AND SEVERAL Joint and several liability, or solidary (*in solido*) liability, is where two or more persons are liable for the same debt, in full. Creditor can claim the full sum from either debtor, but of course cannot recover more than the total due. Where one debtor pays the full debt, he then has a right of recovery against the other debtors for their pro rata share.

JUDICIAL FACTOR A person appointed by the court to administer property, investments etc. for some special reason, e.g. curator bonis.

JURISPRUDENCE (1) Law or legal system, e.g. "jurisprudence of Italy" = Italian law. (2) Philosophy of law. (3) Case law.

JURIDICAL ACT (Also called juristic act.) A lawful act which changes the legal situation, such as the making of a contract, the raising of an action, getting married. Only a person with legal or juristic capacity can do juristic acts. (Contrast a juristic event, which is an event which changes the legal situation but is not a deliberate act, for example death. Also contrast illicit acts, such as delicts.)

JURISTIC PERSON Also called artificial or legal or moral person. Law divides persons into natural (i.e. human beings) and juristic. Some juristic persons exist in public law (e.g. City of Edinburgh Council) and others in private law (e.g. Royal Bank of Scotland).

LAW SOCIETY OF SCOTLAND Professional body to which all Scottish solicitors belong.

LORD ADVOCATE Government minister. Advises Government on matters of Scots law. Represents the Crown in litigation. In criminal cases called "Her Majesty's Advocate".

MORTIS CAUSA By reason of death. A *mortis causa* act takes full effect on death. Main example is a will. Opposite of *inter vivos*.

MOVEABLE PROPERTY All property other than land and buildings. Opposite of heritable.

NOBILE OFFICIUM The power of the Court of Session and High Court to modify the law in technical points, adhering to the spirit of the law. Used only in clear cases.

NOTARY Or notary public. Person authorised to take sworn statements (affidavits) and to authenticate some types of document. Notaries exist in all legal systems. In Scotland all notaries are solicitors.

NULLITY Something is absolutely null (void) if it appears valid but in fact has no legal effect at all, for instance a forged testament, or a contract signed at gunpoint. A thing is relatively null (voidable) if it is valid but can be made null at the option of someone. Thus, a contract entered into by fraud is voidable and the defrauded party can annul (avoid) the contract or not, at his option.

OBITER DICTA "Things said by the way." Singular is *obiter dictum*. Things said by judge which are not necessary to reach her/his decision. Opposite of *ratio*.

OPINION (1) Of judge, explaining her/his decision. Sometimes called judgment or, in the House of Lords, speech. (2) In some cases a law firm will seek opinion of advocate or other independent party to assist with a particular legal problem.

OUTER HOUSE of Court of Session. Judges sit singly to hear cases at first instance.

OVERRULE Where an appellate court says that a decision of a lower court in another earlier unconnected case was wrong.

PLAINTIFF Former English term for pursuer. (Modern term is claimant.)

POINT To be "in point" means to be relevant. Thus if a court "distinguishes" an earlier case it does so because it is not "in point".

PRECEDENT The doctrine of precedent, also called the doctrine of *stare decisis*, is that where the law has been settled in a case, later cases should follow the same rule. A "precedent" is a prior case on which reliance is placed. A "binding precedent" is one which the court must follow. A "persuasive precedent" is one which has weight but is not binding. (For example, English cases are usually only persuasive precedents in Scots law.)

PRESCRIPTION (1) Negative or extinctive prescription means the loss of rights by non-enforcement for a certain period of years. Thus a debt not claimed will eventually prescribe. (2) Positive or acquisitive prescription means acquisition of ownership by possession over a certain period of years.

PRIVATE LAW All law except public law.

PRIVY COUNCIL (1) A body which in theory advises the Queen. "Order in Council" is a royal decree to which this body has nominally assented: in practice a type of government order. (2) Appeal court for certain Commonwealth countries. (3) Under the Scotland Act 1998 certain cases involving devolved matters can be appealed to the Privy Council, but in this respect its jurisdiction is being transferred to the new Supreme Court.

PROOF Court hearing in which the facts are investigated. A "proof before answer" is a proof where disputed points of law are left open until after the proof.

PUBLIC LAW Law concerning the state (Crown) and state organisations (e.g. local authorities). Examples: tax law, planning law, constitutional law, criminal law. Opposite of private law.

PURSUER The person who raises an action, opposite of defender.

QUANTUM "How much." The extent of a loss suffered, in money terms.

QUASI-CONTRACT Another name for the law of unjustified enrichment.

RATIO DECIDENDI Or *ratio* for short. Reason or rule of law on which decision is based. (A case which turns purely on disputed facts will not have any *ratio*.) Contrast *obiter dicta*.

REAL RIGHT A right in a thing, as opposed to a right against a person (personal right). Examples are ownership and servitude.

RELEVANCY One possible defence to an action is that, as stated, it is "irrelevant" that is to say, even if the pursuer can prove all his alleged facts they still would not entitle him to the remedy he seeks.

RESCIND To withdraw from a contract on the ground of the other party's breach of it.

RESILE (1) To withdraw from an agreement before it has become a binding contract. (2) To withdraw from a contract.

RESPONDENT (1) In an appeal, the non-appealing party, i.e. opposite of appellant. (2) In a petition, the respondent corresponds to the defender in an ordinary action.

SEQUESTRATION Main meaning is formal bankruptcy.

SERVITUDE A right held by one landowner in relation to neighbouring property. Thus, a servitude of way is private right of way across someone else's land.

SHERIFF Judge in the Sheriff Court, who has jurisdiction on most matters, civil and criminal.

SIST (Noun and verb.) (1) To sist an action is to suspend all further procedure for the time being. But the action remains in existence, and the sist can be recalled. (2) To sist a party in an action is to bring that party in as additional party. For example, if a pursuer dies, his executor may be "sisted" to carry on action.

SOLATIUM Damages to compensate for suffering, as opposed to patrimonial loss.

SOLICITOR Lawyer qualified to do all legal work but with no right of audience in the Court of Session or High Court. But some solicitors, called solicitor-advocates, have such rights.

SPECIFIC IMPLEMENT Remedy of getting someone to perform his obligation, as opposed to an award of damages for its non-performance.

STARE DECISIS "To stand by the decisions." See Precedent.

STATUTORY INSTRUMENT An SI is subordinate (delegated) legislation, passed not by Act of Parliament but by a procedure authorised by some Act of Parliament. Thus procedural rules of the Court of Session ("Acts of Sederunt") are SIs authorised by the Acts of Parliament regulating the Court of Session.

SUBORDINATE LEGISLATION See statutory instrument.

THIRD PARTY (Also called a *tertius*.) Legal transactions are often between two persons. In that case anyone else is called a third party. For example, third party motor insurance is where an insurance contract between a motorist and an insurance company covers claims against the motorist by third parties (perhaps an injured pedestrian).

TITLE TO SUE One possible defence to a claim is that the pursuer has no title to sue. Thus, even if the defender has acted unlawfully, the right to object is vested in someone else, not in the pursuer. Also called *locus standi*.

TORT English term for delict.

ULTRA VIRES "Beyond the powers". Corporations are often restricted in what they can do. Acts outwith these powers are *ultra vires* and may thus be null. A statutory instrument can also be *ultra vires* if it goes beyond what was authorised by the Act of Parliament in question.

UNJUSTIFIED ENRICHMENT A branch of the law of obligations. In certain cases a person who is "unjustifiably enriched" can be required to return the benefit. To give an example, if A mistakenly pays a bill twice to B, B is unjustifiably enriched and must return the second payment to A. B's obligation to do so is not contractual or delictual, but belongs to this branch of law.

VOID, VOIDABLE See nullity.

Abbreviations

AG: Attorney General

All ER: All England Reports

asp: Act of the Scottish Parliament

c or **ch** or **cap**: Chapter (statute number)

CAB[x]: Citizens Advice Bureau[x]

CB: Curator Bonis

ECHR: European Convention on Human Rights

ECtHR: European Court of Human Rights

ECJ: European Court of Justice

HL: House of Lords

JF: Judicial Factor

LA: (or **Ld Adv**): Lord Advocate

LLP: Limited liability partnership

LJC: Lord Justice Clerk

LP: Lord President

Mor: Morison's Dictionary of Decisions

OJ: Official Journal of the European Communities

PC: Privy Council

QC: Queen's Counsel

s: section

SC: Session Cases

Sch: schedule

SCLR: Scottish Civil Law Reports

SI: Statutory instrument

SSI: Scottish Statutory Instrument

SME: *Stair Memorial Encyclopaedia*

SLT: Scots Law Times

WLR: Weekly Law Reports

Appendix 2   Quick Quiz Answers

Chapter 1—Introduction to the nature and sources of Scots Law

- *Why is it important that a business or accountancy student should know a bit about business law?*
  Students of other disciplines such as business or accountancy may be surprised when they find business or commercial law subjects on their curriculum. Although business and accountancy students are not going to become professional lawyers, business managers will have to work within the legal framework of business, and need to know about certain areas of law that are important for them. Accountants have to have quite a wide knowledge of law, in addition to specialist areas such as the statutory rules for the contents of company annual accounts, as their business clients will seek advice on areas of law that apply to them, such as the differences between operating as a business as a partnership or as a company.
- *What is the essential difference between public law and private law?*

  - Public law governs the relationship between the state and the citizen (constitutional law, administrative law and criminal law).
  - Private law governs relationships between citizens, and has several branches (including the law of contract, the law of delict and the law of persons).

- *Explain the procedure for the enactment of a public bill in the UK Parliament.*
  A bill is drafted by Parliamentary draftsmen and introduced to one of the Houses of Parliament by a government minister or other sponsor of the bill. At the First Reading the title is read out and the bill is printed. At the Second Reading the general principles of the bill are debated. At the Committee Stage the Bill is examined clause by clause and amendments are often made. At the Report Stage the Committee reports back to the House with proposed amendments, which are voted on. At the Third Reading a final discussion will take place and the bill is passed. Once the Bill has been passed in one House, it goes to the other House and is put through the same procedures. It then obtains the Royal assent and becomes an Act.
- *If you wanted to look up a section of an Act of the UK Parliament, where would you look?*
  You could purchase a hard copy of the Act at the Stationery Office. Alternatively, you could look the statute up in Public

General Statutes and Measures. In these places you could find the
Act as it was originally enacted, and not with any later amendments incorporated. It is a good idea to look for the section of the
Act in a source that gives you the law as updated including any
amendments. You can use the UK Statute Law Database
www.statutelaw.gov.uk or one of the subscription databases such
as Westlaw.

- *What are the provisions in the Scotland Act 1998 which fix the
  boundaries of the legislative competence of the Scottish Parliament?*
  Sections 29–30 and Schedule 5 of the Scotland Act 1998.
  The Scottish Parliament may legislate on any matters that are not
  reserved to the Westminster Parliament. It may not legislate in
  ways that are incompatible with the European Convention on
  Human Rights and Fundamental Freedoms or European community law. Also it may not enact legislation with extra-territorial
  scope. And it may not legislate so as to remove the Lord Advocate as head of the system of criminal prosecution or of the
  investigation of deaths in Scotland.
- *What role does the UK Parliament and the Scottish Parliament
  play in relation to delegated legislation?*
  The UK Parliament and the Scottish Parliament must pass an Act
  authorising another body to make delegated legislation, within set
  limits (usually a government department). Depending on what
  that parent Act provides, whichever Parliament enacted the parent Act will have a role in scrutinising the delegated legislation
  before it comes into effect, but will not have power to amend it. In
  the case of some Scottish delegated legislation, both Parliaments
  will scrutinise the delegated legislation.
- *What are the advantages and disadvantages of having a system of
  binding precedent?*
  Advantages:

  - It helps to promote justice by treating like cases alike.
  - It makes the outcomes of litigation more predictable.
  - It provides scope for the law to develop slowly as society's
    needs change by forcing judges to take previous cases into
    account.

  Disadvantages:

  - Bad decisions can hold back the development of the law.
  - There may be a lack of relevant case law in a particular area
    of law, making the law doubtful.
  - There may be conflicting precedents.
  - A precedent may be difficult to interpret because it may be
    badly reported.
  - A court may be overloaded with precedents.

- *In what circumstances must a later court follow the decision of an
  earlier court in Scotland?*

- The precedent must be (1) in point and (2) binding.
- A precedent is in point if the *ratio decidendi* (issue of law on which the earlier case was decided) is the same as the current case.
- A precedent is binding if it comes from a court whose judgments bind the current court (generally courts of appeal bind courts of first instance and higher courts bind lower).

- *To what extent are the institutional writers still of relevance to the decisions of the courts today?*
  The institutional writers did their work over a long period between roughly1800–1830, and were responsible for crafting a modern legal system for Scotland from old Scots customary law, mediaeval writings, Acts of the old Scots Parliament, decisions of the courts, and borrowings from Roman law. Their works were regarded as themselves being formal sources of law, rather than secondary sources.
  Nowadays their influence is declining as their works become superseded by legislation or developments in case law. However, their writings will still be cited in today's courts where still relevant.
- *In what circumstances is custom regarded as a formal source of Scots law?*
  Some old customs are already part of the law because they have been recognised as law by the courts. Their formal source then becomes judicial precedent. Where this has not occurred, the custom must be proved to the court (1) to have been acquiesced in as representing law for a long though undefined period of time; (2) to be definite and certain; (3) to be fair and reasonable; and (4) to be consistent with legal principle.
- *Explain what is meant by the nobile officium of the Court of Session and High Court of Justiciary.*
  The Court of Session and the High Court of Justiciary have an extraordinary equitable jurisdiction to fill in the gaps in the law to provide a remedy if one is not otherwise available.
- *When writing about the law in an essay or an examination, and you have to give the formal source of a legal rule, why would it not usually be correct to refer to a textbook as your authority?*
  When you write about the law, you must give authority for what you say. When you are explaining how a legal rule works, you will need to refer to statutory or case law as authority for what you are asserting. These are the formal sources. A textbook might write about a statute or a case, and the writer might have worthwhile things to say, but is a secondary source. However, you should refer directly to the statute or the case, and only refer to the textbook if you want to refer to the particular opinion of the textbook writer. Never use the textbook as your authority in place of naming the section and the statute, or giving the citation of the case.

Chapter 2—Structure of the Scottish Legal System

- *What does "privative jurisdiction" mean?*
  Cases or issues restricted to a specific court—e.g. the High Court of Justiciary has privative jurisdiction to try cases of murder.
- *What three criteria define the civil jurisdiction of the Sheriff Court?*
  Location; persons; and subject matter.
- *Which court hears applications for judicial review?*
  The Court of Session.
- *What is the maximum prison sentence that can be imposed by the District Court?*
  60 days.
- *How many years must a JP have practised as a lawyer?*
  None, JPs are lay justices and not legally qualified.
- *What is the ultimate court of civil appeal?*
  The House of Lords, or soon to be the UK Supreme Court.
- *What is the ultimate court of criminal appeal?*
  The High Court of Justiciary sitting as a Court of Appeal
- *What is the maximum fine a Sheriff can impose after conviction in a solemn trial?*
  There is no maximum amount, the level is unlimited.
- *How many people sit in a Scottish criminal jury?*
  15
- *What is a judge of the High Court called?*
  Lord Commissioner of Justiciary
- *What does an Advocate Depute do?*
  Prosecute in the High Court of Justiciary
- *Name the offices of the highest civil and criminal judiciary in Scotland?*
  The Lord President of the Court of Session (civil) and The Lord Justice-General (criminal).

Chapter 3—Business Regulation

- *Is the criminal law a branch of public or private law?*
  It is a branch of public law. Although victims' rights are increasingly recognised in the system, the criminal law is essentially concerned with the state exercising the public interest in preventing, resolving and punishing harmful behaviour.
- *What are the elements of a common law offence?*
  Common law offences can only be committed if the accused has engaged in some manner of prohibited behaviour (i.e. carried out the *actus reus* of the crime) while possessing a criminal or blameworthy state of mind (*mens rea*).
- *What kinds of state of mind are capable of satisfying the requirement of mens rea?*
  The *mens rea* differs depending on the particular crime that the accused is charged with. Some crimes require intention; others may be satisfied through recklessness, negligence, or possession of a particular state of knowledge.

- *What is strict liability?*
  A strict liability crime is one which does not require proof of *mens rea*. Thus one can commit a strict liability crime merely by carrying out its *actus reus*. Strict liability is required for all common law crimes, but not all statutory ones. The consequences of imposing strict liability can be very harsh. As a result the courts are somewhat reluctant to hold that a crime is one of strict liability, and the parliament will often temper the effect of strict liability crimes by providing the accused with a due diligence defence.

- *What is vicarious liability?*
  Vicarious liability arises when the courts hold someone guilty of a criminal offence because of something done by someone else, even though the two persons involved did not share a common purpose. Vicarious liability does not arise at common law but can arise in the context of statutory offences. For example, the proprietor of a business may in certain circumstances be made criminally liable for the criminal conduct of his employees.

- *Can corporations be found guilty of a crime?*
  Yes. Corporations can be found vicariously liable for the actings of their employees in appropriate circumstances. In addition, corporations can themselves be found guilty of breaching the criminal law, albeit it can be difficult to establish *mens rea*, particularly against large corporations.

- *What is the mens rea of theft?*
  An intention to deprive the owner of his/her property.

- *What are the elements of the crime of fraud?*
  The *actus reus* of fraud is the use of a false pretence that (a) deceives another and (b) causes a definite practical result. The *mens rea* of the offence is comprised of knowing that the statement made is false, and intending to deceive the person to whom the statement was made.

- *What does the expression "regulatory law" mean?*
  Regulatory law can be defined as the body of law whereby public authorities seek to exercise control over activities which are of importance to the community. This can involve making certain types of activities criminal offences, but also includes other forms of regulatory controls such as demanding that persons obtain a licence before carrying out certain activities.

- *The Health and Safety At Work etc Act 1974 is the main piece of occupational health legislation in the UK. What are the essential features of HSWA?*
  The HSWA itself imposes duties upon employers—most notably the duties to ensure, "so far as is reasonably practicable" the health, safety and welfare at work of all his employees and to ensure that persons not in his employment who may be affected by it are not exposed to risks to their health or safety. HWSA also allows regulations to be issued which impose more detailed and specific duties upon employers. HSWA also created the Health

and Safety Executive, which can enforce HSWA by using a range
of powers, including prosecution for breaches of the Act.
- *What is the purpose of the Corporate Manslaughter and Corporate
  Homicide Act 2007?*
  The Act creates the offence of corporate homicide. This offence
  gives the court no more sentencing power than HSWA, but, given
  the difficulties which have occurred in convicting large corporations of common law homicide, parliament felt that the Act would
  satisfy the public's desire to see companies which kill as a result of
  a serious breach of duty convicted of an offence which obviously
  carries a serious degree of blameworthiness.
- *What are the essential features of the Data Protection Act 1998?*
  The DPA regulates the way in which personal data may be collected and used. It requires organisations which hold personal
  data to notify the Information Commissioner and to abide by a
  series of data protection principles when holding or making use of
  that data. Data subjects (i.e. the person the data concerns) have
  certain rights and can, e.g., ensure that the data held about them
  is correct; the Information Commissioner's Office also has a range
  of powers, including, in certain cases, the right to prosecute, to
  ensure that the Act is complied with.
- *Why do we regulate competition between businesses? Which anti-
  competitive behaviours are regulated by competition law? What are
  the consequences of breaching the prohibitions?*
  Competition between businesses is widely believed to bring benefits to consumers and society as a whole. Any illegitimate
  manipulation of free markets, making them less competitive, is
  therefore seen as a serious matter. Competition law regulates anti-
  competitive behaviours (such as price-fixing agreements), the
  abuse of a dominant position, and the mergers of businesses large
  enough to have a distorting effect upon competition. Those
  breaching these regulations are liable to civil penalties or fines.

Chapter 4—The Law of Contract

- *What is a contract?*
  At its most basic, a contract is as described by Gloag: "an
  agreement intended to create a legal obligation between the
  parties."
- *Are all agreements contractually binding?*
  No; not all agreements are intended to create legal obligations.
  See, e.g. the case of social and domestic arrangements.
- *Is a unilateral gratuitous promise a contract?*
  No, but it will be legally binding if the conditions set out in
  RSWA are met.
- *What is consensus in idem? What is its legal significance?*
  Consensus in idem is a meeting of the minds; agreement by the
  parties on the essential elements of a contract. The moment that
  consensus is reached, a contract comes into existence.

- *What kind of test do the courts use to assess if a consensus in idem has been reached?*
  An objective test. In other words, whether the parties themselves think they have agreement is irrelevant; what matters is what an objective bystander witnessing their discussions and negotiations would think.
- *What is the identifying feature of an offer?*
  An offer must "contemplate acceptance." If a proposition or statement is not of such a nature that it can be met with an unqualified agreement, it is not an offer.
- *What is an invitation to treat? Give examples of common invitations to treat.*
  An invitation to treat is an invitation for someone else to make an offer. Examples include shop displays and (usually) advertisements and invitations to tender.
- *Does an offer not stated to be subject to a time-limit remain open indefinitely?*
  No. It will lapse after the expiry of a reasonable time. It may also be capable of being revoked.
- *What is the identifying feature of an acceptance?*
  It must be an unqualified agreement to an offer.
- *What is the legal effect of a counter-offer?*
  A counter-offer revokes the offer to which it responds, and puts in place a new offer which the original offeror can either accept or decline as he/she chooses.
- *When will the law consider an acceptance to have been effectually communicated to the offeror?*
  In the case of instantaneous forms of communication, when the acceptance is actually received. In the case of delayed forms of communication, upon despatch of the acceptance.
- *"Contracts relating to ____ form the most significant exception to the rule that contracts do not require to be in writing." What is the missing word?*
  Land
- *A and B intend to enter into a contract. B is worried that A may try to include terms contrary to B's interests, but reckons that if he doesn't sign anything, he will be safe enough. Is B's analysis correct?*
  No, it is incorrect and unsafe. Terms *can* be incorporated into a contract by signature, but they will also be incorporated without signature if (i) the offeror brings them to the offeree's attention in time; (ii) they are contained in a contractual document; and (iii) the notice is adequate.
- *Name the two major statutory regimes which regulate contractual terms. Outline their essential features.*
  The Unfair Contract Terms Act 1977 ("UCTA") and The Unfair Terms in Consumer Contracts Regulations 1999 ("UTCCR"). UCTA controls the circumstances in which the courts will enforce exemption clauses. UTCCR applies to consumer contracts only,

but provides that the court may declare unenforceable *any* clause in such a contract if it operates unfairly to the detriment of the consumer. UTCCR also differs from UCTA in that it is policed by the Office of Fair Trading, which can take action to get unfair terms struck out of standard form contracts.

- *Is a contract entered into between a major record company and an 8-year old child prodigy legally binding? What about a 17-year old?*
  No. The 8-year old lacks capacity. The record company would have to contract with his/her legal guardian. The 17-year old has capacity but could subsequently challenge the contract if it was entered into on prejudicial terms. The record company could exclude the possibility of challenge by having the court ratify the contract.

- *If a person suffering from a mental illness, while on a euphoric high, decides to spend £100,000 on designer clothes, is the contract of purchase he/she has apparently entered into legally binding?*
  Yes, unless the purchaser could demonstrate that he/she satisfied the legal test of insanity, and therefore lacked capacity at the time. This would involve demonstrating that he/she was incapable of understanding the legal obligations the contract entailed.

- *A is a fan of the band Pink Floyd. On hearing that "Floyd" is to be appearing live at SECC, A buys a ticket for the event. It transpires that the event is a cooking demonstration by the celebrity chef, Keith Floyd. Is A bound by the contract?*
  Yes. This is a unilateral uninduced error of intention and the ticket purchaser is therefore bound. Matters would be different if the purchaser of the tickets had been tricked into buying the tickets by misrepresentation on the part of the seller.

- *A places a large bet on a horse-race. His horse loses. Disappointed, he decides to cheer himself up by buying a knighthood from a corrupt public official. Happy now, he celebrates by buying a case of vintage champagne and hiring a prostitute. How many binding contracts has A entered into in this sequence of events?*
  Two: the bet is (now, since the Gambling Act 2005 Act entered into legal force) a valid legal contract; so too is the purchase of the champagne. The other two agreements are *pacta illicita*.

- *What is a restrictive covenant? Will such contractual terms be enforced by the courts?*
  A restrictive covenant is a contractual term by which one of the parties agrees that he or she will in some way refrain from competing with the other. They are commonly inserted into contracts of employment and contracts for the sale of a business. Such terms are unenforceable unless the party seeking to enforce it has a legitimate interest to protect, the clause is reasonable in its scope and extent and it is in the public interest.

- *What is a material breach of contract? Which contractual remedies available to someone suffering a material breach of contract are not available to the innocent party in the case of a non-material breach?*

A material breach of contract is a particularly significant breach of contract—one which goes "to the root of the contract." The additional remedies available in the case of a material breach are the self-help remedies: rescission, retention and lien.

- *What is meant by "the duty to mitigate loss"?*
  The legal duty imposed upon the innocent party to take reasonable steps to reduce the loss he/she has suffered as a result of the breach of contract.
- *What is meant by "remoteness of damages"?*
  An innocent party is only entitled to recover such damages as arise naturally from the breach of contract or such as may reasonably supposed to have been in the contemplation of both parties at the time they made the contract. Any other losses will be deemed "too remote" and will not be legally recoverable.
- *What are liquidate damages, and are they legally enforceable?*
  Liquidate damages clauses are terms inserted into contracts by which the parties agree the amount of damages which will be paid in the event of a particular type of breach. They are legally enforceable if they are a genuine attempt at pre-estimating loss but not if they are punitive in nature.
- *After what period of time will the right to enforce a contractual obligation be lost?*
  Five years from the date when the obligation became enforceable unless the contract is one pertaining to land, in which case the relevant period is 20 years.
- *In which circumstances will a contract be brought to an end by "frustration"?*
  If the contract becomes:
  (i) physically impossible to perform e.g. as a result of the destruction of the contractual subject matter;
  (ii) practically impossible to perform; or
  (iii) illegal to perform.

Chapter 5—Sale and Supply of Goods

- *Name three types of contract dealing with the supply of goods.*
  Sale, barter, hire-purchase, hire and contracts for services where goods also are supplied.
- *Which Act of Parliament governs contracts of sale?*
  Sale of Goods Act 1979.
- *How is a contract of sale different from other contracts for the supply of goods?*
  It involves a money consideration called the price and transfer of ownership.
- *There are exceptions to the rule that someone who is not the legal owner of goods cannot pass on a good title to them. State two of them.*
  Personal Bar

  - Sale by a mercantile agent

- Sale under a voidable title
- Sale by a seller in possession after a sale
- Sale by a buyer in possession after a sale
- Sales of motor vehicles subject to hire purchase or conditional sale

- *What terms are implied in contracts of sale?*
  Terms about title, description, satisfactory quality, fitness for a specified purpose, conformity of bulk with sample.
- *When are goods of satisfactory quality?*
  See the general definition in s.14(2A) and the factors set out in s.14(2B) of the Sale of Goods Act 1979.
- *When does the satisfactory quality test not apply?*
  Where defects have been specifically drawn to the attention of the buyer before sale and, where the buyer has examined the goods, defects which that examination ought to have revealed.
- *What remedies are available to a purchaser who buys defective goods?*
  Rejection, damages, specific implement or, in the case of consumers, the alternative remedies of repair or replacement, compensation and rescission.
- *What remedies are available to a seller if the buyer breaks the contract?*

  (i)   action for the price—s.49;
  (ii) damages for non-acceptance—s.50;
  (iii) and in some circumstance:
     (a) right of lien over goods—ss.39(1)(a) and 41;
     (b) stoppage in transit—ss.44–46;
     (c) right of resale—ss.39(1)(c) and 48.

- *What terms are implied in contracts for the transfer of goods governed by the Supply of Goods and Services Act 1982?*
  The same types as are implied in contracts of sale i.e. title, description, satisfactory quality, fitness for specified purpose and correspondence of bulk with sample.

Chapter 6—Consumer Protection

- *Which is the main statute governing consumer credit?*
  Consumer Credit Act 1974.
- *Which two categories of agreement does the Act referred to in the previous question cover?*
  Credit agreements and hire agreements.
- *Name two ways in which the activities of traders in the credit industry are controlled.*
  Licensing, advertising controls, a ban on canvassing off trade premises, a ban on circulars to minors, and a ban on unsolicited distribution of credit cards.
- *Who runs the credit licensing system?*
  The Office of Fair Trading.

- *What is connected lender liability?*
  This describes a situation where a person providing credit is liable for acts or omissions of the person who supplied the goods or services purchased on credit. Examples are in ss.56 and 75 of the Consumer Credit Act 1974.
- *Why were the Consumer Protection from Unfair Trading Regulations 2008 introduced?*
  To implement the EC's Unfair Commercial Practices Directive.
- *As well as a general ban on unfair practices the regulations ban four different types of unfair practice. Name them.*
  Misleading actions, misleading omissions, aggressive practices and those on the banned list in Sch.1.
- *Describe a specific practice banned by the regulations.*
  See the list of 31 practices referred to in the text.
- *What is meant in the regulations by the "average consumer"?*
  In general it means someone "who is reasonably well-informed, reasonably observant and circumspect ...". In addition, where a practice is aimed at a particular group of consumers it is the average member of that group; and the average member of a group who are particularly vulnerable.
- *What methods are used to enforce the Consumer Protection from Unfair Trading Regulations 2008?*
  Informal means, enforcement orders and criminal prosecutions.
- *Name other legislation controlling a trade practice.*
  Consumer Protection (Cancellation of Contracts Concluded away from Business Premises) Regulations 1987, Consumer Protection (Distance Selling) Regulations 2000, Timeshare Act 1992 and The Estate Agents Act 1979.

Chapter 7—E-Commerce

- *Can a contract be concluded electronically in Scots law? What is your authority for this?*
  Yes: The Requirements of Writing (Scotland) Act 1995, as amended by the Automated Title of Land (Electronic Communications) (Scotland) Order 2006 (SSI 2006/431).
- *What are "information society services"?*
  This term is defined in the E-Commerce Regulations as "any service normally provided for remuneration, at a distance, by means of electronic equipment for the processing (including digital compression) and storage of data, and at the individual request of a recipient of the service. It covers online services such as email and webhosting, as well as the sale of goods and services online.
- *What legislation regulates the provision of information society services?*
  The Electronic Commerce (EC Directive) Regulations 2002 (SI 2002/2013), which implements the Electronic Commerce Directive, 2000/31/EC.

- *What obligations are imposed on providers of information society services? (Hint: what information is required?)*
  Regulation 6 requires the provision of certain information, including details as to the geographical location of the service provider and his contact details;
  Regulations 7 and 8 require all "commercial communications", such as an email from an online retailer, to be marked as such;
  Regulation 9 requires the service provider to specify the different technical steps required to conclude the contract online.
- *What is a "distance selling" contract? (Your definition should contain five elements.)*
  A distance selling contract involves:

  - a contract
  - concerning goods or services
  - concluded between a supplier and a consumer
  - under an organised distance sales or service provision scheme
  - which makes exclusive use of one or more means of distance communication up to and including the moment at which the contract is concluded.

- *What legislation regulates distance selling contracts?*
  The Consumer Protection (Distance Selling) Regulations 2000 (SI 2000/2334) which implement the Distance Selling Directive 97/7/EC.
- *What information must be provided by sellers under a distance selling contract?*
  The key information requirements are set out in regs 7 and 8. Regulation 7 deals with pre-contractual information and includes the identity of the supplier and his address; a description of the goods or services; the price and any delivery costs or taxes; and the existence of the right of cancellation. The reg.8 information to be provided mirrors reg.7 but also includes more detail on the right to cancel, and information about after-sales services or guarantee.
- *When does the consumer's right to cancel arise? How does this cancellation affect a related credit agreement?*
  The right to cancel arises in every single case where there is a distance selling contract. Where the consumer exercises his right to cancel, any related credit agreement will also be cancelled.
- *How can these regulations be enforced by a consumer?*
  A consumer has no direct right of redress for breach of the Regulations. They must be enforced through the OFT or local trading standards: the consumer can only make a complaint to these bodies. Alternatively, the consumer can exercise his right to cancel if it is still operative.
- *What other legislation might affect suppliers and customers trading online?*

The Trade Descriptions Act 1968; the Consumer Credit Act 1974; the Unfair Contract Terms Act 1977; the Supply of Goods and Services Act 1982; the Unfair Terms in Consumer Contracts Regulations 1999; the Privacy and Electronic Communications (EC Directive) Regulations 2003; Package Travel, Package Holiday and Package Tours Regulations 1992.

Chapter 8—Employment Law

- *What are the key ingredients for a contract of service?*
  Sufficient mutuality of obligation, personal service, control and other terms being consistent with employment.
- *Can a director who is a controlling shareholder also be an employee?*
  Yes—but only if this genuinely reflects the reality of the situation and is not a sham—the extent of shareholding is a relevant but not decisive factor.
- *When does a written statement of employment particulars have to be provided by an employer?*
  Within two months of employment commencing.
- *What is a collective agreement? How can such agreements be sources of terms and conditions of employment?*
  An agreement between one or more employers (or employers associations) with one or more trade unions. Whilst such agreements are presumed not to be binding as between employer and trade union they can contain terms and conditions of employment which become incorporated in individual contracts of employment.
- *What limit does the Working Time Regulations 1998 place on maximum weekly working hours? Can employees waive their rights to this limit?*
  The Regulations provide for a maximum weekly average of 48 hours calculated over a default 17 week reference period. Individuals can opt-out of this average limit by signing opt-out agreements.
- *What is wrongful dismissal and how is this different from unfair dismissal?*
  Wrongful dismissal is essentially a termination of employment in breach of contract by the employer. The remedy of the employee is to claim damages under common law principles. Unfair dismissal is a separate statutory right not to be unfairly dismissed involving a claim to an employment tribunal.
- *What are the six potentially fair reasons for dismissal in unfair dismissal law?*
  The six potentially fair reasons are: capability/qualifications, conduct, retirement, redundancy, inability to continue working without contravening an enactment, and some other substantial reason.

- *How much continuous service is required to be eligible to claim a redundancy payment?*
  Two years continuous service.
- *Can direct sex discrimination ever be justified?*
  No—direct sex discrimination can never be justified although there are certain genuine occupational qualifications which permit employing one gender for certain roles in exceptional circumstances.
- *What is the general test for "disability" under the Disability Discrimination Act 1995?*
  The Act generally requires a claimant to establish a physical or mental impairment which has a substantial and long-term adverse effect on their ability to carry out normal day-to-day activities.

Chapter 9—Agency

- *What is the purpose of agency?*
  Agency is a mechanism which is often used in business (but is not restricted to business use) which allows one party (the principal) to use an intermediary (the agent) to enter into binding contractual arrangements with third parties. It is often used when the principal requires expertise or advice from the agent or where the principal is too busy or simply prefers that someone else looks after their commercial arrangements.
- *What are the main categories and types of agency?*
  There are many differing types and categories of agency and the labels used are not always a definitive guide to the actual agency involved. The main labels and descriptions used are general and special agency, the less common mercantile and *del credere* agency, and the newer commercial agency.
- *What are the main ways that agency can be created?*
  Agency can be created:

  - Expressly
  - By implication
  - By ratification
  - By necessity
  - By holding out

- *Give an example of agency created by implication*
  A good example arises in partnership where s.5 of the Partnership Act 1890 contains a rule of law which implies agency. If someone can be shown to factually be a partner then that factual situation combined with the rule of law in s.5 impliedly creates agency.
- *What are the conditions needed to establish agency by ratification?*

  - The agent must have been acting as an agent and disclosed this to the third party
  - The principal must have been in existence at the time of the agent's actions

- The principal must have had the necessary legal capacity to take the action in question
- The principal must have known all the facts behind the agent's actions
- The ratifications has to have taken place within any relevant time limits
- The action being ratified must itself been legal

- *What is needed for agency to exist on the basis of holding out?*
  The third party needs to believe that the 'agent' is acting as an agent and has this belief either on the basis of positive encouragement from the principal or because the principal takes no action to contradict this belief.
- *What are the main types of authority an agent may have?*

  - Express
  - Implied
  - Apparent or ostensible

- *How does apparent or ostensible authority differ from implied authority?*
  Apparent or ostensible authority will involve an impression being given to third parties that the 'agent' has authority to act on the basis of action or inaction on the part of the principal. Implied authority can come out on the basis of a broader range of circumstances which simply imply that authority exists.
- *What are the duties owed by an agent to a principal?*

  - The duty to perform instructions
  - A good faith/fiduciary duty
  - The duty to exercise skill and care
  - The duty to keep accounts

- *What rights does an agent enjoy?*

  - To be remunerated and reimbursed
  - To be relieved of liabilities
  - To enjoy rights of lien and security

- *When might an agent become liable to a third party?*
  The main situations when this can arise are when the agent acts in a way which exceeds the authority the agent has been given or the agent acts but does not disclose that he/she is acting as an agent.
- *What happens if an agent exceeds the authority given by a principal?*
  There will be no binding contract between the principal and the third party unless the principal decides to ratify the agent's actions and the agent will almost certainly be liable to the third party.
- *What is a commercial agent?*
  A commercial agent is a self employed intermediary who negotiates the sale or purchase of goods on behalf of a principal.

- *What rights do the Commercial Agents (Council Directive) Regulations give to a commercial agent?*
    - To be provided by the principal with all necessary documentation
    - To be provided by the principal with all information needed to perform the contract
    - To be notified by the principal if it is anticipated if the volume of transactions will be significantly less than the agent could have anticipated
    - To be informed by the principal within a reasonable time of the principal's acceptance or refusal of a transaction which the agent has arranged

- *What duties are owed to a principal by a commercial agent?*
  A commercial agent must act dutifully for the principal and act in good faith and look after the principal's interests.
- *How can commercial agency be terminated?*
  The most straightforward to terminate commercial agency is on the basis of notice given by either the principal or the agent. The Regulations set out the periods of notice which require to be given.

Chapter 10—Delict

- *Explain what is meant by damnum injuria datum?*
  This literally means a loss caused by a legal wrong. This is the essence of delict; the legal obligation to take responsibility for harm caused to another.
- *Which case set out the criteria for the delict of passing off?*
  Erven Warnink BV v J Townend & Sons (Hull) Ltd (No.1).
- *State the five steps used to establish a case of liability for unintentional harm?*
    - There must be a duty of care between pursuer and defender
    - The defender must have breached the duty of care by falling below the standard of care exercised by the reasonable man
    - The pursuer must have sustained a loss
    - The breach of duty of care must have been the factual and legal cause of the loss to the pursuer
    - The loss must not be too remote

- *What is a duty of care and what is the test for identifying whether a duty exists?*
  A duty of care is the responsibility owed by each person to take care in their acts and omissions so as not to cause harm to others. A duty of care can be established where there is foreseeability, proximity and it is fair, just and reasonable to impose a duty. This is the tripartite test set out in *Caparo Industries Plc v Dickman*.
- *How will the court determine whether a duty of care has been breached?*

The court will ascertain whether a pursuer has exercised less care then the reasonable man would in the same situation by applying the calculus of risk.

- *What types of loss will give rise to recovery in delict?*
Physical injury and financial losses resulting from it will give rise to a claim, as will property damage. Psychiatric injury will give rise to a claim for primary victims and for secondary victims where the three criteria set out in *Alcock v Chief Constable of South Yorkshire Police* are fulfilled. Pure economic loss will not give rise to recovery except in very limited circumstances of cases such as *Henderson v Merrett Syndicates Ltd.*

- *Explain the meaning of the term causa causans?*
The *causa causans* is the legal cause, or the dominant, effective or immediate cause, of the pursuer's loss.

- *What is the correct test for remoteness of damage?*
The correct test, following *Simmons v British Steel*, is probably the reasonable foreseeability test set out in *Overseas Tankship (UK) Ltd v Morts Dock & Engineering Co Ltd (The Wagon Mound.)*

- *What will be the effect of a finding of contributory negligence in a case of liability for unintentional harm?*
A finding of contributory negligence will reduce the pursuer's damages by the percentage by which he was found to be contributorily negligent.

- *Name the two conditions which must be satisfied before an employer will be found vicariously liable for the actions of his employee?*
A contract of employment must exist between the two parties and the employee must have been acting in the course of his duties at the time the delictual act took place.

- *What rule was set out by the case of Hunter v Hanley?*
This case set out the test of professional negligence, which is that the professional must have taken a course of action that no other reasonable professional in the same circumstances would have followed.

- *What is an interdict?*
An interdict is a court order prohibiting specific conduct which is either anticipated or ongoing.

Chapter 11—Property

- *What are the main ways in which property can be classified?*
Property may be classified into heritable property (mainly land and buildings) and moveable property (everything else). Moveable property may be classified into corporeal moveable property (things in the physical world that can be seen or touched) and incorporeal moveable property (rights).

- *What is the difference between real rights and personal rights?*
Real rights (e.g. ownership) can be enforced against anyone in the world, whereas personal rights (e.g. contractual rights) can only

be enforced against a particular person, the one who owes the corresponding obligation.

- *What are the main characteristics of registration of title?*
  The main characteristics of registration of title are:

  - the title is registered as a whole and not as a series of individual documents;
  - the validity of the title is backed by a government guarantee;
  - each property is identified on a master Ordnance Survey plan; and
  - records are held electronically, and some transactions can now be carried out electronically, by a system of automated registration of title to land (ARTL).

- *What are the main rights of ownership?*
  The main rights of ownership are:

  - the right to exclusive possession;
  - the right to freedom from interference by neighbours; and
  - rights of support.

- *In what circumstances can a person raise an action under the common law of nuisance and what remedies may be available to him or her?*
  The most common cases of nuisance arise where a person's activities interfere with the peaceful enjoyment of a neighbour's property (e.g. by the creation of noise, vibration, smoke or fumes). A nuisance must be continuing and substantial and it makes no difference that it may have predated the arrival of the complaining owner. The main remedy is interdict. Damages may also be claimed where *culpa* (blame) can be established.

- *In what respects has the law of trespass been modified by the Land Reform (Scotland) Act 2003?*
  Members of the public now have a statutory right of access to private land for recreational, educational and commercial purposes, and also the right to cross land, though subject to certain exceptions. Guidance can be found in the *Scottish Outdoor Access Code*.

- *What are the rules for determining whether or not an item is a heritable fixture?*
  An item may be a heritable fixture:

  - if it cannot be removed without damaging itself or damaging the soil or building to which it is attached;
  - if it was intended to be permanent;
  - if the building or land has been specially adapted to it;
  - if its removal would substantially affect the use and enjoyment of the property; or
  - if it is particularly heavy.

- *What are the main rules of the law of the tenement?*

The statutory law of the tenement under the Tenements (Scotland) Act 2004 provides:

- the boundary between adjacent flats etc is the mid point;
- a door or window serving one flat only is the sole property of that flat's owner;
- a top flat includes the roof over that flat and the air space up to the roof's highest point;
- a bottom flat includes the solum (the site) under the flat;
- the close, stair and landings are common property;
- a lift is normally common property;
- ground is owned by the owner of the immediately adjacent bottom flat; and
- chimney stacks are common property.

Strategic parts of the tenement have to be maintained by all owners on an equitable basis.

- *What are the main legal restrictions upon ownership?*
  The main legal restrictions upon ownership are:

  - servitudes;
  - real burdens;
  - securities; and
  - statutory controls, such as planning or building control.

- *What is meant by saying that a lease confers a real right upon a tenant?*
  A tenant's real right to a property means that, should the landlord sell the property, the lease can be enforced against the new owner.
- *What are the main legal remedies of the parties to a lease in the event of a breach of the lease contract?*
  The main breach of contract remedies of the parties to a lease are:

  - specific implement or interdict;
  - court action for debt;
  - rescission;
  - damages;
  - rent retention (tenant only);
  - hypothec (landlord only); and
  - irritancy (landlord only).

- *What are the main categories of lease and the statutes regulating them?*
  The main categories of lease are:

  - residential leases, including private sector assured and short assured tenancies (regulated by the Housing (Scotland) Acts 1988 and 2006) and social tenancies (regulated by the Housing (Scotland) Act 2001);
  - agricultural leases (regulated by the Agricultural Holdings (Scotland) Acts 1991 and 2003); and

- commercial leases (i.e. of shops, offices, factories or other business premises) which are largely free of statutory regulation in Scotland.

Chapter 12—Intellectual Property

- *What are the elements that a pursuer must establish to constitute the action of passing-off?*

  - Goodwill
  - Misrepresentation
  - Damage.

- *What are the advantages of registering trade marks?*

  - UK registered trade mark protection extends UK-wide and is not limited by the geographical scope of goodwill.
  - A mark need not have been used or acquired goodwill before registration.
  - The registered trade mark owner only needs to prove trade mark rights at application for registration and upon challenges for non-use of the registered mark, not upon every challenge as required for passing-off.
  - Once registered, to gain protection against conflicting registration or infringing use, a mark owner only needs to demonstrate public confusion in the cases of identical marks being registered or used for similar goods and services or cases of similar marks being registered or used for identical or similar goods and services, but not in the other cases of conflicting registration or infringing use.

- *Are written responses to this quick quiz protected by copyright? How?*
  Yes, if it fulfills the legislative requirements:

  - The written responses originated from the responder (hopefully),
  - They are recorded,
  - They are considered "literary works" as a subject matter which attracts copyright, and
  - If they are made by a UK citizen, resident, or domicile.

- *What intellectual property right may accrue in the THOMSON design mark?*

  - Trade mark
  - Right against passing-off
  - Copyright (both economic and moral rights)

- *What moral rights subsist in the written responses to this quick quiz?*

- The right to be identified as the author of the work, if the right has been asserted,
- The right to object to the derogatory treatment of the work, and
- The right not to have the work falsely attributed to someone other than the author of the work.

- *Can an invention which is the subject of a patent attract registered trade mark rights?*

  - No, marks which consist exclusively of shapes which are necessary to obtain a technical result are absolutely barred from registration.

- *Can a copyright work also attract design rights?*
  Yes. For this reason, the CDPA stipulates that where a work attracts copyright as well as design right, only an action in copyright would lie. However, copyright is not infringed for design documents or models recording designs for anything other than an artistic work or type face.

- *What are the advantages to registering design rights?*

  - Registered design rights last longer (up to 25 years) than CDPA design rights (up to 15 years).
  - Registration provides some evidence to the existence and priority of the right.
  - CDPA rights are only infringed where copying is shown. Such showing is not necessary as an element of registered design right infringement.
  - However, not all designs qualify for registration.

- *What are the basic criteria in determining the patentability of an invention?*

  - Novelty
  - Inventive step
  - Capable of industrial application
  - Not contrary to public policy or morality.

- *What are two basic types of patent claims?*

  - A product patent, and
  - A process patent.

Chapter 13—Trusts

- *What is a trust?*
  A trust exists where a truster transfers property to a trustee, who is under no obligation to apply that property for the benefit of the beneficiary.
- *Who owns trust property?*
  The trustee.
- *How is a voluntary trust created?*

By declaring the trust purposes and transferring the property from the truster to the trustee.

- *What restrictions does Scots law place on the validity of trust purposes?*
They must not be criminal, "directly prohibited", *contra bonos mores* or contrary to public policy.
- *Must trust decisions be taken unanimously?*
No, they can be taken by a majority.
- *What general duties does the law impose on trustees?*
A general duty of care, along with duties not to delegate the trust, to secure trust property, to invest trust property, to take advice where appropriate, to meet existing debts and obligations, to keep accounts and to pay the correct beneficiaries.
- *What is meant by the rule against auctor in rem suam?*
A trustee must not place himself in a position where his position as trustee and his interests as an individual conflict.
- *What are the sources of trustees' powers?*
The trust deed, along with the statutory powers implied under s.4 of the Trusts (Scotland) Act 1921. It is possible to apply to the court for additional powers in some cases.
- *When a trustee has been in breach of trust, what remedies are open to the beneficiaries?*
The principal remedies are an action for interdict, damages, or "count, reckoning and payment" ("accounting").
- *How may trustees be protected from liability for breach of trust?*
By an immunity clause in the trust deed, or by relying on statutory defences available to trustees who act honestly and reasonably or commit a breach of trust at a beneficiary's instigation.
- *Are trustees personally liable on trust contracts?*
Yes, unless there is an agreement to the contrary.
- *What requirements must be satisfied before the terms of a private trust can be varied? To what extent is the court involved in this process?*
All the beneficiaries must consent. The court has a power to consent on behalf of beneficiaries who are incapable of doing so if certain conditions are met.

Chapter 14—Choice of Business Medium

- *What is a sole trader?*
A sole trader is an individual involved in the management and control of his/her own business.
- *What is a Partnership?*
A partnership is the relation which subsists between persons carrying on a business in common with a view of profit.
- *How are the sole trader, partnership, LLP and incorporated company distinct?*
Companies and LLPs are both bodies corporate whereas sole traders and partnerships are not. Partnerships and companies

possess legal personality and are legally distinct from their partners, members and managers/directors. This can be contrasted with the sole trader which has no separate legal personality.

- *What is meant by personal liability in this context?*
Personal liability means that the owners or members of an organisation are fully liable for the debts of that organisation.

- *What is meant by limited liability?*
Limited liability means that the owners or members of an organisation enjoy limited liability for the debts of that organisation. The extent of the limitation is regulated by the limited liability partnership agreement in the case of an LLP and in the case of an incorporated company limited by shares, the shareholder's liability is limited to the value which remains unpaid on their shares. In the case of an incorporated company limited by guarantee, the extent of a member's liability is limited to the monetary value which they have agreed to contribute towards the debts of the company on a winding up in terms of the memorandum of association.

- *What does separate legal personality mean?*
An organisation has separate legal personality when it is an organisation which is distinct from its members, partners or owners.

- *Explain the concept of perpetual succession?*
If an organisation possesses perpetual succession, this means that it is not dissolved or terminated by a change in the composition of its membership or management. In other words, it continues to exist notwithstanding such changes.

- *Explain what is meant by a division of ownership and control?*
If an organisation exhibits a separation between ownership and control, this means that a manager of the organisation does not require to be an owner or vice versa and thus it is easier to obtain outside capital investment since investors know that they do not necessarily need to participate in the management of the business.

Chapter 15—The Law of Partnership

- *What is a partnership and what are its main attributes?*
A partnership is the relation which subsists between persons carrying on a business in common with a view of profit. It is a separate legal person distinct from its partners in terms of Scots law—s.4(2) of the Partnership Act 1890. A partnership can be constituted in writing or orally. It may also be inferred from the actions of the parties and in particular the attributes of their relationship towards each other. Where the relationship between partners amounts to a partnership, they are deemed to be fiduciaries.

- *What are the rules for determining whether the partnership or other partners are liable for wrongs, delicts or omissions of a partner which have caused injury or loss to a third party?*

- Where a partner commits a wrongful act or omits to act in the ordinary course of the business of the partnership, or with the authority of his co-partners, loss or injury is caused to a third party, or any penalty is incurred, the partnership is liable to the same extent as the partner so acting or omitting to act.
- Where a partner in a firm of solicitors dishonestly assists a client in perpetrating a fraud by drafting bogus agreements, this will amount to the ordinary course of the business of the partnership, since drafting and advising on agreements is part and portion of the business of a firm of solicitors—*Dubai Aluminium v Salaam* [2003] 2 A.C. 366.
- *Which rules in the Act regulate partnership property?*
  Property purchased with the money of the partnership or on account of the partnership in the ordinary course of the business of the partnership, is deemed to be partnership property. Such property must be held by the partners exclusively for the purposes of the partnership and in accordance with the partnership agreement—s.20(1) of the Act.
- *Can the partners dismiss a partner by majority vote?*
  No. Section 25 of the Act states that unanimity is required. However, the partnership agreement may provide otherwise.
- *Is a partnership legally bound where a third party enters into a contract with the partnership knowing that the partner has no authority to bind the partnership?*
  No. See s.5 of the Act.
- *Is a partner entitled to retain a personal profit?*
  No. A partner is a fiduciary and owes fiduciary obligations to the partnership which involve full disclosure and accounting to the partnership for private profits. See s.29 of the Act.
- *Is a provision in the partnership agreement which provides that the partnership will continue notwithstanding the death of a partner a lawful provision which will be upheld by the courts?*
  Yes. The general rule in s.33(1) of the Act is that the death of a partner automatically dissolves the partnership. However, this rule may be disapplied by the partnership agreement. A prime example of this technique is provided by *W S Gordon & Co. Ltd. v Thomson Partnership* 1985 S.L.T. 122.
- *Section 35(f) of the Act stipulates that a partnership can be dissolved by the court where it is 'just and equitable'. What does this mean?*
  There is no straightforward answer to this question. The concept of "just and equitable" is very wide and flexible. However, one can point to past case law and in particular the case of Sutherland v Barnes (Unreported, October 8, 1997, Vinelott J (CA)) for examples of what the courts have considered to be 'just and equitable' grounds for dissolution. Here it was held that it was "just and equitable" to dissolve a partnership in circumstances where the relationship of trust and confidence had irrevocably broken down between the partners of the partnership.

- *I don't understand the case of Dubai Aluminium v Salaam [2003] 2 A.C. 366. How can it be logical that a partnership is liable to third parties under section 10 of the Act for the fraudulent activities of a partner?*
  The relevant question is not whether fraud is "in the ordinary course of the business of the" partnership in terms of s.10 of the Act. Instead, one must focus on the general acts of the partner in perpetrating the fraud and ask whether they were so closely connected with the acts which that partner was authorised to do that those actions might fairly and properly be considered as done by the partner whilst acting in the ordinary course of the firm's business. In Dubai Aluminium, the House of Lords held that the general acts of the partner in perpetrating the fraud were the drafting and negotiation of bogus agreements. Since the drafting of agreements were acts which partners in law firms were authorized to do as part of the partnership's business, such acts were within the ordinary course of the firm's business and so the partnership was liable to third parties for losses which the latter had sustained as a result of the perpetration of the fraud.
- *What is joint and several liability?*
  Partners are jointly and severally liable for the debts of the partnership. This means that an injured third party may sue one partner, some partners or all of the partners to recover debts, damages or compensation which is due to them by the partnership. The third party also has the right to sue such partners for different amounts and if they do so, s.4(2) of the Act applies to settle matters amongst the partners.

Chapter 16—Company Law

- *What are the sources of company law?*
  The sources of company law may be divided into a number of categories, as follows:

  - Primary legislation
  - Subordinate legislation
  - The common law
  - Extra-legal rules

- *What are the objectives and purposes of company law?*
  Company law is concerned with the regulation of the power, rights, duties and liabilities of companies and constituencies which are closely connected with the company, namely the company's directors, managers, members/shareholders and creditors.
- *What are the core features of companies?*

  - The shareholders of limited liability companies enjoy limited liability for the debts of the company
  - A company is a body corporate having separate legal personality distinct from its constituent members and so can be

sued, sue third parties in its own name, enter into contracts, own property in its own name, etc.

- Companies have the power to issue transferable shares to shareholders/investors as a means of raising corporate finance
- There is a natural division between ownership of the company and its control
- The ease with which a company can replace poorly performing directors with specialised management as a means of turning around the fortunes of the company.
- A company enjoys the attribute of perpetual succession and only on the completion of a liquidation or the implementation of a striking out in terms of the Insolvency Act 1986 or the Companies Act 2006 will a company cease to exist.
- A company has the ability to grant a floating charge which is a kind of enterprise security which can be granted over the entirety of the assets and undertaking of a company to a lender in exchange for debt funding.

- *What are the main types of company?*
  Companies may be divided into three different categories:

    (i) Limited liability companies v unlimited companies
    (ii) Companies limited by shares v companies limited by guarantee
    (iii) Private companies and public

- *What documentation is required to incorporate a company?*

    (i) The company's memorandum of association—s.8 of the Act;
    (ii) The company's articles of association, unless the company is proposing to adopt the model articles of association referred to in s.20 of the Act—s.9(5)(b) of the Companies Act 2006;
    (iii) A statement of compliance—ss.9(1) and 13 of the Act; and
    (iv) An application for registration—s.9 of the Act.

- *What are the constitutional documents of the company?*

    1. Memorandum of Association
    2. Articles of Association

- *What is the memorandum of association?*
  The memorandum of association of a company is a document which states that the subscribers (i) wish to form a company under the Act and (ii) agree to become members of the company and, in the case of a company that is to have a share capital, to take at least one share each. It must be subscribed by each member on incorporation of the company—s.8 of the Act.
- *What are the articles of association of the company?*

The articles regulate the internal affairs of the company and contain provisions on the division of authority between the directors and the members, the powers and responsibilities of directors, decision-making by directors, the appointment of directors, the organisation of, and voting at, general meetings, provisions on shares, transfers of shares and distributions of income amongst the members.

- *What is the legal effect of the articles of association?*
  Section 33 of the Act provides that the articles represent a "contract" entered into between the members and the company and the members inter se. Accordingly, the members of the company can enforce the articles as a "contract" against the company and the company can enforce the articles against the members.

- *What are trading disclosures?*
  Trading disclosures enjoin a company to display, state and provide information about itself in certain locations and communications (e.g. business letters, letters of credit, licences, business correspondence, business communications, invoices, bills of exchange, etc.), including its name and registered office.

- *What is an annual return?*
  A company must complete and submit an annual return to the Registrar of Companies. It includes information about the registered office address of the company, the nature of the company, e.g. whether it is private or public, its principal business activities, details of the directors and company secretary of the company, details of any changes in the members of the company and the share capital of the company (including details of transfers of shares in the company and classes of shares) since the last annual return date—ss.854–859 of the Act.

- *Through what organs can a company act?*
  The company can act through two organs, namely its board of directors and the members in (a) general meeting and (b) in the case of a private company, outwith general meeting by written resolution procedure under the Act.

- *Explain the role of the company secretary.*
  The company secretary performs an administrative role, dealing with official correspondence on behalf of the company, maintaining the statutory registers and ensuring that the filing and other administrative obligations imposed on the company are complied with in accordance with the terms of the Act.

- *What is the role of a company director?*
  A director is the agent of the company and is responsible for the management and direction of the company.

- *How many directors must a company have?*
  Every private company must have at least one director and a public company must have no less than 2 directors—s.154 of the Act.

- *Are there any restrictions on who can be a director?*

Persons under 16 years of age are not eligible for appointment as a director and an undischarged bankrupt cannot be appointed as a director of a company without the prior leave of the court—s.157(1) of the Act and s.11 of the Company Directors Disqualification Act 1986.

- *List the different types of directors.*
  Directors may be:
  (i) executive directors who are involved in the "day-to-day" management of the business, take executive decisions on behalf of the company and
  (ii) non-executive directors who do not directly run or manage the business of the company. Directors may also be shadow directors.

- *Explain how directors can be removed in terms of the law?*
  Directors may be removed by an ordinary resolution of the members of the company by special notice procedure—ss.168(1) and 312 of the Act. At a general meeting, the director has the right to protest his or her removal and has a right to be heard—s.169 of the Act.

- *To whom do directors owe their duties?*
  Directors owe their duties to the company—s.170(1) of the Act. Having said that, the directors will owe their duties to the creditors of the company in terms of the common law where the company is of doubtful solvency or is insolvent.

- *What is the general meeting and what is its purpose?*
  The general meeting is the place where the members of the company can come together to consider the performance of the directors of the company and vote on matters which the Act and the articles of association of the company specify must be passed by ordinary or special resolution.

- *Who has the power to call general meetings?*
  The directors, 10 per cent of the members (in voting terms) and the court have the power to call a general meeting—ss.302, 303 and 306 of the Act.

- *How much notice must be given of general meetings?*
  Subject to any longer period of notice stipulated in the articles, a general meeting of a private company requires 14 days prior notice to the members. In the case of a plc, a general meeting must be called by 21 days' prior notice to the members in the case of an AGM or 14 days' prior notice to the members in the case of any other general meeting.

- *What information must be included in a notice of a general meeting?*
  The time, date and place of the meeting must be detailed, including the general nature of the business to be dealt with at the meeting, but this is subject to any provision in the company's articles—s.311 of the Act. In the case of an AGM of a public company, it is legal requirement for the plc to specify in the notice that the meeting is an annual general meeting—ss.307 and 337 of the Act.

- *What is a Proxy?*

A proxy is a person who attends a general meeting on behalf of a member and has the right to speak and vote at a general meeting on behalf of his appointing member on a show of hands or on a poll. A proxy also has the right to demand a vote on a poll and to be appointed as the chairman of the meeting—ss.324, 328 and 329 of the Act.

- *What is an ordinary resolution?*
An ordinary resolution of the members of a company or of a class of members of a company means a resolution that is passed by a simple majority of the members—s. 282 of the Act.

- *What is a special resolution?*
A special resolution of the members of a company or of a class of members of a company means a resolution that is passed by a majority of not less than 75 per cent—s.283 of the Act.

- *What is a written resolution?*
In the case of a private company only, an ordinary resolution or special resolution may be passed as a written resolution outwith a general meeting of the company in accordance with the written resolution procedure contained in the Act—s.288 of the Act.

- *What is a share?*
A share is the interest of a shareholder in the company measured by a sum of money, for the purpose of liability in the first place, and of interest in the second, but also consisting of a series of mutual covenants entered into by all the shareholders inter se in accordance with the Act—*Borland's Trustee v Steel Bros & Co. Ltd* [1901] 1 Ch. 279, 288 per Farwell J.

- *What is meant by different classes of shares?*
A share belongs to a class where the articles of association attach certain rights to that class which can be distinguished from rights attaching to shares of another class.

- *How can shares be acquired?*
Shares may be acquired by original acquisition, i.e. by an allotment and issue of fresh shares or derivative acquisition, i.e. by the transfer or transmission of shares.

- *What is a prospectus?*
A prospectus is a document which a public company must issue if it is seeking to offer its shares to the public in return for capital investment.

- *What is a debenture?*
A debenture is a debt instrument, sometimes also known as a bond, loan stock or loan notes issued by a company in return for capital investment.

- *What protections are available to minority shareholders?*
Minority shareholders may (i) raise common law derivative proceedings, (ii) statutory derivative proceedings or (iii) present a petition to the court on the basis that they are suffering from unfair prejudice.

Chapter 17—Insolvency

- *Explain briefly what is meant by insolvency.*
  Insolvency is the situation where an individual or other legal entity is incapable of paying its debts.
- *What is a trustee in sequestration's main function?*
  The main function of the trustee in sequestration is to ingather the assets of an individual who has been declared bankrupt and, as far as possible, to use these assets to pay off the individual's debts.
- *After what period of time will a debtor be discharged from bankruptcy?*
  Under s.1 of the Bankruptcy and Diligence etc. (Scotland) Act 2007, a debtor will be discharged from bankruptcy after 1 year.
- *Explain briefly the diligences of arrestment, attachment and inhibition.*
  Arrestment is a process by which certain assets of the debtor being held by third parties are "frozen", and will be handed over in time to the relevant creditor. Attachment is a process by which certain assets of the debtor are seized and sold, with a view to paying off the creditor executing the attachment. Inhibition is where restrictions are put on the debtor's use of his property, with a view to encouraging repayment of a debt.
- *What are the benefits of a company voluntary arrangement to a company that is facing financial difficulty?*
  A CVA (company voluntary arrangement) allows a company to agree, with its creditors, a scheme for repayment of its debts. This is beneficial because it allows the company to continue trading, and affords an opportunity to remedy its financial problems without the normality of other procedures.
- *What is the main purpose of administration?*
  The main purpose of administration is to improve a company's financial position. The ideal situation is that the company is rescued from its financial problems and allowed to continue as a going concern, but this is not always possible.
- *Under what circumstances can a creditor of a company appoint a receiver?*
  A creditor can only appoint a receiver if he holds a floating charge over the company's assets but, since September 2003 and the coming into force of the Enterprise Act 2002, many floating charge holders will now be required to appoint an administrator rather than a receiver.)
- *In terms of insolvency procedures, why is administration often seen as a preferable alternative to receivership?*
  Administration is generally seen as preferable to receivership because it involves an attempt to improve the company's financial position, which is to the benefit of all creditors. Receivership does not have this objective, and aims instead to repay only the floating charge holder.

- *Briefly outline any two circumstances that might justify a company being put into liquidation.*
There are a number of circumstances that would justify a company being put into liquidation. The most common reason is that the company is unable to pay its debts. Other circumstances include: if the company passes a special resolution to this effect; if a plc fails to obtain a trading certificate within 12 months of incorporation; if the company is an "old" public company; if the company has not commenced its business within one year of incorporation, or suspends its business for a year; if the membership of a plc falls below 2; if the court is of the opinion that it is just and equitable that the company should be wound up.
- *What is the essential difference between a members' voluntary winding up and a creditors' voluntary winding up?*
The essential difference between a members' voluntary winding up and a creditors' voluntary winding up is the declaration of solvency. Essentially, if there is no doubt that the company will be able to pay off all of its existing debt, the creditors need not be involved, and the liquidation can proceed as a members' voluntary winding up. However, if there is a possibility that not all debts will be paid, the liquidation must proceed as a creditors' voluntary winding up.

Chapter 18—Negotiable Instruments

- *A bill of exchange is always payable on demand*
True/False
Commercial bills and promissory notes may be payable at a specified date in the future or on demand or on sight. However, a cheque is payable on demand, unless it is post-dated.
- *A bearer bill cannot be negotiated*
False
A bearer bill is negotiated by delivery. On the other hand, a bill made payable to order is negotiated by indorsement and delivery. If no indorsee is named on the bill this is known as a blank indorsement and the bill then becomes a bearer bill.
- *A holder who is also a holder for value and a holder in due course is entitled to be paid even if the person he bought the bill from came by it dishonestly*
True
A bill "stands on its own two feet" and is treated as a cash equivalent. If the holder in due course is unaware of any defect in the title he can enforce payment against the drawer and any indorser. This is an exception to the *nemo dat quem non habet* rule.
- *Overdue bills cannot be paid in any circumstance*
False
Although a commercial bill should be presented for payment on the date specified on the face of the bill if the delay is due to circumstances beyond the control of the bearer he will still be

entitled to payment. In the case of a bill payable on demand it will be held to be overdue if it has been in circulation for an unreasonable length of time. Banking practice, however, sees banks treat a cheque which has not been presented within six months as stale.

- *A crossed cheque must be paid into the payee's bank account*
True
Section 79(2) of the 1882 Act applies. If a bank fails to abide by this stipulation and pays in cash a cheque bearing the words account payee the bank will be liable to the true owner of the cheque if it turns out that the cheque has been stolen.

Chapter 19—Rights in Security

- *A real right in security is always to be preferred to a personal right.*
True
A real right in security differs from a personal right in that it gives the creditor a nexus or a bond, over heritable or moveable property belonging to the debtor. A personal right in security is inferior to that of a real right, given it is only of any practical effect if the guarantor is solvent and in a position to honour the debtor's liability to the creditor.
- *A contract of guarantee is a principal obligation.*
False
A contract of guarantee is an accessory obligation which means that the principal debt must exist or be in the contemplation of the parties, before it can be enforced against the guarantor. It follows that the guarantor's liability to the creditor is in addition to that of the principal debtor and can only be enforced if the debtor fails to pay.
- *The guarantor enjoys no right of relief against the debtor if required to pay the creditor on his behalf.*
False
The guarantor who has paid the debt has a right of relief, which is to claim the sum paid, including expenses, from the debtor. This right will exist for a period of 5 years after the debt has been paid.
- *A guarantee is considered a contract uberrimae fidei.*
False
There is no general duty placed on the creditor to disclose the financial standing of the debtor to the creditor. However, a creditor will be under a duty to act in good faith where a proximate relationship exists between the debtor and the guarantor and the creditor is aware of the nature of the relationship between the parties. This duty is discharged if the creditor takes reasonable steps to enquire whether the party with no financial interest in the venture guaranteed has entered into the guarantee in full knowledge of the risk involved and without undue influence being exerted, or through any misrepresentation made, by the debtor.

- *A real right in security can only be created where there is delivery of the property subject to the security.*
  False
  It is a general rule of Scots law that a real right can only be created if there is delivery from the debtor to the creditor; however there are exceptions to this rule, namely hypothecs and floating charges.
- *A floating charge is said to crystallise if the company concerned goes into liquidation or a receiver is appointed.*
  True
  Until this occurs, the charge floats over the assets of the company undisturbed enabling the company to use the property, dispose of it or add further assets to its holdings.
- *Pledge may only be constituted by actual delivery of the property concerned.*
  False
  Pledge can also be created by constructive or symbolic delivery of the property to the pledgee.
- *A real right in security over incorporeal moveable property can only be created via assignation and intimation.*
  False
  Although this is the general rule, intimation is not always possible. This will arise where there is no actual debtor to inform that assignation has taken place. However, the real right will not be constituted until the assignation is registered, if registration is required by law.

Chapter 20—Dispute Resolution

- *Do the parties to a business dispute have to hire lawyers in the negotiation process?*
  No.
- *What are the main features of mediation?*
  Mediation is an informal dispute resolution where the parties try to reach an agreement with the help of mediator. However, the decision made by the mediator has no binding force on the parties.
- *What are the advantages and disadvantages of using commercial arbitration to resolve business disputes?*
  Advantages: Speedy, confidentiality, privacy, party autonomy and the binding effect of the arbitral awards.
  Disadvantages: Arbitrator's lack of coercive power.
- *What are the statutes regulating domestic arbitration in Scotland?*

  - 25th Act of the Article of Regulation 1695 which lays down grounds on which the validity of awards may be challenged,
  - The Arbitration (Scotland) Act 1894 regulates the naming of arbitrators and the court's power to appoint arbitrators,
  - The Administration of Justice (Scotland) Act 1972 stipulates the stated case procedure,

- The Arbitration Act 1996, ss.89—91 and Schs 3 and 4.
- *What duties does an arbiter have?*
  To act independently, impartially and with due diligence to resolve the disputes.
- *What is the legal effect of an arbitral award?*
  An arbitral award has binding force on the parties.
- *Which form of alternative dispute resolution is widely adopted for construction disputes and which statute provides the legal framework for such method?*
  Adjudication: the Housing, Grants, Construction and Regeneration Act 1996.
- *What is the limit of claim for the Court of Session?*
  A claim over £5,000.
- *What is the limit of claim for an ordinary cause action in a Sheriff court?*
  A claim over £5,000.
- *What is the limit of claim for a summary cause action?*
  A claim between £3,000 and £5,000.
- *What is the limit of claim for a small claim procedure?*
  A claim below £3,000.

Index

Abuse of dominant position
competition law, and, 3–53
Abuse of position
facility and circumvention, 4–57
force and fear, 4–56
introduction, 4–55
undue influence, 4–58
Academic writings
generally, 1–50
importance, 1–51
Acceptance
communication of
delayed, 4–26
instantaneous, 4–25
introduction, 4–25
generally, 4–21
Acceptance of goods
e-commerce, and, 7–16
Access rights
property, and, 11–27
Accounting
trustee liabilities, and, 13–47
Accounts
agents' duties, and, 9–27
Acquisition of own shares
general, 16–60
prohibition against financial assistance,
16–61
Action for debt
breach of contract, and, 4–86
leases, and, 11–60
Action for price
sale of goods, and, 5–23
Actus reus
causation, 3–07
embezzlement, 3–23
extortion, 3–26
fraud, 3–24
generally, 3–06
state of affairs, 3–08
theft, 3–22
uttering, 3–25
Adjudication
generally, 20–23
legal framework, 20–24
Adjudicators
Ombudsmen, and, 2–57
Administration
appointment of administrator
company, by, 17–36
court, by, 17–33

Administration—*cont.*
appointment of administrator—*cont.*
directors, by, 17–36
effect, 17–37
out of court, 17–34—17–36
QFCH, 17–35
ending, 17–39
introduction, 17–31
process, 17–38
purposes, 17–32
**Administrative Justice and Tribunals
Council**
generally, 2–43
Administrative tribunals
generally, 2–46—2–49
Advertising
consumer credit, and, 6–15
Advocate Deputes
generally, 2–64
Advocate General
generally, 2–80
Advocates
Advocate Deputes, 2–64
generally, 2–62
Queens Counsel, 2–63
Agency
accounting, 9–27
agent's authority
apparent authority, 9–22
express authority, 9–20
implied authority, 9–21
introduction, 9–19
ostensible authority, 9–22
agent's duties
account, to, 9–27
act personally, to, 9–26
conflicts of interest, and, 9–29
disclosure of information, and, 9–28
exercise skill and care, 9–30
fiduciary, 9–25
good faith, 9–25—9–29
introduction, 9–23
keep accounts, to, 9–31
performance of instructions, 9–24
agent's rights
introduction, 9–32
lien, 9–35
reimbursement, 9–33
relieved of liabilities, to be, 9–34
remuneration, 9–33
security, 9–35

Agency—*cont.*
  apparent authority, 9–22
  commercial agents
    background to regulation, 9–45
    commission, 9–49
    compensation, 9–51
    duties, 9–47
    indemnity, 9–51
    meaning, 9–46
    remuneration, 9–49
    rights, 9–48
    termination of agency, 9–50
  company directors, and, 9–11
  conflicts of interest, and, 9–29
  disclosure of information, and, 9–28
  creation
    express, 9–13
    holding out, by, 9–17
    implied, 9–14
    introduction, 9–12
    necessity, by, 9–16
    ratification, by, 9–15
  del credere agents, 9–07
  examples
    company directors, 9–11
    introduction, 9–08
    partners, 9–10
    solicitors, 9–09
  express authority, 9–20
  express creation, 9–13
  features, 9–03
  fiduciary duty, 9–25
  frustration, and, 9–44
  general agents, 9–05
  good faith obligation
    account, to, 9–27
    act personally, to, 9–26
    conflicts of interest, and, 9–29
    disclosure of information, and, 9–28
    introduction, 9–25
  holding out, 9–17
  implied authority, 9–21
  implied creation, 9–14
  indemnification of agent, 9–34
  introduction, 9–03
  judicial precedent, and, 1–36
  keeping accounts, 9–31
  lien, 9–35
  meaning, 9–03
  mercantile agents, 9–06
  necessity, 9–16
  ostensible authority, 9–22
  overview, 9–01—9–02
  partners, and, 9–10
  performance of instructions, 9–24
  principal's duties, 9–32—9–35
  principal's rights, 9–23—9–31
  ratification, 9–15
  reimbursement of agent, 9–33

Agency—*cont.*
  relationship
    agent's authority, 9–19—9–22
    agent's duties, 9–23—9–31
    agent's rights, 9–32—9–35
    introduction, 9–18
    principal's duties, 9–32—9–35
    principal's rights, 9–23—9–31
  remuneration of agent, 9–33
  security, 9–35
  solicitors, and, 9–09
  termination
    agent, by, 9–42
    contract, under, 9–43
    frustration, by, 9–44
    introduction, 9–41
    principal, by, 9–42
  third parties, and
    agent acts as an agent, 9–36—9–39
    agent exceeds authority, 9–40
    introduction, 9–36
    principal disclosed and named, 9–37
    principal disclosed but not named,
      9–38
    principal neither disclosed nor named,
      9–39
  types of agent, 9–04—9–07
Agency workers
  employment law, and, 8–06
Aggressive practices
  unfair trading, and, 6–46
Agreement
  lack of formalities, 4–05
  number of parties, 4–04
  relevant circumstances, 4–06
Agricultural leases
  generally, 11–63
Alienation
  leases, and, 11–65
Alternative dispute resolution
  adjudication
    generally, 20–23
    legal framework, 20–24
  advantages, 20–03
  arbitration
    agreements, 20–10
    applicable laws, 20–11
    appointment of arbitrators, 20–12
    arbitral tribunal, 20–12
    award, 20–18—20–21
    duties of arbiters, 20–14
    enforcement of award, 20–21
    immunity of arbiters, 20–15
    introduction, 20–07
    jurisdiction of arbiters, 20–13
    legal framework, 20–08
    party autonomy doctrine, 20–09
    recognition of award, 20–21
    relationship with courts, 20–16
    Scottish Arbitration Code, 20–22

Alternative dispute resolution—*cont.*
  arbitration—*cont.*
    setting aside awards, 20–20
    stated case procedure, 20–17
    types of award, 20–19
  conclusion, 20–33
  court actions
    generally, 20–25
    jurisdiction, 20–26
    value of claim, 20–27—20–32
  disadvantages, 20–03
  employment law, and, 8–21
  mediation
    introduction, 20–05
    process, 20–06
  negotiation, 20–04
  overview, 20–01—20–02
  summary, 20–34
Animals
  delict, and, 10–38
  trusts, and, 13–21
Annual accounts
  audit, 16–17
  introduction, 16–15
  laying documents, 16–16
  submission of accounts, 16–16
Annual general meetings
  calling, 16–38
  general, 16–37
  introduction, 16–36
  notice, 16–40
  ordinary resolutions, 16–44
  procedure, 16–41
  proxies, 16–42
  public companies, of, 16–39
  resolutions
    general, 16–43
    ordinary, 16–44
    special, 16–45
    voting of members, 16–46
    written, 16–47
  special resolutions, 16–45
  voting of members, 16–46
Annual return
  companies, and, 16–14
Antecedent negotiations
  consumer credit, and, 6–28
Anticipatory breach
  breach of contract, and, 4–79
Anti-competitive agreements
  competition law, and, 3–50—3–52
Apparent authority
  agents, and, 9–22
Appeals
  civil courts, and, 2–17
  High Court of Justiciary, and, 2–37
Arbitration
  agreements, 20–10
  applicable laws, 20–11
  appointment of arbitrators, 20–12

Arbitration—*cont.*
  arbitral tribunal, 20–12
  award, 20–18—20–21
  duties of arbiters, 20–14
  enforcement of award, 20–21
  immunity of arbiters, 20–15
  introduction, 20–07
  jurisdiction of arbiters, 20–13
  legal framework, 20–08
  party autonomy doctrine, 20–09
  recognition of award, 20–21
  relationship with courts, 20–16
  Scottish Arbitration Code, 20–22
  setting aside awards, 20–20
  stated case procedure, 20–17
  types of award, 20–19
Arrestment
  diligence, and, 17–21
Art and part liability
  criminal law, and, 3–16
Articles of association
  companies, and, 16–10
Assault
  delict, and, 10–06
Attachment
  diligence, and, 17–22
Auctor in rem suam
  trustees, and, 13–40
Audits
  companies, and, 16–17

B2B contracts
  e-commerce, and, 7–05
Bankruptcy restrictions orders
  sequestration, and, 17–16
Bankruptcy restrictions undertakings
  sequestration, and, 17–16
Banned practices
  unfair trading, and, 6–40
Barter
  See also **Sale of goods**
  generally, 5–03
"Battle of the forms"
  offer and acceptance, and, 4–24
Bills of exchange
  alterations, 18–14
  benefits, 18–04
  definition, 18–07
  form, 18–08
  holders
    for value, 18–11
    generally, 18–10
    in due course, 18–12
  indorsement, 18–09
  liability, 18–13
  lost bills, 18–16
  origins, 18–03
  overdue bills, 18–15
  parties, 18–05
  terminology, 18–06

Breach of contract
action for debt, 4–86
anticipatory breach, 4–79
damages
causation requirement, 4–91
compensatory nature, 4–90
duty to mitigate loss, 4–92
generally, 4–89
liquidate damages, 4–94
remoteness of loss, 4–93
employment contracts, and, 8–17
interdict, 4–88
introduction, 4–78
judicial remedies
action for debt, 4–86
damages, 4–89—4–94
interdict, 4–88
introduction, 4–85
specific implement, 4–87
jus quaesitum tertio, 4–96
lien, 4–84
liquidate damages, 4–94
parties to claims
exception to rule, 4–96
general rule, 4–95
privity of contract, and, 4–95
remedies
introduction, 4–80
judicial remedies, 4–85—4–94
self-help remedies, 4–81—4–84
rescission, 4–82
retention, 4–83
self-help remedies
introduction, 4–81
lien, 4–84
rescission, 4–82
retention, 4–83
specific implement, 4–87
Breach of duty
expense of precautions, 10–22
introduction, 10–19
likelihood of harm, 10–20
likely seriousness of injury, 10–21
purpose of conduct causing harm, 10–23
Breach of statutory duty
animals, 10–38
introduction, 10–36
occupiers' liability, 10–39
product liability, 10–37
Building controls
property, and, 11–55
Business regulation
common law crimes
embezzlement, 3–23
extortion, 3–26
fraud, 3–24
introduction, 3–21
theft. 3–22
uttering, 3–25

Business regulation—*cont.*
competition law
abuse of dominant position, 3–53
anti-competitive agreements,
3–50—3–52
enforcement, 3–54
generally, 3–49
market-sharing agreements, 3–52
merger control, 3–55
price fixing, 3–51
corporate homicide, 3–41
criminal law
actus reus, 3–06—3–08
art and part liability, 3–16
causation, 3–07
common law crimes, 3–21—3–26
corporate liability, 3–18
defences, 3–20
elements of offences, 3–05—3–14
error, 3–14
inchoate offences, 3–19
intention, 3–10
introduction, 3–03
knowledge, 3–12
mens rea, 3–09—3–14
nature, 3–04
omission, 3–06
recklessness, 3–11
state of affairs, 3–08
strict liability, 3–15
vicarious liability, 3–17
data protection
data subjects' rights, 3–47
definitions, 3–45
enforcement, 3–47—3–48
introduction, 3–44
principles, 3–46
environmental law, 3–56
health and safety
corporate homicide, and, 3–41
employers' duties, 3–30—3–34
enforcement, 3–40
introduction, 3–29
regulations, 3–35—3–39
merger control, 3–55
misleading consumer information, 3–42
misuse of data, 3–43
overview, 3–01—3–02
regulatory law and offences
competition law, 3–49—3–54
corporate homicide, 3–41
data protection, 3–44—3–48
environmental law, 3–56
generally, 3–28
health and safety, 3–29—3–40
introduction, 3–27
merger control, 3–55
misleading consumer information,
3–42
misuse of data, 3–43

Business regulation—*cont.*
self-regulation, 3–27
summary, 3–57
Business medium
companies
advantages, 14–10
disadvantages, 14–11
introduction, 14–09
limited liability partnerships
advantages, 14–13
disadvantages, 14–13
introduction, 14–12
overview, 14–01—14–02
partnerships
advantages, 14–07
continuity, 14–05
disadvantages, 14–09
introduction, 14–04
legal personality, 14–05
statutory regulation, 14–06
sole trader, 14–03
summary, 14–14
"But for" test
delict, and, 10–27

Cancellation
consumer credit, and, 6–25
consumer protection, and, 6–52
e-commerce, and, 7–11
Canvassing
consumer credit, and, 6–16
Capacity
basis of contracts, and, 4–03
corporations, 4–54
insanity, 4–52
intoxication, 4–53
introduction, 4–50
non-age, 4–51
Causation
criminal law, and, 3–07
delict, and, 10–27
Cautionary obligations
constitution, 19–05
contra proferentum rule, 19–09
creditors' duty of good faith, 19–11
extent of liability, 19–06
extinction, 19–13
guarantor's rights, 19–07—19–08
grounds to invalidate, 19–10—19–12
introduction, 19–04
overview, 19–01
relief against co-guarantors, 19–08
relief against debtor, 19–07
unenforceable guarantees, 19–12
void guarantees, 19–10
Cheques
clearing, 18–21
crossed, 18–20
generally, 18–17
liability, 18–22

Cheques—*cont.*
parties, 18–18
stale, 18–19
undated, 18–19
Circulars to minors
consumer credit, and, 6–17
Civil courts
appeals, 2–17
Court of Session
generally, 2–18
Inner House, 2–20
Outer House, 2–19
Court of the Lord Lyon, 2–28
House of Lords, 2–21
introduction, 2–06—2–07
Judicial Committee of the Privy Council,
2–22
judicial precedent, and
Court of Session, 1–42
House of Lords, 1–41
introduction, 1–40
jurisdiction, 2–09
key concepts, 2–06
Lands Tribunal for Scotland, 2–27
ordinary cause, 2–14
organisation, 2–08
other courts, 2–24—2–28
persons, 2–10
procedures, 2–13
Scottish Land Court, 2–26
small claims, 2–16
subject matter, 2–12
summary cause, 2–15
Supreme Court, 2–23
terminology, 2–06
VAT and Duties Tribunal, 2–25
Civil law
categories of law, and, 1–15—1–16
Collective agreements
employment law, and, 8–10
Commercial agents
background to regulation, 9–45
commission, 9–49
compensation, 9–51
duties, 9–47
indemnity, 9–51
meaning, 9–46
remuneration, 9–49
rights, 9–48
termination of agency, 9–50
Commercial leases
generally, 11–64—11–65
Common law
categories of law, and, 1–16—1–17
Companies
acquisition of own shares
general, 16–60
prohibition against financial
assistance, 16–61
administrative matters, 16–11—16–17

Companies—*cont.*
advantages, 14–10
annual accounts
　audit, 16–17
　introduction, 16–15
　laying documents, 16–16
　submission of accounts, 16–16
annual general meetings
　calling, 16–38
　general, 16–37
　introduction,16–36
　notice, 16–40
　procedure, 16–41
　proxies, 16–42
　public companies, of, 16–39
annual return, 16–14
articles of association, 16–10
certificate of incorporation, 16–09
choice of business medium, and
　advantages, 14–10
　disadvantages, 14–11
　introduction, 14–09
company secretary, 16–19
constitution, 16–10
corporate decision-making, and
　general meetings, 16–37—16–42
　introduction, 16–36
　resolutions, 16–43—16–47
corporate veil, and, 16–06
debentures
　introduction, 16–55
　register of holders, 16–56
　secured debentures, 16–57
decision-making
　corporations, by, 16–18
　meetings and resolutions, 16–36—16–47
　officers and directors, 16–18—16–35
defective contracts, and, 4–54
directors
　act for proper purpose, 16–27
　appointment, 16.21
　benefits from third parties, 16–31
　care, skill and diligence, 16–33
　conflicts of interest, 16–30
　declaring interest in transaction or
　　arrangement, 16–32
　disqualification, 16–24
　duties, 16–25—16–33
　exercise of independent judgment, 16–29
　generally, 16–20
　obeying constitution, 16–27
　persons to whom duties owed, 16–26
　powers, 16–25
　promoting success of company, 16–28
　removal, 16–23
　statutory obligations, 16–35
　types, 16–22
disadvantages, 14–11

Companies—*cont.*
disclosures
　annual accounts, 16–15—16–17
　annual return, 16–14
　generally, 16–11
　maintenance of statutory registers,
　　16–13
　trading, 16–12
features, 16–05
finance
　capital maintenance, 16–58—16–62
　debentures and loan stock, 16–55—16–57
　minority protection, 16–63—16–67
　share capital, 16–48—16–54
incorporation
　certificate, 16–09
　consequences, 16–06
　generally, 16–09
introduction, 16–03—16–06
loan stock, 16–55—16–57
maintenance of share capital
　acquisition of own shares, 16–60
　general, 16–58
　general restrictions, 16–59
　prohibition against financial
　　assistance, 16–61
　reduction of capital, 16–52
meetings, 16–37—16–42
memorandum of association, 16–10
minority shareholder protection
　common law derivative proceedings,
　　16–64
　introduction, 16–63
　statutory derivative proceedings,
　　16–66
　statutory intervention, 16–65
　unfair prejudice remedy, 16–67
name, 16–08
overview, 16–01—16–02
purposes, 16–04
reduction of capital, 16–52
resolutions
　general, 16–43
　ordinary resolutions, 16–44
　special resolutions, 16–45
　voting of members, 16–46
　written, 16–47
share capital
　acquisition of shares, 16–52
　"called up", 16–50
　classes of shares, 16–51
　generally, 16–48
　maintenance, 16–58—16–62
　minimum capital requirements, 16–53
　nature of share, 16–49
　nominal value, 16–50
　"paid-up", 16–50
　prospectuses, 16–54
sources, 16–03

Companies—*cont.*
statutory registers, 16–13
summary, 16–68
trading disclosures, 16–12
types, 16–07
Company secretary
generally, 16–19
Company directors
act for proper purpose, 16–27
appointment, 16.21
benefits from third parties, 16–31
care, skill and diligence, 16–33
conflicts of interest, 16–30
declaring interest in transaction or
    arrangement, 16–32
disqualification, 16–24
duties, 16–25—16–33
exercise of independent judgment, 16–29
generally, 16–20
obeying constitution, 16–27
persons to whom duties owed, 16–26
powers, 16–25
promoting success of company, 16–28
removal, 16–23
statutory obligations, 16–35
types, 16–22
Company voluntary arrangements
approval of scheme, 17–29
initiating procedure, 17–28
introduction, 17–27
subsequent procedure, 17–30
Compensation
extinction of contracts, and, 4–100
Competition law
abuse of dominant position, 3–53
anti-competitive agreements,
    3–50—3–52
enforcement, 3–54
generally, 3–49
market-sharing agreements, 3–52
merger control, 3–55
price fixing, 3–51
Compulsory winding-up
appointment of liquidator, 17–49
dissolution of company, 17–52
distribution of monies, 17–51
effects of order, 17–48
function of liquidator, 17–50
introduction, 17–46
petition, 17–47
powers of liquidator, 17–50
Conflicts of interest
agents, and, 9–29
directors, and, 16–30
trustees, and, 13–40
Confusion
extinction of contracts, and, 4–102
Connected lender liability
consumer credit, and, 6–27

Consensus ad idem
generally, 4–12
objective nature of test, 4–13
Consent
delict, and, 10–30
Consideration
basis of contracts, and, 4–05
sale of goods, and, 5–04
Conspiracy
delict, and, 10–11
Constructive fixtures
property, and, 11–36
Constructive trusts
generally, 13–23
Consumer credit
advertising, 6–15
antecedent negotiations, 6–28
cancellation, 6–25
canvassing, 6–16
circulars to minors, 6–17
connected lender liability, 6–27
content of agreements, 6–20
controlling business activities
    advertising, 6–15
    canvassing, 6–16
    circulars to minors, 6–17
    credit reference agencies, 6–19
    distribution of credit tokens, 6–18
    introduction, 6–13
    licensing, 6–14
copies of agreements, 6–22
credit agreements
    debtor-creditor agreements, 6–09
    debtor-creditor-supplier agreements,
        6–08
    individual, 6–07
    introduction, 6–06
credit reference agencies, 6–19
default, 6–32
distribution of credit tokens, 6–18
early settlement, 6–31
enforcement orders, 6–33
execution of agreements
    copies of agreements, 6–22
    generally, 6–21
    improper execution, 6–23
exempt agreements, 6–11
extortionate credit transactions, 6–36
form of agreements, 6–20
hire agreements, 6–10
implied terms, 6–16
introduction, 6–04
judicial control
    enforcement orders, 6–33
    return orders, 6–35
    time orders, 6–34
    transfer orders, 6–35
    unfair credit relationships, 6–36
licensing, 6–14
return orders, 6–35

Consumer credit—*cont.*
s 75 liability, 6–29
small agreements, 6–12
statutory basis, 6–05
termination, 6–30
time orders, 6–34
transfer orders, 6–35
unfair credit relationships, 6–36
withdrawal, 6–24
Consumer protection
See also **Sale of goods**
cancellation, 6–52
consumer credit
And see **Consumer credit**
cancellation, 6–25
content of agreements, 6–20
controlling business activities,
6–13—6–19
credit agreements, 6–06—6–09
during agreement, 6–26—6–32
execution of agreements, 6–21—6–23
exempt agreements, 6–11
form of agreements, 6–20
hire agreements, 6–10
introduction, 6–04
judicial control, 6–33—6–36
small agreements, 6–12
statutory basis, 6–05
withdrawal, 6–24
cooling-off period, 6–52
distance selling, 6–53
doorstep selling, 6–51
enforcement orders
enforcers, 6–57
generally, 6–56
estate agency, 6–55
introduction, 6–03
overview, 6–01—6–02
summary, 6–58
timeshare, 6–54
unfair contract terms, and, 6–03
unfair trading practices
And see **Unfair trading**
average consumer, 6–48
enforcement, 6–49
overview, 6–37
prohibited practices, 6–39—6–47
scope, 6–38
Contra bonos mores
trusts, and, 13–20
Contracts
See also **Contracts of employment**
acceptance
communication, 4–25—4–26
generally, 4–21
agreement
lack of formalities, 4–05
number of parties, 4–04
relevant circumstances, 4–06

Contracts—*cont.*
breach of contract
And see **Breach of contract**
action for debt, 4–86
anticipatory breach, 4–79
damages, 4–89—4–94
interdict, 4–88
introduction, 4–78
judicial remedies, 4–85—4–94
lien, 4–84
parties to claims, 4–95—4–96
remedies, 4–80—4–94
rescission, 4–82
retention, 4–83
self-help remedies, 4–81—4–84
specific implement, 4–87
capacity, 4–03
confusion, and, 4–102
consensus ad idem
generally, 4–12
objective nature of test, 4–13
consideration, and, 4–05
contents, 4–29—4–41
course of dealing, and, 4–40
defective contracts
And see **Defective contracts**
abuse of position, 4–55—4–58
bilateral uninduced error in intention,
4–64
commission of crimes, 4–70
commission of delicts, 4–71
contrary to public policy, 4–73
corporations, 4–54
error, 4–59—4–68
error in expression, 4–62
error of law, 4–60
examples, 4–50—4–77
facility and circumvention, 4–57
force and fear, 4–56
fraudulent misrepresentation, 4–66
improper negotiations, 4–55—4–58
induced errors as to fact, 4–65—4–68
innocent misrepresentation, 4–68
insanity, 4–52
intoxication, 4–53
introduction, 4–48
lack of legal capacity, 4–50—4–54
misrepresentation, 4–65—4–68
negligent misrepresentation, 4–67
non-age, 4–51
pacta illicita, 4–69—4–77
promotion of immorality, 4–72
restraint of trade, 4–75—4–77
restrictive covenants, 4–76
solus agreements, 4–77
undue influence, 4–58
unenforceable agreements, 4–49
unilateral uninduced error in
intent: n, 4–63
uninduced error of fact, 4–61—4–64

Contracts—*cont.*
  defective contracts—*cont.*
    void contracts, 4–49
    voidable contracts, 4–49
  discharge by consent, 4–99
  e-commerce, and, 7–04
  exemption clauses, 4–43
  express terms, 4–35
  extinction
    compensation, 4–100
    confusion, 4–102
    discharge by consent, 4–99
    frustration, 4–104—4–107
    impossibility, 4–104
    introduction, 4–97
    novation, 4–101
    performance, 4–98
    physical impossibility, 4–105
    practical impossibility, 4–106
    prescription, 4–103
    rei interitus, 4–105
    supervening illegality, 4–107
  formalities
    introduction, 4–27
    writing, 4–28
  formation
    acceptance, 4–21—4–26
    consensus ad idem, 4–12—4–13
    introduction, 4–11
    offer, 4–14—4–20
  frustration
    introduction, 4–104
    physical impossibility, 4–105
    practical impossibility, 4–106
    rei interitus, 4–105
    supervening illegality, 4–107
  gratuitous promise, 4–10
  implied terms, 4–41
  impossibility
    introduction, 4–104
    physical impossibility, 4–105
    practical impossibility, 4–106
    rei interitus, 4–105
    supervening illegality, 4–107
  incorporation of terms
    course of dealing, by, 4–40
    express agreement, by, 4–35
    implied by law, as, 4–41
    introduction, 4–34
    other cases, in, 4–39
    reference, by, 4–37
    signature, by, 4–38
  intention to create legal relations
    commercial agreements, 4–09
    generally, 4–07
    social and domestic arrangements,
      4–08
  invitations to treat, 4–17
  judicial precedent, and, 1–36

Contracts—*cont.*
  legal regulation of terms
    exemption clauses, 4–43
    introduction, 4–42
    unfair contract terms, 4–44—4–47
  meaning
    agreement, 4–04—4–06
    consideration, and, 4–05
    intention to create legal relations,
      4–07—4–09
    introduction, 4–03
    unilateral gratuitous promise, 4–10
  non-acceptance
    "battle of the forms", 4–24
    counter-offer, 4–23
    rejection, 4–22
  offer
    communication of, 4–18
    counter-offer, 4–23
    generally, 4–14
    invitations to treat, 4–17
    lapse, 4–20
    non-offers, 4–15—4–17
    rejection, 4–22
    revocation, 4–19
    statements of future intent, 4–16
  overview, 4–01—4–02
  promise, 4–10
  summary, 4–108
  supervening illegality, 4–107
  termination
    compensation, 4–100
    confusion, 4–102
    discharge by consent, 4–99
    frustration, 4–104—4–107
    impossibility, 4–104
    introduction, 4–97
    novation, 4–101
    performance, 4–98
    physical impossibility, 4–105
    practical impossibility, 4–106
    prescription, 4–103
    rei interitus, 4–105
    supervening illegality, 4–107
  terms
    examples, 4–30—4–33
    express agreement, 4–35
    implied by law, 4–41
    incorporation of, 4–34—4–41
    insurance, 4–33
    introduction, 4–29
    legal regulation, 4–42—4–47
    provision of services, 4–32
    sale of goods, 4–31
  unfair contract terms
    common law, at, 4–44
    statute, under, 4–45—4–47
    UCTA 1977, 4–46
    UTCCR 1999, 4–47
  unilateral gratuitous promise, 4–10

Contract of employment
agency workers, 8–06
company directors, 8–07
employees, 8–04
formation, 8–08
identification, 8–04
introduction, 8–03
workers, 8–05
Contract of service
employment law, and, 8–04
Contra proferentum rule
cautionary obligations, and, 19–09
Contributory negligence
delict, and, 10–31
Cooling-off period
consumer protection, and, 6–52
Copyright
defences, 12–15
designs, and
defences, 12–19
"design", 12–17
infringement, 12–19
protection, 12–18
infringement, 12–15
introduction, 12–13
moral rights, 12–16
protection, 12–14
Corporate homicide
generally, 3–41
Corporate insolvency
administration
appointment of administrator,
17–33—17–37
ending, 17–39
introduction, 17–31
process, 17–38
purposes, 17–32
company voluntary arrangements
approval of scheme, 17–29
initiating procedure, 17–28
introduction, 17–27
subsequent procedure, 17–30
compulsory winding-up
appointment of liquidator, 17–49
dissolution of company, 17–52
distribution of monies, 17–51
effects of order, 17–48
function of liquidator, 17–50
introduction, 17–46
petition, 17–47
powers of liquidator, 17–50
creditors' voluntary winding-up, 17–56
liquidation
compulsory winding-up, 17–46—
17–52
introduction, 17–45
voluntary winding-up, 17–53—17–56
members' voluntary winding-up, 17–55
receivership
appointment of receiver, 17–41

Corporate insolvency—*cont.*
receivership—*cont.*
distribution of monies, 17–43
introduction, 17–40
powers of receiver, 17–42
termination, 17–44
summary, 17–57
voluntary winding-up
commencement, 17–54
creditors', 17–56
introduction, 17–53
members', 17–55
Corporate liability
criminal law, and, 3–18
Corporate veil
companies, and, 16–06
Corporeal property
introduction, 11–05
moveable property
generally, 11–09
lien, 19–28
pledge, 19–27
Count, reckoning and payment
trustee liabilities, and, 13–48
Counter-offer
generally, 4–23
Course of dealing
incorporation of contract terms, and,
4–40
Court of Session
generally, 2–18
Inner House, 2–20
judicial precedent, and, 1–42
Outer House, 2–19
Court of the Lord Lyon
generally, 2–28
Credit agreements
And see **Consumer credit**
debtor-creditor agreements, 6–09
debtor-creditor-supplier agreements,
6–08
individual, 6–07
introduction, 6–06
Credit reference agencies
consumer credit, and, 6–19
Credit tokens
consumer credit, and, 6–18
Creditors' voluntary winding-up
generally, 17–56
Criminal courts
See also **Criminal law**
District Court
generally, 2–30
reforms, 2–31
High Court of Justiciary
appeal court, as, 2–37
declaratory power, 2–38
extraordinary powers, 2–38—2–39
first instance, at, 2–36
introduction, 2–35

Criminal courts—*cont.*
High Court of Justiciary—*cont.*
nobile officium, 2–39
Trial Court, 2–36
introduction, 2–29
judicial precedent, and
District Court, 1–47
High Court of Justiciary, 1–45
House of Lords, 1–44
introduction, 1–43
Sheriff Court, 1–46
Justice of the Peace Court, 2–31
Sheriff Court
introduction, 2–32
solemn procedure, 2–34
summary procedure, 2–33
Sheriff Summary Court, 2–31
Criminal law
actus reus
causation, 3–07
embezzlement, 3–23
extortion, 3–26
fraud, 3–24
generally, 3–06
state of affairs, 3–08
theft, 3–22
uttering, 3–25
art and part liability, 3–16
categories of law, and, 1–15
causation, 3–07
common law crimes
embezzlement, 3–23
extortion, 3–26
fraud, 3–24
introduction, 3–21
theft, 3–22
uttering, 3–25
corporate liability, 3–18
defences, 3–20
elements of offences
actus reus, 3–06—3–08
introduction, 3–05
mens rea, 3–09—3–14
embezzlement, 3–23
error, 3–14
extortion, 3–26
raud, 3–24
inchoate offences, 3–19
intention, 3–10
introduction, 3–03
knowledge, 3–12
mens rea
embezzlement, 3–23
error, 3–14
extortion, 3–26
fraud, 3–24
generally, 3–09
intention, 3–10
knowledge, 3–12
nature, 3–13

Criminal law—*cont.*
mens rea—*cont.*
recklessness, 3–11
theft, 3–22
uttering, 3–25
nature, 3–04
omission, 3–06
recklessness, 3–11
state of affairs, 3–08
strict liability, 3–15
theft, 3–22
uttering, 3–25
vicarious liability, 3–17
Criminality
trusts, and, 13–18
Custom
sources of law, and, 1–52

Damage
delict, and
causation, 10–27
introduction, 10–24
psychiatric injury, 10–25
pure economic loss, 10–26
remoteness of loss, 10–28
Damages
causation requirement, 4–91
compensatory nature, 4–90
delict, and, 10–43
duty to mitigate loss, 4–92
generally, 4–89
leases, and, 11–60
liquidate damages, 4–94
remoteness of loss, 4–93
sale of goods, and
buyer's remedies, 5–28
seller's remedies, 5–23
trustee liabilities, and, 13–46
Damnum injuria datum
delict, and, 10–03
Data protection
data subjects' rights, 3–47
definitions, 3–45
e-commerce, and, 7–16
enforcement, 3–47—3–48
introduction, 3–44
principles, 3–46
Death
trustees, and, 13–26
Debentures
introduction, 16–55
register of holders, 16–56
secured debentures, 16–57
Decisions
generally, 1–20
making, 1–21
Declaration of trust
trusts, and, 13–11
Declaratory power
High Court of Justiciary, and, 2–38

Defective contracts
abuse of position, 4–55—4–58
bilateral uninduced error in intention,
4–64
commission of crimes, 4–70
commission of delicts, 4–71
contrary to public policy, 4–73
corporations, 4–54
error
expression, in, 4–62
induced error as to fact, 4–65—4–68
introduction, 4–59
law, of, 4–60
uninduced error of fact, 4–61—4–64
error of law, 4–60
examples
error, 4–59—4–68
improper negotiations, 4–55—4–58
lack of legal capacity, 4–50—4–54
facility and circumvention, 4–57
force and fear, 4–56
fraudulent misrepresentation, 4–66
immorality, 4–72
improper negotiations
facility and circumvention, 4–57
force and fear, 4–56
introduction, 4–55
undue influence, 4–58
induced error as to fact
fraudulent misrepresentation, 4–66
innocent misrepresentation, 4–68
introduction, 4–65
negligent misrepresentation, 4–67
innocent misrepresentation, 4–68
insanity, 4–52
intoxication, 4–53
introduction, 4–48
lack of legal capacity
corporations, 4–54
insanity, 4–52
intoxication, 4–53
introduction, 4–50
non-age, 4–51
misrepresentation
fraudulent, 4–66
innocent, 4–68
introduction, 4–65
negligent, 4–67
negligent misrepresentation, 4–67
non-age, 4–51
pacta illicta
commission of crimes, 4–70
commission of delicts, 4–71
contrary to public policy, 4–73
immorality, 4–72
introduction, 4–69
promotion of immorality, 4–72
restraint of trade, 4–75—4–77
statutory, 4–74
promotion of immorality, 4–72

Defective contracts—*cont.*
restraint of trade
introduction, 4–75—4–77
restrictive covenants, 4–76
solus agreements, 4–77
restrictive covenants, 4–76
solus agreements, 4–77
undue influence, 4–58
unenforceable agreements, 4–49
uninduced error of fact
bilateral uninduced error in intention,
4–64
error in expression, 4–62
introduction, 4–61
unilateral uninduced error in
intention, 4–63
void contracts, 4–49
voidable contracts, 4–49
Defences
animals, and, 10–38
criminal law, and, 3–20
occupiers' liability, and, 10–39
product liability, and, 10–37
unintentional delict, and
consent, 10–30
contributory negligence, 10–31
introduction, 10–29
volenti non fit injuria, 10–30
Defenders
delict, and, 10–04
Del credere agents
generally, 9–07
Delegated legislation
forms, 1–32—1–33
generally, 1–30
locating, 1–34
making, 1–31
summary, 1–55
ultra vires, and, 1–31
Delict
animals, 10–38
assault, 10–06
breach of statutory duty
animals, 10–38
introduction, 10–36
occupiers' liability, 10–39
product liability, 10–37
conspiracy, 10–11
damages, 10–43
damnum injuria datum, 10–03
defenders, 10–04
economic delicts
conspiracy, 10–11
induced breach of contract, 10–09
intimidation, 10–10
introduction, 10–08
employment context, in
employers' liability, 10–33
vicarious liability, 10–34
fraud, 10–12

Delict—*cont.*
　induced breach of contract, 10–09
　intentional delicts
　　assault, 10–06
　　conspiracy, 10–11
　　economic delicts, 10–08—10–011
　　fraud, 10–12
　　induced breach of contract, 10–09
　　intimidation, 10–10
　　introduction, 10–05
　　passing off, 10–13
　　trespass, 10–07
　interdict, 10–42
　intimidation, 10–10
　judicial precedent, and, 1–36
　limitation, 10–41
　meaning, 10–03
　modes of liability, 10–44
　nuisance, 10–40
　occupiers' liability, 10–39
　overview, 10–01—10–02
　parties to claims, 10–04
　passing off, 10–13
　prescription, 10–41
　product liability, 10–37
　professional liability, 10–35
　pursuers, 10–04
　remedies
　　damages, 10–43
　　interdict, 10–42
　summary, 10–45
　terminology, 10–04
　trespass, 10–07
　unintentional delicts
　　attribution of fault, 10–32
　　breach of duty, 10–19—10–24
　　"but for" test, 10–27
　　causation, 10–27
　　consent, 10–30
　　contributory negligence, 10–31
　　damage, 10–24—10–28
　　defences, 10–29—10–31
　　difficulty of precautions, 10–22
　　duty of care, 10–15—10–18
　　elements, 10–14
　　expense of precautions, 10–22
　　"fair, just and reasonable", 10–18
　　foreseeability of harm, 10–16
　　introduction, 10–14
　　likelihood of harm, 10–20
　　loss suffered, 10–24—10–28
　　proximity, 10–17
　　psychiatric injury, 10–25
　　pre economic loss, 10–26
　　purpose of conduct causing harm,
　　　10–23
　　remoteness of loss, 10–28
　　seriousness of injury, 10–21
　　volenti non fit injuria, 10–30
　vicarious liability, 10–34

Delivery
　sale of goods, and, 5–18
Derivative proceedings
　common law, 16–64
　introduction, 16–63
　statutory, 16–66
Description
　sale of goods, and, 5–20
Design right
　CDPA, under
　　defences, 12–19
　　"design", 12–17
　　infringement, 12–19
　　protection, 12–18
　　introduction, 12–17
　Registered Designs Act, under
　　defences, 12–23
　　infringement, 12–23
　　introduction, 12–20
　　invalidity, 12–24
　　protection, 12–21
　　registration, 12–22
　　revocation, 12–24
Digital signatures
　e-commerce, and, 7–04
Diligence
　arrestment, 17–21
　attachment, 17–22
　inhibition, 17–23
　introduction, 17–20
　land attachment, 17–24
　money attachment, 17–25
　residual attachment, 17–26
Directives
　generally, 1–20
　making, 1–21
Directors
　act for proper purpose, 16–27
　agency, and, 9–11
　appointment, 16.21
　benefits from third parties, 16–31
　care, skill and diligence, 16–33
　conflicts of interest, 16–30
　declaring interest in transaction or
　　arrangement, 16–32
　disqualification, 16–24
　duties, 16–25—16–33
　employment law, and, 8–07
　exercise of independent judgment, 16–29
　generally, 16–20
　obeying constitution, 16–27
　persons to whom duties owed, 16–26
　powers, 16–25
　promoting success of company, 16–28
　removal, 16–23
　statutory obligations, 16–35
　types, 16–22
Disability discrimination
　employment law, and, 8–40

Discharge by consent
extinction of contracts, and, 4–99
Disclosure of information
agents' duties, and, 9–28
Discrimination
disability, 8–40
introduction, 8–33
race, 8–39
sex, 8–34—8–38
Dispute resolution
adjudication
generally, 20–23
legal framework, 20–24
advantages, 20–03
arbitration
agreements, 20–10
applicable laws, 20–11
appointment of arbitrators, 20–12
arbitral tribunal, 20–12
award, 20–18—20–21
duties of arbiters, 20–14
enforcement of award, 20–21
immunity of arbiters, 20–15
introduction, 20–07
jurisdiction of arbiters, 20–13
legal framework, 20–08
party autonomy doctrine, 20–09
recognition of award, 20–21
relationship with courts, 20–16
Scottish Arbitration Code, 20–22
setting aside awards, 20–20
stated case procedure, 20–17
types of award, 20–19
conclusion, 20–33
court actions
generally, 20–25
jurisdiction, 20–26
value of claim, 20–27—20–32
disadvantages, 20–03
employment law, and, 8–21
mediation
introduction, 20–05
process, 20–06
negotiation, 20–04
overview, 20–01—20–02
summary, 20–34
Disqualification
directors, and, 16–24
Distance selling
consumer protection, and, 6–53
cancellation rights, 7–11
conclusion, 7–14
enforcement, 7–13
information requirements, 7–10
meaning, 7–09
performance of contract, 7–12
relationship with other regulations, 7–15
District Court
generally, 2–30
judicial precedent, and, 1–47

District Court—*cont.*
reforms, 2–31
Domestic arrangements
intention to create legal relations, and,
4–09
Doorstep selling
consumer protection, and, 6–51
Duty of care
delict, and, 10–15—10–18

Early settlement
consumer credit, and, 6–31
EC law
categories of law, and, 1–11
E-commerce
acceptance of goods, and, 7–16
B2B contracts, 7–05
cancellation rights, 7–11
contract law, and, 7–04
data protection, and, 7–16
digital signatures, 7–04
Distance Selling Regulations
cancellation rights, 7–11
conclusion, 7–14
"distance selling", 7–09
enforcement, 7–13
information requirements, 7–10
performance of contract, 7–12
relationship with other regulations,
7–15
Electronic Commerce Regulations
background, 7–05
intermediaries' protection, 7–08
introduction, 7–05
relationship with other regulations,
7–15
service providers' liability, 7–07
service providers' obligations, 7–06
terminology, 7–05
information requirements, 7–10
intermediaries, and, 7–08
introduction, 7–03—7–04
legal regulation
Distance Selling Regulations,
7–09—7–15
Electronic Commerce Regulations,
7–05—7–08
other issues, 7–16
overview, 7–01—7–02
payment, and, 7–16
performance of contract, 7–12
purpose of regulation, 7–03
quality of goods, 7–16
Sale of Goods Act, and, 7–16
service providers, and
liability, 7–07
obligations, 7–06
summary, 7–17
title to goods, 7–16

Economic delicts
  conspiracy, 10–11
  induced breach of contract, 10–09
  intimidation, 10–10
  introduction, 10–08
Embezzlement
  criminal law, and, 3–23
Employment Appeal Tribunal
  generally, 2–45
Employment law
  agency workers, 8–06
  breach of contract, 8–17
  collective agreements, 8–10
  company directors, 8–07
  contract of service, 8–04
  delict, and
    employers' liability, 10–33
    vicarious liability, 10–34
  directors, 8–07
  disability discrimination, 8–40
  discrimination
    disability, 8–40
    introduction, 8–33
    race, 8–39
    sex, 8–34—8–38
  dispute resolution procedures, 8–21
  employees, 8–04
  employment contract
    agency workers, 8–06
    company directors, 8–07
    employees, 8–04
    formation, 8–08
    identification, 8–04
    introduction, 8–03
    workers, 8–05
  family-friendly rights, 8–13
  frustration, 8–18
  hours of work, 8–12
  implied duties, 8–14
  maternity rights, 8–13
  mutual obligations, 8–04
  notice rights, 8–16
  overview, 8–01—8–02
  race discrimination, 8–39
  redundancy
    alternative employment, 8–28
    calculation of payment, 8–27
    claim for payment, 8–30
    consultation requirements, 8–32
    enhanced rights, 8–31
    generally, 8–25
    meaning, 8–26
    time off to look for new employment,
      8–29
  sex discrimination
    complaint, 8–38
    direct discrimination, 8–35
    generally, 8–34
    harassment, 8–37
    indirect discrimination, 8–36

Employment law—*cont.*
  statutory dispute resolution procedures,
    8–21
  summary, 8–41
  termination of employment
    breach of contract, 8–17
    frustration, 8–18
    notice rights, 8–16
    operation of law, 8–18
    redundancy, 8–25—8–32
    unfair dismissal, 8–19—8–24
    wrongful dismissal, 8–17
  terms and conditions
    collective agreements, 8–10
    family-friendly rights, 8–13
    generally, 8–08
    hours of work, 8–12
    implied duties, 8–14
    maternity rights, 8–13
    transfer of undertakings, 8–15
    wages, 8–11
    working hours, 8–12
    written statement of particulars, 8–09
  transfer of undertakings, 8–15
  unfair dismissal
    complaints, 8–24
    "dismissal", 8–20
    generally, 8–19
    potentially fair reasons, 8–22
    reasonableness, 8–23
    statutory dispute resolution
      procedures, 8–21
  wages, 8–11
  workers, 8–05
  working hours, 8–12
  written statement of particulars, 8–09
  wrongful dismissal, 8–17
Employment Tribunals
  generally, 2–44
Enforcement orders
  enforcers, 6–57
  generally, 6–56
English law
  generally, 1–05
  historical development, 1–06
Environmental law
  generally, 3–56
Equity
  sources of law, and, 1–53
Error
  criminal law, and, 3–14
  expression, in, 4–62
  induced error as to fact
    fraudulent misrepresentation, 4–66
    innocent misrepresentation, 4–68
    introduction, 4–65
    negligent misrepresentation, 4–67
  introduction, 4–59
  law, of, 4–60

Error—*cont.*
  uninduced error of fact
    bilateral uninduced error in intention,
      4–64
    error in expression, 4–62
    introduction, 4–61
    unilateral uninduced error in
      intention, 4–63
Estate agency
  consumer protection, and, 6–55
European Convention on Human Rights
  categories of law, and, 1–10
European legislation
  generally, 1–20
  making, 1–21
Exclusion of liability
  sale of goods, and, 5–41
Exclusive possession
  access rights, 11–27
  generally, 11–25
  trespass, 11–26
  unlawful possession, 11–28
Exempt agreements
  consumer credit, and, 6–11
Exemption clauses
  contract terms, and, 4–43
Express terms
  incorporation of contract terms, and,
    4–35
Extortion
  criminal law, and, 3–26
Extortionate credit transactions
  consumer credit, and, 6–36
Extraordinary powers
  High Court of Justiciary, and, 2–38—
    2–39

Facility and circumvention
  defective contracts, and, 4–57
Family-friendly rights
  employment law, and, 8–13
Fiduciary duty
  agents' duties, and, 9–25
Finance tribunals
  generally, 2–48
Financial Ombudsman Service
  generally, 2–56
Financing of companies
  acquisition of own shares
    generally, 16–60
    prohibition against financial
      assistance, 16–61
  capital maintenance
    acquisition of own shares, 16–60
    general, 16–58
    general restrictions, 16–59
    prohibition against financial
      assistance, 16–61
    reduction of capital, 16–52

Financing of companies—*cont.*
  debentures and loan stock
    introduction, 16–55
    register of holders, 16–56
    secured debentures, 16–57
  financial assistance, 16–61
  minority shareholder protection
    common law derivative proceedings,
      16–64
    introduction, 16–63
    statutory derivative proceedings,
      16–66
    statutory intervention, 16–65
    unfair prejudice remedy, 16–67
  reduction of capital, 16–52
  secured debentures, 16–57
  share capital
    acquisition of shares, 16–52
    "called up", 16–50
    classes of shares, 16–51
    generally, 16–48
    maintenance, 16–58—16–62
    minimum capital requirements, 16–53
    nature of share, 16–49
    nominal value, 16–50
    "paid-up", 16–50
    prospectuses, 16–54
Fitness for purpose
  sale of goods, and, 5–22
Fixtures
  constructive, 11–36
  contracting out, and, 11–37
  determination, 11–34
  examples, 11–35
  generally, 11–33
  trade, 11–38
Floating charges
  appointment of receiver, 19–21
  Bankruptcy and Diligence etc (Scotland)
    Act 2007, 19–24
  company in liquidation, 19–20
  introduction, 19–18
  limitation on receiver's powers, 19–22
  meaning, 19–18
  post-14 September 2003 grant, 19–23
  pre-15 September 2003 grant, 19–19
  property, and, 11–52
Force and fear
  defective contracts, and, 4–56
Foreseeability
  delict, and, 10–16
Fraud
  criminal law, and, 3–24
  delict, and, 10–12
Fraudulent misrepresentation
  defective contracts, and, 4–66
Freedom from interference by neighbours
  introduction, 11–29
  nuisance, 11–30
  statutory nuisance, 11–31

Frustration
agency, and, 9–44
employment law, and, 8–18
introduction, 4–104
physical impossibility, 4–105
practical impossibility, 4–106
rei interitus, 4–105
supervening illegality, 4–107

Gambling contracts
generally, 1–04
Good faith
account, to, 9–27
act personally, to, 9–26
cautionary obligations, and, 19–11
conflicts of interest, and, 9–29
disclosure of information, and, 9–28
introduction, 9–25
Gratuitous promise
basis of contracts, and, 4–10
Guarantees
constitution, 19–05
contra proferentum rule, 19–09
creditors' duty of good faith, 19–11
extent of liability, 19–06
extinction, 19–13
guarantor's rights, 19–07—19–08
grounds to invalidate, 19–10—19–12
introduction, 19–04
overview, 19–01
relief against co-guarantors, 19–08
relief against debtor, 19–07
unenforceable guarantees, 19–12
void guarantees, 19–10

Health and safety
corporate homicide, and, 3–41
employers' duties, 3–30—3–34
enforcement, 3–40
introduction, 3–29
regulations, 3–35—3–39
Heritable property
access rights, 11–27
exclusive possession
access rights, 11–27
generally, 11–25
trespass, 11–26
unlawful possession, 11–28
freedom from interference by neighbours
introduction, 11–29
nuisance, 11–30
statutory nuisance, 11–31
historical background, 11–11—11–13
introduction, 11–04
land registration
automated system, 11–23
burdens register, 11–22
charges register, 11–21
first registration, 11–17
historical background, 11–14—11–15

Heritable property—*cont.*
land registration—*cont.*
land certificate, 11–18
Land Register, 11–16
property register, 11–19
proprietorship register, 11–20
overview, 11–03
ownership
exclusive possession, 11–25—11–28
fixtures, 11–33—11–38
freedom from interference by
neighbours, 11–29—11–31
generally, 11–24
introduction, 11–06
support, 11–32
nuisance, 11–30
rights in security, and, 19–26
statutory nuisance, 11–31
support, 11–32
transfer, 11–66
trespass, 11–26
unlawful possession, 11–28
High Court of Justiciary
appeal court, as, 2–37
declaratory power, 2–38
extraordinary powers, 2–38—2–39
first instance, at, 2–36
introduction, 2–35
judicial precedent, and, 1–45
nobile officium, 2–39
Trial Court, 2–36
Hire agreements
consumer credit, and, 6–10
Hire contracts
See also **Sale of goods**
generally, 5–39
implied terms, 5–40
remedies, 5–40
Holding out
agents, and, 9–17
Hours of work
employment law, and, 8–12
House of Lords
civil courts, and, 2–21
judicial precedent, and
civil actions, 1–41
criminal actions, 1–44
Hypothec
conventional, 19–16
introduction, 19–15
landlord's, 19–17
leases, and, 11–60
legal, 19–17
solicitor's, 10–17

Illegality
trusts, and, 13–17—13–21
Immorality
defective contracts, and, 4–72
trusts, and, 13–20

Implied terms
consumer credit agreements, and, 6–16
employment contracts, and, 8–14
generally, 4–41
hire contracts, and, 5–40
transfer of goods, and, 5–37
Impossibility
introduction, 4–104
physical impossibility, 4–105
practical impossibility, 4–106
rei interitus, 4–105
supervening illegality, 4–107
Improper negotiations
facility and circumvention, 4–57
force and fear, 4–56
introduction, 4–55
undue influence, 4–58
Inchoate offences
criminal law, and, 3–19
Income payment agreements
sequestration, and, 17–10
Income payment orders
sequestration, and, 17–10
Incorporation of companies
certificate, 16–09
consequences, 16–06
generally, 16–09
Incorporation of contract terms
course of dealing, by, 4–40
express agreement, by, 4–35
implied by law, as, 4–41
introduction, 4–34
other cases, in, 4–39
reference, by, 4–37
signature, by, 4–38
Incorporeal moveable property
generally, 11–10
rights in security, and, 19–29—19–30
Incorporeal property
introduction, 11–05
moveable property, 11–10
Indemnities
agents' rights, and, 9–34
Induced breach of contract
delict, and, 10–09
Induced error as to fact
fraudulent misrepresentation, 4–66
innocent misrepresentation, 4–68
introduction, 4–65
negligent misrepresentation, 4–67
Information Commissioner
generally, 2–53
Information requirements
e-commerce, and, 7–10
Information Tribunal
generally, 2–47
Inhibition
diligence, and, 17–23
Innocent misrepresentation
defective contracts, and, 4–68

Insanity
defective contracts, and, 4–52
Insolvency
administration
appointment of administrator,
17–33—17–37
ending, 17–39
introduction, 17–31
process, 17–38
purposes, 17–32
bankruptcy restrictions orders, 17–16
bankruptcy restrictions undertakings,
17–16
company voluntary arrangements
approval of scheme, 17–29
initiating procedure, 17–28
introduction, 17–27
subsequent procedure, 17–30
compulsory winding-up
appointment of liquidator, 17–49
dissolution of company, 17–52
distribution of monies, 17–51
effects of order, 17–48
function of liquidator, 17–50
introduction, 17–46
petition, 17–47
powers of liquidator, 17–50
corporate insolvency
administration, 17–31—17–39
company voluntary arrangements,
17–27—17–30
compulsory winding-up, 17–46—
17–52
liquidation, 17–45—17–56
receivership, 17–40—17–44
summary, 17–57
voluntary winding-up, 17–53—17–56
creditors' voluntary winding-up, 17–56
diligence
arrestment, 17–21
attachment, 17–22
inhibition, 17–23
introduction, 17–20
land attachment, 17–24
money attachment, 17–25
residual attachment, 17–26
income payment agreements, 17–10
income payment orders, 17–10
liquidation
compulsory winding-up, 17–46—17–
52
introduction, 17–45
voluntary winding-up, 17–53—17–56
members' voluntary winding-up, 17–55
overview, 17–01—17–02
personal insolvency
diligence, 17–20—17–26
sequestration, 17–03—17–19
summary, 17–57

Insolvency—*cont.*
receivership
appointment of receiver, 17–41
distribution of monies, 17–43
introduction, 17–40
powers of receiver, 17–42
termination, 17–44
sequestration
"absolute insolvency", 17–05
accountant in bankruptcy, 17–04
alternative procedures, 17–17—17–19
"apparent insolvency", 17–05
challengeable transactions, 17–
12—17–14
commencement, 17–06
discharge of debtor, 17–16
distribution of debtor's estate, 17–15
duties of trustee, 17–08
equalisation of diligence, 17–14
gratuitous alienations, 17–12
income received, 17–10
introduction, 17–03
management of debtor's estate, 17–15
prior transactions, 17–11
simplified procedures, 17–19
trust deeds, 17–18
trustee, 17–07
unfair preferences, 17–13
vesting of debtor's estate, 17–09
summary, 17–57
voluntary winding-up
commencement, 17–54
creditors', 17–56
introduction, 17–53
members', 17–55
Institutional writers
generally, 1–50
importance, 1–51
Insurance clause
leases, and, 11–65
Insurance contracts
contract terms, and, 4–33
Intellectual property rights
characteristics, 12–03
copyright
defences, 12–15
infringement, 12–15
introduction, 12–13
moral rights, 12–16
protection, 12–14
design right (CDPA)
defences, 12–19
"design", 12–17
infringement, 12–19
protection, 12–18
designs
CDPA, under, 12–18—12–19
introduction, 12–17
Registered Designs Act, under,
12–20—12–24

Intellectual property rights—*cont.*
moral rights, 12–16
overview, 12–01—12–02
passing off
damage, 12–07
goodwill, 12–05
introduction, 12–04
misrepresentation, 12–06
patents
defences, 12–28
infringement, 12–28
introduction, 12–25
invalidity, 12–29
protection, 12–26
registration, 12–27
revocation, 12–29
registered design right
defences, 12–23
infringement, 12–23
introduction, 12–20
invalidity, 12–24
protection, 12–21
registration, 12–22
revocation, 12–24
summary, 12–30
trade marks
defences, 12–11
infringement, 12–11
introduction, 12–08
invalidity, 12–12
protection, 12–09
registration, 12–10
revocation, 12–12
Intention
criminal law, and, 3–10
Intention to create legal relations
commercial agreements, 4–09
generally, 4–07
social and domestic arrangements, 4–08
Inter vivos trusts
generally, 13–08
Interdict
breach of contract, and, 4–88
delict, and, 10–42
trustee liabilities, and, 13–46
Intermediaries
e-commerce, and, 7–08
Intimidation
delict, and, 10–10
Intoxication
defective contracts, and, 4–53
Involuntary obligations
And see **Delict**
judicial precedent, and, 1–36
Irritancy
leases, and, 11–60

Joint property
generally, 11–41

Judges of the supreme courts of Scotland
generally, 2–70
Judicial Committee of the Privy Council
generally, 2–22
Judicial precedent
advantages, 1–36
binding, 1–39
civil courts, in
Court of Session, 1–42
House of Lords, 1–41
introduction, 1–40
Court of Session, in, 1–42
criminal courts, in
District Court, 1–47
High Court of Justiciary, 1–45
House of Lords, 1–44
introduction, 1–43
Sheriff Court, 1–46
disadvantages, 1–36
District Court, in, 1–47
generally, 1–36
High Court of Justiciary, in, 1–45
House of Lords, in
civil actions, 1–41
criminal actions, 1–44
law reporting, and, 1–49
nature, 1–37—1–39
ratio decidendi, 1–38
Sheriff Court, in, 1–46
summary, 1–55
use in subsequent cases, 1–48
Judiciary
generally, 2–65
judges of the supreme courts of
Scotland, 2–70
justices of the peace, 2–66
Lord Commissioners of the High Court
of Justiciary, 2–72
Lord Justice Clerk, 2–74
Lord Justice-General, 2–73
Lord President, 2–73
senators of the College of Justice, 2–71
sheriffs, 2–68
sheriffs principal, 2–69
stipendiary magistrates, 2–67
Jurisdiction
civil courts, and, 2–09
Jus quaesitum tertio
breach of contract, and, 4–96
Justice of the Peace Court
generally, 2–31
Justices of the peace
generally, 2–66

Knowledge
criminal law, and, 3–12

Lack of legal capacity
corporations, 4–54
insanity, 4–52

Lack of legal capacity—*cont.*
intoxication, 4–53
introduction, 4–50
non-age, 4–51
Land attachment
diligence, and, 17–24
Land registration
automated system, 11–23
burdens register, 11–22
charges register, 11–21
first registration, 11–17
historical background, 11–14—11–15
land certificate, 11–18
Land Register, 11–16
property register, 11–19
proprietorship register, 11–20
Lands Tribunal for Scotland
generally, 2–27
Law officers
Advocate General, 2–80
introduction, 2–76
Lord Advocate, 2–77
Procurators Fiscal, 2–79
Solicitor General, 2–78
Law reporting
judicial precedent, and, 1–49
Leases
action for debt, and, 11–60
agricultural leases, 11–63
alienation, 11–65
commercial leases, 11–64—11–65
damages, and, 11–60
duration, 11–58
essential elements, 11–58
hypothec, and, 11–60
insurance clause, 11–65
irritancy, and, 11–60
nature, 11–56—11–57
parties, 11–58
real rights, and, 11–57
registration, 11–58
remedies, 11–60
rent, 11–58
rent review, 11–65
repairing covenant, 11–65
rescission, and, 11–60
residential leases, 11–62
rights and obligations of the parties,
11–59
service charges, 11–65
statutory protection, 11–57
tenure, 11–57
termination, 11–61
types, 11–62
use clause, 11–65
withholding rent, and, 11–60
Legal profession
Advocate Deputes, 2–64
advocates
Advocate Deputes, 2–64

Legal profession—*cont.*
advocates—*cont.*
generally, 2–62
Queens Counsel, 2–63
complaints, 2–75
introduction, 2–58
judiciary
generally, 2–65
judges of the supreme courts of
Scotland, 2–70
justices of the peace, 2–66
Lord Commissioners of the High
Court of Justiciary, 2–72
Lord Justice Clerk, 2–74
Lord Justice-General, 2–73
Lord President, 2–73
senators of the College of Justice, 2–71
sheriffs, 2–68
sheriffs principal, 2–69
stipendiary magistrates, 2–67
"lawyer", 2–58
Notary Public, 2–60
Queens Counsel, 2–63
Solicitor-Advocate, 2–61
solicitors
generally, 2–59
Notary Public, 2–60
Solicitor-Advocate, 2–61
Legal writing
answering problem questions
applicable law, 21–17
applying law to facts, 21–18
conclusion, 21–19
introduction, 21–15
relevant issue, 21–16
tackling of, 21–20
exam hints
general advice, 21–22
introduction, 21–21
multiple choice questions, 21–24
notes questions, 21–23
legal essays
case citations, 21–07
citation of articles, 21–12
citation of books, 21–11
citation of Stair Memorial
Encyclopedia, 21–10
citation from websites, 32–24
direct quotations, 21–05
EC legislation, 21–09
how to reference, 21–04—21–06
introduction, 21–02
multiple authors, 21–13
paraphrasing, 21–06
statute citations, 21–08
what to reference, 21–03
overview, 21–01
Legally implied trusts
constructive trusts, 13–23
resulting trusts, 13–22

Legislation
delegated
forms, 1–32—1–33
generally, 1–30
locating, 1–34
making, 1–31
summary, 1–55
ultra vires, and, 1–31
European
generally, 1–20
making, 1–21
introduction, 1–19
Royal Prerogative, under, 1–35
Scottish legislation
form, 1–29
generally, 1–27
making, 1–28
Scottish Parliament, 1–12
secondary legislation
forms, 1–32—1–33
generally, 1–30
locating, 1–34
making, 1–31
summary, 1–55
ultra vires, and, 1–31
summary, 1–55
UK Parliament legislation
form, 1–25
generally, 1–22
locating, 1–26
making, 1–23—1–24
Licensing
consumer credit, and, 6–14
Lien
agents' rights, and, 9–35
breach of contract, and, 4–84
rights in security, and, 19–28
sale of goods, and, 5–23
Lifetime trusts
generally, 13–08
Limitation
delict, and, 10–41
Limited liability partnerships
advantages, 14–13
disadvantages, 14–13
introduction, 14–12
Limited partnerships
generally, 15–10
Liquidate damages
breach of contract, and, 4–94
Liquidation
compulsory winding-up
appointment of liquidator, 17–49
dissolution of company, 17–52
distribution of monies, 17–51
effects of order, 17–48
function of liquidator, 17–50
introduction, 17–46
petition, 17–47
powers of liquidator, 17–50

Liquidation—*cont.*
  introduction, 17–45
  voluntary winding-up
    commencement, 17–54
    creditors', 17–56
    introduction, 17–53
    members', 17–55
Living arrangements
  trusts, and, 13–20
Loan stock
  introduction, 16–55
  register of holders, 16–56
  secured debentures, 16–57
Lord Advocate
  generally, 2–77
Lord Commissioners of the High Court of Justiciary
  generally, 2–72
Lord Justice Clerk
  generally, 2–74
Lord Justice-General
  generally, 2–73
Lord President
  generally, 2–73

Maintenance
  property, and, 11–44
Maintenance of share capital
  acquisition of own shares, 16–60
  general, 16–58
  general restrictions, 16–59
  prohibition against financial assistance, 16–61
  reduction of capital, 16–52
Management
  property, and, 11–44
Market-sharing agreements
  competition law, and, 3–52
Marriage
  trusts, and, 13–20
Maternity rights
  employment law, and, 8–13
Mediation
  introduction, 20–05
  process, 20–06
Meetings
  calling, 16–38
  general, 16–37
  introduction,16–36
  notice, 16–40
  ordinary resolutions, 16–44
  procedure, 16–41
  proxies, 16–42
  public companies, of, 16–39
  resolutions
    general, 16–43
    ordinary, 16–44
    special, 16–45
    voting of members, 16–46
    written, 16–47

Meetings—*cont.*
  special resolutions, 16–45
  voting of members, 16–46
Members' voluntary winding-up
  generally, 17–55
Memorandum of association
  companies, and, 16–10
Memorials
  trusts, and, 13–21
Mens rea
  embezzlement, 3–23
  error, 3–14
  extortion, 3–26
  fraud, 3–24
  generally, 3–09
  intention, 3–10
  knowledge, 3–12
  nature, 3–13
  recklessness, 3–11
  theft, 3–22
  uttering, 3–25
Mercantile agents
  generally, 9–06
Merger control
  competition law, and, 3–55
Minority shareholder protection
  common law derivative proceedings, 16–64
  introduction, 16–63
  statutory derivative proceedings, 16–66
  statutory intervention, 16–65
  unfair prejudice remedy, 16–67
Misleading actions
  creating confusion with competitors' products, 6–43
  failing to honour firm commitments, 6–44
  introduction, 6–41
  misleading information, 6–42
  types, 6–41
Misleading consumer information
  generally, 3–42
Misleading information
  unfair trading, and, 6–42
Misleading omissions
  unfair trading, and, 6–45
Misleading practices
  aggressive practices, 6–46
  misleading actions, 6–41—6–44
  misleading omissions, 6–45
Misrepresentation
  fraudulent, 4–66
  innocent, 4–68
  introduction, 4–65
  negligent, 4–67
Misuse of data
  generally, 3–43
Money attachment
  diligence, and, 17–25

Moral rights
generally, 12–16
Mortgages
property, and, 11–04
Mortis causa trusts
generally, 13–08
Moveable property
corporeal moveable property, 11–09
incorporeal moveable property, 11–10
introduction, 11–04
Mutual obligations
employment law, and, 8–04

Negligence
See **Unintentional delicts**
Negligent misrepresentation
defective contracts, and, 4–67
Negotiable instruments
bills of exchange
alterations, 18–14
benefits, 18–04
definition, 18–07
form, 18–08
holders, 18–10—18–12
indorsement, 18–09
liable parties, 18–13
lost bills, 18–16
material alterations, 18–14
origins, 18–03
overdue bills, 18–15
parties, 18–05
terminology, 18–06
cheques
clearing, 18–21
crossed, 18–20
generally, 18–17
liability, 18–22
parties, 18–18
special crossing, 18–20
stale, 18–19
undated, 18–19
overview, 18–01—18–02
promissory notes, 18–23
summary, 18–24
types, 18–01
Negotiation
dispute resolution, and, 20–04
Nemo dat non quod habet
exceptions to rule, 5–11—5–17
general rule, 5–10
motor vehicles subject to hire purchase, 5–16
passing of risk, 5–17
personal bar, 5–11
sale by mercantile agent, 5–12
sale by buyer in possession after sale, 5–15
sale by seller in possession after sale, 5–14
sale under voidable title, 5–13

Nobile officium
High Court of Justiciary, and, 2–39
Non-age
defective contracts, and, 4–51
Notary Public
generally, 2–60
Notice rights
employment law, and, 8–16
Novation
extinction of contracts, and, 4–101
Nuisance
delict, and, 10–40
property, and, 11–30

Occupiers' liability
delict, and, 10–39
Offer
"battle of the forms", and, 4–24
communication of, 4–18
counter-offer, 4–23
generally, 4–14
invitations to treat, 4–17
lapse, 4–20
non-offers, 4–15—4–17
rejection, 4–22
revocation, 4–19
statements of future intent, 4–16
Ombudsmen
adjudicators, and, 2–57
Financial Ombudsman Service, 2–56
Information Commissioner, 2–53
introduction, 2–50
Parliamentary Ombudsman, 2–51
Scottish Information Commissioner, 2–54
Scottish Legal Complaints Commission, 2–55
Scottish Public Services Ombudsman, 2–52
Omission
criminal law, and, 3–06
Ordinary cause
civil courts, and, 2–14
Ordinary resolutions
company meetings, and, 16–44
Ostensible authority
agents, and, 9–22
Ownership of property
exclusive possession
access rights, 11–27
generally, 11–25
trespass, 11–26
unlawful possession, 11–28
fixtures
constructive, 11–36
contracting out, and, 11–37
determination, 11–34
examples, 11–35
generally, 11–33
trade, 11–38

Ownership of property—*cont.*
  freedom from interference by neighbours
    introduction, 11–29
    nuisance, 11–30
    statutory nuisance, 11–31
  generally, 11–24
  introduction, 11–06
  nuisance, 11–30
  statutory nuisance, 11–31
  support, 11–32

Pacta illicta
  commission of crimes, 4–70
  commission of delicts, 4–71
  contrary to public policy, 4–73
  immorality, 4–72
  introduction, 4–69
  promotion of immorality, 4–72
  restraint of trade
    introduction, 4–75—4–77
    restrictive covenants, 4–76
    solus agreements, 4–77
  statutory, 4–74
"Paction"
  property, and, 11–06
Parliamentary Ombudsman
  generally, 2–51
Partnerships
  advantages, 14–07
  agency, and, 9–10
  choice of business medium, and
    advantages, 14–07
    continuity, 14–05
    disadvantages, 14–09
    introduction, 14–04
    legal personality, 14–05
    statutory regulation, 14–06
  disadvantages, 14–09
  dissolution, 15–08
  duties of partners, 15–07
  introduction, 15–03
  law reforms, 15–09
  legal personality, 14–05
  limited partnerships, 15–10
  nature, 15–04
  overview, 15–01—15–02
  property, 15–06
  regulation of internal relations, 15–07
  relationship between partners,
      partnership and third parties, 15–05
  statutory regulation, 14–06
  summary, 15–11
Passing of property
  sale of goods, and, 5–08
Passing of risk
  sale of goods, and, 5–17
Passing off
  damage, 12–07
  delict, and, 10–13
  goodwill, 12–05

Passing off—*cont.*
  introduction, 12–04
  misrepresentation, 12–06
Patents
  defences, 12–28
  infringement, 12–28
  introduction, 12–25
  invalidity, 12–29
  protection, 12–26
  registration, 12–27
  revocation, 12–29
Payment
  e-commerce, and, 7–16
Performance of contract
  agents' duties, and, 9–24
  e-commerce, and, 7–12
  extinction of contracts, and, 4–98
Personal rights
  property, and, 11–07
Planning controls
  property, and, 11–54
Pledge
  property, and, 11–50
  rights in security, and, 19–27
Precedent
  advantages, 1–36
  binding, 1–39
  civil courts, in
    Court of Session, 1–42
    House of Lords, 1–41
    introduction, 1–40
  Court of Session, in, 1–42
  criminal courts, in
    District Court, 1–47
    High Court of Justiciary, 1–45
    House of Lords, 1–44
    introduction, 1–43
    Sheriff Court, 1–46
  disadvantages, 1–36
  District Court, in, 1–47
  generally, 1–36
  High Court of Justiciary, in, 1–45
  House of Lords, in
    civil actions, 1–41
    criminal actions, 1–44
  law reporting, and, 1–49
  nature, 1–37—1–39
  ratio decidendi, 1–38
  Sheriff Court, in, 1–46
  summary, 1–55
  use in subsequent cases, 1–48
Prescription
  delict, and, 10–41
  extinction of contracts, and, 4–103
  property, and, 11–08
Price
  sale of goods, and, 5–06
Price fixing
  competition law, and, 3–51

Price reduction
sale of goods, and, 5–32
Private law
categories of law, and, 1–14
Privity of contract
breach of contract, and, 4–95
Product liability
delict, and, 10–37
Professional liability
delict, and, 10–35
Promise
basis of contracts, and, 4–10
Promissory notes
generally, 18–23
Property
access rights, 11–27
basic concepts, 11–03—11–08
classification
corporeal property, 11–05
heritable property, 11–04
incorporeal property, 11–05
moveable property, 11–04
common rights
common property, 11–40
introduction, 11–39
joint property, 11–41
maintenance, 11–44
management, 11–44
ownership, 11–43
tenement, 11–42
constructive fixtures, 11–36
corporeal property
introduction, 11–05
moveable property, 11–09
exclusive possession
access rights, 11–27
generally, 11–25
trespass, 11–26
unlawful possession, 11–28
fixtures
constructive, 11–36
contracting out, and, 11–37
determination, 11–34
examples, 11–35
generally, 11–33
trade, 11–38
floating charges, 11–52
freedom from interference by neighbours
introduction, 11–29
nuisance, 11–30
statutory nuisance, 11–31
heritable property
historical background, 11–11—11–13
introduction, 11–04
land registration, 11–14—11–23
overview, 11–03
ownership, 11–24—11–38
transfer, 11–66
incorporeal property
introduction, 11–05

Property—*cont.*
incorporeal property—*cont.*
moveable property, 11–10
joint property, 11–41
judicial precedent, and, 1–36
Land Register, 11–16
land registration
automated system, 11–23
burdens register, 11–22
charges register, 11–21
first registration, 11–17
historical background, 11–14—11–15
land certificate, 11–18
Land Register, 11–16
property register, 11–19
proprietorship register, 11–20
leases
action for debt, and, 11–60
agricultural leases, 11–63
alienation, 11–65
commercial leases, 11–64—11–65
damages, and, 11–60
duration, 11–58
essential elements, 11–58
hypothec, and, 11–60
insurance clause, 11–65
irritancy, and, 11–60
nature, 11–56—11–57
parties, 11–58
real rights, and, 11–57
registration, 11–58
remedies, 11–60
rent, 11–58
rent review, 11–65
repairing covenant, 11–65
rescission, and, 11–60
residential leases, 11–62
rights and obligations of the parties, 11–59
service charges, 11–65
statutory protection, 11–57
tenure, 11–57
termination, 11–61
types, 11–62
use clause, 11–65
withholding rent, and, 11–60
maintenance, 11–44
management, 11–44
meaning, 11–03
mortgages, 11–04
moveable property
corporeal moveable property, 11–09
incorporeal moveable property, 11–10
introduction, 11–04
nuisance, 11–30
overview, 11–01—11–02
ownership
exclusive possession, 11–25—11–28
fixtures, 11–33—11–38

Property—*cont.*
 ownership—*cont.*
  freedom from interference by
   neighbours, 11–29—11–31
  generally, 11–24
  introduction, 11–06
  nuisance, 11–30
  statutory nuisance, 11–31
  support, 11–32
  "paction", 11–06
 personal rights, 11–07
 pledge, 11–50
 prescription, 11–08
 real rights, 11–07
 Register of Sasines, 11–14—11–15
 restrictions on rights
  floating charges, 11–52
  introduction, 11–45
  pledge, 11–50
  real burdens, 11–49
  securities, 11–50—11.52
  servitude, 11–46—11–48
 right to exclusive possession
  access rights, 11–27
  generally, 11–25
  trespass, 11–26
  unlawful possession, 11–28
 right to freedom from interference by
  neighbours
  introduction, 11–29
  nuisance, 11–30
  statutory nuisance, 11–31
 right to support, 11–32
 servitudes
  creation, 11–48
  generally, 11–46
  types, 11–47
 statutory controls
  building, 11–55
  introduction, 11–53
  planning, 11–54
 statutory nuisance, 11–31
 summary, 11–67
 tenement, 11–42
 trade fixtures, 11–38
 transfer of heritable property, 11–66
 trespass, 11–26
 unlawful possession, 11–28
Procurators Fiscal
 generally, 2–79
Promissory notes
 generally, 18–23
Promotion of immorality
 defective contracts, and, 4–72
Proxies
 company meetings, and, 16–42
Proximity
 delict, and, 10–17
Psychiatric injury
 delict, and, 10–25

Public law
 categories of law, and, 1–14
Public policy
 trusts, and, 13–21
Pure economic loss
 delict, and, 10–26
Pursuers
 delict, and, 10–04

Quality of goods
 e-commerce, and, 7–16
 sale of goods, and, 5–21—5–22
Queens Counsel
 generally, 2–63

Race discrimination
 employment law, and, 8–39
Ratification
 agency, and, 9–15
Ratio decidendi
 judicial precedent, and, 1–38
Real rights
 corporeal moveable property, over
  lien, 19–28
  pledge, 19–27
 delivery not required, where
  floating charges, 19–18—19–24
  hypothecs, 19–15—19–17
 delivery required, where, 19–25
 floating charges
  appointment of receiver, 19–21
  Bankruptcy and Diligence etc
   (Scotland) Act 2007, 19–24
  company in liquidation, 19–20
  introduction, 19–18
  limitation on receiver's powers, 19–22
  meaning, 19–18
  post-14 September 2003 grant, 19–23
  pre-15 September 2003 grant, 19–19
 heritable property, over, 19–26
 hypothecs
  conventional, 19–16
  introduction, 19–15
  landlord's, 19–17
  legal, 19–17
  solicitor's, 10–17
 incorporeal moveable property, over,
  19–29—19–30
 introduction, 19–14
 leases, and, 11–57
 lien, 19–28
 overview, 19–01
 pledge, 19–27
 property, and, 11–07
 standard security, 19–26
Receivership
 appointment of receiver, 17–41
 distribution of monies, 17–43
 introduction, 17–40
 powers of receiver, 17–42

Receivership—*cont.*
termination, 17–44
Recklessness
criminal law, and, 3–11
Reduction of capital
financing of companies, and, 16–52
Redundancy
alternative employment, 8–28
calculation of payment, 8–27
claim for payment, 8–30
consultation requirements, 8–32
enhanced rights, 8–31
generally, 8–25
meaning, 8–26
time off to look for new employment,
8–29
Register of Sasines
property, and, 11–14—11–15
Registered design right
defences, 12–23
infringement, 12–23
introduction, 12–20
invalidity, 12–24
protection, 12–21
registration, 12–22
revocation, 12–24
Regulations
generally, 1–20
making, 1–21
Regulatory law and offences
competition law
abuse of dominant position, 3–53
anti-competitive agreements,
3–50—3–52
enforcement, 3–54
generally, 3–49
market-sharing agreements, 3–52
merger control, 3–55
price fixing, 3–51
corporate homicide, 3–41
data protection
data subjects' rights, 3–47
definitions, 3–45
enforcement, 3–47—3–48
introduction, 3–44
principles, 3–46
environmental law, 3–56
generally, 3–28
health and safety
corporate homicide, and, 3–41
employers' duties, 3–30—3–34
enforcement, 3–40
introduction, 3–29
regulations, 3–35—3–39
introduction, 3–27
merger control, 3–55
misleading consumer information, 3–42
misuse of data, 3–43
self-regulation, 3–27
summary, 3–57

Rei interitus
extinction of contracts, and, 4–105
Reimbursement
trustees, and, 13–41
Rejection
offers, and, 4–22
sale of goods, and, 5–25—5–27
Religion
trusts, and, 13–20
Remedies
breach of contract (judicial), and
action for debt, 4–86
damages, 4–89—4–94
interdict, 4–88
introduction, 4–85
specific implement, 4–87
breach of contract (self-help), and
introduction, 4–81
lien, 4–84
rescission, 4–82
retention, 4–83
delict, and
damages, 10–43
interdict, 10–42
hire contracts, and, 5–40
leases, and, 11–60
sale of goods (buyer), and
additional, 5–30—5–33
damages, 5–28
enforcement, 5–33
introduction, 5–24
price reduction, 5–32
rejection, 5–25—5–27
repair or replacement, 5–31
rescission, 5–32
specific implement, 5–29
sale of goods (seller), and
action for price, 5–23
damages for non-acceptance, 5–23
lien over goods, 5–23
other, 5–23
resale, 5–23
stoppage in transit, 5–23
supply of goods, and
hire contracts, 5–40
transfer of goods, 5–38
transfer of goods, and, 5–38
Remoteness of loss
delict, and, 10–28
Rent
leases, and, 11–58
Rent review
leases, and, 11–65
Repairs
leases, and, 11–65
sale of goods, and, 5–31
Replacement
sale of goods, and, 5–31
Resale
sale of goods, and, 5–23

Rescission
breach of contract, and, 4–82
leases, and, 11–60
sale of goods, and, 5–32
Residential leases
generally, 11–62
Residual attachment
diligence, and, 17–26
Resignation
trustees, and, 13–25
Resolutions
general, 16–43
ordinary resolutions, 16–44
special resolutions, 16–45
voting of members, 16–46
written, 16–47
Restraint of trade
introduction, 4–75—4–77
restrictive covenants, 4–76
solus agreements, 4–77
Restrictive covenants
defective contracts, and, 4–76
Resulting trusts
generally, 13–22
Retention
breach of contract, and, 4–83
Return orders
consumer credit, and, 6–35
Rights in security
cautionary obligations
constitution, 19–05
contra proferentum rule, 19–09
creditors' duty of good faith, 19–11
extent of liability, 19–06
extinction, 19–13
guarantor's rights, 19–07—19–08
grounds to invalidate, 19–10—19–12
introduction, 19–04
overview, 19–01
relief against co-guarantors, 19–08
relief against debtor, 19–07
unenforceable guarantees, 19–12
void guarantees, 19–10
corporeal moveable property, over
lien, 19–28
pledge, 19–27
delivery not required, where
floating charges, 19–18—19–24
hypothecs, 19–15—19–17
delivery required, where
corporeal moveable property, over,
19–27—19–28
heritable property, over, 19–26
incorporeal moveable property, over,
19–29—19–30
introduction, 19–25
floating charges
appointment of receiver, 19–21
Bankruptcy and Diligence etc
(Scotland) Act 2007, 19–24

Rights in security—*cont.*
floating charges—*cont.*
company in liquidation, 19–20
introduction, 19–18
limitation on receiver's powers, 19–22
meaning, 19–18
post-14 September 2003 grant, 19–23
pre-15 September 2003 grant, 19–19
guarantees
constitution, 19–05
contra proferentum rule, 19–09
creditors' duty of good faith, 19–11
extent of liability, 19–06
extinction, 19–13
guarantor's rights, 19–07—19–08
grounds to invalidate, 19–10—19–12
introduction, 19–04
overview, 19–01
relief against co-guarantors, 19–08
relief against debtor, 19–07
unenforceable guarantees, 19–12
void guarantees, 19–10
heritable property, over, 19–26
hypothecs
conventional, 19–16
introduction, 19–15
landlord's, 19–17
legal, 19–17
solicitor's, 10–17
incorporeal moveable property, over,
19–29—19–30
introduction, 19–03
judicial precedent, and, 1–36
lien, 19–28
overview, 19–01—19–02
personal rights
constitution, 19–05
contra proferentum rule, 19–09
creditors' duty of good faith, 19–11
extent of liability, 19–06
extinction, 19–13
guarantor's rights, 19–07—19–08
grounds to invalidate, 19–10—19–12
introduction, 19–04
overview, 19–01
relief against co-guarantors, 19–08
relief against debtor, 19–07
unenforceable guarantees, 19–12
void guarantees, 19–10
pledge, 19–27
real rights
corporeal moveable property, over,
19–27—19–28
delivery not required, where, 19–
15—19–24
delivery required, where, 19–25
floating charges, 19–18—19–24
heritable property, over, 19–26
hypothecs, 19–15—19–17

Rights in security—*cont.*
real rights—*cont.*
incorporeal moveable property, over, 19–29—19–30
introduction, 19–14
lien, 19–28
overview, 19–01
pledge, 19–27
standard security, 19–26
real rights where delivery not required
floating charges, 19–18—19–24
hypothecs, 19–15—19–17
standard security, 19–26
summary, 19–31
types, 19–01
Roman law
categories of law, and, 1–06
Royal Prerogative
legislation, and, 1–35

Sale of goods
See also **Consumer protection**
See also **Supply of services**
buyer's duties, 5–34
buyer's remedies
additional, 5–30—5–33
damages, 5–28
enforcement, 5–33
introduction, 5–24
price reduction, 5–32
rejection, 5–25—5–27
repair or replacement, 5–31
rescission, 5–32
specific implement, 5–29
contract of sale, 5–04
contract terms, and, 4–31
e-commerce, and, 7–16
exclusion of liability, 5–41
formation of contract, 5–07
goods, 5–05
introduction, 5–03
monetary consideration, 5–04
nemo dat non quod habet
exceptions to rule, 5–11—5–17
general rule, 5–10
motor vehicles subject to hire purchase, 5–16
passing of risk, 5–17
personal bar, 5–11
sale by mercantile agent, 5–12
sale by buyer in possession after sale, 5–15
sale by seller in possession after sale, 5–14
sale under voidable title, 5–13
overview, 5–01—5–02
passing of property, 5–08
passing of risk, 5–17
price, 5–06
property, 5–04

Sale of goods—*cont.*
right to sell
introduction, 5–09
nemo dat non quod habet, 5–10—5–17
seller's duties
delivery, 5–18
description, 5–20
fitness for particular purpose, 5–22
samples, 5–22
satisfactory quality, 5–21—5–22
title, 5–19
seller's remedies
action for price, 5–23
damages for non-acceptance, 5–23
lien over goods, 5–23
other, 5–23
resale, 5–23
stoppage in transit, 5–23
summary, 5–42
title, 5–09—5–17
Samples
sale of goods, and, 5–22
Satisfactory quality
e-commerce, and, 7–16
sale of goods, and, 5–21—5–22
Scots law
academic writings
generally, 1–50
importance, 1–51
background, 1–06—1–12
categories
civil law, 1–15—1–16
common law, 1–16—1–17
criminal law, 1–15
introduction, 1–13
private law, 1–14
public law, 1–14
statute law, 1–17
summary, 1–55
civil law, 1–15—1–16
common law, 1–16—1–17
criminal law, 1–15
custom, 1–52
Decisions
generally, 1–20
making, 1–21
delegated legislation
forms, 1–32—1–33
generally, 1–30
locating, 1–34
making, 1–31
summary, 1–55
ultra vires, and, 1–31
Directives
generally, 1–20
making, 1–21
EC law, and, 1–11
English law, and
generally, 1–05
historical development, 1–06

Scots law—*cont.*
  equity, 1–53
  European Convention on Human
      Rights, 1–10
  European legislation
    generally, 1–20
    making, 1–21
  gambling contracts, and, 1–04
  historical development
    Celtic period, 1–07
    EC law, 1–11
    eighteenth and nineteenth centuries,
        1–09
    European Convention on Human
        Rights, 1–10
    introduction, 1–06
    middle ages, 1–08
    Scottish Parliament, 1–12
    summary, 1–55
    Union of the Parliaments, 1–08—1–09
  institutional writers
    generally, 1–50
    importance, 1–51
  introduction, 1–03—1–05
  judicial precedent
    advantages, 1–36
    binding, 1–39
    civil courts, in, 1–40—1–42
    Court of Session, in, 1–42
    criminal courts, in, 1–43—1–47
    disadvantages, 1–36
    District Court, in, 1–47
    generally, 1–36
    High Court of Justiciary, in, 1–45
    House of Lords, in, 1–41, 1–44
    law reporting, and, 1–49
    nature, 1–37—1–39
    ratio decidendi, 1–38
    Sheriff Court, in, 1–46
    summary, 1–55
    use in subsequent cases, 1–48
  legal rules, 1–04
  legislation
    delegated, 1–30—1–34
    European, 1–20—1–21
    introduction, 1–19
    Royal Prerogative, under, 1–35
    Scottish Parliament, 1–27—1–29
    secondary, 1–30—1–34
    summary, 1–55
    UK Parliament, 1–22—1–26
  non-legal rules, 1–04
  overview, 1–01—1–02
  precedent
    advantages, 1–36
    binding, 1–39
    civil courts, in, 1–40—1–42
    Court of Session, in, 1–42
    criminal courts, in, 1–43—1–47
    disadvantages, 1–36

Scots law—*cont.*
  precedent—*cont.*
    District Court, in, 1–47
    generally, 1–36
    High Court of Justiciary, in, 1–45
    House of Lords, in, 1–41, 1–44
    law reporting, and, 1–49
    nature, 1–37—1–39
    ratio decidendi, 1–38
    Sheriff Court, in, 1–46
    summary, 1–55
    use in subsequent cases, 1–48
  private law, 1–14
  public law, 1–14
  Regulations
    generally, 1–20
    making, 1–21
  Roman law, and, 1–06
  Royal Prerogative, 1–35
  Scottish legislation
    form, 1–29
    generally, 1–27
    making, 1–28
  Scottish Parliament, 1–12
  secondary legislation
    forms, 1–32—1–33
    generally, 1–30
    locating, 1–34
    making, 1–31
    summary, 1–55
    ultra vires, and, 1–31
  sources
    custom, 1–52
    equity, 1–53
    general, 1–54
    institutional writers, 1–50—1–51
    introduction, 1–18
    judicial precedent, 1–36—1–49
    legislation, 1–19—1–35
    summary, 1–55
  statute law, 1–17
  summary, 1–55
  treaties, 1–20
  UK Parliament legislation
    form, 1–25
    generally, 1–22
    locating, 1–26
    making, 1–23—1–24
Scottish Information Commissioner
  generally, 2–54
Scottish Land Court
  generally, 2–26
Scottish Legal Complaints Commission
  generally, 2–55
Scottish legal system
  Advocate Deputes, 2–64
  Advocate General, 2–80
  advocates
    Advocate Deputes, 2–64
    generally, 2–62

Scottish legal system—*cont.*
  Queens Counsel, 2–63
  civil courts
    appeals, 2–17
    Court of Session, 2–18—2–20
    House of Lords, 2–21
    introduction, 2–06—2–07
    Judicial Committee of the Privy
      Council, 2–22
    jurisdiction, 2–09
    key concepts, 2–06
    ordinary cause, 2–14
    organisation, 2–08
    other courts, 2–24—2–28
    persons, 2–10
    procedures, 2–13
    small claims, 2–16
    subject matter, 2–12
    summary cause, 2–15
    Supreme Court, 2–23
    terminology, 2–06
  Court of Session
    generally, 2–18
    Inner House, 2–20
    Outer House, 2–19
  Court of the Lord Lyon, 2–28
  criminal courts
    District Court, 2–30
    High Court of Justiciary, 2–35—2–39
    introduction, 2–29
    Justice of the Peace Court, 2–31
    Sheriff Court, 2–32—2–34
    Sheriff Summary Court, 2–31
  defenders, 2–06
  District Court
    generally, 2–30
    reforms, 2–31
  fact and law, 2–05
  Financial Ombudsman Service, 2–56
  High Court of Justiciary
    appeal court, as, 2–37
    declaratory power, 2–38
    extraordinary powers, 2–38—2–39
    first instance, at, 2–36
    introduction, 2–35
    nobile officium, 2–39
    Trial Court, 2–36
  House of Lords, 2–21
  Information Commissioner, 2–53
  introduction, 2–03
  judges of the supreme courts of
    Scotland, 2–70
  Judicial Committee of the Privy Council,
    2–22
  judiciary
    generally, 2–65
    judges of the supreme courts of
      Scotland, 2–70
    justices of the peace, 2–66

Scottish legal system—*cont.*
  judiciary—*cont.*
    Lord Commissioners of the High
      Court of Justiciary, 2–72
    Lord Justice Clerk, 2–74
    Lord Justice-General, 2–73
    Lord President, 2–73
    senators of the College of Justice, 2–71
    sheriffs, 2–68
    sheriffs principal, 2–69
    stipendiary magistrates, 2–67
  jurisdictions, 2–04
  Justice of the Peace Court, 2–31
  justices of the peace, 2–66
  Lands Tribunal for Scotland, 2–27
  law officers
    Advocate General, 2–80
    introduction, 2–76
    Lord Advocate, 2–77
    Procurators Fiscal, 2–79
    Solicitor General, 2–78
  legal profession
    Advocate Deputes, 2–64
    advocates, 2–62—2–64
    complaints, 2–75
    introduction, 2–58
    judiciary, 2–65—2–74
    "lawyer", 2–58
    Notary Public, 2–60
    Queens Counsel, 2–63
    Solicitor-Advocate, 2–61
    solicitors, 2–59—2–61
  Lord Advocate, 2–77
  Lord Commissioners of the High Court
    of Justiciary, 2–72
  Lord Justice Clerk, 2–74
  Lord Justice-General, 2–73
  Lord President, 2–73
  Notary Public, 2–60
  Ombudsmen
    adjudicators, and, 2–57
    Financial Ombudsman Service, 2–56
    Information Commissioner, 2–53
    introduction, 2–50
    Parliamentary Ombudsman, 2–51
    Scottish Information Commissioner,
      2–54
    Scottish Legal Complaints
      Commission, 2–55
    Scottish Public Services Ombudsman,
      2–52
    senators of the College of Justice, 2–71
    sheriffs, 2–68
    sheriffs principal, 2–69
    stipendiary magistrates, 2–67
  overview, 2–01—2–02
  Parliamentary Ombudsman, 2–51
  Procurators Fiscal, 2–79
  pursuers, 2–06
  Queens Counsel, 2–63

Scottish legal system—*cont.*
  Scottish Information Commissioner,
    2–54
  Scottish Land Court, 2–26
  Scottish Legal Complaints Commission,
    2–55
  Scottish Public Services Ombudsman,
    2–52
  senators of the College of Justice, 2–71
  Sheriff Court
    introduction, 2–32
    solemn procedure, 2–34
    summary procedure, 2–33
  Sheriff Summary Court, 2–31
  sheriffs, 2–68
  sheriffs principal, 2–69
  Solicitor-Advocate, 2–61
  Solicitor General, 2–78
  solicitors
    generally, 2–59
    Notary Public, 2–60
    Solicitor-Advocate, 2–61
  stipendiary magistrates, 2–67
  summary, 2–81
  Supreme Court, 2–23
  tribunals
    Administrative Justice and Tribunals
      Council, 2–43
    administrative tribunals, 2–46—2–49
    Employment Appeal Tribunal, 2–45
    Employment Tribunals, 2–44
    finance tribunals, 2–48
    generally, 2–40—2–41
    Information Tribunal, 2–47
    statutory tribunals, 2–46—2–49
    tax tribunals, 2–48
    Tribunals Service, 2–42
  VAT and Duties Tribunal, 2–25
Scottish Land Court
  generally, 2–26
Scottish legislation
  form, 1–29
  generally, 1–27
  making, 1–28
Scottish Parliament
  generally, 1–12
Scottish Public Services Ombudsman
  generally, 2–52
Secondary legislation
  forms, 1–32—1–33
  generally, 1–30
  locating, 1–34
  making, 1–31
  summary, 1–55
  ultra vires, and, 1–31
Self-help remedies
  introduction, 4–81
  lien, 4–84
  rescission, 4–82
  retention, 4–83

Self-regulation
  generally, 3–27
Senators of the College of Justice
  generally, 2–71
Sequestration
  "absolute insolvency", 17–05
  accountant in bankruptcy, 17–04
  alternative procedures, 17–17—17–19
  "apparent insolvency", 17–05
  challengeable transactions, 17–12—
    17–14
  commencement, 17–06
  discharge of debtor, 17–16
  distribution of debtor's estate, 17–15
  duties of trustee, 17–08
  equalisation of diligence, 17–14
  gratuitous alienations, 17–12
  income received, 17–10
  introduction, 17–03
  management of debtor's estate, 17–15
  prior transactions, 17–11
  simplified procedures, 17–19
  trust deeds, 17–18
  trustee, 17–07
  unfair preferences, 17–13
  vesting of debtor's estate, 17–09
Service charges
  leases, and, 11–65
Service providers
  e-commerce, and
    liability, 7–07
    obligations, 7–06
Servitudes
  creation, 11–48
  generally, 11–46
  types, 11–47
Sex discrimination
  complaint, 8–38
  direct discrimination, 8–35
  generally, 8–34
  harassment, 8–37
  indirect discrimination, 8–36
Share capital
  acquisition of shares, 16–52
  "called up", 16–50
  classes of shares, 16–51
  generally, 16–48
  maintenance
    acquisition of own shares, 16–60
    general, 16–58
    general restrictions, 16–59
    prohibition against financial
      assistance, 16–61
    reduction of capital, 16–52
  minimum capital requirements, 16–53
  nature of share, 16–49
  nominal value, 16–50
  "paid-up", 16–50
  prospectuses, 16–54

Sheriff Court
introduction, 2–32
judicial precedent, and, 1–46
solemn procedure, 2–34
summary procedure, 2–33
Sheriff Summary Court
generally, 2–31
Sheriffs
generally, 2–68
Sheriffs principal
generally, 2–69
Signature
incorporation of contract terms, and, 4–38
Small agreements
consumer credit, and, 6–12
Small claims
civil courts, and, 2–16
Social arrangements
intention to create legal relations, and,
4–08
Sole traders
generally, 14–03
Solemn procedure
Sheriff Court, 2–34
Solicitor-Advocate
generally, 2–61
Solicitor General
generally, 2–78
Solicitors
agency, and, 9–09
generally, 2–59
Notary Public, 2–60
Solicitor-Advocate, 2–61
Solus agreements
defective contracts, and, 4–77
Sources of law
custom, 1–52
equity, 1–53
general, 1–54
institutional writers
generally, 1–50
importance, 1–51
introduction, 1–18
judicial precedent
advantages, 1–36
binding, 1–39
civil courts, in, 1–40—1–42
Court of Session, in, 1–42
criminal courts, in, 1–43—1–47
disadvantages, 1–36
District Court, in, 1–47
generally, 1–36
High Court of Justiciary, in, 1–45
House of Lords, in, 1–41, 1–44
law reporting, and, 1–49
nature, 1–37—1–39
ratio decidendi, 1–38
Sheriff Court, in, 1–46
summary, 1–55
use in subsequent cases, 1–48

Sources of law—*cont.*
legislation
delegated, 1–30—1–34
European, 1–20—1–21
introduction, 1–19
Royal Prerogative, under, 1–35
Scottish Parliament, 1–27—1–29
secondary, 1–30—1–34
summary, 1–55
UK Parliament, 1–22—1–26
summary, 1–55
statute law, 1–17
Special resolutions
company meetings, and, 16–45
Specific implement
breach of contract, and, 4–87
sale of goods, and, 5–29
Standard security
generally, 19–26
Stare decisis
judicial precedent, and, 1–36
State of affairs
criminal law, and, 3–08
Statutory dispute resolution procedures
employment law, and, 8–21
Statutory nuisance
property, and, 11–31
Statutory registers
companies, and, 16–13
Statutory tribunals
generally, 2–46—2–49
Stipendiary magistrates
generally, 2–67
Stoppage in transit
sale of goods, and, 5–23
Strict liability
criminal law, and, 3–15
Summary cause
civil courts, and, 2–15
Summary procedure
Sheriff Court, 2–33
Supervening illegality
extinction of contracts, and, 4–107
Supply of goods
See also **Sale of goods**
hire contracts
generally, 5–39
implied terms, 5–40
remedies, 5–40
introduction, 5–35
transfer of goods
generally, 5–36
implied terms, 5–37
remedies, 5–38
Supply of services
contract terms, and, 4–32
Support
property, and, 11–32
Supreme Court
generally, 2–23

Tax tribunals
　generally, 2–48
Tenement
　property, and, 11–42
Termination of contracts
　agency, and
　　agent, by, 9–42
　　contract, under, 9–43
　　frustration, by, 9–44
　　introduction, 9–41
　　principal, by, 9–42
　compensation, 4–100
　confusion, 4–102
　discharge by consent, 4–99
　employment law, and
　　breach of contract, 8–17
　　frustration, 8–18
　　notice rights, 8–16
　　operation of law, 8–18
　　redundancy, 8–25—8–32
　　unfair dismissal, 8–19—8–24
　　wrongful dismissal, 8–17
　frustration
　　introduction, 4–104
　　physical impossibility, 4–105
　　practical impossibility, 4–106
　　rei interitus, 4–105
　　supervening illegality, 4–107
　impossibility, 4–104
　introduction, 4–97
　novation, 4–101
　performance, 4–98
　physical impossibility, 4–105
　practical impossibility, 4–106
　prescription, 4–103
　rei interitus, 4–105
　supervening illegality, 4–107
Termination of employment
　breach of contract, 8–17
　frustration, 8–18
　notice rights, 8–16
　operation of law, 8–18
　redundancy
　　alternative employment, 8–28
　　calculation of payment, 8–27
　　claim for payment, 8–30
　　consultation requirements, 8–32
　　enhanced rights, 8–31
　　generally, 8–25
　　meaning, 8–26
　　time off to look for new employment,
　　　8–29
　unfair dismissal
　　complaints, 8–24
　　"dismissal", 8–20
　　generally, 8–19
　　potentially fair reasons, 8–22
　　reasonableness, 8–23
　　statutory dispute resolution
　　　procedures, 8–21

Termination of employment—*cont.*
　wrongful dismissal, 8–17
Terms and conditions of employment
　collective agreements, 8–10
　family-friendly rights, 8–13
　generally, 8–08
　hours of work, 8–12
　implied duties, 8–14
　maternity rights, 8–13
　transfer of undertakings, 8–15
　wages, 8–11
　working hours, 8–12
　written statement of particulars, 8–09
Terms of contract
　examples, 4–30—4–33
　express agreement, 4–35
　implied by law, 4–41
　incorporation of
　　course of dealing, by, 4–40
　　express agreement, by, 4–35
　　implied by law, as, 4–41
　　introduction, 4–34
　　other cases, in, 4–39
　　reference, by, 4–37
　　signature, by, 4–38
　insurance, 4–33
　introduction, 4–29
　legal regulation, 4–42—4–47
　provision of services, 4–32
　sale of goods, 4–31
Theft
　criminal law, and, 3–22
Time orders
　consumer credit, and, 6–34
Timeshare
　consumer protection, and, 6–54
Title to goods
　e-commerce, and, 7–16
　introduction, 5–09
　nemo dat non quod habet, 5–10—5–17
Torts
　And see **Delict**
　generally, 10–03
Trade fixtures
　property, and, 11–38
Trade marks
　defences, 12–11
　infringement, 12–11
　introduction, 12–08
　invalidity, 12–12
　protection, 12–09
　registration, 12–10
　revocation, 12–12
Trading disclosures
　companies, and, 16–12
Transfer of goods
　generally, 5–36
　implied terms, 5–37
　remedies, 5–38

Transfer of undertakings
employment law, and, 8–15
Transfer orders
consumer credit, and, 6–35
Treaties
sources of law, and, 1–20
Trespass
delict, and, 10–07
property, and, 11–26
Trial Court
High Court of Justiciary, and, 2–36
Tribunals
Administrative Justice and Tribunals
Council, 2–43
administrative tribunals, 2–46—2–49
Employment Appeal Tribunal, 2–45
Employment Tribunals, 2–44
finance tribunals, 2–48
generally, 2–40—2–41
Information Tribunal, 2–47
statutory tribunals, 2–46—2–49
tax tribunals, 2–48
Tribunals Service, 2–42
Tribunals Service
generally, 2–42
Trustees
appointment, 13–25
auctor in rem suam, 13–40
conflicts of interest, 13–40
death, 13–26
decision-making
court interference, 13–29
introduction, 13–27
quorum, 13–28
duties
care, of, 13–30
existing debts and obligations, as to,
13–36
investment, of, 13–33—13–34
keep accounts, to, 13–38
new debts and obligations, as to, 13–
37
not to delegate the trust, 13–31
pay correct beneficiaries, to, 13–39
secure trust property, to, 13–32
take advice, to, 13–35
eligibility, 13–24
liability to beneficiaries
accounting, 13–48
breach of trust with consent, 13–51
count, reckoning and payment, 13–48
damages, 13–47
honesty and reasonableness, 13–51
interdict, 13–46
introduction, 13–45
protection of trustee, 13–49—13–51
liability to third parties
acquire trust property, who, 13–53
generally, 13–52

Trustees—*cont.*
powers
common law, at, 13–44
generally, 13–42
statute, under, 13–43
reimbursement, 13–41
removal, 13–26
resignation, 13–25
termination of trust, and, 13–62
Trusts
animals, and, 13–21
classifications
inter vivos trusts, 13–08
introduction, 13–06
lifetime trusts, 13–08
mortis causa trusts, 13–08
private trusts, 13–07
public trusts, 13–07
testamentary trusts, 13–08
concept, 13–03
consequences, 13–04
constructive trusts, 13–23
contra bonos mores purposes, 13–20
creation
introduction, 13–09
legally implication, 13–22—13–23
voluntary, 13–10—13–21
criminal purposes, 13–18
cy-pres jurisdiction, 13–56—13–58
declaration of trust, 13–11
directly prohibited purposes, 13–19
illegal purposes, 13–17—13–21
immoral purposes, 13–20
inter vivos trusts, 13–08
legally implied trusts
constructive trusts, 13–23
resulting trusts, 13–22
lifetime trusts, 13–08
living arrangements, and, 13–20
maintenance of animals, and, 13–21
marriage, and, 13–20
memorials, and, 13–21
mortis causa trusts, 13–08
overly wide purposes, 13–16
overview, 13–01—13–02
private trusts
generally, 13–07
variation of purposes, 13–55
public policy, and, 13–21
public trusts
generally, 13–07
variation of purposes, 13–56
purpose, 13–05
religion, and, 13–20
resulting trusts, 13–22
revocation by truster, 13–62
summary, 13–64
termination
beneficiaries, by, 13–63
introduction, 13–60

Trusts—*cont.*
  termination—*cont.*
    revocation by truster, 13–62
    trustees, by, 13–62
  testamentary trusts, 13–08
  transfer of property, 13–12
  trustees
    And see **Trustees**
    appointment, 13–25
    auctor in rem suam, 13–40
    death, 13–26
    decision-making, 13–27—13–29
    duties, 13–30—13–39
    eligibility, 13–24
    liabilities, 13–45—13–53
    powers, 13–42—13–44
    reimbursement, 13–41
    removal, 13–26
  uncertainty of purposes, 13–15
  variation of purposes
    cy-pres jurisdiction, 13–56—13–58
    generally, 13–54
    initial failure, 13–57
    private trusts, 13–55
    public trusts, 13–56
    role of court, 13–59
    subsequent failure, 13–58
  voluntarily created trusts
    animals, and, 13–21
    contra bonos mores purposes, 13–20
    criminal purposes, 13–18
    declaration of trust, 13–11
    directly prohibited purposes, 13–19
    illegal purposes, 13–17—13–21
    immoral purposes, 13–20
    living arrangements, and, 13–20
    maintenance of animals, and, 13–21
    marriage, and, 13–20
    memorials, and, 13–21
    overly wide purposes, 13–16
    position of truster as trustee, 13–13
    public policy, and, 13–21
    purposes of the trust, 13–14—13–21
    religion, and, 13–20
    requirements, 13–10
    transfer of property, 13–12
    trust purposes, 13–14—13–21
    uncertainty of purposes, 13–15

UK Parliament legislation
  form, 1–25
  generally, 1–22
  locating, 1–26
  making, 1–23—1–24
Ultra vires
  secondary legislation, and, 1–31
Undue influence
  defective contracts, and, 4–58
Unenforceable agreements
  defective contracts, and, 4–49

Unfair contract terms
  common law, at, 4–44
  consumer protection, and, 6–03
  statute, under, 4–45—4–47
  UCTA 1977, 4–46
  UTCCR 1999, 4–47
Unfair credit relationships
  consumer credit, and, 6–36
Unfair dismissal
  complaints, 8–24
  "dismissal", 8–20
  generally, 8–19
  potentially fair reasons, 8–22
  reasonableness, 8–23
  statutory dispute resolution procedures, 8–21
Unfair trading practices
  aggressive practices, 6–46
  average consumer, 6–48
  banned practices, 6–40
  commercial practice, 6–38
  creating confusion with competitors' products, 6–43
  enforcement, 6–49
  failing to honour firm commitments, 6–44
  general prohibition, 6–47
  misleading actions
    creating confusion with competitors' products, 6–43
    failing to honour firm commitments, 6–44
    introduction, 6–41
    misleading information, 6–42
    types, 6–41
  misleading information, 6–42
  misleading omissions, 6–45
  misleading practices
    aggressive practices, 6–46
    misleading actions, 6–41—6–44
    misleading omissions, 6–45
  overview, 6–37
  prohibited practices
    banned practices, 6–40
    general prohibition, 6–47
    introduction, 6–39
    misleading practices, 6–41—6–46
  scope, 6–38
Unilateral gratuitous promise
  basis of contracts, and, 4–10
Uninduced error of fact
  bilateral uninduced error in intention, 4–64
  error in expression, 4–62
  introduction, 4–61
  unilateral uninduced error in intention, 4–63
Unintentional delicts
  attribution of fault, 10–32

Unintentional delicts—*cont.*
  breach of duty—*cont.*
    expense of precautions, 10–22
    introduction, 10–19
    likelihood of harm, 10–20
    likely seriousness of injury, 10–21
    purpose of conduct causing harm,
      10–23
  "but for" test, 10–27
  causation, 10–27
  consent, 10–30
  contributory negligence, 10–31
  damage
    causation, 10–27
    introduction, 10–24
    psychiatric injury, 10–25
    pure economic loss, 10–26
    remoteness of loss, 10–28
  defences
    consent, 10–30
    contributory negligence, 10–31
    introduction, 10–29
    volenti non fit injuria, 10–30
  difficulty of precautions, 10–22
  duty of care, 10–15—10–18
  elements, 10–14
  expense of precautions, 10–22
  "fair, just and reasonable", 10–18
  foreseeability of harm, 10–16
  introduction, 10–14
  likelihood of harm, 10–20
  loss suffered
    causation, 10–27
    introduction, 10–24
    psychiatric injury, 10–25
    pure economic loss, 10–26
    remoteness of loss, 10–28
  proximity, 10–17
  psychiatric injury, 10–25
  pure economic loss, 10–26
  purpose of conduct causing harm,
    10–23
  remoteness of loss, 10–28
  seriousness of injury, 10–21
  volenti non fit injuria, 10–30
Unlawful possession
  property, and, 11–28
Use clause
  leases, and, 11–65
Uttering
  criminal law, and, 3–25

VAT and Duties Tribunal
  generally, 2–25
Vicarious liability
  criminal law, and, 3–17
  delict, and, 10–34
Void contracts
  defective contracts, and, 4–49
Voidable contracts
  defective contracts, and, 4–49
Volenti non fit injuria
  delict, and, 10–30
Voluntarily created trusts
  animals, and, 13–21
  contra bonos mores purposes, 13–20
  criminal purposes, 13–18
  declaration of trust, 13–11
  directly prohibited purposes, 13–19
  illegal purposes, 13–17—13–21
  immoral purposes, 13–20
  living arrangements, and, 13–20
  maintenance of animals, and, 13–21
  marriage, and, 13–20
  memorials, and, 13–21
  overly wide purposes, 13–16
  position of truster as trustee, 13–13
  public policy, and, 13–21
  purposes of the trust, 13–14—13–21
  religion, and, 13–20
  requirements, 13–10
  transfer of property, 13–12
  trust purposes, 13–14—13–21
  uncertainty of purposes, 13–15
Voluntary obligations
  And see **Contracts**
  judicial precedent, and, 1–36
Voluntary winding-up
  commencement, 17–54
  creditors', 17–56
  introduction, 17–53
  members', 17–55

Wages
  employment law, and, 8–11
Workers
  employment law, and, 8–05
Working hours
  employment law, and, 8–12
Written statement of particulars
  employment law, and, 8–09
Wrongful dismissal
  employment law, and, 8–17